D0850077

# The Tree of Liberty

# The Tree

A Documentary History of Rebellion
and Political Crime in America

REVISED EDITION

A Legal, Historical, Social, and
Psychological Inquiry into
Rebellions and Political Crimes,
Their Causes, Suppression,
and Punishment in the United States

# of Liberty

edited by Nicholas N. Kittrie
and Eldon D. Wedlock, Jr.

The Johns Hopkins University Press
Baltimore and London

© 1986, 1998 The Johns Hopkins University Press
All rights reserved. First edition 1986
Revised edition 1998
Printed in the United States of America on acid-free paper
07  06  05  04  03  02  01  00  99  98    5  4  3  2  1

The Johns Hopkins University Press
2715 North Charles Street, Baltimore, Maryland 21218-4319
The Johns Hopkins Press Ltd., London

Permissions are on pages 844-45, which are a continuation of the copyright page.

Library of Congress Cataloging-in-Publication Data will be found at the end of this book.
A catalog record for this book is available from the British Library.

ISBN 0-8018-5812-7        ISBN 0-8018-5643-4 (pbk.: v. 1)
ISBN 0-8018-5811-9 (pbk.: v. 2)

For
Leon Felhendler
who led the righteous in rebellion (Sobibor, 1943)

and

in memory of
Eldon D. Wedlock
(1908-1983)
who freed minds and liberated hearts

I hold it that a little rebellion now and
then is a good thing, and as necessary in
the political world as storms in the physical. . . . It is a medicine necessary for the
sound health of government.

God forbid we should ever be twenty
years without such a rebellion.

*        *        *

What signify a few lives lost in a century or
two? The tree of liberty must be refreshed
from time to time with the blood of patriots
and tyrants. It is its natural manure.

—Thomas Jefferson

The struggle between Liberty and Authority
is the most conspicuous feature in . . . history.

—John Stuart Mill

# Contents

# Detailed Contents

## Chapter 2   The Revolutionary War, 1765–1781   37

**Chapter 3  The Dawn of the Republic, 1785–1815**                                  **67**

# Chapter 5    The Civil War, 1861–1870                                            **173**

## Chapter 8   The World War II Era, 1939–1946                                    353

# Chapter 12  International Terrorism and Human Rights, 1961–1985    **641**

# Preface to the Revised Edition

The past decade has witnessed increased communal discontent and an escalation in the incidence of rebellion and public strife, both in the United States and elsewhere. In the Introduction to this book's first edition, published in 1986, we identified major eruptions of political rebellion and militance as expressions of protest against alleged abuses of power by governmental agencies or by powerful elites. The protests have frequently been fueled by the attempts of those excluded from the prevailing "social contract" to gain political, economic, and social empowerment. We further attributed the escalating political tensions to conflicts of allegiance within marginalized groups or individuals. The traditional loyalty that citizens owe their country or state, nourished by appeals to national pride and honor and enforced by the power of the existing law, often finds itself in conflict with allegiances owed to some other community—be it racial, ethnic, tribal, clannish, religious, ideological, economic, sexual, or linguistic. When such competing allegiances cannot be reconciled through existing political institutions, protest, violence, and domestic warfare may erupt. These internal tensions are even more likely to flare up when the existence of external, or international, threats declines, as seen at the conclusion of the cold war.

The emerging domestic struggles consist not merely of resistance, civil disobedience, and martial contests but also of appeals to the minds and hearts of the people. The mass media, with their influence over modern society, are frequently used as a vehicle, or courted as allies, by the combating camps. Ironically, both those in power and their challengers sometimes base the legitimacy of their causes on identical or related sources. This commonality is frequently manifested in the United States by appeals to the Constitution. Opponents often challenge the government, arguing that it and its agents have betrayed their oaths, have strayed from the path of the Founders, and have exceeded the powers devolved upon them by the Constitution. American political offenders, as a consequence, frequently perceive no "disloyalty," "treason," or "fundamental disso-nance" in their quest for the "true meaning of the Constitution" and their struggle to dispossess those in power who have allegedly "abused or perverted" the Constitutional scheme. While in other countries the primary contest might be between such extremes as religious fundamentalism and secular democracy, and the antagonists might agree on no common ideological principles or national objectives, in the United States the hallowed image of the Constitution has made both the government and its political opponents point to that document's language and intent for the legitimation of their claims.

The worldwide political strife of the past decade (in such diverse settings as Afghanistan, Cambodia, Canada, East Timor, Mexico, Liberia, Rwanda, Somalia, and the former Yugoslavia and Soviet Union) helps to demonstrate the many close relationships between the international scene and domestic disorder. Domestic rebellion and militancy are evidently dampened when foreign threats are perceived as more dangerous to the common well-being than the injustices practiced by the existing government in power. Grossly disaffected communities or groups may, nevertheless, succumb to dangerous adventuring and variations of the maxim "The enemy of my enemy is my friend," and may seek to advance their group's causes through questionable foreign alliances. But most will eschew such extremes, to submerge for a time the more militant measures for proclaiming or correcting existing grievances. The relative domestic calm that prevailed within the countries of both the Eastern and Western blocs during much of the twentieth century, an era of mortal confrontations between the proponents of democracy and the forces of Nazism, Fascism, and "Godless Communism," well illustrates this inverse relationship between the presence of external enemies and the emergence of domestic militancy.

It was shortsightedness, therefore, that suggested to many pundits of international affairs that the end of the cold war heralded the arrival of a global peace. Similar lack of vision led to claims that the racial and political struggles of the 1960s and 1970s would lead to domestic tranquility, as well. This optimism was clearly ill-placed. In a world community containing few nation-states (a term suggesting sovereign entities consisting of homogeneous nations or peoples) but composed instead of patchwork countries made up of diverse ethnic, religious, racial, or tribal communities, each with distinct objectives and expectations, the removal of external threats has not brought about conciliation and peace at home. Indeed, when the external threats that cement these pluralistic and diverse communities vanish, new as well as old and long-suppressed grievances surface with renewed vigor and cruelty. The removal of the East-West divide did not begin the end of history but rather renewed the traditional rivalries that have occupied peoples over the millennia.

Evidence of similar developments in the United States, a country made up of an ever-changing pluralistic mix, is abundantly supplied in this revised edition. Not only the rekindling of recent grievances but also the emergence of forgotten concerns, as well as totally new ones, is illustrated. These include the surfacing of both individual and collective militance in the country's heartland, among the "dispossessed" people of the nation's farm belt and the "forgotten" former members of the country's armed services. Accusations that uncontrolled immigration has turned America into an "alien nation" and suspicions that the United Nations is seeking to impose a New World Order have done little to quiet the fears and discontents of a country in the midst of a painful search for a just, appropriate, and broadly encompassing consensus for the third century of its evolution.

The new documents added to this revised edition of *The Tree of Liberty* clearly demonstrate that even the United States, this great leader of the democratic camp, is far from reaching its own peaceful utopia. The struggles in the nation's urban ghettoes and in front of its abortion clinics, the fires that gut religious institutions, the deep discontent in mid-America, and the disorder spreading through streets, schools, and families readily testify to the fact that the ongoing war against authority is likely to continue. To paraphrase Thomas Jefferson's memorable words, the roots of the tree of liberty must continue to be "refreshed" until its fruits truly meet the pluralistic tastes and expectations of America—a country made up of a richly diverse people.

# Acknowledgments to the Revised Edition

The Johns Hopkins University Press is owed a debt of gratitude for its recognition of *The Tree of Liberty*'s unique character and its classic potential as a record of the role of rebellion and political militance in the creation and democratic development of the United States. Particular thanks are due to the press's director, Willis Regier; former director, Jack Goellner; associate director, Doug Armato; and executive editor, Henry Tom. Our deep appreciation is due also to Miriam Kleiger, senior manuscript editor. To make the volume more readily available to history and politics enthusiasts and to facilitate its use as a sourcebook for classroom instruction, this new, updated, and enlarged edition appears in a two-volume paperback edition as well as in a one-volume hardcover edition.

The editors wish to express their deep appreciation to Dean Claudio Grossman and to former dean Elliott Milstein, of American University's Washington College of Law, for the further nourishing of this project. Asnat Davidi, Sharon Maerten, and Lesley Rein, all students at the law school, earned our thanks for their thorough and dedicated research and editing work. Donna Bradley, Elma Gates, Robert Kelso, Christopher Stearns, and Mark Williams, members of the law school staff, carried out the complex production and copying tasks under great pressure and with great devotion.

Alan Fisher, a recent graduate of the Washington College of Law who is currently an attorney working for the United States government, is gratefully acknowledged both as an active participant in and as the chief coordinator of all the research, writing, and editing connected with the preparation of this revised edition.

Georgette J. Sobel has earned special recognition for her selfless and tireless care and feeding of the participating "troops," as well as her timely and exceptional carrying out of all requisite coordination and managerial duties.

# Acknowledgments

This collection was initiated in 1980 during a visiting fellowship extended to Dr. Kittrie by the National Institute of Justice of the United States Department of Justice. A previous grant to him by the National Endowment for the Humanities, in 1973, helped in the initial planting of the seeds for this project. Warm thanks are due to our colleagues at the National Endowment for the Humanities and the National Institute for Justice, particularly Winifred L. Reed and Patrick Langan, for their professional challenges, material support, and personal confidence. Several research assistants worked loyally with Dr. Kittrie in the collection of and commentary on these documents. Patrice Fitzgerald, William Pesch, Eric Pomeranz, Elizabeth Buck, and Daniel B. Seferian are owed a particular debt of gratitude. Beth Levenson, a recent graduate of the American University Law School, carried out the demanding final tasks of review and editing. Several seminar groups at the American University both utilized and analyzed earlier versions of these materials. For their commentary we wish to express our thanks to Mary Schwemle, Jill Rosenfeld, Bob Burkholder, George May, Richard Cohen, Ruth Jamison, May Farber, Tony Bornstein, Ingrid Yellick, Rick Gondelman, Sara Chenetz, Rick Lazio, Tom Kass, Steven Kantor, Keith Costa, Jessica Indig, Karen Shapiro, William Sharp, Bruce Waterhouse, Linda Harrison, Bruce Bender, Joy Schwan, and Sharon Gross. Dean Thomas Buergenthal of the American University has nourished the project, recognizing its contributions to the cause of human rights, and Professor Burton D. Wechsler generously shared with us his sensitive understanding of constitutional law and history. Thanks are also due to Dean Harry M. Lightsey, Jr., and the University of South Carolina for continuing staff and service support to Professor Wedlock during his sabbatical. Finally, we must express our gratitude to Michal R. Belknap of the University of Georgia for a thorough and critical review of the manuscript, to Henry Tom and Carol Ehrlich of the Johns Hopkins University Press for their invaluable editorial contributions, and to Georgette J. Sobel for her untiring effort in supervising the technical production of this volume. Professor Henry Steele Commager supplied enthusiastic encouragement for the comprehensive breadth of this undertaking. Shirley Green was responsible for the creative character of the historical photographs and illustrations; Stina C. Wedlock assisted with the graphic research; and Jonathan Dolger supplied invaluable assistance as the editors' literary agent. Recognition is due also to Norda and Zachary Kittrie for their assistance with the Bibliography and to Elizabeth Kelne and Mary Wason for carrying out the complex typing and photocopying tasks.

# Introduction

The terms *political crime* and *political criminals* are rarely found in the American literature of the social and political sciences, history, criminology, or law. In 1979, *Webster's New Collegiate Dictionary* for the first time defined the political criminal as one "involv[ed] or charged . . . with acts against the government or a political system." This obviously impoverished definition provides a point of departure for the subject matter of this book.

Political criminals need not necessarily engage in acts; their crimes might be their failure to perform legally imposed duties. Failure to swear allegiance or to register for the draft is such a crime. Speech or writing concerning a prohibited subject matter can be criminal. The crimes of sedition and treason are examples. To be political a crime need not seek to overthrow the government or to depose its leaders. Proposing change or attempting reform of entrenched political policies, such as the advocacy of liberty for blacks and the exercise of the franchise by women, may be criminal.

To comprehend political criminality, one must view the term *political* quite liberally. Many actions or omissions motivated by religious, economic, social, or racial concerns may be perceived as threatening the political authority of the state. The recent refusal by Christian ministers in Nebraska to submit their schools to certification by the secular government resulted in court injunctions and the arrests of the offending fundamentalists. Moreover, even an offense against nongovernmental institutions, persons, or practices may be deemed political. Violence or even discrimination against an ethnic or racial group, as well as a proscribed labor strike or picketing against a private employer, can be perceived as a political crime when those in power see such conduct as undermining the political stability of the state.

A political offender, finally, need not be charged with a crime or be dealt with through criminal sanctions. Politically suspect individuals may be subjected to other burdens and liabilities. Restrictions on public employment and officeholding have been imposed not only on Communists but on others whose allegiance to the government was in doubt. Limitations on travel and association, curfew, and exile have been applied not only to the Japanese-Americans during World War II but also to Native Americans throughout our national history.

We have sought in this collection to bring together materials that broadly survey these various aspects of political crime. Our task has been complicated by the fact that the conventional vision of American history and growth strongly rejects the utility of studying the meaning and role of political criminality. Given the paucity of discussion and analysis of the concept of political criminality among American scholars, we have chosen to proceed in a broad exploratory fashion, without a strict definition. We have developed, in the lexicon of the mathematicians, an open rather than a closed set of materials. The boundary of the open set is indefinite, vague, amorphous, and indiscernible, while in the latter it is definitively fixed and firm. It may be possible sometime in the future to elaborate a precise and complete definition of political crime, but to do so at this point in our knowledge would be to truncate prematurely the investigation of this important arena.

## Pilgrims in the Promised Land

The story of America's success in molding a pluralistic society has been told and retold in numerous variations. Most accounts have sought out or dwelled on harmonizing elements and influences. Few have viewed the initial hardships or the continuing internal conflicts as more than temporary roadblocks and digressions on the path toward national unity. Yet one may advance the thesis that America's unique success and its peculiar sensitivity to questions of justice and equality stem from the stress of this historical adversity and strife. It is therefore with no apologies that this account of America's internal tensions and upheavals is presented.

Severe challenges confronted the first English settlers on these shores. When in December of 1606 three small ships—the *Susan Constant*, the *Godspeed*, and the *Discovery*—sailed down the Thames River on their way to settle the distant colony of Virginia, storms prevented them from promptly leaving the English Channel. Numbering approximately 105 men, not including the crews of the three ships, the Virginia settlers later made several stops in the Canaries and in the islands of the West Indies, further delaying their arrival in the New World and diminishing their stores of supplies.

From their very first landing on a spring day in 1607, the settlers, in addition to battling the physical and economic hardships of colonizing a wilderness (for which the gentlemen-adventurers were ill prepared), became embroiled in constant political strife. Natives attacked an exploring party of the English empire builders even before they had selected a place for their permanent colony. Within the first year, George Kendall, one of the seven councillors initially put in charge of the colony by King James's authority, was charged, convicted, and shot for conspiring against the colony. In 1622, the struggling colony was almost obliterated during a mass Indian uprising in which more than 350 white settlers of all ages and both sexes perished (blacks were left unharmed). In 1635 long-brewing controversies between the settlers, their council, and their governor, Sir John Harvey, appointed by the Crown, erupted into open revolt. The critics of the governor and leaders of the opposition were arrested on the governor's orders and were held to be tried under martial law. In the ensuing confrontation with the council, the governor charged a councillor with treason against His Majesty the King. The council summoned forty musketeers previously planted around the chamber into action, and the conflict did not subside until Governor Harvey departed in haste for England—this possibly constituting the first coup d'état in the new colonies. Indeed, not until after the bloody suppression of the popular rebellion of 1676, commanded by Nathaniel Bacon, an aristocratic Cambridge-educated member of the council who led opposition to another royal governor, did Virginia achieve a temporary political respite.[1]

The pattern of remonstrance, rebellion, and response was evident elsewhere in the colonies, if not as dramatically so. It culminated in two civil wars and several insurrections. Challenges to constituted authority in America and the government's need to mold timely response continued with every wave of immigration, with every thrust westward, with every stage in economic development, with every new assertion of racial, gender, or class claims, and with every American involvement in conflicts beyond its boundaries. This volume presents the evidentiary record for the thesis that political criminality is an integral part of an ongoing historical process of challenge and response which accounts for many of the liberties and for much of the societal diversity for which America is most admired.

## The Denial of Political Crime in America

Dissent, protest, disobedience, violence, and rebellion—in pursuit of political change or in opposition to it—have been major forces in the recent history of the nations of the world. This compilation is the first comprehensive documentation of the historical causes and outcomes—from the colonial period to the present—of the political struggle by individuals and groups in America against governmental authority. Although many excellent documentary histories of particular reformist or activist movements and of the United States generally exist, they are either too narrow in the former case or too broad in the latter. The common trends among all resisters to authority—as well as repeated patterns of governmental response—are not treated; or if they are, tend to be lost.

Problems of definition and historical diffusion greatly complicated the task of researching, documenting, and analyzing, under the rubric of political criminality, the phenomena that constitute the core events in this book. One frequently encounters events of political turmoil, kidnappings, bombings, and terrorism in other countries. One is often exposed to the campaigns of the International Red Cross or Amnesty International on behalf of political prisoners elsewhere. But reference to "political crimes and criminals in America" usually brings a puzzled look to the faces of an American audience. Presenting the notion that the concept of political crime might have a place in American social science or law brings forth either a denial of the validity of the concept or the opposite assertion that all crimes are at root political. Neither of these responses is particularly helpful in assessing or addressing the very real problems associated with the existence of unorthodox political beliefs or with the resort to unlawful methods for attaining political ends.

Despite the inability of the public, the social sciences, or the law to articulate some general, neutral, and acceptable definitions of the phenomenon, the archives of United States history are full of evidence of political violence and struggle from the beginning of this continent's colonization. The public's lingering suspicion that political crime—however inadequate its definition—indeed exists in our midst has been fed further by a series of governmental measures designed to combat "royalists," "traitors," "seditionists," "political prisoners," "anarchists," "syndicalists," "communists," and other breeds of dissidents.

Nevertheless, Americans have long adhered to the contradictory belief that the history of this country has differed radically, and for the better, from the heritage of the less civilized countries and even that of other Western nations. Europe, despite its advanced civilization, was conceded to have had a violent foundation and a convulsive history. In both scholarly and public opinion it is admitted, therefore, that

> [a]s comforting as it is for civilized people to think of barbarians as violent and of violence as barbarian, Western civilization and various forms of collective violence have always been close partners. . . . Historically, collective violence has flowed regularly out of the central political processes of Western countries. . . . The oppressed have struck in the name of justice, the privileged in the name of order, those in between in the name of fear. Great shifts in the arrangements of [European] power have ordinarily produced—and have often depended on—exceptional movements of collective violence.[2]

In contrast, both political leaders and social commentators have painted the United States as being endowed with a manifest destiny and a distinct governmental style. "[A]mericans since the Puritans have historically regarded themselves as a latter-day 'chosen people' sent on a holy errand to the wilderness, there to create a new Jerusalem," wrote historian Hugh Davis Graham and political scientist Ted Robert Gurr.[3] On the new continent settlers were to attain the Peaceable Kingdom, the restored Eden that nineteenth-century American

painter Edward Hicks so frequently portrayed. Within its boundaries the true realization of Isaiah's prophetic promise was to occur. "The wolf and lamb shall feed together, and the lion shall eat straw like the bullock; and dust shall be the serpent's food. They shall not hurt nor destroy in all my holy mountain. . . ."[4]

With characteristic faith and optimism the American nation—said by Benjamin Franklin to be founded by the design of providence to cultivate the new earth[5]—was believed to be the agent of destiny in the realization of humanity's utopian ideals and progress. There developed, concurrently, what historian Richard E. Rubenstein called "The Myth of Peaceful Progress."[6] The myth professed that the United States, alone among nations, was the place in which extremely diverse groups had learned to compromise their differences peaceably. American society, it was held, had been blessed by a blurring of divisions between its multiple economic, social, political, and ethnic groups. This achievement was attributed to a combination of factors, including the fertility of the land and the richness of its resources, the tendency of the people to be hardworking, the fact that neither a true aristocracy nor an impoverished proletariat grew roots on this soil, and finally, the ability of the Constitution and the two-party system to provide an ideal instrument for political compromise. There was a general conviction that "any sizeable domestic group could gain its proper share of power, prosperity and respectability merely by playing the game according to the rules."[7] In an America which had, through the design of destiny, constitutional doctrines, and pragmatic politics, perfected the unique art of peaceful power sharing and transference, so necessary for continuing change and progress, there was no need for violent political, social, or economic conflicts.

But the riots in the urban ghettoes and the student and Vietnam-connected unrest of the 1960s produced an awareness of the uses of political dissent and violence and a revision of the traditional or change-through-consensus view of United States history. When black activist H. Rap Brown asserted that mass political violence was "as American as apple pie," the public was shocked. Serious scholars, however, soon joined in debunking the myth of peaceful progress. The Reverend Theodore Parker's voice was a daring and lonely one when he proclaimed in 1848: "We are a rebellious nation; our whole history is treason; our blood was attainted before we were born." Yet, well over a century later, prominent historians and social scientists have embraced his claim.

"For more than two hundred years . . . the United States has experienced regular episodes of serious mass violence related to the social, political, and economic objectives of insurgent groups," Richard E. Rubenstein asserted.[8] The Staff Report to the National Commission on the Causes and Prevention of Violence reached similar conclusions. There has been a vast amount of violence, pointed out the report, "connected with some of the most constructive, positive, and indeed, among the noblest chapters in our national history."[9] But some of the most ignoble, destructive, and undemocratic chapters of American history have likewise been connected with political violence, disorder, and subversion.

The Founding Fathers were political offenders all. But although traitors in contemporary English judgment, they were patriots in their own eyes and in the subsequent view of history. This resort to illegal or extralegal political means, however, did not come to an end in America with the founding of the new nation or the Republic. Crimes committed for political ends manifested by rebellions, treasons, assassinations, homicides, hostage taking, bomb throwings, seditions, draft evasions, and widespread civil disobedience have influenced and continue to affect dramatically the political life of the nation.

Despite America's virtually unbroken tradition of political dissent, crime, and violence, American criminal law and jurisprudence, following the dictum of English Common Law, refuse to take account of assertions of political motive, ideology, conviction, or demands of conscience as a justification, excuse, or defense. Obscured by the precept of criminal law that only intent to commit the prohibited act is important and that motive—evil or benign—has no bearing on guilt, political criminality has not been recognized by the American police, courts, or corrections system as a unique category of offenses.

This has resulted in a failure formally to accord political offenders a differential standing and treatment by the government and its agencies. Thus, while the laws of most European countries, as well as international law generally, grant political offenders a special and "honorable" status—by virtue of which they are exempted from demeaning penalties and from international extradition—the domestic law of the United States has continued to view political offenders no differently from common criminals. The argument that one was acting for a political motive or in adherence to the demands of a higher law or the values of one's conscience and beliefs has not officially penetrated American jurisprudence.

Author Brendan Behan, in his autobiographical *Borstal Boy*, reflected on this peculiarly Anglo-Saxon anomaly. As an adolescent Behan was active with the Irish Republican Army. After his arrest he was placed in confinement together with common offenders. To this he responded: "I knew . . . it was the usual hypocrisy of the English not giving anyone political treatment, and then being able to say that alone among the empires she had no political prisoners."[10]

American law and the American criminal justice system never have denominated any portion of the country's massive criminal problem as "political crime." Even though the only crime defined in the United States Constitution, treason, is a political offense, neither this nor the other criminal offenses erected and used to preserve political order and governmental authority have ever been so designated. Never have these offenses been grouped together for common consideration, analysis, or criticism. Indeed, for a long time the country's legal and criminal justice experts failed to profess any interest in this compelling subject. So little concern have Anglo-American criminal justice scholars manifested for political criminality that when renowned Italian criminologist Cesare Lombroso published his major study of political and revolutionary offenses in 1890 (*Il Delitto Politico e le Rivoluzioni*), the topic was considered so irrelevant that no English translation was undertaken.

## Neither a Nation of Lawlessness nor One of Oppression

American law's resistance to any doctrine of political criminality is not surprising. The colonies were conceived in political exile; the nation was born of treason and midwived by violent revolution. From the perspectives of stability and political order, the United States has not overcome the fear of the skeletons in its closet. It is no wonder that to counter the lessons of its own origins, responsible leaders and politicians fostered the dogma that all evils of the past were the result of the tyrannical monarch, that in a democratic republic obedience to the law was the unquestionable duty of all citizens, and that existing political mechanisms were ample for peaceful reform. The proposition that ends might sometimes justify extralegal means became an intolerable heresy. Nevertheless, our national original sin was never quite expiated, and as is eminently apparent from the materials in this collection, extralegal, illegal, and violent methods are significant factors in weaving freedom, justice, and equality into the fabric of the American social order.

American law over the years has responded vigorously to real as well as to imagined challenges to authority. The law has prohibited various types of political or politically-motivated conduct—from treason and sedition to the education of blacks, from the advocacy of anarchy to voting by women, from office-holding by Communists to picketing and striking by workers, from interstate and international travel by dissidents and subversives to continued residence by suspect aliens and citizens. Diverse mechanisms and criminal or quasi-criminal sanctions for the control of political offenses and the punishment of political offenders likewise have been established. Federal and state laws have relied not only on penal sanctions but also on loyalty oaths, security investigations, the exclusion and expulsion of politically suspect aliens, the calling up of the military, the imposition of martial law, and the confinement of suspect populations in special camps as tools to maintain political order.

Political offenses in America have not necessarily consisted of overt actions. Failure to act, when required under law, has oftentimes constituted an offense. The law not only has prohibited direct opposition or attacks upon the state (by traitors, secessionists, or anarchists) but also has sanctioned those unwilling to render active service or offer verbal adherence to the state and its endeavors (conscientious objectors, refusers of loyalty oaths, and the like). From time to time the state has sought to protect not only its own agencies but also the interests of its power elites. Criminal penalties as well as court injunctions were utilized to ward off attacks against the Southern institution of human bondage and the Northern menace of labor organization. At times the people's resort to rights now considered guaranteed under the Constitution (freedom of speech, assembly, and association) were punished as sedition and criminal conspiracy. Finally, and frequently, political offenses have consisted of nothing more than the very act of being. Singled out on the basis of gender, color, race, ethnicity, or nationality, some populations were selected for adverse treatment—through criminal or other state sanctions—because of their perceived collective threat. Native Americans, blacks, women, and Japanese-Americans thus became political offenders by virtue of their nature rather than their deeds.

Unlike its doctrine, in actual implementation the American justice system frequently has differentiated between political offenses and offenders and common ones. Offenders motivated by political, ideological, or other convictions sometimes have been granted certain benefits, usually through the executive rather than the judicial agencies of government. Most amnesties and pardons granted by American presidents have been issued for the benefit of former political offenders—especially those who criminally resisted the prosecution of international wars or participated in domestic insurrections or civil wars. But differentiation has not necessarily resulted in more lax or benevolent treatment. From time to time, the political nature of the offense has triggered harsher sanctions and more oppressive policing measures. Through reliance on either explicit or implicit constitutional authority, the executive has employed measures against political offenders which are impermissible in the struggle against common crime, including suspension of the writ of habeas corpus, imposition of martial law, use of the militia for quelling mass disorders, trial by military tribunals without the protection of the Bill of Rights, the exclusion of civilian populations from militarily proclaimed defense zones, and the undertaking of comprehensive surveillance programs against suspect populations, without compliance with the warrant requirement or other constitutional safeguards.

We set out to thoroughly collect documents surrounding the major events and actors of political criminality in the United States, whether manifested in purely political or in social, economic, religious, racial, or gender struggles.

The resulting sourcebook unequivocally demonstrates that the vigorous pursuit of life, liberty, and happiness has been a particular and ongoing undertaking of the American people beginning even before the nation's independence. Given endorsement by the Declaration of Independence, this pursuit has not always been satisfied with the available legally prescribed methods for political action and change. American history reflects frequent and continuing resort to unlawful means for political ends. Yet, despite this constant dissidence and fervor, America has become neither a nation of lawlessness nor one of oppression. Instead, spurred by the people's constant vigilance for liberty and equality and protected from severe oppressions of government, many competing nations, ideologies, races, religions, and economic systems have found here their best haven in the memory of human history.

## Approaches to a Definition: Conflicts of Allegiance

The definitional problem of political crime has troubled the editors no less than others, and we do not attempt to present a complete solution to it. Instead, we have sought to provide in one collection basic materials from which further research and reflection may lead to a better understanding, if not a consensus, about political crime in the United States. Of course, the process of selecting documents requires that some parameters be set, and some preliminary analysis is in order.

It may be that an objective and neutral definition of political crime is impossible, because the term seems to involve relativistic relationships between the motives and acts of individuals and the perspectives of government toward their conduct and allegiances. Thus, on the one hand, an individual may claim to be committing acts of violence against the state out of political motivations but be relegated to the status of common criminal by the government. On the other hand, an individual may profess firm allegiance to the state yet be subjected to the pains and penalties of criminality because the government perceives his status or professed ideals to be inimical to its interests. Sometimes the perspectives of the parties coalesce, and a common agreement that particular people are political criminals is reached.

Furthermore, a third party, a neutral country or an eye detached from events by the distance of time, may designate particular activity as a political offense.

Another complication in any attempt to define political criminality revolves around the nature of the act that makes up the crime. Mere membership by birth in a suspect population, or voluntary adherence to a proscribed political party, may suffice as an "act." More frequently, engaging in prohibited speech or, conversely, refusal to swear an oath of allegiance may cause the application of criminal penalties. All these nonviolent activities are usually referred to, in international law, as pure political offenses. In addition, there are common criminal acts, such as murder, assault, and kidnapping, which, when directed against political figures and motivated by political goals, are known as complex political crimes. Finally, there are criminal acts perpetrated against innocent and private parties, allegedly for the purpose of sustaining, financing, or publicizing political opposition, and whose connection with political goals or change is tangential at best.

It should always be remembered that unlike a strict documentary history of a well-defined topic or phenomenon, this collection is charting new territory. Many of the entries relate to incidents that do not result in a direct resort to traditional criminal laws and sanctions; there are documents that relate to activities that many would consider primarily economic, racial, or social rather than political; there are documents regarding unsuccessful attempts by government to regulate conduct and to impose sanctions upon the nonconforming; and there are memoirs, speeches, letters, and other communications intended to give insights into the political offender and his or her pursuits. Not all of these appear immediately and obviously connected with political criminality. However, they all contribute to the understanding of the roles and methods of political criminals and the reciprocal governmental attempts, through resort to penal as well as nonpenal sanctions, to control them.

The power and compulsion of the state have also operated, and do operate, through sanctions other than those contained in penal codes, such as capital or corporal punishment, restraint of liberty, and fines. In many cases exclusion, expulsion, exile, curfews, confiscation, confinement, and diverse licensing burdens become the tools of the coercive power of the state. The withdrawal of passports and licenses and the withholding of eligibility for officeholding, voting, and government employment are resorted to, in addition, to enforce governmentally prescribed norms. The use of restraining orders and civil injunctions further serves to expand the state's coercion into areas of economic and social conflict such as labor and racial disputes. Indeed, in its warfare against political criminality the state possesses the particularly dangerous option of making selective use of these alternative approaches, rather than relying solely on criminal sanctions, for the attainment of its ends.

Economic, social, and racial dissent often is the vanguard of political criminality. Materials relating to the preliminary stages of societal ferment are necessary to establish the matrix from which political criminality arises. After the methods of peaceful change are exhausted (and sometimes before), the proponents of reform often turn to extralegal activity and rebellion. But even before that point is reached, oftentimes the government, in an abundance of caution, takes upon itself the burden of extinguishing even the mildest voices for reform, making otherwise innocuous activities criminal. Prohibiting the education of blacks, making the distribution of abolitionist literature illegal, and proscribing the display of the red flag all fall within this category. Political criminality can thus arise from the most passive manifestations.

The importance of a government's attempt, albeit eventually unsuccessful, to make some political activity illegal must not be overlooked. Many of the selected materials relate to failed efforts to limit political activism and opposition, and we should be alert to the reasons for these failures. In these materials are contained the seeds of a methodology for understanding the processes whereby the state power combating political crime has been constrained in the United States. It is also important to identify these failed state efforts, because in many instances they have continued in effect for long periods of time, exerting a "chilling effect" upon the struggle for political and civil rights in this country.

Ultimately, political crime arises from perceived irreconcilable conflicts of allegiance. Individuals may profess an adherence to different racial, religious, ethnic, familial, or economic groups. There may be philosophical, ethical, social, or political ideals that claim one's attention and passion as well. The need to balance the claims of the various allegiances and ideals is left mostly to the conscience and conduct of the individual. Inevitably, however, conflicts will arise between the central principles and requirements of the different groups making claims upon the individual. The more pluralistic a society is, the more likely these conflicts are. For the most part, these conflicts are resolved within the privacy of the individual's conscience or through efforts within or between groups to remove incompatibilities. Individuals, alternatively, may be expelled from or choose to abandon one or more of the incompatible groups. While often deeply troubling to the individuals involved, the resolution of these conflicts is, nevertheless, generally an informal and private matter.

The conflict of allegiances cannot be as easily resolved when it involves the state. Having access to the power of the law to compel obedience and adherence to its norms, the state is usually unwilling to tolerate an accommodation with a conflicting allegiance. Thus, when an individual to whose allegiance the state makes a claim is confronted with an uncompromisable conflict between the demands of the state and the principles of another group or belief, an informal compromise is not possible. The state demands total obedience and frequently exacts punishment not only for the betrayal but even for doubting the primacy of the allegiance owed to it.

In nation-states evolving from relatively homogeneous ethnic, linguistic, racial, and cultural societies, conflicts of allegiances may not be too evident. In the more recently created nations, where populations may have little in common other than that they share geographical boundaries designated by colonial powers, conflicts may be all too common. The United States is lodged midway between these categories, and this collection well documents the process whereby conflicts of allegiance were resolved in a New World composed of a variety of peoples with many conflicting affiliations and aspirations.

There are in this collection at least two categories of documents that flow unambiguously from conflicts with the demands of the state. Ironically, they represent the opposite ends of the continuum of criminal conduct: the passive type manifested in refusals to offer service demanded by the state (conscientious objection, draft resistance, failing to swear allegiance) and the aggressive type reflecting direct attack upon the state in the interest of a competing group or allegiance (treason, secession, anarchy).

The conflict of allegiances may manifest itself in yet other ways. This collection offers several instances of special state controls and sanctions against groups identified by some attributes that cast doubts upon the political "maturity," "patriotism," or commitment of their members to the state. Slaves, blacks, Native Americans, Japanese-Americans, Communists, and women have been so singled out and thus qualify for attention and study in a volume on political crime. State sanctions and disabilities have been imposed upon these groups whether or not individual members have committed discrete offenses against the law. For an understanding of the reaches of political crime it is important not to confuse one phenomenon, the punishment of individual violations of laws, with the other, the oppression of peoples whose allegiance to the status quo is suspect. While there is a certain interrelationship in a causal sense between actors against the regime and dissatisfied groups who may precipitate such actions, the two are different phenomena. Important items on the agenda of research and analysis in the new arena of political criminality are the connections and disconnections between these distinct manifestations of political crime.

Finally, some of the materials in this collection document the uses of criminal and other state sanctions in upholding certain widely (but not universally) shared principles, ideals, or even biases that might be challenged in the nation's social and economic evolutionary process. The resort to criminal and noncriminal sanctions for the suppression of labor organizations and strikes, the preservation of abolition of slavery and racial discrimination, the prohibition or permission of abortions, illustrate the practice of recruiting the state as arbiter of intracommunity value conflicts. Unlike the earlier classifications, these materials do not deal directly with the issues of allegiance. Instead, they reflect political and legal structures that permit certain groups or interests to utilize the compulsory and sanctioning power of the state to bear upon groups not sharing their particular interests or practices. The documents reflecting the struggles of labor and the civil rights movement fall within this category.

## Rebels, Reformers, Madmen, and Renegades

The study of political criminality in large measure brings together the investigation of two unorthodoxies—unorthodox politics and unorthodox crimes. To students of politics, the political offender is one who deviates from the orthodox or authorized political procedures in order to secure his ends. Since legitimate means of political action have varied throughout the history of the United States, a deviant is a person who resorts to political methods beyond those recognized by the positive law at any given period of time. A political criminal of one period or place therefore may not constitute an offender at another time or location. Yet despite this definitional relativism, the existing authorities continue to prevent and punish criminally any such political unorthodoxy and deviations from the permissible.

Criminologists characterize political offenders as unorthodox criminals, for they often admit to violation of the positive law but deny guilt and culpability—professing adherence to values higher than, or transcending those served by, the law. Political criminals lay claim to the authority of justice and morality, which ordinarily is presumed to lie behind the law. In their unorthodoxy they disown the egotistic mantle of the common criminal and assert the altruistic goal of the social reformer. To counteract this heroic stance, the government often seeks deliberately to trivialize and personalize the goals and deeds of political offenders.

Because of this, we have gone beyond the official portrayal of political offenders and their offenses, as contained in legislation, administrative rulings, and judicial cases, and have sought to elucidate the motivations and present the self-images of those acting in opposition to authority. These considerations dictated the inclusion, among the more traditional historical and legal sources, of materials that reflect sociological, psychological, and philosophical perspectives.

A corollary problem is posed by the instinctive urge for either deification or vilification of political criminality and criminals. The law's failure to recognize the existence of the political offender, or to respond to his or her offer of noble motives, perversely translates into a negative comment upon the system of justice and its punishment of someone who might popularly be accepted as acting for the common good. But it is important to divorce the judgments of morality and history from the day-to-day questions posed by political criminality. Political criminals have been both heroes and villains upon the stage of politics. Thus we have George Washington, traitor to his king, and Benedict Arnold, recanting his treason and adhering once again to his sovereign lord; John Brown, leader of an armed raid upon the armory of the United States at Harpers Ferry, seeking to incite a slave rebellion, and Jefferson Davis, constitutional scholar and leader of the rebellion against the Union. There are other colorful figures in the play as well: Susan B. Anthony, confined to prison for her militant urging of women's suffrage; Eugene V. Debs, labor leader, disobedient to court injunctions and underminer of the World War I effort; Martin Luther King, Jr., leading unlawful demonstrations in Selma, Alabama; Philip Berrigan and Daniel Ellsberg, who broke the law to expose what they saw as the truth about the Vietnam War; Julius and Ethel Rosenberg, convicted of communicating atom bomb secrets to the Soviet Union; and Philip Agee, who sought to divulge the names of America's secret agents abroad. But however these figures ultimately are disposed of by the judgment of the ages, their activities at first glance meet the criteria of political crimes, although it might be said in some cases that such status is tenuous.

Resistance to "oppressive" taxes and to military conscription provided a rich source of political criminality in earlier American history, but can the modern tax protest movement or the opposition to Selective Service registration be so considered? And then there are the psychiatrically borderline assassins—John Wilkes Booth, Sirhan Sirhan, Arthur Bremer, and John Hinckley. Can their crimes be called political?

In eschewing an attempt at definitiveness, we have preferred to err on the side of inclusion rather than exclusion. Since this is not a doctrinaire thesis but an exploratory sourcebook, we urge readers to develop their own views and conclusions as to the meaning of the materials. But we believe that a thorough review will demonstrate that the concept of political crime is not without content, and that we have

cause to regret that the peculiar problems it presents have not, heretofore, been addressed in a dispassionate manner. As the nation moves ahead and encounters new challenges to the existing order, we would do well to have a firmer grasp than we currently do on the role and limits of political crime and the government's response to it.

First, admitting and then understanding our own record of political dissent, disobedience, protest, and violence also may help reshape our perception of political turmoil in other nations. We have frequently been appalled and our foreign policy thrown into imbalance by the sight of internal disruptions in other countries. Our own myth of peaceful change has obscured our vision and made us insensitive and intolerant to the complex moral as well as pragmatic issues raised by the conflict between just ends and unlawful means in a less than perfect world. A more realistic assessment of our past might aid not only in understanding internal conflicts in other places but in the shaping of a more consistent, just, and pragmatic American position in the international arena.

Two characteristics of American political dissent and criminality unambiguously emerge from these materials. First, the resort to unorthodox and extralegal political means in America may be described generally as a manifestation of a reformist rather than an insurrectionary mission. Political disorder in this country has usually been directed to modifying the use of power by government, not overthrowing it.[11] Moreover, much of our political violence, as pointed out by historian Richard Hofstadter, "has taken the form of action by one group of citizens against another group rather than by citizens against the State."[12] When governmental authority is enlisted to defend one group's interests, the strife usually changes from social or economic to political. Undoubtedly the political diffusion and the governmental decentralization of America, coupled with the notion that it is not the government's structure but its abusers that must be guarded against, have caused public dissatisfaction and political crimes to be directed not so much against "government" itself but against its "agents," its subdivisions, or individuals and groups representing some social, political, or economic "establishment" or power base.

Second, this book demonstrates the constant yet dramatic shift from rebellions, violent assemblies, and direct action to militant advocacy in the legislative halls and particularly in the courts. This may be described as a progression from militant deeds to litigiousness. The dominance of judicial cases in the second part of this volume is testimony of this trend.

Finally, the collection readily demonstrates that the ascendancy of nationalism and self-determination cannot be counted on to produce an end to political turmoil and violent fervor, in this country or elsewhere. From the warlike beginnings of Swiss independence and the American revolution to Garibaldi's and the Irish campaigns against foreign rule, and on to the contemporary struggles for national liberation, self-determination rarely has been achieved without illegal and violent means. Yet the hope that once self-determination and self-rule are attained, political continuity and change would be achieved through peaceful means has not been fulfilled in most countries. Discontented political, regional, tribal, ethnic, religious, lingual, economic, and racial factions frequently have set out to accomplish their unsatisfied claims through acts of dissent, subversion, violence, and rebellion, and the record of the present day shows no improvement.

Since they attained independence, during the post–World War II years, some two-thirds of Africa's forty-five nations have seen their regimes toppled by unlawful or extralegal means. In Latin America fourteen out of twenty-eight existing governments have come into power through means other than those constitutionally prescribed. Central America, in particular, has become the virtual powder keg of unor-

thodox political activism. Manifestations of political strife and disorder are evident, not only in Africa, Latin America, and Asia, but also among the European nations claiming long and established traditions of relatively peaceful political life and transition. Basques in Spain, Corsican zealots in France, ethnic dissidents in Yugoslavia, royalist insurgents in Albania, Scottish Nationalists in the United Kingdom, the Red Brigade in Italy, the Bader-Meinhof group in West Germany, and the IRA in Northern Ireland are a mere sampling of the diverse political activists in contemporary Europe.

Although comparisons are inherently suspect, we believe that these materials demonstrate that our experience with manifestations of political crime is not wholly unlike that of other nations. Thus it may be that careful analysis of the treatment of political offenders in foreign countries would be useful in forging a principled American response to domestic political crime. The similarity suggests also that the study of our experience might be fruitful for others, for despite our definitional myopia, our inability to achieve the Peaceable Kingdom, and our failure to solve internal problems without resort to unlawfulness and violence, the stern and severe governmental responses thereto have stayed within civilized boundaries and have never thrown this nation into a reign of terror or long-term irreversible oppression—such as occurred in revolutionary France, in the twentieth-century Soviet Union, Nazi Germany, and Fascist Italy, and in an increasing number of post–World War II regimes worldwide.

---

1. Virginius Dabney, *Virginia: The New Dominion* (Garden City, N.Y.: Doubleday, 1971), 1-68.

2. Charles Tilly, "Collective Violence in European Perspective," in National Commission on the Causes and Prevention of Violence, vol. 1, *Violence in America: Historical and Comparative Perspectives* (Washington, D.C.: U.S. Government Printing Office, 1969), 5.

3. Hugh Davis Graham and Ted Robert Gurr, "Conclusion," in vol. 2, *Violence in America*, 624. *See* n. 2, above.

4. Isaiah 65:25.

5. Rollo May, *Power and Innocence: A Search for the Sources of Violence* (New York: Norton, 1972), 51.

6. Richard E. Rubenstein, *Rebels in Eden: Mass*

*Political Violence in the United States* (Boston: Little, Brown, 1970), 2.

7. Id., 5.

8. Id., 7.

9. Richard Maxwell Brown, "Historical Patterns in Violence in America," in vol. 1, *Violence in America*, 35. *See* n. 2, above.

10. Brendan Behan, *Borstal Boy* (New York: Knopf, 1959), 271.

11. National Advisory Committee on Criminal Justice Standards and Goals, *Disorders and Terrorism* (Washington, D.C.: U.S. Government Printing Office, 1977), 1.

12. Richard Hofstadter and Michael Wallace, eds., *American Violence: A Documentary History* (New York: Vintage Books, 1971), 10.

# Note to Readers and Users

This comprehensive collection offers a historical survey of political criminality (including rebellion and terrorism) and of governmental responses to it in America. The comprehensive approach—which brings together instances of political, social, economic, racial, gender, and religious unrest—is designed to permit discussion and analysis of the common issues raised by various types and forms of political crime.

The chapters as well as the documents in this sourcebook have been organized in chronological order. Only the last three chapters (Chap. 11, "Contemporary Political Conflicts and Domestic Security," Chap. 12, "International Terrorism and Human Rights," and Chap. 13, "Towards the Third Millennium") depart from this pattern. To permit special attention to a number of major contemporary issues (such as government secrecy and related questions of domestic security, or topics raised by the growth of international political criminality), these two chapters have been set apart and include documents that otherwise would have been treated in previous chapters.

Although the ordering of the material is chronological, special efforts were made by the editors to permit the volume's ready utilization by those primarily or exclusively interested in specific issues relating to political crime. To simplify the task of the reader and user who seeks information about a particular topic (e.g., the status of Native Americans or the requirement of loyalty oaths), a subject-matter guide (Concordance), is supplied in addition to the more traditional Proper Name Index and the Table of Cases at the back of the volume. The Concordance is a compilation of major concepts and subjects, each followed by a list of documents (designated by number). For example, one interested in civil disobedience could find all the documents treating the subject listed under that heading. In addition, each document is likely to be listed under more than one heading. A document dealing with the status of blacks, for instance, might appear both under "Blacks, Slavery, and Civil Rights" and "Advocacy of Unlawful Acts or Disobedience to Law." The Concordance headings, moreover, seek to bring together many related subjects. For example, executive clemency is treated under the heading "Amnesty, Pardon, and Clemency." Cross-references are provided for the user's convenience.

## Abridgment

Most of the documents have been abridged. Asterisks indicate deletions of one or more paragraphs—or, in some instances, several pages. The editors sought in these abridgments to maintain the historical flavor of the original writings. Nevertheless, since the goal of this collection has been to focus the reader's attention on matters relating to political dissent and disorder, material extraneous to these ends was deleted.

## Legal Materials—Cases and Statutes

Because the in-text citations typically found in legal documents interfere with the flow of the material and are of limited interest in the context of this collection, we have omitted most of them. We have kept only those that make it easier for the reader to refer to another document in this book and some to relevant materials that we have had to omit. We have similarly deleted most footnotes to the texts. Interested readers may find the fully cited original texts in any law library by utilizing the references or citations given for the document in the Table of Cases.

Most of the cases included are from decisions of the Supreme Court of the United States. These are compiled in the United States Reports and are cited as "U.S." The first number in the citation is the volume, the second number is the page number, and the year of the decision is in parentheses. For example, *Adler v. Board of Education*, 342 U.S. 485 (1952), denotes that the named opinion may be found in the 342d volume of the United States Reports at page 485, and that the case was decided in 1952.

Citations to cases decided by other courts follow the same format of volume, law reporter system, page, and date. In addition to the United States Reporter we have included cases from The Federal Reporter (F.), The Federal Reporter, Second Series (F.2d), The Federal Supplement (F. Supp.), Federal Cases (F. Cas.), and various state reporters, the identity of which is obvious from the abbreviations (Mass., N.H., Va., Ill., Ala., etc.). The second citation for state cases refers to the West regional reporter system—for example, N.E. denotes Northeastern; So., Southern. State cases are from that state's highest court unless otherwise noted.

Citations to the federal reporters include within parentheses the level and territorial jurisdiction of the court rendering the decision. For example, *McSurley v. Ratliff*, 282 F. Supp. 848 (E.D. Ken. 1967) advises, in addition to the location and year of the case, that it was decided by a U.S. district (or trial) court in the Eastern District of Kentucky. *Levy v. Parker*, 478 F.2d 772 (3d Cir. 1973) designates a decision by the United States Court of Appeals for the Third Circuit.

Most of the statutes included are enactments of the United States Congress. We have referenced them to the Statutes at Large (Stat.), the original chronological compilation of all Acts of Congress. Although some of the federal laws in the collection subsequently appeared in the compiled United States Code, we have viewed the original reference as preferable for historical accuracy and research purposes. As with the case citations, the number preceding the "Stat." reference is the volume, and the number following is the page. With the more modern statutes we have parenthetically indicated the current United States Code Sections. The date appears parenthetically. The treatment of state statutory material follows this system.

## Internet Documents

Chapter 13 of this book contains several documents culled from the Internet. Given the ephemeral nature of the medium, the reader is advised that the addresses given for these works may not be valid when this book goes to print. This is regrettable, albeit unavoidable, and it is recommended that the reader use any of the various search engines available to find these documents in their new locations.

## Format, Variant Spellings, Errors, Sources

Certain aspects of diverse formats occurring in the collected documents have been harmonized by the editors (e.g., the styling of salutations and closings in letters, internal headings). Variant and archaic spellings in the earlier documents of the colonial and national periods have been retained, with either a [*sic*] or a bracketed correction if considered necessary. Punctuation was not standardized. Obvious typographical errors in the original documents were corrected without specific notation. The editors have attempted to provide citations to modern sources of material, when available, to assist the interested reader.

# The Tree of Liberty

CHAPTER 1

# The Colonial Heritage

1352-1750

NO sooner did the colonists set out for the shores of the Promised Land in search of liberty than they found it necessary to delineate the boundaries between freedom and authority.

This first set of materials presents some of the organic documents of the English colonial period in America. These fall into two basic categories. The first traces the bases of the assertion of European authority in North America. The king's colonists were given the legal and moral authority to conquer the land and to subjugate all native inhabitants. The Crown's representatives, whether styled as companies under a royal charter or as lords of a proprietary grant, were accorded full authority in the new lands, to be breached only upon pain of the penalty for treason—death and attainder. Secondly, the colonists themselves, in the exercise of considerable self-government and often under royal urging, formed law-making associations of their own to manage their internal and day-to-day affairs.

Ultimate allegiance was always stoutly sworn to the king, but often the more immediate concerns of the colonists were at odds with those of the overseas sovereign. Several of the documents relate to the clashes between the economic interests of the overlords and the survival problem faced by the colonists. The rash of uprisings in Virginia over the colonial governor's abuse and neglect provided the first example of the harsh methods used by the government in America to deal with popular unrest.

The next focus of this chapter is on the use of the law to define the relations among the different ethnic and religious groups newly constituting the population of the eastern seaboard of North America. The religious minorities that founded some colonies erected barriers of religious intolerance of their own. Additionally, the tensions between the Native Americans and the English erupted into open warfare at various points, prompting John Smith to conclude that there was full justification to pursue a policy of extermination toward the Native Americans. Other materials, nevertheless, demonstrate a more congenial, conciliatory, and respectful political attitude toward the aboriginal populations. William Penn's letter and the laws of certain colonies reflected a respect for their right to maintain their self-governing societies. Virginia, in contrast, presumed a more intrusive authority.

Effort was made everywhere, however, to maintain the segregation of the Native American and white populations by imposing burdens, punishments, and restraints upon Native Americans inhabiting the areas of white settlement. At the same time efforts were made to preserve aboriginal lands from unauthorized encroachment. When it became clear the local Native American societies had been weakened, the colonists enacted other legislation exercising paternalistic and quasi-assimilative authority over the remaining communities and individuals. Nevertheless, the strict line between white and Native American remained. Indeed, the law frequently classified the Native Americans together with that other unfortunate race of American history—African blacks.

Race relations have from our earliest times been the object of extensive legislative attention in America's North as well as South. It was extremely important to white society that the relationship between the "colored peoples" and whites be clearly delineated and subject to strict regulation. Detailed laws were enacted to make sure the social interaction between these peoples was highly structured and formalized. The divisions, while ostensibly based on the need to regulate slaves, swept within this stricture all men and women of color—free as well as enslaved. From these beginnings flowed the race wars and riots of our later history, as well as the oppressive use of the law against emerging social and economic groups considered dangerous by the majority.

We have focused on documents defining the crime of treason and recording its use in these early times. It should be noted that this most heinous of crimes was often invoked to assert the righteousness of an interest the government sought to advance or protect rather than merely to guard the safety of government itself. It also should be noted how quickly the appellations "traitor" and "treason" were abandoned when the government perceived the threat to have subsided. Special attention also should be paid to the procedural requirements accompanying this offense—demonstrating awareness of the potential for abuse contained in the accusation of treason, were it to be used against political opponents. The early use of the military in maintaining political order is documented, as well as the traditional American concern regarding the injection of the military into the country's social and political mainstream.

The materials in this section finally expose the roots of the greatest American rebellion and political criminality. Throughout the earlier period God and the Gospels supplied the main foundations for judging the righteousness and accepting the authority of political governance in the colonies. So, too, did divine authority provide much of the justification for contradicting the commands of law. But new, secular standards for judging political authority were increasingly being advanced before the Revolution. The documents in the chapter reflect the intensity of the colonial commitment to righteousness: the remonstrance against practices approved by law but condemned by the rules of a higher morality; the assertion of a duty of disobedience to a government that perpetuates injustice; the use of the press to communicate the odiousness of governmental practices; civil disobedience in the name of religious and political liberty; and riot and rebellion to compel a distant and unheeding government to attend to the needs of the people. These are practices and techniques that we will see repeated and refined throughout future chapters—and so shall we see the corresponding efforts of government to curtail them through the use of law.

---

## 1 King Edward III's Treason Law (1352)

Arriving at the shores of the "New Jerusalem"—an epithet sometimes applied to the English colonies of America—the settlers nevertheless found themselves still bound to the legal commands of the mother country, England. Uppermost among these was the law of treason, which articulated the political loyalty of all the Crown's subjects, whether settled in England or colonizing the new realms, to their sovereign.

King Edward III's statute of 1352—being "A declaration [upon] which offenses shall be adjudged Treason"—was the first codification of the English treason law. The law of treason always stood in the center of the broad legal effort to protect the Crown and the country against external as well as internal enemies. Prior to the statute of 1352, the English courts applied vague and overly broad criteria to this offense, making even mere speech, such as criticism and ridicule of the Crown, tantamount to treason. In the struggle to consolidate royal authority and to wrest political power from the nobility, the Crown frequently resorted to the elastic treason laws as an oppressive weapon against its opponents. Treason was not only a capital offense but also punishable by the forfeiture of the offender's estate to the king.

Intended to reform the abuses of the treason law, the 1352 statute was passed at a time when Edward III was particularly vulnerable. Taking advantage of the king's weakness—the result of financial overextension caused by the support of foreign wars, harlots, and court pageantry—Parliament forced a reform of the treason law. The new statute reflected the close affinity between the state and the sovereign—punishing conduct against the realm as well as against the king's kin. But the effort to curtail the overreach of the treason law was short-lived. The king's courts soon resorted to their old practices of unduly broadening the law through judicial interpretation. Yet the restraining principles of the English statute remained as a model for America's own eventual treason law. Phrases from Edward's law (such as levying war or "adhering" to the enemies, giving them "aid and comfort") were incorporated into the United States Constitution (Art. III, Sec. 3) and have continued in American legal and political language for over three hundred years.

### ☆1 A Declaration Which Offenses Shall Be Adjudged Treason (23 Edward III [1352])

Reprinted in C. Stephenson and F. Marcham, eds., *Sources of English Constitutional History* (New York: Harper & Bros., 1937), 227.

ITEM, Whereas divers Opinions have been before this Time in what Case Treason shall be said, and in what not; (2) the King, at the Request of the Lords and of the Commons, hath made a Declaration in the Manner as hereafter followeth; that is to say, When a Man doth compass or imagine the Death of our Lord the King, or of our Lady his Queen, or of their eldest Son and Heir; (3) or if a Man do violate the King's Companion, or the King's eldest Daughter unmarried, or the Wife of the King's eldest Son and Heir; (4) of if a Man do levy War against our Lord the King in his Realm, or be adherent to the King's Enemies in his Realm, giving to them Aid and Comfort in the Realm, or elsewhere, and thereof be probably attainted of open Deed by the People of their Condition. (5) And if a Man counterfeit the King's Great or

Privy Seal, or his Money; (6) and if a Man bring false Money into this Realm, counterfeit to the Money of *England*, as the Money called *Lushburgh*, or other like to the said Money of England, knowing the Money to be false, to merchandise or make Payment in Deceit of our said Lord the King and of his People; (7) and if a Man flee the Chancellor, Treasurer, or the King's Justices of the one Bench or the other, Justices in Evre, or Justices of Assise, and all other Justices assigned to hear and determine, being in their Places, doing their Offices. (8) And it is to be understood, that in the Cases above rehearsed, that ought to be judged Treason which extends to our Lord the King, and his Royal Majesty: (9) And of such Treason the Forfeiture of the Escheats pertaineth to our Sovereign Lord, as well of the Lands and Tenements holden of other, as of himself. (10) And moreover there is another Manner of Treason, that is to say, when a Servant slayeth his Master, or a Wife her Husband, or when a Man Secular or Religious slayeth his Prelate, to whom he oweth Faith and Obedience; (11) and of such Treason the Escheats ought to pertain to every Lord of his own Fee. (12) And because that many other like Cases of Treason may happen in Time to come, which a Man cannot think nor declare at this present Time; it is accorded, That if any other Case, supposed Treason, which is not above specified, doth happen before any Justices, the Justices shall tarry without any going to Judgment of the Treason, till the Cause be shewed and declared before the King and his Parliament, whether it ought to be judged Treason or other Felony. (13) And if percase any Man of this Realm ride armed covertly or secretly with Men of Arms against any other, to slay him, or rob him, or take him, or retain him till he hath made Fine or Ransom for to have his Deliverance, it is not the Mind of the King nor his Council, that in such Case it shall be judged Treason, but shall be judged Felony or Trespass, according to the Laws of the Land of old Time used, and according as the Case requireth.

*     *     *

## 2 Authority to Subjugate America's Natives (1496)

On March 5, 1496, Henry VII, King of England, France, and Ireland, granted letters patent to Giovanni Caboto, a native of Genoa, who set sail from Bristol to find lands hitherto unknown to the Christians of Europe. These letters authorized Caboto, better known by his anglicized name, John Cabot, to discover the provinces "of the heathens and infidels," subdue them, and take possession of all towns and lands on behalf of the Crown. Overlooking the wishes as well as the potential opposition of the native inhabitants of the unexplored lands, the charter decreed the extension of English sovereignty in the New World (to be administered by Cabot and his company) to English settlers and Native Americans alike. It is against the background of this assertion of authority that the Native American rebellions and wars of the ensuing years must be viewed.

## ☆2 Letters Patent of Henry VII to John Cabot

Reprinted in F. Thorpe, ed., *Federal and State Constitutions* (Washington, D.C.: U.S. Government Printing Office, 1909), 1:46–47.

*The Letters patents of King Henry the seuenth granted vnto Iohn Cabot and his three sonnes, Lewis, Sebastian, and Sancius for the discouerie of new and vnknowen lands.*

Henry, by the grace of God, king of England and France, and lord of Ireland, to all to whom these presents shall come, Greeting.

Be it knowen that we haue giuen and granted, and by these presents do giue and grant for vs and our heires, to our welbeloued Iohn Cabot citizen of Venice, to Lewis, Sebastian, and Santius, sonnes of the sayd Iohn, and to the heires of them, and euery of them, and their deputies, full and free authority, leaue, and power to saile to all parts, countreys, and seas of the East, of the West, and of the North, vnder our banners and ensignes, with fiue ships of what burthen or quantity soeuer they be, and as many mariners or men as they will haue with them in the sayd ships, vpon their owne proper costs and charges, to seeke out, discouer, and finde whatsoeuer isles, countreys, regions or prouinces of the heathen and infidels whatsoeuer they be, and in what part of the world soeuer they be, which before this time haue bene vnknowen to all Christians: we haue granted to them, and also to euery of them, the heires of them, and euery of them, and their deputies, and haue giuen them licence to set vp our banners and ensignes in euery village, towne, castle, isle, or maine land of them newly found. And that the aforesayd Iohn and his sonnes, or their heires and assignes may subdue, occupy and possesse all such townes, cities, castles and isles of them found, which they can subdue, occupy and possesse, as our vassals, and lieutenants, getting vnto vs the rule, title, and iurisdiction of the same villages, townes, castles, & firme land so found. Yet so that the aforesayd Iohn, and his sonnes and heires, and their deputies, be holden and bounden of all the fruits, profits, gaines, and commodities growing of such nauigation, for euery their voyage, as often as they shall arriue at our port of Bristoll (at which port they shall be bound and holden onely to arriue) all manner of necessary costs and charges by them made, being deducted, to pay vnto vs in wares or money the fift part of the capitall gaine so gotten. We giuing and granting vnto them and to their heires and deputies, that they shall be free from all paying of customes of all and singular such merchandize as they shall bring with them from those places so newlie found.

And moreouer, we haue given and granted to them, their heires and deputies, that all the firme lands, isles, villages, townes, castles and places whatsoeuer they be that they shall chance to finde, may not of any other of our subjects be frequented or visited without the licence of the foresayd Iohn and his sonnes, and their deputies, vnder payne of forfeiture as well of their ships as of all and singular goods of all them that shall presume to saile to those places so found. Willing, and most straightly commanding all and singular our subjects as well on land as on sea, appointed officers, to giue good assistance to the aforesaid Iohn, and his sonnes and deputies, and that as well in arming and furnishing their ships or vessels, as in prouision of quietnesse, and in buying of victuals for their money, and all other things by them to be prouided necessary for the sayd nauigation, they do giue them all their help and favour. In Witnesse whereof we have caused to be made these our letters of patents. Witnesse our selfe at Westminster, the fifth day of March, in the eleventh yeere of our reigne.

# 3 "all Liberties, Franchises, and Immunities" (1606)

The actual English colonization of America did not commence until the end of the sixteenth century. In 1584, Sir Walter Raleigh received a royal charter pursuant to which he organized five expeditions to the New World. His short-lived colony on Roanoke Island, Virginia (now part of North Carolina), was the first to demonstrate the practicability of establishing permanent English settlements in America.

In 1606, King James I granted a charter to the Virginia Company, and 120 settlers planted the first permanent English colony in America—at Jamestown on May 14, 1607. The royal charter inaugurated the first English council in North America, which was nevertheless under the supervision of a similar council resident in England. By extending to all settlers, and their children born in the colony all the rights they would enjoy had they been natives and residents of England, the king firmly asserted for the populations of the New World the primacy of the Crown and the allegiance owed to it. Further authority, in the name of evangelism, was granted to the settlers to bring the Indian populations into "civility and . . . settled [English] government."

# ☆3 First Charter of Virginia (April 10, 1606)

Reprinted in B. P. Poore, ed., *The Federal and State Constitutions, Colonial Charters, and Other Organic Laws of the United States* (Washington, D.C.: U.S. Government Printing Office, 1877), pt. 2:1889 ff.

I, JAMES, by the Grace of God, King of England, Scotland, France, and Ireland, Defender of the Faith, &c. WHEREAS our loving and well-disposed Subjects, Sir Thomas Gates, and Sir George Somers, Knights, Richard Hackluit, Clerk, Prebendary of Westminster, and Edward-Maria Wingfield, Thomas Hanham, and Ralegh Gilbert, Esqrs. William Parker, and George Popham, Gentlemen, and divers others of our loving Subjects, have been humble Suitors unto us, that We would vouchsafe unto them our Licence, to make Habitation, Plantation, and to deduce a Colony of sundry of our People into that Part of America, commonly called VIRGINIA, and other Parts and Territories in America, either appertaining unto us, or which are not now actually possessed by any Christian Prince of People, situate, lying, and being all along the Sea Coasts, between four and thirty Degrees of Northerly Latitude from the Equinoctial Line, and five and forty Degrees of the same Latitude, and in the main Land between the same four and thirty and five and forty, and the Islands thereunto adjacent, or within one hundred Miles of the Coast thereof;

And to that End, and for the more speedy Accomplishment of their said intended Plantation and Habitation there, are desirous to divide themselves into two several Colonies and Companies; The one consisting of certain Knights, Gentlemen, Merchants, and other Adventurers, of our City of London and elsewhere, which are, and from time to time shall be, joined unto them, which do desire to begin their Plantation and Habitation in some fit and convenient Place, between four and thirty and one and forty Degrees of the said Latitude, alongst the Coasts of Virginia and Coasts of America aforesaid; And the other consisting of sundry Knights, Gentlemen, Merchants, and other Adventurers, of our Cities of Bristol and Exeter, and of our Town of Plimouth, and of other Places, which do join themselves unto that Colony, which do desire to begin their Plantation and Habitation in some fit and convenient Place, between eight and thirty Degrees and five and forty Degrees of the said Latitude, all alongst the said Coast of Virginia and America, as that Coast lyeth:

We, greatly commending, and graciously accepting of, their Desires for the Furtherance of so noble a Work, which may, by the Providence of Almighty God, hereafter tend to the Glory of his Divine Majesty, in propagating of Christian Religion to such People, as yet live in Darkness and miserable Ignorance of the true Knowledge and Worship of God, and may in time bring the Infidels and Savages, living in those Parts, to human Civility, and to a settled and quiet Government; Do, by these our Letters Patents, graciously accept of, and agree to, their humble and well-intended Desires;

AND do therefore, for US, our Heirs, and SUCCESSORS, GRANT and agree, that the said Sir Thomas Gates, Sir George Somers, Richard Hackluit, and Edward-Maria Wingfield, Adventurers of and for our City of London, and all such others, as are, or shall be, joined unto them of that Colony, shall be called the first Colony....

AND we do likewise ... GRANT and agree, that the said Thomas Hanham, and Ralegh Gilbert, William Parker, and George Popham, and all others of the Town of Plimouth in the County of Devon, or elsewhere, which are, or shall be, joined unto them of that Colony, shall be called the second Colony....

*      *      *

AND we do also ordain ... that each of the said Colonies shall have a Council, which shall govern and order all Matters and Causes, which shall arise, grow, or happen, to or within the same several Colonies, according to such Laws, Ordinances, and Instructions, as shall be, in that behalf, given and signed with Our Hand or Sign Manual, and pass under the Privy Seal of our Realm of England; Each of which Councils shall consist of thirteen Persons, to be ordained, made, and removed, from time to time, according as shall be directed and comprised in the same instructions....

AND that also there shall be a Council established here in England, which shall, in like Manner, consist of thirteen Persons, to be, for that Purpose, appointed by Us, ... which shall be called our Council of Virginia; And shall, from time to time, have the superior Managing and Direction, only of and for all Matters, that shall or may concern the Government, as well of the said several Colonies, as of and for any other Part or Place, within the aforesaid Precincts....

AND moreover, we do GRANT that the said several Councils, of and for the said several Colonies, shall and lawfully may, by Virtue hereof, from time to time, without any Interruption of Us ..., give and take Order, to dig, mine, and search for all Manner of Mines of Gold, Silver, and Copper, as well within any part of their said several Colonies, as for the said main Lands on the Backside of the same Colonies ... YIELDING therefore, to Us ... the fifth Part only of all the same Gold and Silver, and the fifteenth Part of all the same Copper, so to be gotten or had....

Giving and granting, by these Presents, unto the said Sir Thomas Gates ... and their Associates of the said first Colony, and unto the said Thomas Hanham ... and their Associates of the said second Colony ... Power and Authority to take and surprise, by all Ways and Means whatsoever, all and every Person and Persons, with their Ships, Vessels, Goods and other Furniture, which shall be found trafficking, into any Harbour or Harbours, Creek or Creeks, or Place, within the Limits or Precincts of the said several Colonies and Plantations, not being of the same Colony, until such time, as they, being of any Realms or Dominions under our Obedience, shall pay, or agree to pay, to the Hands of the Treasurer of that Colony, within whose Limits and Precincts they shall so traffick, two and a half upon every Hundred, of any thing, so by them trafficked, bought, or sold; And being Strangers, and not Subjects under our Obeysance, until they shall pay five upon every Hundred, of such Wares and Merchandises, as they shall traffick, buy, or sell, within the Precincts of the said several Colonies, wherein they shall so traffick, buy, or sell as aforesaid....

Also we do ... DECLARE ... that all and every the Persons, being our Subjects, which shall dwell and inhabit within every or any of the said several Colonies and Plantations, and every of their children, which shall happen to be born within any of the Limits and Precincts of the said several Colonies and Plantations, shall HAVE and enjoy all Liberties, Franchises, and Immunities, within any of our other Dominions, to all Intents and Purposes, as if they had been abiding and born, within this our Realm of England, or any other of our said Dominions....

*      *      *

## 4 "combine ourselves together into a civil Body Politick" (1620)

A group of London and Yorkshire separatists, religious dissenters who had exiled themselves to Amsterdam and Leyden to escape persecution, applied to the Virginia Company for a patent to immigrate to the New World. To assure the English king of their loyalty and docility, they drafted the Leyden Agreement in 1618:

> The King's Majesty wee acknowledge for Spreame Governer in his Dominion in all causes and over al parsons, and ye none maye decklyne or apeale from his authority or judgement in any cause whatsoever, but y in all thinges obedience is dewe unto him, ether active, if ye thing commanded be not agaynst God's woord, or passive yf itt bee....

Finally securing a patent for a private plantation, the Leyden Pilgrims, reinforced by some seventy persons from London, sailed from Plymouth, England in September 1620. Since some of the London recruits, described as an "undesirable lot," rebelled against the authority of the Virginia Company and threatened to "use their owne libertie," the Pilgrim leaders drew up the Mayflower Compact. Although ultimate allegiance was sworn to the king, the document provided for the formation of a governing unit based on mutual consent of the signatories, to which all would submit. The compact not only advanced for the first time the concept of self-determination in the New World but provided an alternative allegiance to that of the overseas sovereign—one that was more likely to respond to the needs and grievances of the governed.

## ☆ 4 The Mayflower Compact
(November 11, 1620)

Reprinted in B. P. Poore, ed., *The Federal and State Constitutions, Colonial Charters, and Other Organic Laws of the United States* (Washington, D.C.: U.S. Government Printing Office, 1877), pt. 1:931.

IN The Name of God, Amen. We, whose names are underwritten, the Loyal Subjects of our dread Sovereign Lord King James, by the Grace of God, of Great Britain, France, and Ireland, King, Defender of the Faith, &c. Having undertaken for the Glory of God, and Advancement of the Christian Faith, and the Honour of our King and Country, a Voyage to plant the first colony in the northern Parts of Virginia; Do by these Presents, solemnly and mutually in the Presence of God and one another, covenant and combine ourselves together into a civil Body Politick, for our better Ordering and Preservation, and Furtherance of the Ends aforesaid; And by Virtue hereof do enact, constitute, and frame, such just and equal Laws, Ordinances, Acts, Constitutions, and Offices, from time to time, as shall be thought most meet and convenient for the general Good of the Colony; unto which we promise all due Submission and Obedience. In WITNESS whereof we have hereunto subscribed our names at Cape Cod the eleventh of November, in the Reign of our Sovereign Lord King James of England, France, and Ireland, the eighteenth and of Scotland, the fifty-fourth. Anno Domini, 1620.

| | |
|---|---|
| MR. JOHN CARVER | JOSES FLETCHER |
| MR. WILLIAM BRADFORD | JOHN GOODMAN |
| MR. EDWARD WINSLOW | MR. SAMUEL FULLER |
| MR. WILLIAM BREWSTER | MR. CHRISTOPHER MARTIN |
| ISAAC ALLERTON | MR. WILLIAM MULLINS |
| MILES STANDISH | MR. WILLIAM WHITE |
| JOHN ALDEN | MR. RICHARD WARREN |
| JOHN TURNER | JOHN HOWLAND |
| FRANCIS EATON | MR. STEPHEN HOPKINS |
| JAMES CHILTON | DIGERY PRIEST |
| JOHN CRAXTON | THOMAS WILLIAMS |
| JOHN BILLINGTON | GILBERT WINSLOW |

| | |
|---|---|
| EDMUND MARGESSON | JOHN RIDGATE |
| PETER BROWN | EDWARD FULLER |
| RICHARD BITTERIDGE | RICHARD CLARK |
| GEORGE SOULE | RICHARD GARDINER |
| EDWARD TILLY | MR. JOHN ALLERTON |
| JOHN TILLY | THOMAS ENGLISH |
| FRANCIS COOKE | EDWARD DOTEN |
| THOMAS ROGERS | EDWARD LIESTER |
| THOMAS TINKER | |

## 5 We Now Have Just Cause to Destroy Them by All Means (1622)

Seeking in the New World a haven from England's religious, economic, and political oppressions, the settlers did not arrive at a continent barren of populations. A wide range of Native American tribes in various stages of economic, social, and political development inhabited areas throughout most of North America. The Native Americans never were able to articulate effectively or organize their political opposition to the invasion of their lands by alien colonizers, but resistance to assertions of English sovereignty nevertheless was manifested from time to time in acts of violence, which the settlers conceived to be further evidence of the "brutishness" of these "beasts." The apparent cause of the 1622 massacre of 347 settlers in Virginia, recorded by Captain John Smith, describing himself as President of Virginia and Admiral of New England, was the killing of a Native American who resisted arrest and trial for the murder of an Englishman. The uprisings provided the moral justification for the English to oust the Native Americans from their lands.

## ☆ 5 The Massacre upon the Two and Twentieth of March

Reprinted in E. Arber, *Travels and Works of Captain John Smith* (New York: Burt Franklin, 1910), pt. 2:572-79.

THE Prologue to this Tragedy, is supposed was occasioned by *Nemattanow*, otherwise called *Iack of the Feather*, because hee commonly was most strangely adorned with them; and for his courage and policy, was accounted amongst the Saluages their chiefe Captaine, and immortall from any hurt could bee done him by the *English*. This Captaine comming to one *Morgans* house [*in March* 1622], knowing he had many commodities that hee desired, perswaded *Morgan* to goe with him to *Pamau[n]ke* to trucke, but the Saluage murdered him by the way; and after two or three daies returned againe to *Morgans* house, where he found two youths his Seruants, who asked for their Master: *Iack* replied directly he was dead; the Boyes suspecting as it was, by seeing him weare his Cap, would haue had him to Master

*Thorp:* But *Iack* so moued their patience, they shot him; so he fell to the ground, [they] put him in a Boat to haue him before the Gouernor, then seuen or eight miles from them. But by the way *Iack* finding the pangs of death vpon him, desired of the Boyes two things: the one was, that they would not make it knowne hee was slaine with a bullet; the other, to bury him amongst the *English.*

At the losse of this Saluage, *Opechankanough* much grieued and repined, with great threats of reuenge; but the *English* returned him such terrible answers, that he cunningly dissembled his intent, with the greatest signes he could of loue and peace: yet within fourteene daies after he acted what followeth.

Sir *Francis Wyat* at his arriuall [*Oct.* 1621] was aduertised, he found the Countrey setled in such a firme peace, as most men there thought sure and vnuiolable, not onely in regard of their promises, but of a necessitie. The poore weake Saluages being euery way bettered by vs, and safely sheltred and defended, whereby wee might freely follow our businesse: and such was the conceit of this conceited peace, as that there was seldome or neuer a sword, and seldomer a peece [used], except for a Deere or Fowle; by which assurances the most plantations were placed straglingly and scatteringly, as a choice veine of rich ground inuited them, and further from neighbours the better. Their houses [were] generally open to the Saluages, who were alwaies friendly fed at their tables, and lodged in their bed-chambers; which made the way plaine to effect their intents, and the conuersion of the Saluages as they supposed.

Hauing occasion to send to *Opechankanough* about the middle of March, hee vsed the Messenger well, and told him he held the peace so firme, the sky should fall or he dissolued it; yet such was the treachery of those people, when they had contriued our destruction, euen but two daies before the massacre, they guided our men with much kindnesse thorow the woods, and one *Browne* that liued among them to learne the language, they sent home to his Master. Yea, they borrowed our Boats to transport themselues ouer the Riuer, to consult on the deuillish murder that insued, and of our vtter extirpation, which God of his mercy (by the meanes of one of themselues conuerted to Christianitie) preuented; and as well on the Friday morning that fatall day, being the two and twentieth of March [1622], as also in the euening before, as at other times they came vnarmed into our houses, with Deere, Turkies, Fish, Fruits, and other prouisions to sell vs: yea in some places sat downe at breakfast with our people, whom immediatly with their owne tooles they slew most barbarously, not sparing either age or sex, man woman or childe; so sudden in their execution, that few or none discerned the weapon or blow that brought them to destruction. In which manner also

they slew many of our people at seuerall works in the fields, well knowing in what places and quarters each of our men were, in regard of their familiaritie with vs, for the effecting that great master-peece of worke their conuersion: and by this meanes fell that fatall morning vnder the bloudy and barbarous hands of that perfidious and inhumane people, three hundred forty seuen men, women and children; most[l]y by their owne weapons; and not being content with their liues, they fell againe vpon the dead bodies, making as well as they could a fresh murder, defacing, dragging, and mangling their dead carkases into many peeces, and carrying some parts away in derision, with base and brutish triumph.

Neither yet did these beasts spare those amongst the rest well knowne vnto them, from whom they had daily receiued many benefits; but spightfully also massacred them without any remorse or pitie: being in this more fell than Lions and Dragons, as Histories record, which haue preserued their Benefactors; such is the force of good deeds, though done to cruell beasts, to take humanitie vpon them, but these miscreants put on a more vnnaturall brutishnesse then beasts, as by those instances may appeare.

## 6 "to be drawn and hanged" (1630)

Less than one generation passed between the Jamestown settlement in Virginia and the first reported political trial in the colony.

Patterned after the English treason law, with its feudal origins, the colonial treason statutes and court cases similarly reflected the social stratification of the Middle Ages. Treason in England consisted not only of an act of betrayal against the country's highest sovereign (the king, his family, his seal, and his realm) but also of offenses against others in the social order — i.e., those to whom one owed feudal allegiance. Accordingly, petit treason applied when a servant slew his master; or a wife, her husband. The 1630 Virginia conviction of Matthewes not only established the colonial acceptance of petit treason but also demonstrated its gravity by the barbarity of the punishment inflicted — drawing and hanging. The Cugley conviction further reflected the period's intolerance of dissent from governmental policy or administration. The concept of a "loyal opposition" hardly had been broached in either England or the colonies, and speech critical of government officials was viewed as a grave threat to the social and political order. Repentant prodigals, however, were welcomed back.

☆ 6  Extract from the Minutes of the Judicial Proceedings of the Governor and Council of Virginia

Reprinted in W. Hening, ed., *Virginia Statutes at Large, 1619-1660* (Charlottesville: University Press of Virginia, 1969), 146.

July 13th, 1630. William Matthewes servant to Henry Booth, indicted and found guilty of petit treason, by fourteen jurors. Judgment to be drawn and hanged.

For scandalous speeches against Governor and Councell, Daniel Cugley sentenced to be pilloryd, but was forgiven.

## 7  "Subversion of our Fundamental Frame" (1636)

The 1636 laws of New Plymouth reflected the settlers' dual cultural heritage: the biblical Judaeo-Christian and the English. The crimes of idolatry and blasphemy were founded on the biblical prohibitions contained in Exodus, Deuteronomy, and Leviticus. The crime of treason incorporated the 1352 English protection for the person of the king and his estates in the New World. But the New Plymouth statute voiced a new commitment to the preservation of the established government or its "fundamental frame and constitution." Thus the form of government, in addition to the person of the sovereign and his realm, was recognized as deserving of protection by the harsh law of treason.

☆ 7  The Capital Laws of New Plimouth

Reprinted in *The Book of the General Laws of the Inhabitants of the Jurisdiction of New Plymouth* (Boston: Samuel Green, 1685), chap. 4.

It is Enacted by this Court, and the Authority thereof, That if any Person having had the knowledge of the true God, openly and manifestly, have or worship any other God but the Lord God, he shall be put to Death. Exod. 22.20. Deut. 13.6, 10.

2. If any Person within this Jurisdiction professing the True God, shall wittingly and willingly presume to Blaspheme the Holy Name of God the Father, Son, or Holy Ghost, with direct, express, presumptious, high-handed Blasphemy, either by wilful or obstinate denying of the True God, or his Creation, or Government of the World, or shall curse God the Father, Son or Holy Ghost, such Persons shall be put to Death. Levit. 24.15, 16.

3. Treason against the Person of our Soveraigne Lord the King, the Realm and Common-wealth of England, shall be punisht by Death.

4. That whosoever shall Conspire and Attempt any invasion, Insurrection, or publick Rebellion against this Jurisdiction and His Majesties Authority here established, or surprize any Town, Plantation, Fortification or Amunition therein provided for the safety thereof; or shall treacherously and profideously attempt and endeavor the Alteration and Subversion of our Fundamental Frame and Constitution of this Government, every such Person shall be put to Death.

\*        \*        \*

## 8  "to come adhere or confederate with the Indians" (1638)

The Maryland Act for Treasons reflected special colonial concerns. Unlike earlier colonies, which experimented with new, autonomous forms of government, Maryland, established by the English Crown, was a proprietorship of Sir George Calvert, Lord Baltimore. The land was divided into manors, and their "lords" had nearly feudal control over their estates.

The Maryland General Assembly passed the Treasons Act against a background of ever-increasing hostility between its citizens and those of Virginia. The rich fisheries and fertile lands of the Chesapeake region made Virginians covetous of the new colony. The fact that Maryland had been carved from land originally under the Virginia Charter did not diminish the envy, and the "Oyster Wars" resulted.

Marylanders thus were particularly sensitive to treasonous activities of the inhabitants which might adversely affect the feudal inheritance of the "Lord Proprietary." In addition to securing the feudal hierarchy in Maryland, the law also brought association with the Indians within the scope of political betrayal. The act imposed on traitors the most severe penalties known to the English law — drawing, hanging, burning, and quartering, as well as the forfeiture of lands and the corruption of the offenders' bloodline.

☆ 8  An Act for Treasons [Maryland]

Reprinted in W. Brown, ed., *Proceedings and Acts of the General Assembly of Maryland, January 1637-1638* (Baltimore: Press of Isaac Friedenwald, 1883), 70.

AN ACT FOR TREASONS

Be it Enacted By the Lord proprietarie of this Province of and with the advice and approbation of the freemen of the same  That these offences following in this act shall be adjudged offences of Treason within this Province  To Compasse or conspire the death of his Majestie the King of England or the

Queen his wife or of his son and heir or to levie warre against his Majestie or to counterfeit the Kings great or privy Seal or his coin or to come or adhere to any forreine prince or State being a professed and declared enemy of his Majesties in any practice or attempt against his said Majestie

Or to Compass conspire and cause the death of the Lord proprietarie within this Province or of his Leiutenant Generall for the time being (in the absence of the Lord Proprietarie) or to levy warre against the Lord Proprietarie or his Leiutent Generall for the time being (in absence of the Lord proprietarie) or to come adhere or confederate with the Indians of these parts or any forreing prince or Governour to the invadeing of this Province or disheriting the Lord Proprietarie of his Seignory and dominion therein And all offences of treason shall be punished by drawing hanging and quartering of a man by drawing and burning of a Woman and the offenders blood shall be corupted and the offender shall forfeit to the Lord Proprietary all his or her Lands tenements goods franchises and all that may be forfeited Provided That punishment of death shall be inflicted on a Lord of a Mannour by beheading This Act to Continue to the end of the next Generall Assembly.

# 9 The Memory of Charles I in Virginia (1649)

The laws of the remote American colonies frequently reflected the political turmoil and wars of the mother country. At the commencement of the conflict between Charles I and the Parliamentarians under Cromwell, the Virginians asserted their loyalty to the Crown. The Virginia Assembly voiced its concern over the trial, conviction, and execution of Charles I and the resultant disruption to the English Crown. The assembly sought not only to protect the king's memory and honor by prohibiting any "discourse or argument" in defense of the Puritan regime but also to reinforce the royal claim of Charles II (who did not ascend to the throne until 1660) and the authority of Virginia's royalist government by outlawing "false reports and malicious rumors." The arbitrary nature of political offenses is herein demonstrated. While, in England, royalists were traitors to the Cromwell regime, in Virginia, an English colony, it was treasonous to utter any words in favor of the ruling power of England. The problem became even more complex when the Puritan colonies of Connecticut and Massachusetts gave refuge to the regicides who fled England after the Restoration.

## ☆9 Act I of a Grand Assembly (Held at James City the 10th Day of October 1649)

Reprinted in W. Hening, ed., *Virginia Statutes at Large, 1619-1660* (Charlottesville: University Press of Virginia, 1969), 358-61.

WHEREAS divers out of ignorance, others out of malice, schisme and faction, in pursuance of some designe of innovation, may be presumed to prepare mens' minds and inclinations to entertain a good likeing of their contrivement, by casting blemishes of dishonour upon the late most excellent and now undoubtedly sainted king, and to those close ends vindicating and attesting the late proceedings against the said blessed King (though by so much as they may seeme to have colour of law, and forme of justice, they may be truly and really said to have the more and greater height of impudence.) And upon this foundation of asserting the cleerness and legality of the said unparalel'd treasons, perpetrated on the said King, doe build hopes and inferrences to the high dishonour of the regall estate, and in truth to the utter disinherison of his sacred Majesty that now is, and the devesting him of those rights, which the law of nature and nations and the knowne lawes of the kingdom of England have adjudged inherent to his royall line, and the law of God himselfe (if sacred writ may be soe stiled which this age doth loudly call in question) hath consecrated unto him. And as arguments easily and naturally deduced from the aforesaid cursed and destructive principles, with much indeavour, they press and perswade the power of the comission to be void and null, and all magistracy and office thereon depending to have lost their vigor and efficacy, but such means assuredly expecting advantages for the accomplishment of their lawless and tyrranous intentions,

Be it therefore declared and enacted and it is hereby enacted by Governour, Council and Burgesses of this Grand Assembly, and the authority of the same, That what person soever, whether stranger or inhabitant of this collony, after the date of this act, by reasoning, discourse or argument shall go about to defend or maintain the late traiterous proceedings against the aforesaid King of most happy memory, under any notion of law and justice, such person using reasoning, discourse or argument, or uttering any words or speeches to such purpose or effect, and being proved by competent witnes, shall be adjudged an accessory post factum, to the death of the aforesaid King, and shall be proceeded against for the same, according to the knowne lawes of England: or whoever shall go about by irreverent or scandalous words or language to blast the memory and honour of that late most pious King, (deserving ever altars and monuments in the hearts of all good men,) shall, upon conviction, suffer such censure and punishment as shall be thought fitt by the Governour and Council. And be it further enacted, That what person soever shall by words or speeches indeavour to insinuate any doubt, scruple or question of or concerning the undoubted and inherent right of his Majesty that now is to the collony of Virginia, and all other his majesties dominions and countryes as King and Supream Governour, such words and speeches shall be adjudged high treason: And it is also enacted, That what person soever, by false reports and malicious rumors shall spread abroad, among the people, any thing tending to change of government, or to the lessening of the power and authority of the Governor or government either in civill or ecclesiasticall causes (which this Assembly hath and doth declare to be full and plenarie to all intents and purposes) such persons not onely the authors of such reports and rumours, but the reporters and divulgers thereof, (unless it be done by way of legall information before a magistrate) shall be adjudged equally guilty, and shall suffer such punishment even to severity as shall be thought fitt, according to the nature and quality of the offence.

*          *          *

## 10  Popular Agitation in Virginia (1653)

The Virginians' sympathy for King Charles in his war with Parliament was shared by Sir William Berkeley, who had been Virginia's governor since 1641. In 1652, when Parliament sent a fleet to secure the royalist colony, the residents decided the wisest course was to surrender to the mission. Richard Bennett, a Puritan, was appointed governor. He and his Puritan successors continued to govern until Berkeley was restored to office in 1660. Nevertheless, the change of governors did not reduce the growing conflict between the outlying, less privileged populations and the aristocratic plantation families who controlled the House of Burgesses. Popular petitions calling for a freer land-grant system and a more popular governmental assembly chosen by all freeholders were not entertained sympathetically by the oligarchical Burgesses. The tensions that eventually erupted in the rebellion of Nathaniel Bacon were manifested initially in popular agitation followed by repressive legislation. This document prescribed a punishment for "subscription" or signing of a petition critical of the government. Disabling individuals with suspect allegiances from office holding was a common method of preserving political orthodoxy.

### ☆ 10  Laws of Virginia

Reprinted in W. Hening, ed., *Virginia Statutes at Large, 1619-1660* (Charlottesville: University Press of Virginia, 1969), 380.

WHEREAS the paper subscribed by name of the inhabitants of Northampton countie is scandalous and seditious and hath caused much disturbance in the peace and government of that county, It is therefore ordered by this present Grand Assembly, That all the subscribers of the said paper bee disabled from bearing any office in this countrey, and that Leift. Edmund Scarbrough who hath been an assistant and instrument concerneing the subscribeing of the same bee also disabled from bearing any office vntill he hath answered therevnto, and the honourable Governour & Secretarie be intreated to go over to Accomack with such assistants as the house shall think fitt, for the settlement of the peace of that countie, and punishinge delinquents.

## 11  "subversion of the frame of policy" (1656)

The colonial settlers, many of whom were fugitives from the English law of treason or its ecclesiastical counterpart, heresy, sought to create new societies. Nevertheless, they were intent on protecting the security and fundamental structure of their new governments against subversion. New Haven Colony, an offshoot of the Massachusetts settlement, reflected its foundations by relying upon the Bible as authority for its political structure. But in seeking to make every person a bulwark against rebellion, the law punished not only those actively conspiring or attempting rebellion but also those aware of the political threat who failed to report it to the authorities.

### ☆ 11  Capital Laws of New Haven

Reprinted in J. D. Cushing, ed., *The Earliest Laws of the New Haven and Connecticut Colonies, 1639-1673* (Wilmington, Del.: Michael Glazier, 1977), 19-20.

If any person shall conspire, and attempt any invasion, insurrection, or publick Rebellion against this Jurisdiction, or shall endeavour to surprize, or seize any Plantation, or Town, any Fortification, Platform, or any great Guns, provided for the defence of the Jurisdiction, or any Plantation therein; or shall treacherously and perfidiously attempt the alteration and subversion of the frame of policy, or fundamentall Government laid, and setled for this Jurisdiction, he or they shall be put to death. Num. 16. 2 Sam. 18. 2 Sam. 20. Or if any person shall consent unto any such mischievous practice, or by the space of foure and twenty houres conceale it, not giving notice thereof to some Magistrate, if there be any Magistrate in the Plantation, or place where he liveth, or if none, to some Deputy for the Jurisdiction, or to the Constable of the place, that the publick safety may be seasonably provided for, he shall be put to death, or severely punished, as the Court of Magistrates weighing all circumstances shall determine.

## 12 "rebelliously returning" (1660)

The new settlers of Massachusetts Bay and Plymouth colonies were disturbed by the intrusions of members of other dissident sects and the emergence of heresies. Although victims of persecution themselves, their reaction to any threat to their religiously orthodox government was harsh. In 1635 Roger Williams was banished for advocating liberty of conscience, supporting separation of church and state, and denouncing the practice of settling on Native American lands without payment. Ann Hutchinson was banished in 1638 for religious reasons. The settlements they subsequently founded on lands purchased from the Narragansett Indians (Hutchinson's Rhode Island settlement and Williams's Providence Plantations) were chartered specifically as a separate colony by Charles I in 1644. But expulsion and exclusion of those professing unorthodox belief persisted in the older colonies.

With the English Revolution of 1649 and the rise of Puritan power in England, members of the Society of Friends, or Quakers, became the target of persecution. They found little refuge in Puritan New England. In 1656, the first Quakers to arrive in Boston were promptly reembarked to England. That same year the General Court of Massachusetts Bay directed that Quakers be jailed after being "severly whipt." In 1658, government officials banished Quakers from Massachusetts Bay upon pain of death, and in 1660 Mary Dyer, a Quaker, was condemned to death and hanged. Three others suffered her fate. Public reaction to the executions, however, caused the repeal of the law in 1661. While expelling Quakers from their midst the General Court, nevertheless, gave haven in the colony to two of the signers of the death warrant of Charles I; they sought refuge in the colonies after the Restoration in England.

Massachusetts was not the only colony to conduct religious prosecutions. Even Maryland, Catholic and relatively liberal, reserved its religious toleration for Christians professing a belief in the Trinity—excluding Jews, Unitarians, Quakers, and other religious groups from full privileges. Conformity of religious belief was a prime requisite for full enjoyment of political and civil rights.

Only Rhode Island provided refuge for heretics and infidels. In 1659, Dutch Jews who were unwelcome in the colony of New Amsterdam (New York) migrated to Newport, where they established the first synagogue in America in 1763. Even though it had been excluded from the surrounding confederation known as the United Colonies of New England because of its refusal to yield to the hegemony of Massachusetts, Rhode Island prospered, earning its nickname, "Rogue's Island," by welcoming the exiles of the other colonies.

☆ 12 The Second Sentence of Mary Dyer

4 Mass. Ct. Rec., part 1:419 (1660), reprinted in E. Powers, *Crime and Punishment in Early Massachusetts, 1620-1692* (Boston: Beacon Press, 1966), 343.

The whole Court mett together sent for Mary Dyer, who rebelliously, after sentence of death past against hir, returned into this jurisdiction. Being come before the Court, she acknowledged hirself to be Mary Dyer, the person, & was condemned by this Court to death. Being asked what she had to say why the sentence should not be executed, she gave no other answ[r] but that she denied our lawe, came to beare witnes against it, & could not choose but come & doe as formerly. The whole Court mett together voted, that the said Mary Dyer, for hir rebelliously returning into this jurisdiction, (notwithstanding the favor of this Court towards hir,) shall be, by the marshall generall, on the first day of June, about nine of the clocke in the morning, carried to the place of execution, and according to the sentence of the Generall Court in October last, be put to death; that the secretary issue out warrant accordingly; which sentence the Governor declared to hir in open Court; & warrant issued out accordingly to Edward Michelson, marshall generall, & to Captain James Oliver, & his order, as formerly.

## 13 "illegal and clandestine purchases" (1663)

The Indian tribes were generally viewed as independent, self-governing societies. Relations between settlers and Native Americans were under the political control of the colonial governments. Rhode Island, accordingly, outlawed the purchase of Native American lands by its settlers without authorization by the General Assembly. All cession of lands by Native Americans to whites was subject to political negotiation and supervision.

☆ 13 Rhode Island Indian Land Purchase Law

Reprinted in J. D. Cushing, ed., *Rhode Island Colony Laws, 1647-1719* (Wilmington, Del.: Michael Glazier, 1977), 139.

Made and Past by the General Assembly . . . Begun . . . the first day of March 1662. . . .

*          *          *

AN ACT FOR THE PREVENTING OF ILLEGAL AND
CLANDESTINE PURCHASES OF THE NATIVE
INDIANS IN THIS COLONY

Forasmuch as divers persons have made purchases
of lands in this Colony of the Indians, without the
consent or approbation of the General Assembly,
which manifestly tends to the defrauding and manifest injury of such native Indians, as well as defeating the just rights of this Colony:

*Be it therefore enacted by the General Assem-
bly, and the authority of the same,* That no person or
persons, for the future, shall purchase any lands or
islands within this Colony, of or from the native Indians within the same, but such only as are so allowed
to do by the General Assembly, upon penalty of forfeiting all such lands or islands so purchased, to this
Colony; and to pay for every such purchase by them
so made, the sum of twenty pounds, as a fine to and
for the use of the Colony; and all such purchases
shall be esteemed and adjudged null, void, and of
none effect.

## 14  Beginnings of Black Bondage (1664)

The colonists brought the first black "servants" to
Jamestown, Virginia, in 1619, the same year in
which they established the House of Burgesses, the
instrument of their own local government and self-
determination. In the early seventeenth century,
American planters and landlords did not seek black
labor. They preferred white settlers and servants
who would continue the patterns of master-servant
relations familiar to feudal Europe. But in the passage of time the black immigrant, not initially differentiated from other servants, became an important
resource in the land-rich, population-poor New
World.

The scarcity of labor in the colonies tempted
landowners into subjugating the native populations
as well as the African immigrant workers. Although
blacks originally shared with other servants the opportunities for emancipation, the last part of the seventeenth century marked the beginning of a particularly racist policy which inaugurated black bondage
*durante vita* and enforced it through criminal and
civil law.

From this document, it is apparent that some in-
terracial marriages existed. For the betrayal of
their race, free white women who married slaves became slaves themselves, as did their children. They
thus were rendered civilly impotent as well as socially outcast.

## ☆ 14  An Act concerning Negroes and Other Slaves [Maryland]

Proceedings and Acts of the General Assembly of Maryland, September 1664, 28-29, reprinted in Albert P. Blaustein & Robert Zangrando, eds., *Civil Rights and the American Negro: A Documentary History* (New York: Trident
Press, 1968), 8-9.

Be it enacted by the Right Honorable the Lord Proprietary by the advise and consent of the upper and
lower house of this present Generall Assembly, that
all Negroes or other slaves already within the province, and all Negroes and other slaves to be hereafter imported into the province, shall serve *durante
vita.* And all children born of any Negro or other
slave shall be slaves as their fathers were, for the
term of their lives. And forasmuch as divers freeborn English women, forgetful of their free condition and to the disgrace of our nation, marry Negro
slaves, by which also divers suits may arise touching
the issue of such women, and a great damage befalls
the masters of such Negroes for prevention whereof, for deterring such freeborn women from such
shameful matches. Be it further enacted by the authority, advise, and consent aforesaid, that whatsoever freeborn woman shall marry any slave from
and after the last day of this present Assembly shall
serve the master of such slave during the life of her
husband. And that all the issue of such freeborn
women so married shall be slaves as their fathers
were. And be it further enacted, that all the issues of
English or other freeborn women that have already
married Negroes shall serve the masters of their
parents till they be thirty years of age and no longer.

## 15  Native Americans as Rebels (1665)

Despite the general tendency of the Native Americans and the English colonists to live apart, there
were continual interactions between them. While
most colonies had legislation regulating commerce
with Native Americans and punishing them for
crimes against whites within the colony, this Virginia enactment attempted to assert overall political
control over the Native Americans as a people. The
act deprived them of self-government and designated as rebellion any Native American refusal to
obey the commanders appointed by the colonial authorities. It is the first instance of an attempt
through law to break the social and political order of
the Native Americans and supplant it with colonial
control.

## ☆ 15  An Act concerning Indians [Virginia]

Reprinted in W. Hening, ed., *Virginia Statutes at Large,
1660-1682* (Charlottesville: University Press of Virginia,
1969), 21.

WHEREAS, at a Grand Assemblie, held at James City, September 10th, 1663, it was provided that where any murther was committed by the Indians upon the English, the nexte turne of the Indians was, to use their utmost endeavours for discovering the actors and doers thereof, and in regard the said act was only lymited upon the northern Indians: *This Grand Assembly have thought fit to enact, and it being enacted,* That the said law be a generall law against all Indians whatsoever, and where any murthers be committed upon the English, the next turne is to use all their care and diligence in finding the doers and actors of the said murthers.

*And be it further enacted,* That if any Englishmen is murthered, the nexte turne shall be answerable for it with their lives or liberties to the use of the publique.

*And be it further enacted by this Grand Assembly,* That the said Indians shall not have power within themselves to elect or constitute their owne *werowance* or Chiefe Commander, but the present Honourable Governour, and his successors from time to time shall constitute and authorize such persons in whose fidelity they may finde the greatest cause to repose a confidence, to be the Commander of the respective townes, and in case the Indians shall refuse their obedience to, or murther such persons, then that nation of Indians soe refusing or offending to be accompted enemies and rebels and to be proceeded against accordingly.

And whereas the careless manner of the English, in going unarmed into churches, courts, and other publique meetings, may probably in time invite the Indians to make some desperate attempt upon them, *It is further enacted,* That the Honourable the Governour, be requested to issue his commands to the officers of the malitieo to take care to prevent the same.

*And it is further enacted,* That any person or persons that shall harbour, entertaine, or employ any Indian, shall be fined five thousand pounds of tobacco, or suffer one year's imprisonment without baile or maineprise, unless such as shall give sufficient security to the county courts, and upon such security, obteyne a certificate from the said court, and upon that certificate a lysence from the Governour.

And whereas by the former articles of agreement, it was provided, that no Indians which are seated on the South side of James river, should come over the *Black water* or the Southerne branches thereof,

*It is hereby enacted,* That the said bounds, from the head of *Black water* to the Apamatack Indian towne, and thence cross to the Monikon towne, be the bounds of the Indians on the South side of James river.

# 16 Removing "the guilt of blood from the land" (1672)

Although the English Crown claimed dominion over all discovered lands, colonial existence depended on the sufferance and often the assistance of the powerful Native American tribes and nations that inhabited the territory. The colonies traded with and purchased land from the tribes, but as their populations grew, frictions with the Native Americans developed.

The surge of settlers into the Connecticut Valley from both New England and New Amsterdam (and the resulting competition between the English and the Dutch) stirred the Pequot tribe to fight the white migration. After failing to enlist the aid of the powerful Narragansetts or Mohicans, the Pequots undertook the task alone. The Massachusetts colony sent aid to the settlers, and in a surprise raid from the sea upon the Pequot stockade on the Mystic River, the settler forces killed over one thousand men, women, and children of the tribe. Those escaping were hunted down and killed or enslaved. Remnants of the tribe were assimilated into other tribes, and the Pequots' history as a cohesive people came to an end.

The colonists began to regulate more carefully their relations with the Native Americans. It was unusual, nevertheless, for the whites to assert jurisdiction, as here, with respect to affairs that involved Native American aggression upon other Native Americans. More common were the restrictions on trade, particularly of liquor and armaments—and not without cause. In 1675, Metacomet (or King Philip as he was known to the whites), son of Massasoit, who first welcomed the colonists, began a war that was to last three years and to rage through Massachusetts, Rhode Island, and Connecticut. Thirteen towns were destroyed and six hundred whites and three thousand Wampanoags, Narragansetts, and Nipmucks were killed. The war ended when King Philip was assassinated by another Native American. With the defeat, the threat Native Americans posed to the existence of these colonies ended.

## ☆ 16 An Act for the Well Ordering of the Indians [Connecticut]

Reprinted in E. M. Coleman, ed., *Laws of the Colonial And State Governments Relating to Indians and Indian Affairs, from 1633-1831 Inclusive* (Washington, D.C.: Thompson and Homans, 1832), 37-40.

That some means may be used to convey the knowledge of God, and of his word, to the Indians and natives among us,

*Be it enacted by the Governor, Council, and Representatives, in General Court assembled, and by*

*the authority of the same*, That one or more of the teaching Elders of the churches in this jurisdiction, with the help of an able interpreter, shall be desired, as often as he may, in every year, to go among the neighboring Indians, and endeavor to make known to them the councils of the Lord; thereby to draw and stir them up to direct and order all their ways and conversations according to the rules of his word: and the Governor and Deputy Governor, and other magistrates, are desired to take care and see the thing attended, and, with their own presence, so far as may be convenient, to encourage the same.

*And it is further enacted, by the authority aforesaid*, That where any company of Indians do sit down near any town or English plantation, they shall declare who is their Sachem, or Chief; and that the said Sachem, or Chief, shall pay to the English such trespasses as shall be committed by any Indian or Indians in the said plantations adjoining, either by spoiling or killing of cattle or swine, either with guns, traps, dogs, or arrows, or by any other means, although they plead it was done by strangers, unless they can produce the party, and deliver him, or his goods, into the custody of the English; and that they shall pay double damage if it were done wittingly and voluntarily; the like engagement this Court also makes to them, in case of wrong or injury done to them by the English, which shall be paid by the party by whom it was done, if it can be made to appear, or else by the town in whose limits such facts are committed.

And to prevent inconveniences and troubles that may arise by the Indians coming into the English towns and plantations in the night season, and supplying themselves with liquors and prohibited goods,

*It is further enacted by the authority aforesaid*, That all and every Indian and Indians that shall be found passing and repassing in any town in this Colony, after the shutting in of the evening, (except he or they shall give sufficient reason that there was necessity thereof) shall forfeit and pay the sum of *twenty shillings*, whereof *fifteen shillings* shall be to the county treasury, and *five shillings* to the complainer or complainers; or be whipt, not exceeding *six stripes*: any one assistant or justice of the peace, before whom any such complaint shall come, shall be, and is hereby, empowered to secure every such Indian or Indians, by committing them to prison, or setting a watch upon them, till he may hear and issue such complaints.

*And be it further enacted, by the authority aforesaid*, That no person or persons whomsoever, shall, directly or indirectly, sell, truck, barter, give, or deliver, to any Indian, any strong beer, ale, cyder, perry, wine, rum, brandy, or other strong liquors, by what name or names soever called or known, on pain of forfeiting the sum of *twenty shillings* for every

pint, and proportionable for any greater or lesser quantity so sold, trucked, bartered, given, or delivered, to any Indian, directly or indirectly, as aforesaid, upon conviction thereof before any assistant or justice of the peace, where the penalty doth not exceed *forty shillings*, and if it exceed that sum, at the county court to be holden for the same county where the offence is committed; two-third parts of all such forfeitures to be to the county treasury, the remaining third part to him or them that shall prosecute the same by bill, plaint, or information: *Provided*, This act shall not be intended, or extend to restrain any act of charity for relieving any Indian (*bona fide*) in any sudden exigent of faintness, or sickness, not to exceed one or two drams, or by the allowance of an assistant or justice of the peace.

*And it is further enacted, by the authority aforesaid*, That every Indian or negro, servant or slave, that shall be convicted of the breach of this law, shall be openly whipt, not exceeding *ten stripes*, unless the master of such servant or slave shall answer the law by paying his or her fine: and every Indian convicted of drunkenness in the Colony, shall forfeit and pay the sum of *ten shillings*, whereof one half shall be to the complainer or complainers, and the other half to the County Treasury, where the offence is committed, or else be openly whipped, not exceeding *ten stripes* for one offence, as the assistant or justice of the peace, before whom such conviction is, shall determine.

And for preventing of the breach of the Sabbath, by the Indians within this Colony:

*It is further enacted by the authority aforesaid*, That, if any Indian or Indians shall labour or play on the Sabbath day, within the limits of any English town, every such Indian, being thereof duly convicted, shall pay a fine of *five shillings*, whereof the one-half shall be to the complainer, the rest to the county treasury, or else set in the stocks *one hour*; any one assistant or justice of the peace to hear and determine the same.

*And be it further enacted by the authority aforesaid*, That no Indian or Indians shall, at any time, pawaw, or perform outward worship to false gods, or to the devil, within this Colony, on pain of forfeiting the sum of *five pounds* to the public treasury of this Colony, for every time any Indian or Indians shall be convicted of performing or doing the same.

And if any person or persons, of the age of twenty years or upwards, shall, at any time, be present at any Indian play or pawawing, at any of their general meetings, every such person shall forfeit the sum of *forty shillings*; and if any person shall join in playing with any Indian or Indians, or shall lay any wager with, or for, any Indian, about or concerning any such play or game, he shall forfeit and pay a fine of *ten pounds*; one moiety of these fines and forfeitures to be to the complainer, or complainers, and the other moiety to the treasury of the county in which such offence is committed.

And whereas, it is too manifest, that the Indians, notwithstanding all council and advice to the contrary, have committed, and still do proceed to commit murder, and kill one another, within the English plantations in this Colony, and take no course that such justice be executed on such malefactors as may take off the guilt of blood from the land: Which to prevent—

*It is further enacted by the authority aforesaid*, That, if any Indian or Indians, within this Colony, shall wilfully and violently fall upon any Indian or Indians, within this Colony, and upon the English land, (except it be such as they are at open war with) and murder him or them, and be thereof legally convicted, every such Indian and Indians shall suffer the pains of death: And if the Indians shall not do just execution upon such murderer, or murderers, speedily, the next assistant or justice of the peace shall, forthwith, cause him or them to be apprehended, and without bail or mainprize, commit him or them to the common gaol, there to be secured for a trial, at the next court of assistants.

*       *       *

# 17 Nathaniel Bacon's Rebellion (1676-1677)

An aristocratic, English-born Cambridge graduate, Nathaniel Bacon, sailed for Virginia in 1673, where he acquired several estates and received an appointment to the governor's council. Virginia's western settlers were dissatisfied with rule by privileged families and the failure of the government to protect them against Native American raids. (Sir William Berkeley, the royal governor, was alleged to have benefited greatly from the Native American fur trade.) Bacon took up the cause of pacifying the borders. In the Battle of Bloody Run, Bacon's unofficial military expedition defeated and severely punished the Native Americans.

Governor Berkeley quickly outlawed Bacon, who then marched on the colonial capital demanding recognition for his forces as the official colonial army. In the civil war that followed, Berkeley was defeated and Jamestown was burned. But Bacon fell ill in the midst of the campaign, and with his death in October 1676, the rebellion collapsed.

The House of Burgesses declared Bacon and his followers guilty of high treason without trial. The episode concluded with wholesale executions and confiscations of the rebels' estates by the royal governor. To prevent future unrest, the legislature also passed an act prohibiting any spoken or written sentiments supporting Bacon's on any other rebellion or

in any way treating contemptuously the governor, his council, the justices of the peace, or the official militia. The prescribed penalties included fines of one thousand pounds of tobacco, a stint in the pillory, and, for women offenders, whipping on the naked back.

The act of attainder or outlawry was an important tool used to punish individuals for political dissent. An attainder, as here, was usually a legislative adjudgment and punishment for a past treason. Lesser penalties were prescribed prospectively for people engaging in activities not amounting to treason but nevertheless considered inimical to the welfare of the colony.

## ☆ 17 Acts against Wicked and Desolute Persons [Virginia]

W. Hening, ed., *Virginia Statutes at Large, 1660-1682* (Charlottesville: University Press of Virginia, 1969), 366-87.

## ☆ 17a Act II. An Act of Attainder, etc.

WHEREAS Nathaniel Bacon the younger, having by many false and wicked pretences drawn to his party many other wicked and desolute persons within this his majesties collony of Virginia, and haveing together with some other his desperate accomplices plotted and contrived the ruine of this his majesties country, and to draw and persuade many of his most sacred majesties subjects from theire due allegiance and obedience to his majestie, and the government under him established, under which this collony hath bin soe long happy and flourished, in order to which plotts and contrivances, the said Nathaniel Bacon junior, and his desperate accomplices in a most traiterous and rebellious manner, haveing putt themselves in armes and under pretence of the said Indian warr by threats and menaces of killing and destroying the whole grand assembly, haveing by force procured a commission to make the said Nathaniel Bacon generall for the said Indian warr, did in prosecution of the said traytorous and rebellious plotts themselves contrive and take most traiterous and rebellious oathes against and contrary to their allegiance to his most sacred majestie and with their armed men, and otherwayes did inforce many of his majesties subjects to take the same traiterous and rebellious oathes, and proceeded with his said armed acomplices to the seizing and imprisoning many of his majesties loyall subjects, and threatening his majesties governour and many of his loyall subjects with death, soe as they were inforced to departe from their habitations, whereupon the said Nathaniell Bacon did with the said wicked ayders and assisters, robb and dispoile many of his majesties subjects of their estates, and murthered and killed many of them; in the height of their monstrious rebellion, it pleased Almighty God of his infinite mercy and goodnes to this poore country, by a just and most exemplary death, to take the said Nathaniell Bacon out of this world, and his said wicked accomplices still continueing their said treasons and rebellions against his sacred majestie, did prosecute the said rebellion, destroying their estates and endeavouring to kill and destroy many his majesties loyall subjects, untill God Almighty, by his infinite mercy and goodnesse was pleased soe to blesse the just endeavours of the right honourable Sir William Berkeley, his majesties governour of this colony, and the loyall party under his command, that the said traitors and rebells were reduced to their allegiance, and enforced to submit to the right and good government established by his most sacred majestie. *And whereas* the said Nathaniell Bacon the younger died in open rebellion against his most sacred majestie, and Edmund Cheesman a principall ayder and abetter with the said Nathaniell Bacon in the said rebellion, being taken in armes and brought prisoner dyed before his tryall, and William Hunt, another principal ayder and abetter of the said Nathaniell Bacon, dyed alsoe before the rebells were reduced to their allegiance to his majestie by which said meanes the said Nathaniell Bacon, junr. Edmund Cheeseman and William Hunt have escaped their due and just demerritts for their wicked and unheard of treasons and rebellions; *Bee it therefore enacted by the governour, councell and burgesses of this grand assembly, and the authoritie thereof,* that the said Nathaniell Bacon, junr. Edmund Cheesman and William Hunt, and every and either of them shall by vertue of this act be adjudged to be convicted and attainted of high treason to all intents and purposes, as if they and every of them had been attainted respectively in their lives. *And whereas* alsoe Thomas Hansford, Thomas Wilsford, William Carver, Wm. Drummond, James Crewes, John Johnson, George ffarloe, Thomas Hall, Thomas Young, Henry Page, James Wilson, John Baptista, William Cockson and John Digby, all notorious actors and confederates with the said Nathaniell Bacon, junr. in the said rebellions and treasons, and endeavoured to continue the same after his death, who were some of them taken in the height of, and all of them taken in open rebellion against the kings majestie, and were all of them tryed found guilty, and deservedly adjudged to death by the right honourable the governour and a councell of warre of the cheife commanders of the country, which sentance for their said treasons and rebellions against his sacred majestie accordingly executed upon them and every of them. *And be it further enacted by the authority aforesaid,* that the said Thomas Hansford, Thomas Wilsford, William Carver, William Drummond, James Crewes, John Johnson, George ffarloe,

Thomas Hall, Thomas Young, Henry Page, James Wilson, John Baptista, William Cockson and John Digby, and every or either of them, shalby vertue of this act be adjudged to be convicted and attainted of high treason to all intents and purposes. And that William West and John Turner, two notorious actors and confederates with the said Nathaniell Bacon, junr. in the said wicked treasons and rebellions, and endeavoured to continue the same after his death, and were taken in open rebellion against his most sacred majestie, and for such their treasons and rebellions, before the right honourable the governour and a councell of warr, were tryed, found guilty and deservedly adjudged to death, but before justice was executed upon them, they made their escapes out of prison and are fled; *Bee it therefore further enacted by the authority aforesaid,* that the said William West and John Turner, and either of them shall by vertue of this act stand, and be adjudged to be convicted and attainted of high treason to all intents and purposes. And whereas William Rookins, a very notorious actor and confederate with the said Nathaniell Bacon in the said rebellions and treasons, and endeavouring to continue the same after his death, was taken in open rebellion against his most sacred majestie, and for such his treasons and rebellions before the right honourable the governour and a councell of warr, was tryed, found guilty and deservedly adjudged to suffer death, but before justice was executed upon him, he the said William Rookins dyed in prison; *Bee it therefore enacted by the authority aforesaid,* that the said William Rookins shall by vertue of this act be adjudged to be convicted and attainted of high treason to all intents and purposes. And whereas Richard Lawrence, Thomas Whaley and John fforth, three of the most notorious ayders and assisters of the said Nathaniell Bacon in the said horrid rebellions and treasons, and three of the principall actors in continueing of the same, are fled from justice, not dareing to abide a legall tryall; *Bee it further enacted by the authority aforesaid,* that the said Richard Lawrence, Thomas Whaley and John fforth, and either of them, shall by vertue of this act be adjudged to be convicted and attainted of high treason to all intents and purposes, and that all and every the messuages, lands, tenements, rents, remainders, interests and all other the hereditaments, chattles, reall goods, debts and other principall estate, and other things of that nature whatsoever that be of them the said Nathaniell Bacon, junr., Edmund Cheesman, William Hunt, Thomas Hansford, Thomas Wilsford, William Carver, William Drummond, James Crewes, John Johnson, George ffarloe, Thomas Hall, Thomas Younge, Henry Page, James Willson, John Baptista, William Cookson, William West, John Turner, John Digby, William Rookins, Richard Lawrence, Thomas Whaley and John fforth, which they or either of them, or any other person or persons to their or any of their uses or interests, for them or either of them were seized or possessed of the ffirst day of October last past, or at any time since, shall stand and be forfeited to the kings most sacred majestie, his heires and successors, and shalbe deemed vested, and adjudged to be in the actuall and reall possession of the kings majestie without any office or inquisition thereof hereafter to be taken or found.

\*        \*        \*

☆ 17b Act V. An Act for the Reliefe of Such Loyall Persons As Have Suffered Losse by the Late Rebells

\*        \*        \*

*Bee it enacted by this present grand assembly, and the authority thereof, and it is hereby enacted*, that if any person or persons, not being a women covert shall presume to speake, write, disperse or publish by words, writeing or otherwise, any matter or thing tending to rebellion, or in favour of the late rebels or rebellion, and shall thereof be lawfully convict, then such persons for the ffirst such offence shall be fined one thousands pounds of tobacco and caske, and stand upon the pillory two howers with capitall letters of their crimes affixed on their foreheads or brest, and for such second offence pay double the fine and stand in the pillory two howres with capitall letters of their crimes fixed as aforesaid, and for the third such offence be prosecuted as a rebell and a tratour to his most sacred majestie. And if any woman covert that comitt such offence as is before recited, then to be whipped on the bare back with twenty lashes, for the first offence, and for the second offence thirty lashes, except she can redeeme herselfe from the said corporall punishments by payment of the ffine or ffines before mentioned, for such first and second offences. *And be it further enacted*, that if any woman under covert shall a third tyme committ such offence, to be prosecuted against as a rebell and traytor to his most sacred majestie. And whereas it hath beene frequent for rude and ill disposed persons to contemne and revile authority and magistrates, as well in words as in actions; *Bee it therefore enacted by this present grand assembly, and by the authority thereof*, that all and every person and persons that shall from the tyme to come presume to speake and utter mutinous or contemptuous words, or shall by any wayes or meanes abuse the right honourable the governour or any of the councell, justices of the peace or commissionated militia officers, and shall be thereof lawfully convict, shall for his such offence, if against the right honourable the governour, be whipped on the bare back with thirty lashes, or pay eight hundred pounds of

tobacco and caske, if against any of the honourable councell, that then he shalbe whipped on the bare back with twenty fowre lashes, or pay six hundred pounds of tobacco and caske, and if against any justice of the peace or comissionate field officer, then to be whipped on the bare back with twenty lashes, or pay fowre hundred pounds of tobacco and caske, and the like for such second offence, being likewise thereof lawfully convict. And if any person or persons, male or female, shall be convicted a third tyme of such mutany or contemptious or villifying words writeing or otherwise, abuseing or scanduliseing the right honourable the governour or any of the honourable councell or any justice of the peace or commissioned militia ffield officer, then to be whipped on the bare back with thirty nine lashes, and stand in the pillowry two howers, or pay double the before recited ffines, all which said ffines as aforesaid shalbe and belong the one halfe to the informer, if he shall sue for the same, and the other halfe to the county, where the offending party then dwells or resides, which said ffines to be levyed by distresse or otherwise, and collected or destrayned for by the sherriffe or collector for the publique and county levyes.... *And* whereas by a branch of an act of assembly made in March last, liberty is granted to all persons to carry their armes wheresoever they goe, which liberty hath beene found to be very prejudiciall to the peace and wellfaire of this colony. *Bee it therefore further enacted by this present grand assembly, and the authority thereof, and it is hereby enacted*, that if any person or persons shall, from and after publication of this act, presume to assemble together in armes to the number of five or upwards without being legally called together, that for such convention, or assembling together in armes the number of ffive or upwards, they be held deemed and adjudged as riotous and mutinous, and that they be proceeded against and punished accordingly.

\*        \*        \*

## 18 "seduced from their allegiance" (1680)

The brutal sanctions Governor Berkeley imposed on Bacon's followers resulted in Berkeley's censure by Charles II. Berkeley sailed to England to set forth his defense, but he died in London in 1677 without having seen the king. Seeking a reconciliation with the rebels, both Charles II and the General Assembly of Virginia in 1680 granted a comprehensive pardon to those who had participated in Bacon's Rebellion — with certain exceptions. This amnesty set the course for similar reconciliations following future rebellions in America. Nevertheless, this "generall pardon" was unwilling to overlook the "lycentiousnesse" of those who in the future might defame the government and its officials. It prescribed less severe penalties for those who would spread false and scandalous reports or otherwise would dishonor or defame the colony's councillors, judges, or officers.

## ☆ 18 An Act of Free and Generall Pardon, Indennitie and Oblivion [Virginia]

W. Hening, ed., *Virginia Statutes at Large, 1660-1682* (Charlottesville: University Press of Virginia, 1969), 458-64.

THE Kings most excellent majestie haveing taken into his serious and gratious consideration the present state and condition of his colony of Virginia, and reflecting on the late rebellion raised there by Nathaniell Bacon junr. deceased, his complices and abettors, and how many of his good subjects were drawne into the same and seduced from their allegiance by the specious pretences sett forth by the said Nathaniell Bacon, who have since by their dutifull behaviour shewed themselves sencible thereof, and repenting for the same, and to the intent that noe crime whatsoever comitted against his said majestie and government may hereafter rise into judgment or be brought in question against any of them to their least endamagement, either in lives, liberties, estates or to the prejudice of their reputations, by any reproach or terme of distinctions, and to turne all seeds of future discords and the remembrances thereof in utter oblivion, as well in his majesties owne breast as in the breasts of his majesties subjects one towards another, and out of an earnest desire to put an end to all suites, quarrells and controversies whatsoever that by occasion of the said rebellion and late destractions have arisen and may arise betweene any of his majesties subjects and in pursuance of his gratious proclamation of pardon hearing date the seaven and twentyeth day of October 1676, and in the eight and twentyeth yeare of his raigne, is gratiously pleased *that it may be enacted, and be it encted by the kings most excellent majestie by and with the consent of the generall assembly,* that all and all manner of treasons, misprision of treasons, murders, fellonies, crimes and misdeameanors comitted, acted, councelled or done by any person or persons whatsoever upon or at any tyme before the sixteenth day of January, 1676, in the 28th yeare of his majesties raigne, other then the persons hereafter excepted.... *And be it further enacted by the authority aforesaid,* that all and every such person and persons, their and every of their heires, executors and administrators (except as hereafter excepted) that were actually ingaged in ayding, assisting, adviseing, abetting or councelling the said rebellion shall have and enjoy all and every their lands, tenements, hereditaments, goods, and chattells, whatsoever forfeited to his majestie, his heires and successors for any of the crimes aforesaid in the same manner, and as freely to all intents and purposes as if they had not been forfeited, yet soe that they may and every of them and their estates both reall and personall, shalbe subject and lyable to pay all and singuler their just debts in the same manner as if they had comitted noe rebellion, crimes or offences, *except and always foreprized out* of this act, the above named *Nathaniell Bacon, junr.* the principall contriver, beginner and maintainer of the said rebellion who haveing taken up armes under pretence of an Indian warr, assumed unto himselfe the title of generall, and did afterwards chase the then governor, there rob, kill and continue to destroy severall other of his majesties loyall subjects that refused to take the detestible oaths imposed by the said Bacon, untill it pleased the Allmighty to send him the said *Bacon* an infamous and exemplary death, whereby he hath escaped the punishment in this world soe justly due to his person; *Bee it therefore enacted, and it is hereby enacted by the authority aforesaid,* that the said Nathaniell Bacon junior shalbe by virtue of this act, and is hereby adjudged to be convict and attainted of high treason to all intents and purposes as if he had been convict and attainted thereof by due course of law in his life time, and that all the estate reall and personall, whereof he was seized or possessed upon the ffifth day of June 1676, or at any tyme after within the colony of Virginia shalbe forfeited to the kings majestie, his heires and successors, and is hereby declared to be vested in his majesty, his heires and successors without any office or inquisition thereof to be hereafter taken or found; *Provided alwayes, and be it enacted* that this act nor any thing therein contained shall extend to pardon, discharge or give any other benefitt whatsoever unto [certain named individuals] but that the persons last aforesaid and their estates are out of this act wholly excepted and fforeprized.

*Provided alsoe, and it is hereby enacted and declared by the authority aforesaid,* that if Joseph Ingram, Gregory Walklett, Thomas Whaley, John fforth and John Langston shall at any tyme after the passing of this act accept or exercise any publique office whatsoever within the said colony of Virginia, that then such of them as doe soe, accept or exercise aforesaid, shall to all intents and purposes stand as if he or they had beene totally excepted by name out of this act.... *Provided always* that noe further punishment, satisfaction or damages shalbe recovered or inflicted on any christian servants that have deserted their masters or bin active in the late rebellion, then that the time incurring betweene the said ffirst day of May and the said sixteenth of January shalbe accompted noe part of their tyme of service. *And be it further enacted by the authority aforesaid* that noe verdicts, judgments, indictments, informations, decrees, sentences, probatts of wills, administrations, writts or actings, or returne of writts, orders or other proceedings whatsoever in law or equity had, made, given, taken or done or depending in any courts or before any judges whatsoever within the said colony of Virginia. . . . *And whereas* during the lycentiousnesse of the late tymes several ill disposed persons tooke upon them to asperse the government and defame the governor and cheife magistrates of the said colony, raising false and scandalous reports, without which our good subjects there could not have been soe easily led away, which cannot but tend to the future disturbance of the peace and welfare thereof if not tymely prevented, by inflicting punishments proportionate to the greateness of the crime. *Bee it therefore enacted by the authority aforesaid*, that whosoever shall after passing of this act, malitiously and advisedly by writeing, speakeing or otherwise expresse, publish, utter or declare any word, sentence or thing or things to incite or stir up the people to the dislike of any person appointed by his majestie to be governor or comander in cheife of the said colony, or tending to the dishonour or defameing the said governour or comander in cheife for the tyme being, and being thereof legally convicted shalbe imprisoned during one yeare without bayle or mainprize, and incurr such forfeiture as shalbe adjudged, not exceeding the sume of 500*l.* to the kings most excellent majestie, his heires and successors, *And it is in like manner enacted*, that whosoever shall malitiously and advisedly by writing, speaking or otherwise expresse, publish, utter or declare any words, sentences or other things to incite or stirr up the people to the dislike of his majesties councellors, judges, or other principall officers within the said colony, or tending to the dishonour or defameing of the said councellors, judges or principall officers, and being thereof legally convicted shalbe imprisoned three months without bayle or mainprise and incurr such forfeiture as shalbe adjudged, not exceeding the sume of one hundred pounds, to the kings most excellent majestie, his heires and successors, any act or acts, order or orders to the contrary in any wise notwithstanding.

## 19 "not to devour and destroy one another" (1681)

In 1681 Charles II granted a charter to his friend William Penn — in settlement of a debt owed by the king to Penn's father — to permit the founding of a haven for Penn's fellow Quakers in the New World. Originally interested in settling New Jersey, Penn accepted instead the fertile lands along the west bank of the Delaware River. Charles himself bestowed the name *Pennsylvania* upon this territory. Being a remarkable proprietor, Penn set out not only to permit the people of the colony to formulate their own laws but also to seek an accommodation with the land's native people.

References exist to a Great Treaty entered into by Penn with the Native Americans in 1682 to bring about mutual cooperation between the colonizers and the natives. This treaty was to guarantee the founding in America of the Peaceable Kingdom forecast in biblical times by the prophet Isaiah. No copy of the treaty has survived, and its existence is doubted. But Penn's sensitivity toward the native population is reflected in a letter written to the Native Americans of Pennsylvania a year earlier. The communication is in sharp contrast to the attitudes of other colonists (including John Smith, rescued by Pocahontas) and calls for relations based upon mutual respect between equals. Tension between these two fundamentally radical attitudes toward the Native Americans has long persisted.

## ☆ 19 William Penn's Letter to the Native Americans of Pennsylvania (October 18, 1681)

Reprinted in Catherine O. Peare, *William Penn: A Biography* (Ann Arbor: University of Michigan Press, 1956), 223-24.

MY FRIENDS:

There is one great God and power that hath made the world and all things therein, to whom you and I and all people owe their being and well-being, and to whom you and I must one day give an account, for all that we do in the world; this great God hath written His law in our hearts, by which we are taught and commanded to love and help, and do good to one another, and not to do harm and mischief one unto another. Now this great God hath been pleased to make me concerned in your parts of the world, and the King of the country where I live hath given unto me a great province therein; but I desire to enjoy it with your love and consent, that we may always live together as neighbors and friends, else what would the great God say to us, who hath made us not to devour and destroy one another, but live soberly and kindly together in the world? Now I would have you well observe, that I am very sensible of the unkindness and injustice that hath been too much exercised toward you by the people of these parts of the world, who have sought themselves, and to make great advantages by you, rather than be examples of justice and goodness unto you, which I hear, hath been matter of trouble to you, and caused great grudgings and animosities, sometimes to the shedding of blood, which hath made the great God angry. But I am not such a man, as is well known in my own country, I have great love and regard towards you, and I desire to win and gain your love and friendship by a kind, just and peaceable life, and the people I send are of the same mind, and shall in all things behave themselves accordingly; and if in any thing any shall offend you or your people, you shall have a full and speedy satisfaction for the same, by an equal number of just men on both sides, that by no means you may have just occasion of being offended against them. I shall shortly come to you myself, at what time we may more largely and freely confer and discourse of these matters; in the meantime, I have sent my commissioners to treat with you about land, and a firm league of peace; let me desire you to be kind to them and the people, and receive these presents and tokens which I have sent to you, as a testimony of my good will to you, and my resolution to live justly, peaceably and friendly with you.

I am your loving friend,

WILLIAM PENN

## 20  The Tobacco Treason (1684)

Until William and Mary's succession to the British throne in 1688, a bitter struggle continued between the privileged landowners, joined by the English officials, and the poorer population. Popular dissatisfaction frequently was vented by the destruction of the tobacco crop upon which the colonial government relied for revenue. In 1684, the General Assembly of Virginia, during the governorship of Lord Howard, perceived that the cutting up, pulling up, or other destruction of a tobacco plant, primarily an act of protest against private property, was a threat to the political order of the colony. The General Assembly decreed such acts to be treason punishable by death. The economic interests in the state thus were granted special protection from attack by the less fortunate segments of the populace.

## ☆20  An Act for the Better Preservation of the Peace of Virginia, and Preventing Unlawfull and Treasonable Associations

Reprinted in W. Hening, ed., *Virginia Statutes at Large, 1682-1710* (Charlottesville: University Press of Virginia, 1969), 9-12.

*       *       *

WHEREAS, many evill and ill-disposed persons inhabitants of this his majesties collony and dominion of Virginia, contrary to their duty and allegiance, on or about the first of May, in the thirty-fourth yeare of his majesties raigne (1682), and divers other dayes, and times tumultously and mutinously assembled and gathered together to cut up and destroy all tobacco plants, and to perpetrate the same in a trayterous and rebellious manner, with force

and armes entered the plantations of many his majesties good subjects of this his collony, resolving by open force, a generall and totall destruction of all tobacco plants within this his majesties dominion, to the hazarding the subvertion of the whole government, and ruine and destruction of his majesties good subjects. . . . *And bee it enacted by the governour, councill and burgesses of this assembly,* That if any person or persons whatsoever, to the number of eight or above, being assembled together, shall at any time after the first day of June now next ensueing, intend, goe about, practice or put in use with force, unlawfully to cut, pull up or destroy any tobacco plants, either in bedds or hills, growing within the said collony, or to destroy the same, either cureing or cured, either before the same is in hogsheads or afterwards, or to pull downe, burne or destroy the houses or other places where any such tobacco shall be, or to pull downe the fences or enclosures of any tobacco plants, with intent to cut up or destroy the same, (and such person or persons being commanded or required in his majesties name by the governour or other commander in chief, or any one of the councell, or one or more of the justices of the peace of the said collony, commanding and requireing such persons to disperse themselves, and peaceably to depart to their habitations) shall continue together by the space of four houres after such proclamation made, at or nigh the place where such persons shall be soe assembled; that then every such persons soe willingly assembled, in forceable manner, to doe any of the acts before mentioned and soe continuing together as aforesaid, and being thereof lawfully convicted, shall be deemed, declared and adjudged to be traytors, and suffer paines of death, and alsoe and forfeite as in cases of high treason. *Provided always,* that noe person or persons whatsoever shall incurr the pains and penalties hereby inflicted, unlesse he or they be prosecuted and indicted thereupon, within twelve months after the offence committed. Any thing herein contained to the contrary notwithstanding.

*       *       *

## 21  "against the traffic of men-body" (1688)

In William Penn's colony, founded as a haven for the oppressed Quakers and perceived as tolerant of national, ethnic, and religious diversity, the first protest against black enslavement resounded. The Germantown Mennonites argued that the slave trade was inhuman and contrary to Christian principles and should not be permitted in Pennsylvania. Despite the fact that the existing law required subservient acquiescence by the slave to his condition, the

Mennonites stated the moral case justifying breach of the law in defense of one's freedom.

## ☆21 Resolution of the Germantown, Pennsylvania, Mennonites

Reprinted in P. Mode, ed., *Source Book and Bibliographical Guide for American Church History* (Menasha, Wis.: George Banta, 1921), 552-53.

This is to the monthly meeting held at Richard Worrell's:

These are the reasons why we are against the traffic of men-body, as followeth: Is there any that would be done or handled at this manner? viz., to be sold or made a slave for all the time of his life? How fearful and faint-hearted are many at sea, when they see a strange vessel, being afraid it should be a Turk, and they should be taken, and sold for slaves into Turkey. Now, what is *this* better done, than Turks do? Yea, rather it is worse for them, which say they are Christians; for we hear that the most part of such negers are brought hither against their will and consent, and that many of them are stolen. Now, though they are black, we cannot conceive there is more liberty to have them slaves, as it is to have other white ones. There is a saying, that we should do to all men like as we will be done ourselves; making no difference of what generation, descent, or colour they are. And those who steal or rob men, and those who buy or purchase them, are they not all alike? Here is liberty of conscience, which is right and reasonable; here ought to be likewise liberty of the body, except of evil-doers, which is another case. But to bring men hither, or to rob and sell them against their will, we stand against. In Europe there are many oppressed for conscience-sake; and here there are those oppressed which are of a black colour. And we who know that men must not commit adultery—some do commit adultery *in* others, separating wives from their husbands, and giving them to others: and some sell the children of these poor creatures to other men. Ah! do consider well this thing, you who do it, if you would be done at this manner—and if it is done according to Christianity! You surpass Holland and Germany in this thing. This makes an ill report in all those countries of Europe, where they hear of [it], that the Quakers do here handel men as they handel there the cattle. And for that reason some have no mind or inclination to come hither. And who shall maintain this your cause, or plead for it? Truly, we cannot do so, except you shall inform us better hereof, viz.: that Christians have liberty to practice these things. Pray, what thing in the world can be done worse towards us, than if men should rob or steal us away, and sell us for slaves to strange countries; separating husbands from their wives and children. Being now this is not done in the manner we would be done at; therefore, we contradict, and are against this traffic of men-body. And we who profess that it is not lawful to steal, must, likewise, avoid to purchase such things as are stolen, but rather help to stop this robbing and stealing, if possible. And such men ought to be delivered out of the hands of the robbers, and set free as in Europe. Then is Pennsylvania to have a good report, instead, it hath now a bad one, for this sake, in other countries; Especially whereas the Europeans are desirous to know in what manner *the Quakers* do rule in *their* province; and most of them do look upon us with an envious eye. But if this is done well, what shall we say is done evil?

If once these slaves (which they say are so wicked and stubborn men,) should join themselves—fight for their freedom, and handel their masters and mistresses, as they did handel them before; will these masters and mistresses take the sword at hand and war against these poor slaves, like, as we are able to believe, some will not refuse to do? Or, have these poor negers not as much right to fight for their freedom, as you have to keep them slaves?

Now consider well this thing, if it is good or bad. And in case you find it to be good to handel these blacks in that manner, we desire and require you hereby lovingly, that you may inform us herein, which at this time never was done, viz., that Christians have such a liberty to do so. To the end we shall be satisfied on this point, and satisfy likewise our good friends and acquaintances in our native country, to whom it is a terror, or fearful thing, that men should be handelled so in Pennsylvania.

This is from our meeting at Germantown, held yᵉ 18th of the 2d month, 1688, to be delivered to the monthly meeting at Richard Worrell's.

GARRET HENDERICH
DERICK OP DE GRAEFF
FRANCIS DANIEL PASTORIUS
ABRAM OP DE GRAEFF

## 22 No Appearance of Any Domestic Rebellion (1691)

Under a charter granted to the Earl of Clarendon and seven other royal favorites in 1663, Charles II established Carolina as a proprietary colony. Its two early settlements were Albemarle (1670) and Charleston (1680). Theoretically North and South Carolina constituted a single colony, but after 1712 each part of the province had its own governor. For this province, the "Lords Proprietors" were to legislate "by and with the advice, assent, and approbation of the freeman."

The Lords Proprietors' rule met with much popular opposition. In their eagerness to combat popular unrest, the governor of the southern province and several leaders of the military declared martial law over that portion of the colony in 1690. As part of English common law and practice, colonial governments had the power to impose martial law to and suspend the traditional liberties and political rights of citizens whenever an emergency necessitated such measures. Martial law, an exception to the rule of law, permitted the military to resort to whatever measures it deemed necessary to meet the emergency.

Although concerned with the colony's protection against treason and rebellion, Carolina's legislature was mindful of the potential abuses of citizen's rights under the guise of an impending emergency. The colonial legislature, therefore, acted promptly to curtail the military's power. Pointing to the absence of a foreign invasion or a domestic rebellion that would have justified the termination of civil government and the imposition of martial law, the legislators set out to bar the offending officers from holding any future public office, "military or civil." This document then reflected on several subjects relating to political criminality: the temptation to resort to military power to suppress political dissention; the duty of responsible government to sanction those who betray and exceed their political authority; and the beginning of an American policy to keep the military out of political strife.

Proprietary rule in the Carolinas weakened, and in 1719 local dissatisfaction finally led to a rebellion against the existing government in Charleston and to the popular election of James Moore as governor. England accepted this outcome, and the colony, denominated South Carolina, came thereafter under royal rule until it achieved independence and statehood in 1776. Albemarle, denominated North Carolina in 1691, became a royal colony in 1729.

## ☆ 22 An Act for the Disabling of the Several Persons That Did Sett Up & Advise the Setting Up and Executing Martial Law [South Carolina]

Reprinted in T. Cooper, ed., *Statutes of South Carolina, 1682-1716* (Columbia, S.C.: A. S. Johnston, 1837), 49-50.

WHEREAS, Lieut. Col. Ste. Bull, Major Charles Colleton, Paul Grimball, Esq. together with Landgrave James Colleton, late Governor of this part of the Province, did make articles of warr and erect and establish Martiall Law, and the same cause to be published at the head of every company of the militia of this part of the Province, under the paines of death and other penaltys as in the said articles is sett downe and required, and the same did enforce and put in execution against divers of theire Majesties

peaceable subjects inhabiting in this province, to the apparent breach of libertys, propertys and privileges, and to the dread and terrour of theire Majesty's subjects, notwithstanding at the time there was noe appearance of any forraigne invasion or any domestick rebellion, tumult or sedition, and that at the same tyme all the Courts of Justice were opened and always after continued to be so. And whereas, Thomas Smith, senior, Esq. did by composing, inventing, writing and publishing, as by him confest a certaine Petition, entitled The Petition of divers of theire Majesty's subjects and inhabitants of Charlestowne and parts adjacent, and by other means move, stirr, encourage, advise and persuade the said Stephen Bull, Charles Colleton, Paul Grimball and James Colleton, to exercise and establish law martiall, contrary to law and the priviledges of theire Majesty's subjects as aforesaid.

Be it therefore enacted by the Pallatine and the rest of the Lords and absolute Proprietors of this Province, by and with the advice and consent of the Commons of this present Parliament assembled, and by the authority of the same, that the said Stephen Bull, Charles Colleton, Paul Grimball and Thomas Smith, shall not att any tyme after the ratifycation of this Act, exercise any publick office or charge, either military or civill, either of honour, profit or trust in this Province, but shall be utterly disabled and are hereby rendered and made incapable to exercise the same by him or themselves, theire substitutes or deputys. And if any one of the aforesaid persons in any way offend contrary to this Act or any clause therein contained, he or they shall forfeit the summe of one thousand pounds sterling, one moyety whereof shall be disposed of by the Parliament, and the other moyety to him or them that shall sue for the same by any action of debt, bill, plaint, or information. . . .

## 23 "burned with a hot iron on the most visible part of the left cheek" (1704)

The colonial legislatures spelled out in great detail the conduct of slaves and the responsibilities of freemen toward them. Slaves departing from permitted conduct suffered harsh physical punishment, and erring freemen incurred severe financial penalties. In addition, laws were enforced in large measure by offering rewards to informants in the populace, a prime technique in combating political crime. The New Jersey enactment of 1704 was typical of colonial practices, but in 1709 the Lord Commissioners for Trade and Plantations recommended the repeal of this law on the grounds that it imposed "inhumane penalties on Negroes."

## ☆ 23 An Act for Regulating Negro, Indian, and Mulatto Slaves within the Province of New Jersey

Laws of New Jersey, chap. IX (1704).

Whereas it is found by daily experience, that Negro, Indian, and mulatto slaves, under pretense of trade, or liberty of traffic, frequently steal from their masters, mistresses, or others what they expose to sale at a difference from their habitations; and it being a known truth, that without a receiver, the thief would soon desert his practice, be it therefore enacted by the Governor, Council, and Assembly now met and assembled, and by the authority of the same, that all and every person or persons inhabiting within this province, who shall at any time after publication hereof buy, sell, barter, trade, or traffic with any Negro, Indian, or mulatto slaves, for any rum, wine, beer, cider, or other strong drink, or any other chattels, goods, wares, or commodities whatsoever within this province of Nova Casaria, or New Jersey, shall pay for the first offense five pounds, and for the second and every other offense, ten pounds current money of this province, one-half to the informer, the other half to the use of the poor of that place where the fact is committed....

*     *     *

And be it further enacted by the authority aforesaid, that if any Negro, Indian, or mulatto slaves of or belonging to any other province, without license under the hand of his or her master or mistress, shall be taken up by any person within this province, he, she, or they so taken up shall be whipped at the public whipping post belonging to the place where the said Negro, Indian, or mulatto slaves shall be taken up, not exceeding twenty lashes on the bare back, and to be committed by a warrant from a justice of the peace where the fact shall arise to the jail of that county; and the person so taking them up and carrying them to be whipped, shall have for his reward the sum of ten shillings for each slave, paid by the master or mistress of the said slaves, and to remain in prison till it be paid, with all other charges that shall accrue thereby.

And be it further enacted by the authority aforesaid, that if any Negro, Indian, or mulatto slave shall steal to the value of sixpence, or above, and under the sum of five shillings, and be thereof convicted before two justices of the peace, one whereof to be of quorum, upon the oath or solemn affirmation of one or more witnesses, such Negro, Indian, or mulatto slave shall be whipped on the bare back, at the public whipping place, with forty lashes by the constable of such township or place where the offense was committed, or by such person as he shall appoint. And, that if any Negro, Indian, or mulatto slave shall steal to the value of five shillings, or above, and under the sum of forty shillings, and be thereof convicted in manner as aforesaid, such Negro, Indian, or mulatto slave shall be whipped on the bare back with forty stripes, as aforesaid, and be likewise burned with a hot iron on the most visible part of the left cheek, near the nose, with the letter T, by the constable, as aforesaid; the said constable shall receive for the whipping of each Negro, Indian, or mulatto slave five shillings, and for burning each Negro, Indian, or mulatto slave ten shillings, to be paid by the master or mistress of the said slave; and in default of payment, to be levied by warrant from any justice of the peace, out of the goods of the said master or mistress; and that every constable who shall neglect or refuse to do his duty herein shall forfeit the sum of forty shillings, to be levied by warrant of any justice of the peace, directed to whom he shall appoint, out of the goods and chattels of the said constable.

And if any Negro, Indian, or mulatto slave shall attempt by force or persuasion to ravish or have carnal knowledge of any white woman, maid or child, and be thereof convicted by the verdict of twelve men of the neighborhood before two justices of the peace, one whereof to be of the quorum, such Indian, Negro, or mulatto shall be castrated at the care and charge of his master or mistress, and the Negro to continue in jail at the charge of his master or mistress till execution be performed.

And whereas the baptizing of slaves is thought by some to be a sufficient reason to set them at liberty, which being a groundless opinion and prejudicial to the inhabitants of this province, be it further enacted by the authority aforesaid, that the baptizing of any Negro, Indian, or mulatto slave shall not be any reason or cause for setting them, or any of them, at liberty; nor shall they nor any of them have or procure their or any of their liberty by virtue thereof.

And be it enacted by the authority aforesaid, that all the children that have been or shall be born in the county of such Negro, Indian, or mulatto slaves as have been formerly or may hereafter be set at liberty, and all their posterity shall be and are hereby forever after rendered incapable of purchasing or inheriting any lands and tenements within this province.

And be it further enacted by the authority aforesaid, that any person or persons within this province, who shall knowingly keep or entertain any Negro, Indian, or mulatto slave in his or their house, or otherwise, for above the space of two hours, without their master's or mistress' leave, or some other reasonable cause or occasion, shall forfeit the sum of one shilling for each hour to the master or mistress of such slave, to be recovered before any one of Her Majesty's justices of the peace, in the manner aforesaid; and if above forty shillings, then before the Court of Common Pleas, as aforesaid.

## 24 "a convenient dwelling place in this their native country" (1704)

As the population of the colonies grew, the settlers pressed into aboriginal lands with or without the approval of the colonial governments. New legislation was enacted to protect the lands held by Native Americans against incursions by whites. Significantly, while confirming the property rights of the Native Americans, this law also affirmed the higher sovereignty of Maryland's Lord Proprietor, to whom a yearly rent of a beaver skin was to be paid. Under this claim of a dominant sovereignty over the land, Native American self-governance became predicated upon English suffrance.

☆24 An Act for Ascertaining the Bounds of a Certain Tract of Land to the Use of the Nanticoke Indians so Long as They Shall Occupy and Live upon the Same [Maryland]

Reprinted in J. D. Cushing, ed., *Laws of the Province of Maryland (1718)* (Wilmington, Del.: Michael Glazier, 1977), 38.

It being most just that the Indians, the ancient inhabitants of this province, should have a convenient dwelling place in this their native country, free from the encroachments and oppressions of the English, more especially the Nanticoke Indians, in Dorchester county, who, for these many years, have lived in peace and concord with the English; and, in all matters, in obedience to the government of this Province; we, the burgesses and delegates of this present General Assembly, therefore, do pray that it may be enacted,

SEC. 2. *And be it enacted by the Queen's most Excellent Majesty, by and with the advice and consent of Her Majesty's Governor, Council, and Assembly, of this Province, and the authority of the same,* That all the land, [herein described] is confirmed and assured unto Panquash and Annotoughquan, and the people under their government or charge, and their heirs and successors forever, any law, usage, custom, or grant, to the contrary, in anywise, notwithstanding, to be held of the lord proprietary, and his heirs, lord proprietary, or lords proprietaries, of this province, under the yearly rent of one beaver skin, to be paid to his said lordship, and his heirs, as other rents in this province by the English used to be paid.

SEC. 3. *Provided always,* That it shall or may be lawful for any person or persons, that hath formerly taken up and obtained any grants from the Lord Baltimore, for any tracts or parcels of land within the aforesaid boundaries, upon the Indians deserting or leaving the said land, to enter, occupy, and enjoy the same; any thing in this law to the contrary notwithstanding.

SEC. 4. *And be it further enacted by the authority aforesaid,* That it may not, nor shall be lawful for the Lord Baltimore to ask, have, or demand, any rent or service for any of the said tracts or dividends as may or have been taken up as aforesaid, within the said Indian boundaries, until such time that the takers up, or owners aforesaid, do enjoy or possess the same, any law, usage, or custom, to the contrary notwithstanding. . . .

## 25 Sunday Arrests for Treason (1705)

While recognizing the gravity of the offense of treason, the colonists nevertheless insisted upon procedural safeguards for those accused. The 1705 Virginia laws that prohibited any sheriff or other officer from serving a legal writ on the Lord's Day excepted from this limitation the arrest of specified offenders, including those suspected of treason or riot. Extraordinary procedural mechanisms were a hallmark of combating the political offender.

☆25 An Act Prescribing the Method of Appointing Sheriffs; and for Limiting the Time of Their Continuance in Office and Directing Their Duty Therein [Virginia]

Reprinted in W. Hening, ed., *Virginia Statutes at Large, 1682-1710* (Charlottesville: University Press of Virginia, 1969), 250.

\*            \*            \*

VI. *Provided always,* That it shall not be lawful for any sheriff, or his officer, or deputy, to execute any writ or precept upon the Lord's Day, commonly called Sunday, nor upon any person attending or doing his duty at any muster of the militia, or at any election of burgesses. And the execution of any writ or precept, contrary to the true meaning hereof, is hereby declared to be null and void; any thing herein contained, or any law, custom, or usage, to the contrary, notwithstanding.

VII. *Provided nevertheless,* That it shall and may be lawful for the sheriff, his officer, and deputy, at any time and place whatsoever, to arrest and apprehend any person for treason, or felony, or suspicion of felony, or being accessory thereto; or for any riot, or breach of the peace; or upon any escape out of prison; any thing herein contained to the contrary thereof, notwithstanding.

\*            \*            \*

## 26 Any Person May Be Outlawed and Thereby Attainted (1712)

To protect their population against unfounded and false charges of treason, England's lawmakers relied not only on the early statute of Edward III (1352) which narrowly defined the offense but also on a 1696 enactment under William and Mary which established procedural requirements for treason trials. Following the 1696 English reform, South Carolina set out, in 1712, to lessen the "terror and dread" of this accusation by requiring that all treason indictments be returned by a grand jury within three years of the commission of the offense, testimony be given by two lawful witnesses in open court, and the accused be accorded the right to two court-appointed lawyers. Those charged with treason thus were accorded the right to counsel over 250 years before the United States Supreme Court extended this safeguard to felons generally (*Gideon v. Wainwright*, 372 U.S. 335 [1963]).

## ☆26 An Act for Regulating of Trials in Cases of Treason and Misprision of Treason [South Carolina]

Reprinted in T. Cooper, ed., *Statutes of South Carolina, 1682-1716* (Columbia, S.C.: A. S. Johnston, 1837), 539-41.

WHEREAS, nothing is more just and reasonable, than that persons prosecuted for high treason and misprision of treason, whereby the liberties, lives, honour, estates, blood, and posterity of the subjects, may be lost and destroyed, should be justly and equally tried, and that persons accused as offenders therein should not be debarred of all just and equal means for defence of their innocencies in such cases; in order thereunto, and for the better regulation of trials of persons prosecuted for high treason and misprision of such treason, be it enacted by the King's most excellent majesty, by and with the advice and consent of the lord's spiritual and temporal, and the commons, in this present parliament assembled, and by the authority of the same, That from and after the 25th day of March, in the year of our Lord 1696, all and every person and persons whatsoever, that shall be accused and indicted for high treason, whereby any corruption of blood may or shall be made to any such offender or offenders, or to any heir or heirs of any such offender or offenders, or for misprision of such treason, shall have a true copy of the whole indictment, but not the names of the witnesses, delivered unto them, or any of them, five days at the least before he or they shall be tried, for the same, whereby to enable them, and any of them respectively, to advise with counsel thereupon, to plead and make their defence, his or their attorney or attornies, agent or agents, or any of them, requiring the same, and paying the officer his reasonable fees for writing thereof, not exceeding 5s. for the copy of every such indictment; and that every such person so accused and indicted, arraigned or tried for any such treason, as aforesaid, or for misprision of such treason, from and after the said time, shall be

received and admitted to make his and their full defence, by counsel learned in the law, and to make any proof that he or they can produce by lawful witness or witnesses, who shall then be upon oath, for his and their just defence in that behalf; and in case any person or persons so accused or indicted shall desire counsel, the court before whom such person or persons shall be tried, or some judge of that court, shall and is hereby authorized and required immediately, upon his or their request, to assign to such person and persons such and so many counsel, not exceeding two, as the person or persons shall desire, to whom such counsel shall have free access at all seasonable hours; any law or usage to the contrary notwithstanding.

II. And be it further enacted, That from and after the said 25th day of March, in the year of our Lord 1696, no person or persons whatsoever shall be indicted, tried, or attainted, of high treason, whereby any corruption of blood may or shall be made to any such offender or offenders, or to any the heir or heirs of any such offender or offenders, or of misprision of such treason, but by and upon the oaths and testimony of two lawful witnesses, either both of them to the same overt act, or one of them to one, and the other of them to another overt act of the same treason; unless the party indicted, and arraigned, or tried, shall willingly, without violence, in open court, confess the same, or shall stand mute, or refuse to plead, or in cases of high treason shall peremptorily challenge above the number of 35 of the jury; any law, statute, or usage, to the contrary notwithstanding.

III. Provided always, That any person or persons, being indicted, as aforesaid, for any of the treasons, or misprisions of the treasons aforesaid, may be outlawed, and thereby attainted of or for any of the said offences of treason, or misprision of treason; and in cases of the high treasons aforesaid, where by the law, after such outlawry the party outlawed may come in, and be tried, he shall, upon such trial, have the benefit of this Act.

IV. And be it further enacted and declared by the authority aforesaid, That if two or more distinct treasons of divers heads or kinds shall be alleged in one bill of indictment, one witness produced to prove one of the said treasons, and another witness produced to prove another of the said treasons, shall not be deemed or taken to be two witnesses to the same treason, within the meaning of this Act.

V. And to the intent that the terror and dread of such criminal accusations may in some reasonable time be removed, be it further enacted by the authority aforesaid, That ... no person or persons whatsoever shall be indicted, tried or prosecuted, for any such treason ... unless the same indictment be found by a grand jury within three years next after the treason or offence done or committed.

VI. And that no person or persons shall be prosecuted for any such treason, ... always provided and excepted, That if any person or persons whatsoever, shall be guilty of designing, endeavouring or attempting, any assassination on the body of the King, by poison or otherwise, such person or persons may be prosecuted at any time, notwithstanding the aforesaid limitation.

VII. And that all and every person or persons, who shall be accused, indicted, and tried for such treason ... shall have copies of the panel of the jurors who are to try them, ... two days at the least before he or they shall be tried for the same; and that all persons so accused and indicted for any such treason ... shall have the like process of the court where they shall be tried, to compel their witnesses to appear for them at any such trial or trials, as is usually granted to compel witnesses to appear against them.

VIII. And be it further enacted, That no evidence shall be admitted or given of any overt act that is not expressly laid in the indictment, against any person or persons whatsoever.

\*     \*     \*

## 27 To Acquaint Indians with the Laws of Government (1717)

Native American proximity to the colonies not only caused concern regarding their adherence to the white man's law and order but also resulted in an evangelizing effort. While continuing to recognize the self-governing nature of the Native American tribes, the new laws began a movement to undermine aboriginal social order and tribal authority by replacing dependence upon tribal resources with individual and familial "self-reliance."

☆ 27 An Act for the More Effectual Well Ordering of the Indians and for the Bringing of Them to the Knowledge of the Gospel [Connecticut]

Reprinted in *Laws of the Colonial and State Governments, Relating to Indians and Indian Affairs, 1633-1831 Inclusive* (Standfordville, N.Y.: E. M. Coleman, 1979), 42-43.

Whereas, pursuant to an act of the Assembly, holden in Hartford on the ninth day of May, in the present year one thousand seven hundred and seventeen: The Governor and Council have laid before this Assembly several measures for bringing the Indians in this Colony to the knowledge of the gospel, which was the avowed design of those that obtained the patent for this corporation, to hold the land and government of the Colony:

Upon consideration of which measures, the Gov-

ernor and Company of this, his Majestie's colony, in General Court assembled, desirous of pursuing in the best manner the solemn professions of our predecessors, have enacted,

*And it is hereby enacted by the Governor, Council, and Representatives, in General Court assembled, and by the authority of the same*, That care be taken annually, by the authority of each town, to convene the Indians inhabiting in each town, and acquaint them with the laws of the Government for punishing such immoralities as they shall be guilty of, and make them sensible that no exemption from the penalties of such laws lies for them, any more than for other his Majesty's subjects.

\*     \*     \*

And forasmuch as idleness appears to be a great obstruction to the Indians receiving the gospel of truth, and it might very much conduce to their reformation, in that particular, if they were, by easy and agreeable methods, brought off from their pagan manner of living, and encouraged to make settlements in convenient places, in villages, after the Eglish manner:

*It is hereby resolved*, That measures shall be used to form villages of the natives, wherein the several families of them should have suitable portions of land appropriated to them, so that the said portions shall descend from the father to his children, the more to encourage them to apply themselves to husbandry, and good diligence therein, for their support.

\*     \*     \*

## 28 "publishing a false, scandalous, and seditious libel" (1735)

John Peter Zenger's trial generally is considered the first important test for the political freedom of the press in American colonies. It occurred at a time when the right to political opposition was not widely recognized. In 1733, German-born printer Zenger began publishing the *New York Weekly Journal*. Virtually every issue of the *Journal* contained scathing attacks on the policies of the colonial governor, William Cosby. Zenger had been publishing the *Journal* for two months when Governor Cosby decided to silence him.

Chief Justice James DeLancey unsuccessfully sought indictments for seditious libel from a grand jury. The governor's council then carried out the campaign against Zenger on its own. On November 2, 1734, it decided that four issues of the *Journal* were seditious and should be burned, and that the attorney general would be instructed to prosecute the authors of the controversial articles as well as Zenger, the printer. Zenger was arrested on November 17, and bail was set at £400—an unusually large sum. Unable to raise bail, Zenger remained in the city jail until the conclusion of his trial.

Zenger's trial did not take place until August 4, 1735. Prior to that time, the hostile court had disbarred his counsel. New counsel volunteered to represent the accused—including Andrew Hamilton of Philadelphia, then reputed to be the best lawyer in America.

Hamilton offered to prove the truth of the statements that had appeared in Zenger's paper. But the judge, in accordance with English law, instructed the jury that truth was not a defense to seditious libel, and that the legal decision of whether the statements were libelous could be left for the court rather than the jury to decide. Hamilton, nevertheless, urged the jury to consider itself competent to decide not only whether Zenger, in fact, published the statements but also whether they were legally libelous.

When the arguments were concluded at the end of the day, the jury took only a few minutes before returning a verdict of not guilty. Despite the ultimate vindication, the government was successful in silencing Zenger for the period of his incarceration—and similar treatment could be expected for future dissidents, as the law of sedition remained generally viable. This document is one of the few to highlight the role of the jury in nullifying the reach of the law in political cases.

## ☆ 28 The Trial of John Peter Zenger [New York]

Reprinted in James Alexander, *A Brief Narrative of the Case and Trial of John Peter Zenger* (Cambridge, Mass.: Harvard University Press, Belknap Press, 1963), 58-79.

MR. ATTORNEY GENERAL opened as follows: ... May it please Your Honors, and you, gentlemen of the jury; the information now before the Court, and to which the Defendant Zenger has pleaded not guilty, is an information for printing and publishing a false, scandalous and seditious libel, in which His Excellency the Governor of this Province, who is the King's immediate representative here, is greatly and unjustly scandalized as a person that has no regard to law nor justice; with much more, as will appear upon reading the information. This of libeling is what has always been discouraged as a thing that tends to create differences among men, ill blood among the people, and oftentimes great bloodshed between the party libeling and the party libeled. There can be no doubt but you gentlemen of the jury will have the same ill opinion of such practices as the judges have always shown upon such occasions: But I shall say no more at this time until you hear the information, which is as follows:

... Be it remembered that Richard Bradley, Esq., Attorney General of our sovereign lord the King, for

the Province of New York, who for our said lord the King in this part prosecutes ... gives the Court here to understand and be informed that John Peter Zenger, late of the City of New York, printer (being a seditious person and a frequent printer and publisher of false news and seditious libels, ... [designed] to bring into suspicion and the ill opinion of the subjects of our said lord the King residing within the said Province) the twenty-eighth day of January, ... did falsely, seditiously and scandalously print and publish, and cause to be printed and published, a certain false, malicious, seditious scandalous libel, entitled The New York Weekly Journal, containing the Freshest Advices, Foreign and Domestic; in which libel (of and concerning His Excellency the said Governor, and the ministers and officers of our said lord the King, of and for the said Province) among other things therein contained are these words:

*Your appearance in print* at last gives a pleasure to many, though most wish you had come fairly into the open field, and not appeared behind *retrenchments* made of the supposed laws against libeling and of what other men have said and done before; these *retrenchments*, gentlemen, may soon be shown to you and all men to be weak, and to have neither law nor reason for their foundation, so cannot long stand you in stead: Therefore, you had much better as yet leave them, and come to what *the people of this City and Province* ... think are the points in question (to wit) *They* ... *think as matters now stand that their LIBERTIES and PROPERTIES are precarious, and that SLAVERY is like to be entailed on them and their posterity if some past things be not amended, and this they collect from many past proceedings.* (Meaning many of the past proceedings of His Excellency the said Governor, and of the ministers and officers of our said lord the King, of and for the said Province.)

\*    \*    \*

And the said Attorney general ... likewise gives the Court here to understand and be informed that the said John Peter Zenger ... did falsely, seditiously and scandalously print and publish, and cause to be printed and published, another false, malicious seditious and scandalous libel entitled The New York Weekly Journal, containing the Freshest Advices, Foreign and Domestic. In which libel ... among other things therein contained was these words:

*One of our neighbors* (one of the inhabitants of New Jersey meaning) *being in company, observing the strangers* (some of the inhabitants of New York meaning) *full of complaints, endeavored to persuade them to remove into Jersey; to which it was replied that would be leaping out of the frying pan into the fire, for, says he, we both are under the same Governor* (His Excellency the said

Governor meaning) *and your Assembly have shown with a witness what is to be expected from them; one that was then moving to Pennsylvania,* (meaning one that was then removing from New York with intent to reside at Pennsylvania) *to which place it is reported several considerable men are removing* (from New York meaning) *expressed, in terms very moving, much concern for the circumstances of New York* (the bad circumstances of the Province and people of New York meaning) *seemed to think them very much owing to the influence that some men* (whom he called tools) *had in the administration* (meaning the administration of government of the said Province of New York) *said he was now going from them, and was not to be hurt by any measures they should take, but could not help having some concern for the welfare of his countrymen, and should be glad to hear that the Assembly* (meaning the General Assembly of the Province of New York) *would exert themselves as became them, by showing that they have the interest of their country more at heart than the gratification of any private view of any of their members, or being at all affected by the smiles or frowns of a governor* (His Excellency the said Governor meaning), *both which ought equally to be despised when the interest of their country is at stake. You, says he, complain of the lawyers, but I think the law itself is at an end; WE* (the people of the Province of New York meaning) *SEE MEN'S DEEDS DESTROYED, JUDGES ARBITRARILY DISPLACED, NEW COURTS ERECTED WITHOUT CONSENT OF THE LEGISLATURE* (within the Province of New York meaning) *BY WHICH, IT SEEMS TO ME, TRIALS BY JURIES ARE TAKEN AWAY WHEN A GOVERNOR PLEASES* (His Excellency the said Governor meaning), *MEN OF KNOWN ESTATES DENIED THEIR VOTES CONTRARY TO THE RECEIVED PRACTICE, THE BEST EXPOSITOR OF ANY LAW: Who is then in that Province* (meaning the Province of New York) *that call* (can call meaning) *anything his own, or enjoy any liberty* (liberty meaning) *longer than those in the administration* (meaning the administration of government of the said Province of New York) *will condescend to let them do it, for which reason I have left it* (the Province of New York meaning), *as I believe more will.*

To the great disturbance of the peace of the said Province of New York, to the great scandal of our said lord the King, of His Excellency the said Governor, and of all others concerned in the administration of the government of the said Province, and against the peace of our sovereign lord the King his crown and dignity, etc. Whereupon the said Attorney General of our said lord the King, for our said lord the King, prays the advisement of the Court here, in the premises, and the due process of the law, against him the said John Peter Zenger, in this part

to be done, to answer to our said lord the King of and in the premises, etc.

R. Bradley, Attorney General

To this information the Defendant has pleaded not guilty, and we are ready to prove it. . . .

Mr. Hamilton. May it please Your Honor; I cannot think it proper for me (without doing violence to my own principles) to deny the publication of a complaint which I think is the right of every free-born subject to make when the matters so published can be supported with truth; and therefore . . . I do (for my client) confess that he both printed and published the two newspapers set forth in the information, and I hope in so doing he has committed no crime.

\*          \*          \*

Mr. Attorney. [A]s Mr. Hamilton has confessed the printing and publishing these libels, I think the jury must find a verdict for the King; for supposing they were true, the law says that they are not the less libelous for that; nay indeed the law says their being true is an aggravation of the crime.

Mr. Hamilton. Not so neither, Mr. Attorney, there are two words to that bargain. I hope it is not our bare printing and publishing a paper that will make it a libel: You will have something more to do before you make my client a libeler; for the words themselves must be libelous, that is, false, scandalous, and seditious or else we are not guilty.

\*          \*          \*

Mr. Attorney. The case before the Court is whether Mr. Zenger is guilty of libeling His Excellency the Governor of New York, and indeed the whole administration of the government? Mr. Hamilton has confessed the printing and publishing, and I think nothing is plainer than that the words in the information are scandalous, and tend to sedition, and to disquiet the minds of the people of this Province. And if such papers are not libels, I think it may be said there can be no such thing as a libel.

\*          \*          \*

Mr. Chief Justice. Mr. Attorney, you have heard what Mr. Hamilton has said, and the cases he has cited, for having his witnesses examined to prove the truth of the several facts contained in the papers set forth in the information, what do you say to it?

Mr. Attorney. The law in my opinion is very clear; they cannot be admitted to justify a libel; for, by the authorities I have already read to the Court, it is not the less a libel because it is true. I think I need not trouble the Court with reading the cases over again; the thing seems to be very plain, and I submit it to the Court.

Mr. Chief Justice. Mr. Hamilton, the Court is of opinion, you ought not to be permitted to prove the facts in the papers: These are the words of the book, "It is far from being a justification of a libel, that the contents thereof are true, or that the person upon whom it is made had a bad reputation, since the greater appearance there is of truth in any malicious invective, so much the more provoking it is."

MR. HAMILTON. These are Star Chamber cases, and I was in hopes that practice had been dead with the Court.

... MR. HAMILTON. I thank Your Honor. Then, gentlemen of the jury, it is to you we must now appeal for witnesses to the truth of the facts we have offered and are denied the liberty to prove; and let it not seem strange that I apply myself to you in this manner, I am warranted so to do both by law and reason. The law supposes you to be summoned out of the neighborhood where the fact is alleged to be committed; and the reason of your being taken out of the neighborhood is because you are supposed to have the best knowledge of the fact that is to be tried. And were you to find a verdict against my client, you must take upon you to say the papers referred to in the information, and which we acknowledge we printed and published, are false, scandalous and seditious. . . .

*       *       *

MR. CHIEF JUSTICE. No, Mr. Hamilton; the jury may find that Zenger printed and published those papers, and leave it to the Court to judge whether they are libelous; you know this is very common; it is in the nature of a special verdict, where the jury leave the matter of law to the Court.

MR. HAMILTON. I know, may it please Your Honor, the jury may do so; but I do likewise know they may do otherwise. I know they have the right beyond all dispute to determine both the law and the fact, and where they do not doubt of the law, they ought to do so. This of leaving it to the judgment of the Court whether the words are libelous or not in effect renders juries useless (to say no worse) in many cases; ...

For though I own it to be base and unworthy to scandalize any man, yet I think it is even villainous to scandalize a person of public character, and I will go so far into Mr. Attorney's doctrine as to agree that if the faults, mistakes, nay even the vices of such a person be private and personal, and don't affect the peace of the public, or the liberty or property of our neighbor, it is unmanly and unmannerly to expose them either by word or writing. But when a ruler of a people brings his personal failings, but much more his vices, into his administration, and the people find themselves affected by them, either in their liberties or properties, that will alter the case mightily, and all the high things that are said in favor of rulers, and of dignities, and upon the side of power, will not be able to stop people's mouths when they feel themselves oppressed, I mean in a free

government. It is true in times past it was a crime to speak truth, and in that terrible Court of Star Chamber, many worthy and brave men suffered for so doing; and yet even in that Court and in those bad times, a great and good man durst say, what I hope will not be taken amiss of me to say in this place, to wit, The practice of informations for libels is a sword in the hands of a wicked king and an arrant coward to cut down and destroy the innocent; the one cannot because of his high station, and the other dares not because of his want of courage, revenge himself in another manner.

*       *       *

## 29 "A riot, and insult upon the King's government" (1747)

Not all disagreements between the colonists and the English authorities were viewed or were articulated as political conflicts. Many of the conflicts were related, however, to a growing difference between the mother country and its colonies regarding the power of government and the rights of the people. "Pressing" unwilling sailors into service in the British navy gave rise to some early conflicts. Press gangs who seized merchant seamen plagued Boston in the 1740s, and sympathetic townspeople often joined in the resistance to the practice. Despite strong protests at the town meeting, impressment, which hurt Boston's trade, continued. On November 16, 1747, several hundred townspeople made up of sailors, laborers, and blacks seized a navy lieutenant under Commodore Charles Knowles, assaulted a sheriff who came to his aid, and stormed the General Court. The local militia failed to respond to Governor William Shirley's order to put down the riot. Impressment in America, despite popular opposition, continued until after the War of 1812.

A report of the riots was contained in Governor Shirley's letter to the Lords of Trade in London.

☆ 29 Letter by Governor William Shirley to the Lords of Trade regarding the Knowles Riot (December 1, 1747)

Reprinted in Richard Hofstadter and Michael Wallace, eds., *American Violence: A Documentary History* (New York: Knopf, 1970), 60-63.

A riot, and insult upon the King's government lately happen'd here of so extraordinary a nature, that I think it my duty to give your Lordships an account of it.

It was occasion'd by an impress made on the sixteenth of November at night out of all the vessels in this harbour, by order of Commodore Knowles, then on board the Canterbury, for manning his Squadron. . . .

The first notice, I had of the mob, was given me between nine and ten o'clock in the forenoon by the Speaker of the House of Representatives, who had pick'd up in the streets Captain Derby of his Majesty's Ship Alborough, and the Purser of the Canterbury, and brought 'em under his Protection to me for shelter in my house acquainting me at the same time, that the mob consisted of about three hundred seamen, all strangers, (the greatest part Scotch) with cutlasses and clubs, and that they had seiz'd and detain'd in their custody a Lieutenant of the Lark, whom they met with at his lodgins on shoar; The next notice I had was about half an hour after by the Sheriff of the County, who with some of his officers had been in pursuit of the mob in order to recover the Man of War's Lieutenant, and to endeavour to disperse 'em; and who coming up with four of 'em separated from the others, had wrested a cutlass from one and seiz'd two of 'em; but being overtaken by the whole mob, (who were appriz'd of this), as he was carrying those two to goal, was assaulted, and grievously wounded by 'em, and forc'd to deliver up his two prisoners, and leave one of his deputies in their hands, for whose life he assur'd me he was in fear.

Thereupon I immediately sent orders to the Colonel of the Regiment to raise the militia of the town and suppress the mob by force, and, if need was, to fire upon 'em with ball; which were scarcely deliver'd to him, when they appear'd before my gates, and part of 'em advanc'd directly through my court yard up to my door with the Lieutenant, two other sea officers, that part of the mob which stay'd at the outward gate crying out to the party at my door not to give up any of their prisoners to me. Upon this I immediately went out to 'em and demanded the cause of the tumult, to which one of 'em arm'd with a cutlass answer'd me in an insolent manner it was caus'd by my unjustifiable impress warrant; whereupon I told 'em that the impress was not made by my warrant, nor with my knowledge; but that he was a very impudent rascal for his behaviour; and upon his still growing more insolent, my son in law who happen'd to follow me out, struck his hat off his head, asking him if he knew, who he was talking to; this immediately silenced their clamour, when I demanded of 'em, where the King's Officers were, that they had seiz'd; and they being shewn to me, I went up to the Lieutenant and bid him go into my house, and upon his telling me the mob would not suffer him, I took him from among 'em, and putting him before me caus'd him to go in, as I did likewise the other three and follow'd 'em without exchanging more words with the mob, that I might avoid making any promises or terms with 'em. . . .

[T]he mob now increas'd and join'd by some inhabitants came to the Town House (just after candle light) arm'd as in the morning, assaulted the Council Chamber (myself and the Council being then sitting there and the House of Representatives a minute or two before by accident adjourn'd) by throwing stones and brickbatts in at the windows, and having broke all the windows of the lower floor, where a few of the Militia Officers were assembled, forcibly enter'd into it, and oblig'd most of the officers to retire up into the Council Chamber; where the mob was expected soon to follow 'em up; but prevented by some few of the officers below, who behav'd better.

*          *          *

. . . The day following Mr. Knowles upon hearing of these outrages wrote me word, that he purpos'd to bring his whole squadron before the town the next morning, but I dissuaded him from it, by an immediate answer to his letter: In the evening the mob forcibly search'd the Navy Hospital upon the Town Common in order to let out what seamen they could find there belonging to the King's ships; and seven or eight private houses for officers, and took four or five petty officers; but soon releas'd 'em without any ill usage, as they did the same day Captain Erskine, whom they had suffer'd to remain in a gentleman's house upon his parole, their chief intent appearing to be, from the beginning, not to use the officers well any otherwise than by detaining 'em, in hopes of obliging Mr. Knowles to give up the impress'd men.

*          *          *

## 30 "punishing their secret Plots and dangerous Combinations" (1748)

Between 1680 and 1776, the British colonies of America and the West Indies imported more than two million African slaves. The British slave trade reached its peak shortly before the War of American Independence.

During the first half of the eighteenth century, several slave rebellions occurred in South Carolina, Virginia, and New York. Colonial slaveowners attempted to keep news of conspiracies or uprisings from spreading so as not to incite slaves in other places. It is known, however, that thirty-four slave ship revolts took place from 1700 to 1776. Among the colonial rebellions, the Cato uprising of 1739-40 in South Carolina and the New York slave insurrection scare of 1741 are particularly noteworthy. By the mid-eighteenth century, the laws in southern states began to reflect considerable anxiety regarding slave conspiracies and insurrections. In attempting to combat the perceived threat, the law began to sweep within its proscriptions free blacks, who, for reasons of racial affinity, might be in sympathy with the plight of slaves.

## ☆ 30 An Act Directing the Trial of Slaves Committing Capital Crimes, and for the More Effectual Punishing Conspiracies and Insurrections of Them, and for the Better Government of Negroes, Mulattoes, and Indians, Bond or Free [Virginia]

Reprinted in *The Acts of Assembly Now in Force in the Colony of Virginia 1661-1769* (Williamsburg: Rind, Purdie, and Dixon, 1769), 258-59.

I. WHEREAS it is absolutely necessary that effectual Provision should be made for the better ordering and governing of Slaves, free Negroes, Mulattoes, and Indians, and detecting and punishing their secret Plots and dangerous Combinations, and for the speedy Trial of such of them as commit capital Crimes:

II. BE it therefore enacted, by the Lieutenant Governour, Council, and Burgesses of this present General Assembly, and it is hereby enacted, by the Authority of the same, that if any Negro, or other Slaves, shall at any Time consult, advise or conspire to rebel or make Insurrection, or shall plot or conspire the Murder of any Person or Persons whatsoever, every such consulting, plotting, or conspiring, shall be adjudged and deemed Felony, and the Slave or Slaves convicted thereof, in Manner herein after directed, shall suffer Death, and be utterly excluded all Benefit of Clergy.

III. AND whereas many Negroes, under Pretence of practicing Physick, have prepared and exhibited poisonous Medicines, by which many Persons have been murdered, and others have languished under long and tedious Indispositions, and it will be difficult to detect such pernicious and dangerous Practices if they should be permitted to exhibit any Sort of Medicine, Be it therefore further enacted, that if any Negro or other Slave, shall prepare, exhibit, or administer, any Medicine whatsoever, he or she so offending shall be judged guilty of Felony, and suffer Death without Benefit of Clergy.

IV. PROVIDED always, that if it shall appear to the Court, before which such Slave shall be tried, that the Medicine was not prepared, exhibited, or administered, with an ill Intent, not attended with any bad Consequences, such Slave shall have the Benefit of Clergy.

V. PROVIDED also, that nothing herein contained shall be construed to extend to any Slave or Slaves administering Medicines by his or her Master's or Mistress's Order, in his or her Family, or the Family of another, with the mutual Consent of the Owner of such Slave, and the Master or Mistress of such Family.

VI. AND be it further enacted, by the Authority aforesaid, that every Slave committing such Offence as by Law is punishable with Death, or Loss of Member, shall be forthwith committed to the common Gaol of the County wherein such Offence shall be done, there to be safely kept, and upon such Commitment the Sheriff of such County shall certify the same, with the Cause thereof, to the Governour or Commander in Chief of this Dominion for the Time being, who is thereupon desired and empowered to issue a Commission of Oyer and Terminer to such Persons as he shall think fit, which Persons, forthwith after Receipt of such Commission, are empowered and required to cause the Offender to be publickly arraigned and tried at the Courthouse of the said County, and to take for Evidence the Confession of the Offender, the Oath of one or more credible Witnesses, or such Testimony of Negroes, Mulattoes, or Indians, bond or free, with pregnant Circumstances, as to them shall seem convincing, without the Solemnity of a Jury; and the Offender being by them found guilty, to pass such Judgment upon such Offender as the Law directs for the like Crimes, and on such Judgment to award Execution.

VII. PROVIDED always, that if at such Trial the Court be divided in Opinion whether the accused be guilty or not guilty, in that Case he, she, or they, shall be acquitted: Provided also, that when Judgment of Death shall be passed upon any such Offender there shall be ten Days at least between the Time of passing Judgment and the Day of Execution, except in Cases of Conspiracy, Insurrection, or Rebellion.

\*      \*      \*

## 31 "Rulers have no authority from God to do mischief" (1750)

The foundation of the American position on civil disobedience owes much to Jonathan Mayhew, who, from 1747 to 1766, served as minister of Boston's West Church. Mayhew thought of himself as a true and loyal Englishman committed to the beloved, though unwritten, British constitution. Yet he opposed the doctrine of the divine rights of kings. The legitimacy of secular authority, he believed, was contingent on its commitment to advance the happiness and well-being of the people.

Having borrowed his theories from John Locke, Mayhew was not an original thinker but was nevertheless a very prominent and influential speaker in America. Preaching on the anniversary of the death of Charles I, Mayhew spoke in support of the people's right to overthrow a tyrannical government. But his sermon went beyond the question of communal opposition to tyranny and disclosed a sensitivity toward the duties of the individual citizen confronted by unjust rulers. His most succinct support of dissent was contained in an earlier sermon where he stated:

It indeed is often a sin to transgress human laws; but not universally so. It is possible for human legislators who are sometimes wicked, and always fallible, to enact unrighteous laws; to enjoin things that are in their own nature unlawful; and to forbid things that are in their own nature good and commendable. Now when iniquity comes to be thus established by a law, it can not be any iniquity to transgress that law by which it is established. On the contrary, it is a sin not to transgress it.... It is universally better to obey God than Man when the laws of God and Man clash and interfere with one another.

These premises, having firm roots in the colonies' reliance upon biblical authority and their experience with consensual government, provided a process by which to test the legitimacy of law and political authority. In the contest between allegiances, Mayhew advocated the supremacy of God's law and righteousness over the iniquities of the state.

☆ 31 Discourse concerning Unlimited Submission and Non-Resistance to the Higher Powers (Jonathan Mayhew)

Reprinted in J. W. Thornton, ed., *The Pulpit of the American Revolution: Or the Political Sermons of the Period of 1776* (Boston: Gould & Lincoln, 1860), 73-86.

Rulers have no authority from God to do mischief. ... It is blasphemy to call tyrants and oppressors God's ministers. They are more properly "the messengers of Satan to buffet us." No rulers are properly God's ministers but such as are "just, ruling in the fear of God." When once magistrates act contrary to their office, and the end of their institution—when they rob and ruin the public, instead of being guardians of its peace and welfare—, they immediately cease to be the ordinance and ministers of God, and no more deserve that glorious character than common pirates and highwaymen.

If magistrates are unrighteous, ... the main end of civil government will be frustrated. And what reason is there for submitting to that government which does by no means answer the design of government? "Wherefore ye must needs be subject not only for wrath, but also for conscience' sake." Here the apostle [Paul] argues the duty of a cheerful and conscientious submission to civil government from the nature and end of magistracy, as he had before laid it down; *i.e.*, as the design of it was to punish evil-doers, and to support and encourage such as do well; ... if the motive and argument for submission to government be taken from the apparent usefulness of civil authority,—it follows, that when no such good end can be answered by submission, there remains no argument or motive to enforce it; ... And therefore, in such cases, a regard to the public welfare ought to make us withhold from our rulers

that obedience and submission which it would otherwise be our duty to render to them. If it be our duty, for example, to obey our king merely for this reason, that he rules for the public welfare (which is the only argument the apostle makes use of), it follows, by a parity of reason, that when he turns tyrant, and makes his subjects his prey to devour and destroy, instead of his charge to defend and cherish, we are bound to throw off our allegiance to him, and to resist; and that according to the tenor of the apostle's argument in this passage. Not to discontinue our allegiance in this case would be to join with the sovereign in promoting the slavery and misery of that society, the welfare of which we ourselves, as well as our sovereign, are indispensably obliged to secure and promote, as far as in us lies. It is true the apostle puts no case of such a tyrannical prince; but, by his grounding his argument for submission wholly upon the good of civil society, it is plain he implicitly authorizes, and even requires us to make resistance, whenever this shall be necessary to the public safety and happiness....

But, then, if unlimited submission and passive obedience to the higher powers, in all possible cases, be not a duty, it will be asked, "How far are we obliged to submit? If we may innocently disobey and resist in some cases, why not in all? Where shall we stop? What is the measure of our duty? This doctrine tends to the total dissolution of civil government, and to introduce such scenes of wild anarchy and confusion as are more fatal to society than the worst of tyranny."

But ... similar difficulties may be raised with respect to almost every duty of natural and revealed religion. To instance only in two, both of which are near akin, and indeed exactly parallel to the case before us: It is unquestionably the duty of children to submit to their parents, and of servants to their masters; but no one asserts that it is their duty to obey and submit to them in all supposable cases, or universally a sin to resist them. Now, does this tend to subvert the just authority of parents and masters, or to introduce confusion and anarchy into private families? No. How, then, does the same principle tend to unhinge the government of that larger family the body politic? ... Now, there is at least as much difficulty in stating the measure of duty in these two cases as in the case of rulers and subjects; so that this is really no objection—at least, no reasonable one—against resistance to the higher powers. Or, if it is one, it will hold equally against resistance in the other cases mentioned.

We may very safely assert these two things in general, without undermining government: One is, that no civil rulers are to be obeyed when they enjoin things that are inconsistent with the commands of God. All such disobedience is lawful and glorious; ... All commands running counter to the declared will of the Supreme Legislator of heaven and earth are null and void, and therefore disobedience to them is a duty, not a crime. Another thing that may be asserted with equal truth and safety is, that no government is to be submitted to at the expense of that which is the sole end of all government—the common good and safety of society. . . .

Now, as all men are fallible, it cannot be supposed that the public affairs of any state should be always administered in the best manner possible, even by persons of the greatest wisdom and integrity. Nor is it sufficient to legitimate disobedience to the higher powers that they are not so administered, or that they are in some instances very ill-managed; for, upon this principle, it is scarcely supposable that any government at all could be supported, or subsist. Such a principle manifestly tends to the dissolution of government, and to throw all things into confusion and anarchy. But it is equally evident, upon the other hand, that those in authority may abuse their trust and power to such a degree, that neither the law of reason nor of religion requires that any obedience or submission should be paid to them; but, on the contrary, that they should be totally discarded, and the authority which they were before vested with transferred to others, who may exercise it more to those good purposes for which it is given. Nor is this principle, that resistance to the higher

powers is in some extraordinary cases justifiable, so liable to abuse as many persons seem to apprehend it. . . . Mankind in general have a disposition to be as submissive and passive and tame under government as they ought to be. . . . While those who govern do it with any tolerable degree of moderation and justice, and in any good measure act up to their office and character by being public benefactors, the people will generally be easy and peaceable, and be rather inclined to flatter and adore than to insult and resist them. . . . [P]eople know for what end they set up and maintain their governors, and they are the proper judges when they execute their trust as they ought to do it. . . . Till people find themselves greatly abused and oppressed by their governors, they are not apt to complain; and whenever they do, in fact, find themselves thus abused and oppressed, they must be stupid *not* to complain. To say that subjects in general are not proper judges when their governors oppress them and play the tyrant, and when they defend their rights, administer justice impartially, and promote the public welfare, is as great treason as ever man uttered. 'T is treason, not against one *single* man, but the state—against the whole body politic; 't is treason against mankind, 't is treason against common sense, 't is treason against God. . . .

### CHAPTER 2

# The Revolutionary War

1765-1781

THE American Revolution has meant various things to different observers and commentators: some have seen it primarily as a political rebellion, others as an economic protest or a social uprising. But in the context of this collection the Revolution represented the first major collaborative—indeed, nation-wide—manifestation of political crime in America. By and large, the modern conception of the Revolutionary War is that of a unified country fighting a relatively brief war of national liberation against an exploitive and foreign power. Similarly, the Declaration of Independence has been perceived, for the most part, as a domestic preamble for the rights and goals of national self-government. However, a closer examination of contemporary documents reveals wavering and conflicting bonds of allegiance, first to the king and later to the local colonial governing bodies that ultimately promulgated the Revolution. Nowhere is the status of the new national American sovereign clearly defined. The Declaration of Independence likewise represents more than a mere domestic document; it is indeed the first national and international statement articulating the right to lawful revolution.

The years spanning this chapter are replete with well-known instances of political dissent and violence, such as the Boston Tea Party in 1773. Their number and our limited space prevents inclusion of them all. This collection focuses instead on the more revealing though less dramatic documents associated with the enunciation of disobedience to the overseas king and the enforcement of allegiance to the embryonic local political sovereignty. This emphasis, not on acts of dissent and violence, but on the theories and machinery utilized both in support of and in opposition to political criminality, should enhance the understanding of the jurisprudence of political crime.

Both sides of the Atlantic were aware of the law of treason and the requirement of oaths (including adherence to the Articles of War) as mechanisms for the assertion of sovereignty and political dominion over people. The pains and penalties for treason were applied and misapplied in like manner, although for opposite reasons, by the contending powers in North America. Once, it was the colonists who remonstrated against the excesses of General Gage, who, acting in response to Bostonian intransigence, expanded the reach of the law of treason beyond that of the English law. Later, the newly independent states enacted laws that abandoned the jealously guarded procedural protections surrounding those accused of treason for continuing to adhere to the English king. Other methods of investigating the loyalties of an ambivalent citizenry and of purging those suspected of royalist sympathies were utilized by the states as well.

Thus, the requirement of oaths of allegiance and the formulation of the law of treason provide the main instruments for examining the process whereby, in the eighteen-year period from the Stamp Act (1765) to the Treaty of Paris (1783), the loyalties of the citizenry officially and gradually were changed from the king to the sovereign United States. The materials, in addition, relate the asserted grievances that provided the incentive for the colonists' abandoning not only the obligation to obey the laws of Parliament but ultimately the allegiance to the king himself. The chapter, finally, supplies some references to demonstrate that while the Revolutionary War was going on, the foundations for new and future dissent, unrest, and political criminality were beginning to evolve.

---

## 32 "We can no longer forbear" (1765)

In 1760, England's seven-year-long French and Indian War, waged to expand English colonial rule in America, concluded, with France ceding to Britain her territories in Canada in the 1763 Treaty of Paris. Even though the proportion of English to French colonists was approximately fifteen to one, the more numerous but disunited English colonials initially were no match for the Frenchmen and their Native American allies, both superior wilderness fighters. But with his ascension to power in England in 1758, William Pitt made adequate finances and capable commanders available to change the course of events in America. The actual hostilities ceased with the British conquest of Quebec in 1759 under the command of Major General James Wolfe and the surrender of Montreal in 1760 to Colonel Jeffrey Amherst.

The English Parliament's demands for colonial

contributions to the defense costs of the American continent gave rise to a number of conflicts between the colonists and the mother country. Parliament, in March 1765, passed the Stamp Act, imposing a tax on all formal documents such as deeds, diplomas, bills, and newspapers. The artisans and shopkeepers of Boston led the popular resistance to the new tax, and the houses of several government officials were attacked, including that of Andrew Oliver, the Stamp Collector-designate. Although the violence was limited and no one was killed, the tax united the colonies for the first time, in the Stamp Act Congress, in opposition to English law.

The colonial objections to the Stamp Act were summarized in the instructions of the Town of Braintree, Massachusetts, drafted by John Adams.

☆ 32 Instructions of the Town of Braintree

Reprinted in C. F. Adams, ed., *The Works of John Adams* (New York: AMS Press, 1971), 3:465-67.

To EBENEZER THAYER, ESQ.

SIR, — ... We can no longer forbear complaining, that many of the measures of the late ministry, and some of the late acts of Parliament, have a tendency, in our apprehension, to divest us of our most essential rights and liberties. We shall confine ourselves, however, chiefly to the act of Parliament, commonly called the Stamp Act, by which a very burthensome, and, in our opinion, unconstitutional tax, is to be laid upon us all; and we subjected to numerous and enormous penalties, to be prosecuted, sued for, and recovered, at the option of an informer, in a court of admiralty, without a jury.

We have called this a burthensome tax, because the duties are so numerous and so high, and the embarrassments to business in this infant, sparsely-settled country so great, that it would be totally impossible for the people to subsist under it, if we had no controversy at all about the right and authority of imposing it. Considering the present scarcity of money, we have reason to think, the execution of that act for a short space of time would drain the country of its cash, strip multitudes of all their property, and reduce them to absolute beggary. And what the consequence would be to the peace of the province, from so sudden a shock and such a convulsive change in the whole course of our business and subsistence, we tremble to consider. We further apprehend this tax to be unconstitutional. We have always understood it to be a grand and fundamental principle of the constitution, that no freeman should be subject to any tax to which he has not given his own consent, in person or by proxy. And the maxims of the law, as we have constantly received them, are to the same effect, that no freeman can be separated from his property but by his own act or fault. We take it clearly, therefore, to be inconsistent with the spirit of the common law, and of the essential fundamental principles of the British constitution, that we should be subject to any tax imposed by the British Parliament; because we are not represented in that assembly in any sense, unless it be by a fiction of law, as insensible in theory as it would be injurious in practice, if such a taxation should be grounded on it.

But the most grievous innovation of all, is the alarming extension of the power of courts of admiralty. In these courts, one judge presides alone! No juries have any concern there! The law and the fact are both to be decided by the same single judge, whose commission is only during pleasure, and with whom, as we are told, the most mischievous of all customs has become established, that of taking commissions on all condemnations; so that he is under a pecuniary temptation always against the subject. ... We have all along thought the acts of trade in this respect a grievance; but the Stamp Act has opened a vast number of sources of new crimes, which may be committed by any man, and cannot but be committed by multitudes, and prodigious penalties are annexed, and all these are to be tried by such a judge of such a court! ... We cannot help asserting, therefore, that this part of the act will make an essential change in the constitution of juries, and it is directly repugnant to the Great Charter itself; for, by that charter, "no americament shall be assessed, but by the oath of honest and lawful men of the vicinage;" and, "no freeman shall be taken, or imprisoned, or disseized of his freehold, or liberties of free customs, nor passed upon, nor condemned, but by lawful judgment of his peers, or by the law of the land." So that this act will "make such a distinction, and create such a difference between" the subjects in Great Britain and those in America, as we could not have expected from the guardians of liberty in "both."

As these, sir, are our sentiments of this act, we, the freeholders and other inhabitants, legally assembled for this purpose, must enjoin it upon you, to comply with no measures or proposals for countenancing the same, or assisting in the execution of it, but by all lawful means, consistent with our allegiance to the King, and relation to Great Britain, to oppose the execution of it, till we can hear the success of the cries and petitions of America for relief.

We further recommend the most clear and explicit assertion and vindication of our rights and liberties to be entered on the public records, that the world may know, in the present and all future generations, that we have a clear knowledge and a just sense of them, and, with submission to Divine Providence, that we never can be slaves. ...

## 33 " 'you shall die then' " (1766)

Colonial America witnessed several instances of domestic economic struggle. The accumulation of large estates in New York created a quasi-feudal class with single-family possessions sometimes exceeding one million acres. The owners of these estates often were granted criminal jurisdiction, the authority to appoint magistrates, and the right to name representatives to the assembly of the colony. Cultivated by tenants who paid rent in kind, the estates flourished while the workers chafed against the system. Tenant complaints at times erupted into violence. The climax came in the Agrarian Rebellion of 1766, when the sheriff of Albany County attempted to dispossess settlers on the John Van Renselear land. Some seventeen hundred armed settlers closed the courts and opened the jails in Poughkeepsie. In response to the landowners' call for help, the government declared the insurrection's leaders guilty of high treason.

An account of the initial June 26, 1766, confrontation between the settlers and the forces of law was printed in the *Boston Gazetteer*.

☆ 33 New York Agrarian Rebellion
(July 14, 1766)

*Boston Gazetteer* or *Country Journal*, reprinted in Richard Hofstadter and Michael Wallace, eds., *American Violence: A Documentary History* (New York: Knopf, 1970), 116-17.

. . . [T]he inhabitants of a place called Nobletown and a place called Spencer-Town lying west of Sheffield, Great Barrington, and Stockbridge, who has purchased of the Stockbridge Indians the lands they now possess; by virtue of an order of the General Court of this province, and settled about two hundred families; John Van Renselear Esq., pretending a right to said lands, had treated the inhabitants very cruelly, because they would not submit to him as tenants, he claiming a right to said lands by virtue of a patent from the Government of New York; that said Van Renselear some years ago raised a number of men and came upon the poor people, and pulled down some houses killed some people, imprisoned others, and has been constantly vexing and injuring the people. That on the 26th of last month said Renselear came down with between two and three hundred men, all armed with guns, pistols and swords; that upon intelligence that 500 men armed were coming against them, about forty or fifty of the inhabitants went out unarmed, except with sticks, and proceeded to a fence between them and the assailants, in order to compromise the matter between them. That the assailants came up to the fence, and Hermanus Schuyler the Sheriff of the County of Albany, fired his pistol down . . . upon them and three

others fired their guns over them. The inhabitants thereupon desired to talk with them, and they would not harken; but the Sheriff, it was said by some who knew him, ordered the men to fire, who thereupon fired, and killed one of their own men, who had got over the fence and one of the inhabitants likewise within the fence. Upon this the chief of the inhabitants, unarmed as aforesaid, retreated most of them into the woods, but twelve betook themselves to the house from whence they set out and there defended themselves with six small arms and some ammunition that were therein. The two parties here fired upon each other. The assailants killed one man in the house, and the inhabitants wounded several of them, whom the rest carried off and retreated, to the number of seven, none of whom at the last accounts were dead. That the Sheriff shewed no paper, nor attempted to execute any warrant, and the inhabitants never offered any provocation at the fence, excepting their continuing there, nor had any one of them a gun, pistol or sword, till they retreated to the house. At the action at the fence one of the inhabitants had a leg broke, whereupon the assailants attempted to seize him and carry him off. He therefore begged they would consider the misery he was in, declaring he had rather die than be carried off, whereupon one of the assailants said "you shall die then" and discharging his pistol upon him as he lay on the ground, shot him to the body, as the wounded man told the informant; that the said wounded man was alive when he left him, but not like to continue long. The affray happened about sixteen miles distant from Hudson's River. It is feared the Dutch will pursue these poor people for thus defending themselves, as murderers; and keep them in great consternation.

## 34 "The alarming cries of the oppressed" (1769)

Colonial America was not a classless society, and the dissatisfaction of the backcountry and its nonslaveholding small farmers with the aristocratic and privileged landed gentry frequently surfaced. Economically deprived, politically unrepresented, and religiously unorthodox, the dissenting frontiersmen were particularly vocal in North and South Carolina. The political history during the colonial period can be depicted as a constant struggle between representatives of the people and the representatives of the crown. These disputes were over local government corruption, scarcity of money, stiff taxation, restraints on commerce, burdensome land policies, and religious intolerance. Organized into formal associations known as the "Regulators," these country yeomen from the Blue Ridge Mountain settlements petitioned the authorities for reform, but in the eyes of the officials the demands constituted sedition. When the 1769 Regulator petitions (calling for ballot voting, taxation in proportion to wealth, collection of taxes in local commodities, and the regular publishing of laws) were ignored, the exasperated Regulators interfered with the collection of rents and taxes and with the operation of the courts. The assembly responded by imposing the death penalty upon members of any crowd of ten or more who failed to disperse when so ordered.

Even earlier, armed partisans in 1765 and 1766 prevented the enforcement of the Stamp Act in North and South Carolina, whose population numbered less than three hundred thousand. There were several other armed conflicts that culminated in the Battle of Alamance (1771) between the Regulators and the forces of Governor William Tryon, the Crown representative. The Regulators forced the governor to lead two military expeditions against them in 1768 and in 1771. The latter campaign required a government force of approximately one thousand men and officers. The Regulator troops consisted of twice that number, but their lack of arms and discipline resulted in defeat. Seven rebel prisoners were executed for treason. Thousands of frontiersmen were required to take an oath of allegiance to the colonial government, and many moved further west to avoid the requirement. The hostility between the western settlers and the eastern seaboard establishment led many of the backcountry population to support the Loyalists rather than their exploitative local gentry at the time of the revolution.

## ☆ 34 Petition of the Inhabitants of Anson County, North Carolina (October 9, 1769)

Reprinted in W. Saunders, ed., *The Colonial Records of North Carolina* (Raleigh: Josephus Daniel, 1890), 3:75.

MR. SPEAKER AND GENTLEMEN OF THE ASSEMBLY:

*The Petition of the Inhabitants of Anson County, being part of the Remonstrance of the Province of North Carolina*, HUMBLY SHEWETH, That the Province in general labour under general grievances, and the Western part thereof under particular ones; which we not only see but very sensibly feel, being crouch'd beneath our sufferings: and, notwithstanding our sacred priviledges, have too long yielded ourselves slaves to remorseless oppression.—Permit us to conceive it to be our inviolable right to make known our grievances, and to petition for redress; as appears in the Bill of Rights pass'd in the reign of King Charles the first, as well as the act of Settlement of the Crown of the Revolution. We therefore beg leave to lay before you a specimen

thereof, that your compassionate endeavours may tend to the relief of your injured Constituents, whose distressed condition calls aloud for aid. The alarming cries of the oppressed possibly may reach your Ears; but without your zeal how shall they ascend the throne. How relentless is the breast without sympathy, the heart that cannot bleed on a View of our calamity; to see tenderness removed, cruelty stepping in; and all our liberties and priviledges invaded and abridg'd by (as it were) domesticks who are conscious of their guilt and void of remorse. O how daring! how relentless! whilst impending Judgments loudly threaten and gaze upon them, with every emblem of merited destruction.

A few of the many grievances are as follows, viz.,

1. That the poor Inhabitants in general are much oppress'd by reason of disproportionate Taxes, and those of the western Counties in particular; as they are generally in mean circumstances.

2. That no method is prescribed by Law for the payment of the Taxes of the Western counties in produce (in lieu of a Currency) as is in other Counties within this Province; to the Peoples great oppression.

3. That Lawyers, Clerks, and other pentioners, in place of being obsequious Servants for the Country's use, are become a nuisance, as the business of the people is often transacted without the least degree of fairness, the intention of the law evaded, exorbitant fees extorted, and the sufferers left to mourn under their oppressions.

4. That an Attorney should have it in his power, either for the sake of ease or interest or to gratify their malevolence and spite, to commence suits to what Courts he pleases, however inconvenient it may be to the Defendant: is a very great oppression.

5. That all unlawful fees taken on Indictment, where the Defendant is acquitted by his Country (however customary it may be) is an oppression.

6. That Lawyers, Clerks, and others extorting more fees than is intended by law; is also an oppression.

7. That the violation of the King's Instructions to his delegates, their artfulness in concealing the same from him; and the great Injury the People thereby sustains: is a manifest oppression.

And for remedy whereof, we take the freedom to recommend the following mode of redress, not doubting audience and acceptance; which will not only tend to our relief, but command prayers as a duty from your humble Petitioners.

1. That at all elections each suffrage be given by Ticket & Ballot.

2. That the mode of Taxation be altered, and each person to pay in proportion to the profits arising from his Estate.

3. That no future tax be laid in Money, untill a currency is made.

4. That there may be established a Western as

well as a Northern and Southern District, and a Treasurer for the same.

5. That when a currency is made it may be let out by a Loan office on Land security, and not to be call'd in by a Tax.

6. That all debts above 40s. and under £10 be tried and determined without Lawyers, by a jury of six freeholders impanneled by a Justice, and that their verdict be enter'd by the said Justice, and be a final judgment.

7. That the Chief Justice have no perquisites, but a Sallary only.

8. That Clerks be restricted in respect to fees, costs, and other things within the course of their office.

9. That Lawyers be effectually Barr'd from exacting and extorting fees.

10. That all doubts may be removed in respect to the payment of fees and costs on Indictments where the Defendant is not found guilty by the jury, and therefore acquitted.

11. That the Assembly make known by Remonstrance to the King, the conduct of the cruel and oppressive Receiver of the Quit Rents, for omitting the customary easie and effectual method of collecting by distress, and pursuing the expensive mode of commencing suits in the most distant Courts.

12. That the Assembly in like manner make known that the Governor and Council do frequently grant Lands to as many as they think proper without regard to head rights, notwithstanding the contrariety of His Majesties Instructions; by which means immense sums has been collected and numerous Patents granted, for much of the most fertile lands in this Province, that is yet uninhabited and uncultivated, environed by great numbers of poor people who are necessitated to toil in the cultivation of bad Lands whereon they hardly can subsist, who are thereby deprived of His Majesties liberality and Bounty: nor is there the least regard paid to the cultivation clause in said Patent mentioned, as many of the said Council as well as their friends and favorites enjoy large Quantities of Lands under the above-mentioned circumstances.

\*       \*       \*

16. That every denomination of People may marry according to their respective Mode, Ceremony, and custom, after due publication or Licence.

17. That Doctr Benjamin Franklin or some other known patriot be appointed Agent, to represent the unhappy state of this Province to His Majesty, and to solicit the several Boards in England. . . .

\*       \*       \*

# 35 "I heard the word 'fire'" (1770)

The repeal of the Stamp Act reduced tensions temporarily. But the colonies met the Townshend Acts, which imposed new import duties and created both customs boards and vice-admiralty courts for their collection and enforcement, with new hostility. A boycott against the importation of British goods was instituted, and the Massachusetts House of Representatives called for united colonial resistance. Five British regiments were sent to Boston in response.

On March 5, 1770, a local crowd attacked some British sentries. The evidence of what happened was contradictory; in response to the hurling of snowballs the soldiers shot into the crowd, killing three people instantly, with two others dying shortly thereafter. The leader of the troops, Captain Thomas Preston, and six of his men were arrested and tried for murder. Preston and four soldiers, defended by John Adams and Josiah Quincy, were acquitted, and the remaining two were convicted of manslaughter. To the local patriots the incident supplied a major focus for anti-British propaganda.

☆ 35  The Horrid Massacre in Boston

Richard Palmes, "A Short Narrative of the Horrid Massacre in Boston (1770)," reprinted in Richard Hofstadter and Michael Wallace, eds., *American Violence: A Documentary History* (New York: Knopf, 1970), 116–17.

I, Richard Palmes, of Boston, of lawful age, testify and say, that between the hours of nine and ten o'clock of the fifth instant, I heard one of the bells ring, which I supposed was occasioned by fire, and enquiring where the fire was, was answered that the soldiers were abusing the inhabitants; I asked where, was first answered at Murray's barracks. I went there and spoke to some officers that were standing at the door, I told them I was surprised they suffered the soldiers to go out of the barracks after eight o'clock; I was answered by one of the officers, pray do you mean to teach us our duty; I answered I did not, only to remind them of it. One of them then said, you see that the soldiers are all in their barracks, and why do you not go to your homes. Mr. James Lamb and I said, Gentlemen, let us go home, and were answered by some, home, home. Accordingly I asked Mr. William Hickling if he was going home, he said he was; I walked with him as far as the post-office, upon my stopping to talk with two or three people, Mr. Hickling left me; I then saw Mr. Pool Spear going towards the town-house, he asked me if I was going home, I told him I was; I asked him where he was going that way, he said he was going to his brother David's. But when I got to the town-pump, we were told there was a rumpus at the Custom-house door; Mr. Spear said to me you had better not go, I told him I would go and try to make peace. I immediately went there and saw Capt. Preston at the head of six or eight soldiers in a circular form, with guns breast high and bayonets fixed; the said Captain stood almost to the end of their guns. I went immediately to Capt. Preston (as soon as Mr. Bliss had left him), and asked him if their guns were loaded, his answer was they are loaded with powder and ball; I then said to him, I hope you do not intend they shall fire upon the inhabitants, his reply was, by no means. When I was asking him these questions, my left hand was on his right shoulder; Mr. John Hickling had that instant taken his hand off my shoulder, and stepped to my left, then instantly I saw a piece of snow or ice fall among the soldiers on which the soldier at the officer's right hand stepped back and discharged his gun at the space of some seconds the soldier at his left fired next, and the others one after the other. After the first gun was fired, I heard the word "fire," but who said it I know not. After the first gun was fired, the said officer had full time to forbid the other soldiers not to fire, but I did not hear him speak to them at all; then turning myself to the left I saw one man dead, distant about six feet; I having a stick in my hand made a stroke at the soldier who fired, and struck the gun out of his hand. I then made a stroke at the officer, my right foot slipped, that brought me on my knee, the blow falling short; he says I hit his arm; when I was recovering myself from the fall, I saw the soldier that fired the first gun endeavoring to push me through with his bayonet, on which I threw my stick at his head, the soldier starting back, gave me an opportunity to jump from him into Exchange lane, or I must been inevitably run through my body. I looked back and saw three persons laying on the ground, and perceiving a soldier stepping round the corner as I thought to shoot me, I ran down Exchange lane, and so up the next into King Street, and followed Mr. Gridley with several other persons with the body of Capt. Morton's apprentice, up to the prison house, and saw he had a ball shot through his breast; at my return I found that the officers and soldiers were gone to the main guard. To my best observation there were not seventy people in King street at the time of their firing, and them very scattering; but in a few minutes after the firing there were upwards of a thousand. . . .

# 36 "enemy to the liberties of America" (1773-1774)

The East Indian Company's importation and sale of tea in the colonies was greatly assisted by Parliamentary concessions as well as by effective merchandizing practices. An act of May 1773 authorized the East India Company to sell tea directly to the colonies free from other duties except a three-penny tax payable in America. The distribution of the imported tea in the colonies was through the company's exclusive agents. Both the local tax and the monopolistic distribution system aroused suspicion and hostility. The colonists devised opposition tactics, as the accompanying document illustrates. In Philadelphia and New York, ships bearing tea were forced to turn back. In Boston, attempts to land tea resulted in the Boston Tea Party of December 16, 1773. In response to these disturbances the British Parliament passed a number of emergency measures, known collectively in the colonies as the "Intolerable Acts"; one of these, the Administration of Justice Act, permitted the transfer of controversial trials from local courts to England.

## ☆ 36 The Boston Tea Party and Its Aftermath

### ☆ 36a Sons of Liberty Resolutions on Tea (December 15, 1773)

Reprinted in Hezekiah Niles, *Chronicles of the American Revolution*, ed. Alden T. Vaughn. (New York: Grosset & Dunlap, 1965), 66-67.

. . . To prevent a calamity which, of all others, is the most to be dreaded — slavery, and its terrible concomitants — we, subscribers being influenced from a regard to liberty, and disposed to use all lawful endeavors in our power, to defeat the pernicious project, and to transmit to our posterity, those blessings of freedom which our ancestors have handed down to us; and to contribute to the support of the common liberties of America, which are in danger to be subverted, *do*, for those important purposes, agree to associate together, under the name and style of the *sons of liberty of New York*, and engage our honor to, and with each other, faithfully to observe and perform the following *resolutions, viz.*

1st. *Resolved*, That whoever shall aid, or abet, or in any manner assist in the introduction of tea, from any place whatsoever, into this colony, while it is subject, by a British act to parliament, to the payment of a duty, for the purpose of raising a revenue in America, he shall be deemed an enemy to the liberties of America.

2d. *Resolved*, That whoever shall be aiding, or assisting, in the landing, or carting, of such tea, from any ship or vessel, or shall hire any house, storehouse, or cellar or any place whatsoever to deposit the tea, subject to a duty as aforesaid, he shall be deemed an enemy to the liberties of America.

3d. *Resolved*, That whoever shall sell, or buy, . . . tea, or shall aid . . . in transporting such tea, . . . from this city, until the . . . revenue act shall be totally and clearly repealed, he shall be deemed an enemy to the liberties of America.

4th. *Resolved*, That whether the duties on tea, imposed by this act, be paid in Great Britain or in America, our liberties are equally affected.

5th. *Resolved*, That whoever shall transgress any of these resolutions, we will not deal with, or employ, or have any connection with him.

☆ 36b  Administration of Justice Act (May 20, 1774)

Reprinted in H. S. Commager, ed., *Documents of American History* (New York: Meredith Corp., 1973), 1:73-74.

*An act for the impartial administration of justice in the cases of persons questioned for any acts done by them in the execution of the law, or for the suppression of riots and tumults, in the province of the* Massachuset's Bay, *in* New England.

WHEREAS *in his Majesty's province of* Massachuset's Bay, *in* New England, *an attempt hath lately been made to throw off the authority of the parliament of* Great Britain *over the said province, and an actual and avowed resistance, by open force, to the execution of certain acts of parliament, hath been suffered to take place, uncontrouled and unpunished* ...: *and whereas, in the present disordered state of the said province, it is of the utmost importance* ... *to the reestablishment of lawful authority throughout the same, that neither the magistrates acting in support of the laws, nor any of his Majesty's subjects aiding and assisting them therein, or in the suppression of riots and tumults,* ... *should be discouraged from the proper discharge of their duty, by an apprehension, that in case of their being questioned for any acts done therein, they may be liable to be brought to trial for the same before persons who do not acknowledge the validity of the laws, in the execution thereof, or the authority of the magistrate in support of whom, such acts had been done: in order therefore to remove every such discouragement from the minds of his Majesty's subjects, and to induce them, upon all proper occasions, to exert themselves in support of the public peace of the province, and of the authority of the King and Parliament of* Great Britain *over the same;* be it enacted ... , That if any inquisition or indictment shall be found, or if any appeal shall be sued or preferred against any person, for murther, or other capital offence, in the province of the *Massachuset's Bay,* and it shall appear, by information given upon oath to the governor ... of the said province, that the fact was committed by the person against whom such inquisition or indictment shall be found, or against whom such appeal shall be sued or preferred, as aforesaid, either in the execution of his duty as a magistrate, for the suppression of riots, or in the support of the laws of revenue, or in acting in his duty as an officer of revenue, or in acting under the direction and order of any magistrate, for the suppression of riots, or for the carrying into effect the laws of revenue, or in aiding and assisting in any of the cases aforesaid; and if it shall also appear, to the satisfaction of the said governor ... that an indifferent trial cannot be had within the said province, in that case, it shall and may be lawful for the governor ... , to direct, with the advice and consent of the council, that the inquisition, indictment, or appeal, shall be tried in some other of his Majesty's colonies, or in *Great Britain;* and for that purpose, to order the person against whom such inquisition or indictment shall be found, ... to be sent, under sufficient custody, to the place appointed for his trial, or to admit such person to bail, taking a recognizance ... from such person, with sufficient sureties, ... in such sums of money as the said governor ... shall deem reasonable, for the personal appearance of such person, if the trial shall be appointed to be had in any other colony, before the governor, ... of such colony; and if the trial shall be appointed to be had in *Great Britain,* then before his Majesty's court of *King's Bench,* at a time to be mentioned in such recognizances; and the governor, ... or court of *King's Bench,* where the trial is appointed to be had in *Great Britain,* upon the appearance of such person, according to such recognizance, or in custody, shall either commit such person, or admit him to bail, until such trial. ...

# 37  "our lawful and rightful Sovereign" (1774)

Colonial dissatisfaction with taxes imposed by a Parliament with no colonial representation mounted. In 1772, Boston and other Massachusetts towns, at the proposal of Samuel Adams, organized Committees of Correspondence to formulate American rights and grievances. Other colonies followed suit, and relations with England worsened. By 1774, General Thomas Gage, commander in chief of the English colonial troops, arrived to govern Massachusetts. The Committees of Correspondence called for an intercolonial congress. The First Continental Congress convened in Philadelphia on September 5, 1774.

Although the Instructions by the Virginia Convention to Their Delegates expressed "true Allegiance to his Majesty King George the Third, our lawful and rightful Sovereign," they sounded a new and more independent chord concerning the political relationship between England and her American colonies. The Instructions laid the grievances at the feet of a malevolent Parliament. But while seeking royal relief, the Instructions' endorsement of a total embargo conveyed an assertion of political sovereignty.

Particular note should be taken of the reaction of the English to these threats. Although not a time of generalized civil disorder, the civil authorities had been supplanted by General Gage's military authority. In addition, the crime of treason had, by military edict, been extended beyond the provisions of the existing English statutory authority contained in 25 Edward III. These two responses—imposition of military rule and expansion of the crime of treason (or its surrogate)—have characterized governmental response to political crime ever since.

☆ 37 Instructions by the Virginia Convention to Their Delegates in Congress (August 1-6, 1774)

Reprinted in J. Boyd, ed., *The Papers of Thomas Jefferson* (Princeton: Princeton University Press, 1950) 1:141-43.

THE unhappy Disputes between Great Britain and her American Colonies, which began about the third Year of the Reign of his present Majesty, and since, continually increasing, have proceeded to Lengths so dangerous and alarming as to excite just Apprehensions in the Minds of his Majesty's faithful Subjects of this Colony that they are in Danger of being deprived of their natural, ancient, constitutional, and chartered Rights, have compelled them to take the same into their most serious Consideration; and, being deprived of their usual and accustomed Mode of making known their Grievances, have appointed us their Representatives to consider what is proper to be done in this dangerous Crisis of American Affairs. It being our Opinion that the united Wisdom of North America should be collected in a General Congress of all the Colonies, we have appointed the Honourable PEYTON RANDOLPH, Esquire, RICHARD HENRY LEE, GEORGE WASHINGTON, PATRICK HENRY, RICHARD BLAND, BENJAMIN HARRISON, and EDMUND PENDLETON, Esquires, Deputies to represent this Colony in the said Congress, to be held at Philadelphia on the first Monday in September next.

And that they may be the better informed of our Sentiments touching the Conduct we wish them to observe on this important Occasion, we desire that they will express, in the first Place, our Faith and true Allegiance to his Majesty King George the Third, our lawful and rightful Sovereign; and that we are determined, with our Lives and Fortunes, to support him in the legal Exercise of all his just Rights and Prerogatives. And however misrepresented, we sincerely approve of a constitutional Connexion with Great Britain, and wish most ardently a Return of that Intercourse of Affection and commercial Connexion that formerly united both Countries, which can only be effected by a Removal of those Causes of Discontent which have of late unhappily divided us.

It cannot admit of a Doubt but that British Subjects in America are entitled to the same Rights and Privileges as their Fellow Subjects possess in Britain; and therefore, that the Power assumed by the British Parliament to bind America by their Statutes, in all Cases whatsoever, is unconstitutional, and the Source of these unhappy Differences.

The End of Government would be defeated by the British Parliament exercising a Power over the Lives, the Property, and the Liberty of the American Subject; who are not, and, from their local Circumstances, cannot, be there represented. Of this

Nature we consider the several Acts of Parliament for raising a Revenue in America, for extending the Jurisdiction of the Courts of Admiralty, for seizing American Subjects and transporting them to Britain to be tried for Crimes committed in America, and the several late oppressive Acts respecting the Town of Boston and Province of the Massachusetts Bay.

The original Constitution of the American Colonies possessing their Assemblies with the sole Right of directing their internal Polity, it is absolutely destructive of the End of their Institution that their Legislatures should be suspended, or prevented, by hasty Dissolutions, from exercising their legislative Powers.

Wanting the Protection of Britain, we have long acquiesced in their Acts of Navigation restrictive of our Commerce, which we consider as an ample Recompense for such Protection; but as those Acts derive their Efficacy from that Foundation alone, we have Reason to expect they will be restrained so as to produce the reasonable Purposes of Britain, and not injurious to us.

To obtain Redress of these Grievances, without which the People of America can neither be safe, free, nor happy, they are willing to undergo the great Inconvenience that will be derived to them from stopping all Imports whatsoever from Great Britain after the first Day of November next, and also to cease exporting any Commodity whatsoever to the same Place after the tenth Day of August 1775. . . . [I]t is our Desire that you cordially co-operate with our Sister Colonies in General Congress in such other just and proper Methods as they, or the Majority, shall deem necessary for the Accomplishment of these valuable Ends.

The Proclamation issued by General Gage, in the Government of the Province of the Massachusetts Bay, declaring it Treason for the Inhabitants of that Province to assemble themselves to consider of their Grievances and form Associations for their common Conduct on the Occasion, and requiring the Civil Magistrates and Officers to apprehend all such Persons to be tried for their supposed Offences, is the most alarming Process that ever appeared in a British Government; that the said General Gage hath thereby assumed and taken upon himself Powers denied by the Constitution to our legal Sovereign; that he, not having condescended to disclose by what Authority he exercises such extensive and unheard of Powers, we are at a Loss to determine whether he intends to justify himself as the Representative of the King or as the Commander in Chief of his Majesty's Forces in America. If he considers himself as acting in the Character of his Majesty's Representative, we would remind him that the Statute 25th Edward III has expressed and defined all treasonable Offences, and that the Legislature of

Great Britain hath declared that no Offence shall be construed to be Treason but such as is pointed out by that Statute, and that this was done to take out of the Hands of tyrannical Kings, and of weak and wicked Ministers, that deadly Weapon which constructive Treason had furnished them with, and which had drawn the Blood of the best and honestest Men in the Kingdom; and that the King of Great Britain hath no Right by his Proclamation to subject his People to Imprisonment, Pains, and Penalties.

That if the said General Gage conceives he is empowered to act in this Manner, as the Commander in Chief of his Majesty's Forces in America, this odious and illegal Proclamation must be considered as a plain and full Declaration that this despotick Viceroy will be bound by no Law, nor regard the constitutional Rights of his Majesty's Subjects, whenever they interfere with the Plan he has formed for oppressing the good People of the Massachusetts Bay; and therefore, that the executing, or attempting to execute, such Proclamation, will justify Resistance and Reprisal.

# 38 "whereas hostilities have actually been commenced" (1775)

The First Continental Congress, convened in Philadelphia on September 5, 1774, approved resistance to the Intolerable Acts of Parliament and expressed the view that all colonies should support Massachusetts if the British sought execution of their laws by force. It also approved the Declaration of Rights and Resolves, which called for rights of assembly and petition, trial by peers, freedom from a standing army, and the right to be consulted on the imposition of taxes. The Congress threatened to reconvene in Philadelphia in May 1775 unless the British redressed colonial grievances. When Parliament met at the close of 1774, the king and his ministers expressed the view that the First Continental Congress constituted illegal assembly and that Massachusetts was, in fact, in a state of rebellion.

As a conciliatory measure, former prime minister William Pitt, now earl of Chatham, proposed that Parliament agree not to levy any tax upon the colonies. Lord North, then prime minister, secured passage of another conciliatory resolution, but these efforts proved futile. The two parties drifted steadily toward war. Suspecting the Massachusetts militia was gathering arms, British General Gage directed 700 troops to Concord on April 18, 1775, to seize military stores. The following day, at Lexington, the Minutemen stood their ground against the approaching force, and the first blood of the American Revolution was shed.

The Second Continental Congress met on May 10, 1775. The previous month the revolution had begun in Lexington and Concord. On June 17, fighting resumed at the Battle of Bunker Hill, and George Washington took command of the Continental Army on June 23, 1775.

The Preamble to the Articles of War, a proclamation of fidelity to the English king, preceded the regulations for the new army that would fight the royal forces. The Articles dramatically illustrated the Revolutionary War's conflict of loyalties—the old loyalty to the Crown versus the new loyalty to the emerging United States.

☆ 38 Articles of War for the Continental Army (June 30, 1775)

Reprinted in W. C. Ford, ed., *Journals of the Continental Congress* (Washington, D.C.: U.S. Government Printing Office, 1906), 2:120.

The Congress met according to adjournment.

The consideration of the articles of war being resumed, Congress agreed to the same:

RULES AND REGULATIONS

Whereas his Majesty's most faithful subjects in these Colonies are reduced to a dangerous and critical situation, by the attempts of the British Ministry, to carry into execution, by force of arms, several unconstitutional and oppressive acts of the British parliament for laying taxes in America, to enforce the collection of these taxes, and for altering and changing the constitution and internal police of some of these Colonies, in violation of the natural and civil rights of the Colonies.

And whereas hostilities have been actually commenced in Massachusetts Bay, by the British troops, under the command of General Gage, and the lives of a number of the inhabitants of that Colony destroyed; the town of Boston not only having been long occupied as a garrisoned town in an enemy's country, but the inhabitants thereof treated with a severity and cruelty not to be justified even towards declared enemies.

And whereas large reinforcements have been ordered, and are soon expected, for the declared purpose of compelling these colonies to submit to the operation of the said acts, which hath rendered it necessary, and an indispensable duty, for the express purpose of securing and defending these Colonies, and preserving them in safety against all attempts to carry the said acts into execution; that an armed force be raised sufficient to defeat such hostile designs, and preserve and defend the lives, liberties and immunities of the Colonists: for the due regulating and well ordering of which;—

Resolved, That the following Rules and Orders be attended to, and observed by such forces as are or may hereafter be raised for the purpose aforesaid.

Article I. That every officer who shall be retained, and every soldier who shall serve in the Continental Army, shall, at the time of his acceptance of his commission or inlistment, subscribe these rules and regulations.

Article II. It is earnestly recommended to all officers and soldiers, diligently to attend Divine Service; and all officers and soldiers who shall behave indecently or irreverently at any place of Divine Worship, shall, if commissioned officers, be brought before a court-martial.

*        *        *

Article IV. Any officer or soldier, who shall behave himself with contempt or disrespect towards the General or Generals, or Commanders in chief of the Continental Forces, or shall speak false words, tending to his or their hurt or dishonour, shall be punished according to the nature of his offence, by the judgment of a general court-martial.

Art. V. Any officer or soldier, who shall begin, excite, cause, or join in any mutiny or sedition, in the regiment, troop or company to which he belongs, or in any other regiment, troop or company of the Continental Forces, either by land or sea, or in any party, post, detachment, or guard, on any pretence whatsoever, shall suffer such punishment, as by a general court-martial shall be ordered.

Art. VI. Any officer, non-commissioned officer, or soldier, who being present at any mutiny or sedition, does not use his utmost endeavours to suppress the same, or coming to the knowledge of any mutiny, or intended mutiny, does not, without delay, give information thereof to the commanding officer, shall be punished by order of a general court-martial, according to the nature of his offence.

Art. VII. Any officer or soldier, who shall strike his superior officer, or draw, or offer to draw, or shall lift up any weapon, or offer any violence against him, being in the execution of his office, on any pretence whatsoever, or shall disobey any lawful commands of his superior officer, shall suffer such punishment as shall, according to the nature of his offence, be ordered by the sentence of a general court-martial.

*        *        *

Art. XII. Every officer, commanding in quarters or on a march, shall keep good order, and, to the utmost of his power, redress all such abuses or disorders which may be committed by any officer or soldier under his command: If upon any complaint [being] made to him, of officers or soldiers beating, or otherwise ill-treating any person, or of committing any kind of riot, to the disquieting of the inhabitants of this Continent: he the said commander, who shall refuse or omit to see justice done on the offender or offenders, and reparation made to the party or parties injured, as far as the offender's

wages shall enable him or them, shall, upon due proof thereof, be punished as ordered by a general court-martial, in such manner as if he himself had committed the crimes or disorders complained of.

Art. XIII. If any officer should think himself to be wronged by his colonel or the commanding officer of the regiment, and shall, upon due application made to him, be refused to be redressed, he may complain to the General or Commander in chief of the Continental Forces, in order to obtain justice, who is hereby required to examine into said complaint, and see that justice be done.

*        *        *

Art. XXV. Whatsoever officer or soldier shall shamefully abandon any post committed to his charge, or shall speak words inducing others to do the like, in time of an engagement, shall suffer death immediately.

Art. XXVI. Any person belonging to the Continental Army, who shall make known the watch-word to any person who is not entitled to receive it, according to the rules and discipline of war, or shall presume to give a parole, or watch-word, different from what he received, shall suffer death, or such other punishment as shall be ordered by the sentence of a general court-martial.

Art. XXVII. Whosoever belonging to the Continental Army, shall relieve the enemy with money, victuals, or ammunition, or shall knowingly harbour or protect an enemy, shall suffer such punishment as by a general court-martial shall be ordered.

Art. XXVIII. Whosoever belonging to the Continental Army, shall be convicted of holding correspondence with, or of giving intelligence to, the enemy, either directly or indirectly, shall suffer such punishment as by a general court-martial shall be ordered.

*        *        *

Art. XXXI. If any commander of any post, intrenchment, or fortress, shall be *compelled*, by the officers or soldiers under his command, to give it up to the enemy, or to abandon it, the commissioned officer, non-commissioned officers, or soldiers, who shall be convicted of having so offended, shall suffer death, or such other punishment as may be inflicted upon them by the sentence of a general court-martial.

*        *        *

Art. LI. That no persons shall be sentenced by a court-martial to suffer death, except in the cases expressly mentioned in the foregoing articles; nor shall any punishment be inflicted at the discretion of a court-martial, other than degrading, cashiering, drumming out of the army, whipping not exceeding thirty-nine lashes, fine not exceeding two months pay of the offender, imprisonment not exceeding one month.

*        *        *

# 39 "We have pursued every temperate, every respectful measure" (1775)

Shortly after granting the command of the Continental Army to George Washington and drafting Articles of War for the army's conduct, the Continental Congress established a committee to draw up a justification for the colonies' resort to arms. Benjamin Franklin of Pennsylvania, John Jay of New York, Edward Rutledge of South Carolina, Robert R. Livingston of New York, William Samuel Johnson of Connecticut, Thomas Jefferson of Virginia, and John Dickinson of Delaware constituted the committee. The final document, addressing the "Necessity of Taking up Arms," was the work of Dickinson and Jefferson.

## ☆ 39 Declaration of the Causes and Necessity of Taking Up Arms (July 6, 1775)

Reprinted in W. C. Ford, ed., *Journals of the Continental Congress* (Washington, D.C.: U.S. Government Printing Office, 1906), 2:140.

If it was possible for men, who exercise their reason to believe, that the divine Author of our existence intended a part of the human race to hold an absolute property in, and an unbounded power over others, marked out by his infinite goodness and wisdom, as the objects of a legal domination never rightfully resistible, however severe and oppressive, the inhabitants of these colonies might at least require from the parliament of Great Britain some evidence, that this dreadful authority over them, has been granted to that body. But a reverence for our great Creator, principles of humanity, and the dictates of common sense, must convince all those who reflect upon the subject, that government was instituted to promote the welfare of mankind, and ought to be administered for the attainment of that end. The legislature of Great Britain, however, stimulated by an inordinate passion for a power not only unjustifiable, but which they know to be peculiarly reprobated by the very constitution of that kingdom, and desperate of success in any mode of contest, where regard should be had to truth, law, or right, have at length, deserting those, attempted to effect their cruel and impolitic purpose of enslaving these colonies by violence, and have thereby rendered it necessary for us to close with their last appeal from reason to arms. Yet, however blinded that assembly may be, by their intemperate rage for unlimited domination, so to slight justice and the opinion of mankind, we esteem ourselves bound by obligations of respect to the rest of the world, to make known the justice of our cause.

Our forefathers, inhabitants of the island of Great Britain, left their native land, to seek on these shores a residence for civil and religious freedom. At the expense of their blood, at the hazard of their fortunes, without the least charge to the country from which they removed, by unceasing labour, and an unconquerable spirit, they effected settlements in the distant and inhospitable wilds of America, then filled with numerous and warlike nations of barbarians. Societies or governments, vested with perfect legislatures, were formed under charters from the crown, and an harmonious intercourse was established between the colonies and the kingdom from which they derived their origin.

... [But] these devoted colonies were judged to be in such a state, as to present victories without bloodshed, and all the easy emoluments of statuteable plunder. The uninterrupted tenor of their peaceable and respectful behaviour from the beginning of colonization, their dutiful, zealous, and useful services during the [French and Indian] war, though so recently and amply acknowledged in the most honourable manner by his majesty, by the late king, and by parliament, could not save them from the meditated innovations. Parliament [has] undertaken to give and grant our money without our consent, though we have ever exercised an exclusive right to dispose of our own property; statutes have been passed for extending the jurisdiction of courts of admiralty, and vice-admiralty beyond their ancient limits; for depriving us of the accustomed and inestimable privilege of trial by jury, in cases affecting both life and property; for suspending the legislature of one of the colonies; for interdicting all commerce to the capital of another; and for altering fundamentally the form of government established by charter, and secured by acts of its own legislature solemnly confirmed by the crown; for exempting the "murderers" of colonists from legal trial, and in effect, from punishment; for erecting in a neighbouring province, acquired by the joint arms of Great Britain and America, a despotism dangerous to our very existence; and for quartering soldiers upon the colonists in time of profound peace. It has also been resolved in parliament, that colonists charged with committing certain offences, shall be transported to England to be tried.

But why should we enumerate our injuries in detail? By one statute it is declared, that parliament can "of right make laws to bind us in all cases whatsoever." What is to defend us against so enormous, so unlimited a power? Not a single man of those who assume it, is chosen by us; or is subject to our controul or influence; but, on the contrary, they are all of them exempt from the operation of such laws, and an American revenue, if not diverted from the ostensible purposes for which it is raised, would actually lighten their own burdens in proportion, as they increase ours. . . .

We have pursued every temperate, every respectful measure: we have even proceeded to break off our commercial intercourse with our fellow subjects, as the last peaceable admonition, that our attachment to no nation upon earth should supplant our attachment to liberty. This, we flattered ourselves, was the ultimate step of the controversy: but subsequent events have shewn, how vain was this hope of finding moderation in our enemies.

*     *     *

Fruitless were all the entreaties, arguments, and eloquence of an illustrious band of the most distinguished peers, and commoners, who nobly and stren[u]ously asserted the justice of our cause, to stay, or even to mitigate the heedless fury with which these accumulated and unexampled outrages were hurried on. . . .

. . . General Gage, who in the course of the last year had taken possession of the town of Boston, in the province of Massachusetts Bay, . . . on the 19th day of April, sent out from that place a large detachment of his army, who made an unprovoked assault on the inhabitants of the said province, at the town of Lexington . . . murdered eight of the inhabitants, and wounded many others. From thence the troops proceeded in warlike array to the town of Concord, where they set upon another party of the inhabitants of the same province, killing several and wounding more, until compelled to retreat by the country people suddenly assembled to repel this cruel aggression. Hostilities, thus commenced by the British troops, have been since prosecuted by them without regard to faith or reputation. The inhabitants of Boston being confined within that town by the general their governor, and having, in order to procure their dismission, entered into a treaty with him . . . but in open violation of honour, in defiance of the obligation of treaties, which even savage nations esteemed sacred, . . . detained the greatest part of the inhabitants in the town, and compelled the few who were permitted to retire, to leave their most valuable effects behind. . . .

The General . . . proceeds to "declare them all, either by name or description, to be rebels and traitors, to supersede the course of the common law, and instead thereof to publish and order the use and exercise of the law martial." His troops have butchered our countrymen, have wantonly burnt Charlestown, besides a considerable number of houses in other places; our ships and vessels are seized; the necessary supplies of provisions are intercepted, and he is exerting his utmost power to spread destruction and devastation around him.

We have received certain intelligence, that General Carleton, the Governor of Canada, is instigating the people of that province and the Indians to fall upon us; and we have but too much reason to apprehend, that schemes have been formed to excite domestic enemies against us. In brief, a part of these colonies now feel, and all of them are sure of feeling, as far as the vengeance of administration can inflict them, the complicated calamities of fire, sword, and famine. We are reduced to the alternative of choosing an unconditional submission to the tyranny of irritated ministers, or resistance by force. The latter is our choice. We have counted the cost of this contest, and find nothing so dreadful as voluntary slavery. Honour, justice, and humanity, forbid us tamely to surrender that freedom which we received from our gallant ancestors, and which our innocent posterity have a right to receive from us. We cannot endure the infamy and guilt of resigning succeeding generations to that wretchedness which inevitably awaits them, if we basely entail hereditary bondage upon them.

Our cause is just. Our union is perfect. Our internal resources are great, and, if necessary, foreign assistance is undoubtedly attainable. We gratefully acknowledge, as signal instances of the Divine favour towards us, that his Providence would not permit us to be called into this severe controversy, until we were grown up to our present strength, had been previously exercised in warlike operation, and possessed of the means of defending ourselves. . . . The arms we have been compelled by our enemies to assume, we will, in defiance of every hazard, with unabating firmness and perseverance, employ for the preservation of our liberties; being with one mind resolved to die freemen rather than to live slaves.

Lest this declaration should disquiet the minds of our friends and fellow subjects in any part of the empire, we assure them that we mean not to dissolve that union which has so long and so happily subsisted between us, and which we sincerely wish to see restored. Necessity has not yet driven us into that desperate measure, or induced us to excite any other nation to war against them. We have not raised armies with ambitious designs of separating from Great Britain, and establishing independent states. We fight not for glory or for conquest. We exhibit to mankind the remarkable spectacle of a people attacked by unprovoked enemies, without any imputation or even suspicion of offence. They boast of their privileges and civilization, and yet proffer no milder conditions than servitude or death.

In our own native land, in defence of the freedom that is our birth-right, and which we ever enjoyed till the late violation of it — for the protection of our property, acquired solely by the honest industry of our fore-fathers and ourselves, against violence actually offered, we have taken up arms. We shall lay them down when hostilities shall cease on the part of the aggressors, and all danger of their being renewed shall be removed, and not before.

# 40 "misled by dangerous and ill designing men" (1775)

Despite continuing pitched battles, the moderates in the Continental Congress continued to hope for a peaceful solution. On June 18, 1775, two days after Bunker Hill, John Dickinson of Delaware, the leader of the moderates, introduced the draft of a final petition to the king. After approval of the draft on July 8, William Penn was to present it in London. Nevertheless, the conciliatory voices in England were growing weak, and the news of American resistance moved the king on August 23, 1775, to proclaim a state of rebellion, declaring its adherents to be traitors and ordering his loyal subjects to inform upon those who corresponded or expressed sympathy with the rebels.

☆ 40 A Proclamation by the King for Suppressing Rebellion and Sedition (August 23, 1775)

Reprinted in P. Force, ed., *American Archives*, 4th ser. (Washington, D.C.: M. St. Clair Clarke & P. Force, 1837), 3:240.

Whereas many of our subjects in divers parts of our Colonies and Plantations in North America, misled by dangerous and ill designing men, and forgetting the allegiance which they owe to the power that has protected and supported them; after various disorderly acts committed in disturbance of the publick peace, to the obstruction of lawful commerce and to the oppression of our loyal subjects carrying on the same; have at length proceeded to open and avowed rebellion, by arraying themselves in a hostile manner, to withstand the execution of the law, and traitorously preparing, ordering and levying war against us: And whereas, there is reason to apprehend that such rebellion hath been much promoted and encouraged by the traitorous correspondence, counsels and comfort of divers wicked and desperate persons within this realm: To the end therefore, that none of our subjects may neglect or violate their duty through ignorance thereof, or through any doubt of the protection which the law will afford to their loyalty and zeal, we have thought fit, by and with the advice of our Privy Council, to issue our Royal Proclamation, hereby declaring, that not only all our Officers, civil and military, are obliged to exert their utmost endeavours to suppress such rebellion, and to bring the traitors to justice, but that all our subjects of this Realm, and the dominions thereunto belonging, are bound by law to be aiding and assisting in the suppression of such rebellion, and to disclose and make known all traitorous conspiracies and attempts against us, our crown and dignity; and we do accordingly strictly charge and command all our Officers, as well civil as military, and all others

our obedient and loyal subjects, to use their utmost endeavours to withstand and suppress such rebellion, and to disclose and make known all treasons and traitorous conspiracies which they shall know to be against us, our crown and dignity; and for that purpose, that they transmit to one of our principal Secretaries of State, or other proper officer, due and full information of all persons who shall be found carrying on correspondence with, or in any manner or degree aiding or abetting the persons now in open arms and rebellion against our Government, within any of our Colonies and Plantations in North America, in order to bring to condign punishment the authors, perpetrators, and abetters of such traitorous designs.

\*　　　\*　　　\*

God save the King.

# 41 Amendments to the Articles of War (1775)

The American War of Independence began on April 19, 1775, with the skirmishes at Lexington and Concord. In May, Ethan Allen's Green Mountain Boys took Fort Ticonderoga; the conquest became America's first military victory. George Washington was named commander in chief of the Continental Army in June, and the British issued the Royal Proclamation of Rebellion on August 23. The establishment of an American navy followed in October.

The original Articles of War, enacted on June 30, 1775, appeared inadequate for the conduct of an independent and wartime army. The colonies were no longer willing to proclaim their loyalty to the Crown. The Amendments to the Articles of War, dated November 7, 1775, extended the death penalty to offenses not so punished originally, including treacherous correspondence, sedition, desertions, and mutiny.

☆ 41 Additions and Alterations to the Rules of the Continental Army (November 7, 1775)

*Papers of the Continental Congress*, 1, no. 152:155, reprinted in W. C. Force, ed., *Writings of George Washington* (New York: Putnam 1889), 190.

A letter from General Washington, No. 11, was read.

The secretary having digested in order the resolutions of Congress, as far as they have gone on the report of the Committee of Conference, produced the same, which being read, and agreed to as follows:

Resolved, That the following additions and alterations or amendments, be made in the RULES and REGULATIONS of the continental Army, viz.

1. All persons convicted of holding a treacherous correspondence with, or giving intelligence to the enemy, shall suffer death, or such other punishment as a general court-martial shall think proper.

\*          \*          \*

4. In all cases where a commissioned officer is cashiered for cowardice or fraud, it be added in the punishment, that the crime, name, place of abode, and punishment of the delinquent be published in the news papers, in and about the camp, and of that colony from which the offender came, or usually resides: after which it shall be deemed scandalous in any officer to associate with him.

5. Any officer or soldier, who shall begin, excite, cause, or join in any mutiny or sedition in the regiment, troop, or company to which he belongs, or in any other regiment, troop, or company of the continental forces, either by land or sea, or in any party, post, detachment or guard, on any pretence whatsoever, shall suffer death, or such other punishment, as a general court-martial shall direct.

6. Any officer or soldier, who shall desert to the enemy, and afterwards be taken, shall suffer death, or such other punishment, as a general court-martial shall direct.

7. Whatsoever commissioned officer shall be found drunk on his guard, party, or other duty under arms, shall be cashiered and drummed out of the army with infamy; any non-commissioned officer or soldier, so offending, shall be sentenced to be whipt, not less than twenty, nor more than thirty-nine lashes, according to the nature of the offence.

\*          \*          \*

10. Whatsoever officer or soldier shall misbehave himself before the enemy, or shamefully abandon any post committed to his charge, or shall speak words inducing others to do the like, shall suffer death.

\*          \*          \*

16. All officers and soldiers who shall wilfully, or through negligence, disobey any general or special orders, shall be punished at the discretion of a regimental court-martial, where the offence is against a regimental order, and at the discretion of a general court-martial, where the offence is against an order given from the commander in chief, or the commanding officer of any detachment or post, and such general court-martial can be had.

## 42 "Ye that dare oppose not only the tyranny but the tyrant" (1776)

When the time arrived, the cause of the American Revolution had many willing and courageous soldiers and an even greater number of supporters. But no one had a larger role in the planting and nour-ishment of the seeds of independence than Patrick Henry, a native Virginian who came to be called "The Tongue of the Revolution," and Thomas Paine, a transplanted Englishman who best articulated the need for the break from the mother country in *Common Sense*.

Patrick Henry's (1736-99) fame was derived from his initial 1765 oration against the Stamp Act, when shouts of "treason" resounded from his fellow burgesses at Williamsburg. A decade later in Richmond, his cry for "liberty or death" helped galvanize further the emerging nation. After the Revolution Thomas Paine (1737-1809) became a French citizen and a member of the National Convention. But the French revolutionary upheaval resulted in Paine's disaffection; and labeled a reactionary, he was imprisoned and condemned by Robespierre. Upon the fall of Robespierre, Paine was released from jail; and after a six-year stay in France, he returned to America in 1802 at the invitation of President Jefferson. Paine died alone and neglected.

## ☆ 42 Common Sense

Reprinted in R. Heffner, ed., *A Documentary History of the United States* (New York: Mentor, 1952), 13-15.

Volumes have been written on the subject of the struggle between England and America. Men of all ranks have embarked in the controversy, from different motives, and with various designs; but all have been ineffectual, and the period of debate is closed. Arms as the last resource decide the contest; the appeal was the choice of the King, and the Continent has accepted the challenge. . . .

The Sun never shined on a cause of greater worth. 'Tis not the affair of a City, a County, a Province, or a Kingdom; but of a Continent—of at least one-eighth part of the habitable Globe. 'Tis not the concern of a day, a year, or an age; posterity are virtually involved in the contest, and will be more or less affected even to the end of time, by the proceedings now. Now is the seedtime of Continental union, faith and honour. The least fracture now will be like a name engraved with the point of a pin on the tender rind of a young oak; the wound would enlarge with the tree, and posterity read in it full grown characters. . . .

I have heard it asserted by some, that as America has flourished under her former connection with Great Britain, the same connection is necessary towards her future happiness, and will always have the same effect. Nothing can be more fallacious than this kind of argument. We may as well assert that because a child has thrived upon milk, that it is never to have meat, or that the first twenty years of our lives is to become a precedent for the next twenty. But even this is admitting more than is true; for I answer roundly that America would have flourished as much, and probably much more, had no European power taken any notice of her. The commerce by which she hath enriched herself are the necessaries of life, and will always have a market while eating is the custom of Europe.

But she has protected us, say some. That she hath engrossed us is true, and defended the Continent at our expense as well as her own, is admitted; and she would have defended Turkey from the same motive, *viz.* for the sake of trade and dominion.

Alas! we have been long led away by ancient prejudices and made large sacrifices to superstition. We have boasted the protection of Great Britain, without considering, that her motive was *interest* not *attachment*; and that she did not protect us from *our enemies* on *our account*; but from *her enemies* on *her own account*, from those who had no quarrel with us on any *other account*, and who will always be our enemies on the *same account*. Let Britain waive her pretentions to the Continent, or the Continent throw off the dependence, and we should be at peace with France and Spain, were they at war with Britain. . . .

But Britain is the parent country, say some. Then the more shame upon her conduct. Even brutes do not devour their young, nor savages make war upon their families. . . . Europe, and not England, is the parent Country of America. . . .

I challenge the warmest advocate for reconciliation to show a single advantage that this Continent can reap by being connected with Great Britain. I repeat the challenge; not a single advantage is derived. Our corn will fetch its price in any market in Europe, and our imported goods must be paid for, buy them where we will.

But the injuries and disadvantages which we sustain by that connection, are without number; and our duty to mankind at large, as well as to ourselves, instructs us to renounce the alliance: because, any submission to, or dependence on, Great Britain, tends directly to involve this Continent in European wars and quarrels, and set us at variance with nations who would otherwise seek our friendship, and against whom we have neither anger nor complaint. As Europe is our market for trade, we ought to form no partial connection with any part of it. It is the true interest of America to steer clear of European contentions, which she never can do, while, by her dependence on Britain, she is made the makeweight in the scale of British politics. . . .

'Tis repugnant to reason, to the universal order of things, to all examples from former ages, to suppose that this Continent can long remain subject to any external power. The most sanguine in Britain doth not think so. The utmost stretch of human wisdom cannot, at this time, compass a plan, short of separation, which can promise the Continent even a year's security. Reconciliation is *now* a fallacious dream. Nature hath deserted the connection, and art cannot supply her place. For, as Milton wisely expresses, "never can true reconcilement grow where wounds of deadly hate have pierced so deep." . . .

To talk of friendship with those in whom our reason forbids us to have faith, and our affections wounded thro' a thousand pores instruct us to detest, is madness and folly. Every day wears out the little remains of kindred between us and them; and can there be any reason to hope, that as the relationship expires, the affection will encrease, or that we shall agree better when we have ten times more and greater concerns to quarrel over than ever?

Ye that tell us of harmony and reconciliation, can ye restore to us the time that is past? Can ye give to prostitution its former innocence? neither can ye reconcile Britain and America. The last cord now is broken, the people of England are presenting addresses against us. There are injuries which nature cannot forgive; she would cease to be nature if she did. As well can the lover forgive the ravisher of his mistress, as the Continent forgive the murders of Britain. . . .

O! ye that love mankind! Ye that dare oppose not only the tyranny but the tyrant, stand forth! Every spot of the old world is overrun with oppression. Freedom hath been hunted round the Globe. Asia and Africa have long expelled her. Europe regards her like a stranger, and England hath given her warning to depart. O! receive the fugitive, and prepare in time an asylum for mankind. . . .

## 43 "required to take the following Oath" (1776)

Not all colonists favored the war against the English sovereign. A significant portion of the colonial population was English-born. Many others belonged to the Tory ranks and continued to profess their allegiance to the king.

Still other Americans, sympathetic to the cause of independence, were reluctant to risk a failed revolution and trial for treason. Until almost its very close, the colonial military campaign of 1776 appeared to be a disheartening failure. By the end of the year, the colonies possessed only five thousand poorly equipped troops.

But others who were more ambivalent in their support apparently desired to modify this zeal in the hopes of not altogether forswearing a reconciliation. This North Carolina oath requirement reflected these competing claims on the allegiance of the civil population. In addition, it recorded the fact that the old backwoods parochial conflicts were not subsumed totally by the greater rebellion.

☆ 43 Resolution of the Provincial Council of
North Carolina, March 5, 1776

Reprinted in W. Saunders, ed., *The Colonial Records of
North Carolina* (Raleigh: Josephus Daniel, 1890), 10:475-76.

The [Provincial Council of North Carolina] met according to Adjournment Tuesday, 5th March 1776.

\*        \*        \*

Resolved, That all persons who shall be disarmed
by the Town and County Committees and other suspected persons who have not taken up Arms against
this Colony shall be required to take the following
Oath on pain of imprisonment viz:

I do solemnly and sincerely swear on the holy
Evangelists of Almighty God that during the present unhappy contest between Great Britain and
America, I will not under any pretence whatever oppose or take up Arms to oppose the Measures of the
Continental or provincial Congresses or any Troops
raised by or acting under the Authority of either,
nor will I directly or indirectly, either personally or
by letter, Counsel, advise or give Intelligence to any
of his Majesty's Governors, General Officers, Soldiers, or others employed by Land or sea to carry
into execution and enforce Obedience to the several
Acts of British Legislature, deemed oppressive to
these Colonies: I will not by example, opinion, advice
or persuasion, endeavour to prejudice the people or
any of them in favour of Parliamentary Measures or
against those recommended by the General and provincial Congresses until it shall please God to restore peace and good understanding to the contending powers.

\*        \*        \*

That the thanks of this Council be given to Col.
James Moore and all the Brave Officers and Soldiers
of every denomination for their late very important
services rendered their country in effectually suppressing the late daring and dangerous insurrection
of the Highlanders and Regulators, and that this Resolve be published in the North Carolina gazette.

Resolved, That Col. Robert Howe is justly intitled to the most honourable Testimony of the Approbation of this Council for his important services
while in the Colony of Virginia rendered in the common cause of American Liberty, and that the President transmit the warmest thanks of this Board in
the fullest and most honorable terms to Colonel
Howe and all the Brave Officers and Soldiers under
his command for their spirited conduct, having acquitted themselves greatly to their Country.

## 44 "all persons abiding within any of the United Colonies" (1776)

Not until the adoption of the United States Constitution in 1787 was there a nationwide law respecting

treason against the newly created American political entity. At the start of the Revolution, the laws of
various colonies defined treason as adherence to the
enemies of the English sovereign. Thus, there was
no law prohibiting treason against the United Colonies or any individual colony by supporters of the
Loyalist cause. The Second Continental Congress
acted to remedy this legal anachronism by setting
forth the foundations of allegiance and treason for
the several colonies.

The Resolution on Spies, passed before the Declaration of Independence, acknowledged the preeminence of the colonial governments over the Crown in
America by referring to those adhering to the king
as "guilty of treason." The document also reflected
the incompetence of the Continental Congress to
pass laws binding within the various colonies.

☆ 44 Resolution on Spies (June 24, 1776)

Reprinted in W. C. Ford, ed., *Journals of the Continental
Congress* (Washington, D.C.: U.S. Government Printing Office, 1906), 5:475.

The Congress took into consideration the report of
the Committee on Spies; Whereupon,

Resolved, That all persons abiding within any of
the United Colonies, and deriving protection from
the laws of the same, owe allegiance to the said laws,
and are members of such colony; and that all persons
passing through, visiting, or make a temporary stay
in any of the said colonies, being entitled to the protection of the laws during the time of such passage,
visitation or temporary stay, owe, during the same
time, allegiance thereto:

That all persons, members of, or owing allegiance
to any of the United Colonies, as before described,
who shall levy war against any of the said colonies
within the same, or be adherent to the king of Great
Britain, or others the enemies of the said colonies, or
any of them, within the same, giving to him or them
aid and comfort, are guilty of treason against such
colony:

That it be recommended to the legislatures of the
several United Colonies, to pass laws for punishing,
in such manner as to them shall seem fit, such persons before described, as shall be proveably attainted of open deed, by people of their condition, of
any of the treasons before described.

\*        \*        \*

## 45 "the right of the people to alter or to abolish" Forms of Government (1776)

The country had not yet attained an international
standing, and its independence could not be secured

without military victories against the world's greatest naval power, Britain, well-supported by veteran British armies. To some, a claim of independence seemed an act of utmost recklessness. Yet on June 4, Richard Henry Lee of Virginia introduced in the Continental Congress a resolution that "these united Colonies are and of right ought to be free and independent states" and that a plan of confederation should be carried out. A committee to prepare such a declaration formed, consisting of John Adams, Benjamin Franklin, Thomas Jefferson, Robert R. Livingston, and Roger Sherman. On July 4, 1776, the Congress adopted the declaration, substantially as drafted by Thomas Jefferson, and John Hancock as president of the Congress signed it. The New York delegation abstained from the vote, and two delegates from Pennsylvania stayed away so as not to have to cast votes.

The abuses heretofore blamed on Parliament and wicked ministers were laid directly to the king. The Declaration gave effect to the twin political themes articulated from earliest colonial times: that governments derive their just powers from the consent of the governed and that the people have a right and a duty to revolt against abusive government.

## ☆ 45 Declaration of Independence (July 4, 1776)

### THE UNANIMOUS DECLARATION OF THE THIRTEEN UNITED STATES OF AMERICA

WHEN, in the course of human events, it becomes necessary for one people to dissolve the political bands which have connected them with another, and to assume, among the powers of the earth, the separate and equal station to which the laws of nature and of nature's God entitle them, a decent respect to the opinions of mankind requires that they should declare the causes which impel them to the separation.

We hold these truths to be self-evident: that all men are created equal; that they are endowed, by their Creator, with certain unalienable rights; that among these are life, liberty, and the pursuit of happiness. That to secure these rights, governments are instituted among men, deriving their just powers from the consent of the governed; that whenever any form of government becomes destructive of these ends, it is the right of the people to alter or to abolish it, and to institute a new government, laying its foundation on such principles, and organizing its powers in such form, as to them shall seem most likely to effect their safety and happiness. Prudence, indeed, will dictate, that governments long established, should not be changed for light and transient causes; and accordingly all experience hath shown, that mankind are more disposed to suffer, while evils are sufferable, than to right themselves by abolishing the forms to which they are accustomed. But when a long train of abuses and usurpations, pursuing invariably the same object, evinces a design to reduce them under absolute despotism, it is their right, it is their duty, to throw off such government, and to provide new guards for their future security. Such has been the patient sufferance of these colonies; and such is now the necessity which constrains them to alter their former systems of government. The history of the present King of Great Britain is a history of repeated injuries and usurpations, all having in direct object the establishment of an absolute tyranny over these states.

\*          \*          \*

## 46 The Revolution in Literature (1776-1777)

Described as the First American Civil War, the contest between the competing American political forces — the Patriots and the Loyalists — took place in the streets, the legislative arenas, and the artistic and religious forums. But even here, the references often were to legal rights and obligations. A Loyalist song of 1776 warned against the sedition of the Continental Congress and foresaw "scenes of blood," while Patriot literature, taking the text of Judges 5:23, drew biblical support for violent opposition to oppression.

## ☆ 46 Loyalists and Patriots

## ☆ 46a The Congress

*A Song*
wrote in the spring of the year 1776
TUNE: "Nancy Dawson"

Reprinted in W. Sargent, *The Loyalist Poetry of the Revolution* (Boston: Milford House, 1972), 70-74.

YE Tories all rejoice and sing
Success to George our gracious king;
The faithful subjects tribute bring
    And execrate the Congress.

These hardy knaves and stupid fools;
Some apish and pragmatic mules;
Some servile acquiescing tools;
    These, these compose the Congress.

\*          \*          \*

Time serving priests to zealots preach,
Who king and parliament impeach,
Seditious lessons to us teach
    At the command of Congress.

Good Lord! disperse this venal tribe;
Their doctrine let no fools imbibe;
Let Balaam no more asses ride
    Nor burdens bear to Congress.

\*          \*          \*

There's Washington and all his men—
Where Howe had one, the goose had ten—
March'd up the hill, and down again;
    And sent returns to Congress.

Prepare, prepare, my friends prepare,
For scenes of blood, the field of war;
To royal standard we'll repair,
    And curse the haughty Congress.

☆ 46b  An Antidote against Toryism (Nathaniel Whittaker)

Reprinted in L. F. S. Upton, ed., *Revolutionary versus Loyalist: The First American Civil War, 1774-1784* (Waltham: Blaisdell, 1968), 85.

JUDGES V, 23

Curse ye Meroz, said the Angel of the Lord,
Curse ye bitterly the inhabitants thereof,
  because they came not to the help of the Lord,
  to the help of the Lord, against the mighty. . . .
      *        *        *

From this view of the text and context, we may deduce the following doctrinal observations:

I. That the cause of Liberty is the cause of God and Truth.

II. That to take arms and repel force by force, when our Liberties are invaded, is well pleasing to God.

III. That it is lawful to levy war against those who oppress us, even when they are not in arms against us.

IV. That indolence and backwardness in taking arms, and exerting ourselves in the service of our Country, when called thereto by the public voice in order to recover and secure our freedoms, is a heinous sin in the sight of God.

V. That God requires a people, struggling for their Liberties, to treat such of the community who will not join them, as open enemies, and to reject them as unworthy of the privileges which others enjoy. . . .
      *        *        *

# 47  "dark and criminal designs of enslaving America" (1777)

The law passed by the Maryland General Assembly in 1777 sought to punish those who were "still pursuing their dark and criminal designs of enslaving America." The act coincided with similar attempts throughout the states to clarify the duties as well as the rights of the citizenry by means of state treason laws, bills of rights, and constitutions.

Pockets of Toryism remained strong, particularly in states like Maryland where pro-British populations and economic interests were pronounced.

The new law prohibited any citizen, under penalty of five years' imprisonment or banishment for life, from maintaining that the king or Parliament had any authority over the United States. Oaths of allegiance were imposed on all voters. Citizens adjudged guilty of treason against the state were to be put to death without benefit of clergy, and their estates were forfeited to the state. The 1777 law was replete with several of the controversial practices which were reenacted in later periods of political stress in America: the requirement of loyalty oaths; the prohibition of seditious speech; the limitation of travel; the detention of suspicious individuals; and the suspension of habeas corpus—the legal writ that serves to protect individuals from unlawful imprisonment.

☆ 47  An Act to Punish Certain Crimes and Misdemeanors, and Prevent the Growth of Toryism [Maryland]

*1777-80 Maryland Laws* (Annapolis: Frederick Green, 1777), chapter 20.

WHEREAS the clemency of this state towards such of its subjects and inhabitants as are inimical to its freedom and independence, has not had the desired effect of reclaiming them from their evil practices, but still pursuing their dark and criminal designs of enslaving America, they continue to encourage and promote the operations of our enemies: And whereas every hope of uniting to the interest of their country the affections of these its unnatural and implacable enemies is extinguished, and great disadvantages have arisen, and still more dangerous consequences may be apprehended, from a delay of effectual measures to suppress or remove them from the society of a free people, constrained by oppression to declare their independence, and determined at all events to maintain the fame;

II. BE it therefore enacted, by the General Assembly of Maryland, That if any subject or inhabitant of this state shall, within or without the same, and if any person whatever, being an inhabitant of any other of the United States; shall, within this state, levy war against the United States, or any of them, or shall adhere to any person bearing arms, or employed in the service of Great Britain, against the United States, or any of them, or shall afford such persons, or any of them, any aid or comfort, or shall give them, or any of them, or any subject of Great Britain, any intelligence of the warlike preparations or designs of the United States, or any of them, and shall be thereof convicted in the general court of this state, or shall stand mute, or peremptorily challenge above the number of twenty of the pannel [*sic*], shall be adjudged guilty of treason against this state, and shall suffer death without benefit of clergy, and forfeit all the estate which he had at the time of the commission of the crime, to the use of this state; and the several crimes aforesaid shall receive the same constructions that have been given to each of the said crimes as are enumerated in the statute of Edward the third, commonly called the statute of treasons. . . .

III. AND be it enacted, That if any subject or inhabitant of this state has knowledge of the actual commission of any of the crimes aforesaid, about to be treason, shall conceal the same, and shall not, as soon as convenient be, disclose and make the same known to the governor, or some one of the judges or justices of this state for the time being, such person, on conviction thereof in the general court, shall be adjudged guilty of a misprision of treason, and shall forfeit all the estate which he had, at the time of the commission of the crime, to the use of this state.

IV. AND be it enacted, That if any subject or inhabitant of this state shall, by any word, open deed, writing, printing, or other act, advisedly and willingly declare, affirm, maintain or defend, that the king or parliament of Great Britain hath any authority, power or jurisdiction, in or over the United States, or any of them, or that any allegiance is due from any of the subjects or inhabitants of the United States, or any of them, to the king of Great Britain, his heirs or successors, or shall wickedly, corruptly or seditiously, persuade or entice any of the subjects or inhabitants of this state, to return to or acknowledge any dependence on the crown and parliament of Great Britain, or to own any allegiance or obedience to the King of Great Britain, his heirs or successors, and shall be thereof convicted in the general court, such person shall be fined not exceeding ten thousand pounds current money, and be imprisoned not more than five years, in the discretion of the court, or be banished from this state for ever.

V. AND be it enacted, That if any subject or inhabitant of this state shall, by any word, open deed, writing, printing, or other act, persuade or excite any of the inhabitants of this state to resist the present government thereof by force, or to oppose, or in any manner obstruct, with force, the execution of any of the laws of this state, such person being convicted thereof in the general court, shall be fined not exceeding two thousand pounds current money, and be imprisoned not more than two years, in the discretion of the court.

VI. AND be it enacted, That if any subject or inhabitant of this state shall know of any intention, design or attempt, to commit any of the crimes declared by this act to be treason against this state, and shall not reveal the same, as soon as conveniently may be, to the governor, or some one of the judges or justices of this state for the time being, such person, on conviction thereof in the general court, shall be fined not exceeding one thousand pounds current money, and imprisoned not more than one year, in the discretion of the court.

VII. AND be it enacted, That if any subject or inhabitant of this state, shall advisedly and maliciously, with an intention to obstruct the service, dissuade, discourage or obstruct, any person from enlisting or engaging in the army or navy of the United States, or any of them, such person, on conviction thereof in the general court, shall be fined not exceeding one thousand pounds current money, in the discretion of the court.

VIII. AND be it enacted, That if any subject or inhabitant of this state shall, by any word, open deed, writing, printing or other act, wickedly, corruptly or seditiously, dissuade, discourage or terrify, any of the people of this state from supporting the independency of the United States, or any of them, or shall directly or indirectly endeavour to support or justify the measures taken by the king and parliament of Great Britain against the United States, or any of them, and shall be thereof convicted in the general court, such person shall be fined not exceeding one thousand pounds current money, in the discretion of the court.

IX. AND be it enacted, That if any subject or inhabitant of this state, shall write or convey any letter, or send or carry any message, to any person employed in the service of Great Britain against the United States, or any of them, without the leave of the governor of this state, or some one of the general officers of the army of the United States, or shall knowingly receive or bring any letter or message from any such person, and shall not deliver or communicate the same, as soon as conveniently may be, to the governor, or some one of the judges or justices of the peace within this state, and shall be thereof convicted in any county court of this state, such person shall be fined not exceeding one hundred pounds current money, in the discretion of the court.

\* \* \*

XII. AND be it enacted, That in case this state shall be invaded by the enemy, the governor for the time being, with the advice of the council, shall have full power and authority to arrest, or order to be arrested, all persons whose going at large the governor and council shall have good grounds to believe may be dangerous to the safety of this state, and the same persons to confine during such invasion, to such places as the governor and the council shall think proper, or to limit such persons to particular districts in this state, or in their discretion to discharge such persons on security; and that during any invasion of this state by the enemy, the habeas corpus act shall be suspended, as to all such persons arrested by the order of the governor and council.

\* \* \*

XV. AND be it enacted, That every voter for delegates of sheriffs, or for electors of the senate, if required, and every other person required by law to take the oath of fidelity and support to this state, shall take, repeat and subscribe, the same oath, or if a quaker, menonist or dunker, shall solemnly, sincerely and truly, declare and affirm thereto in the words thereof.

XVI. AND be it enacted, That if any person shall travel into or pass through or from this state to any other, without a pass of safe conduct, signed by some member of congress, or by the governor, or some judge or justice of this state, or of the state of which he is a subject or resident, he shall be liable to be apprehended and carried before some judge or justice for examination, who may commit him to the public gaol, if an offender against the laws, or dangerous person to this state, or to the United States, or any of them, there to remain till discharged by due course of law, and if not an offender or dangerous as aforesaid, the said judge or justice may discharge him and give him a pass.

XVII. WHEREAS several persons, late inhabitants of this state, have, since the fourteenth day of August, seventeen hundred and seventy-five, deserted the defence of this country in the present just and necessary war, BE IT ENACTED, That no person whatsoever, who hath deserted as aforesaid, or any person who since the said time hath left this state without leave, shall at any time hereafter (unless he returns to this state within twelve months, and during the present war, and takes and subscribes the oath of fidelity aforesaid within ten days after his return) be capable of holding any office of trust or profit within this state; nor shall any person, now a resident of this state, who hath refused or neglected to subscribe the association, and shall not take the said oath of fidelity on or before the first day of August next, be capable of holding any office as aforesaid.

XVIII. PROVIDED always, That nothing herein contained shall extend to such persons who from religious principles have not subscribed or shall not subscribe the association.

XIX. AND be it enacted, That this act shall be publicly read by the clerk of the general court, and by the clerk of every county court in this state, at their next court respectively, immediately after empannelling the grand jury, and also by every minister, teacher or preacher of the gospel, immediately after divine service, at every church, chapel or meeting-house, where they officiate, on some Sunday in the month of May next; and every clerk, minister, teacher or preacher, failing so to do, shall forfeit and pay the sum of five pounds, to be recovered with costs by the informer before any justice of the peace of the county where the offence shall be committed.

\*          \*          \*

# 48 "Dangers Which May Arise from Persons Disaffected to the State" (1777-1780)

In 1777, North Carolina responded to the Continental Congress's Resolution on Spies by stiffening its oath-taking requirement and making continued allegiance to the English sovereign an act of treason. The law prohibited the continuation of the public debate on the issues of war and independence and made treasonous any efforts to persuade people "to return to a dependence on the Crown" or to spread "false and dispiriting news." Although attending to the forms of earlier English treason law, the act broadened the definitions of treason and misprision of treason. The General Assembly also established an elaborate oath-taking procedure for those suspected of Loyalist connections. Individuals who continued to acknowledge allegiance to the king were subject to exile from the state. By 1780, so many were accused of treason that problems arose in the administering of the statute. In response, the legislature simplified the legal process for the trial of alleged traitors by eliminating many procedural protections of the accused.

## ☆ 48 All Persons Accused of Treason

### ☆ 48a An Act to Amend an Act for Declaring What Crimes and Practices against the State Shall Be Treason, and What Shall Be Misprision of Treason, and Providing Punishments Adequate to Crimes of Both Classes, and for Preventing the Dangers Which May Arise from Persons Disaffected to the State [North Carolina]

Chap. 3, 1777 N.C. Sess. Laws 11.

I. Be it Enacted by the General Assembly of the State of North Carolina, and it is hereby Enacted by the Authority of the same, That all and every Person or Persons (Prisoners of War excepted) now inhabiting or residing within the Limits of the State of North Carolina, or who shall voluntarily come into the same hereafter to inhabit or reside, do owe and shall pay Allegiance to the State of North Carolina.

II. And be it further Enacted, by the Authority aforesaid, That if any Person or Persons belonging to, or residing within this State, and under the protection of its Laws, shall take a Commission or Commissions from the King of Great Britain, or any under his Authority, or other the Enemies of this State, or the United States of America, or shall levy War against this State, or the Government thereof, or knowingly and wilfully shall aid or assist any Enemies at open War against this State, or the United States of America, by joining their Armies, or by inlisting, or procuring or persuading others to inlist for that Purpose, or by furnishing such Enemies with Arms, Ammunition, Provision, or any other Article for their Aid or Comfort, or shall form, or be in any wise concerned in forming, any Combination, Plot or Conspiracy, for betraying this State, or the United States of America, into the Hands or Power of any Foreign Enemy, or shall give any Intelligence to the Enemies of this State for that Purpose, every Person so offending, and being thereof legally convicted by the Evidence of Two sufficient Witnesses, or standing mute, or peremptorily challenging more than Thirty Five Jurors, in any Court of Oyer and Terminer, or other Court that shall and may be established for the Trial of such Offences, shall be adjudged guilty of High Treason, and shall suffer Death without the Benefit of Clergy, and his or her Estate shall be forfeited to the State. Provided, That the Judge or Judges of the Court wherein such Conviction may be, shall and may order and appropriate so much of the Traitor's Estate as to him or them may appear sufficient for the Support of his or her Family.

III. And be it further Enacted, by the Authority aforesaid, That if any Person or Persons within this State shall attempt to convey intelligence to the Enemies of this State, or of the United States, or shall Publickly and deliberately speak or write against the Public Defence, or shall maliciously and advisedly endeavour to excite the People to resist the Government of this State, or persuade them to return to a Dependence on the Crown of Great Britain, or shall knowingly spread false and dispiriting News, or maliciously and advisedly terrify and discourage the People from inlisting into the Service of this State, or the United States, or shall stir up or excite Tumults, Disorders, or Insurrections in the State, or dispose the People to favour the Enemy, or oppose, or endeavour to prevent the Measures carrying on in Support of the Election of the Freedom and Independence of the said United States, every such Person or Persons, being thereof legally convicted by the Evidence of Two or more creditable Witnesses, or other sufficient Testimony, shall be adjudged guilty of Misprision of Treason, and shall suffer Imprisonment during the War, and forfeit to the State one Half of his, her, or their Lands, Tenements, Goods and Chattels.

\* \* \*

V. And whereas the safety of the State, and the present critical Situation of Affairs, make it necessary that all Persons who owe or acknowledge Allegiance or Obedience to the King of Great Britain should be removed out of the State; Be it Enacted, by the Authority aforesaid, That all the late Officers of the King of Great Britain, and all Persons (Quakers excepted) [Quakers to make a similar Affirmation], being Subjects of this State, and now living therein, or who shall hereafter come to live therein, who have traded immediately to Great Britain or Ireland within Ten Years last Past, in their own Right, or acted as Factors, Storekeepers or Agents, here or in any of the United States of America or Ireland, shall take the following Oath of Abjuration or Allegiance, or depart out of the State, viz.

I will bear faithful and true Allegiance to the State of North Carolina, and will truly endeavour to support, maintain, and defend the independent Government thereof, against George the Third, King of Great Britain, and his Successors, and the Attempts of any other Person, Prince, Power, State or Potentate, who by secret Arts, Treasons, Conspiracies, or by open Force, shall attempt to subvert the same, and will in every Respect conduct myself as a peaceful orderly Subject; and that I will disclose and make known to the Governor, some Member of the Council of State, or some Justice of the Superior Courts or of the Peace, all Treasons, Conspiracies, and Attempts, committed or intended against the State, which shall come to my knowledge.

\* \* \*

And the said Oath or Affirmation shall be taken and subscribed in open Court, in the County where the Person or Persons taking the same shall or do usually reside.

VI. And be it further Enacted, by the Authority aforesaid, That the County Courts in each and every County, and every Justice of the Peace in each respective County, shall have full Power to issue Citations against Persons coming within the above Description. . . .

And if any Person so cited (due proof being made thereof), shall fail or neglect to attend, or attending shall refuse to take the said Oath or Affirmation (as the Case may be) then the said Court shall and may have full Power and Authority to order such Person to depart out of this State, to Europe or the West Indies, within Sixty Days. . . .

VII. And be it further Enacted, That if any Person so departing, or sent off from this State, shall return to the same, then such Persons shall be adjudged guilty of Treason against the State, and shall and may be proceeded against in like Manner as is herein directed in Cases of Treason. . . .

VIII. And whereas . . . some Scruples have arisen with Respect to the Manner by Law required for the Service of such Citations [for appearance at the court for the taking of the oath] and as by many it has been held that a Service upon the Person of him intended to be cited was necessary, before his Attendance in Court could be legally compelled, as many suspected Persons, by continual Absence from their Place of Abode, or frequently removing from thence, have rendered the Service of such personal Citations difficult, and in some Cases impracticable, whereby they evade the Intentions of the said Act, and cannot be obliged to take the said Oath prescribed, nor be made subject to the Penalties ordained for neglecting or refusing the same: And whereas there is great Reason to believe that there are divers persons whose intentions are inimical to the State, who would in Case of Invasion by our Enemies, or the Expectation of immediate Support of them, carry such Intentions into Practice, but who artfully in their open Demeanor and Deportment betray no such Design, whereby from not incurring particular Suspicion, they have escaped being cited; ... Be it further Enacted, by the Authority aforesaid, That [there be established districts in each county in] which said Justices within their respective Districts are hereby enjoined and required to administer such Oath of Allegiance or Affirmation, as the Case may be, to all free Male Persons above Sixteen Years of Age (Persons non compos Mentis, Prisoners of War, only excepted) and ... post and publish a Notice in Writing of the Places and Times when and where he or they will attend within their respective Districts to administer such Oath or Affirmation; and all such Persons who are inhabitants of the said Districts respectively (and it is declared that a Residence of one Week shall in this Instance constitute any Person an Inhabitant, seafaring Persons and foreign Traders excepted) being above the Age of Sixteen Years, and of sound Mind, shall at such Time attend upon such Justice of the Peace, and take the Oath or Affirmation required, as the case may be, and subscribe the same in a Book ..., and if any Person (such only as are by this Act excepted) shall fail to attend, or attending at such Time and Place as he shall have been warned by such public Notice, shall refuse to take the Oath, or make such Affirmation, as the case may be, except as excused by Sickness or unavoidable Necessity, or other sufficient Reason ... , [he] shall be ordered by the said County Court next after such Failure or Neglect, to take the said Oath, or quit the State, and depart to the West Indies or Europe in Sixty Days; or permit[ted] to remain within the State.

IX. And be it further Enacted, by the Authority aforesaid, That all Persons failing or refusing to take the Oath of Allegiance, and permitted by the County Courts, as immediately aforesaid, to remain in the State, shall be adjudged incapable and disabled in Law to have, occupy or enjoy, any Office, Appointment, Licence, or Election of Trust or Profit, civil or Military, within this State, and shall not be capable of being elected to, or aiding by their Votes to elect another to be a Member of Assembly, and shall not by themselves, or by Deputy, Attorney or Trustee, execute any such Office, Trust or Appointment, and shall be disabled to prosecute any Suit at Law or Equity, or to be Guardians, Executors or Administrators, or capable of any Legacy, or Deed of Gift of Lands, and shall be disabled from taking any Lands by Descent or Purchase, or conveying Lands to oth-

ers for any Term longer than for one year, and shall not keep Guns or other Arms within his or their house, but the same may be seized by a written Order of a Justice of the County in which he or they reside; and after the Expiration of the said Sixty Days, he or they shall not be permitted to depart this State without Permission first had and obtained from the Governor and Council; and in Case of being suffered to depart, shall give Bond and sufficient Security, if such shall be required, not to be aiding to the Enemies of the State during his or their Absence; and in Case of their Departure without such Permission had, he or they shall forfeit all their Goods and Chattels, Lands and Tenements, to the Use of the State. ...

X. And be it further Enacted, by the Authority aforesaid, That if any Person who has been banished this State for not having taken the Oath of Allegiance, or made the Affirmation agreeable to the aforesaid Act ... shall return hither, or who may be banished in Consequence of this Act, then such Persons shall and may be dealt with in like Manner as is herein directed in Cases of Treason.

*       *       *

☆ 48b  An Act for the Speedy Trial of All Persons Accused of Treason against This and the United States and for Other Purposes [North Carolina]

Chap. 3, 1780 N.C. Sess. Laws 4.

I. Whereas most of the county gaols in this State are insufficient to contain any number of prisoners, as well with respect to their size as their strength, and where there are district gaols, the most of them are already crowded with prisoners of divers kinds, and whereas the armies of the enemy, now in the State of South Carolina, preparing to carry the war into this State, makes it highly necessary that some method for the speedy trial of traitors should be adopted and enforced.

II. Be it therefore enacted by the General Assembly of the State of North Carolina, and it is hereby enacted by the authority of the same, that when any person or persons, shall hereafter be accused of treason ... it shall be lawful for the magistrates of any county in this State, although such county shall be distant from, or in a different district, from that in which such person or persons may be taken, or have committed such treasonable crime, or any three of them ... to hear, try and determine, all treasons against this State, and against the United States, which shall be committed within their jurisdiction, and shall pass sentence on, and order immediate execution, if necessary, of all such offenders who shall be convicted or stand mute.

III. And be it further enacted, by the authority aforesaid, that in case of a default of jurors attending at any of the said courts, it shall be lawful for such courts to direct the sheriff or coroner of the county, as the case may require, to summon of the bystanders other persons, being freeholders, to complete the said juries or any of them; and that on the trial by the petit jury no challenges shall be allowed, unless the causes be shewn, any law or usage to the contrary notwithstanding.

IV. And be it further enacted, by the authority aforesaid, that counsel shall not be allowed on trial in any of the said courts either for or against the prisoner, nor shall any prisoner arrest judgment for any defect or want of form in the bill of indictment, or other proceedings so that there is sufficient substance to convict such prisoner. Provided always, that every prisoner shall be at liberty to make his own defence, and to demand summonses to inforce the attendance of his witnesses, and a reasonable time to prepare for his trial.

*        *        *

## 49  To Invite Tribes to Form a State (1778)

After the Declaration of Independence, the Continental Congress appointed commissioners to carry out the relations of the new nation with the several Native American tribes. Some tribes, including the powerful Cherokee Nation, fought on the side of the Crown in the Revolutionary War. Other tribes fought with the rebels. Securing Native American sympathy and support was important to both parties in the conflict.

In 1778, the United States ratified its first treaty with a Native American nation, complying with the forms of international law and plainly speaking in the terms of equal sovereignty which had been the basis of William Penn's attitude toward Native American relations. The hint of statehood appeared to offer an additional incentive for Native American collaboration. The premises of this treaty, however, did not provide the foundation for subsequent policy of the United States toward the Native Americans.

☆ 49  United States Treaty with the Delawares, September 17, 1778

7 Stat. 13 (1778).

*Articles of agreement and confederation, made and entered into by Andrew and Thomas Lewis, Esquires, Commissioners for, and in Behalf of the United States of North-America of the one Part, and Capt. White Eyes, Capt. John Kill Buck, Junior, and Capt. Pipe, Deputies and Chief Men of the Delaware Nation of the other Part.*

Article I. That all offences or acts of hostilities by one, or either of the contracting parties against the other, be mutually forgiven, and buried in the depth of oblivion, never more to be had in remembrance.

Article II. That a perpetual peace and friendship shall from henceforth take place, and subsist between the contracting parties aforesaid, through all succeeding generations: and if either of the parties are engaged in a just and necessary war with any other nation or nations, that then each shall assist the other in due proportion to their abilities, till their enemies are brought to reasonable terms of accommodation: and that if either of them shall discover any hostile designs forming against the other, they shall give the earliest notice thereof, that timeous measures may be taken to prevent their ill effect.

Article III. And whereas the United States are engaged in a just and necessary war, in defence and support of life, liberty and independence, against the King of England and his adherents, and as said King is yet possessed of several posts and forts on the lakes and other places, the reduction of which is of great importance to the peace and security of the contracting parties, and as the most practicable way for the troops of the United States to some of the posts and forts is by passing through the country of the Delaware nation, the aforesaid deputies, on behalf of themselves and their nation, do hereby stipulate and agree to give a free passage through their country to the troops aforesaid, and the same to conduct by the nearest and best ways to the posts, forts or towns of the enemies of the United States, affording to said troops such supplies of corn, meat, horses, or whatever may be in their power for the accommodation of such troops....

*        *        *

Article VI. Whereas the enemies of the United States have endeavored, by every artifice in their power, to possess the Indians in general with an opinion, that it is the design of the States aforesaid, to extirpate the Indians and take possession of their country: to obviate such false suggestion, the United States do engage to guarantee to the aforesaid nation of Delawares, and their heirs, all their territorial rights in the fullest and most ample manner, as it hath been bounded by former treaties, as long as they the said Delaware nation shall abide by, and hold fast the chain of friendship now entered into. And it is further agreed on between the contracting parties should it for the future be found conducive for the mutual interest of both parties to invite any other tribes who have been friends to the interest of the United States, to join the present confederation, and to form a state whereof the Delaware nation shall be the head, and have a representation in Congress: Provided, nothing contained in this article to be considered as conclusive until it meets with the approbation of Congress. And it is also the intent and meaning of this article, that no protection or countenance shall be afforded to any who are at present our enemies, by which they might escape the punishment they deserve.

In witness whereof, the parties have hereunto interchangeably set their hands and seals, at Fort Pitt, September seventeenth, anno Domini one thousand seven hundred and seventy-eight.

ANDREW LEWIS,                    [L. S.]
THOMAS LEWIS,                    [L. S.]
WHITE EYES, HIS X MARK,          [L. S.]
THE PIPE, HIS X MARK,            [L. S.]
JOHN KILL BUCK, HIS X MARK,      [L. S.]

In presence of—
LACH'N MCINTOSH, brigadier-general, commander the Western Department
DANIEL BRODHEAD, colonel Eighth Pennsylvania Regiment
W. CRAWFORD, colonel
JOHN CAMPBELL
JOHN STEPHENSON
JOHN GIBSON, colonel Thirteenth Virginia Regiment
A. GRAHAM, brigade major
LACH. MCINTOSH, JR., major brigade
BENJAMIN MILLS
JOSEPH L. FINLEY, captain Eighth Pennsylvania Regiment
JOHN FINLEY, captain Eighth Pennsylvania Regiment

## 50  The Treason of Malin (1778)

Pennsylvania indicted Malin, a British sympathizer, for the crime of treason. Malin's prosecution furnished one of the early American judicial decisions demonstrating the strict evidentiary requirements necessary to prove this offense. The laconic acquittal in the face of the evidence indicates a reluctance on the part of the jury to convict one of treason in these times of ambivalent loyalties.

☆ 50  *Respublica v. Malin*

1 U.S. (1 Dall.) 33 (1778).

INDICTMENT for High Treason. The prisoner, mistaking a corps of American troops for British, went over to them. And now the Attorney-General offered evidence of words spoken by the defendant, to prove this mistake, and his real intention of joining and adhering to the enemy.

This was opposed by the counsel for the defendant, who contended that, as words did not amount to treason, no general evidence could be given of a man's sentiments; but that the intention expressed by any words offered in evidence, must relate immediately to the overt act laid and proved on the indictment; that although an adherence to the British

troops was treason, yet, an adherence to American troops, even under a supposition that they were British, did not amount to that crime; and that the opinion, that words joined with actions made treason, however ingeniously supported, failed in point of law.

The Attorney-General, on the other hand, admitted that words alone do not amount to treason; but, he insisted that they were proper evidence to explain the defendant's actions on a trial for that crime. For, though barely being within the enemy's camp might be innocent, yet, if it could be shown that the intention of going thither was to join and adhere to them, the evidence ought to be received.

BY THE COURT. No evidence of words, relative to the mistake of the American troops, can be admitted, for any adherence to them, though contrary to the design of the party, cannot possibly come within the idea of treason. But, as it appears that the prisoner was actually with the enemy, at another time, words indicating his intention to join them are proper testimony, to explain the motives upon which that intention was afterwards carried into effect.

The Attorney-General then called a witness to prove that the defendant was seen parading with the enemy's light horse in the city of Philadelphia. But to this, also, his counsel objected; for, they urged, that every criminal act must be tried in the county in which it is committed. And that the circumstance of merely joining the enemy's army, being neither treason, nor misprision of treason, unless done with a traitorous intention, no overt act had been proved in Chester, which was a pre-requisite to any evidence being heard of an overt act committed in any other county. To evince that this was, likewise, the sense of the legislature, the defendant's counsel read the act of assembly giving the supreme court a special power to try offenders in Lancaster, for crimes committed in the counties of Chester and Philadelphia.

The Attorney-General answered, that when an overt act is proved in the county where the trial is held, corroborative evidence may be given of overt acts committed in any other county. And that having established the prisoner's presence with the British army, nothing, but the proof of actual force, and its continuance, could excuse him from the charge of adhering to the enemies of the commonwealth. [J]oining the army of an enemy, has always been held prima facie evidence of an overt act. And—

BY THE COURT, it was accordingly ruled, that evidence might be given of an overt act, committed in another county, after an overt act was proved to have been committed in the county where the indictment was laid and tried.

*The defendant was acquitted.*

# 51  The Execution of Abraham Carlisle (1778)

Abraham Carlisle served as a gatekeeper for the city of Philadelphia while it was under British occupation. The Commonwealth's laws made it an act of treason to take a commission from the king of Great Britain. Carlisle was tried, promptly convicted, and executed. The case demonstrates the perils confronting one's choice of loyalties during the Revolution, even as to discharging a civil office under the wrong authority.

## ☆51  *Respublica v. Carlisle*

1 U.S. (1 Dall.) 35 (1778).

This was an indictment for high treason which was set forth in the following words:

"The jurors for the commonwealth of Pennsylvania, upon their oaths and affirmations do present, That Abraham Carlisle, late of the city of Philadelphia, in the county of Philadelphia, carpenter; being an inhabitant of and belonging to and residing within the state of Pennsylvania, and under the protection of its laws, and owing allegiance to the same state he owed wholly withdrawing, and with all his might intending the peace and tranquility of this commonwealth of Pennsylvania to disturb, and war and rebellion against the same to raise and move, and the government and independency thereof, as by law established, to subvert, and to raise again and restore the government and tyranny of the king of Great Britain within the same commonwealth: On the first day of January, in the year of our Lord one thousand seven hundred and seventy-eight, and at divers days and times, as well before as after, at the city of Philadelphia, in the county aforesaid, with force and arms, did falsely and traitorously take a commission or commissions from the king of Great Britain, and then and there, with force and arms did falsely and treacherously also take a commission or commissions from Gen. Sir William Howe, then and there acting under the said king of Great Britain, and under the authority of the same king, to wit, a commission to watch over and guard the gates of the city of Philadelphia, by the said Sir William Howe, erected and set up for the purpose of keeping and maintaining the possession of the said city, and of shutting and excluding the faithful and liege inhabitants and subjects of this state and of the United States from the said city: And then and there also maliciously and traitorously, with a great multitude of traitors and rebels, against the said commonwealth, (whose names are as yet unknown to the jurors) being armed and arrayed in a hostile manner, with force and arms did falsely and traitorously assemble and join himself against this commonwealth, and then and there, with force and arms, did falsely

and traitorously, and in a warlike and hostile manner, array and dispose himself against this commonwealth; and then and there in pursuance and execution of such his wicked and traitorous intentions and purposes aforesaid, did falsely and traitorously prepare, order, wage and levy a public and cruel war against this commonwealth; then and there committing and perpetrating a miserable and cruel slaughter of and amongst the faithful and liege inhabitants thereof, and then and there did, with force and arms, falsely and traitorously aid and assist the king of Great Britain being an enemy at open war against this state, by joining his armies, to wit, his army under the command of Gen. Sir William Howe, then actually invading this state; and then and there maliciously and traitorously (with divers other traitors to the jurors aforesaid unknown) with force and arms, did combine, plot and conspire to betray this state and the United States of America into the hands and power of the king of Great Britain being a foreign enemy to this state and to the United States of America, at open war against the same; and then and there did with force and arms, maliciously and traitorously give and send intelligence to the same enemies for that purpose, against the duty of his allegiance, against the form of the act of Assembly in such case made and provided and against the peace and dignity of the commonwealth of Pennsylvania."

The Attorney General offering a witness to prove, that the defendant had taken a quantity of salt from persons, whom he termed rebels, as they were passing out of the city of Philadelphia; and that he had a power of granting passes; his Counsel objected, that this was impertinent to the overt act laid in the indictment, and therefore not admissible. It was urged that at common law, no evidence could be given of a fact, which was not stated in the declaration. And that this caution, with respect to the allegata et probata, in a civil cause, ought, a fortiori, to be exercised in a capital prosecution. The overt act must be particularly laid, and strictly proved. For, justice requires that the Defendant should be fully apprized of the charge, so that he may have an opportunity of encountering it with his evidence.

The Attorney General, in reply, observed that by the pleadings in a civil action, the issue must be reduced to a single point, and he admitted that in all indictments for treason, an overt act must be laid and proved. But, he contended, that it was unnecessary to fill the indictment with a detail of the whole evidence in support of the prosecution; for, if the charge is reduced to a reasonable certainty, it is all that justice can require, and it is all that is to be found in any former precedent. Divers overt acts may, also, be laid in the same indictment; and, though, some of them are faulty, if one be well proved, it is sufficient to entitle the commonwealth to a verdict.

THE CHIEF JUSTICE delivered the opinion of the Court to the following effect:

M'KEAN, Chief Justice. There are three species of treason in Pennsylvania; First, To take a commission or commissions from the king of Great Britain or any under his authority; second, To levy war against the state or government thereof; and third, Knowingly and willingly to aid and assist any enemies at open war against this state or the United States of America. With respect to this third species of treason, the legislature has further explained the meaning of the words, aiding and assisting, to be, "by joining the armies of the enemy, or by enlisting, or procuring, or persuading others to enlist for that purpose; or by furnishing such enemies with arms or ammunition, provision, or any other article, or articles, for their aid or comfort, or by carrying on a traitorous correspondence with them." All these several species of treason are laid in this indictment.

It is here particularly stated, that the defendant took a commission, under the king of Great Britain, to watch and guard the gates of the city of Philadelphia; and the offense is certain enough in this description, though, without some overt act, it would not be sufficient for a conviction. In order to prove an overt act however, evidence has been offered to show, that the prisoner had a power of granting passes into, and out of the city, which was at that time in the possession of the enemy.... The court, on the present occasion ... are of opinion, that the evidence which is offered, ought to be received, but not as conclusive proof of the defendant's having taken a commission. Nor will the evidence of seizing the salt, or any act of disarming the inhabitants whom the defendant called rebels, apply to this species of treason; however they may support the allegation, of his having joined the armies of the king of Great Britain.

We think it is sufficient, also, to lay in the indictment, that the defendant sent intelligence to the enemy, without setting forth the particular letter, or its contents: And, though the charge of levying war is not, of itself, sufficient; yet assembling, joining and arraying himself with the forces of the enemy, is a sufficient overt act levying war.

BY THE COURT: Let the witness be sworn.

The Attorney General and Reed for the commonwealth—Ross and Wilson for the defendant.

The defendant being convicted by the verdict of the jury, his counsel filed the following reasons in arrest of judgment:

1st. For that the indictment is vague and uncertain, there being no overt act expressly or particularly ascertained, as the prisoner is advised it ought to be.

2d. For that the formal part of the indictment is not drawn with sufficient precision.

3d. For that the several facts are so uncertainly charged, that the prisoner could not be apprized of the particulars urged against him. And

4th. That the whole wants form and substance.

These reasons were elaborately discussed on the 5th of October, 1778, by the same counsel on both sides: But, upon mature consideration, they were finally overruled by the court, who gave judgment for the commonwealth; and the defendant, a short time afterwards, was accordingly executed.

## 52 The Treason of Benedict Arnold (1780)

From the first proclamation of the Declaration of Independence in Philadelphia on July 9, 1776, the road to victory over the English army and the Loyalist faction was long and painful. Throughout the war, the allegiances of the people, and even of the leading patriots, were often in doubt.

At the end of 1777, General William Howe captured Philadelphia, driving Congress out of the city. A group of disgruntled army officers and members of Congress plotted to remove Washington from his command, hoping to place General Horatio Gates in charge of the American forces. The plot was exposed, and Washington retired his army into winter quarters at Valley Forge, Pennsylvania.

In 1778 Sir Henry Clinton, the newly appointed British commander, organized a new offensive, abandoning Philadelphia and attempting to reach New York. The American troops dashed out in pursuit, but American general Charles Lee ordered a retreat, thus permitting Clinton to extricate his English troops. Rumors of treason by General Lee circulated. The British once again sought support from Native Americans and Loyalists. In 1779, they moved the major scene of the battle into the southern states, where substantial Loyalist sympathy prevailed. The American troops spent their winter in Morristown in great gloom. The British gained substantial control over Georgia and South Carolina in the beginning of 1780, but the substantial support expected from southern Loyalists failed to materialize. Difficulties within the American ranks greatly troubled General Washington.

On September 21, 1780, with the arrest by New York militiamen of Major John Andre, an adjutant of General Clinton, the plot of Benedict Arnold to deliver his command, West Point, to the British was exposed. Arnold fled to the British ranks. They commissioned him a brigadier general, and he led a British raiding expedition into Virginia. He moved to London at the end of 1781, then immigrated to Canada, and from there returned to England, where he lived on a military pension and the six hundred pounds that he had received for his treason.

## ☆ 52 Correspondence of Washington

Reprinted in S. Commins, ed., *Basic Writings of George Washington* (New York: Random House, 1948), 406-7.

[To General William Heath, September 26, 1780.]

DR SIR: In the present situation of things I think it necessary that You should join the Army, and request that You will do it. I write to the Count de Rochambeau by this conveyance and I trust that your coming away now will not be attended with any material inconvenience to him.

I cannot conclude without informing You of an event which has happened here which will strike You with astonishment and indignation. Major General Arnold has gone to the Enemy. He had had an interview with Major Andre, Adjutant Genl. of the British Army, and had put into his possession a state of our Army; of the Garrison at this post; of the number of Men considered as necessary for the defence of it; a Return of the Ordnance, and the disposition of the Artillery Corps in case of an Alarm. By a most providential interposition, Major Andre was taken in returning to New York with all these papers in General Arnold's hand writing, who hearing of the matter kept it secret, left his Quarters immediately under pretence of going over to West point on Monday forenoon, about an hour before my arrival, then pushed down the river in the barge, which was not discovered till I had returned from West point in the Afternoon and when I received the first information of Mr. Andre's captivity. Measures were instantly taken to apprehend him, but before the Officers sent for the purpose could reach Verplank's point, he had passed it with a Flag and got on board the Vulture Ship of War, which lay a few miles below. He knew of my approach and that I was visiting with the Marquiss, the North and Middle Redoubts, and from this circumstance was so strained in point of time that I believe, he carried with him but very few if any material papers, tho he has a very precise knowledge of the Affairs of the post.

The Gentlemen of General Arnold's family, I have the greatest reason to believe, were not privy in the least degree to the measures he was carrying on, or to his escape. I am etc.

G? WASHINGTON

[To Count de Rochambeau, September 27, 1780.]

SIR: General Arnold, who has sullied his former glory by the blackest treason, has escaped to the enemy. This is an event that occasions me equal regret and mortification; but traitors are the growth of every country and in a revolution of the present nature, it is more to be wondered at, that the catalogue is so small than that there have been found a few.

The situation of the army at this time will make General Heath's presence with us useful. . . . I hope

his removal will be attended with no inconvenience to your Excellency. With the greatest regard etc.

G? WASHINGTON

## 53 Sentence to Be Served on a Ship of War (1781)

During the early part of 1781, the British controlled the seas and occupied or blockaded most major American ports. But toward August two powerful French fleets appeared, breaking the British siege. By September the forces of Washington and Rochambeau had combined to form a sixteen-thousand-man American-French army, which the British mistakenly believed to be intent on striking New York. The American-French troops instead traveled down the Chesapeake Bay to Yorktown, where they surprised General Cornwallis and his seven thousand British troops. Cornwallis's surrender on October 19 sealed the English hopes of recapturing rebellious America.

Yet, American gloom and destitution had marked much of the earlier part of the year. The English held the city of New York, and the American lack of naval support made recapture impossible. The American army suffered from mutiny and desertion. Although the country's Articles of Confederation and Perpetual Union had been declared in effect after Maryland entered its ratification, the Loyalists continued challenging the revolutionary cause. The New York law of March 30, 1781, supplemented its existing treason law by creating a new felony. At the same time, a special penalty provision was enacted to meet the shortage of seamen in the naval service of the United States as well as to mitigate the sentence of death for the offense. This practice of mitigating the harshness of declared sentences is a recurring theme of political criminality.

Despite the surrender of General Cornwallis, the war continued along the eastern seaboard, in the west, and in the northwest. Indeed, remnants of a stubborn British army lingered, refusing to evacuate New York completely until the end of 1783.

## ☆ 53 An Act More Effectually to Punish Adherence to the King of Great Britain within This State [New York]

Reprinted in *Laws of the State of New York, 1777-1784* (Albany: Weed, Parsons, 1886), 1:370-71.

WHEREAS, altho' adhering to the enemies of this State is by law high treason against the people of this State: yet in order more effectually to prevent an adherence to the king of Great Britain it is deemed requisite that farther provision should be made by law.

Be it therefore enacted by the People of the State of New York represented in Senate and Assembly and it is hereby enacted by the authority of the same. That if any person, being a citizen or subject of this State or of any of the United States of America and abiding or residing within this State, shall maliciously advisedly and directly be preaching, teaching speaking writing or printing declare or maintain that the king of Great Britain hath or of right ought to have any authority or dominion in or over this State or the inhabitants thereof, or shall maliciously and advisedly seduce or persuade or attempt to seduce or persuade any inhabitant of this State to renounce his or her allegiance to this State or to acknowledge allegiance or subjection to the king or crown of Great Britain, or shall maliciously and advisedly declare or affirm that he or she doth owe allegiance to the king or crown of Great Britain, and be convicted thereof shall he be adjudged guilty of felony and shall suffer the pains and penalties pre-scribed by law in cases of felony without benefit of clergy. . . .

Provided nevertheless that it shall and may be lawful for the court before whom such offender shall be convicted if such court shall deem it proper instead of giving judgment of death to order and direct that such offender shall be sent as soon as conveniently may be to serve for the term of three years on board of any ship of war belonging to this State or to the United States or to an ally of the United States and if any offender so ordered by any such court to be sent to serve on board any such ship of war for the term aforesaid shall desert from such service and be found within this State or any other of the United States the person so deserting shall be liable to be punished as a person attainted of felony without benefit of clergy and execution may and shall be awarded against such offender accordingly any thing in this act to the contrary notwithstanding.

### CHAPTER 3

# The Dawn of the Republic

———

## 1785-1815

A S the United States emerged victorious from the Revolution, new and difficult problems faced the loosely allied peoples of the nation. Foremost among these was the structure of the federal government and its relationship to the several states. Fearful that the recently experienced excesses of government under the king of England might be repeated, the new country's political leaders originally opted for a confederation with a virtually powerless central government. When this arrangement proved unsatisfactory, the Constitution of the United States was drafted and adopted. But since the document was one of compromise, many questions were left unanswered concerning the reach of the federal government's power.

Many of the documents in this chapter relate to the disputes concerning the extension of federal authority. To the extent that actions of the federal government were perceived as exceeding its delegated authority and therefore as unconstitutional, they were considered void, and at times were defied openly, a reaction not without some contemporary parallels. As the concept of judicial review for constitutionality was not yet established firmly, the major forums for testing the validity of federal law were the state legislatures, the political arena (including the press), and the battlefield.

The materials in this chapter trace the developments of the central dispute over the primacy of sovereignty (state versus federal) through the remonstrances of the legislatures, state flirtations with secession, fulminations of the press, and open rebellions in defiance of the law. Mostly, these materials reflect on the nature of the governmental response to these perceived threats to national security. The Alien and Sedition Laws, the resort to the military to suppress insurrections, and the trials of rebellion leaders for treason and their eventual pardons by executive authority reflect the many ways in which the government responded to political crime.

In reading these materials, one should be alert to the contrasting attitudes of the executive at the beginning and the end of a particular incident. Also, the judicial and executive responses to the treatment of participants in the various insurrections should be compared. In addition, the reader should note how the early and fearfully expansive interpretations of the law of treason were truncated and constrained in the later *Burr* case when national security seemed less threatened. Overall, it was an uncertain and fractious thirty years; the people and governments of the United States sorted out the balance of power between the federal and state authority, often through breaches of the criminal law and responses thereto. Although the bitterness in the debate drained away as the Jeffersonian ideals of a democratic republic were victorious at the ballot box, the ultimate issues of state and federal power, as well as the question of the individual's and the community's right to resist oppression, were not resolved—only stored away.

---

## 54 "restore all the prisoners taken" (1785)

Although the 1783 Treaty of Paris had terminated all English claims to the territory of the former colonies, as well as to the territory east of the Mississippi, it did not determine the status of the Native American nations residing therein. The Cherokees, in particular, did not recognize the Treaty of Paris as concluding the war with them, and they continued to maintain their ties with the English Crown. In a 1763 proclamation, George III had previously guaranteed to Native Americans protection of their lands from pressure by western settlers. This guarantee was affirmed by the United States in the Treaty of Hopewell, in return for Native American consent in concluding the war and relinquishing land titles. It was around this treaty and its guarantees that United States policy toward the Native Americans evolved over the next half-century, culminating in the Trail of Tears.

☆ 54 United States Treaty with the Cherokees, November 28, 1785

7 Stat. 18 (1785).

*Articles concluded at Hopewell on the Keowee, between Benjamin Hawkins, Andrew Pickens, Joseph Martin and Lachlan M'Intosh, Commissioners Plenipotentiary of the United States of America, of the one part, and the head men and warriors of all the Cherokees of the other.*

*The Commissioners* Plenipotentiary of the United States, in Congress assembled, give peace to all the Cherokees, and receive them into the favour and protection of the United States of America, on the following conditions:

ARTICLE I. The Head-Men and Warriors of all the Cherokees shall restore all the prisoners, citizens of the United States, or subjects of their allies, to their entire liberty: They shall also restore all the Negroes, and all other property taken during the late war from the citizens, to such person, and at such time and place, as the Commissioners shall appoint.

ARTICLE II. The Commissioners of the United States in Congress assembled, shall restore all the prisoners taken from the Indians, during the late war, to the Head-Men and Warriors of the Cherokees, as early as is practicable.

ARTICLE III. The said Indians for themselves and their respective tribes and towns do acknowledge all the Cherokees to be under the protection of the United States of America, and of no other sovereign whosoever.

*       *       *

ARTICLE IX. For the benefit and comfort of the Indians, and for the prevention of injuries or oppressions on the part of the citizens or Indians, the United States in Congress assembled shall have the sole and exclusive right of regulating the trade with the Indians, and managing all their affairs in such manner as they think proper.

ARTICLE X. Until the pleasure of Congress be known, respecting the ninth article, all traders, citizens of the United States, shall have liberty to go to any of the tribes or towns of the Cherokees to trade with them, and they shall be protected in their persons and property, and kindly treated.

*       *       *

ARTICLE XIII. The hatchet shall be forever buried, and the peace given by the United States, and friendship re-established between the said states on the one part, and all the Cherokees on the other, shall be universal; and the contracting parties shall use their utmost endeavours to maintain the peace given as aforesaid, and friendship re-established.

In witness of all and every thing herein determined, between the United States of America, and all the Cherokees, We, their underwritten Commissioners, by virtue of our full powers, have signed this definitive treaty, and have caused our seals to be hereunto affixed.

Done at Hopewell, on the Keowee, this twenty-eighth of November, in the year of our Lord one thousand seven hundred and eighty-five.

BENJAMIN HAWKINS
ANDW. PICKENS

JOS. MARTIN
LACH'N M'INTOSH
KOATOHEE, OR CORN TASSEL OF TOQUE
SCHOLAUETTA, OR HANGING MAN OF CHOTA
OOSK-WHA, OR ABRAHAM OF CHILKOWA
KOLAKUSTA, OR PRINCE OF NOTH
NEWOTA, OR THE GRITZS OF CHICAMAGA
KONATOTA, OR THE RISING FAWN OF HIGHWASSAY
CHOKASATAHE, CHICASAW KILLER TASONTA
ONANOOTA, OF KOOSOATEE
OOKOSETA, OR SOWER MUSH OF KOOLOQUE
UMATOOETHA, THE WATER HUNTER, CHOIKAMAWGA
WYUKA, OF LOOKOUT MOUNTAIN
TULCO, OR TOM OF CHATUGA
WILL, OF AKOHA
NECATEE, OF SAWTA
AMOKONTAKONA, KUTCLOA
TUCKASEE, OR YOUNG TARRAPIN OF ALLAJOY
TOOSTAKA, OR THE WAKER OF OOSTANAWA
UNTOOLA, OR GUN ROD OF SETECO
UNSUOKANAIL, BUFFALO WHITE CALF NEW CUFFEE
KOSTAYEAK, OR SHARP FELLOW WATAGA
CHONOSTA, OF COWE
CHESCOONWHO, BIRD IN CLOSE OF TOMOTLUG
TUCKASEE, OR TARRAPIN OF HIGHTOWA
CHESETOA, OR THE RABBIT OF TLACOA
CHESECOTETONA, OF YELLOW BIRD OF THE PINE LOG
SKETALOSKA, SECOND MAN OF TILLICO
KOWETATAHEE, IN FROG TOWN
KEUKUCH, TALKOA
TULATISKA, OF CHAWAY
WOOALUKA, THE WAY-LAYER, CHOTA
TATLIUSTA, OR PORPUS OF TILASSI
JOHN, OF LITTLE TALLICO
SKELELAK
AKONOLUCHTA, THE CABIN
CHEANODA, OF KAWETAKAC
YELLOW BIRD

IN PRESENCE OF
WM. BLOUNT
SAML. TAYLOR, *Major*
JOHN OWEN
JESS WALTON
JNO. COWAN, *Capt. Commandant*
THOS. GEGG
W. HAZZARD
*Sworn Interpreters*, JAMES MADISON, ARTHUR COODEY

## 55  Shays's Rebellion (1786)

In April of 1783, some seven thousand loyalists sailed from the port of New York, heading for Canada. Altogether, over 120,000 loyalists departed from the United States during the War of Independence. On September 3, Great Britain and the United States signed the Treaty of Paris, formally ending the war. Although independent, the United States was united in name only. A loose confederation of thirteen states with competing economic interests, strong tariff barriers, and a deep distaste for centralized power, the country could not meet its growing obligations—domestic and international. When the revolutionary forces disbanded at the end of 1783, the nation remained obligated to them for unpaid wages.

The nation's central government proved ineffectual. Under the Articles of Confederation, Congress had no power to levy or collect taxes. In 1785, inflation reached new heights. By 1786, a major depression severely afflicted the country's business. Currency was considered unstable, prices were falling, and the shipping industry was at a standstill. From the following documents, it is evident that the newly won independence had done little to remedy the grievances of the unprivileged. Note also the disclaimer that the grievances were British-inspired.

In the fall of 1786, against this backdrop of economic near-chaos and governmental indifference, Captain Daniel Shays led a rebellion to stop court foreclosures of the farms of impoverished soldiers and farmers who failed to pay taxes. The rebellion threatened the federal arsenal at Springfield, Massachusetts, and demonstrated further the weakness of the Confederation. The uprising was declared to be treason by Massachusetts, and the state militia crushed it. Nevertheless, all participants were pardoned for their offense by 1788, and many of the reforms here advocated eventually were enacted by the Massachusetts legislature.

## ☆ 55 Communications regarding the Insurrection

### ☆ 55a An Address to the People of the Several Towns in the County of Hampshire, Now at Arms [Massachusetts]

Reprinted in G. R. Minot, *History of the Insurrection in Massachusetts* (Boston: James W. Burditt, 1810), 82.

GENTLEMEN,

We have thought proper to inform you of some of the principal causes of the late risings of the people, and also of their present movement, viz.

1st. The present expensive mode of collecting debts, which by reason of the great scarcity of cash, will of necessity fill our gaols with unhappy debtors; and thereby a reputable body of people rendered incapable of being serviceable either to themselves or the community.

2d. The monies raised by impost and excise being appropriated to discharge the interest of governmental securities, and not the foreign debt, when these securities are not subject to taxation.

3d. A suspension of the writ of Habeas Corpus, by which those persons who have stepped forth to assert and maintain the rights of the people, are liable to be taken and conveyed even to the most distant part of the Commonwealth, and thereby subjected to an unjust punishment.

4th. The unlimited power granted to Justices of the Peace and Sheriffs, Deputy Sheriffs, and Constables, by the Riot Act, indemnifying them to the prosecution thereof; when perhaps, wholly actuated from a principle of revenge, hatred, and envy.

Furthermore, Be assured, that this body, now at arms, despise the idea of being instigated by British emissaries, which is so strenuously propagated by the enemies of our liberties: And also wish the most proper and speedy measures may be taken, to discharge both our foreign and domestic debt.

Per Order,

DANIEL GRAY, Chairman of the Committee

### ☆ 55b To the Printer of the Hampshire Herald

Reprinted in G. R. Minot, *History of the Insurrection in Massachusetts* (Boston: James W. Burditt, 1810), 82.

SIR,

It has some how or other fallen to my lot to be employed in a more conspicuous manner than some others of my fellow citizens, in stepping forth on defense of the rights and privileges of the people, more especially of the county of Hampshire.

Therefore, upon the desire of the people now at arms, I take this method to publish to the world of mankind in general, particularly the people of this Commonwealth, some of the principal grievances we complain of. . . .

In this first place, I must refer you to a draught of grievances drawn up by a committee of the people, now at arms, under the signature of Daniel Gray, chairman, which is heartily approved of; some others also are here added, viz.

1st. The General Court, for certain obvious reasons, must be removed out of the town of Boston.

2d. A revision of the constitution is absolutely necessary.

3d. All kinds of governmental securities, now on interest, that have been bought of the original owners for two shillings, and the highest for six shillings and eight pence on the pound, and have received more interest than the principal cost the speculator who purchased them—that if justice was done, we verily believe, nay positively know, it would save this Commonwealth thousands of pounds.

4th. Let the lands belonging to this Commonwealth, at the eastward, be sold at the best advantage to pay the remainder of our domestick debt.

5th. Let the monies arising from impost and excise be appropriated to discharge the foreign debt.

6th. Let that act, passed by the General Court last June by a small majority of only seven, called the Supplementary Act, for twenty-five years to come, be repealed.

7th. The total abolition of the Inferiour Court of Common Pleas and General Sessions of the Peace.

8th. Deputy Sheriffs totally set aside, as a useless set of officers in the community; and Constables who are really neccessay, be empowered to do the duty, by which means a large swarm of lawyers will be banished from their wonted haunts, who have been more damage to the people at large, especially the common farmers, than the savage beasts of prey.

To this I boldly sign my proper name, as a hearty well-wisher to the real rights of the people.

THOMAS GROVER
*Worcester, December 7, 1786*


## 56 The Constitution and Political Crime (1787)

To many, it was intolerable that the Commonwealth of Massachusetts had to relieve the national arsenal at Springfield, Massachusetts, from Shays's forces. The growing recognition of the inadequacy of the Confederation, reinforced by this event, soon produced a movement for the reform of the national government. In 1787, a convention, with George Washington presiding, met in Philadelphia "for the sole and express purpose of revising the Articles of Confederation." The result was a new United States Constitution.

The Constitution, in its various articles, set up the branches of a unified and stronger central government. But safeguards against federal abuse of power abounded throughout the document. Article I limited the arbitrary power of government by guaranteeing to citizens the protection of the writ of habeas corpus. Article III purposefully defined treason against the United States, thus making that offense the only constitutionally defined crime, as a safeguard against the overreach of the federal government. As for the states, each was obliged to aid the others in the apprehension of traitors, criminals, and runaway slaves. The new Constitution ordained the republican form of government as the new political orthodoxy for members of the Union.

☆ 56 United States Constitution

\* \* \*

Art. I, Section 9, cl. 2. The Privilege of the Writ of Habeas Corpus shall not be suspended, unless when in Cases of Rebellion or Invasion the public Safety may require it.

\* \* \*

Art. III, Section 3. Treason against the United States, shall consist only in levying War against them, or in adhering to their Enemies, giving them Aid and Comfort. No Person shall be convicted of Treason unless on the Testimony of two Witnesses to the same overt Act, or on Confession in open Court.

The Congress shall have Power to declare the Punishment of Treason, but no Attainder of Treason shall work Corruption of Blood, or Forfeiture except during the Life of the Person attained.

\* \* \*

Art. IV, Section 2. A Person charged in any State with Treason, Felony, or other Crime, who shall flee from Justice, and be found in another State, shall on Demand of the executive Authority of the State from which he fled, be delivered up, to be removed to the State having Jurisdiction of the Crime.

No Person held to Service or Labour in one State, under the Laws thereof, escaping into another, shall, in Consequence of any Law or Regulation therein, be discharged from such Service or Labour, but shall be delivered up on Claim of the Party to whom such Service or Labour may be due.

\* \* \*

Art. VI, Section 4. The United States shall guarantee to every State in this Union a Republican Form of Government, and shall protect each of them against Invasion; and on Application of the Legislature, or of the Executive (when the Legislature cannot be convened) against domestic Violence.


## 57 "a general constitution, in subversion of that of the state" (1787)

The convention that assembled in Philadelphia on May 25, 1787, to revise the Articles of Confederation had representatives from all the original states except Rhode Island. The fifty-five delegates were described as "clear-headed, moderate men, with positive views of their own and firm purpose but with a willingness to compromise." The document that was produced differed from that of the Confederation in many respects, principally by giving the national government direct power over individual citizens. Some of the delegates, including Edmund Randolph and George Mason of Virginia and Elbridge Gerry of Massachusetts, refused to sign the Constitution. Of New York's three delegates, two walked out prior to the signing of the Constitution, and Alexander Hamilton alone from that state gave his consent. The two New York dissenters, Robert Yates and John Lansing, represented the intense opposition which existed in New York to the proposed Constitution. In the end, New York ratified the document after the requisite nine states already had done so. To these opponents, participating in the presentation of the proposed Constitution would amount to an act of subversion against the state. Allegiance to the primary sovereignty of the several states thus provided the legal justification for refusal to support the new order. Despite its apparent resolution by the ratification of the new Constitution, this is a theme that echoes and reechoes for the next two centuries and provides much authority for resistance to the federal government.

## ☆ 57 Letter from Robert Yates and John Lansing to the Governor of New York

Reprinted in J. Elliot, ed., *Debates in the Several State Conventions on the Adoption of the Federal Constitution* (Philadelphia: Lippincott, 1907), 1:480-82.

\*        \*        \*

... We beg leave, briefly, to state some cogent reasons, which, among others, influenced us to decide against a consolidation of the states. These are reducible into two heads:—

1st. The limited and well-defined powers under which we acted, and which could not on any possible construction, embrace an idea of such magnitude as to assent to a general constitution, in subversion of that of the state.

2nd. A conviction of the impracticability of establishing a general government, pervading every part of the United States, and extending essential benefits to all.

Our powers were explicit, and confined to the sole and express purpose of revising the Articles of Confederation, and reporting such alterations and provisions therein, as should render the Federal Constitution adequate to the exigencies of government, and the preservation of the Union.

From these expressions, we were led to believe that a system of consolidated government could not, in the remotest degree, have been in contemplation of the legislature of this state; for that so important a trust, as the adopting measures which tended to deprive the state government of its most essential rights of sovereignty, and to place it in a dependent situation, could not have been confided by implication; and the circumstance, that the acts of the Convention were to receive a state approbation in the last resort, forcibly corroborated the opinion that our powers could not involve the subversion of a Constitution which, being immediately derived from the people, could only be abolished by their express consent, and not by a legislature, possessing authority vested in them for its preservation. Nor could we suppose that, if it had been the intention of the legislature to abrogate the existing confederation, they would, in such pointed terms, have directed the attention of their delegates to the revision and amendment of it, in total exclusion of every other idea.

Reasoning in this manner, we were of opinion that the leading feature of every amendment ought to be the preservation of the individual states in their uncontrolled constitutional rights, and that, in reserving these, a mode might have been devised of granting to the Confederacy, the moneys arising from a general system of revenue, the power of regulating commerce and enforcing the observance of foreign treaties, and other necessary matters of less moment.

Exclusive of our objections originating from the want of power, we entertained an opinion that a general government, however guarded by declarations of rights, or cautionary provisions, must unavoidably, in a short time, be productive of the destruction of the civil liberty of such citizens who could be effectually coerced by it, by reason of the extensive territory of the United States, the dispersed situation of its inhabitants, and the insuperable difficulty of controlling or counteracting the views of a set of men (however unconstitutional and oppressive their acts might be) possessed of all the powers of government, and who, from their remoteness from their constituents, and necessary permanency of office, could not be supposed to be uniformly actuated by an attention to their welfare and happiness; that, however wise and energetic the principles of the general government might be, the extremities of the United States could not be kept in due submission and obedience to its laws, at the distance of many hundred miles from the seat of government; that, if the general legislature was composed of so numerous a body of men as to represent the interests of all the inhabitants of the United States, in the usual and true ideas of representation, the expense of supporting it would become intolerably burdensome; and that, if a few only were vested with a power of legislation, the interests of a great majority of the inhabitants of the United States must necessarily be unknown; or, if known, even in the first stages of the operations of the new government, unattended to.

These reasons were, in our opinion, conclusive against any system of consolidated government: to that recommended by the Convention, we suppose most of them very forcibly apply....

\*        \*        \*

## 58 "to put to death or capture the said Indians" (1787)

Native Americans were subject to the white man's rules when visiting his territory and, according to federal treaty, they were purportedly autonomous in their own territory. But the states sought to exercise jurisdiction over Native Americans within their boundaries as well.

Particularly with regard to the western territory England ceded to the United States in the Treaty of Paris, the controversy between the federal government, the state authorities, and the indigenous populations grew extremely intense. The federal government claimed the territory as the sovereign successor to the king of England. This position was accepted by those states (Rhode Island, New Hampshire, New Jersey, Pennsylvania, Delaware, and Maryland) that, as colonies, had fixed western boundaries. The states without a colonial western border claimed sovereignty over the same territory at least as far as Mississippi. This dispute accounted in part for the delay between the adoption of the Articles of Confederation in 1777 and their ratification in 1781. Most of the states finally ceded their claims to the lands west of the Eastern Continental Divide to the federal government during the 1780s. Georgia, nevertheless, did not relinquish its claim until 1802.

With the jurisdiction over these lands in dispute, western settlers moved into aboriginal territories, an act that produced skirmishes with Native Americans. Despite the protection accorded by treaty to Native American territory by the United States, Georgia, in effect, declared war in 1787 on the Creek Nation that occupied most of what is now Georgia and Alabama.

## ☆ 58  An Act for Suppressing the Violences of the Indians

Reprinted in E. M. Coleman, ed., *Laws of the Colonial and State Governments Relating to Indians and Indian Affairs, from 1633-1831 Inclusive* (Washington: Thompson and Homans, 1832), 186-87.

*Be it enacted by the Representatives of the Freemen of the state of Georgia, in General Assembly met, and by the authority of the same,* That from and immediately after the passing of this act, the Creek Indians shall be considered as without the protection of this state; and it shall be lawful for the government and people of the same to put to death or capture the said Indians wheresoever they may be found within the limits of this state, except such tribes of the said Indians which have not, or shall not hereafter, commit hostilities against the people of this state, or which the commanding officer shall judge.

SEC. 2. *And be it further enacted,* That fifteen hundred men be enlisted as soon as may be, to serve until peace is established with the Indians. . . .

*               *               *

SEC. 8. And whereas, it may so happen, that certain persons have run and surveyed lands without

the limits of the respective counties of this State, as established by law, and for which grants may have been surreptitiously claimed: *Be it enacted,* That all lands without the limits aforesaid, are hereby declared to be vacant, any warrant, survey, or grant, to the contrary notwithstanding; and that a tract of land herein described shall be reserved, and, at the cessation of the hostilities with the Indians, appropriated to and for the allowances and bounties of and for the said officers and troops; and no warrant, survey, or grant, shall be obtained for any part of the lands within the said reserve, by any person whatever, until such hostilities shall cease; and all such officers or troops shall have a preference in laying their bounties within the said reserve.

SEC. 9. *And be it also enacted,* That the said bounties shall not interfere with a certain quantity of land in the vicinity of those Indian towns which are, and shall continue to be, friendly, which quantity shall be determined by a future legislature. . . .

*               *               *

# 59  The United States Treason Statute (1790)

In the new American nation, the political leadership consisted of persons formerly condemned as traitors by the British as well as by some of their fellow Americans. Having been so tarred, these political leaders responded to the issue of loyalty with some delicacy. The question of where primary allegiance lay—to the United States or to a particular state— remained unresolved for a long time. The United States Congress enacted the Treason Statute of 1790 in accordance with the power granted to it in the Constitution. The Constitution had defined the crime of treason, but not its punishment. Although the statute retained the death penalty for treason, it ordained hanging as a less barbaric sanction than the English drawing and quartering, and abolished corruption of blood and forfeiture. The enactment implemented the procedural safeguards previously developed under English and colonial law. The statute also created and defined other offenses against the government of the United States, including the lesser crime of misprision of treason and piracy.

## ☆ 59  An Act for the Punishment of Certain Crimes against the United States

1 Stat. 112 (1790).

SECTION 1. *Be it enacted by the Senate and House of Representatives of the United States of America in Congress assembled,* That if any person or persons, owing allegiance to the United States of America, shall levy war against them, or shall adhere to their enemies, giving them aid and comfort within the United States or elsewhere, and shall be thereof convicted, on confession in open court, or on the testimony of two witnesses to the same overt act of the treason whereof he or they shall stand indicted, such person or persons shall be adjudged guilty of treason against the United States, and shall suffer death.

SEC. 2. *And be it [further] enacted,* That if any person or persons, having knowledge of the commission of any of the treasons aforesaid, shall conceal and not as soon as may be disclose and make known the same to the President of the United States, or some one of the judges thereof, or to the president or governor of a particular state, or some one of the judges or justices thereof, such person or persons on conviction shall be judged guilty of misprision of treason, and shall be imprisoned not exceeding seven years, and fined not exceeding one thousand dollars.

\* \* \*

SEC. 8. *And be it [further] enacted,* That if any person or persons shall commit upon the high seas, or in any river, haven, basin or bay, out of the jurisdiction of any particular state, murder or robbery, or any other offence which if committed within the body of a county, would by the laws of the United States be punishable with death; or if any captain or mariner of any ship or other vessel, shall piratically and feloniously run away with such ship or vessel, or any goods or merchandise to the value of fifty dollars, or yield up such ship or vessel voluntarily to any pirate; or if any seaman shall lay violent hands upon his commander, thereby to hinder and prevent his fighting in defence of his ship or goods committed to his trust, or shall make a revolt in the ship; every such offender shall be deemed, taken and adjudged to be a pirate and felon, and being thereof convicted, shall suffer death; and the trial of crimes committed on the high seas, or in any place out of the jurisdiction of any particular state, shall be in the district where the offender is apprehended, or into which he may first be brought.

SEC. 9. *And be it [further] enacted,* That if any citizen shall commit any piracy or robbery aforesaid, or any act of hostility against the United States, or any citizen thereof, upon the high seas, under colour of any commission from any person, such offender shall, notwithstanding the pretence of any such authority, be deemed, adjudged and taken to be a pirate, felon, and robber, and on being thereof convicted shall suffer death.

\* \* \*

SEC. 24. *Provided always,* and be it enacted, That no conviction or judgment for any of the offences aforesaid, shall work corruption of blood, or any forfeiture of estate.

\* \* \*

SEC. 29. *And be it [further] enacted,* That any person who shall be accused and indicted of treason, shall have a copy of the indictment, and a list of the jury and witnesses, to be produced on the trial for proving the said indictment, mentioning the names and places of abode of such witnesses and jurors, delivered unto him at least three entire days before he shall be tried for the same; and in other capital offences, shall have such copy of the indictment and list of the jury two entire days at least before the trial: And that every person so accused and indicted for any of the crimes aforesaid, shall also be allowed and admitted to make his full defence by counsel learned in the law; and the court before whom such person shall be tried, or some judge thereof, shall, and they are hereby authorized and required immediately upon his request to assign to such person such counsel, not exceeding two, as such person shall desire, to whom such counsel shall have free access at all seasonable hours; and every such person or persons accused or indicted of the crimes aforesaid, shall be allowed and admitted in his said defence to make any proof that he or they can produce, by lawful witness or witnesses, and shall have the like process of the court where he or they shall be tried, to compel his or their witnesses to appear at his or their trial, as is usually granted to compel witnesses to appear on the prosecution against them.

SEC. 30. *And be it further enacted,* That if any person or persons be indicted of treason against the United States, and shall stand mute or refuse to plead, or shall challenge peremptorily above the number of thirty-five of the jury; or if any person or persons be indicted of any other of the offences herein before set forth, for which the punishment is declared to be death, if he or they shall also stand mute or will not answer to the indictment, or challenge peremptorily above the number of twenty persons of the jury; the court, in any of the cases aforesaid, shall notwithstanding proceed to the trial of the person or persons so standing mute or challenging, as if he or they had pleaded not guilty, and render judgment thereon accordingly.

SEC. 31. *And be it further enacted,* That the benefit of clergy shall not be used or allowed, upon conviction of any crime, for which, by any statute of the United States, the punishment is or shall be declared to be death.

SEC. 32. *And be it further enacted,* That no person or persons shall be prosecuted, tried or punished for treason or other capital offence aforesaid, wilful murder or forgery excepted, unless the indictment for the same shall be found by a grand jury within three years next after the treason or capital offence aforesaid shall be done or committed; . . . *Provided,* That nothing herein contained shall extend to any person or persons fleeing from justice.

SEC. 33. *And be it further enacted,* That the

manner of inflicting the punishment of death, shall be by hanging the person convicted by the neck until dead.

*Approved, April 30, 1790.*

## 60 The Bill of Rights (1791)

Fears of abuse of power by the stronger central government proposed in the Constitution led many states to ratify the Constitution with requests for the adoption of a declaration of rights (restraints) upon the exercise of federal power. On September 25, 1789, Congress placed twelve proposals before the states as amendments to the Constitution. The first two, dealing respectively with the ratio of representatives to population and the compensation of members of Congress, never received the requisite number of ratifications. Thus, the first amendment to the Constitution was actually the third one that Congress proposed. On December 15, 1791, Virginia became the eleventh of fourteen states to ratify the Bill of Rights, completing the amendment process.

Although ultimately a supporter of the Bill of Rights, James Madison earlier had expressed doubts regarding its wisdom. He was concerned that the specific definitions of rights would lend themselves to narrowing constructions and that, in any event, "experience proves the inefficacy of a bill of rights on those occasions when its control is most needed. Repeated violations of these parchment barriers have been committed by overbearing majorities in every state. . . . Whenever there is an interest and power to do wrong, wrong will generally be done and not less readily by a powerful and interested party than by a powerful and interested prince." Apparently, Jefferson's response to Madison, particularly the argument that a bill of rights would place an instrument in the hands of a hopefully independent, learned, and honest judicial department which would check overreaching legislative and executive authorities, persuaded Madison to change his position. The change was probably due also to political consideration: Madison's desire to weaken the cause of the anti-Federalists, who agitated for the recognition of these rights, and to forestall demands for a second constitutional convention which might weaken the new central government.

In conformity with Jefferson's views, the speech and press clauses of the First Amendment as well as the procedural protections of the Fourth, Fifth, and Sixth Amendments have sometimes played an important role in limiting the government's reaction to political crimes. At other times Madison's more cynical view has prevailed.

## ☆ 60 United States Constitution, Amendments I-X

### AMENDMENT I

Congress shall make no law respecting an establishment of religion, or prohibiting the free exercise thereof; or abridging the freedom of speech, or of the press; or the right of the people peaceably to assemble, and to petition the Government for a redress of grievances.

### AMENDMENT II

A well regulated Militia, being necessary to the security of a free State, the right of the people to keep and bear Arms, shall not be infringed.

### AMENDMENT III

No Soldier shall, in time of peace be quartered in any house, without the consent of the Owner, nor in time of war, but in a manner to be prescribed by law.

### AMENDMENT IV

The right of the people to be secure in their persons, houses, papers, and effects, against unreasonable searches and seizures, shall not be violated, and no Warrants shall issue, but upon probable cause, supported by Oath or affirmation, and particularly describing the place to be searched, and the persons or things to be seized.

### AMENDMENT V

No person shall be held to answer for a capital, or otherwise infamous crime, unless on a presentment or indictment of a Grand Jury, except in cases arising in the land or naval forces, or in the Militia, when in actual service in time of War or public danger; nor shall any person be subject for the same offence to be twice put in jeopardy of life or limb; nor shall be compelled in any criminal case to be a witness against himself, nor be deprived of life, liberty, or property, without due process of law; nor shall private property be taken for public use, without just compensation.

### AMENDMENT VI

In all criminal prosecutions, the accused shall enjoy the right to a speedy and public trial, by an impartial jury of the State and district wherein the crime shall have been committed, which district shall have been previously ascertained by law, and to be informed of the nature and cause of the accusation; to be confronted with the witness against him; to have compulsory process for obtaining witnesses in his favor, and to have the Assistance of Counsel for his defense.

### AMENDMENT VII

In Suits at common law, where the value in controversy shall exceed twenty dollars, the right of trial by jury shall be preserved, and no fact tried by jury, shall be otherwise re-examined in any Court of the United States, than according to the rules of the common law.

### AMENDMENT VIII

Excessive bail shall not be required, nor excessive fines imposed, nor cruel and unusual punishments inflicted.

### AMENDMENT IX

The enumeration in the Constitution, of certain rights, shall not be construed to deny or disparage others retained by the people.

### AMENDMENT X

The powers not delegated to the United States by the Constitution, nor prohibited by it to the States, are reserved to the States respectively, or to the people.

## 61 Fugitives from Law and from Slavery (1793)

The United States Constitution gave legal validity to slavery, restrained states from emancipating slaves escaped from other states, and articulated the right to repossess fugitive slaves. The detailed machinery for the execution of this right, the Fugitive Slave Act, was created by the Second Congress on February 12, 1793. Upheld by the Supreme Court in *Prigg v. Pennsylvania*, 41 U.S. (16 Pet.) 539 (1842), the 1793 act was later amended by the Fugitive Slave Law of 1850, a more severe measure resulting from a series of compromise resolutions proposed by Senator Henry Clay of Kentucky.

Congress relied on state authorities for rendering fugitives from the law but invoked federal process for the repossession of runaway slaves. Thus, the power of the United States government sustained the institution of slavery outside the boundaries of the slave states. Additionally, those who acted to hinder the recapture of slaves were subject to criminal punishment by the United States. The vigor with which this law was or was not enforced provided one point of friction between the Union and the various states, as well as among states.

☆ 61 An Act respecting Fugitives from Justice, and Persons Escaping from the Service of Their Masters

1 Stat. 302 (1793).

SECTION 1. *Be it enacted by the Senate and House of Representatives of the United States of America in Congress assembled*, That whenever the executive authority of any state in the Union, or of either of the territories northwest or south of the river Ohio, shall demand any person as a fugitive from justice, of the executive authority of any such state or territory to which such person shall have fled, and shall moreover produce the copy of an indictment found, or an affidavit made before a magistrate of any state or territory as aforesaid, charging the person so demanded, with having committed treason, felony, or other crime, certified as authentic by the governor or chief magistrate of the state or territory from whence the person so charged fled, it shall be the duty of the executive authority of the state or territory to which such person shall have fled, to cause him or her to be arrested and secured, and notice of the arrest to be given to the executive authority appointed to receive the fugitive, and to cause the fugitive to be delivered to such agent when he shall appear. . . .

SEC. 2. *And be it further enacted*, That any agent, appointed as aforesaid, who shall receive the fugitive into his custody, shall be empowered to transport him or her to the state or territory from which he or she shall have fled. And if any person or persons shall by force set at liberty, or rescue the fugitive from such agent while transporting, as aforesaid, the person or persons so offending shall, on conviction, be fined not exceeding five hundred dollars, and be imprisoned not exceeding one year.

SEC. 3. *And be it also enacted*, That when a person held to labour in any of the United States, or in either of the territories on the northwest or south of the river Ohio, under the laws thereof, shall escape into any other of the said states or territory, the person to whom such labour or service may be due, his agent or attorney, is hereby empowered to seize or arrest such fugitive from labour, and to take him or her before any judge of the circuit or district courts of the United States, residing or being within the state, or before any magistrate of a county, city or town corporate, wherein such seizure or arrest shall be made, and upon proof to the satisfaction of such judge or magistrate, either by oral testimony or affidavit taken before and certified by a magistrate of any such state or territory, that the person so seized or arrested, doth, under the laws of the state or territory from which he or she fled, owe service or labour to the person claiming him or her, it shall be the duty of such judge or magistrate to give a certificate thereof to such claimant, his agent or attorney, which shall be sufficient warrant for removing the said fugitive from labour, to the state or territory from which he or she fled.

SEC. 4. *And be it further enacted*, That any person who shall knowingly and willingly obstruct or hinder such claimant, his agent or attorney in so seizing or arresting such fugitive from labour, or shall rescue such fugitive from such claimant, his agent or attorney when so arrested pursuant to the authority herein given or declared; or shall harbor or conceal such person after notice that he or she was a fugitive from labour, as aforesaid, shall, for either of the said offences, forfeit and pay the sum of five hundred dollars. Which penalty may be recovered by and for the benefit of such claimant, by action of debt, in any court proper to try the same, saving moreover to the person claiming such labour or service, his right of action for or on account of the said injuries or either of them.

*Approved, February 12, 1793.*

# 62 The Whiskey Rebellion (1791-1794)

In 1790, at the suggestion of Secretary of the Treasury Alexander Hamilton, the federal government assumed the entire domestic debt from the Revolutionary War, which the states had not been able to service. The undertaking of this substantial load compelled government to seek new revenues.

The March 3, 1791, excise tax on domestically produced spirits stirred up the western counties of Pennsylvania, which contained a quarter of the nation's stills. The backcountry farmers considered the tax, ranging from nine to twenty-five cents per gallon, particularly unjust, because it affected the sole product that they were able to transport profitably over the rugged Alleghany mountains to the markets of Philadelphia and the East Coast. The tax also reminded the settlers of hated English excises including the odious Stamp Act, opposition to which had fueled the movement toward revolution. The fact that western distillers accused of violating the excise law were to be tried in Philadelphia aggravated the situation. The trip was time consuming and expensive, and the law was reminiscent of the acts of Parliament requiring that certain crimes in the colonies be tried in England. In 1794, Congress provided that these charges could be heard in the local state court, as well as the federal court in Philadelphia, but it was too late. A series of summonses commanding appearance in Philadelphia had already been issued and subsequently served. Angry western settlers directed their wrath at the federal marshals seeking to serve process. Several were tarred and feathered and forced to swear not to serve federal process in the western counties. The following report from a trial arising out of the Whiskey Rebellion sets out subsequent events in graphic detail. Prior to his appointment as a tax inspector, General Neville had been a popular state politician.

In reading this and the documents that follow, it should be kept in mind that these events occurred a scant few years after the ratification of the Constitution, characterized by its opponents as vesting in a central government powers that could as easily be abused as those previously held by the English king and Parliament.

☆ 62 *United States v. Insurgents*

26 F. Cas. 449 (C.C.D. Pa. 1795) (No. 15,443).

The act of congress of the 3rd of March, 1791, which imposed a duty upon spirits distilled within the United States, produced at once great opposition, both in and out of congress.... It was branded with the name of excise, a term very hateful to the people, as connected with the former oppressions of the British government. It was declared unnecessary and tyrannical. The legislatures of Maryland, Pennsylvania, Virginia, and North Carolina united in solemn declarations of rooted dislike, and of resistance, in some cases hardly to be reconciled with constitutional opposition; and by the latter state a position was assumed, which in later days would have been called nullification. But it was in the western parts of Pennsylvania and Virginia, and particularly in the counties of Alleghany, Washington, Fayette, and Westmoreland, in the first-mentioned state, that resistance to the bill was most violent, and it was there an agitation was started which, in the course of a few years, ripened into an organized insurgation and involved its leaders in the crime of treason.

\*     \*     \*

The act of 1791 came up for revision before the congress which assembled in October of the same year. By an act passed May 8, 1792, several material alterations were thereto made; the duties were reduced to so moderate a rate as to obviate any complaint on that score. The other changes were also favourable to distillers.

The act of 1792 required that there should be an office for collection in every county. It was therefore supposed, on the part of the discontented, that if the establishment of these offices was prevented, a material point would be gained. A plan of intimidation was accordingly pursued, directed against those who might be disposed to allow their houses to be used for the obnoxious purpose. Threats of personal violence and of destruction of property were made, and in some cases actually executed. It became, therefore, in a short time, almost impossible to obtain suitable places for the revenue offices. After much difficulty, in August, 1792, General Neville obtained the house of one William Faulkner, a captain in the army, for an office of inspection in Washington county. Soon after this, Captain Faulkner was met by a large number of people, in the same neighbourhood where Johnson had been maltreated the preceding year. A knife was put at his throat, and the assailants threatened to scalp, tar and feather him, and to burn his house, unless he would promise to prevent its further use as an office. He was compelled to make the promise; and, in consequence, wrote a letter to the inspector, countermanding the permission to use his house.

General Neville had received warnings for some time previous, that an attack was intended on his house. . . . Acting on these intimations, he had had his house prepared for resistance. The windows were filled up with thick plank, and the negroes abundantly supplied with arms and ammunition. These precautions were not idle. About day-break on the 10th [July, 1794], the party from the meeting [at Couche's Fort] under the command of one John Holcroft, counting about forty guns, appeared at the house of the inspector. On being asked what they wanted, and replying in a suspicious manner, they were fired upon from the house. They returned the fire, but being unexpectedly attacked by the negroes in the out-houses, they precipitately retired, with six of their number wounded and one killed. The inspector's family received no injury. Though thus far entirely successful, General Neville had every reason to suppose that the business would not terminate thus, and to anticipate a renewed and more dangerous attack. He accordingly made application to the judges, generals of militia, and sheriff of the county for protection. A reply to this application, on the part of these officers, informed him that the laws could not be executed, so as to afford him protection, owing to the too general combination of the people in that part of Pennsylvania, to oppose the revenue law; and expressed a fear, that should the posse comitatus be ordered out in support of the civil authority, very few could be found who were not of the party of the rioters. A detachment of eleven men, regulars, was obtained, however, from Fort Pitt, and command was taken by Major Kirkpatrick, a relative of General Neville. On the day following the attack, the rioters assembled again at Couche's Fort, a few miles from the residence of General Neville, to the number of five or six hundred men. [They conceived a plan to march to the General's house, compel his resignation, and seize the tax records. Upon arriving at the house, they sent a messenger with a flag to demand the papers. Informed that the General had left,] the flag was sent a second time, requiring the inspector to resign, and that six good, reputable citizens should be admitted to examine and seize the papers, promising that in that case no further injury should be done. This was refused at once. Notice was given, by a third flag, for the women and children to withdraw. The attack then commenced.

In about a quarter of an hour the defenders of the house was ceased firing, and a call was heard thence, which was mistaken by the assailants for a parley. Their leader, McFarlane, then stepped from behind a tree, where he had for greater safety posted himself, to order the firing to stop, when he was hit in the groin by a musket-ball from the house, and instantly killed. The firing then recommenced, and a message was sent to the committe to know whether the house should not be stormed. In the meantime the out-houses and the adjacent buildings were set fire to. The intensity of the heat, and the danger of an immediate communication of the conflagration to the house, compelled Major Kirkpatrick and his small party to come out and surrender themselves. The attack lasted for about an hour, during which the assailants had two killed and several wounded; and three of the soldiers were wounded. The privates were suffered to depart without injury, but Major Kirkpatrick was arrested, and ordered to give up his musket. He refused to do so, whereupon one presented a gun at his breast, and was about to fire, when he dropped upon his knees and asked quarter. The mansion was then set on fire, and it and the out-buildings were consumed, except a small out-house, which was preserved at the request of the negroes, as containing their bacon. While the house was burning, the rioters broke open the cellar, and drunk up the wine, and many things of value were supposed to be stolen therefrom. The marshal, with Colonel Presley Neville (the son of General Neville) and several others, were taken on their way to the house. They were arrested and put under guard. After a short time, all but the two former were permitted to escape. Colonel Neville begged to be permitted to go on, and engaged that all their demands should be complied with. He was refused, however, and was compelled to remain during the period of the attack in sight of the house; in painful uncertainty as to the fate of his father and family. [The insurgents finally forced General Neville and the Marshall to leave Pittsburgh. The insurgents threatened to attack the town in an attempt to compel Neville's resignation and forced the surrender of the processes held by the Marshall.]

Before separating, after the attack on the inspector's, the insurgents appointed a meeting to be held on the 23rd of July, at Mingo Creek Meeting House, in Washington county. At this meeting, which was composed of those who had been engaged in the attack, and a large number from the neighbouring counties . . . managed to show them that they had committed acts of treason, and to persuade them against any precipitate action, without endangering his safety, and without appearing to be adverse to their cause. It was finally determined to postpone their final determination to a more general assemblage. The following call for another meeting was made, and published in the Pittsburgh Gazette of the 26th July: "By a respectable number of citizens who met on Wednesday, the 23rd instant, it is recommended to the townships of the four Western

Pennsylvania counties, and its neighbouring counties of Virginia to meet and choose representatives, to meet at Parkinson's Ferry, on the Monongahela, on the 11th of August next to take into consideration the situations of the Western country."

*              *              *

## 63 "combinations to defeat the execution of the laws" (1794)

Under the leadership of David Bradford, a deputy state's attorney, the masses of the Whiskey Army mustered at Braddock's Field and marched into Pittsburgh. Note that while the state officials could not provide protection for the federal officers, the uprising was limited to opposition to the enforcement of a single law. The civil authorities were otherwise in control of matters, and presumably there was no generalized disorder. Nevertheless, President Washington characterized the situation as insurrection and anarchy. Clearly the resistance was a test of the newly created government's ability to enforce federal law. In his first proclamation, Washington exhorted the insurgents to disperse. The ultimate calling of the militia was in acquiescence to Hamilton's recommendation that forceful action was necessary or else the "spirit of disobedience will naturally extend."

☆ 63 Proclamations of President Washington on the Whiskey Rebellion

☆ 63a August 7, 1794

Reprinted in J. Richardson, ed., *A Compilation of the Messages and Papers of the Presidents* (New York: Bureau of National Literature, 1897), 150-52.

Whereas combinations to defeat the execution of the laws laying duties upon spirits distilled within the United States and upon stills have from the time of the commencement of those laws existed in some of the western parts of Pennsylvania; and

Whereas the said combinations, proceeding in a manner subversive equally of the just authority of government and of the rights of individuals, have hitherto effected their dangerous and criminal purpose by the influence of certain irregular meetings whose proceedings have tended to encourage and uphold the spirit of opposition by misrepresentations of the laws calculated to render them odious; by endeavors to deter those who might be so disposed from accepting offices under them through fear of public resentment and of injury to person and property, and to compel those who had accepted such offices by actual violence to surrender or forbear the execution of them; by circulating vindictive menaces against all those who should otherwise, directly or indirectly, aid in the execution of the said laws, or who, yielding to the dictates of conscience and to a sense of obligation, should themselves comply therewith, by actually injuring and destroying the property of persons who were understood to have so complied; by inflicting cruel humiliation punishments upon private citizens for no other cause than that of appearing to be the friends of the laws; by intercepting the public officers on the highways, abusing, assaulting, and otherwise ill treating them; by going to their houses in the night, gaining admittance by force, taking away their papers, and committing other outrages, employing for these unwarrantable purposes the agency of armed banditti disguised in such manner as for the most part to escape discovery; and

Whereas the endeavors of the Legislature to obviate objections to the said laws by lowering the duties and by other alterations conducive to the convenience of those whom they immediately affect ... and the endeavors of the executive officers to conciliate a compliance with the laws by explanations, by forbearance, and even by particular accommodations founded on the suggestion of local considerations, have been disappointed of their effect by the machinations of persons whose industry to excite resistance has increased with every appearance of a disposition among the people to relax in their opposition and to acquiesce in the laws, insomuch that many persons in the said western parts of Pennsylvania have at length been hardy enough to perpetrate acts which I am advised amount to treason, being overt acts of levying war against the Unites States, ... avowing as the motives of these outrageous proceedings an intention to prevent by force of arms the execution of the said laws, ... to withstand by open violence the lawful authority of the Government of the United States, and to compel thereby an alteration in the measures of the Legislature and a repeal of the laws aforesaid; and

Whereas by a law of the United States entitled "An act to provide for calling forth the militia to execute the laws of the Union, suppress insurrections, and repel invasions," it is enacted "that whenever the laws of the United States shall be opposed or the execution thereof obstructed in any State by combinations too powerful to be suppressed by the ordinary course of judicial proceedings ... it shall be lawful for the President of the United States to call forth the militia of such State to suppress such combinations and to cause the laws to be duly executed. And if the militia of a State where such combinations may happen shall refuse or be insufficient to suppress the same, it shall be lawful for the President, if the Legislature of the United States shall not be in session, to call forth and employ such numbers of the militia of any other State or States most convenient thereto as may be necessary; ... Provided always, that whenever it may be necessary in the judgment of the President to use the military force hereby directed to be called forth, the President shall forthwith, and previous thereto, by proclamation, command such insurgents to disperse and retire peaceably to their respective abodes within a limited time," ... and

Whereas it is in my judgment necessary under the circumstances of the case to take measures for calling forth the militia in order to suppress the combinations aforesaid, and to cause the laws to be duly executed; and I have accordingly determined so to do, feeling the deepest regret for the occasion, but withal the most solemn conviction that the essential interests of the Union demand it, that the very existence of Government and the fundamental principles of social order are materially involved in the issue, and that the patriotism and firmness of all good citizens are seriously called upon, as occasions may require, to aid in the effectual suppression of so fatal a spirit:

Wherefore, and in pursuance of the proviso above recited, I, George Washington, President of the United States, do hereby command all persons being insurgents as aforesaid, and all others whom it may concern, on or before the 1st day of September next to disperse and retire peaceably to their respective abodes. And I do moreover warn all persons whomsoever against aiding, abetting, or comforting the perpetrators of the aforesaid treasonable acts, and do require all officers and other citizens, according to their respective duties and the laws of the land, to exert their utmost endeavors to prevent and suppress such dangerous proceedings....

G.° WASHINGTON

☆ 63b September 25, 1794

Reprinted in J. Richardson, ed., *A Compilation of the Messages and Papers of the Presidents* (New York: Bureau of National Liberature, 1897), 1:153-54.

Whereas from a hope that the combinations against the Constitution and laws of the United States in certain of the western counties of Pennsylvania would yield to time and reflection I thought it sufficient in the first instance rather to take measures for calling forth the militia than immediately to embody them, but the moment is now come when the overtures of forgiveness, with no other condition than a submission to law, have been only partially accepted; when every form of conciliation not inconsistent with the being of Government has been adopted without effect; ... when the opportunity of examining the serious consequences of a treasonable opposition has been employed in propagating principles of anarchy, ... and inviting similar acts of insurrection; when it is manifest that violence would

continue to be exercised upon every attempt to enforce the laws; when, therefore, Government is set at defiance, the contest being whether a small portion of the United States shall dictate to the whole Union, and, at the expense of those who desire peace, indulge a desperate ambition:

Now, therefore, I, George Washington, President of the United States, in obedience to that high and irresistible duty consigned to me by the Constitution "to take care that the laws be faithfully executed," deploring that the American name should be sullied by the outrages of citizens on their own Government, ... resolved to reduce the refractory to a due subordination to the law, do hereby declare and make known that, ... a force which, according to every reasonable expectation, is adequate to the exigency is already in motion to the scene of disaffection; that those who have confided or shall confide in the protection of Government shall meet full succor under the standard and from the arms of the United States; that those who, having offended against the laws, have since entitled themselves to indemnity will be treated with the most liberal good faith if they shall not have forfeited their claim by any subsequent conduct, and that instructions are given accordingly.

And I do moreover exhort all individuals, officers, and bodies of men to contemplate with abhorrence the measures leading directly or indirectly to those crimes which produce this resort to military coercion; to check in their respective spheres the efforts of misguided or designing men to substitute their misrepresentation in the place of truth and their discontents in the place of stable government, and to call to mind that, as the people of the United States have been permitted, under the Divine favor, in perfect freedom, after solemn deliberation, and in an enlightened age, to elect their own government, so will their gratitude for this inestimable blessing be best distinguished by firm exertions to maintain the Constitution and the laws.

And, lastly, I again warn all persons whomsoever and wheresoever not to abet, aid, or comfort the insurgents aforesaid, as they will answer the contrary at their peril, and I do also require all the officers and other citizens, according to their several duties, as far as may be in their power, to bring under the cognizance of the laws all offenders....

G.° WASHINGTON

## 64 The Treasons of Mitchell and Vigol (1795)

Thirteen thousand troops advanced to crush the Whiskey Rebellion. Alexander Hamilton secured George Washington's permission to join the punitive expedition and wrote: "Those ... who preach doctrines or set examples which underwrite or subvert the authority of the law, lead us from freedom to slavery. They incapacitate us from a government of laws and consequently prepare the way for one of force, for mankind must have government of one sort or another."

Prepared for a protracted war, the federal army arrived to find that most of the insurgents had departed. Many former rebels were seeking the benefits of an amnesty offer that required subscription to a loyalty oath. By and large, the more moderate forces had established control. While the use of military force to suppress the resistance was not untoward, the incident exemplified some of the perils of using the military to support domestic authority. (One historical commentator claims that "[t]he conduct of the Army in the disaffected territory is a sorry page in United States military history. Wholesale and indiscriminate arrests, harsh treatment of prisoners, inhumanity as Standard Operating Procedure—best describes it.")

The main leaders of the rebellion had either escaped or received amnesty. (David Bradford sought refuge in the Spanish territory, and although pardoned in 1799, he continued the life of a planter in Natchez.) The federal troops took twenty prisoners to Philadelphia. Only two lowly members of the rebellious forces were convicted of treason: John Mitchell, who came voluntarily before General Daniel Morgan to confess his guilt; and Philip Weigel, appearing in the court records as Vigol, who was reportedly a mad Pennsylvania Dutchman. Although the events of the rebellion were well established, questions remained whether these individuals had participated in the rebellion and whether their conduct was treasonous or merely riotous. Note how the court characterized organized resistance to the operation of a law as constituting treason and the distinction between conspiracy and treason.

Mitchell and Vigol were sentenced to hang. Nevertheless, President Washington pardoned them because of their obvious incapacities.

## ☆ 64 A Madman and a Moron

☆ 64a *United States v. Mitchell*

26 F. Cas. 1277 (C.C.D. Pa. 1795) (No. 15,788).

Indictment for high treason, by levying war against the United States. It was alleged that the prisoner was one of the party that assembled at Couche's Fort, armed; that he proceeded thence to Gen. Neville's and assisted at the burning of the general's house; that he attended with great zeal at the meeting at Bradock's field; and that on the day prescribed for signing a submission to the government he was intoxicated, refused to sign himself, and was active in dissuading others from signing.

PATERSON, Circuit Justice. . . . Let it be granted that to compel Congress to repeal a law, by . . . violence, or intimidation, is treason . . . it does not follow, that resisting the execution of a law, or attempting to coerce an officer into the resignation of this commission, will amount to the same offence. Let it be granted, also, that an insurrection, for the avowed purpose of suppressing all the excise offices in the United States, may be construed into an act of levying war against the government . . . it does not follow that an attempt to oblige one officer to resign, or to suppress all the offices in one district, will be a crime of the same denomination.

*            *            *

[I]t has been argued, that Congress has provided a specific punishment for the offence of resisting or obstructing the service of process, obviously distinguishing it from treason; and that it is as much treason to resist the execution of one law as another; to resist the marshall of a court, as much as the supervisor of a district. The analogy is, in a great measure, just. In either case, if the resistance is made by a few persons, in a particular instance, and under the impulse of a particular interest, the offence would not amount to high treason; but, if, in either case, there is a general rising of a whole county, to prevent the officer from discharging his duty in relation to the public at large, the offence is, unquestionably, high treason.

Again, it has been urged, that the criminal intention must point to the suppression of all the excise offices in the United States, or it cannot amount to high treason. If it is meant by this argument, that the insurgents of Pennsylvania must have contemplated a march from Georgia to New Hampshire, it is extravagant and absurd: but, in another view, it is perfectly correct; for, if it was intended that, by their lawless career and example, congress should be forced into a repeal of the obnoxious law, it necessarily followed, that, from the same cause, the offices of excise would be suppressed throughout the Union. That universality of object, which the books require, was inseparable from the nature of the opposition; for, it was impossible to contemplate the repeal of the excise law in one survey, or in one state, without effecting it in every survey, and in every state. The truth is, however, that the insurgents did not entertain a personal dislike for Gen. Neville; but in every stage of their proceedings at Couche's Fort, at the general's house, and at Bradock's field, they were actuated by one single, traiterous motive, a determination, if practicable, to frustrate and prevent the execution of the excise law. The whole was one great insurrection; and it is immaterial at what point of time, or place, from its commencement to its termination, any man became an agent in carrying it on. Many persons, indeed, may have attended innocently at Couche's Fort, as was the case with Porter; but those would not remain long, after the purpose of the meeting was developed. To render any man criminal, he must not only have been present, but he must have taken part with the insurgents; yet, whether he was present at Couche's Fort on the march to Gen. Neville's, or at the burning of the general's house, if his intention was traiterous, his offence was treason.... The overt act laid in the indictment ... is levying war; and war may be levied, though not actually made.... It is agreed that this overt act must be proved by two witnesses; but there is a difference as to what constitutes the act itself. Now, it is manifest from every authority, that to assemble in a body, armed and arrayed, for some treasonable purpose, is an act of levying war; this was the case at Couche's Fort; and the prisoner's active attendance there is proved by a number of witnesses. It is not required that every witness should have seen him at the same spot, at the same moment, and in the same act; but if they see him at the place and time of rendezvous, exhibiting the same species of traiterous conduct, the law is satisfied. The conspiracy to levy war being effected, all the conspirators are guilty, though, they did not all attend at Gen. Neville's house.... Besides, the meeting at Bradock's field is a distinct and substantive act of treason: and the prisoner is proved by four witnesses to have been there. The design of the meeting, was, avowedly, to oppose the execution of the excise law, to over-awe the government, to involve others in the guilt of the insurrection, to prevent the punishment of the delinquents, to banish unpopular individuals from the town, and to attack the garrison of Pittsburgh. The hasty declarations of the quo animo, proceeding from the prisoner himself, ought not to have much weight, were they not so strongly corroborated by other testimony.

PATERSON, Circuit Justice (charging jury). The first question to be considered is, what was the general object of the insurrection? If its object was to suppress the excise offices, and to prevent the execution of an act of congress, by force and intimidation, the offence, in legal estimation, is high treason; it is an usurpation of the authority of government; it is high treason by levying of war. Taking the testimony in a rational and connected point of view, this was the object: It was of a general nature, and of national concern.

Let us attend, for a moment, to the evidence. With what view was the attack made on General Neville's house? Was it to gratify a spirit of revenge against him as a private citizen, as an individual? No: as a private citizen he had been highly respected and beloved; it was only by becoming a public officer that he became obnoxious: and it was on account of his holding the excise office alone, that his house had been assailed, and his person endangered. On the

first day of attack, the insurgents were repulsed; but they rallied, returned with greater force, and fatally succeeded in the second attempt. They were arrayed in a military manner; they affected the military forms of negotiation by a flag; they pretended no personal hostility to General Neville; but they insisted on the surrender of his commission. Can there be a doubt, then, that the object of the insurrection was of a general and public nature?

The second question to be considered, is — how far was the prisoner traiterously connected with the insurgents? It is proved by four witnesses, that he was at Couche's Fort, at a great distance from his own home, and that he was armed.... Of the overt act of treason, there must, undoubtedly, be proof by two witnesses: and it is equally clear, that the intention and the act, the will and the deed, must concur; for, a bare conspiracy is not treason.

## ☆ 64b  *United States v. Vigol*

28 F. Cas. 376 (C.C.D. Pa. 1795) (No. 16,621).

Indictment for high treason, in levying war against the United States. The prisoner was one of the most active of the insurgents in the western counties of Pennsylvania, and had accompanied the armed party, who attacked the house of the excise officer (Reigan) in Westmoreland, with guns, drum, &c., insisted upon his surrendering his official papers, and extorted an oath from him, that he would never act again in the execution of the excise law. The same party then proceeded to the house of Wells, the excise officer in Fayette county, swearing that the excise law should never be carried into effect, and that they would destroy Wells and his house. On their arrival, Wells had fled and concealed himself; whereupon they ransacked the house: burned it, with all its contents, including the public books and papers; and afterwards discovering Wells, seized, imprisoned, and compelled him to swear, that he would no longer act as excise officer. Witnesses were, likewise, examined to establish that the general combination and scope of the insurrection, were to prevent the execution of the excise law by force; and in the course of the evidence, the duress of the marshal of the district, the assembling at Couche's, the burning of General Neville's house, &c., were prominent features.

As no question of law arose upon the trial, but the case rested entirely on a proof of the overt acts by two witnesses, M. Levy and Lewis, for the defendant, and the attorney of the district agreed, without argument, to submit to the decision of the jury, under the charge of the court, which was delivered to the following effect:

PATERSON, Circuit Justice. The first point for consideration is the evidence which has been given to establish the case stated in the indictment; the second point turns upon the criminal intention of the party; and from these points, — the evidence and intention — the law arises.

With respect to the evidence, the current runs one way. It harmonizes in all its parts. It proves that the prisoner was a member of the party who went to Reigan's house, and, afterwards, to the house of Wells, in arms, marshalled and arrayed; and who, at each place, committed acts of violence and devastation.

With respect to the intention, likewise, there is not, unhappily, the slightest possibility of doubt. To suppress the office of excise in the Fourth survey of this state, and particularly, in the present instance, to compel the resignation of Wells, the excise officer, so as to render null and void, in effect, an act of congress, constituted the apparent — the avowed — object of the insurrection, and of the outrages which the prisoner assisted to commit. Combining these facts and this design, the crime of high treason is consummate in the contemplation of the constitution and law of the United States.

The counsel for the prisoner have endeavored, in the course of a faithful discharge of their duty, to extract from the witnesses some testimony which might justify a defence upon the ground or duress and terror. But in this they have failed, for the whole scene exhibits a disgraceful unanimity; and, with regard to the prisoner, he can only be distinguished for a guilty pre-eminence in zeal and activity. It may not, however, be useless on this occasion to observe that the fear which the law recognizes as an excuse for the perpetration of an offence must proceed from an immediate and actual danger, threatening the very life of the party. The apprehension of any loss of property, by waste or fire, or even an apprehension of a slight or remote injury to the person, furnish no excuse. If, indeed, such circumstances could avail, it would be in the power of every crafty leader of tumults and rebellion to indemnify his followers by uttering previous menaces; an avenue would be forever open for the escape of unsuccessful guilt, and the whole fabric of society must, inevitably, be laid prostrate.

A technical objection has, also, been suggested in favor of the prisoner. It is said that the offence is not proved to have been committed on the day, nor the number of the insurgent party to be so great, as the indictment states. But both these exceptions, even if well founded in fact, are immaterial in point of law. The crime is proved, and laid to have been committed, before the charge was presented; and whether it was committed by one hundred or five hundred cannot alter the guilt of the defendant. If, however, the jury entertain any doubt upon the matter, they may find it specially.

*Verdict, guilty.*

# 65  "a full, free, and entire pardon" (1795)

President Washington had proved the presidential authority granted under the new Constitution in the campaign against the Whiskey rebels. The speedy and successful quashing of the rebellion demonstrated that the new federal government's power extended to all citizens throughout the nation, and that national laws could be enforced. Having survived the test, the new government could afford to be magnanimous. In 1795, the president issued a general amnesty to all those who gave bona fide assurance of allegiance to the United States. He restored tranquility in western Pennsylvania without the shedding of blood or the exacting of vengeance.

☆ 65  Washington's Presidential Proclamation (July 10, 1795)

Reprinted in J. Richardson, ed., *A Compilation of the Messages and Papers of the Presidents* (New York: Bureau of National Literature, 1897), 1:173.

PROCLAMATION

Whereas the commissioners appointed by the President of the United States to confer with the citizens in the western counties of Pennsylvania during the late insurrection which prevailed therein, by their act and agreement bearing date the 2d day of September last, in pusuance of the powers in them vested, did promise and engage that, if assurances of submission to the laws of the United States should be bona fide given by the citizens resident in the fourth survey of Pennsylvania, in the manner and within the time in the said act and agreement specified, a general pardon should be granted on the 10th day of July then next ensuing of all treasons and other indictable offenses against the United States committed within the said survey before the 22d day of August last, excluding therefrom, nevertheless, every person who should refuse or neglect to subscribe such assurance and engagement in manner aforesaid, or who should after such subscription violate the same, or willfully obstruct or attempt to obstruct the execution of the acts for raising a revenue on distilled spirits and stills, or be aiding or abetting therein; and

Whereas I have since thought proper to extend the said pardon to all persons guilty of the said treasons, misprisions of treasons, or otherwise concerned in the late insurrection within the survey aforesaid who have not since been indicted or convicted thereof, or of any other offense against the United States:

Therefore be it known that I, George Washington, President of the said United States, have granted, and by these presents to grant, a full, free, and entire pardon to all persons (excepting as is hereinafter excepted) of all treasons, misprisions of treason, and other indictable offenses against the United States committed within the fourth survey of Pennsylvania before the said 22d day of August last past, excepting and excluding therefrom, nevertheless, every person who refused or neglected to give and subscribe the said assurances in the manner aforesaid (or having subscribed hath violated the same) and now standeth indicted or convicted of any treason, misprision of treason, or other offense against the said United States, hereby remitting and releasing unto all persons, except as before excepted, all penalties incurred, or supposed to be incurred, for or on account of the premises.

## 66 "the doctrine of nonresistance is . . . slavish" (1797)

Despite the dramatic suppression of the Whiskey Rebellion, the revolutionary tradition of the United States continued, finding authority not only in the Declaration of Independence but also in Article X of the New Hampshire Constitution. This article is a clear reminder that at the conclusion of the first decade of the federal government's existence—a decade of political strife—the American people's commitment to the "Social Contract" continued to be reserved and conditional.

The legal efficacy of New Hampshire's permissiveness must be weighed, however, against the federal Constitution's provision in Article VI, Section 2, that laws made "under the authority of the United States, shall be the supreme law of the land; . . . any thing in the Constitution or laws of any state to the contrary notwithstanding." Nevertheless, New Hampshire's "Right of Revolution" might provide the foundation for a defense to charges of treason against the state for resisting the enforcement of some "odious" law.

☆ 66  New Hampshire Constitution, Article X

*          *          *

10th [Right of Revolution]. Government being instituted for the common benefit, protection, and security, of the whole community, and not for the private interest or emolument of any one man, family, or class of men; therefore, whenever the ends of government are perverted, and public liberty manifestly endangered, and all other means of redress are ineffectual, the doctrine of nonresistance against arbitrary power, and oppression, is absurd, slavish, and destructive of the good and happiness of mankind.

*          *          *

## 67 "dangerous to the peace and safety of the United States" (1798)

The French Revolution, a rebellion in Ireland, and political unrest in England caused an influx of large numbers of political activists into the new American nation. The administration of President John Adams was preparing for war with France. In domestic politics, the relations between the Federalist and the Jeffersonian Republicans grew tense. Thus, seven years after the adoption of the First Amendment protection of free speech, press, and assembly, Congress passed a series of laws which seriously punished expression of views critical of the government or its laws. Some argued that the acts were compatible with the First Amendment, since they imposed no prior restraint on what might be expressed.

Collectively known as the Alien and Sedition Acts, these laws "concerning aliens" (June 25), "respecting alien Enemies" (July 6), and "for the punishment of certain crimes against the United States" (July 14) reflected fears of threats to American security. The Alien Acts gave the president unbridled discretion to deport "dangerous" aliens. The Sedition Act prohibited not only the counseling of or the attempt "to procure any insurrection, riot, unlawful assembly" but also the printing and uttering of any "false" and "scandalous" writings with intent to defame the president, congress, or the government.

The sedition law was enforced vigorously and discriminatorily against newspaper editors and officeholders who challenged the policies of Adams's Federalist administration. It expired by its own terms on March 3, 1801.

☆ 67  Alien and Sedition Laws (June 25-July 14, 1798)

☆ 67a  An Act concerning Aliens

1 Stat. 570 (1798).

Section 1. *Be it enacted by the Senate and House of Representatives of the United States of America in Congress assembled,* That it shall be lawful for the President of the United States at any time during the continuance of this act, to *order* all such *aliens* as he shall judge dangerous to the peace and safety of the United States, or shall have reasonable grounds to suspect are concerned in any treasonable or secret machinations against the government thereof, to depart out of the territory of the United States, within such time as shall be expressed in such order, which order shall be served on such alien by delivering him a copy thereof, or leaving the same at his usual abode.... *Provided always, and be it further enacted,* that if any alien so ordered to depart shall prove to the satisfaction of the President

... that no injury or danger to the United States will arise from suffering such alien to reside therein, the President may grant a *license* to such alien to remain within the United States for such time as he shall judge proper, and at such place as he may designate. ...

\*       \*       \*

*Approved, June 25, 1798.*

☆ 67b  An Act respecting Alien Enemies

1 Stat. 577 (1798).

SECTION 1. *Be it enacted by the Senate and House of Representatives of the United States of America in Congress assembled*, That whenever there shall be a declared war between the United States and any foreign nation or government, or any invasion or predatory incursion shall be perpetrated, attempted, or threatened against the territory of the United States, by any foreign nation or government, ... all natives, citizens, denizens, or subjects of the hostile nation or government, being males of the age of fourteen years and upwards, who shall be within the United States, and not actually naturalized, shall be liable to be apprehended, restrained, secured and removed, as alien enemies. And the President of the United States shall be, and he is hereby authorized, in any event, as aforesaid, by his proclamation thereof, or other public act, to direct the conduct to be observed, on the part of the United States, towards the aliens who shall become liable, as aforesaid; the manner and degree of the restraint to which they shall be subject, and in what cases, and upon what security their residence shall be permitted, and to provide for the removal of those, who, not being permitted to reside within the United States, shall refuse or neglect to depart therefrom; and to establish any other regulations which shall be found necessary in the premises and for the public safety: Provided, that aliens resident within the United States, who shall become liable as enemies, in the manner aforesaid, and who shall not be chargeable with actual hostility, or other crime against the public safety, shall be allowed, for the recovery, disposal, and removal or their goods and effects, and for their departure, the full time which is, or shall be stipulated by any treaty, ... and where no such treaty shall have existed, the President of the United States may ascertain and declare such reasonable time as may be consistent with the public safety, and according to the dictates of humanity and national hospitality. ... And the President may also require of such alien to enter into a bond to the United States, in such penal sum as he may direct, with one or more sufficient sureties to the satisfaction of the person authorized by the President to take the same, conditioned for the good behavior of such alien during his residence in the United States,

and not violating his license, which license the President may revoke, whenever he shall think proper.

\*       \*       \*

*Approved, July 6, 1798.*

☆ 67c  An Act for the Punishment of Certain Crimes against the United States

1 Stat. 596 (1798).

SECTION 1. *Be it enacted by the Senate and House of Representatives of the United States of America, in Congress assembled*, That if any persons shall unlawfully combine or conspire together, with intent to oppose any measure or measures of the government of the United States, which are or shall be directed by proper authority, or to impede the operation of any law of the United States, or to intimidate or prevent any person holding a place or office in or under the government of the United States, from undertaking, performing or executing his trust or duty; and if any person or persons, with intent as aforesaid, shall counsel, advise or attempt to procure any insurrection, riot, unlawful assembly, or combination, whether such conspiracy, threatening, counsel, advice, or attempt shall have the proposed effect or not, he or they shall be deemed guilty of a high misdemeanor, and on conviction, before any court of the United States having jurisdiction thereof, shall be punished by a fine not exceeding five thousand dollars, and by imprisonment during a term not less than six months nor exceeding five years; and further, at the discretion of the court may be holden to find sureties for his good behaviour in such sum, and for such time, as the said court may direct.

SEC. 2. *And be it further enacted*, That if any person shall write, print, utter or publish, or shall cause or procure to be written, printed, uttered or published, or shall knowingly and willingly assist or aid in writing, printing, uttering or publishing any false, scandalous and malicious writing or writings against the government of the United States, or either house of the Congress of the United States, or the President of the United States, with intent to defame the said government, or either house of the said Congress, or the said President, or to bring them, or either of them, into contempt or disrepute; or to excite against them, or either or any of them, the hatred of the good people of the United States, or to stir up sedition within the United States, or to excite any unlawful combinations therein, for opposing or resisting any law of the United States, or any act of the President of the United States, done in pursuance of any such law, or of the powers in him vested by the constitution of the United States, or to resist, oppose, or defeat any such law or act, or to aid, encourage or abet any hostile designs of any foreign nation against the United States, their people or government, then such person, being thereof convicted before any court of the United States having jurisdiction thereof, shall be punished by a fine not exceeding two thousand dollars, and by imprisonment not exceeding two years.

SEC. 3. *And be it further enacted and declared,* That if any person shall be prosecuted under this act, for the writing or publishing any libel aforesaid, it shall be lawful for the defendant, upon the trial of the cause, to give in evidence in his defence, the truth of the matter contained in the publication charged as a libel. And the jury who shall try the cause, shall have a right to determine the law and the fact, under the direction of the court, as in other cases.

SEC. 4. *And be it further enacted,* That this act shall continue and be in force until the third day of March, one thousand eight hundred and one, and no longer: *Provided,* that the expiration of the act shall not prevent or defeat a prosecution and punishment of any offence against the law, during the time it shall be in force.

*Approved, July 14, 1798.*

# 68 "blush and weep over our sedition law" (1798)

Jefferson's early wariness of federal power was exemplified in his letter to John Taylor, a member of the Virginia House of Delegates and a leading political philosopher. It was Taylor, the foremost apologist for Jeffersonian democracy, who introduced the doctrine of state's rights (manifested in the Kentucky and Virginia Resolutions) into the Virginia legislature. At this point in the history of the new republic, the Constitution seemed ineffective in constraining its exercise of powers. The worst fears of the Jeffersonian Republicans were becoming reality.

☆ 68 Letter from Thomas Jefferson to John Taylor

Reprinted in W. Parker, ed., *Letters and Addresses of Thomas Jefferson* (New York: United Book Publishing, 1905), 126.

Monticello, November 26, 1798

I wish it were possible to obtain a single amendment to our Constitution. I would be willing to depend on that alone for the reduction of the administration of our government to the genuine principles of its Constitution; I mean an additional article, taking from the federal government the power of borrowing.

For the present, I should be for resolving the alien and sedition laws to be against the Constitution and merely void, and for addressing the other States to obtain similar declarations. . . .

I inclose you a column, cut out of a London paper, to show you that the English, though charmed with our making their enemies our enemies, yet blush and weep over our sedition law.

\*     \*     \*

# 69 "ridiculous pomp, foolish adulation, and selfish avarice" (1798)

The first case brought under the Sedition Act was against Matthew Lyon, a Republican congressman from Vermont. He was charged with publishing two letters critical of the Adams administration's domestic and foreign policies. Lyon's newspaper, *The Scourge of Aristocracy,* labeled the president a bully.

At Lyon's trial, the presiding judge's charge to the jury reflected the fear that the jury, which lacked sympathy with the law, might acquit the defendant. The judge's sentence plainly favored enhancement of the punishment because of the political nature of the controversy and the defendant. Lyon was fined one thousand dollars and jailed for four months. The prosecution and the resultant public outcry subsequently helped to reelect Lyon to Congress by an overwhelming majority. When Jefferson assumed the presidency, he pardoned Lyon and all others convicted under the act.

☆ 69 *Lyon's Case*

15 F. Cas. 1183 (C.C.D. Vt. 1798) (No. 8,646).

[This was an indictment, under the act of July 14, 1798, against Matthew Lyon, for the publication of a seditious libel.]

The indictment which was found on October 5, 1798, contained three counts, the first of which, after averring the intent to be "to stir up sedition, and to bring the president and government of the United States into contempt," laid the following libelous matter:

"As to the executive, when I shall see the efforts of that power bent on the promotion of the comfort, the happiness, and accommodation of the people, that executive shall have my zealous and uniform support: but whenever I shall, on the part of the executive, see every consideration of the public welfare swallowed up in a continual grasp for power, in an unbounded thirst for ridiculous pomp, foolish adulation, and selfish avarice; when I shall behold men of real merit daily turned out of office, for no other cause but independency of sentiment; when I shall see men of firmness, merit, years, abilities, and experience, discarded in their applications for office, for fear they possess that independence, and men of meanness preferred for the ease with which they take up and advocate opinions, the consequence of which they know but little of—when I shall see the sacred name of religion employed as a state engine to make mankind hate and persecute one another, I shall not be their humble advocate."

The second count consisted of having maliciously, &c., and with intent, &c., published a letter, said to be a letter from a diplomatic character in France, containing two paragraphs in the words following:

"The misunderstanding between the two governments (France and the United States), has become extremely alarming; confidence is completely destroyed, mistrusts, jealousy, and a disposition to a wrong attribution of motives, are so apparent, as to require the utmost caution in every word and action that are to come from your executive. I mean, if your object is to avoid hostilities. Had this truth been understood with you before the recall of Monroe, before the coming and second coming of Pinckney; had it guided the pens that wrote the bullying speech of your president, and stupid answer of your senate, at the opening of congress in November last, I should probably had [*sic*] no occasion to address you this letter.—But when we found him borrowing the language of Edmund Burke, and telling the world that although he should succeed in treating with the French, there was no dependence to be placed on any of their engagements, that their religion and morality were at an end, that they would turn pirates and plunderers, and it would be necessary to be perpetually armed against them, though you were at peace: we wondered that the answer of both houses had not been an order to send him to a mad house. Instead of this the senate have echoed the speech with more servility than ever George III experienced from either house of parliament."

The third count was for assisting, counseling, aiding, and abetting the publication of the same.

*          *          *

PATERSON, Circuit Justice (charging jury). "You have nothing whatever to do with the constitutionality or unconstitutionality of the sedition law. Congress has said that the author and publisher of seditious libels is to be punished; and until this law is declared null and void by a tribunal competent for the purpose, its validity cannot be disputed. Great would be the abuses were the constitutionality of every statute to be submitted to a jury, in each case where the statute is to be applied. The only question you are to determine is, that which the record submits to you. Did Mr. Lyon publish the writing given in the indictment? Did he do so seditiously? On the first point, the evidence is undisputed, and in fact, he himself concedes the fact of publication as to a large portion of libellous matter. As to the second point, you will have to consider whether language such as

that here complained of could have been uttered with any other intent than that of making odious or contemptible the president and government, and bringing them both into disrepute. If you find such is the case, the offence is made out, and you must render a verdict of guilty. Nor should the political rank of the defendant, his past services, or the dependent condition of his family, deter you from this duty. Such considerations are for the court alone in adjusting the penalty they will bestow. The fact of guilt is for you, for the court, the grade of punishment. As to yourselves, one point, in addition, in exercising the functions allotted to you, you must keep in mind; and that is, that in order to render a verdict of guilty, you must be satisfied beyond all reasonable substantial doubt that the hypothesis of innocence is unsustainable. Keeping these instructions in your mind, you will proceed to deliberate on your verdict."

At about eight o'clock in the evening of the same day, after about an hour's absence, the jury returned with a verdict of guilty.

The defendant being called up for sentence, a postponement was obtained till the next morning, when, after upon a representation of his circumstances, it appearing that he was almost insolvent, Judge PATERSON addressed him as follows: "Matthew Lyon, as member of the federal legislature, you must be well acquainted with the mischiefs which flow from an unlicensed abuse of government, and of the motives which led to the passage of the act under which this indictment is framed. No one, also, can be better acquainted than yourself with the existence and nature of the act. Your position, so far from making the case one which might slip with a minimal fine through the hands of the court, would make impunity conspicuous should such a fine alone be imposed. What, however, has tended to mitigate the sentence which would otherwise have been imposed, is, what I am sorry to hear of, the reduced condition of your estate. The judgment of the court is, that you stand imprisoned four months, pay the costs of prosecution, and a fine of one thousand dollars, and stand committed until this sentence be complied with."

*          *          *

## 70 "no rampart now remains against the passions and the power of a majority of Congress" (1798)

The Alien and Sedition Acts, noted historian Nathaniel Weyl, were weapons of internal political warfare designed to disintegrate the opposition party. Although the Supreme Court never addressed the constitutionality of the Alien and Sedition Acts, three Supreme Court justices sitting on circuit upheld the Sedition Act as merely codifying the existing common law of seditious libel. Supporters also argued that authority to pass the law derived from Article I, Section 8 (18) of the Constitution, the "necessary and proper" clause, and claimed that it did not violate the First Amendment's proscription, since it imposed no prior restraint upon speech.

Twenty years after the Revolution, the problems of sovereignty which caused the near collapse of the government under the Articles of Confederation remained unresolved. The case for states' rights, or, more properly, the primacy of state sovereignty and a limited national government, was strongly stated in the resolution drafted by Jefferson and passed by the Kentucky Legislature. James Madison drafted a similar resolution for the state of Virginia. Primarily, these resolutions declared that federal legislation was void whenever Congress assumed "undelegated powers"; the First Amendment was only secondarily relied upon as a limit on congressional authority to pass the Sedition Act.

The opposition by the states proved unsuccessful. Not until June 23, 1800, after the inauguration of Thomas Jefferson and the Republican-dominated Congress, were these laws allowed to expire. Even some Federalists joined the opposition. Speaking out against the Sedition Law, Hamilton warned, "Let us not establish a tyranny," and John Marshall broke party discipline to cast the deciding vote against the law's extension.

Beyond the assertion of the states' rights theory of the Constitution that provided the legal justification for secession, the resolution identified two features of the Alien Act which made it particularly adaptable for political uses: the resting of discretionary deportation power in the executive branch and the elimination of procedural safeguards. These two aspects of the Alien Act reappeared in other assertions of political power through the use of criminal and quasi-criminal law. Particularly noteworthy was the expressed fear that the restraints of the Alien and Sedition Acts would not long be confined only to "the friendless alien . . . selected as the safest subject of a first experiment."

## ☆ 70 Resolution of the Kentucky Legislature

J. Madison and T. Jefferson, *Resolutions of Virginia and Kentucky* (Richmond: Shepherd, 1835), 64-69.

[T]wice read and agreed to by the House.

Resolved, That the several States composing the United States of America, are not united on the principle of unlimited submission to their General Government; but that by compact under the style and title of a Constitution for the United States, and of amendments thereto, they constituted a General Government for special purposes, delegated to that Government certain definite powers, reserving each State to itself, the residuary mass of right to their own self-Government; and that whensoever the General Government assumes undelegated powers, its acts are unauthoritative, void, and of no force: That to this compact each State acceded as a State, and is an integral party, its Co-States forming as to itself, the other party: That the Government created by this compact was not made the exclusive or final judge of the extent of the powers delegated to itself; since that would have made its discretion, and not the Constitution, the measure of its powers; but that as in all other cases of compact among parties having no common judge, each party has an equal right to judge for itself, as well of infractions, as of the mode and measure of redress.

2. Resolved, That the Constitution of the United States having delegated to Congress a power to punish treason, counterfeiting the securities and current coin of the United States, piracies and felonies committed on the high seas, and offences against the laws of nations, and no other crimes whatever . . . [the Alien and Sedition Acts are] altogether void and of no force, and that the power to create, define, and punish such other crimes is reserved, and of right, appertains solely and exclusively to the respective States, each within its own territory.

3. Resolved, That it is true as a general principle, and is also expressly declared by one of the amendments to the Constitution, that "the powers not delegated to the United States by the Constitution, nor prohibited by it to the States, are reserved to the States respectively, or to the people;" and that no power over the freedom of religion, freedom of speech, or freedom of the press, being delegated to the United States by the Constitution, nor prohibited by it to the States, all lawful powers respecting the same did of right remain, and were reserved to the States, or to the people. . . .

And that in addition to this general principle and express declaration, another and more special provision has been made by one of the amendments to the Constitution, which expressly declares, that "Congress shall make no law respecting an establishment of religion, or prohibiting the free exercise thereof, or abridging the freedom of speech, or of the press." . . . That therefore the act of the Congress of the United States, passed on the 14th day of July, 1798, entitled "an act, in addition to the act, for the punishment of certain crimes against the United States," which does abridge the freedom of the press, is not law, but is altogether void and of no effect.

4. Resolved, That alien friends are under the jurisdiction and protection of the laws of the State wherein they are; that no power over them has been delegated to the United States, nor prohibited to the individual States distinct from their power over citizens; . . . [accordingly] the act of the Congress of the United States, passed on the 22nd day of June, 1798, entitled "an act concerning aliens," which assumes

power over alien friends not delegated by the Constitution, is not law, but is altogether void and of no force.

*         *         *

6. Resolved, That the imprisonment of a person under the protection of the laws of the Commonwealth on his failure to obey the simple order of the President, to depart out of the United States, as is undertaken by the said act, entitled "an act concerning aliens," is contrary to the Constitution, one amendment to which has provided, that "no person shall be deprived of liberty without due process of law," and that another having provided, "that in all criminal prosecutions, the accused shall enjoy the right to a public trial by an impartial jury, to be informed of the nature and cause of the accusation, to be confronted with the witnesses against him, to have compulsory process for obtaining witnesses in his favour, and to have the assistance of counsel for his defence," the same act undertaking to authorise the President to remove a person out of the United States who is under the protection of the law, on his own suspicion, without accusation, without jury, without public trial, without confrontation of the witnesses against him; without having witnesses in his favour, without defence, without counsel, is contrary to these provisions also of the Constitution, is therefore not law, but utterly void and of no force.

That transferring the power of judging any person who is under the protection of the laws, from the Courts to the President of the United States, as is undertaken by the same act, concerning aliens, is against the article of the Constitution, which provides, that "the judicial power of the United States, shall be vested in Courts, the Judges of which shall hold their offices during good behaviour," and that the said act is void. . . .

7. Resolved, That the construction applied by the General Government, (as is evinced by sundry of their proceedings,) to those parts of the Constitution of the United States which delegates to Congress a power . . . to make all laws which shall be necessary and proper for carrying into execution the powers vested by the Constitution in the Government of the United States, or any department thereof, goes to the destruction of all the limits prescribed to their power by the Constitution—That words meant by that instrument to be subsidiary only to the execution of the limited powers, ought not to be so construed as themselves to give unlimited powers, nor a part so to be taken, as to destroy the whole residue of the instrument. . . .

*         *         *

Resolved, lastly, . . . And that therefore, this Commonwealth is determined, as it doubts not its Co-States are, tamely to submit to undelegated and consequently unlimited powers in no man or body of men on earth: that if the acts before specified should stand, these conclusions would flow from them; that the General Government may place any act they think proper on the list of crimes, and punish it themselves, whether enumerated or not enumerated by the Constitution as cognizable by them; that they may transfer its cognizance to the President or any other person, who may himself be the accuser, counsel, judge and jury, whose suspicions may be the evidence, his order the sentence, his officer, the executioner, and his breast the sole record of the transaction; that . . . the barrier of the Constitution thus swept away from us all, no rampart now remains against the passions and the power of a majority of Congress, to protect from a like exportation or other more grievous punishment the minority of the same body, the Legislatures, Judges, Governors and Counsellors of the States, nor their other peaceable inhabitants who may venture to re-claim the Constitutional rights and liberties of the States and people, or who for other causes, good or bad, may be obnoxious to the views, or marked by the suspicions of the President, or be thought dangerous to his or their elections or other interests public or personal: that the friendless alien has indeed been selected as the safest subject of a first experiment; but the citizen will soon follow, or rather has already followed; for, already has a Sedition Act marked him as its prey: that these successive acts of the same character, unless arrested on the threshold, may tend to drive these States into revolution and blood; . . . free government is founded in jealousy and not in confidence; it is jealousy and not confidence which prescribes limited Constitutions to bind down those whom we are obliged to trust with power. . . . In questions of power, then let no more be heard of confidence in man, but bind him down from mischief, by the chains of the Constitution. That this Commonwealth does therefore call on its Co-States for an expression of their sentiments on the acts concerning aliens, and for the punishment of certain crimes herein-before specified, plainly declaring whether these acts are or are not authorized by the Federal Compact?

*         *         *

EDMUND BULLOCK, S.H.R.
JOHN CAMPBELL, S.S.P.T.

*Passed the House of Representatives, November 10th, 1798. Attest,*

THOMAS TODD, C.H.R.

*In Senate, November 13th, 1798, unanimously concurred in. Attest,*

B. THRUSTON, Clk. Sen.

*Approved, November 16th, 1798.*

JAMES GARRARD, G.K.

*By the Governor.*

HARRY TOULMIN, Secretary of State

## 71 Appeals to the Federal Judiciary — No Suits against One of the States (1798)

Article III, Section 2 of the Constitution provides that "The Judicial Power of the United States shall extend to . . . Controversies . . . between a State and Citizens of another State. . . ." Under the authority of this provision, the United States Supreme Court accepted jurisdiction in *Chisholm v. Georgia*, 2 U.S. (2 Dall.) 419 (1793). The decision prompted an angry reaction in the states, which saw such authority as another step toward the assertion of federal control over the affairs of the sovereign states. The response was swift. Congress met following the decision. It drafted, and the states quickly ratified, the Eleventh Amendment. Although the amendment by its terms speaks only of suits by citizens of other states and foreign subjects, the Supreme Court has construed the amendment to bar suits by citizens against their own states. Citizen applications to the federal judiciary to seek relief against abusive state laws and practices were thus constitutionally forbidden until after adoption of the Fourteenth Amendment. Meanwhile, conflicts between citizens and their states were left to be resolved on the local level.

## ☆71 United States Constitution, Amendment XI

The Judicial power of the United States shall not be construed to extend to any suit in law or equity, commenced or prosecuted against one of the United States by Citizens of another State, or by Citizens or Subjects of any Foreign State.

## 72 John Fries's Rebellion (1799-1800)

The first federal excise tax imposed on spirits (1791) led to the Whiskey Rebellion. A different tax imposed within the same decade, to satisfy Hamilton's desire to strengthen the federal government and to finance an expected war with France, gave rise to the similar rebellion of John Fries in 1799. A venue cryer with quickness of wit, Fries became a leader in the opposition. He represented the German-speaking populations of northern and southeastern Pennsylvania by opposing the collection of the new tax "based on the evaluation of lands and dwelling houses and the enumeration of slaves within the United States." When disorderly resistance to the tax led to the mobbing and threatening of the tax collectors, the federal authorities made several arrests. The rebels held local meetings and decided to rescue the prisoners.

Their elected leader, John Fries, proceeded to Bethlehem at the head of an ill-equipped column of about 140 men. Under the threat of arms, the marshall released the prisoners and the irregulars dispersed. But reports of the events reached President John Adams, and although all resistance to the law had ceased, Adams convened his cabinet and issued a proclamation accusing the insurgents of treason and ordering them to lay down their arms. John Fries was arrested, and federal troops proceeded to harass the local inhabitants suspected of opposition to the government. With peace restored, John Adams issued a general pardon.

## ☆72 Proclamations of President John Adams

### ☆72a By the President of the United States of America: Proclamation (March 12, 1799)

Reprinted in C. F. Adams, *The Works of John Adams* (New York: AMS Press, 1971), 9:174-75.

WHEREAS, combinations, to defeat the execution of the laws for the valuation of lands and dwelling houses within the United States, have existed within the counties of Northampton, Montgomery and Bucks, in the State of Pennsylvania, have proceeded in a manner subversive of the just authority of the government, by misrepresentations to render the laws odious, by deterring the officers of the United States to forbear the execution of their functions, and by openly threatening their lives. And whereas the endeavors of the well-effected citizens as well as of the executive officers to conciliate compliance with these laws, have failed of success, and certain persons in the county of Northampton, aforesaid, have been hardy enough to perpetrate certain acts, which, I am advised, amount to treason, being overt acts of levying war against the United States, the said persons exceeding one hundred in number, and armed and arrayed in warlike manner, having, on the seventh day of the present month of March, proceeded to the house of Abraham Levering, in the town of Bethlehem, and there compelled William Nichols, Marshal of the United States, for the District of Pennsylvania, to desist from the execution of certain legal processes in his hands to be executed, and having compelled him to discharge and set at liberty, certain persons whom he had arrested by virtue of a criminal process, duly issued for offenses against the United States, and having impeded and prevented the commissioners and assessor, in conformity with the laws aforesaid, by threats of personal injury, from executing the said laws, avowing, as the motive of these illegal and treasonable proceedings, an intention to prevent, by force of arms, the execution of the said laws, and to withstand, by open violence, the lawful authority of the United States. And, whereas, by the Constitution and laws of the United States, I am authorized, whenever the laws of the United States shall be opposed, or the execution thereof obstructed in any State, by combinations too powerful to be suppressed by the ordinary course of judicial proceedings, or by powers, vested in the Marshal, to call forth military force to suppress such combinations, and to cause the laws to be duly executed, and I have accordingly determined so to do, under the solemn conviction that the essential interest of the United States demand it.

Therefore, I, John Adams, President of the United States, do hereby command all persons, being insurgents as aforesaid, and all others whom it may concern, on or before Monday next being the eighteenth day of the present month, to disperse and retire peaceably to their respective abodes: and I do, moreover, warn all persons whomsoever, against aiding, abetting or comforting the perpetrators of the aforesaid treasonable acts, and I do require all officers and others, good and faithful citizens, according to their respective duties and laws of the land, to exert their utmost endeavors to prevent and suppress such dangerous and unlawful proceedings.

\*　　　\*　　　\*

☆72b  Proclamation by John Adams, President of the United States of America (May 21, 1800)

Reprinted in C. F. Adams, *The Works of John Adams* (New York: AMS Press, 1971), 9:178-79.

WHEREAS The late wicked and treasonable insurrection against the just authorities of the United States . . . in the State of Pennsylvania, in the year 1799, having been speedily suppressed without any of the calamities usually attending rebellion, whereupon peace, order, and submission to the laws of the United States were restored in the aforesaid counties, and the ignorant, misguided and misinformed in the counties have returned to a proper sense of their duty; whereby it is become unnecessary for the public good that any future prosecutions should be commenced or carried on against any person or persons, by reason of their being concerned in the said insurrection; wherefore be it known that I, John Adams, President of the United States of America, have granted, and by these presents do grant, a full free and absolute pardon, to all and every person or persons concerned in the said insurrection, excepting as hereinafter excepted, of all felonies, misdemeanors and other crimes by them respectively done or committed against the United States; in either of the said counties, before the 12th day of March, in the year 1799; excepting and excluding therefrom any person who now standeth indicted or convicted of any treason, misprision of treason, or other offence against the United States. . . .

# 73 The Greatest Crime That Any Man Can Commit (1800)

John Fries, leader of the antitax rebellion, was indicted and tried for treason. Alexander Dallas, a leading Jeffersonian who later would become Madison's secretary of the treasury, defended Fries. His first trial ended in a mistrial, but at the second trial before Justice Samuel Chase and Judge Richard Peters, Fries was convicted and sentenced to death. John Fries's lawyers withdrew from the trial on the grounds that Judge Chase's injudicious conduct made it impossible for them to defend their client. On advice of counsel, Fries rejected substitute counsel and defended himself. Justice Chase's final comment before imposing sentence represents the classic statement on the nonlegitimacy of disobedience to oppressive laws in the United States.

☆73  *Case of Fries*

9 F. Cas. 924 (C.C.D. Pa. 1800) (No. 5,127).

CHASE, Circuit Justice (charging jury):—"Gentlemen of the Jury: John Fries, the prisoner at the bar, stands indicted for the crime of treason, of levying war against the United States, contrary to the constitution. . . . It is the opinion of the court, that any insurrection or rising of any body of the people, within the United States, to attain or effect by force or violence any object of a great public nature, or of public and general (or national) concern, is a levying of war against the United States, within the contemplation and construction of the constitution. On this general position the court are of opinion, that any such insurrection or rising to resist, or to prevent by force or violence, the execution of any statute of the United States, . . . under any pretence, as that the statute was unjust, burthensome, oppressive, or unconstitutional, is a levying war against the United States, within the contemplation and construction of the constitution. The reason for this opinion is, that an insurrection to resist or prevent, by force, the execution of any statute of the United States, has a direct tendency to dissolve all the bands of society, to destroy all order and all laws, and also all security for the lives, liberties and property of the citizens of the United States. . . . The legal guilt of levying war may be incurred without the use of military weapons or military array. The court are of opinion that the assembling bodies of men, armed and arrayed in a warlike manner, for purposes only of a private nature, is not treason, although the judges, or other peace officers, should be insulted or resisted. . . .

"The true criterion to determine whether acts committed are treason, or a less offence (as a riot), is the quo animo, or the intention, with which the people did assemble. When the intention is universal or general, as to effect some object of a general public nature, it will be treason, and cannot be considered construed, or reduced to a riot. . . .

\*          \*          \*

"The court are of opinion, that if a body of people conspire and meditate an insurrection to resist or oppose the execution of any statute of the United States by force, that they are only guilty of a high misdemeanour; but if they proceed to carry such intention into execution by force, that they are guilty of the treason of levying war, and the quantum of the force employed neither lessens nor increases the crime—whether by one hundred or one thousand persons, is wholly immaterial. The court are of opinion, that a combination or conspiracy to levy war against the United States is not treason, unless combined with an attempt to carry such combination or conspiracy into execution; some actual force or violence must be used, in pursuance of such design to levy war; but that it is altogether immaterial whether the force used is sufficient to effectuate the object—any force connected with the intention will constitute the crime of levying war. . . ."

\*          \*          \*

The jury retired for the space of two hours, and brought in their verdict, "Guilty."

After the verdict was given, Judge CHASE, with great feeling and sensibility, addressed the prisoner, observing that, as he had no counsel on the trial, if he, or any person for him, could point out any flaw in the indictment, or legal ground for arrest of judgment, ample time would be allowed for that purpose.

\*          \*          \*

The prisoner being set at the bar, Judge CHASE, after observing to the other defendants that what he had to say to Fries would apply generally to them, proceeded:—

"John Fries, you have been already informed, that you stood convicted of the treason, charged upon you by the indictment on which you have been arraigned, of levying war against the United States. You have had a legal, fair, and impartial trial, with every indulgence that the law would permit. Of the whole panel, you peremptorily challenged thirty-four, and with truth I may say, that the jury who tried you were of your own selection and choice. Not one of them before had ever formed and delivered any opinion respecting your guilt or innocence. The verdict of the jury against you was founded on the testimony of many creditable and unexceptionable witnesses. It was apparent from the conduct of the jury, when they delivered their verdict, that if innocent, they would have acquitted you with pleasure; and that they pronounced their verdict against you with great concern and reluctance, from a sense of duty to their country, and a full conviction of your

guilt. The crime of which you have been found guilty is treason; a crime considered, in the most civilized and the most free countries in the world, as the greatest that any man can commit. It is a crime of so deep a dye, and attended with such a train of fatal consequences, that it can receive no aggravation; yet the duty of my station requires that I should explain to you the nature of the crime of which you are convicted; to show the necessity of that justice which is this day to be administered, and to awaken your mind to proper reflections and a due sense of your own condition, which, I imagine, you must have reflected upon during your long confinement. You are a native of this country—you live under a constitution (or form of government) framed by the people themselves; and under laws made by your representatives, faithfully executed by independent and impartial judges. Your government secures to every member of the community equal liberty and equal rights; by which equality of liberty and rights, I mean, that every person, without any regard to wealth, rank, or station, may enjoy an equal share of civil liberty, and equal protection of law, and an equal security for his person and property. You enjoyed, in common with your fellow-citizens, all those rights. If experience should prove that the constitution is defective, it provides a mode to change or amend it, without any danger to public order, or any injury to social rights. If congress, from inattention, error in judgment, or want of information, should pass any law in violation of the constitution, or burdensome or oppressive to the people, a peaceable, safe and ample remedy is provided by the constitution. The people themselves have established the mode by which such grievances are to be redressed; and no other mode can be adopted without a violation of the constitution and of the laws. If congress should pass a law contrary to the constitution, such law would be void, and the courts of the United States possess complete authority, and are the only tribunal to decide, whether any law is contrary to the constitution. If congress should pass burdensome or oppressive laws, the remedy is with their constituents, from whom they derive their existence and authority. If any law is made repugnant to the voice of a majority of their constituents, it is in their power to make choice of persons to repeal it; but until it is repealed, it is the duty of every citizen to submit to it, and to give up his private sentiments to the public will. If a law which is burdensome, or even oppressive in its nature or execution, is to be opposed by force; and obedience cannot be compelled, there must soon be an end to all government in this country. . . .

"The insurrection in 1794, in the four western counties of this state (particularly in Washington), to oppose the execution of the laws of the United

States, which laid duties on stills, and spirits distilled, within the United States, is still fresh in memory: it originated from prejudices and misrepresentations industriously disseminated and diffused against those laws. Either persons disaffected to our government, or wishing to aggrandize themselves, deceived and misled the ignorant and uninformed class of the people. The opposition commenced in meetings of the people, with threats against the officers, which ripened into acts of outrage against them, and were extended to private citizens. Committees were formed to systematize and inflame the spirit of opposition. Violence succeeded to violence, and the collector of Fayette county was compelled to surrender his commission and official books; the dwelling house of the inspector (in the vicinity of Pittsburgh) was attacked and burnt; and the marshal was seized and obtained his liberty on a promise to serve no other process on the west side of the Alleghany mountains. To compel submission to the laws, the government were obliged to march an army against the insurgents, and the expense was above one million one hundred thousand dollars. Of the whole number of insurgents (many hundreds) only a few were brought to trial; and of them only two were sentenced to die (Vigol and Mitchell), and they were pardoned by the late president. Although the insurgents made no resistance to the army sent against them, yet not a few of our troops lost their lives, in consequence of their great fatigue, and exposure to the severity of the season. This great and remarkable clemency of the government had no effect upon you, and the deluded people in your neighbourhood. The rise, progress, and termination of the late insurrection bear a strong and striking analogy to the former; and it may be remembered that it has cost the United States 80,000 dollars. It cannot escape observation, that the ignorant and uninformed are taught to complain of taxes, which are necessary for the support of government, and yet they permit themselves to be seduced into insurrections which have so enormously increased the public burthens, of which their contributions can scarcely be calculated. When citizens combine and assemble with intent to prevent by threats, intimidation and violence, the execution of the laws, and they actually carry such traitorous designs into execution, they reduce the government to the alternative of prostrating the laws before the insurgents, or of taking necessary measures to compel submission. No government can hesitate. The expense, and all the consequences, therefore, are not imputable to the government, but to the insurgents. The mildness and lenity of our government are as striking on the late as on the former insurrection. Of nearly one hundred and thirty persons who might have been put on their trial for treason, only five have been prosecuted and tried for that crime.

"In the late insurrection, you, John Fries, bore a conspicuous and leading part. If you had reflected, you would have seen that your attempt was as weak as it was wicked. It was the height of folly in you to suppose that the great body of our citizens, blessed in enjoyment of a free republican government of their own choice, and of all rights civil and religious; secure in their persons and property; and conscious that the laws are the only security for their preservation from violence, would not rise up as one man to oppose and crush so ill-founded, so unprovoked an attempt to disturb the public peace and tranquillity. If you could see in a proper light your own folly and wickedness, you ought now to bless God that your insurrection was so happily and speedily quelled by the vigilance and energy of our government, aided by the patriotism and activity of your fellow-citizens, who left their homes and business and embodied themselves in the support of its laws. The annual, necessary expenditures for the support of any extensive government like ours must be great; and the sum required can only be obtained by taxes, or loans. In all countries the levying taxes is unpopular, and a subject of complaint. It appears to me that there was not the least pretence of complaint against, much less of opposition and violence to, the law for levying taxes on dwelling-houses; and it becomes you to reflect that the time you chose to rise up in arms to oppose the laws of your country, was when it stood in a very critical situation with regard to France, and on the eve of a rupture with that country. . . . In your serious hours of reflection, you ought to consider the consequences that would have flowed from the insurrection, which you incited, encouraged, and promoted. . . . Violence, oppression and rapine, destruction, waste, and murder, always attend the progress of insurrection and rebellion; the arm of the father would have been raised against the son; that of the son against the father; a brother's hand would have been stained with brother's blood; the sacred bands of friendship would have been broken, and all the ties of natural affection would have been dissolved.

"The end of all punishment is example; and the enormity of your crime requires that a severe example should be made to deter others from the commission of like crimes in future. You have forfeited your life to justice. . . . The judgment of the law is, and this court doth award, "that you be hanged by the neck until dead," and I pray God Almighty to be merciful to your soul!"

# 74 How Should the Pennsylvania Insurgents Be Treated? (1800)

Fries submitted a petition requesting forgiveness. He raised objections on the grounds that Justice

Chase had tried the case in Philadelphia, in contradiction of the United States' laws requiring a crime to be judged in the county in which it was committed. He also claimed Justice Chase unreasonably limited the arguments of counsel, precipitating their resignation from the case.

The Adams cabinet, taking refuge in the letter of this law, unanimously advised that Fries be hanged. Secretary of the Treasury Wolcott urged that the whole state should be cleansed, since Pennsylvania was "the most villainous compound of heterogeneous matter conceivable." President Adams, however, overruled his cabinet and pardoned John Fries and his followers. Adams's questions provide a glimpse of the broad factors that surround political criminality. He considered not only the penitence and the character of the condemned men, as in any other pardon, but also the public effect of the decision and the degree of danger to the country posed by the crime.

## ☆74 The Offender, the President, and the Cabinet

Reprinted from C. F. Adams, ed., *The Works of John Adams* (New York: AMS Press, 1971), 9:56-61.

☆74a The Petition of John Fries (Philadelphia Prison, May 1800)

TO THE PRESIDENT OF THE UNITED STATES:

The petition of John Fries respectfully showeth; that your prisoner is one of those deluded and unfortunate men, who, at the Circuit Court of this district, has been convicted of treason against the United States, for which offense he is pressed with a just sense of the crime which he has committed, and with the sincerity of a penitent offender, he entreats mercy and pardon from him on whose determination rests the fate of an unfortunate man. He solicits the interference of the President to save him from an ignominious death, and to rescue a large, and hitherto happy family, from future misery and ruin. If the prayer of his petition should be granted, he will show, by a future course of good conduct, his gratitude to his offended country by a steady and active support of that excellent Constitution and laws, which it has been his misfortune to violate and oppose.

JOHN FRIES

\*          \*          \*

☆74b To the Heads of Departments (President's Communication, May 20, 1800)

Philadelphia, 20 May 1800

1. Among the three criminals under sentence of death, is there any discrimination in the essential circumstances of their cases, which would justify a determination to pardon or reprieve one or two, and execute the other?

2. Is the execution of one or more so indispensably demanded by public justice and by the security of the public peace, that mercy cannot be extended to all three, or any two, or one?

3. Will the national Constitution acquire more confidence in the minds of the American people by the execution than by the pardon of one or more of the offenders?

4. Is it clear beyond all reasonable doubt that the crime of which they stand convicted, amounts to a levying of war against the United States, or, in other words, to treason?

5. Is there any evidence of a secret correspondence or combination with other anti-federalists of any denomination in other States in the Union, or in other parts of this State, to rise in force against the execution of the law for taxing houses, &c., or for opposing the commissioners in general in the execution of their offices?

6. *Quo animo* was this insurrection? Was it a design of general resistance to all law, or any particular law? Or was it particular to the place and persons?

7. Was it any thing more than a riot, high-handed, aggravated, daring, and dangerous indeed, for the purpose of a rescue? This is a high crime, but can it strictly amount to treason?

8. Is there not great danger in establishing such a construction of treason, as may be applied to every sudden, ignorant, inconsiderate heat, among a part of the people, wrought up by political disputes, and personal or party animosities?

9. Will not a career of capital executions for treason, once opened, without actual bloodshed or hostility against any military force of government, inflict a deep wound in the minds of the people, inflame their animosities, and make them more desperate in sudden heats, and thoughtless riots in elections, and on other occasions where political disputes run high, and introduce a more sanguinary disposition among them?

10. Is not the tranquillity in the western counties, since the insurrection there, and the subsequent submission to law, a precedent in favor of clemency?

11. Is there any probability that a capital execution will have any tendency to change the political sentiments of the people?

12. Will not clemency have a greater tendency to correct their errors?

13. Are not the fines and imprisonments, imposed and suffered, a sufficient discouragement, for the present, of such crimes?

JOHN ADAMS

☆ 74c The Heads of the Departments to the President (May 20, 1800)

Philadelphia, 20 May 1800

Having considered the questions proposed by the President for our consideration, we respectfully submit the following opinions.

That the intent of the insurgents in Pennsylvania, in 1798, was to prevent the execution of the law, directing the valuation of houses and lands, and the enumeration of slaves, in the particular district of country where they resided. That we know of no combination in other States, and presume that no combination, pervading the whole State of Pennsylvania, was actually formed. We believe, however, that if the government had not adopted prompt measures, the spirit of insurrection would have rapidly extended.

We are of opinion that the crime committed by Fries, Heyney, and Getman, amounted to treason, and that no danger can arise to the community from the precedents already established by the judges upon this subject. We cannot form a certain judgment of the effect upon public opinion, of suffering the law to have its course, but we think it must be beneficial, by inspiring the well disposed with confidence in the government, and the malevolent and factious with terror.

The Attorney-General and the Secretary of the Navy, however, believe that the execution of one will be enough to show the power of the laws to punish, and may be enough for example, the great end of punishment, and that Fries deserves most to suffer; because though all are guilty, and all have forfeited their lives to the justice of their country, he was the most distinguished in the commission of the crime. The Secretary of the Treasury perceives no good ground for any distinction in the three cases, and he believes that a discrimination, instead of being viewed as an act of mercy, would too much resemble a sentence against an unfortunate individual. He also believes that the mercy of government has been sufficiently manifested by the proceedings of the Attorney of the United States, and that the cause of humanity will be most effectually promoted by impressing an opinion that those who are brought to trial, and convicted of treason, will not be pardoned.

CHARLES LEE
OLIVER WOLCOTT
BEN. STODDERT

## 75 "lose the respect both of friends and foes" (1800)

President Adams's pardon of Fries and other participants in the rebellion outraged Alexander Hamilton, who had suggested Adams's earlier hard-line

position. Hamilton's letter criticized the decision and focused on Adams's previous opinion that Washington's clemency in the Whiskey Rebellion "had been the cause of the second insurrection and that Adams would take care there should not be a third." Hamilton speculated regarding the "novel doctrine" presented by Fries's counsel that treason required more than resistance to and interference with law — it required an act of a military nature.

☆ 75 Letter from Alexander Hamilton Opposing the Fries Pardon

Case of Fries, 9 F. Cas. 924, 944 N. 2 (C.C.D. Pa. 1800) (No. 5,127).

The last material occurrence in the administration of Mr. Adams of which I shall take notice, is the pardon of Fries, and other principals in the late insurrection in Pennsylvania. It is a fact, that a very refractory spirit has long existed in the western counties of that state. Repeatedly, have its own laws been opposed with violence, and as often, according to my information, with impunity. It is also a fact which everybody knows, that the laws of the Union, in the vital article of revenue, have been twice resisted in the same state, by combinations so extensive and under circumstances so violent, as to have called for the employment of military force.... Two insurrections in the same state, the one upon the heels of the other, demonstrated a spirit of insubordination or disaffection which required a strong corrective. It is a disagreeable fact, forming a weighty argument in the question, that a large part of the population of Pennsylvania, is of a composition which peculiarly fits it for the intrigues of factious men, who may disturb or overthrow the government. And it is an equally disagreeable fact, that disaffection to the national government is in no other state more general, more deeply rooted, or more envenomed.... It ought to be added, that the impunity so often experienced, had made it an article in the creed of those, who were actuated by the insurgent spirit, that neither the general not [_sic_] the state government dared to inflict capital punishment. To destroy this persuasion, to repress this dangerous spirit, it was essential that a salutary rigour should have been exerted, and that those who were under the influence of the one and the other, should be taught that they were the dupes of a fatal illusion. Of this Mr. Adams appeared so sensible [declaring] ... with no small ostentation, that the mistaken clemency of Washington on the former occasion, had been the cause of the second insurrection, and that he would take care there should not be a third, giving the laws their full course against the convicted offenders. Yet he thought proper, as if distrusting the courts and officers of the United States, to resort, through the attorney general, to the counsel of the culprits, for a statement of their cases; in which was found, besides some objections of form, the novel doctrine, disavowed by every page of our law books, that treason does no [sic] consist of resistance by force to a public law, unless it be an act relative to the militia, or other military force. And upon this, or some other ground not easy to be comprehended, he of a sudden departed from all his former declarations, and against the unanimous advice of his ministers, with the attorney general, came to the resolution, which he executed, of pardoning all those which had received sentence of death. No wonder that the public was thunder-struck at such a result, that the friends of government regarded it as a virtual dereliction; it was impossible to commit a greater error. This particular situation of Pennsylvania, the singular posture of human affairs, in which there is so strong a tendency to the disorganization of the government, the turbulent and malignant humours which exist, and are so industriously nourished throughout the United States; everything loudly demanded that the executive should have acted with exemplary vigour, and should have given a striking demonstration, that condign punishment would be the lot of the violent opposers of the laws.... It is by temporizings like these, that men at the head of affairs, lose the respect both of friends and foes; it is by temporizings like these, that in times of fermentation and commotion, governments are prostrated, which might easily have been upheld by an erect and imposing attitude.

*          *          *

## 76 "to regain the road which alone leads to peace, liberty, and safety" (1801)

In the 1800 elections, the Federalists, in popular disfavor since the Alien and Sedition Acts, lost power in Congress as well as the presidency. Thomas Jefferson, the Republican candidate, won the presidential election. (Aaron Burr, who introduced the machinery of modern American politics in New York, was elected vice-president.) The new dominant party stood for the primacy of state authority in areas of power not explicitly delegated to the central government, and the inaugural address reflected the principles of the Virginia and Kentucky resolutions as well as Jefferson's belief in the importance of tolerating political dissent and opposition.

Although he placed the will of the majority at the pinnacle of our protections of liberty, Jefferson noted, "To be rightful, it must be reasonable." He also rested the liberties of the people on the procedural protections of the Bill of Rights. Jefferson acted on his beliefs by releasing all those convicted under the Alien and Sedition Acts. In his speech, he

nevertheless expressed a hope for, and presumed a unity of loyalty among, the citizens.

## ☆ 76 First Inaugural Address by Thomas Jefferson (March 4, 1801)

Reprinted in J. Richardson, ed., *A Compilation of the Messages and Papers of the Presidents* (New York: Bureau of National Literature, 1897), 1:321-24.

FRIENDS AND FELLOW CITIZENS: Called upon to undertake the duties of the first executive office of our country, I avail myself of the presence of that portion of my fellow citizens which is here assembled, to express my grateful thanks for the favor with which they have been pleased to look toward me....

During the contest of opinion through which we have passed, the animation of discussion and of exertions has sometimes worn an aspect which might impose on strangers unused to think freely and to speak and to write what they think; but this being now decided by the voice of the nation, announced according to the rules of the constitution, all will, of course, arrange themselves under the will of the law, and unite in common efforts for the common good. All, too, will bear in mind this sacred principle, that though the will of the majority is in all cases to prevail, that will, to be rightful, must be reasonable; that the minority possess their equal rights, which equal laws must protect, and to violate which would be oppression. Let us, then, fellow citizens, unite with one heart and one mind. Let us restore to social intercourse that harmony and affection without which liberty and even life itself are but dreary things. And let us reflect that having banished from our land that religious intolerance under which mankind so long bled and suffered, we have yet gained little if we countenance a political intolerance as despotic, as wicked, and capable of as bitter and bloody persecutions.... But every difference of opinion is not a difference of principle. We have called by different names brethren of the same principle. We are all republicans—we are federalists. If there be any among us who would wish to dissolve this Union or to change its republican form, let them stand undisturbed as monuments of the safety with which error of opinion may be tolerated where reason is left free to combat it. I know, indeed, that some honest men fear that a republican government cannot be strong; that this government is not strong enough. But would the honest patriot, in the full tide of successful experiment, abandon a government which has so far kept us free and firm, on the theoretic and visionary fear that this government, the world's best hope, may by possibility want energy to preserve itself? I trust not. I believe this, on the contrary, the strongest government on earth. I believe it is the only one where every man, at the call of the laws, would fly to the standard of the law, and would meet invasions of the public order as his own personal concern....

... [W]hat more is necessary to make us a happy and prosperous and frugal government, which shall restrain men from injuring one another, which shall leave them otherwise free to regulate their own pursuits of industry and improvement, and shall not take from the mouth of labor the bread it has earned. This is the sum of good government, and this is necessary to close the circle of our felicities.

About to enter, fellow citizens, on the exercise of duties which comprehend everything dear and valuable to you, it is proper that you should understand what I deem the essential principles of our government, and consequently those which ought to shape its administration. I will compress them within the narrowest compass they will bear, stating the general principle, but not all its limitations. Equal and exact justice to all men, of whatever state or persuasion, religious or political; peace, commerce and honest friendship with all nations—entangling alliances with none; the support of the State governments in all their rights, as the most competent administrations for our domestic concerns and the surest bulwarks against anti-republican tendencies; the preservation of the general government in its whole constitutional vigor, as the sheet anchor of our peace at home and safety abroad; a jealous care of the right of election by the people—a mild and safe corrective of abuses of which are lopped by the sword of the revolution where peaceable remedies are unprovided; absolute acquiescence in the decisions of the majority—the vital principle of republics, from which there is no appeal but to force, the vital principle and immediate parent of despotism; ... the diffusion of information and the arraignment of all abuses at the bar of public reason; freedom of religion; freedom of the press; freedom of person under the protection of the habeas corpus; and trial by juries impartially selected—these principles form the bright constellation which has gone before us, and guided our steps through an age of revolution and reformation. The wisdom of our sages and the blood of our heroes have been devoted to their attainment. They should be the creed of our political faith—the text of civil instruction—the touchstone by which to try the services of those we trust; and should we wander from them in moments of error or alarm, let us hasten to retrace our steps and to regain the road which alone leads to peace, liberty, and safety....

*       *       *

... I ask so much confidence only as may give firmness and effect to the legal administration of your affairs. I shall often go wrong through defect of judgment. When right, I shall often be thought wrong by those whose positions will not command a view of the whole ground. I ask your indulgence for my own errors, which will never be intentional; and your support against the errors of others, who condemn what they would not if seen in all its parts.

*       *       *

## 77 Not Acting under the Government's Secret Patronage (1807)

In 1800, the Constitution provided that the person who received the second highest vote in the Electoral College was to serve as vice-president. Although the Jeffersonian Republicans won the elections of 1800, the vote in the Electoral College produced a tie between Jefferson and Aaron Burr of New York—Jefferson's supposed running mate—throwing the election into the House of Representatives. There, the still powerful Federalist faction rallied around Burr as a more acceptable president than their bitter foe, Jefferson. But Federalist Alexander Hamilton's implacable opposition to Burr, stemming from political infighting in New York, finally secured the election for Jefferson. (Burr subsequently killed Hamilton in a duel in 1804.) Although Burr did not campaign actively in the House for the presidency, Jefferson harbored an opinion that Burr had a treacherous streak.

At the conclusion of his term in office as vice-president, this unusually gifted leader found himself politically and financially ruined. President Jefferson used the power of his office to reduce Burr's support among the Republicans in his New York base. Hamilton, the leader of the Federalists, blocked any rapproachement between Burr and that party in New York. These activities frustrated Burr's ambitions, and his duel with Alexander Hamilton, whom he sought to dethrone in order to assume leadership of the Federalists, turned him into a social pariah and a fugitive from justice.

When word reached President Jefferson of Burr's enterprises, he was prepared to believe the worst. On November 27, 1806, Jefferson assembled his cabinet and issued a proclamation charging unidentified "sundry persons" with conspiracy to attack the possessions of the king of Spain and ordering that all men and property engaged in this enterprise be seized and detained. The following message to Congress expounded the government's position with regard to Burr's activities.

☆ 77 Jefferson's Message on the Burr Conspiracy to the Senate and House of Representatives of the United States (January 22, 1807)

Reprinted in J. Richardson, ed., *A Compilation of the Messages and Papers of the Presidents* (New York: Bureau of National Literature, 1897), 195-97.

Agreeably to the request of the House of Representatives communicated in their resolution of the 16th instant, I proceed to state, under the reserve therein expressed, information received touching an illegal combination of private individuals against the peace and safety of the Union, and a military expedition planned by them against the territories of a power in amity with the United States, with the measures I have pursued for suppressing the same. . . .

Some time in the latter part of September I received intimations that designs were in agitation in the Western country unlawful and unfriendly to the peace of the Union, and that the prime mover in these was Aaron Burr, heretofore distinguished by the favor of his country. . . .

*          *          *

. . . [I]t was known that many boats were under preparation, stores of provisions collecting, and an unusual number of suspicious characters in motion on the Ohio and its waters. Besides dispatching the confidential agent to that quarter, orders were at the time sent to the governors of the Orleans and Mississippi Territories and to the commanders of the land and naval forces there to be on their guard against surprise and in constant readiness to resist any enterprise which might be attempted on the vessels, posts, or other objects under their care; and on the 8th of November instructions were forwarded to General Wilkinson to hasten an accommodation with the Spanish commandant on the Sabine, and as soon as that was effected to fall back with his principal force to the hither bank of the Mississippi for the defense of the interesting points on that river. By a letter received from that officer on the 25th of November, we learnt that a confidential agent of Aaron Burr had been deputed to him with communications, partly written in cipher and partly oral, explaining his designs, exaggerating his resources, and making such offers of emolument and command to engage him and the army in his unlawful enterprise as he had flattered himself would be successful. The General, . . . immediately dispatched a trusty officer to me with information of what had passed. . . .

The General's letter . . . and some other information received a few days earlier, when brought together developed Burr's general design. . . . It appeared that he contemplated two distinct objects, which might be carried on either jointly or separately, and either the one or the other first, as circumstances should direct. One of these was the severance of the Union of these States by the Alleghany Mountains; the other an attack on Mexico. . . .

He found at once that the attachment of the Western country to the present Union was not to be shaken; that its dissolution could not be effected with the consent of its inhabitants, and that his re-

sources were inadequate as yet to effect it by force. He took his course then at once, determined to seize on New Orleans, plunder the bank there, possess himself of the military and naval stores, and proceed on his expedition to Mexico, and to this object all his means and preparations were now directed. He collected from all the quarters where himself or his agents possessed influence all the ardent, restless, desperate, and disaffected persons who were ready for any enterprise analogous to their characters. He seduced good and well-meaning citizens, some by assurances that he possessed the confidence of the Government and was acting under its secret patronage, a pretense which procured some credit from the state of our difference with Spain, and others by offers of land in Bastrop's claim on the Washita. . . .

*          *          *

Surmises have been hazarded that this enterprise is to receive aid from certain foreign powers; but these surmises are without proof or probability. . . .

By letters from General Wilkinson . . . I received the important affidavit [by which] it will be seen that of three of the principal emissaries of Mr. Burr whom the General had caused to be apprehended, one had been liberated by habeas corpus, and two others . . . have been embarked by him for ports in the Atlantic states. . . . As soon as these persons shall arrive they will be delivered to the custody of the law and left to such course of trial, both as to place and process, as the functionaries of the law may direct. . . .

TH. JEFFERSON

## 78 "conspiracy is not treason" (1807)

Burr instructed Erick Bollman and Samuel Swartwout to carry copies of his own coded letter to General Wilkinson. After their arrest, they were charged with treason and taken to Washington where they filed a petition for a writ of habeas corpus from the United States Supreme Court. After preliminary arguments in which the government contended that the Supreme Court did not have jurisdiction to issue the Great Writ, the following opinion was written. The questions in the cases were difficult for the court to resolve, as only four members were sitting, and there was a two-two split on central evidentiary issues.

☆ 78 *Ex Parte Bollman and Swartwout*

8 U.S. (4 Cranch) 75 (1807).

MARSHALL, CH. J., delivered the opinion of the court, — The prisoners having been brought before this court on a writ of *habeas corpus*, . . . the question to be determined is, whether the accused shall be discharged or held to trial. . . .

The specific charge brought against the prisoners is treason, in levying war against the United States.

\*          \*          \*

To constitute that specific crime for which the prisoners now before the court have been committed, war must be actually levied against the United States. However flagitious may be the crime of conspiring to subject by force the government of our country, such conspiracy is not treason. To conspire to levy war, and actually to levy war, are distinct offences. The first must be brought into open action, by the assemblage of men for a purpose treasonable itself, or the fact of levying war cannot have been committed. . . .

It is not the intention of the court to say, that no individual can be guilty of this crime, who has not appeared in arms against his country. On the contrary, if war be actually levied, that is, if a body of men be actually assembled, for the purpose of effecting by force a treasonable purpose, all those who perform any part, however minute, or however remote from the scene of action, and who are actually leagued in the general conspiracy, are to be considered as traitors. But there must be an actual assembling of men, for the treasonable purpose, to constitute a levying of war.

\*          \*          \*

To complete the crime of levying war against the United States, there must be an actual assemblage of men for the purpose of executing a treasonable design. In the case now before the court, a design to overturn the government of the United States, in New Orleans, by force, would have been unquestionably a design which, if carried into execution, would have been treason, and the assemblage of a body of men for the purpose of carrying it into execution, would amount to levying of war against the United States; but no conspiracy for this object, no enlisting of men to effect it, would be an actual levying of war.

. . . That the letter from Col. Burr to General Wilkinson relates to a military enterprise meditated by the former, has not been questioned. If this enterprise was against Mexico, it would amount to a high misdemeanor; if against any of the territories of the United States, or if, in its progress, the subversion of the government of the United States, in any of their territories, was a mean, clearly and necessarily, to be employed, if such mean formed a substantive part of the plan, the assemblage of a body of men to effect it, would be levying war against the United States.

\*          \*          \*

The letter is in language which furnishes no distinct view of the design of the writer. The co-opera-

tion, however, which is stated to have been secured, points strongly to some expedition against the territories of Spain. After making these general statements, the writer becomes rather more explicit, and says, "Burr's plan of operations is to move down rapidly from the falls, on the 15th of November, with the first 500 or 1000 men, in light boats now constructing for that purpose, to be at Natchez, between the 5th and 15th of December, there to meet Wilkinson; then to determine whether it will be expedient, in the first instance, to seize on, or to pass by, Baton Rouge. The people of the country to which we are going are prepared to receive us. Their agents, now with Burr, say, that if we will protect their religion, and will not subject them to a foreign power, in three weeks, all will be settled."

There is no expression in these sentences, which would justify a suspicion, that any territory of the United States was the object of the expedition. For what purpose, seize on Baton Rouge? Why engage Spain against this enterprise, if it was designed against the United States?

\*          \*          \*

There certainly is not in the letter delivered to General Wilkinson, so far as the letter is laid before the court, one syllable which has a necessary or a natural reference to an enterprise against any territory of the United States. That the bearer of this letter must be considered as acquainted with its contents, is not to be controverted. The letter and his own declarations evince the fact. . . . [H]e states their object to be, "to carry an expedition to the Mexican provinces." This statement may be considered as explanatory of the letter of Col. Burr, if the expressions of that letter could be thought ambiguous.

But there are other declarations made by Mr. Swartwout, which constitute the difficulty of this case. On an inquiry from General Wilkinson, he said, "this territory would be revolutionized, where the people were ready to join them, and that there would be some seizing, he supposed, at New Orleans." If these words import that the government established by the United States in any of its territories, was to be revolutionized by force, although merely as a step to, or a mean of executing some greater projects, the design was unquestionably treasonable, and any assemblage of men for that purpose would amount to a levying of war. But on the import of the words, a difference of opinion exists. Some of the judges suppose, they refer to the territory against which the expedition was intended; others to that in which the conversation was held. Some consider the words, if even applicable to a territory of the United States, as alluding to a revolution to be effected by the people, rather than by the party conducted by Col. Burr.

But whether this treasonable intention be really imputable to the plan or not, it is admitted, that it must have been carried into execution by an open assemblage of men for that purpose, previous to the arrest of the prisoner, in order to consummate the crime as to him; and a majority of the court is of opinion, that the conversation of Mr. Swartwout affords no sufficient proof of such assembling.

*     *     *

... The mere enlisting of men, without assembling them, is not levying war. The question then, is, whether this evidence proves Col. Burr to have advanced so far in levying an army, as actually to have assembled them.

It is argued, that since it cannot be necessary that the whole 7000 men should have assembled, their commencing their march, by detachments, to the place of rendezvous, must be sufficient to constitute the crime. This position is correct, with some qualification. It cannot be necessary, that the whole army should assemble, and that various parts which are to compose it should have combined. But it is necessary, that there should be an actual assemblage, and therefore, the evidence should make the fact unequivocal. The travelling of individuals to the place of rendezvous would, perhaps, not be sufficient. This would be an equivocal act, and has no warlike appearance. The meeting of particular bodies of men, and their marching from places of partial to a place of general rendezvous, would be such an assemblage.

The particular words used by Mr. Swartwout are, that Col. Burr "was levying an armed body of 7000 men." If the term levying, in this place, imports that they were assembled, then such fact would amount, if the intention be against the United States, to levying war. If it barely imports that he was enlisting or engaging them in his service, the fact would not amount to levying war. It is thought sufficiently apparent, that the latter is the sense in which the term was used. The fact alluded to, if taken in the proper sense, is of a nature so to force itself upon the public view, that if the army had then actually assembled, either together or in detachments, some evidence of such assembling would have been laid before the court.

The words used by the prisoner, in reference to seizing at New Orleans, and borrowing, perhaps by force, from the bank, though indicating a design to rob, and consequently, importing a high offence, do not designate the specific crime of levying war against the United States.

It is, therefore, the opinion of a majority of the court, that in the case of Samuel Swartwout there is not sufficient evidence of his levying war against the United States to justify his commitment on the charge of treason.

Against Erick Bollman, there is still less testimony. Nothing has been said by him, to support the charge that the enterprise in which he was engaged had any other object than stated in the letter of Col. Burr. Against him, therefore, there is no evidence to support a charge of treason.

*     *     *

## 79 "obviously a military enterprise" (1807)

"The conspiracies of Aaron Burr remain one of the greatest enigmas in American history," wrote historian Nathaniel Weyl. A member of a distinguished family, graduate of Princeton at age sixteen, a leader of New York's Society of Tammany as well as United States Senator from New York, and vice-president in 1800, Burr had little in his history to suggest that he would become the supreme conspirator in American history.

Burr's conspiracy was an act of grandeur as well as desperation. Some historians believe that his aim was to dismember the United States and establish an independent nation, west of the Alleghanies. Talk of secession from the young United States, whether by the mercantile interests of New England or the populists of the West, dominated American political discussion. Others suggest that he was intent on conquering Mexico and making himself its emperor. Holding secret meetings with the British minister to Washington, conspiring with Major General James Wilkinson—governor of the northern part of the newly acquired Louisiana Territory—and building alliances with such western expansionists as Andrew Jackson, Henry Clay, and John C. Calhoun, Burr had one or more enterprises on his mind.

An Irish expatriate supporter of Burr owned Blennerhassett's Island in the Ohio River. It was used as a base of operations for recruitment, and provisions for a military force were established. But on November 25, 1806, General Wilkinson denounced the plan to Jefferson, describing it as an imperial expedition aginst Vera Cruz. Jefferson issued a proclamation warning the citizenry of the Burr conspiracy. On January 17, 1807, Burr surrendered to the acting governor of the Louisiana Territory. In Richmond, Virginia, circuit-riding John Marshall, chief justice of the United States Supreme Court and a bitter opponent of Jefferson, tried Aaron Burr in 1807. The first determination was whether enough evidence existed to require Burr to undergo trial for treason. Marshall, scrupulously adhering to constitutional language, held that Burr could not be indicted for treason, only for the lesser charge of mounting "a military expedition against a nation with whom the United States was at peace."

☆ 79  *United States v. Burr* (April 1807)

25 F. Cas. 2 (C.C.D. Va. 1807) (No. 14,692a).

MARSHALL, Chief Justice. I am required on the part of the attorney for the United States to commit the accused on two charges: (1) For setting on foot and providing the means for an expedition against the territories of a nation at peace with the United States. (2) For committing high treason against the United States.

\*      \*      \*

The first charge stands upon the testimony of General Eaton and General Wilkinson.... To make the testimony of General Wilkinson bear on Colonel Burr, it is necessary to consider as genuine the letter stated by the former to be, as nearly as he can make it, an interpretation of one received in cypher from the latter. Exclude this letter, and nothing remains in the testimony which can in the most remote degree affect Colonel Burr....

\*      \*      \*

... The enterprise described in this letter is obviously a military enterprise, and must have been intended either against the United States, or against the territories of some other power on the continent, with all of whom the United States were at peace. The expressions of this letter must be admitted to furnish at least probable cause for believing that the means for the expedition were provided. In every part of it we find declarations indicating that he was providing the means for the expedition; and as these means might be provided in secret, I do not think that further testimony ought to be required to satisfy me that there is probable cause for committing the prisoner on this charge....

The second charge exhibited against the prisoner is high treason against the United States in levying war against them. As this is the most atrocious offence which can be committed against the political body, so is it the charge which is most capable of being employed as the instrument of those malignant and vindictive passions which may rage in the bosoms of contending parties struggling for power. It is that of which the people of America have been most jealous, and therefore, while other crimes are unnoticed, they have refused to trust the national legislature with the definition of this, but have themselves declared in their constitution that "it shall consist only in levying war against the United States, or in adhering to their enemies, giving them aid and comfort." This high crime consists of overt acts, which must be proved by two witnesses, or by the confession of the party in open court. Under the control of this constitutional regulation, I am to inquire whether the testimony laid before me furnishes probable cause in support of this charge....

That part of [General Eaton's] deposition which bears upon this charge is the plan disclosed by the prisoner for seizing upon New Orleans, and revolutionizing the Western states. That this plan, if consummated by overt acts, would amount to treason, no man will controvert. But it is equally clear that an intention to commit treason is an offence entirely distinct from the actual commission of that crime. War can only be levied by the employment of actual force. Troops must be embodied, men must be assembled, in order to levy war. If Colonel Burr had been apprehended on making these communications to General Eaton, could it have been alleged that he had gone further than to meditate the crime? Could it have been said that he had actually collected forces and had actually levied war? Most certainly it could not. The crime really complete was a conspiracy to commit treason, not an actual commission of treason. If these communications were not treason at the instant they were made, no lapse of time can make them so. They are not in themselves acts. They may serve to explain the intention with which acts were committed, but they cannot supply those acts if they be not proved. The next testimony is the deposition of General Wilkinson, which consists of the letter already noticed, and of the communications made by the bearer of that letter. This letter has already been considered by the supreme court of the United States, and has been declared to import, taken by itself or in connection with Eaton's deposition, rather an expedition against Mexico than the territories of the United States. [Upon the meaning of Mr. Swartwout's testimony] ... it appears that the supreme court was divided. I therefore hold myself at liberty to pursue my own opinion, which was, that the words "this territory must be revolutionized" did not so clearly apply to a foreign territory as to reject that sense which would make them applicable to a territory of the United States, at least so far as to admit of further inquiry into their meaning. And if a territory of the United States was to be revolutionized, though only as a means for an expedition against a foreign power, the act would be treason. This reasoning leads to the conclusion that there is probable cause for the allegation that treasonable designs were entertained by the prisoner so late as July last, when this letter was written.

It remains to inquire whether there is also probable cause to believe that these designs have been ripened into the crime itself, by actually levying war against the United States. It has been already observed that, to constitute this crime, troops must be embodied, men must be actually assembled; and these are facts which cannot remain invisible. Treason may be machinated in secret, but it can be perpetrated only in open day, and in the eye of the world. Testimony of a fact which in its own nature is so notorious ought to be unequivocal. The testimony now offered has been laid before the supreme court of the United States and has been determined in the Cases of Bollman and Swartwout not to furnish probable cause for the opinion that war had been actually levied.... The first piece of testimony relied on to render this fact probable is the declaration of Mr. Swartwout, that "Colonel Burr was levying an armed body of 7,000 men...." The term "levying" has been said, according to the explanation of the lexicons, to mean the embodying of troops, and therefore to prove what is required. Although I do not suppose that Mr. Swartwout had consulted a dictionary, I have looked into Johnson for the term, and find its first signification to be "to raise"; its second, "to bring together." In common parlance, it may signify the one or the other. But its sense is certainly decided by the fact. If when Mr. Swartwout left Colonel Burr, which must be supposed to have been in July, he was actually embodying men from New York to the Western states, what could veil his troops from human sight? An invisible army is not the instrument of war, and had these troops been visible, some testimony relative to them could have been adduced. I take the real sense, then, in which this term was used to be, that Colonel Burr was raising, or in other words engaging or enlisting, men through the country described, for the enterprise he meditated.... I shall readily avow my opinion, that the strength of the presumption arising from this testimony ought to depend greatly on the time at which the application is made. If soon after the period at which the troops were to assemble, when full time had not elapsed to ascertain the fact, these circumstances had been urged as the ground for a commitment on the charge of treason, I should have thought them entitled to great consideration. I will not deny that, in the Cases of Bollman and Swartwout, I was not perfectly satisfied that they did not warrant an inquiry into the fact. But I think every person must admit that the weight of these circumstances daily diminishes....

The fact to be proved in this case is an act of public notoriety. It must exist in the view of the world, or it cannot exist at all. The assembling of forces to levy war is a visible transaction, and numbers must witness it. It is therefore capable of proof; and when time to collect this proof has been given, it ought to be adduced, or suspicion becomes ground too weak to stand upon. Several months have elapsed since this fact did occur, if it ever occurred. More than five weeks have elapsed since the opinion of the supreme court has declared the necessity of proving the fact, if it exists. Why is it not proved? ... I ought not to believe that there has been any remissness on the part of those who prosecute on this important and interesting subject; and consequently, when at this

late period no evidence that troops have been actually embodied is given. I must say that the suspicion which in the first instance might have been created ought not to be continued, unless this want of proof can be in some manner accounted for.

\* \* \*

... I shall not therefore insert in the commitment the charge of high treason. I repeat, that this is the less important, because it detracts nothing from the right of the attorney to prefer an indictment for high treason, should he be furnished with the necessary testimony.

The CHIEF JUSTICE, having delivered his opinion, observed that ... the case was of course bailable.... The sum was finally fixed at ten thousand dollars....

## 80 Marshall Meets Burr in the Courtroom a Second Time (1807)

Burr was reindicted on a second and more specific charge of treason by levying of war in moving to seize New Orleans. As he had done previously, Chief Justice Marshall imposed such stringent requirements in his charge to the jury that a conviction was unlikely. In his opinion, Marshall discussed in great detail the highly technical requirements that must be met to satisfy a charge of treason.

After several other lesser trials and acquittals, Aaron Burr went into exile in Europe. His dreams of western conquests continued to haunt him. In 1812, a charitable United States government permitted his return. At age seventy-seven he married again, and three years later his wife divorced him on grounds of adultery. Burr was an adventurer to the end.

☆ 80 *United States v. Burr* (October 1807)

25 F. Cas. 201 (C.C.D. Va. 1807) (No. 14,694a).

[MARSHALL, C. J.] ...

The charges against the accused are: 1st, that they have levied war against the United States at the mouth of Cumberland river, in Kentucky; and, 2dly, that they have begun and provided the means for a military expedition against a nation with which the United States were at peace.

\* \* \*

Both charges are supported by the same transaction and the same testimony. The assemblage at the mouth of Cumberland is considered as an act of levying war against the United States, and as a military armament collected for the invasion of a neighboring power with whom the United States were at peace. From the evidence which details that transaction, it appears that from sixty to one hundred men, who were collected from the upper parts of the Ohio under the direction of Tyler and Floyd, had descended the river and reached the mouth of Cumberland about the 25th of December, 1806. The next day they went on shore, and formed a line, represented by some somewhat circular, to receive Colonel Burr, who was introduced to them, and who said that he had intended to impart something to them, or that he had intended to communicate his views, but that reasons of his own had induced him to postpone this communication; or, as others say, that there were then too many bystanders to admit of a communication of his objects. The men assembled at the mouth of Cumberland appear to have considered Colonel Burr as their chief. . . . There was no act of disobedience to the civil authority, nor were there any military appearances. There were some arms, and some boxes which might or might not contain arms. There were also some implements of husbandry, but they were purchased at the place. These men assembled under contracts to settle a tract of country on the Red river. No hostile objects were avowed; and, after continuing a day or two on an island in the mouth of the river, the party proceeded down the Ohio. . . . That the men should have been armed with rifles was to be expected, had their single object been to plant themselves in the Wachita; but the musket and bayonet are, perhaps, not the species of arms which are most usually found in our frontier settlements; nor were the individuals who were assembled of that description of persons who would most naturally be employed for such a purpose. The engagement for six months, too, is a stipulation for which it is difficult to account upon the principle that a settlement of lands was the sole or principal object in contemplation. These are circumstances which excite suspicion. How far they may be accounted for by saying that ulterior eventual objects were entertained, and that the event on which those objects depended was believed to be certain or nearly certain, I need not determine; but I can scarcely suppose it possible that it would be contended by any person that the transactions at the mouth of Cumberland do, in themselves, amount to an act of levying war. There was neither an act of hostility committed, nor any intention to commit such act avowed.

Very early in the proceedings which preceded this motion, I declared the opinion that war might be levied without a battle, or the actual application of force to the object on which it was designed to act; that a body of men assembled for the purpose of war, and being in a posture of war, do levy war; and from that opinion I have certainly felt no disposition to recede. But the intention is an indispensable ingredient in the composition of the fact; and if war may be levied without striking the blow, the intention to strike must be plainly proved. To prove this intention, the prosecutor for the United States offers evidence of conversations held by the accused. . . . That conversations or actions at a different time and place might be given in evidence as corroborative of the overt act of levying war, after that had been proved in such a manner as to be left to a jury, I never doubted for an instant. But that in a case where the intent could not be inferred from the fact, and was not proved by declarations connected with the fact, . . . this defect could be entirely supplied by extrinsic testimony, not applying the intend conclusively to the particular fact, is a point on which I have entertained doubts which are not yet entirely removed. . . .

*          *          *

The first question which arises on the evidence is: With what objects did those men convene who assembled at the mouth of Cumberland? Was it to separate the Western from the Eastern states by seizing and holding New Orleans? Was it to carry on an expedition against Mexico, making the embarkation at New Orleans? Was this expedition to depend on a war with Spain? The conversation held by Colonel Burr with Commodore Decatur stated his object to be an expedition against Mexico, which would be undertaken, as the commodore understood, with the approbation of government in the event of war. To General Eaton, he unfolded, in his various conversations, plans for invading Mexico, and also for severing the Western from the Atlantic states. To Commodore Truxton, he spoke of the invasion and conquest of Mexico in the event of a war, as a plan which he had digested in concert with General Wilkinson, and into which he was extremely desirous to draw the commodore. A circumstance is narrated by this witness. . . . It is the declaration of Colonel Burr that he was about to despatch two couriers with letters to General Wilkinson relative to the expedition. It was at this time that Messrs. Bollman and Swartwout are said to have left Philadelphia, carrying each a copy of the ciphered letter which has constituted so important a document in the various motions that have been made on this occasion. This letter, though expressed in terms of some ambiguity, has been understood by the supreme court, and is understood by me, to relate to a military expedition against the territories of a foreign prince.

*          *          *

. . . The supreme court has said that to revolutionize a territory by force, although merely as a step to or a means of executing some greater projects is treason. But an embarkation of troops against a foreign country may be made without revolutionizing the government of the place, and without subverting the legitimate authority. . . . If the object of the assemblage at the mouth of Cumberland was to embark at New Orleans for the purpose of invading Mexico, the law relative to that assemblage would be essentially different from what it might be if their direct object was to subvert the government of New Orleans by force. If, in prosecuting their purpose at New Orleans, war should be levied, this would be treason at New Orleans when the fact was committed, but it could not, I think, be said to be treason by levying war at the mouth of Cumberland, where the fact was neither committed nor intended. It might be otherwise, if at the mouth of Cumberland the determination to subvert the government of a territory by force had been formed.

*　　*　　*

... The reason why men in a posture of war may be said to levy war before a blow is struck, is that they are ready to strike, and war consists in the various movements of a military force, as well as in actual fighting. But these men were not ready nor willing to strike, nor could their chief be ready to strike without them. He had yet to prevail upon them to come into his measures. This is not a meeting for the purpose of executing a formal design, but a meeting for the purpose of forming a design. It is, therefore, more in the nature of conspiracy than actual war.

*　　*　　*

Believing, then, the weight of testimony to be in favor of the opinion that the real and direct object of the expedition was Mexico, and inclining, also, to the opinion that, in law, either acts of hostility and resistance to the government, or a hostile intention in the body assembled, is necessary to convert a meeting of men with ordinary appearances into an act of levying war, it would, in my judgement, be improper in me to commit the accused on the charge of treason.

*　　*　　*

# 81 Protecting America's Neutrality (1809)

The European wars of the early nineteenth century directly affected the distant American nation. The British and the French, America's largest trading partners, sought to disrupt each other's maritime supply lines. By 1806, the British had seized some 120 American vessels engaged in trade with the French and their colonies. In retaliation for the English interference with neutral commerce, Napoleon responded with his own blockade measures, thus interrupting American trade with Britain.

America's pride, honor, and economy suffered from the interference with its shipping. The growing conflict with England over the freedom of open sea routes resulted in Jefferson's 1807 Embargo Act, which prohibited any vessel — American or foreign — from leaving domestic ports to engage in international trade. The embargo reportedly struck New England and its ports "like a thunderbolt." When the Embargo Act proved unenforceable, Congress passed the Non-Intercourse Act on March 1, 1809, which closed American harbors to English and French ships and prohibited Americans from engaging in any commercial transactions with the English and the French. Congress expected the shipping interests to comply with this economic burden it imposed on them out of a sense of allegiance to the United States and her interests. The government prescribed sanctions for those who did not obey. For reasons of international politics, the United States had criminalized the act of participating in useful commercial relations between individuals of specified nationalities.

## ☆ 81 The Non-Intercourse Act

2 Stat. 539 (1809).

*Be it enacted,* That from and after the passing of this act, the entrance of the harbors and waters of the United States and of the territories thereof, be, and the same is hereby interdicted to all public ships and vessels belonging to Great Britain or France....

SEC. 2. That it shall not be lawful for any citizen or citizens of the United States or the territories thereof, nor for any person or persons residing or being in the same, to have any intercourse with, or to afford any aid or supplies to any public ship or vessel as aforesaid, which shall, contrary to the provisions of this act, have entered any harbor or waters within the jurisdiction of the United States or the territories thereof; and if any person shall, contrary to the provisions of this act, have any intercourse with such ship or vessel, or shall afford any aid to such ship or vessel, either in repairing the said vessel or in furnishing her, her officers and crew with supplies of any kind or in any manner whatever, ... every person so offending, shall forfeit and pay a sum not less than one hundred dollars, nor exceeding ten thousand dollars; and shall also be imprisoned for a term not less than one month, nor more than one year.

SEC. 3. That from and after the twentieth day of May next, the entrance of the harbors and waters of the United States and the territories thereof be, and the same is hereby interdicted to all ships or vessels sailing under the flag of Great Britain or France, or owned in whole or in part by any citizen or subject of either.

SEC. 4. That from and after the twentieth day of May next, it shall not be lawful to import into the United States or the territories thereof, any goods, wares or merchandise whatever, from any port or place situated in Great Britain or Ireland, or in any of the colonies or dependencies of Great Britain, nor from any port or place situated in France, or in any of her colonies or dependencies, nor from any port or place in the actual possession of either Great Britain or France. Nor shall it be lawful to import into the United States, or the territories thereof, from any foreign port or place whatever, any goods, wares or merchandise whatever, being of the growth, produce or manufacture of France, or of any of her colonies or dependencies, or being of the growth, produce or manufacture of Great Britain or Ireland, or of any of the colonies or dependencies of Great Britain, or being of the growth, produce or manufacture of any place or country in the actual possession of either France or Great Britain. . . .

*Approved, March 1, 1809.*

# 82 Winds of Secession (1815)

The War of 1812 put almost unbearable stress on the fledgling Republic. Regional, economic, and political tension reached a peak, and the dissatisfaction of the aristocratic, sophisticated Federalist leaders of New England with the more populist Republican rule in Washington ("government by the worst") led the Federalists to consider the possibility of secession from the Union.

As early as 1808, Jefferson, in a private letter, predicted that "the Federalists may attempt insurrection." When war was declared, furious rioting broke out in various parts of the country—for and against the war. Resistance to the war and its measures was highest in the North. In Massachusetts, recruiting offices were mobbed and an American privateer was sunk. By 1814, the key New England states refused to furnish men or money for the conduct of a war which they considered "iniquitous." The avowed strategy of some of the Federalists, claims historian Nathaniel Weyl, "was to precipitate the military defeat of the United States, thus dissolving the republic and establishing an independent New England Confederacy under English protection."

The fortunes of the national government reached new depths at the end of 1814. On October 17, the Massachusetts legislature issued an invitation of the New England states to convene at Hartford "to lay the foundation for a radical reform in the national compact." Delegates from Massachusetts, Connecticut, Rhode Island, Vermont, and New Hampshire attended the Hartford Convention. But the moderating influence of the chairman, George Cabot of Massachusetts, prevailed, and the resolutions adopted were neither radical nor treasonable.

In early 1815, Andrew Jackson repelled the Brit-

ish naval assault on Louisiana, and the United States signed a favorable peace treaty at Ghent. The secessionist sentiments of New England were forgotten. Regional differences were not to mature into actual conflict until the Civil War.

## ☆ 82 Report and Resolutions of the Hartford Convention (January 4, 1815)

Reprinted in T. Dwight, *History of the Hartford Convention* (New York: Da Capo Press, 1970), 368.

. . . To investigate and explain the means whereby this fatal reverse has been effected, would require a voluminous discussion. Nothing more can be attempted in this report than a general allusion to the principal outlines of the policy which has produced this vicissitude. Among these may be enumerated—

*First.* — A deliberate and extensive system for effecting a combination among certain states, by exciting local jealousies and ambition, so as to secure to popular leaders in one section of the Union, the controul of public affairs in perpetual succession. To which primary object most other characteristics of the system may be reconciled.

*Secondly.* — The political intolerance displayed and avowed in excluding from office men of unexceptionable merit, for want of adherence to the executive creed.

\*         \*         \*

*Fourthly.* — The abolition of existing taxes, requisite to prepare the country for those changes to which nations are always exposed, with a view of the acquisition of popular favour.

*Fifthly.* — The influence of patronage in the distribution of offices, which in these states has been almost invariably made among men the least entitled to such distinction. . . .

*Sixthly.* — The admission of new states into the Union formed at pleasure in the western region, has destroyed the balance of power which existed among the original States, and deeply affected their interest.

*Seventhly.* — The easy admission of naturalized foreigners, to places of trust, honour or profit, operating as an inducement to the malcontent subjects of the old world to come to these States, in quest of executive patronage, and to repay it by an abject devotion to executive measures.

*Eighthly.* — Hostility to Great Britain, and partiality to the late government of France, adopted as coincident with popular prejudice, and subservient to the main object, party power. Connected with these must be ranked erroneous and distorted estimates of the power and resources of those nations, of the probable results of their controversies, and of our political relations to them respectively.

*Lastly and principally.* — A visionary and superficial theory in regard to commerce, accompanied by a real hatred but a feigned regard to its interests, and a ruinous perseverance in efforts to render it an instrument of coercion and war.

But it is not conceivable that the obliquity of any administration could, in so short a period, have so nearly consummated the work of national ruin, unless favoured by defects in the constitution.

To enumerate all the improvements of which that instrument is susceptible, and to propose such amendments as might render it in all respects perfect, would be a task which this convention has not thought proper to assume. They have confined their attention to such as experience has demonstrated to be essential, and even among these, some are considered entitled to a more serious attention than others. . . .

THEREFORE RESOLVED, That it be and hereby is recommended to the legislatures of the several states represented in this Convention, to adopt all such measures as may be necessary effectually to protect the citizens of said states from the operation and effects of all acts which have been or may be passed by the Congress of the United States, which shall contain provisions, subjecting the militia or other citizens to forcible drafts, conscriptions, or impressments, not authorised by the constitution of the United States.

*Resolved*, That it be and hereby is recommended to the said Legislatures, to authorize an immediate and earnest application to be made to the government of the United States, requesting their consent to some arrangement, whereby the said states may, separately or in concert, be empowered to assume upon themselves the defence of their territory against the enemy; and a reasonable portion of the taxes, collected within said States, may be paid into the respective treasuries thereof. . . .

*Resolved*, That the following amendments of the constitution of the United States be recommended to the states. . . .

*First.* Representatives and direct taxes shall be apportioned among the several states which may be included within this Union, according to their respective numbers of free persons, including those bound to serve for a term of years, and excluding Indians not taxed, and all other persons.

*Second.* No new state shall be admitted into the Union by Congress, in virtue of the power granted by the constitution, without the concurrence of two thirds of both houses.

*Third.* Congress shall not have power to lay any embargo on the ships or vessels of the citizens of the United States, in the ports or harbours thereof, for more than sixty days.

*Fourth.* Congress shall not have power, without the concurrence of two thirds of both houses, to interdict the commercial intercourse between the United States and any foreign nation, or the dependencies thereof.

*Fifth.* Congress shall not make or declare war, or authorize acts of hostility against any foreign nation, without the concurrence of two thirds of both houses, except such acts of hostility be in defence of the territories of the United States when actually invaded.

*Sixth.* No person who shall hereafter be naturalized, shall be eligible as a member of the senate or house of representatives of the United States, nor capable of holding any civil office under the authority of the United States.

*Seventh.* The same person shall not be elected president of the United States a second time; nor shall the president be elected from the same state two terms in succession.

*Resolved*, That if the application of these states to the government of the United States, recommended in a foregoing resolution, should be unsuccessful and peace should not be concluded, and the defence of these states should be neglected, as it has since the commencement of the war, it will, in the opinion of this convention, be expedient for the legislatures of the several states to appoint delegates to another convention, to meet at Boston . . . with such powers and instructions as the exigency of a crisis so momentous may require.

## 83 I Humbled the Insurgents at a Trifling Expense (1815)

The first quarter-century of the United States was beset by competition and conflict between different political persuasions, feelings of sectional chauvinism, and tension amidst the diverse social and economic elements in the population. Despite almost continual threats of insurrection, secession, and resistance to the national law, America's political leaders readily displayed a spirit of forgiveness against dissidents and rebels once the immediate crises passed. In 1815, former president John Adams, reflecting on his decisions in office, finally spelled out his reasoning behind the pardon of John Fries: national integration was served more by charity than by ruthlessness.

### ☆ 83 Letter from John Adams to James Lloyd (March 31, 1815)

Reprinted in C. F. Adams, ed., *The Works of John Adams* (New York: AMS Press, 1971), 10:152-55.

\*　　　\*　　　\*

I had suppressed an insurrection in Pennsylvania, and effectually humbled and punished the insurgents; not by assembling an army of militia from three or four States, and marching in all the pride, pomp, and circumstance of war, at an expense of millions, but silently, without noise, and at a trifling expense. I pardoned Fries . . . . What good, what example would have been exhibited to the nation by the execution of three or four obscure, miserable Germans, as ignorant of our language as they were of our laws, and the nature and definition of treason? Pitiful puppets danced upon the wires of jugglers behind the scene or under ground. Had the mountebanks been in the place of he puppets, mercy would have had a harder struggle to obtain absolution for them.

The verdict of a jury, and the judgement of the court, would, to be sure, have justified me in the opinion of the nation, and in the judgement of the world, if I had signed the warrant for their execution; but neither, nor both, could have satisfied my conscience, nor tranquillized my feelings. If I had en-

tertained only a doubt of their guilt, notwithstanding verdicts and judgements, it was my duty to pardon them. But my determination did not rest upon so wavering a foundation as a doubt.

My judgement was clear, that their crime did not amount to treason. They had been guilty of a high-handed riot and rescue, attended with circumstances hot, rash, violent, and dangerous, but all these did not amount to treason. And I thought the officers of the law had been injudicious in indicting them for any crime higher than riot, aggravated by rescue. Here I rest my cause on this head, and proceed to another.

### CHAPTER 4

\*     \*     \*

# Consolidation and Schism

Suffrage, Citizenship,
and the Right of Secession
1821-1861

THE regulation of blacks and Native Americans, respectively, forms the main theme of this chapter. The period produced stringent state regulations of slaves as apprehension grew over the danger this population posed to the security of life, property, and the economic system of the South. The documents demonstrate the use of the criminal law to suppress abolitionist and insurrectionist sentiments. Close regulations also were imposed on free blacks and whites who might associate with and assist slaves in their search for revenge or freedom.

The materials relating to Native Americans run almost in counterpoint to those regarding blacks. While the tensions between blacks and whites found expression in the law through tight regulation of the interactions between these populations, the conflict between whites and Native Americans gave rise to the isolation, betrayal, and exile of the Native Americans from their homelands. This chapter documents the resettlement of the Five Civilized Tribes of the southeast in the Indian Territory of what is now Oklahoma. Even in this haven the Native Americans could not maintain long-term refuge, since the government withdrew its promised protection and left them without recourse to the law to safeguard their recognized interests. Martial force finally was utilized to compel their further withdrawal.

These are the bare facts reported by the documents. But there are more subtle messages as well. Although the law treated blacks and Native Americans quite differently, it regulated them for the same reason. These groups constituted identifiable populations whose allegiance to the ruling authority could not be assumed. Blacks were necessary to the economic survival of the South, and their continued presence was essential. The effort was directed instead toward criminalizing the education and organization of blacks, and prohibiting any kind of social intercourse which might kindle a spark of opposition or rebellion.

Native Americans, in contrast, were organized into coherent societies that concededly owed no allegiance to the federal government or to any state. Oppression of individual Native Americans by state law clearly could not operate within the tribal lands. As long as the federal government protected Native American sovereignty over the territory that they inhabited, these societies were immune from disintegration or control by the white society. The direction America's Native American policy took, therefore, was to banish the entire expendable suspect population whose social and political order could not be tolerated within the American Manifest Destiny.

Sprinkled among the documents are items that hint at the major arenas of political criminality in the next few decades. Despite the earlier American articulation of the right of revolution, the prevailing American view no longer justified recourse to political crime or rebellion, since government was considered subject to the will of the people and the ballot box was to be the tool for curbing oppression. This note strikes flat, however, when one observes that vast numbers of people were not only disenfranchised but also held in isolation and bondage. Blacks and Native Americans (not to mention women) were totally excluded from the electoral process, and the working class, likewise, largely was denied political and economic power.

It is difficult to see how, for those on the outside, major reforms could be expected through the conventional political process. Perceived injustice, therefore, was countered through various acts of criminality and violence. Correspondingly, government and its allies utilized the criminal and martial law to suppress and punish those who resisted their assigned roles and conditions.

The documents in this chapter also begin to chart the interaction between federal and state laws with regard to political crime. Electoral dominance throughout the period covered in this chapter gave prominence to Southern and western interests. For the most part the federal law supported the political interests of the Southern states, thereby facilitating the survival of slavery. The Native American-related documents also largely demonstrate a pattern of federal subversion of its treaty obligations in favor of the expanding western populations. Federal failure to prevent the incursions of white settlers into Native American territories placed the Native Americans under continuing duress, which culminated in the Trail of Tears.

Finally, as in earlier periods, the documents of this chapter foreshadow the major arenas of future political criminality: secession, labor, and women's suffrage.

## 84 Bowing before "the idol of universal suffrage" (1821)

In 1820, the census results showed a total United States population of 9,638,453. Slightly more than half of these Americans lived in the Northern states. The black population, of which nearly 90 percent were slaves, totaled 1,771,656. In most states the circle of political power was narrow, and the right of suffrage was guarded jealously. Slaves, women, and nonpropertied laborers were excluded totally from the political process. State electoral restrictions limited access to the federal ballot as well.

Yet, given the fact that the United States was a federation of democratic republics, any oppressive laws theoretically could be remedied through the political process. Also America's settled frontier reached to the Mississippi River, and the new states exported not only corn and tobacco but also liberal, democratic policies, including the abolition of the property qualification for suffrage. The following excerpt from an address by James Kent, president of the Court of Chancery and a leading American legal scholar, to the New York Constitutional Convention expressed the concerns of the more conservative easterners regarding the widening of the suffrage to include all white males.

### ☆84 Remarks of Chancellor Kent to the New York Constitutional Convention

Reprinted in H. Carter, W. Stone, and M. Gould, eds., *Reports of the Proceedings and Debates of the Convention of 1821* (New York: Da Capo Press, 1970), § 219.

Chancellor Kent.... [W]e are engaged in the bold and hazardous experiment of remodelling the constitution.... [W]e should pause in our career, and reflect well on the immensity of the innovation in contemplation....

The senate has hitherto been elected by the farmers of the state—by the free and independent lords of the soil, worth at least $250 in freehold estate, over and above all debts charged thereon. The governor has been chosen by the same electors, and we have hitherto elected citizens of elevated rank and character. Our assembly has been chosen by freeholders, possessing a freehold of the value of $50, or by persons renting a tenement of the yearly value of $5, and who have been rated and actually paid taxes to the state. By the report before us, we propose to annihilate, at one stroke, all those property distinctions and to bow before the idol of universal suffrage. That extreme democratic principle, when applied to the legislative and executive departments of the government, has been regarded with terror, by the wise men of every age, because

in every European republic, ancient and modern, in which it has been tried, it has terminated disastrously, and been productive of corruption, injustice, violence, and tyranny. And dare we flatter ourselves that we are a peculiar people, who can run the career of history, exempted from the passions which have disturbed and corrupted the rest of mankind? If we are like other races of men, with similar follies and vices, then I greatly fear that our posterity will have reason to deplore in sackcloth and ashes, the delusion of the day....

Now sir, I wish to preserve our senate as the representative of the landed interest.... I wish them to be always enabled to say that their freeholds cannot be taxed without their consent. The men of no property, together with the crowds of dependents connected with great manufacturing and commercial establishments, and the motley and undefinable population of crowded ports, may, perhaps, at some future day, under skilful management predominate in the assembly, and yet we should be perfectly safe if no laws could pass without the free consent of the owners of the soil. That security we at present enjoy; and it is that security which I wish to retain.

... The tendency of universal suffrage, is to jeopardize the rights of property, and the principles of liberty. There is a constant tendency in human society, and the history of every age proves it; there is a tendency in the poor to covet a share in the plunder of the rich; in the debtor to relax or avoid the obligation of contracts; in the majority to tyrannize over the minority, and trample down their rights; in the indolent and profligate, to cast the whole burthens of society upon the industrious and the virtuous; and *there is a tendency in ambitious and wicked men, to inflame these combustible materials*. It requires a vigilant government, and a firm administration of justice, to counteract that tendency. Thou shalt not covet; thou shalt not steal; are divine injunctions induced by this miserable depravity of our nature. Who can undertake to calculate with any precision, how many millions of people, this great state will contain in the course of this and the next century, and who can estimate the future extent and magnitude of our commercial ports? The disproportion between the men of property, and the men of no property, will be in every society in a ratio of its commerce, wealth, and population.

... We are fast becoming a great nation, with great commerce, manufactures, population, wealth, luxuries, and with the vices and miseries that they engender. One seventh of the population of the city of Paris at this day subsists on charity, and one third of the inhabitants of that city die in the hospitals; what would become of such a city with universal suffrage? France has upwards of four, and England upwards of five millions of manufacturing and commercial labourers without property. Could these Kingdoms sustain the weight of universal suffrage? The radicals in England, with the force of that mighty engine, would at once sweep away the property, the laws, and the liberties of that island like a deluge.

The growth of the city of New-York is enough to startle and awaken those who are pursuing the IGNIS FATUUS of universal suffrage. . . .

## 85 The Crime of Being Black (1823)

An 1820 South Carolina statute required that free blacks aboard vessels entering the harbors of the state be imprisoned on shore for the duration of their ship's stay in port. This assertion of state power to exclude "undesirable" aliens from its territory on racial or other grounds was tested in 1823 before Justice William Johnson, a member of the United States Supreme Court riding circuit. Although the decision primarily rested on the supremacy of the Constitution's commerce clause, it contained other themes. In asserting federal protection for a foreign nation's black seamen, *Elkison* began the process of resorting to federal, as well as international, laws and obligations as the basis for erecting civil and human rights barriers against enforcement of criminal and quasi-criminal laws.

☆85 *Elkison v. Deliesseline*

8 F. Cas. 493 (C.C.D.S.C. 1823) (No. 4,366).

JOHNSON, CIRCUIT JUSTICE.

\* \* \*

. . . On the unconstitutionality of the law under which this man is confined, it is not too much to say, that it will not bear argument. . . . Neither of the gentlemen has attempted to prove that the power therein assumed by the state can be exercised without clashing with the general powers of the United States to regulate commerce; but they have both strenuously contended, that ex necessitate it was a power which the state must and would exercise, and, indeed, Mr. Holmes concluded his argument with the declaration, that, if a dissolution of the Union must be the alternative, he was ready to meet it. Nor did the argument of Col. Hunt deviate at all from the same course. Giving it in the language of his own summary, it was this: South Carolina was a sovereign state when she adopted the constitution; a sovereign state cannot surrender a right of vital importance; South Carolina, therefore, either did not surrender this right, or still possesses the power to resume it, and whether it is necessary, or when it is necessary, to resume it, she is herself the sovereign judge. But it was not necessary to give this candid exposé of the grounds which this law assumes; for it

is a subject of positive proof, that it is altogether irreconcilable with the powers of the general government; that it necessarily compromits the public peace, and tends to embroil us with, if not separate us from, our sister states; in short, that it leads to a dissolution of the Union, and implies a direct attack upon the sovereignty of the United States.

Let it be observed that the law is, "if any vessel (not even the vessels of the United States excepted) shall come into any port or harbor of this state," etc., bringing in free colored persons, such persons are to become "absolute slaves," and that, without even a form of trial, as I understand the act, they are to be sold. By the next clause the sheriff is vested with absolute power, and expressly enjoined to carry the law into effect, and is to receive the one half of the proceeds of the sale. The object of this law, and it has been so acknowledged in argument, is to prohibit ships coming into this port employing colored seamen, whether citizens or subjects of their own government or not. But if this state can prohibit Great Britain from employing her colored subjects (and she has them of all colors on the globe), or if at liberty to prohibit the employment of her subjects of the African race, why not prohibit her from using those of Irish or of Scottish nativity? If the color of his skin is to preclude the Lascar or the Sierra Leone seaman, why not the color of his eye or his hair exclude from our ports the inhabitants of her other territories? In fact it amounts to the assertion of the power to exclude the seamen of the territories of Great Britain, or any other nation, altogether. With regard to various friendly nations it amounts to an actual exclusion in its present form. . . . [A]nd even the state of Massachusetts might lately, and may perhaps now, expedite to this port a vessel with her officers black, and her crew composed of Nantucket Indians, known to be among the best seamen in our service. These might all become slaves under this act. If this law were enforced upon such vessels, retaliation would follow; and the commerce of this city, feeble and sickly, comparatively, as it already is, might be fatally injured. . . .

Apply the law to the particular case before us, and the incongruity will be glaring. [The] offense, it will be observed, for which this individual is supposed to forfeit his freedom, is that of coming into this port in the ship, Homer, in the capacity of a seaman. . . . The seaman's crime is complete, and the forfeiture incurred by the single act of coming into port; and this even though driven into port by stress of weather, or forced by a power which he cannot control into a port for which he did not ship himself; the law contains no exception to meet such contingencies. The seaman's offense, therefore, is coming into the state in a ship or vessel; that of the captain consists in bringing him in, and not taking him out of the state, and paying all expenses. Now, according to the laws and treaties of the United States, it was both lawful for this seaman to come into this port, in this vessel, and for the captain to bring him in the capacity of a seaman; and yet these are the very acts for which the state law imposes these heavy penalties. Is there no clashing in this? It is in effect a repeal of the laws of the United States, pro tanto, converting a right into a crime.

And here it is proper to notice that part of the argument against the motion, in which it was insisted on that this law was passed by the state in exercise of a concurrent right. "Concurrent" does not mean "paramount," and yet, in order to divest a right conferred by the general government, it is very clear that the state right must be more than concurrent. But the right of the general government to regulate commerce with the sister states and foreign nations is a paramount and exclusive right; and this conclusion we arrive at, whether we examine it with reference to the words of the constitution, or the nature of the grant. . . .

But the case does not rest here. In order to sustain this law, the state must also possess a power paramount to the treaty-making power of the United States, expressly declared to be a part of the supreme legislative power of the land; for the seizure of this man, on board a British ship, is an express violation of the commercial convention with Great Britain of 1815. . . . Such a law as this could not be passed even by the general government, without furnishing a just cause of war.

But to all this the plea of necessity is urged; and of the existence of that necessity we are told the state alone is the judge. Where is this to land us? Is it not asserting the right in each state to throw off the federal constitution at its will and pleasure? If it can be done as to any particular article it may be done as to all; and, like the old confederation, the Union becomes a mere rope of sand. But I deny that the state surrendered a single power necessary to its security, against this species of property. What is to prevent their being confined to their ships, if it is dangerous for them to go abroad? This power may be lawfully exercised. To land their cargoes, take in others, and depart, is all that is necessary to ordinary commerce, and is all that is properly stipulated for in the convention of 1815, so far as relates to seamen. If our fears extend also to the British merchant, the supercargo, or master, being persons of color, I acknowledge that, as to them, the treaty precludes us from abridging their rights to free ingress and egress, and occupying houses and warehouses for the purposes of commerce. As to them, this law is an express infraction of the treaty. No such law can be passed consistently with the treaty, and unless sanctioned by diplomatic arrangement, the

passing of such a law is tantamount to a declaration of war. . . .

*            *            *

Upon the whole, I am decidedly of the opinion that the third section of the state act now under consideration is unconstitutional and void, and that every arrest made under it subjects the parties making it to an action of trespass.

*            *            *

## 86 "the Indians . . . have retained their savage habits" (1829)

Georgia ultimately compromised its early claims to sovereignty and title over all lands westward to the Mississippi by its cession to the United States of whatever interest it had in the land west of its present borders. Georgia's 1802 cession, nevertheless, included the requirement that the United States "should, at their own expense, extinguish, for the use of Georgia, as early as the same can be peaceably obtained, on reasonable terms, the Indian title to lands within the state of Georgia." The motive behind Georgia's insistence on this provision was the desire for the good farmland which, under the Treaty of Hopewell and subsequent treaties, belonged to the Cherokee and Creek nations.

The United States had taken some measures to remove the Native Americans from Georgia. They did not want to leave, however, and the government could do little to make them move—short of force. Yet settlers continually were intruding upon their lands and establishing themselves in violation of the treaties. The pressures on the Cherokees were not lessened with the discovery of gold in their territory in 1828.

That year, the Georgia legislature passed a series of laws which carved up the Native American-occupied territory and established a system of apportioning land. In addition, the jurisdiction of the laws of the state was extended to include all Native American territory. The administration of President John Quincy Adams intervened on behalf of the Cherokees, much to the anger of the Georgians. The political climate soon changed, however, when Andrew Jackson, who had made a considerable portion of his reputation as a fighter against the Creeks, became President in 1829. In his First Annual Message to Congress, he addressed the need to remove the Native Americans to regions west of the Mississippi. Five months later, Congress passed the Indian Removal Act, which authorized the president to negotiate with the Native Americans for a trade of their lands for lands west of the Mississippi and appropriated $500,000 for that purpose.

Thus began the process whereby an entire people was forced, through operation of law, to choose between self-perpetuation and self-government and their dominion over their homeland. Describing the policies behind the Removal Act, the Comte de Tocqueville commented in 1831: "[The Native Americans] were isolated in their own country, and their race only constituted a little colony of troublesome strangers in the midst of a numerous and dominant people." Their status *as Native Americans* become the grounds for their exile.

## ☆ 86 First Annual Message from President Jackson to Congress: Indian Removal

Reprinted in J. Richardson, ed., *A Compilation of the Messages and Papers of the Presidents* (New York: Bureau of National Literature, 1897), 2:456-59.

*         *         *

The condition and ulterior destiny of the Indian tribes within the limits of some of our States have become objects of much interest and importance. It has long been the policy of Government to introduce among them the arts of civilization, in the hope of gradually reclaiming them from a wandering life. This policy has, however, been coupled with another wholly incompatible with its success. Professing a desire to civilize and settle them, we have at the same time lost no opportunity to purchase their lands and thrust them farther into the wilderness. By this means they have not only been kept in a wandering state, but been led to look upon us as unjust and indifferent to their fate. Thus, though lavish in its expenditures upon the subject, Government has constantly defeated its own policy, and the Indians in general, receding farther and farther to the west, have retained their savage habits. A portion, however, of the Southern tribes having mingled much with the whites and made some progress in the arts of civilized life, have lately attempted to erect an independent government within the limits of Georgia and Alabama. These States, claiming to be the only sovereigns within their territories, extended their laws over the Indians, which induced the latter to call upon the United States for protection.

Under these circumstances the question presented was whether the General Government had a right to sustain those people in their pretensions. The Constitution declares that "no new State shall be formed or erected within the jurisdiction of any other State" without the consent of its legislature. If the General Government is not permitted to tolerate the erection of a confederate State within the territory of one of the members of this Union against her consent, much less could it allow a foreign and independent government to establish itself there. Georgia became a member of the Confederacy which eventuated in

our Federal Union as a sovereign State, always asserting her claim to certain limits, which, having been originally defined in her colonial charter and subsequently recognized in the treaty of peace, she has ever since continued to enjoy, except as they have been circumscribed by her own voluntary transfer of a portion of her territory to the United States in the articles of cession of 1802. Alabama was admitted into the Union on the same footing with the original States, with boundaries which were prescribed by Congress. There is no constitutional, conventional, or legal provision which allows them less power over the Indians within their borders than is possessed by Maine or New York. Would the people of Maine permit the Penobscot tribe to erect an independent government within their State? And unless they did would it not be the duty of the General Government to support them in resisting such a measure? Would the people of New York permit each remnant of the Six Nations within her borders to declare itself an independent people under the protection of the United States? Could the Indians establish a separate republic on each of their reservations in Ohio? And if they were so disposed would it be the duty of this Government to protect them in the attempt? If the principle involved in the obvious answer to these questions be abandoned, it will follow that the objects of this Government are reversed, and that it has become a part of its duty to aid in destroying the States which it was established to protect.

Actuated by this view of the subject, I informed the Indians inhabiting parts of Georgia and Alabama that their attempt to establish an independent government would not be countenanced by the Executive of the United States, and advised them to emigrate beyond the Mississippi or submit to the laws of those States.

*         *         *

... Surrounded by the whites with their arts of civilization, which by destroying the resources of the savage doom him to weakness and decay, the fate of the Mohegan, the Narragansett, and the Delaware is fast overtaking the Choctaw, the Cherokee, and the Creek. That this fate surely awaits them if they remain within the limits of the States does not admit of a doubt. Humanity and national honor demand that every effort should be made to avert so great a calamity....

As a means of effecting this end I suggest for your consideration the propriety of setting apart an ample district west of the Mississippi, and without the limit of any State or Territory now formed, to be guaranteed to the Indian tribes as long as they shall occupy it, each tribe having a distinct control over the portion designated for its use. There they may be secured in the enjoyment of governments of their own choice, subject to no other control from the United States than such as may be necessary to preserve peace on the frontier and between the several tribes. There the benevolent may endeavor to teach them the arts of civilization, and, by promoting union and harmony among them, to raise up an interesting commonwealth, destined to perpetuate the race and to attest the humanity and justice of this Government.

This emigration should be voluntary, for it would be as cruel as unjust to compel the aborigines to abandon the graves of their fathers and seek a home in a distant land. But they should be distinctly informed that if they remain within the limits of the States they must be subject to their laws. In return for their obedience as individuals they will without doubt be protected in the enjoyment of those possessions which they have improved by their industry. But it seems to me visionary to suppose that in this state of things claims can be allowed on tracts of country on which they have neither dwelt nor made improvements, merely because they have seen them from the mountain or passed them in the chase. Submitting to the laws of the States, and receiving, like other citizens, protection in their persons and property, they will ere long become merged in the mass of our population.

\*       \*       \*

## 87  School-Houses as Unlawful Assembly (1831)

A growing preoccupation in the Southern states with the management and control of their slave populations began to surface at the end of the first quarter of the nineteenth century. Because of the Southern aristocracy's concern for the protection of its individual rights, the Jeffersonian theories of the primacy of state sovereignty became the rallying point for its effort to insulate the slave system against external influences.

After the plot of Denmark Vesey, a free black, in South Carolina in 1822, state "Slave Codes" became more and more stringent for free blacks and slaves alike. Whites also were regulated more strictly in their relations with blacks. By isolating its members in ignorance, the state sought to neutralize this politically unadhering population.

The Virginia law was passed in April 1831. In August of that year, Nat Turner's rebellion erupted in Southampton County, Virginia.

☆ 87  An Act Prohibiting Education of Free Negroes and Mulattoes [Virginia]

1831 Va. Acts 107.

\*       \*       \*

4. Be it further enacted, That all meetings of free negroes or mulattoes, at any school-house, church, meeting-house or other place for teaching them reading or writing, either in the day or night, under whatsoever pretext, shall be deemed and considered as an unlawful assembly; and any justice of the county or corporation, wherein such assemblage shall be, either from his own knowledge, or on the information of others, of such unlawful assemblage or meeting, shall issue his warrant, directed to any sworn officer or officers, authorizing him or them, to enter the house or houses where such unlawful assemblage or meting may be, for the purpose of apprehending or dispersing such free negroes or mulattoes, and to inflict corporal punishment on the offender or offenders, at the discretion of any justice of the peace, not exceeding twenty lashes.

5. Be it further enacted, That if any white person or persons assemble with free negroes or mulattoes, at any school-house, church, meeting-house, or other place for the purpose of instructing such free negroes or mulattoes to read or write, such person or persons shall, on conviction thereof, be fined in a sum not exceeding fifty dollars, and moreover may be imprisoned at the discretion of a jury, not exceeding two months.

6. Be it further enacted, That if any white person, for pay or compensation, shall assemble with any slaves for the purpose of teaching, and shall teach any slave to read or write, such person, or any white person or persons contracting with such teacher so to act, who shall offend as aforesaid, shall, for each offence, be fined at the discretion of a jury, in a sum not less than ten, nor exceeding one hundred dollars, to be recovered on an information or indictment.

## 88  The Motives of the "late insurrection" (1831)

Violence by masters against slaves was a common occurrence in America. Slave revolts and reprisals were relatively infrequent and were usually harshly suppressed. In 1712 when some blacks and Native Americans planned to revolt in New York City and attacked their masters, the governor sent out troops to end the uprising. After trial, eighteen slaves were put to death, some by hanging and others by torture and fire.

A century later more than 150 whites and blacks were killed during a Virginia slave rebellion and subsequent manhunt. Twenty rebels, including leader Nat Turner, a black preacher, were executed after trial.

Thomas Gray claimed to have taken Nat Turner's confession prior to his trial and conviction. Turner, according to Gray, made no attempt to exculpate himself but frankly acknowledged his full participation in the uprising. This observation was consistent with Turner's views on the rightness, or perhaps righteousness, of his course. In answer to the question, "Do you find yourself mistaken now?" he responded without hesitation, "Was not Christ crucified?" Despite the bloodshed of innocents during the insurrection, he remained steadfast in his belief that his cause and actions were morally justified.

## ☆ 88  Thomas Gray's Introduction and Nat Turner's Confession

Reprinted in Nat Turner, *The Confession, Trial, and Execution of Nat Turner, the Negro Insurrectionist* (New York: AMS Press, 1975), 1-15.

TO THE PUBLIC

The late insurrection in Southampton has greatly excited the public mind, and led to a thousand idle, exaggerated, and mischievous reports. It is the first instance in our history of an open rebellion of the slaves, and attended with such atrocious circumstances of cruelty and destruction, as could not fail to leave a deep impression, not only upon the minds of the community where this fearful tragedy was wrought, but throughout every portion of our country, in which this population is to be found. Public curiosity has been on the stretch to understand the origin and progress of this dreadful conspiracy, and the motives which influence its diabolical actors. The insurgent slaves had all been destroyed, or apprehended, tried, and executed (with the exception of the leader), without revealing anything at all satisfactory as to the motives which governed them, or the means by which they expected to accomplish their object. Every thing connected with the sad affair was wrapt in mystery, until Nat Turner, the leader of this ferocious band, whose name has resounded throughout our widely extended empire, was captured. This "great Bandit" was taken by a single individual, in a cave near the residence of his late owner, on Sunday, the thirtieth of October, without attempting to make the slightest resistance, and on the following day safely lodged in the jail of the County. His captor was Benjamin Phipps, armed with a shotgun well charged. Nat's only weapon was a small light sword which he immediately surrendered, and begged that his life might be spared. Since his confinement, by permission of the Jailor, I have had ready access to him, and finding that he was willing to make a full and free confession of the origin, progress, and consummation of the insurrectory movements of the slaves of which he was the contriver and head, I determined for the gratification of public curiosity to commit his statements to writing, and publish them, with little or no variation, from his own words. That this is a faithful record of

his confessions, the annexed certificate of the County Court of Southampton, will attest. They certainly bear one stamp of truth and sincerity. He makes no attempt (as all the other insurgents who were examined did), to exculpate himself, but frankly acknowledges his full participation in all the guilt of the transaction. He was not only the contriver of the conspiracy, but gave the first blow towards its execution. . . .

Believing the following narrative, by removing doubts and conjectures from the public mind which otherwise must have remained, would give general satisfaction, it is respectfully submitted to the public by their ob't serv't,

T. R. GRAY

CONFESSION

Sir, You have asked to me to give a history of the motives which induced me to undertake the late insurrection, as you call it. To do so I must go back to the days of my infancy, and even before I was born. . . . In my childhood a circumstance occurred which made an indelible impression on my mind, and laid the groundwork of that enthusiasm which has terminated so fatally to many, both white and black, and for which I am about to atone at the gallows. . . . Being at play with other children, when three or four years old, I was telling them something, which my mother overhearing, said it had happened before I was born. I stuck to my story, however, and related some things which went, in her opinion, to confirm it. Others being called on were greatly astonished, knowing that these things had happened, and caused them to say in my hearing, I surely would be a prophet, as the Lord had shewn me things that had happened before my birth. And my father and mother strengthened me in this my first impression, saying in my presence, I was intended for some great purpose, which they had always thought from certain marks on my head and breast. . . . My grandmother, . . . my master, . . . and other religious persons . . . remarked I had too much sense to be raised, and if I was, I would never be of any service to any one as a slave. To a mind like mine, restless, inquisitive, and observant of everything that was passing, . . . there was nothing I saw or heard of to which my attention was not directed. . . . I have no recollection whatever of learning the alphabet; but to the astonishment of the family, one day, when a book was shewn to me to keep me from crying, I began spelling the names of different objects—this was a source of wonder to all in the neighborhood, particularly the blacks—and this learning was constantly improved at all opportunities. . . . I was not addicted to stealing in my youth, nor have ever been. Yet such was the confidence of the negroes in the neighborhood, even at this early period of my life, in my superior judgment, that they would often carry me with them when they were going on any roguery, to plan for them.

*     *     *

QUESTION: Do you not find yourself mistaken now?

ANSWER: Was not Christ crucified? And by signs in the heavens that it would make known to me when I should commence the great work—and until the first sign appeared, I should conceal if from the knowledge of men. And on the appearance of the sign (the eclipse of the sun last February), I should arise and prepare myself, and slay my enemies with their own weapons. And immediately on the sign appearing in the heavens, the seal was removed from my lips, and I communicated the great work laid out for me to do, to four in whom I had the greatest confidence (Henry, Hark, Nelson, and Sam). It was intended by us to have begun the work of death on the 4th July last. Many were the plans formed and rejected by us, and it affected my mind to such a degree, that I fell sick; and the time passed without our coming to any determination how to commence. Still forming new schemes and rejecting them, when the sign appeared again, which determined me not to wait longer.

... On Saturday evening, the 20th of August, it was agreed between Henry, Hark, and myself to prepare a dinner the next day for the men we expected, and then to concert a plan, as we had not yet determined on any. Hark, on the following morning, brought a pig, and Henry brandy, and being joined by Sam, Nelson, Will, and Jack, they prepared in the woods a dinner, where, about three o'clock, I joined them.

Q. Why were you so backward in joining them?

A. The same reason that had caused me not mix with them for years before.

I saluted them on coming up and asked Will how came he there; he answered, his life was worth no more than others, and his liberty as dear to him. I asked him if he thought to obtain it? He said he would, or lose his life. This was enough to put him in full confidence. Jack, I knew, was only a tool in the hands of Hark; it was quickly agreed we should commence at home (Mr. J. Travis' [Turner's master]) on that night, and until we had armed and equipped ourselves and gathered sufficient force, neither age nor sex was to be spared (which was invariably adhered to). We remained at the feast, until about two hours in the night, when we went to the house and found Austin; they all went to the cider press and drank, except myself. On returning to the house, Hark went to the door with an axe for the purpose of breaking it open, as we knew we were strong enough to murder the family if they were awaked by the noise; but reflecting that it might create an alarm in the neighborhood, we determined to enter the house

secretly, and murder them whilst sleeping. Hark got a ladder and set it against the chimney, on which I ascended, and hoisting a window, entered and came downstairs, unbarred the door, and removed the guns from their places. It was then observed that I must spill the first blood. On which, armed with a hatchet and accompanied by Will, I entered my master's chamber; it being dark, I could not give a deathblow. The hatchet glanced from his head; he sprang from the bed and called his wife. It was his last word. Will laid him dead with a blow of his axe, and Mrs. Travis shared the same fate as she lay in bed. The murder of this family, five in number, was the work of a moment; not one of them awoke. There was a little infant sleeping in a cradle, that was forgotten, until we had left the house and gone some distance, when Henry and Will returned and killed it; we got here four guns that would shoot and several old muskets, with a pound or two of powder. We remained some time at the barn, where we paraded. I formed them in a line as soldiers, and after carrying them through all the manoeuvres I was master of, marched them off to Mr. Salathul Francis', about six hundred yards distant. Sam and Will went to the door and knocked. Mr. Francis asked who was there. Sam replied it was him, and he had a letter for him; on which he got up and came to the door. They immediately seized him, and dragging him out a little from the door, he was dispatched by repeated blows on the head. There was no other white person in the family. We started from there for Mrs. Reese's, maintaining the most perfect silence on our march, where finding the door unlocked, we entered, and murdered Mrs. Reese in her bed, while sleeping; her son awoke, but it was only to sleep the sleep of death. He had only time to say who is that, and was no more.

*     *     *

Our number amounted now to fifty or sixty, all mounted and armed with guns, axes, swords, and clubs....

*     *     *

## 89 "to annihilate the Cherokee as a political society" (1831)

From the beginning of the European colonization of America, the status of the Native American populations caused both philosophical and practical concern. In the early sixteenth century, serious questions arose regarding the capacity of these aboriginal people to be free, to govern themselves, and to own property. By 1539, Spanish theologian Francisco de Vitoria proclaimed the human rights of the native people; and in 1542, Spanish Law of the Indies decreed that Native Americans were free people not to be enslaved nor have their property taken except in fair trade. Other colonizers as well generally accepted these principles.

By their very existence, the English colonies established along the Atlantic seaboard encroached on Native American occupation and sovereignty. Nevertheless, resistance to Europeans, like King Philip's War in 1675, was largely ineffective. From an early date, the colonies sought to reduce tensions by establishing special areas for exclusive Native American use. In these enclaves, the Native American nations were to exist as "distinct, independent, political communities, retaining their original natural rights." In 1827, the Cherokees in northwestern Georgia declared themselves an independent nation and established a government. The Georgia legislature responded by claiming dominion over all Cherokee territory. The Cherokee Nation sued to enjoin the act of Georgia. In his technical decision that the Cherokee Nation was neither a state of the Union nor a foreign state entitled to sue, Chief Justice Marshall withheld the protection of the federal judiciary from the Cherokees, leaving the protection of their rights to the disposition of the executive branch.

☆ 89  *Cherokee Nation v. Georgia*

29 U.S. (5 Pet.) 1 (1831).

MARSHALL, C. J. This bill is brought by the Cherokee nation, praying an injuction to restrain the state of Georgia from the execution of certain laws of the state, which, as is alleged, go directly to annihilate the Cherokee as a political society, and to seize for the use of Georgia, the lands of the nation which have been assured to them by the United States, in solemn treaties repeatedly made and still in force.

If courts were permitted to indulge their sympathies, a case better calculated to excite them can scarcely be imagined. A people, once numerous, powerful, and truly independent, found by our ancestors in the quiet and uncontrolled possession of an ample domain, gradually sinking beneath our superior policy, our arts and our arms, have yielded their lands by successive treaties, each of which contains a solemn guarantee of the residue, until they retain no more of their formerly extensive territory than is deemed necessary to their comfortable subsistence. To preserve this remnant, the present application is made.

Before we can look into the merits of the case, a preliminary inquiry presents itself. Has this court jurisdiction of the cause? The third article of the constitution ... closes an enumeration of the cases to which it is extended, with "controversies between a state or citizens thereof, and foreign states, citizens or subjects." A subsequent clause of the same section gives the supreme court original jurisdiction, in all cases in which a state shall be a party. The party

defendant may then unquestionably be sued in this court. May the plaintiff sue in it? Is the Cherokee nation a foreign state, in the sense in which that term is used in the constitution?

... So much of the argument as was intended to prove the character of the Cherokees as a state, as a distinct political society, ... has in the opinion of a majority of the judges, been completely successful. They have been uniformly treated as a state, from the settlement of our country. The numerous treaties made with them by the United States, recognise them as a people capable of maintaining the relations of peace and war, of being responsible in their political character for any violation of their engagements, or for any aggression committed on the citizens of the United States, by any individual of their community. Laws have been enacted in the spirit of these treaties. The acts of our government plainly recognise the Cherokee nation as a state, and the courts are bound by those acts.

A question of much more difficulty remains. Do the Cherokees constitute a foreign state in the sense of the constitution? The counsel have shown conclusively, that they are not a state of the Union, and have insisted that, individually, they are aliens, not owing allegiance to the United States. An aggregate of aliens composing a state must, they say, be a foreign state; each individual being foreign, the whole must be foreign.

This argument is imposing, but we must examine it more closely, before we yield to it. The condition of the Indians in relation to the United States is, perhaps, unlike that of any other two people in existence.... The Indian territory is admitted to compose a part of the United States. In all our maps, geographical treaties, histories and laws, it is so considered. In all our intercourse with foreign nations, in our commercial regulations, in any attempt at intercourse between Indians and foreign nations, they are considered as within the jurisdictional limits of the United States, subject to many of those restraints which are imposed upon our own citizens. They acknowledge themselves, in their treaties, to be under the protection of the United States; they admit, that the United States shall have the sole and exclusive right of regulating the trade with them, and managing all their affairs as they think proper; and the Cherokees in particular were allowed by the treaty of Hopewell, which preceded the constitution, "to send a deputy of their choice, whenever they think fit, to congress." ...

... [I]t may well be doubted, whether those tribes which reside within the acknowledged boundaries of the United States can, with accuracy, be denominated foreign nations. They may, more correctly, perhaps, be denominated domestic dependent nations. They occupy a territory to which we assert a title independent of their will, which must take effect in point of possession, when their right of possession ceases. Meanwhile, they are in a state of pupilage; their relation to the United States resembles that of a ward to his guardian. They look to our government for protection: rely upon its kindness and its power; appeal to it for relief to their wants; and address the president as their great father. They and their country are considered by foreign nations, as well as by ourselves, as being so completely under the sovereignty and dominion of the United States, that any attempt to acquire their lands, or to form a political connection with them would be considered by all as an invasion of our territory and an act of hostility. These considerations go far to support the opinion, that the framers of our constitution had not the Indian tribes in view, when they opened the courts of the Union to controversies between a state or the citizens thereof and foreign states.

\*          \*          \*

[T]he eighth section of the third article ... empowers congress to "regulate commerce with foreign nations, and among the several states, and with the Indian tribes." In this clause, they are as clearly contradistinguished, by a name appropriate to themselves, from foreign nations, as from the several states composing the Union. They are designated by a distinct appellation; and as this appellation can be applied to neither of the others, neither can the application distinguishing either of the others be, in fair construction, applied to them. The objects to which the power of regulating commerce might be directed, are divided into three distinct classes — foreign nations, the several states, and Indian tribes. When forming this article, the convention considered them as entirely distinct. We cannot assume that the distinction was lost, in framing a subsequent article, unless there be something in its language to authorize the assumption.

\*          \*          \*

We perceive plainly, that the constitution, in this article, does not comprehend Indian tribes in the general term "foreign nations;" not, we presume, because a tribe may not be a nation, but because it is not foreign to the United States. When, afterwards, the term "foreign state" is introduced, we cannot impute to the convention, the intention to desert its former meaning, and to comprehend Indian tribes within it, unless the context force that construction on us. We find nothing in the context, and nothing in the subject of the article, which leads to it.

The court has bestowed its best attention on this question, and, after mature deliberation, the majority is of opinion, that an Indian tribe or nation within the United States is not a foreign state, in the sense of the constitution, and cannot maintain an action in the courts of the United States.

A serious additional objection exists to the juris-

diction of the court. Is the matter of the bill the proper subject for judicial inquiry and decision? It seeks to restrain a state from the forcible exercise of legislative power over a neighboring people, asserting their independence; their right to which the state denies. On several of the matters alleged in the bill, for example, on the laws making it criminal to exercise the usual powers of self-government in their own country, by the Cherokee nation, this court cannot interpose; at least, in the form in which those matters are presented.

That part of the bill which respects the land occupied by the Indians, and prays the aid of the court to protect their possession, may be more doubtful. The mere question of right might, perhaps, be decided by this court, in a proper case, with proper parties. But the court is asked to do more than decide on the title. The bill requires us to control the legislature of Georgia, and to restrain the exertion of its physical force. The propriety of such an interposition by the court may be well questioned; it savors too much of the exercise of political power, to be within the proper province of the judicial department. But the opinion on the point respecting parties makes it unnecessary to decide this question.

If it be true, that the Cherokee nation have rights, this is not the tribunal in which those rights are to be asserted. If it be true, that wrongs have been inflicted, and that still greater are to be apprehended, this is not the tribunal which can redress the past or prevent the future. The motion for an injunction is denied.

## 90 "I will not retreat a single inch" (1831)

A man of limited formal education, yet skillful in the startling and militant use of language and the press, William Lloyd Garrison began publishing the abolitionist *Liberator* in Boston in 1831. Garrison believed moral persuasion rather than force or the ballot was the most effective means in the campaign for the immediate and complete abolition of slavery. Though its circulation never exceeded two thousand, *The Liberator* became famous nationwide for its inflammatory language and uncompromising call for abolition.

Garrison's bitter attacks on the moderate antislavery movement earned him enemies in both the North and the South. His zeal led him to advocate Northern secession from the Union because the Constitution permitted slavery, and at a public meeting in Framingham, Massachusetts on July 4, 1854, he burned the Constitution. *The Liberator* and other incendiary publications sparked Southern reaction mostly through the passage of laws prohibiting the advocation of abolition, similar to those laws of an earlier generation which punished the expression of sentiments regarding the illegitimacy of the ruling authorities. After Nat Turner's insurrection, an attempt was made to have Garrison extradited as a criminal from his home state of Massachusetts, and Georgia offered five thousand dollars for his apprehension.

## ☆90 The Liberator

Reprinted in W. Garrison and F. Garrison, *William Lloyd Garrison, 1805-1879: The Story of His Life Told by His Children* (New York: Arno Press, 1969), 1:224-26.

TO THE PUBLIC.

> \*      \*      \*

During my recent tour for the purpose of exciting the minds of the people by a series of discourses on the subject of slavery, every place that I visited gave fresh evidence of the fact, that a greater revolution in public sentiment was to be effected in the free states—*and particularly in New England*—than at the south. I found contempt more bitter, opposition more active, detraction more relentless, prejudice more stubborn, and apathy more frozen, than among slave owners themselves. Of course, there were individual exceptions to the contrary. This state of things afflicted, but did not dishearten me. I determined, at every hazard, to lift up the standard of emancipation in the eyes of the nation, *within sight of Bunker Hill and in the birth place of liberty.* That standard is now unfurled; and long may it float, unhurt by the spoliations of time or the missiles of a desperate foe—yea, till every chain be broken, and every bondman set free! Let Southern oppressors tremble—let their secret abettors tremble—let their Northern apologists tremble—let all the enemies of the persecuted blacks tremble.

... I shall not array myself as the political partisan of any man. In defending the great cause of human rights, I wish to derive the assistance of all religions and of all parties.

Assenting to the "self evident truth" maintained in the American Declaration of Independence, "that all men are created equal, and endowed by their Creator with certain inalienable rights—among which are life, liberty and the pursuit of happiness," I shall strenuously contend for the immediate enfranchisement of our slave population. In Park-Street Church, on the Fourth of July, 1829, in an address on slavery, I unreflectingly assented to the popular but pernicious doctrine of *gradual* abolition. I seize this opportunity to make a full and unequivocal recantation, and thus publicly to ask pardon of my God, of my country, and of my brethren the poor slaves, for having uttered a sentiment so full of timidity, injustice and absurdity....

I am aware, that many object to the severity of my language; but is there not cause for severity? I *will be* as harsh as truth, and as uncompromising as justice. On this subject, I do not wish to think, or speak, or write, with moderation. No! No! Tell a man whose house is on fire, to give a moderate alarm; tell him to moderately rescue his wife from the hands of the ravisher; tell the mother to gradually extricate her babe from the fire into which it has fallen;—but urge me not to use moderation in a cause like the present. I am in earnest—I will not equivocate—I will not excuse—I will not retreat a single inch—AND I WILL BE HEARD. The apathy of the people is enough to make every statue leap from its pedestal, and to hasten the resurrection of the dead.

It is pretended, that I am retarding the cause of emancipation by the coarseness of my invective, and the precipitancy of my measures. *The charge is not true.* On this question my influence,—humble as it is,—is felt at this moment to a considerable extent, and shall be felt in coming years—not perniciously, but beneficially—not as a curse, but as a blessing; and posterity will bear testimony that I was right. I desire to thank God, that he enables me to disregard "the fear of man which bringeth a snare," and to speak his truth in its simplicity and power....

WILLIAM LLOYD GARRISON

# 91 Independent Political Communities (1832)

The Georgia law extending state jurisdiction over Native American country also included a provision exacting a loyalty oath to the state of Georgia from any white person "residing within the limits of the Cherokee nation." For failure to take this oath, Samuel A. Worcester, a missionary from Vermont holding a commission from the United States to proselytize among the Native Americans, was sentenced to four years at hard labor—the maximum penalty under the law.

At issue was the constitutionality of Georgia's enforcement of its law within the territory occupied by Cherokees in the state—sovereignty over the inhabitants of that land. The court rejected all of Georgia's arguments and recognized the Cherokees to be a distinct, sovereign, and self-governing community with the rights to possess a definable tract of land over which they had dominion and authority, except to the extent that they voluntarily ceded it away. The laws of Georgia were ineffective therein, and the citizens of Georgia could not enter the territory without the assent of the Cherokee Nation. The decision was the high-water mark of the legal recognition accorded to the political independence of the Native American nations. There was no language of "pupilage" or "tutelage" as there was in the court's decision in *Cherokee Nation* the term before.

But this legal protection was available only insofar as assaults upon Native American rights were by way of state authority. Native American relations with the United States were not scrutinized in this case, and Justice McLean's concurring opinion, while supportive of the existing rights of the Cherokee Nation, contemplated them as being predicated more upon policy choices of the United States rather than matters of natural right. But these opinions deserve careful reading because they touch upon matters that are at the root of understanding political criminality: the coherence of a people, the exercise of territorial dominion, and the power to demand allegiance. The Cherokees as a people were considered politically independent of Georgia (and the United States), since they were self-governing. Allegiance was not owed by the Cherokee to the United States, and, as Justice McLean pointed out, "We have recognized in them the right to make war. No one has ever supposed that the Indians could commit treason against the United States ... we have inflicted punishment on them as a nation, and not on individual offenders among them as traitors." Attention also should be directed to his assertion that "the abstract right of every section of the human race to a reasonable portion of the soil, by which to acquire the means of subsistence, cannot be controverted."

☆ 91  *Worcester v. Georgia*

31 U.S. (6 Pet.) 515 (1832).

Mr. Chief Justice MARSHALL delivered the opinion of the Court. The extra-territorial power of every legislature being limited in its action to its own citizens or subjects, the very passage of this act is an assertion of jurisdiction over the Cherokee nation, and of the rights and powers consequent on jurisdiction.

The first step, then, in the inquiry, which the Constitution and laws impose on this Court, is an examination of the rightfulness of this claim.

America, separated from Europe by a wide ocean, was inhabited by a distinct people, divided into separate nations, independent of each other and of the rest of the world, having institutions of their own, and governing themselves by their own laws. It is difficult to comprehend the proposition, that the inhabitants of either quarter of the globe could have rightful original claims of dominion over the inhabitants of the other, or over the lands they occupied; or that the discovery of either by the other should give the discoverer rights in the country discovered, which annulled the pre-existing right of its ancient possessors.

\*      \*      \*

But power, war, conquest, give rights, which, after possession, are conceded by the world; and

which can never be controverted by those on whom they descend. ...

The great maritime powers of Europe discovered and visited different parts of this continent at nearly the same time. The object was too immense for any one of them to grasp the whole; and the claimants were too powerful to submit to the exclusive or unreasonable pretensions of any single potentate. To avoid bloody conflicts, which might terminate disastrously to all, it was necessary for the nations of Europe to establish some principle which all would acknowledge, and which should decide their respective rights as between themselves. This principle, suggested by the actual state of things, was, "that discovery gave title to the government by whose subjects or by whose authority it was made, against all other European governments, which title might be consummated by possession."

This principle, acknowledged by all Europeans, because it was the interest of all to acknowledge it, gave to the nation making the discovery, as its inevitable consequence, the sole right of acquiring the soil and of making settlements on it. It was an exclusive principle which shut out the right of competition among those who had agreed to it; not one which could annul the previous rights of those who had not agreed to it. It regulated the right given by discovery among the European discoverers; but could not affect the rights of those already in possession, either as aboriginal occupants, or as occupants by virtue of a discovery made before the memory of man. It gave the exclusive right to purchase, but did not found that right on a denial of the right of the possessor to sell.

The relation between the Europeans and the natives was determined in each case by the particular government which asserted and could maintain this pre-emptive privilege in the particular place. The United States succeeded to all the claims of Great Britain, both territorial and political; but no attempt, so far as is known, has been made to enlarge them. ...

Soon after Great Britain determined on planting colonies in America, the king granted charters to companies of his subjects who associated for the purpose of carrying the views of the crown into effect, and of enriching themselves. The first of these charters was made before possession was taken of any part of the country. They purport, generally, to convey the soil, from the Atlantic to the South Sea. This soil was occupied by numerous and warlike nations, equally willing and able to defend their possessions. The extravagant and absurd idea, that the feeble settlements made on the sea-coast, or the companies under whom they were made, acquired legitimate power by them to govern the people, or occupy the lands from sea to sea, did not enter the mind of any man. They were well understood to convey the title which, according to the common law of European sovereigns respecting America, they might rightfully convey, and no more. This was the exclusive right of purchasing such lands as the natives were willing to sell. The crown could not be understood to grant what the crown did not affect to claim; nor was it so understood.

The power of making war is conferred by these charters on the colonies, but defensive war alone seems to have been contemplated. . . .

\* \* \*

The charter to Georgia professes to be granted for the charitable purpose of enabling poor subjects to gain a comfortable subsistence by cultivating lands in the American provinces "at present waste and desolate." It recites: "And whereas our provinces in North America have been frequently ravaged by Indian enemies, more especially that of South Carolina, which, in the late war by the neighbouring savages, was laid waste by fire and sword, and great numbers of the English inhabitants miserably massacred; and our loving subjects, who now inhabit there, by reason of the smallness of their numbers, will, in case of any new war, be exposed to the like calamities, inasmuch as their whole southern frontier continueth unsettled, and lieth open to the said savages."

These motives for planting the new colony are incompatible with the lofty ideas of granting the soil and all its inhabitants from sea to sea. They demonstrate the truth, that these grants asserted a title against Europeans only, and were considered as blank paper so far as the rights of the natives were concerned. The power of war is given only for defence, not for conquest.

The charters contain passages showing one of their objects to be the civilization of the Indians, and their conversion to Christianity — objects to be accomplished by conciliatory conduct and good example; not by extermination.

. . . Fierce and warlike in their character, [the Indians] might be formidable enemies, or effective friends. Instead of rousing their resentments, by asserting claims to their lands, or to dominion over their persons, their alliance was sought by flattering professions, and purchased by rich presents. The English, the French, and the Spaniards, were equally competitors for their friendship and their aid. Not well acquainted with the exact meaning of words, nor supposing it to be material whether they were called the subjects, or the children of their father in Europe; lavish in professions of duty and affection, in return for the rich presents they received; so long as their actual independence was untouched, and their right to self-government acknowledged, they were willing to profess dependence on the power which furnished supplies of which they were in absolute need, and restrained dangerous intruders from entering their country; and this was probably the sense in which the term was understood by them.

Certain it is, that our history furnishes no example, from the first settlement of our country, of any attempt on the part of the crown to interfere with the internal affairs of the Indians, farther than to keep out the agents of foreign powers, who, as traders or otherwise, might seduce them into foreign alliances. The king purchased their lands when they were willing to sell, at a price they were willing to take; but never coerced a surrender of them. He also purchased their alliance and dependence by subsidies; but never intruded into the interior of their affairs, or interfered with their self-government, so far as respected themselves only.

\* \* \*

Such was the policy of Great Britain towards the Indian nations inhabiting the territory from which she excluded all other Europeans . . . : she considered them as nations capable of maintaining the relations of peace and war; of governing themselves, under her protection; and she made treaties with them, the obligation of which she acknowledged.

\* \* \*

During the war of the revolution, the Cherokees took part with the British. After its termination, the United States, though desirous of peace, did not feel its necessity so strongly as while the war continued. Their political situation being changed, they might very well think it advisable to assume a higher tone, and to impress on the Cherokees the same respect for Congress which was before felt for the King of Great Britain. This may account for the language of the treaty of Hopewell. There is the more reason for supposing that the Cherokee chiefs were not very critical judges of the language, from the fact that every one makes his mark; no chief was capable of signing his name. It is probable the treaty was interpreted to them.

The treaty is introduced with the declaration, that "the commissioners plenipotentiary of the United States give peace to all the Cherokees, and receive them into the favour and protection of the United States of America, on the following conditions."

When the United States gave peace, did they not also receive it? Were not both parties desirous of it? If we consult the history of the day, does it not inform us that the United States were at least as anxious to obtain it as the Cherokees? We may ask, further: did the Cherokees come to the seat of the American government to solicit peace; or, did the American commissioners go to them to obtain it? The treaty was made at Hopewell, not at New York.

The word "give," then, has no real importance attached to it.

\* \* \*

The third article acknowledges the Cherokees to be under the protection of the United States of America, and of no other power.... The Indians perceived in [an earlier] protection only what was beneficial to themselves—an engagement to punish aggressions on them. It involved, practically, no claim to their lands, no dominion over their persons. It merely bound the nation to the British crown, as a dependent ally, claiming the protection of a powerful friend and neighbour, and receiving the advantages of that protection, without involving a surrender of their national character.

This is the true meaning of the stipulation, and is undoubtedly the sense in which it was made. Neither the British government nor the Cherokees ever understood it otherwise.

The same stipulation entered into with the United States, is undoubtedly to be construed in the same manner. They receive the Cherokee nation into their favour and protection. The Cherokees acknowledge themselves to be under the protection of the United States, and of no other power. Protection does not imply the destruction of the protected....

\* \* \*

The ninth article is in these words: "for the benefit and comfort of the Indians, and for the prevention of injuries or oppressions on the part of the citizens or Indians, the United States, in Congress assembled, shall have the sole and exclusive right of regulating the trade with the Indians, and managing all their affairs, as they think proper."

To construe the expression "managing all their affairs," into a surrender of self-government, would be, we think a perversion of their necessary meaning, and a departure from the construction which has been uniformly put on them. The great subject of the article is the Indian trade.... Is it credible, that they should have considered themselves as surrendering to the United States the right to dictate their future cessions, and the terms on which they should be made? or to compel their submission to the violence of disorderly and licentious intruders? It is equally inconceivable that they could have supposed themselves, by a phrase thus slipped into an article, on another and most interesting subject, to have divested themselves of the right of self-government on subjects not connected with trade.... Such a construction ... would convert a treaty of peace covertly into an act, annihilating the political existence of one of the parties. Had such a result been intended, it would have been openly avowed.

This treaty ... treat[s] the Cherokees as a nation capable of maintaining the relations of peace and war; and ascertain[s] the boundaries between them and the United States.

The treaty of Hopewell seems not to have established a solid peace. To accommodate the differences still existing between the state of Georgia and the Cherokee nation, the treaty of Holston was negotiated in July, 1791....

\* \* \*

By the fifth article, the Cherokees allow the United States a road through their country, and the navigation of the Tennessee river. The acceptance of these cessions is an acknowledgment of the right of the Cherokees to make or withhold them....

\* \* \*

This treaty, thus explicitly recognising the national character of the Cherokees, and their right of self-government; thus guarantying their lands; assuming the duty of protection, and of course pledging the faith of the United States for that protection; has been frequently renewed and is now in full force....

\* \* \*

In 1819, Congress passed an act for promoting those humane designs of civilizing the neighbouring Indians, which had long been cherished by the executive....

This act avowedly contemplates the preservation of the Indian nations as an object sought by the United States, and proposes to effect this object by civilizing and converting them from hunters into agriculturists....

\* \* \*

The Indian nations had always been considered as distinct, independent political communities, retaining their original natural rights, as the undisputed possessors of the soil, from time immemorial, with the single exception of that imposed by irresistible power, which excluded them from intercourse with any other European potentate than the first discoverer of the coast of the particular region claimed; and this was a restriction which those European potentates imposed on themselves, as well as on the Indians. The very term "nation," so generally applied to them, means "a people distinct from others." The Constitution, by declaring treaties already made, as well as those to be made, to be the supreme law of the land, has adopted and sanctioned the previous treaties with the Indian nations, and consequently admits their rank among those powers who are capable of making treaties. The words "treaty" and "nation" are words of our own language, selected in our diplomatic and legislative proceedings, by ourselves, having each a definite and well understood meaning. We have applied them to Indians, as we have applied them to the other nations of the earth. They are applied to all in the same sense.

* * *

In opposition to this original right, possessed by the undisputed occupants of every country; to this recognition of that right, which is evidenced by our history, in every change through which we have passed; is placed the charters granted by the monarch of a distant and distinct region, parcelling out a territory in possession of others whom he could not remove and did not attempt to remove, and the cession made of his claims by the treaty of peace.

The actual state of things at the time, and all history since, explain these charters; and the King of Great Britain, at the treaty of peace, could cede only what belonged to his crown.... [T]he settled doctrine of the law of nations is, that a weaker power does not surrender its independence—its right to self-government, by associating with a stronger, and taking its protection. A weak state, in order to provide for its safety, may place itself under the protection of one more powerful, without stripping itself of the right of government, and ceasing to be a state. Examples of this kind are not wanting in Europe. "Tributary and feudatory states," says Vattel, "do not thereby cease to be sovereign and independent states, so long as self-government and sovereign and independent authority are left in the administration of the state."...

The Cherokee nation, then, is a distinct community, occupying its own territory, with boundaries accurately described, in which the laws of Georgia can have no force, and which the citizens of Georgia have no right to enter, but with the assent of the Cherokees themselves, or in conformity with treaties, and with the acts of Congress. The whole intercourse between the United States and this nation, is, by our Constitution and laws, vested in the government of the United States.

* * *

[The laws of Georgia] are in direct hostility with treaties, repeated in a succession of years, which mark out the boundary that separates the Cherokee country from Georgia; guaranty to them all the land within their boundary; solemnly pledge the faith of the United States to restrain their citizens from trespassing on it; and recognise the pre-existing power of the nation to govern itself.

They are in equal hostility with the acts of Congress for regulating this intercourse, and giving effect to the treaties.

The forcible seizure and abduction of the plaintiff in error, who was residing in the nation with its permission, and by authority of the President of the United States, is also a violation of the acts which authorize the chief magistrate to exercise this authority.

* * *

It is the Opinion of this Court that the judgment of the Superior Court for the county of Gwinnett, in the state of Georgia, condemning Samuel A. Worcester to hard labour in the penitentiary of the state of Georgia, for four years, was pronounced by that Court under colour of a law which is void, as being repugnant to the Constitution, treaties, and laws of the United States, and ought, therefore, to be reversed and annulled.

Mr. Justice MCLEAN. As this case involves principles of the highest importance, and may lead to consequences which shall have an enduring influence on the institutions of this country; and as there are some points in the case on which I wish to state, distinctly, my opinion, I embrace the privilege of doing so.

With the decision just given, I concur.

* * *

The abstract right of every section of the human race to a reasonable portion of the soil, by which to acquire the means of subsistence, cannot be controverted. And it is equally clear, that the range of nations or tribes, who exist in the hunter state, may be restricted within reasonable limits. They shall not be permitted to roam, in the pursuit of game, over an extensive and rich country, whilst in other parts, human beings are crowded so closely together as to render the means of subsistence precarious....

In this view, perhaps, our ancestors, when they first migrated to this country, might have taken possession of a limited extent of the domain, had they been sufficiently powerful, without negotiation or purchase from the native Indians. But this course is believed to have been nowhere taken. A more conciliatory mode was preferred, and one which was better calculated to impress the Indians, who were then powerful, with a sense of the justice of their white neighbours. The occupancy of their lands was never assumed, except upon the basis of contract, and on the payment of a valuable consideration.

* * *

... Some cessions of territory may have been made by the Indians, in compliance with the terms on which peace was offered by the whites; but the soil, thus taken, was taken by the laws of conquest, and always as an indemnity for the expenses of the war, commenced by the Indians.

At no time has the sovereignty of the country been recognised as existing in the Indians, but they have been always admitted to possess many of the attributes of sovereignty. All the rights which belong to self-government have been recognised as vested in them. Their right of occupancy has never been questioned, but the fee in the soil has been considered in the government. This may be called the right to the ultimate domain, but the Indians have a present right of possession.

In some of the old states, Massachusetts, Connecticut, Rhode Island, and others, where small remnants of tribes remain, surrounded by white population, and who, by their reduced numbers, had lost the power of self-government, the laws of the state have been extended over them, for the protection of their persons and property.

\*       \*       \*

It must be admitted, that the Indians sustain a peculiar relation to the United States. They do not constitute, as was decided at the last term, a foreign state, so as to claim the right to sue in the Supreme Court of the United States: and yet, having the right of self-government, they, in some sense, form a state. In the management of their internal concerns, they are dependent on no power. They punish offences under their own laws, and, in doing so, they are responsible to no earthly tribunal. They make war, and form treaties of peace. The exercise of these and other powers, gives to them a distinct character as a people, and constitutes them, in some respects, a state, although they may not be admitted to possess the rights of soil.

\*       \*       \*

Every state is more or less dependent on those which surround it: but, unless this dependence shall extend so far as to merge the political existence of the protected people into that of their protectors, they may still constitute a state. They may exercise the powers not relinquished, and bind themselves as a distinct and separate community.

\*       \*       \*

The question may be asked, is no distinction to be made between a civilized and savage people? Are our Indians to be placed upon a footing with the nations of Europe, with whom we have made treaties?

The inquiry is not, what station shall now be given to the Indian tribes in our country? but what relation have they sustained to us, since the commencement of our government?

We have made treaties with them; and are those treaties to be disregarded on our part, because they were entered into with an uncivilized people? Does this lessen the obligation of such treaties? By entering into them, have we not admitted the power of this people to bind themselves, and to impose obligations on us?

The President and Senate, except under the treaty-making power, cannot enter into compacts with the Indians, or with foreign nations. This power has been uniformly exercised in forming treaties with the Indians.

Nations differ from each other in condition, and that of the same nation may change by the revolutions of time, but the principles of justice are the same. They rest upon a base which will remain beyond the endurance of time.

\*       \*       \*

By numerous treaties with the Indian tribes, we have acquired accessions of territory, of incalculable value to the Union. Except by compact, we have not even claimed a right of way through the Indian lands. We have recognised in them the right to make war. No one has ever supposed that the Indians could commit treason against the United States. We have punished them for their violation of treaties; but we have inflicted the punishment on them as a nation, and not on individual offenders among them as traitors.

\*       \*       \*

It is important, on this part of the case, to ascertain in what light Georgia has considered the Indian title to lands, generally, and particularly, within her own boundaries; and also, as to the right of the Indians to self-government.

\*       \*       \*

In a memorial to the President of the United States, by the legislature of Georgia, in 1819, they say, "it has long been the desire of Georgia, that her settlements should be extended to her ultimate limits." "That the soil within her boundaries should be subjected to her control; and, that her police organization and government should be fixed and permanent." "That the state of Georgia claims a right to the jurisdiction and soil of the territory within her limits." "She admits, however, that the right is inchoate — remaining to be perfected by the United States, in the extinction of the Indian title; the United States pro hac vice as their agents."

\*       \*       \*

Neither Georgia, nor the United States, when the cession was made, contemplated that force should be used in the extinguishment of the Indian title; nor that it should be procured on terms that are not reasonable....

\*       \*       \*

Much has been said against the existence of an independent power within a sovereign state; and the conclusion has been drawn, that the Indians, as a matter of right, cannot enforce their own laws within the territorial limits of a state. The refutation of this argument is found in our past history.

Might not the same objection to this interior independent power, by Georgia, have been urged, with as much force as at present, ever since the adoption of the Constitution? Her chartered limits, to the extent claimed, embraced a great number of different nations of Indians, all of whom were governed by their own laws, and were amenable only to them. Has not this been the condition of the Indians within Tennessee, Ohio, and other states?

The exercise of this independent power surely does not become more objectionable, as it assumes the basis of justice and the forms of civilization. Would it not be a singular argument to admit, that, so long as the Indians govern by the rifle and the tomahawk, their government may be tolerated; but, that it must be suppressed, so soon as it shall be administered upon the enlightened principles of reason and justice?

Are not those nations of Indians who have made some advances in civilization better neighbours than those who are still in a savage state? And is not the principle, as to their self-government, within the jurisdiction of a state, the same?

*          *          *

The exercise of the power of self-government by the Indians, within a state, is undoubtedly contemplated to be temporary. This is shown by the settled policy of the government, in the extinguishment of their title, and especially by the compact with the ,tate of Georgia. It is a question, not of abstract right, but of public policy. I do not mean to say, that the same moral rule which should regulate the affairs of private life, should not be regarded by communities or nations. But, a sound national policy does require that the Indian tribes within our states should exchange their territories, upon equitable principles, or eventually consent to become amalgamated in our political communities.

At best they can enjoy a very limited independence within the boundaries of a state, and such a residence must always subject them to encroachments from the settlements around them; and their existence within a state, as a separate and independent community, may seriously embarrass or obstruct the operation of the state laws. If, therefore, it would be inconsistent with the political welfare of the states, and the social advance of their citizens, that an independent and permanent power should exist within their limits, this power must give way to the greater power which surrounds it, or seek its exercise beyond the sphere of state authority.

This state of things can only be produced by a cooperation of the state and federal governments. The latter has the exclusive regulation of intercourse with the Indians; and, so long as this power shall be exercised, it cannot be obstructed by the state. It is a power given by the Constitution, and sanctioned by the most solemn acts of both the federal and state governments: consequently, it cannot be abrogated at the will of a state....

*          *          *

## 92  The Nullifying Laws of South Carolina (1832)

The Southern states considered Northern opposition to slavery an attack on the vested property rights of Southern citizens. They perceived Northern economic developments and political trends as inimical to Southern interests, and particularly so as these developments found their way into federal legislation. Following earlier patterns of resistance to central authority, Southern legislatures declared certain federal duties and imposts to be invalid under the United States Constitution, making it unlawful for the laws to be enforced and threatening secession. Many of the arguments against the validity of these Northern-inspired economic regulations are reminiscent of the abolitionist denunciations of the South's repressive laws against blacks.

President Andrew Jackson ignored these enactments, endorsing the position that the determination of the constitutionality of United States laws was a judicial function, not state legislative function.

### ☆92  Proclamation by Andrew Jackson, President of the United States (December 10, 1832)

11 Stat. 771 (1832).

WHEREAS, a convention assembled in the State of South Carolina, have passed an ordinance, by which they declare, "That the several acts and parts of acts of the Congress of the United States, purporting to be laws for the imposing of duties and imposts on the importation of foreign commodities, and now having actual operation and effect within the United States ... are unauthorized by the Constitution of the United States, and violate the true meaning and intent thereof, and are null and void, and no law," nor binding on the citizens of that State, or its officers; and by the said ordinance, it is further declared to be unlawful for any of the constituted authorities of the State, or of the United States, to enforce the payment of the duties imposed by the said acts, within the same State, and that it is the duty of the legislature to pass such laws as may be necessary to give full effect to the said ordinance:

*          *          *

And, finally, the said ordinance declares that the people of South Carolina will maintain the said ordinance at every hazard; and that they will consider the passage of any act, by Congress, abolishing or closing the ports of the said State, or otherwise obstructing the free ingress or egress of vessels to and from the said ports, or any other act of the Federal Government to coerce the State, shut up her ports, destroy or harass her commerce, or to enforce the said acts otherwise than through the civil tribunals of the country, as inconsistent with the longer continuance of South Carolina in the Union; and that the people of the said State will thenceforth hold themselves absolved from all further obligation to maintain or preserve their political connection with the people of the other States, and will forthwith proceed to organize a separate government, and do all other acts and things which sovereign and independent States may of right do:

And whereas the said ordinance prescribes to the people of South Carolina a course of conduct in direct violation of their duty as citizens of the United States, contrary to the laws of their country, subversive of its constitution, and having for its object the destruction of the Union — that Union, which, coeval with our political existence, led our fathers, without any other ties to unite them than those of patriotism and a common cause, through a sanguinary struggle to a glorious independence, — that sacred Union hitherto inviolate, which, perfected by our happy Constitution, has brought us, by the favor of Heaven, to a state of prosperity at home, and high consideration abroad, rarely, if ever, equalled in the history of nations — To preserve this bond of our political existence from destruction, to maintain inviolate this state of national honor and prosperity, and to justify the confidence my fellow-citizens have reposed in me, I, ANDREW JACKSON, President of the United States, have thought proper to issue this my proclamation, stating my views of the Constitution and laws applicable to the measures adopted by the convention of South Carolina, and to the reasons they have put forth to sustain them....

\*          \*          \*

The ordinance is founded, not on the indefeasible right of resisting acts which are plainly unconstitutional, and too oppressive to be endured; but on the strange position that any one State may not only declare an act of Congress void, but prohibit its execution — that they may do this consistently with the Constitution — that the true construction of the instrument permits a State to retain its place in the Union, and yet be bound by no other of its laws than those it may choose to consider as constitutional. It is true, they add, that to justify this abrogation of a law, it must be palpably contrary to the Constitution; but it is evident, that to give the right of resisting laws of the description, coupled with the uncontrolled right to decide what laws deserve that character, is to give the power of resisting all laws. For, as by the theory, there is no appeal, the reasons alleged by the State, good or bad, must prevail. If it should be said that public opinion is a sufficient check against the abuse of this power, it may be asked why it is not deemed a sufficient guard

against the passage of an unconstitutional act by Congress? ...

If this doctrine had been established at an earlier day, the Union would have been dissolved in its infancy. The excise law in Pennsylvania, the embargo and non-intercourse law in the Eastern States, the carriage tax in Virginia, were all deemed unconstitutional, and were more unequal in their operation than any of the laws now complained of; but fortunately, none of those States discovered that they had the right now claimed by South Carolina. The war [of 1812] ... might have ended in defeat and disgrace, instead of victory and honor, if the States who supposed it a ruinous and unconstitutional measure, had thought they possessed the right of nullifying the act by which it was declared, and denying supplies for its prosecution.... To the statesmen of South Carolina belongs [this] invention, and upon the citizens of that State will unfortunately fall the evils of reducing it to practice.

If the doctrine of a State veto upon the laws of the Union carries with it internal evidence of its impracticable absurdity, our constitutional history will also afford abundant proof that it would have been repudiated with indignation had it been proposed to form a feature in our government.

\*          \*          \*

Under the confederation, no State could legally annul a decision of the Congress, or refuse to submit to its execution; but no provision was made to enforce these decisions. Congress made requisitions, but they were not complied with. The government could not operate on individuals. They had no Judiciary, no means of collecting revenue.

But the defects of the confederation need not be detailed. Under its operation we could scarcely be called a nation. We had neither prosperity at home nor consideration abroad. This state of things could not be endured, and our present happy Constitution was formed, but formed in vain, if this fatal doctrine prevails.... [C]an it be conceived, that an instrument made for the purpose of *"forming a more perfect Union,"* than that of the confederation, could be so constructed by the assembled wisdom of our country, as to substitute for that confederation a form of government dependent for its existence on the local interest, the party spirit of a State, or of a prevailing faction in a State? Every man of plain, unsophisticated understanding, who hears the question, will give such an answer as will preserve the Union. Metaphysical subtlety, in pursuit of an impracticable theory could alone have devised one that is calculated to destroy it.

I consider, then, the power to annul a law of the United States, assumed by one State, *incompatible with the existence of the Union, contradicted ex-*

*pressly by the letter of the Constitution, unauthorized by its spirit, inconsistent with every principle on which it was founded, and destructive of the great object for which it was formed.*

*      *      *

## 93 "Slavery is contrary to the principles of natural justice" (1833)

William Lloyd Garrison sought to channel abolitionist sentiments by organizing the Anti-Slavery Society in 1833. A handful of delegates met in Philadelphia for the event. Garrison not only fought in the United States for abolition but also traveled throughout the world to foster support for his campaign. Taunted by his fellow citizens who once raised a gallows for him in front of his Boston home, Garrison observed in 1851, "The truth is, he who commences any reform which at last becomes one of transcendent importance and is crowned with victory is always ill-judged and unfairly estimated. At the outset he is looked upon with contempt and treated in the most opprobrious manner as a wild fanatic or a dangerous organizer. In the clear light of Reason, it will be seen that he simply stood up to discharge a duty which he owed to his God, to his fellow-men, to the land of his nativity."

While these documents call for immediate action, they eschew physical force as a legitimate means of accomplishing their ends. Despite the claim they did only that which was lawful in service of their cause, many of their actions were illegal under the laws of the slave states. But of course *those* laws were declared utterly null and void. The document also relates the nature in which the federal government supported the institution, if not the spread, of slavery.

### ☆ 93 Documents of the American Anti-Slavery Society (December 4, 1833)

Reprinted in W. Garrison and F. Garrison, *William Lloyd Garrison, 1805-1879: The Story of His Life Told by His Children* (New York: Arno Press, 1969), 1:3-4, 408.

### ☆ 93a Constitution

Whereas the Most High God "hath made of one blood all nations of men to dwell on all the face of the earth," and hath commanded them to love their neighbors as themselves; and whereas, our National Existence is based upon this principle, as recognized in the Declaration of Independence, "that all mankind are created equal, and that they are endowed by their Creator with certain inalienable rights, among which are life, liberty, and the pursuit of happiness"; and whereas, after the lapse of nearly sixty years, since the faith and honor of the American people were pledged to this avowal, before Almighty God and the World, nearly one-sixth part of the nation are held in bondage by their fellow-citizens; and whereas, Slavery is contrary to the principles of natural justice, of our republican form of government, and of the Christian religion, and is destructive of the prosperity of the country, while it is endangering the peace, union, and liberties of the States; and whereas, we believe it the duty and interest of the masters immediately to emancipate their slaves, and that no scheme of expatriation, either voluntary or by compulsion, can remove this great and increasing evil; and whereas, we believe that it is practicable, by appeals to the consciences, hearts, and interests of the people, to awaken a public sentiment throughout the nation that will be opposed to the continuance of Slavery in any part of the Republic, and by effecting the speedy abolition of Slavery, prevent a general convulsion; and whereas, we believe we owe it to the oppressed, to our fellow-citizens who hold slaves, to our whole country, to posterity, and to God, to do all that is lawfully in our power to bring about the extinction of Slavery, we do hereby agree, with a prayerful reliance on the Divine aid, to form ourselves into a society, to be governed by the following Constitution:—

ART. I.—This Society shall be called the AMERICAN ANTI-SLAVERY SOCIETY.

ART. II.—The object of this Society is the entire abolition of Slavery in the United States....

[I]t shall aim to convince all our fellow-citizens ... that Slave-holding is a heinous crime in the sight of God, and that the duty, safety, and best interests of all concerned, require its *immediate abandonment without expatriation.*...

ART. III.—This Society shall aim to elevate the character and condition of the people of color, ... but this Society will never, in any way, countenance the oppressed in vindicating their rights by resorting to physical force.

*      *      *

### ☆ 93b Declaration of Sentiments

*      *      *

We have met together for the achievement of an enterprise without which that of our fathers is incomplete....

Their grievances, great as they were, were trifling in comparison with the wrongs and sufferings of those for whom we plead. Our fathers were never slaves—never bought and sold like cattle—never shut out from the light of knowledge and religion—never subjected to the lash of brutal taskmasters.

But those, for whose emancipation we are striving—constituting at the present time at least one-sixth part of our countrymen—are recognized by law, and treated by their fellow-beings, as brute beasts; are plundered daily of the fruits of their toil without redress; really enjoy no constitutional nor legal protection from licentious and murderous outrages upon their persons; and are ruthlessly torn asunder—the tender babe from the arms of its frantic mother—the heartbroken wife from her weeping husband—at the caprice or pleasure of irresponsible tyrants. For the crime of having a dark complexion, they suffer the pangs of hunger, the infliction of stripes, the ignominy of brutal servitude. They are kept in heathenish darkness by laws expressly enacted to make their instruction a criminal offence.

\*        \*        \*

[W]e maintain—that, in view of the civil and religious privileges of this nation, the guilt of its oppression is unequalled by any other on the face of the earth; and, therefore, that it is bound to repent instantly, to undo the heavy burdens, and to let the oppressed go free....

It is piracy to buy or steal an native African, and subject him to servitude. Surely, the sin is as great to enslave an American as an African.

[W]e believe and affirm—that there is no difference, in principle, between the African slave trade and American slavery:

That every American citizen, who detains a human being in involuntary bondage as his property, is, according to Scripture (Ex. xxi, 16), a man-stealer.

That the slaves ought instantly to be set free, and brought under the protection of law:

\*        \*        \*

That if they had lived from the time of Pharaoh down to the present period, and had been entailed through successive generations, their right to be free could never have been alienated, but their claims would have constantly risen in solemnity:

That all those laws which are now in force, admitting the right of slavery, are therefore, before God, utterly null and void; being an audacious usurpation of the Divine prerogative, a daring infringement on the law of nature, a base overthrow of the very foundations of the social compact, a complete extinction of all the relations, endearments and obligations of mankind, and a presumptuous transgression of all the holy commandments; and that therefore they ought instantly to be abrogated.

\*        \*        \*

We maintain that no compensation should be given to the planters emancipating their slaves:

Because it would be a surrender of the great fundamental principle, that man cannot hold property in man:

Because slavery is a crime, and therefore is not an article to be sold:

Because the holders of slaves are not the just proprietors of what they claim; freeing the slave is not depriving them of property, but restoring it to its rightful owner; it is not wronging the master, but righting the slave—restoring him to himself:

\*        \*        \*

Because, if compensation is to be given at all, it should be given to the outraged and guiltless slaves, and not to those who have plundered and abused them.

We regard as delusive, cruel and dangerous, any scheme of expatriation which pretends to aid, either directly or indirectly, in the emancipation of the slaves, or to be a substitute for the immediate and total abolition of slavery.

We fully and unanimously recognise the sovereignty of each State, to legislate exclusively on the subject of the slavery which is tolerated within its limits; we concede that Congress, under the present national compact, has no right to interfere with any of the slave States, in relation to this momentous subject:

But we maintain that Congress has a right, and is solemnly bound, to suppress the domestic slave trade between the several States, and to abolish slavery in those portions of our territory which the Constitution has placed under its exclusive jurisdiction.

We also maintain that there are, at the present time, the highest obligations resting upon the people of the free States to remove slavery by moral and political action, as prescribed in the Constitution of the United States. They are now living under a pledge of their tremendous physical force, to fasten the galling fetters of tyranny upon the limbs of millions in the Southern States; they are liable to be called at any moment to suppress a general insurrection of the slaves; they authorize the slave owner to vote for three-fifths of his slaves as property, and thus enable him to perpetuate his oppression; they support a standing army at the South for its protection; and they seize the slave, who has escaped into their territories, and send him back to be tortured by an enraged master or a brutal driver. This relation to slavery is criminal, and full of danger: IT MUST BE BROKEN UP.

These are our views and principles—these our designs and measures. With entire confidence in the overruling justice of God, we plant ourselves upon the Declaration of our Independence and the truths of Divine Revelation, as upon the Everlasting Rock....

## 94 Reward for Laying Violent Hands (1835)

Abolitionist newspapers, such as William Lloyd Garrison's *Liberator*, were blamed by many Southerners for Nat Turner's rebellion. Despite bans on the literature, Garrison and his adherents continued to mail newspapers and other antislavery propaganda throughout the nation, particularly to the South. But the supporters of slavery resorted to illegal actions as well. In July 1835 abolitionist literature was taken from post offices in Charleston, South Carolina, and was burned. Northerners, too, were hostile to abolition, seeing it as inimical to the peaceful continuation of the Union. On October 21, Garrison was paraded around Boston in a noose during a riot directed against visiting English abolitionist George Thompson that this poster advertised.

## ☆94 Thompson, the Abolitionist

Reprinted from a poster of October 21, 1835.

# THOMPSON,
## THE ABOLITIONIST.

That infamous foreign scoundrel THOMPSON, will hold forth *this afternoon*, at the Liberator Office, No. 48, Washington Street. The present is a fair opportunity for the friends of the Union to *snake Thompson out!* It will be a contest between the Abolitionists and the friends of the Union. A purse of **$100** has been raised by a number of patriotic citizens to reward the individual who shall first lay violent hands on Thompson, so that he may be brought to the tar kettle before dark. Friends of the Union, be vigilant!

*Boston, Wednesday, 12 o'clock.*

## 95 The Removal of the "aboriginal people" (1835)

The Supreme Court decision in *Worcester v. Georgia* was immensely unpopular, and Georgia officials continued to exercise jurisdiction in Cherokee territory. Although Worcester was set free, the case's lofty language went unenforced. The federal executive made every effort to convince the Native Americans they could not be safeguarded and protected under the terms of the federal treaties unless they removed themselves beyond the Mississippi. President Jackson's Seventh Annual Message to Congress reiterated that the Native Americans "cannot live in contact with a civilized community and prosper." Faced with the choice of relinquishing their lands in hostile Georgia but retaining self-government in the West, the Cherokees finally ceded their lands east of the Mississippi. The New Echota Treaty with the Cherokees specified the terms of their removal. The "Trail of Tears" ensued, as virtually the entire Cherokee Nation marched under military "escort" from Georgia to Oklahoma. An estimated twenty-five thousand died in the forced

migrations during the decade of the 1830s. Although they had violated neither federal nor state criminal laws, many Native Americans were treated much like traitors receiving the punishment of exile under martial law. The United States sought to justify this disposition of the Native American "problem" by asserting paternalistic motives.

Not all the Five Civilized Tribes (Choctaw, Chickasaw, Cherokee, Seminole, and Creek) went as peacefully as the Cherokees. Dissatisfied with the land chosen for them west of the Mississippi, the Seminoles, under the leadership of Osceola, refused to migrate. When federal troops were sent to remove them forcibly, a war began that lasted seven years and cost forty million dollars and the lives of two thousand United States troops and an unknown number of Seminoles and their escaped-slave allies. At first the Seminoles were on the offensive, but with the capture of Osceola in 1837 while ostensibly protected by a flag of truce, the Seminoles retreated to the Florida swamps and fought a defensive war for another five years. Osceola died in prison in 1838, and the Seminoles capitulated in 1842, effectively ending the existence of the independent and self-governing Indian nations east of the Mississippi.

## ☆95 A Home in a Country Selected by Their Forefathers

## ☆95a President Jackson's Seventh Annual Message on Indian Removal (December 7, 1835)

Reprinted in J. Richardson, ed., *A Compilation of the Messages and Papers of the Presidents* (New York: Bureau of National Literature, 1897), 3:171.

... The plan of removing the aboriginal people who yet remain within the settled portions of the United States to the country west of the Mississippi River approaches its consummation. It was adopted on the most mature consideration of the condition of this race, and ought to be persisted in till the object is accomplished, and prosecuted with as much vigor as a just regard to their circumstances will permit, and as fast as their consent can be obtained. All preceding experiments for the improvement of the Indians have failed. It seems now to be an established fact that they can not live in contact with a civilized community and prosper. Ages of fruitless endeavors have at length brought us to a knowledge of this principle of intercommunication with them. The past we can not recall, but the future we can provide for. Independently of the treaty stipulations into which we have entered with the various tribes for the usufructuary rights they have ceded to us, no one can doubt the moral duty of the Government of the United States to protect and if possible to preserve and perpetuate the scattered remnants of this race which are left within our borders. In the discharge of this duty an extensive region in the West has been assigned for their permanent residence....

The plan ... has been dictated by a spirit of enlarged liberality. A territory exceeding in extent that relinquished has been granted to each tribe. Of its climate, fertility, and capacity to support an Indian population the representations are highly favorable. To these districts the Indians are removed at the expense of the United States, and with certain supplies of clothing, arms, ammunition, and other indispensable articles; they are also furnished gratuitously with provisions for the period of a year after their arrival at their new homes. In that time, from the nature of the country and of the products raised by them, they can subsist themselves by agricultural labor, if they choose to resort to that mode of life; if they do not they are upon the skirts of the great prairies, where countless herds of buffalo roam, and a short time suffices to adapt their own habits to the changes which a change of the animals destined for their food may require. Ample arrangements have also been made for the support of schools; in some instances council houses and churches are to be erected, dwellings constructed for the chiefs, and mills for common use. Funds have been set apart for the maintenance of the poor; the most necessary mechanical arts have been introduced, and blacksmiths, gunsmiths, wheelwrights, millwrights, etc., are supported among them. Steel and iron, and sometimes salt, are purchased for them, and plows and other farming utensils, domestic animals, looms, spinning wheels, cards, etc., are presented to them.... [A]s a stimulus for exertion, it is now provided by law that "in all cases of the appointment of interpreters or other persons employed for the benefit of the Indians a preference shall be given to persons of Indian descent, if such can be found who are properly qualified for the discharge of the duties."

Such are the arrangements for the physical comfort and for the moral improvement of the Indians. The necessary measures for their political advancement and for their separation from our citizens have not been neglected. The pledge of the United States has been given by Congress that the country destined for the residence of this people shall be forever "secured and guaranteed to them." A country west of Missouri and Arkansas has been assigned to them, into which the white settlements are not to be pushed. No political communities can be formed in that extensive region, except those which are established by the Indians themselves or by the United States for them and with their concurrence. A barrier has thus been raised for their protection against the encroachment of our citizens, and guarding the Indians as far as possible from those evils which have brought them to their present condition.

☆ 95b  Treaty of New Echota with the Cherokees (December 29, 1835)

7 Stat. 478 (1835).

*Articles of a treaty concluded at New Echota in the State of Georgia on the 29th day of December 1835 by General William Carroll and John F. Schermerhorn, Commissioners on the part of the United States, and the Chiefs, Head Men and people of the Cherokee tribe of Indians.*

WHEREAS THE CHEROKEE are anxious to make some arrangements with the Government of the United States whereby the difficulties they have experienced by a residence within the settled parts of the United States under the jurisdiction and laws of the State Governments may be terminated and adjusted; and with a view to reuniting their people in one body and securing a permanent home for themselves and their posterity in the country selected by their forefathers without the territorial limits of the State sovereignties, and where they can establish and enjoy a government of their choice and perpetuate such a state of society as may be most consonant with their views, habits and condition; and as may tend to their individual comfort and their advancement in civilization.

\*          \*          \*

Therefore the following articles of a treaty are agreed upon and concluded between William Carroll and John F. Schermerhorn commissioners on the part of the United States and the chiefs and head men and people of the Cherokee nation in general council assembled this 29th day of Dec. 1835.

ARTICLE I. The Cherokee nation hereby cede relinquish and convey to the United States all the lands owned claimed or possessed by them east of the Mississippi river, and hereby release all their claims upon the United States for spoliations of every kind for and in consideration of the sum of five millions of dollars to be expended paid and invested in the manner stipulated and agreed upon in the following articles. But as a question has arisen between the commissioners and the Cherokees whether the Senate in their resolution by which they advised "that a sum not exceeding five millions of dollars be paid to the Cherokee Indians for all their lands and possessions east of the Mississippi river" have included and made any allowance or consideration for claims for spoliations it is therefore agreed on the part of the United States that this question shall be again submitted to the Senate for their consideration and decision and if no allowance was made for spoliations that then an additional sum of three hundred thousand dollars be allowed for the same.

\*          \*          \*

ARTICLE V. The United States hereby covenant and agree that the lands ceded to the Cherokee nation in the foregoing article shall, in no future time without their consent, be included within the territorial limits or jurisdiction of any State or Territory. But they shall secure to the Cherokee nation the right by their national councils to make and carry into effect all such laws as they may deem necessary for the government and protection of the persons and property within their own country belonging to their people or such persons as have connected themselves with them: provided always that they shall not be inconsistent with the constitution of the United States and such acts of Congress as have been or may be passed regulating trade and intercourse with the Indians; and also, that they shall not be considered as extending to such citizens and army of the United States as may travel or reside in the Indian country by permission according to the laws and regulations established by the Government of the same.

ARTICLE VI. Perpetual peace and friendship shall exist between the citizens of the United States and the Cherokee Indians. The United States agree to protect the Cherokee nation from domestic strife and foreign enemies and against intestine wars between the several tribes. The Cherokees shall endeavor to preserve and maintain the peace of the country and not make war upon their neighbors they shall also be protected against interruption and intrusion from citizens of the United States, who may attempt to settle in the country without their consent; and all such persons shall be removed from the same by order of the President of the United States. But this is not intended to prevent the residence among them of useful farmers mechanics and teachers for the instruction of Indians according to treaty stipulations.

ARTICLE VII. The Cherokee nation having already made great progress in civilization and deeming it important that every proper and laudable inducement should be offered to their people to improve their condition as well as to guard and secure in the most effectual manner the rights guarantied to them in this treaty, and with a view to illustrate the liberal and enlarged policy of the Government of the United States towards the Indians in their removal beyond the territorial limits of the States, it is stipulated that they shall be entitled to a delegate in the House of Representatives of the United States whenever Congress shall make provision for the same.

\*       \*       \*

ARTICLE XVI. It is hereby stipulated and agreed by the Cherokees that they shall remove to their new homes within two years from the ratification of this treaty and that during such time the United States shall protect and defend them in their posses-

sions and property and free use and occupation of the same and such persons as have been dispossessed of their improvements and houses; and for which no grant has actually issued previously to the enactment of the law of the State of Georgia, of December 1835 to regulate Indian occupancy shall be again put in possession and placed in the same situation and condition, in reference to the laws of the State of Georgia, as the Indians that have not been dispossessed; and if this is not done, and the people are left unprotected, then the United States shall pay the several Cherokees for their losses and damages sustained by them in consequence thereof. . . .

\*       \*       \*

ARTICLE XVIII. Whereas in consequences of the unsettled affairs of the Cherokee people and the early frosts, their crops are insufficient to support their families and great distress is likely to ensue and whereas the nation will not, until after their removal be able advantageously to expend the income of the permanent funds of the nation it is therefore agreed that the annuities of the nation which may accrue under this treaty for two years, the time fixed for their removal shall be expended in provision and clothing for the benefit of the poorer class of the nation; and the United States hereby agree to advance the same for that purpose as soon after the ratification of this treaty as an appropriation for the same shall be made. It is however not intended in this article to interfere with that part of the annuities due the Cherokees west by the treaty of 1819.

ARTICLE XIX. This treaty after the same shall be ratified by the President and Senate of the United States shall be obligatory on the contracting parties.

In testimony whereof the commissioners and the chiefs head men and people whose names are hereunto annexed being duly authorized by the people in general council assembled have affixed their hands and seals for themselves and in behalf of the Cherokee nation.

I have examined the foregoing treaty and although not present when it was made, I approve its provisions generally, and therefore sign it.

| | |
|---|---|
| WM. CARROLL | CAE-TE-HEE |
| J. F. SCHERMERHORN | TE-GAH-E-SKE |
| | ROBERT ROGERS |
| MAJOR RIDGE | JOHN GUNTER |
| JAMES FOSTER | JOHN A. BELL |
| TESA-TA-ESKY | CHARLES F. FOREMAN |
| CHARLES MOORE | WILLIAM ROGERS |
| GEORGE CHAMBERS | GEORGE W. ADAIR |
| TAH-YESKE | ELIAS BOUDINOT |
| ARCHILLA SMITH | JAMES STARR |
| ANDREW ROSS | JESSE HALF-BREED |
| WILLIAM LASSLEY | |

Signed and sealed in presence of

Western B. Thomas, Secry.
Ben F. Currey, Special Agent
M. Wolfe Bateman, 1st Lt. 6th U.S.A. inf.,
    Disbg. Agent
Jno. L. Hooper, Lt. 4th inf.
C. M. Hitchcock, M.D., Assist. Surg. U.S.A.
G. W. Currey
Wm. H. Underwood
Cornelius D. Terhune
John W. H. Underwood

## 96 "acts and doings of certain fanatics" (1835-1836)

Southern states met abolitionist propaganda with regulation and repression of the press. Several states asserted the obligation of the Northern members of the Union to suppress, within their boundaries, activities that adversely affected the peace and security of other members of the "common league" and the duty of the federal government to close the mails to "incendiary" literature.

### ☆ 96 Opposition to Abolition Societies

☆ 96a South Carolina Resolutions on Abolition Societies (December 16, 1835)

1835 S.C. Acts 26.

1. *Resolved,* That the formation of the abolition societies, and the acts and doings of certain fanatics, calling themselves abolitionists, in the non-slaveholding states of this confederacy, are in direct violation of the obligations of the compact of the union, dissocial, and incendiary in the extreme.

2. *Resolved,* That no state having a just regard for her own peace and security can acquiesce in a state of things by which such conspiracies are engendered within the limits of a friendly state, united to her by the bonds of a common league of political association, without either surrendering or compromising her most essential rights.

3. *Resolved,* That the Legislature of South Carolina, having every confidence in the justice and friendship of the non-slaveholding states, announces to her co-states her confident expectation, and she earnestly requests that the governments of these states will promptly and effectually suppress all those associations within their respective limits, purporting to be abolition societies, and that they will make it highly penal to print, publish, and distribute newspapers, pamphlets, tracts and pictorial representations calculated and having an obvious tendency to excite the slaves of the southern states to insurrection and revolt.

4. *Resolved,* That, regarding the domestic slavery of the southern states as a subject exclusively within the control of each of the said states, we shall consider every interference, by any other state of the general government, as a direct and unlawful interference, to be resisted at once, and under every possible circumstance.

5. *Resolved,* In order that a salutary negative may be put on the mischievous and unfounded assumption of some of the abolitionists—the non-slaveholding states are requested to disclaim by legislative declaration, all right, either on the part of themselves or the government of the United States, to interfere in any manner with domestic slavery, either in the states, or in the territories where it exists.

\*          \*          \*

7. *Resolved,* That the legislature of South Carolina, regards with decided approbation, the measures of security adopted by the Post Office Department of the United States, in relation to the transmission of incendiary tracts. But if this highly essential and protective policy, be counteracted by congress, and the United States mail becomes a vehicle for the transmission of the mischievous documents, with which it was recently freighted, we, in this contingency, expect that the Chief Magistrate of our state, will forthwith call the legislature together, that timely measures may be taken to prevent its traversing our territory.

\*          \*          \*

☆ 96b An Act to Suppress the Circulation of Incendiary Publications and for Other Purposes (March 23, 1836) [Virginia]

1836 Va. Acts 44.

*Whereas* attempts have been recently made by certain abolition or anti-slavery societies and evil disposed persons, being and residing in some of the non-slaveholding states, to interfere with the relations existing between master and slave in this state, and to excite in our coloured population a spirit of insubordination, rebellion and insurrection, by distributing among them, through the agency of the United States mail and other means, certain incendiary books, pamphlets, or other writings of an inflammatory and mischievous character and tendency: For remedy whereof, and to provide against the dangers thence arising,

1. *Be it enacted by the general assembly,* That any member of an abolition or anti-slavery society, or agent of an abolition or anti-slavery society, who shall come into this state, and shall here maintain, by speaking or writing, that the owners of slaves have no property in the same, or advocate or advise the abolition of slavery, shall be deemed guilty of a high

misdemeanor, and on conviction thereof shall be fined in a sum of not less than fifty dollars nor more than two hundred dollars, and shall suffer a term of imprisonment of not less than six months nor more than three years, at the discretion of a jury.

2. *And be it further enacted,* That if any person shall hereafter write, print, or cause to be written or printed, any book, pamphlet, or other writing, with intent of advising, enticing, or persuading persons of colour within this commonwealth to make insurrections, or to rebel, or denying the right of masters to property in their slaves, and inculcating the duty of resistance to such right, or shall, with intent to aid the purposes aforesaid of such book, pamphlet, or other writing, knowingly circulate, or cause to be circulated, any such book, pamphlet, or other writing, such person shall, if a slave or other coloured person, be punished by stripes, not exceeding thirty-nine, and transported and sold beyond the limits of the United States, under the orders of the executive of this commonwealth; and if a free white person, shall be deemed guilty of felony, and on conviction thereof be punished by imprisonment in the penitentiary of this commonwealth for a term not less than two years nor more than five years.

3. *Be it further enacted,* That if any post-master or deputy post-master within this commonwealth, shall give notice to any justice of the peace that any book, pamphlet, or other writing, hath been received at his office through the medium of the mail, of the character and description mentioned in the section of this act immediately preceding, it shall be the duty of such justice of the peace to enquire into the circumstances of the case, and to have such book, pamphlet, or other writing, burned in his presence; and if it shall appear to him by satisfactory evidence that the person to whom the same is directed, subscribed for the said book, pamphlet, or other writing, knowing its character and tendency, or agreed to receive it with an intention of circulating it, thereby to aid the purposes of the abolitionists or anti-slavery societies, the said justice shall commit him or her to the jail of his county, to be dealt with according to law.

*         *         *

## 97 Twenty Journeymen Tailors (1836)

In an 1834 letter to the Workingmen, a radical political party of Massachusetts, American historian George Bancroft wrote: "The Feud between the capitalist and laborer, the House of Have and the House of Want, is as old as the social union and can never be entirely quitted." Toward the middle of the nineteenth century, European immigrants — especially on the eastern seaboard — combined with American craftsmen to create a laboring class sensitive to fair wages and humane working conditions. Their efforts to organize the workers as a prerequisite for exerting the power of collective bargaining nevertheless triggered criminal prosecutions on charges of conspiracy to violate the established law of the land.

The 1836 New York trial of twenty journeymen tailors exemplified the courts' practice of resorting to the common law or statutory crime of conspiracy as a means of interfering with the organization of labor unions. The court in *People v. Faulkner* relied on Supreme Court precedent, as it announced to the jury that such organizations were "a conspiracy and injurious to trade." By 1846, confronted with a similar case, a Massachusetts court reached the opposite conclusion in *Commonwealth v. Hunt.* Justice Shaw acknowledged that the purpose of the organization was neither criminal nor carried out by criminal means.

## ☆ 97 They Formed Themselves into a Society

☆ 97a *People v. Faulkner* [New York]

Reprinted in J. R. Commons and E. Gillmore, eds., *A Documentary History of American Industrial Society* (New York: Russell & Russell, 1958), 4:315-33.

*         *         *

From the New York *Courier and Enquirer,* May 31, 1836.

The accused, who are journeymen tailors, and members of the Union Society of Journeymen Tailors, were indicted for a conspiracy to injure trade and commerce, and for riot, and assault and battery, &c.

*         *         *

The Court has been occupied several days with the trial of twenty-one [*sic*] journeymen tailors for combination.... It will be remembered that some months back there was a strike for wages amongst a large number of journeymen Tailors in this city, and that a certain body called the Trades Union Society, who undertook to make laws and regulations for the trade, made several rules [for the fair distribution of work] which they insisted on being observed by the master tailors, and on their refusing to comply with these rules, a number of journeymen left their employment and had recourse to threats, and promises, and various other modes [picketing] to prevent journeymen tailors from woring for any master tailor who did not conform to the rules, and pay the prices laid down by this association. The charges were fully substantiated by evidence.

The Court charged the jury.

*         *         *

The offence committed by the present defendants, if an offence at all, is against the Statute, which says that if any man enter into a combination injurious to trade or commerce, that constitutes a conspiracy; but at the same time the Act says— "That no agreement, except to commit a felony on the person of another, or to commit arson or burglary, shall be deemed a conspiracy unless some act, besides such agreement, shall be done to effect the object thereof, by one or more of the parties." If then there is a conspiracy against trade or commerce, and any act in furtherance of it, if done by one of the parties it renders them all guilty.

In criminal cases the jury were judges of the law and the facts, this was their constitutional right, but the court trusted that as a discreet jury they would pay proper respect to the opinions of the highest tribunal of the country, which had unanimously concurred as to what was the exposition of the Act, and the Supreme Court had said in a case similar to the present one, that it was a conspiracy and injurious to trade. . . .

*          *          *

Such was the law, and how stood the facts.

The Court then summed up the leading facts of the case.

It was unnecessary for the Court to state more. It would be insulting the understanding of the jury to suppose they could imagine for one moment, that the prisoners had not taken measures to carry their combination into effect; and if they did form a combination and take measures to carry it into effect, and that the law was as the supreme court decided it, then the prisoners were indubitably guilty.

The combination had been of so extensive a character and created so great an excitement that it might possibly have involved some persons for whom the jury might directly or indirectly feel some interest—but the court and jury must raise themselves above all feelings of friendship or sympathy and be true to their oaths, and the well being of the public at large; and it was impossible that the acts of the defendants could escape with impunity unless the court and jury violate their duty in order to take them out of the operation of the law. The Court would again impress upon the minds of the jury that the present question was not to be considered a mere struggle between the masters and journeymen. It was one upon which the harmony of the whole community depended. Let these societies only arise from time to time and they would at last extend to every trade in this city and we should have as many governments as there were societies.

*          *          *

The jury retired for a short time and returned a verdict of guilty against all the defendants. Counsel for the prisoners made a motion for time to put in exceptions to the charge, but the Court stated its determination to sentence the prisoners on Monday next.

*          *          *

From the New York *Evening Post*, June 13, 1836, copied from the *Times*.

COURT OF OYER AND TERMINER. Present—Judge Edwards, Aldermen Banks, Ingraham, Benson and Randall.

SENTENCE OF THE TAILORS. . . . A large number of persons, who had previously assembled in the passages of the hall, immediately entered, and completely filled the large room. There appeared to be no peculiar excitement however. There was no assembling in the Park as had been predicted. . . .

*          *          *

On enquiring of Mr. Western, one of the counsel, that gentleman informed us that eleven of these were native born citizens; and of the other nine, five were naturalized. Of the native born, he could only call to mind Henry Faulkner, Howell Vail, Livingston, Smith, Gray, Keating, and Delong. Another gentleman stated that Busey and the Douglases were also native born; that eleven of the twenty were born in the United States, two in Ireland, three in Scotland, and four in England.

Mr. Western moved for an arrest of judgment on three grounds. 1st, that no crime was contained in the indictment. 2nd, that even if so, the crime consisted in the men endeavoring to prevent others from working, which had not been proved. And 3d, that the judge took from the jury the decision of the case, by stating what was the law and what the facts.

*          *          *

The Judge then proceeded to pass sentence, which was done in the following words:

You have been convicted of a conspiracy. The bill of indictment charges substantially that you and others, being journeymen tailors, did perniciously form and unite yourselves into an unlawful club or combination to injure trade, and did make certain arbitrary bylaws, rules and orders, intending to govern not only yourselves but other journeymen tailors, and persons engaged in the business of tailors, and to oppress and injure them, and to injure trade and commerce. And also to prevent any journeymen tailors from working for any tailor who would not assent to said by-laws. . . .

*          *          *

Combining to do an act injurious to trade, is declared by a statute of this State, to be a misdemeanor.

That an offence, of the description of the one with which you are charged, is one within the act, has been unanimously decided by the Supreme Court of this State, and for reasons which are deemed by the Court perfectly satisfactory. That such combinations are injurious to trade, has been fully verified in this city. Various trades have from time to time been brought to a stand, and the community extensively inconvenienced and embarrassed by them. . . . [The Legislature has], therefore, re-enacted the common law upon the subject with the additional provision, that some act shall be done to effect the object of it by one or more of the parties, in order to render it a misdemeanor.

The law leaves every individual master of his own individual acts. But it will not suffer him to encroach upon the rights of others. He may work or not, as suits his pleasure, but he shall not enter into a confederacy with a view of controlling others, and take measures to carry it into effect. The reason for the distinction is manifest. So long as individual members of the community do not resort to any acts of violence, their hostility can be guarded against. But who can withstand an extensive combination to injure him in his calling? When such cases, therefore, occur, the law extends its protecting shield.

*    *    *

☆ 97b *Commonwealth v. Hunt* [Massachusetts]

45 Mass. (4 Met.) 45 (1842).

SHAW, C. J. . . . We have no doubt, that by the operation of the constitution of this Commonwealth, the general rules of the common law, making conspiracy an indictable offence, are in force here, and that this is included in the description of laws which had, before the adoption of the constitution, been used and approved in the Province, Colony, or State of Massachusetts Bay, and usually practised in the courts of law. . . . Still it is proper in this connexion to remark, that although the common law in regard to conspiracy in this Commonwealth is in force, yet it will not necessarily follow that every indictment at common law for this offence is a precedent for a similar indictment in this State. The general rule of the common law is, that it is a criminal and indictable offence, for two or more to confederate and combine together, by concerted means, to do that which is unlawful or criminal, to the injury of the public, or portions or classes of the community, or even to the rights of an individual. This rule of law may be equally in force as a rule of the common law, in England and in this Commonwealth; and yet it must depend upon the local laws of each country to determine, whether the purpose to be accomplished by the combination, or the concerted means of accomplishing it, be unlawful or criminal in the respective countries. All those laws of the parent country, whether rules of the common law, or early English statutes, which were made for the purpose of regulating the wages of laborers, the settlement of paupers, and making it penal for anyone to use a trade or handicraft to which he had not served a full apprenticeship — not being adapted to the circumstances of our colonial condition — were not adopted, used or approved, and therefore do not come within the description of the laws adopted and confirmed by the provision of the constitution already cited. . . .

Stripped then of these introductory recitals and alleged injurious consequences, and of the qualifying epithets attached to the facts, the averment is this; that the defendants and others formed themselves into a society, and agreed not to work for any person who should employ any journeyman or other person, not a member of such society, after notice given him to discharge such workman. The manifest intent of the association is, to induce all those engaged in the same occupation to become members of it. Such a purpose is not unlawful. It would give them a power which might be exerted for useful and honorable purposes, or for dangerous and pernicious ones. If the latter were the real and actual object, and susceptible of proof, it should have been specially charged. Such an association might be used to afford each other assistance in times of poverty, sickness and distress; or to raise their intellectual, moral and social condition; or to make improvement in their art; or for other proper purposes. Or the association might be designed for purposes of oppression and injustice. . . .

Nor can we perceive that the objects of this association, whatever they may have been, were to be attained by criminal means. The means which they proposed to employ, as averred in this count, and which, as we are now to presume, were established by the proof, were, that they would not work for a person, who, after due notice, should employ a journeyman not a member of their society. Supposing the object of the association to be laudable and lawful, or at least not unlawful, are these means criminal? The case supposes that these persons are not bound by contract, but free to work for whom they please, or not to work, if they so prefer. In this state of things, we cannot perceive, that it is criminal for men to agree together to exercise their own acknowledged rights, in such a manner as best to subserve their own interests. One way to test this is, to consider the effect of such an agreement, where the object of the association is acknowledged on all hands to be a laudable one. Suppose a class of workmen, impressed with the manifold evils of intemperance, should agree with each other not to work in a shop in which ardent spirit was furnished, or not to work in a shop with any one who used it, or not to work for an employer, who should, after notice, employ a journeyman who habitually used it. The consequences might be the same. A workman, who should still persist in the use of ardent spirit, would find it more difficult to get employment; a master employing such an one might, at times, experience inconvenience in his work, in losing the services of a skilful but intemperate workman. Still it seems to us, that as the object would be lawful, and the means not unlawful, such an agreement could not be pronounced a criminal conspiracy. . . .

We think, therefore, that associations may be entered into, the object of which is to adopt measures that may have a tendency to impoverish another, that is, to diminish his gains and profits, and yet so far from being criminal or unlawful, the object may be highly meritorious and public spirited. The legality of such an association will therefore depend upon the means to be used for its accomplishment. . . .

*       *       *

## 98 "the encroachments of military despots" (1836)

On June 30, 1835, Texas colonists led by William B. Travis seized the Mexican garrison at Fort Anahuac at the mouth of the Trinity River. Three months later the first major battle of the Texas revolution took place between the American settlers of Gonzales and the Mexican cavalry. A Mexican army of some six thousand under Santa Anna crossed into Texas in early 1836, and the war for independence escalated. On March 1, 1836, at a convention held at Washington, on the Brazos, Texas drew up a declaration of independence. At the same time Travis and his 188 men were preparing to defend the Alamo.

### ☆ 98 Texas Declaration of Independence

Reprinted in B. P. Poore, ed., *The Federal and State Constitutions, Colonial Charters, and Other Organic Laws of the United States* (Washington, D.C.: U.S. Government Printing Office, 1877), pt. 2:1752.

WHEREAS, General Antonio Lopez de Santa Anna and other Military Chieftains have, by force of arms, overthrown the Federal Institutions of Mexico, and dissolved the Social Compact which existed between Texas and the other Members of the Mexican Confederacy—Now, the good People of Texas, availing themselves of their natural rights,

SOLEMNLY DECLARE

1st. That they have taken up arms in defence of their Rights and Liberties, which were threatened by the encroachments of military despots, and in defence of the Republican Principles of the Federal Constitution of Mexico of eighteen hundred and twenty-four.

2d. That Texas is no longer, morally or civilly, bounded by the compact of Union; yet, stimulated by the generosity and sympathy common to a free people they offer their support and assistance to such of the Mexicans of the Mexican Confederacy as will take up arms against their military despotism.

3d. That they do not acknowledge, that the present authorities of the nominal Mexican Republic have the right to govern within the limits of Texas.

4th. That they will not cease to carry on war against the said authorities, whilst their troops are within the limits of Texas.

5th. That they hold it to be their right, during the disorganization of the Federal System and the reign of despotism, to withdraw from the Union, to establish an independent Government, or to adopt such measures as they may deem best calculated to protect their rights and liberties; but that they will continue faithful to the Mexican Government so long as that nation is governed by the Constitution and Laws that were formed for the government of the Political Association.

6th. That Texas is responsible for the expenses of their Armies now in the field.

7th. That the public faith of Texas is pledged for the payment of any debts contracted by her Agents.

8th. That she will reward by donations in Land, all who volunteer their services in her present struggle, and receive them as Citizens.

These DECLARATIONS we solemnly avow to the world, and call GOD to witness their truth and sincerity; and invoke defeat and disgrace upon our heads should we prove guilty of duplicity.

RICHARD ELLIS, President

## 99 "prompted by the pure spirit of christianity" (1837)

The clash between abolitionists and proslavery groups grew violent. In Illinois, newspaper editor Elijah Paris Lovejoy, who held abolitionist views, was shot and killed for his persistence in refurbishing his printing press after mobs twice destroyed it. In Philadelphia, in the summer of 1837, proslavery activities resulted in riots.

The case of *State v. M'Donald* involved an 1812 statute that prohibited aiding in the rebellion of slaves. The judge pointedly remarked, "Even he who professing to be prompted by the pure spirit of christianity shall proclaim to our slaves the doctrine of universal emancipation . . . renders himself a subject for criminal justice." Although the opinion demonstrated the court's attitude toward the defense of moral justification for disobedience to law, it also showed how procedural protections could limit the reach of an overzealous prosecution.

### ☆ 99 *State v. M'Donald* [Alabama]

4 Port. 499 (Alabama, 1837).

*       *       *

The prisoner was indicted in the Circuit Court of Lowndes, in an indictment with four counts:

In the first and third it was charged that he "did maliciously, feloniously and traitorously advise, plot and consult with Moses, a slave belonging to one Jesse H. Robertson, for the purpose of encouraging, exciting and aiding an insurrection against the laws and government of the State of Alabama, &c."

In the second and fourth counts, the term "rebellion" was substituted for "insurrection."

The second concluded as the first; and the third and fourth charged the offence to have been committed "against the people," instead of "against the laws and government."

The prisoner plead not guilty, and the case went to the jury....

[From the record:] "The State's counsel introduced witnesses, who gave evidence, that the master of the slave Moses, in consequence of suspicions entertained by him, directed the slave Moses, that if the prisoner should come to him, that he should conduct him to a particular spot, and there hold the conversation with him. That in consequence of this the negro [Moses] did conduct the defendant to that spot, and held the conversation with the defendant, which was detailed in evidence, in the hearing of his master and another.... In this conversation the defendant said the negroes ought to rise, and if they would he would head them;—that they had hard masters. That they must raise five hundred men, but he would start with three hundred men. That a negro in the neighborhood, named Frank, was to furnish him with a horse. The defendant promised to give the rifle he had with him to Moses, when they started: he shewed him how to cock it, and snapped it two or three times. The defendant told the slave Moses, that they would go to Mobile, and that if they did not like that, they would then go to Pensacola— that, that was a weaker place. That they could get arms and ammunition there, and could press a ship, with which they could go to Texas. That Texas was a free place, and that they might have their freedom there. That they would be joined by other slaves on their way to Mobile. The defendant urged the slave to go home with him, which the negro declined, but promised to come next evening to his house.... [Subsequently] the slave acted under the direction of his master and others, and his questions to the defendant were prompted by instructions from them, and were for the purpose of discovering the defendant. The defendant then told the slave that he must get him one thousand men, but he would start with five hundred. That they would make a forced march to Pensacola, take that, press a ship, and sail to Texas. That it was not safe to stay in Florida, as the United States would reach them:—that he knew how to man a ship:—they could enjoy freedom in Texas. He stated they could get guns from their masters, with ammunition and horses, and escape to Pensacola, and that Moses should have his rifle. The defendant said there was no white men engaged— he would head them, and that Frank should be second in command, and Moses third in command."

\*       \*       \*

COLLIER, J.—The first inquiry which invites our consideration, in examining this case, is this—What offence does the indictment charge?

... [The] statute is as follows: "If any free person shall be aiding and assisting, or in any wise concerned with any slave or slaves, in any actual or mediated rebellion or conspiracy against the laws, government or people of this territory, or shall in any manner advise, plot or consult with any slave or slaves, for the purpose of encouraging, exciting, aiding or assisting any such insurrection or rebellion, or intended insurrection or rebellion, such free person so offending, and being thereof convicted, shall suffer death."

The first branch of the act embraces two distinct descriptions of offence.

1st. For a free person to be aiding and assisting, or in any wise concerned with a slave or slaves, in any actual rebellion or conspiracy.

2d. For a free person to be similarly concerned in any meditated rebellion or conspiracy.

The second branch of the act, is alike comprehensive, and subjects to punishment—

1st. Any free person who shall in any manner advise, plot or consult with any slave or slaves, for the purpose of encouraging, exciting, aiding or assisting any such insurrection or rebellion.

2d. Any free person who shall in any manner advise, plot, &c. an intended insurrection or rebellion.

To make "a free person" guilty of the first offence prescribed by the first branch of the statute, it is necessary that there should be an "actual rebellion." To make out the second offence, it is necessary that the offence should not have developed itself by action ... [and] it is necessary that a *slave or slaves* should lend to it a favorable ear.

\*       \*       \*

The terms "rebellion or insurrection," employed in the second branch of the act, are used as synonymous; this is sufficiently indicated by the terms "any such insurrection or rebellion,"—and are referable as the words "any such" prove, to the first branch of the act.

To make a *free person* guilty of *advising, plotting or consulting with any slave or slaves, for the purpose of encouraging, &c. any insurrection or rebellion,* such as the first branch of the act contemplates, it would be necessary to shew that a *slave or slaves* have already assumed a rebellious or insurrectionary attitude, or else, that they *meditate* the assumption of such a position.

It has been already shewn what would constitute a *meditated* rebellion, let us now inquire what is essential to an *actual rebellion or insurrection*. These terms, in their ordinary acceptation, mean a resistance to the established order of things.

However regardless one may be of the dictates of social duty, or reckless of civil order, so long as he locks up, in his own breast, his unpatriotic and wicked feelings, or merely gives vent to them by words, he rebels not against the laws and government of his country. But, when, having indulged these sentiments, for a period sufficiently long to prepare him for active movements, setting at defiance the duties of the man and the citizen, he places himself in hostile array to the quiet and security which society professes to guarantee to its members — he is then, and not sooner, in a state of rebellion to the *laws, government or people of the State*.

In regard to the second offence, denounced by the second branch of the statute, it may be remarked, that a mere intention, undiscovered by any thing said or done, or shewn merely by loose and casual remarks, would not prove an *intended rebellion*.

\*          \*          \*

... If a *free person* shall *in any manner advise*, &c. *with any slave or slaves, for the purpose of encouraging,* &c. *a rebellion or insurrection intended by him only*, he is guilty of this offence, though the arguments addressed to the slave may not have been such as to command his approbation.

\*          \*          \*

The *free person*, whether white or colored, who seeks to sow in the bosom of our slaves, the seeds of disaffection, and urges them to resist by force, the authority of their legitimate masters, renders himself obnoxious to the penalties of the law. And even he who professing to be prompted by the *pure spirit of christianity*, shall proclaim to our slaves the doctrine of universal emancipation, and denounce slavery as incompatible with the sublime and elevated morality of revelation, and thus scatter broad-cast the seeds of discontent, and estrange the affections of the slave from his master, with the intention of arousing him to the effort to break by force the bonds of servitude, renders himself *a subject* for criminal justice. He whose course is thus characterised, must be supposed *Quixotic indeed*, who, when he had employed the means directly calculated to achieve a result so disastrous, could hope to escape the retribution of justice, by declaring to a jury the purity of his purpose — the integrity of his motive. The intention here, as in every other offence of which it is a constituent, need not be shown by direct and positive proof, where it is inferable from facts and circumstances, in themselves manifest.

\*          \*          \*

Having thus determined the proper interpretation of the statute, let us next inquire whether the evidence warranted the conviction of the prisoner, and whether the charge of the judge was proper, considering the indictment, against him....

The words, "any such," it has been said, refer the terms insurrection or rebellion, to the first branch of the act, and are to be taken to mean an actual or meditated rebellion.... There was no proof of an actual rebellion, nor none of a meditated rebellion; but every thing of the kind, is directly disproved, so far as it is possible to shew the non-existence of a fact.

The witnesses all state that there was no insurrection or rebellion, or preparation for it, so far as they could learn — that they had no knowledge of the prisoner tampering with any other slave than Moses. The master of Moses stated that he was faithful and obedient; and that he gave him the earliest information of the advances of the prisoner. — From all this it is clear, that Moses never participated in any criminal design of the prisoner.

\*          \*          \*

... [T]here is error; for the indictment before us, charges offences, — to complete which, it is necessary to shew the participation of slaves, as has been sufficiently shewn in considering the different parts of the act.

Had the indictment charged an advising, &c., for the purpose of encouraging, &c., an intended rebellion, &c. — we will not say that the proof would have been sufficient to authorise a conviction. Such an expression by this Court, might prejudice the prisoner, should he be indicted hereafter for that offence; but we cannot forbear the opinion, that such indictment would much better suit the proof than any that could be framed under the statute.

... It was argued for the prisoner, that as the advising, plotting or consulting, for the purpose of encouraging, exciting, aiding or assisting an insurrection or rebellion, against the laws, government or people, was treason in other countries, and particularly in England, — these could not be indicted as a distinct and substantive offence here.

\*          \*          \*

Our Legislature ... exercises all [powers] as are compatible with the social compact, unless restrained by express inhibition or clear implication.

[T]he right of protection belongs to man in a state of nature — and he may exert this right, as a member of society, in cases of emergency, where there is neither time nor opportunity to apply to the government. This right of protection extends itself to communities, and is the foundation of the moral power to punish crimes, or provide against their commission. Society owes to each of its members a security for those rights, which he retains upon entering into it: among these stands first, the right of personal security. If this right is assailed, the assailant is obnoxious to punishment. And the right to punish crime, actually committed, includes the right to prevent it, by punishing him who contemplates it, without waiting for an act of personal aggression. This is preventive justice—the right to exercise which, is unquestionable, at this day.

We do not deem it necessary to enquire, if an actual rebellion or insurrection had taken place, whether the indictment should have been for *treason*; or whether *treason* can be committed against the laws, government or people of a State—as neither of these questions arise in this case: "Sufficient unto the day, is the evil thereof."

*     *     *

Our conclusion is, that the conviction of the prisoner was unauthorised—that the judgment of the Circuit Court must be reversed, and that the prisoner remain in custody, until he be discharged by due course of law.

## 100  An Incendiary Petition to Congress (1839)

The Virginia law against incendiary publications was applied not only to books, journals, pamphlets, and other circulars but also to citizens' petitions. The court in *Barrett* avoided the question concerning the state's power to restrain a petition to Congress. Nevertheless, the court overturned Barrett's conviction on procedural grounds, thus frustrating law enforcement officials in their attempt to enforce the law.

☆100  *Commonwealth v. Barrett* [Virginia]

36 Va. 233 (9 Leigh 655) (1839).

At September term 1839, the attorney prosecuting for the commonwealth in the said court moved for rules against *Lysander Barrett* and ten other persons, to shew cause why criminal informations should not be filed against them respectively, for violations of the "act to suppress the circulation of incendiary publications, and for other purposes," passed March 23, 1836. . . . In support of the motion, the attorney for the commonwealth produced affidavits of several witnesses, proving that the said *Lysander Barrett* had caused to be circulated in the county of *Lewis*, for the purpose of procuring signatures, and that the ten other persons aforesaid had signed, a memorial to congress, which prayed the abolition of slavery in the district of *Columbia*, and contained the following expressions: "In the opinion of your petitioners, slavery and the slave trade, as at present existing in the district of *Columbia*, where congress has sole jurisdiction ought not so to be,—as

a sin against God, a foul stain upon our national character, and contrary to the spirit of our republican institutions." *Lysander Barrett* appeared, and contested the motion for the said rule against him: whereupon, with his consent, the circuit court adjourned to this court, for novelty and difficulty, the following questions: 1. Is circulating the aforesaid memorial to congress, and procuring subscribers thereto, an offence under the provisions of the aforesaid act to suppress the circulation of incendiary publications, and for other purposes, passed March 23, 1836? 2. Is the signing of the said memorial an offence by the signers thereof, under the said statute? 3. Is it necessary, in order to furnish the foundation of a rule for a criminal information against the said *Lysander Barrett* for the causes aforesaid, that there should be proof that he was a member or agent of an abolition or antislavery society?

The response of the general court was as follows:

"This court is unanimously of opinion and doth decide, in answer to the 3d question adjourned, that to sustain a prosecution for the offence created by the first section of the act to suppress the circulation of incendiary publications, and for other purposes, passed March 23, 1836, the person accused must be a member or agent of an abolition or antislavery society.

"This court is also of opinion that the offence created by the 2d section of the aforesaid statute, being a felony, cannot be prosecuted by information; and that consequently the 1st and 2d questions adjourned by the circuit court to this court do not properly arise in this case."

## 101  "the dreadful acts by which they asserted their liberty" (1841)

Occasionally, the United States courts had to adjudicate the rights of alien blacks. In 1841, the Supreme Court considered a case involving a captured Spanish schooner, *Amistad*, and its cargo of blacks. Taken in Africa, sold in Cuba, and en route to another port, the blacks, under the leadership of Cinque, had seized the vessel and sailed into United States waters. Were they to be treated as slaves to be surrendered to their masters or as liberty-seeking free men? Justice Joseph Story concluded that they were not pirates but "free native Africans" who, unlike slaves, possessed the same rights to use violence to defend or regain liberty as any other kidnapped persons. Although the Supreme Court decision stirred Southern frustration because it seemed to subordinate the property rights of the owners of slaves to a slave's "right to escape," no recourse to abolitionist arguments was made, and the court clearly stated that if these blacks were recognized to be slaves by international and Spanish law, they would be subject to recapture. But such was not the case, since Spanish law prohibited the taking of slaves in Africa. The incident, which caused nation-wide attention at the time, was lost to the public until Cinque's namesake in the Symbionese Liberation Army caused a recollection of the incident in the 1970s.

☆ 101 *United States v. Amistad*

40 U.S. (15 Pet.) 518 (1841).

MR. JUSTICE STORY delivered the opinion of the court.

\*       \*       \*

... The vessel, with the negroes and other persons on board, was brought by [Naval] Lieutenant Gedney into the district of Connecticut, and there libelled for salvage [by the United States] in the district court of the United States. A libel for salvage was also filed by Henry Green and Pelatiah Fordham, of Sag Harbor, Long Island. On the 18th of September, Ruiz and Montez filed claims and libels, in which they asserted their ownership of the negroes as their slaves, and of certain parts of the cargo, and prayed that the same might be "delivered to them, or to the representatives of her Catholic Majesty, as might be most proper." ...

On the 7th of January 1840, the negroes ... filed an answer, denying that they were slaves, or the property of Ruiz and Montez, or that the court could, under the constitution or laws of the United States, or under any treaty, exercise any jurisdiction over their persons, by reason of the premises; and praying that they might be dismissed. They specially set forth and insisted in this answer, that they were native-born Africans; born free, and still, of right, ought to be free and not slaves. ... The main controversy is, whether these negroes are the property of Ruiz and Montez, and ought to be delivered up. ... It has been argued on behalf of the United States, that the court are bound to deliver them up, according to the treaty of 1795, with Spain. The ninth article [of the treaty] provides, "that ... all ships and merchandize, of what nature soever, which shall be rescued out of the hands of any pirates or robbers, on the high seas, shall be brought into some port of either state, and shall be delivered to the custody of the officers of that port, in order to be taken care of and restored, entire, to the true proprietor, as soon as due and sufficient proof shall be made concerning the property thereof." This is the article on which the main reliance is placed on behalf of the United States, for the restitution of these negroes. To bring the case within the article, it is essential to establish: 1st, That these negroes, under all the circumstances, fall within the description of merchandize, in the sense of the treaty. 2d, That there has been a rescue

of them on the high seas, out of the hands of the pirates and robbers; which, in the present case, can only be, by showing that they themselves are pirates and robbers: and 3d, That Ruiz and Montez, the asserted proprietors, are the true proprietors, and have established their title by competent proof.

If these negroes were, at the time, lawfully held as slaves, under the laws of Spain, and recognised by those laws as property, capable of being lawfully bought and sold; we see no reason why they may not justly be deemed, within the intent of the treaty, to be included under the denomination of merchandize, and as such ought to be restored to the claimants; for upon that point the laws of Spain would seem to furnish the proper rule of interpretation. But admitting this, it is clear, in our opinion, that neither of the other essential facts and requisites has been established in proof; and the *onus probandi* of both lies upon the claimants to give rise to the *casus foederis*. It is plain, beyond controversy, if we examine the evidence, that these negroes never were the lawful slaves of Ruiz or Montez, or of any other Spanish subjects. They are natives of Africa, and were kidnapped there, and were unlawfully transported to Cuba, in violation of the laws and treaties of Spain, and the most solemn edicts and declarations of that government. By those laws and treaties, and edicts, the African slave-trade is utterly abolished; the dealing in that trade is deemed a heinous crime; and the negroes thereby introduced into the dominions of Spain, are declared to be free. ... The supposed proprietary interest of Ruiz and Montez is completely displaced, if we are at liberty to look at the evidence, or the admissions of the district-attorney.

If then, these negroes are not slaves, but are kidnapped Africans, who, by the laws of Spain itself, are entitled to their freedom, and were kidnapped and illegally carried to Cuba, and illegally detained and restrained on board the Amistad; there is no pretence to say, that they are pirates or robbers. We may lament the dreadful acts by which they asserted their liberty, and took possession of the Amistad, and endeavored to regain their native country; but they cannot be deemed pirates or robbers, in the sense of the law of nations, or the treaty with Spain, or the laws of Spain itself; at least, so far as those laws have been brought to our knowledge. Nor do the libels of Ruiz or Montez assert them to be such.

This posture of the facts would seem, of itself, to put an end to the whole inquiry upon the merits. But it is argued, on behalf of the United States that the ship and cargo, and negroes, were duly documented as belonging to Spanish subjects, and this court have no right to look behind these documents; that full faith and credit is to be given to them; and that they are to be held conclusive evidence in this cause, even although it should be established by the most satisfactory proofs, that they have been obtained by the grossest frauds and impositions upon the constituted authorities of Spain. To this argument, we can, in no wise, assent. There is nothing in the treaty which justifies or sustains the argument.... [A]lthough public documents of the government, accompanying property found on board of the private ships of a foreign nation, certainly are to be deemed *prima facie* evidence of the facts which they purport to state, yet they are always open to be impugned for fraud; and whether that fraud be in the original obtaining of these documents, or in the subsequent fraudulent and illegal use of them, when once it is satisfactorily established, it overthrows all their sanctity, and destroys them as proof. Fraud will vitiate any, even the most solemn, transactions; and an asserted title to property, founded upon it is utterly void. This is not a mere rule of municipal jurisprudence. Nothing is more clear in the law of nations ... than the doctrine, that the ship's papers are but prima facie evidence, and that, if they are shown to be fraudulent, they are not to be held proof of any valid title....

It is also a most important consideration, in the present case, which ought not to be lost sight of, that, supposing these African negroes not to be slaves, but kidnapped, and free negroes, the treaty with Spain cannot be obligatory upon them; and the United States are bound to respect their rights as much as those of Spanish subjects. The conflict of rights between the parties, under such circumstances, becomes positive and inevitable, and must be decided upon the eternal principles of justice and international law. If the contest were about any goods on board of this ship, to which American citizens asserted a title, which was denied by the Spanish claimants, there could be no doubt of the right of such American citizens to litigate their claims before any competent American tribunal, notwithstanding the treaty with Spain. A fortiori, the doctrine must apply, where human life and human liberty are in issue, and constitute the very essence of the controversy. The treaty with Spain never could have intended to take away the equal rights of all foreigners, who should contest their claims before any of our courts, to equal justice; or to deprive such foreigners of the protection given them by other treaties, or by the general law of nations. Upon the merits of the case, then, there does not seem to us to be any ground for doubt, that these negroes ought to be deemed free; and that the Spanish treaty interposes no obstacle to the just assertion of their rights.

*　　　*　　　*

# 102 The Recognition of Political Crime (1843)

An 1843 commercial treaty between France and the United States provided the first documented recognition by the United States of a difference between common criminals and those who commit offenses of a "purely political character." Article V stated that the extradition obligations under the treaty were not to apply to the latter class. Although not defined in the treaty, the recognition of such crimes and the propriety of differential treatment for such offenders corresponded with the European jurisprudence of the period. The political offender exception originated in an earlier treaty between France and Belgium (1833) and is attributed to the period of political instability, revolutions, and coups d'état in Europe which the French Revolution inaugurated. The United States, unlike several Continental countries, never extended the political crime differentiation from the treaty to domestic criminal law, but the exception has continued unaffected for extradition purposes to this day.

## ☆ 102 Convention for the Surrender of Criminals between the United States of America and His Majesty the King of the French

8 Stat. 585 (1843).

The United States of America and His Majesty the King of the French having judged it expedient, with a view to the better administration of justice, and to the prevention of crime within their respective territories and jurisdictions, that persons charged with the crimes hereinafter enumerated, and being fugitives from justice, should, under certain circumstances, be reciprocally delivered up....

ARTICLE I. It is agreed that the High Contracting Parties shall ... deliver up to justice persons who, being accused of the crimes enumerated in the next following article, committed within the jurisdiction of the requiring party, shall seek an asylum, or shall be found within the territories of the other: *Provided*, That this shall be done only when the fact of the commission of the crime shall be so established as that the laws of the country in which the fugitive or the person so accused shall be found would justify his or her apprehension and commitment for trial, if the crime had been there committed.

ARTICLE II. Persons shall be so delivered up who shall be charged, according to the provisions of this Convention, with any of the following crimes, to wit: murder, (comprehending the crimes designated in the French Penal Code by the terms, assassination, parricide, infanticide, and poisoning,) or with an attempt to commit murder, or with rape, or with forgery, or with arson, or with embezzlement by public officers, when the same is punishable with infamous punishment.

\*          \*          \*

ARTICLE V. The provisions of the present Convention shall not be applied in any manner to the crimes enumerated in the second article, committed anterior to the date thereof, nor to any crime or offence of a purely political character.

\*          \*          \*

# 103 "No Union with Slaveholders" (1844)

Garrison and the American Anti-Slavery Society went so far in support of abolitionism as to contend that morally, abolitionists could not vote or hold office under the United States Constitution. Garrison considered the Constitution, which permitted slavery and repression of blacks, a covenant with death and an agreement with hell. Conscientious objection to slavery was so strong among the abolitionists that they viewed it as a justification for their breaking the laws of the states and their repudiation of the authority of the Union and its social compact—the Constitution.

☆ 103 Resolution—Can Abolitionists Vote or Take Office under the United States Constitution? American Anti-Slavery Society Annual Meeting

Reprinted in W. Garrison and F. Garrison, *William Lloyd Garrison: The Story of His Life Told by His Children* (New York: Arno Press, 1969), 3:96-133.

*Resolved*, That secession from the present United States government is the duty of every abolitionist; since no one can take office, or throw a vote for another to hold office, under the United States Constitution, without violating his anti-slavery principles, and rendering himself an abettor of the slaveholder in his sin.

The passage of this Resolution has caused two charges to be brought against the Society: *First*, that it is a no-government body, and that the whole doctrine of non-resistance is endorsed by this vote; and *secondly*, that the Society transcended its proper sphere and constitutional powers by taking such a step.

The logic which infers that because a man thinks the Federal Government bad, he must necessarily think *all* government so, has at least, the merit and the charm of novelty. There is a spice of arrogance just perceptible, in the conclusion that the Constitution of these United States is so perfect, that one

who dislikes it could never be satisfied with any form of government whatever!

\*          \*          \*

The Society is not opposed to government, but only to *this* Government based upon and acting for slavery.

With regard to the second charge, of exceeding its proper limits and trespassing on the rights of the minority, it is enough to say, that the object of the American Anti-Slavery Society is the "entire abolition of slavery in the United States." Of course it is its duty to find out all the sources of pro-slavery influence in the land. It is its right, it is its duty to try every institution in the land, no matter how venerable, or sacred, by the touch-stone of anti-slavery principle.... It has tried the Constitution, and pronounced it unsound.

... The qualification for membership remains the same, "the belief that slave-holding is a heinous crime." ...

No one who did not vote for the Resolution is responsible for it. No one is asked to quit our platform. We, the majority, only ask him to extend to our opinions the same toleration that we extend to him, and agreeing to differ on this point, work together where we can. We proscribe no man for difference of opinion.

\*          \*          \*

I am aware that we non-voters are rather singular. But history, from the earliest Christians downwards, is full of instances of men who refused all connection with government, and all the influence which office could bestow, rather than deny their principles, or aid in doing wrong. Yet I never heard them called either idiots or over-scrupulous. Sir Thomas More need never have mounted the scaffold, had he only consented to take the oath of supremacy. He had only to tell a lie with solemnity, as we are asked to do, and he might not only have saved his life, but, as the trimmers of his day would have told him, doubled his influence. Pitt resigned his place as Prime Minister of England, rather than break faith with the Catholics of Ireland. Should I not resign a petty ballot rather than break faith with the slave? But I was specially glad to find a distinct recognition of the principle upon which we have acted, applied to a different point, in the life of that Patriarch of the Anti-Slavery enterprise, Granville Sharpe. It is in a late number of the *Edinburgh Review*. While an underclerk in the War Office, he sympathized with our fathers in their struggle for independence. "Orders reached his office to ship munitions of war to the revolted colonies. If his hand had entered the account of such a cargo, it would have contracted in his eyes the stain of innocent blood. To avoid this pollution, he resigned his place and his means of subsistence at a period of life when he could no longer hope to find any other lucrative employment." ...

One friend proposes to vote for men who shall be pledged not to take office unless the oath of the Constitution is dispensed with, and who shall then go on to perform in their offices only such duties as we, their constituents, approve. ... Waiving all other objections, this plan seems to me mere playing at politics, and an entire waste of effort. It loses our high position as moral reformers; it subjects us to all that malignant opposition and suspicion of motives which attend the array of parties; and while thus closing up our access to the national conscience, it wastes in fruitless caucussing and party tactics, the time and the effort which should have been directed to efficient agitation.

The history of our Union is lesson enough, for every candid mind, of the fatal effects of every, the least, compromise with evil. ... The trial of fifty years only proves that it is impossible for free and slave States to unite on any terms, without all becoming partners in the guilt and responsible for the sin of slavery. Why prolong the experiment? Let every honest man join in the outcry of the American Anti-Slavery Society, NO UNION WITH SLAVEHOLDERS.

WENDELL PHILLIPS

## 104 Franchise for Men of Color (1846)

The Southern states were not alone in passing laws to maintain their social, racial, and political order. The New York Constitution imposed stringent qualifications for the enfranchisement of black citizens despite virtually nonexistent requirements for whites. Additional proof of allegiance was required before free blacks were considered sufficiently adherent to the state to be allowed to participate publicly. Such provisions were common.

## ☆104 New York Constitution of 1846, Article III, Section 1

Reprinted in F. Thorpe, ed., *Federal and State Constitutions* (Washington, D.C.: U.S. Government Printing Office, 1909), 5:2656.

SECTION 1. Every male citizen of the age of twenty-one years, who shall have been a citizen for ten days, and an inhabitant of this State one year next preceding any election, and for the last four months a resident of the county where he may offer his vote, shall be entitled to vote ... ; but such citizen shall have been for thirty days next preceding the election, a resident of the district from which the officer is to be chosen for whom he offers his vote. But no man of color, unless he shall have been for three years a citizen of this State, and for one year next preceding

any election shall have been seized and possessed of a freehold estate of the value of two hundred and fifty dollars, over and above all debts and incumbrances charged thereon, and shall have been actually rated and paid a tax thereon, shall be entitled to vote at such election. And no person of color shall be subject to direct taxation unless he shall be seized and possessed of such real estate as aforesaid.

\*          \*          \*

## 105 Maintaining That "owners have not right of property in their slaves" (1848)

As a result of Nat Turner's insurrection and similar incidents, fear of a widespread black rebellion spread among Southern authorities. Each Southern state embarked on a course of harsh repression of slaves, free blacks, and white sympathizers seeking to ameliorate the black condition. The laws were designed specifically to deter whites and free blacks who felt they had a moral obligation to speak against the status quo. The Slave Codes were perhaps the most extreme example of political and racial suppression in American history and relied on a reward and bounty system for enforcement.

## ☆105 Virginia Slavery Law

1848 Va. Acts 113-21.

\*          \*          \*

24. Any free person who, by speaking or writing, shall maintain that owners have not right of property in their slaves, shall be punished by confinement in the jail not more than twelve months, and by fine not exceeding five hundred dollars; and such person may be arrested by any white person and carried before a judge or justice to be dealt with according to law.

25. Any free person who shall write, print, or cause to be written or printed, any book, pamphlet, or other writing, with intent to advise or incite persons of colour within this commonwealth to rebel or make insurrection, or denying the rights of masters to property in their slaves, and inculcating the duty of resistance to such right, or shall, with intent to aid the purposes aforesaid of such book, pamphlet or other writing, knowingly circulate the same, shall be punished by confinement in the penitentiary for a term not less than one nor more than five years.

26. If any postmaster or deputy postmaster shall know that any such book, pamphlet or other writing mentioned in the preceding section has been received at his office, through the medium of the mail, it shall be his duty to give notice thereof to some justice of the peace, whose duty it shall be to enquire

into the circumstances, and to have such book, pamphlet or other writing burned in his presence; and if it shall appear to him by satisfactory evidence that the person to whom the same is directed, subscribed therefor, knowing its character and tendency, or agreed to receive with intention to circulate it, thereby to aid the purposes of the abolitionists, the said justice shall commit him to the jail to be dealt with according to law. Any postmaster or deputy postmaster who shall knowingly violate the provisions of this section shall be punished by fine not exceeding two hundred dollars.

27. It shall be the duty of any judge, justice of the peace, or mayor, before whom any person may be brought for the offence mentioned in the preceding section, to cause such person to enter into a recognizance, with sufficient security, to appear before the circuit superior court of law and chancery having jurisdiction of the offence, at the next term thereof, to answer for the same; and in default of such recognizance, to commit such offender to jail, there to remain until discharged by order of the said court.

*     *     *

39. Every assemblage of slaves, free negroes or mulattoes, at any meeting house or other place for the purpose of public religious worship, where such worship shall be conducted by a slave, free negro or mulatto, and every such assemblage for the purpose of instruction in reading or writing, by whomsoever conducted, and every such assemblage in the night time under whatsoever pretext, shall be unlawful assembly, and it shall be the duty of all magistrates to suppress all such assemblies which occur within their respective jurisdictions; and as often as any slaves, free negroes or mulattoes shall be unlawfully assembled, it shall be the duty of each magistrate within whose jurisdiction the assemblage may be, forthwith to disperse the same, and to that end he may issue his warrant directed to any sheriff, constable, sergeant, or other person specially designated, commanding him to enter the house or place where such assemblage may be, and seize any slave, free negro or mulatto there found, and it shall be lawful for the magistrate giving such warrant, or any other magistrate before whom the same may be returned, to order any slave, free negro or mulatto so seized to be punished by stripes not exceeding thirty-nine.

40. Any white person who shall assemble with slaves, free negroes or mulattoes for the purpose of instructing them to read or write, or shall associate with slaves, free negroes and mulattoes in an unlawful assembly thereof, shall be punished by confinement in the jail not exceeding six months, and by fine not exceeding one hundred dollars; and it shall be lawful for any magistrate in whose jurisdiction

such assemblage may be, to cause any white person found so associated with slaves, free negroes or mulattoes, to enter into a recognizance with sufficient security to appear before the circuit superior court of law and chancery, or county or corporation court having jurisdiction of the offence, at the next term thereof, to answer for the same, and in the meantime to keep the peace and be of good behaviour; and in default of such recognizance, to commit such person to jail, there to remain until discharged by order of said court.

*     *     *

## 106 "that all men and women are created equal" (1848)

The first Women's Rights Convention convened in Seneca Falls, New York, in July 1846. Freed slave and political reformer Frederick Douglass described its declaration as "the basis of a grand movement for attaining the civil, social, political, and religious rights of women."

The choice of the Declaration of Independence as a model for the convention's manifesto testifies to the ambitions of the movement. The new declaration, which resorted to natural rights to justify disobedience of unjust manmade laws and deny allegiance to the governments that make them, furnished the theoretical foundation for the illegal actions of suffragist Susan B. Anthony and the modern feminist movement.

### ☆ 106 Declaration of Sentiments and Resolutions of the First Women's Rights Convention

Reprinted in E. Stanton, S. Anthony, and M. Gage, eds., *History of Woman Suffrage* (New York: Fowler & Wells, 1881), 1:70–73.

When, in the course of human events, it becomes necessary for one portion of the family of man to assume among the people of the earth a position different from that which they have hitherto occupied, but one to which the laws of nature and of nature's God entitle them, a decent respect to the opinions of mankind requires that they should declare the causes that impel them to such a course.

We hold these truths to be self-evident: that all men and women are created equal; that they are endowed by their Creator with certain inalienable rights; that among these are life, liberty, and the pursuit of happiness; that to secure these rights governments are instituted, deriving their just powers from the consent of the governed. Whenever any form of government becomes destructive of these ends, it is the right of those who suffer from it to refuse allegiance to it, and to insist upon the institution of a new government, laying its foundation on such principles, and organizing its powers in such form, as to them shall seem most likely to effect their safety and happiness. Prudence, indeed, will dictate that governments long established should not be changed for light and transient causes; and accordingly all experience hath shown that mankind are more disposed to suffer, while evils are sufferable, than to right themselves by abolishing the forms to which they were accustomed. But when a long train of abuses and usurpations, pursuing invariably the same object evinces a design to reduce them under absolute despotism, it is their duty to throw off such government, and to provide new guards for their future security. Such has been the patient sufferance of the women under this government, and such is now the necessity which constrains them to demand the equal station to which they are entitled.

The history of mankind is a history of repeated injuries and usurpations on the part of man toward woman, having in direct object the establishment of an absolute tyranny over her. To prove this, let facts be submitted to a candid world.

He has never permitted her to exercise her inalienable right to the elective franchise.

He has compelled her to submit to laws, in the formation of which she had no voice.

       \*       \*       \*

Now, in view of this entire disfranchisement of one-half the people of this country, their social and religious degradation—in view of ... unjust laws ..., and because women do feel themselves aggrieved, oppressed, and fraudulently deprived of their most sacred rights, we insist that they have immediate admission to all the rights and privileges which belong to them as citizens of the United States.

In entering upon the great work before us, we anticipate no small amount of misconception, misrepresentation, and ridicule; but we shall use every instrumentality within our power to effect our object. We shall employ agents, circulate tracts, petition the State and National legislatures, and endeavor to enlist the pulpit and the press in our behalf. We hope this Convention will be followed by a series of Conventions embracing every part of the country.

#### RESOLUTIONS

WHEREAS, The great precept of nature is conceded to be, that "man shall pursue his own true and substantial happiness." Blackstone in his Commentaries remarks, that this law of Nature being coeval with mankind, and dictated by God himself, is of course superior in obligation to any other. It is binding over all the globe, in all countries and at all times; no human laws are of any validity if contrary

to this, and such of them as are valid, derive all their force, and all their validity, and all their authority, mediately and immediately, from this original; therefore,

*Resolved*, That such laws as conflict, in any way, with the true and substantial happiness of woman, are contrary to the great precept of nature and of no validity, for this is "superior in obligation to any other."

*Resolved*, That all laws which prevent woman from occupying such a station in society as her conscience shall dictate, or which place her in a position inferior to that of man, are contrary to the great precept of nature, and therefore of no force or authority.

*Resolved*, That woman is man's equal—was intended to be so by the Creator, and the highest good of the race demands that she should be recognized as such.

       \*       \*       \*

*Resolved*, That the same amount of virtue, delicacy, and refinement of behavior that is required of woman in the social state, should also be required of man, and the same transgressions should be visited with equal severity on both man and woman.

*Resolved*, That the objection of indelicacy and impropriety, which is so often brought against woman when she addresses a public audience, comes with a very ill-grace from those who encourage, by their attendance, her appearance on the stage, in the concert, or in feats of the circus.

       \*       \*       \*

*Resolved*, That it is the duty of the women of this country to secure themselves their sacred right to the elective franchise.

       \*       \*       \*

## 107 Rhode Island's Dorr Rebellion (1849)

The struggle for political power between the established regime and popular forces erupted in Rhode Island in the early 1840s and tested the capacity of America's legal system to resolve revolutionary conflicts. Based on a charter issued by Charles II in 1663, the Rhode Island Constitution enfranchised less than half of the state's male population. As a consequence, the election of the state legislature was within the power of fewer than four thousand voters out of a state population exceeding one hundred thousand.

In 1841, the Rhode Island Peoples' Party, a group organized by Thomas Dorr, convened in Providence and framed a new state constitution, declaring the old charter constitution null and void. The new constitution was ratified in a statewide referendum, and Dorr was elected governor of Rhode Island by the newly franchised voters.

Dorr's supporters unsuccessfully attempted to seize the state's arsenal, and the old charter government declared a state of insurrection and imposed martial law. In the face of the inability of his supporters to gain a military victory, Dorr fled to Connecticut to continue the struggle. Dorr was arrested upon his return a year and a half later, tried for treason, convicted, and sentenced to life imprisonment. The following year the State Assembly ordered his release on the condition that he take an oath of allegiance to the existing state constitution. Stalwartly refusing to do so, Dorr was nevertheless unconditionally released soon thereafter by a more sympathetic legislature.

A new constitution was proposed by the charter legislature and adopted in 1843. The legitimacy of Dorr's regime vis-à-vis the charter government eventually was tested before the United States Supreme Court. Martin Luther, a shoemaker and supporter of the Dorr regime, brought suit for trespass against the defendants who broke into his house without a civil warrant to arrest him under orders from their military commander. Luther contended the charter government was not the lawful government of Rhode Island at the time and therefore had no authority to search and arrest. Further, he argued that the declaration of martial law was improper and that therefore the military had no authority to conduct searches and arrests without warrants. The case reached the Supreme Court in 1849. Chief Justice Roger B. Taney, a supporter of Andrew Jackson and an advocate of state's rights, avoided the issue by writing that the court lacked the authority to pass upon the legitimacy of a state government; that question must be left to the Congress and the president. This approach effectively upheld the charter government. Luther, in his pursuit of wider suffrage, could not shed the cloak of treason.

## ☆ 107 *Luther v. Borden*

48 U.S. (7 How.) 1 (1849).

Mr. Chief Justice TANEY delivered the opinion of the court:

\*      \*      \*

The charter government ... passed resolutions declaring that all acts done for the purpose of imposing [Dorr's] constitution upon the State to be an assumption of the powers of government, in violation of the rights of the existing government and of the people at large; and that it would maintain its authority and defend the legal and constitutional rights of the people.

But, notwithstanding the determination of the charter government, and of those who adhered to it, to maintain its authority, Thomas W. Dorr, who had been elected governor under the new constitution, prepared to assert the authority of that government by force, and many citizens assembled in arms to support him. The charter government thereupon passed an act declaring the State under martial law, and at the same time proceeded to call out the militia, to repel the threatened attack and to subdue those who were engaged in it. In this state of the contest, the house of the plaintiff, who was engaged in supporting the authority of the new government, was broken and entered in order to arrest him. The defendants were, at the time, in the military service of the old government, and in arms to support its authority.

\*      \*      \*

The Circuit Court ... instructed the jury that the charter government and laws under which the defendants acted were, at the time the trespass is alleged to have been committed, in full force and effect as the form of government and paramount law of the State, and constituted a justification of the acts of the defendants as set forth in their pleas.

It is this opinion of the Circuit Court that we are now called upon to review.

\*      \*      \*

Certainly, the question which the plaintiff proposed to raise by the testimony he offered has not heretofore been recognized as a judicial one in any of the State courts....

In Rhode Island, the question has been directly decided. Prosecutions were there instituted against some of the persons who had been active in the forcible opposition to the old government. And in more than one of the cases evidence was offered on the part of the defense similar to the testimony offered in the Circuit Court, and for the same purpose; that is, for the purpose of showing that the proposed constitution had been adopted by the people of Rhode Island, and had, therefore, become the established government, and consequently that the parties accused were doing nothing more than their duty in endeavoring to support it.

But the courts uniformly held that the inquiry proposed to be made belonged to the political power and not to the judicial; that it rested with the political power to decide whether the charter government had been displaced or not: and when that decision was made, the Judicial Department would be bound to take notice of it as the paramount law of the State, without the aid of oral evidence or the examination of witnesses; that, according to the laws and institutions of Rhode Island, no such change had been recognized by the political power; and that the charter government was the lawful and established government of the State during the period in contest, and that those who were in arms against it were insurgents, and liable to punishment. This doctrine is clearly and forcibly stated in the opinion of the Supreme Court of the State in the trial of Thomas W. Dorr, who was the governor elected under the opposing constitution, and headed the armed force which endeavored to maintain its authority.

* * *

It is worthy of remark ... when we are referring to the authority of State decisions, that the trial of Thomas W. Dorr took place after the constitution of 1843 went into operation. The judges who decided that case held their authority under that constitution; and it is admitted on all hands that it was adopted by the people of the State, and is the lawful and established government....

The point, then raised here has been already decided by the courts of Rhode Island. The question relates, altogether, to the constitution and laws of that State; and the well settled rule in this court is, that the courts of the United States adopt and follow the decisions of the State courts in questions which concern merely the constitution and laws of the State.

Upon what ground could the Circuit Court of the United States which tried this case have departed from this rule, and disregarded and overruled the decisions of the courts of Rhode Island? ... [T]he power of determining that a State government has been lawfully established, which the courts of the State disown and repudiate, is not one of them. Upon such a question the courts of the United States are bound to follow the decisions of the State tribunals, and must therefore regard the charter government as the lawful and established government during the time of this contest.

* * *

Moreover, the Constitution of the United States, as far as it has provided for an emergency of this kind, and authorized the general government to interfere in the domestic concerns of a State, has treated the subject as political in its nature, and placed the power in the hands of that department.

* * *

Under ... the Constitution it rests with Congress to decide what government is the established one in a State. For as the United States guarantee to each State a republican government, Congress must necessarily decide what government is established in the State before it can determine whether it is republican or not. And when the senators and representatives of a State are admitted into the councils of the Union, the authority of the government under which they are appointed, as well as its republican character, is recognized by the proper constitutional

authority. And its decision is binding on every other department of the government, and could not be questioned in a judicial tribunal....

So, too, as relates to the clause in the above mentioned article of the Constitution.... Congress ... provided that, "in case of an insurrection in any State against the government thereof, it shall be lawful for the President of the United States, on application of the Legislature of such State or of the executive (when the Legislature cannot be convened), to call forth such number of the militia of any other State or States, as may be applied for, as he may judge sufficient to suppress such insurrection."

By this act, the power of deciding whether the exigency had arisen upon which the government of the United States is bound to interfere, is given to the President.... [H]e must determine what body of men constitute the Legislature, and who is the governor, before he can act.... If there is an armed conflict, like the one of which we are speaking, it is a case of domestic violence, and one of the parties must be in insurrection against the lawful government. And the President must, of necessity, decide which is the government, and which party is unlawfully arrayed against it, before he can perform the duty imposed upon him by the act of Congress.

After the President has acted and called out the militia, is a circuit court of the United States authorized to inquire whether his decision was right? Could the court, while the parties were actually contending in arms for the possession of the government, call witnesses before it and inquire which party represented a majority of the people? ... If the judicial power extends so far, the guarantee contained in the Constitution of the United States is a guarantee of anarchy, and not of order. Yet if this right does not reside in the courts when the conflict is raging, if the judicial power is at that time bound to follow the decision of the political, it must be equally bound when the contest is over. It cannot, when peace is restored, punish as offenses and crimes the acts which it before recognized, and was bound to recognize, as lawful.

It is true that in this case the militia were not called out by the President. But upon the application of the governor under the charter government, the President recognized him as the executive power of the State, and took measures to call out the militia to support his authority if it should be found necessary for the general government to interfere; and it is admitted in the argument, that it was the knowledge of this decision that put an end to the armed opposition to the charter government, and prevented any further efforts to establish by force the proposed constitution. The interference of the President, therefore, by announcing his determination, was as effectual as if the militia had been assembled under his orders. And it should be equally authoritative. For certainly no court of the United States, with a knowledge of this decision, would have been justified in recognizing the opposing party as the lawful government; or in treating as wrong-doers or insurgents the officers of the government which the President had recognized, and was prepared to support by an armed force. In the case of foreign nations, the government acknowledged by the President is always recognized in the courts of justice. And this principle has been applied by the act of Congress to the sovereign States of the Union.

* * *

The remaining question is whether the defendants, acting under military orders issued under the authority of the government, were justified in breaking and entering the plaintiff's house.... Unquestionably a military government, established as the permanent government of the State, would not be a republican government and it would be the duty of Congress to overthrow it. But the law of Rhode Island evidently contemplated no such government. It was intended merely for the crisis, and to meet the peril in which the existing government was placed by the armed resistance to its authority. ... And if the government of Rhode Island deemed armed opposition so formidable, and so ramified throughout the State, as to require the use of its military force and the declaration of martial law, we see no ground upon which this court can question its authority. It was a state of war; and the established government resorted to the rights and usages of war to maintain itself, and to overcome the unlawful opposition. And in that state of things the officers engaged in its military service might lawfully arrest anyone, who, from the information before them, they had reasonable grounds to believe was engaged in the insurrection; and might order a house to be forcibly entered and searched, when there were reasonable grounds for supposing he might be there concealed.... No more force, however, can be used than is necessary to accomplish the object. And if the power is exercised for the purposes of oppression, or any injury willfully done to person or property, the party by whom, or by whose order, it is committed would undoubtedly be answerable.

* * *

Upon the whole, we see no reason for disturbing the judgment of the Circuit Court. The admission of evidence to prove that the charter government was the established government of the State was an irregularity, but is not material to the judgment....

Much of the argument on the part of the plaintiff turned upon political rights and political questions, upon which the court has been urged to express an opinion. We decline doing so. The high power has been conferred on this court of passing judgment upon the acts of the State sovereignties, and of the legislative and executive branches of the federal government, and of determining whether they are beyond the limits of power marked out for them respectively by the Constitution of the United States. This tribunal, therefore, should be the last to overstep the boundaries which limit its own jurisdiction. And while it should always be ready to meet any question confided to it by the Constitution, it is equally its duty not to pass beyond its appropriate sphere of action, and to take care not to involve itself in discussions which properly belong to other forums. No one, we believe, has ever doubted the proposition, that, according to the institutions of this country, the sovereignty in every State resides in the people of the State, and that they may alter and change their form of government at their own pleasure. But whether they have changed it or not by abolishing an old government, and establishing a new one in its place, is a question to be settled by the political power. And when that power has decided, the courts are bound to take notice of its decision, and to follow it.

*The judgment of the Circuit Court must therefore be affirmed.*

Mr. Justice WOODBURY, dissenting:

* * *

[The] difference ... between me and my brethren extends only to the points in issue concerning martial law.... I concur with the rest of the court in the opinion, that the other leading question, the validity of the old charter at that time, is not within our constitutional jurisdiction.... It must be very obvious, on a little reflection that the last is a mere political question.... For they extend to the power of the people, independent of the Legislature, to make constitutions—to the right of suffrage among different classes of them in doing this—to the authority of naked majorities—and other kindred questions, of such high political interest as during a few years to have agitated much of the Union no less than Rhode Island.

But, fortunately for our freedom from political excitements in judicial duties, this court can never with propriety be called on officially to be the umpire in questions merely political. The adjustment of these questions belongs to the people and their political representatives, either in the State or general government. These questions relate to matters not to be settled on strict legal principles. They are adjusted rather by inclination—or prejudice or compromise, often. Some of them succeed or are defeated even by public policy alone, or mere naked power, rather than intrinsic right.

* * *

If it be asked what redress have the people, if wronged in these matters, unless by resorting to the judiciary, the answer is, they have the same as in all other political matters. In those, they go to the ballot boxes, to the Legislature or executive, for the redress of such grievances as are within the jurisdiction of each, and, for such as are not, to conventions and amendments of constitution. And when the former fail, and these last are forbidden by statutes, all that is left in extreme cases, where the suffering is intolerable and the prospect is good of relief by action of the people without the forms of law, is to do as did Hampden and Washington, and venture action without those forms, and abide the consequences. Should strong majorities favor the change, it generally is completed without much violence.

*         *         *

[A]ll which ... is left for us to decide is ... whether the statute establishing martial law over the whole State, and under which the acts done by the defendants are sought to be justified, can be deemed constitutional.

To decide a point like this last is clearly within judicial cognizance, it being a matter of private personal authority and right, set up by the defendants under constitutions and laws, and not of political power, to act in relation to the making of the former.

*         *         *

The Legislature evidently meant to be understood in that sense by using words [martial law] of such well settled construction, without any limit or qualification, and covering the whole State with its influence, under a supposed exigency and justification for such an unusual course. I do not understand this to be directly combated in the opinion just delivered by the Chief Justice. That they could mean no other than the ancient martial law often used before the Petition of Right, and sometimes since, is further manifest from the fact that they not only declared "martial" law to exist over the State, but put their militia into the field to help, by means of them and such a law, to suppress the action of those denominated "insurgents" and this without any subordination to the civil power, or any efforts in conjunction and in co-operation with it.

*         *         *

[I]n every country which makes any claim to political or civil liberty, "martial law," as here attempted and as once practiced in England against her own people, has been expressly forbidden there for near two centuries, as well as by the principles of every other free constitutional government. And it would be not a little extraordinary, if the spirit of our institutions, both State and national, was not much stronger than in England against the unlimited exercise of martial law over a whole people, whether attempted by any chief magistrate or even by a Legislature.

*         *         *

[H]ow under the general principles of American jurisprudence in modern times, [can such a law] properly exist, or be judicially upheld [?]. A brief retrospect of the gradual, but decisive, repudiation of it in England will exhibit many of the reasons why such a law cannot be rightfully tolerated anywhere in this country.

*         *         *

It appears, also, that nobody has dared to exercise it, in war or peace, on the community at large, in England, for the last century and a half, unless specially enacted by Parliament, in some great exigency and under various restrictions, and then under the theory, not that it is consistent with bills of rights and constitutions, but that Parliament is omnipotent, and for sufficient cause may override and trample on them all, temporarily.

After the civil authorities have become prostrated in particular places, and the din of arms has reached the most advanced stages of intestine commotions, a Parliament which alone furnishes the means of war — a Parliament unlimited in its powers — has, *in extremis*, on two or three occasions, ventured on martial law beyond the military; but it has usually confined it to the particular places thus situated, limited it to the continuance of such resistance, and embraced in its scope only those actually in arms.... When speaking of the absence of other and sound precedents to justify such martial law in modern times here, I am aware that something of the kind may have been attempted in some of the doings of the British Colonial governors towards this country at the Revolution.

*         *         *

Having thus seen that "martial law" like this, ranging over a whole people and State, was not by our fathers considered proper at all in peace or during civil strife, and that, in the country from which we derive most of our jurisprudence, the king has long been forbidden to put it in force in war or peace, and that Parliament never, in the most extreme cases of rebellion, allows it, except as being sovereign and unlimited in power, and under peculiar restrictions, the next inquiry is, whether the Legislature of Rhode Island could, looking to her peculiar situation as to a constitution, rightfully establish such a law under the circumstances existing there in 1842. And, to meet this question broadly, whether she could do it, regarding those circumstances, first, as constituting peace, and next, as amounting to war.

*         *         *

All our social usages and political education, as well as our constitutional checks, are the other way. It would be alarming enough to sanction here an unlimited power, exercised either by Legislatures, or the executive, or courts, when all our governments are themselves governments of limitations and checks, and of fixed and known laws, and the people a race above all others jealous of encroachments by those in power. And it is far better that those persons should be without the protection of the ordinary laws of the land who disregard them in an emergency, and should look to a grateful country for indemnity and pardon, than to allow, beforehand, the whole frame of jurisprudence to be overturned, and everything placed at the mercy of the bayonet.

No tribunal or department in our system of governments ever can be lawfully authorized to dispense with the laws, like some of the tyrannical Stuarts, or to repeal, or abolish, or suspend the whole body of them; or, in other words, appoint an unrestrained military dictator at the head of armed men.

*            *            *

In short, then, there was nothing peculiar in the condition of Rhode Island as to a constitution in 1842, which justified her Legislature in peace, more than the Legislature of any other State, to declare martial law over her whole people; but there was much in her ancient charter, as well as in the plainest principles of constitutional liberty, to forbid it. ... [T]he State Legislature alone possessed no constitutional authority to establish martial law, of this kind and to this extent, over her people generally, whether in peace or civil strife. But some of the members of this court seem to consider the pleadings broad enough to cover the justification, under some rights of war, independent of the act of the Assembly, or, as the opinion just read by the Chief Justice seems to imply, under the supposed authority of the State, in case of domestic insurrection like this, to adopt an act of martial law over its whole people, or any war measure deemed necessary by its Legislature for the public safety.

It looks, certainly, like pretty bold doctrine in a constitutional government, that, even in time of legitimate war, the Legislature can properly suspend or abolish all constitutional restrictions, as martial law does, and lay all the personal and political rights of the people at their feet. But bolder still is it to justify a claim to this tremendous power in any State, or in any of its officers, on the occurrence merely of some domestic violence.

*            *            *

It may not be useless to refresh our minds a tittle on this subject. The Congress [*sic*] expressly provides that "the Congress shall have power to declare war. (Art. 1, sec. 8.) This is not the States, nor the President, and much less the Legislature of a State. Nor is it foreign war alone that Congress is to declare, but "war"—war of any kind existing legitimately or according to the law of nations.

*            *            *

Some mistake has arisen here, probably from not adverting to the circumstance that Congress alone can declare war, and that all other conditions of violence are regarded by the Constitution as but ordinary cases of private outrage, to be punished by prosecutions in the courts; or as insurrections, rebellions, or domestic violence, to be put down by the civil authorities, aided by the militia; or, when these prove incompetent, by the general government, when appealed to by a State for aid, and matters appear to the general government to have reached the extreme stage, requiring more force to sustain the civil tribunals of a State, or requiring a declaration of war, and the exercise of all its extraordinary rights. Of these last, when applied to as here, and the danger has not been so imminent as to prevent an application, the general government must be the judge, and the general government is responsible for the consequences. ...

Carry these constitutional provisions with us, and the facts which have existed, that there had been no war declared by Congress, no actual invasion of the State by a foreign enemy, no imminent danger of it, no emergency of any kind, which prevented time or delay to apply to the general government, and remember that, in this stage of things, Congress omitted or declined to do anything, and that the President also declined to consider a civil violence or insurrection as existing so as to justify his ordering out troops to suppress it. The State, then, in and of itself, declared martial law, and the defendants attempted to enforce it. In such a condition of things, I am not prepared to say that the authorities of a State alone can exercise the rights of war against their own citizens; persons, too, who, it is to be remembered, were for many purposes at the same time under the laws and protection of the general government. ...

Under all these circumstances, then, to imply a power like this declaration of martial law over a State as still lawfully existing in its Legislature would be to imply what is forbidden by all constitutional checks, forbidden by all the usages of free governments, forbidden by an exclusive grant of the war power to Congress, forbidden by the fact that there were no exceptions or exigencies existing here which could justify it, and, in short, forbidden by the absence of any necessity in our system for a measure so dangerous and unreasonable, unless in some great extremity, if at all, by the general government, which alone holds the issues of war and the power and means of waging it.

*            *            *

There having been, then, no rights of war on the part of the State when this act of Assembly passed, and certainly none which could justify so extreme a measure as martial law over the whole State as incident to them, and this act being otherwise unconstitutional, the justification set up under it must, in my opinion, fail. If either government, on the 24th of June, possessed authority to pass an act establishing martial law to this extent, it was, of course, that of the United States—the government appointed in our system to carry on war and suppress rebellion or domestic violence when a State is unable to do it by her own powers. But as the general government did not exercise this authority, and probably could not have done it constitutionally in so sweeping a manner, and in such an early stage of resistance, if at all, this furnishes an additional reason why the State alone could not properly do it.

*     *     *

... Under the worst insurrections, and even wars, in our history, so strong a measure as this is believed never to have been ventured on before by the general government, and much less by any one of the States, as within their constitutional capacity, either in peace, insurrection, or war. And if it is to be tolerated, and the more especially in civil feuds like this, it will open the door in future domestic dissensions here to a series of butchery, rapine, confiscation, plunder, conflagration, and cruelty, unparalleled in the worst contests in history between mere dynasties for supreme power. It would go in practice to render the whole country—what Bolivar at one time seemed to consider his—a camp, and the administration of the government a campaign.

It is to be hoped we have some national ambition and pride, under our boasted dominion of law and order, to preserve them by law, by enlightened and constitutional law, and the moderation of superior intelligence and civilization, rather than by appeals to any of the semibarbarous measures of the darker ages, and the unrelenting, lawless persecutions of opponents in civil strife which characterized and disgraced those ages.

Again, when belligerent measures do become authorized by extreme resistance, and a legitimate state of war exists, and civil authority is prostrate, and violence and bloodshed seem the last desperate resort, yet war measures must be kept within certain restraints in all civil contests in all civilized communities.

*     *     *

# 108 "appeals to passion, and denunciations of the law" (1851)

One outcome of the Compromise of 1850 was the Fugitive Slave Act, which required the return of alleged slaves on the presentation of an affidavit by a person claiming ownership. Northerners severely criticized the act, and its enforcement was uneven.

An incident in eastern Pennsylvania raised suspicions of an organized resistance to enforcement of the act. Judge Kane's charge to the grand jury, impaneled to investigate and possibly charge the individuals involved, stated the law's position regarding justifications of disobedience based on claims of morality and conscience and gave considerable breadth to the definition of treason.

## ☆ 108  Charge to the Grand Jury—Treason [Pennsylvania]

30 F. Cas. 1047 (C.C.E.D. Pa. 1851) (No. 18,276).

... Mr. Edward Gorsuch, a citizen of Maryland, who had come to Christiana, in Lancaster county, Pennsylvania, to reclaim his slaves, was met by a body of armed men, assaulted, beaten and murdered.... And it was stated that for some time before this, gatherings of people had been held from time to time at West-Chester, a town near the place of the outbreak, at which denunciations of the law were made as unconstitutional and of no obligation against "the higher law of every man's conscience:" the judges of the United States who would enforce it denounced ... , and exhortations made and pledges given to defy its execution to the last. The murder of Mr. Gorsuch, under such circumstances, caused a deep feeling throughout the whole country; and it being stated to the court that several bills of indictment for treason against the United States would be laid before the grand jury, that body was thus charged on the law of treason, by

KANE, District Judge. Treason against the United States is defined by the constitution (article 3, § 3, cl. 1) to consist in "levying war against them, or in adhering to their enemies, giving them aid and comfort." This definition is borrowed from the ancient law of England (St. 25 Edw. III., St. 5, c. 2), and its terms must be understood of course in the sense which they bore in that law, and which obtained here when the constitution was adopted. The expression "levying war," so regarded, embraces not merely that act of formal or declared war, but any combination forcibly to prevent or oppose the execution or enforcement of a provision of the constitution or of a public statute, if accompanied or followed by an act of forcible opposition in pursuance of such combination....

The definition, as you will observe, includes two particulars, both of them indispensable elements of the offence. There must have been a combination or conspiring together to oppose the law by force, and some actual force must have been exerted; or the crime of treason is not consummated. The highest, or at least the direct proof of the combining may be found in the declared purposes of the individual party before the actual outbreak; or it may be derived from the proceedings of meeting, in which he took part openly, or which he either prompted, or made effective by his countenance or sanction,— commending, counselling or instigating forcible resistance, to the law. I speak, of course, of a conspiring to resist a law, not the more limited purpose to violate it, or to prevent its application and enforcement in a particular case, or against a particular individual. The combination must be directed against the law itself. But such a direct proof of this element of the offence is not legally necessary to establish its existence. The concert of purpose may be deduced from the concerted action itself, or it may be inferred from facts concurring at the time, or afterwards, as well as before. Beside this, there must be some act of violence, as the result or consequence of the combining. But here again, it is not necessary to prove that the individual accused, was a direct, personal actor in the violence. . . . In treason there are no accessories. There has been, I fear, an erroneous impression on this subject among a portion of our people. If it has been thought safe, to counsel and instigate others to acts of forcible oppugnation to the provisions of a statute,—to inflame the minds of the ignorant, by appeals to passion, and denunciations of the law as oppressive, unjust, revolting to the conscience, and not binding on the actions of men,—to represent the constitution of the land as a compact of iniquity, which it were meritorious to violate or subvert,—the mistake has been a grievous one; and they who have fallen into it may rejoice, if their appeals and their counsels have been hitherto without effect. The supremacy of the constitution, in all its provisions, is at the very basis of our existence as a nation. He, whose conscience, or whose theories of political or individual right forbid him to support and maintain it in its integrity, may relieve himself from the duties of citizenship, by divesting himself of its rights. But while he remains within our borders, he is to remember, that successfully to instigate treason, is to commit it.

It is declared in the article of the constitution which I have already cited, that "no person shall be convicted of treason, unless on the testimony of two witnesses to the same overt act, or on confession in open court." This and the corresponding language in the act of congress of April 30, 1790, seems to refer to the proofs on the trial, and not to the preliminary hearing before the committing magistrate, or the proceeding before the grand inquest. There can be no conviction until after arraignment on bill found. The previous action in the case is not a trial, and cannot convict, whatever be the evidence or the number of witnesses. I understand this to have been the opinion entertained by Chief Justice Marshall, and though it differs from that expressed by Judge Iredell, on the indictment of Fries, I feel authorized to recommend it to you, as within the terms of the constitution, and involving no injustice to the accused.

I have only to add, that treason against the United States may be committed by any one resident or sojourning within its territory and under the protection of its laws, whether he be a citizen or alien.

\*        \*        \*

## 109 The Treason of Giving Shelter (1851)

The federal grand jury indicated one Castner Hanway for treason for not aiding an officer of the United States in executing a fugitive slave warrant. Hanway told the federal officer trying to enforce the law that "he would not assist—that he did not care for that act of Congress or any other act." The case reflects on the particular character of treason as a manifestation of moral or political protest. In the face of the traditional insistence on strict construction of the elements of the offense of treason, the charge of treason against Hanway, who at most violated the Fugitive Slave Law, was trumped-up.

☆ 109  *United States v. Hanway* [Pennsylvania]

26 F. Cas. 105 (C.C.E.D. Pa. 1851) (No. 15,299).

Hanway was indicted for treason against the United States, the punishment for which is death. A number of other persons also stood indicted at this term for the same offence in which he was said to be engaged. The bill charged Hanway with intending to resist, in a treasonable way, the execution of an act of congress passed September 16, 1850, and commonly called the "Fugitive Slave Law." . . .

\*        \*        \*

. . . On the 9th of September, 1851, Mr. Gorsuch, of Maryland, having procured . . . certain warrants to arrest some fugitive slaves of his, went with Kline, an officer, appointed by the commissioner, to Christiana, in Lancaster county, Pennsylvania, to take them. The place was inhabited by people who, in general, were strongly opposed to the fugitive slave law. . . . The fact that the writs had issued, became known to Williams, a negro in Philadelphia, who . . . gave notice that the arrests were to be made, leaving with another person the names of some of Mr. Gorsuch's slaves, on a piece of paper. On the 11th, the officer and the others went over to Parker's, which they reached about daylight. While proceeding along the road, their attention was arrested by the sound of horns and the blowing of a bugle. After watching about Parker's house for a short time, one or two negroes were seen coming out of it. On discovering Kline and his party, they fled back into the house, and on pursuit being made by him, ran up stairs. These negroes were recognized by Mr. Gorsuch as his slaves. Kline entered the house, and almost immediately ascertained that a large number of negroes were concealed in the upper part of it; he nevertheless went to the stairway and called the keeper of the house to come down, stating that he was desirous of speaking to him. The negroes at this time were heard loading their guns. Kline, hearing the noise, said to them that there was no occasion for arming themselves,—that he designed to hurt no one, but meant to arrest two men who were in the house, and for whom he had warrants. Some one replied they would not come down. Mr. Gorsuch then went to the stairway, called his slaves by name, and stated that if they would come down and return home, he would treat them kindly, and forgive the past. Kline then read the warrants three times, and afterwards attempted to go up stairs, when a sharp-pointed instrument was thrust at him, and an axe afterwards thrown down, which struck two of the party below. Mr. Gorsuch then went to the front door of the house, and looking up to the window, again called to his slaves by name, when a shot was fired at him from the window. To show that his party was armed, Kline fired his pistol. At this period a horn was blown in the house, which was answered by other horns from the outside, as if by preconcerted action. The negroes then asked fifteen minutes time for consideration, which was granted to them. At this moment a white man was seen approaching the house on horseback. It turned out to be Hanway. . . . [Kline] called upon him, in the name of the United States, to assist in making the arrests. Hanway replied "he would not assist— that he did not care for that act of congress or any other act,—that the negroes had rights and could defend themselves, and that he need not come there to make arrests, for he could not do it." By this time another white man had arrived on the ground (Lewis), who walked up to Kline, and asked him for his authority to be there. Kline showed his papers to him also. Lewis then read the warrants, passed them to Hanway, who returned them to the marshal. Lewis, after reading the warrants, said, "the negroes had a right to defend themselves." . . . By this time the blacks had gathered in very large numbers around the house, armed with guns, which they commenced pointing towards the marshal. At this juncture, Kline implored Hanway and Lewis to keep the negroes from firing, and he would withdraw his men, leave the ground, and let the negroes go. Hanway instantly replied, "they had a right to defend themselves, and he would not interfere." Kline's answer was, "they were not good citizens, or they never would permit the laws to be set at defiance in this way." One of Mr. Gorsuch's family then remarked, "that all they wanted was their property, and that they did not wish to hurt a hair of any one's head." Lewis replied, "that negroes were not property;" and then walked away. By this time another

gang of negroes had arrived, armed with guns and clubs, and Hanway rode up to them and said something which was not heard. He moved his horse out of the way of the guns; the negroes shouted, and immediately fired from every direction. Hanway rode a short distance down the lane leading from Parker's house, and sat on his horse watching the blacks. Kline then called to Lewis, telling him a man was shot, and begging him to come and assist, which Lewis refused to do. . . . In the effort to escape, these last of Kline's men rushed towards Hanway, who was on his horse which was yet standing still. They besought him to prevent the negroes from pursuing farther. He said he could not. They then asked for permission to get upon his horse, which would afford the means of making their escape. He refused their request, and putting whip to his horse rode off at full speed. . . . In connexion with these facts it appeared from Kline's testimony (1) that so soon as Hanway appeared at the bars, the negroes in Parker's house appeared to be encouraged, and gave a shout of satisfaction, when before that they had appeared discouraged, and had asked for time; (2) that before the firing commenced, Kline had given orders to his party to retreat, and they were actually engaged in the retreat when the attack was made; (3) that Mr. Gorsuch, who was killed, had no weapon of any kind in his hands.

\*        \*        \*

*For the United States.* Levying war against the United States, is a phrase, the meaning of which is settled, both in England and the United States. . . . The matter is settled by our own decisions. In the Cases of the Western Insurgents, in 1795, Judge Patterson says: "If the object of insurrection was to prevent the execution of an act of congress by force and intimidation, the offence in legal estimation is high treason; it is an usurpation of the authority of the government. It is high treason by levying war." In Fries' Case Judge Iredell, in his charge to the grand jury (A.D. 1799), says: "I am warranted in saying, that if in the case of the insurgents who may come under your consideration, the intention was to prevent by force the execution of any act of the congress of the United States altogether, any forcible opposition calculated to carry that intention into effect, was a levying of war against the United States, and of course an act of treason. But if its intention was merely to defeat its operation in a particular instance, or through the agency of a particular officer, from some private or personal motive, though a high offence may have been committed, it did not amount to the crime of treason. The particular motive, must however, be the sole ingredient in the case, for if committed with a general view to obstruct the execution of the act, the offence must be deemed treason."

\*        \*        \*

*For the Prisoner.* If the issue were on the fugitive slave law, and the question was, whether Hanway disapproved it? he could not be convicted even of that. There is no certain evidence which shows that he has an opinion about that law. Admitting that he disapproved the law, as he had a right to, there is no evidence which shows what motive brought him to this spot on the morning of the 11th. The sounding of a horn about breakfast time (an usual signal in the country for breakfast) shows nothing; and if it were clearly shown to be a signal for concourse, it follows not that it was a concourse for at treasonable purpose. There is evidence that there was in the neighbourhood a gang of professional kidnappers, who, on recent occasions, without any authority, had seized black men and carried them away, so that they were never heard of again. And that in consequence of this, there was a general alarm and feeling of indignation in the neighbourhood — not against lawful authority, but against man-stealers. Lewis was informed exactly, that there were "kidnappers at Parker's house," and he gave that information and none other to Hanway. And it does not matter, that by the word "kidnappers" slave owners were sometimes called, since there had recently been people in the neighbourhood to whom the word strictly and legally applied. Now who can say on the evidence what took Hanway to this spot? It is the intent which here is every thing. For if Hanway came there with a lawful intent, it is no treason, even though he did afterwards see with composure the laws violated, or even commit a murder.

... "Treason against the United States, shall consist only in levying war against them, or in adhering to their enemies, giving them aid and comfort." This definition was framed by men who, in the exercise of the right of revolution, had risked the penalties of treason, and studied the subject on the steps of the scaffold. Indignant at the wrongs that had been perpetrated, and the blood that had been shed for fictitious offences made treason by ingenious construction, they determined to deprive both faction and power of so potent an engine of mischief, long used and abused by demagogues and despots. They cut off at one blow, that once flourishing and fatal branch of interpretative treason. They defined the crime by terms severely strict and rigorously exact. ... The offence requires the existence of war. Its sole element is war. It cannot be committed in time of peace. To be guilty of the crime, a person must be actually engaged in the war, or giving aid to those that are. To contemplate, or to advise war, or even to conspire to wage it, is not enough. The war must be actually levied. It must not be a mere tumult — a fight — a struggle in arms between individuals or companies, or violence offered to an executive or military officer of the government, in a matter relat-

ing only to individual interest or private right, but it must be national in its scope and object. It must possess that dignity in mischievous design that aims at the life of the government, or at least at the prostration of some branch of its power, by an armed opposition. It must have the impress of universality. ...

\*       \*       \*

GRIER, Circuit Justice (charging jury).

\*       \*       \*

The bill charges the defendant with "wickedly and traitorously intending to levy war against the United States:" and the jury must find the act or acts to have been committed with such intention. For although the prisoner may have been guilty of riot, robbery, murder, or any other felony, he cannot be found guilty under this bill of indictment, unless you find that he intended to levy war against the United States, or that the acts were committed by himself and others in pursuance of some conspiracy or preconcert for that purpose; and this is a question of fact for the decision of the jury. ...

... [S]ome actual force or violence must be used in pursuance of such design to levy war; but it is altogether immaterial whether the force used is sufficient to effectuate the object; any force, connected with the intention, will constitute the crime of 'levying war.'" ...

... But there must be a conspiracy to resist by force, and an actual resistance by force of arms of intimidation by numbers. The conspiracy and the insurrection connected with it must be to effect something of a public nature, to overthrow the government, or to nullify some law of the United States, and totally to hinder its execution, or compel its repeal. A band of smugglers may be said to set the laws at defiance, and to have conspired together for that purpose, and to resist by armed force, the execution of the revenue laws; they may have battles with the officers of the revenue, in which numbers may be slain on both sides, and yet they will not be guilty of treason, because it is not an insurrection of a public nature, but merely for private lucre or advantage. ... A number of fugitive slaves may infest a neighbourhood, and may be encouraged by the neighbours in combining to resist the capture of any of their number; they may resist with force and arms, their master or the public officer, who may come to arrest them; they may murder and rob them; they are guilty of felony and liable to punishment, but not as traitors. Their insurrection is for a private object, and connected with no public purpose. It is true that constructively they may be said to resist the execution of the fugitive slave law, but in no other sense than the smugglers resist the revenue laws, and the anti-renters the execution laws. Their insurrection, their violence, however great their numbers may be, so long as it is merely to attain some personal or private end of their own, cannot be called levying war. Alexander the Great may be classed with robbers by moralists, but still the political distinction will remain between war and robbery. One is public and national, the other private and personal.

*      *      *

*[The jury found for the defendant.]*

# 110 Teaching Colored Children to Read (1853)

Although Mrs. Margaret Douglas knew that it was against the law to teach slaves, she was unaware that the law forbade the education of free blacks. She and her daughter held school for free black children in a back room in her house in Norfolk, Virginia. City constables searched the house, and she was indicted by the grand jury. Refusing the services of a lawyer, Mrs. Douglas defended herself. She was convicted, but the jury set the penalty at a one-dollar fine. The judge nevertheless disagreed with this leniency, and Mrs. Douglas served a one-month prison sentence.

## ☆ 110 Remarks by the Judge at the Sentencing of Mrs. Margaret Douglas (January 10, 1854)

*State v. Douglas*, 7 Am. State Trials 45 (1853).

Judge Baker [remarks at sentencing]. . . . There are persons, I believe, in our community, opposed to the policy of the law in question. They profess to believe that universal intellectual culture is necessary to religious instruction and education, and that such culture is suitable to a state of slavery; and there can be no misapprehension as to your opinions on this subject, judging from the indiscreet freedom with which you spoke of your regard for the colored race in general. Such opinions in the present state of our society I regard as manifestly mischievous. It is not true that our slaves cannot be taught religious and moral duty, without being able to read the Bible and use the pen. . . .

A valuable report or document recently published in the city of New York by the Southern Aid Society sets forth many valuable and important truths upon the condition of the Southern slaves, and the utility of moral and religious instruction, apart from a knowledge of books. I recommend the careful perusal of it to all whose opinions concur with your own. It shows that a system of catechetical instruction, with a clear and simple exposition of Scripture, has been employed with gratifying success; that the slave population of the South are peculiarly susceptible of good religious influences. Their mere residence among a Christian people has

wrought a great and happy change in their condition: they have been raised from the night of heathenism to the light of Christianity, and thousands of them have been brought to a saving knowledge of the Gospel.

Of the one hundred millions of the negro race, there cannot be found another so large a body as the three millions of slaves in the United States, at once so intelligent, so inclined to the Gospel, and so blessed by the elevating influence of civilization and Christianity. Occasional instances of cruelty and oppression, it is true, may sometimes occur, and probably will ever continue to take place under any system of laws: but this is not confined to wrongs committed upon the negro; wrongs are committed and cruelly practiced in a like degree by the lawless white man upon his own color; and while the negroes of our town and State are known to be surrounded by most of the substantial comforts of life, and invited both by precept and example to participate in proper, moral and religious duties, it argues, it seems to me, a sickly sensibility towards them to say their persons, feelings, and interests are not sufficiently respected by our laws, which, in effect, tend to nullify the act of our Legislature passed for the security and protection of their masters.

. . . Bold and open opposition to [this law] is a matter not to be slightly regarded, especially as we have reason to believe that every Southern slave state in our country, as a measure of self-preservation and protection, has deemed it wise and just to adopt laws with similar provisions.

There might have been no occasion for such enactments in Virginia, or elsewhere, on the subject of negro education, but as a matter of self-defense against the schemes of Northern incendiaries, and the outcry against holding our slaves in bondage. Many now living well remember, how, and when, and why the anti-slavery fury began, and by what means its manifestations were made public. Our mails were clogged with abolition pamphlets and inflammatory documents, to be distributed among our Southern negroes to induce them to cut our throats. Sometimes, it may be, these libelous documents were distributed by Northern citizens professing Southern feelings, and at other times by Southern people professing Northern feelings. These, however, were not the only means resorted to by the Northern fanatics to stir up insubordination among our slaves. They scattered far and near pocket handkerchiefs, and other similar articles, with frightful engravings, and printed over with anti-slavery nonsense, with the view to work upon the feeling and ignorance of our negroes, who otherwise would have remained comfortable and happy. Under such circumstances there was but one measure of protection for the South, and that was adopted. . . .

For these reasons, as an example to all others in

like cases disposed to offend, and in vindication of the policy and justness of our laws, which every individual should be taught to respect, the judgment of the Court is, in addition to the proper fine and costs, that you will be imprisoned for the period of one month in the jail of this city.

## 111 Cutting the Iron Chain or Collar of Any Runaway Slave (1856)

The slavery controversy inspired both words and action from many Americans. Harriet Beecher Stowe's *Uncle Tom's Cabin*, published in 1851, went through 120 United States printings that year alone. In 1854, the Wisconsin Supreme Court released a Wisconsin man convicted of rescuing a runaway slave in violation of the 1850 Fugitive Slave Act and ruled that law unconstitutional. That same year, a mob in Boston attacked the federal courthouse in an attempt to rescue a fugitive slave from return to his Southern owner. In 1856, "Free-Soil" leaders in the territory of Kansas were indicted for treason by their legislature, and raids and lynchings occurred on the Missouri-Kansas border. Slave insurrection and escape to the North became more common.

Louisiana passed its Black Code covering offenses by and against blacks. It established a totally distinct system of criminal justice for slaves and blacks, thereby instituting the first comprehensive system of legal racial apartheid in modern history. The code provided the death penalty for those who wrote, printed, published, or distributed anything "having the tendency to produce discontent among the free colored population or insubordination among the slaves."

### ☆ 111 Louisiana Black Code

1856 La. Acts 1-105.

#### CRIMES AND OFFENCES COMMITTED BY SLAVES AND FREE COLORED PERSONS

Section 1. Any slave who shall commit the crime of wilful murder, on conviction thereof, shall be punished with death.

Sec. 2. Any slave who shall with a dangerous weapon, and with intent to kill, cut or otherwise wound any person, or who shall attempt maliciously to kill by drowning, or strangling, on conviction thereof, shall suffer death.

Sec. 3. Any slave who shall wilfully and maliciously strike his master or mistress, or his master's or mistress' child, or any white overseer appointed by his owner, to superintend said owner's slaves, so as to cause a contusion or shedding of blood, shall be punished with death or imprisonment at hard labor for a term not less than ten years.

Sec. 4. If a slave shall shoot at or stab any person with intent to kill, such slave, on conviction of either of said offences, shall suffer death.

Sec. 5. If any slave or free colored person shall wilfully and maliciously poison or attempt to poison any person, he shall, on conviction thereof, suffer death.

Sec. 6. If any slave or free colored person shall commit a rape, or attempt to do so, upon the body of any white female, he shall, upon conviction thereof, suffer death.

Sec. 7. Any slave who shall encourage or excite any insurrection or revolt in this State, or who shall be in any wise concerned in instigating to the same, on due conviction thereof, shall suffer death.

Sec. 8. If any slave or free colored person shall wilfully and maliciously burn or destroy any building or house, or shall attempt to burn any house or building, he shall on conviction thereof, suffer death.

Sec. 9. If any slave shall strike a white person, for the first and second offence he shall receive such punishment as the jury shall think proper, but for the third offence, the said slave shall suffer death; and whenever any slave shall have grievously and wilfully wounded or mutilated any white person, although it prove to be the first offence, such slave shall suffer death; provided the blow, wound, mutilation or bruises are not made or committed in defence of the person or property of his master, or of some member of his family, or of the person having charge of him, or in whose care he then may be, in which case the said slave shall be excused.

Sec. 10. Any slave who shall feloniously and forcibly take any goods or money from the person of another, by violence or by putting him in fear, shall, upon conviction, be punished with death or otherwise, at the discretion of the court.

*        *        *

Sec. 14. Any slave who shall revolt or rebel against any white overseer, appointed by his owner to superintend the conduct of his slaves, when being punished by him, or another, by his orders, shall, on conviction thereof, be punished at the discretion of the court.

Sec. 15. If a slave, or free person of color, insult or assault and beat any white person, such offender, on conviction of either of said offences, shall be punished at the discretion of the court.

*        *        *

Sec. 18. Whoever shall inflict, or cause to be inflicted, any cruel treatment upon any slave, whether by maltreating, flogging, failing to clothe and feed in a proper manner, by imprisoning, by putting in irons, or by ill treating in any other manner, to be judged of by the court and jury, shall be fined not less than fifty nor more than two hundred dollars. The court and jury shall have power in all cases, whether they convict or not, to decree the sale of the slave at public auction. The owner shall not be allowed to purchase either directly or indirectly, or to have under his control the said slave, under the penalty of one thousand dollars. The price of the slave thus sold, shall be paid over to the owner after deducting all costs....

Sec. 19. Any free person who shall play at any game of chance, or make any bet, or in any manner gamble with any slave, on conviction thereof, be fined not less than one hundred nor more than one thousand dollars, and be imprisoned in the parish jail not less than one month nor more than one year; and on a second or any subsequent conviction for a similar offence, shall be fined one thousand dollars and be imprisoned in the parish jail one year.

Sec. 20. Any master or other person having the charge or government of any slave accused of any capital crime who shall conceal or convey him away, so that he cannot be brought to trial and punishment, shall forfeit the sum of one thousand dollars. But if such slave be accused of a crime not capital, then he shall forfeit the sum of five hundred dollars.

Sec. 21. If any person shall harbor or conceal any runaway slave, knowing him to be such, or shall cut or break any iron chain or collar which any master of slaves may have used, he shall, on conviction thereof, be fined not less than two hundred nor more than one thousand dollars; and in default of payment, he shall be imprisoned not less than three nor more than six months.

*          *          *

Sec. 27. If any person shall, by words, actions, writing, or in any other manner whatsoever, persuade, encourage, or advise any slave to insurrection, against his lawful proprietor, or against the white inhabitants of the State or the government thereof, such person, on conviction, shall suffer death or imprisonment at hard labor at the discretion of the court.

Sec. 28. Whoever shall, with the intent to produce discontent among the free colored population, or insubordination among the slaves, write, print, publish or distribute, anything having a tendency to produce discontent among the free colored population, or insubordination among the slaves therein, shall, on conviction, be sentenced to imprisonment at hard labor or suffer death, at the discretion of the court.

Sec. 29. Whoever, with the intent aforesaid, shall make use of language in any public discourse, from the bar, the bench, the stage, the pulpit, or in any place whatsoever, or whoever shall make use of language in private discourses or conversations, or of signs or actions, having a tendency to produce discontent among the free colored population of this State, or to excite insubordination among the slaves

therein; or whosoever shall knowingly be instrumental in bringing into this State any paper, pamphlet or book having such tendency, shall, on conviction thereof, suffer imprisonment at hard labor not less than three nor more than twenty-one years, or death, at the discretion of the court.

Sec. 30. It shall be the duty of Judges in this State to give the two preceding sections in charge to the Grand Jury at each term of their respective courts.

*          *          *

## RUNAWAY SLAVES

Sec. 82. It shall be lawful to fire upon runaway negroes who may be armed, when pursued, if they refuse to surrender.

Sec. 83. Every person taking up a runaway slave shall immediately convey him before the nearest Justice of the Peace, who shall either commit the slave to the parish prison or send him to the owner, employer, or overseer, if known, who shall pay the person taking him up the rates herafter specified, to wit:

For taking up a slave in the woods, six dollars.

For taking up on the road or plantation, three dollars.

For mileage in all cases, going and returning, ten cents per mile.

For Magistrates' committing, one dollar.

For Jailer receiving and placing in confinement, one dollar.

For feeding slave while confined, twenty-five cents per day.

For Magistrate, for receiving proof of ownership, one dollar.

For delivery by Jailer to owner, fifty cents.

These fees and no others shall be charged.

Sec. 84. The Jailer shall have every slave by him placed in confinement as a runaway, advertised in the nearest newspaper three times, making the advertisment as brief as possible so as to give a full description of the slave confined, with his name, the name of the owner and place of residence, if known, or as given by the slave; and on the owner's payment of the same the Jailer shall produce the printer's receipt for the payment of the advertisement, or the paper with the advertisement therein contained.

## 112 "executors of the will of the majority of our citizens" (1856)

In January of 1848 gold was discovered in California. The subsequent mass migration of American settlers (the Forty-Niners) drastically changed the character of the territory, which had expanded greatly through recent acquisitions from Mexico. Upon President Zachary Taylor's urging, the people of California formed a government and adopted a constitution prohibiting slavery. In his 1849 message to Congress, Taylor proposed that California immediately be admitted into the Union, but Southerners opposed the move for fear of upsetting the congressional and electoral college balance between free and slave states. Both the turbulent nature of the settling population and the absence of federal authority hampered the operation of lawful authority in California.

Self-appointed executors of the will of the people, vigilante committees, formed throughout the territory to substitute for civil law enforcement. Despite their pledge to disassociate themselves from all political activities, the vigilantes frequently disregarded the finer details of legal process and exerted great influence upon the political process.

## ☆ 112 Constitution of the Committee of Vigilantes of San Francisco (May 15, 1856)

Reprinted in J. D. Lawson, ed., *American State Trials* (St. Louis: Thomas Lawbook Co., 1856), 15:65.

*        *        *

Whereas, it has become apparent to the citizens of San Francisco that there is no security for life and property, either under the regulations of society, as it at present exists, or under the laws as now administered; and that by the association together of bad characters, our ballot boxes have been stolen and others substituted, or stuffed with votes that were not polled, and thereby our elections nullifed, our dearest rights violated, and no other method left by which the will of the people can be manifested; therefore, the citizens whose names are hereunto attached, do unite themselves into an association for maintenance of peace and good order of society — the preservation of our lives and property, and to insure that our ballot boxes shall hereafter express the actual and unforged will of the majority of our citizens . . . we are determined that no thief, burglar, incendiary, assassin, ballot-box stuffer, or other disturbers of the peace, shall escape punishment, either by the quibbles of the law, the insecurity of prisons, the carelessness or corruption of police, or a laxity of those who pretend to administer justice; and to secure the objects of this association, we do hereby agree:

1st. That the name and style of this association shall be the Committee of Vigilance, for the protection of the ballot-box, the lives, liberty and property of the citizens and residents of the City of San Francisco.

2d. That there shall be rooms for the deliberations of the Committee, at which there shall be some one or more members of the Committee appointed for that purpose, in constant attendance . . . and if, in the judgment of the member or members of the Committee present, it be such an act as justifies or demands the interference of this Committee, either in aiding in the execution of the laws, or the prompt and summary punishment of the offender, the Committee shall be at once assembled for the purpose of taking such action as the majority of them, when assembled, shall determine upon.

*        *        *

7th. That the action of this body shall be entirely and vigorously free from all consideration of, or participation in the merits or demerits, or opinion or acts, of any and all sects, political parties, or sectional divisions in the community; and every class of orderly citizens, of whatever sect, party, or nativity, may become members of this body. No discussion of political, sectional, or sectarian subjects shall be allowed in the rooms of the association.

8th. That no persons, accused before this body, shall be punished until after fair and impartial trial and conviction.

9th. That whenever the General Committee have assembled for deliberation, the decision of the majority, upon any question that may be submitted to them by the Executive Committee, shall be binding upon the whole; provided nevertheless, that when the delegates are deliberating upon the punishment to be awarded to any criminals, no vote inflicting the death penalty shall be binding, unless passed by two-thirds of those present and entitled to vote.

10th. That all good citizens shall be eligible for admission to this body, under such regulations as may be prescribed by a committee on qualifications; and if any unworthy persons gain admission, they shall on due proof be expelled; and believing ourselves to be executors of the will of the majority of our citizens, we do pledge our sacred honor, to defend and sustain each other in carrying out the determined action of this committee, at the hazard of our lives and our fortunes.

## 113 "a subordinate and inferior class of beings" (1857)

Efforts to resolve, through legislation or resort to the courts, some of the public conflicts derived from the institution of slavery usually were not successful. The proslavery forces controlled the Southern state legislatures. In the federal Congress, the Southern delegations likewise exerted great power. The Supreme Court of the United States was unwilling to undertake radical reforms of the original institutions of the country, including the property right in slaves. In the Dred Scott decision the court reiterated that slaves or their descendants, in bondage or liberated, were not United States citizens and therefore were not entitled to access to the federal judicial system.

## ☆ 113 *Dred Scott v. Sandford*

60 U.S. (19 How.) 393, 400-54 (1857).

Mr. Chief Justice TANEY. . . .

\* \* \*

The plaintiff . . . was, with his wife and children, held as slaves by the defendant, in the State of Missouri, and he brought this action in the Circuit Court of the United States for that district, to assert the title of himself and his family to freedom.

The declaration is . . . that he and the defendant are citizens of different States; that is, that he is a citizen of Missouri, and the defendant a citizen of New York.

The defendant pleaded in abatement to the jurisdiction of the court, that the plantiff was not a citizen of the State of Missouri, as alleged in his declaration, being a Negro of African descent whose ancestors were of pure African blood, and who were brought into this country and sold as slaves.

\* \* \*

That plea denies the right of the plaintiff to sue in a court of the United States, for the reasons therein stated.

\* \* \*

The question is simply this: Can a Negro, whose ancestors were imported into this country, and sold as slaves, become a member of the political community formed and brought into existence by the Constitution of the United States, and as such become entitled to all the rights, and privileges, and immunities, guaranteed by that instrument to the citizen? One of which rights is the privilege of suing in a court of the United States in the cases specified in the Constitution.

It will be observed, that the plea applies to that class of persons only whose ancestors were Negroes of the African race, and imported into this country, and sold and held as slaves. The only matter in issue before the court, therefore, is whether the descendants of such slaves, when they shall be emancipated, or who are born of parents who had become free before their birth, are citizens of a State, in the sense in which the word citizen is used in the Constitution of the United States. . . .

\* \* \*

The words "people of the United States" and "citizens" are synonymous terms, and mean the same thing. They both describe the political body who, according to our republican institutions, form the sovereignty, and who hold the power and conduct the government through their representatives. They are what we familarily call the "sovereign people,"

and every citizen is one of this people, and a constituent member of this sovereignty. The question before us is, whether the class of persons described in the plea in abatement compose a portion of this people, and are constituent members of this sovereignty? We think they are not, and that they are not included, and were not intended to be included, under the word "citizens" in the Constitution, and can, therefore, claim none of the rights and privileges which that instrument provides for and secures to citizens of the United States. On the contrary, they were at that time considered as a subordinate and inferior class of beings, who had been subjugated by the dominant race, and whether emancipated or not, yet remained subject to their authority, and had no rights or privileges but such as those who held the power and the government might choose to grant them.

\* \* \*

In discussing this question, we must not confound the rights of citizenship which a State may confer within its own limits, and the rights of citizenship as a member of the Union. It does not by any means follow, because he has all the rights and privileges of a citizen of a State, that he must be a citizen of the United States. He may have all of the rights and privileges of the citizen of a State, and yet not be entitled to the rights and privileges of a citizen in any other State. For, previous to the adoption of the Constitution of the United States, every State had the undoubted right to confer on whomsoever it pleased the character of a citizen, and to endow him with all rights. But this character, of course, was confined to the boundaries of the State, and gave him no rights or privileges in other States beyond those secured to him by the laws of nations and the comity of States. Nor have the several States surrendered the power of conferring these rights and privileges by adopting the Constitution of the United States. . . .

It is very clear, therefore, that no State can, by any Act or law of its own, passed since the adoption of the Constitution, introduce a new member into the political community created by the Constitution of the United States. It cannot make him a member of this community by making him a member of its own. And for the same reason it cannot introduce any person, or description of persons, who were intended to be embraced in this new political family, which the Constitution brought into existence, but were intended to be excluded from it.

The question then arises, whether the provisions of the Constitution, in relation to the personal rights and privileges to which the citizen of a State should be entitled, embraced the Negro African race, at that time in this country, or who might afterwards be imported, who had then or should afterwards be made free in any State; and to put within the power of a single State to make him a citizen of the United States, and endue him with the full rights of citizenship in every other State without their consent. Does the Constitution of the United States act upon him whenever he shall be made free under the laws of a State, and raised there to the rank of a citizen, and immediately clothe him with all the privileges of a citizen in every other State, and in its own courts?

The court think the affirmative of these propositions cannot be maintained. And if it cannot, the plaintiff in error could not be a citizen of the State of Missouri, within the meaning of the Constitution of the United States, and, consequently, was not entitled to sue in its courts.

It is true, every person, and every class and description of persons, who were at the time of the adoption of the Constitution recognized as citizens in the several States, became also citizens of this new political body; but none other; it was formed by them, and for them and their posterity, but for no one else. And the personal rights and privileges guaranteed to citizens of this new sovereignty were intended to embrace those only who were then members of the several state communities, or who should afterwards, by birthright or otherwise, become members, according to the provisions of the Constitution and the principles on which it was founded. . . .

\*         \*         \*

In the opinion of the court, the legislation and histories of the times, and the language used in the Declaration of Independence show, that neither the class of persons who had been imported as slaves, nor their descendants, whether they had become free or not, were then acknowledged as a part of the people, nor intended to be included in the general words used in that memorable instrument.

\*         \*         \*

They had for more than a century before been regarded as beings of an inferior order and altogether unfit to associate with the white race, either in social or political relations, and so far inferior that they had no rights which the white man was bound to respect; and that the Negro might justly and lawfully be reduced to slavery for his benefit. He was bought and sold and treated as an ordinary article of merchandise and traffic whenever a profit could be made by it. This opinion was at that time fixed and universal in the civilized portion of the white race. It was regarded as an axiom in morals as well as in politics, which no one thought of disputing, or supposed to be open to dispute; and men in every grade and position in society daily and habitually acted upon it in their private pursuits, as well as in matters of public concern, without doubting for a moment the correctness of this opinion.

\*         \*         \*

[T]he men who framed this declaration were great men — high in literary acquirements — high in their sense of honor, and incapable of asserting principles inconsistent with those on which they were acting. They perfectly understood the meaning of the language they used and how it would be understood by others; and they knew that it would not in any part of the civilized world be supposed to embrace the Negro race, which, by common consent, had been excluded from civilized governments and the family of nations and doomed to slavery. They spoke and acted according to the then established doctrine and principles and in the ordinary language of the day, and no one misunderstood them. The unhappy black race were separated from the white by indelible marks, and laws long before established, and were never thought of or spoken of except as property and when the claims of the owner or the profit of the trader were supposed to need protection.

This state of public opinion had undergone no change when the Constitution was adopted, as is equally evident from its provisions and language.

\*         \*         \*

[T]here are two clauses in the Constitution which point directly and specifically to the Negro race as a separate class of persons, and show clearly that they were not regarded as a portion of the people or citizens of the Government then formed.

One of these clauses reserves to each of the thirteen States the right to import slaves until the year 1808, if it thinks it proper. And the importation which it thus sanctions was unquestionably of persons of the race of which we are speaking, as the traffic in slaves in the United States had always been confined to them. And by the other provision the States pledge themselves to each other to maintain the right of property of the master, by delivering up to him any slave who may have escaped from his service, and be found within their respective territories. . . . And these two provisions show, conclusively, that neither the description of persons therein referred to, nor their descendants, were embraced in any of the other provisions of the Constitution; for certainly these two clauses were not intended to confer on them or their posterity the blessings of liberty, or any of the personal rights so carefully provided for the citizen.

\*         \*         \*

. . . Upon a full and careful consideration of the subect, the court is of opinion that, upon the facts stated in the plea in abatement, Dred Scott was not a citizen of Missouri within the meaning of the Constitution of the United States, and not entitled as such to sue in its courts; and, consequently that the Circuit Court had no jurisdiction of the case. . . .

\*      \*      \*

We proceed, therefore, to inquire whether the facts relied on by the plaintiff entitled him to his freedom.

\*      \*      \*

The Act of Congress, upon which the plaintiff relies, declares that slavery and involuntary servitude, except as a punishment for crime, shall be forever prohibited in all that part of the territory ceded by France, under the name of Louisiana. ... [T]his part of the inquiry is, whether Congress was authorized to pass this law under any of the powers granted to it by the Constitution; for if the authority is not given by that instrument, it is the duty of this court to declare it void and inoperative, and incapable of conferring freedom upon any one who is held as slave under the laws of any one of the States.

The counsel for the plaintiff has laid much stress upon that article in the Constitution which confers on Congress the power "to dispose of and make all needful rules and regulations respecting the territory or other property belonging to the United States;" but, in the judgment of the court, that provision has no bearing on the present controversy, and the power there given, whatever it may be, is confined, and was intended to be confined, to the territory which at that time belonged to, or was claimed by, the United States, and was within their boundaries as settled by the treaty with Great Britain, and can have no influence upon a territory afterwards acquired from a foreign Government. ...

\*      \*      \*

... [A]n Act of Congress which deprives a person of the United States of his liberty or property merely because he came himself or brought his property into a particular Territory of the United States, and who had committed no offense against the laws, could hardly be dignified with the name of due process of law.

\*      \*      \*

Now ... the right of property in a slave is distinctly and expressly affirmed in the Constitution. The right to traffic in it, like an ordinary article of merchandise and property, was guaranteed to the citizens of the United States, in every State that might desire it, for twenty years. And the Government in express terms is pledged to protect it in all future time, if the slave escapes from his owner. ... And no word can be found in the Constitution which gives Congress a greater power over slave property, or which entitles property of that kind to less protection than property of any other description. The only power conferred is the power coupled with the duty of guarding and protecting the owner in his rights.

\*      \*      \*

## 114 "threats of assassination" (1858)

Founded by Joseph Smith, the Prophet of Latter-Day Saints, the Mormon church and its members encountered savage persecution wherever they went. Hounded out of Missouri in 1838, Joseph Smith founded the all-Mormon city of Nauvoo on the Mississippi River in Illinois. By 1840, Nauvoo was more populous than Chicago. The murder of Joseph Smith by a mob and the destruction of Nauvoo elevated Brigham Young and resulted in the Mormon move west. In their proposed State of Desert—which would have contained present-day Utah, Nevada, half of California and Arizona, and parts of Oregon, Idaho, Wyoming, Colorado, and New Mexico—the Mormons sought to maintain cultural and religious purity as well as political hegemony.

Assuming the presidency in 1850, Millard Fillmore named Brigham Young territorial governor of Utah. But tensions mounted between the Mormons and the Gentiles in the territory; Brigham Young and his followers were charged by federal officials with establishing an absolute dictatorship in the Utah territory, discrimination against non-Mormons, and disloyalty to Washington. In June of 1857, President Buchanan dispatched an expeditionary force of twenty-six hundred men from Fort Leavenworth to Utah to install non-Mormon officials in the territory. In mid-September Brigham Young ordered his forces to "forbid all armed forces of every description from coming into this territory under any pretense whatever." He further instructed his followers to put the torch to all structures in the line of march of the federal force. Historian Nathaniel Weyl wrote: "The founders of Mormonism in Utah were unquestionably guilty of treason against the United States. They levied an army, declared martial law in Utah Territory, prepared to repel an American expeditionary force, raided its supply depots, attempted to starve its enemy in the desert, and carried out the first scorched earth program in American history."

In 1858 President Buchanan issued a clear and unemotional proclamation in an effort to stop what he thought was "the first rebellion which has existed in our territories."

Although Young planned to burn down Salt Lake City and to retreat into the southern wilderness, the spirit of compromise finally prevailed. Alfred Cumming, the newly appointed territorial governor, counseled negotiations, and in return for Young's recognition of his authority, President Buchanan issued a general amnesty to the rebels of the "Utah War." The decisive action by Washington brought an end to Mormon separatism, yet the costly "Utah War" has continued to be viewed as "Buchanan's Blunder."

☆ 114  President James Buchanan's
Proclamation on the Rebellion in Utah (April 6,
1858)

11 Stat. 796 (1858).

Whereas, the Territory of Utah was settled by certain emigrants from the States, and from foreign
countries, who have for several years past manifested a spirit of insubordination to the Constitution
and laws of the United States, The great mass of
those settlers, acting under the influence of leaders
to whom they seem to have surrendered their judgment, refuse to be controlled by any other authority.
They have been often advised to obedience, and
these friendly counsels have been answered with defiance. Officers of the federal government have been
driven from the Territory for no offense but an effort to do their sworn duty. Others have been prevented from going there by threats of assassination.
Judges have been violently interrupted in the performance of their functions, and the records of the
courts have been seized and either destroyed or concealed. Many other acts of unlawful violence have
been perpetrated, and the right to repeat them has
been openly claimed by the leading inhabitants, with
at least the silent acquiescence of nearly all the others. Their hostility to the lawful government of the
country has at length become so violent that no officer bearing a commission from the Chief Magistrate
of the Union can enter the Territory or remain there
with safety; and all the officers recently appointed
have been unable to go to Salt Lake or anywhere
else in Utah beyond the immediate power of the
army. Indeed, such is believed to be the condition to
which a strange system of terrorism has brought the
inhabitants of that region, that no one among them
could express an opinion favorable to this government, or even propose to obey its laws, without exposing his life and property to peril.

... I accordingly ordered a detachment of the
army to march for the City of Salt Lake, or within
reach of that place, and to act, in case of need, as a
posse for the enforcement of the laws. But, in the
meantime, the hatred of that misguided people for
the just and legal authority of the government had
become so intense that they resolved to measure
their military strength with that of the Union. They
have organized an armed force far from contemptible in point of numbers, and trained it, if not with
skill, at least with great assiduity and perseverance.
While the troops of the United States were on their
march, a train of baggage wagons, which happened
to be unprotected, was attacked and destroyed by a
portion of the Mormon forces, and the provisions
and stores with which the train was laden were wantonly burnt. In short, their present attitude is one of
decided and unreserved enmity to the United States

and to all their loyal citizens. Their determination to
oppose the authority of the government by military
force has not only been expressed in words, but
manifested in overt acts of the most unequivocal
character.

Fellow-citizens of Utah! this is rebellion against
the government to which you owe allegiance. It is
levying war against the United States, and involves
you in the guilt to treason. Persistence in it will
bring you to condign punishment, to ruin, and to
shame; for it is mere madness to suppose that, with
your limited resources, you can successfully resist
the force of this great and powerful nation.

If you have calculated upon the forbearance of
the United States—if you have permitted yourselves to suppose that this government will fail to
put forth its strength and bring you to submission—
you have fallen into a grave mistake. You have settled upon territory which lies geographically in the
heart of the Union. The land you live upon was purchased by the United States and paid for out of their
treasury; the proprietary right and title to it is in
them, and not in you. Utah is bounded on every side
by States and Territories whose people are true to
the Union. It is absurd to believe that they will or
can permit you to erect in their very midst a government of your own, not only independent of the authority which they all acknowledge, but hostile to
them and their interests.

Do not deceive yourselves nor try to mislead others by propagating the idea  that this is a crusade
against your religion. The Constitution and laws of
this country can take no notice of your creed,
whether it be true or false. That is a question between your God and yourselves, in which I disclaim
all right to interfere. If you obey the laws, keep the
peace, and respect the just rights of others, you will
be perfectly secure, and may live on in your present
faith or change it for another at your pleasure.
Every intelligent man among you knows very well
that this government has never, directly, or indirectly, sought to molest you in your worship, to control you in your ecclesiastical affairs, or even to influence you in your religious opinions.

This rebellion is not merely a violation of your legal duty; it is without just cause, without reason,
without excuse. You never made a complaint that
was not listened to with patience. You never exhibited a real grievance that was not redressed as
promptly as it could be. The laws and regulations enacted for your government by Congress have been
equal and just, and their enforcement was manifestly necessary for your own welfare and happiness. You have never asked their repeal. They are
similar in every material respect to the laws which
have been passed for the other Territories of the
Union, and which everywhere else (with one partial
exception) have been cheerfully obeyed. No people

ever lived who were freer from unnecessary legal restraints than you. Human wisdom never devised a political system which bestowed more blessings or imposed lighter burdens than the government of the United States in its operation upon the Territories.

But being anxious to save the effusion of blood, and to avoid the indiscriminate punishment of a whole people for crimes of which it is not probable that all are equally guilty, I offer now a free and full pardon to all who will submit themselves to the authority of the federal government. If you refuse to accept it, let the consequences fall upon your own heads. But I conjure you to pause deliberately, and reflect well, before you reject this tender of peace and good will.

*Now, therefore*, I, James Buchanan, *President of the United States*, have thought proper to issue this, my Proclamation, enjoining upon all public officers in the Territory of Utah to be diligent and faithful, to the full extent of their power, in the execution of the laws; commanding all citizens of the United States in said Territory to aid and assist the officers in the performance of their duties; offering to the inhabitants of Utah, who shall submit to the laws, a free pardon for the seditions and treasons heretofore by them committed; warning those who shall persist, after notice of this proclamation, in the present rebellion against the United States, that they must expect no further lenity, but look to be rigorously dealt with according to their deserts; and declaring that the military forces now in Utah, and hereafter to be sent there, will not be withdrawn until the inhabitants of that Territory shall manifest a proper sense of the duty which they owe to this government.

JAMES BUCHANAN

## 115 John Brown's Constitution (1858)

In 1857, the Supreme Court decided *Dred Scott v. Sandford*, crushing hopes of moderate abolitionists for the gradual emancipation of slaves through national legislation. The radical wing of the abolitionists had been proven right. A native of Torrington, Connecticut, John Brown attended many antislavery meetings, read William Lloyd Garrison's *Liberator* and other abolitionist literature, and knew several of the antislavery leaders of his day. To him, the failure of peaceful means to liberate slaves was evident. "Brown had learned that slavery was an institution based upon force and terror . . ." wrote historian Louis Ruchames, "[a]nd that against men who never hesitated to use force and violence to keep their slaves . . . the only recourse left to anyone with a sense of justice and compassion for the slave was forceful liberation."

John Brown fought as a guerrilla leader seeking to retain Kansas as a free state. But preparing for a revolution that was designed, ultimately, to overcome slavery in the South, Brown also pressed his adherents to adopt a Provisional Constitution to govern the territories liberated by his forces. The forty-eight-article constitution was adopted at a convention held in Chatham, Canada, on May 8-10, 1858, with participation by forty-six Brown followers of both races. Contrary to the prevailing law of the land, Brown's constitution branded slavery as "perpetual imprisonment" and condemned it to "absolute extermination." As in other movements, these organized resisters to lawful authority presented a document that both enshrined their objective and provided a point of cohesion for the group.

## ☆ 115 Provisional Constitution and Ordinances for the People of the United States

Reprinted in L. Ruchames, *John Brown: The Making of a Revolutionary* (New York: Grosset & Dunlap, 1969), 119-21.

PREAMBLE

Whereas slavery, throughout its entire existence in the United States, is none other than a most barbarous, unprovoked, and unjustifiable war of one portion of its citizens upon another portion—the only conditions of which are perpetual imprisonment and hopeless servitude or absolute extermination—in utter disregard and violation of those eternal and self-evident truths set forth in our Declaration of Independence:

Therefore we, citizens of the United States, and the oppressed people who, by a recent decision of the Supreme Court, are declared to have no rights which the white man is bound to respect, together with all other people degraded by the laws thereof, do, for the time being, ordain and establish for ourselves the following Provisional Constitution and Ordinances, the better to protect our persons, property, lives, and liberties, and to govern our actions:

ARTICLE I

*Qualifications for membership.* All persons of mature age . . . who shall agree to sustain and enforce the Provisional Constitution and Ordinances of this organization, together with all minor children of such persons, shall be held to be fully entitled to protection under the same.

\*        \*        \*

ARTICLE III

*Legislative.* The legislative branch shall be a Congress or House of Representatives, composed of not less than five nor more than ten members, who shall be elected by all citizens of mature age and of sound mind connected with this organization, and who shall remain in office for three years, unless sooner removed for misconduct, inability, or by death. . . .

### ARTICLE IV

*Executive.* The executive branch of this organization shall consist of a President and Vice-President, who shall be chosen by the citizens or members of this organization, and each of whom shall hold his office for three years, unless sooner removed by death or for inability or misconduct.

### ARTICLE V

*Judicial.* The judicial branch of this organization shall consist of one Chief Justice of the Supreme Court and of four associate judges of said court, each constituting a circuit court. They shall each be chosen in the same manner as the President, and shall continue in office until their places have been filled in the same manner by election of the citizens. Said court shall have jurisdiction in all civil or criminal causes arising under this constitution, except breaches of the rules of war.

\*          \*          \*

### ARTICLE VII

*Commander-in-chief.* A Commander-in-chief of the army shall be chosen by the President, Vice-President, a majority of the Provisional Congress, and of the Supreme Court . . . and he shall hold his office for three years, unless removed by death or on proof of incapacity or misbehavior. He shall, unless under arrest, (and until his place is actually filled as provided for by this constitution,) direct all movements of the army and advise with any allies. He shall, however, be tried, removed, or punished, on complaint of the President, by at least three general officers, or a majority of the House of Representatives, or of the Supreme Court; which House of Representatives, (the President presiding,) the Vice-President, and the members of the Supreme Court, shall constitute a court-martial for his trial; with power to remove or punish, as the case may require, and to fill his place, as above provided.

\*          \*          \*

## 116 "guilty of a great wrong against God and humanity" (1859)

On Sunday night, October 16, 1859, John Brown and twenty-one others set out to attack the United States arsenal at Harper's Ferry, Virginia. Their goal was to seize the armory and to arm the multitudes of slaves expected to flock to his standard. The raid was a military success, but the slave uprising failed to materialize. Brown and his men found themselves surrounded by the Virginia militia. On Tuesday, October 18, the United States Marines, under the command of Colonel Robert E. Lee, stormed the engine house in which the surviving members of Brown's "Army of Liberation" had taken refuge. Ten of Brown's army were killed in the Harper's Ferry raid, five escaped, and seven, including Brown, were captured and later convicted of three crimes: conspiring with slaves to rebel, murder, and treason.

Several Southern leaders interviewed Brown, who was slightly wounded in the battle, the day after his capture.

## ☆ 116 John Brown's Interview with Southern Leaders (October 19, 1859)

Reprinted in L. Ruchames, *John Brown: The Making of a Revolutionary* (New York: Grosset & Dunlap, 1969), 133–34.

"Old Brown," or "Ossawattomie Brown," as he is often called, the hero of a dozen fights or so with the "border ruffians" of Missouri, in the days of "bleeding Kansas," is the head and front of this offending — the commander of the abolition filibuster army. . . .

Brown is fifty-five years of age, rather small sized, with keen and restless gray eyes, and a grizzly beard and hair. He is a wiry, active man, and should the slightest chance for an escape be afforded, there is no doubt that he will yet give his captors much trouble. His hair is matted and tangled, and his face, hands and clothes all smouched and smeared with blood. Colonel [Robert E.] Lee stated that he would exclude all visiters from the room if the wounded men were annoyed or pained by them, but Brown said he was by no means annoyed; on the contrary he was glad to be able to make himself and his motives clearly understood. He converses freely, fluently and cheerfully, without the slightest manifestation of fear or uneasiness, evidently weighing well his words, and possessing a good command of language. His manner is courteous and affable, and he appears to make a favorable impression upon his auditory, which, during most of the day yesterday, averaged about ten or a dozen men.

When I arrived in the armory . . . Brown was answering questions put to him by Senator [J. M.] Mason [of Virginia], who had just arrived from his residence at Winchester, thirty miles distant; Colonel [Charles James] Faulkner, member of Congress, who lives but a few miles off; Mr. [Clement L.] Vallandigham, member of Congress from Ohio; and several other distinguished gentlemen. The following is a verbatim report of the conversation: —

#### BROWN'S INTERVIEW WITH MASON, VALLANDIGHAM, AND OTHERS

SENATOR MASON. Can you tell us who furnished money for your expedition?

JOHN BROWN. I furnished most of it myself; I cannot implicate others. It is by my own folly that I have been taken. I could easily have saved myself from it, had I exercised my own better judgment rather than yielded to my feelings.

MASON. You mean if you had escaped immediately?

BROWN. No. I had the means to make myself secure without any escape; but I allowed myself to be surrounded by a force by being too tardy. I should have gone away; but I had thirty-odd prisoners, whose wives and daughters were in tears for their safety, and I felt for them. Besides, I wanted to allay the fears of those who believed we came here to burn and kill. For this reason I allowed the train to cross the bridge, and gave them full liberty to pass on. I did it only to spare the feelings of those passengers and their families, and to allay the apprehensions that you had got here in your vicinity a band of men who had no regard for life and property, nor any feelings of humanity.

MASON. But you killed some people passing along the streets quietly.

BROWN. Well, sir, if there was anything of that kind done, it was without my knowledge. Your own citizens who were my prisoners will tell you that every possible means was taken to prevent it. I did not allow my men to fire when there was danger of killing those we regarded as innocent persons, if I could help it. They will tell you that we allowed ourselves to be fired at repeatedly, and did not return it.

*          *          *

MASON. If you would tell us who sent you here,—who provided the means,—that would be information of some value.

BROWN. I will answer freely and faithfully about what concerns myself,—I will answer anything I can with honor,—but not about others.

*          *          *

VALLANDIGHAM. How long have you been engaged in this business?

BROWN. From the breaking out of the difficulties in Kansas. Four of my sons had gone there to settle, and they induced me to go. I did not go there to settle, but because of the difficulties.

MASON. How many are there engaged with you in this movement?

BROWN. Any questions that I can honorably answer I will,—not otherwise. So far as I am myself concerned, I have told everything truthfully. I value my word, sir.

MASON. What was your object in coming?

BROWN. We came to free the slaves, and only that.

A VOLUNTEER. How many men, in all, had you?

BROWN. I came to Virginia with eighteen men only, besides myself.

VOLUNTEER. What in the world did you suppose you could do here in Virginia with that amount of men?

*          *          *

MASON. How do you justify your acts?

BROWN. I think, my friend, you are guilty of a great wrong against God and humanity,—I say it without wishing to be offensive,—and it would be perfectly right for any one to interfere with you so far as to free those you wilfully and wickedly hold in bondage. I do not say this insultingly.

MASON. I understand that.

BROWN. I think I did right, and that others will do right who interfere with you at any time and at all times. I hold that the Golden Rule, "Do unto others as ye would that others should do unto you," applies to all who would help others to gain their liberty.

LIEUTENANT [J. E. B.] STUART. But don't you believe in the Bible?

BROWN. Certainly I do.

*          *          *

MASON. Did you consider this a military organization in this Constitution? I have not yet read it.

BROWN. I did, in some sense. I wish you would give that paper close attention.

MASON. You consider yourself the commander-in-chief of these "provisional" military forces?

BROWN. I was chosen, agreeably to the ordinance of a certain document, commander-in-chief of that force.

MASON. What wages did you offer?

BROWN. None.

STUART. "The wages of sin is death."

BROWN. I would not have made such a remark to you if you had been a prisoner, and wounded, in my hands.

*          *          *

VALLANDIGHAM. Have you had correspondence with parties at the North on the subject of this movement?

BROWN. I have had correspondence.

A BYSTANDER. Do you consider this a religious movement?

BROWN. It is, in my opinion, the greatest service man can render to God.

BYSTANDER. Do you consider yourself an instrument in the hands of Providence?

BROWN. I do.

BYSTANDER. Upon what principle do you justify your acts?

BROWN. Upon the Golden Rule. I pity the poor in bondage that have none to help them: that is why I am here; not to gratify any personal animosity, revenge, or vindictive spirit. It is my sympathy with the oppressed and the wronged, that are as good as you and as precious in the sight of God. . . . I want you to understand that I respect the rights of the poorest and weakest of colored people, oppressed by the slave system, just as much as I do those of the most wealthy and powerful. This is the idea that has moved me, and that alone. We expected no reward except the satisfaction of endeavoring to do for those in distress and greatly oppressed as we would be done by. The cry of distress of the oppressed is my reason, and the only thing that prompted me to come here.

BYSTANDER. Why did you do it secretly?

BROWN. Because I thought that necessary to success; no other reason.

\*       \*       \*

BYSTANDER. The "New York Herald" of yesterday, in speaking of this affair, mentions a letter in this way:—

. . . "[O]ne of Gerrit Smith's letters . . . speaks of the folly of attempting to strike the shackles off the slaves by the force of moral suasion or legal agitation, and predicts that the next movement made in the direction of negro emancipation would be an insurrection in the South."

BROWN. . . . I agree with Mr. Smith that moral suasion is hopeless. I don't think the people of the slave States will ever consider the subject of slavery in its true light till some other argument is resorted to than moral suasion.

VALLANDIGHAM. Did you expect a general rising of the slaves in case of your success?

BROWN. No, sir; nor did I wish it. I expected to gather them up from time to time and set them free.

VALLANDIGHAM. Did you expect to hold possession here till then?

BROWN. Well, probably I had quite a different idea. I do not know that I ought to reveal my plans. I am here a prisoner and wounded, because I foolishly allowed myself to be so. You overrate your strength in supposing I could have been taken if I had not allowed it. I was too tardy after commencing the open attack—in delaying my movements through Monday night, and up to the time I was attacked by the Government troops. It was all occasioned by my desire to spare the feelings of my prisoners and their families and the community at large. . . .

\*       \*       \*

REPORTER. I do not wish to annoy you; but if you have anything further you would like to say, I will report it.

BROWN. I have nothing to say, only that I claim to be here in carrying out out a measure I believe perfectly justifiable, and not to act the part of an incendiary or ruffian, but to aid those suffering great

wrong. I wish to say, furthermore, that you had better—all you people at the South—prepare yourselves for a settlement of this question, that must come up for settlement sooner than you are prepared for it. The sooner you are prepared the better. You may dispose of me very easily,—I am nearly disposed of now; but this question is still to be settled,—this negro question I mean; the end of that is not yet. These wounds were inflicted upon me—both sabre cuts on my head and bayonet stabs in differents parts of my body—some minutes after I had ceased fighting and had consented to surrender, for the benefit of others, not for my own. I believe the Major would not have been alive; I could have killed him just as easy as a mosquito when he came in, but I supposed he only came in to receive our surrender. There had been loud and long calls of "surrender" from us,—as loud as men could yell; but in the confusion and excitement I suppose we were not heard. I do not think the Major, or any one, meant to butcher us after we had surrendered.

AN OFFICER. Why did you not surrender before the attack?

BROWN. I did not think it was my duty or interest to do so. We assured the prisoners that we did not wish to harm them, and they should be set at liberty. I exercised my best judgment, not believing the people would wantonly sacrifice their own fellow-citizens, when we offered to let them go on condition of being allowed to change our position about a quarter of a mile. The prisoners agreed by a vote among themselves to pass across the bridge with us. We wanted them only as a sort of guarantee of our own safety,—that we should not be fired into. We took them, in the first place, as hostages and to keep them from doing any harm. We did kill some men in defending ourselves, but I saw no one fire except directly in self-defence. Our orders were strict not to harm any one not in arms against us.

Q. Brown, suppose you had every nigger in the United States, what would you do with them? A. Set them free.

Q. Your intention was to carry them off and free them? A. Not at all.

A BYSTANDER. To set them free would sacrifice the life of every man in this community.

BROWN. I do not think so.

BYSTANDER. I know it. I think you are fanatical.

BROWN. And I think you are fanatical. "Whom the gods would destroy they first make mad," and you are mad.

Q. Was it your only object to free the negroes? A. Absolutely our only object.

Q. But you demanded and took Colonel [Lewis] Washington's silver and watch? A. Yes; we intended freely to appropriate the property of slaveholders to carry out our object. It was for that, and only that, and with no design to enrich ourselves with any plunder whatever.

*        *        *

## 117 "remember them that are in bonds" (1859)

On November 2, 1859, after deliberating for three-quarters of an hour, the jury convicted John Brown of murder, treason, and conspiring with slaves to rebel. Responding to the question of whether he had anything to say or why the sentence of death should not be imposed on him, Brown made his last address.

On December 2, 1859, prior to his execution, John Brown handed a final written statement to the guards:

> Charlestown, Va., 2d December, 1859
>
> I John Brown am now quite *certain* that the crimes of *this guilty* land: will never be purged *away*; but with Blood. I had *as I now think: vainly* flattered myself that without *verry much* bloodshed; it might be done.

## ☆ 117 John Brown's Last Speech to the Court (November 2, 1859)

Reprinted in L. Ruchames, *John Brown: The Making of a Revolutionary* (New York: Grosset & Dunlap, 1969), 125–26.

I have, may it please the Court, a few words to say.

In the first place, I deny everything but what I have all along admitted,—the design on my part to free the slaves. . . . That was all I intended. I never did intend murder, or treason, or the destruction of property, or to excite or incite slaves to rebellion, or to make insurrection.

I have another objection; and that is, it is unjust that I should suffer such a penalty. Had I interfered in the manner which I admit, . . . in behalf of the rich, the powerful, the intelligent, the so-called great, or in behalf of any of their friends,—either father, mother, brother, sister, wife, or children, or any of that class,—and suffered and sacrificed what I have in this interference, it would have been all right; and every man in this court would have deemed it an act worthy of reward rather than punishment.

This court acknowledges, as I suppose, the validity of the law of God. I see a book kissed here which I suppose to be the Bible, or at least the New Testament. That teaches me that all things whatsoever I would that men should do to me, I should do even so to them. It teaches me, further, to "remember them that are in bonds, as bound with them." I endeavored to act up to that instruction. I say, I am yet too young to understand that God is any respecter of persons. I believe that to have interfered as I have done—as I have always freely admitted I have done—in behalf of His despised poor, was not wrong, but right. Now, if it is deemed necessary that I should forfeit my life for the furtherance of the ends of justice, and mingle my blood further with the blood of my children and with the blood of millions in this slave country whose rights are disregarded by wicked, cruel, and unjust enactments,—I submit; so let it be done!

Let me say one word further.

I feel entirely satisfied with the treatment I have received on my trial. Considering all the circumstances, it has been more generous than I expected. But I feel no consciousness of guilt. I have stated from the first what was my intention, and what was not. I never have had any design against the life of any person, nor any disposition to commit treason, or excite slaves to rebel, or make any general insurrection. I never encouraged any man to do so, but always discouraged any idea of that kind.

Let me say, also, a word in regard to the statements made by some of those connected with me. I hear it has been stated by some of them that I have induced them to join me. But the contrary is true. I do not say this to injure them, but as regretting their weakness. There is not one of them but joined me of his own accord, and the greater part of them at their own expense. A number of them I never saw, and never had a word of conversation with, till the day they came to me; and that was for the purpose I have stated.

Now I have done.

## 118 On the Right of Secession (1860)

Abraham Lincoln's election as president in 1860 greatly aggravated the tensions between South and North. With less than 40 percent of the popular vote (compared with nearly 30 percent for Democrat Stephen A. Douglas and 18.2 percent for Southern Democrat John C. Breckenridge), Lincoln carried eighteen free states against Breckenridge's eleven slave states.

On December 3, 1860, President James Buchanan observed in his fourth State of the Union Message that "the different sections of the Union are now arrayed against each other, and the time has arrived, so much dreaded by the Father of his Country, when hostile geographical parties have been formed." Many local and county resolutions on secession preceded the state enactments. The resolution from Floyd County, Georgia, reflected not only the intensity of Southern regionalism but also the fear of a black takeover. Many of these expressions were more eloquently phrased in the state resolutions.

On December 20, 1860, a special state convention

held in Columbia, South Carolina, passed by a unanimous vote an ordinance dissolving the union between South Carolina and the other states of the United States. A few days later the state convention called on the federal government to restore Forts Moultrie and Sumter, the Charleston Arsenal, and Castle Pinckney to state authority. The convention next issued a "Declaration of Immediate Causes" for its decision to secede in legal and political terms. On December 27, 1860, South Carolina troops occupied Fort Moultrie and Castle Pinckney. The *William Aiken*, a federal revenue cutter, was also seized. South Carolina troops occupied the United States arsenal on December 30, thus completing the takeover of all federal facilities in the Charleston area except Fort Sumter. Before Lincoln's inauguration, six states had seceded from the Union: Mississippi, South Carolina, Florida, Alabama, Georgia, and Louisiana.

## ☆ 118  Resolutions on Secession

### ☆ 118a  Floyd County, Georgia

Reprinted in A. Candler, ed., *The Confederate Records of the State of Georgia* (Atlanta: C. P. Byrd, 1909), 1:115.

Whereas, the abolition sentiment of the *Northern States* first openly manifested in 1820, has for the last forty years, steadily and rapidly increased in volume, and in the intensity of hostility to the form of society, existing in the *Southern States*, and to the rights of these States as equal, independent and sovereign members of the Union; has led to long continued and ever increasing abuse and hatred of the Southern people; to ceaseless war upon their plainest Constitutional rights; to an open and shameless nullification of that provision of the constitution intended to secure the rendition of fugitive slaves, and of the laws of Congress to give it effect; ... has prompted the armed invasion of Southern soil, by stealth ... for the diabolical purpose of inaugurating a ruthless war of the blacks against the whites throughout the Southern States; has prompted large masses of Northern people openly to sympathize with the treacherous and traitorous invaders of our country, and elevate the leader of a band of midnight assassins, and robbers ... to the rank of a hero and a martyr ...; has disrupted the churches, and destroyed all national parties, and has now finally organized a party confined to a *hostile section*, and composed even there of those only who have encouraged, sympathized with, instigated, or perpetuated their long series of insults, outrages and wrongs, for the avowed purpose of making a common government, armed by us with power only for our protection, an instrument, in the hands of enemies of our destruction.

Therefore we, a portion of the people of Floyd County ... do hereby declare:

1st. That Georgia is and of right ought to be a free, sovereign and independent State.

2d. That she came into the union with the other States, as a sovereignty, and by virtue of that sovereignty, has the right to secede whenever, in her sovereign capacity, she shall judge such a step necessary.

3d. That in our opinion, she ought not to submit to the inauguration of Abraham Lincoln and Hannibal Hamlin, as her President and Vice-President; but should leave them to rule over those by whom alone they were elected.

4th. That we request the Legislature to announce this opinion ... and to co-operate with the Governor in calling a Convention of the people to determine on the mode and measures of redress....

     *        *        *

6th. That we respectfully suggest to the Legislature to take immediate steps to organize and arm the forces of the State....

### ☆ 118b  South Carolina Declaration of Causes of Secession (December 24, 1860)

Reprinted in F. Moore, ed., *The Rebellion Record* (New York: Putnam, 1861-63), 1:3.

The people of the State of South Carolina in Convention assembled, on the 2d day of April, A.D. 1852, declared that the frequent violations of the Constitution of the United States by the Federal Government, and its encroachments upon the reserved rights of the States, fully justified this State in their withdrawal from the Federal Union; but in deference to the opinions and wishes of the other Slaveholding States, she forbore at that time to exercise this right. Since that time these encroachments have continued to increase, and further forbearance ceases to be a virtue.

And now the State of South Carolina having resumed her separate and equal place among nations, deems it due to herself, to the remaining United States of America, and to the nations of the world, that she should declare the immediate causes which have led to this act.

In 1787, Deputies were appointed by the States to revise the articles of Confederation; and on 17th September, 1787, these Deputies recommended, for the adoption of the States, the Articles of Union, known as the Constitution of the United States.... We hold that the [Federal] Government thus established is subject to the ... law of compact. We maintain that in every compact between two or more parties, the obligation is mutual; that the failure of one of the contracting parties to perform a material part of the agreement, entirely releases the obligation of the other; and that, where no arbiter is provided, each party is remitted to his own judgment to determine the fact of failure, with all its consequences.

In the present case, that fact is established with certainty. . . .

The Constitution of the United States, in its fourth Article, provides as follows:

No person held to service or labor in one State under the laws thereof, escaping into another, shall, in consequence of any law or regulation therein, be discharged from such service or labor, but shall be delivered up, on claim of the party to whom such service or labor may be due.

This stipulation was so material to the compact that without it that compact would not have been made. . . . The States of Maine, New Hampshire, Vermont, Massachusetts, Connecticut, Rhode Island, New York, Pennsylvania, Illinois, Indiana, Michigan, Wisconsin and Iowa, have enacted laws which either nullify the acts of Congress, or render useless any attempt to execute them. . . . [I]n none of them has the State Government complied with the stipulation made in the Constitution. . . . Thus the constitutional compact has been deliberately broken and disregarded by the non-slaveholding States; and the consequence follows that South Carolina is released from her obligation. . . .

We affirm that these ends for which this Government was instituted have been defeated. . . .

. . . Observing the *forms* of the Constitution, a sectional party has found within that article establishing the Executive Department, the means of subverting the Constitution itself. A geographical line has been drawn across the Union, and all the States north of that line have united in the election of a man to the high office of President of the United States whose opinions and purposes are hostile to Slavery. He is to be intrusted with the administration of the common Government, because he has declared that "Government cannot endure permanently half slave, half free," and that the public mind must rest in the belief that Slavery is in the course of ultimate extinction.

This sectional combination for the subversion of the Constitution has been aided, in some of the States, by elevating to citizenship persons who, by the supreme law of the land, are incapable of becoming citizens; and their votes have been used to inaugurate a new policy, hostile to the South, and destructive of its peace and safety.

\* \* \*

Sectional interest and animosity will deepen the irritation; and all hope of remedy is rendered vain, by the fact that the public opinion at the North has invested a great political error with the sanctions of a more erroneous religious belief.

We, therefore, the people of South Carolina, by our delegates in Convention assembled, appealing to the Supreme Judge of the world for the rectitude of our intentions, have solemnly declared that the Union heretofore existing between this State and the other States of North America is dissolved, and that the State of South Carolina has resumed her position among the nations of the world, as a separate and independent state, with full power to levy war, conclude peace, contract alliances, establish commerce, and to do all other acts and things which independent States may of right do.

## 119 New York as a Free City (1861)

Opposition to secession was not unanimous in the North, and it was unclear whether the Union would respond with force. Protective of New York City's heavy investments in and trade with the Southern states, Mayor Fernando Wood's sentiments toward "the odious and oppressive connection" with the Union were due also in great part to the fact that his city alone contributed "in revenue two-thirds of the expenses of the United States." He considered the independence of New York City from the state and the Union as a potential benefit of disunion.

☆ 119 Mayor Wood's Recommendation for the Secession of New York City (January 6, 1861)

Reprinted in E. McPherson, ed., *The Political History of the United States during the Great Rebellion* (Washington, D.C.: Philip and Solomons, 1865), 42.

To the Honorable the Common Council:

Gentlemen: We are entering upon the public duties of the year under circumstances as unprecedented as they are gloomy and painful to contemplate. . . .

It would seem that a dissolution of the Federal Union is inevitable. . . .

\* \* \*

. . . [W]e must rely upon our own resources and assume a position predicated upon the new phase which public affairs will present, and upon the inherent strength which our geographical, commercial, political, and financial preëminence imparts to us.

With our aggrieved brethren of the Slave States, we have friendly relations and a common sympathy. We have not participated in the warfare upon their constitutional rights or their domestic institutions. . . . Our ships have penetrated to every clime, and so have New York capital, energy, and enterprise found their way to every State, and, indeed, to almost every county and town of the American Union. . . . Therefore, New York has a right to expect, and should endeavor to preserve a continuance of uninterrupted intercourse with every section.

It is, however, folly to disguise the fact that, judging from the past, New York may have more cause of apprehension from the aggressive legislation of our own State than from external dangers. We have already suffered largely from this cause. For the past five years, our interests and corporate [municipal] rights have been repeatedly trampled upon....

...[T]he political connection between the people of the city and the State has been used by the latter to our injury. The Legislature, in which the present partizan majority has the power, has become an instrument by which we are plundered to enrich their speculators, lobby agents, and Abolition politicians....

How we shall rid ourselves of this odious and oppressive connection, it is not for me to determine. It is certain that a dissolution cannot be peacefully accomplished, except by the consent of the Legislature itself. Whether this can be obtained or not, is, in my judgement, doubtful....

Much, no doubt, can be said in favor of the justice and policy of a separation.... Why should not New York city, instead of supporting by her contributions in revenue two-thirds of the expenses of the United States, become also equally independent? As a free city, with but nominal duty on imports, her local Government could be supported without taxa-

tion upon her people. Thus we could live free from taxes, and have cheap goods nearly duty free....

\*          \*          \*

When Disunion has become a fixed and certain fact, why may not New York disrupt the bands which bind her to a venal and corrupt master—to a people and a party that have plundered her revenues, attempted to ruin her commerce, taken away the power of self-government, and destroyed the Confederacy of which she was the proud Empire City?...

But I am not prepared to recommend the violence implied in these views. In stating this argument in favor of freedom "peaceably if we can, forcibly if we must," let me not be misunderstood. The redress can be found only in appeals to the magnanimity of the people of the whole State. The events of the past two months have no doubt effected a change in the popular sentiment of the State and National politics. This change may bring us the desired relief, and we may be able to obtain a repeal of the law to which I have referred, and a consequent restoration of our corporate rights.

FERNANDO WOOD, Mayor

### CHAPTER 5

# The Civil War

1861-1870

The conflagration known as the Civil War or the War between the States provides a unique, concentrated historical laboratory for observing the phenomenon of political criminality in the United States. The very choice of nomenclature reflects the contrasting perspectives on the war: was it to be viewed as a domestic event in which the offenders were engaging in treason and were subject therefore to punishment as criminals, or was it in fact a conflict between sovereign equals with the combatants therefore entitled to be treated as prisoners of war? Beyond the strains of open warfare between contending armies, each swearing allegiance to different sovereigns, the North also had to confront the problem of controlling a population that was not always sympathetic to the goals of the Washington government. In the so-called border states that had not seceded, sentiment ran high in favor of allowing the Southern states to go their own way, if not actually accompanying them in the secession from the Union. Finally, the law had to address not only the combatants during the war but also prisoners, Confederacy officials, and the population of the Southern states — both black and white — after the conflict concluded. The documents in this chapter detail the processes used to deal with these difficult problems.

The core issues of the chapter relate to the legally ambiguous status of the rebel states and their populations. The legislatures of the Confederate states stood in open defiance of the laws and the Constitution of the United States. From the Northern perspective, the act of secession was unlawful and treasonous. By raising armies and seizing United States garrisons, post offices, and arsenals, the leaders of the Southern states and their followers were traitors. But this was not a relatively harmless treasonous insurrection of the type encountered in the early days of the Republic. These actions were undertaken, as in the American Revolution, by the leading political figures of the region. The decisions of secession were enacted into law by fitting forms of legislation, and the new political entity of the Confederate States of America was forged through voluntary adherence.

A government new in form and substance replaced that of the United States throughout the South, but the preexisting governments of the various seceding states went unchanged. Furthermore, the seceding states were not attempting a coup, but rather a partition of the United States of America. Their hostile actions were initially limited to the territory of their newly founded nation, as they sought to divest the federal authority of the United States and to transfer control to the Confederacy. Were the Southern populations who obeyed the laws of their legally constituted state governments implicated as traitors when their legislatures altered their allegiance from the United States to the Confederate States of America? Or should they, instead, have been accorded the status of enemy aliens who under international law remained innocent parties entitled to humane consideration? Should the leaders of the Confederacy then be deemed traitors, or should the high and noble purposes from which they claimed to act — the right of self-government and opposition to the breach of the original compact of the Constitution — immunize them from the ignominy of treason? How should captured rebel combatants be treated — as criminals or as prisoners of war?

At the outbreak of hostilities, President Lincoln engaged in several extraordinary activities intended to secure the lines of defense against the actions of those sympathetic to the Southern cause. The slow and procedurally difficult process of accusing, trying, and convicting people of treason for aiding the South was replaced by military arrest, trial, and execution, facilitated by the suspension of the writ of habeas corpus. These actions were originally accomplished without the approval of Congress, but that body later assented to all of the president's measures undertaken in the face of the perceived threat to the nation's security. The courts, however, were more critical of the unilateral executive supplanting of civilian authority with martial law.

Congress likewise was dissatisfied with the existing law of treason and defined new "treasonous" offenses, which relieved the prosecution of its heavy burden in proving the crime. Congressional authorization of the confiscation of Southern property and Southern sympathizers' property by the military demonstrated confusion over whether these actions constituted criminal penalties for treason or the seizure of the property of innocent enemy aliens under the normal usages of the law of war. Whichever the case, the protections accorded to the suspect individual were far less than either body of law would have provided.

Resort to the law of treason and confiscation also was important in the deliverance of slaves from bondage. This chapter demonstrates that the emancipation of slaves was in response to the political transgressions of their masters in engaging in treasonous activities. Slavery as an institution was not affected in the slave states that remained in the Union. Not until the ratification of the Thirteenth Amendment was slavery abolished throughout the United States.

That abolition, nevertheless, did not put an end to attempts by the remnants of the old Southern political order to assert control over the recently emancipated and therefore increasingly suspect black populations. Special regulation of black activities continued until the imposition of Reconstruction—which was more a program of political and social purging than of economic rebuilding. The quest for political control by the new Reconstruction elites was manifested through the classic techniques: resort to

military rule, the requirement of loyalty oaths, the restriction of the franchise, and the imposition of strict qualifications for officeholding. The response to these controls was similarly classic: the emergence of a resistance underground that attempted to maintain, through illegal activity and terror, the status quo ante.

The ultimate grant of amnesty to those connected with the Confederacy, a common accompaniment to political criminality throughout American history, began the official reassertion of the white power structure in the South. This also was the beginning of the growing tensions emanating from the unfulfilled promises of the Fourteenth Amendment and the Civil Rights Acts. The struggle for the realization of these promises gave rise to new political criminality for the attainment, and at times the containment, of racial justice. Against these major institutional conflicts and transitions flash also the sparks of assassination and anticonscription riots—mere flare-ups of political and sometimes pseudo-political criminality.

---

## 120 "the inviolability of the sovereign power" (1861)

During late 1860 and early 1861, eleven slaveholding states seceded from the Union. Southern congressmen, politicians, and military officers left the North to stand with their own states. The Southern states seized federal facilities, including forts, arsenals, barracks, ports, custom houses, and mint offices. On April 20, Colonel Robert E. Lee, who had captured John Brown on charges of treason less than two years earlier, resigned his United States commission as the first step toward assuming command of the seceding Virginia troops.

On February 18, 1861, three weeks before Abraham Lincoln's inauguration as the sixteenth president of the United States, Jefferson Davis assumed the provisional presidency of the Confederate States of America. On April 12, the Civil War opened with the attack by four thousand Confederate troops on Fort Sumter, which was defended by a Union force of eighty-five officers and men and forty-three workmen. President Lincoln declared a state of insurrection on April 15, 1861. The onset of the Civil War brought before the courts the question of whether secession was in fact treasonous. This discourse on the law of treason was presented to a grand jury summoned to consider evidence

against persons accused of treason. Despite the consistency of the judicial holding that secession was treasonous, few Confederates were tried and convicted of the charge.

☆ 120 Charge to the Grand Jury—Treason [Massachusetts]

30 F. Cas. 1039 (D.C.D. Ma. 1861) (No. 18,273).

SPRAGUE, District Judge. It is the duty of the court to give you some instructions upon the criminal jurisprudence of the United States.

\*        \*        \*

The highest crime known to our law is treason.

"Treason against the United States shall consist only in levying war against them, or in adhering to their enemies, giving them aid and comfort."

These terms, "levying war," "adhering to enemies," "giving them aid and comfort," were not new. . . .

The question what amounts to levying war, arose soon after the adoption of our constitution. . . .

It is settled that if a body of men be actually assembled for the purpose of effecting a treasonable purpose by force, that is levying war. But it must be an assemblage in force, a military assemblage in a condition to make war. A mere conspiracy to overthrow the government, however atrocious such conspiracy may be, does not of itself amount to the crime of treason. Thus, if a convention, legislature, junto, or other assemblage, entertain the purpose of subverting the government, and to that end pass acts, resolves, ordinances or decrees, even with the view of raising a military force to carry their purpose into effect, this alone does not constitute a levying of war.

What is a treasonable purpose? If the object be to prevent by force the execution of any public law of the United States, generally and in all cases, that is a treasonable purpose, for it is entirely to overthrow the government as to one of its laws. And if there be such an assemblage as I have already described, for the purpose of carrying such an intention into effect by force, it will constitute levying war.

But the sudden outbreak of a mob, or the assembling of men in order, by force, to defeat the execution of the law, in a particular instance, and then to disperse, without the intention to continue together, or to re-assemble for the purpose of defeating the law generally, in all cases, is not levying war.

If the purpose be entirely to overthrow the government at any one place, by force, that is a treasonable purpose.

*        *        *

The constitution has not only defined the crime of treason, but prescribed a rule of evidence: "No person shall be convicted of treason, unless on the testimony of two witnesses to the same overt act, or on confession in open court."

The reason of these extraordinary safeguards is to be found in the nature of the offence, and in the pages of history. An attempt to overthrow the government excites the deepest indignation in great numbers, especially in those who are imbued with a warm and devoted patriotism, the cherished sentiment of a life-time, strengthened by a matured conviction of the vastness of the interests which are wrapped up in the inviolability of the sovereign power, that power which is the guardian of their safety, the daily dispenser of blessings, and the object of their prayers. A traitorous assault arouses the strongest passions, and in the keenness of their resentment, and the eager pursuit of the guilty, they are apt to break down the barriers which are essential to the protection of innocence. Our fathers, therefore, endeavored to render some of these safeguards impregnable, by imbedding them in the fundamental law.

*        *        *

It has been, at a former period, and is now a momentous question, whether, under our complex system, there is any power extrinsic to that of the national government by which its laws can be

rightfully resisted, or their obligation impaired. There is no such power.

As I have already said to you, the authority of the United States, within their sphere, is supreme. . . . And to render this effectual, they provided that the government which they created should be the final judge of the extent of its own powers and the meaning of its own laws. And to this end, they established a judicial department as a co-ordinate branch of the government, to expound and enforce the provisions of the constitution and the acts of congress. . . .

This supremacy has not always been acquiesced in. The legislation of a great country can never meet with universal approbation. And it has sometimes happened that acts of congress have been adverse to the opinions or supposed interests of many persons, sometimes constituting a majority in particular states.

And in such cases, unwilling to submit, they have eagerly sought for some mode of resistance which should wear the semblance of legality, and to this end have invoked state interposition, and the cover of state authority.

Such was nullification. That doctrine did not deny the paramount obligation of laws constitutionally enacted, but it arrogated for a state the right to determine, in the last resort, whether a law was constitutional or not. It sought to overthrow the judicial power by denying its supremacy, and claimed for every state the right to judge of the extent of the powers of the general government, and of the validity of its laws, and to limit, restrain, or annul them, according to the views of each state.

This doctrine, once formidable, has now few adherents.

*        *        *

The disaffected, at different times, and in various sections of the Union, have earnestly sought for some legal mode of resisting legitimate authority. But it has been in vain. There is no such anomalous middle ground between submission and rebellion; and this last extreme has at length been reached. Secession is but another name for revolution; for it is vain to contend for a constitutional right to overthrow the constitution, and a legal right to destroy all law.

*        *        *

## 121 "affording aid and comfort to rebels" (1861–1864)

The writ of habeas corpus serves to protect individuals from unlawful imprisonment. One form of such imprisonment consists of detention before trial without a judicial officer's determination of the existence of "probable cause" that the individual held had committed a crime.

Article I, Section 9 of the United States Constitution provides that "The Privilege of the Writ of Habeas Corpus shall not be suspended, unless when in Cases of Rebellion or Invasion the public safety may require it." Even though this section is contained in the portion of the Constitution dealing with legislative powers and thus may be considered suspendable only by an act of Congress, President Lincoln unilaterally proclaimed several suspensions of habeas corpus. This action by the president, without congressional approval, was condemned judicially as unconstitutional. The president ignored that decision, but the issue subsequently became moot with congressional authorization and ratification of the suspensions.

President Lincoln's impatience with habeas corpus demonstrated the suspension's utility as a method of suppressing political crime. The initial suspension was limited to parts of Maryland, in order to protect the capital and its lines of communication against the threats of local resistance and Southern invasion. But the president also authorized the writ's selective suspension with regard to particular persons and for those suspected by military authorities of encouraging draft resistance or otherwise obstructing the war effort. In concert with proclamations authorizing military tribunals to try, convict, and sentence war resisters or Southern sympathizers, the suspension of the writ eliminated the difficulties associated with convicting individuals of specific crimes before regularly constituted courts and with attendant procedural protections. The military arrested over ten thousand suspects during the course of the war and denied them the benefit of a habeas corpus hearing. The technique of supplanting civilian authority with military rule is a common response to political criminality.

## ☆ 121  President Lincoln's Correspondence and Proclamations Suspending Habeas Corpus

Reprinted in J. Richardson, ed., *A Compilation of the Messages and Papers of the Presidents* (Washington, D.C.: U.S. Government Printing Office, 1897), 3:18, 19, 98-99, 170-74, 219-21.

### ☆ 121a  April 27, 1861

THE COMMANDING GENERAL OF THE ARMY OF THE UNITED STATES:

You are engaged in suppressing an insurrection against the laws of the United States. If at any point on or in the vicinity of any military line which is now or which shall be used between the city of Philadelphia and the city of Washington you find resistance which renders it necessary to suspend the writ of *habeas corpus* for the public safety, you personally, or

through the officer in command at the point where resistance occurs, are authorized to suspend that writ.

Given under my hand and the seal of the United States, at the city of Washington, this 27th day of April, 1861, and of the Independence of the United States the eighty-fifth.

ABRAHAM LINCOLN

By the President of the United States:

WILLIAM H. SEWARD, Secretary of State

### ☆ 121b  June 20, 1861

THE LIEUTENANT-GENERAL COMMANDING THE ARMIES OF THE UNITED STATES:

You or any officer you may designate will, in your discretion, suspend the writ of *habeas corpus* so far as may relate to Major Chase, lately of the Engineer Corps of the Army of the United States, now alleged to be guilty of treasonable practices against this Government.

ABRAHAM LINCOLN

By the President:

WILLIAM H. SEWARD

### ☆ 121c  September 24, 1862

BY THE PRESIDENT OF THE UNITED STATES OF AMERICA

*A Proclamation*

Whereas it has become necessary to call into service not only volunteers, but also portions of the militia of the States by draft in order to suppress the insurrection existing in the United States, and disloyal persons are not adequately restrained by the ordinary processes of law from hindering this measure and from giving aid and comfort in various ways to the insurrection:

Now, therefore, be it ordered, first, that during the existing insurrection, and as a necessary measure for suppressing the same, all rebels and insurgents, their aiders and abettors, within the United States, and all persons discouraging volunteer enlistments, resisting militia drafts, or guilty of any disloyal practice affording aid and comfort to rebels against the authority of the United States, shall be subject to martial law and liable to trial and punishment by courts-martial or military commissions; second, that the writ of *habeas corpus* is suspended in respect to all persons arrested or who are now or hereafter during the rebellion shall be imprisoned in any fort, camp, arsenal, military prison, or other place of confinement by any military authority or by the sentence of any court-martial or military commission.

In witness whereof I have hereunto set my hand and caused the seal of the United States to be affixed.

Done at the city of Washington, this 24th day of September, A.D. 1862, and of the Independence of the United States the eighty-seventh.

ABRAHAM LINCOLN

By the President:

WILLIAM H. SEWARD, Secretary of State

☆ 121d  September 15, 1863

BY THE PRESIDENT OF THE UNITED STATES OF AMERICA

*A Proclamation*

Whereas the Constitution of the United States has ordained that the privilege of the writ of *habeas corpus* shall not be suspended unless when, in cases of rebellion or invasion, the public safety may require it; and

Whereas a rebellion was existing on the 3d day of March, 1863, which rebellion is still existing; and

Whereas by a statute which was approved on that day it was enacted by the Senate and House of Representatives of the United States in Congress assembled that during the present insurrection the President of the United States, whenever in his judgment the public safety may require, is authorized to suspend the privilege of the writ of *habeas corpus* in any case throughout the United States or any part thereof; and

Whereas, in the judgment of the President, the public safety does require that the privilege of the said writ shall now be suspended throughout the United States in the cases where, by the authority of the President of the United States, military, naval, and civil officers of the United States, or any of them, hold persons under their command or in their custody, either as prisoners of war, spies, or aiders or abettors of the enemy, or officers, soldiers, or seamen enrolled or drafted or mustered or enlisted in or belonging to the land or naval forces of the United States, or as deserters therefrom, or otherwise amenable to military law or the rules and articles of war or the rules or regulations prescribed for the military or naval services by authority of the President of the United States, or for resisting a draft, or for any other offense against the military or naval service:

Now, therefore, I, Abraham Lincoln, President of the United States, do hereby proclaim and make known to all whom it may concern that the privilege of the writ of *habeas corpus* is suspended throughout the United States in the several cases before mentioned, and that this suspension will continue throughout the duration of the said rebellion or until this proclamation shall, by a subsequent one to be issued by the President of the United States, be modified or revoked....

In testimony whereof I have hereunto set my hand and caused the seal of the United States to be affixed this 15th day of September, A.D 1863, and of the Independence of the United States of America the eighty-eighth.

ABRAHAM LINCOLN

By the President:

WILLIAM H. SEWARD, Secretary of State

☆ 121e  July 5, 1864

BY THE PRESIDENT OF THE UNITED STATES OF AMERICA

*A Proclamation*

\*       \*       \*

Whereas the said insurrection and rebellion still continue, endangering the existence of the Constitution and Government of the United States; and

Whereas the military forces of the United States are now actively engaged in suppressing the said insurrection and rebellion in various parts of the States where the said rebellion has been successful in obstructing the laws and public authorities, especially in the States of Virginia and Georgia; and

\*       \*       \*

Whereas many citizens of the State of Kentucky have joined the forces of the insurgents, and such insurgents have on several occasions entered the said State of Kentucky in large force, and, not without aid and comfort furnished by disaffected and disloyal citizens of the United States residing therein, have not only greatly disturbed the public peace, but have overborne the civil authorities and made flagrant civil war, destroying property and life in various parts of that State; and

Whereas it has been made known to the President of the United States by the officers commanding the national armies that combinations have been formed in the said State of Kentucky with a purpose of inciting rebel forces to renew the said operations of civil war within the said State and thereby to embarrass the United States armies now operating in the said States of Virginia and Georgia and even to endanger their safety:

Now, therefore, I, Abraham Lincoln, President of the United States, by virtue of the authority vested in me by the Constitution and laws, do hereby declare that in my judgment the public safety especially requires that the suspension of the privilege of the writ of *habeas corpus*, so proclaimed in the said proclamation on the 15th September 1862 be made effectual and be duly enforced in and throughout the said State of Kentucky, and that martial law be for the present established therein. I do therefore hereby require of the military officers in the said State that the privileges of the writ of *habeas corpus* be effectually suspended within the said State, according to the aforesaid proclamation, and that martial law be established therein, to take effect from the date of this proclamation, the said suspension and establishment of martial law to continue until this proclamation shall be revoked or modified, but not beyond the period when the said rebellion shall have been suppressed or come to an end. . . .

The martial law herein proclaimed and the things in that respect herein ordered will not be deemed or taken to interfere with the holding of lawful elections, or with the proceedings of the constitutional legislature of Kentucky, or with the administration of justice in the courts of law existing therein between citizens of the United States in suits or proceedings which do not affect the military operations or the constituted authorities of the Government of the United States.

In testimony whereof I have hereunto set my hand and caused the seal of the United States to be affixed.

Done at the city of Washington, this 5th day of July, A.D. 1864, and of the Independence of the United States the eighty-ninth.

ABRAHAM LINCOLN

By the President:

WILLIAM H. SEWARD, Secretary of State

## 122 "regal and absolute power" (1861)

Military authorities arrested John Merryman in his home in Baltimore, Maryland, for his participation in antiwar riots and brought him to Fort McHenry. Military officials ignored his requests to have a hearing before a magistrate. They claimed that the president's proclamation suspending the writ of habeas corpus in all offenses against the United States government authorized his detention.

The United States Circuit Court decision in Merryman's case became known as the *Taney Decision* after Chief Justice Taney of the United States Supreme Court, who was sitting as justice for the Maryland circuit. Taney repudiated the authority of the executive to suspend the writ. Both Lincoln and the military, nevertheless, ignored his decision and Merryman remained in Fort McHenry. Congress did not authorize the president to suspend the writ (itself a dubious delegation of authority) until March 3, 1863.

☆ 122 *Ex Parte Merryman*

17 F. Cas. 144 (C.C.D. Md. 1861) (No. 9,487).

TANEY, Circuit Justice.

\*          \*          \*

The case, then, is simply this: a military officer, residing in Pennsylvania, issues an order to arrest a citizen of Maryland, upon vague and indefinite charges, without any proof, so far as appears; under this order, his house is entered in the night, he is seized as a prisoner, and conveyed to Fort McHenry, and there kept in close confinement; and when a habeas corpus is served on the commanding officer, requiring him to produce the prisoner before a justice of the supreme court, in order that he may examine into the legality of the imprisonment, the answer of the officer, is that he is authorized by the president to suspend the writ of habeas corpus at his discretion, and in the exercise of that discretion, suspends it in this case, and on that ground refuses obedience to the writ.

As the case comes before me, therefore, I understand that the president not only claims the right to suspend the writ of habeas corpus himself, at his discretion, but to delegate that discretionary power to a military officer, and to leave it to him to determine whether he will or will not obey judicial process that may be served upon him. No official notice has been given to the courts of justice, or to the public, by proclamation or otherwise, that the president claimed this power, and had exercised it in the manner stated in the return. And I certainly listened to it with some surprise, for I had supposed it to be one of those points of constitutional law upon which there was no difference of opinion, and that it was admitted on all hands, that the privilege of the writ could not be suspended, except by act of congress.

\*          \*          \*

The clause of the constitution, which authorizes the suspension of the privilege of the writ of habeas corpus, is in the 9th section of the first article. This article is devoted to the legislative department of the United States, and has not the slightest reference to the executive department. . . .

\*          \*          \*

. . . The great importance which the framers of the constitution attached to the privilege of the writ of habeas corpus, to protect the liberty of the citizen, is proved by the fact, that its suspension, except in cases of invasion or rebellion, is first in the list of prohibited [legislative] powers; and even in these cases the power is denied, and its exercise prohibited, unless the public safety shall require it.

It is true, that in the cases mentioned, congress is, of necessity, the judge of whether the public safety does or does not require it; and their judgment is conclusive. But the introduction of these words is a standing admonition to the legislative body of the danger of suspending it, and of the extreme caution they should exercise, before they give the government of the United States such power over the liberty of a citizen.

It is the second article of the constitution that provides for the organization of the executive department, enumerates the powers conferred on it, and prescribes its duties. And if the high power over the liberty of the citizen now claimed, was intended to be conferred on the president, it would undoubtedly be found in plain words in this article; but there is not a word in it that can furnish the slightest ground to justify the exercise of the power.

*         *         *

So too [the President's] powers in relation to the civil duties and authority necessarily conferred on him are carefully restricted.... He is not empowered to arrest any one charged with an offence against the United States, and whom he may, from the evidence before him, believe to be guilty; nor can he authorize any officer, civil or military, to exercise this power, for the fifth article of the amendments to the constitution expressly provides that no person "shall be deprived of life, liberty or property, without due process of law"—that is, judicial process.

Even if the privilege of the writ of habeas corpus were suspended by act of congress, and a party not subject to the rules and articles of war were afterwards arrested and imprisoned by regular judicial process, he could not be detained in prison, or brought to trial before a military tribunal, for the [sixth] article in the amendments to the constitution [would thereby be violated].

*         *         *

The only power, therefore, which the president possesses, where the "life, liberty or property" of a private citizen is concerned, is the power and duty ... which requires "that he shall take care that the laws shall be faithfully executed." He is not authorized to execute them himself, ... but he is to take care that they be faithfully carried into execution, as they are expounded and adjudged by the co-ordinate branch of the government to which that duty is assigned by the constitution. It is thus made his duty to come in aid of the judicial authority, if it shall be resisted by a force too strong to be overcome without the assistance of the executive arm; but in exercising this power he acts in subordination to judicial authority, assisting it to execute its process and enforce its judgments.

... I can see no ground whatever for supposing that the president, in any emergency, or in any state of things, can authorize the suspension of the privileges of the writ of habeas corpus, or the arrest of a citizen, except in aid of the judicial power. He certainly does not faithfully execute the laws, if he takes upon himself legislative power, by suspending the writ of habeas corpus, and the judicial power also, by arresting and imprisoning a person without due process of law.

Nor can any argument be drawn from the nature of sovereignty, or the necessity of government, for self-defence in times of tumult and danger. The gov-ernment of the United States is one of delegated and limited powers; it derives it existence and authority altogether from the constitution, and neither of its branches, executive, legislative or judicial can exercise any of the powers of government beyond those specified and granted....

Indeed, the security against imprisonment by executive authority [is like the ancient common law of England]. Blackstone states it in the following words: "To make imprisonment lawful, it must be either by process of law from the courts of judicature, or by warrant from some legal officer having authority to commit to prison."

*         *         *

... [T]he value set upon this writ in England [for protecting rights] has been ... the object of the most jealous care. Accordingly, no power in England short of that of parliament can suspend or authorize the suspension of the writ of habeas corpus.... If the president of the United States may suspend the writ, then the constitution of the United States has conferred upon him more regal and absolute power over the liberty of the citizen, than the people of England have thought it safe to entrust to the crown; a power which the queen of England cannot exercise at this day, and which could not have been lawfully exercised by the sovereign even in the reign of Charles the First.

*         *         *

[T]he Commentaries on the Constitution of the United States of the late Mr. Justice Story, ... and also the clear and authoritative decision of [the supreme] court itself, given more than half a century since, and conclusively establishing the principles I have above stated.

*         *         *

But the documents before me show, that the military authority in this case has gone far beyond the mere suspension of the privilege of the writ of habeas corpus. It has, by force of arms, thrust aside the judicial authorities and officers to whom the constitution has confided the power and duty of interpreting and administering the laws, and substituted a military government in its place, to be administered and executed by military officers. For, at the time these proceedings were had against John Merryman, the district judge of Maryland, the commissioner appointed under the act of congress, the district attorney and the marshal, all resided in the city of Baltimore, a few miles only from the home of the prisoner. Up to that time, there had never been the slightest resistance or obstruction to the process of any court or judicial officer of the United States, in Maryland, except by the military authority.... There was no danger of any obstruction or resistance to the action of the civil authorities, and therefore no reason whatever for the interposition of the military.

Yet, under these circumstances, a military officer, stationed in Pennsylvania, without giving any information to the district attorney, and without any application to the judicial authorities, assumes to himself the judicial power in the district of Maryland; undertakes to decide what constitutes the crime of treason or rebellion; what evidence (if indeed he required any) is sufficient to support the accusation and justify the commitment; and commits the party, without a hearing, even before himself, to close custody, in a strongly garrisoned fort, to be there held, it would seem, during the pleasure of those who committed him.

*          *          *

[The Bill of Rights], which congress itself could not suspend, ha[s] been disregarded and suspended, like the writ of habeas corpus, by a military order, supported by force of arms. Such is the case now before me, and I can only say that if the authority which the constitution has confided to the judiciary department and judicial officers, may thus, upon any pretext or under any circumstances, be usurped by the military power, at its discretion, the people of the United States are no longer living under a government of laws, but every citizen holds life, liberty and property at the will and pleasure of the army officer in whose military district he may happen to be found.

In such a case, my duty was too plain to be mistaken. I have exercised all the power which the constitution and laws confer upon me, but that power has been resisted by a force too strong for me to overcome. It is possible that the officer who has incurred this grave responsibility may have misunderstood his instructions, and exceeded the authority intended to be given him; I shall, therefore, order all the proceedings in this case, with my opinion, to be filed and recorded ... and direct the clerk to transmit a copy, under seal, to the president of the United States. It will then remain for that high officer, in fulfilment of his constitutional obligation to "take care that the laws be faithfully executed," to determine what measures he will take to cause the civil process of the United States to be respected and enforced.

# 123 "to resist force ... by force" (1861)

President Lincoln delivered this address to Congress at a special session on July 4, 1861, three months after the attack on Fort Sumter. Lincoln's purpose was threefold: (1) to defend his suspension of habeas corpus, (2) to request money and troops for

the preservation of the Union, and (3) to repudiate secession.

Lincoln justified his executive suspension of the writ of habeas corpus on the doctrines of exigency, national security, and lesser evil. "To state the question more directly, 'are all the laws but one to go unexecuted and the government itself go to pieces lest that one be violated?' " he asked. The themes herein had been sounded before and were to be replayed again. But this was the first time that they had been applied directly to the constitutional protection of the Great Writ.

☆ 123 Lincoln's Message to Congress in Special Session (July 4, 1861)

Reprinted in R. P. Basler, ed., *The Collected Works of Abraham Lincoln* (New Brunswick, N.J.: Rutgers University Press, 1959), 1860-61:421-41.

*Fellow-citizens of the Senate and House of Representatives:* Having been convened on an extraordinary occasion, as authorized by the Constitution, your attention is not called to any ordinary subject of legislation.

At the beginning of the present presidential term, four months ago, the functions of the Federal Government were found to be generally suspended within the several States of South Carolina, Georgia, Alabama, Mississippi, Louisiana, and Florida, excepting only those of the Post-office Department.

*          *          *

... By the affair at Fort Sumter ... the assailants of the government began the conflict of arms, without a gun in sight or in expectancy to return their fire. ... In this act, discarding all else, they have forced upon the country the distinct issue, "immediate dissolution or blood."

And this issue embraces more than the fate of these United States. It presents to the whole family of man the question whether a constitutional republic or democracy—a government of the people by the same people—can or cannot maintain its territorial integrity against its own domestic foes. It presents the question whether discontented individuals, too few in numbers to control administration according to organic law in any case, can always, upon the pretenses made in this case, or on any other pretenses, or arbitrarily without any pretense, break up their government, and thus practically put an end to free government upon the earth. It forces us to ask: "Is there, in all republics, this inherent and fatal weakness?" "Must a government, of necessity, be too strong for the liberties of its own people, or too weak to maintain its own existence?"

So viewing the issue, no choice was left but to call out the war power of the government; and so to resist force employed for its destruction, by force for its preservation.

\*　　　\*　　　\*

... [C]alls were made for volunteers to serve for three years, unless sooner discharged, and also for large additions to the regular army and navy. These measures, whether strictly legal or not, were ventured upon, under what appeared to be a popular demand and a public necessity; trusting then, as now, that Congress would readily ratify them. It is believed that nothing has been done beyond the constitutional competency of Congress.

Soon after the first call for militia, it was considered a duty to authorize the commanding general in proper cases, according to his discretion, to suspend the privilege of the writ of *habeas corpus*, or, in other words, to arrest and detain, without resort to the ordinary processes and forms of law, such individuals as he might deem dangerous to the public safety. This authority has purposely been exercised but very sparingly. Nevertheless, the legality and propriety of what has been done under it are questioned, and the attention of the country has been called to the proposition that one who has sworn to "take care that the laws be faithfully executed" should not himself violate them. Of course some consideration was given to the questions of power and propriety before this matter was acted upon. The whole of the laws which were required to be faithfully executed were being resisted and failing of execution in nearly one third of the States. Must they be allowed to finally fail of execution, even had it been perfectly clear that by the use of the means necessary to their execution some single law, made in such extreme tenderness of the citizen's liberty that, practically, it relieves more of the guilty than of the innocent, should to a very limited extent be violated? To state the question more directly, are all the laws but one to go unexecuted, and the government itself go to pieces lest that one be violated? Even in such a case, would not the official oath be broken if the government should be overthrown, when it was believed that disregarding the single law would tend to preserve it? But it was not believed that this question was presented. It was not believed that any law was violated. The provision of the Constitution that "the privilege of the writ of *habeas corpus* shall not be suspended, unless when, in cases of rebellion or invasion, the public safety may require it," is equivalent to a provision—is a provision—that such privilege may be suspended when, in case of rebellion or invasion, the public safety does require it. It was decided that we have a case of rebellion, and that the public safety does require the qualified suspension of the privilege of the writ which was authorized to be made. Now it is insisted that Congress, and not the executive, is vested with

this power. But the Constitution itself is silent as to which or who is to exercise the power; and as the provision was plainly made for a dangerous emergency, it cannot be believed the framers of the instrument intended that in every case the danger should run its course until Congress could be called together, the very assembling of which might be prevented, as was intended in this case, by the rebellion.

\*　　　\*　　　\*

It might seem, at first thought, to be of little difference whether the present movement at the South be called "secession" or "rebellion." The movers, however, well understand the difference. At the beginning they knew they could never raise their treason to any respectable magnitude by any name which implies violation of law.... Accordingly, they commenced by an insidious debauching of the public mind. They invented an ingenious sophism which, if conceded, was followed by perfectly logical steps, through all the incidents, to the complete destruction of the Union. The sophism itself is that any State of the Union may consistently with the National Constitution, and therefore lawfully and peacefully, withdraw from the Union without the consent of the Union or of any other State. The little disguise that the supposed right is to be exercised only for just cause, themselves to be the sole judges of its justice, is too thin to merit any notice.

With rebellion thus sugar-coated they have been drugging the public mind of their section for more than thirty years, and until at length they have brought many good men to a willingness to take up arms against the government the day after some assemblage of men have enacted the farcical pretense of taking their State out of the Union, who could have been brought to no such thing the day before.

This sophism derives much, perhaps the whole, of its currency from the assumption that there is some omnipotent and sacred supremacy pertaining to a State—to each State of our Federal Union. Our States have neither more nor less power than that reserved to them in the Union by the Constitution—no one of them ever having been a State out of the Union. The original ones passed into the Union even before they cast off their British colonial dependence; and the new ones each came into the Union directly from a condition of dependence, excepting Texas. And even Texas, in its temporary independence, was never designated a State.... Much is said about the "sovereignty" of the States; but the word even is not in the National Constitution, nor, as is believed, in any of the State constitutions. What is "sovereignty" in the political sense of the term? Would it be far wrong to define it "a political community without a political superior"? Tested by this, no one of our States except Texas ever was a sovereignty. And even Texas gave up the character on coming into the Union; by which act she acknowledged the Constitution of the United States, and the laws and treaties of the United States made in pursuance of the Constitution, to be for her the supreme law of the land. The States have their status in the Union, and they have no other legal status. If they break from this, they can only do so against law and by revolution. The Union, and not themselves separately, procured their independence and their liberty. By conquest or purchase the Union gave each of them whatever of independence or liberty it has. The Union is older than any of the States, and, in fact, it created them as States. . . .

Unquestionably the States have the powers and rights reserved to them in and by the National Constitution; but among these surely are not included all conceivable powers, however mischievous or destructive, but, at most, such only as were known in the world at the time as governmental powers; and certainly a power to destroy the government itself had never been known as a governmental . . . power. . . .

*            *            *

What is now combated is the position that secession is consistent with the Constitution—is lawful and peaceful. It is not contended that there is any express law for it; and nothing should ever be implied as law which leads to unjust or absurd consequences. The nation purchased with money the countries out of which several of these States were formed. Is it just that they shall go off without leave and without refunding? . . .

This is essentially a people's contest. . . .

I am most happy to believe that the plain people understand and appreciate this. It is worthy of note that while in this, the government's hour of trial, large numbers of those in the army and navy who have been favored with the offices have resigned and proved false to the hand which had pampered them, not one common soldier or common sailor is known to have deserted his flag.

Great honor is due to those officers who remained true, despite the example of their treacherous associates; but the greatest honor, and most important fact of all, is the unanimous firmness of the common soldiers and common sailors. To the last man, so far as known, they have successfully resisted the traitorous efforts of those whose commands, but an hour before, they obeyed as absolute law. This is the patriotic instinct of the plain people. They understand, without an argument, that the destroying of the government which was made by Washington means no good to them.

Our popular government has often been called an experiment. Two points in it our people have already settled—the successful establishing and the successful administering of it. One still remains—its successful maintenance against a formidable internal attempt to overthrow it. It is now for them to demonstrate to the world that those who can fairly carry an election can also suppress a rebellion; that ballots are the rightful and peaceful successors of bullets; and that when ballots have fairly and constitutionally decided, there can be no successful appeal back to bullets; that there can be no successful appeal, except to ballots themselves, at succeeding elections. Such will be a great lesson of peace: teaching men that what they cannot take by an election, neither can they take it by a war; teaching all the folly of being the beginners of a war.

*            *            *

And having thus chosen our course, without guile and with pure purpose, let us renew our trust in God, and go forward without fear and with manly hearts.

ABRAHAM LINCOLN
*July 4, 1861*

## 124 "a government that thus tramples on all the principles of constitutional liberty" (1861)

Jefferson Davis delivered this message to the Provisional Congress of the Confederate States of America, which met in its new capital of Richmond, Virginia, two weeks after Lincoln's Fourth of July message to Congress. Davis's focus on resolution of the status of prisoners was particularly timely. The Battle of Manassas was fought the day after his address, and the number of captured soldiers on both sides was greatly increased. Although on May 13, 1861, Great Britain had recognized both sides in the Civil War as belligerents, the captives on both sides were not accorded formal prisoner-of-war status until February 14, 1862. Despite this resolution, questions of the status of those enlisted in the Southern cause lingered throughout and after the war.

Ironically, while urging the actual existence of a state of war, which the Confederate Congress had declared on May 6, Davis denounced Lincoln for his imposition of martial law in the border states. The Confederacy, although it too had to confront pockets of population disenchanted with the prosecution of the war, never did suspend habeas corpus.

☆ 124 Jefferson Davis's Message to the Provisional Congress, Third Session (July 20, 1861)

Reprinted in J. Richardson, ed., *A Compilation of Messages and Papers of the Confederacy* (Nashville: United States Publishing Co., 1905), 1:117-22.

To the Congress of the Confederate States of America.

*Gentlemen*:

\*　　　\*　　　\*

[T]he true policy and purposes of the Government of the United States had been previously concealed; their odious features now stand fully revealed; the message of their President and the action of their Congress during the present month confess the intention of subjugating these States by war.... [T]he President of the United States and his advisers succeeded in deceiving the people of those States into the belief that the purpose of this Government was not peace at home, but conquest abroad; not the defense of its own liberties, but the subversion of those of the people of the United States.

\*　　　\*　　　\*

Mankind will shudder to hear the tales of outrages committed on defenseless females by soldiers of the United States now invading our homes; yet these outrages are prompted by inflamed passions and the madness of intoxication. But who shall depict the horror with which they will regard the cool and deliberate malignity which, under pretext of suppressing an insurrection, said by themselves to be upheld by a minority only of our people, makes special war on the sick, including the women and the children....

\*　　　\*　　　\*

[But] they admit of no retaliation. The humanity of our people would shrink instinctively from the bare idea of waging a like war upon the sick, the women, and the children of the enemy.

But there are other savage practices which have been resorted to by the Government of the United States, which do admit of repression by retaliation. ... The prisoners of war taken by the enemy on board the armed schooner Savannah, sailing under our commission, were, as I was credibly advised, treated like common felons; put in irons; confined in a jail usually appropriated to criminals of the worst dye, and threatened with punishment as such.... I have informed President Lincoln of my resolute purpose to check all barbarities on prisoners of war, by such severity of retaliation on the prisoners held by us as should secure the abandonment of the practice.

... I have directed your attention ... to the peculiar relations which exist between this Government and the States usually termed the border slave States, which cannot properly be withheld from notice.

The hearts of our people are animated by sentiments toward the inhabitants of these States, which found expression in your enactment refusing to consider them as enemies, or to authorize hostilities against them. That a very large portion of the people of those States regard us as brethren; that if unrestrained by the actual presence of large armies, the subversion of civil authority and the declaration of martial law, some of them at least would joyfully unite with us; that they are with almost entire unanimity opposed to the prosecution of the war waged against us, are facts of which daily recurring events fully warrant the assertion.

\*　　　\*　　　\*

... [A]nother assertion of the message [to Congress is] that the Executive possesses the power of suspending the writ of *habeas corpus*, and of delegating that power to military commanders, at his discretion; and both these propositions claim a respect equal to that which is felt for the additional statement of opinion in the same paper, that it is proper, in order to execute the laws, that "some single law, made in such extreme tenderness of the citizen's liberty, that practically it relieved more of the guilty than the innocent, should, to a very limited extent, be violated."

We may well rejoice that we have forever severed our connection with a government that thus tramples on all the principles of constitutional liberty, and with a people in whose presence such avowals could be hazarded....

\*　　　\*　　　\*

JEFFERSON DAVIS
*Richmond, July 20, 1961*

## 125 "to overthrow ... by force, the Government of the United States" (1861)

On July 31, 1861, Congress passed "An Act to Define and Punish Certain Conspiracies." Those representatives opposed to the act feared it would nullify the constitutional safeguards regarding treason prosecutions by creating new crimes "kindred to treason" which required lesser evidentiary proof. The act was passed ten days after the first Battle of Bull Run, when defeated Union troops were streaming into Washington — a reminder of the precariousness not only of the nation's capital but also of the Union.

☆ 125 Conspiracies Act

12 Stat. 284 (1861).

*Be it enacted by the Senate and House of Representatives of the United States of America in Congress assembled*, That if two or more persons within any State or Territory of the United States shall conspire together to overthrow, or to put down, or to destroy by force, the Government of the United States, or to levy war against the United States, or to oppose by force the authority of the Government of the United States; or by force to prevent, hinder, or delay the execution of any law of the United States; or by force to seize, take, or possess any property of the United States against the will or contrary to the authority of the United States; or by force, or intimidation, or threat to prevent any person from accepting or holding any office, or trust, or place of confidence, under the United States; each and every person so offending shall be guilty of a high crime, and upon conviction thereof . . . shall be punished by a fine not more than five thousand dollars; or by imprisonment, with or without hard labor, as the court shall determine, for a period not less than six months nor greater than six years, or by both such fine and imprisonment.

*Approved, July 31, 1861.*

## 126 "aiding . . . insurrection or resistance to the laws" (1861)

The first emancipation of slaves by the Union was not the result of abolitionist sentiment but a function of the criminal law. The earliest treason laws mandated forfeiture of property by traitors and rebels, but the treason statute of 1790 did not include forfeiture as a punishment. Relying on tradition, Congress reinstated limited forfeiture of rebels' property by expropriating any "property," including slaves employed in the insurrectionary effort. The institution of slavery itself, therefore, was unaffected in the so-called border states of Delaware, Maryland, Kentucky, and Missouri, and the Fugitive Slave Law continued in force.

### ☆ 126 An Act to Confiscate Property Used for Insurrectionary Purposes

12 Stat. 319 (1861).

*Be it enacted by the Senate and House of Representatives of the United States of America in Congress assembled*, That if, during the present or any future insurrection against the Government of the United States, . . . any person or persons, his, her, or their agent, attorney or employee, shall purchase or acquire, sell or give, any property of whatsoever kind or description, with intent to use or employ the same . . . in aiding, abetting, or promoting such insurrection or resistance to the laws, or . . . shall knowingly use or employ, or consent to the use or employment of the same as aforesaid, all such property is hereby declared to be lawful subject of prize and capture wherever found; and it shall be the duty of the President of the United States to cause the same to be seized, confiscated, and condemned.

*            *            *

SEC. 3. And be it further enacted, That the Attorney-General, or any district attorney of the United States in which said property may at the time be, may institute the proceedings of condemnation, . . . or any person may file an information with such attorney, in which case the proceedings shall be for the use of such informer and the United States in equal parts.

SEC. 4. And be it further enacted, That whenever hereafter, during the present insurrection against the Government of the United States, any person claimed to be held to labor or service under the law of any State shall be required or permitted by the person to whom such labor or service is claimed to be due to take up arms against the United States, or . . . to work or to be employed against the Government and lawful authority of the United States, then and in every such case the person to whom such labor or service is claimed to be due shall forfeit his claim to such labor, any law of the State or of the United States to the contrary notwithstanding. . . .

*Approved, August 6, 1861.*

## 127 "furthering the work of disunion" (1862)

On February 14, 1862, President Lincoln granted amnesty to all persons then held by the United States as suspected insurgents. Seized by authority of the president in an unprecedented exercise of power, Lincoln referred to the detainees as "political prisoners."

This document offered an apology for the president's actions based upon the chaos of the early stages of the Civil War. He argued that the Civil War was an insurrection that required resort to "extraordinary powers which the Constitution confides . . . [in the president] in cases of insurrection." There is, however, no mention in the Constitution of the "extraordinary powers" to which Lincoln referred. The Article II powers of the president, although open-ended, make no reference to special events or to conditional authority to meet emergencies.

Lincoln's gesture of amnesty, suggesting the withholding of punishment if the rebels gave up secession, was in vain. The Civil War was to continue until 1865, becoming the bloodiest military conflict in United States history. Despite the general release and grant of amnesty, Lincoln's order did not repudiate the actions previously exercised or forswear their reoccurrence. Rather, it affirmed the claim of the existence of "extraordinary powers."

## ☆127 President Lincoln's Executive Order Number One relating to Political Prisoners (February 14, 1862)

Reprinted in J. Richardson, *A Compilation of the Messages and Papers of the Presidents* (Washington, D.C.: U.S. Government Printing Office, 1897), 6:102-4.

The breaking out of a formidable insurrection based on a conflict of political ideas, being an event without precedent in the United States, was necessarily attended by great confusion and perplexity of the public mind. Disloyalty before unsuspected suddenly became bold, and treason astonished the world by bringing at once into the field military forces superior in number to the standing Army of the United States.

Every department of the Government was paralyzed by treason. Defection appeared in the Senate, in the House of Representatives, in the Cabinet, in the Federal courts; ministers and consuls returned from foreign countries to enter the insurrectionary councils or land or naval forces; commanding and other officers of the Army and in the Navy betrayed our councils or deserted their posts for commands in the insurgent forces. Treason was flagrant in the revenue and in the post-office service, as well as in the Territorial governments and in the Indian reserves.

Not only governors, judges, legislators, and ministerial officers in the States, but even whole States rushed one after another with apparent unanimity into rebellion. The capital was besieged and its connection with all the States cut off.

Even in the portions of the country which were most loyal political combinations and secret societies were formed furthering the work of disunion, while, from motives of disloyalty or cupidity or from excited passions or perverted sympathies, individuals were found furnishing men, money, and materials of war and supplies to the insurgents' military and naval forces. Armies, ships, fortifications, navy-yards, arsenals, military posts, and garrisons one after another were betrayed or abandoned to the insurgents.

Congress had not anticipated, and so had not provided for, the emergency. The municipal authorities were powerless and inactive. The judicial machinery seemed as if it had been designed, not to sustain the Government, but to embarrass and betray it.

*          *          *

In this emergency the President felt it his duty to employ with energy the extraordinary powers which the Constitution confides to him in cases of insurrection. He called into the field such military and naval forces, unauthorized by the existing laws, as seemed necessary. He directed measures to prevent the use of the post-office for treasonable correspondence. He subjected passengers to and from foreign countries to new passport regulations, and he instituted a blockade, suspended the writ of *habeas corpus* in various places, and caused persons who were represented to him as being or about to engage in disloyal and treasonable practices to be arrested by special civil as well as military agencies and detained in military custody when necessary to prevent them and deter others from such practices. Examinations of such cases were instituted, and some of the persons so arrested have been discharged from time to time under circumstances or upon conditions compatible, as was thought, with the public safety.

Meantime a favorable change of public opinion has occurred. The line between loyalty and disloyalty is plainly defined. The whole structure of the Government is firm and stable. Apprehension of public danger and facilities for treasonable practices have diminished with the passions which prompted heedless persons to adopt them. The insurrection is believed to have culminated and to be declining.

The President, in view of these facts, and anxious to favor a return to the normal course of the Administration as far as regard for the public welfare will allow, directs that all political prisoners or state prisoners now held in military custody be released on their subscribing to a parole engaging them to render no aid or comfort to the enemies in hostility to the United States.

The Secretary of War will, however, in his discretion, except from the effect of this order any persons detained as spies in the service of the insurgents, or others whose release at the present moment may be deemed incompatible with the public safety.

To all persons who shall be so released and who shall keep their parole the President grants an amnesty for any past offenses of treason or disloyalty which they may have committed.

Extraordinary arrests will hereafter be made under the direction of the military authorities alone.

By order of the President:

EDWIN M. STANTON, Secretary of War

## 128 "denying our right to self-government" (1862)

On February 22, 1862, Jefferson Davis was sworn in as the first president under a Confederate Constitution authorizing one six-year presidential term. Detailing the abuses of power and disregard for constitutional rights by Lincoln and his troops and asserting the Confederacy's claim to the true heritage of the Revolution, Davis overlooked slavery's impairment of personal liberty and the Southern curbs on abolitionist sentiment.

☆128 Jefferson Davis's Inaugural Address
(February 22, 1862)

Reprinted in J. Richardson, ed., *A Compilation of Messages
and Papers of the Confederacy* (Nashville: United States
Publishing Co., 1905), 1:184-88.

FELLOW CITIZENS:

... [W]e have assembled to usher into existence the
Permanent Government of the Confederate States.
Through this instrumentality, under the favor of Divine Providence, we hope to perpetuate the principles of our revolutionary fathers....

\*     \*     \*

When a long course of class legislation, directed
not to the general welfare, but to the aggrandizement of the Northern section of the Union, culminated in a warfare on the domestic institutions of
the Southern States, ... six of those States, withdrawing from the Union, confederated together to
exercise the right and perform the duty of instituting a Government which would better secure the liberties for the preservation of which that Union was
established.

Whatever of hope [there was of reunion] ... must
have been dispelled by the malignity and barbarity
of the Northern States in the prosecution of the existing war. The confidence of the most hopeful
among us must have been destroyed by the disregard they have recently exhibited for all the time-honored bulwarks of civil and religious liberty. Bastiles filled with prisoners, arrested without civil
process or indictment duly found; the writ of *habeas
corpus* suspended by Executive mandate; a State
Legislature controlled by the imprisonment of members whose avowed principles suggested to the Federal Executive that there might be another added to
the list of seceded States; elections held under
threats of a military power; civil officers, peaceful
citizens, and gentlewomen incarcerated for opinion's
sake—proclaimed the incapacity of our late associates to administer a Government as free, liberal, and
humane as that established for our common use.

For proof of the sincerity of our purpose to maintain our ancient institutions, we may point to the
Constitution of the Confederacy and the laws enacted under it, as well as to the fact that through all
the necessities of an unequal struggle there has
been no act on our part to impair personal liberty or
the freedom of speech, of thought, or of the press.
The courts have been open, the judicial functions
fully executed, and every right of the peaceful citizen maintained as securely as if a war of invasion
had not disturbed the land.

\*     \*     \*

... To save ourselves from a revolution which, in
its silent but rapid progress, was about to place us
under the despotism of numbers, and to preserve in

spirit, as well as in form, a system of government we
believed to be peculiarly fitted to our condition, and
full of promise for mankind, we determined to make
a new association, composed of States homogeneous
in interest, in policy, and in feeling.

True to our traditions of peace and our love of
justice, we sent commissioners to the United States
to propose a fair and amicable settlement of all questions of public debt or property which might be in
dispute. But the Government at Washington, denying our right to self-government, refused even to listen to any proposals for a peaceful separation. Nothing was then left to do but to prepare for war.

\*     \*     \*

The period is near at hand when our foes must
sink under the immense load of debt which they
have incurred, a debt which in their effort to subjugate us has already attained such fearful dimensions
as will subject them to burdens which must continue
to oppress them for generations to come.

\*     \*     \*

... This great strife has awakened in the people
the highest emotions and qualities of the human
soul. It is cultivating feelings of patriotism, virtue,
and courage. Instances of self-sacrifice and of generous devotion to the noble cause for which we are contending are rife throughout the land. Never has a
people evinced a more determined spirit than that
now animating men, women, and children in every
part of our country. Upon the first call the men flew
to arms, and wives and mothers send their husbands
and sons to battle without a murmur of regret.

It was, perhaps, in the ordination of Providence
that we were to be taught the value of our liberties
by the price which we pay for them.

\*     \*     \*

Fellow-citizens, after the struggle of ages had
consecrated the right of the Englishman to constitutional representative government, our colonial ancestors were forced to vindicate that birthright by
an appeal to arms. Success crowned their efforts,
and they provided for their posterity a peaceful remedy against future aggression.

The tyranny of an unbridled majority, the most
odious and least responsible form of despotism, has
denied us both the right and the remedy. Therefore
we are in arms to renew such sacrifices as our fathers made to the holy cause of constitutional
liberty....

To show ourselves worthy of the inheritance bequeathed to us by the patriots of the Revolution, we
must emulate that heroic devotion which made reverse to them but the crucible in which their patriotism was refined.

... With humble gratitude and adoration, acknowledging the Providence which has so visibly
protected the Confederacy during its brief but

eventful career, to thee, O God, I trustingly commit myself, and prayerfully invoke thy blessing on my country and its cause.

## 129 Freeing the Slaves of Those Committing Treason (1862)

Economic sanctions were a central feature of the Union strategy in the Civil War. On April 19, 1861, Lincoln proclaimed a blockade of the Confederate states. The first Confiscation Act of August 6, 1861, ordered the freeing of all slaves used by the Confederates either in labor or in arms. On August 16, 1861, Lincoln proclaimed an end to commercial relations with inhabitants of the areas in rebellion. On July 17, 1862, he signed the second Confiscation Act, which recognized the need for a different disposition of "confiscated" slaves than the customary transfer of ownership to the government provided in the law of forfeiture, and authorized the freeing of slaves in areas taken by Union arms.

Congress wanted to maintain the support of proslavery elements in the North and continued to be unwilling to address the problem of slavery in general. But two months later, on September 22, 1862, President Lincoln finally issued the Emancipation Proclamation. This proclamation, nevertheless, only declared the freedom of slaves within the rebel states, exempting parts thereof not deemed to be in rebellion. In the four slave states of Delaware, Kentucky, Maryland, and Missouri, the institution of slavery was unaffected. Not until the adoption of the Thirteenth Amendment was the issue resolved.

☆ 129 An Act to Suppress Insurrection, to Punish Treason and Rebellion and Confiscate the Property of Rebels . . .

12 Stat. 589 (1862).

*Be it enacted by the Senate and House of Representatives of the United States of America in Congress assembled*, That every person who shall hereafter commit the crime of treason against the United States, and shall be adjudged guilty thereof, shall suffer death, and all his slaves, if any, shall be declared and made free; or, at the discretion of the court, he shall be imprisoned for not less than five years and fined not less than ten thousand dollars, and all his slaves, if any, shall be declared and made free; said fine shall be levied and collected on any or all of the property, real and personal, excluding slaves, of which the said person so convicted was the owner. . . .

SEC. 2. *And be it further enacted*, That if any person shall hereafter incite, set on foot, assist, or engage in any rebellion or insurrection against the au-

thority of the United States, or the laws thereof, or shall give aid or comfort thereto, or shall engage in, or give aid and comfort to, any such existing rebellion or insurrection, and be convicted thereof, such person shall be punished by imprisonment for a period not exceeding ten years, or by a fine not exceeding ten thousand dollars, and by the liberation of all his slaves, if any he have; or by both of said punishments, at the discretion of the court.

SEC. 3. *And be it further enacted*, That every person guilty of either of the offences described in this act shall be forever incapable and disqualified to hold any office under the United States.

\*　　　\*　　　\*

SEC. 5. *And be it further enacted*, That, to insure the speedy termination of the present rebellion, it shall be the duty of the President of the United States to cause the seizure of all the estate and property, money, stocks, credits, and effects of the persons hereinafter named in this section, and to apply and use the same and the proceeds thereof for the support of the army of the United States, that is to say: [army and navy officers, government officials and others giving aid and comfort to the "so called confederate states of America"].

\*　　　\*　　　\*

SEC. 9. *And be it further enacted*, That all slaves of persons who shall hereafter be engaged in rebellion against the government of the United States, or who shall in any way give aid or comfort thereto, escaping from such persons and taking refuge within the lines of the army; and all slaves captured from such persons or deserted by them and coming under the control of the government of the United States; and all slaves of such persons found *on* [or] being within any place occupied by rebel forces and afterwards occupied by the forces of the United States, shall be deemed captives of war, and shall be forever free of their servitude, and not again held as slaves.

SEC. 10. *And be it further enacted*, That no slave escaping into any State, Territory, or the District of Columbia, from any other State, shall be delivered up, or in any way impeded or hindered of his liberty, except for crime, or some offence against the laws, unless the person claiming said fugitive shall first make oath that the person to whom the labor or service of such fugitive is alleged to be due is his lawful owner, and has not borne arms against the United States in the present rebellion, nor in any way given aid and comfort thereto; and no person engaged in the military or naval service of the United States shall, under any pretence whatever, assume to decide on the validity of the claim of any person to the service or labor of any other person, or surrender up any such person to the claimant, on pain of being dismissed from the service.

SEC. 11. *And be it further enacted*, That the

President of the United States is authorized to employ as many persons of African descent as he may deem necessary and proper for the suppression of this rebellion, and for this purpose he may organize and use them in such manner as he may judge best for the public welfare.

SEC. 12. *And be it further enacted*, That the President of the United States is hereby authorized to make provision for the transportation, colonization, and settlement, in some tropical country beyond the limits of the United States, of such persons of the African race, made free by the provisions of this act, as may be willing to emigrate, having first obtained the consent of the government of said country to their protection and settlement within the same, with all the rights and privileges of freemen.

*   *   *

*Approved, July 17, 1862.*

## 130 "no service can be more praiseworthy or honorable" (1863)

The combination of enlistments and the impression of the state militias into the Union forces was insufficient to meet the manpower needs of the federal army. On March 3, 1863, Congress passed an act authorizing conscription and punishing speech and conduct resistant to this measure. There was no provision exempting conscientious objectors, although there were exemptions for men who were the sole support of women and children. In addition, men could avoid the service by finding a substitute or paying the government a fee of three hundred dollars.

Opposition to unfair draft laws, combined with race tensions, labor unrest, religious and ethnic conflict, and class antagonism erupted into violence. While the violence was at first directed against the draft offices, the discontent vented itself upon the black population, which was viewed as the cause of the war. In a week of riots in July 1863, as many as one thousand to twelve hundred persons were killed or wounded in New York City alone. Eventually troops were detached from Gettysburg to restore order. Riots occurred also in many other Northern cities, including Newark, Jersey City, Troy, Boston, Toledo, and Evansville. The New York account is from an official army record.

☆ 130  Resistance to Military Conscription

☆ 130a  An Act for Enrolling and Calling out the National Forces, and for Other Purposes

12 Stat. 731 (1863).

Whereas there now exist in the United States an insurrection and rebellion against the authority thereof, and it is, under the Constitution of the United States, the duty of the government to suppress insurrection and rebellion, to guarantee to each State a republican form of government, and to preserve the public tranquillity; and whereas, for these high purposes, a military force is indispensable, to raise and support which all persons ought willingly to contribute; and whereas no service can be more praiseworthy and honorable than that which is rendered for the maintenance of the Constitution and Union, and the consequent preservation of free government: Therefore—

*Be it enacted by the Senate and House of Representatives of the United States of America in Congress assembled*, That all able-bodied male citizens of the United States, and persons of foreign birth who shall have declared on oath their intention to become citizens under and in pursuance of the laws thereof, between the ages of twenty and forty-five years, except as hereinafter excepted, are hereby declared to constitute the national forces, and shall be liable to perform military duty in the service of the United States when called out by the President for that purpose.

*   *   *

SEC. 13. *And be it further enacted*, That any person drafted and notified to appear as aforesaid, may, on or before the day fixed for his appearance, furnish an acceptable substitute to take his place in the draft; or he may pay to such person as the Secretary of War may authorize to receive it, such sum, not exceeding three hundred dollars, as the Secretary may determine, for the procuration of such substitute; which sum shall be fixed at a uniform rate by a general order made at the time of ordering a draft for any state or territory; and thereupon such person so furnishing the substitute, or paying the money, shall be discharged from further liability under that draft. And any person failing to report after due service of notice, as herein prescribed, without furnishing a substitute, or paying the required sum therefor, shall be deemed a deserter, and shall be arrested by the provost-marshal and sent to the nearest military post for trial by court-martial, unless, upon proper showing that he is not liable to do military duty, the board of enrolment shall relieve him from the draft.

*   *   *

SEC. 24. *And be it further enacted*, That every person not subject to the rules and articles of war who shall procure or entice, or attempt to procure or entice, a soldier in the service of the United States to desert; or who shall harbor, conceal, or give employment to a deserter, or carry him away, or aid in carrying him away, knowing him to be such; or who shall purchase from any soldier his arms, equipments, ammunition, uniform, clothing, or any part thereof; and any captain or commanding officer of any ship or vessel, or any superintendent or conductor of any railroad, or any other public conveyance, carrying away any such soldier as one of his crew or otherwise, knowing him to have deserted, or shall refuse to deliver him up to the orders of his commanding officer, shall, upon legal conviction, be fined, at the discretion of any court having cognizance of the same, in any sum not exceeding five hundred dollars, and he shall be imprisoned not exceeding two years nor less than six months.

SEC. 25. *And be it further enacted*, That if any person shall resist any draft of men enrolled under this act into the service of the United States, or shall counsel or aid any person to resist any such draft; or shall assault or obstruct any officer in making such draft, or in the performance of any service in relation thereto; or shall counsel any person to assault or obstruct any such officer, or shall counsel any drafted men not to appear at the place of rendezvous, or wilfully dissuade them from the performance of military duty as required by law, such person shall be subject to summary arrest by the provost-marshal, and shall be forthwith delivered to the civil authorities, and, upon conviction thereof, be punished by a fine not exceeding five hundred dollars, or by imprisonment not exceeding two years, or by both of said punishments.

*          *          *

*Approved, March 3, 1863.*

☆ 130b  Troops Attacked by Armed Mob

Reprinted in Richard Hofstadter and Michael Wallace, *American Violence: A Documentary History* (New York: Knopf, 1970), 213-14.

. . . About six o'clock P.M., General Dodge and Colonel Mott informed General Brown, that the troops at Grammercy Park had marched down Twenty-second Street, and been attacked by an armed mob; that they had been driven back, leaving their dead in the street. The general ordered me to take my company, and a portion of the Twentieth and Twenty-eighth New York volunteer batteries, about eighty men, armed as infantry, commanded by Lieutenant B. F. Ryer. Lieutenant Ryer had with him Lieutenant Robert F. Joyce and Lieutenant F. M. Chase, Twenty-eighth New York battery. My whole command amounted to one hundred and sixty men.

With this force I marched to the Grammercy Hotel. At a short distance from the hotel, I saw some of the rioters fire from a house on some of Colonel Mott's command. I immediately sent Lieutenant Joyce with a few men to search the house. The search was fruitless, the men having escaped to the rear. I then told the women in the house that the artillery would open on the house, if any more shots

were fired from it. We then marched down Twenty-second Street, between Second and Third Avenues, found the body of a sergeant of Davis' Cavalry, who had been killed two hours before. I ordered a livery-stable keeper to put his horses to a carriage, and accompany me, for the purpose of carrying the dead and wounded. He replied that the mob would kill him if he did, and that he dare not do it. He was informed that he would be protected if he went, but if he refused he would be instantly shot. The horses were speedily harnessed, and the body put into the carriage. The mob at this time commenced firing on us from the houses. We at once commenced searching the houses, while my skirmishers drove the rioters back from every window and from the roofs. The houses were searched from cellar to the roof. The mob made a desperate fight, and evidently seemed to think they could whip us. Every house that was used to conceal these rioters was cleared. A large number was killed, and several prisoners taken. We then marched to Second Avenue, where we found the mob in great force and concealed in houses. They fired on us from house-tops, and from windows, and also from cross streets. We soon cleared the streets, and then commenced searching the houses. We searched thirteen houses, killed those within that resisted, and took the remainder prisoners. Some of them fought like incarnate fiends, and would not surrender. All such were shot on the spot. The soldiers captured a large number of revolvers of large size, which I allowed them to keep. The mob at this place were well armed; nearly every one had some kind of fire-arms, and had one blunderbuss which they fired on us.

If they had been cool and steady, they might have done us great harm. As it was, they fired wildly, running to a window and firing, and then retreating back out of danger.

When my soldiers once got into a house they made short work of it. The fight lasted about forty minutes and was more severe than all the rest in which my company was engaged. There were none of my men killed. Sergeant Cadro, of company F, Twelfth Infantry (my own), was slightly wounded in the hand; private Krouse was also slightly wounded.

The mob being entirely dispersed, we returned to head-quarters.

# 131  "Treating captured rebels as prisoners of war" (1863)

The exigencies of the American Civil War produced the first attempt to codify the international laws of war, which had by custom been considered to be binding upon all civilized nations. Prepared by Francis Lieber, a professor at Columbia College in New

York, and promulgated by President Lincoln on April 24, 1863, this General Order No. 100 is the forerunner of the Hague Conventions of 1899 and 1907 and the Geneva Convention of 1949.

Although the main part of these instructions pertained to wars between nations, articles 149 to 157 concerned civil wars and insurrections. The instructions did not exempt participants in such domestic armed conflicts from punishment under treason and other domestic criminal laws. But the instructions recognized humanitarian considerations (not to mention the pragmatic impossibility of trying and punishing large numbers of rebels) as a justification for the application of the regular rules of international warfare to domestic insurgents. The Union army thus was given the option of treating Confederate captives as prisoners of war rather than traitors. Yet the instructions hastened to reiterate that such practices were not to constitute a recognition of the rebels as a "sovereign power," nor were they to preclude the trial of the "chief rebels for high treason."

## ☆ 131 Instructions for the Government of Armies of the United States in the Field (April 24, 1863)

General Order No. 100, Adjutant General's Office, 1863, reprinted in D. Schindler and J. Toman, eds., *The Laws of Armed Conflicts* (Alphen aan den Rijn, The Netherlands: Sijthoff & Noordhoff, 1981), 21-23.

\*　　　\*　　　\*

### SECTION IX

#### *Assassination*

Art. 148. The law of war does not allow proclaiming either an individual belonging to the hostile army, or a citizen, or a subject of the hostile government, an outlaw, who may be slain without trial by any captor, any more than the modern law of peace allows such intentional outlawry; on the contrary, it abhors such outrage. The sternest retaliation should follow the murder committed in consequence of such proclamation, made by whatever authority. Civilized nations look with horror upon offers of rewards for the assassination of enemies as relapses into barbarism.

### SECTION X

#### *Insurrection—Civil War—Rebellion*

Art. 149. Insurrection is the rising of people in arms against their government, or a portion of it, or against one or more of its laws, or against an officer or officers of the government. It may be confined to mere armed resistance, or it may have greater ends in view.

Art. 150. Civil war is war between two or more portions of a country or state, each contending for the mastery of the whole, and each claiming to be the legitimate government. The term is also sometimes applied to war of rebellion, when the rebellious provinces or portions of the state are contiguous to those containing the seat of government.

Art. 151. The term rebellion is applied to an insurrection of large extent, and is usually a war between the legitimate government of a country and portions of provinces of the same who seek to throw off their allegiance to it and set up a government of their own.

Art. 152. When humanity induces the adoption of the rules of regular war toward rebels, whether the adoption is partial or entire, it does in no way whatever imply a partial or complete acknowledgment of their government, if they have set up one, or of them, as an independent and sovereign power. Neutrals have no right to make the adoption of the rules of war by the assailed government toward rebels the ground of their own acknowledgment of the revolted people as an independent power.

Art. 153. Treating captured rebels as prisoners of war, exchanging them, concluding of cartels, capitulations, or other warlike agreements with them; addressing officers of a rebel army by the rank they may have in the same; accepting flags of truce; or, on the other hand, proclaiming Martial Law in their territory, or levying war-taxes or forced loans, or doing any other act sanctioned or demanded by the law and usages of public war between sovereign belligerents, neither proves nor establishes an acknowledgment of the rebellious people, or of the government which they may have erected, as a public or sovereign power. Nor does the adoption of the rules of war toward rebels imply an engagement with them extending beyond the limits of these rules. It is victory in the field that ends the strife and settles the future relations between the contending parties.

Art. 154. Treating, in the field, the rebellious enemy according to the law and usages of war has never prevented the legitimate government from trying the leaders of the rebellion or chief rebels for high treason, and from treating them accordingly, unless they are included in a general amnesty.

Art. 155. All enemies in regular war are divided into two general classes—that is to say, into combatants and noncombatants, or unarmed citizens of the hostile government.

The military commander of the legitimate government, in a war of rebellion, distinguishes between the loyal citizen in the revolted portion of the country and the disloyal citizen. The disloyal citizens may further be classified into those citizens known to sympathize with the rebellion without positively aiding it, and those who, without taking up arms, give positive aid and comfort to the rebellious enemy without being bodily forced thereto.

Art. 156. Common justice and plain expediency

require that the military commander protect the manifestly loyal citizens, in revolted territories, against the hardships of the war as much as the common misfortune of all war admits.

The commander will throw the burden of the war, as much as lies within his power, on the disloyal citizens, of the revolted portion or province, subjecting them to a stricter police than the noncombatant enemies have to suffer in regular war; and if he deems it appropriate, or if his government demands of him that every citizen shall, by an oath of allegiance, or by some other manifest act, declare his fidelity to the legitimate government, he may expel, transfer, imprison, or fine the revolted citizens who refuse to pledge themselves anew as citizens obedient to the law and loyal to the government.

Whether it is expedient to do so, and whether reliance can be placed upon such oaths, the commander or his government have the right to decide.

Art. 157. Armed or unarmed resistance by citizens of the United States against the lawful movements of their troops is levying war against the United States, and is therefore treason.

## 132 "that he has never given any aid or comfort to the present rebellion" (1863)

The Abandoned Property Act served two Union objectives: the economic punishment of rebels and the financing of the war through confiscations. The act allowed the government to confiscate property of Southerners without cumbersome legal proceedings and sanctioned the summary collection and sale of property abandoned or captured in any of the rebellious states, with the proceeds going into the United States Treasury. Perhaps in recognition of the Fifth Amendment guarantees against the taking of property without due process of law, the act provided that owners could recover a standardized value of confiscated property two years after the conclusion of the insurrection. But unlike earlier enactments in which the government had the burden of showing some support of the rebellion by the property owner, this act shifted the burden of proof to the claimant to prove he had not supported the rebellion. While Confederate soldiers were accorded prisoner-of-war status, civilians in the South were still held to loyalty to the United States. After the war the United States Supreme Court held the act to be constitutional as a valid exercise of the government's war powers.

## ☆ 132 An Act to Provide for the Collection of Abandoned Property

12 Stat. 820 (1863).

*Be it enacted by the Senate and House of Representatives of the United States of America in Congress assembled,* That it shall be lawful for the Secretary of the Treasury ... to receive and collect all abandoned or captured property in any state or territory ... designated as in insurrection against the lawful Government of the United States. ...

Sec. 2. *And be it further enacted,* That any part of the goods or property received or collected by such agent or agents may be appropriated to public use on due appraisement and certificate thereof, or forwarded to any place of sale within the loyal states, as the public interests may require; and all sales of such property shall be at auction to the highest bidder, and the proceeds thereof shall be paid into the treasury of the United States.

Sec. 3. *And be it further enacted,* That ... any person claiming to have been the owner of any such abandoned or captured property may, at any time within two years after the suppression of the rebellion, prefer his claim to the proceeds thereof in the court of claims; and on proof to the satisfaction of said court of his ownership of said property, of his right to the proceeds thereof, and that he has never given any aid or comfort to the present rebellion, to receive the residue of such proceeds, after the deduction of any purchase-money which may have been paid, together with the expense of transportation and sale of said property, and any other lawful expenses attending the disposition thereof.

Sec. 4. *And be it further enacted,* That all property coming into any of the United States not declared in insurrection as aforesaid, from within any of the states declared in insurrection, through or by any other person than any agent duly appointed under the provisions of this act, or under a lawful clearance by the proper officer of the Treasury Department, shall be confiscated to the use of the Government of the United States. ...

\*         \*         \*

*Approved, March 12, 1863.*

## 133 "too few arrests rather than too many" (1863)

The Albany Democratic Convention voiced complaints that certain military arrests were unconstitutional, particularly the arrest of Congressman Clement L. Vallandigham of Ohio, a famous Copperhead. (This term was first applied to Lincoln's Northern opponents by the *New York Tribune* in 1861.) Lincoln, in defense of his asserted power, wrote to Erastus Corning, a New York political leader. This letter presents a most eloquent defense of the "inherent power" of the executive, in the absence of specific legislative or constitutional authority, to use whatever force necessary to suppress activities deemed inimical to the national security.

Professing a personal distaste for the suspension of the writ of habeas corpus, Lincoln nevertheless asserted its necessity and constitutionality, and the view that it would have no lasting effect on civil liberties. The letter reiterated Lincoln's defiant refusal to accept the court's ruling in *Ex Parte Merryman* that Congress alone had the authority to suspend the writ. Attention should also be given to Lincoln's recitation of the resolution of General Andrew Jackson's brush with civil authorities during an earlier period of martial law.

☆ 133  Letter from Abraham Lincoln to Erastus Corning and Others (June 12, 1863)

Reprinted in J. Nicolay and J. Hay, eds., *Complete Works of Lincoln* (New York: F. D. Tandy, 1905), 8:298-314.

Executive Mansion, June 12, 1863

GENTLEMEN:

Your letter of May 19, inclosing the resolutions of a public meeting held at Albany, New York, on the 16th of the same month, was received several days ago.

                    *       *       *

... The resolutions promise to support me in every constitutional and lawful measure to suppress the rebellion; and I have not knowingly employed, nor shall knowingly employ, any other. But the meeting, by their resolutions, assert and argue that certain military arrests and proceedings following them, for which I am ultimately responsible are unconstitutional. I think they are not. The resolutions quote from the Constitution the definition of treason, and also the limiting safeguards and guarantees therein provided for the citizen on trials for treason, and on his being held to answer for capital or otherwise infamous crimes, and in criminal prosecutions his right to a speedy and public trial by an impartial jury. They proceed to resolve "that these safeguards of the rights of the citizen against the pretensions of arbitrary power were intended more especially for his protection in times of civil commotion." And, apparently to demonstrate the proposition, the resolutions proceed: "They were secured substantially to the English people after years of protracted civil war, and were adopted into our Constitution at the close of the revolution." Would not the demonstration have been better if it could have been truly said that these safeguards had been adopted and applied during the civil wars and during our revolution, instead of after the one and at the close of the

other? I, too, am devotedly for them after civil war and before civil war, and at all times, "except when, in cases of rebellion or invasion, the public safety may require" their suspension.... But these provisions of the Constitution have no application to the case we have in hand, because the arrests complained of were not made for treason—that is, not for the treason defined in the Constitution, and upon the conviction of which the punishment is death—nor yet were they made to hold persons to answer for any capital or otherwise infamous crimes; nor were the proceedings following, in any constitutional or legal sense, "criminal prosecutions." The arrests were made on totally different grounds, and the proceedings following accorded with the grounds of the arrests.... [The rebel] sympathizers pervaded all departments of the government and nearly all communities of the people. From this material, under cover of "liberty of speech," "liberty of the press," and "*habeas corpus,*" they hoped to keep on foot amongst us a most efficient corps of spies, informers, suppliers and aiders and abettors of their cause in a thousand ways. They knew that in times such as they were inaugurating, by the Constitution itself the "*habeas corpus*" might be suspended; but they also knew they had friends who would make a question as to who was to suspend it; meanwhile their spies and others might remain at large to help on their cause. Or if, as has happened, the Executive should suspend the writ without ruinous waste of time, instances of arresting innocent persons might occur, as are always likely to occur in such cases; and then a clamor could be raised in regard to this.... Yet ... I was slow to adopt the strong measures which [are] ... indispensable to the public safety. Nothing is better known to history than that courts of justice are utterly incompetent to such cases. Civil courts are organized chiefly for trials of individuals, or, at most, a few individuals acting in concert—and this in quiet times, and on charges of crimes well defined in the law. Even in times of peace bands of horse-thieves and robbers frequently grow too numerous and powerful for the ordinary courts of justice. But what comparison, in numbers, have such bands ever borne to the insurgent sympathizers even in many of the loyal States? Again, a jury too frequently has at least one member more ready to hang the panel than to hang the traitor. And yet again, he who dissuades one man from volunteering, or induces one soldier to desert, weakens the Union cause as much as he who kills a Union soldier in battle. Yet this dissuasion or inducement may be so conducted as to be no defined crime of which any civil court would take cognizance.

Ours is a case of rebellion.... [The Suspension Clause] plainly attests the understanding of those who made the Constitution that ordinary courts of justice are inadequate to "cases of rebellion"—attests their purpose that, in such cases, men may be held in custody whom the courts, acting on ordinary rules, would discharge. *Habeas corpus* does not discharge men who are proved to be guilty of defined crime; and its suspension is allowed by the Constitution on purpose that men may be arrested and held who cannot be proved to be guilty of defined crime, "when, in cases of rebellion or invasion, the public safety may require it."

This is precisely our present case—a case of rebellion wherein the public safety does require the suspension.... Arrests in cases of rebellion do not proceed altogether upon the same basis. In the latter case arrests are made not so much for what has been done, as for what probably would be done. The latter is more for the preventive and less for the vindictive than the former. In such cases the purposes of men are much more easily understood than in cases of ordinary crime. The man who stands by and says nothing when the peril of his government is discussed, cannot be misunderstood. If not hindered, he is sure to help the enemy; much more if he talks ambiguously—talks for his country with "buts," and "ifs" and "ands." [Several Confederate leaders] were all within the power of the government since the rebellion began, and were nearly as well known to be traitors then as now. Unquestionably if we had seized and held them, the insurgent cause would be much weaker. But no one of them had then committed any crime defined in the law. Every one of them, if arrested, would have been discharged on *habeas corpus* were the writ allowed to operate. In view of these and similar cases, I think the time not unlikely to come when I shall be blamed for having made too few arrests rather than too many.

By the third resolution the meeting indicate their opinion that military arrests may be constitutional in localities where rebellion actually exists, but that such arrests are unconstitutional in localities where rebellion or insurrection does not actually exist. They insist that such arrests shall not be made "outside of the lines of necessary military occupation and the scenes of insurrection." Inasmuch, however, as the Constitution itself makes no such distinction, I am unable to believe that there is any such constitutional distinction. I concede that the class of arrests complained of can be constitutional only when, in cases of rebellion or invasion, the public safety may require them; and I insist that in such cases they are constitutional wherever the public safety does require them, as well in places to which they may prevent the rebellion extending, as in those where it may be already prevailing; as well where they may restrain mischievous interference with the raising and supplying of armies to suppress the rebellion, as where the rebellion may actually be; as well where they may restrain the enticing men out of the army, as where they would prevent mutiny in the army;

equally constitutional at all places where they will conduce to the public safety, as against the dangers of rebellion or invasion. Take the particular case mentioned by the meeting. It is asserted in substance, that Mr. Vallandigham was, by a military commander, seized and tried "for no other reason than words addressed to a public meeting in criticism of the course of the administration, and in condemnation of the military orders of the general." Now, if there be no mistake about this, if this assertion is the truth and the whole truth, if there was no other reason for the arrest, then I concede that the arrest was wrong. But the arrest, as I understand, was made for a very different reason. Mr. Vallandigham avows his hostility to the war on the part of the Union; and his arrest was made because he was laboring, with some effect, to prevent the raising of troops, to encourage desertions from the army, and to leave the rebellion without an adequate military force to suppress it. He was not arrested because he was damaging the political prospects of the administration or the personal interests of the commanding general but because he was damaging the army, upon the existence and vigor of which the life of the nation depends. He was warring upon the military, and this gave the military constitutional jurisdiction to lay hands upon him.... Long experience has shown that armies cannot be maintained unless desertion shall be punished by the severe penalty of death.... Must I shoot a simple-minded soldier boy who deserts, while I must not touch a hair of a wily agitator who induces him to desert? This is none the less injurious when effected by getting a father, or brother, or friend into a public meeting, and there working upon his feelings till he is persuaded to write the soldier boy that he is fighting in a bad cause, for a wicked administration of a contemptible government, too weak to arrest and punish him if he shall desert. I think that, in such a case, to silence the agitator and save the boy is not only constitutional, but withal a great mercy.

If I be wrong ... my error lies in believing ... that the Constitution is not in its application in all respects the same in cases of rebellion or invasion involving the public safety, as it is in times of profound peace and public security. The Constitution itself makes the distinction, and I can no more be persuaded that the government can constitutionally take no strong measures in times of rebellion, because it can be shown that the same could not be lawfully taken in time of peace, than I can be persuaded that a particular drug is not good medicine for a sick man because it can be shown to not be good food for a well one. Nor am I able to appreciate the danger apprehended by the meeting, that the American people will by means of military arrests during the rebellion lose the right of public discussion, the liberty of speech and the press, the law of evidence, trial by jury, and *habeas corpus* throughout the indefinite peaceful future which I trust lies before them, any more than I am able to believe that a man could contract so strong an appetite for emetics during temporary illness as to persist in feeding upon them during the remainder of his healthful life.

... I cannot overlook the fact that the meeting speak as "Democrats." Nor can I ... suppose that this occurred by accident, or in any way other than that they preferred to designate themselves "Democrats" rather than "American citizens." ... He on whose discretionary judgment Mr. Vallandigham was arrested and tried is a Democrat, having no old party affinity with me, and the judge who rejected the constitutional view expressed in these resolutions, by refusing to discharge Mr. Vallandigham on *habeas corpus*, is a Democrat of better days than these, having received his judicial mantle at the hands of President Jackson. And still more, of all those Democrats who are nobly exposing their lives and shedding their blood on the battle-field, I have learned that many approve the course taken with Mr. Vallandigham, while I have not heard of a single one condemning it. I cannot assert that there are none such. And the name of President Jackson recalls an instance of pertinent history. After the battle of New Orleans, ... General Andrew Jackson still maintained martial or military law.... [A] Mr. Louaillier published a denunciatory newspaper article. General Jackson arrested him. A lawyer by the name of Morel procured the United States Judge Hall to order a writ of *habeas corpus* to release Mr. Louaillier. General Jackson arrested both the lawyer and the judge. A Mr. Hollander ventured to say of some part of the matter that "it was a dirty trick." General Jackson arrested him. When the officer undertook to serve the writ of *habeas corpus*, General Jackson took it from him, and sent him away with a copy.... [When] the ratification of the treaty of peace was regularly announced, ... the judge and others were fully liberated. A few days more, and the judge called General Jackson into court and fined him $1000 for having arrested him and the others named. The general paid the fine, and then the matter rested for nearly thirty years, when Congress refunded principal and interest....

It may be remarked—first, that we had the same Constitution then as now; secondly, that we then had a case of invasion, and now we have a case of rebellion; and, thirdly, that the permanent right of the people to public discussion, the liberty of speech and of the press, the trial by jury, the law of evidence, and the *habeas corpus*, suffered no detriment whatever by that conduct of General Jackson, or its subsequent approval by the American Congress.

\*       \*       \*

I am specifically called on to discharge Mr. Vallandigham.... In response to such appeal I have to say ... it will afford me great pleasure to discharge him so soon as I can by any means believe the public safety will not suffer by it.

\*       \*       \*

A. LINCOLN

# 134  Enemies or Traitors (1863)

On March 15, 1863, Union forces seized the schooner *J. M. Chapman* in the harbor of San Francisco. The officers and crew were arrested and indicted for treason on the grounds that they had procured and armed a boat to conduct hostilities under a letter of marque from Jefferson Davis against the United States on the high seas.

In his charge to the jury, Judge Field defined the constitutional meaning of "enemies" and contrasted the judicial conclusion that the rebels were traitors with the ambivalent posture of the executive branch, which accorded prisoner-of-war status to the rebel soldiers. In the courts, civilian supporters of the Southern cause were held to standards expected of citizens of the United States, even though they held a commission from the president of the rebel government.

☆ 134  *United States v. Greathouse*

26 F. Cas. 21 (C.C.N.D. Ca. 1863) (No. 15,254).

FIELD, Circuit Justice (charging jury).... There prevails a very general, but an erroneous opinion, that in all criminal cases the jury are the judges as well of the law as of the fact—that is, that they have a right to disregard the law as laid down by the court, and to follow their own notions on the subject. Such is not the right of the jury. They have the power ... but they have no moral right to adopt their own views of the law. It is their duty to take the law from the court and apply it to the facts of the case....

The defendants are indicted for engaging in, and giving aid and comfort to, the existing rebellion against the government of the United States. The indictment is framed under the second section of the act of congress of July 17, 1862, ... and it charges the commission of acts, which, in the judgment of the court, amount to treason within the meaning of the constitution. "Treason against the United States," is the language adopted, "shall consist only in levying war against them, or adhering to their enemies, giving them aid and comfort." No other acts can be declared to constitute the offense. Congress can neither extend, nor restrict, nor define the crime. Its power over the subject is limited to prescribing the punishment.

\*       \*       \*

The term "enemies" ... applies only to the subjects of a foreign power in a state of open hostility with us. It does not embrace rebels in insurrection against their own government. An enemy is always the subject of a foreign power who owes no allegiance to our government or country. We may, therefore, omit all consideration of this second clause in the constitutional definition of treason. To convict the defendants they must be brought within the first clause of the definition. They must be shown to have committed acts which amount to a levying of war against the United States. To constitute a levying of war there must be an assemblage of persons in force, to overthrow the government, or to coerce its conduct.... The offense is complete, whether the force be directed to the entire overthrow of the government throughout the country, or only in certain portions of the country, or to defeat the execution and compel the repeal of one of its public laws.

It is not, however, necessary that I should go into any close definition of the words "levying war," for it is not sought to apply them to any doubtful case. War has been levied against the United States. War of gigantic proportions is now waged against them, and the government is struggling with it for its life. War being levied, all who aid in its prosecution, whether by open hostilities in the field, or by performing any part in the furtherance of the common object, "however minute or however remote from the scene of action," are equally guilty of treason within the constitutional provision. In treason there are no accessories; all who engage in the rebellion at any stage of its existence, or who designedly give to it any species of aid and comfort, in whatever part of the country they may be, stand on the same platform; they are all principals in the commission of the crime; they are all levying war against the United States.

*     *     *

The indictment in the present case, as I have already stated, is based upon the second section of the act of July 17, 1862. The constitution, although defining treason, leaves to congress the authority to prescribe its punishment. In 1790, congress passed an act fixing to the offense the penalty of death. By the first section of the act of July, 1862, congress gave a discretionary power to the courts to inflict the penalty of death, or fine and imprisonment, providing that in either case the slaves of the party convicted, if any he have, shall be liberated. The second section of the act declares "that if any person shall hereafter incite, set on foot, assist, or engage in any rebellion or insurrection against the authority of the United States, or the laws thereof, or shall give aid or comfort thereto, or shall engage in or give aid and comfort to any such existing rebellion or insurrection, and be convicted thereof, such person shall be pun-

ished by imprisonment for a period not exceeding ten years, or by a fine not exceeding $10,000...."

There would seem, upon a first examination, to be an inconsistency between the first and second sections of this act—the first section declaring a particular punishment for treason, and the second declaring, for acts which may constitute treason, a different punishment. It appears from the debate in the senate of the United States, when the second section was under consideration, that it was the opinion of several senators that the commission of the acts which it designates might, under some circumstances, constitute an offense less than treason. ... Rebels not being enemies within the Constitution's meaning, an indictment alleging the giving of aid and comfort to them had been, as it was stated, held defective. But ... not because the giving of aid and comfort to rebels was not treason, but because the parties giving such aid and comfort were equally involved in guilt with those in open hostilities and should have been indicted for levying war; for every species of aid and comfort which, if given to a foreign enemy, would constitute treason within the second clause of the constitutional provision—adhering to the enemies of the United States—would, if given to the rebels in insurrection against the government, constitute a levying of war under the first clause. The second section of the act, however, relieves the subject from any difficulty.... But we are unable to conceive of any act designated in the second section which would not constitute treason, except perhaps as suggested by my associate, that of inciting to a rebellion.... Looking at the act alone, we conclude that congress intended: 1. To preserve the act of 1790, which prescribes the penalty of death, in force for the prosecution and punishment of offenses committed previous to July 17, 1862, unless the parties accused are convicted under the act of the latter date for subsequent offenses; 2. To punish treason thereafter committed with death, or fine and imprisonment in the discretion of the court, unless the treason consist in engaging in or assisting a rebellion or insurrection against the authority of the United States, or the laws thereof, in which event the death penalty is to be abandoned, and a less penalty inflicted. By this construction, the apparent inconsistency in the provisions of the different sections is avoided, and effect given to each clause of the act. The defendants are therefore in fact on trial for treason, and they have had all the protection and privileges allowed to parties accused of treason, without being liable, in case of conviction, to the penalty which all other civilized nations have awarded to this, the highest of crimes known to the law.

*     *     *

[T]he indictment alleges: 1. The existence of a rebellion against the United States, their authority and laws; 2. That the defendants traitorously engaged in and gave aid and comfort to the same; 3. That in the execution of their treasonable and traitorous purposes, they procured, fitted out, and armed a vessel to cruise in the service of the rebellion upon the high seas, and commit hostilities against the citizens, property and vessels of the United States; 4. That they sailed in their vessel from the port of San Francisco upon such cruise in the service of the rebellion.

The existence of the rebellion is a matter of public notoriety, and like matters of general and public concern to the whole country, may be taken notice of by judges and juries without that particular proof which is required of the other matters charged. The public notoriety, the proclamations of the president, and the acts of congress are sufficient proof of the allegation of the indictment in this respect. The same notoriety and public documents are also sufficient proof that the rebellion is organized and carried on under a pretended government, called the Confederate States of America.

As to the treasonable purposes of the defendants there is no conflict in the evidence. . . . I do not propose to say anything to you upon the much disputed questions whether or not the vessel ever did, in fact, sail from the port of San Francisco, or whether, if she did sail, she started on the hostile expedition. In the judgment of the court they are immaterial, if you find the facts to be what I have said the evidence tends to establish.

When Harpending received the letter of marque, with the intention of using it, . . . he became leagued with the insurgents — the conspiracy between him and the chiefs of the rebellion was complete. . . . The subsequent purchasing of the vessel, and the guns, and the ammunition, and the employment of the men to manage the vessel, if these acts were done in furtherance of the common design, were overt acts of treason. Together, these acts complete the essential charge of the indictment. In doing them, the defendants were performing a part in aid of the great rebellion. They were giving it aid and comfort.

It is not essential to constitute the giving of aid and comfort that the enterprise commenced should be successful and actually render assistance. . . .

Wherever overt acts have been committed which, in their natural consequence, if successful, would encourage and advance the interests of the rebellion, in judgment of law aid and comfort are given. Whether aid and comfort are given — the overt acts of treason being established — is not left to the balancing of probabilities — it is a conclusion of law.

If the defendants obtained a letter of marque from the president of the so-called Confederate States, the fact does not exempt them from prosecution in the tribunals of the country for the acts charged in the indictment. The existence of civil war, and the application of the rules of war to particular cases, under special circumstances, do not imply the renunciation or waiver by the federal government of any of its municipal rights as sovereign toward the citizens of the seceded states.

As [a] matter of policy and humanity, the government of the United States has treated the citizens of the so-called Confederate States, taken in open hostilities, as prisoners of war, and has thus exempted them from trial for violation of its municipal laws. But the courts have no such dispensing power; they can only enforce the laws as they find them upon the statute-book. They cannot treat any new government as having authority to issue commissions or letters of marque which will afford protection to its citizens until the legislative and executive departments have recognized its existence. The judiciary follows the political department of the government in these particulars. By that department the rules of war have been applied only in special cases; and notwithstanding the application, congress has legislated in numerous instances for the punishment of all parties engaged in or rendering assistance in any way to the existing rebellion. The law under which the defendants are indicted was passed after captives in war had been treated and exchanged as prisoners of war, in numerous instances.

But even if full belligerent rights had been conceded to the Confederate States, such rights could not be invoked for the protection of persons entering within the limits of states which have never seceded, and secretly getting up hostile expeditions against our government and its authority and laws. The local and temporary allegiance, which every one — citizen or alien — owes to the government under which he at the time lives, is sufficient to subject him to the penalties of treason.

These, gentlemen, constitute all the instructions I have to give. My associate, Judge HOFFMAN, will submit some further observations to you. . . .

HOFFMAN, District Judge (charging jury). At the request of the presiding judge, I have prepared some observations which . . . [are] to be taken as the expression of my individual opinion. The charge of the presiding judge is to be exclusively received as the opinion and instructions of the court.

\*          \*          \*

In the constitution of the United States it is declared that the crime of treason shall consist only in levying war against the United States, and in adhering to their enemies, giving them aid and comfort. The last branch of this definition has always been admitted to apply only to cases of adhering, and giving aid and comfort to, foreign public enemies. It was therefore held that an indictment charging the defendant with having given aid and comfort to domestic rebels was bad, and that the acts should be charged as "a levying of war against the United

States." It appears, however, to have been considered by congress that some acts might be committed which would constitute an "engaging in the present rebellion, and giving it aid and comfort," which would not amount to a levying of war, or to the crime of treason, within the meaning of the constitution. Under this idea, the act of 1862, in its first section, re-enacts the former statute against treason eo nomine, but modifies, in some respects, the penalty, while the second section denounces, as if it were a different offense, the "engaging in, and giving aid and comfort to, the existing rebellion." We have not been able to concur in the view which congress seems to have taken of the offenses created by these sections.

*     *     *

... As the framers of the constitution restricted the crime of treason to two classes of cases only, the one "adhering to the public enemy, giving him aid and comfort;" the other "levying war against the United States," what motive can be suggested for attaching any less guilt to him who aids and comforts a rebellion, than to him who aids and comforts a public enemy? A moment's consideration of the magnitude and power of the present rebellion, its aim not merely to change the form of government, or to resist the laws, but to dismember the country, and to destroy forever our integrity as a nation, and to inflict a fatal blow on the cause of human progress and civilization, will convince us that the dangers to be apprehended are as great, and the guilt of the actors as deep, when aid and comfort are given to a domestic rebellion, as when given to a public enemy....

*     *     *

It is unnecessary to repeat what has already been said in regard to the letter of marque. The question is not whether the commission, or letter of marque, was in all respects regular or formally executed. Emanating from the rebel government, it could, of course, confer no authority to levy war on the United States, or to destroy or rob the vessels of her citizens....

*     *     *

I have endeavored, gentlemen, to consider the questions involved in this cause in the calm spirit of judicial inquiry, and unaffected by the excitements of the hour or the fierce passions necessarily aroused by the stupendous contest in which the country is engaged. For the accused, personally, I feel a deep regret, and especially for one of them, who appears to have been animated rather by a zeal for the cause which he has unhappily espoused than by the more unworthy motive of enriching himself by the plunder of his fellow-citizens. It is deeply to be regretted that the courage and willingness to sacrifice himself for the benefit of his associates, slight

glimpses of which have been revealed by the evidence, have been wasted on an enterprise which is as indefensible in morals, or even under any political theory ever proclaimed by the advocates of secession, as it is criminal in law.

# 135 "They were terribly mutilated" (1864)

The North-South hostilities and bloodshed of the Civil War in no way lessened the other tensions between the west-bound white settlers and the native occupants of the western lands. The southern Cheyenne and Arapaho Indians had considered central Kansas and the Rocky Mountains their domain since the early part of the nineteenth century. The increasing number of settlers who came to the territory as part of the Pike's Peak gold rush began encroaching on the Indian lands. Government officials persuaded the Indians, who were located in the very center of the white emigration route, to sell their land to the United States and to move to the arid southeastern sections of the Colorado Territory. Claiming that they were cheated by the transaction, some of the tribes rebelled and attacked the neighboring settlers. The Cheyenne, nevertheless, adhered to a peace policy and were promised federal protection against the revenging Colorado militia.

A contingent of the Colorado militia under Colonel J. M. Chivington, a Methodist preacher in private life, attacked the unsuspecting Cheyenne camp, in spite of the assurance of protection by federal troops. The soldiers ignored the Indians' white flag of surrender, and as many as 450 men, women, and children were slain and mutilated. The soldiers scalped the dead and dying, and the genitals of the women were cut out and stuck on poles or worn on the soldiers' hats. Chivington later remarked that the children had to be killed because "nits make lice." A local newspaper described the attack as "a brilliant feat of arms."

The following document contains the testimony of John S. Smith, an Indian agent.

☆ 135 Massacre of the Cheyenne Indians

Testimony of John S. Smith before the Joint Committee on the Conduct of the War: Massacre of the Cheyenne Indians, 38th Congress, 2d Session, III (1865), reprinted in Richard Hofstadter and Michael Wallace, eds., *American Violence: A Documentary History* (New York: Knopf, 1970), 276-77.

*     *     *

QUESTION. Were the women and children slaughtered indiscriminately, or only so far as they were with the warriors?

ANSWER. Indiscriminately.

QUESTION. Were there any acts of barbarity perpetrated there that came under your own observation?

ANSWER. Yes, sir; I saw the bodies of those lying there cut all to pieces, worse multilated than any I ever saw before; the women cut all to pieces.

By Mr. Buckalew:

QUESTION. How cut?

ANSWER. With knives; scalped; their brains knocked out; children two or three months old; all ages lying there, from sucking infants up to warriors.... They were terribly mutilated, lying there in the water and sand; most of them in the bed of the creek, dead and dying, making many struggles. They were so badly mutilated and covered with sand and water that it was very hard for me to tell one from another....

By Mr. Gooch:

QUESTION. Did you see it done?

ANSWER. Yes, sir; I saw them fall.

QUESTION. Fall when they were killed?

ANSWER. Yes, sir.

QUESTION. Did you see them when they were mutilated?

ANSWER. Yes, sir.

QUESTION. By whom were they mutilated?

ANSWER. By the United States troops.

QUESTION. Do you know whether or not it was done by the direction or consent of any of the officers?

ANSWER. I do not; I hardly think it was....

QUESTION. Were there any other barbarities or atrocities committed there other than those you have mentioned, that you saw?

ANSWER. Yes, sir; I had a half-breed son there, who gave himself up. He started at the time the Indians fled; being a half-breed he had but little hope of being spared, and seeing them fire at me, he ran away with the Indians for the distance of about a mile. During the fight up there he walked back to my camp and went into the lodge. It was surrounded by soldiers at the time. He came in quietly and sat down; he remained there that day, that night, and the next day in the afternoon; about four o'clock in the evening, as I was sitting inside the camp, a soldier came up outside of the lodge and called me by name. I got up and went out; he took me by the arm and walked towards Colonel Chivington's camp, which was about sixty yards from my camp. Said he, "I am sorry to tell you, but they are going to kill your son Jack." I knew the feeling towards the whole camp of Indians, and that there was no use to make any resistance. I said, "I can't help it." I then walked on towards where Colonel Chivington was standing by his camp-fire; when I had got within a few feet of him I heard a gun fired, and saw a crowd run to my lodge, and they told me that Jack was dead.

QUESTION. What action did Colonel Chivington take in regard to that matter?

ANSWER. Major Anthony, who was present, told Colonel Chivington that he had heard some remarks made, indicating that they were desirous of killing Jack; and that he (Colonel Chivington) had it in his power to save him, and that by saving him he might make him a very useful man, as he was well acquainted with all the Cheyenne and Arapahoe country, and he could be used as a guide or interpreter. Colonel Chivington replied to Major Anthony, as the Major himself told me, that he had no orders to receive and no advice to give.

# 136 "[I] have never hated nor wronged any one" (1864-1865)

On April 11, 1865, in his last public address, delivered to an audience gathered in front of the White House, President Lincoln discussed his hopes for the early return of the Southern states to the Union. Two days later, while attending a comedy at Ford's Theater, the president was shot by actor John Wilkes Booth. Secretary of State William H. Seward was stabbed in his bed the same night by an accomplice of Booth. Lincoln died on April 15 of the wound inflicted by the assassin.

Assassination of the head of state is considered by most to be the paradigm political crime and would, of course, be high treason under common law. Although Booth viewed Lincoln as a tyrant set on destroying the country, the excerpts from Booth's letter and diary supply glimpses into the more personal passions and motives of the man who killed Lincoln. After his hasty escape from Washington, Booth was killed in Virginia in an encounter with his pursuers.

☆ 136 Writings of John Wilkes Booth

☆ 136a Letter to the *Philadelphia Enquirer* (1864; published April 19, 1865)

Reprinted in Stanley Kimmel, *The Mad Booths of Maryland* (New York: Dover, 1969), 396.

1864

MY DEAR SIR:

You may use this as you think best. But as *some* may wish to know *when*, who and *why* as I know not *how* to direct, I give it (in the words of your master) — "To whom it may concern."

Right or wrong, God judge me, not man. For be my motives good or bad, of one thing I am sure, the lasting condemnation of the North.... All hope for peace is dead. My prayers have proved as idle as my hopes. God's will be done. I go to see and share the bitter end.

*       *       *

The country was formed for the white, not for the black man. And looking upon African slavery from the same standpoint held by the noble framers of our Constitution, I, for one, have ever considered it one of the greatest blessings (both for themselves and us) that God ever bestowed upon a favored nation. Witness heretofore our wealth and power: witness their elevation and enlightenment above their race elsewhere. I have lived among it most of my life, and I have seen *less* harsh treatment from master to man than I have beheld in the North from father to son. Yet, heaven knows, *no one* would be willing to do *more* for the Negro race than I, could I but see the way to *still better their condition.*

But Lincoln's policy is only preparing a way for their total annihilation. The south *are not, nor have they* been fighting for the continuation of slavery. The first battle of Bull Run did away with that idea. Their causes for war have been *as noble and greater far than those that urged our fathers on. Even* should we allow they were wrong at the beginning of this contest, *cruelty and injustice* have made the wrong become the right, and they stand now (before the wonder and admiration of the world) as a noble band of patriotic heroes. Hereafter, reading of their deeds, Thermopylæ will be forgotten.

When I aided in the capture and execution of John Brown (who was a murderer on our Western border and who was fairly tried and convicted before an impartial judge and jury, of treason, and who, by the way, has since been made a god) I was proud of my little share in the transaction, for I deemed it my duty that it was helping our common country to perform an act of justice. But what was a crime in poor John Brown is considered (by themselves) as the greatest and only virtue of the whole Republican party. Strange transmigration. *Vice so* becomes a *virtue*, simply because more indulged in. I thought then as *now* that the Abolitionists were the *only traitors* in the land and that the entire party deserved the fate of poor John Brown, not because they wish to abolish slavery, but on account of the means they have ever used to effect that abolition. If Brown were living I doubt whether he *himself* would set slavery against the Union. Most or many in the North do, and openly curse the Union, if the South are to return and retain a *single right* guaranteed to them by every tie which we once revered as sacred.

The South can make no choice. It is either extermination or slavery for *themselves* (worse than death) to draw from. I know my choice.

I have also studied hard to know upon what grounds the right of a state to secede has been de-

nied, when our very name United States, and the Declaration of Independence *both* provide for secession.

But there is no time for words. I write in haste. I know how foolish I shall be deemed for taking such a step as this. . . .

*       *       *

. . . My love (as things stand to-day) is for the South alone. Nor do I deem it a dishonor in attempting to make for her a prisoner of this man to whom she owes so much misery.

If success attends me, I go penniless to her side. They say she has found that "last ditch" which the North has so long derided and has been endeavoring to force her in, forgetting they are our brothers, and that it's impolitic to force on an enemy to madness. Should I reach her in safety and find it true, I will proudly beg permission to triumph or die in that same "ditch" by her side.

A Confederate doing duty on his own responsibility.

J. WILKES BOOTH

☆ 136b Booth's Diary

Reprinted in L. A. Weichmann, *A True History of the Assassination of Abraham Lincoln and of the Conspiracy of 1865* (New York: Knopf, 1975), 209-38.

April 13, 14, Friday, The Ides [1865]

Until to-day nothing was ever thought of sacrificing to our country's wrongs. For six months we had worked to capture. But, our cause being almost lost, something decisive and great must be done. But its failure was owing to others who did not strike for their country with a heart. I struck boldly, and not as the papers say. I walked with a firm step through a thousand of his friends, was stopped, but pushed on. A colonel was at his side. I shouted "Sic semper" before I fired. In jumping broke my leg. I passed all his pickets, rode sixty miles that night, with the bone of my leg tearing the flesh at every jump.

I can never repent it, though we hated to kill. Our country owed all our [her] troubles to him, and God simply made me the instrument of his punishment.

The country is not what it was. This forced union is not what I have loved. I care not what becomes of me. I have no desire to outlive my country. This night before the deed, I wrote a long article and left it for one of the editors of the *National Intelligencer*, in which I fully set forth our reasons for our proceedings. He or the gov'r — [South].

Friday 21

*       *       *

I am here in despair. And why? For doing what Brutus was honored for — what made Tell a hero. And yet I, for striking down a greater tyrant than they ever knew, am looked [up]on as a common cut-throat. My action [act] was purer than either of theirs. One hoped to be great [himself], the other had not only his country's but his own wrongs to avenge. I hoped for no gain[s]. I knew no private wrong. I struck for my country and that alone. A country groaned beneath this tyranny, and prayed for this end, and yet now behold the cold hand they extend [to] me.

I do not repent the blow I struck, I may before [my] God, but not to man. I think I have done well, though I am abandoned with the curse of Cain upon me, when if the world knew my heart, that one blow would have made me great, thought [*sic*] I did desire no greatness.

To-night I try to escape these blood-hounds once more. Who, who read his fate? God's will be done.

"I have too great a soul to die like a criminal. O, may He spare me that, and let me die bravely!"

I bless the entire world. [I] have never hated nor wronged any one. This last was not a wrong, unless God deems it so. And it's with [for] Him to damn or bless me. And for this brave boy with me, who often prays (yes, before and since) with a true and sincere heart,—was it crime in him, if so, why can he pray the same? I do not wish to shed a drop of blood, but "I must fight the course." "T'is all that's left to me."

. . . God cannot pardon me if I have done wrong. Yet I cannot see my [any] wrong, except in serving a degenerate people. The little, the very little, I left behind to clear [bear] my name, the Government will not allow to be printed. So ends all. For my country I have given up all that makes life sweet and holy, brought misery upon my family, and am sure there is no pardon in [the] Heaven for me since man condemns me so. I have only heard of what has been done, (except what I did myself), and it fills me with horror. God!, try and forgive me, and bless my mother. To-night I will once more try the river with [the] intention to cross, though I have a greater desire and almost a mind to return to Washington, and in a measure clear my name, which I feel I can do.

## 137 "The civil tribunals . . . can not rightfully interfere with the military" (1865)

Under advice from his attorney general, President Andrew Johnson, on May 1, 1865, ordered the trial by a military commission of the eight persons accused of conspiracy in the Lincoln assassination. Since the civil courts in Washington, D.C., were open at the time, public arguments were raised against a military trial for the accused. Attorney General James Speed's opinion recited the legal position supporting a military trial, devoid of the traditional criminal procedure

safeguards, for the civilians accused of the president's murder. On June 30, 1865, the military commission found all eight guilty: Mary E. Surratt and three other coconspirators were sentenced to hang, Samuel A. Mudd and two accomplices were sentenced to life imprisonment, and Edward Spangler was given six years' imprisonment.

## ☆ 137 Opinion on the Constitutional Power of the Military by Attorney General James Speed

Reprinted in B. Pitman, ed., *The Assassination of President Lincoln and the Trial of the Conspirators* (Cincinnati: Moore, Wilstach & Baldwin, 1865), 403-9.

SIR:

You ask me whether the persons charged with the offense of having assassinated the President can be tried before a military tribunal, or must they be tried before a civil court.

The President was assassinated at a theater in the city of Washington. At the time of the assassination a civil war was flagrant, the city of Washington was defended by fortifications regularly and constantly manned, the principal police of the city was by Federal soldiers, the public offices and property in the city were all guarded by soldiers, and the President's House and person were, or should have been, under the guard of soldiers. Martial law had been declared in the District of Columbia, but the civil courts were open and held their regular sessions, and transacted business as in times of peace.

Such being the facts, the question is one of great importance—important, because it involves the constitutional guarantees thrown about the rights of the citizen, and because the security of the army and the government in time of war is involved; important, as it involves a seeming conflict between the laws of peace and of war.

Having given the question propounded the patient and earnest consideration its magnitude and importance require, I will proceed to give the reasons why I am of the opinion that the conspirators not only may but ought to be tried by a military tribunal.

A civil court of the United States is created by a law of congress, under and according to the Constitution. To the Constitution and the law we must look to ascertain how the court is constituted, the limits of its jurisdiction, and what its mode of procedure.

A military tribunal exists under and according to the Constitution in time of war. Congress may prescribe how all such tribunals are to be constituted, what shall be their jurisdiction and mode of procedure. Should Congress fail to create such tribunals, then, under the Constitution, they must be constituted according to the laws and usages of civilized warfare. They may take cognizance of such offenses as the laws of war permit; they must proceed according to the customary usages of such tribunals in time of war, and inflict such punishments as are sanctioned by the practice of civilized nations in time of war. In time of peace, neither Congress nor the military can create any military tribunals, except such as are made in pursuance of that clause of the Constitution which gives to Congress the power "to make rules for the government of the land and naval forces." I do not think that Congress can, in time of war or peace, under this clause of the Constitution, create military tribunals for the adjudication of offenses committed by persons not engaged in, or belonging to, such forces. This is a proposition too plain for argument. But it does not follow that because such military tribunals can not be created by Congress under this clause, that they can not be created at all. . . . That the law of nations constitutes a part of the laws of the land, must be admitted. . . . But very soon after the organization of the Federal Government, Mr. Randolph, then Attorney General, said: "The law of nations, although not specifically adopted by the Constitution, is essentially a part of the law of the land. Its obligation commences and runs with the existence of a nation, subject to modification on some points of indifference." . . .

. . . The framers of the Constitution knew that a nation could not maintain an honorable place among the nations of the world that does not regard the great and essential principles of the law of nations as a part of the law of the land. Hence Congress may define those laws, but can not abrogate them, or as Mr. Randolph says, may "modify on some points of indifference."

*        *        *

But the laws of war constitute much the greater part of the law of nations. Like the other laws of nations, they exist and are of binding force upon the departments and citizens of the Government, though not defined by any law of Congress. . . .

Congress can declare war. When war is declared, it must be, under the Constitution, carried on according to the known laws and usages of war among civilized nations. . . . The Constitution does not permit this Government to prosecute a war as an uncivilized and barbarous people.

*        *        *

All wars against a domestic enemy or to repel invasions, are prosecuted to preserve the Government. If the invading force can be overcome by the ordinary civil police of a country, it should be done without bringing upon the country the terrible scourge of war; if a commotion or insurrection can be put down by the ordinary process of law, the military should not be called out. A defensive foreign war is declared and carried on because the civil police is inadequate to repel it; a civil war is waged because the laws can not be peacefully enforced by the ordinary tribunals of the country through civil process and by civil officers. . . . Peace is the normal condition of a country, and war abnormal, neither being without law, but each having laws appropriate to the condition of society. The maxim *enter arma silent leges* is never wholly true. The object of war is to bring society out of its abnormal condition; and the laws of war aim to have that done with the least possible injury to persons or property.

*        *        *

. . . Non-combatants are not to be disturbed or interfered with by the armies of either party except in extreme cases. Armies are called out and organized to meet and overcome the active, acting public enemies.

. . . [E]nemies with which an army has to deal are of two classes:

1. Open, active participants in hostilities, as soldiers who wear the uniform, move under the flag, and hold the appropriate commission from their government. Openly assuming to discharge the duties and meet the responsibilities and dangers of soldiers, they are entitled to all belligerent rights, and should receive all the courtesies due to soldiers. The true soldier is proud to acknowledge and respect those rights, and ever cheerfully extends those courtesies.

2. Secret, but active participants, as spies, brigands, bushwhackers, jayhawkers, war rebels and assassins. In all wars, and especially in civil wars, such secret, active enemies rise up to annoy and attack an army, and must be met and put down by the army. When lawless wretches become so impudent and powerful as not to be controlled and governed by the ordinary tribunals of a country, armies are called out, and the laws of war invoked. Wars never have been and never can be conducted upon the principle that an army is but a *posse comitatus* of a civil magistrate.

An army, like all other organized bodies, has a right, and it is its first duty, to protect its own existence and the existence of all its parts, by the means and in the mode usual among civilized nations when at war. Then the question arises, do the laws of war authorize a different mode of proceeding, and the use of different means against secret active enemies from those used against open active enemies?

As has been said, the open enemy or soldier in time of war may be met in battle and killed, wounded or taken prisoner, or so placed by the lawful strategy of war as that he is powerless. Unless the law of self-preservation absolutely demands it, the life of a wounded enemy or a prisoner must be spared. Unless pressed thereto by the extremest necessity, the laws of war condemn and punish with great severity harsh or cruel treatment to a wounded enemy or a prisoner.

Certain stipulations and agreements, tacit or express, betwixt the open belligerent parties, are permitted by the laws of war, and are held to be of very high and sacred character. Such is the tacit understanding, or it may be usage, of war, in regard to flags of truce. Flags of truce are resorted to as a means of saving human life, or alleviating human suffering. When not used with perfidy, the laws of war require that they should be respected. The Romans regarded ambassadors betwixt belligerents as persons to be treated with consideration and respect. Plutarch, in his *Life of Cæsar*, tells us that the barbarians in Gaul having sent some ambassadors to Cæsar, he detained them, charging fraudulent practices, and led his army to battle, obtaining a great victory.

When the Senate decreed festivals and sacrifices for the victory, Cato declared it to be his opinion that Cæsar ought to be given into the hands of the barbarians, that so the guilt which this breach of faith might otherwise bring upon the State might be expiated by transferring the curse on him who was the occasion of it.

Under the Constitution and laws of the United States, should a commander be guilty of such a flagrant breach of law as Cato charged upon Cæsar, he would not be delivered to the enemy, but would be punished after a military trial. The many honorable gentlemen who hold commissions in the army of the United States, and have been deputed to conduct war according to the laws of war, would keenly feel it as an insult to their profession of arms for any one to say that they could not or would not punish a fellow-soldier who was guilty of wanton cruelty to a prisoner, or perfidy toward the bearers of a flag of truce.

The laws of war permit capitulations of surrender and paroles. They are agreements betwixt belligerents, and should be scrupulously observed and performed. They are contracts wholly unknown to civil tribunals. Parties to such contracts must answer any breaches thereof to the customary military tribunals in time of war. If an officer of rank, possessing the pride that becomes a soldier and a gentleman, who should capitulate to surrender the forces and property under his command and control, be charged with a fraudulent breach of the terms of surrender, the laws of war do not permit that he should be punished without a trial, or, if innocent, that he shall have no means of wiping out the foul imputation. If a paroled prisoner is charged with a breach of his parole, he may be punished if guilty, but not without a trial. He should be tried by a military tribunal, constituted and proceeding as the laws and usages of war prescribe.

The law and usage of war contemplate that sol-diers have a high sense of personal honor. The true soldier is proud to feel and know that his enemy possesses personal honor, and will conform and be obedient to the laws of war. In a spirit of justice, and with a wise appreciation of such feelings, the laws of war protect the character and honor of an open enemy. When by the fortunes of war one open enemy is thrown into the hands and power of another, and is charged with dishonorable conduct and a breach of the laws of war, he must be tried according to the usages of war. Justice and fairness say that an open enemy to whom dishonorable conduct is imputed, has a right to demand a trial. If such a demand can be rightfully made, surely it can not be rightfully refused. It is to be hoped that the military authorities of this country will never refuse such a demand, because there is no act of Congress that authorizes it. In time of war the law and usage of war authorize it, and they are a part of the law of the land.

One belligerent may request the other to punish for breaches of the laws of war, and, regularly, such a request should be made before retaliatory measures are taken. Whether the laws of war have been infringed or not, is of necessity a question to be decided by the laws and usages of war, and is cognizable before a military tribunal. When prisoners of war conspire to escape, or are guilty of a breach of appropriate and necessary rules of prison discipline, they may be punished, but not without trial. The commander who should order every prisoner charged with improper conduct to be shot or hung, would be guilty of a high offense against the laws of war, and should be punished therefor, after a regular military trial. If the culprit should be condemned and executed, the commander would be as free from guilt as if the man had been killed in battle.

It is manifest, from what has been said, that military tribunals exist under and according to the laws and usages of war, in the interest of justice and mercy. They are established to save human life, and to prevent cruelty as far as possible. The commander of an army in time of war has the same power to organize military tribunals and execute their judgments that he has to set his squadrons in the field and fight battles. His authority in each case is from the law and usage of war.

Having seen that there must be military tribunals to decide questions arising in time of war betwixt belligerents who are open and active enemies, let us next see whether the laws of war do not authorize such tribunals to determine the fate of those who are active, but secret, participants in the hostilities.

\*          \*          \*

... That the laws of war authorized commanders to create and establish military commissions, courts or tribunals, for the trial of offenders against the laws of war, whether they be active or secret partici-pants in the hostilities, can not be denied. That the judgments of such tribunals may have been some-times harsh, and sometimes even tyrannical, does not prove that they ought not to exist, nor does it prove that they are not constituted in the interest of justice and mercy. Considering the power that the laws of war give over secret participants in hostili-ties, such as banditti, guerrillas, spies, etc., the posi-tion of a commander would be miserable indeed if he could not call to his aid the judgments of such tribu-nals; he would become a mere butcher of men, with-out the power to ascertain justice, and there can be no mercy where there is no justice. . . . Impartial his-tory will record the fact that the Bureau of Military Justice, regularly organized during this war, has saved human life and prevented human suffering. The greatest suffering, patiently endured by sol-diers, and the hardest battles gallantly fought dur-ing this protracted struggle, are not more creditable to the American character than the establishment of this bureau. This people have such an educated and profound respect for law and justice — such a love of mercy — that they have, in the midst of this greatest of civil wars, systematized and brought into regular order, tribunals that before this war existed under the law of war, but without general rule. To con-demn the tribunals that have been established un-der this bureau, is to condemn and denounce the war itself, or justifying the war, to insist that it shall be prosecuted according to the harshest rules, and without the aid of the laws, usages and customary agencies for mitigating those rules. If such tribunals had not existed before, under the laws and usages of war, the American citizen might as proudly point to their establishments as to our inimitable and inesti-mable constitutions. It must be constantly borne in mind that such tribunals and such a bureau can not exist except in time of war, and can not then take cognizance of offenders or offenses where the civil courts are open, except offenders and offenses against the laws of war.

But it is insisted by some, and doubtless with honesty, and with a zeal commensurate with their honesty, that such military tribunals can have no constitutional existence. The argument against their constitutionality may be shortly, and I think fairly, stated thus:

Congress alone can establish military or civil ju-dicial tribunals. As Congress has not established military tribunals, except such as have been created under the articles of war, and which articles are made in pursuance of that clause in the Constitution which gives to Congress the power to make rules for the government of the army and navy, any other tri-bunal is and must be plainly unconstitutional, and all its acts void.

This objection thus stated, or stated in any other

way, begs the question. It assumes that Congress alone can establish military judicial tribunals. Is that assumption true?

*          *          *

. . . The Constitution was framed by great men — men of learning and large experience, and it is a wonderful monument of their wisdom. Well versed in the history of the world, they knew that the na-tion for which they were forming a government would, unless all history was false, have wars, for-eign and domestic. Hence the government framed by them is clothed with the power to make and carry on war. As has been shown, when war comes, the laws of war come with it. Infractions of the laws of nations are not denominated *crimes*, but *offenses*. Hence the expression in the Constitution that "Con-gress shall have power to define and punish *offenses* against the law of nations." . . .

There is, then, an apparent but no real conflict in the constitutional provisions. *Offenses* against the laws of war must be dealt with and punished under the Constitution, as the laws of war, they being part of the law of nations direct; *crimes* must be dealt with and punished as the Constitution, and laws made in pursuance thereof, may direct.

*          *          *

That portion of the Constitution which declares that "no person shall be deprived of his life, liberty or property without due process of law," has such direct reference to, and connection with, trials for *crime* or *criminal* prosecutions, that comments upon it would seem to be unnecessary. Trials for offenses against the laws of war are not embraced or in-tended to be embraced in those provisions. . . .

The fact that the civil courts are open does not affect the right of the military tribunal to hold as a prisoner and to try. The civil courts have no more right to prevent the military, in time of war, from trying an offender against the laws of war than they have a right to interfere with and prevent a battle. A battle may be lawfully fought in the very view and presence of a court; so a spy, a bandit or other of-fender against the law of war, may be tried, and tried lawfully, when and where the civil courts are open and transacting the usual business.

*          *          *

. . . The civil tribunals of the country can not rightfully interfere with the military in the perfor-mance of their high, arduous and perilous, but lawful duties. That Booth and his associates were secret ac-tive public enemies, no mind that contemplates the facts can doubt. The exclamation used by him when he escaped from the box onto the stage, after he had fired the fatal shot, *sic semper tyrannis*, and his dying message, "Say to my mother that I died for my country," show that he was not an assassin from private malice, but that he acted as a public foe.

Such a deed is expressly laid down by Vattel, in his work on the law of nations, as an offense against the laws of war, and a great crime. . . .

My conclusion, therefore, is, that if the persons who are charged with the assassination of the President committed the deed as public enemies, as I believe they did, and whether they did or not is a question to be decided by the tribunal before which they are tried, they not only can, but ought to be tried before a military tribunal. If the persons charged have offended against the laws of war, it would be as palpably wrong for the military to hand them over to the civil courts, as it would be wrong in a civil court to convict a man of murder who had, in time of war, killed another in battle.

I am, sir, most respectfully, your obedient servant,

JAMES SPEED, Attorney General

To the President

## 138 "The relation of husband and wife amongst persons of color" (1865)

The first Emancipation Proclamation, issued on September 22, 1862, allowed slaveholders the opportunity of giving up the war and thereby keeping their human property. The second and better-known Emancipation Proclamation was issued on January 1, 1863. The Thirteenth Amendment, abolishing slavery, was submitted to the states on January 31, 1865, and ratified on December 6 of that year. During the process of ratification, the former slave states were legislating to regulate the status and conduct of blacks under the new regime. The codes related to all aspects of black life from labor and wages to marriage and social intercourse.

Sections of three Black Codes are reproduced here. Although varying in harshness, the purpose of the codes was the same: maintenance of the pre-Civil War social and political order between blacks and whites. Northern reaction to these codes gave rise to the new civil rights acts and the Fourteenth Amendment, which would criminalize the adherence to these state laws.

☆ 138 Southern Black Codes

☆ 138a South Carolina Black Code

1865 S.C. Acts 291-304.

*Be it enacted by the Senate and House of Representatives, now met and sitting in General Assembly, and by the authority of the same, as follows:*

### HUSBAND AND WIFE

I. The relation of husband and wife amongst persons of color is established.

II. Those who now live as such, are declared to be husband and wife.

III. In case of one man having two or more reputed wives, or one woman two or more reputed husbands, the man shall, by the first of April next, select one of his reputed wives, or the woman one of her reputed husbands, and the ceremony of marriage, between this man or woman, and the person so selected, shall be performed.

IV. Every colored child, heretofore born, is declared to be the legitimate child of his mother, and also of his colored father, if he is acknowledged by such a father.

\*          \*          \*

VIII. One who is a pauper, or a charge to the public, shall not be competent to contract marriage. Marriage between a white person and a person of color, shall be illegal and void.

IX. The marriage of an apprentice shall not, without the consent of the master, be lawful.

\*          \*          \*

XVIII. Males of the age of twelve years, and females, of the age of ten years, shall sign the indenture of apprenticeship and be bound thereby.

\*          \*          \*

### CONTRACTS FOR SERVICE

XXXV. All persons of color who make contracts for service or labor, shall be known as servants, and those with whom they contract shall be known as masters.

\*          \*          \*

XLV. On farms or in out-door service, the hours of labor, except on Sunday, shall be from sun-rise to sun-set, with a reasonable interval for breakfast and dinner. . . .

\*          \*          \*

XLVII. The master may give to a servant a task at work about the business of the farm which shall be reasonable. If the servant complain of the task, the District Judge, or a Magistrate, shall have power to reduce or increase it. . . .

\*          \*          \*

XLVIII. Visitors or other persons shall not be invited, or allowed by the servant, to come or remain upon the premises of the master, without his express permission.

XLIX. Servants shall not be absent from the premises without the permission of the master.

### RIGHTS OF MASTER AS BETWEEN HIMSELF AND HIS SERVANT

L. . . . The servant shall obey all lawful orders of the master or his agent, and shall be honest, truthful, sober, civil, and diligent in his business. The master may moderately correct servants who have made contracts, and are under eighteen years of age....

\*          \*          \*

### MECHANICS, ARTISANS AND SHOP-KEEPERS

LXXII. No person of color shall pursue or practice the art, trade or business of an artisan, mechanic or shop-keeper, or any other trade, employment or business (besides that of husbandry, or that of a servant under a contract for services or labor) on his own account and for his own benefit, or in partnership with a white person, or as agent or servant of any person, until he shall have obtained a license therefor from the Judge of the District Court, which license shall be good for one year only. This license the Judge may grant upon petition of the applicant, and upon being satisfied of his skill and fitness, and of his good moral character, and upon payment, by the applicant, to the Clerk of the District Court of one hundred dollars, if a shop-keeper or pedlar, to be paid annually, and ten dollars if a mechanic artisan, or to engage in any other trade, also to be paid annually: *Provided, however,* That upon complaint being made and proved to the District Judge of an abuse of such license, he shall revoke the same, and: *Provided, also,* That no person of color shall practice any mechanical art or trade, unless he shows that he has served an apprenticeship in such trade or art, or is now practicing such trade or art.

\*          \*          \*

### VAGRANCY AND IDLENESS

XCV. These are public grievances, and must be punished as crimes.

XCVI. All persons who have not some fixed and known place of abode, and some lawful and reputable employment; those who have not some visible and known means of a fair, honest and reputable livelihood ... those who, (whether or not they own lands, or are lessees or mechanics,) do not provide a reasonable and proper maintenance for themselves and families....

\*          \*          \*

☆ 138b  Black Code of Louisiana

1865 La. Acts 3.

### 1. AN ACT TO PROVIDE FOR AND REGULATE LABOR CONTRACTS FOR AGRICULTURAL PURSUITS

Sec. 1. Be it enacted ... That all persons employed as laborers in agricultural pursuits shall be required, during the first ten days of the month of January of each year, to make contracts for labor for the then ensuing year, or for the year next ensuing the termination of their present contracts....

Sec. 2. Every laborer shall have full and perfect liberty to choose his employer, but, when once cho-

sen, he shall not be allowed to leave his place of employment until the fulfillment of his contract ... and if they do so leave, without cause or permission, they shall forfeit all wages earned to the time of abandonment....

\*          \*          \*

Sec. 8. Be it further enacted, &c., That in case of sickness of the laborer, wages for the time lost shall be deducted, and where the sickness is feigned for purposes of idleness, and also on refusal to work according to contract, double the amount of wages shall be deducted for the time lost; and also where rations have been furnished; and should the refusal to work continue beyond three days, the offender shall be reported to a Justice of the Peace, and shall be forced to labor on roads, levees, and other public works, without pay, until the offender consents to return to his labor.

Sec. 9. Be it further enacted, &c., That, when in health, the laborer shall work ten hours during the day in summer, and nine hours during the day in winter, unless otherwise stipulated in the labor contract; he shall obey all proper orders of his employer or his agent, ... and employers shall have the right to make a reasonable deduction from the laborer's wages for injuries done to animals or agricultural implements committed to his care, or for bad or negligent work. Bad work shall not be allowed. Failing to obey reasonable orders, neglect of duty, and leaving home without permission will be deemed disobedience.... For all absence from home without leave he will be fined at the rate of two dollars per day. Laborers will not be required to labor on the Sabbath unless by special contract. For all thefts of the laborer from the employer ... or willful destruction of property or injury, the laborer shall pay the employer double the amount of the value of the property stolen, destroyed, or injured.... No live stock shall be allowed to laborers without the permission of the employer. Laborers shall not receive visitors during work-hours. All difficulties arising between the employers and laborers, under this section, shall be settled by the former; if not satisfactory to the laborers, an appeal may be had to the nearest Justice of the Peace and two freeholders, citizens, one of said citizens to be selected by the employer and the other by the laborer....

\*          \*          \*

☆ 138c  Black Code of Mississippi

1865 Miss. Laws 82.

### 1. CIVIL RIGHTS OF FREEDMEN

\*          \*          \*

Sec. 3. ... All freedmen, free negroes, or mulattoes who do now and have herebefore lived and cohabited together as husband and wife shall be taken and held in law as legally married, and the issue shall be taken and held as legitimate for all purposes; that it shall not be lawful for any freedman, free negro, or mulatto to intermarry with any white person; nor for any white person to intermarry with any freedman, free negro, or mulatto; and any person who shall so intermarry, shall be deemed guilty of felony, and on conviction thereof shall be confined in the State penitentiary for life; and those shall be deemed freedmen, free negroes, and mulattoes who are of pure negro blood, and those descended from a negro to the third generation, inclusive, though one ancestor in each generation may have been a white person.

\*       \*       \*

Sec. 7. . . . Every civil officer shall, and every person may, arrest and carry back to his or her legal employer any freedman, free negro, or mulatto who shall have quit the service of his or her employer before the expiration of his or her term of service without good cause, and said officer and person shall be entitled to receive for arresting and carrying back every deserting employe aforesaid the sum of five dollars, and ten cents per mile from the place of arrest to the place of delivery. . . .

\*       \*       \*

Sec. 9. . . . If any person shall persuade or attempt to persuade, entice, or cause any freedman, free negro, or mulatto to desert from the legal employment of any person before the expiration of his or her term of service, or shall knowingly employ any such deserting freedman, free negro, or mulatto, or shall knowingly give or sell to any such deserting freedman, free negro, or mulatto, any food, raiment, or other thing, he or she shall be guilty of a misdemeanor, and, upon conviction, shall be fined not less than twenty-five dollars and not more than two hundred dollars and the costs; and if said fine and costs shall not be immediately paid, the court shall sentence said convict to not exceeding two months' imprisonment in the county jail, and he or she shall moreover be liable to the party injured in damages: *Provided*, if any person shall, or shall attempt to, persuade, entice, or cause any freedman, free negro, or mulatto to desert from any legal employment of any person, with the view to employ said freedman, free negro, or mulatto without the limits of this State, such person, on conviction, shall be fined not less than fifty dollars, and not more than five hundred dollars and costs; and if said fine and costs shall not be immediately paid, the court shall sentence said convict to not exceeding six months imprisonment in the county jail.

\*       \*       \*

## 2. APPRENTICE LAW

Sec. 1. . . . It shall be the duty of all sheriffs, justices of the peace, and other civil officers . . . to report to the probate courts of their respective counties semi-annually, at the January and July terms of said courts, all freedmen, free negroes, and mulattoes, under the age of eighteen, in their respective counties, beats or districts, who are orphans, or whose parent or parents have not the means or who refuse to provide for and support said minors; and thereupon it shall be the duty of said probate court to order the clerk of said court to apprentice said minors to some competent and suitable person, on such terms as the court may direct, having a particular care to the interest of said minor: *Provided*, that the former owner of said minors shall have the preference when, in the opinion of the court, he or she shall be a suitable person for that purpose.

\*       \*       \*

Sec. 3. . . . In the management and control of said apprentice, said master or mistress shall have the power to inflict such moderate corporate chastisement as a father or guardian is allowed to inflict on his or her child or ward at common law: *Provided*, that in no case shall cruel or inhuman punishment be inflicted.

## 3. VAGRANT LAW

\*       \*       \*

Sec. 2. . . . All freedmen, free negroes and mulattoes in this State, over the age of eighteen years, found on the second Monday in January, 1866, or thereafter, with no lawful employment or business, or found unlawfully assembling themselves together, either in the day or night time, and all white persons so assembling themselves with freedmen, free negroes or mulattoes, or usually associating with freedmen, free negroes or mulattoes, on terms of equality, or living in adultery or fornication with a freed woman, free negro or mulatto, shall be deemed vagrants, and on conviction thereof shall be fined in a sum not exceeding, in the case of a freedman, free negro or mulatto, fifty dollars, and a white man two hundred dollars, and imprisoned at the discretion of the court, the free negro not exceeding ten days, and the white man not exceeding six months. . . .

\*       \*       \*

## 4. PENAL LAWS

Sec. 1. *Be it enacted* . . . That no freedman, free negro or mulatto, not in the military service of the United States government, and not licensed so to do by the board of police of his or her county, shall keep or carry fire-arms of any kind, or any ammunition, dirk or bowie knife, and on conviction thereof in the county court shall be punished by fine, not exceeding ten dollars, and pay the costs of such proceedings, and all such arms or ammunition shall be forfeited to the informer. . . .

Sec. 2. . . . Any freedman, free negro, or mulatto committing riots, routs, affrays, trespasses, malicious mischief, cruel treatment to animals, seditious speeches, insulting gestures, language, or acts, or assaults on any person, disturbance of the peace, exercising the function of a minister of the Gospel without a license from some regularly organized church, vending spirituous or intoxicating liquors, or committing any other misdemeanor, the punishment of which is not specifically provided for by law, shall, upon conviction thereof in the county court, be fined not less than ten dollars, and not more than one hundred dollars, and may be imprisoned at the discretion of the court, not exceeding thirty days.

Sec. 3. . . . If any white person shall sell, lend, or give to any freedman, free negro, or mulatto any fire-arms, dirk or bowie knife, or ammunition, or any spirituous or intoxicating liquors, such person or persons so offending, upon conviction thereof in the county court of his or her county, shall be fined not exceeding fifty dollars, and may be imprisoned, at the discretion of the court, not exceeding thirty days.

*          *          *

Sec. 5. . . . If any freedman, free negro, or mulatto, convicted of any of the misdemeanors provided against in this act, shall fail or refuse for the space of five days, after conviction, to pay the fine and costs imposed, such person shall be hired out by the sheriff or other officer, at public outcry, to any white person who will pay said fine and all costs, and take said convict for the shortest time.

## 139 "the late wicked Rebellion" (1866)

With Lee's surrender to Grant on April 9, 1865, the Civil War hostilities concluded. In August 1866 the new president, Andrew Johnson, declared that the emergency was over. In the same year, the United States Supreme Court asserted its authority by imposing limitations on the power of the executive to resort to martial law and to suspend the writ of habeas corpus safeguards.

Under the authority of Lincoln's proclamations, military authorities arrested Lambden P. Milligan, a civilian, and others in Indiana, a Union state, in October of 1864. A military commission tried Milligan (without the protections of Article III or the Bill of Rights), found him guilty of treason, and sentenced him to hang. After this conviction, a federal grand jury convened to investigate the same charges, but they returned no indictment. Milligan's challenge to the jurisdiction of the military tribunal to try a civil-

ian found its way to the Supreme Court after President Andrew Johnson restored the writ of habeas corpus.

In *Ex Parte Milligan* the court held that the suspension of the writ of habeas corpus permitted the military to arrest and hold persons without charge. The suspension of the writ, nevertheless, did not empower the military commissions to try and to sentence persons so held. The judicial branch alone had jurisdiction to try and to sentence civilians accused of crimes. Only when civil authority had been disrupted and martial law properly declared could military commissions, out of necessity, try and sentence accused persons. Although some justices suggested Congress could suspend civil authority and declare martial law in effect in peaceful zones, they held that the executive could not do so. Only when events precluded the operation of civilian courts could the military authorities unilaterally declare martial law and try civilians. The court concluded that Milligan's trial by military commission was constitutionally invalid.

The case delimits the executive's unilateral supplanting of local civilian authority in the absence of actual hostilities or perhaps a congressional determination of necessity. By so doing, the case acts as a restraint on the use of military authority to combat political crime.

## ☆ 139 *Ex Parte Milligan*

71 U.S. (4 Wall.) 2 (1866).

December 17, 1866, Mr. Justice DAVIS delivered the opinion of the court: . . .

During the late wicked Rebellion, the temper of the times did not allow that calmness in deliberation and discussion so necessary to a correct conclusion of a purely judicial question. Then, considerations of safety were mingled with the exercise of power; and feelings and interests prevailed which are happily terminated. Now that the public safety is assured, this question, as well as all others, can be discussed and decided without passion or the admixture of any element not required to form a legal judgment. We approach the investigation of this case, fully sensible of the magnitude of the inquiry and the necessity of full and cautious deliberation.

*          *          *

The controlling question in the case is this: Upon the facts stated in Milligan's petition, and the exhibits filed, had the Military Commission mentioned in it jurisdiction, legally, to try and sentence him? Milligan, not a resident of one of the rebellious States, or a prisoner of war, but a citizen of Indiana for twenty years past, and never in the military or naval service, is, while at his home, arrested by the military power of the United States, imprisoned and, on certain criminal charges preferred against him, tried, convicted and sentenced to be hanged by a military commission, organized under the direction of the military commander of the military district of Indiana. Had this tribunal the legal power and authority to try and punish this man?

No graver question was ever considered by this court, nor one which more nearly concerns the rights of the whole people; for it is the birthright of every American citizen when charged with crime, to be tried and punished according to law. The power of punishment is alone through the means which the laws have provided for that purpose, and if they are ineffectual, there is an immunity from punishment, no matter how great an offender the individual may be, or how much his crimes may have shocked the sense of justice of the country, or endangered its safety. By the protection of the law human rights are secured; withdraw that protection, and they are at the mercy of wicked rulers, or the clamor of an excited people. If there was law to justify this military trial, it is not our province to interfere; if there was not, it is our duty to declare the nullity of the whole proceedings. The decision of this question does not depend on argument or judicial precedents, numerous and highly illustrative as they are. . . .

The provisions of [the Constitution] on the administration of criminal justice are too plain and direct to leave room for misconstruction or doubt of their true meaning. Those applicable to this case are found in that clause of the original Constitution which says, "That the trial of all crimes, except in case of impeachment, shall be by jury;" and in the fourth, fifth and sixth articles of the amendments. . . .

Have any of the rights guarantied by the Constitution been violated in the case of Milligan? and if so, what are they?

Every trial involves the exercise of judicial power; and from what source did the Military Commission that tried him derive their authority? Certainly no part of the judicial power of the country was conferred on them; because the Constitution expressly vests it "in one Supreme Court and such inferior courts as the Congress may from time to time ordain and establish," and it is not pretended that the commission was a court ordained and established by Congress. They cannot justify on the mandate of the President; because he is controlled by law, and has his appropriate sphere of duty, which is to execute, not to make, the laws; and there is "no unwritten criminal code to which resort can be had as a source of jurisdiction."

But it is said that the jurisdiction is complete under the "laws and usages of war."

It can serve no useful purpose to inquire what those laws and usages are, whence they orginated, where found, and on whom they operate; they can never be applied to citizens in States which have upheld the authority of the government, and where the courts are open and their process unobstructed. This court has judicial knowledge that in Indiana the federal authority was always unopposed, and its courts always open to hear criminal accusations and redress grievances; and no usage of war could sanction a military trial there for any offense whatever of a citizen in civil life, in nowise connected with the military service. Congress could grant no such power; and to the honor of our National Legislature be it said, it has never been provoked by the state of the country even to attempt its exercise. One of the plainest constitutional provisions was, therefore, infringed when Milligan was tried by a court not ordained and established by Congress, and not composed of judges appointed during good behavior.

It is claimed that martial law covers with its broad mantle the proceedings of this Military Commission. The proposition is this: that in a time of war the commander of an armed force (if in his opinion the exigencies of the country demand it, and of which he is to judge), has the power, within the lines of his military district, to suspend all civil rights and their remedies, and subject citizens as well as soldiers to the rule of his will; and in the exercise of his lawful authority cannot be restrained, except by his superior officer or the President of the United States.

\*         \*         \*

The statement of this proposition shows its importance; for, if true, republican government is a failure, and there is an end of liberty regulated by law. Martial law, established on such a basis, destroys every guaranty of the Constitution, and effectually renders the "military independent of and superior to the civil power." . . . Civil liberty and this kind of martial law cannot endure together; the antagonism is irreconcilable and, in the conflict, one or the other must perish.

It is essential to the safety of every government that, in a great crisis, like the one we have just passed through, there should be a power somewhere of suspending the writ of *habeas corpus*. In every war, there are men of previously good character, wicked enough to counsel their fellow citizens to resist the measures deemed necessary by a good government to sustain its just authority and overthrow its enemies; and their influence may lead to dangerous combinations. In the emergency of the times, an immediate public investigation according to law may not be possible; and yet, the peril to the country may be too imminent to suffer such persons to go at large. Unquestionably, there is then an exigency which demands that the government, if it should see fit, in the exercise of a proper discretion, to make arrests, should not be required to produce tne person arrested in answer to a writ of *habeas corpus.* The Constitution goes no further. It does not say after a writ of *habeas corpus* is denied a citizen, that he shall be tried otherwise than by the course of common law. If it had intended this result, it was easy by the use of direct words to have accomplished it.

It is difficult to see how the safety of the country required martial law in Indiana. If any of her citizens were plotting treason, the power of arrest could secure them, until the government was prepared for their trial, when the courts were open and ready to try them. . . .

It follows, from what has been said on this subject, that there are occasions when martial rule can be properly applied. If, in foreign invasion or civil war, the courts are actually closed, and it is impossible to administer criminal justice according to law, then, on the theater of active military operations, where war really prevails, there is a necessity to furnish a substitute for the civil authority, thus overthrown, to preserve the safety of the army and society; and as no power is left but the military, it is allowed to govern by martial rule until the laws can have their free course. As necessity creates the rule, so it limits its duration; for, if this government is continued after the courts are reinstated, it is a gross usurpation of power. Martial rule can never exist where the courts are open, and in the proper and unobstructed exercise of their jurisdiction. It is also confined to the locality of actual war. Because, during the late Rebellion it could have been enforced in Virginia, where the national authority was overturned and the courts driven out, it does not follow that it should obtain in Indiana, where that authority was never disputed, and justice was always administered. And so in the case of a foreign invasion, martial rule may become a necessity, in one State, when, in another, it would be "mere lawless violence."

\*          \*          \*

. . . If these averments were true (and their truth is conceded for the purposes of this case), the court was required to liberate him on taking certain oaths prescribed by the law, and entering into recognizance for his good behavior.

But it is insisted that Milligan was a prisoner of war and, therefore, excluded from the privileges of the statute. It is not easy to see how he can be treated as a prisoner of war, when he lived in Indiana for the past twenty years, was arrested there, and had not been, during the late troubles, a resident of any of the States in rebellion. If in Indiana he conspired with bad men to assist the enemy, he is punishable for it in the courts of Indiana; but, when tried for the offense, he cannot plead the rights of war; for he was not engaged in legal acts of hostility against the government, and only such persons, when captured, are prisoners of war. If he cannot enjoy the immunities attaching to the character of a prisoner of war, how can he be subject to their pains and penalties?

\*          \*          \*

## 140 "any office of honor, trust, or profit" (1867)

Federal and state loyalty oaths were not new, but after the war they became widespread. These all-encompassing oaths were a prerequisite for voting, for holding public office or employment, and for engaging in certain occupations. Those of uncertain political loyalties were to be relegated to second-class citizenship.

Cummings was a Roman Catholic priest convicted of treason and preaching without complying with Missouri's oath requirement. In *Cummings* the Supreme Court struck down the oath as unconstitutional, because it violated Article I, Section 9, which prohibits bills of attainder (legislative acts that inflict punishments without a judicial trial) and ex post facto laws (laws that impose punishment for acts not punishable at the time committed).

In *Garland* the court scrutinized a similar federal oath for the practice of law in federal courts. Protective of the rights of dissenters and private citizens, these decisions also produced adverse side effects. The apparent judicial leniency provided ammunition to the new members of the Radical Republican party in Congress. They argued that the moderate treatment of the postwar South, begun by Lincoln and continued by Johnson—who on June 6, 1865, released the bulk of the Confederate prisoners of war—enabled the South to escape the rebellion without punishment or retribution. Beginning in March 1867 the Congress passed a series of reconstruction acts, which placed portions of the South under martial law, restricted the power of the president, encouraged the reign of the "carpetbaggers," and brought about the impeachment of Andrew Johnson.

☆ 140 The Loyalty Oath Cases

☆ 140a *Cummings v. Missouri*

71 U.S. (4 Wall.) 356 (1867).

. . . The indictment was under the . . . 6th . . . section of the Constitution of Missouri, which [is] as follows:

Sec. 6. "The oath to be taken as aforesaid, shall be known as the oath of loyalty, and shall be in the following terms:

'I, A. B., do solemnly swear that I am well acquainted with the terms of the 3d section of the 2d article of the Constitution of the State of Missouri, adopted in the year 1865, and have carefully considered the same; that I have never, directly or indirectly, done any of the acts in said section specified; that I have always been truly and loyally on the side of the United States against all enemies thereof, foreign and domestic; that I will bear true faith and allegiance to the United States, and will support the Constitution and laws thereof as the supreme law of the land, any law or ordinance of any State to the contrary notwithstanding; that I will, to the best of my ability, protect and defend the Union of the United States, and not allow the same to be broken up and dissolved, or the government thereof to be distroyed or overthrown under any circumstances, if in my power to prevent it; that I will support the Constitution of the State of Missouri; that I make this oath without any mental reservation or evasion, and hold it to be binding on me.' "

*               *               *

Mr. Justice FIELD delivered the opinion of the court:

This case ... involves a consideration of the test oath imposed by the Constitution of [Missouri]. The plaintiff in error is a priest of the Roman Catholic Church, and was indicted and convicted in one of the circuit courts of the State of the crime of teaching and preaching as a priest and minister of that religious denomination without having first taken the oath, and was sentenced to pay a fine of $500....

The oath prescribed by the [Missouri] Constitution, divided into its separable parts, embraces more than thirty distinct affirmations or tests.... It requires the affiant to deny not only that he has ever "been in armed hostility to the United States, or to the lawful authorities thereof," but, among other things, that he has ever, "by act or word," manifested his adherence to the cause of the enemies of the United States, foreign or domestic, or his desire for their triumph over the arms of the United States; or his sympathy with those engaged in rebellion, or has ever harbored or aided any person engaged in guerilla warfare against the loyal inhabitants of the United States; or has ever entered or left the State for the purpose of avoiding enrollment or draft in the military service of the United States; or, to escape the performance of duty in the militia of the United States; has ever indicated, in any terms, his disaffection to the Government of the United States in its contest with the Rebellion.

Every person who is unable to take this oath is declared incapable of holding in the State, "any office of honor, trust or profit under its authority, or of being an officer, councilman, director or trustee, or other manager of any corporation, public or private, now existing or hereafter established by its authority, or of acting as a professor or teacher in any educational institution, or in any common or other school, or of holding any real estate or other prop-

erty in trust for the use of any church, religious society or congregation."

*               *               *

Qualifications relate to the fitness or capacity of the party for a particular pursuit or profession.... It is evident from the nature of the pursuits and professions of the parties, placed under disabilities by the Constitution of Missouri, that many of the acts, from the taint of which they must purge themselves, have no possible relation to their fitness for those pursuits and professions. There can be no connection between the fact that Mr. Cummings entered or left the State of Missouri to avoid enrollment or draft in the military service of the United States, and his fitness to teach the doctrines or administer the sacraments of his church.... [The oath] was exacted, not from any notion that the several acts designated indicated unfitness for the callings, but because it was thought that the several acts deserved punishment, and that for many of them there was no way to inflict punishment except by depriving the parties who had committed them of some of the rights and privileges of the citizen.

The clauses in the Missouri Constitution ... were intended especially to operate upon parties who, in some form or manner, by actions or words directly or indirectly, had aided or countenanced the Rebellion, or sympathized with parties engaged in the Rebellion, or had endeavored to escape the proper responsibilities and duties of a citizen in time of war; and they were intended to operate by depriving such persons of the right to hold certain offices and trusts, and to pursue their ordinary and regular avocations.... To make the enjoyment of a right dependent upon an impossible condition is equivalent to an absolute denial of the right under any condition, and such denial, enforced for a past act, is nothing less than punishment imposed for that act. It is a misapplication of terms to call it anything else.

Now, some of the acts to which the expurgatory oath is directed were not offenses at the time they were committed. It was no offense against any law to enter or leave the State of Missouri for the purpose of avoiding enrollment or draft in the military service of the United States, however much the evasion of such service might be the subject of moral censure. Clauses which prescribe a penalty for an act of this nature are within the terms of the definition of an *ex post facto* law — "they impose a punishment for an act not punishable at the time it was committed."

*               *               *

And this is not all. The clauses in question subvert the presumptions of innocence, and alter the rules of evidence.... They assume that the parties are guilty; they call upon the parties to establish their innocence; and they declare that such innocence can be shown only in one way — by an inquisition, in the form of an expurgatory oath, into the consciences of the parties.

[*Reversed.*]

☆ 140b *Ex Parte Garland*

71 U.S. (4 Wall.) 333 (1867).

FIELD, J.

* * *

The petitioner . . . now produces his pardon, and asks permission to continue to practise as an attorney and counsellor of the court without taking the oath required by the act of January 24, 1865, and the rule of the court, which he is unable to take, by reason of the offices he held under the Confederate government. He rests his application principally upon two grounds:

1st. That the act of January 24, 1865, so far as it affects his status in the court, is unconstitutional and void; and,

2. That, if the act be constitutional, he is released from compliance with its provisions by the pardon of the President. . . .

The statute is directed against parties who have offended in any of the particulars embraced by these clauses. And its object is to exclude them from the profession of the law, or at least from its practice in the courts of the United States. As the oath prescribed cannot be taken by these parties, the act, as against them, operates as a legislative decree of perpetual exclusion. And exclusion from any of the professions or any of the ordinary avocations of life for past conduct can be regarded in no other light than as punishment for such conduct. The exaction of the oath is the mode provided for ascertaining the parties upon whom the act is intended to operate, and instead of lessening, increases its objectionable character. All enactments of this kind partake of the nature of bills of pains and penalties, and are subject to the constitutional inhibition against the passage of bills of attainder, under which general designation they are included.

* * *

. . . They are officers of the court, admitted as such by its order, upon evidence of their possessing sufficient legal learning and fair private character. . . . They hold their office during good behavior, and can only be deprived of it for misconduct ascertained and declared by the judgment of the court after opportunity to be heard has been afforded. Their admission or their exclusion is not the exercise of a mere ministerial power. It is the exercise of judicial power, and has been so held in numerous cases. . . .

. . . The question, in this case, is not as to the power of Congress to prescribe qualifications, but whether that power has been exercised as a means for the infliction of punishment, against the prohibition of the Constitution. . . .

This view is strengthened by a consideration of the effect of the pardon produced by the petitioner, and the nature of the pardoning power of the President.

The Constitution provides that the President "shall have power to grant reprieves and pardons for offenses against the United States, except in cases of impeachment."

The power thus conferred is unlimited, with the exception stated. It extends to every offense known to the law, and may be exercised at any time after its commission, either before legal proceedings are taken, or during their pendency, or after conviction and judgment. This power of the President is not subject to legislative control. Congress can neither limit the effect of his pardon, nor exclude from its exercise any class of offenders. The benign prerogative of mercy reposed in him cannot be fettered by any legislative restrictions.

. . . A pardon reaches both the punishment prescribed for the offense and the guilt of the offender; and when the pardon is full, it releases the punishment and blots out of existence the guilt, so that in the eye of the law the offender is as innocent as if he had never committed the offense. . . . The pardon produced by the petitioner is a full pardon "for all offenses by him committed, arising from participation, direct or implied, in the Rebellion," and is subject to certain conditions which have been complied with. The effect of this pardon is to relieve the petitioner from all penalties and disabilities attached to the offense of treason, committed by his participation in the Rebellion. So far as that offense is concerned, he is thus placed beyond the reach of punishment of any kind. But to exclude him, by reason of that offense, from continuing in the enjoyment of a previously acquired right, is to enforce a punishment for that offense notwithstanding the pardon. If such exclusion can be effected by the exaction of an expurgatory oath covering the offense, the pardon may be avoided, and that accomplished indirectly which cannot be reached by direct legislation. It is not within the constitutional power of Congress to inflict punishment beyond the reach of executive clemency. From the petitioner, therefore, the oath required by the act of January 24th, 1865, could not be exacted, even if that act were not subject to any other objection than the one thus stated.

It follows, from the views expressed, that the prayer of the petitioner must be granted. . . . And it is so ordered.

# 141 "until loyal and republican State governments can be legally established" (1867)

Despite the conciliatory actions of presidents Lincoln and Johnson, the Congress of the United States, controlled by the Radical Republicans, undertook to suspend the still-functioning governments of the states that had joined the Confederacy. In addition to establishing military governments in place of state civil authority, these acts provided the terms for the states' "readmission" into the Union. The principal feature of these reconstruction acts was to require the rebellious states to adopt new constitutions drawn up by conventions elected by universal manhood suffrage, excepting those who had supported the rebellion. The conventions, as a result, were loaded with blacks and newly arrived whites from the North—carpetbaggers. Moreover, the states were not to be readmitted until they had ratified the then-proposed Fourteenth Amendment to the United States Constitution.

Once again, the use of military government, loyalty oaths, and restrictions on the franchise provided the mechanisms by which the ascendant political power attempted to insulate and enshrine itself in power over a recalcitrant population.

☆ 141 An Act to Provide for the More Efficient Government of the Rebel States

14 Stat. 428 (1867).

WHEREAS no legal State governments or adequate protection for life or property now exists in the rebel States of Virginia, North Carolina, South Carolina, Georgia, Mississippi, Alabama, Louisiana, Florida, Texas, and Arkansas; and whereas it is necessary that peace and good order should be enforced in said States until loyal and republican State governments can be legally established: Therefore,

*Be it enacted by the Senate and House of Representatives of the United States of America in Congress assembled,* That said rebel States shall be divided into military districts and made subject to the military authority of the United States as hereinafter prescribed, and for that purpose Virginia shall constitute the first district; North Carolina and South Carolina the second district; Georgia, Alabama, and Florida the third district; Mississippi and Arkansas the fourth district; and Louisiana and Texas the fifth district.

SEC. 2. *And be it further enacted,* That it shall be the duty of the President to assign to the command of each of said districts an officer of the army, not below the rank of brigadier-general, and to detail a sufficient military force to enable such officer to perform his duties and enforce his authority within the district to which he is assigned.

SEC. 3. *And be it further enacted,* That it shall be the duty of each officer assigned as aforesaid, to protect all persons in their rights of person and property, to suppress insurrection, disorder, and violence, and to punish, or cause to be punished, all disturbers of the public peace and criminals; and to this end he may allow local civil tribunals to take jurisdiction of and to try offenders, or, when in his judgment it may be necessary for the trial of offenders, he shall have power to organize military commissions or tribunals for that purpose, and all interference under color of State authority with the exercise of military authority under this act, shall be null and void.

SEC. 4. *And be it further enacted,* That all persons put under military arrest by virtue of this act shall be tried without unnecessary delay, and no cruel or unusual punishment shall be inflicted, and no sentence of any military commission or tribunal hereby authorized, affecting the life or liberty of any person, shall be executed until it is approved by the officer in command of the district, and the laws and regulations for the government of the army shall not be affected by this act, except in so far as they conflict with its provisions: *Provided,* That no sentence of death under the provisions of this act shall be carried into effect without the approval of the President.

*        *        *

# 142 The Caged Eagle (1867-1871)

After the conclusion of the Civil War, federal troops apprehended Confederate president Jefferson Davis, Mrs. Davis, and several officials of the secessionist government. An editorial in the *New York Times* called for Jefferson Davis's trial on treason charges in order to establish that "the attempted secession was not only a failure but a crime." Lengthy political discussions led to the decision that Davis should be tried for treason in a federal circuit court in Virginia. But Chief Justice Salmon P. Chase refused to hold court in Richmond, which was under martial law. Davis was confined at Fort Monroe for two years before the formal charges were pressed. Although his wife and family accompanied him, and his friends freely visited him (in the European tradition of Festungs arrest—confinement without the usual ardors of prison—accorded to political offenders), he complained of the continuing uncertainty and sought parole, speedy trial, or release on bail. The following excerpt from an argument of Davis's lawyer, Charles O'Conor, urged that the circumstances of the Civil War were such that treason was not a proper charge. Of importance to the distinction between traitor and failed patriot was the assertion of the powers of war by the victorious party.

Davis was released on $100,000 bail on May 13, having been the last of the confined captives. After argument, a motion to quash his indictment was certified to the Supreme Court. The Court rendered no decision on the question. Johnson's proclamation of amnesty in 1868 mooted the possibility of a judicial resolution of the question, and the government took no further action. Davis died in New Orleans twenty-two years later at age eighty-one.

## ☆ 142 On Behalf of Jefferson Davis—Seeking Bail or Parole

*Case of Davis*, 7 F. Cas. 63 (C.C.D. Va., 1867-71) (No. 3,621a).

[Argument of Charles O'Conor, Davis's lawyer]

\*          \*          \*

When traitors and rebels oppose their government by open violence, and are summarily put down, those not slain in the combat may fairly be tried for treason in the civil courts and dealt with as ordinary criminals. The transaction constitutes only a species of riot. But far different results ensue when rebellion maintains itself so long and so effectively as to compel between itself, its people and their territory, on the one hand, and the lawful government on the other, an institution and acceptance of the rules and usages which obtain in regular wars between independent nations. Amongst men claiming to have attained a high civilization, war is recognized as a state or condition governed by law. In its conduct or at its close, morality and justice are not lost sight of. If successful, the rebels acquire the power of establishing an independent state, which all men regard as not only legitimate but honorable in its origin; if they fail, the victor may be as indulgent as he will, or as far as he dare may consecrate to his revenge the field of their ruin. Whatever severity can be justified at the bar of public opinion, may be practiced; and certainty no more should be exercised. To the latter proposition every magnanimous spirit will assent. Washington might have failed: Kosciuszko did fail. Trials for treason in the civil courts are not remedies adapted to the close of a great civil war. Honor forbids a resort to them after combatants in open war have recognized each other as soldiers and gentlemen engaged in a legitimate conflict. After they have established truces, exchanged prisoners, and thus made applicable to their hostile intercourse, the laws of chivalry, based upon an acknowledgment of mutual confidence and respect, the rules and usages of war can not in any event be departed from by either. It would be shockingly indecorous for the ultimate victor in such a conflict to send his vanquished opponent before the civil magistrate to be tried as if he were a mere thief or rioter.

\*          \*          \*

... After an open territorial war of this kind had existed for four years, it might be thought by some that the rebels were still simply criminal violators of the municipal law; and that they ought to be dealt with as such. By the way of reasoning it might be urged that the extent of their operations merely intensified their guilt, and should not in any way affect the question. But this reasoning, if such it may be called, proves too much. On the fall of a rebellious state, after sustaining a belligerent attitude for one hundred years, its chiefs and leaders might, with equal propriety, be brought to trial as traitors in civil courts, although they and their ancestors had for several generations, been uniformly regarded and treated as public enemies carrying on against the ultimate victor a regular national war. This can not be admitted. The law of nature forbids it; and there are broad and comprehensive doctrines deducible from the universal practice of nations which forbid it. And these doctrines are founded in necessity as well as in reason and justice.

Taking, under positive written law, the narrowest technical view of the subject, one is led to a like result. ...

\*          \*          \*

... Once the lawful government acknowledges the actual existence of public territorial belligerency, and exercises the rights consequent thereon, including the conversion of the opposite party into a public enemy whose acts, as those of a sovereign de facto, are imputable to all within his territory however innocent, thus impressing upon such persons a hostile character, the preliminary action which may have been treason when it occurred, is divested of that character, and is no longer judicially cognizable as such. It is no longer susceptible of a separate consideration and must thenceforth be regarded only as an introductory step which has become part and parcel of the supervening war thus regularly instituted. Technically it is regarded as an incident merged in the principal transaction. A conflict marked by the features alluded to, is to be deemed a regular and formal public war, because it has been clothed with that character by the government itself.

\*          \*          \*

## 143 "who ... shall have engaged in insurrection" (1868)

The Fourteenth Amendment not only recognizes the privilege of federal citizenship and affirms the right to equal justice, it also contains punitive features. Section 4 prohibits the United States or any state from assuming or paying any debt or obligation incurred in aid of the Southern war effort. Thus, those who engaged in commercial transactions with the Confederacy and lent money or accepted Confederate specie for payment were penalized economically. Section 3 also exacts a political penalty, which President Andrew Johnson's subsequent full pardon could not lift. The provision stripped the South of most of its mature and proven political leadership.

## ☆ 143 United States Constitution, Amendment XIV

Section 1. All persons born or naturalized in the United States and subject to the jurisdiction thereof, are citizens of the United States and of the State wherein they reside. No State shall make or enforce any law which shall abridge the privileges or immunities of citizens of the United States; nor shall any state deprive any person of life, liberty, or property, without due process of law, nor deny to any person within its jurisdiction the equal protection of the laws.

*             *             *

Section 3. No person shall be a Senator or Representative in Congress, or elector of President and Vice President, or hold any office, civil or military, under the United States, or under any State, who, having previously taken an oath, as a member of Congress, or as an officer of the United States, or as a member of any State legislature, or as an executive or judicial officer of any State, to support the Constitution of the United States, shall have engaged in insurrection against the same, or given aid or comfort to the enemies thereof. But Congress may by a vote of two-thirds of each House, remove such disability.

*             *             *

## 144 "unconditionally, and without reservation, ... a full pardon" (1868)

On December 8, 1863, in the midst of the Civil War, President Lincoln issued a Proclamation of Amnesty and Reconstruction, a leniency program for pardoning all rebels (except high officials of the Confederacy and military officers who had joined the South) upon their taking a loyalty oath to the federal government. That proclamation also set out to restore self-government in the seceded states when one-tenth of the voting population took the prescribed oath and organized a loyal regime.

President Andrew Johnson followed Lincoln's lenient yet conditional policies in his first amnesty proclamation of May 29, 1865. Johnson announced the final, comprehensive pardon on Christmas Day, 1868. By so doing he reenfranchised those who had

been excluded from the political process by virtue of the reconstruction acts. Their renewed political power would soon assert itself against the federally supported governments of the Southern states.

## ☆ 144 President Andrew Johnson's Amnesty Proclamation (December 25, 1868)

15 Stat. 711 (1868).

*             *             *

[W]hereas, the authority of the Federal Government having been re-established in all the States and Territories within the jurisdiction of the United States, ... and that a universal amnesty and pardon for participation in said rebellion extended to all who have borne any part therein will tend to secure permanent peace, order, and prosperity throughout the land, and to renew and fully restore confidence and fraternal feeling among the whole people, and their respect for and attachment to the National Government, designed by its patriotic founders for the general good:

Now, therefore, be it known that I, ANDREW JOHNSON, ... hereby proclaim and declare unconditionally, and without reservation, to all and to every person who directly or indirectly participated in the late insurrection or rebellion, a full pardon and amnesty for the offence of treason against the United States, or of adhering to their enemies during the late civil war, with restoration of all rights, privileges, and immunities under the Constitution and the laws which have been made in pursuance thereof.

In testimony whereof, I have signed these presents with my hand, and have caused the seal of the United States to be hereunto affixed.

*             *             *

ANDREW JOHNSON

By the President:

F. W. SEWARD, Acting Secretary of State

## 145 "are you opposed to negro equality, both social and political?" (1868)

The Ku Klux Klan, founded at Pulaski, Tennessee, in 1865, was one of the largest secret organizations flourishing in the South during Reconstruction. The Order was effective in combating the emergence of black rights in the South and undercutting federal Reconstruction policies. Following reports of lawlessness and violence, the organization formally disbanded in 1869, although its clandestine operations continued.

The Knights of the White Camelia, a lower order of the K.K.K., similarly were dedicated, through violence and intimidation, to preventing blacks from exercising the newly won rights of citizenship. The charge to initiates began by stressing the evidence of white superiority and declaring the objective of "regenerating" the United States "from the humiliating condition to which it has lately been reduced."

These organizing documents are a curious blend of high principle and low purpose — much of it illegal. Nevertheless, these organizations were dedicated to the maintenance of the social and political status quo ante and may be regarded as an underground resistance wing of a broader political movement. They reflect as well the principle of providing a fundamental organizational framework to which allegiance, beyond that owed to the state, may be expected mutually from each member and against which claims of illegality provide an ineffective and illegitimate defense to nonadherence.

## ☆ 145 The Secret Organizations of the Reconstruction

### ☆ 145a Organization and Principles of the Ku Klux Klan

Reprinted in W. L. Fleming, ed., *The Ku Klux Klan: Its Origin, Growth, and Disbandment* (New York: Neale, 1905), 154.

#### CHARACTER AND OBJECTS OF THE ORDER

This is an institution of Chivalry, Humanity, Mercy, and Patriotism; embodying in its genius and its principles all that is chivalric in conduct, noble in sentiment, generous in manhood, and patriotic in purpose; its peculiar objects being

First: To protect the weak, the innocent, and the defenseless, from the indignities, wrongs, and outrages of the lawless, the violent, and the brutal; to relieve the injured and oppressed; to succor the suffering and unfortunate, and especially the widows and orphans of Confederate soldiers.

Second: To protect and defend the Constitution of the United States, and all laws passed in conformity thereto, and to protect the States and the people thereof from all invasion from any source whatever.

Third: To aid and assist in the execution of all constitutional laws, and to protect the people from unlawful seizure, and from trial except by their peers in conformity to the laws of the land.

#### INTERROGATIONS TO BE ASKED

\*          \*          \*

4th. Did you belong to the Federal army during the late war, and fight against the South during the existence of the same?

5th. Are you opposed to negro equality, both social and political?

6th. Are you in favor of a white man's government in this country?

7th. Are you in favor of Constitutional liberty, and a Government of equitable laws instead of a Government of violence and oppression?

8th. Are you in favor of maintaining the Constitutional rights of the South?

### ☆ 145b Charge to Initiates of the Knights of the White Camelia

Reprinted in W. L. Fleming, ed., *Documents Relating to Reconstruction* (Morgantown: University of West Virginia, 1904), 22-29.

#### [QUESTIONS ASKED THE CANDIDATE]

1. Do you belong to the white race? Ans. — I do.

2. Did you ever marry any woman who did not, or does not, belong to the white race? Ans. — No.

3. Do you promise never to marry any woman but one who belongs to the white race? Ans. — I do.

4. Do you believe in the superiority of your race? Ans. — I do.

5. Will you promise never to vote for any one for any office of honor, profit or trust, who does not belong to your race? Ans. — I do.

6. Will you take a solemn oath never to abstain from casting your vote at any election in which a candidate of the negro race shall be opposed to a white man attached to your principles, unless prevented by severe illness or any other physical disability? Ans. — I will.

7. Are you opposed to allowing the control of the political affairs of this country to go in whole or in part, into the hands of the African race, and will you do everything in your power to prevent it? Ans. — Yes.

8. Will you devote your intelligence, energy and influence to a furtherance and propagation of the principles of our Order? A. — I will.

9. Will you, under all circumstances, defend and protect persons of the white race in their lives, rights and property, against all encroachments or invasions from any inferior race, and especially the African? A. — Yes.

10. Are you willing to take an oath forever to cherish these grand principles, and to unite yourself with others who, like you, believing in their truth, have firmly bound themselves to stand by and defend them against all? Ans. — I am.

The C[ommander] shall then say: If you consent to join our Association, raise your right hand and I will administer to you the oath which we have all taken: . . .

#### [CHARGE TO INITIATES]

Brothers: You have been initiated into one of the most important Orders which have ever been established on this continent: an Order, which, if its principles are faithfully observed and its objects diligently carried out, is destined to regenerate our unfortunate country and to relieve the White Race from the humiliating condition to which it has lately been reduced in this Republic....

As you may have already gathered from the questions which were propounded to you, and which you have answered so satisfactorily, and from the clauses of the Oath which you have taken, our main and fundamental object is the MAINTENANCE OF THE SUPREMACY OF THE WHITE RACE in this Republic. History and physiology teach us that we belong to a race which nature has endowed with an evident superiority over all other races, and that the Maker, in thus elevating us above the common standard of human creation, has intended to give us over inferior races, a dominion from which no human laws can permanently derogate. The experience of ages demonstrates that, from the origin of the world, this dominion has always remained in the hands of the Caucasian Race; whilst all the other races have constantly occupied a subordinate and secondary position; a fact which triumphantly confirms this great law of nature. Powerful nations have succeeded each other on the face of the world, and have marked their passage by glorious and memorable deeds; and among those who have thus left on this globe indelible traces of their splendor and greatness, we find none but descended from the Caucasian stock. We see, on the contrary, that most of the countries inhabited by the other races have remained in a state of complete barbarity; whilst the small number of those who have advanced beyond this savage existence, have, for centuries, stagnated in a semi-barbarous condition of which there can be no progress or improvement. And it is a remarkable fact that as a race of men is more remote from the Caucasian and approaches nearer to the black African, the more fatally that stamp of inferiority is affixed to its sons, and irrevocably dooms them to eternal imperfectibility and degradation.

Convinced that we are of these elements of [white supremacy], we know, besides, that the government of our Republic was established by white men, for white men alone, and that it never was in the contemplation of its founders that it should fall into the hands of an inferior and degraded race. We hold, therefore, that any attempt to wrest from the white race the management of its affairs in order to transfer it to control of the black population, is an invasion of the sacred prerogatives vouchsafed to us by the Constitution, and a violation of the laws established by God himself; that such encroachments are subversive of the established institutions of our Republic, and that no individual of the white race can submit to them without humiliation and shame.

It, then, becomes our solemn duty, as white men, to resist strenuously and persistently those attempts against our natural and constitutional rights, and to do everything in our power in order to maintain, in this Republic, the supremacy of the Caucasian race, and restrain the black or African race to that condition of social and political inferiority for which God has destined it. This is the object for which our Order was instituted; and, in carrying it out, we intend to infringe no laws, to violate no rights, and to resort to no forcible means, except for purposes of legitimate and necessary defense.

As an essential condition of success, this Order proscribes absolutely all social equality between the races. If we were to admit persons of African race on the same level with ourselves, a state of personal relations would follow which would unavoidably lead to political equality; for it would be a virtual recognition of *status*, after which we could not consistently deny them an equal share in the administration of our public affairs. The man who is good enough to be our familiar companion, is good enough also to participate in our political government; and if we were to grant the one, there could be no good reason for us not to concede the other of these two privileges.

... [T]herefore, we take the obligation TO OBSERVE A MARKED DISTINCTION BETWEEN THE TWO RACES, not only in the relations of public affairs, but also in the more intimate dealings and intercourse of private life....

[L]et me charge you specially in relation to one of your most important duties as one of its members. Our statutes make us bound to respect sedulously the rights of the colored inhabitants of this Republic, and in every instance, to give to them whatever lawfully belongs to them. It is an act of simple justice not to deny them any of the privileges to which they are legitimately entitled.... Besides, it would be ungenerous for us to undertake to restrict them to the narrowest limits as to the exercise of certain rights, without conceding to them, at the same time, the fullest measure of those which we recognize as theirs....

From the brief explanation which I have just given you, you must have satisfied yourselves that our Association is not a political party, and has no connection with any of the organized parties of the day.... You may meet here, congregated together, men who belong to all the political organizations which now divide, or may divide, this country; you see some whom embittered feuds and irreconcilable hatred have long and widely separated; they have all cast away these rankling feelings to unite cordially and zealously in the labors of our great undertaking. Let their example be to you a useful lesson of the disinterestedness and devotedness which should characterize our efforts for the success of our cause!

## 146 "citizens . . . of every race and color" (1866-1875)

Between 1866 and 1875, Congress passed seven acts (including one reenactment) protecting the freed slaves from hostile social and political conditions. Congress would not legislate any further significant civil rights measures until 1957, eighty-two years later.

The first Civil Rights Act, passed on April 9, 1866, in response to the enactment of the Black Codes, declared that all persons born in the United States, whatever their race or color, were citizens thereof and entitled to the same rights in every state as white citizens. Doubts were raised concerning the power of Congress to enact such a law, there being no provision in the Constitution giving Congress the power to define citizenship or to regulate the civil rights of state citizens. Despite the Civil War and the Thirteenth Amendment, the *Dred Scott* case was still the law on the subject of citizenship. Only with the Fourteenth Amendment, which was ratified on July 9, 1868, were the issues of both national and state citizenship resolved and an injunction imposed upon the states to respect the privileges and immunities of United States citizens and not deny any person due process or the equal protection of the laws. Thus *Dred Scott* was overturned, and the great question of primacy of sovereignty—a major cause of political dissension and the Civil War—supposedly was resolved. Conflicts between the commands of state and federal laws governing the social and political relations of whites and blacks nevertheless continued.

☆ 146  The Civil Rights Acts

☆ 146a  Civil Rights Act of 1866

14 Stat. 27 (1866).

*Be it enacted by the Senate and House of Representatives of the United States of America in Congress assembled,* That all persons born in the United States and not subject to any foreign power, excluding Indians not taxed, are hereby declared to be citizens of the United States; and such citizens, of every race and color, without regard to any previous condition of slavery or involuntary servitude, except as a punishment for crime whereof the party shall have been duly convicted, shall have the same right, in every State and Territory in the United States, to make and enforce contracts, to sue, be parties, and give evidence, to inherit, purchase, lease, sell, hold, and convey real and personal property, and to full and equal benefit of all laws and proceedings for the security of person and property, as is enjoyed by white citizens, and shall be subject to like punishment, pains, and penalties, and to none other, any law, statute, ordinance, regulation, or custom, to the contrary notwithstanding.

SEC. 2. *And be it further enacted,* That any person who, under color of any law, statute, ordinance, regulation, or custom, shall subject, or cause to be subjected, any inhabitant of any State or Territory to the deprivation of any right secured or protected by this act, or to different punishment, pains, or penalties on account of such person having at any time been held in a condition of slavery or involuntary servitude, except as a punishment for crime whereof the party shall have been duly convicted, or by reason of his color or race, than is prescribed for the punishment of white persons, shall be deemed guilty of a misdemeanor, and, on conviction, shall be punished by fine not exceeding one thousand dollars, or imprisonment not exceeding one year, or both, in the discretion of the court.

\*          \*          \*

SEC. 6. *And be it further enacted,* That any person who shall knowingly and wilfully obstruct, hinder, or prevent any officer, or other person charged with the execution of any warrant or process issued under the provisions of this act . . . [shall] be subject to a fine not exceeding one thousand dollars, and imprisonment not exceeding six months. . . .

\*          \*          \*

☆ 146b  Civil Rights Act of 1870
(The Enforcement Act)

16 Stat. 140 (1870).

*Be it enacted by the Senate and House of Representatives of the United States of America in Congress assembled,* That all citizens of the United States who are or shall be otherwise qualified by law to vote at any election . . . shall be entitled and allowed to vote at all such elections, without distinction of race, color, or previous condition of servitude. . . .

SEC. 2. *And be it further enacted,* That it shall be the duty of every . . . person and officer to give to all citizens of the United States the same and equal opportunity to perform [any] prerequisite, and to become qualified to vote without distinction of race, color, or previous condition of servitude; and if any . . . person or officer shall refuse or knowingly omit to give full effect to this section, he shall . . . be deemed guilty of a misdemeanor, and shall, on conviction thereof, be fined not less than five hundred dollars, or be imprisoned not less than one month and not more than one year, or both, at the discretion of the court.

\*          \*          \*

SEC. 6. *And be it further enacted,* That if two or more persons shall band or conspire together, or go in disguise upon the public highway, or upon the premises of another, with intent to violate any provision of this act, or to injure, oppress, threaten, or intimidate any citizen with intent to prevent or hinder his free exercise and enjoyment of any right or privilege granted or secured to him by the Constitution or laws of the United States, or because of his having exercised the same, such persons shall be held guilty of felony, and, on conviction thereof, shall be fined or imprisoned, or both, at the discretion of the court,—the fine not to exceed five thousand dollars, and the imprisonment not to exceed ten years,—and shall, moreover, be thereafter ineligible to, and disabled from holding, any office or place of honor, profit, or trust created by the Constitution or laws of the United States.

\*          \*          \*

SEC. 17. *And be it further enacted,* That any person who, under color of any law, statute, ordinance, regulation, or custom, shall subject, or cause to be subjected, any inhabitant of any State or Territory to the deprivation of any right secured or protected by the last preceding section [giving all persons the same rights as white citizens] of this act, or to different punishment, pains, or penalties on account of such person being an alien, or by reason of his color or race, than is prescribed for the punishment of citizens, shall be deemed guilty of a misdemeanor, and, on conviction, shall be punished by fine not exceeding one thousand dollars, or imprisonment not exceeding one year, or both, in the discretion of the court.

☆ 146c  Civil Rights Act of 1871

17 Stat. 13 (1871).

\*          \*          \*

SEC. 2. That if two or more persons within any State or Territory of the United States shall conspire together to overthrow, or to put down, or to destroy by force the government of the United States, or to levy war against the United States, or to oppose by force the authority of the government of the United States, or by force, intimidation, or threat to prevent, hinder, or delay the execution of any law of the United States, or by force to seize, take, or possess any property of the United States contrary to the authority thereof, or by force, intimidation, or threat to prevent any person from accepting or holding any office or trust or place of confidence under the United States, or from discharging the duties thereof, or by force, intimidation, or threat to induce any officer of the United States to leave any State, district, or place where his duties as such officer might lawfully be performed, or to injure him in his person or property on account of his lawful discharge of the duties of his office, or to injure his person while engaged in the lawful discharge of the duties of his office, or to injure his property so as to molest, interrupt, hinder, or im-

pede him in the discharge of his official duty, or by force, intimidation, or threat to deter any party or witness in any court of the United States from attending such court, or from testifying in any matter pending in such court fully, freely, and truthfully, or to injure any such party or witness in his person or property on account of his having so attended or testified, or by force, intimidation, or threat to influence the verdict, presentment, or indictment, of any juror or grand juror in any court of the United States, or to injure such juror in his person or property on account of any verdict, presentment, or indictment lawfully assented to by him, or on account of his being or having been such juror, or shall conspire together, or go in disguise upon the public highway or upon the premises of another for the purpose, either directly or indirectly, of depriving any person or any class of persons of the equal protection of the laws, or of equal privileges or immunities under the laws, or for the purpose of preventing or hindering the constituted authorities of any State from giving or securing to all persons within such State the equal protection of the laws, or shall conspire together for the purpose of in any manner impeding, hindering, obstructing, or defeating the due course of justice in any State or Territory, with intent to deny to any citizen of the United States the due and equal protection of the laws, or to injure any person in his person or his property for lawfully enforcing the right of any person or class of persons to the equal protection of the laws, or by force, intimidation, or threat to prevent any citizen of the United States lawfully entitled to vote from giving his support or advocacy in a lawful manner towards or in favor of the election of any lawfully qualified person as an elector of President or Vice-President of the United States, or as a member of the Congress of the United States, or to injure any such citizen in his person or property on account of such support or advocacy, each and every person so offending shall be deemed guilty of a high crime, and, upon conviction thereof in any district or circuit court of the United States or district or supreme court of any Territory of the United States having jurisdiction of similar offences, shall be punished by a fine not less than five hundred nor more than five thousand dollars, or by imprisonment, with or without hard labor, as the court may determine, for a period of not less than six months nor more than six years, as the court may determine, or by both such fine and imprisonment as the court shall determine....

\*          \*          \*

☆ 146d  Civil Rights Act of 1875

18 Stat. 335 (1875).

Whereas, it is essential to just government we recognize the equality of all men before the law, and hold that it is the duty of government in its dealings with the people to mete out equal and exact justice to all, of whatever nativity, race, color, or persuasion, religious or political; and it being the appropriate object of legislation to enact great fundamental principles into law: Therefore,

*Be it enacted by the Senate and House of Representatives of the United States of America in Congress assembled*, That all persons within the jurisdiction of the United States shall be entitled to the full and equal enjoyment of the accommodations, advantages, facilities, and privileges of inns, public conveyances on land or water, theaters, and other places of public amusement; subject only to the conditions and limitations established by law, and applicable alike to citizens of every race and color, regardless of any previous condition of servitude.

SEC. 2. That any person who shall violate the foregoing section by denying to any citizen, except for reasons by law applicable to citizens of every race and color, and regardless of any previous condition of servitude, the full enjoyment of any of the accommodations, advantages, facilities, or privileges in said section enumerated, or by aiding or inciting such denial, shall, for every such offense, forfeit and pay the sum of five hundred dollars to the person aggrieved thereby, to be recovered in an action of debt, with full costs; and shall also, for every such offense, be deemed guilty of a misdemeanor and, upon conviction thereof, shall be fined not less than five hundred nor more than one thousand dollars, or shall be imprisoned not less than thirty days nor more than one year....

\*     \*     \*

SEC. 4. That no citizen possessing all other qualifications which are or may be prescribed by law shall be disqualified for service as a grand or petit juror in any court of the United States, or of any State, on account of race, color, or previous condition of servitude; and any officer or other person charged with any duty in the selection or summoning of jurors who shall exclude or fail to summon any citizen for the cause aforesaid shall, on conviction thereof, be deemed guilty of a misdemeanor and be fined not more than five thousand dollars.

\*     \*     \*

# 147  Rebel Property and Due Process (1870)

In *Miller v. United States*, the Supreme Court upheld the 1861 and 1862 acts providing for the confiscation of the properties of rebels and of their aiders and abettors against complaints that the acts had violated the Fifth and Sixth amendment safeguards of due process of law and fair trial. Miller argued that

the confiscation acts were penal laws under the municipal power of Congress and, accordingly, subject to the constitutional limitations on criminal law. The court, nevertheless, found the acts to be exercises of the war powers upon which, it was conceded, the Constitution imposed no restrictions.

Pointing out that the acts were aimed not at external enemies of the United States but at citizens committing acts of treason, the dissenting justices urged that the acts should be considered not under the war powers but as domestic legislation subject to the Fifth and Sixth amendments. While there was no disagreement that the United States could treat the people of the South as *either* enemy aliens or traitors, it was doubtful whether Congress could escape its choice, once made. The confiscation acts did not, as in a foreign war, authorize the appropriation of all property, only that of people engaging in certain acts. Hence the laws were not in aid of the war, but punitive of persons of suspect loyalties. The case demonstrated, again, the ambiguous position of the supporters of the Confederate cause: enemies or traitors?

☆ 147  *Miller v. United States*

78 U.S. (6 Wall.) 268 (1870).

Mr. Justice STRONG delivered the opinion of the court.

\*     \*     \*

It remains to consider the objection urged on behalf of the plaintiff in error that the acts of Congress under which these proceedings to confiscate the stock have been taken are not warranted by the Constitution, and that they are in conflict with some of its provisions. The objection starts with the assumption that the purpose of the acts was to punish offences against the sovereignty of the United States, and that they are merely statutes against crimes.... But if the assumption of the plaintiff in error is not well made, if the statutes were not enacted under the municipal power of Congress to legislate for the punishment of crimes against the sovereignty of the United States, if, on the contrary, they are an exercise of the war powers of the government, it is clear they are not affected by the restrictions imposed by the fifth and sixth amendments. This we understand to have been conceded in the argument. The question, therefore, is, whether the action of Congress was a legitimate exercise of the war power. The Constitution confers upon Congress expressly power to declare war, grant letters of marque and reprisal, and make rules respecting captures on land and water. Upon the exercise of these powers no restrictions are imposed....

[W]hen the acts of 1861 and 1862 were passed, there was a state of war existing between the

United States and the rebellious portions of the country.... War existing, the United States were invested with belligerent rights in addition to the sovereign powers previously held.... Mr. Wheaton, in his work on international law, asserts the doctrine to be that "the general usage of nations regards such a war as entitling both the contending parties to all the rights of war as against each other, and even as it respects neutral nations." It would be absurd to hold that, while in a foreign war [the] enemy's property may be captured and confiscated, ... in a civil war of equal dimensions, ... the right to confiscate the property ... does not exist.... Every reason for the allowance of a right to confiscate in case of foreign wars exists in full force when the war is domestic or civil....

\*     \*     \*

Mr. Justice FIELD, with whom concurred Mr. Justice CLIFFORD, dissenting.

\*     \*     \*

The authority for the legislation in question must be found in what are termed the war powers of the government; ... or, in what is termed the municipal power of the government to legislate for the punishment of offences against the United States.

... The question is, not as to the right of the United States to adopt either course against the inhabitants of the Confederate States engaged in the rebellion; that is, the right to treat them as public enemies, and to apply to them all the harsh measures justified by the rules of war; or the right to prosecute them in the ordinary modes of criminal procedure for the punishment of treason; but what course has Con-

gress, by its legislation, authorized. For it is evident that legislation founded upon the war powers of the government, and directed against the public enemies of the United States, is subject to different considerations and limitations from those applicable to legislation founded upon the municipal power of the government and directed against criminals. Legislation in the former case is subject to no limitations, except such as are imposed by the law of nations in the conduct of war. Legislation in the latter case is subject to all the limitations prescribed by the Constitution for the protection of the citizen....

\*     \*     \*

If we turn now to the act of July 17th, 1862, we find that its provisions are not directed against enemies at all, but against persons who have committed certain overt acts of treason....

\*     \*     \*

It would seem clear, therefore, that the provisions of the act were not passed in the exercise of the war powers of the government, but in the exercise of the municipal power of the government to legislate for the punishment of offences against the United States....

\*     \*     \*

As the act is highly penal in its nature, it would seem that, according to well-received rules, it should be strictly construed, and a rigid compliance with its provisions exacted. But the very opposite course in the construction of the act appears to have been adopted by the majority of the court.

\*     \*     \*

*Top,* Doc. 4: The Pilgrims signing the Mayflower Compact on board the ship. Engraving by Gauthier, 1857, after H. Matteson. *Middle, left,* Doc. 17: Nathaniel Bacon, aristocratic Englishman and leader of the Virginia Rebellion (1676). From an original at Lord Viscount Grimston's, at Gorhambury. *Middle, right,* Doc. 5: Indian massacre of early Virginia settlers. Engraving by Theodore DeBry. *Bottom,* Doc. 19: William Penn entering a treaty of mutual respect with the Native Americans upon the founding of the province of Pennsylvania (1681).

*Top*, Doc. 35: The Boston Massacre. Engraving by Paul Revere. *Middle*, Doc. 45: Ratification of the Declaration of Independence (1776). *Bottom*, Doc. 52: Captured British Major John André, liaison for the Benedict Arnold conspiracy, seeking to bribe a patriotic member of the New York militia to release him (September 23, 1780). From *Harper's Weekly*, September 29, 1860.

## Negroes for Sale.

A Cargo of very fine stout Men and Women, in good order and fit for immediate service, just imported from the Windward Coast of Africa, in the Ship Two Brothers.—

Conditions are one half Cash or Produce, the other half payable the first of January next, giving Bond and Security if required.

The Sale to be opened at 10 o'Clock each Day, in Mr. Bourdeaux's Yard, at No, 48, on the Bay.

May 19, 1784.     JOHN MITCHELL.

## Thirty Seasoned Negroes

*To be Sold for Credit, at Private Sale.*

AMONGST which is a Carpenter, none of whom are known to be dishonest.

Also, to be sold for Cash, a regular bred young Negroe Man-Cook, born in this Country, who served several Years under an exceeding good French Cook abroad, and his Wife a middle aged Washer-Woman, (both very honest) and their two Children. Likewise, a young Man a Carpenter.

For Terms apply to the Printer.

*Top*, Doc. 61: Advertisement for the sale of slaves in America (1784). *Bottom*, Doc. 88: Virginia slaves, under the leadership of Nat Turner, rebel against their masters. Woodcut from an abolitionist tract by S. Warner, 1831.

# HORRID MASSACRE IN VIRGINIA.

The Scenes which the above Plate is designed to represent, are—Fig 1. a Mother intreating for the lives of her children.—2. Mr. Travis, cruelly murdered by his own Slaves.—3. Mr. Barrow, who bravely defended himself until his wife escaped.—4. A comp. of mounted Dragoons in pursuit of the Blacks.

*Top*, Doc. 95: Native Americans on the "Trail of Tears," prodded along by United States soldiers (1843). Original painting by Robert Lindneux. *Bottom*, Doc. 95: Seminole Chief Osceola, who led a seven-year war in opposition to the federal resettlement of Native Americans west of the Mississippi (1835).

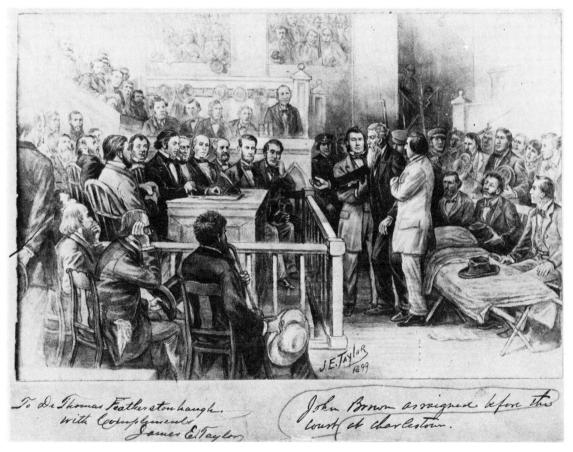

# ANTI-TEXAS MEETING
## AT FANEUIL HALL!

### *Friends of Freedom!*

A proposition has been made, and will soon come up for consideration in the United States Senate, to annex Texas to the Union. This territory has been wrested from Mexico by violence and fraud. Such is the character of the leaders in this enterprise that the country has been aptly termed "that valley of rascals." It is large enough to make *nine* or *ten* States as large as Massachusetts. It was, under Mexico, a free territory. The freebooters have made it a slave territory. The design is to annex it, with its load of infamy and oppression, to the Union. The immediate result may be a war with Mexico—the ultimate result *will be* some 18 or 20 more slaveholders in the Senate of the United States, a still larger number in the House of Representatives, and the balance of power in the hands of the South! And if, when in a minority in Congress, slaveholders browbeat the North, demand the passage of gag laws, trample on the Right of Petition, and threaten, in defiance of the General Government, to hang every man, caught at the South, who dares to speak against their "domestic institutions,"what limits shall be set to their intolerant demands and high handed usurpations, when they are in the majority ?

All opposed to this scheme, of whatever sect or party, are invited to attend the meeting at the Old Cradle of Liberty, to-morrow, ( Thursday Jan. 25, )at 10 o'clock, A. M., at which time addresses are expected from several able speakers.

Bostonians ! Friends of Freedom !! Let your voices be heard in loud remonstrance against this scheme, fraught with such ruin to yourselves and such infamy to your country.

January 24, 1838.

*Top*, Doc. 98: Appeal to the "Friends of Freedom" to oppose the admission into the Union of Texas, which was "wrested from Mexico by violence and fraud" (1838). *Bottom*, Doc. 116: The trial of John Brown for his rebellion in Harper's Ferry.

*Top*, Doc. 114: The assassination of Mormon leaders Joseph and Hiram Smith in the Carthage, Illinois, jail (1844). Lithograph by C. G. Crehen (1851). *Bottom*, Doc. 114: The march of the United States Army, across the snowy plains of Utah Territory, against the rebellious Mormons (1858). From *Harper's Weekly*, April 24, 1858.

Top, *left*, Doc. 130: Antidraft rioters in New York City (1863). Wood engraving in *Leslie's Illustrated News*, July 25, 1863. Top, *right*, Doc. 124: Hostile portrayal of Jefferson Davis, the provisional president of the seceding Confederate States of America (1861). *Bottom*, Doc. 134: Confederate President Jefferson Davis portrayed in a "family reunion" with Benedict Arnold (1865).

SATAN TEMPTING BOOTH TO THE MURDER OF THE PRESIDENT.

*Top, left*, Doc. 145: Two members of the Ku Klux Klan in their disguises (1868). Woodcut from *Harper's Weekly*, December 19, 1868. *Top, right*, Doc. 136: Satan tempting John Wilkes Booth, the assassin of President Lincoln (1865). *Bottom*, Doc. 131: Confederate troops engaging in an indiscriminate massacre of white and black Union troops and followers, including the wounded, children, and women, after the conquest of Fort Pillow, Kentucky (April 12, 1864). From *Harper's Weekly*, April 30, 1864.

### CHAPTER 6

# Social and Industrial Stress

---

### The Struggles of Native
### Americans, Women,
### and Labor
### 1871-1916

The close of the Civil War permitted some longstanding but temporarily dormant social and political movements to come to the fore. The war concluded with a basic restructuring of the state-federal system through the passage of the Fourteenth Amendment, which authorized federal scrutiny of the conduct of the states' legal relations with their citizenry. Other forms of restructuring were now to occupy the nation's sociopolitical agenda after the half-century, as various factions of the population pressed for access to political power—often through illegal and violent means. Southern whites regrasped political control of their states to maintain social and racial hegemony, women sought the franchise and access to public office and the professions, Native Americans fought a losing battle against expatriation and western resettlement, and the labor movement struggled to reform the economic order and to accord workers access to the safeguards, rather than the hostility, of the law.

In all these arenas the existing laws, both criminal and quasi-criminal, shaped the character of the debate and either facilitated or retarded change. This chapter thus focuses on the interactions of the law, particularly the federal law, with these reform and retrenchment movements. To be sure, there was considerable criminal conduct associated with all of the groups included in this chapter: nightriders engaged in acts of terrorism; women sought to cast illegal votes; Native Americans frequently rose in defense of their land and social order; and workers illegally struck, boycotted, and rioted. But this chapter is replete with the richer material of political criminality as well.

The recurring themes of loyalty and allegiance to the social, economic, and political order echoed through these years, but new phenomena came into existence as well. Despite the general amnesty, the confiscation measures of the Civil War continued in effect, and a white man's rights depended on his wartime loyalties. But as franchise restrictions on former Confederate officers and soldiers were lifted, the white Southern political structure asserted itself against the federally supported Reconstruction governments. With the federal presence reduced, many white Southerners undertook terrorist acts to diminish the political power of blacks—

to which neither the new state authorities nor those of federal government effectively responded. The passive attitude of both state and federal criminal law enforcement officials thus permitted the subjugation of blacks through private conspiracies and terrorism.

In contrast to the passive posture of the governments with regard to the enforcement of civil rights stands the active federal role in addressing another resurging social concern—the destiny of the Native American population. The federal government, first through the use of military force to contain and isolate Native Americans on reservations and then through a policy of "assimilation," undertook, through punitive laws and regulations, the ethnocide of a socially and politically distinct people.

Passive and active involvements also marked the federal government's approach to the women's and the labor movements, respectively. A narrow construction of the recently enacted Fourteenth Amendment withheld from women access to federal authority to challenge state restrictions on their political and social rights. Conversely, capital and management often invoked federal power, military and judicial, to neutralize and punish the exercise of economic and political power by organized labor.

In these materials, once again there is a pattern of political criminality arising in and around groups that are excluded from equal participation in the ordinary political processes, yet are held accountable to the demands of the law. The severity of the governmental response to such criminality seems to be related to the perceived loyalty of the offending group. The Native Americans were affected the most directly and heavily by state and federal government policies. They were attacked and held in captivity, and their social cohesion was broken violently. The duplicitous policy of the United States was to recognize the Native Americans as sovereign, and therefore to see them as disloyal to the United States. Before they could be granted politically protected rights they were required to demonstrate their "assimilation"—adherence to the order of the white society.

Workers, especially noncraft laborers, received the next most severe treatment at the hands of government. Many, if not most, of this sector of the working class consisted of immigrants, ineligible to vote, who spoke foreign languages and adhered to foreign customs and ideologies. The government and the general public perceived their organizations as suspiciously foreign and as opposed to the principles of the American Republic, as a threat to the interests of capital.

Women were denied the franchise and could not directly influence policy, but otherwise their deprivation was more evident in economic than in political realms. They were punished when they breached the law to demonstrate their disaffection with the existing order; otherwise their political subjugation was more a matter of exclusion than direct oppression. Blacks were in the most peculiar position of all with regard to governmental authority. Unlike the other groups they were specifically entitled to the special protection of the United States under the Fourteenth Amendment, yet they were victimized through terrorism and state-sanctioned discrimination more than any other group. The United States laws that guaranteed black voting rights proved ineffectual in protecting the

exercise of that right in the face of violent, politically motivated local opposition. The resulting political disenfranchisement, reinforced by blacks' social reisolation, continued at the federal as well as the state level, since federal and state electors were one and the same.

It is the struggle of these groups—Native Americans, women, blacks, and labor—for political and civil rights which constituted a major portion of political criminality in post-Civil War America. None of these groups sought to do anything that was inherently or fundamentally criminal: *malum in se*. Living on one's ancestral property in conformity with traditional cultural values, organizing and collectively asserting economic power and the need for reform, and discharging civic and political responsibilities through the elective process are not usually deemed inimical to the social order. Yet people were for those reasons subjected to punishment, deprivation, and even death, through the use or the nonuse of governmental power.

---

## 148 "no Indian nation . . . shall be acknowledged or recognized as an independent nation" (1871)

The new federal policies regarding Native Americans were hampered severely by the sovereign status of the Indian nations, entitling them to bilateral and consensual treaty relations. The cumbersome treaty form of managing Native American affairs also was objectionable to the House of Representatives, which was excluded from the treaty ratification process. In 1867, Congress passed a bill (which was plainly unconstitutional and was quickly repealed) that purported to strip the president of treaty negotiating power with the Native Americans. Finally, in 1871 an amendment was tacked on to the appropriations bill terminating this time-honored procedure. The Native American nations, thereafter, were no longer entitled to the procedural trappings of independent nations. Their status had been defined one year earlier when the Supreme Court ruled in the *Cherokee Tobacco Case*, 78 U.S. (11 Wall.) 616 (1870), that an act of Congress could abrogate a treaty obligation.

This loss of treaty-making status provided the foundation for the assertion of federal law-making authority over the heretofore inviolable internal affairs of the various Native American societies. Although often coerced, regulation of internal Native

American affairs had always been based on the consent of the tribal authority. Thereafter this authority existed only at the sufferance of Congress, and the individual Native American, rather than the nation or tribe, became the legitimate object of regulation by Congress. Membership in a Native American society nevertheless precluded individuals from asserting any voice in the enactment of the regulation, even though they were directly subject to penalties.

☆ 148  An Act Making Appropriation for the Indian Department and for Other Purposes

16 Stat. 544 (1871).

BE IT ENACTED *by the Senate and House of Representatives of the United States of America in Congress assembled,* That the following sums be, and they are hereby, appropriated, out of any money in the treasury not otherwise appropriated, for the purpose of paying the current and contingent expenses of the Indian department, and fulfilling treaty stipulations with the various Indian tribes:—

\*         \*         \*

For insurance and transportation of goods for the Yanktons, one thousand five hundred dollars: *Provided,* That hereafter no Indian nation or tribe within the territory of the United States shall be acknowledged or recognized as an independent nation, tribe, or power with whom the United States may contract by treaty: *Provided further*, That nothing herein contained shall be construed to invalidate or impair the obligation of any treaty heretofore lawfully made and ratified with any such Indian nation or tribe. . . .

* * *

## 149 "grudging obedience to the most reasonable requirements of the Government" (1872)

The final removal of the Seminoles to lands west of the Mississippi temporarily mitigated the tension between Native Americans and whites. But with the westward press of white settlement, the nomadic Native Americans' habit of "straying off the reservation" in pursuit of game engendered more and more friction and brought military intervention. In 1862, Sioux facing semistarvation rose in Minnesota. After the uprising was quelled, thirty-eight Sioux leaders were hanged the day after Christmas in Mankato, Minnesota, by order of President Lincoln. It was clear that the earlier policy of removal could not be repeated. The so-called peace policy finally prevailed, and the reservation system, which segregated the Native American population, was strictly enforced through the use of military.

The implementation of the new federal peace policy—the virtual confinement of the Native Americans—was described starkly in the report of the Commissioner of the Indian Affairs. Pursuit of this policy resulted in several noted events in United States military history, including Custer's Last Stand (1876); the thousand-mile, orderly trek of the Nez Perce under Chief Joseph while pursued by superior United States forces (1877); the guerrilla war of the Chiracawa Apaches and other southwestern tribes, which ended with the capture of Geronimo (1886); and the Ghost Dance Uprising, a combined effort of several tribes, which ended with the massacre at Wounded Knee (1890).

☆ 149 Annual Report of the Commissioner of Indian Affairs

H.R. Exec. Doc. No. 1, 42d Cong., 3d Sess. 391 (1872), reprinted in Francis Paul Prucha, ed., *Documents of United States Indian Policy* (Lincoln: University of Nebraska Press, 1975), 137-41.

THE INDIAN POLICY

The Indian policy, so called, of the Government, is a policy, and it is not a policy, or rather it consists of

two policies, entirely distinct, seeming, indeed, to be mutually inconsistent and to reflect each upon the other: the one regulating the treatment of the tribes which are potentially hostile, that is, whose hostility is only repressed just so long as, and so far as, they are supported in idleness by the Government; the other regulating the treatment of those tribes which, from traditional friendship, from numerical weakness, or by the force of their location, are either indisposed toward, or incapable of, resistance to the demands of the Government. . . . It is, of course, hopelessly illogical that the expenditures of the Government should be proportioned not to the good but to the ill desert of the several tribes; that large bodies of Indians should be supported in entire indolence by the bounty of the Government simply because they are audacious and insolent, while well-disposed Indians are only assisted to self-maintenance, since it is known they will not fight. It is hardly less than absurd, on the first view of it, that delegations from tribes that have frequently defied our authority and fought our troops, and have never yielded more than a partial and grudging obedience to the most reasonable requirements of the Government, should be entertained at the national capital, feasted, and loaded with presents. . . . And yet, for all this, the Government is right and its critics wrong; and the "Indian policy" is sound, sensible, and beneficent, because it reduces to the minimum the loss of life and property upon our frontier, and allows the freest development of our settlements and railways possible under the circumstances.

. . . It is not a whit more unreasonable that the Government should do much for hostile Indians and little for friendly Indians than it is that a private citizen should, to save his life, surrender all the contents of his purse to a highwayman; while on another occasion, to a distressed and deserving applicant for charity, he would measure his contribution by his means and disposition at the time. . . . It is not, of course, to be understood that the Government of the United States is at the mercy of Indians; but thousands of its citizens are, even thousands of families. . . . There are innumerable little rifts of agricultural or mining settlements all over the western country which, if unmolested, will in a few years become self-protecting communities, but which, in the event of a general Indian war occurring at the present time, would utterly and instantly disappear, either by abandonment or massacre. . . . It is right that those who criticise the policy of the Government toward the Indians . . . should fairly face the one alternative which is presented. There is no question of national dignity, be it remembered, involved in the treatment of savages by a civilized power. With wild men, as with wild beasts, the question whether in a given situation one shall fight, coax, or run, is a question merely of what is easiest and safest.

### THE USE OF THE MILITARY ARM

The system now pursued in dealing with the roving tribes dangerous to our frontier population and obstructing our industrial progress, is entirely consistent with, and, indeed, requires the occasional use of the military arm, in restraining or chastising refractory individuals and bands. Such a use of the military constitutes no abandonment of the "peace policy," and involves no disparagement of it. It was not to be expected—it was not in the nature of things—that the entire body of wild Indians should submit to be restrained in their Ishmaelitish proclivities without a struggle on the part of the more audacious to maintain their traditional freedom. In the first announcement made of the reservation system, it was expressly declared that the Indians should be made as comfortable on, and as uncomfortable off, their reservations as it was in the power of the Government to make them; that such of them as went right should be protected and fed, and such as went wrong should be harassed and scourged without intermission. It was not anticipated that the first proclamation of this policy to the tribes concerned would effect the entire cessation of existing evils; but it was believed that persistence in the course marked out would steadily reduce the number of the refractory, both by the losses sustained in actual conflict and by the desertion of individuals as they should become weary of a profitless and hopeless struggle, until, in the near result, the system adopted should apply without exception to all then roving and hostile tribes. Such a use of the strong arm of the Government is not war, but discipline. . . .

It will be sufficient, perhaps, to mark the distinction, to say that a general Indian war could not be carried on with the present military force of the United States, or anything like it. Regiments would be needed where now are only companies, and long lines of posts would have to be established for the protection of regions which, under the safeguard of the feeding system, are now left wholly uncovered. On the other hand, by the reservation system and the feeding system combined, the occasions for collision are so reduced by lessening the points of contact, and the number of Indians available for hostile expeditions involving exposure, hardship, and danger is so diminished through the appeal made to their indolence and self-indulgence, that the Army in its present force is able to deal effectively with the few marauding bands which refuse to accept the terms of the Government.

### THE FORBEARANCE OF THE GOVERNMENT

It is unquestionably true that the Government has seemed somewhat tardy in proceeding under the second half of the reservation policy, and in applying the scourge to individuals and bands leaving their prescribed limits without authority, or for hostile purposes. This has been partly from a legitimate deference to the conviction of the great body of citizens that the Indians have been in the past unjustly and cruelly treated, and that great patience and long forbearance ought to be exercised in bringing them around to submission to the present reasonable requirements of the Government, and partly from the knowledge on the part of the officers of the Government charged with administering Indian affairs, that, from the natural jealousy of these people, their sense of wrongs suffered in the past, and their suspiciousness arising from repeated acts of treachery on the part of the whites; from the great distance of many bands and individuals from points of personal communication with the agents of the Government, and the absence of all means of written communication with them; from the efforts of abandoned and degraded whites, living among the Indians and exerting much influence over them, to misrepresent the policy of the Government, and to keep alive the hostility and suspicion of the savages; and lastly, from the extreme untrustworthiness of many of the interpreters on whom the Government is obliged to rely for bringing its intentions to the knowledge of the Indians: that by the joint effect of all these obstacles, many tribes and bands could come very slowly to hear, comprehend, and trust the professions and promises of the Government. . . .

The patience and forbearance exercised have been fully justified in their fruits. The main body of the roving Indians have, with good grace or with ill grace, submitted to the reservation system. Of those who still remain away from the assigned limits, by far the greater part are careful to do so with as little offense as possible. . . .

### THE BEGINNING OF THE END

It belongs not to a sanguine, but to a sober view of the situation, that three years will see the alternative of war eliminated from the Indian question, and the most powerful and hostile bands of to-day thrown in entire helplessness on the mercy of the Government. Indeed, the progress of two years more, if not of another summer, on the Northern Pacific Railroad will of itself completely solve the great Sioux problem, and leave the ninety thousand Indians ranging between the two trans-continental lines as incapable of resisting the Government as are the Indians of New York or Massachusetts.

*            *            *

. . . The railroads now under construction, or projected with a reasonable assurance of early completion, will multiply fourfold the striking force of the Army in that section; the little rifts of mining settlement, now found all through the mountains of the southern Territories will have become self-protecting communities; the feeble, wavering line of agricultual occupation, now sensitive to the faintest breath of Indian hostility, will then have grown to be the powerful "reserve" to lines still more closely advanced upon the last range of the intractable tribes.

### SUBMISSION THE ONLY HOPE OF THE INDIANS

No one certainly will rejoice more heartily than the present Commissioner when the Indians of this country cease to be in a position to dictate, in any form or degree, to the Government; when, in fact, the last hostile tribe becomes reduced to the condition of suppliants for charity. This is, indeed, the only hope of salvation for the aborigines of the continent. If they stand up against the progress of civilization and industry, they must be relentlessly crushed.

### THE CLAIMS OF THE INDIAN

The people of the United States can never without dishonor refuse to respect these two considerations: 1st. That this continent was originally owned and occupied by the Indians, who have on this account a claim somewhat larger than the privilege of one hundred and sixty acres of land, and "find himself" in tools and stock, which is granted as a matter of course to any newly-arrived foreigner who declares his intention to become a citizen; that something in the nature of an endowment, either capitalized or in the form of annual expenditures for a series of years for the benefit of the Indians, though at the discretion of the Government as to the specific objects, should be provided for every tribe or band which is deprived of its roaming privilege and confined to a diminished reservation: such an endowment being not in the nature of a gratuity, but in common honesty the right of the Indian on account of his original interest in the soil. 2d. That inasmuch as the progress of our industrial enterprise has cut these people off from modes of livelihood entirely sufficient for their wants, and for which they were qualified, in a degree which has been the wonder of more civilized races, by inherited aptitudes and by long pursuit, and has left them utterly without resource, they have a claim on this account again to temporary support and to such assistance as may be necessary to place them in a position to obtain a livelihood by means which shall be compatible with civilization.

*      *      *

... Surely there is obligation found in considerations like these, requiring us in some way, and in the best way, to make good to these original owners of the soil the loss by which we so greatly gain.

Can any principle of national morality be clearer than that, when the expansion and development of a civilized race involve the rapid destruction of the only means of subsistence possessed by the members of a less fortunate race, the higher is bound as of simple right to provide for the lower some substitute for the means of subsistence which it has destroyed? That substitute is, of course, best realized, not by systematic gratuities of food and clothing continued beyond a present emergency, but by directing these people to new pursuits which shall be consistent with the progress of civilization upon the continent; helping them over the first rough places on "the white man's road," and, meanwhile, supplying such subsistence as is absolutely necessary during the period of initiation and experiment....

## 150 "The paramount destiny and mission of woman . . . " (1872)

Activist women were a bulwark of the abolitionist movement, even though they maintained a lowered profile. After the Civil War and the emancipation of blacks, many of these American women turned their energies toward improving the professional and political opportunities of their gender. In early 1866, Elizabeth Cady Stanton alerted the American public to the fact that the proposed Fourteenth Amendment to the Constitution, by making reference to the "male inhabitants" and "male citizens," threatened the Women's Movement toward enfranchisement. Two years later, the national convention of the American Equal Rights Association sent a message to Congress that declared "Women and the colored men are loyal, patriotic, property-holding, taxpaying, liberty-loving citizens, and we cannot believe that sex or complexion should be any ground for civil or political degradation . . . [but] one-half of the citizens are disenfranchised by their sex and about one-eighth by the color of their skin."

The privileges and immunities clause of the newly-passed Fourteenth Amendment appeared to be the appropriate vehicle for pressing against state denial of equal rights to women. Overall, the effort was a failure. Myra Colby Bradwell applied for admission to the Illinois bar in 1869 after sitting for and passing the requisite examination. When the Illinois Supreme Court denied her admission on the grounds that she was a woman, Bradwell took her cause to the United States Supreme Court, arguing the right of all citizens to pursue an occupation. The court denied her relief. The concurring opinion by Justice Bradley set the court's approach to feminist issues for nearly a century by declaring that "the paramount destiny and mission of women are to fulfill the noble and benign offices of wife and mother. This is the law of the Creator."

## ☆ 150 *Bradwell v. Illinois*

83 U.S. ( 16 Wall.) 130 (1872).

Mr. Justice MILLER delivered the opinion of the court.

The record in this case is not very perfect, but it may be fairly taken that the plaintiff asserted her right to a license [to practice law] on the grounds, among others, that she was a citizen of the United States.

\*       \*       \*

In regard to that [fourteenth] amendment counsel for the plaintiff in this court truly says that there are certain privileges and immunities which belong to a citizen of the United States as such; otherwise it would be nonsense for the fourteenth amendment to prohibit a State from abridging them, and he proceeds to argue that admission to the bar of a State of a person who possesses the requisite learning and character is one of [the privileges and immunities of United States citizenship] which a State may not deny.

In this latter proposition we are not able to concur with counsel. We agree with him that there are privileges and immunities belonging to citizens of the United States. . . . But the right to admission to practice in the courts of a State is not one of them. This right in no sense depends on citizenship of the United States. It has not, as far as we know, ever been made in any State, or in any case, to depend on citizenship at all. . . . [S]o far as it can have any relation to citizenship at all, it would seem that, as to the courts of a State, it would relate to citizenship of the State, and as to Federal courts, it would relate to citizenship of the United States. . . .

. . . [T]he right to control and regulate the granting of license to practice law in the courts of a State is one of those powers which are not transferred for its protection to the Federal government, and its exercise is in no manner governed or controlled by citizenship of the United States in the party seeking such license. . . .

*Judgment affirmed.*

Mr. Justice BRADLEY:

I concur in the judgment of the court in this case, by which the judgment of the Supreme Court of Illinois is affirmed, but not for the reasons specified in the opinion just read.

The claim of the plaintiff, who is a married woman, to be admitted to practice as an attorney and counsellor-at-law, is based upon the supposed right of every person, man or woman, to engage in any lawful employment for a livelihood. The Supreme Court of Illinois denied the application on the ground that, by the common law, which is the basis of the laws of Illinois, only men were admitted to the bar, and the legislature had not made any change in

this respect. . . . In other respects it was left to the discretion of the court to establish the rules by which admission to the profession should be determined. The court, however, regarded itself as bound by at least two limitations. One was . . . that it should not admit any persons, or class of persons, not intended by the legislature to be admitted, even though not expressly excluded by statute. In view of this latter limitation the court felt compelled to deny the application of females to be admitted as members of the bar. Being contrary to the rules of the common law and the usages of Westminster Hall from time immemorial, it could not be supposed that the legislature had intended to adopt any different rule.

The claim . . . under the fourteenth amendment . . . assumes that [the right to pursue any lawful employment] is one of the privileges and immunities of women as citizens. . . .

It certainly cannot be affirmed, as an historical fact, that this has ever been established as one of the fundamental privileges and immunities of the sex. On the contrary, the civil law, as well as nature herself, has always recognized a wide difference in the respective spheres and destinies of man and woman. Man is, or should be, woman's protector and defender. The natural and proper timidity and delicacy which belongs to the female sex evidently unfits it for many of the occupations of civil life. The constitution of the family organization, which is founded in the divine ordinance, as well as in the nature of things, indicates the domestic sphere as that which properly belongs to the domain and functions of womanhood. The harmony, not to say identity, of interests and views which belong, or should belong, to the family institution is repugnant to the idea of a woman adopting a distinct and independent career from that of her husband. So firmly fixed was this sentiment in the founders of the common law that it became a maxim of that system of jurisprudence that woman had no legal existence separate from her husband, who was regarded as her head and representative in the social state; and, notwithstanding some recent modifications of this civil status, many of the special rules of law flowing from and dependent upon this cardinal principle still exist in full force in most States. One of these is, that a married woman is incapable, without her husband's consent, of making contracts which shall be binding on her or him. This very incapacity was one circumstance which the Supreme Court of Illinois deemed important in rendering a married woman incompetent fully to perform the duties and trusts that belong to the office of an attorney and counsellor.

It is true that many women are unmarried and not affected by any of the duties, complications, and incapacities arising out of the married state, but these are exceptions to the general rule. The paramount destiny and mission of woman are to fulfill the noble and benign offices of wife and mother. This is the law of the Creator. And the rules of civil society must be adapted to the general constitution of things, and cannot be based upon exceptional cases.

The humane movements of modern society, which have for their object the multiplication of avenues for woman's advancement, and of occupations adapted to her condition and sex, have my heartiest concurrence. But I am not prepared to say that it is one of her fundamental rights and privileges to be admitted into every office and position.... [I]n my opinion, in view of the peculiar characteristics, destiny, and mission of woman, it is within the province of the legislature to ordain what offices, positions, and callings shall be filled and discharged by men, and shall receive the benefit of those energies and responsibilities, and that decision and firmness which are presumed to predominate in the sterner sex.

For these reasons I think that the laws of Illinois now complained of are not obnoxious to the charge of abridging any of the privileges and immunities of citizens of the United States.

*     *     *

# 151 Defendant Is Indicted for Having Voted (1873)

Feminists claimed the Fourteenth Amendment's privileges and immunities clause abolished all state restrictions on the franchise. They argued that voting for a United States Congressman was a privilege of United States citizenship and that women were undeniably citizens. Women in several states attempted to vote in 1871 and 1872. Although the state of New York had limited the vote to members of the male sex, Susan B. Anthony and thirteen other women deliberately went to the polls in Rochester and succeeded in either registering or casting their ballots in the congressional elections. Ironically, the women were charged criminally under the 1870 Civil Rights Act for "having voted without the lawful right to vote." This prohibition was designed to prevent white voters from canceling out black votes by repeat voting and was never intended to be used against women suffragists. Anthony unsuccessfully set up the privileges and immunities clause as a defense to the crime, which carried a maximum jail term of three years.

☆ 151 *United States v. Anthony*

24 F. Cas. 829 (C.C.D. N.Y. 1873) (No. 14,459).

HUNT, Circuit Justice, after argument had been heard on the legal questions involved, ruled as follows:

*     *     *

It is charged that the defendant thus voted, she not having a right to vote, because she is a woman. The defendant insists that she has a right to vote; and that the provision of the constitution of this state, limiting the right to vote to persons of the male sex, is in violation of the fourteenth amendment of the constitution of the United States, and is void.

*     *     *

The right of voting, or the privilege of voting, is a right or privilege arising under the constitution of the state, and not under the constitution of the United States. The qualifications are different in the different states. Citizenship, age, sex, residence, are variously required in the different states, or may be so. If the right belongs to any particular person, it is because such person is entitled to it by the laws of the state where he offers to exercise it, and not because of citizenship of the United States. If the state of New York should provide that no person should vote until he had reached the age of thirty years, or after he had reached the age of fifty, or that no person having gray hair, or who had not the use of all his limbs, should be entitled to vote, I do not see how it could be held to be a violation of any right derived or held under the constitution of the United States. We might say that such regulations were unjust, tyrannical, unfit or the regulation of an intelligent state; but, if rights of a citizen are thereby violated, they are of that fundamental class, derived from his position as a citizen of the state, and not those limited rights belonging to him as a citizen of the United States....

*     *     *

... If the fifteenth amendment had contained the word "sex," the argument of the defendant would have been potent. She would have said, that an attempt by a state to deny the right to vote because one is of a particular sex is expressly prohibited by that amendment. The amendment, however, does not contain that word. It is limited to race, color, or previous condition of servitude. The legislature of the state of New York has seen fit to say, that the franchise of voting shall be limited to the male sex. In saying this, there is, in my judgment, no violation of the letter, or of the spirit, of the fourteenth or of the fifteenth amendment.

This view is assumed in the second section of the fourteenth amendment [reducing the representation of a state restricting the male franchise]. Not only does this section assume that the right of male inhabitants to vote was the especial object of its protection, but it assumes and admits the right of a state ... to deny to classes or portions of the male inhabitants the right to vote which is allowed to other male inhabitants. The regulation of the suffrage is thereby conceded to the states as a state's right.

\*         \*         \*

If she believed she had a right to vote, and voted in reliance upon that belief, does that relieve her from the penalty? . . . Two principles apply here: First, ignorance of the law excuses no one; second, every person is presumed to understand and to intend the necessary effects of his own acts. Miss Anthony knew that she was a woman, and that the constitution of this state prohibits her from voting. She intended to violate that provision—intended to test it, perhaps, but certainly intended to violate it. The necessary effect of her act was to violate it, and this she is presumed to have intended. There was no ignorance of any fact, but, all the facts being known, she undertook to settle a principle in her own person. She takes the risk, and she can not escape the consequences. . . . She voluntarily gave a vote which was illegal, and this is subject to the penalty of the law. . . .

\*         \*         \*

THE COURT declined to submit the case to the jury, on any question, and directed the jury to find a verdict of guilty. A request, by the defendant's counsel, that that jury be polled, was denied by THE COURT, and a verdict of guilty was recorded. . . .

HUNT, Circuit Justice, in denying the motion [for a new trial] said, in substance:

\*         \*         \*

. . . It is the duty of the jury to act upon the facts. It is the duty of the court to decide the law. The facts being specially found by the jury, it is the duty of the court, and not of the jury, to pronounce the judgment of guilty or not guilty. The facts being fully conceded, it is the duty of the court to announce and direct what the verdict shall be, whether guilty or not guilty. Therefore, I cannot doubt the power and the duty of the court to direct a verdict of guilty, whenever the facts constituting guilt are undisputed.

. . . Every fact in the case was undisputed. There was no inference to be drawn or point made on the facts, that could, by possibility, alter the result. It was, therefore, not only the right, but it seems to me, upon the authorities, the plain duty of the judge to direct a verdict of guilty. The motion for a new trial is denied.

## 152 "The Court orders the prisoner to sit down" (1873)

Prior to sentencing, Susan B. Anthony articulated the inequities of the judicial process which she had experienced as well as the ultimate justice of the cause for which she had acted. In conformity with her principles, she refused to pay the one-hundred-dollar fine imposed. The judge, in turn, refused to jail Anthony for failure to pay the fine, precluding an appeal to the Supreme Court which she greatly desired.

## ☆ 152  Susan B. Anthony's Statement to the Court (1873)

Reprinted in E. C. Stanton, S. B. Anthony, and M. J. Gage, eds., *History of Woman Suffrage* (New York: Fowler & Wells, 1881), 2:687-89.

\*         \*         \*

[JUDGE HUNT]: The prisoner will stand up. Has the prisoner anything to say why sentence shall not be pronounced?

MISS ANTHONY: Yes, your honor, I have many things to say; for in your ordered verdict of guilty, you have trampled underfoot, every vital principle of our government. My natural rights, my civil rights, my political rights, are all alike ignored. Robbed of the fundamental privilege of citizenship, I am degraded from the status of a citizen to that of a subject; and not only myself individually, but all of my sex, are, by your honor's verdict, doomed to political subjection under this so-called republican government.

JUDGE HUNT: The Court can not listen to a rehearsal of arguments the prisoner's counsel has already consumed three hours in presenting.

MISS ANTHONY: May it please your honor, I am not arguing the question, but simply stating the reasons why sentence can not, in justice, be pronounced against me. Your denial of my citizen's right to vote is the denial of my right of consent as one of the governed, the denial of my right of representation as one of the taxed, the denial of my right to a trial by a jury of my peers as an offender against the law, therefore, the denial of my sacred rights to life, liberty, property, and—

JUDGE HUNT: The Court can not allow the prisoner to go on.

\*         \*         \*

MISS ANTHONY: Of all my prosecutors, . . . not one is my peer, but each and all are my political sovereigns; and had your honor submitted my case to the jury, as was clearly your duty, even then I should have had just cause of protest, for not one of those men was my peer; but, native or foreign, white or black, rich or poor, educated or ignorant, awake or asleep, sober or drunk, each and every man of them was my political superior; hence, in no sense, my peer. . . . [J]ury, judge, counsel, must all be of the superior class.

JUDGE HUNT: The Court must insist—the prisoner has been tried according to the established forms of law.

MISS ANTHONY: Yes, your honor, but by forms of law all made by men, interpreted by men, administered by men, in favor of men, and against women; and hence, your honor's ordered verdict of guilty, against a United States citizen for the exercise of "that citizen's right to vote," simply because that citizen was a woman and not a man. But, yesterday, the same man-made forms of law declared it a crime punishable with $1,000 fine and six months' imprisonment, for you, or me, or any of us, to give a cup of cold water, a crust of bread, or a night's shelter to a panting fugitive as he was tracking his way to Canada. And every man or woman in whose veins coursed a drop of human sympathy violated that wicked law, reckless of consequences, and was justified in so doing. As then the slaves who got their freedom [had to] take it over, or under, or through the unjust forms of law, precisely so now must women, to get their right to a voice in this Government, take it; and I have taken mine, and mean to take it at every possible opportunity.

JUDGE HUNT: The Court orders the prisoner to sit down. It will not allow another word.

MISS ANTHONY: When I was brought before your honor for trial, I hoped for a broad and liberal interpretation of the Constitution and its recent amendments, that should declare all United States citizens under its protecting aegis—that should declare equality of rights the national guarantee to all persons born or naturalized in the United States. But failing to get this justice—failing, even, to get a trial by a jury *not* of my peers—I ask not leniency at your hands—but rather the full rigors of the law.

JUDGE HUNT: The Court must insist—[Here the prisoner sat down.]

JUDGE HUNT: The prisoner will stand up. [Here Miss Anthony arose again.] The sentence of the Court is that you pay a fine of one hundred dollars and the costs of the prosecution.

MISS ANTHONY: May it please your honor, I shall never pay a dollar of your unjust penalty. All the stock in trade I possess is a $10,000 debt, incurred by publishing my paper—*The Revolution*—four years ago, the sole object of which was to educate all women to do precisely as I have done, rebel against your man-made, unjust, unconstitutional forms of law, that tax, fine, imprison, and hang women, while they deny them the right of representation in the Government; and I shall work on with might and main to pay every dollar of that honest debt, but not a penny shall go to this unjust claim. And I shall earnestly and persistently continue to urge all women to the practical recognition of the old revolutionary maxim, that "Resistance to tyranny is obedience to God."

JUDGE HUNT: Madam, the Court will not order you committed until the fine is paid.

## 153 "The government of the Confederate States. . . . had no existence" (1874)

Sprott, a purchaser of cotton from the Confederate government, sought to recover the proceeds of the sale of that cotton after its capture by Union forces. The stridency of the majority opinion, nine years after the cessation of hostilities, demonstrated that the wounds of the war had not healed. Noting that Sprott had given "aid and assistance to the rebellion," and that the Confederacy had no legal status, the court denied the claim.

☆ 153  *Sprott v. United States*

87 U.S. (20 Wall.) 459 (1874).

Mr. Justice MILLER delivered the opinion of the court. . . . Whether the temporary government of the Confederate States . . . is to be recognized as having been a *de facto* government, and if so, what consequences follow in regard to its transactions . . . is [of] no necessity in the present case.

\*            \*            \*

. . . [C]otton was the principal support of the rebellion, so far as pecuniary aid was necessary to its support. . . . So long as the imperfect blockade of the Southern ports and the unguarded condition of the Mexican frontier enabled them to export this cotton, they were well supplied in return with arms, ammunition, medicine, and the necessaries of life not grown within their lines, as well as with that other great sinew of war, gold. If the rebel government could freely have exchanged the cotton of which it was enabled to possess itself, for the munitions of war or for gold, it seems very doubtful if it could have been suppressed. So when the rigor of the blockade prevented successful export of this cotton, their next resource was to sell it among their own people, or to such persons claiming outwardly to be loyal to the United States, as would buy of them, for the money necessary to support the tottering fabric of rebellion which they called a government.

The cotton which is the subject of this controversy was of this class. It had been in the possession and under the control of the Confederate government, with claim of title. It was captured . . . and sold . . . and the money deposited in the treasury.

The claimant now asserts a right to this money . . . by showing that he purchased it of the Confederate government and paid them for it in money. In doing this he gave aid and assistance to the rebellion in the most efficient manner he possibly could. He could not have aided that cause more acceptably if he had entered its service and become a blockade-runner, or under the guise of a privateer had preyed upon the unoffending commerce of his country. It is asking too much of a court of law sitting under the authority of the government then struggling for existence against a treason respectable only for the numbers and the force by which it was supported, to hold that one of its own citizens, owing and acknowledging to it allegiance, can by the proof of such a transaction establish a title to the property so obtained. . . . A clearer case of turpitude in the consideration of a contract can hardly be imagined unless treason be taken out of the catalogue of crimes.

The case is not relieved of its harsh features by the finding of the court that the claimant did not *intend* to aid the rebellion, but only to make money. It might as well be said that the man who would sell for a sum far beyond its value to a lunatic, a weapon with which he knew the latter would kill himself, only intended to make money and did not intend to aid the lunatic in his fatal purpose. . . .

The recognition of the existence and the validity of the acts of the so called Confederate government, and that of the States which yielded a temporary support to that government, stand on very different grounds, and are governed by very different considerations.

. . . [The laws of the States] were the same, with slight exceptions, whether the authorities of the State acknowledged allegiance to the true or the false Federal power. They . . . must be respected in their administration under whatever temporary dominant authority they may be exercised. It is only when in the use of these powers substantial aid and comfort was given or intended to be given to the rebellion, when the functions necessarily reposed in the State for the maintenance of civil society were perverted to the manifest and intentional aid of treason against the government of the Union, that their acts are void.

The government of the Confederate States can receive no aid from this course of reasoning. It had no existence, except as a conspiracy to overthrow lawful authority. Its foundation was treason against the existing Federal government. . . .

When it was overthrown it perished totally. It left no laws, no statutes, no decrees, no authority which can give support to any contract, or any act done in its service, or in aid of its purpose, or which contributed to protract its existence. So far as the actual exercise of its physical power was brought to bear upon individuals, that may, under some circumstances, constitute a justification or excuse for acts otherwise indefensible, but no validity can be given in the courts of this country to acts voluntarily performed in direct aid and support of its unlawful purpose. . . .

*Judgment affirmed.*

\*          \*          \*

Mr. Justice FIELD, dissenting.

\*          \*          \*

. . . The question, and the only question, is whether the cotton . . . was at the time the property of the claimant. . . . [W]e are not concerned with the consideration of his loyalty or disloyalty. He was a citizen of Mississippi and resided within the lines of the Confederacy, and the act forbidding intercourse with the enemy does not apply to his case. He was subject to be treated, in common with other citizens of the Confederacy, as a public enemy during the continuance of the war. And if he were disloyal in fact, [he was pardoned] and if by his purchase of the cotton he gave aid and comfort to the rebellion, as this court adjudges, the impediment which such conduct previously interposed to the prosecution of his claim was removed by the proclamation of pardon and amnesty made by the President on the 25th day of December, 1868. . . . In legal contemplation the executive pardon not merely releases an offender from the punishment prescribed for his offence, but it obliterates the offence itself.

\*          \*          \*

Now, . . . the confiscation of private property of persons engaged in the rebellion require[s] legal proceedings resulting in a judicial decree of condemnation before the title of the owner can be divested. . . . No proceedings for the condemnation and forfeiture of the cotton seized, or of its proceeds, have ever been instituted by the government. The title of the claimant remains, therefore, at this day, as perfect as it did on the day the cotton was seized.

\*          \*          \*

## 154 "all citizens . . . were not invested with the right of suffrage" (1874)

Despite the inability of Susan B. Anthony to appeal her conviction to the Supreme Court, the issue of women's suffrage was presented to the court in 1874. Virginia L. Minor and her husband, Francis, instituted legal action against Reese Happersett, a Missouri registering officer, for refusal to register the wife as a lawful voter. When the case, which relied on the Fourteenth Amendment to press Mrs. Minor's claim, reached the Supreme Court, the court construed the amendment narrowly, denying that it had any impact on the status of women. Significantly, the court made no reference to the equal protection requirement that had figured so prominently in Anthony's case.

☆ 154 *Minor v. Happersett*

88 U.S. (21 Wall.) 162 (1874).

The CHIEF JUSTICE delivered the opinion of the court.

The question is presented in this case, whether, since the adoption of the fourteenth amendment, a woman, who is a citizen of the United States and of the State of Missouri, is a voter in that State, notwithstanding the provision of the constitution and laws of the State, which confine the right of suffrage to men alone. We might, perhaps, decide the case upon other grounds, but this question is fairly made. From the opinion we find that it was the only one decided in the court below, and it is the only one which has been argued here. The case was undoubtedly brought to this court for the sole purpose of having that question decided by us, and in view of the evident propriety there is of having it settled, so far as it can be by such a decision, we have concluded to waive all other considerations and proceed at once to its determination.

It is contended that the provisions of the constitution and laws of the State of Missouri which confine the right of suffrage and registration therefor to men, are in violation of the Constitution of the United States, and therefore void. The argument is, that as a woman, born or naturalized in the United States and subject to the jurisdiction thereof, is a citizen of the United States and of the State in which she resides, she has the right of suffrage as one of the privileges and immunities of her citizenship, which the State cannot by its laws or constitution abridge.

There is no doubt that women may be citizens. They are persons, and by the fourteenth amendment "all persons born or naturalized in the United States and subject to the jurisdiction thereof" are expressly declared to be "citizens of the United States and of the State wherein they reside." But, in our opinion, it did not need this amendment to give them that position. Before its adoption the Constitution of the United States did not in terms prescribe who should be citizens of the United States or of the several States, yet there were necessarily such citizens without such provision. There cannot be a nation without a people. The very idea of a political community, such as a nation is, implies an association of persons for the promotion of their general welfare. Each one of the persons associated becomes a member of the nation formed by the association. He owes it allegiance and is entitled to its protection. Allegiance and protection are, in this connection, reciprocal obligations. The one is a compensation for the other; allegiance for protection and protection for allegiance.

For convenience it has been found necessary to give a name to this membership. The object is to designate by a title the person and the relation he bears to the nation. For this purpose the words "subject," "inhabitant," and "citizen" have been used, and the choice between them is sometimes made to depend upon the form of the government. Citizen is now more commonly employed, however, and as it has been considered better suited to the description of one living under a republican government, it was adopted by nearly all of the States upon their separation from Great Britain and was afterwards adopted in the Articles of Confederation and in the Constitution of the United States. When used in this sense it is understood as conveying the idea of membership of a nation, and nothing more.

To determine, then, who were citizens of the United States before the adoption of the amendment it is necessary to ascertain what persons originally associated themselves together to form the nation, and what were afterwards admitted to membership.

\*          \*          \*

... [S]ex has never been made one of the elements of citizenship in the United States. In this respect men have never had an advantage over women. The same laws precisely apply to both. The fourteenth amendment did not affect the citizenship of women any more than it did of men. In this particular, therefore, the rights of Mrs. Minor do not depend upon the amendment. She has always been a citizen from her birth, and entitled to all the privileges and immunities of citizenship. The amendment prohibited the State, of which she is a citizen, from abridging any of her privileges and immunities as a citizen of the United States; but it did not confer citizenship on her. That she had before its adoption.

If the right of suffrage is one of the necessary privileges of a citizen of the United States, then the constitution and laws of Missouri confining it to men are in violation of the Constitution of the United States, as amended, and consequently void. The direct question is, therefore, presented whether all citizens are necessarily voters.

The Constitution does not define the privileges and immunities of citizens. For that definition we must look elsewhere. In this case we need not determine what they are, but only whether suffrage is necessarily one of them.

It certainly is nowhere made so in express terms. . . .

\*          \*          \*

The [fourteenth] amendment did not add to the privileges and immunities of a citizen. It simply furnished an additional guaranty for the protection of such as he already had. No new voters were necessarily made by it. Indirectly it may have had that effect, because it may have increased the number of citizens entitled to suffrage under the constitution and laws of the States, but it operates for this purpose, if at all, through the States and the State laws, and not directly upon the citizen.

It is clear, therefore, we think, that the Constitution has not added the right of suffrage to the privileges and immunities of citizenship as they existed at the time it was adopted. This makes it proper to inquire whether suffrage was coextensive with the citizenship of the States at the time of its adoption.

\*       \*       \*

... [A]ll the citizens of the States were not invested with the right of suffrage. In all, save perhaps New Jersey, this right was only bestowed upon men and not upon all of them.... Women were excluded from suffrage in nearly all the States by the express provision of their constitutions and laws.

\*       \*       \*

Certainly, if the courts can consider any question settled, this is one. For nearly ninety years the people have acted upon the idea that the Constitution, when it conferred citizenship, did not necessarily confer the right of suffrage. If uniform practice long continued can settle the construction of so important an instrument as the Constitution of the United States confessedly is, most certainly it has been done here. Our province is to decide what the law is, not to declare what it should be.

We have given this case the careful consideration its importance demands. If the law is wrong, it ought to be changed; but the power for that is not with us. The arguments addressed to us bearing upon such a view of the subject may perhaps be sufficient to induce those having the power, to make the alteration but they ought not to be permitted to influence our judgment in determining the present rights of the parties now litigating before us. No argument as to woman's need of suffrage can be considered. We can only act upon her rights as they exist. It is not for us to look at the hardship of withholding. Our duty is at an end if we find it is within the power of a State to withhold.

Being unanimously of the opinion that the Constitution of the United States does not confer the right of suffrage upon any one, and that the constitutions and laws of the several States which commit that important trust to men alone are not necessarily void, we

*Affirm the judgment.*

## 155 "the rights of one citizen as against another" (1876)

In *United States v. Cruikshank* the United States Supreme Court had before it the convictions of three whites who were among a mob that had broken up a meeting of blacks, killing two participants. The meeting had been called to discuss local Louisiana elections. The fundamental question was whether newly enfranchised blacks would be able to rely on the power of the federal government to protect their exercise of political rights or whether that protection would be withdrawn.

The defendants were convicted in federal court for their politically motivated act of terrorism under Section 6 of the 1866 Civil Rights Act. The Supreme Court reversed the convictions. In its decision, the court relied on the State Action Doctrine, that is, that the Fourteenth Amendment guaranteed the rights of citizens only against encroachment by the state or its agents, not against actions by private individuals. While the language of Section 6 was left intact, its protective application was limited to safeguarding federally- rather than state-derived rights. The State Action Doctrine subsequently was used to invalidate major provisions of the 1875 Civil Rights Act which imposed penalties on private individuals who discriminated against blacks. The grounds for invalidation were that Congress did not intend such a broad grant of legislative power in the Fourteenth Amendment, which was only to be restrictive of the states. Thus, the judicial branch eliminated the authority of the federal law to protect racial minorities from resurgent white domination as Reconstruction ended and the franchise was extended to former rebels. Blacks could resort only to unsympathetic state officials to remedy terrorist violations of their rights by private parties.

☆ 155  *United States v. Cruikshank*

92 U.S. 542 (1876).

MR. CHIEF JUSTICE WAITE delivered the opinion of the court.

\*       \*       \*

The general charge in the first eight counts is that of "banding," and in the second eight, that of "conspiring" together to injure, oppress, threaten, and intimidate Levi Nelson and Alexander Tillman, citizens of the United States, of African descent and persons of color, with the intent thereby to hinder and prevent them in their free exercise and enjoyment of rights and privileges "granted and secured" to them "in common with all other good citizens of the United States by the constitution and laws of the United States."

\*       \*       \*

We have in our political system a government of the United States and a government of each of the several States. Each one of these governments is distinct from the others, and each has citizens of its own who owe it allegiance, and whose rights, within its jurisdiction, it must protect. The same person may be at the same time a citizen of the United States and a citizen of a State, but his rights of citizenship under one of these governments will be different from those he has under the other.

\*       \*       \*

The first and ninth counts state the intent of the defendants to have been to hinder and prevent the citizens named in the free exercise and enjoyment of their "lawful right and privilege to peaceably assemble together with each other and with other citizens of the United States for a peaceful and lawful purpose."...

\*　　\*　　\*

The particular amendment [the first] now under consideration assumes the existence of the right of the people to assemble for lawful purposes, and protects it against encroachment by Congress. The right was not created by the amendment; neither was its continuance guaranteed, except as against congressional interference. For their protection in its enjoyment, therefore, the people must look to the States. The power for that purpose was originally placed there, and it has never been surrendered to the United States.

The right of the people peaceably to assemble for the purpose of petitioning Congress for a redress of grievances, or for any thing else connected with the powers of the duties of the national government, is an attribute of national citizenship, and, as such, under the protection of, and guaranteed by, the United States.... If it had been alleged in these counts that the object of the defendants was to prevent a meeting for such a purpose, the case would have been within the statute, and within the scope of the sovereignty of the United States. Such, however, is not the case. The offence, as stated in the indictment, will be made out, if it be shown that the object of the conspiracy was to prevent a meeting for any lawful purpose whatever.

\*　　\*　　\*

The fourteenth amendment prohibits a State from depriving any person of life, or property, without due process of law; but this adds nothing to the rights of one citizen as against another....

... When stripped of its verbiage, the case as presented amounts to nothing more than that the defendants conspired to prevent certain citizens of the United States, being within the State of Louisiana, from enjoying the equal protection of the laws of the State and of the United States.

[B]ut [the equal protection clause] does not ... add any thing to the rights which one citizen has ... against another.

\*　　\*　　\*

The seventh and fifteenth counts are no better than the sixth and fourteenth. The intent here charged is to put the parties named in great fear of bodily harm, and to injure and oppress them, because, being and having been in all things qualified, they had voted.... There is nothing to show that the elections voted at were any other than State elections, or that the conspiracy was formed on account of the race of the parties against whom the conspirators were to act. The charge as made is re-

ally of nothing more than a conspiracy to commit a breach of the peace within a State. Certainly it will not be claimed that the United States have the power or are required to do mere police duty in the States. If a State cannot protect itself against domestic violence, the United States may, upon the call of the executive, when the legislature cannot be convened, lend their assistance for that purpose. This is a guaranty of the Constitution (art. 4, sect. 4); but it applies to no case like this.

\*　　\*　　\*

*The order of the Circuit Court arresting the judgment upon the verdict is, therefore, affirmed; and the cause remanded, with instructions to discharge the defendants.*

## 156  Rifle Clubs (1876)

With the post-Civil War disenfranchisement of nearly all the native white populations of the Southern states, political power rested in the hands of blacks and whites sympathetic to the Radical Republican powers in Washington. President Grant's administration was not known for its integrity, and the corruption of the national party infected the "occupation" administrations in the former Confederate states. One by one, as civil disabilities were gradually removed from Confederate soldiers and officers, and as the growth of the Ku Klux Klan and other terrorist organizations increasingly intimidated the black population, states were returning to native white rule. By 1876, the remaining strictly Republican Southern states were Florida, Louisiana, and South Carolina. In South Carolina the Republican officeholders were severely challenged both in the community and at the polls by the Democratic "Red Shirts" led by General Wade Hampton. Ostensibly a faction of the Democratic party, the "Red Shirts" (named for their "uniform") were an irregular militia whose purpose was to protect Democratic whites and blacks from official militias and unofficial mobs controlled by the Republicans. In the face of the armed clashes between blacks and whites—some political and some racial—and the growing tensions of the impending political campaign, Governor Chamberlain appealed to President Grant to permit the use of the federal troops stationed in South Carolina. Grant obliged, and martial law was declared in several counties shortly before the election.

## ☆ 156 Grant's Proclamation of Insurrection in South Carolina

Reprinted in J. Richardson, ed., *A Compilation of the Messages and Papers of the Presidents* (New York: Bureau of National Literature, 1917), 396.

Whereas it has been satisfactorily shown to me that insurrection and domestic violence exist in several counties of the State of South Carolina, and that certain combinations of men against law exist in many counties of said State known as "rifle clubs," who ride up and down by day and night in arms, murdering some peaceable citizens and intimidating others, which combinations, though forbidden by the laws of the State, can not be controlled or suppressed by the ordinary course of justice; and

Whereas it is provided in the Constitution of the United States that the United States shall protect every State in this Union, on application of the legislature, or of the executive (when the legislature can not be convened), against domestic violence; and

Whereas by laws in pursuance of the above it is provided (in the laws of the United States) that in all cases of insurrection in any State or of obstruction to the laws thereof it shall be lawful for the President of the United States, on application of the legislature of such State, or of the executive (when the legislature can not be convened), to call forth the militia of any other State or States, or to employ such part of the land and naval forces as shall be judged necessary, for the purpose of suppressing such insurrection or causing the laws to be duly executed; and

Whereas the legislature of said State is not now in session and can not be convened in time to meet the present emergency, and the executive of said State, under section 4 of Article IV of the Constitution of the United States and the laws passed in pursuance thereof, has therefore made due application to me in the premises for such part of the military force of the United States as may be necessary and adequate to protect said State and the citizens thereof against domestic violence and to enforce the due execution of the laws; and

Whereas it is required that whenever it may be necessary, in the judgment of the President, to use the military force for the purpose aforesaid, he shall forthwith, by proclamation, command such insurgents to disperse and retire peaceably to their respective homes within a limited time:

Now, therefore, I, Ulysses S. Grant, President of the United States, do hereby make proclamation and command all persons engaged in said unlawful and insurrectionary proceedings to disperse and retire peaceably to their respective abodes within three days from this date, and hereafter abandon said combinations and submit themselves to the laws and constituted authorities of said State.

And I invoke the aid and cooperation of all good citizens thereof to uphold the laws and preserve the public peace.

\*     \*     \*

U. S. GRANT

By the President:

JOHN L. CADWALADER, Acting Secretary of State

## 157 "insurrectionary forces too powerful to be resisted" (1877)

1876 witnessed not only the hotly contested Hayes-Tilden presidential election but also a virtual coup d' état in South Carolina. Disputed election returns from South Carolina counties previously declared by President Grant to be in a state of rebellion caused the division of the state legislature into two factions. Each side met separately, claimed to be the legitimate authority of the state, and installed its own governor in December of 1876. For over three months there were two rival governments in the state, each promulgating the illegality of the other. The federal troops, on the orders of Grant, supported the administration of Republican D. H. Chamberlain against the claims of Democrat Wade Hampton. Congress implicitly seconded this acknowledgment of Chamberlain as the governor of South Carolina by its recognition of the Republican delegates to the Electoral College.

Although Chamberlain thus had been recognized by the United States as the legitimate governor of South Carolina, President Hayes's administration (in exchange, for congressional Democratic acquiescence to his election) decided to withdraw the federal troops from South Carolina as of April 10, 1877. Without federal support, Chamberlain's administration fell, and he retired to self-imposed exile in his native Massachusetts. Wade Hampton acceded to the undisputed governorship of the state on April 11. The resignation of Republican legislators gave the Democrats full control of the legislature. Several indictments were issued against Chamberlain and officeholders under his administration for fraud, graft, and corruption, but since they had fled, they were never tried. Subsequently, the actions and obligations of the "unlawful" Chamberlain regime were repudiated by the new government. The following documents relate to the transfer of lawful authority from "Governor" Chamberlain to "Governor" Hampton. Even while graciously abdicating, Chamberlain's parting message excoriated the federal government for failing to support his "lawful" administration against "insurrectionary forces."

## ☆ 157 Abdication of Governor D. H. Chamberlain

Reprinted in W. Allen, *Governor Chamberlain's Administration in South Carolina* (New York: Negro Universities Press, 1969), 480.

## ☆ 157a Letter from the Heads of Departments

Executive Department
Office of Attorney General
Columbia, S. C., April 10, 1877

To His Excellency, D. H. Chamberlain, Governor of South Carolina, Columbia, S. C.:

DEAR SIR—...

Whilst we are no less inspired with admiration for the dignified and resolute manner in which you have consistently maintained your claims to the gubernatorial chair, by virtue of the election held in November last, than we are solemnly impressed with the validity of your title to the office, we are unanimous in the belief that to prolong the contest, in the absence of that moral aid to which we feel ourselves and our party justly entitled at the hands of a National Administration installed, in large measure, through the same agencies which are now held to be insufficient for our maintenance, will be to incur the responsibility of keeping alive partisan prejudices which are in the last degree detrimental to the best interests of the people of the State; and perhaps of precipitating a physical conflict that could have but one result to our defenceless constituency. We cannot afford to contribute, however indirectly, to such a catastrophe, even in the advocacy of what we know to be our right.

We are agreed, therefore, in counselling you to discontinue the struggle for the occupancy of the gubernatorial chair, convinced as we are that, in view of the disastrous odds to which its maintenance has been subjected by the action of the National Administration, your retirement will involve no surrender of principle, nor its motive be misapprehended by the great body of that political party to which, in common with ourselves, you are attached, and whose success in the past in this State has been ennobled by your intelligent and unselfish services.

We have the honor to be, very respectfully, yours,

ROBERT B. ELLIOTT, Attorney General
JOHN R. TOLBERT, Superintendent of Education
JAMES KENNEDY, Adjutant and Inspector General
THOMAS C. DUNN, Comptroller General
F. L. CARDOZO, Treasurer
H. E. HAYNES, Secretary of State

## ☆ 157b Correspondence between the Governors

State of South Carolina
Executive Chamber
Columbia, S. C., April 10, 1877

SIR—

Having learned that you now purpose to turn over to me the Executive Chamber, with the records and papers belonging to the Executive Office, now in your possession, I beg to inform you that I will send a proper officer to receive the same at any hour you may indicate as most convenient to yourself.

I am, very respectfully, your obedient servant,

WADE HAMPTON, Governor

State of South Carolina
Executive Chamber
Columbia, S. C., April 10, 1877

SIR—

Replying to your note of this date, I have to say that my Private Secretary will meet such officer as you may designate, at twelve meridian to-morrow, at the Executive Chamber, for the purpose indicated in your note.

Very respectfully,

D. H. CHAMBERLAIN, Governor S. C.

## ☆ 157c Chamberlain's Abdication Address

TO THE REPUBLICANS OF SOUTH CAROLINA:

By your choice I was made Governor of this State in 1874. At the election on the 7th of November last, I was again, by your votes, elected to the same office. My title to the office, upon every legal and moral ground, is to-day clear and perfect. By the recent decision and action of the President of the United States, I find myself unable longer to maintain my official rights, and I hereby announce to you that I am unwilling to prolong a struggle which can only bring further suffering upon those who engage in it.

In announcing this conclusion, it is my duty to say for you, that the Republicans of South Carolina entered upon their recent political struggle for the maintenance of their political and civil rights. Constituting, beyond question, a large majority of the lawful voters of the State, you allied yourselves with that political party whose central and inspiring principle has hitherto been the civil and political freedom of all men under the Constitution and laws of our country. By heroic efforts and sacrifices which the just verdict history will rescue from the cowardly scorn now cast upon them by political placemen and traders, you secured the electoral vote of South Carolina for Hayes and Wheeler. In accomplishing this result, you became the victims of every form of persecution and injury. From authentic evidence it is shown that not less than one hundred of your number were murdered because they were faithful to their principles and exercised rights solemnly guaranteed to them by the nation. You were denied employment, driven from your homes, robbed of the earnings of years of honest industry, hunted for your lives like wild beasts, your families outraged and scattered, for no offence except your peaceful and firm determination to exercise your political rights. You trusted, as you had a right to trust, that if by such efforts you established the lawful supremacy of your political party in the nation, the Government of the United States, in the discharge of its constitutional duty, would protect the lawful Government of the State from overthrow at the hands of your political enemies. From causes patent to all men, and questioned by none who regard truth, you have been unable to overcome the unlawful combinations and obstacles which have opposed the practical supremacy of the Government which your votes have established.

... To-day—April 10, 1877—by the order of the President whom your votes alone rescued from overwhelming defeat, the Government of the United States abandons you, deliberately withdraws from you its support, with the full knowledge that the lawful Government of the State will be speedily overthrown. By a new interpretation of the Constitution of the United States at variance alike with the previous practice of the Government and with the decisions of the Supreme Court, the Executive of the United States evades the duty of ascertaining which of two rival State Governments is the lawful one, and by the withdrawal of troops now protecting the State from domestic violence, abandons the lawful State Government to a struggle with insurrectionary forces too powerful to be resisted. ...

No effective means of resistance to the consummation of the wrong are left. The struggle can be prolonged. My strict legal rights are, of course, wholly unaffected by the action of the President. No Court of the State has jurisdiction to pass upon the title of my office. No lawful Legislature can be convened except at my call. If the use of these powers promised ultimate success to our cause, I should not shrink from any sacrifices which might confront me. It is a cause in which by the light of reason and conscience a man might well lay down his life.

But, to my mind, my present responsibility involves the consideration of the effect of my action upon those whose representative I am. I have hitherto been willing to ask you, Republicans, to risk all dangers and endure all hardships until relief should come from the Government of the United States. That relief will never come. I cannot ask you to follow me further. In my best judgment I can no longer serve you by further resistance to the impending calamity.

With gratitude to God for the measure of endurance with which He has hitherto inspired me, with gratitude to you for your boundless confidence in me, with profound admiration for your matchless fidelity to the cause in which we have struggled, I now announce to you and to the people of the State that I shall no longer actively assert my right to the office of Governor of South Carolina.

The motives and purposes of the President of the United States in the policy which compels me to my present course are unquestionably honorable and patriotic. I devoutly pray that events may vindicate the wisdom of his action, and that peace, justice, freedom, and prosperity may hereafter be the portion of every citizen of South Carolina.

D. H. CHAMBERLAIN, Governor of South Carolina

## 158 To Secure to the Toilers a Proper Share of the Wealth (1878)

American labor's dissatisfaction with the economic conditions of the working men and women gave rise, from time to time, to concerted economic and political action. In 1860, Massachusetts shoemakers in Lynn and Natick struck for higher wages, and the strike spread to some twenty thousand New England workers.

The labor movement in the United States underwent a marked transition during the decade of the 1870s. During the economic depression of 1873-74, employer opposition to trade unions became bitter. Union workers suffered lockouts and blacklists. Concerted activity and strikes by workers often were prosecuted under criminal conspiracy laws. Since open unions could not survive, labor leaders met secretly and formed "nonpublic" labor societies. The leading organization of this type in the 1870s was the Noble Order of the Knights of Labor, formed in Philadelphia by Uriah Smith in 1869. At the society's convention at Reading in January of 1878, the Knights of Labor organized as a national labor union, which, at its height in the mid-1880s, claimed membership of over 700,000 workers. In the organization's constitution, which proclaimed adherence to democratic and egalitarian doctrines, the Knights focused their attention on the manner in which the law gave unfair advantage to the forces of capital in its resistance to the social and economic agenda of labor. The perceived injustice of these laws provided the foundation for common and honorable disobedience to them and their enforcers.

## ☆ 158 Constitution of the Knights of Labor: Preamble (January 1, 1878)

Reprinted in T. V. Powderly, *Thirty Years of Labor* (Columbus, Ohio: Excelsior, 1980), 243.

The alarming development and aggressiveness of the power of money and corporations under the present industrial and political systems will inevitably lead to the hopeless degradation of the people. It is imperative, if we desire to enjoy the full blessings of life, that unjust accumulation and this power for evil of aggregated wealth shall be prevented. This much-desired object can be accomplished only by the united efforts of those who obey the divine injunction: "In the sweat of thy face shalt thou eat bread." Therefore we have formed the order of the Knights of Labor for the purpose of organizing, educating, and directing the power of the industrial masses.

It is not a political party; it is more, for in it are crystallized sentiments and measures for the benefit of the whole people; but it should be borne in mind, when exercising the right of suffrage, that most of the objects herein set forth can only be obtained through legislation, and that it is the duty, regardless of party, of all to assist in nominating and supporting with their votes such candidates as will support these measures. No one shall, however, be compelled to vote with the majority.

Calling upon all who believe in securing "the greatest good to the greatest number" to join and assist us, we declare to the world that our aims are:

I. To make industrial and moral worth, not wealth, the true standard of individual and national greatness.

II. To secure to the workers the full enjoyment of the wealth they create; sufficient leisure in which to develop their intellectual, moral, and social faculties; all of the benefits, recreations, and pleasures of association; in a word, to enable them to share in the gains and honor of advancing civilization.

In order to secure these results, we demand at the hands of the law-making power of municipality, State, and nation:

III. The establishment of the referendum in the making of all laws.

IV. The establishment of bureaus of labor statistics, that we may arrive at a correct knowledge of the educational, moral, and financial condition of the laboring masses, and the establishment of free State labor bureaus.

V. The land, including all the natural sources of wealth, is the heritage of all the people, and should not be subject to speculative traffic. Occupancy and use should be the only title to the possession of land. The taxes upon land should be levied upon its full value for use, exclusive of improvements, and should be sufficient to take for the community all unearned increment.

VI. The abrogation of all laws that do not bear equally upon capitalists and laborers, and the removal of unjust technicalities, delays, and discriminations in the administration of justice.

VII. The adoption of measures providing for the health and safety of those engaged in mining, manufacturing, and building industries, and for indemnification to those engaged therein for injuries received through lack of necessary safeguards.

VIII. The recognition, by incorporation, of orders and other associations organized by the workers to improve their condition and to protect their rights.

IX. The enactment of laws to compel corporations to pay their employees weekly, in lawful money, for the labor of the preceding week, and giving mechanics and laborers a first lien upon the product of their labor to the extent of their full wages.

X. The abolition of the contract system on national, State, and municipal works.

XI. The enactment of laws providing for arbitration between employers and employed, and to enforce the decision of the arbitrators.

XII. The prohibition by law of the employment of children under fifteen years of age; the compulsory attendance at school for at least ten months in the year of all children between the ages of seven and fifteen years; and the furnishing at the expense of the State of free text-books.

XIII. That a graduated tax on incomes and inheritances be levied.

XIV. To prohibit the hiring out of convict labor.

*        *        *

## 159 "a removal and not an assassination" (1881)

Charles Jules Guiteau resided for a considerable time in the utopian Oneida Community. Upon departing he engaged in successive careers in law, bill collecting, theological writing, public lecturing, and politics. Guiteau joined the Stalwart faction of the Republican party and supported Garfield's election effort. He subsequently moved to Washington, slept on park benches, and petitioned the State Department for a post either in Vienna or in Paris. Disappointed in the lack of official response, Guiteau's criticism of Garfield's policies grew. In 1881 he decided Garfield's alignment with the Half-Breed faction of the Republican party, the enemies of the Stalwarts, called for Garfield's elimination from the political scene. After considerable planning, Guiteau finally shot Garfield on July 2 in the Washington railroad station. The President died on September 19. Guiteau was tried, pleaded the then still novel defense of insanity, but was found guilty and was executed on July 30, 1882.

The accompanying document provides Guiteau's own account of the assassination.

## ☆ 159  The Account of Garfield's Assassin

H. H. Alexander, "The Life of Guiteau and the Official History of the Most Exciting Case on Record" (1882), reprinted in Richard Hofstadter and Michael Wallace, eds., *American Violence: A Documentary History* (New York: Knopf, 1970), 413.

I have not . . . used the words "assassination" or "assassin" in this work. These words grate on the mind and produce a bad feeling. I think of General Garfield's condition as a removal and not as an assassination. My idea simply stated was to remove as easily as possible Mr. James A. Garfield, a quiet and good-natured citizen of Ohio, who temporarily occupied the position of President of the United States, and substitute in his place Mr. Chester A. Arthur, of New York, a distinguished and highly estimable gentleman. . . .

Two weeks after I conceived the idea my mind was thoroughly settled on the intention to remove the President. I then prepared myself. I sent to Boston for a copy of my book, "The Truth," and I spent a week in preparing that. I cut out a paragraph and a line and a word here and there and added one or two new chapters, put some new ideas in it and I greatly improved it. I knew that it would probably have a large sale on account of the notoriety that the act of removing the President would give me, and I wished the book to go out to the public in proper shape. That was one preparation for it.

Another preparation was to think the matter all out in detail and to buy a revolver and to prepare myself for executing the idea. This required some two or three weeks, and I gave my entire time and mind in preparing myself to execute the conception of removing the President. . . . My mind was perfectly clear in regard to removing the President; I had not the slightest doubt about my duty to the Lord and to the American people in trying to remove the President, and I want to say here, as emphatically as words can make it, that, from the moment when I fully decided to remove the President, I have never had the slightest shadow on my mind; my purpose had been just as clear and just as determined as anything could be. I believed that I was acting under a special Divine authority to remove him, and this Divine pressure was upon me from the time when I fully resolved to remove him until I actually shot him. It was only by nerving myself to the utmost that I did it at all, and I never had the slightest doubt as the Divine inspiration of the act, and that it was for the best interest of the American people.

## 160  "to solve the Indian problem" (1881)

The "Indian problem," somewhat submerged during the Civil War and Reconstruction, was a central concern to President Chester A. Arthur in his first State of the Union Message. The earlier "peace policy," a separatist approach that sought to contain Native American tribes within assigned territories, had not eliminated the tensions within the Native American communities or the conflicts with the expanding white populations. The assimilationist measures suggested by Arthur were directed toward reforming the internal structures of Native American life. Seeking to vest ownership of land in individual members of the tribes, these measures were, in part, a benevolent gesture motivated by humanitarian concerns for providing individual Native Americans with the means for their self-support. But the thrust of the recommendations was to render the tribes and nations superfluous units and to subject Native Americans to local and state law.

Quite clearly, the ultimate goal of this policy was the elimination of a people, not through genocide, but rather by destroying the identity and cohesion of the ethnic or racial group and rendering them politically ineffectual. It was a policy of ethnocide.

## ☆ 160  President Arthur's First Annual Message (December 6, 1881)

Reprinted in J. Richardson, *A Compilation of the Messages and Papers of the Presidents* (New York: Bureau of National Literature, 1897), 8:54.

\*     \*     \*

. . . Prominent among the matters which challenge the attention of Congress at its present session is the management of our Indian affairs. While this question has been a cause of trouble and embarrassment from the infancy of the Government, it is but recently that any effort has been made for its solution at once serious, determined, consistent, and promising success.

\*     \*     \*

It was natural, at a time when the national territory seemed almost illimitable and contained many millions of acres far outside the bounds of civilized settlements, that a policy should have been initiated which more than aught else has been the fruitful source of our Indian complications.

I refer, of course, to the policy of dealing with the various Indian tribes as separate nationalities, of relegating them by treaty stipulations to the occupancy of immense reservations in the West, and of encouraging them to live a savage life, undisturbed by any earnest and well-directed efforts to bring them under the influences of civilization.

\*     \*     \*

As the white settlements have crowded the borders of the reservations, the Indians, sometimes contentedly and sometimes against their will, have been transferred to other hunting grounds, from which they have again been dislodged whenever their new-found homes have been desired by the adventurous settlers.

These removals and the frontier collisions by which they have often been preceded have led to frequent and disastrous conflicts between the races.

\*          \*          \*

We have to deal with the appalling fact that though thousands of lives have been sacrificed and hundreds of millions of dollars expended in the attempt to solve the Indian problem, it has until within the past few years seemed scarcely nearer a solution than it was half a century ago. . . .

For the success of the efforts now making to introduce among the Indians the customs and pursuits of civilized life and gradually to absorb them into the mass of our citizens, sharing their rights and holden to their responsibilities, there is imperative need for legislative action.

My suggestions in that regard will be chiefly such as have been already called to the attention of Congress and have received to some extent its consideration.

First. I recommend the passage of an act making the laws of the various States and Territories applicable to the Indian reservations within their borders and extending the laws of the State of Arkansas to the portion of the Indian Territory not occupied by the Five Civilized Tribes.

The Indian should receive the protection of the law. He should be allowed to maintain in court his rights of person and property. He has repeatedly begged for this privilege. Its exercise would be very valuable to him in his progress toward civilization.

Second. Of even greater importance is a measure which has been frequently recommended by my predecessors in office, and in furtherance of which several bills have been from time to time introduced in both Houses of Congress. The enactment of a general law permitting the allotment in severalty, to such Indians, at least, as desire it, of a reasonable quantity of land secured to them by patent, and for their own protection made inalienable for twenty or twenty-five years, is demanded for their present welfare and their permanent advancement.

In return for such considerate action on the part of the Government, there is reason to believe that the Indians in large numbers would be persuaded to sever their tribal relations and to engage at once in agricultural pursuits. Many of them realize the fact that their hunting days are over and that it is now for their best interests to conform their manner of life to the new order of things. By no greater inducement than the assurance of permanent title to the soil can they be led to engage in the occupation of tilling it.

The well-attested reports of their increasing interest in husbandry justify the hope and belief that the enactment of such a statute as I recommend would be at once attended with gratifying results. A resort to the allotment system would have a direct and powerful influence in dissolving the tribal bond, which is so prominent a feature of savage life, and which tends so strongly to perpetuate it.

Third. I advise a liberal appropriation for the support of Indian schools, because of my confident belief that such a course is consistent with the wisest economy.

\*          \*          \*

## 161  The Fire of the Mob (1884)

Opposition to authority and acts of violence against the police or courts were not always triggered by, nor were they in response to, outright manifestations of public policy and power. At times the object of hostility was a private individual or group, and the assault on public authority was merely a means for voicing general dissatisfaction with the system of law and justice. Various activities of the vigilante organizations fell into this category.

When on March 28, 1884, William Berner, a confessed murderer, was sentenced to twenty years in prison instead of the customary death penalty, ten thousand indignant citizens held a mass protest in Cincinnati against the "disgraceful verdict." Unaware that Berner had been transferred to the state penitentiary, the mob broke into the jail and the next day burned down the courthouse. General rioting followed. At least fifty people were killed in the course of the three days of disturbances, which necessitated the calling up of the militia. At the end the mayor of Cincinnati called on the city's "leading two hundred businessmen" and the officers of the Grand Army of the Republic to help extinguish the riot.

### ☆ 161  The Cincinnati Riot

J. S. Tunison, "The Cincinnati Riot: Its Causes and Results" (1886), reprinted in Richard Hofstadter and Michael Wallace, eds., *American Violence: A Documentary History* (New York: Knopf, 1970), 467-69.

The crowd had been dense all day, and it gathered numbers and confidence as dark fell. The barricades looked ugly, and the crowd gathered chiefly in front of the Court-house. The riot began with the throwing of bowlders and brick-bats at the Court-house, while some fired pistols and shot-guns at the windows. Gaining confidence, a storming party was formed, and the iron doors in the Court-house front were battered down in a few minutes. About the same time a crowd of boys began breaking in the County Treasurer's office, which was in the northwest corner of the basement. The idea of firing the Court-house began with this crowd of boys and half-grown men, who are said to have been led by men and boys from Kentucky. The furniture and broken counters were piled up in the middle of the room, and coal-oil was poured upon them. The match was applied, and a small flame shot forth. It leaped from one article to another, gathered head, and roared with increasing strength. The crowd cheered and yelled. One office after another was fired, and soon the flames were dancing in every apartment of the front basement. When the crowd reached South Court Street it rushed along the side of the Courthouse, intending to fire the offices on that side. It was met by a volley of musketry which made it stagger and rush around the corner again. Soon after a white handkerchief tied to a stick was waved, and then a number of the rioters cautiously appeared and carried off the dead and wounded. In a few minutes afterward the sheriff's red auction flag, through which the crowd had been firing bullets, was waved and again the mob surged around the corner, emptying its fire-arms at the barricade. "Fire!" Another crash made every wall in the narrow street tremble, and the multitude rushed back, some reeling and falling, others tripping over them, then picking themselves up and continuing the flight. Again the white flag was waved. "Make way, gentlemen, make way for the wounded," called out several surgeons, whom a sense of professional duty had called to the scene. "Make way," and the crowd opened lanes through which was carried many a poor fellow who had rushed around the corner but a minute before. Soon the tables of the Debolt Exchange were covered with mangled bodies, some from which life had fled, others which were gasping with feeble and perishing breath. The surgeons busied themselves with these while the battle went on without. After this the militia kept up a dropping fire on the crowd whenever it showed itself, and continually the number of the wounded grew. The Debolt could not hold them all. Burdsal's drug-store, below Canal, and a saloon on Ninth Street were turned into temporary hospitals. This sort of skirmishing continued for hours, and amid it all the Court-house burned slowly. Slowly the flames crept from room to room through a building alleged to be fire-proof. Anon the flames pierced the roof, dense volumes of smoke roared through the ventilator over the rotunda, iron shutters bent in the heat, iron girders sprang from their seats on iron pillars with loud explosions, records which were eloquent with human joys and sorrows turned into bright flame and vanished, while passions as hot as the fire raged around the devoted pile. Nothing could be done to stay the flames—the mob would not allow it.

But another turning point had been reached, and the insulted majesty of law and order began to assert itself with greater force. Soldiers began to arrive from other parts of the State who a few hours before had been plying the peaceful arts of the citizen. First came the Fourth Regiment, but only to teach Dayton how little reliance she might place in her citizen-soldiery. Appalled by the hostility of the crowd, which would have made respectful room before a gleaming line of bayonets, this regiment halted within sight almost of the building, which was only beginning to burn then, and ingloriously returned to the depot from which it came. Captain Frank Brown, of Company A, after trying vainly to rally the command, returned with several members of his Dayton company to the lines the next day and did good service. The remainder of that company left for their homes in Dayton. Companies of the regiment from Springfield and other points retrieved their fame by assisting in quelling the following day, and some of the Daytonians were forced to return by the scorn of their wives and fellow-townsmen. But most of them would not risk their precious lives.

*          *          *

... Occasionally some section of the mob, with reckless daring, sprang from behind a sheltering corner to fire on the troops. The troops returned the fire, not in volley, now, for the discharge of two or three guns was enough to disperse the crowd, and almost every such episode added to the list of the dead and wounded. Thus the night wore away, and with the gray dawn the firing gradually ceased.

## 162  To Be "let out of the state of pupilage" (1884)

More than a year before his application to register as a voter, John Elk had severed all relations with the tribe into which he had been born, relinquished the privileges based on his Native American ancestry, become a bona fide resident of the state of Nebraska, and submitted himself to the full jurisdiction of the laws of Nebraska and the United States. His application was rejected. Elk sued, claiming the denial of registration violated the Fourteenth and Fifteenth amendments.

Although the avowed policy of the United States toward the Native Americans involved "civilizing them so they would disestablish their tribal relations and join the mass of the population," the law deemed them unacceptable for admission to citizenship, withholding from them access to the political process that decided their fate.

☆ 162  *Elk v. Wilkins*

112 U.S. 94 (1884).

MR. JUSTICE GRAY delivered the opinion of the court.

*          *          *

The petition, while it does not show of what Indian tribe the plaintiff was a member, yet, by the allegations that he "is an Indian, and was born within the United States," and that "he had severed his tribal relation to the Indian tribes," clearly implies that he was born a member of one of the Indian tribes within the limits of the United States, which still exists and is recognized as a tribe by the government of the United States. Though the plaintiff alleges that he "had fully and completely surrendered himself to the jurisdiction of the United States," he does not allege that the United States accepted his surrender, or that he has ever been naturalized, or taxed, or in any way recognized or treated as a citizen, by the State or by the United States. Nor is it contended by his counsel that there is any statute or treaty that makes him a citizen.

The question then is, whether an Indian, born a member of one of the Indian tribes within the United States, is, merely by reason of his birth within the United States, and of his afterwards voluntarily separating himself from his tribe and taking up his residence among white citizens, a citizen of the United States, within the meaning of the first section of the Fourteenth Amendment of the Constitution.

Under the Constitution of the United States, as originally established, "Indians not taxed" were excluded from the persons according to whose numbers representatives and direct taxes were apportioned among the several States; and Congress had and exercised the power to regulate commerce with the Indian tribes, and the members thereof, whether within or without the boundaries of one of the States of the Union. The Indian tribes, being within the territorial limits of the United States, were not, strictly speaking, foreign States; but they were alien nations, distinct political communities, with whom the United States might and habitually did deal, as they thought fit, either through treaties made by the President and Senate, or through acts of Congress in the ordinary forms of legislation. The members of those tribes owed immediate allegiance to their several tribes, and were not part of the people of the United States. They were in a dependent condition, a state of pupilage, resembling that of a ward to his guardian. Indians and their property, exempt from taxation by treaty or statute of the United States, could not be taxed by any State. General acts of Congress did not apply to Indians, unless so expressed as to clearly manifest an intention to include them.

The alien and dependent condition of the members of the Indian tribes could not be put off at their own will, without the action or assent of the United States. They were never deemed citizens of the United States, except under explicit provisions of treaty or statute to that effect, either declaring a certain tribe, or such members of it as chose to remain behind on the removal of the tribe westward,

to be citizens, or authorizing individuals of particular tribes to become citizens on application to a court of the United States for naturalization, and satisfactory proof of fitness for civilized life....

... The main object of the opening sentence of the Fourteenth Amendment was to settle the question, upon which there had been a difference of opinion throughout the country and in this court, as to the citizenship of free negroes (*Scott v. Sandford*); and to put it beyond doubt that all persons, white or black, and whether formerly slaves or not, born or naturalized in the United States, and owing no allegiance to any alien power, should be citizens of the United States and of the State in which they reside....

This section contemplates two sources of citizenship, and two sources only: birth and naturalization. The persons declared to be citizens are "all persons born or naturalized in the United States, and subject to the jurisdiction thereof." The evident meaning of these last words is, not merely subject in some respect or degree to the jurisdiction of the United States, but completely subject to their political jurisdiction, and owing them direct and immediate allegiance. And the words relate to the time of birth in the one case, as they do to the time of naturalization in the other. Persons not thus subject to the jurisdiction of the United States at the time of birth cannot become so afterwards, except by being naturalized, either individually, as by proceedings under the naturalization acts, or collectively, as by the force of a treaty by which foreign territory is acquired.

Indians born within the territorial limits of the United States, members of, and owing immediate allegiance to, one of the Indian tribes (an alien, though dependent, power), although in a geographical sense born in the United States, are no more "born in the United States and subject to the jurisdiction thereof," within the meaning of the first section of the Fourteenth Amendment, than the children of subjects of any foreign government born within the domain of that government, or the children born within the United States, of ambassadors or other public ministers of foreign nations.

\*          \*          \*

Such Indians, then, not being citizens by birth, can only become citizens in the second way mentioned in the Fourteenth Amendment, by being "naturalized in the United States," by or under some treaty or statute.

\*          \*          \*

Since the ratification of the Fourteenth Amendment, Congress has passed several acts for naturalizing Indians of certain tribes, which would have been superfluous if they were, or might become, without any action of the government, citizens of the United States.

\*          \*          \*

The national legislation has tended more and more towards the education and civilization of the Indians, and fitting them to be citizens. But the question whether any Indian tribes, or any members thereof, have become so far advanced in civilization, that they should be let out of the state of pupilage, and admitted to the privileges and responsibilities of citizenship, is a question to be decided by the nation whose wards they are and whose citizens they seek to become, and not by each Indian for himself.

\*          \*          \*

The condition of the tribe from which he derived his origin, so far as any fragments of it remained within the State of New York, resembled the condition of those Indian nations of which Mr. Justice Johnson said in *Fletcher v. Peck* that they "have totally extinguished their national fire, and submitted themselves to the laws of the States;" and which Mr. Justice McLean had in view, when he observed in *Worcester v. Georgia* that in some of the old States, "where small remnants of tribes remain, surrounded by white population, and who, by their reduced numbers, had lost the power of self-government, the laws of the State have been extended over them, for the protection of their persons and property." See also, as to the condition of Indians in Massachusetts, remnants of tribes never recognized by the treaties or legislative or executive acts of the United States as distinct political communities. . . .

\*          \*          \*

The law upon the question before us has been well stated by Judge Deady in the District Court of the United States for the District of Oregon. . . . [H]e said: "But an Indian cannot make himself a citizen of the United States without the consent and co-operation of the government. The fact that he has abandoned his nomadic life or tribal relations, and adopted the habits and manners of civilized people, may be a good reason why he should be made a citizen of the United States, but does not of itself make him one. To be a citizen of the United States is a political privilege which no one, not born to, can assume without its consent in some form. The Indians in Oregon, not being born subject to the jurisdiction of the United States, were not born citizens thereof, and I am not aware of any law or treaty by which any of them have been made so since."

The plaintiff, not being a citizen of the United States under the Fourteenth Amendment of the Constitution, has been deprived of no right secured by the Fifteenth Amendment, and cannot maintain this action.

*Judgment affirmed.*

MR. JUSTICE HARLAN, with whom concurred MR. JUSTICE WOODS, dissenting.

\*          \*          \*

. . . Is it conceivable that the statesmen who framed, the Congress which submitted, and the people who adopted that amendment, intended to confer citizenship, national and State, upon the entire population in this country of African descent (the larger part of which was shortly before held in slavery), and by the same constitutional provision to exclude from such citizenship Indians who had never been in slavery, and who, by becoming *bona fide* residents of States and Territories within the complete jurisdiction of the United States, had evinced a purpose to abandon their former mode of life and become a part of the People of the United States? If this question be answered in the negative, as we think it must be, then we are justified in withholding our assent to the doctrine which excludes the plaintiff from the body of citizens of the United States, upon the ground that his parents were, when he was born, members of an Indian tribe. . . .

Our brethren, it seems to us, construe the Fourteenth Amendment as if it read: "All persons *born subject* to the jurisdiction of, or naturalized in, the United States, are citizens of the United States and of the State in which they reside;" whereas the amendment, as it is, implies in respect of persons born in this country, that they may claim the rights of national citizenship from and after the moment they become subject to the complete jurisdiction of the United States. This would not include the children, born in this country, of a foreign minister, for the reason that, under the fiction of extra-territoriality as recognized by international law, such minister, "though actually in a foreign country, is considered still to remain within the territory of his own State," and, consequently, he continues "subject to the laws of his own country, both with respect to his personal status, and his rights of property; and his children, though born in a foreign country, are considered as natives." Halleck's International Law, ch. 10, § 12.

\*          \*          \*

## 163 "Revenge! Workingmen! To Arms!" (1886)

During an 1886 strike at the McCormick Harvesting Machine Company, the Chicago police fired into a crowd of strikers. Angered, anarchist August Spies composed the circular reproduced below, with the exception of the heading "Revenge," and circulated it that night. The flyer heaped particular calumny upon the police as the enforcers of the capitalist will. At a protest meeting the following day in Haymarket Square, a bomb thrown at the closing of the demonstration killed seven policemen and four other persons. Eight anarchists, including August

Spies, were arrested, tried, and convicted despite the absence of any direct evidence that they had made or thrown the bomb. The theory of the prosecution, adopted by the court, was codified subsequently in Illinois' extremely broad Merritt Conspiracy Act. Four of the convicts, including Spies, were hanged, and one committed suicide. After the passage of five years, the Merritt Act was repealed; and after seven years' imprisonment the surviving three convicts were pardoned by Illinois' governor, John Peter Altgeld.

## ☆163 The Haymarket Conspiracy

Reprinted in H. David, *The History of the Haymarket Affair* (New York: Farrar & Rinehart, 1936), 191-92.

*          *          *

### ☆163a The Spies Circular

#### REVENGE! WORKINGMEN! TO ARMS!

Your masters sent out their bloodhounds—the police—they killed six of your brothers at McCormick's this afternoon. They killed the poor wretches, because they, like you, had courage to disobey the supreme will of your bosses. They killed them because they dared ask for the shortening of the hours of toil. They killed them to show you "free American citizens" that you must be satisfied and contented with whatever your bosses condescend to allow you, or you will get killed!

You have for years endured the most abject humiliations; you have for years suffered immeasurable iniquities; you have worked yourselves to death; you have endured the pangs of want and hunger; your children you have sacrificed to the factory lords—in short, you have been miserable and obedient slaves all these years. Why? To satisfy the insatiable greed and fill the coffers of your lazy thieving masters! When you ask him now to lessen your burden, he sends his bloodhounds out to shoot you, to kill you!

If you are men, if you are the sons of your grandsires, who have shed their blood to free you, then you will rise in your might, Hercules, and destroy the hideous monster that seeks to destroy you.

To arms, we call you, to arms!

YOUR BROTHERS

### ☆163b Merritt Conspiracy Act

1887 Ill. Laws 168, *repealed*, May 28, 1891.

*          *          *

Sec. 2. If any person shall, by speaking to any public or private assemblage of people or in any public place, or shall, by writing, printing or publishing or by causing to be written, printed, published or circulated any written or printed matter, advise, encourage, aid, abet, or incite a local revolution, or the overthrowing or destruction of the existing order of society by force or violence, or the resistance to, and destruction of, the lawful power and authority of the legal authorities of this State, . . . or advise, abet, encourage, or incite the disturbance of the public peace, and by such disturbance an attempt at revolution or destruction of public order, or resistance to such authorities shall therefore ensue, and human life is taken, or any person injured or property destroyed, every person so aiding, etc., shall be deemed as having conspired with the person or persons who actually commit the crime, and shall be deemed a principal in the perpetration of the same, and shall be punished accordingly, and it shall not be necessary for the prosecution to show that the speaking was heard or the written or printed matter was read or communicated to the person or persons actually committing the crime, if such speaking, writing, etc., is shown to have been done in a public manner.

*          *          *

## 164 "even though you erect a gibbet on every street corner" (1886)

Michael Schwab, in addition to August Spies, was one of the anarchists tried, convicted, and sentenced to death for his part in the Haymarket Affair. Schwab's sentence was commuted to life imprisonment, and in 1893 he was granted a pardon.

The Spies and Schwab views on anarchism and violence were set forth before the court. In particular, they equated anarchism with a higher and more peaceful human condition and eschewed the use of violence except in defense against the violence inherent in the capitalist system.

### ☆164 Speeches of Michael Schwab and August Spies before the Court

Reprinted in *The Chicago Martyrs: The Famous Speeches of Eight Anarchists in Judge Gary's Court* (San Francisco: Free Society, 1899), 14, 19-20.

*          *          *

SCHWAB. "Anarchy" is Greek, and means, verbatim, without rulership; not being ruled. According to our vocabulary, anarchy is a state of society in which the only government is reason; a state of society in which all human beings do right for the simple reason that it is right, and hate wrong because it is wrong. In such a society, no laws, no compulsion will be necessary. The attorney of the State was wrong when he said: "Anarchy is dead." Anarchy, up to the present day, has existed only as a doctrine, and Mr. Grinnell has not the power to kill any doctrine whatever. You may call anarchy, as defined by us, an idle dream, but that dream was dreamed by Gotthold Ephraim Lessing, one of the three great German poets and the most celebrated German critic of the last century. If anarchy were the thing the State's attorney makes it out to be, how could it be that such eminent scholars as Prince Kropotkine and the greatest living geographer, Elisee Reclus, were avowed anarchists, even editors of anarchistic newspapers? Anarchy is a dream, but only in the present. It will be realized. Reason will grow in spite of all obstacles. Who is the man that has the cheek to tell us that human development has already reached its culminating point? I know that our ideal will not be accomplished this or next year, but I know that it will be accomplished as near as possible, some day, in the future. It is entirely wrong to use the word anarchy as synonymous with violence. Violence is one thing and anarchy another. In the present state of society violence is used on all sides, and, therefore, we advocated the use of violence against violence, but against violence only, as a necessary means of defence.

SPIES. Society will reclaim its own, even though you erect a gibbet on every street corner. And anarchism, this terrible "ism," deduces that under a cooperative organization of society, under economic equality and individual independence, the "state"—the political state—will pass into barbaric antiquity. And we will be where all are free, where there are no longer masters and servants, where intellect stands for brute force; there will no longer be any use for the policemen and militia to preserve the so-called "peace and order"—the order that the Russian general speaks of when he telegraphed to the Czar after he had massacred half of Warsaw, "Peace reigns in Warsaw." Anarchism does not mean bloodshed; does not mean, robbery, arson, etc. These monstrosities are, on the contrary, the characteristic features of capitalism. Anarchism means peace and tranquillity to all. Anarchism means the reorganization of society upon scientific principles and the abolition of causes which produce vice and crime.

## 165 The Indian Soil Is under United States Political Control (1886)

Prior to 1885, Native American offenses against Native Americans within Native American territory were tried and punished under tribal law. Treaties always had recognized this authority. In that year, Congress passed the Major Crimes Act, which explicitly extended federal court jurisdiction over seven crimes when both the victim and the alleged perpetrator were Native Americans and the crime

was committed on a Native American reservation. Despite the abolition in 1871 of the treaty-making status of Native American tribes, this was the first time Congress actually had regulated the internal affairs of Native Americans without the consent, through treaty, of the tribe or nation affected. In 1886, the Supreme Court considered the constitutionality of the legislation. Initially determining the act was not based on the commerce clause or the apportionment clauses of Article I and the Fourteenth Amendment, the court nevertheless upheld Congress's power to regulate Native Americans directly and without their consent through either organized tribal negotiation or individual participation in the electoral process. In the final analysis, the political and civil rights of Native Americans rested within the unilateral power of Congress.

☆ 165 *United States v. Kagama*

118 U.S. 375 (1886).

MILLER, J. . . .

\*          \*          \*

. . . [W]e are not able to see, in either of these clauses of the Constitution and its amendments, any delegation of power to enact a code of criminal law for the punishment of the worst class of crimes known to civilized life when committed by Indians. . . .

But these Indians are within the geographical limits of the United States. The soil and the people within these limits are under the political control of the Government of the United States, or of the States of the Union. There exist within the broad domain of sovereignty but these two. There may be cities, counties, and other organized bodies with limited legislative functions, but they are all derived from, or exist in, subordination to one or the other of these. The territorial governments owe all their powers to the statutes of the United States conferring on them the powers which they exercise, and which are liable to be withdrawn, modified, or repealed at any time by Congress. . . . But this power of Congress to organize territorial governments, and make laws for their inhabitants, arises not so much from the clause in the Constitution in regard to disposing of and making rules and regulations concerning the Territory and other property of the United States, as from the ownership of the country in which the Territories are, and the right of exclusive sovereignty which must exist in the National Government, and can be found nowhere else.

\*          \*          \*

The Indian reservation in the case before us is land bought by the United States from Mexico by the treaty of Guadaloupe Hidalgo, and the whole of

California, with the allegiance of its inhabitants, many of whom were Indians, was transferred by that treaty to the United States.

The relation of the Indian tribes living within the borders of the United States, both before and since the Revolution, to the people of the United States has always been an anomalous one and of a complex character.

... They were, and always have been, regarded as having a semi-independent position when they preserved their tribal relations; not as States, not as nations, not as possessed of the full attributes of sovereignty, but as a separate people, with the power of regulating their internal and social relations, and thus far not brought under the laws of the Union or of the State within whose limits they resided.

Perhaps the best statement of their position is found in the two opinions of this court by Chief Justice Marshall in the case of the *Cherokee Nation v. Georgia* and in the case of *Worcester v. State of Georgia*. These opinions are exhaustive; and in the separate opinion of Mr. Justice Baldwin, in the former, is a very valuable résumé of the treaties and statutes concerning the Indian tribes previous to and during the confederation.

In the first of the above cases it was held that these tribes were neither States nor nations, had only some of the attributes of sovereignty, and could not be so far recognized in that capacity as to sustain a suit in the Supreme Court of the United States. In the second case it was said that they were not subject to the jurisdiction asserted over them by the State of Georgia, which, because they were within its limits, where they had been for ages, had attempted to extend her laws and the jurisdiction of her courts over them.

In the opinions in these cases they are spoken of as "wards of the nation," "pupils," as local dependent communities. In this spirit the United States has conducted its relations to them from its organization to this time. But, after an experience of a hundred years of the treaty-making system of government, Congress has determined upon a new departure — to govern them by acts of Congress. This is seen in the act of March 3, 1871, embodied in § 2079 of the Revised Statutes:

"No Indian nation or tribe, within the territory of the United States shall be acknowledged or recognized as an independent nation, tribe, or power, with whom the United States may contract by treaty; but no obligation of any treaty lawfully made and ratified with any such Indian nation or tribe prior to March third, eighteen hundred and seventy one, shall be hereby invalidated or impaired."

... The decision in [*Ex Parte Crow Dog*] admits that if the intention of Congress had been to punish, by the United States courts, the murder of one Indian by another, the law would have been valid. . . . The passage of the act now under consideration was designed to remove that objection, and to go further by including such crimes on reservations lying within a State.

Is this latter fact a fatal objection to the law? . . .

... It does not interfere with the process of the State courts within the reservation, nor with the operation of State laws upon white people found there. Its effect is confined to the acts of an Indian of some tribe, of a criminal character, committed within the limits of the reservation.

It seems to us that this is within the competency of Congress. These Indian tribes *are* the wards of the nation. They are communities *dependent* on the United States. Dependent largely for their daily food. Dependent for their political rights. They owe no allegiance to the States, and receive from them no protection. Because of the local ill feeling, the people of the States where they are found are often their deadliest enemies. From their very weakness and helplessness, so largely due to the course of dealing of the Federal Government with them and the treaties in which it has been promised, there arises the duty of protection, and with it the power. This has always been recognized by the Executive and by Congress, and by this court, whenever the question has arisen.

*              *              *

The power of the General Government over these remnants of a race once powerful, now weak and diminished in numbers, is necessary to their protection, as well as to the safety of those among whom they dwell. It must exist in that government, because it never has existed anywhere else, because the theatre of its exercise is within the geographical limits of the United States, because it has never been denied, and because it alone can enforce its laws on all the tribes.

*We answer the questions propounded to us, that the 9th section of the act of March, 1885, is a valid law in both its branches, and that the Circuit Court of the United States for the District of California has jurisdiction of the offence charged in the indictment in this case.*

## 166 "rights, privileges, and immunities" (1887)

Native Americans were unalterably opposed to the idea of individual allocation of lands, recognizing that loss of the tribal lands would, as intended, undermine and diminish tribal authority and culture. But lingering doubts concerning the authority of the United States directly to affect internal tribal affairs had been dispelled by *United States v. Kagama*, and the Dawes Act, allotting Native American lands to be held in severalty, was passed the following year.

The Dawes Act was not self-executing, and the allotment program was gradual. Under the act, 118 reservations were broken up, and because of the terms of Section 5, some eighty-six million acres of Native American-held lands (62 percent of the total) were opened to white settlement and homesteading. Subsequent amendments extended the allotment policy to the Five Civilized Tribes, delayed acquisition of citizenship, and extended the trust periods. The policies behind the act led to the adoption of other ethnocidal measures by the Bureau of Indian Affairs, including the prohibition of certain religious practices and the refusal to teach Native American children their own language.

## ☆166 An Act to Provide for the Allotment of Lands in Severalty to Indians (Dawes Act)

24 Stat. 388 (1887).

BE IT ENACTED *by the Senate and House of Representatives of the United States of America in Congress assembled*, That in all cases where any tribe or band of Indians has been, or shall hereafter be, located upon any reservation created for their use, either by treaty stipulation or by virtue of an act of Congress or executive order setting apart the same for their use, the President of the United States be, and he hereby is, authorized, whenever in his opinion any reservation or any part thereof of such Indians is advantageous for agricultural and grazing purposes, to cause said reservation, or any part thereof, to be surveyed, or resurveyed if necessary, and to allot the lands in said reservation in severalty to any Indian located thereon in quantities as follows: . . .

\*       \*       \*

SEC. 2. That all allotments set apart under the provisions of this act shall be selected by the Indians, heads of families selecting for their minor children, and the agents shall select for each orphan child, and in such manner as to embrace the improvements of the Indians making the selection. Where the improvements of two or more Indians have been made on the same legal subdivision of land, unless they shall otherwise agree, a provisional line may be run dividing said lands between them, and the amount to which each is entitled shall be equalized in the assignment of the remainder of the land to which they are entitled under this act: *Provided*, That if any one entitled to an allotment shall fail to make a selection within four years after the President shall direct that allotments may be made on a particular reservation, the Secretary of the Interior may direct the agent of such tribe or band, if

such there be, and if there be no agent, then a special agent appointed for that purpose, to make a selection for such Indian, which election shall be allotted as in cases where selections are made by the Indians, and patents shall issue in like manner.

\*       \*       \*

SEC. 4. That where any Indian not residing upon a reservation, or for whose tribe no reservation has been provided by treaty, act of Congress, or executive order, shall make settlement upon any surveyed or unsurveyed lands of the United States not otherwise apropriated, he or she shall be entitled, upon application to the local land-office for the district in which the lands are located, to have the same allotted to him or her, and to his or her children, in quantities and manner as provided in this act for Indians residing upon reservations. . . .

SEC. 5. That upon the approval of the allotments provided for in this act by the Secretary of the Interior, he shall cause patents to issue therefor in the name of the allottees, which patents shall be of the legal effect, and declare that the United States does and will hold the land thus allotted, for the period of twenty-five years, in trust for the sole use and benefit of the Indian to whom such allotment shall have been made, or, in case of his decease, of his heirs according to the laws of the State or Territory where such land is located, and that at the expiration of said period the United States will convey the same by patent to said Indian, or his heirs as aforesaid, in fee, discharged of said trust and free of all charge or incumbrance whatsoever: *Provided*, That the President of the United States may in any case in his discretion extend the period. . . . *And provided further*, That at any time after lands have been allotted to all the Indians of any tribe as herein provided, or sooner if in the opinion of the President it shall be for the best interests of said tribe, it shall be lawful for the Secretary of the Interior to negotiate with such Indian tribe for the purchase and release by said tribe, in conformity with the treaty or statute under which such reservation is held, of such portions of its reservation not allotted as such tribe shall, from time to time, consent to sell, on such terms and conditions as shall be considered just and equitable between the United States and said tribe of Indians, which purchase shall not be complete until ratified by Congress, and the form and manner of executing such release shall also be prescribed by Congress: *Provided however*, That all lands adapted to agriculture, with or without irrigation so sold or released to the United States by any Indian tribe shall be held by the United States for the sole purpose of securing homes to actual settlers and shall be disposed of by the United States to actual and bona fide settlers only in tracts not exceeding one hundred and sixty acres to any one person, on such terms as Congress shall prescribe, subject to grants which Congress may make in aid of education: ... And the sums agreed to be paid by the United States as purchase money for any portion of any such reservation shall be held in the Treasury of the United States for the sole use of the tribe or tribes of Indians; to whom such reservations belonged; and the same, with interest thereon at three per cent per annum, shall be at all times subject to appropriation by Congress for the education and civilization of such tribe or tribes of Indians or the members thereof. ...

SEC. 6. That upon the completion of said allotments and the patenting of the lands to said allottees, each and every member of the respective bands or tribes of Indians to whom allotments have been made shall have the benefit of and be subject to the laws, both civil and criminal, of the State or Territory in which they may reside; and no Territory shall pass or enforce any law denying any such Indian within its jurisdiction the equal protection of the law. And every Indian born within the territorial limits of the United States to whom allotments shall have been made under the provisions of this act, or under any law or treaty, and every Indian born within the territorial limits of the United States who has voluntarily taken up, within said limits, his residence separate and apart from any tribe of Indians therein, and has adopted the habits of civilized life, is hereby declared to be a citizen of the United States, and is entitled to all the rights, privileges, and immunities of such citizens, whether said Indian has been or not, by birth or otherwise, a member of any tribe of Indians within the territorial limits of the United States without in any manner impairing or otherwise affecting the right of any such Indian to tribal or other property.

*      *      *

SEC. 8. That the provision of this act shall not extend to the territory occupied by the Cherokees, Creeks, Choctaws, Chickasaws, Seminoles, and Osage, Miamies and Peorias, and Sacs and Foxes, in the Indian Territory, nor to any of the reservations of the Seneca Nation of New York Indians in the State of New York, nor to that strip of territory in the State of Nebraska adjoining the Sioux Nation on the south added by executive order.

# 167 "combination ... in restraint of trade" (1890)

Enacted for the purpose of combating commercial monopolistic practices, the Sherman Antitrust Act and the remedies provided therein served as a major "union-busting" device. Management was able to invoke the sanctions of the act against union-directed strikes and boycotts. While the sanctions were civil in form, they had a highly punitive and quasi-criminal flavor. In 1902 the courts held that union effort to boycott Loewe Hats violated the Sherman Act and assessed triple damages in the amount of $240,000 against the union. In *Gompers v. Buck's Stove and Range Co.*, management succeeded in obtaining a sweeping injunction forbidding a boycott by the American Federation of Labor, and when AFL officials defied the order, they were jailed for contempt of court. To labor, these applications of the Sherman Act were another example of the law unjustly siding with capital on the economic battleground. Disobedience of the labor injunction became union policy.

## ☆ 167 Sherman Antitrust Act

26 Stat. 209 (1890).

*Be it enacted by the Senate and House of Representatives of the United States of America in Congress assembled,*

SEC. 1. Every contract, combination in the form of trust or otherwise, or conspiracy, in restraint of trade or commerce among the several States, or with foreign nations, is hereby declared to be illegal. Every person who shall make any such contract or engage in any such combination or conspiracy, shall be deemed guilty of a misdemeanor, and, on conviction thereof, shall be punished by fine not exceeding five thousand dollars, or by imprisonment not exceeding one year, or by both said punishments, in the discretion of the court.

SEC. 2. Every person who shall monopolize, or attempt to monopolize, or combine or conspire with any other person or persons, to monopolize any part of the trade or commerce among the several States, or with foreign nations, shall be deemed guilty of a misdemeanor, and, on conviction thereof, shall be punished by fine not exceeding five thousand dollars, or by imprisonment not exceeding one year, or by both said punishments, in the discretion of the court.

SEC. 3. Every contract, combination in form of trust or otherwise, or conspiracy, in restraint of trade or commerce in any Territory of the United States or of the District of Columbia, or in restraint of trade or commerce between any such Territory and another, or between any such Territory or Territories and any State or States or the District of Columbia, or with foreign nations, or between the District of Columbia and any State or States or foreign nations, is hereby declared illegal. Every person who shall make any such contract or engage in any such combination or conspiracy, shall be deemed guilty of a misdemeanor, and, on conviction thereof, shall be punished by fine not exceeding five thousand dollars, or by imprisonment not exceeding one year, or by both said punishments, in the discretion of the court.

SEC. 4. The several circuit courts of the United States are hereby invested with jurisdiction to prevent and restrain violations of this act.... Such proceedings may be by way of petition setting forth the case and praying that such violation shall be enjoined or otherwise prohibited....

\*             \*             \*

SEC. 7. Any person who shall be injured in his business or property by any other person or corporation by reason of anything forbidden or declared to be unlawful by this act, may sue therefor ... and shall recover three fold the damages by him sustained, and the costs of suit, including a reasonable attorney's fee.

\*             \*             \*

## 168 "The President of the United States of America to Eugene V. Debs" (1894)

In 1893, the United States had three million unemployed workers and more than six hundred bank failures. After years of bustling economic growth with rampant speculation in the stock market and overextended industrial production, corporate profits fell rapidly and wages dropped drastically. Labor, acknowledging the depressed economic conditions, submitted to management's stringent measures. The economy showed some improvement the following year, but it failed to make a substantial recovery. Restless, labor responded with an explosion of strikes and disturbances. In 1894, the nation was confronted with the Pullman strike, or "Debs's Rebellion," in which George Mortimer Pullman and the railroads were pitted against labor leader Eugene Victor Debs and the American Railway Union.

The strike paralyzed transportation from Chicago to the Pacific Coast, and the railroad operators beseeched President Grover Cleveland to intervene. He did, sending two thousand troops to keep the trains moving. The power of the United States was enlisted further in aid of management, which sought and obtained injunctions under the Sherman Antitrust Act to restrain Debs and his union from their activities. When Debs defied the law, which he viewed as being favorable to management, the court cited him for criminal contempt and ordered him jailed for six months as punishment.

☆ 168 Debs's Rebellion

☆ 168a *In re Debs Injunction*

S. Ex. Doc. No. 7, 53d Cong., 3d Sess. 179-80 (1894).

UNITED STATES CIRCUIT COURT,
DISTRICT OF INDIANA

The President of the United States of America to Eugene V. Debs ... [et al.] and the American Railway Union. And all other persons combining and conspiring with them, and to all other persons whomsoever:

You are hereby restrained, commanded, and enjoined absolutely to desist and refrain from in any way or manner interfering with, hindering, obstructing, or stopping any of the business of any of the following-named railroads: [23 named] As common carriers of passengers and freight between or among any States of the United States, and from in any way interfering with, hindering, obstructing, or stopping any mail trains, express trains, whether freight or passenger, engaged in interstate commerce, or carrying passengers or freight between or among the States; ... and from compelling or inducing, or attempting to compel or induce, by threats, intimidation, persuasion, force, or violence, any of the employees of any of said railroads to refuse or fail to perform any of their duties as employees of any of said railroads in connection with the interstate business or commerce of such railroads, or the carriage of the United States mail by such railroads, or the transportation of passengers or property between or among the States; ... and from doing any act whatever in furtherance of any conspiracy or combination to restrain either of said railroad companies in the free and unhindered control and handling of interstate commerce over the lines of said railroads, and of transportation of persons and freight between and among the States; and from ordering, directing, aiding, assisting, or abetting, in any manner whatever, any person or persons to commit any or either of the acts aforesaid.

And Eugene V. Debs and all other persons are hereby enjoined and restrained from sending out any letters, messages, or communications directing, inciting, encouraging, or instructing any person whatsoever to interfere with the business or affairs, directly or indirectly, of any of the railway companies hereinabove named, or from persuading any of the employees of said railway companies while in the employment of their respective companies to fail or refuse to perform the duties of their employment....

\*             \*             \*

☆ 168b *United States v. Debs*

64 F. 724 (C.C.N.D. Ill. 1894).

WOODS, Circuit Judge....

\*             \*             \*

[T]he question now to be considered [is] whether or not the injunction was authorized by the [Sherman Antitrust A]ct of July 2, 1890.... [I]t has been seriously questioned in this proceeding, as well as by an eminent judge and by lawyers elsewhere, whether the statute is by its terms applicable. . . .

*     *     *

. . . The position of the defendants in respect to this statute, as stated in one of the briefs, is that it "is directed at capital", "at dangers very generally supposed to result from vast aggregations of capital", that "the evil aimed at is one of a contractual character, and not of force and violence." . . .

. . . [T]he original measure, as proposed in the senate, "was directed wholly against trusts, and not at organizations of labor in any form". But . . . it is worthy of note that a proviso to the effect that the act should not be construed to apply "to any arrangements, agreements or combinations made between laborers with a view of lessening hours of labor or of increasing their wages, nor to any arrangements, agreements or combinations among persons engaged in agriculture made with the view of enhancing the price of agricultural . . . products" was not adopted. . . . [T]he offering of the proposition shows that the possible application of the statute to cases not in the nature of trusts or monopolies, and in which workmen or farmers should be concerned, was not overlooked. But it is more significant that, upon the introduction of the bill into the house, the chairman of the judiciary committee . . . made the following statement: "Now just what contracts, what combinations in the form of trusts, or what conspiracies will be in restraint of trade or commerce, mentioned in the bill, will not be known until the courts have construed and interpreted this provision."

It is therefore the privilege and duty of the court, uncontrolled by considerations drawn from other sources, to find the meaning of the statute in the terms of its provisions, interpreted by the settled rules of construction. That the original design to suppress trusts and monopolies created by contract or combination in the form of trust, which of course would be of a "contractual character" was adhered to, is clear; but it is equally clear that a further and more comprehensive purpose came to be entertained, and was embodied in the final form of the enactment. Combinations are condemned, not only when they take the form of trusts, but in whatever form found, if they be in restraint of trade. That is the effect of the words "or otherwise." . . . Any proposed restraint of trade, though it be in itself innocent, if it is to be accomplished by conspiracy, is unlawful. . . .

*     *     *

I have not failed, I think, to appreciate the just force of the argument to the contrary, of my opinion,—it has sometimes entangled me in doubt,—but my conclusion is clear, that under the act of 1890, the

court had jurisdiction of the case presented in the application, and that the injunction granted was not without authority of law, nor for any reason invalid.

*     *     *

## 169 "keeping those highways of interstate commerce free from obstruction" (1894)

Eugene V. Debs sought a writ of habeas corpus from the United States Supreme Court to review the lawfulness of his imprisonment for violating the injunction against participation in the railroad strike. Clarence Darrow, Debs's lawyer, argued that the United States had no power to intervene in matters of local peacekeeping, that the Sherman Act was not intended to cover labor activities, and that the imprisonment of Debs without a jury trial (suits for injunctions, as well as all equity proceedings, are conducted without a jury) violated the Sixth Amendment. Darrow also made an impassioned plea for the justice of the labor cause. The plea fell on deaf ears. Despite the fact that no law of the United States was defied, the court concluded that the government's interest in the movement of the mails was sufficient cause to uphold Debs's imprisonment through the invocation of the quasi-criminal law. Of particular note is the court's reiteration of the dogma that all social wrongs were to be addressed through the ballot box or the courts—not through mob violence.

☆ 169 *In re Debs*

158 U.S. 564 (1894).

MR. JUSTICE BREWER, after stating the case, delivered the opinion of the court.

The case presented by the bill is this: The United States, finding that the interstate transportation of persons and property, as well as the carriage of the mails, is forcibly obstructed, and that a combination and conspiracy exists to subject the control of such transportation to the will of the conspirators, applied to one of their courts, sitting as a court of equity, for an injunction to restrain such obstruction and prevent carrying into effect such conspiracy. Two questions of importance are presented: First. Are the relations of the general government to interstate commerce and the transportation of the mails such as authorize a direct interference to prevent a forcible obstruction thereof? Second. If authority exists, as authority in governmental affairs implies both power and duty, has a court of equity jurisdiction to issue an injunction in aid of the performance of such duty[?]

First. What are the relations of the general government to interstate commerce and the transportation of the mails? They are those of direct supervision, control, and management.

\*            \*            \*

As, under the Constitution, power over interstate commerce and the transportation of the mails is vested in the national government, and Congress by virtue of such grant has assumed actual and direct control, it follows that the national government may prevent any unlawful and forcible interference therewith. But how shall this be accomplished? Doubtless, it is within the competency of Congress to prescribe by legislation that any interference with these matters shall be offences against the United States, and prosecuted and punished by indictment in the proper courts. But is that the only remedy? Have the vast interests of the nation in interstate commerce, and in the transportation of the mails, no other protection than lies in the possible punishment of those who interfere with it? To ask the question is to answer it. . . .

. . . The entire strength of the nation may be used to enforce in any part of the land the full and free exercise of all national powers and the security of all rights entrusted by the Constitution to its care. The strong arm of the national government may be put forth to brush away all obstructions to the freedom of interstate commerce or the transportation of the mails. If the emergency arises, the army of the Nation, and all its militia, are at the service of the Nation to compel obedience to its laws.

But passing to the second question, is there no other alternative than the use of force on the part of the executive authorities whenever obstructions arise to the freedom of interstate commerce or the transportation of the mails? . . . [T]he existence of this right of forcible abatement is not inconsistent with nor does it destroy the right of appeal in an orderly way to the courts for a judicial determination, and an exercise of their powers by writ of injunction and otherwise to accomplish the same result. . . .

So, in the case before us, the right to use force does not exclude the right of appeal to the courts for a judicial determination and for the exercise of all their powers of prevention. . . .

Neither can it be doubted that the government has such an interest in the subject-matter as enables it to appear as party plaintiff in this suit. . . . [T]he United States have a property in the mails, the protection of which was one of the purposes of this bill. . . .

We do not care to place our decision upon this ground alone. Every government, entrusted, by the very terms of its being, with powers and duties to be exercised and discharged for the general welfare, has a right to apply to its own courts for any proper assistance in the exercise of the one and the discharge of the other, and it is no sufficient answer to

its appeal to one of those courts that it has no pecuniary interest in the matter. The obligations which it is under to promote the interest of all, and to prevent the wrongdoing of one resulting in injury to the general welfare, is often of itself sufficient to give it a standing in court. . . .

\*            \*            \*

The national government, given by the Constitution power to regulate interstate commerce, has by express statute assumed jurisdiction over such commerce when carried upon railroads. It is charged, therefore, with the duty of keeping those highways of interstate commerce free from obstruction, for it has always been recognized as one of the powers and duties of a government to remove obstructions from the highways under its control.

\*            \*            \*

It is said that seldom have the courts assumed jurisdiction to restrain by injunction in suits brought by the government, either state or national, obstructions to highways, either artificial or natural. This is undoubtedly true, but the reason is that the necessity for such interference has only been occasional. Ordinarily the local authorities have taken full control over the matter, and by indictment for misdemeanor, or in some kindred way, have secured the removal of the obstruction and the cessation of the nuisance. . . .

That the bill filed in this case alleged special facts calling for the exercise of all the powers of the court is not open to question. The picture drawn in it of the vast interests involved, not merely of the city of Chicago and the State of Illinois, but of all the States, and the general confusion into which the interstate commerce of the country was thrown; the forcible interference with that commerce; the attempted exercise by individuals of powers belonging only to government, and the threatened continuance of such invasions of public right, presented a condition of affairs which called for the fullest exercise of all the powers of the courts. If ever there was a special exigency, one which demanded that the court should do all that courts can do, it was disclosed by this bill. . . .

The difference between a public nuisance and a private nuisance is that the one affects the people at large and the other simply the individual. The quality of the wrong is the same, and the jurisdiction of the courts over them rests upon the same principles and goes to the same extent. . . .

. . . Of course, circumstances may exist in one case, which do not in another, to induce the court to interfere or to refuse to interfere by injunction, but the jurisdiction, the power to interfere, exists in all cases of nuisance. True, many more suits are brought by individuals than by the public to enjoin nuisances, but there are two reasons for this. First, the instances are more numerous of private than of public nuisances; and, second, often that which is in fact a public nuisance is restrained at the suit of a private individual, whose right to relief arises because of a special injury resulting therefrom.

Again, it is objected that it is outside of the jurisdiction of a court of equity to enjoin the commission of crimes. This, as a general proposition, is unquestioned. A chancellor has no criminal jurisdiction. Something more than the threatened commission of an offence against the laws of the land is necessary to call into exercise the injunctive powers of the court. There must be some interferences, actual or threatened, with property or rights of a pecuniary nature, but when such interferences appear the jurisdiction of a court of equity arises, and is not destroyed by the fact that they are accompanied by or are themselves violations of the criminal law....

... [T]he acts of the defendants may or may not have been violations of the criminal law. If they were, that matter is for inquiry in other proceedings. The complaint made against them in this is of disobedience to an order of a civil court, made for the protection of property and the security of rights. If any criminal prosecution be brought against them for the criminal offences ... it will be no defence to such prosecution that they disobeyed the orders of injunction served upon them and have been punished for such disobedience.

Nor is there in this any invasion of the constitutional right of trial by jury. We fully agree with counsel that "it matters not what form the attempt to deny constitutional right may take. It is vain and ineffectual, and must be so declared by the courts." ... But the power of a court to make an order carries with it the equal power to punish for a disobedience of that order, and the inquiry as to the question of disobedience has been, from time immemorial, the special function of the court.

*        *        *

A most earnest and eloquent appeal was made to us in eulogy of the heroic spirit of those who threw up their employment, and gave up their means of earning a livelihood, not in defence of their own rights, but in sympathy for and to assist others whom they believed to be wronged. We yield to none in our admiration of any act of heroism or self-sacrifice, but we may be permitted to add that it is a lesson which cannot be learned too soon or too thoroughly that under this government of and by the people the means of redress of all wrongs are through the courts and at the ballot-box, and that no wrong, real or fancied, carries with it legal warrant to invite as a means of redress the coöperation of a mob, with its accompanying acts of violence.

We have given to this case the most careful and anxious attention, for we realize that it touches closely questions of supreme importance to the people of this country. Summing up our conclusions, we hold that ... the Circuit Court had power to issue its process of injunction; that it having been issued and served on these defendants, the Circuit Court had authority to inquire whether its orders had been disobeyed, and when it found that they had been, to proceed under section 725, Revised Statutes, which grants power "to punish, by fine or imprisonment, ... disobedience, ... by any party ... or other person, to any lawful writ, process, order, rule, decree or command," and enter the order of punishment complained of; and, finally, that, the Circuit Court, having full jurisdiction in the premises, its finding of the fact of disobedience is not open to review on *habeas corpus* in this or any other court....

We enter into no examination of the [Sherman Antitrust Act], upon which the Circuit Court relied mainly to sustain its jurisdiction. It must not be understood from this that we dissent from the conclusions of that court in reference to the scope of the act, but simply that we prefer to rest our judgment on the broader ground which has been discussed in this opinion, believing it of importance that the principles underlying it should be fully stated and affirmed.

*The petition for a writ of habeas corpus is denied.*

## 170 "this raid was part of 'a political movement' " (1896)

A band of over 130 armed men raided the village of San Ygnacio in Mexico, then returned to Texas. The Mexican government sought the extradition of the alleged bandits. Warrants for their arrest were issued by a United States commissioner, and they were confined to await the decision of the executive branch on whether they were extraditable under the treaty between Mexico and the United States. The treaty contained the usual provisions making extradition inapplicable to any crime or offense of a purely political character. The detainees applied to the district court for release under a writ of habeas corpus. The writ was granted. The Mexican government, through its counsel, Ornelas, appealed. The Supreme Court upheld the commissioner's arrest warrant and reversed the district court. Although the outcome hinged on procedural considerations, the Supreme Court's decision reflected the judiciary's reluctance to entertain claims based on the political offense exception to the law of extradition.

☆ 170  *Ornelas v. Ruiz*

161 U.S. 502 (1896).

*        *        *

The release of petitioners was ordered on the sole ground that, as appears from the portion of the opinion of the learned District Judge contained in the record, this raid was part of "a political movement, having for its purpose the overthrow of the existing government in Mexico, and that the offences committed by the petitioners and their associates in their vain and visionary attempt to accomplish their purpose were purely political offences within the meaning of the sixth article of the treaty of extradition." The evidence before the commissioner, from which this conclusion was deduced, tended to show that on December 10, 1892, a band of armed men to the number of one hundred and thirty or forty, under the leadership of one Francisco Benevides, passed over the Rio Grande from Texas into Mexico, and attacked about forty Mexican soldiers stationed at the village of San Ygnacio; killing and wounding some of them, and capturing others, who were afterwards released; burning their barracks and taking away their horses and equipments; that private citizens were also violently assaulted; horses belonging to them taken; houses burned; small sums of money extorted from women; clothes, provisions, and goods appropriated; and three citizens kidnapped and carried over the river to the Texas side, finally escaping; that these men were bandits, without uniforms or flag, but with a red band on their hats; and that Garza was not there and had nothing to do with the expedition. The band remained on the Mexican side of the river about six hours and recrossed at the village ford. Petitioners were members of the band, and citizens of Mexico, as appeared from the complaints and testimony, though one of them at least had resided a large part of the time, for many years, in Texas. Evidence on behalf of petitioners was adduced indicating that there had been a revolutionary movement on that border under one Garza in 1891; that indictments had been found against the participants for violation of the neutrality laws; and that the aim, object and purpose of Benevides' men was the same as Garza's, "to cross over the river and fight against the government."

In the course of his opinion the District Judge referred to the views of the State Department as to the transaction at San Ygnacio.... The Secretary [of State] concluded his résumé with these words: "The idea that these acts were perpetrated with *bona fide* political or revolutionary designs is negatived by the fact that immediately after this occurrence, though no superior armed force of the Mexican government was in the vicinity to hinder their advance into the country, the bandits withdrew with their booty across the river into Texas." ...

The District Judge entertained different views from those of the Secretary, and arrived at a different result from that reached by the commissioner on the evidence on which the latter proceeded, and so was induced to substitute his judgment for that of the commissioner, in whom was reposed the authority of decision....

Can it be said that the commissioner had no choice on the evidence but to hold, in view of the character of the foray, the mode of attack, the persons killed or captured, and the kind of property taken or destroyed, that this was a movement in aid of a political revolt, an insurrection or a civil war, and that acts which contained all the characteristics of crimes under the ordinary law were exempt from extradition because of the political intentions of those who committed them? In our opinion this inquiry must be answered in the negative.

... [I]f it appear that there was legal evidence on which the commissioner might properly conclude that the accused had committed offences within the treaty as charged, [he is] justified in exercising his power to commit them to await the action of the Executive Department. The rule as to probable cause was thus laid down by Mr. Chief Justice Marshall, sitting as a committing magistrate, in *Burr's case*....

We are of opinion that it cannot be held that there was substantially no evidence calling for the judgment of the commissioner....

*The final order of the District Court is therefore reversed and the case remanded for further proceedings in conformity to law.*

## 171 "an invention of the devil" (1898)

In Oshkosh, Wisconsin, in 1898, the woodworkers at the Paine Lumber Company, the country's largest manufacturer of sashes, doors, and blinds, walked off their jobs and demanded higher wages, the abolition of child and woman labor, the recognition of the union, and a weekly paycheck. A warrant was issued against Thomas I. Kidd, general secretary of the union, whose headquarters were in Chicago. He, along with others, was accused of "criminal conspiracy" to injure the business of the Paine Lumber Company.

After a three-week trial, defense attorney Clarence Darrow's argument to the jury lasted two entire days and detailed the grievances of the workers against Paine Lumber Company, the history of trade unionism, and the justification for fighting oppression. Darrow delivered his argument without notes. Stating, "Whenever a king wanted to get rid of somebody, whenever a political disturber was in someone's way, then they brought a charge of conspiracy," Darrow urged that personal rights should take precedence over property rights. The jury took fifty minutes to return a verdict of "not guilty."

## ☆171 Clarence Darrow's Argument to the Jury in the *Kidd Case*

Reprinted in A. Weinberg, ed., *Attorney for the Damned* (New York: Simon & Schuster, 1957), 267-326.

\*          \*          \*

GENTLEMEN OF THE JURY: The defendants in this case, Thomas I. Kidd, George Zentner and Michael Troiber, are on trial charged with a conspiracy to injure the business of the Paine Lumber Company, by means of a strike, and the incidents arising therefrom. . . . [I]t is impossible to present the case to you without a broad survey of the great questions that are agitating the world today. For whatever its form, this is really not a criminal case. It is but an episode in the great battle for human liberty, a battle which was commenced when the tyranny and oppression of man first caused him to impose upon his fellows and which will not end so long as the children of one father shall be compelled to toil to support the children of another in luxury and ease.

\*          \*          \*

Ordinarily men are brought into a criminal court for the reason that they are bad. Thomas I. Kidd is brought into this court because he is good, and they understand it well. If Thomas I. Kidd had been mean and selfish and designing, if he had held out his hand to take the paltry bribes that these men pass out wherever they find one so poor and weak as to take their dirty gold, this case would not be here today. Kidd is a defendant in these criminal proceedings because he loves his fellow-men. This is not the first case of its kind in the history of the world, and I am afraid it will not be the last. It is not the first time that evil men, men who are themselves criminals, have used the law for the purpose of bringing righteous ones to death or to jail. . . .

Let us understand exactly who are the parties to this case. Counsel for the prosecution will stand before this jury with hypocritical voice and false words, and say it is the great state of Wisconsin on the one hand and these three defendants upon the other. I say that this is not true, and every person in the hearing of my voice knows that it is not true.

Who is the state of Wisconsin, and how does the state of Wisconsin act? It moves only through its officers, ordinary men, strong in some ways, weak in others, subject to all those influences that move you and me and every other man that lives. Mr. Quartermass, the District Attorney, represents the state of Wisconsin. He comes into court, moved and influenced by the people of the community where he lives, by some more, by some less. He is persuaded to file an information charging a crime or offense against his fellow-citizens, and he haltingly complies with the request. He is simply the tool that is used, nothing more and nothing less; and the seal of the state of Wisconsin is not broad enough and heavy enough to cover up the infamy which caused this information to be filed branding these three men as criminals before the law.

\*          \*          \*

Gentlemen, George M. Paine is not supporting these men. These men and women and little children are supporting him. It is through their labor and their toil that he has grown rich and prosperous and great. Here are some of the things that are expected of a man who goes to work for Paine:

"The following rules are made in the interest of good order and strict attention to business [recitation of restraints upon workers]:

\*          \*          \*

Why, gentlemen, the only difference that I can see between the state's prison and George M. Paine's factory is that Paine's men are not allowed to sleep on the premises. American citizens do not exactly relish the idea of being locked up even in a factory; they have inherited certain foolish traditions of liberty that make them object, but they doubtless get over these prejudices in time. Don't be in such a hurry, gentlemen—give them a little time, a little time.

And because these men dared to go to Paine and ask for higher wages, because they had the effrontery to ask for a few more pennies of that wealth that they are grinding out at his machines, because they asked a little more of that money which comes from the sashes and the doors and the blinds which he sends to fourteen states of this great union, he wants to send them to jail.

Gentlemen of the jury, it is the theory of the State in this case, so far as they have a theory, that Mr. Kidd was responsible for this strike. Now, there is one beauty about a conspiracy case; there is one thing that made it valuable to ancient tyrants, and that makes it equally valuable to modern tyrants, and that is that you do not need much of any theory to carry it on. . . . [I]f there happens to be someone you are after, then you make a charge of conspiracy, and you are allowed to prove what the defendant said and did, and what everybody else said and did over any length of time that you see fit to carry it, and there you get your conspiracy. Conspiracy is the child of the Star Chamber [secret] Court of England, and it has come down to us, like most bad things and many good ones, from the remote past, without much modification. Whenever a king wanted to get rid of somebody, whenever a political disturber was in someone's way, then they brought a charge of conspiracy, and they not only proved everything he said, but everything everyone else said and everyone else did.

\*          \*          \*

When these manufacturers set out to get rid of Kidd they started for injunctions. Now, an injunction is a sort of an invention of the devil. But they evidently could not find a judge in Oshkosh that could be used for that purpose. Not one. George M. Paine, when he was on the stand, admitted, although his memory is very faulty—excepting in matters that he wishes to tell—but he admitted that he did try to get these men enjoined, but he could not do it. The judges would not do it; and then he sought to have them arrested, and he went to Quartermass, and he hired lawyers.... They could not prosecute him for vagrancy, and so they unearthed this old Star Chamber proceeding, the same proceedings that in every age of the world have been used to condemn patriots and heretics and the great and the humane of the earth because miserable tyrants desired their blood....

\*          \*          \*

Now, gentlemen, I want to say a few words in relation to the labor question, which is really the controversy involved in this case, because that is all there is of it. Back of all this prosecution is the effort on the part of George M. Paine to wipe these labor organizations out of existence, and you know it. That's all there is of it.

You have heard a great deal of evidence as to whether Thomas I. Kidd provoked this strike. I do not care whether he did or did not. Gentlemen, if it was in my power tomorrow to provoke another strike in this city that would succeed, I would do it, even though the jail opened to receive me. I would do it for the duty I owe to my fellow-men. I do not care whether Kidd provoked this strike or not. I know, gentlemen, that he did what he could in his poor way, with his poor strength, to fight those great monopolies in the interest of the men and women and little children that he loves; and for that you are asked to send him to jail.

\*          \*          \*

Let me tell you something of labor organizations. I have studied this question because I believe in it, because I love it as I do my very life; because it has been the strongest passion of my years; because in this great battle between the powerful and the weak I have ever been and will ever be with the weak so long as the breath is left in my body to speak. I have read it—not, gentlemen, for this case, not for the dirty gold of Paine—but I have read it because I loved it, and because in my own way I wished to do what I could for the thousands—aye, the millions of people who are yet poorer than myself. I know the history of the labor movement; I know what it has come through. I know the difficulties it is in today.

\*          \*          \*

The first step in the conspiracy was forming this organization; the next step was making this request

for wages. The letter containing the request was courteous, it was kind; it was not altogether true because it was too kind; but if any man ever received a courteous letter from a body of his employees, then George M. Paine received such a letter from his men. They respectfully asked him to do four things. First, to raise wages—a terrible crime. Next, to have a weekly pay day. Mr. Houghton [Paine's lawyer] had told them that they had a right to do this. Of course, when he said that he did not get a retainer, so perhaps the advice was not good. You cannot trust a lawyer unless you pay him, and you had better watch him even then. The next request was that he should not employ women, and I think that was right. And then they asked that the union be recognized, although they did not make that as a demand; and I think that was right. But it is not what I think. It is not what you think. These men were employees: they had as much at stake in the running of this factory as George M. Paine. They at least had the right to make these respectful requests in a respectful way; and were they not courteous and decent?

\*          \*          \*

This organization addressed a respectful letter to George M. Paine, and he received it.... And they gave him two days to answer their respectful letter; and he received the letter and put it in the wastebasket. He is a nice man, is he not?

\*          \*          \*

These workmen struck, and this was another conspiracy....

\*          \*          \*

But now let us see what took place. We have heard a great deal about riot and bloodshed and violation of the law. Let me talk with you and reason with you for a moment about that. How much disorder was there in the city of Oshkosh? First, let me call your attention to the fact that sixteen hundred men, honest workingmen of your town, were on a strike; that this strike lasted for fourteen weeks. Of course there was excitement; it could not have been otherwise. Men were taking the places of some of the workers; men were idle on the streets; the matter was the chief topic of thought and discussion. The militia was called out, and of course the tension was extreme during those long fourteen weeks. And yet, gentlemen, aside from these riots ... there was but one single act of violence in the whole fourteen weeks.

\*          \*          \*

Thomas I. Kidd is to be made responsible upon two theories. First, that he knew of and had to do with these unlawful acts, although no human being has yet brought that home to him; not one. Next, because he advised and counseled them.

\*          \*          \*

But did Kidd advise riot?

*          *          *

Gentlemen, the overwhelming evidence in this case shows that from the beginning to the end Kidd counseled peace and order and quiet, and told the men that only in this way could they gain their ends. . . .

*          *          *

Men do not build for today; they do not build for tomorrow. They build for the centuries, for the ages; and when we look back it is the despised criminal and outlaw, the man perhaps without home or country or friend, who has lifted the world upward and onward toward the blessed brotherhood which one day will come. Here is Thomas I. Kidd. He draws a salary of twenty dollars a week. This is more than the Oshkosh woodworkers are paid. It is not a munificent salary, gentlemen. It is not too large for a man who goes up and down the land to help his fellowmen. . . . Gentlemen, it is not a bed of roses in which the agitator sleeps. He may hear himself make speeches, but he often feels that the crowd draws back and shuns him as they would a leper's touch. He may hear himself speak and may receive applause, but it means social ostracism. Aye, gentlemen, it means more. The man who undertakes to serve humanity consecrates his life and he must endure all things, and risk all things, for the cause he serves.

*          *          *

Gentlemen, the world is dark; but it is not hopeless. Here and there through the past some man has ever risen, some man like Kidd, willing to give the devotion of his great soul to humanity's holy cause. Here and there all through the past these men have come, and through the future they will come again. They will come to move the world onward and upward; they will come beckoning their fellow-men to follow in their lead; they will point to a sunrise far away, so distant that the ordinary mortal cannot see, but which is clear to their prophetic eye.

*          *          *

## 172 To Establish "White Supremacy" (1898)

Toward the end of the century, political activity among North Carolina blacks increased. A fusion of Populists and Republicans elected a Republican governor in 1896, and growing numbers of blacks were appointed to federal and state offices. Ousted from power, the Democrats grew hostile, resorting to inflammatory propaganda and violence against black voters. A vigilante group, the Red Shirts, was particularly instrumental in the terrorist campaign that resulted in a Democratic electoral victory in 1898. Emboldened by the victory, the white population of Wilmington on November 8 burned down the office of a black newspaper, then proceeded to riot and attack local blacks. The number of those killed is estimated between twenty and one hundred. The rioters deposed the mayor and forced all black officials to resign, thereby forcing the formation of a new government. Resort to the poll tax and a grandfather clause by the state assembly completed the process of divesting blacks of political power.

The document records the reminiscences of Gunner Jessie Blake, a participant in the riot.

## ☆ 172 The Wilmington Rebellion

Account by Gunner Jessie Blake in Harry Hayden, *The Wilmington Rebellion* (1938), reprinted in Richard Hofstadter and Michael Wallace, *American Violence: A Documentary History* (New York: Knopf, 1970), 231-34.

"You boys were too young to remember much about the Wilmington Rebellion, November 10, 1898," began Mr. Blake, an unreconstructed Rebel who to this day *holds that the South fought for Independence, not Slavery*, and who continues to use the ante- and post-bellum by-word, damnedyank, as a single word without even dignifying the appellation with a capital "D."

"So, I am going to give you the inside story of this insurrection," he proceeded, "wherein the white people of Wilmington overthrew the constituted municipal authority overnight and substituted a reform rule, doing all this legally and with some needless bloodshed, to be sure, but at the same time they eliminated the Negroes from the political life of the city and the state. This Rebellion was the very beginning of Negro disfranchisement in the South and an important step in the establishment of 'White Supremacy' in the Southland. . . .

"The Rebellion was an organized resistance," Mr. Blake said, "on the part of the white citizens of this community to the established government, which had long irked them because it was dominated by 'Carpet Baggers' and Negroes, and also because the better element here wished to establish 'White Supremacy' in the city, the state and throughout the South, and thereby remove the then stupid and ignorant Negroes from their numerically dominating position in the government. . . .

"The older generation of Southern born men were at their wits' end. They had passed through the rigors of the North-South war and through the tyrannies of Reconstruction when Confiscation (the latter the most hated word in the conquered Confederacy next to damnedyankee) of properties without due process of law, was the rule rather than the exception. They had seen 'Forty Acres and a Mule' buy many a Negro's vote.

"Black rapists were attacking Southern girls and women, those pure and lovely creatures who graced the homes in Dixie Land, and the brutes were committing this dastardly crime with more frequency while the majority of them were escaping punishment through the influence of the powers that be.

\*　　\*　　\*

"A group of nine citizens met at the home of Mr. Hugh MacRae and there decided that the attitude and actions of the Negroes made it necessary for them to take some steps towards protecting their families and homes in their immediate neighborhood, Seventh and Market Streets. . . .

"This group of citizens, who will hereafter be referred to as the 'Secret Nine,' divided the city into sections, placing a responsible citizen as captain in charge of each area, and they named Messrs. Lathrop and Manning as their contact men, who were the only ones of the 'Secret Nine' known to the divisional captains. . . .

"The better element planned to gain relief from Negro impudence and domination, from grafting and from immoral conditions; the 'Secret Nine' and the white leaders marked time, hoping something would happen to arouse the citizenry to concerted action.

"But the 'watch-and-wait policy' of the 'Secret Nine' did not obtain for long, as during the latter part of October (1898) there appeared in the columns of The Wilmington (Negro) Daily Record an editorial, written by the Negro editor, Alex Manly, which aroused a state-wide revulsion to the city and state administrations then in the hands of the Republicans and Fusionists. The editorial attempted to justify the Negro rape fiends at the expense of the virtue of Southern womanhood."

Mr. Blake walked over to the library table, stooped and picked up an old scrap book that was reposing on the table's shelf, and then he read the following obnoxious editorial from The Wilmington Record:

> Poor whites are careless in the matter of protecting their women, especially on the farm. They are careless of their conduct towards them, and our experience among the poor white people in the county teaches us that women of that race are not more particular in the matter of clandestine meetings with colored men, than are the white man and colored women.
>
> Meetings of this kind go on for some time until the woman's infatuation, or the man's boldness, bring attention to them, and the man is lynched for rape.
>
> Every Negro lynched is called a "big, burly, black brute," when in fact, many of those who have been thus dealt with had white men for their fathers, and were not only not "black" and "burly," but were sufficiently attractive for white girls of culture and refinement to fall in love with them, as is very well known to all.

"That editorial," Mr. Blake declared with some vehemence as he banged the closed scrap book with his fist, "is the straw that broke Mister Nigger's political back in the Southland." . . .

"A thousand or more white citizens, representative of all walks of life from the minister to the merchant, the mariner to the mendicant, attended the mass meeting in the New Hanover county court house the next morning, November 10, at 11 o'clock.

"Colonel Alfred Moore Waddell, a mild mannered Southern gentleman, noted for his extremely conservative tendencies, was called upon to preside over the gathering. In addressing this meeting, Colonel Waddell said: . . . 'We will not live under these intolerable conditions. No society can stand it. We intend to change it, if we have to choke the current of Cape Fear River with (Negro) carcasses!'

"*That* declaration," Mr. Blake said, "brought forth tremendous applause from the large gathering of white men at the mass meeting. His speech, other than the two paragraphs I have just quoted, was largely a statement of facts, but he was a silver tongued orator and the crowd cheered this distinguished white haired and bearded Southern gentleman throughout the course of his address." (He was as much respected by the Negroes as he was admired by the whites; his character was unimpeachable.)

"Colonel Waddel [*sic*], in concluding his address, announced that he heartily approved the set of resolutions which had been prepared by Mr. Hugh MacRae and which included the latter's 'Declaration of White Independence.'

"These resolutions were unanimously approved by the meeting, followed by a wonderful demonstration, the assemblage rising to its feet and cheering: 'Right! Right! Right!' and there were cries of 'Fumigate' the city with 'The Record' and 'Lynch Manly.' "

Mr. Blake then read the resolutions from the scrap book, as follows:

> Believing that the Constitution of the United States contemplated a government to be carried on by an enlightened people; believing that its framers did not anticipate the enfranchisement of an ignorant population of African origin, and believing that those men of the state of North Carolina, who joined in framing the union, did not contemplate for their descendants subjection to an inferior race.
>
> We, the undersigned citizens of the city of Wilmington and county of New Hanover, do hereby declare that we will no longer be ruled and will never again be ruled, by men of African origin.
>
> This condition we have in part endured because we felt that the consequences of the war of secession were such as to deprive us of the fair consideration of many of our countrymen. . . .

# 173 "a lifetime in the handling of dynamite" (1899-1900)

Dissatisfied with the available relief from their grievances against management, and seeing the law enlisted against them, workers sometimes resorted to violence. An important western mining center, Shoshone County, Idaho, had been in a state of unrest since 1892. In 1899, following the events reported below, the governor of Idaho declared martial law and called for federal assistance in suppressing the insurrection. The local populace and officials allegedly were sympathetic to the miners. President McKinley dispatched two hundred troops, who were accused of active brutality and unconstitutional activity. Pursuant to a resolution of the House of Representatives, the Committee on Military Affairs investigated these charges and exonerated the military force of wrongdoing. Nevertheless, both the propriety of the use of federal military force in connection with this essentially local violent act against management and Congress's conclusion concerning the interaction of martial and civil law remain questionable.

☆ 173 Coeur D'Alene Labor Troubles Report

H.R. Rep. No. 1999, 56th Cong., 1st Sess. (1900).

[SYLLABUS]

\*        \*        \*

Under the circumstances the governor of Idaho was warranted in making application to the President for troops to aid the civil authorities in executing the laws of the State.

It is conceded on all sides that the President of the United States was justified in sending troops to Shoshone County, Idaho, in response to the application of the governor.

Since October, 1899, the troops, not over 200 in number, have performed no duty in enforcing martial law or guarding prisoners, and the prison has been torn down. The troops are now in garrison in Osborne, 8 miles from the scene of the riot. They are there at the official request of the governor of Idaho, supported by a petition signed by 1,500 citizens of that community.

Under the conditions prevailing in Shoshone County in May, 1899, it was not necessary for the President to proclaim martial law under section 5300, Revised Statutes of the United States, and he did not declare martial law.

None of the charges preferred against the United States Army and its officers in Idaho, as set forth in the various paragraphs of the resolution, have been sustained by the testimony.

The military force in Shoshone County, under command of General Merriam, was used strictly in aid of the civil authorities. The sheriff and other county officials were in collusion with the rioters, and therefore civil authority could not be enforced. Some of the county officials were afterwards duly removed from office by judicial process because of said collusion and malfeasance in office.

The United States Army and its officers acted strictly within their instructions and the law.

President McKinley and the War Department exercised every precaution that the military act solely within the Constitution and not encroach in the distinct sphere of the civil authorities. The President exhibited his deep interest and solicitude in the cause of labor by his instruction "that the military must have nothing whatever to do with enforcing rules for the government of miners or miners' unions."

The writ of habeas corpus was not suspended in Shoshone County by the governor in 1899. The supreme court of Idaho refused to issue the writ on the facts presented, and the finding of the highest court of the State on this point, not having been reversed, is binding on this committee.

The proof is positive that the "right of free speech, free press, and peaceable assemblages" were not denied to the peaceable citizens of that community by the use of military power.

The so-called "permit system" is an extreme measure, devised and administered by the State authorities alone, and which they justify by the necessities of martial law. It was not directed against organized labor, but against the criminal members of certain organizations masquerading under the cloak of organized labor, who have for years conducted a reign of terror and lawlessness in the Cœur d'Alene mining district of that county.

The prisoners confined in the temporary prison in Shoshone County were civil prisoners under guard of the military forces. The military commander was authorized to enforce prison discipline against prisoners violating prison rules. The punishments inflicted were not excessive, and the treatment of the prisoners by the soldiers was humane and considerate.

As to all other charges in the resolution not hereinbefore referred to, reference is made to the statement hereinafter set forth.

Martial law and the administration of justice by civil courts can proceed side by side in a community which is in a state of insurrection and riot when the courts can not perform their proper functions without military protection.

Martial law ceases when the necessity for it ceases. It ceases when the civil authorities resume their unobstructed functions, although the military may be present to aid them if the need of such aid should arise.

When the United States Army is called upon to

protect the State against "domestic violence," the military forces act in aid of the State authorities to the extent that the purpose is to reestablish the civil authorities; but the military forces of the United States are not under the command of the State authorities, but of the military officers, under the President. To this extent it is an independent force, operating under the order of the President to perform the guaranty imposed upon the United States by the Constitution.

\*        \*        \*

On the 8th day of December, 1899, Mr. Lentz introduced House resolution No. 31, to provide a committee to investigate the conduct of the United States Army and its officers in Idaho, which, as amended, was adopted January 8, 1900. Said resolution reads as follows:

> Whereas it is a matter of general information given out by the public press and charged by the industrial organization known as the Western Federation of Miners that United States troops have been sent into the State of Idaho in defiance of and contrary to the provisions of Article IV, section 4, of the Constitution of the United States, in that it was done at the individual request of the governor of Idaho, without the authority of the legislature, and at a time when there was no condition of insurrection or riot, and when the legislature could have been called together without danger or delay from any source whatever; and, further, without even consultation by the governor with the sheriff of Shoshone County, where it was desired that the troops should be, and actually were, sent; and
>
> Whereas, in defiance of section 9, Article I, of the Constitution, martial law was declared and the writ of habeas corpus suspended in said county in a time of profound peace, when there was no condition of rebellion or invasion or any menace to the public safety; and
>
> Whereas it is charged that Brig. Gen. H. C. Merriam [acted in violation of the sixth and fourth amendments]; and
>
> Whereas it is charged that the said military commander arbitrarily and in defiance of the civil law ordered the arrest of the sheriff of the county and the board of county commissioners, and subsequently deposed them from office on the unproved pretext of neglect of duty; and
>
> Whereas it is charged that the said Brigadier-General Merriam, immediately upon the arrival of the troops, ordered the arrest of every man who was a member of the miners' union, and also of all citizens who were supposed to sympathize with the cause of organized labor; and
>
> Whereas it is charged that those citizens were imprisoned in what was known as the "bull pen," a place unfit for human habitation ...; and
>
> Whereas the imprisoned citizens ... were held in this vile and inhuman imprisonment for several months without charge or indictment against them, although two sessions of the grand jury were held in the meantime ...; and
>
> Whereas it is charged that by the use of the military power the writ of habeas corpus was suspended for months in Shoshone County, and the right of free speech, free press, and peaceable assemblages were denied to the peaceable citizens of that community without any excuse or justification whatever; and
>
> Whereas when the Industrial Commission sat in Wallace all union men who had been long residents of the county were in the "bull pen" and had no opportunity to appear before the commission; others were arrested while on their way to Wallace to appear before the commission, and thrown into the "bull pen" until after the commission adjourned....

\*        \*        \*

The population of the county of Shoshone is about 10,000, the greater portion of which is engaged in mining.

The towns and mining camps involved in the crimes of April 29, 1899, are Burke, Gem, Mullan, Kellogg, and Wardner. Out of 1,500 miners living in these camps, 1,000 were implicated, directly or indirectly, in the riot. The following extract from the Idaho State Tribune, published at Wallace, May 3, 1899, was written by James R. Sovereign, its editor, who was an eyewitness to the affair. It gives a graphic account of the occurrences of April 29, 1899, which were the immediate cause of the declaration of martial law [by the Governor of Idaho] and the call for United States troops:

> Saturday last witnessed what might properly be considered the close of a seven years' war.... About 10.30 a man on horseback came galloping down Bank street from Canyon Creek, and ... said, "They are coming." ... Five minutes later the whistle on the Northern Pacific engine pulling the train from Burke and Gem resounded with its usual regularity.... On its 9 freight and ore cars were packed 1,000 men, half of whom were masked and armed with Winchester rifles. After a short halt the train proceeded ... toward Wardner.
>
> [B]efore the train proceeded to Wardner with its human freight on its mission of destruction, armed men walked the streets in quest of an abundant supply of ammunition. It was evident to all that some of the scenes of 1892 were to be repeated, and this time the Bunker Hill and Sullivan Mining Company at Wardner, 12 miles below Wallace, was to be the victim of a forceful demonstration on the part of the organized miners of the Cœur d'Alenes....
>
> The train reached Wardner at 1 o'clock, and the work of clearing the country of all opposition was begun. A detachment of union miners armed with Winchester rifles was dispatched to the mountain side beyond the mill, and the work of placing under the mill 3,000 pounds of dynamite,

taken from the magazine of the Frisco mine at Gem, was commenced. At no time did the demonstration assume the appearance or the attitude of a disorganized mob. All the details were managed with the discipline and precision of a perfectly trained military organization. Each miner participating in the affair either wore a strip of white handkerchief in the buttonhole of his coat or a strip of white cloth tied on his right arm. Sixty armed scabs in the employ of the Bunker Hill company offered the only resistance, and they only gave expression to the most pitiable and lamentable cowardice. Only a few desultory shots from the miners were necessary to send them fleeing over the mountains. At the same time Mr. Burbidge, manager of the mine, might have been seen running [away] toward Kingston, skulking behind every conceivable object and wringing his hands in the desperation of fear. Probably a more humiliating spectacle has not presented itself to the world since the capture of King Charles, nor a more striking evidence of supreme cowardice than was shown by Mr. Burbidge, who heretofore has displayed the defiant air of a tyrant equaled only by Sir Henry Morgan, the leader of the buccaneers of the Spanish Main.

At 2.30 the arrangements were complete, the dynamite was placed under the mill in three departments, the fuse attached, and all was in readiness for the destruction of one of the largest concentrators in the world, costing the company the enormous sum of $250,000. All miners and friends of the miners were warned to take a safe distance from the work of destruction about to begin. The fuses were lighted, and at 2.26 there was an awful crash, and broken machinery and fragments of the building were hurled high into the air. Fifteen seconds later another followed, and in about the same time a third. From the force of the third shot débris was hurled in every direction, and a huge canopy was formed in the heavens. Fragments of machinery and broken timbers rained down upon the ruins for several seconds. The shock of each explosion was terrific and was heard 20 miles away. The work of destruction was complete. The great concentrator was as completely demolished as it could have been if months had been spent in preparing the giant explosives for that purpose. The work was planned and executed by men who have received the training of a lifetime in the handling of dynamite.

*       *       *

The explosion was indeed an awe-inspiring scene, and to the eyewitness, were it not for the horrors of destruction, presented a pyrotechnical display which would satisfy the most expert critic of Fourth of July fireworks.

. . . [An] ominous stillness of a few minutes followed. Winchesters and revolvers were everywhere in evidence. The silence was broken by a single shot from a Winchester from some person on top of one of the cars, followed by a deafening fusillade. For five minutes the rattle of musketry

was incessant. It was evident, however, from the beginning of the firing that no harm was intended; that the men were simply celebrating the victory they had secured in the destruction of the Bunker Hill concentrator. In the midst of the firing the enemies gave the starting signal and the train moved slowly toward Wallace. . . .

. . . Ranchers and laboring people living in the valley congregated along the track and cheered the men lustily as they passed along. The train reached Wallace about 4 o'clock, and about a hundred of the people of the city were congregated at the depot to witness its arrival. Mayor Smith had taken the precaution to temporarily close the saloons. . . .

During the desultory firing at Wardner, shortly after the train from Wallace arrived, Jack Smythe, a miner at the Frisco mine, was shot and instantly killed. How it happened or by whom he was shot is not definitely known. Some say he was shot by scabs in the employ of the Bunker Hill company, others that he was shot by the striking miners through mistake. James Cheyne, a vanner man at the Bunker Hill mill, was shot through the hip and died at the Sacred Heart Hospital in Spokane yesterday morning. R. R. Rogers, the stenographer of the Bunker Hill company, was slightly wounded in the upper lip. So far as known, this constitutes all the casualties of the day's doings in connection with the Bunker Hill explosion.

## 174 "that organized government should be overthrown" (1902)

Toward the end of the nineteenth century, violence at the hands of anarchists spread throughout Europe. America was not immune from this terror. A Polish-born anarchist, Leon Czolgosz, assassinated President McKinley on September 6, 1901. In that same year, the United Mine Workers staged a five-month strike, which crippled the nation. Public confusion existed over the difference between militant unionism and anarchism, particularly since the joint strike by anarchists and unionists which had resulted in the Haymarket Riot of 1886. Reacting to fears of anarchism, the New York law set out to suppress not only violent conduct but also the doctrine itself and all political activity connected with it.

### ☆ 174 New York Criminal Anarchy Law

New York Penal Code 1881, § 468(a), (b), (c), (d), (e), added L. 1902, c. 371, § 1.

#### CHAP. 371

AN ACT to amend the penal code by inserting therein five additional sections. . . .

Became a law, April 3, 1902, with the approval of the Governor. . . .

§ 468-a. *Criminal anarchy defined.* — Criminal anarchy is the doctrine that organized government should be overthrown by force or violence, or by assassination of the executive head or of any of the executive officials of government, or by any unlawful means. The advocacy of such doctrine either by word of mouth or writing is a felony.

§ 468-b. *Advocacy of criminal anarchy.* — Any person who:

1. By word of mouth or writing advocates, advises or teaches the duty, necessity or propriety of overthrowing or overturning organized government by force or violence, or by assassination of the executive head or of any of the executive officials of government, or by any unlawful means; or

2. Prints, publishes, edits, issues or knowingly circulates, sells, distributes or publicly displays any book, paper, document, or written or printed matter in any form, containing or advocating, advising or teaching the doctrine that organized government should be overthrown by force, violence or any unlawful means; or,

3. Openly, willfully and deliberately justifies by word of mouth or writing the assassination or unlawful killing or assaulting of any executive or other officer of the United States or of any state or of any civilized nation having an organized government because of his official character, or any other crime, with intent to teach, spread or advocate the propriety of the doctrines of criminal anarchy; or

4. Organizes or helps to organize or becomes a member of or voluntarily assembles with any society, group or assembly of persons formed to teach or advocate such doctrine;

is guilty of a felony and punishable by imprisonment for not more than ten years, or by a fine of not more than five thousand dollars, or both.

§ 468-c. *Liability of editors and others.* — Every editor or proprietor of a book, newspaper or serial and every manager of a partnership or incorporated association by which a book, newspaper or serial is issued, is chargeable with the publication of any matter contained in such book, newspaper or serial. But in every prosecution therefor, the defendant may show in his defense that the matter complained of was published without his knowledge or fault and against his wishes, by another who had no authority from him to make the publication and whose act was disavowed by him so soon as known.

§ 468-d. *Assemblages of anarchists.* — Whenever two or more persons assemble for the purpose of advocating or teaching the doctrines of criminal anarchy, . . . such an assembly is unlawful, and every person voluntarily participating therein by his presence, aid or instigation, is guilty of a felony and punishable by imprisonment for not more than ten

years, or by a fine of more than five thousand dollars, or both.

§ 468-e. *Permitting premises to be used for assemblages of anarchists.* — The owner, agent, superintendent, janitor, caretaker or occupant of any place, building or room, who willfully and knowingly permits therein any assemblage of persons prohibited . . . is guilty of a misdemeanor, and punishable by imprisonment for not more than two years, or by a fine of not more than two thousand dollars, or both.

# 175 "person[s] . . . opposed to all organized government" (1903)

After McKinley died from the bullet of Leon Czolgosz, President Theodore Roosevelt directed his attention to tightening America's immigration laws. In an address to the Fifty-seventh Congress, he called for excluding all anarchists or members of anarchistic societies. He also called for excluding persons who were of "low moral tendency" or "unsavory reputation." Representative Shattuc of Ohio introduced the new immigration act, which contained several of Roosevelt's suggestions, in addition to exclusion of the mentally impaired, epileptics, paupers, beggars, and the contagiously diseased. While exempting "purely political" offenders from exclusion, it nevertheless provided for the debarment of the advocates of anarchy and provided criminal penalties for those who aided an anarchist's entry into the country.

☆ 175 Immigration Act of 1903

32 Stat. 1213 (1903).

\* \* \*

SEC. 2. That the following classes of aliens shall be excluded from admission into the United States: All . . . persons who have been convicted of a felony or other crime or misdemeanor involving moral turpitude. . . .

*Provided*, That nothing in this Act shall exclude persons convicted of an offense purely political, not involving moral turpitude. . . .

\* \* \*

SEC. 38. That no person who disbelieves in or who is opposed to all organized government, or who is a member of or affiliated with any organization entertaining and teaching such disbelief in or opposition to all organized government, or who advocates or teaches the duty, necessity, or propriety of the unlawful assaulting or killing of any officer or officers, either of specific individuals or of officers generally, of the Government of the United States or of any other organized government, because of his or their official character, shall be permitted to enter the United States. . . .

That any person who knowingly aids or assists any such person to enter the United States . . . or who connives or conspires with any person or persons to allow, procure, or permit any such person to enter therein . . . shall be fined not more than five thousand dollars, or imprisoned for not less than one nor more than five years, or both.

## 176 "undesirable additions to our population" (1904)

John Turner, an Englishman alleging to be a paid labor organizer, entered the United States in order to deliver a series of lectures on the "Essentials of Anarchism," the "General Strike," and the "Legal Murder of 1887" (the Haymarket trials). Arrested within ten days of his arrival on a warrant charging him with being an anarchist, Turner was sent to and detained at Ellis Island. Turner challenged his detention by means of a writ of habeas corpus, arguing that the immigration law of 1903 was unconstitutional.

In upholding Turner's arrest and deportation, Chief Justice Fuller noted that "the deportation of an alien who is found to be here in violation of law is not a deprivation of liberty without due process of law, and that the provisions of the Constitution securing the right of trial by jury have no application."

### 176 *Turner v. Williams*

194 U.S. 279 (1904).

Statement by Mr. Chief Justice FULLER: John Turner filed in the United States circuit court for the southern district of New York, October 26, 1903, a petition alleging —

"First. That on October 23, in the city of New York, your relator was arrested by divers persons claiming to be acting by authority of the government of the United States, and was by said persons conveyed to the United States immigration station at Ellis island, in the harbor of New York, and is now there imprisoned by the commissioner of immigration of the port of New York.

"Second. Your relator is so imprisoned by virtue of a warrant sworn out by the Secretary of the Department of Commerce and Labor, which warrant charges your relator with being an anarchist, and being unlawfully within the United States, in violation of § 2 and § 20 of the immigration laws of the United States. . . .

*          *          *

"Fourth. Your relator denies that he is an anarchist within the meaning of the immigration laws of the United States, and states to the court that about six years ago he took out his first papers of application for citizenship in this country, and that he has at no times been engaged as a propagandist of doctrines inciting to, or advising, violent overthrow of government, but for about six years last past he has been the paid organizer of the retail clerks of Great Britain, and his business in this country is solely to promote the interests of organized labor, and that he has at all times conducted himself as a peaceful and law-abiding citizen."

*          *          *

. . . Turner testified that he was an Englishman; that he had been in the United States ten days, and that he did not come through New York, but declined to either affirm or deny that he arrived via Canada; that he would not undertake to deny that he had, in the lecture delivered in New York, October 23, declared himself to be an anarchist, which, he said, was a statement that he would make; and that the testimony of the inspectors was about correct. That evidence gave extracts from the address referred to, including these: "Just imagine what a universal tie-up would mean. What would it mean in New York city alone if this idea of solidarity were spread through the city? If no work was being done, if it were Sunday for a week or a fortnight, life in New York would be impossible, and the workers, gaining audacity, would refuse to recognize the authority of their employer, and eventually take to themselves the handling of the industries. . . . All over Europe they are preparing for a general strike, which will spread over the entire industrial world. Everywhere the employers are organizing, and to me, at any rate, as an anarchist, as one who believes that the people should emancipate themselves, I look forward to this struggle as an opportunity for the workers to assert the power that is really theirs."

Certain papers were found on Turner, one of them being a list of his proposed series of lectures (which, when the warrant was in execution, he rolled up and threw away), the subjects including: "The Legal Murder of 1887," and "The Essentials of Anarchism;" notices of meetings, one of a mass meeting November 9, at which "speeches will be delivered by John Turner in English, John Most in German, and several other speakers. Don't miss this opportunity to hear the truth expressed about the great Chicago tragedy on the eleventh of November, 1887;" and another, stating: "It may be interesting to all that Turner has recently refused to accept a candidacy to Parliament because of his anarchistic principles."

*          *          *

Mr. Chief Justice FULLER delivered the opinion of the court:

*          *          *

It is contended that the act of March 3, 1903, is unconstitutional because in contravention of the 1st, 5th, and 6th articles of amendment of the Constitution, and of § 1 of article 3 of that instrument; and because no power "is delegated by the Constitution to the general government over alien friends with reference to their admission into the United States or otherwise, or over the beliefs of citizens, denizens, sojourners, or aliens, or over the freedom of speech or of the press."

Repeated decisions of this court have determined that Congress has the power to exclude aliens from the United States; to prescribe the terms and conditions on which they may come in; to establish regulations for sending out of the country such aliens as have entered in violation of law, and to commit the enforcement of such conditions and regulations to executive officers; that the deportation of an alien who is found to be here in violation of law is not a deprivation of liberty without due process of law, and that the provisions of the Constitution securing the right of trial by jury have no application.

\*          \*          \*

Whether rested on the accepted principle of international law, that every sovereign nation has the power, as inherent in sovereignty and essential to self-preservation, to forbid the entrance of foreigners within its dominions, or to admit them only in such cases and upon such conditions as it may see fit to prescribe; or on the power to regulate commerce with foreign nations, which includes the entrance of ships, the importation of goods, and the bringing of persons into the ports of the United States, the act before us is not open to constitutional objection. . . .

\*          \*          \*

. . . [I]t is said that the act violates the 1st Amendment, which prohibits the passage of any law "respecting an establishment of religion, or prohibiting the free exercise thereof; or abridging the freedom of speech, or of the press; or the right of the people peaceably to assemble, and to petition the government for a redress of grievances."

We are at a loss to understand in what way the act is obnoxious to this objection. It has no reference to an establishment of religion, nor does it prohibit the free exercise thereof; nor abridge the freedom of speech or of the press; nor the right of the people to assemble and petition the government for a redress of grievances. It is, of course, true, that if an alien is not permitted to enter this country, or, having entered contrary to law, is expelled, he is in fact cut off from worshiping or speaking or publishing or petitioning in the country; but that is merely because of his exclusion therefrom. He does not become one of the people to whom these things are secured by our Constitution by an attempt to enter, forbidden by law. . . .

Appellant's contention really comes to this: that the act is unconstitutional so far as it provides for the exclusion of an alien because he is an anarchist.

The argument seems to be that, conceding that Congress has the power to shut out any alien, the power, nevertheless, does not extend to some aliens, and that if the act includes all alien anarchists, it is unconstitutional, because some anarchists are merely political philosophers, whose teachings are beneficial rather than otherwise.

\*          \*          \*

If the word "anarchists" should be interpreted as including aliens whose anarchistic views are professed as those of political philosophers, innocent of evil intent, it would follow that Congress was of opinion that the tendency of the general exploitation of such views is so dangerous to the public weal that aliens who hold and advocate them would be undesirable additions to our population, whether permanently or temporarily, whether many or few; and, in the light of previous decisions; the act, even in this aspect, would not be unconstitutional, as applicable to any alien who is opposed to all organized government.

\*          \*          \*

*Order affirmed.*

# 177 The Assassination of Governor Steunenberg (1905)

On December 30, 1905, Governor Frank Steunenberg of Idaho was killed by a bomb. Steunenberg was the carrier of a union card and was elected governor in 1896 and again in 1898 with heavy labor support, but he later became instrumental in the crushing of the Coeur d'Alene strike. It was a common belief that the Western Federation of Miners, which viewed Steunenberg as a betrayer of labor, was responsible for his murder.

While the W.F.M. denied the accusation, the apprehended assassin, Harry Orchard, confessed to a police informant that the leaders of the union instigated the crime. The three named by Orchard, including William D. Haywood, the secretary-treasurer of the union, were arrested in Colorado and were brought to Idaho without legal extradition. The events touched off an uproar in labor and radical circles. Public protests were held in Boston, New York, and San Francisco. Clarence Darrow served as defense counsel at Haywood's trial. After eighteen months in jail and eleven weeks of trial, Haywood was found not guilty. The second union leader also was acquitted, and the third was never tried.

Orchard was sentenced to death, but the sentence was commuted by the Pardons Board. He died in jail in 1954, at age eighty-eight, having spent nearly fifty years in prison.

Portions of Clarence Darrow's summation before the Boise jury in the Haywood trial are contained in the accompanying document.

## ☆ 177 The Defense Summation in the Trial of William D. "Big Bill" Haywood

Reprinted in A. Weinberg, ed., *Attorney for the Damned* (New York: Simon & Schuster, 1957), 483-86.

I don't claim that this man is an angel. The Western Federation of Miners could not afford to put an angel at their head. Do you want to hire an angel to fight the Mine Owners' Association and the Pinkerton detectives, and the power of wealth? Oh, no, gentlemen; you better get a first-class fighting man who has physical courage, who has mental courage, who has strong devotion, who loves the poor, who loves the weak, who hates iniquity and hates it more when it is with the powerful and the great; and you cannot win without it, and I believe that down in your hearts there is not one of you would wish him to be an angel. You know an angel would not be fitted for that place, and I make no claim of that; but he is not a demon. If he were a demon or a bad man he would never be working in this cause, for the prizes of the world are somewhere else. The man who enters the labor movement, either as an organizer, a member, or a lawyer, and who enters it in the hope of reward, is a foolish man indeed. The rewards are on the other side — unless you look for your reward to your conscience and to your consciousness of a duty well done. I presume that this big, strong man is a man, a man that has strength and has power, and has weakness; a man of love and affection, a man of strong nature, of strong purposes — I don't know about that, and I don't care about it; I don't look for anything else in man; I want the man of courage and brains and devotion and strength.

\* \* \*

I have known Haywood — I have known him well and I believe in him. God knows it would be a sore day to me if he should go upon the scaffold. The sun would not shine or the birds would not sing on that day — for me. It would be a sad day, indeed, if any such calamity would come to him. I would think of him, I would think of his wife, of his mother, I would think of his children, I would think of the great cause that he represents. It would be a sore day for me, but, gentlemen, he and his mother, and his wife and his children, are not my chief concern in this great case. If you should decree that he must die, ten thousand men will work in the mines and send a portion of the proceeds of their labor to take care of that widow and these orphan children, and a million people throughout the length and breadth of the civilized world will send their messages of kindness and good cheer to comfort them in their bereavement and to heal their wounds. It is not for them I plead. Other men have died before. Other men have died in the same cause in which Bill Haywood has risked his life. Men strong with devotion, men who loved liberty, men who loved their fellow-men, patriots who have raised their voices in defense of the poor, in defense of right, have made their good fight and have met death on the scaffold, on the rack, in the flame, and they will meet it again and again until the world grows old and gray. William Haywood is no better than the rest. He can die if die he must. He can die if this jury decrees it; but, oh, gentlemen, do not think for a moment that if you hang him you will crucify the labor movement of the world; do not think that you will kill the hopes and the aspirations and the desires of the weak and poor. You men of wealth and power, you people anxious for his blood, are you so blind as to believe that liberty will die when he is dead? Think you there are no other brave hearts, no other strong arms, no other devoted souls who will risk all in that great cause which has demanded martyrs in every land and age?

## 178 *Mother Earth* (1906)

Emma Goldman (1869-1940), born in Russia, moved to St. Petersburg at age thirteen, one year after the assassination of Czar Alexander II. After arriving in the United States in 1886, she worked in clothing factories in Rochester, New York. Goldman became active in the anarchist movement after 1889, and her speeches received widespread attention. In 1892, she helped Alexander Berkman in his assassination attempt on Henry Clay Frick of United States Steel during the Homestead Strike in Pittsburgh. She was imprisoned for inciting to riot in 1893. She and Berkman published the anarchist paper *Mother Earth*.

Arrested in June 1917 for obstructing the draft and sedition, she was deported to Russia two years later. Goldman left Russia in 1921 because of her disagreement with the Bolshevik government. Although an advocate of political change through violence in her early years, she eventually came to condemn it. In 1928, she wrote to Berkman that she wished she could adopt the nonviolent attitude of Gandhi and Tolstoy: "I feel that violence in whatever form never had and probably never will bring constructive results." Nevertheless, in this essay Goldman distinguished the general political philosophy of anarchism from the ultimate resort to terrorism in the face of tyranny, suggesting that terrorist acts are the natural response of normal people to stresses of intolerable oppressions.

## ☆178 The Psychology of Political Violence (Emma Goldman)

Reprinted in E. Goldman, *Anarchism and Other Essays* (Port Washington, N.Y.: Kennikat Press, 1969), 85–114.

\*     \*     \*

The ignorant mass looks upon the man who makes a violent protest against our social and economic iniquities as upon a wild beast, a cruel, heartless monster, whose joy it is to destroy life and bathe in blood; or at best, as upon an irresponsible lunatic. Yet nothing is further from the truth. As a matter of fact, those who have studied the character and personality of these men, or who have come in close contact with them, are agreed that it is their supersensitiveness to the wrong and injustice surrounding them which compels them to pay the toll of our social crimes. The most noted writers and poets, discussing the psychology of political offenders, have paid them the highest tribute. . . .

[I]t is among the Anarchists that we must look for the modern martyrs who pay for their faith with their blood, and who welcome death with a smile, because they believe, as truly as Christ did, that their martyrdom will redeem humanity.

\*     \*     \*

[The] indisputable fact is that homicidal outrages have, from time immemorial, been the reply of goaded and desperate classes, and goaded and desperate individuals, to wrongs from their fellowmen, which they felt to be intolerable. Such acts are the violent recoil from violence, whether aggressive or repressive; they are the last desperate struggle of outraged and exasperated human nature for breathing space and life. And their cause lies not in any special conviction, but in the depths of that human nature itself. The whole course of history, political and social, is strewn with evidence of this fact. To go no further, take the three most notorious examples of political parties goaded into violence during the last fifty years: the Mazzinians in Italy, the Fenians in Ireland, and the Terrorists in Russia. Were these people Anarchists? No. Did they all three even hold the same political opinions? No. The Mazzinians were Republicans, the Fenians political separatists, the Russians Social Democrats or Constitutionalists. But all were driven by desperate circumstances into this terrible form of revolt. And when we turn from parties to individuals who have acted in like manner, we stand appalled by the number of human beings goaded and driven by sheer desperation into conduct obviously violently opposed to their social instincts.

\*     \*     \*

That every act of political violence should nowadays be attributed to Anarchists is not at all surprising. Yet it is a fact known to almost everyone familiar with the Anarchist movement that a great number of acts, for which Anarchists had to suffer, either originated with the capitalist press or were instigated, if not directly perpetrated, by the police.

\*     \*     \*

Can one doubt the logic, the justice of these words:

> Repression, tyranny, and indiscriminate punishment of innocent men have been the watchwords of the government of the alien domination in India ever since we began the commercial boycott of English goods. The tiger qualities of the British are much in evidence now in India. They think that by the strength of the sword they will keep down India! It is this arrogance that has brought about the bomb, and the more they tyrannize over a helpless and unarmed people, the more terrorism will grow. We may deprecate terrorism as outlandish and foreign to our culture, but it is inevitable as long as this tyranny continues, for it is not the terrorists that are to be blamed, but the tyrants who are responsible for it. It is the only resource for a helpless and unarmed people when brought to the verge of despair. It is never criminal on their part. The crime lies with the tyrant.

\*     \*     \*

Anarchism, more than any other social theory, values human life above things. All Anarchists agree with Tolstoy in this fundamental truth: if the production of any commodity necessitates the sacrifice of human life, society should do without that commodity, but it can not do without that life. That, however, nowise indicates that Anarchism teaches submission. How can it, when it knows that all suffering, all misery, all ills, result from the evil of submission?

Has not some American ancestor said, many years ago, that resistance to tyranny is obedience to God? And he was not an Anarchist even. I would say that resistance to tyranny is man's highest ideal. So long as tyranny exists, in whatever form, man's deepest aspiration must resist it as inevitably as man must breathe.

Compared with the wholesale violence of capital and government, political acts of violence are but a drop in the ocean. That so few resist is the strongest proof how terrible must be the conflict between their souls and unbearable social iniquities.

High strung, like a violin string, they weep and moan for life, so relentless, so cruel, so terribly inhuman. In a desperate moment the string breaks.

Untuned ears hear nothing but discord. But those who feel the agonized cry understand its harmony, they hear in it the fulfillment of the most compelling moment of human nature.

Such is the psychology of political violence.

# 179 "desperate men are now securing dynamite" (1907)

The United States experienced serious financial panic in 1907. In the West, unrest in the mines of Nevada gave rise once more to calls for federal military action in suppression of labor militancy. The telegraphic communications between Governor Sparks of Nevada and President Roosevelt reflected state efforts to obtain unlawfully the presence of federal military authority as a preventive police measure in order to maintain the peace between the rival economic forces — labor and management. It was perhaps not totally coincidental that the federal presence would chill the use of violence by labor and therefore maintain the status quo favorable to management. Nevertheless, after initially acceding to Nevada's alarm, Washington insisted on strict adherence to the constitutional standards for federal intervention and removed the troops.

☆ 179 Telegraphic Correspondence between Nevada Governor John Sparks and President Theodore Roosevelt

Reprinted in Report on Labor Troubles at Goldfield, Nevada, H.R. Doc. No. 607, 60th Cong., 1st Sess. 2 (1908), Ser. 5374.

Carson City, Nev.
December 3-4, 1907

Hon. Theodore Roosevelt
President of the United States

MR. PRESIDENT:

It now seems apparent that in the near future Nevada may expect serious labor troubles in the district of Goldfield and adjoining camps, which may result in violence and great destruction of both life and property. The State has no enrolled militia and if it had I doubt very much whether it would be effective in maintaining law and order. I am this day in communication with our Congressional representatives urging them to consult with you concerning conditions above stated, and as we now see them, it appears to me as governor of Nevada that it is my duty to ask if you can consistently give us assurance that we may depend upon immediate relief from the Presidio Barracks. I assure you Mr. President I am aware of the fact and consider it an extraordinary request to be made by any governor of the United States, but the existence of the case seems to require it at this time. I am informed that desperate men are now securing dynamite and arms to destroy property and human life. The sheriff of the county seems to be absolutely unable to cope with the situation. A committee of mine owners, mine operators and mill operators from the Goldfield district is now in consultation with me and I assure you, Mr. President, that they are well satisfied that we need relief. We have no military garrison in the State of Nevada and a small detachment of Federal troops stationed at Goldfield would certainly relieve the situation.

Very respectfully,

JOHN SPARKS, Governor of Nevada
R. C. STODDARD, Attorney General

---

The White House, Washington
December 4, 1907

Hon. John Sparks, Governor
Carson City, Nev.

Telegram received 3.05 o'clock this afternoon. The Federal Government is prepared to send detachment of troops at any moment subject of course to your making call under conditions prescribed by the United States Constitution. . . . I have ordered not to exceed two companies to be ready to move immediately if you make such request, as two companies would, I suppose, amount to the small detachment of which you speak.

THEODORE ROOSEVELT

---

Carson City, Nev.
December 5, 1907

His Excellency Theodore Roosevelt
President of the United States
Washington, D.C.

At Goldfield, Esmeralda County, State of Nevada, there does now exist domestic violence and unlawful combinations and conspiracies which do now so obstruct . . . the laws of the State of Nevada and now deprive and continue to deprive the people of said section of the State of the rights, privileges, immunities, and protection named in the Constitution of the United States and of the State of Nevada. . . .

The lawfully constituted authorities of this State are unable to apprehend and punish the perpetrators of . . . crimes and to prevent the commission of other threatened crimes and unless the relief hereinafter requested is granted this State and the lives and property of large numbers of its people will be irreparably affected and damaged, contrary to the peace and dignity of the United States and of the State of Nevada.

Therefore, pursuant to Article IV, section 4 of the Constitution of the United States, . . . I, John Sparks, governor, do hereby respectfully request that Your Excellency Theodore Roosevelt, President, do immediately sent to Goldfield, Esmeralda County, Nev., two companies of the troops of the Army of the United States to suppress unlawful disorder and violence, to protect life and property, to restore peace, and to insure protection of law to the people of the State of Nevada.

*        *        *

JOHN SPARKS, Governor

   Attest

W. G. DOUGLASS, Secretary of State

_____

The White House, Washington
December 5, 1907

Hon. John Sparks, Governor
Carson City, Nev.

I have received your request for troops made in accordance with the Constitution and laws of the United States and will accordingly immediately direct that a sufficient number of troops be sent to Nevada. The number must be determined by the military authorities.

THEODORE ROOSEVELT

_____

December 14, 1907

Hon. John Sparks, Governor
Carson City, Nev.

... The President has instructed me to advise you officially that he has caused several companies of the Regular Army to proceed to the locality in which such disturbances exist or are anticipated, to the end that they may be available in case the occasion contemplated by the Constitution and the laws of the United States for their interposition shall arise.

   The calls upon the President on the part of the government of Nevada for the interposition of troops do not at present satisfy the requirements of the Constitution and the laws so as to justify orders that the military force now at Goldfield shall take any affirmative action. If such action should be desired under the Constitution ... to suppress an insurrection a call must be made by the legislature of the State unless circumstances are such that the legislature can not be convened, and no statement or intimation has been made that the legislature of Nevada can not be convened....

   A mere statement of domestic disturbance would not seem to be sufficient.

   The facts thus far stated in the telegraphic communications from the governor of Nevada, high and unimpeachable as is the source, do not seem sufficient....

   It therefore appears that the communications thus far received from the government of Nevada do not constitute or furnish the basis for authority on the part of the President to direct the use of the armed forces of the United States in the maintenance of public order at Goldfield.

   I respectfully suggest that if in your judgment such interposition is needed you furnish further evidence of facts justifying action by the President to enforce the laws of the United States, or cause the legislature of Nevada to be convened and to make the necessary call in accordance with the Constitution....

ELIHU ROOT

_____

Goldfield, Nev.
December 15, 1907
(Received December 16 — 9.20 A.M.)

The President, Washington, D.C.

Fourteenth from Secretary of State. Submit that conditions in Goldfield necessitates presence but does not warrant active intervention of United States troops. However, am prepared to submit affidavits of more than one hundred representative citizens that they have been deprived of their rights as citizens of the United States and of State of Nevada. Arrival of troops in Goldfield undoubtedly prevented rioting and other disorder, as is shown by statements of same people, including sheriff. Although active intervention of United States troops not now necessary, withdrawal at present would unquestionably precipitate disorder which local and State authorities would be unable to control. In the event of rioting and other disorder justifying military intervention will make requisition in accordance with statutes.

*        *        *

JOHN SPARKS, Governor

_____

The White House, Washington
December 17, 1907

Hon. John Sparks, Governor of Nevada
Goldfield, Nev.

I sent the troops at your request because from the tenor of your telegrams and from the representations made me by the two Senators from Nevada it appeared that an insurrection was imminent against which the State authorities would be powerless. The troops have now been in Goldfield ten days and no insurrection has occurred, and seemingly no circumstances exist to justify your now calling on me for action by the troops under the provision of the Constitution. The troops were sent to Goldfield to be ready to meet a grave emergency which seemed likely at once to arise and to provide a substitute for the exercise by the State of its police function. I do not feel at liberty to leave them indefinitely under such circumstances that they will in effect be performing on the part of the United States those ordinary duties of maintaining public order in the State of Nevada which rest upon the State government. As the legislature of Nevada has not been convened, I am bound to assume that the powers already vested in the peace officers of the State are adequate, and that if they choose to do so they can maintain order themselves. Under these circumstances, unless there be forthwith further cause shown to justify keeping the troops at Goldfield, I shall direct that they return to their former station.

THEODORE ROOSEVELT

---

Goldfield, Nev.
December 20, 1907

The President, Washington, D.C.

We do find no warrant for statement that there has been or is a complete collapse of civil authority here. All the machinery of civil government has been in operation, but has been ineffective in dealing with certain forms of crime because local sentiment has nullified its action. . . . Our investigation so far completely has failed to sustain the general and sweeping allegations in the governor calling for troops, and the impression as to conditions here given in that call is misleading and without warrant. We do find no evidence that any condition then existed not easily controlled by the local authorities. Neither immediately preceding nor since the arrival of troops has there been any particular disorder, but immediately after arrival of troops mine owners announced reduction of wages from $5 to $4, and positively refused employment to all men who do not agree to renounce in writing the local union, although a law of Nevada prohibits such requirement. Large majority of our witnesses assert very earnestly that if troops should be withdrawn now and owners insist upon above requirements there will result serious violence directed against life and property. Rifles in considerable numbers brought in by both sides sometime ago are still believed to be in their possession. Many say they will leave as soon as possible if troops should be withdrawn, and we believe that many of them are sincere in these assertions. . . .

So far as can be learned no county officer was consulted by governor previous to calling for troops. All still resent his action and consider it was unnecessary. They do not believe there has been any need for troops here up to date, but they all further agree and have given us signed statement to the effect that the new element brought into situation since arrival of troops create a dangerous condition, and they recommend troops be left here until present difficulties are adjusted. . . . These men are trying to secure the benefit of Federal assistance to more easily maintain the public order for which they are responsible and at the same time place the responsibility on the President. The governor states to us in writing that he will not convene the legislature to consider call for troops nor will he take the necessary steps to form a State military, as is legally provided for, and that if the [troops] should be withdrawn he will do substantially nothing. In other words, the State authorities propose to do nothing but wholly rely on the Federal authorities. There has been substantial agreement by everybody who

appeared before us that the number of violent or [criminal] men in the organization here is certainly less than 200. With a population of about 14,000 people there would seem to be no good reason why the civil authorities here can not take care of their own city. . . .

MURRAY, NEILL, SMITH

---

Carson City, Nev.
December 26, 1907

The President, Washington

As chief magistrate of the State of Nevada, I have been of the opinion for the past year that a condition bordering on domestic violence and insurrection has existed in the Goldfield mining district. There has been an almost constant state of war between the miners' union and the mine owners, who employ the members of the union. . . . [T]he entire district became divided into two hostile camps—on the one hand the miners with their adherents and sympathizers, and on the other hand the mine owners with their adherents and sympathizers. The union alone claimed a membership of 3,000, and fully one-half of the membership were constantly armed. Arms and ammunition were purchased and kept by the union as a body. On the other hand the mine owners had in their employ a large number of watchmen and guards who were constantly armed and on duty. In addition to these forces were an unusually large number of the criminal element attracted to the new and booming mining camp. Under such conditions the civil authorities were practically powerless. They could attend to the ordinary petty offenders from day to day, but at the first conflict between the real armies of labor and capital they would have been swept away.

. . . A state of domestic violence and insurrection arises, in my judgment, when armed bodies are in existence with sufficient power to overcome the civil authorities, and continual threats were made of the destruction of life and property. This condition has existed in the Goldfield mining districts the past year and exists there now. It calls for the presence of the troops to keep the peace. As this condition has been of slow growth it will take time to remove it. . . . The communist and anarchist must seek new fields; the laboring man be convinced that arbitration and peaceful methods are more certain and lasting methods of improving his condition than by dynamite and the shotgun. This can only come about with time, and for the present and sometime in the future the strong arm of the military must be in evidence to convince all that no other method will be tolerated. . . . I called for the opinions of different representatives and individual citizens of the State generally as to the advisability of convening a special session to act upon a then existing emergency, which, however, did not relate to the present situation. The expressions received at that time indicated that 95 percent of the people were opposed to such an extra session. For geographical reasons and on account of the customary ten days' notice to members it would be impossible to convene and organize a special session of the legislature in less than three weeks, presuming on the most expeditious action on the part of the members. For these reasons I deem it impossible to convene the legislature in special session to meet the present emergency and still think it highly inadvisable.

JOHN SPARKS, Governor

The White House
December 28, 1907

Hon. John Sparks, Governor
Carson City, Nev.

Your telegram December 26 received. It in effect declares that you have failed to call the legislature together because, in your judgment, the legislature would not call upon the Government of the United States for the use of troops, although in your opinion it ought to do so. The Constitution of the United States imposes, not upon you, but upon the legislature, if it can be convened, the duty of calling upon the Government of the United States to protect the State of Nevada against domestic violence. You now request me to use the armed forces of the United States in violation of the Constitution because in your judgment the legislature would fail to perform its duty under the Constitution. The State government certainly does not appear to have made any serious effort to do its duty by the effective enforcement of its police functions. I repeat again what I have already said to you several times, that under the circumstances now existing in the State of Nevada as made known to me, an application from the legislature of the State is an essential condition to the indefinite continuance of the troops at Goldfield. Circumstances may change, and if they do I will take whatever action the needs of the situation require so far as my constitutional powers permit. But the first need is that the State authorities should do their duty, and the first step toward this is the assembling of the legislature. It is apparent from your telegram that the legislature of Nevada can readily be convened. You have fixed the period of three weeks as the time necessary to convene and organize a special session. If within five days from the receipt of this telegram you shall have issued the necessary notice to convene the legislature of Nevada, I shall continue the station of the troops at Goldfield during such period of three weeks. If within the term of five days such notice has not been issued, the troops will be immediately returned to their former stations.

THEODORE ROOSEVELT

## 180  Triple Damages and the Danbury Hatters Union (1908)

Although no one denied the right of labor to organize in local and in nationwide trade unions, concerted labor action in the form of strikes and boycotts frequently came under attack. Management and government resorted to both the common law of conspiracy and the Sherman Anti-Trust Act in efforts to curtail labor activism. In 1908, The Supreme Court approved the applicability of the antitrust laws to the activities of the hatters union of Danbury, Connecticut. The court rendered a verdict of seventy-four thousand dollars in damages against the union, which had attempted to boycott the products of a local hat manufacturer.

Later, in the case of *Gompers v. Buck's Stove and Range Co.*, Samuel Gompers, president of the American Federation of Labor, was held to have been properly cited for contempt of court under the Sherman Act for disobeying a court injunction to abandon the listing of the company as "unfair to labor" in union publications.

☆180  *Loewe v. Lawlor*

208 U.S. 274 (1908).

Mr. Chief Justice FULLER delivered the opinion of the Court:

\*          \*          \*

The question is whether [a treble damage action against a union for its boycott] can be maintained under the Anti-Trust Act.

\*          \*          \*

In our opinion, the combination described in the [complaint] is a combination "in restraint of trade or commerce among the several States," in the sense in which whose words are used in the act, and the action can be maintained accordingly.

And that conclusion rests on many judgments of this court, to the effect that the act prohibits any combination whatever to secure action which essentially obstructs the free flow of commerce between the States, or restricts, in that regard, the liberty of a trader to engage in business.

The combination charged falls within the class of restraints of trade aimed at compelling third parties and strangers involuntarily not to engage in the course of trade except on conditions that the combination imposes; and there is no doubt that (to quote from the well-known work of Chief Justice Erle on Trade Unions) "at common law every person has individually, and the public also has collectively, a right to require that the course of trade should be kept free from unreasonable obstruction. . . ."

\*          \*          \*

The averments here are that there was an existing interstate traffic between plaintiffs and citizens of other States, and that for the direct purpose of destroying such interstate traffic defendants combined not merely to prevent plaintiffs from manufacturing articles then and there intended for transportation beyond the State, but also to prevent the vendees from reselling the hats which they had imported from Connecticut, or from further negotiating with plaintiffs for the purchase and intertransportation of such hats from Connecticut to the various places of destination. So that, although some of the means whereby the interstate traffic was to be destroyed were acts within a State, and some of them were in themselves as a part of their obvious purpose and effect beyond the scope of Federal authority, still, as we have seen, the acts must be considered as a whole, and the plan is open to condemnation, notwithstanding a negligible amount of intrastate business might be affected in carrying it out. If the purposes of the combination were, as alleged, to prevent any interstate transportation at all, the fact that the means operated at one end before physical transportation commenced and at the other end after the physical transportation ended was immaterial.

Nor can the act in question be held inapplicable because defendants were not themselves engaged in interstate commerce. The act made no distinction between classes. It provided that "every" contract, combination or conspiracy in restraint of trade was illegal. The records of Congress show that several efforts were made to exempt, by legislation, organizations of farmers and laborers from the operation of the act and that all these efforts failed, so that the act remained as we have it before us.

*     *     *

[The complaint alleges] that defendants were members of a vast combination called The United Hatters of North America, comprising about 9,000 members and including a large number of subordinate unions, and that they were combined with some 1,400,000 others into another association known as The American Federation of Labor, of which they were members, whose members resided in all the places in the several States where the wholesale dealers in hats and their customers resided and did business; that defendants were "engaged in a combined scheme and effort to force all manufacturers of fur hats in the United States, including the plaintiffs, against their will and their previous policy of carrying on their business, to organize their workmen in the departments of making and finishing, in each of their factories, into an organization, to be part and parcel of the said combination known as The United Hatters of North America, or as the defendants and their confederates term it, to unionize

their shops, with the intent thereby to control the employment of labor in and the operation of said factories, and to subject the same to the direction and control of persons, other than the owners of the same, in a manner extremely onerous and distasteful to such owners, and to carry out such scheme, effort and purpose, by restraining and destroying the interstate trade and commerce of such manufacturers, by means of intimidation of and threats made to such manufacturers and their customers in the several States, of boycotting them, their product and their customers, using therefor all the powerful means at their command, as aforesaid, until such time as, from the damage and loss of business resulting therefrom, the said manufacturers should yield to the said demand to unionize their factories."

*     *     *

We think a case within the statute was set up and that the demurrer should have been overruled.

*Judgment reversed and cause remanded with a direction to proceed accordingly.*

## 181 Liability for Imposing Martial Law (1909)

The power of state officials, in cases of labor disputes, to declare a state of insurrection and to order imprisonments by the military was challenged in *Moyer v. Peabody*. Invoking a provision of the Civil Rights Act of 1871 (the Ku Klux Klan Act), a member of the Western Federation of Miners claimed damages from the governor of Colorado and officers of the National Guard of Colorado for having deprived him of his constitutional rights while acting under color of state law. Writing for the Supreme Court, Justice Holmes denied relief: "When it comes to a decision by the head of the state upon a matter involving its life, the ordinary rights of individuals must yield to what he deems the necessities of the moment." While management had ready access to the courts and the law to protect its interests, individuals were abandoned by the judiciary when asserting that their civil rights had been violated by government forces suppressing labor unrest.

☆ 181 *Moyer v. Peabody*

212 U.S. 78 (1909).

MR. JUSTICE HOLMES delivered the opinion of the court.

This is an action for damages, brought by the plaintiff in error against the former Governor of the State of Colorado et al. for an imprisonment of the plaintiff by them while in office. . . .

The complaint alleges that the imprisonment was continued from the morning of March 30, 1904, to the afternoon of June 15, and . . . was without probable cause, that no complaint was filed against the plaintiff, and that (in that sense) he was prevented from having access to the courts of the State, although they were open during the whole time; but it sets out proceedings on *habeas corpus*, instituted by him before the Supreme Court of the State, in which that court refused to admit him to bail and ultimately discharged the writ. *In re Moyer*, 35 Colorado, 154 and 159. In those proceedings it appeared that the Governor had declared a county to be in a state of insurrection, had called out troops to put down the trouble, and had ordered that the plaintiff should be arrested as a leader of the outbreak, and should be detained until he could be discharged with safety, and that then he should be delivered to the civil authorities to be dealt with according to law.

*          *          *

The plaintiff's position, stated in a few words, is that the action of the Governor, sanctioned to the extent that it was by the decision of the Supreme Court, was the action of the State and therefore within the Fourteenth Amendment; but that if that action was unconstitutional the Governor got no protection from personal liability for his unconstitutional interference with the plaintiff's rights. It is admitted, as it must be, that the Governor's declaration that a state of insurrection existed is conclusive of that fact. It seems to be admitted also that the arrest alone would not necessarily have given a right to bring this suit. But it is said that a detention for so many days, alleged to be without probable cause, at a time when the courts were open, without an attempt to bring the plaintiff before them, makes a case on which he has a right to have a jury pass.

. . . Of course the plaintiff's position is that he has been deprived of his liberty without due process of law. But it is familiar that what is due process of law depends on circumstances. . . . What, then, are the circumstances of this case? . . . The facts that we are to assume are that a state of insurrection existed and that the Governor, without sufficient reason but in good faith, in the course of putting the insurrection down held the plaintiff until he thought that he safely could release him.

. . . In such a situation we must assume that he had a right under the state constitution and laws to call out troops, as was held by the Supreme Court of the State. . . . That means that he shall make the ordinary use of the soldiers to that end; that he may kill persons who resist and, of course, that he may use the milder measure of seizing the bodies of those whom he considers to stand in the way of restoring peace. Such arrests are not necessarily for punishment, but are by way of precaution to prevent the exercise of hostile power. So long as such arrests are made in good faith and in the honest belief that they

are needed in order to head the insurrection off, the Governor is the final judge and cannot be subjected to an action after he is out of office on the ground that he had not reasonable ground for his belief. If we suppose a Governor with a very long term of office, it may be that a case could be imagined in which the length of the imprisonment would raise a different question. But there is nothing in the duration of the plaintiff's detention or in the allegations of the complaint that would warrant submitting the judgment of the Governor to revision by a jury. It is not alleged that his judgment was not honest, if that be material, or that the plaintiff was detained after fears of the insurrection were at an end.

. . . When it comes to a decision by the head of the State upon a matter involving its life, the ordinary rights of individuals must yield to what he deems the necessities of the moment. Public danger warrants the substitution of executive process for judicial process. . . . As no one would deny that there was immunity for ordering a company to fire upon a mob in insurrection, and that a state law authorizing the Governor to deprive citizens of life under such circumstances was consistent with the Fourteenth Amendment, we are of opinion that the same is true of a law authorizing by implication what was done in this case. . . .

*Judgment affirmed.*

# 182 "an instrument of tyranny" (1909)

In its struggle for greater social and economic justice, the American labor movement was limited to strikes and boycotts. Management could invoke the forces of government through prosecutions, damage actions, and proceedings in equity, but organized labor had no comparable mechanism to air its grievances before the courts. Labor viewed the judicial intervention in the economic conflict as favoring capital and management, and sought legislative measures to redress the perceived imbalance.

Before being elected president, William Howard Taft had been the nation's solicitor general and a circuit court judge. His judicial decisions had aroused the unions' wrath. He predicated his extreme position on injunctions in labor disputes and his hostility to the secondary boycott outlined in his inaugural address upon a view of the labor movement as threatening to governmental authority.

☆182 President Taft's Inaugural Address: The Use of Injunctions in Labor Disputes (March 4, 1909)

Reprinted in J. Richardson, *Supplement to the Messages and Papers of the Presidents Covering the Administration of W. H. Taft* (New York: Bureau of National Literature, 1912), 17:7378.

*        *        *

... Another labor question has arisen which has awakened the most excited discussion. That is in respect to the power of the federal courts to issue injunctions in industrial disputes. As to that, my convictions are fixed. Take away from the courts, if it could be taken away, the power to issue injunctions in labor disputes, and it would create a privileged class among the laborers and save the lawless among their number from a most needful remedy available to all men for the protection of their business against lawless invasion. The proposition that business is not a property or pecuniary right which can be protected by equitable injunction is utterly without foundation in precedent or reason. The proposition is usually linked with one to make the secondary boycott lawful. Such a proposition is at variance with the American instinct, and will find no support, in my judgment, when submitted to the American people. The secondary boycott is an instrument of tyranny, and ought not to be made legitimate.

*        *        *

# 183 "unlawful obstructions" (1914)

On November 5, 1912, Woodrow Wilson, having compiled impressive academic credentials as a professor and president of Princeton University, and a liberal record as governor of New Jersey, was elected president of the United States. He defeated incumbent president William Howard Taft and former president Theodore Roosevelt, running again as the Bull Moose party candidate. Despite his mild manner, Wilson did not hesitate to use the military arm of the government. When General Victoriano Huerta overthrew the moderate government of Mexico in 1913, Wilson refused to recognize Huerta's military regime and announced instead United States support for the revolutionary regime under Venustiano Carranza. A year later, when Mexico failed to make the demanded apologies for the temporary arrest of nine American sailors in Tampico, President Wilson ordered a United States naval force to Tampico Bay. He also ordered the taking of Vera Cruz, where German infiltration was suspected.

The same week the Marines were taking Vera Cruz with a loss of fifteen men, a smoldering miners' strike in Colorado erupted into a pitched battle between striking miners and the combined forces of the state militia and John D. Rockefeller's mine guards. In ten days of fighting, before federal troops restored order sixty-six people died, including some women and children of the striking miners who perished when the strikers' tent city at Ludlow was set on fire. The delay in the arrival of the federal troops was due to troop shortages caused by the Mexican

intervention. Six months later, Wilson acted more swiftly in responding to a call for military aid when a federal judge sought help to enforce a labor injunction against a miners' strike in Arkansas.

Despite Wilson's decisiveness both domestically and internationally, he issued a proclamation of neutrality and later called on Americans to be neutral "in thought as well as action" when war broke out in Europe on August 4, 1914. The United States did not enter World War I until 1917.

## ☆ 183 President Wilson and the Labor Wars

### ☆ 183a Suppressing Insurrection in Colorado

38 Stat. 1994 (1914).

BY THE PRESIDENT OF THE UNITED STATES OF
AMERICA

### A Proclamation

Whereas it is provided by the Constitution of the United States that the United States shall protect every State in this Union, on application of the legislature, or of the executive (when the legislature can not be convened), against domestic violence; and

Whereas the Governor of the State of Colorado has represented that domestic violence exists in said State which the authorities of said State are unable to suppress; and has represented that it is impossible to convene the legislature of the State in time to meet the present emergency; and

Whereas the laws of the United States require that in all cases of insurrection in any State or of obstruction to the laws thereof, whenever in the judgment of the President it becomes necessary to use the military forces to suppress such insurrection or obstruction to the laws, he shall forthwith by proclamation command such insurgents to disperse and retire peaceably to their respective abodes within a limited time:

Now, therefore, I, Woodrow Wilson, President of the United States, do hereby admonish all good citizens of the United States and all persons within the territory and jurisdiction of the United States against aiding, countenancing, abetting, or taking part in such unlawful proceedings; and I do hereby warn all persons engaged in or connected with said domestic violence and obstruction of the laws to disperse and retire peaceably to their respective abodes on or before the thirtieth day of April, instant.

In testimony whereof I have hereunto set my hand and caused the seal of the United States to be affixed.

*        *        *

WOODROW WILSON

By the President:

W. J. BRYAN, Secretary of State

☆ 183b  Dispersion of Unlawful
Assemblages in Arkansas

38 Stat. 2035 (1914).

BY THE PRESIDENT OF THE UNITED STATES OF
AMERICA

*A Proclamation*

Whereas by reason of unlawful obstructions, combinations, and assemblages of persons, it has become
impracticable in the judgment of the President to
enforce by the ordinary course of judicial proceedings the laws of the United States within the State
of Arkansas and especially within the western Federal district and in the neighborhood of the towns of
Hartford, Midland, and Fort Smith in said district;
and whereas for the purpose of enforcing the faithful
execution of the laws of the United States and protecting property in the charge of the courts of the
United States, the President deems it necessary to
employ a part of the military forces of the United
States, in pursuance of the statute in that case made
and provided:

Now, therefore, I, Woodrow Wilson, President of
the United States, do hereby admonish all persons
who may be or come within the State, district, or
towns aforesaid against doing, countenancing, encouraging, or taking any part in such unlawful obstructions, combinations, and assemblages, and I
hereby warn all persons in any manner connected
therewith to disperse and retire peaceably to their
respective abodes on or before 12 o'clock noon of the
6th day of November instant.

Those who disregard this warning and persist in
taking part with a riotous mob in forcibly resisting
and obstructing the execution of the laws of the
United States or interfering with the functions of
the Government or destroying or attempting to destroy property in the custody of the courts of the
United States or under its direction can not be regarded otherwise than as public enemies.

Troops employed against such combinations and
assemblages of persons will act with all the moderation and forbearance consistent with the accomplishment of their duty in the premises; but all citizens
must realize that, if they mingle with or become a
part of such riotous assemblages, there will be no opportunity for discrimination in the methods employed in dealing with such assemblages. The only
safe course, therefore, for those not intentionally
participating in such unlawful procedure is to abide
at their homes or, at least, not to go or remain in the
neighborhood of such riotous assemblages.

In testimony whereof I have hereunto set my
hand and caused the seal of the United States to be
affixed.

\*            \*            \*

WOODROW WILSON

By the President:

ROBERT LANSING, Acting Secretary of State

# 184  "the labor of a human being is not a commodity" (1914)

The Clayton Antitrust Act reflected in large part
President Wilson's 1912 campaign ideology, originally
advanced by future Supreme Court justice Louis D.
Brandeis, which called for the tightening of federal
policy toward capital and management and a liberali-
zation of attitudes toward labor. The Act's exemption
of labor organizations from the prohibitions of the
Sherman Act, its recognition of union strikes, boycotts, and picketing, and the limitations it placed upon
the use of federal injunctions against strikes and boycotts helped to neutralize federal law as an instrument of management and resulted in a major legislative victory for labor. By the time the Clayton Act
passed, President Wilson had moved closer to the antitrust approach embodied in the Federal Trade Commission Act of 1914 and articulated by Theodore
Roosevelt during the 1912 campaign.

☆ 184  Clayton Antitrust Act

38 Stat. 730 (1914).

\*            \*            \*

SEC. 6. That the labor of a human being is not a commodity or article of commerce. Nothing contained in
the anti-trust laws shall be construed to forbid the
existence and operation of labor, agricultural, or hor-
ticultural organizations, instituted for the purposes
of mutual help, and not having capital stock or con-
duced for profit, or to forbid or restrain individual
members of such organizations from lawfully carrying out the legitimate objects thereof; nor shall such
organizations, or the members thereof, be held or
construed to be illegal combinations or conspiracies
in restraint of trade, under the anti-trust laws.

\*            \*            \*

SEC. 20. That no restraining order or injunction
shall be granted by any order of the United States,
or a judge or the judges thereof, in any case between
an employer and employees or between employers
and employees, or between employees, or between
persons employed and persons seeking employment, involving, or growing out of, a dispute concerning terms or conditions of employment, unless
necessary to prevent irreparable injury to property,
or to a property right, of the party making the application, for which injury there is no adequate remedy
at law, and such property or property right must be

described with a particularity in the application, which must be in writing and sworn to by the applicant or by his agent or attorney.

And no such restraining order or injunction shall prohibit any person or persons, whether singly or in concert, from terminating any relation of employment, or from ceasing to perform any work of labor, or from recommending, advising, or persuading others by peaceful means so to do; or from attending at any place where any such person or persons may lawfully be, for the purpose of peacefully obtaining or communicating information, or from peacefully persuading any person to work or to abstain from working; or from ceasing to patronize or to employ any party to such dispute, or from recommending, advising, or persuading others by peaceful and lawful means so to do; or from paying or giving to, or withholding from, any person engaged in such dispute, any strike benefits or other moneys or things of value; or from peaceably assembling in a lawful manner, and for lawful purposes; or from doing any act or thing which might lawfully be done in the absence of such dispute by any party thereto; nor shall any of the acts specified in this paragraph be considered or held to be violations of any law of the United States.

## 185  The Execution of Joe Hill (1915)

"Murdered by the Authorities of the State of Utah." So read the banner over Joe Hill's coffin during his funeral in Chicago.

It has been alleged that Joe Hill was killed by a firing squad of Salt Lake County for political reasons because he was a member of the "fighting section of the American working class, the I.W.W." Whether Hill received a fair trial for the first-degree murder of a grocery store owner (wounded in a similar attack long before Hill came to Utah) will continue to be debated by labor sympathizers and legal scholars. The Supreme Court of Utah's opinion makes little reference to his leadership in the Industrial Workers of the World. Although the IWW never developed into a major rival of the AFL, its organizers brought the plight of the migrant worker of the western United States and the immigrant factory worker of the East to the attention of the craft-dominated union movement. The IWW demonstrated that unskilled workers, speaking in many tongues, could combine to form a militant labor organization.

The careful review of the evidence by the Utah Supreme Court was unconvincing to Hill's followers. They could easily believe Joe Hill was framed, considering their inherent mistrust of the law and courts, which had so often acted to frustrate their goals. Joe Hill's body received a hero's funeral in Chicago, and a judge detailed the legal errors of the

Utah courts during the funeral oration. In his life, as well as his songs, Joe Hill, born Joseph Hillstrom, greatly enriched American folklore.

☆ 185  *State v. Hillstrom*

46 Utah 341, 150 P. 935 (1915).

STRAUP, C. J. . . . The claim made is that there is not sufficient evidence to identify the defendant, to connect him with the commission of the offense, nor to show motive.

In the information it is charged that he with a revolver shot and killed J. G. Morrison. . . . As the deceased and his two sons [Arling, 17; Merlin, 13] were preparing to close the store, two men with red bandana handkerchiefs over their faces as masks, and with revolvers in their hands, suddenly entered the store. . . . Merlin, the only living witness to the shooting, testified that as the two assailants entered the store and approached his father they said, "We have got you now," and immediately shot. He gave it as his best judgment that about seven shots in all were fired, when the assailants fled, without attempting to take anything from the cash register or elsewhere. The father and Arling were both killed. . . . Two bullet marks were found in shelving or the counter where the deceased was killed, another on the inside of the ice chest, where the deceased kept his revolver, and two or three where lay the body of Arling, behind the counter, and one bullet hole through his body and straight down through the floor. Merlin testified he did not see the first shot fired, which hit his father, but saw the second, which was shot by the taller of the two assailants, who then directed his attention towards the ice chest. Merlin retreated into a little storeroom, where he no longer saw Arling nor the assailants, but heard shots. After the assailants had fled, Merlin first went to his father, and then to Arling. He found the latter dead behind the south counter, and but a short distance from the ice chest. Near [Arling's] outstretched hand lay the revolver which was kept in the ice chest, with one chamber discharged. . . . From this it is quite evident that at some period during the shooting Arling went to the ice chest, got the gun, and discharged it at the assailants.

Another witness . . . saw the taller of the two assailants come out of the store in a rather stooped position, with his hands drawn over his chest, and heard him exclaim as if in great pain, "Oh, Bob!" Another witness saw the taller of the two assailants run from the store . . . and heard him in a clear voice say, "I am shot." . . . The blood [on the sidewalk] had the appearance, as described by the witnesses, as coughed up and spat on the sidewalk. . . .

The defendant and Applequist [a friend] . . . left [the Eselius house in Murray] that evening some time between 6 and 9; the exact time is not made to appear. Applequist did not return, and has not been seen nor heard of since. That night between 11:30 and 12 o'clock the defendant called at a Dr. McHugh's office on Fourteenth South and State streets, about 2-1/2 miles south of the place of the homicide, and about midway between the place of the homicide and Murray. . . . [T]he defendant [said] that he was shot, and stated: "I wish this kept private." The doctor removed the defendant's clothes, and found him suffering from a gunshot wound through the chest and lungs. . . . From the appearance of the wound the doctors [a Dr. Bird had arrived] gave it as their opinion that the bullet causing the wound was shot from a 38 caliber gun. They further testified that such a wound would cause internal hemorrhages, coughing, and spitting of blood. After the wound was attended the doctors assisted the defendant in dressing. In doing that a revolver in a holster with shoulder straps fell from the defendant's clothes to the floor. . . . The doctors saw but the handle of the gun sticking out of the holster. From the appearance of the handle they gave it as their opinion that the gun was a 38 caliber automatic gun, and that the handle was similar to a Colt's automatic 38 gun exhibited to them. While the defendant was there at the office he told the doctors that "he had had a quarrel with some one over a woman, and that in the quarrel he was shot, and that he was as much to blame as the other fellow, and wanted it kept quiet, kept private." That was all that was said by him concerning the manner in which he received the wound. . . . [Dr. Bird offered the defendant a ride.] As Dr. Bird and the defendant approached the Eselius place the defendant requested the doctor to turn down the lights of the automobile. Dr. Bird did so. As they neared the house the defendant, "with a combination of the teeth, tongue, and lips, gave two shrill, penetrating whistles." Dr. Bird assisted the defendant to the kitchen or back door. As the defendant and Dr. Bird entered "a number of men seemed to have just gone from the back room that we first entered into the next room, and all were standing or walking in that direction as we entered the door, and turned and recognized the defendant, and, seeing him with me, expressed surprise, and asked if he was hurt." . . . Two or three days after that the defendant was arrested. In his room on a table was found a red bandana handkerchief similar to that worn by the assailants. The defendant's coat and clothing worn by him on the night of the homicide were seized and put in evidence. They were similar in appearance to those worn by the taller assailant. One of the officers asked the defendant where his gun was. He told him that Dr. Bird, on the way from Dr. McHugh's office to the Eseliuses [*sic*], had trouble with his automobile, and as Dr. Bird got out to crank it the defendant threw the gun away. No gun was found. The defendant was not a witness in the

case, and at no time explained or offered to explain the place where, nor the circumstances under which he received his wound, except as stated by him to the doctors, that he received it in a quarrel over a woman; nor did he offer any evidence whatever to show his whereabouts or movements on the night of the homicide.

A Mrs. Seeley . . . testified that she met two men with red bandana handkerchiefs tied around their necks. One of the men was tall and slender. In passing they crowded her off the sidewalk. She turned and looked at them. The taller turned and looked at her. She gave this description of him. . . .

\*　　　　\*　　　　\*

When the defendant stood erect with his coat on and his arms down the bullet hole where the bullet entered the coat was four inches lower than the wound where the bullet entered his body. From this it is argued by defendant's counsel that the defendant received the shot causing his wound when his hand and arm were raised above his head drawing his coat up, and that the arms of the assailant in the store were at no time in such a position, and therefore the defendant's wound was not received in the store. Such argument does not demonstrate that the defendant was not the man who was shot in the store by Arling. At most, it is but an inference of fact, which, and the weight of it, were for the jury. That Arling shot one of the assailants in the store is sufficiently shown; indeed, that fact is not seriously controverted. But no one at that moment saw either the assailant or Arling. In what position Arling was when he shot or the assailant when he received the shot is not disclosed. . . . [C]ounsel base a positive conclusion upon nonexisting premises, at least upon premises wholly conjectural and speculative—the position the assailant or Arling was in at the time the former was shot. The argument that the defendant, if he was one of the assailants, must, when he was shot, have been in the middle of the room with his hands raised above his head, is not the only deducible inference. . . . It also can be inferred that Arling may have shot the assailant as the latter was leaning and reaching over the counter, which position would account for the upraised arm and coat of the defendant and the course the bullet took through his coat and body. That, of course, is but an inference, but it is as probable as the argument of counsel that the defendant, when he was shot, must have had his hands in the air above his head. . . . But all this is mere matter of inference and argument, and was for the jury.

It further is claimed that no bullet shot from the deceased's gun was found in the store . . . from which, and from the further fact that the bullet which produced the defendant's wound went clear through his body, it is argued that it was not the defendant, but another, who was shot in the store by

Arling.... These also are positive conclusions based on but conjectural or speculative premises.... Such argument is proper enough addressed to a jury; but it has no foundation when addressed to a court....

Evidence also was given to show that the red bandana handkerchief ... was given him by Mrs. Eselius the next morning after the defendant was shot.... The credibility and weight of her testimony were for the jury, not for us.

*     *     *

But the claim of insufficiency of the evidence is chiefly based on the fact that none of the witnesses who saw the assailant at or about the store on the night of the homicide testified positively that the defendant was one of them; and for that reason it is argued that the case is no stronger than the case of *State v. Hill*, where the evidence was held insufficient to connect the accused with the commission of that offense. We think the cases on the facts dissimilar. The testimony of Merlin ... is alone not sufficient. But there is the testimony of the witnesses who saw the taller of the two assailants ... heard his voice, and that the voice, size, and appearance of that man were similar to those of the defendant. Though it be conceded that that also was insufficient, still there is the further testimony of the witness who but a few minutes prior to the homicide, close to one of the assailants, in a bright light nearly as light as day, looked him directly in the face.... That man and the defendant, as testified to by her, were similar in size and features, had the same slim face, sharp nose, and large nostrils, and the same "defection" or scar on the side of the face and neck. True, that witness would not testify positively that the defendant was that man; but the facts testified to by her as to the description of that man pointed most strikingly to the defendant.... In addition to all this was the fresh bullet wound on the defendant. That wound, unexplained, or unsatisfactorily explained by him, was, in connection with other evidence that one of the perpetrators of the crime answering the defendant's description was shot in the store, a relevant mark of identification, especially in light of the defendant's effort to have the fact of his wound concealed, and in view of his statement that he threw his gun away, of his request that the lights of the automobile be turned down, and of no apparent good reason for his giving two sharp penetrating whistles before he entered the Eselius house with Dr. Bird. Gunshot wounds such as had the defendant are unusual and extraordinary. Under all the circumstances the defendant's wound, unexplained, was quite as much a distinguishing mark as though one of the assailants in the assault had one of his ears chopped off. The only explanation the defendant gave of his wound was that he received it at some undisclosed place in a quarrel with some undescribed man over some undescribed woman, in

which he "was to blame as much as the other fellow." ... One suffering from such a wound as did the defendant — a wound of such serious and oft-fatal consequences — ordinarily does not walk around the country seeking surgical aid until, from loss of blood, he is about to collapse. Generally such aid is promptly summoned and brought to such a sufferer.... [An] officer after the defendant's arrest stated to him that, if the defendant would tell him the place where and the circumstances under which he received his wound, ... and if true that the defendant received his wound in a quarrel over a woman, he would be given his liberty. The defendant declined to give the officer any information.... The defendant, of course, was not required to make any statement to the officer. His refusal to make any or to answer any question cannot, though the fact was brought out by the defendant, be considered as an admission of guilt. He had a right to remain silent. Nor can his neglect or refusal to be a witness in any manner prejudice him or be used against him. The state, as in all other criminal cases, was required to prove the defendant's guilt beyond a reasonable doubt. But the defendant, without some proof tending to rebut them, may not avoid the natural and reasonable inferences deducible from proven facts by merely declining to stay off the stand or remaining silent.... While the proven facts and inferences against him are neither strengthened nor weakened by his mere silence or failure to take the stand, yet when he, with peculiar knowledge of facts remains silent, or has evidence in his power by which he may repel or rebut such proven facts and inferences, and chooses not to avail himself of it, he must suffer the consequences of whatever the facts and inferences adduced against him tend fairly and reasonably to prove.

We think the evidence sufficient to justify a finding that the defendant was one of the perpetrators of the crime. To hold otherwise is to hold that the accused must be identified or connected with the commission of the offense by direct testimony of eyewitnesses who unerringly are able to testify positively and unequivocally that he was the perpetrator.... To ... place ourselves in the jury box ... is to ignore the law and to usurp a function not possessed by us. And yet the import of their argument ... is on mere weight and worthiness of testimony, arguments such as the witnesses had not positively identified the defendant and had not sufficient means or opportunity of observing and giving a reliable description of the assailants; that of discrepancies as to the description of the hat and clothes worn by one of them; that the defendant was not shot in the store, because the bullet hole in his coat was four inches lower than the wound on his body, and because no bullet shot from the gun near the outstretched hand of Arling's body was found; ... that the handkerchief found in defendant's room was given him the day after he was shot; and that no motive was shown for the defendant to mask himself and with gun in hand to enter the store and shoot to death his victim, with whom it was not shown he had any acquaintance. All this, it is contended, when properly considered and weighed, so clearly repelled whatever testimony there may be to point to the defendant's guilt as to leave no evidence to connect him with the commission of the offense. It is apparent all this was for the jury.

With this conclusion it is unnecessary to inquire into the question of motive. . . . Since the evidence is sufficient to show that the defendant was one of the perpetrators who, with his face masked and gun in hand, entered the store and deliberately shot his victim to death, it is immaterial to inquire whether the motive was assassination or robbery. Nothing but a wicked motive emanating from a depraved and malignant heart is attributable to the commission of such a crime as is here indisputably shown.

*          *          *

## 186  This Struggle Will Go On (1915)

William ("Big Bill") Haywood (1869-1928) was born in Salt Lake City, Utah, and lost an eye at the age of nine in a mining accident. Haywood was a leader of the Western Federation of Miners during a series of violent strikes and also helped organize the Industrial Workers of the World in 1905. He ran as a socialist candidate for governor of Colorado while imprisoned on the charge of assassinating the former governor of Idaho. Haywood opposed America's entry into World War I and in 1917 was arrested for sedition. He jumped bail and went to the Soviet Union in 1921. Like Emma Goldman before him, he became disillusioned with Russia's revolution.

Haywood and the IWW envisioned a future society in which workers would control the means of production and their own destinies. This goal was to be achieved through the direct action of a general strike. In his testimony before the Industrial Relations Commission Haywood also called for "filling the jails" as an antiestablishment tactic.

☆ 186  William Haywood: Testimony before the Industrial Relations Commission

Reprinted in S. Lynd, ed., *Nonviolence in America: A Documentary History* (New York: Bobbs-Merrill, 1966), 217-40.

CHAIRMAN WALSH: Are you familiar with the formation of the Western Federation of Miners?

MR. HAYWOOD: Yes; being a miner, of course I kept acquainted with what the miners were doing and remember when that federation of miners was

organized, and have since become acquainted with all of the circumstances that brought about the federation of miners.

CHAIRMAN WALSH: Will you please describe the conditions that led to the formation of the Western Federation of Miners?

MR. HAYWOOD: It was organized as the result of a strike that occurred in the Coeur d'Alene.

*          *          *

. . . In 1902 and 1903 came the strike that is so well known as the Cripple Creek strike, and that strike was in the nature of a sympathetic strike. The men who were working in the mills in Colorado City, although entitled to the benefits of the 8-hour law which had been passed in Colorado at that time, were working 12 hours a day 11 hours on the day shift and 13 hours on the night shift.

This condition prevails in the smelting plants of Colorado at the present time, and in some of the milling plants. They went out on strike in September, I think, 1902.

CHAIRMAN WALSH: Was the attention of the authorities called to the condition—that is, that the law was being violated with reference to the hours of labor?

MR. HAYWOOD: Oh, yes, indeed.

CHAIRMAN WALSH: Was the law inoperative, or why didn't they prosecute the officials?

MR. HAYWOOD: The smelter officials, or mine owners, do you mean?

CHAIRMAN WALSH: Yes.

MR. HAYWOOD: Did you ever hear of a mine owner or of a manufacturer being prosecuted for violation of a law? Well, they were not, anyway. The courts don't work that way.

*          *          *

They were striking as they struck ten years before, for the enforcement of a state law. The laws at that time were inoperative at Cripple Creek. The militia ran the district. They threw the officers out of office. Sheriff Robinson, I remember, had a rope thrown at his feet and was told to resign or they would hang him. . . . Habeas corpus was denied. I recall Judge Seed's court, where he had three men brought in that were being held by the militia. While his court was in session it was surrounded by soldiers who had their gatling guns and rifles trained on the door. He ordered those three prisoners released, and the soldiers went after them and they were taken back to trial. That strike was not won. . . .

*          *          *

. . . The authorities of the city took up the side of the employment sharks, and between 500 and 600 men and women, members of the organization, were thrown into prison.

*          *          *

... [E]verywhere, I might say, that I have seen courts in action; they took the side of the capitalists.

\* \* \*

... [T]here is a class struggle in society, with workers on one side of that struggle and the capitalists on the other; that the workers have nothing but their labor power and the capitalists have the control of and the influence of all branches of government — legislative, executive, and judicial; that they have on their side of the question all of the forces of law; they can hire detectives, they can have the police force for the asking or the militia, or the Regular Army.

There are workers who have come to the conclusion that there is only one way to win this battle. We don't agree at all with the statement that you heard reiterated here day after day — that there is an identity of interests between capital and labor. We say to you frankly that there can be no identity of interests between labor, who produces all by their own labor power and their brains, and such men as John D. Rockefeller, Morgan, and their stockholders, who neither by brain or muscle or by any other effort contribute to the productivity of the industries that they own.

\* \* \*

COMMISSIONER WEINSTOCK: Well then, summing up, we find that I.W.W.'ism teaches the following: . . .

MR. HAYWOOD: Read me that over again.

COMMISSIONER WEINSTOCK: "(a) that the workers are to use any and all tactics that will get the results sought with the least possible expenditure of time and energy."

MR. HAYWOOD: Yes; I believe in the worker using any kind of tactics that will get results. . . .

COMMISSIONER WEINSTOCK: "(b) The question of right or wrong is not to be considered."

MR. HAYWOOD: What is right and wrong? What I think is right in my mind or what you think is right in your mind?

COMMISSIONER WEINSTOCK: "(c) The avenging sword is to be unsheathed, with all hearts resolved on victory or death."

MR. HAYWOOD: What that means is a general strike.

COMMISSIONER WEINSTOCK: "(d) The workman is to help himself when the proper time comes."

MR. HAYWOOD: When the proper time comes, when he needs it let him go and get it.

COMMISSIONER WEINSTOCK: "(e) No agreement with an employer of labor is to be considered by the worker as sacred or inviolable."

\* \* \*

MR. HAYWOOD: . . . You can let that about contract and agreement stand.

COMMISSIONER WEINSTOCK: "(f) The worker is to produce inferior goods and kill time" — we will cut that out, that which relates to the production of inferior goods and killing time; that is out of the subject.

MR. HAYWOOD: Yes.

COMMISSIONER WEINSTOCK: "(g) The worker is to look forward to the day when he will confiscate the factories and drive out the owners."

MR. HAYWOOD: I would drive them in instead of out.

\* \* \*

COMMISSIONER WEINSTOCK: And the last is, "(i) Strikers are to disobey and treat with contempt all judicial injunctions."

MR. HAYWOOD: Well, I have been plastered up with injunctions until I do not need a suit of clothes, and I have treated them with contempt.

COMMISSIONER WEINSTOCK: And you advocate that?

MR. HAYWOOD: I do not believe in that kind of law at all. I think that is a usurpation on the part of the courts of a function that was never vested in the courts by the Constitution.

\* \* \*

COMMISSIONER WEINSTOCK: . . . As I understand it, I.W.W.'ism is socialism, with this difference —

MR. HAYWOOD (interrupting): With its working clothes on.

COMMISSIONER WEINSTOCK: As an I.W.W., are you a believer in free speech?

MR. HAYWOOD: Yes, sir.

COMMISSIONER WEINSTOCK: Are you a believer in free press?

MR. HAYWOOD: Yes, sir.

COMMISSIONER WEINSTOCK: Now, if your idea prevails and you went to bed tonight under the capitalistic system and woke up tomorrow morning under your system, the machinery of production and distribution would belong to all the people.

MR. HAYWOOD: Under our system it would be under the management of the working class.

\* \* \*

COMMISSIONER WEINSTOCK: . . . [W]ill you briefly outline to us, Mr. Haywood, how would you govern and direct the affairs under your proposed system of 100,000,000 of people, as we are in this country today?

MR. HAYWOOD: Well, how are the affairs of the hundred million people conducted at the present time? The workers have no interest, have no voice in anything except the shops. Many of the workers are children. They certainly have no interest and no voice in the franchise. They are employed in the shops, and of course my idea is that children who work should have a voice in the way they work — in the hours they work, in the wages that they should receive—that is, children who labor. The same is true of women. The political state, the Government, says that women are not entitled to vote—that is, except in the 10 free States of the West; but they are industrial units; they are productive units.... My idea is that they should have a voice in the control or disposition of their labor power, and the only place where they can express themselves to the fullest as citizens of industry, if you will, as to the purpose of their work and the conditions under which they will labor. Now, you recognize that in conjunction with women and children.

The black men of the South are on the same footing. They are all citizens of this country, but they have no voice in its government. Millions of black men are disfranchised, who if organized would have a voice in saying how they should work and how the conditions of labor should be regulated. But unorganized they are as helpless and in the same condition of slavery as they were before the [Civil W]ar. This is not only true of women and children and black men, but it extends to the foreigner who comes to this country and is certainly a useful member of society. Most of them at once go into industries, but for five years they are not citizens. They plod along at their work and have no voice in the control or use of their labor power. And as you have learned through this commission there are corporations who direct the manner in which these foreigners shall vote. Certainly you have heard something of that in connection with the Rockefeller interests in the Southern part of Colorado. You know that the elections there were never carried on straight, and these foreigners were directed as to how their ballot should be placed.

They are not the only ones who are disfranchised, but there is also the workingman who is born in this country, who is shifted about from place to place by industrial depressions; their homes are broken up and they are compelled to go from one city to another, and each State requires a certain period of residence before a man has the right to vote. Some States say he must be a resident 1 year, others say 2 years; he must live for a certain length of time in the county; he must live for 30 days or such a matter in the precinct before he has any voice in the conduct of government. Now, if a man was not a subject of a State or Nation, but a citizen of industry, moving from place to place, belonging to his union, wherever he went he would step in the union hall, show his card, register, and he at once has a voice in the conduct of the affairs pertaining to his welfare. That is the form of society I want to see, where the men who do the work, and who are the only people who are worth while—understand me, Mr. Weinstock, I think that the workingman, even doing the meanest

kind of work, is a more important member of society than any judge on the Supreme Bench and other useless members of society. I am speaking for the working class, and I am a partisan to the workers....

COMMISSIONER HARRIMAN: Mr. Haywood, I understand that you do not believe in war. Now, if you don't believe in war, why do you believe in violence in labor disputes? One is war between nations, and the other is war between—

MR. HAYWOOD (interrupting): You say I believe in violence?

*          *          *

COMMISSIONER HARRIMAN: I thought you did.

MR. HAYWOOD: Probably I do; but I don't want it to be taken for granted without giving me an opportunity to explain what violence means. I think you will agree that there is nothing more violent that you can do to the capitalist than to drain his pocketbook. In that sort of violence I believe, and we are trying to make it impossible for the growth of more capitalists and to make useful citizens out of the existing capitalists.

*          *          *

## 187 "use a little direct action" (1916, 1918, 1927-1930)

On Saturday afternoon, July 22, 1916, a bomb was thrown into a San Francisco crowd during a Preparedness Day parade, designed to stimulate popular support for the national and state war effort. Nine spectators were killed by the explosion, which was viewed as the work of left-wing, antimilitary anarchists. Five local labor leaders, some with radical reputations, were arrested and indicted for murder. Of the four who were tried, two were convicted: Warren Billings, sentenced to life imprisonment; and Tom Mooney, a self-proclaimed Marxist and labor organizer, sentenced to death. Rena Mooney, Tom's wife, was found not guilty. Celebrated as a labor martyr and victim of militarist capitalism, Tom Mooney gained national and international prominence. Anarchist and labor organizations demonstrated on his behalf in Russia and England and on the Continent. His sentence was commuted to life imprisonment a year later, two weeks before the scheduled execution. After twenty-one years in prison, Tom Mooney and Warren Billings were released and pardoned in 1939 by California governor Culbert L. Olsen.

## ☆ 187 The San Francisco Preparedness Day Bombing and the Mooney Case

### ☆ 187a An Anonymous Warning Received by San Francisco Newspapers (July 21, 1916)

Reprinted in R. Frost, *The Mooney Case* (Stanford: Stanford University Press, 1968), 82-83.

Our protests have been in vain in regards to this preparedness proppaganda, so we are going to use a little direct action on the 22nd which will echo around the earth and show that Frisco really knows how, and that militarism cant be forced on us and our children without a violent protest. Things are going to happen to show that we will go to any extreme, the same as the controlling class, to preserve what little democracy we still have, Dont take this as a joke or you will be rudely awaken, *We have sworn to do our duty to the masses*, and only send this warning to those who are wise but are forced to march to hold their jobs, as we want to give only *the hypocritical patriots who shout for war but never go*, a real taste of w[ar.] Kindly ask the Chamber of Commerce to march [in] a solid body, *if they want to prove they [are] not cowards*. Our duty has been done so far, Thank Mr Older for his great work of the past in enlightening the masses and ho[pe] he will never allow himself to become the intellectual prostitute as the other dailys. . . .

TH[E] DETERMINED EXILES FROM MILITARISTIC
GOVERNMENT
U.S.
Holland
Italy
Russia
Italy
Germany

### ☆ 187b Excerpts from the Police Interrogation of Tom Mooney (July 28, 1916)

Reprinted in R. Frost, *The Mooney Case* (Stanford: Stanford University Press, 1968), 106-8.

Q. [Prosecutor JAMES F. BRENNAN] How long have you known Billings?

A. [MOONEY] *I insist that I have the right to counsel.* There is [no] fair minded, honest, liberty loving men that can deny me that right.

MR. FICKERT: We thought you wanted to make a statement.

*       *       *

MR. BRENNAN: There are some circumstances can be cleared up. How long do you know Billings?

A. Listen Mr. Brennan, — Well, you don't intend to give us our rights?

Q. You sent a telegram for the purpose of making the people believe you are an innocent man.

A. To let you and Mr. Fickert and Chief of Police White know where I was.

Q. You knew we were right on your tail with five or six officers, right after you all the time. You knew you couldn't step ten feet without an officer being on top of you.

A. Why did you put in the paper a state wide search — a nation wide search —

*       *       *

Q. [BRENNAN] (Int'g) Let me tell you something. One of the most dastardly crimes that has been committed in this country has been committed in the last ten days.

A. *I know that. The most fiendish crime, the most heinous crime.*

Q. *Yes, and you are guilty of that crime.*

A. *Is that so!* [At this point Mooney rushed Brennan, calling him a "S.O.B." Police hauled him off and quieted him down.]

*       *       *

A. . . . I am only a working man and there are many tricks in this game and I want my rights all safe guarded and I realize they cannot be safe guarded under these circumstances. I realize the seriousness of this charge that has been lodged against me. There is no provocation or justification for it, absolutely none, and you know it.

Q. Then if there is absolutely none your conscience is clear.

A. Absolutely.

Q. There is no reason why you should fear — have any fear of being contradicted.

A. I saw what was in the Examiner [local paper] today.

Q. Then you are fore-warned of what might be asked of you?

A. I saw what was in the Examiner. I know why it was there and who put it there. *I am going to have counsel.*

MR. BRENNAN: Q. What was in the Examiner that came to your notice?

A. The whole paper.

Q. Give us just one idea of it, just one thing or suggestion.

A. All of it. All of my past. My trials at Martinez in connection with strikes and being tried for dynamite, which was not true, and all that stuff. It was to prejudice the minds of the people and inflame them, to make them believe I actually committed this dirty, dastardly crime. That is what it was done for.

*       *       *

Q. [BRENNAN] In this case, of course, nobody claims you, well known as you are, actually placed the bomb, . . . but if you are responsible for this crime at all it is because of the fact [that] you aided and abetted in its perpetration, and therefore, the

only way to connect you up is to connect you with
certain people who are claimed to be perpetrators.
... As soon as we touch on any dangerous ground,
that is, your connection with any of the parties who
are responsible for this outrage, why, you immediately refuse to answer.

☆187c  Reports of President Wilson's Mediation
Commission (January 28, 1918)

Reprinted in R. Frost, *The Mooney Case* (Stanford: Stanford University Press, 1968), 293-94.

... We conceived it to be our duty merely to determine whether a solid basis exists for a feeling that
an injustice was done ... and that an irreparable injustice would be committed to allow such conviction
to proceed to execution. ...

                    *         *         *

... It is now well known that the attention to the
situation in the East was first aroused through
meetings of protest against the Mooney conviction
in Russia. From Russia and the Western States protest spread to the entire country until it has gathered momentum from many sources, sources whose
opposition to violence is unquestioned, whose devotion to our cause in the war is unstinted. The liberal
sentiment of Russia was aroused, the liberal sentiment of the United States was aroused, because the
circumstances of Mooney's prosecution, in the light
of his history, led to the belief that the terrible and
sacred instruments of criminal justice were consciously or unconsciously made use of against labor
by its enemies in an industrial conflict.

However strange or however unexpected it may
be, the just disposition of the Mooney case thus affects influences far beyond the confines of California, and California can be depended upon to see the
wider implications of the case. With the mere local
aspects, with the political and journalistic conflicts
which the case has occasioned, neither the commission nor the country at large is concerned. But the
feeling of disquietude aroused by the case must be
heeded, for if unchecked, it impairs the faith that our
democracy protects the lowliest and even the unworthy against false accusations. War is fought with
moral as well as material resources. We are in this
war to vindicate the moral claims of unstained processes of law, however slow at times, such processes
may be. These claims must be tempered by the fire
of our own devotion to them at home.

Your Commission, therefore respectfully recommends in case the Supreme Court of California should
find it necessary (confined as it is by jurisdictional limitations) to sustain the conviction of Mooney on the
record of the trial, that the President use his good offices to invoke action by the governor of California
and the cooperation of its prosecuting officers to the

end that a new trial may be had for Mooney whereby
guilt or innocence may be put to the test of unquestionable justice. This result can easily be accomplished by postponing the execution of the sentence
of Mooney to await the outcome of a new trial, based
upon prosecution under one of the untried indictments against him.

☆187d  Excerpts of Letters to Governor Clement C.
Young of California Opposing Proposed Pardon for
Tom Mooney (1927-1930)

Reprinted in R. Frost, *The Mooney Case* (Stanford: Stanford University Press, 1968), 383-84.

"MY DEAR GOVERNOR:" "HONORABLE SIR:"
"MY DEAR GOVERNOR YOUNG:"

"Stand firm, Mr. Governor." "Too many criminals in
the whole United States are having leniency extended to them." "I remember, and so do you, the
agitation that was gotten up on behalf of the Mc-
Namara brothers who destroyed the Times Building
in Los Angeles. It was claimed that they were the
innocent victims of capitalistic conspiracy under the
direction of Harrison Gray Otis. The agitators knew
nothing more about the facts of that affair than do
the present excitable friends of Mr. Mooney."
"[Mooney] was caught out in Suisun Bay with a boat-
load of dynamite." "If Mooney was not a strong
union radical there wouldn't be all this fuss made
over him to liberate him."

"Pardoning Mooney would mean that the preparedness parade [was] unpatriotic and wrong and
should not have been held." "One of my childhood
friends was killed in that frightful affair." "Emma
Goldman was in the city at the same time, and I regard them all as accessories to crime." "The Department of Labor during the Wilson administration
seems never to have missed a single opportunity for
unwarranted interference with due process of state
law where agitators were involved." "We hope you
will be courageous enough to hold your own ground
(as Calvin Coolidge did when the Police and Firemen
of Boston wanted to unionize) and not be politically
influenced by the murderers and rough necks of the
country." "None of these petitioners have suggested
who might have been guilty of this crime, and some
doubtless have inside information. In my judgment
his sentence should be relentlessly carried out."

"These men are not Savanarolas. The class to
which they belong is entitled to the same consideration we give mad dogs, hydrophobia skunks, and
rattlesnakes." "Sympathy should not thwart the
purpose of our people in meting out appropriate
punishment to a misguided Russian, posing under an
Irish name." "If Tom Mooney ever be Pardoned or
released, He should by all means be deported because every body knows, he has been working
against our flag. Tom and his Brother has allways

been an I.W.W." "Mrs. Mooney was also as vicious as her husband." "Many of the anarchist-Communist-American Civil Liberties Union crowd would like to see them released." "The Communists wish to get these prisoners out of jail to advance the cause of communism, which is exactly what their pardon would do." "I commend you for not allowing the Hearst mud slinging machine to rail Road you into making a decision on the Mooney Billings cases." "I have just been talking to a few spies and if the Mooney methods of political threats are successful the whole state will soon be worse than Chicago."

"Have you noticed since Mooney and Billings have been locked up that there has been no dynamiting of buildings?" "Do you believe for one moment that money in great sums has not been used to bring about their release?" "Dont be a 'jellyfish' again by liberating this convicted assassin. You were fooled as to the Whitney female but dont repeat that mistake in the Mooney case." "The idea of such notariety hunters such as Sinclair Lewis going out and retrying the case and playing Judge and Jury and declaring him innocent." "They cry for his release like those of old cried for Barabas's release."

"Stick to your guns like the good soldier that the people of this great State believe you to be." "If I have helped just a little to stiffen your backbone I'll feel repaid." "This republic would crumble to pieces if it wasnt for the courageous fellows like you." "It is unfortunate that the matter came up now, but I am sure you have the approbation of our best people."

### CHAPTER 7

# World War I
# and the
# Rise of Totalitarianism

1917-1940

The steady political pressure from women to secure the right to vote finally resulted in the adoption of the Nineteenth Amendment to the United States Constitution. Success did not come without dramatic confrontations between suffragists and the forces of law and order, which resulted in the arrest, conviction, and imprisonment of women activists for the zealous pursuit of their cause.

The second and more central focus of this chapter is on America's response to World War I, a war in which the Old World nations had a vested interest. Pacifists, socialists, partisans of the various European camps, and America Firsters strongly opposed the New World's involvement in this conflagration. The resistance to America's involvement gave rise to a new class of political offenders — antiwar activists.

The wartime and postwar fears and anxieties also gave rise to a movement for the purification of the American melting pot by eliminating "un-American" influences. United States entry into World War I and the success of the Russian Revolution had a dramatic effect upon the American public. Socialism and communism were not mere idle notions expounded by foreign philosophers but could provide a stimulus for conspiracies on American soil. In addition, the call to arms, which previously had been resisted in instances of domestic conflict, was likely to encounter even greater opposition in cases of foreign wars. In short, the suspicion grew that the nation's pluralistic population was not as committed to the American Way as had been assumed and could be manipulated by foreign agitators.

The criminal law was invoked directly to punish war and draft resisters, as well as those who advocated the forceful overthrow of government. Other quasi-criminal methods for purging the country of the disloyal, such as the exclusion and deportation of politically suspect aliens — often associated with the labor movement — were also utilized. Ideological dissidents were subject to punishment for political associations, and several documents reflect less a concern with the enforcement of traditional justice than the desire of the authorities to convey a symbolic message to left-leaning aliens to watch their step.

This chapter documents as well the first resorts to the Constitution, particularly the First Amendment, as a judicially enforceable protection against the criminalizing of unorthodox political belief and advocacy.

Although it was at the height of World War I and shortly thereafter that the movement toward enforcing American homogeneity reached its peak, its legacies lingered on for several decades and are still evident today.

The labor movement continued to be a focus for much of the material in this chapter. In its quest for legitimacy, labor finally achieved its long-sought goal of preventing federal power, in the form of the labor injunction, from playing a partisan role in the contest between labor and capital. It ultimately succeeded in having the federal government cast as an impartial referee of labor disputes, and several long-standing management techniques for curbing labor's power were determined to be illegal. The changing relations between capital and labor are reflected further in the increased sophistication of labor tactics, including the sit-down strike, which led to many violent confrontations with local police.

Greatly diminished from the labor scene, federal force was evident, nevertheless, in Washington, D.C., during the Depression, as the encampment of the Bonus Marchers was dispersed by military force. But tensions continued between state and federal authorities in several other arenas of political and civil rights. The power of the state to resort to martial law in order to avoid the command of a federal injunction was tested and denied. But federal involvement in protecting blacks in the South from terrorist attacks was as passive as before. Also, the failure of the assimilationist policies toward Native Americans accounted in large part for the new grant of limited powers of self-determination to them.

At the close of this chapter, with the blowing winds of World War II, one can observe the beginning of the government's renewed attempts to curb political and related activities motivated by sympathy to various foreign causes. With mounting tensions overseas, the authorities set out once again, as they had done a quarter-century earlier, to enforce the American Way.

# 188  How Long Must Women Wait for Liberty? (1917)

The suffragist movement contributed to Woodrow Wilson's continuing political education. Before he secured reelection in 1916, Wilson had decided that women's right to vote could be denied no longer. Yet he was reluctant to assume an active role in securing suffrage for them.

The militant suffragists were convinced that only a strong exercise of presidential power could overcome congressional resistance, and they set out to spur Wilson into action. They picketed the White House throughout 1917. After the United States declared war on Germany, banners continued to point out to "Kaiser Wilson!" that "20,000,000 American women are not self-governed."

After six months of picketing, the authorities stepped in to suppress the embarrassing demonstrations. The following contemporaneous account of the events reported the escalation of government response from toleration to arrest and release to the filing of charges, fines, and imprisonment. Those arrested received sentences of up to sixty days. The prosecutions only served to stiffen the resolve of the suffragists. They engaged in more alarming tactics: hunger strikes, public burnings of Wilson's lofty speeches on democracy, and the burning of the president in effigy.

It was not until September 1918 that Wilson directly urged Congress to pass the National Suffrage Amendment. Though gravely ill, Wilson worked hard to ensure that women could vote in the presidential election of 1920.

## ☆ 188  Militant Suffragists Picket President Wilson

Reprinted in D. Stevens, *Jailed for Freedom* (New York: Boni and Liveright, 1920), 93–111.

... The Chief of Police, Major Pullman, was detailed to "request" us to stop "picketing" and to tell us that if we continued to picket, we would be arrested.

"We have picketed for six months without interference," said Miss Paul. "*Has the law been changed?*"

"No," was the reply, "but you must stop it."

"But, Major Pullman, we have consulted our lawyers and know we have a legal right to picket."

"I warn you, you will be arrested if you attempt to picket again."

The following day Miss Lucy Burns and Miss Katherine Morey of Boston carried to the White House gates "We shall fight for the things we have always held nearest our hearts, for democracy, for the right of those who submit to authority to have a voice in their own government," and were arrested.

News had spread through the city that the pickets were to be arrested. A moderately large crowd had gathered to see the "fun." One has only to come into conflict with prevailing authority, whether rightly or wrongly, to find friendly hosts vanishing with lightning speed. To know that we were no longer wanted at the gates of the White House and that the police were no longer our "friends" was enough for the mob mind.

Some members of the crowd made sport of the women. Others hurled cheap and childish epithets at them. Small boys were allowed to capture souvenirs, shreds of the banners torn from non-resistant women, as trophies of the sport.

Thinking they had been mistaken in believing the pickets were to be arrested, and having grown weary of their strenuous sport, the crowd moved on its way. Two solitary figures remained, standing on the sidewalk, flanked by the vast Pennsylvania Avenue, looking quite abandoned and alone, when suddenly without any warrant in law, they were arrested on a completely deserted avenue.

Miss Burns and Miss Morey upon arriving at the police station, insisted to the great surprise of all the officials, upon knowing the charge against them. Major Pullman and his entire staff were utterly at a loss to know what to answer. . . .

. . . Hours passed. Finally the two prisoners were pompously told that they had "obstructed the traffic" on Pennsylvania Avenue, were dismissed on their own recognizance, and never brought to trial.

The following day, June 23rd, more arrests were made; two women at the White House, two at the Capitol. All carried banners with the same words of the President. There was no hesitation this time. They were promptly arrested for "obstructing the traffic." They, too, were dismissed and their cases never tried. It seemed clear that the Administration hoped to suppress picketing merely by arrests. When, however, women continued to picket in the face of arrest, the Administration quickened its advance into the venture of suppression. It decided to bring the offenders to trial.

On June 26, six American women were tried, judged guilty on the technical charge of "obstructing the traffic," warned by the court of their "unpatriotic, almost treasonable behavior," and sentenced to pay a fine of twenty-five dollars or serve three days in jail.

"Not a dollar of your fine will we pay," was the answer of the women. "To pay a fine would be an admission of guilt. We are innocent."

Independence Day, July 4, 1917, is the occasion for two demonstrations in the name of liberty. Champ Clark, late Democratic speaker of the House, is declaiming to a cheering crowd behind the White House, "Governments derive their just powers from the consent of the governed." In front of the White

House thirteen silent sentinels with banners bearing the same words, are arrested. It would have been exceedingly droll if it had not been so tragic. Champ Clark and his throng were not molested. The women with practically a deserted street were arrested and served jail terms for "obstructing traffic."

It is Bastille Day, July fourteenth. . . .

The proud banner is scarcely at the gates when the leader is placed under arrest. Her place is taken by another. She is taken. Another, and still another steps into the breach and is arrested.

Meanwhile, the crowd grows, attracted to the spot by the presence of the police and the patrol wagon. Applause is heard. There are cries of "shame" for the police, who, I must say, did not always act as if they relished carrying out what they termed "orders from higher up." An occasional hoot from a small boy served to make the mood of the hostile ones a bit gayer. But for the most part an intense silence fell upon the watchers, as they saw not only younger women, but white-haired grandmothers hoisted before the public gaze into the crowded patrol, their heads erect, their eyes a little moist and their frail hands holding tightly to the banner until wrested from them by superior brute force. . . .

The stuffy court room is packed to overflowing. . . . The prosecuting attorney now elaborately proves that we walked, that we carried banners, that we were arrested by the aforesaid officers while attempting to hold banners at the White House gates.

Each woman speaks briefly in her own defense. She denounces the government's policy with hot defiance. The blame is placed squarely at the door of the Administration, and in unmistakable terms. Miss Anne Martin opens for the defense:

"This is what we are doing with our banners before the White House, petitioning the most powerful representative of the government, the President of the United States, for a redress of grievances; we are asking him to use his great power to secure the passage of the national suffrage amendment.

"As long as the government and the representatives of the government prefer to send women to jail on petty and technical charges, we will go to jail. Persecution has always advanced the cause of justice. The right of American women to work for democracy must be maintained. . . . We would hinder, not help, the whole cause of freedom for women, if we weakly submitted to persecution now. Our work for the passage of the amendment must go on. It *will* go on."

Mrs. John Rogers, Jr., descendant of Roger Sherman, one of signers of the Declaration of Independence, speaks: "We are not guilty of any offence, not even of infringing a police regulation. We know full well that we stand here because the President of the United States refuses to give liberty to American women. We believe, your Honor, that the wrong persons are before the bar in this Court. . . ."

"I object, your Honor, to this woman making such a statement here in Court," says the District Attorney.

"We believe the President is the guilty one and that we are innocent."

Mrs. Florence Bayard Hilles speaks in her own defense: . . . "I am a Democrat, and to a Democratic President I went with my appeal. . . . What a spectacle it must be to the thinking people of this country to see us urged to go to war for democracy in a foreign land, and to see women thrown into prison who plead for that same cause at home.

\*　　　\*　　　\*

"My services as an American woman are being conscripted by order of the President of the United States to help win the world war for democracy, . . . 'for the right of those who submit to authority to have a voice in their own government.' I shall continue to plead for the political liberty of American women — and especially do I plead to the President, since he is the one person who . . . can end the struggles of American women to take their proper places in a true democracy."

There is a continuous objection from the prosecutor, eager advice from the judge, "you had better keep to the charge of obstructing traffic." . . . And how utterly puny the "charge" is! If it were true that the prisoners actually obstructed the traffic, how grotesque that would be. The importance of their demand, the purity of their reasoning, the nobility and gentle quality of the prisoners at the bar; all conspire to make the charge against them, and the attorney who makes it, and the judge who hears it, petty and ridiculous.

But justice must proceed.

Mrs. Gilson Gardner of Washington, D.C., a member of the Executive Committee of the National Woman's party, and the wife of Gilson Gardner, a well-known Liberal and journalist, speaks:

"It is impossible for me to believe that we were arrested because we were obstructing traffic or blocking the public highway.

"We have been carrying on activities of a distinctly political nature, and these political activities have seemingly disturbed certain powerful influences. Arrest followed. I submit that these arrests are purely political and that the charge of an unlawful assemblage and of obstructing traffic is a political subterfuge. Even should I be sent to jail which, I could not, your Honor, anticipate, I would be in jail, not because I obstructed traffic, but because I have offended politically, because I have demanded of this government freedom for women."

## 189 Suffragists as Political Prisoners (1917)

The country's preoccupation with winning World War I did not deter the suffragists. Arrested for their persistent picketing, the suffragists carried their struggle to the jails. Although segregated from each other, they collectively managed to frame and sign the earliest known claim in the United States for special treatment, in the European tradition, as political prisoners. Refusal of the authorities to accede to the demands led to hunger strikes and forced feeding.

### ☆ 189 Suffragists, Letters from Prison

Reprinted in D. Stevens, *Jailed for Freedom* (New York: Boni & Liveright, 1920), 175.

To the Commissioners of the District of Columbia:

As political prisoners, we, the undersigned, refuse to work while in prison. We have taken this stand as a matter of principle after careful consideration, and from it we shall not recede.

This action is a necessary protest against an unjust sentence. In reminding President Wilson of his pre-election promises toward woman suffrage we were exercising the right of peaceful petition, guaranteed by the Constitution. . . .

Conscious, therefore, of having acted in accordance with the highest standards of citizenship, we ask the Commissioners of the District to grant us the rights due political prisoners. We ask that we no longer be segregated and confined under locks and bars in small groups, but permitted to see each other, and that Miss Lucy Burns, who is in full sympathy with this letter, be released from solitary confinement in another building and given back to us.

We ask exemption from prison work, that our legal right to consult counsel be recognized, to have food sent to us from outside, to supply ourselves with writing material for as much correspondence as we may need, to receive books, letters, newspapers, our relatives and friends.

Our united demand for political treatment has been delayed, because on entering the workhouse we found conditions so very bad that before we could ask that the suffragists be treated as political prisoners, it was necessary to make a stand for the ordinary rights of human beings for all the inmates. Although this has not been accomplished we now wish to bring the important question of the status of political prisoners to the attention of the commissioners, who, we are informed, have full authority to make what regulations they please for the District prison and workhouse.

The Commissioners are requested to send us a written reply so that we may be sure this protest has reached them.

Signed by,

Mary Winsor
Lucy Branham
Ernestine Hara
Hilda Blumberg
Maud Malone
Pauline F. Adams
Eleanor A. Calnan
Edith Ainge
Annie Arneil
Dorothy J. Bartlett
Margaret Fotheringham

\*            \*            \*

The Commissioners' only answer to this was a hasty transfer of the signers and the leader, Miss Burns, to the District Jail, where they were put in solitary confinement. The women were not only refused the privileges asked but were denied some of the usual privileges allowed to ordinary criminals.

## 190 "war is wrong" (1917)

John Haynes Holmes served as minister of the Community Church of New York from 1907 to 1949. An outspoken pacifist, he reaffirmed his unwavering opposition to all wars in the immediate aftermath of Pearl Harbor in 1941. In his 1917 "Statement to My People," he unequivocally condemned America's imminent entry into World War I and affirmed his support for draft resistance. Recognizing that "statements of this kind, made on the eve of War, seem to many persons to be treasonable," Holmes insisted, nevertheless, that the "whole fabric of democracy is threatened" by war, conscription, the national war fever, and the "orgy of bigotry, intolerance, and persecutions for opinions' sake as America has not seen since the days of the Salem witches." The trustees of Holmes's church were nearly unanimous in disavowing his antiwar positions, but they also defended his right to speak freely from the pulpit. The Secret Service placed agents in the congregation to monitor his sermons. The federal government subsequently imposed criminal sanctions on individuals who refused to be inducted because of their adherence to the principles of conscientious objection as summarized in the following document.

### ☆ 190 A Statement to My People on the Eve of War (John Haynes Holmes)

The Messiah Pulpit, May 1917, 4-5, 6, 8-9, 10-12, 15-16 (The Community Church of New York), reprinted in David R. Weber, ed., *Civil Disobedience in America* (Ithaca: Cornell University Press, 1978), 234-39.

... You have a right to know what I shall say and do in the event of war, upon what road of doctrine I shall set my feet, into what hazards of pain and peril I shall lead this church. The pew is always entitled to the full confession of the pulpit, but never so urgently as at the time when such confession touches the deep issues of life and death. If there be any here who is tempted to question the wisdom or the sincerity of what I am now doing, let him think for a moment of how easy it would have been for me to keep silent, avoid the questions which are to-day setting the son "at variance against his father, the daughter against her mother, the daughter-in-law against her mother-in-law," ... before the bugles sing and the flags are lifted high, I ask you to hear me....

... War is in open and utter violation of Christianity. If war is right, then Christianity is wrong, false, a lie. If Christianity is right, then war is wrong, false, a lie. The God revealed by Jesus, and by every great spiritual leader of the race, is no God of battles. He lifts no sword—he asks no sacrifice of blood. He is the Father of all men, Jew and Gentile, bond and free. His spirit is love, his rule is peace, his method of persuasion is forgiveness. His law, as interpreted and promulgated by the Nazarene, is "love one another," "resist not evil with evil," "forgive seventy times seven," "overcome evil with good," "love your enemies, bless them that curse you, do good to them that hate you, pray for them which despitefully use you and persecute you." Such a God and such a law, others may reconcile with war, if they can. I cannot—and what I cannot do, I will not profess to do.

But I must go farther—I must speak not only of war in general, but of this war in particular. Most persons are quite ready to agree, especially in the piping times of peace, that war is wrong. But let a war cloud no bigger than a man's hand, appear on the horizon of the nation's life, and they straightway begin to qualify their judgment, and if the war cloud grow until it covers all the heavens, they finally reverse it. This brings the curious situation of all war being wrong in general, and each war being right in particular....

In its ultimate causes, this war is the natural product and expression of our unchristian civilization. Its armed men are grown from the dragon's teeth of secret diplomacy, imperialistic ambitions, dynastic pride, greedy commercialism, economic exploitation at home and abroad. In the sowing of these teeth, America had had her part; and it is therefore only proper, perhaps, that she should have her part also in the reaping of the dreadful harvest. ... Any honor, dignity, or beauty which there may be in our impending action, is to be found in the impulses, pure and undefiled, which are actuating many patriotic hearts to-day, and not at all in the real facts of the situation. The war itself is wrong.

Its prosecution will be a crime. There is not a question raised, an issue involved, a cause at stake, which is worth the life of one blue-jacket on the sea or one khaki-coat in the trenches.... I say to you that when, years hence, the whole of this story has been told, it will be found that we have been tragically deceived, and all our sacrifices been made in vain.

... Nothing that America can do, can quench my passion for her beauty, or divert my loyalty from her service. She is the only country I have, or shall ever have, and I propose that she shall be mine forever, in war or peace, in storm or calm, in evil or good. In this impending crisis with Germany, I believe that she is wrong. She seems to me to be faithless to her own supreme calling among the nations of the earth, disloyal to high interests of humanity long since committed to her care, guilty for a selfish motive of a grievous fault. But her infidelity shall not shake my faith, her disloyalty shall not change my loyalty, her guilt shall not discharge my obligation. I shall decline to become, or to be made, "a man without a country." America has committed wrongs in the past, and she will undoubtedly commit other wrongs in the future. But she is mine....

And how shall I, a pacifist, serve my country in time of war?

When hostilities begin, it is universally assumed that there is but a single service which a loyal citizen can render to the state—that of bearing arms and killing the enemy. Will you understand me if I say, humbly and regretfully, that this I cannot, and will not, do. If any man or boy in this church answers the call to arms, I shall bless him as he marches to the front. When he lies in the trenches, or watches on the lonely sentinel post, or fights in the charge, I shall follow him with my prayers. If he is brought back dead from hospital or battlefield, I shall bury him with all the honors not of war but of religion. He will have obeyed his conscience and thus performed his whole duty as a man. But I also have a conscience, and that conscience I also must obey. When, therefore, there comes a call for volunteers, I shall have to refuse to heed. When, or if, the system of conscription is adopted, I shall have to decline to serve. If this means a fine, I will pay my fine. If this means imprisonment, I will serve my term. If this means persecution, I will carry my cross. No order of president or governor, no law of nation or state, no loss of reputation, freedom or life, will persuade me or force me to this business of killing. On this issue, for me at least, there is "no compromise." Mistaken, foolish, fanatical, I may be; I will not deny the charge. But false to my own soul I will not be. [S]o long as I am your minister, the Church of the Messiah will answer no military summons. Other pulpits may preach recruiting sermons; mine will not. Other parish houses may be turned into drill halls and rifle ranges; ours will not. Other clergymen may pray to God for victory for our arms; I will not. In this church, if nowhere else in all America, the Germans will still be included in the family of God's children. No word of hatred shall be spoken against them — no evil fate shall be desired upon them. ... [I]t remains for us who cannot take up arms at her behest, to keep it in her stead. How better can we serve our country than by restoring to her, or fulfilling for her, that high mission of peace-making, which is so uniquely and divinely hers! ...

No nation is worthy the allegiance of even the meanest of her citizenry, which is not dedicated to the establishment of that larger and more inclusive life of universal association, which is the glad promise of mankind. America, for more than a hundred years, has been first among the countries of the world, in recognition and service of this ideal. She has been a gathering place of all the tribes of earth — a melting-pot into which the ingredients of every race, religion and nationality have been poured. And out of it has come not so much a new nation as a new idea — the idea of brotherhood. This idea has stamped our people a chosen people. It has set our land apart as a holy land. It has exalted our destiny as a divine destiny. And now, with the plunge into the welter of contending European nationalities, all this is gone. Gone, at least, if those of us who see not today's quarrel but tomorrow's prophecy, do not dedicate ourselves unfalteringly to the forgotten vision! This I am resolved to do. ...

## 191  " 'Extreme Penalty for Traitors' " (1917)

Ammon Hennacy opposed World War I as being contrary to his socialist political beliefs. He refused to register for the draft and was imprisoned in Atlanta for speaking out in opposition to war. He entered prison "an atheist and not a pacifist. I would fight in a revolution but not in a capitalist war." His religious conversion while in prison turned him from violence — but not from militancy.

This account of Hennacy's prison experience portrays many of the difficulties which the correctional system faces when dealing with political offenders and the manner in which traditional penal techniques of appealing to an inmate's self-interest (either to avoid punishment or to obtain reward) have little impact upon the "politicals." Resistance and obstinance yield harsher punishment but also greater respect from officials. The superintendent of federal prisons wanted to co-opt this stiff-necked man and make him a Secret Service agent. Hennacy turned down the job and was paroled nevertheless. He eventually became a leader of the Catholic Worker movement, founded in 1933, which encouraged non-payment of taxes and civil disobedience in opposition to war.

## ☆ 191  Atlanta Prison (Ammon Hennacy)

A. Hennacy, ed., *Two Agitators: Peter Maurin — Ammon Hennacy* (New York: Catholic Worker, 1959), 6-19.

I was arrested when I spoke against the coming war at Broad and High in Columbus, Ohio before about 10,000 people on the evening of April 5, 1917. The next day war was declared and I was released for trial May 30. Meanwhile I distributed leaflets over Ohio for the Socialist Party, advising young men to refuse to register for the draft. When I was picked up again I asked to see a lawyer but was told I could not see one. Detective Wilson said that unless I registered for the draft by June 5th, which was registration day, I was to be shot on orders from Washington. I was shown a copy of the local paper with headlines "Extreme Penalty for Traitors." I only saw it through the bars and was not allowed to read it. ... Spike Moore, ... from Pittsburgh who was in Columbus, sneaked me a note and a clipping from the paper in which a reporter asked my mother if she was not frightened because I was to be shot soon. Her reply was that the only thing she was afraid of was that they might scare me to give in. This gave me added courage. June 5th passed and no move was made to shoot me. ... My partner and I each got 2 years in Atlanta. After this term was served I was to do 9 months in Delaware, Ohio, County Jail nearby for refusal to register.

\*         \*         \*

The conscientious objectors were scattered in different gangs and cell houses over the prison. The warden told me that the orders from Washington were to put us all in one place, but he knew better and scattered us out, for if we were in one place we would plot. This reminded me of the farmer who caught the ground-mole and said, "Hanging's too good; burning's too good; I'll bury you alive." So we conscientious objectors were scattered around where we could do propaganda instead of being segregated where we would argue among ourselves.

\*         \*         \*

... A white man and a Negro had been killed by guards and I was incensed about it. My cell mates laughed and said I should worry about the living, for the dead were dead and no one could do anything about it. That if I wanted anything to do I should raise a fuss about the poor fish served on Fridays by the new mess guard, who was accused of making his rake by charging for good food and giving us junk. Accordingly I got cardboard from John Dunn and painted signs which I put up in all of the toilets around the place telling the prisoners to work on Fridays, but to stay in their cells and refuse to go to dinner or to eat the rotten fish. The guards and stoolpigeons tore the signs down, but I made others and put them up. The last Friday 20 of us stayed in our cells. The guards came around and asked us if we were sick. We said we were sick of that damn fish. The next Friday 200 stayed in their cells; and the next Friday 600. That was too many people thinking alike, as on the next Thursday the warden came to the second mess and said that those who did not come to dinner the next day would be put in the hole. Some kid squeaked out in a shrill voice: "You can't do it warden; there's only 40 solitary cells and there's a thousand of us." The next day 900 out of the 1,100 who ate at this shift stayed in their cells.

The next Monday I was called to the office and was told that I had been seen plotting to blow up the prison with dynamite, and was promptly sent to the dark hole.

*         *         *

Once when I was going to get a shave I saw Popoff entering his cell with his head bandaged. This must have been the result of the blows which I had heard faintly the day before. He was mistreated for a year or more until he went insane. Selma and I visited him in 1921 at St. Elizabeth's Hospital in Washington, D.C. He did not recognize me until I said "Johnson, the guard." I sent notes to my sister Lola for the newspapers about the treatment of Popoff. I heard the chains fall which bound him to the bars and then the thump of his body to the floor. I was told that papers in Atlanta printed something about it but no official investigation was ever made. . . .

It was now nearly three months that I had been in solitary. Fred Zerbst, the warden, came in and asked me to sign a paper. It was registration for the second war draft. I told him that I had not changed my mind about the war. He said I wouldn't get anything around here acting that way. I told him that I wasn't asking for anything around here: I was just doing time. He said that I would get another year back in the hole for this second refusal to register. I told him that was o.k. It was September 21, 1918. The warden came in again and said this was all the longer they kept prisoners in solitary and that he would let me out in the regular prison the next day, if I would not plot to blow up any more prisons.

"You know I didn't do that," I said.

"I know you didn't," he replied, "but what do you suppose I am warden for? If I had told the prisoners that you were put in solitary for leading in that food sit-down, all of them would be your friends. When you are accused of plotting to blow up the prison they are all afraid to know you. Why didn't you come and tell me about the food?"

"Why didn't you come in the kitchen and find out? No one but stoolies go to your office," I answered. He left hurriedly.

In about five minutes he returned, saying, "I forgot to ask you something, Hennacy. I'll leave you out tomorrow just the same."

"What's on your mind?" I asked.

"Have you been sneaking any letters out of this prison?" he asked in an angry tone.

"Sure," I replied, smiling.

"Who is doing it for you?" he demanded.

"A friend of mine," I answered.

"What is his name?" was the query.

"That is for you and your guards and stool pigeons to find out."

He stormed around my cell, somewhat taken back by the fact that I had not lied or given in.

"You'll stay in here all your good time and get another year, you stubborn fool," he said as he left.

*         *         *

. . . I could not see anywhere except across the hall to the solid door of another cell, but I could hear Popoff in the next cell groaning and calling for water. He was still hanging from his hands for the eight hours a day as he had been for months. As the guard came down the hall he opened Popoff's door, dipping his tin cup in the toilet and threw the dirty water in Popoff's face. . . .

Two months later I heard the whistles blow and shouts resound throughout the prison. The war was over. The Armistice had been signed. It was not until then that I was informed in a [secret] note from [fellow prisoner and anarchist Alexander] Berkman that November 11 was also an anarchist anniversary: the date of the hanging of the Chicago anarchists of the Haymarket in 1887. . . .

[I decided that] the remainder of my two years in solitary must result in a clear-cut plan whereby I could go forth and be a force in the world. I could not take any half-way measures. If assassination, violence and revolution was the better way, then military tactics must be studied and a group of fearless rebels organized. . . . I also remembered what Berkman had said about being firm, but quiet. He had tried violence but did not believe in it as a wholesale method. I read of the wars and hatred in the Old Testament. I also read of the courage of Daniel and the Hebrew children who would not worship the golden image; of Peter who chose to obey God rather than the properly constituted authorities who placed him in jail; and of the victory of these men by courage and peaceful methods. I read of Jesus, who was confronted with a whole world empire of tyranny and chose not to overturn the tyrant and make Himself King, but to change the hatred in the hearts of men to love and understanding—to overcome evil with goodwill.

I had called loudly for the sword and mentally listed those whom I desired to kill when I was free. Was this really the universal method which should be used? . . . Gradually I came to gain a glimpse of what

Jesus meant when He said, "The Kingdom of God is within you." In my heart now after six months I could love everybody in the world but the warden, but if I did not love him then the Sermon on the Mount meant nothing at all. I really saw this and felt it in my heart but I was too stubborn to admit it in my mind. One day ... the thought came to me: "Here I am locked up in a cell. The warden was never locked up in any cell and he never had a chance to know what Jesus meant. Neither did I until yesterday. So I must not blame him. I must love him." ... The warden had said that he did not understand political prisoners. He and the deputy, in plain words, did not know any better; they had put on the false face of sternness and tyranny because this was the only method which they knew. It was my job to teach them another method: that of goodwill overcoming their evil intentions, or rather habits. The opposite of the Sermon on the Mount was what the whole world had been practicing, in prison and out of prison; and hate piled on hate had brought hate and revenge. It was plain that this system did not work....

I fancied what my radical friends in and out of prison would say when I spoke of the above teachings of Jesus. I knew that I would have to bear their displeasure, just as I had born the hysteria of the patriots and the silence of my friends when I was sent to prison. This did not mean that I was going to "squeal" and give in to the officials, but in my heart I would try to see the good in them and not hate them. Jesus did not give in to His persecutors. He used strong words against the evil doers of His time, but He had mercy for the sinner. I now was not alone fighting the world for I had Him as my helper. I saw that if I held this philosophy for myself I could not engage in violence for a revolution—a good war, as some might call it—but would have to renounce violence even in my thought. Would I be ready to go the whole way? At that time I had not heard of Tolstoy and his application of Christ's teachings to society. Berkman had just mentioned his name along with other anarchists and he might have told me more if I had had a lengthy conversation with him; but I never saw him again....

*        *        *

It was now in February of 1919 and I had been in solitary for 7½ months. Mr. Duehay, Superintendent of Federal Prisons from Washington, and his secretary, and Warden Zerbst came to my cell. Duehay wanted to know why I was being held so long here. I told him I was telling the world of evil conditions in the prison and would not divulge the source of my outlet for contraband mail....

*        *        *

The next morning a runner came down from the office to measure me for an outgoing suit, saying· "The warden told us 'that damn Hennacy wouldn't

tell anything in 7½ months; he won't tell anything in 7½ years. Get him the hell out of hole give him back his good time and let him go to his other jail. He is too much of a nuisance.' "

The next month went very quickly. It was now March 19, 1919, and I was to be released the next day. That night the deputy came in and said:

"Going out tomorrow, Hennacy?"

"That's what they say; sure a fine feeling," I replied.

"We give; we take. You tell who is getting out your contraband mail or you'll stay here another 5½ months and lose your good time and then another year for refusing to register. You don't think we will allow anyone to get on by bucking us, do you?"

Tears came to my eyes as I chokingly replied, "I can do it. Go away and don't bother me any more." After he left I wept, but I was at the stage where I felt strong enough to take it.

The next morning after breakfast I wrote on the wall that I was beginning to do the "good time" that I had lost, when the door opened suddenly and old Johnson smiled for once, saying, "Going out of this jail, Hennacy." I did not believe him; and even while the barber was shaving me I thought it was some trick to bedevil me. I was given my out-going suit and an overcoat. It is customary for the warden to shake hands with those who leave and to admonish them to live a good life out in the world. A guard gave me my $10 outgoing money and a bundle of letters that had come to me while I was in solitary, but the warden never appeared.

When I walked out of prison a plain clothes man met me saying that I was being arrested for refusing to register for the draft in August 1918 and would be taken to the county tower to await trial....

*        *        *

... Sam Castelton, who was to be Debs' lawyer in Atlanta, was also my lawyer. My case came up for trial after seven weeks. Castleton told me that if I was not too radical he might get me off with six months. I was asked if I had really refused to register for the first and second drafts and if I had not changed my mind and would I be ready to register for the third draft if and when it came along. I replied that I had entered prison an atheist and not a pacifist. I would fight in a revolution but not in a capitalist war. I had got locked up with the Bible in solitary and read it and become a Christian and a pacifist.... [M]y study of the Bible had made me see that Christ was the greatest Revolutionist. And a few weeks ago I had read Tolstoy [while awaiting trial] and had become an anarchist.

"What's an anarchist?" asked the judge. My lawyer shook his head and put his finger to his lips as a warning for me not to be too radical.

"An anarchist is one who doesn't have to have a

cop to make him behave. It is the individual, the family, or the small co-operative group as a unit rather than the State." And, I continued for about ten minutes to quote Tolstoy to the effect that one had to obey God rather than man. The District Attorney, Hooper Alexander, an old fashioned looking southerner, came up to the judge and whispered, and the judge said, "case dismissed." I looked around to see whose case it was and it was mine. My lawyer seemed bewildered and so was I. I had approached the court this time with love for my enemy and had never thought I would get my freedom, for he allowed me to go 10 days on my own before I reported to the court in Columbus, Ohio, to do my 9 months in Delaware County jail for my first refusal to register.

## 192 "false reports or false statements" (1917)

On June 15, 1917, Congress passed the Espionage Act giving the United States broad powers to punish acts of gathering, transmitting, or negligently handling information that would be injurious to the defense of the United States if in the hands of a foreign nation or enemy. The act also imposed penalties for certain antiwar commentary and opinions. Congress enacted the law in large part to check enemy sympathizers residing in the United States. A widespread propaganda campaign had stirred up Germanophobia, and German immigrants throughout the country were accused of supporting the kaiser and spying for him.

President Woodrow Wilson, apparently recognizing the potential for abuse, approved the Espionage Act with the statement that "I shall not permit . . . any part of this law to apply to me . . . as a shield against criticism."

### ☆ 192  The Espionage Act

40 Stat. 217 (1917).

CHAP. 30—An Act to punish acts of interference with the foreign relations, the neutrality, and the foreign commerce of the United States, to punish espionage, and better to enforce the criminal laws of the United States, and for other purposes.

Be it enacted by the Senate and House of Representatives of the United States of America in Congress assembled:

#### TITLE I. ESPIONAGE

*      *      *

SEC. 3. Whoever, when the United States is at war, shall willfully make or convey false reports or false statements with intent to interfere with the operation or success of the military or naval forces of the United States or to promote the success of its enemies and whoever, when the United States is at war, shall willfully cause or attempt to cause insubordination, disloyalty, mutiny, or refusal of duty, in the military or naval forces of the United States, or shall willfully obstruct the recruiting or enlistment service of the United States, to the injury of the service or of the United States, shall be punished by a fine of not more than $10,000 or imprisonment for not more than twenty years, or both.

SEC. 4. If two or more persons conspire to violate the provisions of sections two or three of this title, and one or more of such persons does any act to effect the object of the consipiracy, each of the parties to such conspiracy shall be punished as in said sections. . . .

SEC. 5. Whoever harbors or conceals any person who he knows, or has reasonable grounds to believe or suspect, has committed, or is about to commit, an offense under this title shall be punished by a fine of not more than $10,000 or by imprisonment for not more than two years, or both.

*      *      *

## 193 "I do not believe that I am seeking martyrdom" (1917-1918)

Some conscientious objectors declined to register for the draft and were prosecuted in regular civilian courts. But in 1917 and 1918 the army inducted more than twenty thousand men who previously had filed claims to be classified as objectors. Of these, some four thousand declined to perform military service. The conscription bill made liberal provisions for members of recognized religious sects to choose a noncombatant corps. In addition, conscientious objectors whom a presidential board of inquiry deemed to be "sincere" were eligible for noncombatant service or for agricultural furloughs. But some men refused all forms of alternative service. The military court-martialed several hundred such men, together with the "insincere" objectors who professed no religious or moral antipathy to war.

The statements of three objectors illustrate the variety of motives for refusing conscription. Carl Haessler, a Rhodes Scholar and a professor of philosophy, objected on political grounds. Maurice Hess, voicing religious objections, also later became a college professor. Roger Baldwin, who founded the American Civil Liberties Union, articulated moral grounds. These men and the others were punished for refusing to accommodate their political, religious, or moral beliefs to the duties of allegiance owed to their government. Their criminality lay not in any affirmative deed against the government but rather in refusing to act in accordance with the demands of the authorities.

## ☆ 193  Statements of Conscientious Objection

Reprinted in N. Thomas, *The Conscientious Objector in America* (New York: B. W. Heubsch, 1923), 23-28.

### ☆ 193a  Carl Haessler

I, Carl Haessler, Recruit, Machine Gun Company, 46th Infantry, respectfully submit the following statement in extenuation in connection with my proposed plea of guilty to the charge of violation of the 64th Article of War, the offense having been committed June 22, 1918, in Camp Sheridan, Ala.

The offense was not committed from private, secret, personal, impulsive, religious, pacifist or pro-German grounds.

The willful disobedience of my Captain's and of my Lieutenant-Colonel's orders to report in military uniform arose from a conviction ... that America's participation in the World War was unnecessary, of doubtful benefit (if any) to the country and to humanity, and accomplished largely, though not exclusively, through the pressure of the Allied and American commercial imperialists.

Holding this conviction, I conceived my part as a citizen to be opposition to the war before it was declared, active efforts for a peace without victory after the declaration, and a determination so far as possible to do nothing in aid of the war while its character seemed to remain what I thought it was. I hoped in this way to help bring the war to an earlier close and to help make similar future wars less probable in this country.

I further believe that I shall be rendering the country a service by helping to set an example for other citizens to follow in the matter of fearlessly acting on unpopular convictions instead of forgetting them in time of stress. . . .

. . . I regret that I have been forced to make myself a nuisance. . . . Although officers have on three occasions offered me noncombatant service if I would put on the uniform, I have regretfully refused each time on the ground that "bomb-proof" service on my part would give the lie to my sincerity. . . . If I am to render any war services, I shall not ask for special privileges.

I wish to conclude this long statement by reiterating that I am not a pacifist or pro-German, not a religious or private objector, but regard myself as a patriotic political objector, acting largely from public and social grounds.

I regret that, while my present view of this war continues, I cannot freely render any service in aid of the war. I shall not complain about the punishment that the court may see fit to mete out to me.

### ☆ 193b  Maurice Hess

I do not believe that I am seeking martyrdom. As a young man, life and its hopes and freedom and opportunities for service are sweet to me. . . .

But I know that I dare not purchase these things at the price of eternal condemnation. I know the teaching of Christ, my Savior. He taught us to resist not evil, to love our enemies, to bless them that curse us, and do good to them that hate us. Not only did he teach this, but he also practiced it. . . .

. . . We know that obedience to Christ will gain for us the glorious prize of eternal life. We cannot yield, we cannot compromise, we must suffer.

Two centuries ago our people were driven out of Germany by religious persecution, and they accepted the invitation of William Penn to come to his colony where they might enjoy the blessing of religious liberty which he promised them. This religious liberty was later confirmed by the Constitution of Pennsylvania, and the Constitution of the United States.

If the authorities now see fit to change those fundamental documents and take away our privilege of living in accordance with the teaching of the scriptures of God, then we have no course but to endure persecution as true soldiers of Christ.

If I have committed anything worthy of bonds or death, I do not refuse to suffer or to die.

I pray God for strength to remain faithful.

### ☆ 193c  Roger N. Baldwin

The compelling motive for refusing to comply with the draft act is my uncompromising opposition to the principle of conscription of life by the state for any purpose whatever, in time of war or peace. I not only refuse to obey the present conscription law, but I would in future refuse to obey any similar statute which attempts to direct my choice of service and ideals. I regard the principle of conscription of life as a flat contradiction of all our cherished ideals of individual freedom, democratic liberty, and Christian teaching.

I am the more opposed to the present act, because it is for the purpose of conducting war. I am opposed to this and all other wars. I do not believe in the use of physical force as a method of achieving any end, however good. . . .

But, I believe most of us are prepared even to die for our faith, just as our brothers in France are dying for theirs. To them we are comrades in spirit — we understand one another's motive, though our methods are wide apart. We both share deeply the common experience of living up to the truth as we see it, whatever the price.

Though at the moment I am of a tiny minority, I feel myself just one protest in a great revolt surging up from among the people — the struggle of the masses against the rule of the world by the few — profoundly intensified by the war. It is a struggle against the political state itself, against exploitation, militarism, imperialism, authority in all forms. . . .

Having arrived at the state of mind in which

those views mean the dearest things in life to me, I cannot consistently, with self-respect, do other than I have, namely, to deliberately violate an act which seems to me to be a denial of everything which ideally and in practice I hold sacred.

## 194 "any profane, scurrilous, or abusive language about the form of government" (1918)

The Espionage Act of 1917 proved unable to curtail all criticism of the war effort. Attorney General Gregory requested amendments prohibiting attempts to obstruct recruitment and efforts to discredit war loans. The Senate Judiciary Committee responded by revamping Section Three provisions in order to eliminate all disloyal utterances. There were nearly two thousand prosecutions and nine hundred convictions under the combined espionage acts, including that of motion picture producer Robert Goldstein, sentenced to ten years in prison for his unbecoming portrayal of the British, now United States allies, in a film about the American Revolution. Socialist leader Eugene V. Debs was convicted as the result of a speech at a Socialist party state convention in which he criticized former president Theodore Roosevelt's support of the war and praised the moral courage of our revolutionary forefathers who "opposed the social system of their time."

☆ 194  The Espionage Act (as Amended)†

40 Stat. 555 (1918).

\*　　　\*　　　\*

Sec. 3. Whoever, when the United States is at war, shall willfully make or convey false reports or false statements with intent to interfere with the operation or success of the military or naval forces of the United States, or to promote the success of its enemies, or shall willfully make or convey false reports or false statements, *or say or do anything except by way of bona fide and not disloyal advice to an investor or investors, with intent to obstruct the sale by the United States of bonds or other securities of the United States or the making of loans by or to the United States,* and whoever, when the United States is at war, shall willfully cause or attempt to cause, *or incite or attempt to incite,* insubordination, disloyalty, mutiny, or refusal of duty, in the military or naval forces of the United States, or shall willfully obstruct *or attempt to obstruct* the recruiting or enlistment service of the United States [to the injury of the service or of the United States], *and whoever, when the United States is at war, shall willfully utter, print, write, or publish any disloyal, profane, scurrilous, or abusive language about the form of government of the*

*United States, or the Constitution of the United States or the military or naval forces of the United States, or the flag of the United States, or the uniform of the Army or Navy of the United States, or any language intended to bring the form of government of the United States, or the Constitution of the United States, or the military or naval forces of the United States, or the flag of the United States, or the uniform of the Army or Navy of the United States into contempt, scorn, contumely, or disrepute, or shall willfully utter, print, write or publish any language intended to incite, provoke, or encourage resistance to the United States, or to promote the cause of its enemies, or shall willfully display the flag of any foreign enemy, or shall willfully by utterance, writing, printing, publication, or language spoken, urge, incite, or advocate any curtailment of production in this country of any thing or things, product or products, necessary or essential to the prosecution of the war in which the United States may be engaged, with intent by such curtailment to cripple or hinder the United States in the prosecution of the war, and whoever shall willfully advocate, teach, defend, or suggest the doing of any of the acts or things in this section enumerated, and whoever shall by word or act support or favor the cause of any country with which the United States is at war or by word or act oppose the cause of the United States therein,* shall be punished by a fine of not more than $10,000 or imprisonment for not more than twenty years, or both: *Provided, That any employee or official of the United States Government who commits any disloyal act or utters any unpatriotic or disloyal language, or who, in an abusive and violent manner criticizes the Army or Navy or the flag of the United States shall be at once dismissed by the head of the department in which the employee may be engaged, and any such official shall be dismissed by the authority having power to appoint a successor to the dismissed official.*

\*　　　\*　　　\*

---

† Language added to the 1917 Espionage Act is in italics; language deleted is in brackets. In 1920 the amendments were repealed, leaving the original 1917 act in effect.

## 195 "any unlawful method of terrorism" (1919)

In essence, California's antisedition law, similar to laws passed by some two-thirds of the states, was directed not against overt acts but against seditious doctrines and their advocacy. The law was enacted against the background of the Red Scare. Communists had succeeded in Russia, and Germany and other industrialized countries seemed in danger.

The California law defined criminal syndicalism as a doctrine that advocated resort to force and violence for effectuating changes in the political arena or in industrial ownership. Syndicalism, an anticapitalist, working class ideology, held that any form of the state was an instrument of oppression. In a syndicalist society, a universal union, in which membership would entitle one to vote regardless of age, sex, race, property, or residence, would make all social and political decisions. Until its demise in the 1920s, the Industrial Workers of the World (IWW) was the chief syndicalist-oriented organization in the United States.

The sense of urgency regarding communist and syndicalist infiltration and power led to the anti-Red "Palmer Raids" (named after U.S. Attorney General A. Mitchell Palmer, assisted by a twenty-four-year-old lawyer, J. Edgar Hoover) against political and labor activists. Arrested aliens, including Emma Goldman and Alexander Berkman, were deported summarily. On January 2, 1920, twenty-seven hundred people in thirty-three cities were seized. The raids, which ceased in May 1920, were a major impetus for the organization of the American Civil Liberties Union.

## ☆ 195 California Criminal Syndicalism Law

1919 Cal. Stat. 281-82.

### CHAPTER 188

An act defining criminal syndicalism and sabotage, proscribing certain acts and methods in connection therewith and in pursuance thereof and providing penalties and punishments therefor.

[*Approved, April 30, 1919.*]

The people of the State of California do enact as follows:

SECTION 1. The term "criminal syndicalism" as used in this act is hereby defined as any doctrine or precept advocating, teaching or aiding and abetting the commission of crime, sabotage (which word is hereby defined as meaning wilful and malicious physical damage or injury to physical property), or unlawful acts of force and violence or unlawful methods of terrorism as a means of accomplishing a change in industrial ownership or control, or effecting any political change.

SECTION 2. Any person who:

1. By spoken or written words or personal conduct advocates, teaches or aids and abets criminal syndicalism or the duty, necessity or propriety of committing crime, sabotage, ... violence or any unlawful method of terrorism as a means of accomplishing a change in industrial ownership or control, or effecting any political change; or

2. Wilfully and deliberately by spoken or written words justifies or attempts to justify criminal syndicalism or the commission or attempt to commit crime, sabotage, violence or unlawful methods of terrorism with intent to approve, advocate or further the doctrine of criminal syndicalism; or

3. Prints, publishes, edits, issues or circulates or publicly displays any book, paper, pamphlet, document, poster or written or printed matter in any other form, containing or carrying written or printed advocacy, teaching, or aid and abetment of, or advising, criminal syndicalism; or

4. Organizes or assists in organizing, or is or knowingly becomes a member of, any organization, society, group or assemblage of persons organized or assembled to advocate, teach or aid and abet criminal syndicalism; or

5. Wilfully by personal act or conduct, practices or commits any act advised, advocated, taught or aided and abetted by the doctrine or precept of criminal syndicalism, with intent to accomplish a change in industrial ownership or control, or effecting any political change;

is guilty of a felony and punishable by imprisonment in the state prison not less than one nor more than fourteen years.

\*       \*       \*

SECTION 4. Inasmuch as this act concerns and is necessary to the immediate preservation of the public peace and safety, for the reason that at the present time large numbers of persons are going from place to place in this state advocating, teaching and practicing criminal syndicalism, this act shall take effect upon approval by the governor.

\*       \*       \*

## 196 "an aid to propaganda" (1919)

Between 1917 and 1921, thirty-three states supplemented their syndicalism or antisedition legislation with prohibitions against the display of red flags or other symbols of forceful or violent opposition to organized government. The laws manifested the authorities' fear of the communist propaganda threat. In 1931, the Supreme Court, in *Stromberg v. California*, declared California's Red Flag Law unconstitutional.

## ☆ 196 California Red Flag Law

Cal. Penal Code § 403a (1919).

An act to add a new section to the Penal Code ... prohibiting the use of a red flag in aid of anarchistic or seditious activities.

[*Approved, April 30, 1919. In effect, July 22, 1919.*]

The people of the State of California do enact as follows: ...

403a. Any person who displays a red flag, banner or badge or any flag, badge, banner, or device of any color or form whatever in any public place or in any meeting place or public assembly, or from or on any house, building or window as a sign, symbol or emblem of opposition to organized government or as an invitation or stimulus to anarchistic action or as an aid to propaganda that is of a seditious character is guilty of a felony.

# 197 "falsely shouting fire" (1919)

In *Schenck v. United States*, a convicted draft resistance organizer attacked the constitutionality of the 1917 Espionage Act on First Amendment grounds. The Supreme Court reviewed this wartime law in an opinion by Justice Oliver Wendell Holmes, Jr., in which he enunciated the famous "clear and present danger" doctrine. Justice Holmes pronounced, "The question in every case is whether the words used are used in such circumstances and are of such a nature as to create a clear and present danger that they will bring about the substantive evils that Congress has a right to prevent." The Supreme Court upheld Schenck's conviction.

☆ 197 *Schenck v. United States*

249 U.S. 47 (1919).

Mr. Justice HOLMES delivered the opinion of the Court.

This . . . indictment . . . charges a conspiracy to violate the Espionage Act of June 15, 1917 by causing and attempting to cause insubordination . . . in the military and naval forces of the United States, and to obstruct the recruiting and enlistment service of the United States, when the United States was at war with the German Empire, to-wit, that the defendant wilfully conspired to have printed and circulated to men who had been called and accepted for military service . . . a document set forth and alleged to be calculated to cause such insubordination and obstruction. The count alleges overt acts in pursuance of the conspiracy, ending in the distribution of the document set forth. . . . They set up the First Amendment to the Constitution forbidding Congress to make any law abridging the freedom of speech, or of the press. . . .

\*　　\*　　\*

The document in question upon its first printed side recited the first section of the Thirteenth Amendment, said that the idea embodied in it was violated by the conscription act and that a conscript is little better than a convict. In impassioned language it intimated that conscription was despotism in its worst form and a monstrous wrong against humanity in the interest of Wall Street's chosen few. It said, "Do not submit to intimidation," but in form at least confined itself to peaceful measures such as a petition for the repeal of the act. The other and later printed side of the sheet was headed "Assert Your Rights." It stated reasons for alleging that any one violated the Constitution when he refused to recognize "your right to assert your opposition to the draft," and went on, "If you do not assert and support your rights, you are helping to deny or disparage rights which it is the solemn duty of all citizens and residents of the United States to retain." It described the arguments on the other side as coming from cunning politicians and a mercenary capitalist press, and even silent consent to the conscription law as helping to support an infamous conspiracy. It denied the power to send our citizens away to foreign shores to shoot up the people of other lands, and added that words could not express the condemnation such cold-blooded ruthlessness deserves, &c., &c., winding up, "You must do your share to maintain, support and uphold the rights of the people of this country." Of course the document would not have been sent unless it had been intended to have some effect, and we do not see what effect it could be expected to have upon persons subject to the draft except to influence them to obstruct the carrying of it out. The defendants do not deny that the jury might find against them on this point.

But it is said, suppose that that was the tendency of this circular, it is protected by the First Amendment to the Constitution. . . . We admit that in many places and in ordinary times the defendants in saying all that was said in the circular would have been within their constitutional rights. But the character of every act depends upon the circumstances in which it is done. The most stringent protection of free speech would not protect a man in falsely shouting fire in a theatre and causing a panic. It does not even protect a man from an injunction against uttering words that may have all the effect of force. The question in every case is whether the words used are used in such circumstances and are of such a nature as to create a clear and present danger that they will bring about the substantive evils that Congress has a right to prevent. It is a question of proximity and degree. When a nation is at war many things that might be said in time of peace are such a hindrance to its effort that their utterance will not be endured so long as men fight and that no Court could regard them as protected by any constitutional right. It seems to be admitted that if an actual obstruction of the recruiting service were proved, liability for words that produced that effect might be enforced. The statute of 1917 punishes conspiracies to obstruct as well as actual obstruction. If the act, (speaking, or circulating a paper) its tendency and the intent with which it is done are the same, we perceive no ground for saying that success alone warrants making the act a crime.

\*　　\*　　\*

*Judgments affirmed.*

## 198 "There can be no peace" (1919)

In 1905, the Industrial Workers of the World organized in Chicago as an industrial union uniting skilled and unskilled workers for the purpose of overthrowing capitalism and building a socialist society. Committed to total class warfare, the IWW opposed arbitration and collective bargaining. IWW members, nicknamed "Wobblies," were vocally anti-militaristic during World War I, and their union's uncompromising rhetoric led to zealous federal and state suppression during the postwar era. The IWW led a total of 150 strikes, including the 1919 general strike in Seattle, before internal rifts and a loss of members to the Communist Party accounted for its demise.

### ☆ 198 Preamble of the Industrial Workers of the World

Reprinted in S. Lynd, ed., *Nonviolence in America: A Documentary History* (New York: Bobbs-Merrill, 1966), 240-41.

The working class and the employing class have nothing in common.

There can be no peace so long as hunger and want are found among millions of the working people, and the few who make up the employing class have all the good things of life.

Between these two classes a struggle must go on until the workers of the world organize as a class, take possession of the earth, and the machinery of production, and abolish the wage system.

We find that the centering of the management of industries into fewer and fewer hands makes the trade-unions unable to cope with the ever-growing power of the employing class.

The trade-unions foster a state of affairs which allows one set of workers to be pitted against another set of workers in the same industry, thereby helping to defeat one another in wage wars.

Moreover the trade-unions aid the employing class to mislead the workers into the belief that the working class have interests in common with their employers.

These conditions can be changed and the interests of the working class upheld only by an organization formed in such a way that all its members in any one industry, or in all industries, if necessary, cease work whenever a strike or lockout is on in any department thereof, thus making an injury to one an injury to all.

Instead of the conservative motto, "A fair day's wage for a fair day's work," we must inscribe on our banner the revolutionary watchword, "Abolition of the wage system."

It is the historic mission of the working class to do away with capitalism.

The army of production must be organized, not only for the everyday struggle with the capitalists, but also to carry on production when capitalism shall have been overthrown.

By organizing industrially we are forming the structure of a new society within the shell of the old.

## 199 The "cowardly silence about the intervention in Russia" (1919)

In March 1918, Russia signed a peace treaty with Germany and withdrew from the "capitalist war." Internal warfare soon was raging in Russia between the Red Army under Lenin and Trotsky and the White Army led by General Anton Denikin, which had Allied support. A seven-thousand-man American army contingent occupied the Russan Pacific port of Vladivostok, ostensibly as a watch over the Japanese threat to the shipping lanes, but also as a possible spearhead for an armed suppression of the Bolshevik revolution. The British likewise occupied the ports of Murmansk and Archangel on Russia's northern Barents Sea and White Sea coasts.

To the revolutionaries around the world, it was reasonable that the capitalist countries would unite to suppress the new hope of the workers. Anarchists, socialists, and workers generally strongly protested. The protest resulted in prosecutions under the 1918 amendments to the Espionage Act. *Abrams v. United States* reached the Supreme Court.

### ☆ 199 *Abrams v. United States*

250 U.S. 616 (1919).

MR. JUSTICE CLARKE delivered the opinion of the court.

*         *         *

It was charged in each count of the indictment that it was a part of the conspiracy that the defendants would attempt to accomplish their unlawful purpose by printing, writing and distributing in the City of New York many copies of a leaflet or circular, printed in the English language, and of another printed in the Yiddish language, copies of which, properly identified, were attached to the indictment.

All of the five defendants were born in Russia. They were intelligent, had considerable schooling, and at the time they were arrested they had lived in the United States terms varying from five to ten years, but none of them had applied for naturalization. Four of them testified as witnesses in their own behalf and of these, three frankly avowed that they were "rebels," "revolutionists," "anarchists," that they did not believe in government in any form, and they declared that they had no interest whatever in the Government of the United States. The fourth defendant testified that he was a "socialist" and believed in "a proper kind of government, not capitalistic," but in his classification the Government of the United States was "capitalistic."

It was admitted on the trial that the defendants had united to print and distribute the described circulars and that five thousand of them had been printed and distributed....

\* \* \*

Thus the conspiracy and the doing of the overt acts charged were largely admitted and were fully established.

On the record thus described it is argued, somewhat faintly, that the acts charged against the defendants were not unlawful because within the protection of that freedom of speech and of the press which is guaranteed by the First Amendment to the Constitution of the United States, and that the entire Espionage Act is unconstitutional because in conflict with that Amendment.

This contention is sufficiently discussed and is definitely negatived in *Schenck v. United States....*

The first of the two articles attached to the indictment is conspicuously headed, "The Hypocrisy of the United States and her Allies." After denouncing President Wilson as a hypocrite and a coward because troops were sent into Russia, it proceeds to assail our Government in general, saying:

"His [the President's] shameful, cowardly silence about the intervention in Russia reveals the hypocrisy of the plutocratic gang in Washington and vicinity."

It continues:

"He [the President] is too much of a coward to come out openly and say: 'We capitalist nations cannot afford to have a proletarian republic in Russia.'"

Among the capitalistic nations Abrams testified the United States was included.

Growing more inflammatory as it proceeds, the circular culminates in:

"The Russian Revolution cries: Workers of the World! Awake! Rise! Put down your enemy and mine!

"Yes! friends, there is only one enemy of the workers of the world and that is CAPITALISM."

This is clearly an appeal to the "workers" of this country to arise and put down by force the Government of the United States which they characterize as their "hypocritical," "cowardly" and "capitalistic" enemy.

It concludes:

"Awake! Awake, you Workers of the World!
"REVOLUTIONISTS."

The second of the articles was printed in the Yiddish language and in the translation is headed, "Workers—Wake up." After referring to "his Majesty, Mr. Wilson, and the rest of the gang; dogs of all colors!", it continues:

"Workers, Russian emigrants, you who had the least belief in the honesty of *our* Government," which defendants admitted referred to the United States Government, "must now throw away all confidence, must spit in the face the false, hypocritic, military propaganda which has fooled you so relentlessly, calling forth your sympathy, your help, to the prosecution of the war."

Ths purpose of this obviously was to persuade the persons to whom it was addressed to turn a deaf ear to patriotic appeals in behalf of the Government of the United States, and to cease to render it assistance in the prosecution of the war.

It goes on:

"With the money which you have loaned, or are going to loan them, they will make bullets not only for the Germans, but also for the Workers Soviets of Russia. *Workers in the ammunition, factories, you are producing bullets, bayonets, cannon, to murder not only the Germans, but also your dearest, best, who are in Russia and are fighting for freedom.*"

It will not do to say, as is now argued, that the only intent of these defendants was to prevent injury to the Russian cause.... [T]he obvious effect of this appeal, if it should become effective, as they hoped it might, would be to persuade persons of character such as those whom they regarded themselves as addressing, not to aid government loans and not to work in ammunition factories, where their work would produce "bullets, bayonets, cannon" and other munitions of war, the use of which would cause the "murder" of Germans and Russians.

Again, the spirit becomes more bitter as it proceeds to declare that—

"America and her Allies have betrayed (the Workers). Their robberish aims are clear to all men. The destruction of the Russian Revolution, that is the politics of the march to Russia.

"*Workers, our reply to the barbaric intervention has to be a general strike! An open challenge* only will let the Government know that not only the Russian Worker fights for freedom, but also *here in America lives the spirit of Revolution.*"

... [T]he manifest purpose of such a publication was to create an attempt to defeat the war plans of the Government of the United States, by bringing upon the country the paralysis of a general strike, thereby arresting the production of all munitions and other things essential to the conduct of the war.

This purpose is emphasized in the next paragraph, which reads:

"Do not let the Government scare you with their wild punishment in prisons, hanging and shooting. We must not and will not betray the splendid fighters of Russia. *Workers, up to fight.*"

After more of the same kind, the circular concludes:

"Woe unto those who will be in the way of progress. Let solidarity live!"

It is signed, "The Rebels."

... [T]he additional writings found in the meeting place of the defendant group and on the person of one of them [support our interpretation]. One of these circulars is headed: "Revolutionists! Unite for Action!"

After denouncing the President as "Our Kaiser" and the hypocrisy of the United States and her Allies, this article concludes:

"Socialists, Anarchists, Industrial Workers of the World, Socialists, Labor party men and other revolutionary organizations *Unite for action* and let us save the Workers' Republic of Russia!

"*Know you lovers of freedom that in order to save the Russian revolution, we must keep the armies of the allied countries busy at home.*"

Thus was again avowed the purpose to throw the country into a state of revolution if possible and to thereby frustrate the military program of the Government.

The remaining article, after denouncing the President for what is characterized as hostility to the Russian revolution, continues:

"We, the toilers of America, who believe in real liberty, shall *pledge ourselves*, in case the United States will participate in that bloody conspiracy against Russia, *to create so great a disturbance that the autocrats of America shall be compelled to keep their armies at home, and not be able to spare any for Russia.*"

It concludes with this definite threat of armed rebellion:

"If they will use arms against the Russian people to enforce their standard of order, *so will we use arms*, and they shall never see the ruin of the Russian Revolution." ... A technical distinction may perhaps be taken between disloyal and abusive language applied to the *form* of our government or language intended to bring the *form* of our government into contempt and disrepute, and language of like character and intended to produce like results directed against the President and Congress, the agencies through which that form of government must function in time of war. But it is not necessary to a decision of this case to consider whether such distinction is vital or merely formal, for the language of these circulars was obviously intended to provoke and to encourage resistance to the United States in the war, ... and, the defendants, in terms, plainly urged and advocated a resort to a general strike of workers in ammunition factories for the purpose of curtailing the production of ordnance and munitions necessary and essential to the prosecution of the war....

*Affirmed.*

MR. JUSTICE HOLMES dissenting.

This indictment is founded wholly upon the publication of two leaflets....

\*     \*     \*

No argument seems to me necessary to show that these pronunciamentos in no way attack the form of government of the United States.... [T]he suggestion to workers in the ammunition factories that they are producing bullets to murder their dearest, and the further advocacy of a general strike, both in the second leaflet, do urge curtailment of production of things necessary to the prosecution of the war within the meaning of the Act. But to make the conduct criminal that statute requires that it should be "with intent by such curtailment to cripple or hinder the United States in the prosecution of the war." It seems to me that no such intent is proved.

I am aware of course that the word intent as vaguely used in ordinary legal discussion means no more than knowledge at the time of the act that the consequences said to be intended will ensue.... But, when words are used exactly, a deed is not done with intent to produce a consequence unless that consequence is the aim of the deed....

It seems to me that this statute must be taken to use its words in a strict and accurate sense. They would be absurd in any other. A patriot might think that we were wasting money on aeroplanes, or making more cannon of a certain kind than we needed, and might advocate curtailment with success, yet even if it turned out that the curtailment hindered and was thought by other minds to have been obviously likely to hinder the United States in the prosecution of the war, no one would hold such conduct a crime. I admit that my illustration does not answer all that might be said but it is enough to show what I think and to let me pass to a more important aspect of the case. I refer to the First Amendment to the Constitution that Congress shall make no law abridging the freedom of speech.

I never have seen any reason to doubt that the questions of law that alone were before this Court in the cases of *Schenck*, *Frohwerk* and *Debs* were rightly decided. I do not doubt for a moment that by the same reasoning that would justify punishing persuasion to murder, the United States constitutionally may punish speech that produces or is intended to produce a clear and imminent danger that it will bring about forthwith certain substantive evils that the United States constitutionally may seek to prevent. The power undoubtedly is greater in time of war than in time of peace because war opens dangers that do not exist at other times.

But as against dangers peculiar to war, as against others, the principle of the right to free speech is always the same. It is only the present danger of immediate evil or an intent to bring it about that warrants Congress in setting a limit to the expression of opinion where private rights are not concerned. Congress certainly cannot forbid all effort to change the mind of the country. . . . Publishing those opinions for the very purpose of obstructing however, might indicate a greater danger and at any rate would have the quality of an attempt. . . . [But] an actual intent in the sense that I have explained is necessary to constitute an attempt where a further act of the same individual is required to complete the substantive crime. . . . An intent to prevent interference with the revolution in Russia might have been satisfied without any hindrance to carrying on the war in which we were engaged.

I do not see how anyone can find the intent required by the statute in any of the defendants' words. . . . [T]he only object of the paper is to help Russia and stop American intervention there against the popular government — not to impede the United States in the war that it was carrying on. . . .

\*          \*          \*

In this case sentences of twenty years imprisonment have been imposed for the publishing of two leaflets that I believe the defendants had as much right to publish as the Government has to publish the Constitution of the United States now vainly invoked by them. . . .

Persecution for the expression of opinions seems to me perfectly logical. . . . [T]he best test of truth is the power of the thought to get itself accepted in the competition of the market, and that truth is the only ground upon which their wishes safely can be carried out. That at any rate is the theory of our Constitution. It is an experiment, as all life is an experiment. Every year if not every day we have to wager our salvation upon some prophecy based upon imperfect knowledge. While that experiment is part of our system I think that we should be eternally vigilant against attempts to check the expression of opinions that we loathe and believe to be fraught with death, unless they so imminently threaten immediate interference with the lawful and pressing purposes of the law that an immediate check is required to save the country. I wholly disagree with the argument of the Government that the First Amendment left the common law as to seditious libel in force. History seems to me against the notion. I had conceived that the United States through many years had shown its repentance for the Sedition Act of 1798, by repaying fines that it imposed. Only the emergency that makes it immediately dangerous to leave the correction of evil counsels to time warrants making any exception to the sweeping command, "Congress shall make no law . . . abridging the freedom of speech." Of course I am speaking only of expressions of opinion and exhortations, which were all that were uttered here, but I regret that I cannot put into more impressive words my belief that in their conviction upon this indictment the defendants were deprived of their rights under the Constitution of the United States.

MR. JUSTICE BRANDEIS concurs with the foregoing opinion.

## 200 "using the bullet, the assassin's dagger, the torch, or the bomb" (1919)

On November 10, 1919, the same day that the Supreme Court upheld the convictions in *Abrams v. United States*, the United States House of Representatives voted to exclude Socialist Victor L. Berger from its membership. Berger had been active in the Socialist party and in Milwaukee politics. He had been an alderman in Milwaukee and had served as a member of the United States House of Representatives from Wisconsin in the Sixty-second Congress (1911-13).

When the United States declared war upon Germany in 1917, America's Socialist party called a convention in St. Louis to consider the posture of the party toward the war. Although the Socialists opposed the United States' entry into the war, some believed they should support the country in its efforts now that war had been declared. Berger led the extreme antiwar faction, which controlled the convention. The extremists expelled the nationalist socialists from the party, claiming that the government's declaration of war was a crime against the people of the United States and against the nations of the world and arguing for "continuous, active, and public opposition to the war through demonstrations, mass petitions and all other means within our power."

For editing war-resistant editorials published in the *Milwaukee Leader* (the postmaster general of the United States banned the paper from the mails), Berger and four others were convicted under the Espionage Act of 1917. Prior to his conviction, Berger had won election to the Sixty-sixth Congress from the Fifth District of Wisconsin (Milwaukee). On May 19, 1919, House members objected to the seating of Berger on the grounds that the third section of the Fourteenth Amendment prevented him from serving. Six months later, after a special committee recommended his exclusion, the matter reached the floor of the House. The following excerpt is from the five-and-one-half-hour debate on the motion to exclude Berger. Only one member spoke for three minutes against the motion, defending Berger's right to make such statements on First Amendment grounds. The motion carried 319 to 1.

☆ 200 Remarks of Representative Monahan on the Seating of Victor L. Berger

58 Cong. Rec. 8257 (Nov. 10, 1919).

MR. MONAHAN of Wisconsin. Mr. Speaker, shall Victor L. Berger be given the seat in the House to which he was elected in 1918 or shall he, because of his own words and deeds, be denied the right to sit as a Member in this Congress? Stripped of all legal verbiage that is really the issue before the House.

No question is raised by the Government concerning the regularity of his election nor of the correctness of the election returns, and Berger practically admits the acts and deeds charged against him by the United States, but holds they were in no sense treasonable and that he was strictly within his rights in saying and doing what he did; that the Constitution and laws of the United States gave him that unqualified right.

Victor L. Berger is a living example of that old saying, "A leopard can not change his spots nor the Ethiopian his skin," and of the further fact that we are largely the creatures of heredity and environment.

Sixty years ago he was born in autocratic Austria, where for 18 years, during the time when the heart was young and the mind plastic, he drank deeply from the poisoned waters of autocracy. But seeing no opportunity for himself to become an autocrat in the land of the Hapsburg he came to America, landing at Bridgeport, Conn., in 1878, and in 1881 he, to the everlasting misfortune of Wisconsin, made Milwaukee his home. He had found a way and a place to become an autocrat that gave promise of enabling him to wield a power undreamed of by king, prince, or potentate of ancient or modern times.

To appreciate fully the foregoing sentence, one must know Mr. Berger as we in Wisconsin know him. He is large, well proportioned, has ideal Teutonic features, a mentality above the average, and in many ways is a natural leader of men. Had these great gifts been used in safe and sane methods for the uplifting of the race, Berger would have lived in history as a great and good man, but never as an autocrat or one striving for autocracy.

But all these great qualities are lost in the immensity of his colossal egoism. The gibes leveled at the late Kaiser as being called "the all highest" and the senior member of the firm of "Me und Gott" would have in no sense been pleasing to Berger, who, had he possessed the power, would probably have dissolved the firm and hung out a new sign reading, "Me und Victor."

The foregoing is, I believe, a fair and honest description of the man as the world knows him.

Berger early in life became a Marxian disciple, and continued to be until his ego told him he was a far wiser, much greater man than Marx ever was. When he discovered that Marx was only a man, while he was a really-truly superman, he sought for a land as boundless in resources as his own ego was measureless and all prevailing.

Hence, he came to America, took the oath of allegiance to this Government, swore fealty to the flag and support to the Constitution, and, having done this, adopted the red flag of socialism, communism, anarchy, the I.W.W., and Bolshevism, and began the spreading of a propaganda which he hoped would ultimately lead to the undermining of the Constitution, the destruction of the Government, the breaking down of all commercial and social laws and customs, the tearing down of Old Glory from her place in the skies, and the raising of the red flag in its stead.

All students of history know that socialism and all attending schools of political economy invariably lead to autocracy, and thus Berger intended to become an autocrat who could sit in his office and by pushing a button call a strike in certain industries (as has been done recently in the coal fields) unless their demands were immediately complied with.

Here Berger and his codestructionists met with an unlooked-for obstruction. They found the task much more difficult than they anticipated. They found that the Civil War was ended and the country rapidly recovering from its horrors and devastation. They found the men behind the industrial guns were largely made up of soldiers of the late war, and whether they wore the blue or the gray each carried a loyal American heart, whether he had been born here or across the sea.

So strong was Americanism in those days that Bergerism was a foul weed of slow growth.

Then the soldier began to grow old with increasing years. The foreigner, who had grown up in the blighting atmosphere of autocracy, came to this country in ever increasing numbers and gradually took the jobs formerly held by the Americans.

They could not speak our language, neither did they understand our institutions. They were oftimes despondent and homesick, and too often fell an easy prey to the propaganda of the Bergers, who, like hookworms, worked in the dark to weaken and destroy this Government.

These people were not naturally vicious, but they were ignorant of our laws, language, and customs, and blindly followed when and where the Bergers led. For how could they reason when they did not know? . . .

Many of the socialists never intended to become anarchists, nor the anarchists I.W.W.'s nor Bolshevists, and Mr. Berger in his latest pamphlet, which reached my desk on Saturday, says in effect that there are differences and distinctions in the aims, objects, and methods of these various camps, and that they have in fact no common grounds of union, yet it is also in the record of the trial that when an I.W.W. was indicted for crime Berger sent him $10 to aid in his defense and addressed him as "My dear comrade."

The innocent socialist, having in view only the betterment of his material conditions, away from the land of his birth, unable to read or speak our language, falls an easy prey to the harpings of these ravens of discontent. Beautiful Eutopian dreams are painted for them. The harshness of their physical conditions is magnified and harped upon, until they honestly believe that they have a grievance, whether it be true or not. When they reach this condition of mind it is easy to lead them from socialism to anarchy and to I.W.W.'ism and finally to Bolshevism.

\*     \*     \*

The transition has been easy. First, from socialism — the wet nurse of anarchy — then to anarchy, then to I.W.W.'ism, then to Bolshevism, which means the destruction of all civilization, all laws, all liberties, with the establishment of an autocracy, headed by the Bergers of these various movements, and all bound together by an underlying, overlapping, intertwining system of signals and sympathies, with the trial of the serpent of destruction over all.

Let me plead with you here and now to get away from these false ideas and false teachings. Get back to the teachings of Washington and the founders of the Constitution and become in heart what you really profess to be — American citizens, standing for American ideals.

The laws, customs, and usages that are in force to-day are not here by accident. They are an evolution of all the best the past has given us — a survival of the fittest — the sole hope of the race. Whenever these laws and customs become obsolete, caused by changing conditions and higher ideals, let such laws be changed or modified to meet present conditions, but make those changes by peaceful and constitutional methods and not attempt it by using the bullet, the assassin's dagger, the torch, or the bomb.

Mr. Speaker, we to-day stand at the parting of the ways. One road leads to the land of justice, hope, constitutional law, progress, and enlightenment; the other to the fetid slough of dishonor, where, fed by the foul streams of autocracy, treason, and disloyalty, the reign of Bolshevism becomes a horrible reality, where civilization will be crucified and human hopes destroyed. Are we going to stand for Americanism or Bergerism?

You can not serve two masters. You can not be for the Stars and Stripes, which represents the greatest democracy on the globe, and for the red flag of the Bergers. "Ye can not serve God and mammon," says Holy Writ.

\*     \*     \*

Victor L. Berger once occupied a seat in this House as a Member of Congress from Milwaukee. Before taking his seat he raised his right hand and took a solemn oath to support the laws and Constitution of this country. Yet when the hour came and the existence of this Nation and the liberties of the world were at stake he wretchedly failed in every test of loyalty to the country of his adoption.

\*     \*     \*

He opposed enlistments; he opposed conscriptions; he opposed, wherever and whenever he could with safety, the buying of Liberty bonds, and all efforts of the Government to carry on the war.

His paper, the Milwaukee Leader, was so virulent in its attacks upon the Government that the Postmaster General took away from him the right of using the United States mails, and finally he was indicted under the espionage act, tried for treason in the city of Chicago by a jury of his peers, found guilty, and sentenced by Judge Landis to 20 years in the Federal penitentiary, and has several other indictments for these or similar offenses now pending against him. Yet, in the face of all this, he comes to this Congress, glorifying in his past record, offering no apologies for his past misdeeds, and asks to be seated as a Member of this House, the greatest lawmaking body of the Nation, to take the same oath which he took eight years ago, only to violate, and to become an active lawmaker for the Nation which for years he has sought to destroy.

\*     \*     \*

The proper place for Berger is a cell in the Federal penitentiary — not a seat in Congress. Neither have I any patience or sympathy with these anemic patriots who prattle about: "Now that the war is over, all war prisoners should be released." Why? Are they not just as guilty now as the day they were convicted? Were not their offenses of the blackest of crimes? Were they not rounded up and convicted by our Government at great expense and at an hour when all the man power of the Nation was needed to save the civilization of the globe?

A man steals a horse and is arrested; after several days the horse is found and returned to the owner. Would any of you advocate that, now the horse has been recovered, the thief should be given his liberty? Not one of you. When a man commits as heinous a crime as treason to his country the spirit of the law says: "He shall be punished."

\*     \*     \*

Wisconsin is to-day eagerly awaiting the result of our deliberations on the question now before the House. Shall we by our vote send a message to the heroic men of the Badger State . . . ; to the mothers who gave their boys for human liberty, that liberty might live; to that innumerable army of Red Cross workers and trained nurses who suffered and worked, and with tearful eyes, on bended knees, prayed to God while our Armies fought; and to our invincible soldiers, who maintained the highest traditions of American Armies in the past, a message of appreciation for their valor and soldierly deeds which aided in crushing the Hun and rolling back the waves of gray seeking world dominion, and who to-night will stand in groups with uncovered heads and say, "God bless the House of Representatives! Our comrades who made the supreme sacrifice have not died in vain"?

Or shall we say by our vote, "Now that the war is ended, give this traitor to our country a seat among America's most loyal and patriotic"?

If the former, it will mean that Old Glory will continue to wave o'er the land, beloved, honored, and respected.

If the latter, that Berger's red flag, which to him is greater and dearer than the Stars and Stripes, shall become not only the emblem of this country and perhaps the world, but that the civilization of the ages will be lost in chaos and ruin.

The foregoing is the only issue in this case. Mr. Berger pretends to believe that he is to be kept out of Congress because he is a Socialist. This is the sheerest nonsense. Mr. Berger was not kept out of Congress before when he was elected, nor has any Socialist been denied a seat because of his political belief. It is not because he is a Socialist but because he, as an individual, working through the Socialist Party, in which organization he held a commanding position, was recognized as one of the leaders, and as such proved disloyal to his country in time of war. This is the reason.

                    *            *            *

... It can not be that the people of the fifth congressional district of Wisconsin will ever again elect Berger to any office; but if they do, now that he stands convicted by a jury, sentenced by a judge, and his case thoroughly gone into by a committee of this Congress, it will only show that a majority of the voters of the fifth congressional district are just as disloyal as Berger himself. That is unbelievable.

But if they should send Berger back he will come bearing the same burden of disloyalty and treason that he does to-day, and in my opinion no Congress would ever seat him, for while he might be the choice of the fifth congressional district of Wisconsin and that district sends him back I believe that the Members of this House will reach out their hands to the struggling loyalists of that district and say: "If you are unable to clean house within we will assist you by giving your district a dry cleaning from without."

Mr. Speaker, to-day the powers of the evil, the emissaries of darkness, the foes of constitutional law and the civilization of the Nazarene, are knocking at the door of the House of Representatives, demanding admission for their representative, Victor L. Berger. Let us answer that challenge by hurling back the answer of heroic France at Verdun, and say to him, "You shall not pass." [Applause.]

Let us here to-day figuratively engrave those words over the door, so that the Bergers of to-day, to-morrow, a hundred or a thousand years hence,

when they with traitorous hands knock at that door demanding admission, will be met with that sign, ablaze with patriotic justice: "You shall not pass. You shall not pass." [Great applause.]

## 201  " 'Let our people go' " (1920)

The ruling of the district court judge in *United States v. Steene* demonstrated the reach of the 1918 Amended Espionage Act (generally known as the 1918 Sedition Act), even for events occurring after the Armistice of November 11, 1918. The court held the distribution of handbills (containing pictures of torture), which called a mass meeting to protest the imprisonment of conscientious objectors, was calculated "to inflame and arouse the ignorant and vicious," and resistance to the United States therefore could have been expected.

☆ 201  *United States v. Steene*

263 F. 130 (D.C.N.Y. 1920).

GARVIN, District Judge. Defendants have been indicted for conspiracy to violate and for a violation of section 3 of title 1 of the Espionage Act approved June 15, 1917, and amended May 16, 1918. The indictment is in three counts and charges briefly:

First, a conspiracy to utter, publish, and distribute disloyal, profane, scurrilous, and abusive language about the form of government of the United States and the Constitution....

The second count alleges a violation of said section 3 in the manner above mentioned, by the distribution of said handbills.

The third count sets forth that the defendants did utter, print, write, and publish language intending to incite and promote resistance to the United States and to promote the success of its enemies by distributing the aforesaid handbills.

The defendants pleaded not guilty, and later by permission of the court withdrew that plea, and have filed a demurrer setting forth numerous grounds of objection to the indictment, which may be summarized thus:

                    *            *            *

(2) No offense was committed, because the United States was not at the time at war with the Imperial German government and the Austrian-Hungarian government.

This contention cannot be sustained. The Supreme Court of the United States has recently held otherwise in the war-time prohibition cases.

                    *            *            *

(4) The circulation of the handbill complained of by the government is not a violation of law.

This is the real question involved. The handbills

contain four pictures: One representing a man suspended by his wrists, apparently in a cell, under which appears "Hung by the wrists from ceiling for 8 Hours a Day. McNeil's Island, Washington." A second, the picture of a man whose appearance gives the impression of one being brutally struck with a club; under this appears "Political Prisoners Beaten with a Baseball Bat at Leavenworth Penitentiary." The third is that of a man chained to prison bars, under which is "Chained to the Bars 8 Hours a Day for Two Weeks on Bread and Water." The last is a representation of a man, barefoot, stripped to the waist, being lifted off his feet by a rope around his neck, which runs up over a beam and back into the hands of a man who stands near him, who is pulling it. This man who holds the rope, wears the style of hat common in the army. Near by is another man, with pistol in belt and wearing a similar hat, who is kicking the hapless victim. This is described as "Punishment of a Conscientious Objector in Disciplinary Barracks." These pictures appear in the four corners. The handbill is as follows:

> Attend the Mass Meeting, Moose Hall 235 East Genesse Street Friday, November 21 8:00 P.M. To Protest Against These Atrocities and Voice the Following Demand: Mr President—Let our people go. American Citizens, charged with no crime against persons or property and guilty only of expressing their political, industrial and religious beliefs, are subjected to these tortures in your prisons. These people were convicted in violation of the spirit of the Declaration of Independence and the Constitution of the United States. Their conviction was made possible only by the war hysteria prevailing at that time. Whatever justification those conditions gave no longer exists. The war is over. No justification exists, or ever did exist, for these brutal and inhuman tortures inflicted on defenseless victims by your agents and representatives. In the name of Liberty and Justice we demand the release of all prisoners whose alleged crimes consisted in the peaceable expression and maintenance of their political opinions, industrial activities or religious beliefs. Come to the meeting. Everybody Invited to Join in the above Demand. George R. Kirkpatrick will lecture on Political Prisoners in America. Under the Auspices of the Socialist Party. Admission 25 cents.

The Espionage Act—so called—... provides in part that—

> Whoever, when the United States is at war, shall willfully utter, print, write, or publish any disloyal, profane, scurrilous, or abusive language about the form of government of the United States, or the Constitution of the United States, or the military or naval forces of the United States, or the flag of the United States, or the uniform of the army or navy of the United States, or any language intended to bring the form of government of the United States, or the Constitution of the United States, or the military or naval forces of the United States, or the flag of the United States, or the uniform of the army or navy of the United States, into contempt, scorn, contumely, or disrepute, or shall willfully utter, print, write, or publish any language intended to incite, provoke, or encourage resistance to the United States, or to promote the cause of its enemies, ... shall be punished by a fine of not more than $10,000 or imprisonment for not more than twenty years, or both.

It will be observed that these provisions go much further than the preceding portion of the section, which is designed to prevent any act openly directed against the successful conduct of the war by the United States. The provisions here involved are obviously for the purpose of preventing the sort of abuse of the form of government which, harmless in itself, though usually not the utterance of those who believe in our national institutions, is calculated to inflame and arouse the ignorant and vicious to an actual attempt to bring about open disloyalty. The constitutional guaranty of free speech is unaffected by the conclusion that the pamphlet or handbill involved, rendered conspicuous by the pictures described (which are entirely unnecessary to announce a mass meeting), must be taken to mean that the form of government of the United States and the Constitution upon which it rests have proved inadequate to secure justice for American citizens, who have been not only unjustly convicted (the insinuation is clear that they have been convicted of no offense whatever), but during incarceration have been subjected to most inhuman tortures. Such an allegation, made during a period of war, when loyalty is to a great extent predicated upon belief that the form of government of the United States rests upon liberty and justice, is calculated to bring into disrepute the form of government and its Constitution, under which such conditions could exist, and likewise its military forces, whose members are responsible for the brutalities portrayed in the last-described picture.

When a mass meeting is assembled as a result of an invitation of this character, we may expect that resistance to the United States itself will follow, if the meeting is addressed in the manner outlined by the call, and that the demand upon the President to "Let our people go" will be followed by such action during and after the meeting as indicates a contempt for the Constitution and for the form of government which will not grant the demand so made. That the utterance be an open attack on the form of government or Constitution is not necessary. Indeed, the care with which the pamphlet seems to have been written suggests the desire to accomplish the result forbidden by the act without incurring the penalty involved in a violation. But, even if this was meant as a mere announcement of a public meeting, its form was well calculated to have the effect of arousing the contempt, scorn, contumely, and disrepute which Congress sought to prevent, and under the well-settled principle that one is presumed to intend the natural consequences of his act the indictment charges a crime.

*Demurrer overruled.*

## 202 "There was no disorder save that of the raiders" (1920)

In 1918 and 1919, employers' agents, federal agents, and uniformed soldiers raided several meetings of the Butte Union of the Industrial Workers of the World and obtained certain IWW pamphlets without a warrant. The literature formed the basis or deportation proceedings against Jackson on the grounds that he advocated the unlawful destruction of property. In *Ex Parte Jackson*, the federal district court in Montana demonstrated the value of the provisions of the Bill of Rights and the writ of habeas corpus, which are available to aliens and citizens alike. The court stated that "[n]o emergency in war or peace warrants the violation of the rights of personal security and safety and order and due process of law." The court also held that the defendant had the right to confront all witnesses at the deportation proceeding—a right the lower court had denied him.

Banishment and transportation (to a penal colony) are classic penal sanctions that generally are not utilized today. Exile is also a convenient way of eliminating political adversaries. In the United States these sanctions have only rarely been imposed (including the banishment of Anne Hutchinson and Roger Williams from Massachusetts during the colonial period and Clement Vallandigham's expulsion to the Confederacy during the Civil War). Nevertheless, aliens are subject to deportation for certain violations of the law. Technically not exile, such deportations have the same effect; and in 1920, the nation was actively engaged in purging the country of undesirable, especially politically undesirable, aliens.

☆ 202 *Ex Parte Jackson*

263 F. 110 (D. Mont. 1920).

BOURQUIN, District Judge. Petitioner, held for deportation as an alien "found advocating or teaching the unlawful destruction of property," ... seeks habeas corpus, for that evidence against him in the deportation proceedings was unlawfully secured, the proceedings were unfair, and the findings quoted

without support. Respondent returns the record of said proceedings. Therefrom it appears that from August, 1918, to February, 1919, the Butte Union of the Industrial Workers of the World was dissatisfied with working places, conditions, and wages in the mining industry, and to remedy them was discussing ways and means, including strike if necessary. In consequence, its hall and orderly meetings were several times raided and mobbed by employers' agents, and federal agents and soldiers duly officered, acting by federal authority and without warrant or process. The union members, men and women, many of them citizens, limited themselves to oral protests, though in the circumstances the inalienable right and law of self-defense justified resistance to the last dread extremity. There was no disorder save that of the raiders. These, mainly uniformed and armed, overawed, intimidated, and forcibly entered, broke, and destroyed property, searched persons, effects, and papers, arrested persons, seized papers and documents, cursed, insulted, beat, dispersed, and bayoneted union members by order of the commanding officer. They likewise entered petitioner's adjacent living apartment, insulted his wife, searched his person and effects, arrested him, and seized his papers and documents, and in general, in a populous and orderly city, perpetrated a reign of terror, violence, and crime against citizen and alien alike, and whose only offense seems to have been peaceable insistence upon and exercise of a clear legal right.

The raid of February, 1919, three months after practical end of the war, was upon a union meeting in discussion of the condition created by a reduction of $1 per day made in miners' wages. Petitioner, arrested, for several days was imprisoned and denied bail and counsel. He was then taken before immigration inspector, flanked by a policeman and a soldier, and, these four alone present, was interrogated. He objected generally, but finally answered, and also in respect to pamphlets seized as aforesaid and introduced in evidence against him. At later appearances before the inspector, petitioner was permitted to have counsel. At these, statements made by raiders, without petitioner's presence, identifying papers and pamphlets so seized, and somewhat in respect to petitioner's conduct of a union meeting, were introduced in evidence against him. . . . Objections by petitioner throughout the proceedings are excluded from the record and are now forgotten.

The facts in respect to the condition and objections aforesaid appear ex necessitate by oral testimony in the instant proceeding. The record further discloses that petitioner ... was assistant secretary of the Butte union, and also janitor of the hall for a Finnish society, its owner. He disclaims advocacy, teaching, or belief in unlawful destruction of property, admits having seen some of the pamphlets in the hall and for sale, admits having sold any thereof asked for and on hand for sale, admits having read some thereof, but, disremembering contents, cannot say he indorses them. These pamphlets are assumed to advocate and teach sabotage, and because thereof, and of petitioner's status and relation to them as aforesaid, in the deportation proceedings it is inferred and found that he advocated and taught unlawful destruction of property. Without these pamphlets, and brought home to petitioner, there is no evidence against him.

[I]t is believed the deportation proceedings are unfair and invalid, in that they are based upon evidence and procedure that violate the search and seizure and due process clauses of the Constitution. . . . The law and courts no more sanction such evidence than such methods, and no more approve either than the thumbscrew and the rack. Otherwise the vicious circle of age-old tyranny — to subject to and convict by unlawful means because guilty, and to condemn as guilty because subjected to and convicted by unlawful means, to which both alien and citizen fall victim. The Declaration of Independence, the writings of the fathers, the Revolution, the Constitution, and the Union, all were inspired to overthrow and prevent like governmental despotism. They are yet living, vital, and potential forces to those ends, to safeguard all domiciled in the country, alien as well as citizen.

For the inalienable rights of personal security and safety, orderly and due process of law, are the fundamentals of the social compact, the basis of organized society, the essence and justification of government, the foundation, key, and capstones of the Constitution. They are limited to no man, race, or nation, to no time, place, or occasion, but belong to man, always, everywhere, and in all circumstances. Every nation demands them for its people from all other nations. No emergency in war or peace warrants their violation, for in emergency, real or assumed, tyrants in all ages have found excuse for their destruction. Without them, democracy perishes, autocracy reigns, and the innocent suffer with the guilty. . . .

Assuming petitioner is of the so-called "Reds" and of the evil practice charged against him, he and his kind are less a danger to America than are those who indorse or use the methods that brought him to deportation. These latter are the mob and the spirit of violence and intolerance incarnate, the most alarming manifestation in America today. Far worse than the immediate wrongs to individuals that they do, they undermine the morale of the people, excite the latter's fears, distrust of our institutions, doubts of the sufficiency of law and authority; they incline the people toward arbitrary power, which for protection cowards too often seek, and knaves too readily grant, and subject to which the people cease to be

courageous and free, and become timid and enslaved. They advocate and teach, not only unlawful destruction of property, but in addition unlawful destruction of persons, and they engage in the practice of both. They lay the ax to the root of all government. Doubtless some of those, of some variety of prestige, who horrify the thoughtful lovers of America by their loose suggestion and advocacy of stone walls, shootings at sunrise, and other lynch law, are animated by sincere, but mistaken, concern for national welfare; but equally doubtless many of them are incited by unholy desire for personal advantage — money profit, popular approval, or political preferment. They are breeders of suspicion, fear, anger, revenge, riot, crime, class hatred, "Reds," despotism, threatening, if aught can, civil anarchy and revolution, and they and the government by hysteria that they stimulate are more to be feared than all the miserable, baited, bedeviled "Reds" that are their ostensible occasion and whose sins they exaggerate.

The application of the principle that convicted the Haymarket anarchists may hold guilty these advocates of lynch law, if their recommendations be followed, unless, indeed, there are distinctions in administration of criminal law. They are no new thing, these present excesses. They are the reactions of all great wars, and in due time run their course. In his Constitutional History of England, Freeman describes much the same following the Napoleonic wars, viz. that in England those who ventured to raise their voice to reform corrupt politics and oppressive government, or to improve conditions for the working class, were bitterly denounced as pro-French, charged and tried for treason, popular clamor and violence directed against them, and the bar intimidated from defending them. How history doth repeat itself! . . . And yet confidence in the Constitution and national sanity is justified. All extremists will fail to overthrow them. Even as the "Reds," the advocates of arbitrary power, whether within or without law, will in due time pass away. It is for the courts to restrain both, when brought within jurisdiction.

. . . Whether fair or not in ordinary cases, in a case wherein the alien's rights have been infringed to the extent here, the court will take note of it, . . . and hold the proceedings unfair. . . .

*The writ is granted.*

## 203 "make America safe for democracy first" (1920)

Dissent against World War I, much like the opposition to earlier and later wars, came from many and diverse sources: the faint at heart and confirmed pacifists; supporters of foreign interests and America Firsters. The pursuit of the war effort was made not only a federal task but a state undertaking as well. In the *Gilbert* case, which reached the United States Supreme Court after the war's conclusion, a citizen of Minnesota was convicted under state law for speaking in public against the war with Germany. The right of free speech, the nation's highest judicial tribunal ruled, did not protect Gilbert, because "every word that he uttered in denunciation of the war was false, was deliberate misrepresentation of the motives which impelled it, and the objects for which it was prosecuted."

## ☆ 203 *Gilbert v. Minnesota*

254 U.S. 325 (1920).

MR. JUSTICE MCKENNA delivered the opinion of the court.

A statute of Minnesota makes it unlawful "to interfere with or discourage the enlistment of men in the military or naval forces of the United States or of the State of Minnesota."

Its second and third sections are as follows:

"Sec. 2. Speaking by word of mouth against enlistment unlawful. — It shall be unlawful for any person in any public place, or at any meeting where more than five persons are assembled, to advocate or teach by word of mouth or otherwise that men should not enlist in the military or naval forces of the United States or the state of Minnesota.

"Sec. 3. Teaching or advocating by written or printed matters against enlistment unlawful. — It shall be unlawful for any person to teach or advocate by any written or printed matter whatsoever, or by oral speech, that the citizens of this state should not aid or assist the United States in prosecuting or carrying on war with the public enemies of the United States."

Section 4 defines a citizen to be "any person within the confines of the state," and § 5 declares violations of the act to be gross misdemeanors and punishable by fine and imprisonment.

The indictment charged that Gilbert at a time and place designated in the State, and under the conditions prohibited by § 2, the United States being then and there at war with the Kingdom and Imperial Government of Germany, used the following language:

"We are going over to Europe to make the world safe for democracy, but I tell you we had better make America safe for democracy first. You say, what is the matter with our democracy. I tell you what is the matter with it: Have you had anything to say as to who should be president? Have you had anything to say as to who should be Governor of this state? Have you had anything to say as to whether we would go into this war? You know you have not.

If this is such a great democracy, for Heaven's sake why should we not vote on conscription of men. We were stampeded into this war by newspaper rot to pull England's chestnuts out of the fire for her. I tell you if they conscripted wealth like they have conscripted men, this war would not last over forty-eight hours...."

A demurrer to the indictment was overruled, and Gilbert was tried and convicted. The judgment was that he pay a fine of $500 and be imprisoned in the county jail of the County of Goodhue for one year, and pay the costs of the prosecution. The judgment was affirmed by the Supreme Court of the State.

\*          \*          \*

The ... contention is, that the statute is violative of the right of free speech, and therefore void.... In *Schaefer v. United States*, ... it was said that the curious spectacle was presented of the Constitution of the United States being invoked to justify the activities of anarchy or of the enemies of the United States, and by a strange perversion of its precepts it was adduced against itself. And we did more than reject the contention, we forestalled all repetitions of it, and the contention in the case at bar is a repetition of it. It is a direct assault upon the statute of Minnesota, and a direct assertion in spite of the prohibition of the statute that one can by speech, teach or advocate that the citizens of the State should not aid or assist "the United States in prosecuting or carrying on war with the public enemies of the United States," and be protected by the Constitution of the United States.

[A] condition of war and its emergency existed, and there was explicit limitation to § 3 in the charge of the trial court to the jury. The court read §§ 2 and 3 of the statute to the jury and said, "I take it from the reading of the whole indictment that it is prosecuted under Section 3, which I have just read to you."

Gilbert's speech had the purpose they denounce. The Nation was at war with Germany, armies were recruiting, and the speech was the discouragement of that — its purpose was necessarily the discouragement of that. It was not an advocacy of policies or a censure of actions that a citizen had the right to make. The war was flagrant; it had been declared by the power constituted by the Constitution to declare it, and in the manner provided for by the Constitution. It was not declared in aggression, but in defense, in defense of our national honor, in vindication of the "most sacred rights of our Nation and our people."

This was known to Gilbert for he was informed in affairs and the operations of the Government, and every word that he uttered in denunciation of the war was false, was deliberate misrepresentation of the motives which impelled it, and the objects for which it was prosecuted. He could have had no purpose other than that of which he was charged. It would be a travesty on the constitutional privilege he invokes to assign him its protection.

*Judgment affirmed.*

## 204 "a so-called political conscience" (1921)

In the early 1920s pleas arose for the extension of a general amnesty to the conscientious objectors and the other political offenders of the war and Red Scare eras. President Harding appointed Harry Daugherty attorney general for leading Harding's successful 1920 Republican nomination campaign. Harry Daugherty's address to the American Bar Association demonstrated the government's official position on the subject. The speech articulated a policy of law and order and warned against the lenient treatment of those asserting defenses of conscience. Daugherty later was implicated in the Teapot Dome Scandal (the secret leasing of naval oil reserves to private companies), and in 1924 President Coolidge forced his resignation. Daugherty's prosecution for alleged conspiracy to defraud the United States government ended in two hung juries, and the case eventually was dismissed.

## ☆ 204  Respect for Law

Attorney General H. M. Daugherty's Address to the Joint Session of the American Bar Association and the Ohio State Bar Association, Cincinnati

7 A.B.A. J. 505 (1921).

\*          \*          \*

[I]t seems fitting to speak to you on the general subject of *respect for law*, or rather, to enumerate to you, for your consideration, some of the things that tend to *undermine respect for law*.

. . . My purpose will be mainly to call attention to certain theories of political philosophy advanced by those who either violate the law or sympathize with law violators as a defense and justification of their course. Some of these theories are as old as constitutional government and have been advanced from time to time by those who have sought to evade the penalties of the law.

\*          \*          \*

Respect for law is the one essential fact of our civilization. Without it life, liberty and property are insecure. Without it civilization falls back to the chaos and anarchy of primitive times. . . .

The history of civilization has been a continuous struggle for law and order. Through all the centuries men have striven for that protection of life, liberty and property that comes through well-ordered government. Mankind has paid allegiance to lords and overlords who were able to give this protection.

\*          \*          \*

. . . [T]he supremacy of the law, though challenged, is not undermined by the ordinary criminal who commits murder, robbery, larceny, etc. To the contrary, every occurrence of crimes of this sort tends to impress upon society the profound importance of the supremacy of the law and its vigorous enforcement. The supremacy of the law is and has been challenged mainly in that class of legislation where there exists a difference of opinion as to governmental policy in enacting the legislation in question.

. . . At the present time among the forces that are undermining respect for law are the following: The doctrine of so-called political offenses, erroneous conceptions of personal liberty, and false doctrines as to the rights of individuals and minorities. These may not be the only sources of disrespect for law, but they are deserving of attention at this time because their proponents have been especially active in asserting them since the world war.

\*          \*          \*

Political offenses is a term, as you know, of international law used to denote certain classes of offenses which are excepted from the operation of treaties of extradition between States. The offenses comprehended under this term for which extradition will not be granted are usually those involving matters pertaining to civil, religious or political liberty. The state in which the fugitive has found asylum frequently reserves to itself the right to refuse to surrender such fugitive on the ground that it is one of the excepted cases under the extradition treaty. . . .

\*          \*          \*

The term is unknown in the domestic law of this country. However, in the debates in Congress, in the few years subsequent to the Civil War, the term is found in the discussions pertaining to the status of persons in the Southern Confederacy who gave allegiance to their particular state as against the Union. Here, again, the term has an international rather than a domestic character.

\*          \*          \*

From the history of the origin of the doctrine of political offenses, it will be seen that there can be no recognition of that doctrine in the municipal law of this country. Why? Because when the sovereign will of the state expresses itself through duly enacted law it is repugnant to the very nature of the supremacy of the law and its uniform application to recognize the doctrine of political offenses. Again, the reason for this doctrine is not present under municipal law—that is, the domestic law of a State.... It would destroy the sovereignty of the state to permit two standards, one repugnant to the other, to exist side by side—the standard of the law and the standard of some individual, or group acting as individuals to set up a so-called political conscience at variance therewith. Such a doctrine has never been recognized in the municipal law of this country. It is one of the most dangerous cloaks that has yet been devised by the enemies of our constitutional system of government to cover lawlessness and disrespect for law. It is dangerous because it is a term incapable of definition. If sought to be applied, it would be as omnibus in meaning as the various shades of elasticity of the political conscience of those who sought to apply it. By the propaganda before us, we can readily imagine how elastic this political conscience would be when we are asked to apply it to the idealists such as anarchists, I.W.W.'s and socialists.

There might have been some excuse, or even justification, for the recognition of such a doctrine in the schisms and controversies, rebellions, revolts, and revolutions of the old world, whose history has been in some states one continuous struggle between the arbitrary exercise of tyrannical power on the one hand, and the just fight for civil, political or religious liberty on the other. Again, no organ of government existed in many of these states for the sovereign will of the people to express itself. Hence, revolution, rebellion, revolt, and feud within the state were the agencies that necessity compelled them to invoke in order that the spirit of liberty and democracy might express itself. In view of this, the various factions within the state frequently had the *de facto* status of belligerents. Hence, the development of the doctrine after the analogy of international law within the government of these countries. No such justification for the doctrine can exist in this country. Our constitutional system is so organized that at the ballot box the sovereign elector expresses his will. Changes are to be wrought through the constitutional organs of government and by the orderly processes of law. The constitution by the rights, privileges and immunities granted therein amply protects any citizen in his religious or political liberty. The limitations of the powers of legislation in the Constitution under its Bill of Rights, together with the judiciary system as the agency for protecting the individual against the invasion of these rights by government, furnish ample security for even the most conscientious. In addition thereto, our government during the late war, as it always has in other wars, adopted a considerate and liberal policy toward conscientious objectors. Hence, there is no occasion to engraft this so-called doctrine of political offenses, the child of the struggles against arbitrary power in the old world, upon our American political philosophy.

One word more upon this subject.... A man may have a certain religious or political opinion, but one who not only violates the laws his country imposes, but uses his full power to induce others to violate law, to break down peace and order in society, is going too far to excuse himself on the ground that he obeyed his political conscience and thereby committed only a political offense for which he should not be punished. Such a plea offered as a defense or justification, or even extenuation of his conduct, is not consistent with the uniform application and enforcement of law. This subject could not be more forcibly or tersely expressed than by the present President of the United States in a speech delivered at Omaha, Nebraska, October 7, 1920, in which he said:

> No true American will argue that our laws should not be enforced. I refer to laws, no matter of what nature, whether they be those which deal with ordinary crimes and misdemeanors, or those which deal with acts of treason to the United States, threatening to the Constitution and the fabric of our social organization.
>
> I wish no one to misunderstand me, and, therefore, I will say as plainly as I can that for my part I can see no essential difference between ordinary crimes on the one hand and political crimes and political prisoners on the other hand. If there is a distinction, surely it is not a distinction which favors political crimes or political prisoners. The thief, or any ordinary criminal, is surely less a menace to those things which we hold dear than the man or woman who conspires to destroy our American institutions.

*            *            *

Those who do not believe in our government and the enforcement of our laws should go to a country which gives them their *peculiar liberty.*

To those who come to our shores to take advantage of American opportunities it is becoming to wave the hands of welcome. But it is our duty to warn them to stay away unless they intend to observe our customs and obey our laws.

My duty is clear. As long as I am the responsible head of the Department of Justice the law will be enforced with all the power possessed by the Government which I am at liberty to call to my command.

## 205 "The civil functions and processes ... will not be interfered with" (1921)

President Warren G. Harding dispatched federal troops in 1921 to pacify a festering labor dispute in the coal mines of West Virginia. During the previous decade the disagreements between the union miners and the operators of coal mines had produced disorders requiring intervention by the state's National Guard. The President's ordering of the guard into federal service in 1917 had left West Virginia without a military force. At the governor's request federal troops were sent to the state, both in 1920 and in 1921. In the 1921 disorder, authorities estimated the insurgents to number at least five thousand. The United States government dispatched a total of two thousand federal troops to the region, and they met no resistance. Some fourteen hundred insurgents who surrendered to the troops were returned to their homes. The troops disarmed some three hundred who bore arms and turned their weapons over to the state.

States have the authority to maintain law and quell domestic violence within their borders. Nevertheless, when the disruption goes beyond the control of the state police and National Guard, a state may resort to federal assistance under Title 10, Section 331 of the U.S. Code. Enacted to implement Article IV, Section 4 of the United States Constitution, in which the federal government assumes protection of every state against "invasion" and "domestic violence," the statute provides:

Whenever there is an insurrection in any State against its government, the President may, upon the request of its legislature or of its governor if the legislature cannot be convened, call into Federal service such of the militia of the other States, in the number requested by that State, and use such of the armed forces as he considers necessary to suppress the insurrection.

In recent history, President Johnson invoked his authority on the request of the governor of Michigan during the 1967 Detroit riots; and in April 1968, the statute justified the deployment of troops to Washington, D.C., Baltimore, and Chicago.

## ☆205 Protection against Domestic Violence in West Virginia

### ☆205a President Harding's Proclamation

42 Stat. 2247 (1921).

Whereas the Governor of the State of West Virginia has represented that domestic violence exists in said State which the authorities of said State are unable to suppress; and

Whereas it is provided in the Constitution of the United States that the United States shall protect each State in this Union, on application of the legislature, or of the executive when the legislature cannot be convened, against domestic violence; and

Whereas by the law of the United States in pursuance of the above it is provided that in all cases of insurrection in any State or of obstruction to the laws thereof it shall be lawful for the President of the United States on application of the legislature of such State, or of the executive when the legislature

cannot be convened, to call forth the militia of any other State or States or to employ such part of the land and naval forces of the United States as shall be judged necessary for the purpose of suppressing such insurrection and causing the laws to be duly executed; and

Whereas the Legislature of the State of West Virginia is not now in session and can not be convened in time to meet the present emergency, and the executive of said State, under Section 4 of Article IV of the Constitution of the United States and the laws passed in pursuance thereof, has made due application to me in the premises for such part of the military forces of the United States as may be necessary and adequate to protect the State of West Virginia and the citizens thereof against domestic violence and to enforce the due execution of the laws; and

Whereas it is required that whenever it may be necessary, in the judgment of the President, to use the military forces of the United States for the purposes aforesaid he shall forthwith by proclamation command such insurgents to disperse and retire peaceably to their respective homes within a limited time;

Now, therefore, I, Warren G. Harding, President of the United States, do hereby make proclamation and I do hereby command all persons engaged in said unlawful and insurrectionary proceedings to disperse and retire peaceably to their respective abodes on or before 12 o'clock noon of the 1st day of September, 1921, and hereafter abandon said combinations and submit themselves to the laws and constituted authorities of said State;

And I invoke the aid and cooperation of all good citizens thereof to uphold the laws and preserve the public peace.

In witness whereof I have hereunto set my hand and caused the seal of the United States to be affixed.

Done at the City of Washington, this thirtieth day of August, in the year of our Lord one thousand nine hundred and twenty-one, and of the Independence of the United States the one hundred and forty-sixth.

WARREN G. HARDING
CHARLES E. HUGHES, Secretary of State

### ☆205b Instructions to General H. H. Bandholtz

Office of the Chief of Staff
Washington, August 31, 1921

FROM: THE DEPUTY CHIEF OF STAFF
TO: BRIG. GEN. H. H. BANDHOLTZ, UNITED STATES ARMY
SUBJECT: INSTRUCTIONS

Copies of the President's proclamation and orders covering your movements have been sent to you.

Your primary object is to suppress domestic violence and to establish and maintain order in the disturbed areas. You will cause to be obeyed the command of the proclamation that all persons engaged in unlawful and insurrectionary proceedings disperse and retire to their abodes, and thereafter submit to the laws and constituted authorities of the State. You will make such dispensations as shall appear proper with respect to those who commit or may be about to commit physical violence. Any conduct on the part of any person, group, or association whatever which in your judgment is contributory to or likely to be productive of domestic violence or the continuance of disorder, where such conduct is apparently lawful and would not be interfered with under normal conditions, will be immediately communicated to the War Department and you will await specific instructions, unless the emergency is so grave as to necessitate a departure from that course. In achieving your object necessity is the measure of your authority. You will always countenance and support the civil officers in executing their laws, and if necessary you will protect and support and aid them in the execution of their duties. The civil functions and processes of the State will not be interfered with, nor superseded, if exercised effectually in the suppression of violence and the restoration of order. Persons arrested should either be admonished and sent home, or if detained they should be delivered to the State authorities as soon as practicable. Where that course results in the release and return to scenes of disorder of persons whose presence there impedes the accomplishment of your purpose, such persons may be retained in military custody so long as the necessity exists. Persons in military custody will be held by authority of the United States and with respect to writs of habeas corpus the directions of section 477, 478, and 479, court-martial manual, will be followed, reporting each such case by telegraph direct to the Adjutant General of the Army.

By order of the Secretary of War:

J. G. HARBORD, Major General

## 206 "to foster a homogeneous people" (1923)

During World War I, the United States' efforts to consolidate the home front behind the martial campaign created widespread prejudice not only against the German nation but also against German immigrants and their culture. At the time, many immigrant families still spoke their mother tongue at home and wished that it be taught to their children.

In 1919, Nebraska, like many states, passed an "emergency measure" making it a crime to teach a language other than English in any school, public or private, to students who had not completed the eighth grade. Meyer was convicted of teaching German to a ten-year-old boy enrolled in a parochial school. The Supreme Court overturned the conviction on the grounds that the law invaded the right of the teacher to pursue a useful occupation—a right protected by the due process clause—and that limits existed on the exercise of the state's power to foster a patriotic population.

☆ 206 *Meyer v. Nebraska*

262 U.S. 390 (1923).

MR. JUSTICE MCREYNOLDS delivered the opinion of the Court.

\*            \*            \*

The Supreme Court of the State affirmed the judgment of conviction. It declared the offense charged and established was "the direct and intentional teaching of the German language as a distinct subject to a child who had not passed the eighth grade," in the parochial school maintained by Zion Evangelical Lutheran Congregation, a collection of Biblical stories being used therefor. And it held that the statute forbidding this did not conflict with the Fourteenth Amendment, but was a valid exercise of the police power. The following excerpts from the opinion sufficiently indicate the reasons advanced to support the conclusion.

"The salutary purpose of the statute is clear. The legislature had seen the baneful effects of permitting foreigners, who had taken residence in this country, to rear and educate their children in the language of their native land. The result of that condition was found to be inimical to our own safety. To allow the children of foreigners, who had emigrated here, to be taught from early childhood the language of the country of their parents was to rear them with that language as their mother tongue. It was to educate them so that they must always think in that language, and, as a consequence, naturally inculcate in them the ideas and sentiments foreign to the best interests of this country. The statute, therefore, was intended not only to require that the education of all children be conducted in the English language, but that, until they had grown into that language and until it had become a part of them, they should not in the schools be taught any other language. The obvious purpose of this statute was that the English language should be and become the mother tongue of all children reared in this state. The enactment of such a statute comes reasonably within the police power of the state."

\*            \*            \*

The problem for our determination is whether the statute as construed and applied unreasonably infringes the liberty guaranteed to the plaintiff in error by the Fourteenth Amendment. "No State shall ... derive any person of life, liberty, or property, without due process of law."

\*          \*          \*

The American people have always regarded education and acquisition of knowledge as matters of supreme importance which should be diligently promoted....

Practically, education of the young is only possible in schools conducted by especially qualified persons who devote themselves thereto. The calling always has been regarded as useful and honorable, essential, indeed, to the public welfare. Mere knowledge of the German language cannot reasonably be regarded as harmful. Heretofore it has been commonly looked upon as helpful and desirable. Plaintiff in error taught this language in school as part of his occupation. His right thus to teach and the right of parents to engage him so to instruct their children, we think, are within the liberty of the Amendment.

\*          \*          \*

It is said the purpose of the legislation was to promote civil development by inhibiting training and education of the immature in foreign tongues and ideals before they could learn English and acquire American ideals; and "that the English language should be and become the mother tongue of all children reared in this State." It is also affirmed that the foreign born population is very large, that certain communities commonly use foreign words, follow foreign leaders, move in a foreign atmosphere, and that the children are thereby hindered from becoming citizens of the most useful type and the public safety is imperiled.

That the State may do much, go very far, indeed, in order to improve the quality of its citizens, physically, mentally and morally, is clear; but the individual has certain fundamental rights which must be respected. The protection of the Constitution extends to all, to those who speak other languages as well as to those born with English on the tongue. Perhaps it would be highly advantageous if all had ready understanding of our ordinary speech, but this cannot be coerced by methods which conflict with the Constitution—a desirable end cannot be promoted by prohibited means.

\*          \*          \*

... In order to submerge the individual and develop ideal citizens, Sparta assembled the males at seven into barracks and intrusted their subsequent education and training to official guardians. Although such measures have been deliberately approved by men of great genius, their ideas touching the relation between individual and State were wholly different from those upon which our institutions rest; and it hardly will be affirmed that any legislature could impose such restrictions upon the people of a State without doing violence to both letter and spirit of the Constitution.

The desire of the legislature to foster a homogeneous people with American ideals prepared readily to understand current discussions of civil matters is easy to appreciate. Unfortunate experiences during the late war and aversion toward every characteristic of truculent adversaries were certainly enough to quicken that aspiration. But the means adopted, we think, exceed the limitations upon the power of the State and conflict with rights assured to plaintiff in error. The interference is plain enough and no adequate reason therefor in time of peace and domestic tranquility has been shown.

The power of the State to compel attendance at some school and to make reasonable regulations for all schools, including a requirement that they shall give instructions in English, is not questioned.... No emergency has arisen which renders knowledge by a child of some language other than English so clearly harmful as to justify its inhibition with the consequent infringement of rights long freely enjoyed. We are constrained to conclude that the statute as applied is arbitrary and without reasonable relation to any end within the competency of the State.

\*          \*          \*

*Reversed.*

## 207 "The Left Wing Manifesto" (1925)

Published and distributed in New York, "The Left Wing Manifesto" advocated militant revolution and urged "the proletariat of the world to the final struggle!" Against the background of the Red Scare in America and the post-Lenin power struggle between Stalin and Trotsky in Russia, the Supreme Court agreed that "[s]uch utterances by their very nature involve danger to the public peace and to the security of the State."

*Gitlow v. New York* marked the first time the First Amendment principles of free speech and press were assumed to circumscribe state legislation through the Fourteenth Amendment. Although the court upheld the convictions under the 1902 New York Criminal Anarchy Law, state laws and prosecutions, henceforth, were subject to review by federal authority when they involved claims that the rights of expression or assembly had been abridged.

☆ 207 *Gitlow v. New York*

268 U.S. 652 (1925).

MR. JUSTICE SANFORD delivered the opinion of the Court.

*          *          *

The contention here is that the statute, by its terms and as applied in this case, is repugnant to the due process clause of the Fourteenth Amendment. Its material provisions are:

*          *          *

"§ 161. *Advocacy of criminal anarchy.* Any person who:

"1. By word of mouth or writing advocates, advises or teaches the duty, necessity or propriety of overthrowing or overturning organized government by force or violence, or by assassination of the executive head or of any of the executive officials of government, or by any unlawful means; or,

"2. Prints, publishes, edits, issues or knowingly circulates, sells, distributes or publicly displays any book, paper, document, or written or printed matter in any form, containing or advocating, advising or teaching the doctrine that organized government should be overthrown by force, violence or any unlawful means . . . ,

"Is guilty of a felony and punishable" by imprisonment or fine, or both.

The indictment was in two counts. The first charged that the defendant had advocated, advised and taught the duty, necessity and propriety of overthrowing and overturning organized government by force, violence and unlawful means, by certain writings therein set forth entitled "The Left Wing Manifesto"; the second that he had printed, published and knowingly circulated and distributed a certain paper called "The Revolutionary Age," containing the writings set forth in the first count advocating, advising and teaching the doctrine that organized government should be overthrown by force, violence and unlawful means.

[There was no dispute that the defendant had published the material.]

The following facts were established on the trial by undisputed evidence and admissions: The defendant is a member of the Left Wing Section of the Socialist Party, a dissenting branch or faction of that party formed in opposition to its dominant policy of "moderate Socialism." Membership in both is open to aliens as well as citizens. The Left Wing Section was organized nationally at a conference in New York City in June, 1919, attended by ninety delegates from twenty different States. The conference elected a National Council, of which the defendant was a member, and left to it the adoption of a "Manifesto." This was published in The Revolutionary Age, the official organ of the Left Wing. . . .

*          *          *

. . . The sole contention here is, essentially, that as there was no evidence of any concrete result flowing from the publication of the Manifesto or of circumstances showing the likelihood of such result,

the statute as construed and applied by the trial court penalizes the mere utterance, as such, of "doctrine" having no quality of incitement, without regard either to the circumstances of its utterance or to the likelihood of unlawful sequences; and that, as the exercise of the right of free expression with relation to government is only punishable "in circumstances involving likelihood of substantive evil," the statute contravenes the due process clause of the Fourteenth Amendment. . . .

The precise question presented, and the only question which we can consider under this writ of error, then is, whether the statute, as construed and applied in this case by the state courts, deprived the defendant of his liberty of expression in violation of the due process clause of the Fourteenth Amendment.

The statute does not penalize the utterance or publication of abstract "doctrine" or academic discussion having no quality of incitement to any concrete action. It is not aimed against mere historical or philosophical essays. It does not restrain the advocacy of changes in the form of government by constitutional and lawful means. What it prohibits is language advocating, advising or teaching the overthrow of organized government by unlawful means. . . .

The Manifesto, plainly, is neither the statement of abstract doctrine nor, as suggested by counsel, mere prediction that industrial disturbances and revolutionary mass strikes will result spontaneously in an inevitable process of evolution in the economic system. It advocates and urges in fervent language mass action which shall progressively foment industrial disturbances and through political mass strikes and revolutionary mass action overthrow and destroy organized parliamentary government. It concludes with a call to action in these words: "The proletariat revolution and the Communist reconstruction of society — *the struggle for these* — is now indispensable. . . . The Communist International calls the proletariat of the world to the final struggle!" This is not the expression of philosophical abstraction, the mere prediction of future events; it is the language of direct incitement.

*          *          *

That a State in the exercise of its police power may punish those who abuse this freedom by utterances inimical to the public welfare, tending to corrupt public morals, incite to crime, or disturb the public peace, is not open to question. . . .

*          *          *

By enacting the present statute the State has determined, through its legislative body, that utterances advocating the overthrow of organized government by force, violence and unlawful means, are so inimical to the general welfare and involve such danger of substantive evil that they may be penalized in the exercise of its police power. That determination must be given great weight.... That utterances inciting to the overthrow of organized government by unlawful means, present a sufficient danger of substantive evil to bring their punishment within the range of legislative discretion, is clear. Such utterances, by their very nature, involve danger to the public peace and to the security of the State. They threaten breaches of the peace and ultimate revolution. And the immediate danger is none the less real and substantial, because the effect of a given utterance cannot be accurately foreseen. The State cannot reasonably be required to measure the danger from every such utterance in the nice balance of a jeweler's scale. A single revolutionary spark may kindle a fire that, smouldering for a time, may burst into a sweeping and destructive conflagration. It cannot be said that the State is acting arbitrarily or unreasonably when in the exercise of its judgment as to the measures necessary to protect the public peace and safety, it seeks to extinguish the spark without waiting until it has enkindled the flame or blazed into the conflagration....

\* \* \*

And finding, for the reasons stated, that the statute is not in itself unconstitutional, and that it has not been applied in the present case in derogation of any constitutional right, the judgment of the Court of Appeals is

*Affirmed.*

MR. JUSTICE HOLMES [with BRANDEIS, J.], dissenting.

... If I am right, then I think that the criterion sanctioned by the full Court in *Schenck v. United States* applies. "The question in every case is whether the words used are used in such circumstances and are of such a nature as to create a clear and present danger that they will bring about the substantive evils that [the State] has a right to prevent." ... If what I think the correct test is applied, it is manifest that there was no present danger of an attempt to overthrow the government by force on the part of the admittedly small minority who shared the defendant's views. It is said that this manifesto was more than a theory, that it was an incitement. Every idea is an incitement. It offers itself for belief and if believed it is acted on unless some other belief outweighs it or some failure of energy stifles the movement at its birth. The only difference between the expression of an opinion and an incitement in the narrower sense is the speaker's enthusiasm for the result. Eloquence may set fire to reason. But whatever may be thought of the redundant discourse before us it had no chance of starting a present conflagration. If in the long run the beliefs expressed in proletarian dictatorship are destined to be accepted by the dominant forces of the commu-

nity, the only meaning of free speech is that they should be given their chance and have their way.

If the publication of this document had been laid as an attempt to induce an uprising against government at once and not at some indefinite time in the future it would have presented a different question. The object would have been one with which the law might deal, subject to the doubt whether there was any danger that the publication could produce any result, or in other words, whether it was not futile and too remote from possible consequences. But the indictment alleges the publication and nothing more.

## 208 Conduct of a Nature to Bring Discredit upon the Military Service (1925)

Colonel William Mitchell accumulated a distinguished record during World War I. He foresaw the potential for the effective use of air power and urged the buildup of the nation's armed forces and the creation of an independent air service. He was highly critical of the Navy and War Departments' reliance on battleships to secure the national defense and believed this policy was based on personal and venal motives of high military and government officials. He also charged that belittlement of the prowess of well-developed air power — especially Japanese — was fostering a false sense of security in the public. For earlier criticism he had been relieved of his post as assistant chief of the Air Service and its temporary rank of brigadier general. After two unrelated concurrent aircraft disasters in 1925, Billy Mitchell issued the following statement: "These accidents are the result of the incompetency, the criminal negligence, and the almost treasonable negligence of our national defense by the Navy and War Departments.

Mitchell was court-martialed and convicted for this and other critical assessments of his superiors. He was charged with "conduct prejudicial to good order and military discipline and of a nature to bring discredit upon the military service by uttering insubordinate and highly contemptuous and disrespectful statements intended to discredit the Navy and War Departments." The sentence of five years' suspension of rank and forfeiture of all pay and allowances was approved by President Coolidge. Mitchell resigned his commission within the week. "Had he lived through World War II he would have seen the fulfillment of many of his prophecies," one of his judges, Douglas MacArthur, wrote later.

☆ 208 Excerpts from the Billy Mitchell
Trial Transcript

Reprinted in D. Davis, *The Billy Mitchell Affair* (New York: Random House, 1967), 249-51, 291-92.

[Opening statement of defense counsel Frank R. Reid, explaining the reasons for Mitchell's San Antonio statements after the Shenandoah disaster:]

*          *          *

"His heart was sad due to the distresses of his brave brethren and the thought of his companions who had passed one by one into the Great Beyond, and feeling it his overwhelming duty to do so he issued the statements of September 5, in the hope that it would arouse the conscience of the American people, and that they would . . . through their representatives, cause the evils to be corrected. . . .

. . . Colonel Mitchell, after exhausting every usual means to safeguard the aerial defense of the United States, without result, took the only way possible that would cause a study of the conditions of the national defense to be made."

*          *          *

One of the first defense witnesses was Major Carl ("Tooey") Spaatz, the thirty-five-year-old tactical chief of the Air Service, who wore the Distinguished Service Cross, had shot down three German planes and commanded a training school in France. In World War II he was to become commander of the U.S. Strategic Air Forces in Europe and the Pacific. Spaatz told the court of a pathetically small air force, short of men and planes and almost at a standstill in training.

All told, there were 1820 planes, but 1300 of these were obsolete—and only 400 were "standard." Of these 400, more than half were left over from the war. Only 26 bombers and 39 observation planes were rated as standard, and Spaatz insisted that only 59 planes in the United States were modern and fit for duty. As for properly equipped pursuit planes, with oxygen tanks, synchronized guns, radios and bomb racks, there were none.

By dragging all administrative officers from their desks at his post, Spaatz said, he could put 15 pursuit planes into the air: "It is very disheartening to attempt to train or do work under such circumstances."

Reid asked him if he thought aviation was being retarded by the War Department. The prosecution objected, since that called for a conclusion by the witness, but Spaatz managed to shout: "I do!" The crowd applauded.

*          *          *

[Cross-examination of William Mitchell by assistant prosecutor Allen W. Gullion:]

*          *          *

". . . Now, Colonel Mitchell, in one of your statements you speak of 'we in the air fraternity'—do you recall the expression?"

"Yes."

"Is this 'we in the air fraternity' an incorporated organization?"

"Unquestionably, it is not."

"What does this air fraternity consist of?"

"It means the people who fly in the air."

"Is there an organized air fraternity?"

"No. Just a community of spirit and a community of interest."

"Has this community of spirit and community of interest been recognized by anybody as an official organization?"

"No."

"Who are the leaders of this air fraternity?"

"Everybody that flies has an equal voice in it."

". . . How are the funds raised to support this air fraternity?"

"There are no funds raised."

"Who is this 'we' you refer to in the air fraternity that 'then and there decided to put the issue squarely up to Congress and the people'?"

"We talked it over and discussed what had gone on and decided we would stand that sort of stuff no longer."

*          *          *

[Gullion read from Mitchell's charges on the *Shenandoah*:] " 'Her survivors are muzzled by the Navy Department, pending a whitewash board. Are these things so, or are they not? I'm down here in Texas and have not all the data at hand, but I'm sure the facts are practically as stated.' "

"Are you still sure the facts are practically as stated?"

"More so than ever. I know they are now."

The examination turned to the Army's "propaganda service": "Did you ever give any information to the press, while Assistant Chief of the Air Service?"

"Often. There was no other way of getting the truth out, I found."

*          *          *

## 209 No Right to Strike (1926)

Despite the Clayton Act's withdrawal of federal judicial power to penalize labor for exercising economic sanctions against employers, state laws continued to deny labor's right to resort to strikes to gain concessions from management. *Dorchy v. Kansas* involved the criminal conviction of a United Mine Workers vice-president under the Kansas Industrial Relations Act, which made it an unlawful conspiracy to induce others to quit their employment for the purpose of hindering mining operations. The Supreme Court unequivocally upheld the states' authority to maintain a balance between the competing interests of labor and management, continuing the latter's access to the force of law to support its interests.

## ☆ 209 *Dorchy v. Kansas*

272 U.S. 306 (1926).

MR. JUSTICE BRANDEIS delivered the opinion of the Court.

Section 17 of the Court of Industrial Relations Act, while reserving to the individual employee the right to quit his employment at any time, makes it unlawful to conspire "to induce others to quit their employment for the purpose and with the intent to hinder, delay, limit or suspend the operation of" mining. Section 19 makes it a felony for an officer of a labor union wilfully to use the power or influence incident to his office to induce another person to violate any provision of the act. Dorchy was prosecuted criminally for violating § 19. The jury found him guilty through inducing a violation of § 17.... Dorchy duly claimed ... that § 19 as applied was void because it prohibits strikes; and that to do so is a denial of the liberty guaranteed by the Fourteenth Amendment....

\*    \*    \*

... The question requiring decision is not, however, the broad one whether the legislature has power to prohibit strikes. It is whether the prohibition of § 19 is unconstitutional as here applied. The special facts out of which the strike arose must, therefore, be considered.

... So far as appears, there was no trade dispute. ... The ... strike was called to compel the company to pay a claim of one Mishmash for $180. The men were told this; and they were instructed not to return to work until they should be duly advised that the claim had been paid.... The claim was disputed. It had been pending nearly two years. So far as appears, Mishmash was not in the company's employ at the time of the strike order. The men went out in obedience to the strike order.... While the men were out on strike this criminal proceeding was begun.

\*    \*    \*

The right to carry on business — be it called liberty or property — has value. To interfere with this right without just cause is unlawful. The fact that the injury was inflicted by a strike is sometimes a justification. But a strike may be illegal because of its purpose, however orderly the manner in which it is conducted. To collect a stale claim due to a fellow member of the union who was formerly employed in the business is not a permissible purpose.... To enforce payment by a strike is clearly coercion. The legislature may make such action punishable criminally, as extortion or otherwise. And it may subject to punishment him who uses the power or influence

incident to his office in a union to order the strike. Neither the common law, nor the Fourteenth Amendment, confers the absolute right to strike.

*Affirmed.*

## 210 "fight . . . for your rights" (1926)

In September of 1925, Dr. Ossian H. Sweet, a black gynecologist with an M.D. from Howard University, moved into a newly purchased home in a lower-middle-class white neighborhood in Detroit. The black population of Detroit had grown dramatically from about six thousand in 1910 to some seventy thousand at the time of the Sweets' arrival. It was the World War I boom in the automobile industry which accounted for the influx of black workers from the South into the city. Black housing was limited, and the city's white population violently opposed black expansion into their neighborhoods.

On the first night after the Sweets' arrival, an intimidating white crowd gathered in front of the house. A larger crowd — estimated at several hundred — gathered on the third night, and eight policemen were placed on duty to prevent disorder. Dr. Sweet, his wife, two brothers, and seven friends were in the house at the time. Suddenly, several shots were fired from the Sweet house, and a white man, Leon Breiner, sitting nearby, was killed. The eleven blacks in the house were charged with first-degree murder. Clarence Darrow served as defense counsel. After forty-six hours of deliberation, the jury could not reach a verdict. Five months later, Dr. Sweet's younger brother, Henry Sweet, was tried again. On May 19, 1926, the jury returned a verdict of not guilty. Portions of the Darrow summation in the trial of Henry Sweet appear in the document.

## ☆ 210 The Final Arguments in the Sweet Murder Trial

Reprinted in A. Weinberg, ed., *Attorney for the Damned* (New York: Simon & Schuster, 1957), 241-42.

\*    \*    \*

Gentlemen, lawyers are very intemperate in their statements. My friend, Moll, said that my client here was a coward. A coward, gentlemen. Here, he says, were a gang of gunmen, and cowards — shot Breiner through the back. Nobody saw Breiner, of course. If he had his face turned toward the house, while he was smoking there, waiting for the shooting to begin, it wasn't our fault. It wouldn't make any difference which way he turned. I suppose the bullet would have killed him just the same, if he had been in the way of it. If he had been at home, it would not have happened. Who are the cowards in this case? Cowards, gentlemen! Eleven people with black skins, eleven people, gentlemen, whose ancestors did not come to America because they wanted to, but were brought here in slave ships, to toil for nothing, for the whites — whose lives have been taken in nearly every state in the Union — they have been victims of riots all over this land of the free. They have had to take what is left after everybody else had grabbed what he wanted. The only place where he has been put in front is on the battlefield. When we are fighting we give him a chance to die, and the best chance. But, everywhere else, he has been food for the flames, and the ropes, and the knives, and the guns and hate of the white, regardless of law and liberty, and the common sentiments of justice that should move men. Were they cowards?

No, gentlemen, they may have been gunmen. They may have tried to murder. But they were not cowards. Eleven people, knowing what it meant, with the history of the race behind them, with the knowledge of shootings and killings and insult and injury without end, eleven of them go into a house, gentlemen, with no police protection, in the face of a mob, and the hatred of a community, and take guns and ammunition and fight for their rights, and for your rights and for mine, and for the rights of every being that lives. They went in and faced a mob seeking to tear them to bits. Call them something besides cowards. The cowardly curs were in the mob gathered there with the backing of the law. A lot of children went in front and threw the stones. They stayed for two days and two nights in front of this home, and by their threats and assault were trying to drive the Negroes out. Those were the cowardly curs, and you know it. I suppose there isn't any ten of them that would come out in the open daylight against those ten. Oh no, gentlemen, their blood is too pure for that. They can only act like a band of coyotes baying some victim who has no chance. And then my clients are called cowards.

All right, gentlemen, call them something else. These blacks have been called many names along down through the ages, but there have been those through the sad years who believed in justice and mercy and charity and love and kindliness, and there have been those who believed that a black man should have some rights, even in a country where he was brought in chains. There are those even crazy enough to hope and to dream that sometime he will come from under this cloud and take his place amongst the people of the world. If he does, it will be through his courage and his culture. It will be by his intelligence and his scholarship and his effort, and I say, gentlemen of the jury, no honest, right-feeling man, whether on a jury or anywhere else, would place anything in his way in this great struggle behind him and before him.

\*          \*          \*

# 211 Revolutionary Class Struggle (1927)

*Whitney v. California* was the most notable case prosecuted under the 1919 California Criminal Syndicalism Law. The defendant, Anita Whitney, was a niece of the late United States Supreme Court justice Stephen J. Field. A member of the Oakland branch of the Socialist party, she attended a 1919 party convention in Chicago at which a schism developed between party factions. The more militant faction formed the Communist Labor party, which called for "a revolutionary class struggle." Whitney joined the new party and participated in its meetings but actively opposed the adoption of a call for revolutionary tactics. At her trial, she testified that she did not favor the use of terrorism or violence by the Communist Labor party of California. She claimed in the Supreme Court the syndicalism law violated her rights under the Fourteenth Amendment. Nevertheless, the court upheld her conviction.

Most Americans in 1927 were enjoying the economic boom of the postwar decade, and talk of class struggle seemed anomalous. The Crash of 1929 and the ensuing depression gave these ideas more importance within the large numbers of the unemployed.

☆ 211 *Whitney v. California*

274 U.S. 357 (1927).

Mr. Justice SANFORD delivered the opinion of the Court.

\*          \*          \*

The pertinent provisions of the Criminal Syndicalism Act are:

"Section 1. The Term 'criminal syndicalism' as used in this act is hereby defined as any doctrine or precept advocating, teaching or aiding and abetting the commission of crime, sabotage (which word is hereby defined as meaning willful and malicious physical damage or injury to physical property), or unlawful acts of force and violence or unlawful methods of terrorism as a means of accomplishing a change in industrial ownership or control, or effecting any political change.

"Sec. 2. Any person who: . . . 4. Organizes or assists in organizing, or is or knowingly becomes a member of, any organization, society, group or assemblage of persons organized or assembled to advocate, teach or aid and abet criminal syndicalism; . . .

"Is guilty of a felony and punishable by imprisonment."

\*          \*          \*

The Act, plainly, meets the essential requirement of due process that a penal statute be "sufficiently explicit to inform those who are subject to it what conduct on their part will render them liable to its penalties," and be couched in terms that are not "so vague that men of common intelligence must necessarily guess at its meaning and differ as to its application." ...

*     *     *

Neither is the Syndicalism Act repugnant to the equal protection clause, on the ground that as its penalties are confined to those who advocate a resort to violent and unlawful methods as a means of changing industrial and political conditions, it arbitrarily discriminates between such persons and those who may advocate a resort to these methods as a means of maintaining such conditions.

*     *     *

The Syndicalism Act is not class legislation; it affects all alike, no matter what their business associations or callings, who come within its terms and do the things prohibited. ...

Nor is the Syndicalism Act as applied in this case repugnant to the due process clause as a restraint of the rights of free speech, assembly, and association.

That the freedom of speech which is secured by the Constitution does not confer an absolute right to speak, without responsibility, whatever one may choose, ... and that a State in the exercise of its police power may punish those who abuse this freedom ... is not open to question.

By enacting the provisions of the Syndicalism Act the State has declared, through its legislative body, that to knowingly be or become a member of or assist in organizing an association to advocate, teach or aid and abet the commission of crimes or unlawful acts of force, violence or terrorism as a means of accomplishing industrial or political changes, involves such danger to the public peace and the security of the State, that these acts should be penalized in the exercise of its police power. That determination must be given great weight. ...

The essence of offense denounced by the Act is the combining with others in an association for the accomplishment of the desired ends through the advocacy and use of criminal and unlawful methods. It partakes of the nature of a criminal conspiracy. That such united and joint action involves even greater danger to the public peace and security than the isolated utterances and acts of individuals is clear. We cannot hold that, as here applied, the Act is an unreasonable or arbitrary exercise of the police power of the State, unwarrantably infringing any right of free speech, assembly or association. ...

*     *     *

*Affirmed.*

Mr. Justice BRANDEIS, concurring.

*     *     *

Those who won our independence ... knew that order cannot be secured merely through fear of punishment for its infraction; that it is hazardous to discourage thought, hope and imagination; that fear breeds repression; that repression breeds hate; that hate menaces stable government; that the path of safety lies in the opportunity to discuss freely supposed grievances and proposed remedies; and that the fitting remedy for evil counsels is good ones. Believing in the power of reason as applied through public discussion, they eschewed silence coerced by law — the argument of force in its worst form. Recognizing the occasional tyrannies of governing majorities, they amended the Constitution so that free speech and assembly should be guaranteed.

Fear of serious injury cannot alone justify suppression of free speech and assembly. Men feared witches and burnt women. It is the function of speech to free men from the bondage of irrational fears. To justify suppression of free speech there must be reasonable ground to fear that serious evil will result if free speech is practiced. There must be reasonable ground to believe that the danger apprehended is imminent. There must be reasonable ground to believe that the evil to be prevented is a serious one. ... The wide difference between advocacy and incitement, between preparation and attempt, between assembling and conspiracy, must be borne in mind. In order to support a finding of clear and present danger it must be shown either that immediate serious violence was to be expected or was advocated, or that the past conduct furnished reason to believe that such advocacy was then contemplated.

*     *     *

... Whenever the fundamental rights of free speech and assembly are alleged to have been invaded, it must remain open to a defendant to present the issue whether there actually did exist at the time a clear danger, whether the danger, if any, was imminent, and whether the evil apprehended was one so substantial as to justify the stringent restriction interposed by the Legislature. The legislative declaration, like the fact that the statute was passed and was sustained by the highest court of the State, created merely a rebuttable presumption that these conditions have been satisfied.

Whether in 1919, when Miss Whitney did the things complained of, there was in California such clear and present danger of serious evil, might have been made the important issue in the case. She might have required that the issue be determined either by the court or the jury. She claimed below that the statute as applied to her violated the federal Constitution; but she did not claim that it was void because there was no clear and present danger of serious evil, nor did she request that the existence of these conditions of a valid measure thus restricting the rights of free speech and assembly be passed upon by the court or a jury. On the other hand, there was evidence on which the court or jury might have found that such danger existed. I am unable to assent to the suggestion in the opinion of the court that assembling with a political party, formed to advocate the desirability of a proletarian revolution by mass action at some date necessarily far in the future, is not a right within the protection of the Fourteenth Amendment. In the present case, however, there was other testimony which tended to establish the existence of a conspiracy, on the part of members of the International Workers of the World, to commit present serious crimes, and likewise to show that such a conspiracy would be furthered by the activity of the society of which Miss Whitney was a member. Under these circumstances the judgment of the State court cannot be disturbed.

\*                 \*                 \*

Mr. Justice HOLMES joins in this opinion.

## 212 "violence . . . impelled by persecution and self-defense" (1923-1927)

The 1920s were a period of widespread anti-alien and anti-radical hysteria. Nicola Sacco, a shoemaker, and Bartolomeo Vanzetti, a fish peddler, were tried and convicted in connection with the murders of Alessandro Berardelli, a guard, and F. A. Parmenter, paymaster of a shoe factory, in South Braintree, Massachusetts. Sacco and Vanzetti were Italian-born members of the Galleani anarchist group. The alleged motive for the crime was the robbery of the shoe factory payroll. To distribute some radical literature, they had borrowed a car identified as the vehicle used in the earlier hold-up and murder. The worldwide popular interest in the case stemmed from a belief that the men were denied a fair trial because of their political and social views. Many petitions were filed for clemency after Judge Webster Thayer imposed the death sentence on April 9, 1927. Governor Alvan T. Fuller appointed a committee to investigate charges of prejudice against the defendants. The committee characterized the judge's hostile private statements as "a grave breach of decorum" but decided they had not affected his conduct or influenced the jury. The defendants were executed on August 23, 1927.

Vanzetti's letters and his last statement in court reflect the political overtones of the case.

## ☆ 212 Bartolomeo Vanzetti's Ideology

### ☆ 212a Vanzetti's Letters

Reprinted in M. D. Frankfurter and G. Jackson, eds., *The Letters of Sacco and Vanzetti* (New York: Viking Press, 1928), 96.

May 26, 1923
Charlestown Prison

DEAR COMRADE [MRS. ELSIE] HILLSMITH:

\*                 \*                 \*

. . . I decided not to enter into a discussion [of politics with you] before . . . the answer to the following questions: Are you contrary or in favor of the Anarchistic view and aim? — of a real physical equality in ownership, in rights and duties among the human beings? Did you mean to possess relatively and humanly speaking, the whole truth and reason? If it were that humans should be compelled to the violence either for justice or for injustice, then would you approve those who would use the violence against the violence that compel them to be unjust and violent? Did you ever study Kropotkin, Reclus, Bakunin, Proudhon, or Tolstoy and compare their doctrines with those of liberals or authority Socialists? [Unfinished]

—————

Reprinted in Louis Joughin and E. M. Morgan, *The Legacy of Sacco and Vanzetti* (New York: Harcourt, Brace, 1948), 493-94.

May 23, 1926
Charlestown Prison

[TO THE INTERNATIONAL LABOR DEFENSE:]

\*                 \*                 \*

. . . I repeat, I will repeat to the last, only the people, our comrades, our friends, the world revolutionary proletariat can save us from the powers of the capitalist reactionary hyenas, or vindicate our names and our blood before history. . . .

There are some who think that our case is a trial for a common crime; that our friends should contest our innocence but not turn the case into a political issue, because it would only damage us. Well, I could answer to them all that our case is more than a political case, is a case of class war in which our enemies are personally interested to lose us — not only for class purposes but for personal passions, resentments, and fear. . . .

\*                 \*                 \*

—————

Joughin and Morgan, 490.

May 4, 1927
Dedham Jail

[PETITION FOR CLEMENCY TO GOVERNOR ALVAN T. FULLER:]

\*　　　\*　　　\*

... We cannot deny that acts of violence have been committed by men calling themselves anarchists, and sometimes by men who had a right to call themselves that. But they were impelled by persecution and self-defence, or provoked by violence, oppression and intolerance on the part of persons in power.

\*　　　\*　　　\*

---

Frankfurter and Jackson, 306-7.

July 22, 1927
Charlestown Prison

DEAR COMRADE [HARRY] DRAGAN:

\*　　　\*　　　\*

As long as the several schools of socialism will look for power to themselves, be fatalist and authoritarian, and the workers follow their leaders, there will always be brotherly strife and hatred among them, instead of brothers and harmony. This was clearly seen at the beginning of the Socialist movement, by men who had eyes to see.

Power and abuse of power are synonyms. The working class shall smash all the powers against it, not create a power for itself, except for self defense.

... From what I can understand, we are doomed. Maybe I am wrong; I would be wrong, but things look like that.

... Anyhow, even if they will kill us, they cannot kill all of us; all the good men and women, and still less, kill ideas, rights, necessities, aspirations and ideals. So the cause of freedom and justice, of class and of human emancipation will not be destroyed not stopped by the bodies, burnt, of two more victims of our foes.

So have heart, be cheerful, victory is ahead, and do your share with a glad heart.

BARTOLOMEO VANZETTI

☆ 212b  Vanzetti's Last Statement in Court

Reprinted in O. K. Fraenkel, *The Sacco-Vanzetti Case* (New York: Knopf, 1931), 138.

Yes. What I say is that I am innocent.... [I]n all my life I have never stole and I have never killed and I have never spilled blood.... I have struggled all my life, since I began to reason, to eliminate crime from the earth.

\*　　　\*　　　\*

...[N]ot only have I not been in Braintree to steal and kill and have never steal or kill or spilt blood in all my life, not only have I struggled hard against crimes, but I have refused myself the commodity or glory of life, the pride of life of a good position because in my consideration it is not right to exploit man....

Now, I should say that I am not only innocent of all these things, not only have I never committed a real crime in my life to eliminate crimes that the official law and the official moral condemns, but also the crime that the official moral and the official law sanctions and sanctifies, — the exploitation and the oppression of the man by the man, and if there is a reason why I am here as a guilty man, if there is a reason why you in a few minutes can doom me, it is this reason and none else.

\*　　　\*　　　\*

We have proved that there could not have been another Judge on the face of the earth more prejudiced and more cruel than you have been against us. We have proved that. Still they refuse the new trial. We know, and you know in your heart, that you have been against us from the very beginning, before you see us. Before you see us you already know that we were radicals, that we were underdogs, that we were the enemy of the institution that you can believe in good faith in their goodness — I don't want to condemn that — and that it was easy on the time of the first trial to get a verdict of guiltiness.

We know that you have spoke yourself and have spoke your hostility against us, and your despisement against us with friends of yours on the train, at the University Club, of Boston, on the Golf Club of Worcester, Massachusetts. I am sure that if the people who know all what you say against us would have the civil courage to take the stand, maybe your Honor — I am sorry to say this because you are an old man, and I have an old father — but maybe you would be beside us in good justice at this time.

\*　　　\*　　　\*

We were tried during a time that has now passed into history. I mean by that, a time when there was hysteria of resentment and hate against the people of our principles, against the foreigner, against slackers, and it seems to me — rather, I am positive, that both you and Mr. Katzmann has done all what it were in your power in order to work out, in order to agitate still more the passion of the juror, the prejudice of the juror, against us....

Well, I have already say that I not only am not guilty of these crimes, but I never commit a crime in my life, — I have never steal and I have never kill and I have never spilt blood, and I have fought and I have sacrificed myself even to eliminate the crimes that the law and the church legitimate and sanctify.

\*　　　\*　　　\*

But my conviction is that I have suffered for things that I am guilty of. I am suffering because I am a radical and indeed I am a radical; I have suffered because I was an Italian, and indeed I am an Italian; I have suffered more for my family and for my beloved than for myself; but I am so convinced to be right that if you could execute me two times, I would live again to do what I have done already. I have finished. Thank you.

## 213 " 'peaceful and orderly opposition to government' " (1931)

By 1931, political hysteria, which had subsided somewhat, once more was reawakened as a result of Depression-connected hunger marches by the unemployed and the resultant violent police responses. Nevertheless, many of the measures for controlling dissent fell into desuetude, and when they were invoked, the courts viewed them with a more skeptical eye. *Stromberg v. California* was the first Supreme Court case to uphold a challenge, based on the First Amendment, to political prosecution and is noteworthy for its tacit recognition of "symbolic speech" and its application of what has come to be called the "overbreadth doctrine." The court opinion contained no general condemnation of the legislation in question, only the requirement that it be sufficiently explicit so as not to be construed to apply to peaceful opposition to government.

☆ 213  *Stromberg v. California*

283 U.S. 359 (1931).

MR. CHIEF JUSTICE HUGHES delivered the opinion of the Court.

*          *          *

The information . . . charged [in the statutory language] that the appellant and other defendants, at the time and place set forth, "did wilfully, unlawfully and feloniously display a red flag and banner in a public place and in a meeting place as a sign, symbol and emblem of opposition to organized government and as an invitation and stimulus to anarchistic action and as an aid to propaganda that is and was of a seditious character."

*          *          *

. . . It appears that the appellant, a young woman of nineteen, a citizen of the United States by birth, was one of the supervisors of a summer camp for children, between ten and fifteen years of age, in the foothills of the San Bernardino mountains. Appellant led the children in their daily study, teaching them history and economics. "Among other things, the children were taught class consciousness, the solidarity of the workers, and the theory that the workers of the world are of one blood and brothers all." Appellant was a member of the Young Commu-

nist League, an international organization affiliated with the Communist Party. The charge against her concerned a daily ceremony at the camp, in which the appellant supervised and directed the children in raising a red flag, "a camp-made reproduction of the flag of Soviet Russia, which was also the flag of the Communist Party in the United States." In connection with the flag-raising, there was a ritual at which the children stood at salute and recited a pledge of allegiance "to the worker's red flag, and to the cause for which it stands; one aim throughout our lives, freedom for the working class." The stipulation further shows that "a library was maintained at the camp containing a large number of books, papers and pamphlets, including much radical communist propaganda, specimens of which are quoted in the opinion of the state court." These quotations abundantly demonstrated that the books and pamphlets contained incitements to violence and to "armed uprisings," teaching "the indispensability of a desperate, bloody, destructive war as the immediate task of the coming action." Appellant admitted ownership of a number of the books, some of which bore her name. It appears from the stipulation that none of these books or pamphlets were used in the teaching at the camp.

*          *          *

. . . [D]oubting the constitutionality of the first clause, the state court rested its decision upon the remaining clauses. The basis of the decision, as more fully stated in the opinion of the two concurring justices, was this: "The constitutionality of the phrase of this section, 'of opposition to organized government' is questionable. This phrase can be eliminated from the section without materially changing its purposes, . . ." Accordingly, disregarding the first clause of the statute, and upholding the other clauses, the conviction of the appellant was sustained.

We are unable to agree with this disposition of the case. The verdict against the appellant was a general one. It did not specify the ground upon which it rested. . . . If any one of these clauses, which the state court has held to be separable, was invalid, it cannot be determined upon this record that the appellant was not convicted under that clause. . . .

*          *          *

. . . We have no reason to doubt the validity of the second and third clauses of the statute as construed by the state court to relate to such incitements to violence.

The question is thus narrowed to that of the validity of the first clause, that is, with respect to the display of the flag "as a sign, symbol or emblem of opposition to organized government," and the construction which the state court has placed upon this clause removes every element of doubt. The state court recognized the indefiniteness and ambiguity of the clause. The court considered that it might be construed as embracing conduct which the State could not constitutionally prohibit. Thus it was said that the clause "might be construed to include the peaceful and orderly opposition to a government as organized and controlled by one political party by those of another political party equally high minded and patriotic, which did not agree with the one in power. It might also be construed to include peaceful and orderly opposition to government by legal means and within constitutional limitations." The maintenance of the opportunity for free political discussion to the end that government may be responsive to the will of the people and that changes may be obtained by lawful means, an opportunity essential to the security of the Republic, is a fundamental principle of our constitutional system. A statute which upon its face, and as authoritatively construed, is so vague and indefinite as to permit the punishment of the fair use of this opportunity is repugnant to the guaranty of liberty contained in the Fourteenth Amendment. The first clause of the statute being invalid upon its face, the conviction of the appellant, which so far as the record discloses may have rested upon that clause exclusively, must be set aside.

*  *  *

*Judgment reversed.*

MR. JUSTICE BUTLER, dissenting.

*  *  *

. . . It seems to me that on this record the Court is not called on to decide whether the mere display of a flag as the emblem of a purpose, whatever its sort, is speech within the meaning of the constitutional protection of speech and press or to decide whether such freedom is a part of the liberty protected by the Fourteenth Amendment or whether the anarchy that is certain to follow a successful "opposition to organized goverment" is not a sufficient reason to hold that all activities to that end are outside the "liberty" so protected. . . .

*  *  *

## 214 "jurisdiction to issue a restraining order" (1932)

Industry and business management's ability to secure (through the labor injunction) the power and authority of the law to combat strikes, collective bargaining, and other techniques that the modern labor movement used to gain its demands gave rise to labor's argument that the government was partial to capital, and hence unjust. The Norris-La Guardia Act was the climax of the movement toward stricter limitations on the use of the labor injunction, which began when the earlier attempt in the Clayton Act proved ineffective. The declaration of public policy

in section two of the Norris-La Guardia Act showed a marked shift from earlier pronouncements in positioning the federal government as a more neutral player in the labor-management bouts of the future, thus reducing the inclination of labor to view government authority as the co-opted tool of capital. The goal was a concomitant reduction in the frequency and degree of organized violence surrounding labor disputes.

By its terms, the act prohibited the issuance of an injunction against certain conduct; most notably, striking, picketing and/or publicizing, advocating, and advising or agreeing to engage in collective activity in a labor dispute "without fraud or violence." In addition, management forces had to overcome stricter procedural requirements, including an adversary hearing, before they could obtain an injunction. Finally, courts could impose punishments for contempt (committed outside the presence of the court) only after a speedy trial by jury. The 1947 Taft-Hartley Act modified the Norris-La Guardia Act by again broadening the availability of the labor injunction.

## ☆ 214 The Norris-La Guardia Act

47 Stat. 70 (1932).

An Act to amend the Judicial Code and to define and limit the jurisdiction of courts sitting in equity, and for other purposes.

*Be it enacted by the Senate and House of Representatives of the United States of America in Congress assembled,* That no court of the United States, as herein defined, shall have jurisdiction to issue any restraining order or temporary or permanent injunction in a case involving or growing out of a labor dispute, except in a strict conformity with the provisions of this Act; nor shall any such restraining order or temporary or permanent injunction be issued contrary to the public policy declared in this Act.

SEC. 2. In the interpretation of this Act and in determining the jurisdiction and authority of the courts of the United States, as such jurisdiction and authority are herein defined and limited, the public policy of the United States is hereby declared as follows:

Whereas under prevailing economic conditions, developed with the aid of governmental authority for owners of property to organize in the corporate and other forms of ownership association, the individual unorganized worker is commonly helpless to exercise actual liberty of contract and to protect his freedom of labor, and thereby to obtain acceptable terms and conditions of employment, wherefore, though he should be free to decline to associate with his fellows, it is necessary that he have full freedom of association, self-organization, and designation of representatives of his own choosing, to negotiate the terms and conditions of his employment, and that he shall be free from the interference, restraint, or coercion of employers of labor, or their agents, in the designation of such representatives or in self-organization or in other concerted activities for the purpose of collective bargaining or other mutual aid or protection; therefore, the following definitions of, and limitations upon, the jurisdiction and authority of the courts of the United States are hereby enacted.

SEC. 3. Any undertaking or promise, such as is described in this section, or any other undertaking or promise in conflict with the public policy declared in section 2 of this Act, is hereby declared to be contrary to the public policy of the United States, shall not be enforceable in any court of the United States and shall not afford any basis for the granting of legal or equitable relief by any such court, including specifically the following:

Every undertaking or promise hereafter made, whether written or oral, express or implied, constituting or contained in any contract or agreement of hiring or employment between any individual, firm, company, association, or corporation, and any employee or prospective employee of the same, whereby

(a) Either party to such contract or agreement undertakes or promises not to join, become, or remain a member of any labor organization or of any employer organization; or

(b) Either party to such contract or agreement undertakes or promises that he will withdraw from an employment relation in the event that he joins, becomes, or remains a member of any labor organization or of any employer organization.

SEC. 4. No court of the United States shall have jurisdiction to issue any restraining order or temporary or permanent injunction in any case involving or growing out of any labor dispute to prohibit any person or persons participating or interested in such dispute (as these terms are herein defined) from doing, whether singly or in concert, any of the following acts:

(a) Ceasing or refusing to perform any work or to remain in any relation of employment;

(b) Becoming or remaining a member of any labor organization or of any employer organization, regardless of any such undertaking or promise as is described in section 3 of this Act;

(c) Paying or giving to, or withholding from, any person participating or interested in such labor dispute, any strike or unemployment benefits or insurance, or other moneys or things of value;

(d) By all lawful means aiding any person participating or interested in any labor dispute who is being proceeded against in, or is prosecuting, any action or suit in any court of the United States or of any State;

(e) Giving publicity to the existence of, or the facts involved in, any labor dispute, whether by advertising, speaking, patrolling, or by any other method not involving fraud or violence;

(f) Assembling peaceably to act or to organize to act in promotion of their interests in a labor dispute;

(g) Advising or notifying any person of an intention to do any of the acts heretofore specified;

(h) Agreeing with other persons to do or not to do any of the acts heretofore specified; and

(i) Advising, urging, or otherwise causing or inducing without fraud or violence the acts heretofore specified, regardless of any such undertaking or promise as is described in section 3 of this Act.

SEC. 5. No court of the United States shall have jurisdiction to issue a restraining order or temporary or permanent injunction upon the ground that any of the persons participating or interested in a labor dispute constitute or are engaged in an unlawful combination or conspiracy because of the doing in concert of the acts enumerated in section 4 of this Act.

SEC. 6. No officer or member of any association or organization, and no association or organization participating or interested in a labor dispute, shall be held responsible or liable in any court of the United States for the unlawful acts of individual officers, members, or agents, except upon clear proof of actual participation in, or actual authorization of, such acts, or of ratification of such acts after actual knowledge thereof.

SEC. 7. No court of the United States shall have jurisdiction to issue a temporary or permanent injunction in any case involving or growing out of a labor dispute, as herein defined, except after hearing the testimony of witnesses in open court (with opportunity for cross-examination) in support of the allegations of a complaint made under oath, and testimony in opposition thereto, if offered, and except after findings of fact by the court, to the effect—

(a) That unlawful acts have been threatened and will be committed unless restrained or have been committed and will be continued unless restrained, but no injunction or temporary restraining order shall be issued on account of any threat or unlawful act excepting against the person or persons, association, or organization making the threat or committing the unlawful act or actually authorizing or ratifying the same after actual knowledge thereof;

(b) That substantial and irreparable injury to complainant's property will follow;

(c) That as to each item of relief granted greater injury will be inflicted upon complainant by the denial of relief than will be inflicted upon defendants by the granting of relief;

(d) That complainant has no adequate remedy at law; and

(e) That the public officers charged with the duty

to protect complainant's property are unable or unwilling to furnish adequate protection.

*       *       *

*Approved, March 23, 1932.*

## 215 "Government cannot be coerced by mob rule" (1932)

At the end of World War I, each veteran of military service received sixty dollars as a special gratuity. The veterans lobbied and demanded an additional bonus for the difference between military and civilian salaries during their service time. On May 19, 1924, President Coolidge signed the "adjusted compensation" bill under which each veteran received a certificate that would entitle him and his family to about five hundred dollars in 1945. In May 1932, somewhere between fifteen thousand and twenty-five thousand unemployed veterans formed the "Bonus Expeditionary Force," which encamped in Washington, D.C., demanding that Congress immediately honor the certificates. In mid-June, Congress failed to pass the necessary appropriation but authorized transportation funds for the men. About two-thirds left the city. On July 28 an uneasy President Hoover, fearing a communist-led insurrection, ordered federal troops to remove the remaining bonus marchers from federal property after the District of Columbia police failed in their attempt to do so. Chief of Staff Douglas MacArthur ordered an attack, led by Majors Dwight D. Eisenhower and George S. Patton and employing tanks, tear gas, machine guns, cavalry, and fixed bayonets. The demonstrators were routed; two veterans and two policemen were left dead. On January 24, 1936, Congress, over President Franklin D. Roosevelt's veto, passed a law providing for the exchange of the bonus certificates for cashable bonds.

☆ 215  The Bonus Army March on Washington

Reprinted in W. Myles, ed., *The State Papers and Other Public Writings of Herbert Hoover* (Garden City, N.Y.: Doubleday, Doran, 1934), 2:244–45.

☆ 215a  President Hoover's Letter to Commissioner Reichelderfer

The White House, Washington
July 29, 1932

Honorable Luther H. Reichelderfer
Commissioner, District of Columbia
Washington, D.C.

MY DEAR MR. COMMISSIONER:

In response to your information that the police of the District were overwhelmed by an organized attack by several thousand men, and were unable to maintain law and order, I complied with your request for aid from the Army to the police. It is a matter of satisfaction that, after the arrival of this assistance, the mobs which were defying the municipal government were dissolved without the firing of a shot or the loss of a life.

I wish to call attention of the District Commissioners to the fact that martial law has not been declared; that responsibility for order still rests upon your commission and the police. The civil government of Washington must function uninterrupted. The Commissioners, through their own powers, should now deal with this question decisively.

It is the duty of the authorities of the District to at once find the instigators of this attack on the police and bring them to justice. It is obvious that, after the departure of the majority of the veterans, subversive influences obtained control of the men remaining in the District, a large part of whom were not veterans, secured repudiation of their elected leaders and inaugurated and organized this attack.

They were undoubtedly led to believe that the civil authorities could be intimidated with impunity because of attempts to conciliate by lax enforcement of city ordinances and laws in many directions. I shall expect the police to strictly enforce every ordinance of the District in every part of the city. I wish every violator of the law to be instantly arrested and prosecuted under due process of law.

I have requested the law enforcement agencies of the Federal Government to coöperate with the District authorities to this end.

There is no group, no matter what its origins, that can be allowed either to violate the laws of this city or to intimidate the Goverment.

Yours faithfully,

HERBERT HOOVER

☆ 215b  President Hoover's Press Conference
(July 20, 1932)

The President said:

A challenge to the authority of the United States Government has been met, swiftly and firmly.

After months of patient indulgence, the Government met overt lawlessness as it always must be met if the cherished processes of self-government are to be preserved. We cannot tolerate the abuse of Constitutional rights by those who would destroy all government, no matter who they may be. Government cannot be coerced by mob rule.

The Department of Justice is pressing its investigation into the violence which forced the call for Army detachments, and it is my sincere hope that those agitators who inspired yesterday's attack upon the Federal authority may be brought speedily to trial in the civil courts. There can be no safe harbor in the United States of America for violence.

Order and civil tranquillity are the first requisites in the great task of economic reconstruction to which our whole people now are devoting their heroic and noble energies. This national effort must not be retarded in even the slightest degree by organized lawlessness. The first obligation of my office is to uphold and defend the Constitution and the authority of the law. This I propose always to do.

## 216 "oil and gas producers . . . in a state of insurrection" (1932)

The power of the United States president or a state governor to declare martial law in response to public disorder has not been subject to much judicial review. In 1932, the governor of Texas proclaimed martial law over several oil-producing counties to stop wasteful production. Without denying that a state governor had the power to declare martial law, the Supreme Court held that the propriety of the exercise of that power was subject to judicial scrutiny when private rights were in jeopardy. This judicial review could address the question of whether the facts justified an exertion of a military power. Another thread of political criminality running through this document is the attempt by the lawfully constituted state officials, Governor Sterling and General Wolters, to defy the orders of the federal district court.

☆ 216 *Sterling v. Constantin*

287 U.S. 378 (1932).

MR. CHIEF JUSTICE HUGHES delivered the opinion of the Court.

\*          \*          \*

In August, 1931, the Legislature of Texas passed an amended oil and conservation act. The Governor in issuing his proclamation of August 16th recited the provisions of the constitution and statutes of Texas for the conservation of oil and gas and the existence in the East Texas oil field, the territory in question, of an organized group of oil and gas producers who were said to be in a state of insurrection against the conservation laws; that the civil officers did not have a sufficient force to compel them to obey; that by reason of their reckless production enormous physical waste was being created; that this condition had brought about such a state of public feeling that if the state government could not protect the public's interest they would take the law into their own hands; that this condition had caused threats of acts of violence; that it was necessary to give the Railroad Commission time to have hearings and promulgate proper orders to put the law into force; that a state of "insurrection, tumult, riot and breach of the

peace existed in the defined area" and that there was "serious danger threatening to citizens and property, not only there, but in other oil producing areas of the State"; and that it was necessary "that the reckless and illegal exploitation" should be stopped until such time as the said resources might be properly conserved and developed under the protection of the civil authorities. The troops were then called out and the oil wells were shut down. In September, after the Commission had made its order limiting production, while the proclamation of martial law was not rescinded nor the troops entirely withdrawn, the military occupation in force ended. The wells were opened and continued to produce daily under the order of the Railroad Commission. General Wolters, with the assistance of the "Rangers," the civil officers of the community, and "the few military still remaining in the field," and in aid of the Commission, patrolled the territory to see that its orders were complied with; that from time to time the Commission, sometimes with the approval, and sometimes with the disapproval, of the Governor made its orders further limiting production, and these orders were obeyed.

[Complainants filed suit against the Railroad Commission and secured a temporary restraining order against the production limits. The Commission obeyed the order.]

[A]fter the restraining order against the Commission had been issued in this suit, the defendants, Governor Sterling and General Wolters, "determined not to brook court interference with the program of restricted production which they determined to continue." . . . [T]hey "ousted the Commission from the fixing of and superintendence over the daily production allowed, and have since controlled production by purported military orders."

As to the actual conditions in the area affected by these orders the District Court made the following finding:

"It was conceded that at no time has there been any actual uprising in the territory. At no time has any military force been exerted to put riots or mobs down. At no time, except in the refusal of defendant Wolters to observe the injunction in this case, have the civil authorities or courts been interfered with or their processes made impotent. Though it was testified to by defendants that from reports which came to them they believed that, if plaintiff's wells were not shut in, there would be dynamiting of property in the oil fields, and efforts to close them and any others which opened by violence, and that, if that occurred, there would be general trouble in the field, no evidence of any dynamite having been used, or show of violence practiced or actually attempted, or even threatened against any specific property in the field, was offered. We find, therefore, that not only was there never any actual riot, tumult, or insurrection, which would create a state of war existing in the field, but that, if all of the conditions had come to pass, they would have resulted merely in breaches of the peace to be suppressed by the militia as a civil force, and not at all in a condition constituting, or even remotely resembling, a state of war."

\*   \*   \*

... As the State has no more important interest than the maintenance of law and order, the power it confers upon its Governor as Chief Executive and Commander in Chief of its military forces to suppress insurrection and to preserve the peace is of the highest consequence. The determinations that the Governor makes within the range of that authority have all the weight which can be attributed to state action, and they must be viewed in the light of the object to which they may properly be addressed and with full recognition of its importance. It is with appreciation of the gravity of such an issue that the governing principles have been declared.

By virtue of his duty to "cause the laws to be faithfully executed," the Executive is appropriately vested with the discretion to determine whether an exigency requiring military aid for that purpose has arisen. His decision to that effect is conclusive. That construction, this Court has said, in speaking of the power constitutionally conferred by the Congress upon the President to call the militia into actual service, "necessarily results from the nature of the power itself, and from the manifest object contemplated." The power "is to be exercised upon sudden emergencies, upon great occasions of state, and under circumstances which may be vital to the existence of the Union." Similar effect, for corresponding reasons, is ascribed to the exercise by the Governor of a State of his discretion in calling out its military forces to suppress insurrection and disorder. The nature of the power also necessarily implies that there is a permitted range of honest judgment as to the measures to be taken in meeting force with force, in suppressing violence and restoring order, for without such liberty to make immediate decisions, the power itself would be useless. Such measures, conceived in good faith, in the face of the emergency and directly related to the quelling of the disorder or the prevention of its continuance, fall within the discretion of the Executive in the exercise of his authority to maintain peace....

It does not follow from the fact that the Executive has this range of discretion, deemed to be a necessary incident of his power to suppress disorder, that every sort of action the Governor may take, no matter how unjustified by the exigency or subversive of private right and the jurisdiction of the courts, otherwise available, is conclusively supported by mere executive fiat. The contrary is well established. What are the allowable limits of military discretion, and whether or not they have been overstepped in a particular case, are judicial questions....

We need not undertake to determine the intended significance of the expression "martial law," and all its possible connotations, as it was employed in the Governor's proclamation.... The question before us is simply with respect to the Governor's attempt to regulate by executive order the lawful use of complainant's properties in the production of oil. ... The assertion that such action can be taken as conclusive proof of its own necessity and must be accepted as in itself due process of law has no support in the decisions of this Court.

Appellant's contentions find their appropriate answer in what was said by this Court in *Ex Parte Milligan*, a statement as applicable to the military authority of the State in the case of insurrection as to the military authority of the Nation in time of war:

" ... Martial law established [at the discretion of executive authority] destroys every guarantee of the Constitution, and effectually renders the military independent of and superior to the civil power. ... Civil liberty and this kind of martial law cannot endure together; the antagonism is irreconcilable; and, in the conflict, one or the other must perish."

\*   \*   \*

In the present case, the findings of fact made by the District Court are fully supported by the evidence. They leave no room for doubt that there was no military necessity which, from any point of view, could be taken to justify the action of the Governor in attempting to limit complainants' oil production, otherwise lawful. Complainants had a constitutional right to resort to the federal court to have the validity of the Commission's orders judicially determined. There was no exigency which justified the Governor in attempting to enforce by executive or military order the restriction which the District Judge had restrained pending proper judicial inquiry. If it be assumed that the Governor was entitled to declare a state of insurrection and to bring military force to the aid of civil authority, the proper use of that power in this instance was to maintain the federal court in the exercise of its jurisdiction and not to attempt to override it; to aid in making its process effective and not to nullify it; to remove, and not to create, obstructions to the exercise by the complainants of their rights as judicially declared....

*The judgment of the District Court is affirmed.*

## 217 "The San Francisco *débacle*"
(1934)

In 1934, a general strike failed to materialize in San
Francisco. The general strike was practically unknown in the United States, although it had been a
powerful weapon in the hands of European labor.
General strikes were instrumental in winning universal manhood suffrage in Belgium, in stopping the
use of troops to break up strikes in Italy, and in the
issuance of the liberal Czarist October Manifesto
(1905) in Russia. In more recent times the general
strike, as a tool of political protest, spread particularly to the Middle East and Latin America.

In this article, "The Revolutionary Logic of the
General Strike," Wilfred H. Crook argued that
whether economic, political, or revolutionary, the
general strike tended to overthrow constituted political authority and supplant it with *de facto* government by the workers. It was perhaps this feature
of labor power which caused the instruments of government to concern themselves with labor's revolutionary rather than economic potential.

☆ 217 The Revolutionary Logic of
the General Strike

Wilfred H. Crook, *American Political Science Review* 28
(1934): 655-63.

### THE REVOLUTIONARY LOGIC OF THE
### GENERAL STRIKE

Spanish and Cuban events during the past three
years, and the recent labor disputes on the Pacific
coast, have once again brought the general strike
into the limelight. The abdication of King Alphonso
and the flight of President Machado showed the po-
tentialities of a successful general strike when labor
faces the revolutionary logic of that weapon. The
San Francisco *débacle* proved the futility of that
method when labor refuses to admit its revolutionary implications.

. . . The writer is concerned in this article with exposing the implicit revolutionary logic contained in
even the most peaceable general strike.

In every general strike, organized labor sets up a
dual or rival government, by the purposeful and general cessation of its normal functions. When workers
in a single trade or industry go on strike, this revolutionary logic is seldom involved, unless a vital public
service is affected, such as the police force or hospital and medical service. It is when a strike takes on
the gravity of a general cessation of work that it contains a tacit challenge to the continued functioning
of social life and thereby brings in against it the
forces of the existing government. It is then that an
incipient rival government can be found, no matter

how orderly the strike may be, nor how fervently its
leaders proclaim their non-political aims.

*        *        *

For purposes of discussion, the writer has classified general strikes, so defined, into three types, (1)
economic, (2) political, and (3) revolutionary. . . . The
economic general strike is, in its inception, a protest
against some real or imagined economic injustice to
fellow workers. . . . [A] real distinction is made by
strike leaders themselves between the *political* general strike, which "directs its efforts against the
State," yet "does not seek to transform society, but
rather to make the political masters yield," and the
*revolutionary* general strike, in which the leaders aim
from the outset to introduce confusion into the life of
the State and overthrow the existing order. . . .

It would be superfluous, by the very definitions
used above, to argue the existence of a rival government where a revolutionary general strike is concerned. . . . It is not so simple a matter to prove the
implicit revolutionary logic behind the political general strike. . . .

. . . Despite the careful limitation . . . set to the
use of the general strike as a political weapon, in
many, if not in all, such strikes there can be found an
undercurrent of criticism of the existing form of government, with the implication that stronger, perhaps even more revolutionary, methods would be
used if the more orderly political strike should fail.

*        *        *

It is far more difficult to prove the economic general strike revolutionary in its basic logic. . . . The
economic general strike grows out of a smaller dispute, where it is possible to make very clear to vast
numbers of workers in other industries the economic injustice involved in the original struggle. A
sympathy strike of this type calls for more undiluted
sacrifice by all workers not concerned in the original
dispute, for in this type of general strike the vast
majority stand to lose a great deal in wages and insecurity of employment, but to gain nothing for themselves, not even the right to vote. The issue, therefore, must so clearly appeal to all wage-workers as
to approach closely to the issue of the class struggle.

The purpose underlying an economic general
strike . . . [is] to force the general public, who are not
taking part in the strike, to become umpires between the ranks of striking workers on the one side
and the massed forces of capital and the government
on the other. . . .

The leaders of an economic general strike do not
have to act as if they felt themselves to be a rival
government. It is enough that the strike orders,
given by them to the labor ranks, should in effect
select the essential public services that shall continue to function. To discover the rival government

in action, it is therefore necessary to turn to the interpretation of the general strike orders by the ranks of labor. Evidence will be found most abundantly in the granting or withholding of permits to work issued by the various strike committees, and in the conception of their own function held by those committees.

Four outstanding examples of a strictly economic general strike provide ample data for the discussion in hand, occurring in Sweden in 1909, in Seattle and Winnipeg in 1919, and in Great Britain in 1926. . . .

\*          \*          \*

In Seattle, a startling editorial appeared in the daily labor paper, the *Union Record*, shortly before the strike broke out: "Labor will feed the people! Twelve great kitchens have been offered, and from them food will be distributed by the provision trades at low cost to all. Labor will care for the babies and the sick! . . . Not the withdrawal of labor, but the power of the strikers to manage, will win this strike. Labor will not only shut down the industries, but labor will reopen, under the management of the appropriate trades, such activities as are needed to preserve public health and public peace. If the strike continues, labor may feel led to avoid public suffering by reopening more and more activities, under its own management."

City firemen were instructed to stay at their posts, garbage-wagon drivers were told to collect garbage, but to leave ashes and paper. Auto drivers might drive the mail and answer emergency calls for funerals and hospitals, if those calls were made through the office of their trade union. A police force of unarmed war veterans was organized to aid the strike committee in the preservation of order.

Popular recognition of the de facto government of the strike committee was evident, the *Nation* reported: "Before the committee appeared a long succession of business men, city officials, and the mayor himself, not to threaten or bully, but to discuss the situation and ask the approval of the committee for this or that step. . . ."

During a speaking tour in the East, Mayor Ole Hanson declared of the struggle in his city: "The general strike, as practised in Seattle, is of itself the weapon of revolution, all the more dangerous because quiet. To succeed, it must suspend everything; stop the entire life stream of a community. That is to say, it puts the government out of operation. And that is all there is revolt, no matter how achieve."

\*          \*          \*

The greatest economic general strike in labor history occurred in Great Britain in May, 1926, the result of long-standing troubles in the coal-mining industry. Responsible leaders of the general council of the Trades Union Congress emphatically denied that they were attacking either the government or

the general public. Constantly the strike sheet, the *Daily Worker*, emphasized the purely industrial aspect of the dispute. Nevertheless, the same evidence of the existence of a rival government can be found in the acts of the various strike committees .

The Rt. Hon. Winston Churchill declared that British labor was prepared with a scheme for paralyzing the nation. Nothing was farther from the truth. The government itself was thoroughly prepared and at least two strong citizens' groups had been organized to meet the general strike peril many weeks before it occurred. Labor alone was appallingly unready to face the logic of its action. Its plans were in chaos until two days before the strike actually commenced. Even then, a further forty-eight hours were required to untangle the maze of orders and counter-orders issued from the London headquarters of the strike.

The London labor leaders offered to run enough trains and road transportation to feed the nation, a sample of their refusal to face the problems of a really effective general strike, and yet in itself a significant instance of their tacit assumption of authority. Churchill's reply indicated that the government, of which he was an important part, had no illusions as to such an offer. "What government in the world," he asked, "could enter into a partnership with a rival government, against which it is endeavoring to defend itself and society, and allow that rival government to sit in judgment on every train that runs and on every lorry on the road?

\*          \*          \*

The common attitude of the strike committees toward their own function during the strike can best be seen in a naïve comment of a strike-leader in one of Arnold Bennett's *Five Towns*. Referring to the employers who were coming to the strike committee "cap in hand" to ask for permits to move their goods, he said: "Most of them turned empty away after a most humiliating experience, for one and all were put through a stern questioning, just to make them realize that we and not they were the salt of the earth."

The British government and the press promptly raised the issue of "civil war," and the government organ, the *British Gazette*, spoke glibly of the strikers as "the enemy." Yet no impartial student of the British national strike can question that the vast majority of the strike leaders had not the slightest desire to overthrow the existing form of government, A. J. Cook, the radical leader of the miners, notwithstanding. At the same time no student can doubt that the orders of the the the strike leaders, as interpreted and practised by the local strike committees and the ranks of the strikers, did logically constitute an attempt to set up a rival authority to that of the legitimate local and national governing bodies. If that contention be granted in the case of so peaceable an economic general strike, it would seem that the revolutionary logic of all three types of the general strike has been proved.

\*　　　\*　　　\*

It seems, therefore, that in these days a successful general strike in Western civilization is likely to occur only where the labor forces have faced the full revolutionary logic of that weapon, and where the ruling class or the government has at the same time remained so blind to progress and so unjust to the masses of the people that anything, even revolution, is preferable. Even at that, success in the use of the weapon demands that the cause be so clear that most of the citizens outside the ranks of labor, and the majority of the military and naval forces, express strong sympathy with the strikers. This was evidently the situation in the recent Spanish and Cuban general strikes, where the revolutionary aim of the method was successfully achieved.

## 218 "the right to organize for its common welfare" (1934)

Both the individual and the communal political rights of the Native Americans finally stabilized during the post-World War I era as the earlier policies of ethnocide through assimilation proved ineffective in eliminating their culture. In 1924, Congress granted United States citizenship to all Native Americans in the United States, whether they wanted it or not. Congress had long wavered between policies encouraging tribalism and those supporting assimilation. In 1934 the Indian Reorganization Act reestablished the Native Americans' right to limited self-determination, permitting the tribes to reorganize as corporate entities for their collective benefit.

### ☆218　The Indian Reorganization Act

48 Stat. 984 (1934).

*Be it enacted by the Senate and House of Representatives of the United States of America in Congress assembled*, That hereafter no land of any Indian reservation, created or set apart by treaty or agreement with the Indians, Act of Congress, Executive order, purchase, or otherwise, shall be allotted in severalty to any Indian.

\*　　　\*　　　\*

SEC. 15. Nothing in this Act shall be construed to impair or prejudice any claim or suit or any Indian tribe against the United States. It is hereby declared to be the intent of Congress that no expenditures for the benefit of Indians made out of appropriations authorized by this Act shall be considered as offsets in any suit brought to recover upon any claim of such Indians against the United States.

SEC. 16. Any Indian tribe, or tribes, residing on the same reservation, shall have the right to organize for its common welfare, and may adopt an appropriate constitution and bylaws, which shall become effective when ratified by a majority vote of the adult members of the tribe, or of the adult Indians residing on such reservation, as the case may be, at a special election authorized and called by the Secretary of the Interior under such rules and regulations as he may prescribe. Such constitution and bylaws when ratified as aforesaid and approved by the Secretary of the Interior shall be revocable by an election open to the same voters and conducted in the same manner as hereinabove provided. Amendments to the constitution and bylaws may be ratified and approved by the Secretary in the same manner as the original constitution and bylaws.

In addition to all powers vested in any Indian tribe or tribal council by existing law, the constitution adopted by said tribe shall also vest in such tribe or its tribal council the following rights and powers: To employ legal counsel, the choice of counsel and fixing fees to be subject to the approval of the Secretary of the Interior; to prevent the sale, disposition, lease, or encumbrance of tribal lands, interests in lands, or other tribal assets without the consent of the tribe; and to negotiate with the Federal, State, and local Governments. The Secretary of the Interior shall advise such tribe or its tribal counsel of all appropriation estimates or Federal projects for the benefit of the tribe prior to the submission of such estimates to the Bureau of the Budget and the Congress.

SEC. 17. The Secretary of the Interior may, upon petition by at least one-third of the adult Indians, issue a charter of incorporation to such tribe: *Provided*, That such charter shall not become operative until ratified at a special election by a majority vote of the adult Indians living on the reservation. Such charter may convey to the incorporated tribe the power to purchase, take by gift, or bequest, or otherwise, own, hold, manage, operate, and dispose of property of every description, real and personal, including the power to purchase restricted Indian lands and to issue in exchange therefor interests in corporate property, and such further powers as may be incidental to the conduct of corporate business, not inconsistent with law, but no authority shall be granted to sell, mortgage, or lease for a period exceeding ten years any of the land included in the limits of the reservation. Any charter so issued shall not be revoked or surrendered except by Act of Congress.

SEC. 18. This Act shall not apply to any reservation wherein a majority of the adult Indians, voting at a special election duly called by the Secretary of the Interior, shall vote against its application. It shall be the duty of the Secretary of the Interior, within one year after passage and approval of this Act, to call such an election, which election shall be held by secret ballot upon thirty days' notice.

SEC. 19. The term "Indian" as used in this Act shall include all persons of Indian descent who are members of any recognized Indian tribe now under Federal jurisdiction, and all persons who are descendants of such members who were, on June 1, 1934, residing within the present boundaries of any Indian reservation, and shall further include all other persons of one-half or more Indian blood. For the purpose of this Act, Eskimos and other aboriginal peoples of Alaska shall be considered Indians. The term "tribe" wherever used in this Act shall be construed to refer to any Indian tribe, organized band, pueblo, or the Indians residing on one reservation. The words "adult Indians" wherever used in this Act shall be construed to refer to Indians who have attained the age of twenty-one years.

*           *           *

*Approved, June 18, 1934.*

# 219 "strikes and other forms of industrial strife" (1935)

With the passage of the National Industrial Recovery Act (NIRA) which, among other things, legalized union organization and collective bargaining, labor disputes increased dramatically. The Bureau of Labor Statistics reported a fivefold increase from 1932 to 1933. The 1933-34 New Deal strikers were concerned primarily with union recognition rather than disputes over wages, hours, and working conditions. The wave of unrest which began in 1933 continued into 1935. That year the NIRA was held unconstitutional. Congress reacted by passing the National Labor Relations Act (NLRA), popularly known as the Wagner Act after its chief sponsor. The NLRA was designed to guarantee workers' rights to associate, organize, and choose representatives to negotiate with management. To this end, it defined employer actions hindering organization as unfair labor practices and created an independent agency, the National Labor Relations Board, to conduct secret ballot elections by employees, settle controversies regarding union representation, oversee collective bargaining, investigate unfair labor practices, and issue cease and desist orders to restrain them. The selected sections of the act convey the flavor of the legislation placing governmental authority behind the rights of workers. The Supreme Court upheld the NLRA as constitutional in *NLRB v. Jones & Laughlin Steel Corp.*, 301 U.S. 1 (1937).

Whereas previously only the acts of workers were subject to government sanction, this act positions the federal government as an overseer of management tactics as well. Importantly, these new declarations of public authority were placed largely outside the reach of a judiciary that was still perceived by many as promanagement. Altogether, the government was now viewed as a referee rather than a participant in labor-management conflicts.

## ☆ 219  The National Labor Relations Act (The Wagner Act)

49 Stat. 449 (1935).

*Be it enacted by the Senate and House of Representatives of the United States of American in Congress assembled,*

### FINDINGS AND POLICY

SECTION 1. The denial by employers of the right of employees to organize and the refusal by employers to accept the procedure of collective bargaining lead to strikes and other forms of industrial strife, or unrest, which have the intent or the necessary effect of burdening or obstructing [interstate] commerce. . . .

The inequality of bargaining power between employees who do not possess full freedom of association or actual liberty of contract, and employers who are organized in the corporate or other forms of ownership association substantially burdens and affects the flow of [interstate] commerce, and tends to aggravate recurrent business depressions, by depressing wage rates and the purchasing power of wage earners in industry and by preventing the stabilization of competitive wage rates and working conditions within and between industries.

Experience has proved that protection by law of the right of employees to organize and bargain collectively safeguards commerce from injury, impairment, or interruption, and promotes the flow of [interstate] commerce by removing certain recognized sources of industrial strife and unrest, by encouraging practices fundamental to the friendly adjustment of industrial disputes arising out of differences as to wages, hours, or other working conditions, and by restoring equality of bargaining power between employers and employees.

It is hereby declared to be the policy of the United States to eliminate the causes of certain substantial obstructions to the free flow of [interstate] commerce and to mitigate and eliminate these obstructions when they have occurred by encouraging the practice and procedure of collective bargaining and by protecting the exercise by workers of full freedom of association, self-organization, and designation of representatives of their own choosing, for the purpose of negotiating the terms and conditions of their employment or other mutual aid or protection.

\*         \*         \*

### RIGHTS OF EMPLOYEES

SEC. 7. Employees shall have the right to self-organization, to form, join, or assist labor organizations, to bargain collectively through representatives of their own choosing, and to engage in concerted activities, for the purpose of collective bargaining or other mutual aid or protection.

SEC. 8. It shall be an unfair labor practice for an employer —

(1) To interfere with, restrain, or coerce employees in the exercise of the rights guaranteed in section 7.

(2) To dominate or interfere with formation or administration of any labor organization or contribute financial or other support to it: *Provided*, That subject to rules and regulations made and published by the Board . . . , an employer shall not be prohibited from permitting employees to confer with him during working hours without loss of time or pay.

(3) By discrimination in regard to hire or tenure of employment or any term or condition of employment to encourage or discourage membership in any labor organization: *Provided*, That nothing in this Act, or in the National Industrial Recovery Act . . . or in any other statute of the United States, shall preclude an employer from making an agreement with a labor organization . . . to require as a condition of employment membership therein, if such labor organization is the representative of the employees as provided in section 9 (a), in the appropriate collective bargaining unit covered by such agreement when made.

(4) To discharge or otherwise discriminate against an employee because he has filed charges or given testimony under this Act.

(5) To refuse to bargain collectively with the representatives of his employees. . . .

\*         \*         \*

### LIMITATIONS

SEC. 13. Nothing in this Act shall be construed so as to interfere with or impede or diminish in any way the right to strike.

\*         \*         \*

*Approved, July 5, 1935.*

## 220 "combined resistance to the lawful authority of the State" (1936)

The 1930s reflected a renewed concern with the spread of alien doctrines and political activities in the United States. While the initial attention was directed towards communism, other forms of totalitarianism — fascism and nazism — later gave rise to governmental concern. Efforts to organize whites and blacks in Georgia in the name of the Communist party resulted in Angelo Herndon's indictment and conviction in the state courts. His sentence was eighteen to twenty years' imprisonment. On appeal, the United States Supreme Court reversed the conviction and held the Georgia insurrection statute violated protections of the Fourteenth Amendment.

☆ 220 *Herndon v. Lowry*

301 U.S. 242 (1936).

MR. JUSTICE ROBERTS delivered the opinion of the Court.

\*         \*         \*

. . . The charge was founded on § 56 of the Penal Code, one of four related sections. Section 55 defines insurrection, § 56 defines an attempt to incite insurrection, § 57 prescribes the death penalty for conviction of the offenses described in the two preceding sections unless the jury shall recommend mercy, and § 58 penalizes, by imprisonment, the introduction and circulation of printed matter for the purpose of inciting insurrection, riot, conspiracy, etc. The sections are copied in the margin.[1]

The appellant was brought to trial and convicted. He appealed on the ground that, under the statute as construed by the trial court in its instructions to the jury, there was no evidence to sustain a verdict of guilty.

\*         \*         \*

The evidence on which the judgment rests consists of appellant's admissions and certain documents found in his possession. The appellant told the state's officers that some time prior to his arrest he joined the Communist Party in Kentucky and later came to Atlanta as a paid organizer for the party, his duties being to call meetings, to educate and disseminate information respecting the party, to distribute literature, to secure members, and to work up an organization of the party in Atlanta; and that he had held or attended three meetings called by him. He made no further admission as to what he did as an organizer, or what he said or did at the meetings. When arrested he carried a box containing documents. After he was arrested he conducted the officers to his room where additional documents and bundles of newspapers and periodicals were found, which he stated were sent him from the headquarters of the Communist Party in New York. He gave the names of persons who were members of the organization in Atlanta, and stated he had only five or six actual members at the time of his apprehension. The stubs of membership books found in the box indicated he had enrolled more members than he stated. There was no evidence that he had distributed any of the material carried on his person and found in his room, or had taken any of it to meetings, save two circulars or appeals respecting county relief which are confessedly innocuous.

... Certain documents in his possession when he was arrested were placed in evidence. They fall into five classes: first, receipt books showing receipts of small sums of money, pads containing certificates of contributions to the Communist Party's Presidental Election Campaign Fund, receipts for rent of a post office box, and Communist Party membership books; secondly, printed matter consisting of magazines, pamphlets, and copies of the "Daily Worker," styled the "Central Organ of the Communist Party," and the "Southern Worker," also, apparently, an official newspaper of the party; thirdly, two books, one "Life and Struggles of Negro Toilers," by George Padmore, and the other "Communism and Christianism Analyzed and Contrasted from the Marxian and Darwinian Points of View" by Rt. Rev. William Montgomery Brown, D. D.; fourthly, transcripts of minutes of meetings apparently held in Atlanta; fifthly, two circulars, one of which was prepared by the appellant and both of which had been circulated by him in Fulton County. All of these may be dismissed as irrelevant except those falling within the first and second groups. No inference can be drawn from the possession of the books mentioned, either that they embodied the doctrines of the Communist Party or that they represented views advocated by the appellant. The minutes of meetings contain nothing indicating the purposes of the organization or any intent to overthrow organized government; on the contrary, they indicate merely discussion of relief for the unemployed. The two circulars, admittedly distributed by the appellant, had nothing to do with the Communist Party, its aims or purposes, and were not appeals to join the party but were concerned with unemployment relief in the county and included appeals to the white and negro unemployed to organize and represent the need for further county aid. They were characterized by the Supreme Court of Georgia as "more or less harmless."

*     *     *

The matter appearing upon the membership blanks is innocent upon its face however foolish and pernicious the aims it suggests. Under the heading "What is the Communist Party?" this appears:

"The Party is the vanguard of the working class and consists of the best, most class conscious, most active, the most courageous members of that class. It incorporates the whole body of experience of the proletarian struggle, basing itself upon the revolutionary theory of Marxism and representing the general and lasting interests of the whole of the working class, the Party personifies the unity of proletarian principles, of proletarian will and of proletarian revolutionary action.

"We are the Party of the working class. Consequently, nearly the whole of that class (in time of war and civil war, the whole of that class) should work under the guidance of our Party, should create the closest contacts with our Party."

This vague declaration falls short of an attempt to bring about insurrection either immediately or within a reasonable time but amounts merely to a statement of ultimate ideals. The blanks, however, indicate more specific aims for which members of the Communist Party are to vote. They are to vote Communist for

"1. Unemployment and Social Insurance at the expense of the State and employers.

"2. Against Hoover's wage-cutting policy.

"3. Emergency relief for the poor farmers without restrictions by the government and banks; exemption of poor farmers from taxes and from forced collection of rents or debts.

"4. Equal rights for the Negroes and self-determination for the Black Belt.

"5. Against capitalistic terror: against all forms of suppression of the political rights of the workers.

"6. Against imperialist war; for the defense of the Chinese people and of the Soviet Union."

None of these aims is criminal upon its face. . . .

*     *     *

Section 56, under which the indictment is laid, makes no reference to force or violence except by the phrase "combined resistance to the lawful authority of the State." . . .

To ascertain how the Act is held to apply to the appellant's conduct we turn to the rulings of the state courts in his case. The trial court instructed the jury: "In order to convict the defendant, . . . it must appear clearly by the evidence that immediate serious violence against the State of Georgia was to be expected or advocated." The jury rendered a verdict of guilty. . . .

*     *     *

The appellant had a constitutional right to address meetings and organize parties unless in so doing he violated some prohibition of a valid statute. The only prohibition he is said to have violated is that of § 56 forbidding incitement or attempted incitement to insurrection by violence. If the evidence fails to show that he did so incite, then, as applied to him, the statute unreasonably limits freedom of speech and freedom of assembly and violates the Fourteenth Amendment. We are of opinion that requisite proof is lacking. From what has been said above with respect to the evidence offered at the trial it is apparent that the documents found upon the appellant's person were certainly, as to some of the aims stated therein, innocent and consistent with peaceful action for a change in the laws or the constitution. The proof wholly fails to show that the appellant had read these documents; that he had distributed any of them; that he believed and advocated any or all of the principles and aims set forth in them, or that those he had procured to become members of the party knew or approved of any of these documents.

*     *     *

*Reversed.*

---

[1.] Insurrection shall consist in any combined resistance to the lawful authority of the State, with intent to the denial thereof, when the same is manifested or intended to be manifested by acts of violence. . . .

## 221 " 'mob or riotous assemblage' " (1937)

The atrocious murder of two blacks by a mob at Duck Hill, Mississippi, on April 13, 1937, rekindled national concern for the quality of justice for blacks in the South. A sheriff was transporting two black prisoners accused of the murder of a country merchant to the county jail when a mob forced him to surrender them. They took the two prisoners to the scene of the murder, lashed them, tied them to trees, tortured them with blow torches, riddled them with bullets, and burned them.

The antilynching bill introduced by New York congressman Joseph Gavagan passed the House but failed in the Senate owing to a Southern filibuster founded on states' rights arguments. The proposed law would have imposed penalties upon the political subdivision in which a lynching occurred as well as upon delinquent peace officers. Later antilynching bills sought direct punitive action against members of the mob.

☆ 221  The Gavagan Antilynching Bill

H.R. 1507, 75th Cong., 1st Sess. (1973).

*An Act.* To assure to persons within the jurisdiction of every State the equal protection of the laws, and to punish the crime of lynching.

*Be it enacted by the Senate and House of Representatives of the United States of America in Congress assembled,* That, for the purposes of this Act, the phrase "mob or riotous assemblage," when used in this Act, shall mean an assemblage composed of three or more persons acting on concert, without authority of law, to kill or injure any person in the custody of any peace officer, with the purpose or consequence of depriving such person of due process of law or the equal protection of the laws.

SEC. 2. If any State or governmental subdivision thereof fails, neglects, or refuses to provide and maintain protection to the life or person of any individual within its jurisdiction against a mob or riotous assemblage, whether by way of preventing or punishing the acts thereof, such State shall by reason of such failure, neglect, or refusal be deemed to have denied to such person due process of law and the equal protection of the laws of the State, and to the end that the protection guaranteed to persons within the jurisdiction of the several States, or to citizens of the United States, by the Constitution of the United States, may be secured, the provisions of this Act are enacted.

SEC. 3. (a) Any officer or employee of any State or governmental subdivision thereof who is charged with the duty or who possesses the power or authority as such officer or employee to protect the life or person of any individual injured or put to death by any mob or riotous assemblage or any officer or employee of any State or governmental subdivision thereof having any such individual in his custody, who fails, neglects, or refuses to make all diligent efforts to protect such individual from being so injured or being put to death, or any officer or employee or any State or governmental subdivision thereof charged with the duty of apprehending, keeping in custody, or prosecuting any person participating in such mob or riotous assemblage who fails, neglects, or refuses to make all diligent efforts to perform his duty in apprehending, keeping in custody, or prosecuting to final judgment under the, laws of such State all persons so participating, shall be guilty of a felony, and upon conviction thereof shall be punished by a fine not exceeding $5,000 or by imprisonment not exceeding five years, or by both such fine and imprisonment.

*     *     *

SEC. 4. The District Court of the United States judicial district wherein the person is injured or put to death by a mob or riotous assemblage shall have jurisdiction to try and to punish, in accordance with the laws of the State where the injury is inflicted or the homicide is committed, any and all persons who participate therein: *Provided,* that it is first made to appear to such court (1) that the officers of the State charged with the duty of apprehending, prosecuting, and punishing such offenders under the laws of the State shall have failed, neglected, or refused to apprehend, prosecute, or punish such offenders; or (2) that the jurors obtainable for service in the State court having jurisdiction of the offense are so strongly opposed to such punishment that there is probability that those guilty of the offense will not be punished in such State court. A failure for more than thirty days after commission of such an offense to apprehend or to indict the persons guilty thereof, or a failure diligently to prosecute such persons, shall be sufficient to constitute prima face evidence of the failure, neglect, or refusal described in the above proviso.

SEC. 5. Any county in which a person is seriously injured or put to death by a mob or riotous assemblage shall be liable to the injured person or the legal representatives of such person for a sum not less than $2,000 nor more than $10,000 as liquidated damages, which sum may be recovered in a civil action against such county in the United States District Court of the judicial district wherein such person is put to the injury or death....

SEC. 6. In the event that any person so put to death shall have been transported by such mob or riotous assemblage from one county to another county during the time intervening between his seizure and putting to death, the country in which he is seized and the county in which he is put to death shall be jointly and severally liable to pay the forfeiture herein provided....

*Passed the House of Representatives, April 15, 1937.*

# 222 "Obeying the Rules" (1937)

The Congress of Industrial Organizations (CIO) adopted the sit-down strike as a technique to organize workers in mass production industries. The label "sit-down" derived from the method employed—strikers quit working and "sat" at their work stations until management met their demands. Between September 1936 and May 1937, sit-down strikes proliferated, and as many as 485,000 male and female workers remained in plants, eating food supplied by outside friends and relatives and sleeping in makeshift quarters. Charged with trespassing, the strikers asserted that human rights came first. The following account was printed in a publication of the socialist-oriented League for Industrial Democracy.

## 222 Sit Down (1937)

Joel Seidman, *Sit Down* (New York: League for Industrial Democracy, 1937), 3, 5–19, 22–31.

\*       \*       \*

When they tie the can to a union man,
  Sit down! Sit down!
When they give him the sack, they'll take him back,
  Sit down! Sit down!
        *Chorus*
Sit down, just take a seat,
Sit down, and rest your feet,
Sit down, you've got 'em beat.
  Sit down! Sit down!

A new strike technique has swept the country, arousing enthusiasm among workers, and bewilderment among employers. In industry after industry, in state after state, the workers remain at their posts but refuse to work. No longer is it possible to introduce strikebreakers, for the workers are in possession. Nor are the workers readily dispersed, for they can barricade themselves in a strong defensive position. If strikebreakers or police storm the factory gate, they are clearly responsible in the eyes of the public for whatever violence may occur. The employer cannot too easily afford to alienate public opinion, nor risk damage to his machinery. And so the workers remain in possession of the plant, in much more comfort and security than on the picket line....

\*       \*       \*

### EARLY USES OF THE SIT-DOWN IN AMERICA

It is impossible to determine accurately when and where the sit-down strike was first used. It seems such a logical tactic for workers to employ that there are probably many unrecorded instances, each one short in duration, going back almost as far as our modern industrial civilization. The wonder is that its use did not become widespread much earlier.

\*       \*       \*

### KEEPING COMFORTABLE

Sit-downers have had a host of new problems to solve, not the least of which have been living in factory buildings. Food, sleeping quarters, and sanitation are matters that must be properly attended to if morale is to be kept up and health maintained for long. The necessary work must be done, and facilities for recreation provided. In all of these respects our experience with sit-downs, brief though it has been, is illuminating.

With hundreds or perhaps several thousands of sit-downers in a plant, the problem of food becomes urgent. The union must assume responsibility for seeing that the workers receive three meals a day. This is a severe strain on the union treasury, but thus far adequate meals have been furnished. Indeed, in some strikes most of the sit-downers have gained weight. One of the most important committees in many sit-down strikes is the chiseling committee, which seeks donations from food merchants. It calls for resourcefulness when the committee is unable to obtain the food for the menu as planned, and the cook must prepare whatever is brought back. The Midland Steel Products Company sit-downers in Detroit were aided by a daily donation of 30 gallons of milk by the milk drivers' union. Often the means furnished by the union are supplemented by food brought to individual strikers by their families or friends.

Usually the food is cooked in a nearby hall or restaurant, and brought in milk cans, kettles, or other large containers to the plant. In the case of the Wahl-Eversharp Pen Company of Chicago, police refused to allow friends of the strikers to bring food into the plant. The sit-downers then lowered a rope from an upper window to the roof of an adjoining bakery, and obtained food in this fashion. The menu of sit-downers is usually simple, but adequate. Barrels, kegs, and whatever else is suitable are used for chairs, and tables are likewise improvised. Newspapers sometimes serve as tablecloths. Liquor is strictly forbidden.

Usually the cooking is done by a committee of the strikers' wives. In large strikes, however, a professional cook may be obtained. The cook in the Flint strike, for example, was sent there to help by the Cooks' Union of Detroit. He had previously cooked for four other sit-down strikes. For the Flint strike the union installed new kitchen equipment worth more than $1,000.

"The food goes into the factories in twenty kettles of various sizes," the cook reported. "The amount of food the strikers use is immense. Five hundred pounds of meat, one thousand pounds of potatoes, three hundred loaves of bread, one hundred pounds of coffee, two hundred pounds of sugar, thirty gallons of fresh milk, four cases of evaporated milk!"

In Detroit a cooperative kitchen was established to feed 800 sit-down strikers in the Bohn Aluminum, Cadillac, and Fleetwood plants:

> The kitchen runs on efficient lines, not speed-up, in two shifts. About 50 men and women comprise the working crew; the first shift working from 7:00 until 2:00 in the afternoon, the second from 11:00 in the morning until 6:00 in the afternoon. Everyone attends the meetings held at 2:00 o'clock daily at I.A.S. Hall where the various committees make their reports. There is the kitchen committee, which takes care of preparing the food, with a chef from the Cooks' Union, Local No. 234, to supervise the preparation of it. Then there is a finance committee, with two treasurers, working in shifts, one from the Cadillac plant and one from the Bohn Aluminum plant.

Other important committees were the drivers' committee, which delivered the food, and the chiseling committee, which covered the city for donations of food or money. About two-thirds of the supplies were obtained in this fashion.

\*       \*       \*

Most visitors to sit-down strikes have been impressed by the neatness of the men and the tidy appearance of the plants. One of the important jobs is to see that the factories are kept clean. The machinery is kept in good order, for the sit-downers wish to

return to work as soon as possible after the strike ends. Often a former barber is found among the strikers, and he is made to resume his old trade. In the Kelsey-Hayes plant a wheelbarrow on a platform served as a barber chair. In one sit-down strike where there were women employees, a beauty parlor was opened for them by a former worker in such an establishment. Washing is often a problem, however, for in most plants only ordinary washbowls are available. One sit-down, in the Detroit plant of the Aluminum Company of America, had to be transformed into a walk-out because a number of the men became ill and lack of sufficient sanitary facilities made further stay in the plant hazardous to health.

### OBEYING THE RULES

A certain amount of work is required, for meals must be served, the place kept clean, a watch kept, and discipline maintained. . . .

\*       \*       \*

Discipline and morale are of vital importance. Those who do not conform to the rules may be sentenced to extra clean-up duty for minor offenses, and ejected for serious violations. In the General Motors strike in Flint, court was held each morning, with bringing in liquor and circulating rumors the most frequent offenses. Elsewhere it may be overstaying leaves that is most frequently punished. In the Standard Cotton Products Company strike in Flint the judge himself was twice convicted of breaking the rules, and had to do extra dish washing as the penalty. Sometimes foremen and other company officials are allowed to converse only with union officers, for fear that they may adversely affect the strikers' morale. In some instances subterfuges have been employed by strikers or their wives in order to get out of the plant. Serious illness has been reported at home, or a birth in the family. Where too many such cases seemed to be reported a check was made, and the member immediately dropped. In some cases foremen have visited wives of sit-downers, making false reports of illness or hardships within the plant, in order to break down morale.

Except when trouble is feared, sit-downers are usually permitted to leave the plant for short intervals, under rules that they decide upon. In most cases they are required to return by a specified hour, and a check is made as they go and come. If an outside picket line is maintained as well, the strikers take turns staying within the plant. In one case a sit-downer who belonged to the National Guard was released for strike duty with the Guard.

Visitors are admitted only after a careful check of their credentials. Usually a pass signed by a responsible union officer is required. In many plants everyone who enters must submit to a search for weapons, and a similar search is made of all who leave. A communications system calls to the gate those who have visitors. A post office is sometimes set up to handle the mail, which may be censored. Gates and doors are often barricaded against a surprise attack, with guards on duty at all times. In Flint, sentries, in six-hour watches, were on duty twenty-four hours a day, with an alarm system to warn quickly of impending danger. Sometimes metal strips are welded across doorways and windows, to make police entry more difficult, and to provide protection from gas bombs and bullets. In some plants pickets assigned to make the rounds have had to punch the time clock as they went on or off duty.

*     *     *

Race relations may be another problem faced by sit-downers. In the Midland plant in Detroit both whites and negroes were employed. Workers of both races occupied the plant, and worked together in harmony throughout the strike.

*     *     *

### A TYPICAL SET OF RULES

Sit-downers must govern their community, and solve each problem as it arises. Fundamentally these problems are similar, though new situations will arise in each plant. The rules adopted by the sit-down strikers in the Standard Cotton Products Company in Flint, Michigan, may be taken as fairly typical. With fewer than a hundred strikers, they were able to transact business in a full meeting held at 10 o'clock each morning, without the more complex and elaborate organization that a large plant would require. A strike committee of five members was placed in charge. Other officers included a chairman, a secretary, a judge, a press agent, and three clerks. There was a patrol committee of two, a food committee of two, a clean-up committee of three, and an entertainment committee of one.

Posted on the wall of the mess hall were the following rules, which were added to from time to time by majority vote:

### Rules and Regulations

Rule No. 1. Any man who disturbs anyone while sleeping without good reason will have to wash the dishes and mop floor for one day.

Rule No. 2. Any man found drinking or looking for arguments will wash dishes and mop floor for one day — 1st offense.

Rule No. 3. Every man who leaves must get a pass from the committee and check with the clerk. Passes must be shown to the doorman when going in and out, and on returning must check with the clerk. The doorman must obey these rules very strictly.

Rule No. 4. Doormen answer the phone and if the call is important he calls a committee man. No long-distance calls shall be made. All local calls are allowed. No profane language used over phone.

Rule No. 5. When photographers or outsiders come in no one speaks to them but a committee man.

Rule No. 6. Everyone must line up single file before meals are served. Dishwashers will be appointed before each meal by the clean-up committee. Every man must serve his turn.

Rule No. 7. Anyone eating between meals must wash his own dishes.

Rule No. 8. Every man must attend meetings.

Rule No. 9. No standing on tables.

Rule No. 10. No passes will be issued after 12:00 P.M. — except emergency calls.

Rule No. 11. Judge's decision on all broken rules will be regarded as final.

Rule No. 12. No conversation about the strike to the management. Any information concerning the strike will be furnished by the committee.

Rule No. 13. No more than a two-hour grace period allowed on passes. No grace period on a 20-minute leave.

Rule No. 14. No women allowed in the plant at any time.

Rule No. 15. No passes issued during meals and not until the dishes are done unless it is business.

Rule No. 16. All committees must attend meetings and report their activities.

Rule No. 17. No card playing or walking around or any disturbance during meetings.

### WHAT OF THE LAW?

Unquestionably most judges will hold the sit-down strike illegal, under the law of trespass. The fact that the law of trespass was developed in a different social situation will be of no avail. Yet labor need not be unduly disturbed, for most weapons used by it were first held illegal. That was true both of the strike and the boycott. . . .

Attacks upon the sit-down strike have already begun, and many more may be expected. Governor Hoffman of New Jersey, for example, has warned that the entire resources of the state, if necessary, would be used to eject sit-downers. In his view, workers have no more right to take possession of a factory than gangsters have to take possession of a bank. Early in 1937, legislation to outlaw the sit-down strike was being considered in Alabama and Vermont. . . .

Wyndham Mortimer, vice-president of the United Automobile Workers, has thus stated the case for the sit-down strike:

Is it wrong for a worker to stay at his job? The laws of the state and nation recognize, in a hundred ways, that the worker has a definite claim upon his job; more fundamentally, it is recognized that every workman has a moral right to continue on his job unless some definite misconduct justifies his discharge. These sit-down strikers are staying at their work-places; no one has a better right to be there than have these men themselves. No one else, certainly, has any right to those positions. But the sit-down strikers have performed valuable services in those factories; General Motors and the public alike have profited by those services. To call them trespassers now, and to deny their right as human beings to remain with their jobs, is logically unsound and is manifestly unjust.

The union asserts that the workers have a property right in their jobs which is superior to the company's right to the use of the property....

The sit-down strike has served notice on society that mere ownership does not carry with it all possible rights with reference to a factory. Those who work in it, who make it produce with their labor and who depend upon it for their livelihood, should likewise have a voice in its control. Those who invest their lives in an industry have at least as much at stake as those who merely invest their money. The sit-down strike brings these facts forcibly to public attention. It is interesting to note that, in the sit-down strike, workers are re-establishing the control over the tools of production that they lost with the Industrial Revolution.

The ethical case for the sit-down strike has well been presented by Rabbi Edward L. Israel, former chairman of the Social Justice Commission of the Central Conference of American Rabbis. The problem involved, Rabbi Israel asserts, is one of the comparative emphasis of human rights over against property rights. The entire struggle of the human race from bondage toward freedom, he points out, has been a constant battling against vested interests.

*        *        *

The argument that a worker has a property right in his job has thus been stated by Homer Martin, president of the automobile workers union:

What more sacred property right is there in the world than the right of a man in his job? This property right involves the right to support his family, feed his children and keep starvation away from the door. This property right is the very foundation stone of American homes. It is the most sacred, most fundamental property right in America. It means more to the stabilization of American life, morally, socially and economically, than any other property right.

*        *        *

## 223 Peaceful Assembly Cannot Be Made a Crime (1937)

In 1937 President Franklin Delano Roosevelt revealed his plan to "pack" the Supreme Court, which had been holding unconstitutional the New Deal social welfare and economic recovery programs enacted by Congress. Roosevelt proposed to increase the court's membership from nine to a maximum of fifteen by adding one new justice for each member past age seventy who failed to retire. It was the conservative court, nevertheless, that denied to Oregon the right to interfere with the legitimate rights of syndicalist militants. The repudiation of Oregon's criminal syndicalism statute, which made it a crime to assist in conducting a meeting of an organization that advocated the overthrow of the government by unlawful means, illustrated the technique whereby the Supreme Court applied the safeguards of the Bill of Rights to the states via the Fourteenth Amendment.

☆ 223 *De Jonge v. Oregon*

299 U.S. 353 (1937).

MR. CHIEF JUSTICE HUGHES delivered the opinion of the Court.

Appellant, Dirk De Jonge, was indicted in Multnomah County, Oregon, for violation of the Criminal Syndicalism Law of that State. The Act... defines "criminal syndicalism" as "the doctrine which advocates crime, physical violence, sabotage or any unlawful acts or methods as a means of accomplishing or effecting industrial or political change or revolution."...

... The charge is that appellant assisted in the conduct of a meeting which was called under the auspices of the Communist Party, an organization advocating criminal syndicalism....

*        *        *

The stipulation [of facts] set forth various extracts from the literature of the Communist Party to show its advocacy of criminal syndicalism. The stipulation does not disclose any activity by the defendant as a basis for his prosecution other than his participation in the meeting in question. Nor does the stipulation show that the Communist literature distributed at the meeting contained any advocacy of criminal syndicalism or of any unlawful conduct....

*        *        *

The broad reach of the statute as thus applied is plain. While defendant was a member of the Communist Party, that membership was not necessary to conviction on such a charge. A like fate might have attended any speaker, although not a member, who "assisted in the conduct" of the meeting. However innocuous the object of the meeting, however lawful the subjects and tenor of the addresses, however reasonable and timely the discussion, all those assisting in the conduct of the meeting would be subject to imprisonment as felons if the meeting were held by the Communist Party. . . . Thus if the Communist Party had called a public meeting in Portland to discuss the tariff, or the foreign policy of the Government, or taxation, or relief, or candidacies for the offices of President, members of Congress, Governor, or State legislators, every speaker who assisted in the conduct of the meeting would be equally guilty with the defendant in this case, upon the charge as here defined and sustained. The list of illustrations might be indefinitely extended to every variety of meetings under the auspices of the Communist Party although held for the discussion of political issues or to adopt protests and pass resolutions of an entirely innocent and proper character.

While the States are entitled to protect themselves from the abuse of the privileges of our institutions through an attempted substitution of force and violence in the place of peaceful political action in order to effect revolutionary changes in government, none of our decisions go to the length of sustaining such a curtailment of the right of free speech and assembly as the Oregon statute demands in its present application. . . .

Freedom of speech and of the press are fundamental rights which are safeguarded by the due process clause of the Fourteenth Amendment of the Federal Constitution. . . . The right of peaceable assembly is a right cognate to those of free speech and free press and is equally fundamental. As this Court said in *United States v. Cruikshank,* "The very idea of a government, republican in form, implies a right on the part of its citizens to meet peaceably for consultation in respect to public affairs and to petition for a redress of grievances." The First Amendment of the Federal Constitution expressly guarantees that right against abridgment by Congress. But explicit mention there does not argue exclusion elsewhere. For the right is one that cannot be denied without violating those fundamental principles of liberty and justice which lie at the base of all civil and political institutions — principles which the Fourteenth Amendment embodies in the general terms of its due process clause.

These rights may be abused by using speech or press or assembly in order to incite to violence and crime. The people through their legislatures may protect themselves against that abuse. But the legislative intervention can find constitutional justification only by dealing with the abuse. The rights themselves must not be curtailed. The greater the importance of safeguarding the community from incitements to the overthrow of our institutions by

force and violence, the more imperative is the need to preserve inviolate the constitutional rights of free speech, free press and free assembly in order to maintain the opportunity for free political discussion, to the end that government may be responsive to the will of the people and that changes, if desired, may be obtained by peaceful means. Therein lies the security of the Republic, the very foundation of constitutional government.

It follows from these considerations that, consistently with the Federal Constitution, peaceable assembly for lawful discussion cannot be made a crime. The holding of meetings for peaceable political action cannot be proscribed. Those who assist in the conduct of such meetings cannot be branded as criminals on that score. The question, if the rights of free speech and peaceable assembly are to be preserved, is not as to the auspices under which the meeting is held but as to its purpose; not as to the relations of the speakers, but whether their utterances transcend the bounds of the freedom of speech which the Constitution protects. If the persons assembling have committed crimes elsewhere, if they have formed or are engaged in a conspiracy against the public peace and order, they may be prosecuted for their conspiracy or other violation of valid laws. But it is a different matter when the State, instead of prosecuting them for such offenses, seizes upon mere participation in a peaceable assembly and a lawful public discussion as the basis for a criminal charge.

\* \* \*

We hold that the Oregon statute as applied to the particular charge as defined by the State court is repugnant to the due process clause of the Fourteenth Amendment. . . .

## 224 "the prohibition of the export of arms" (1937)

The belief of many Americans that the United States' involvement in World War I was a mistake led to several legislative enactments designed to keep the country uninvolved in the brewing European conflicts. The Neutrality Act of 1935 banned shipments of war materials to belligerents at the discretion of the president. The Neutrality Act of 1936 prohibited sending arms to nations at war but did not apply to civil wars. In 1936 a civil war erupted in Spain, and the following year the United States placed an embargo on all arms shipments to Spain.

The push for neutrality culminated in the Neutrality Act of 1937. Motivated by the spectacle of American volunteers fighting for the Spanish Republic in the Abraham Lincoln Brigade, Congress extended the act to cover all civil wars, granted broader discretion to the president, excised the distinction between aggressor and victim nations, and imposed severe restrictions on citizens engaging in commercial activity in foreign countries at war. Although the act did not prohibit Americans from participating personally in foreign wars, those who sought to assist a foreign nation through arms, commerce, or financial aid were subject to criminal penalties, regardless of their motivations.

## ☆ 224 The Neutrality Act

50 Stat. 121 (1937).

*Resolved by the Senate and House of Representatives of the United States of America in Congress assembled,* That the joint resolution entitled "Joint resolution providing for the prohibition of the export of arms, ammunition, and implements of war to belligerent countries; the prohibition of the transportation of arms, ammunition, and implements of war by vessels of the United States for the use of belligerent states; for the registration and licensing of persons engaged in the business of manufacturing, exporting, or importing arms, ammunition, or implements of war; and restricting travel by American citizens on belligerent ships during war," approved August 31, 1935, as amended, is amended to read as follows:

### "EXPORT OF ARMS, AMMUNITION, AND IMPLEMENTS OF WAR

"SECTION 1. (a) Whenever the President shall find that there exists a state of war between, or among, two or more foreign states, the President shall proclaim such fact, and it shall thereafter be unlawful to export, or attempt to export, or cause to be exported, arms, ammunition, or implements of war from any place in the United States to any belligerent state named in such proclamation, or to any neutral state for transshipment to, or for the use of, any such belligerent state.

"(b) The President shall, from time to time, by proclamation, extend such embargo upon the export of arms, ammunition, or implements of war to other states as and when they may become involved in such war.

"(c) Whenever the President shall find that a state of civil strife exists in a foreign state and that such civil strife is of a magnitude or is being conducted under such conditions that the export of arms, ammunition, or implements of war from the United States to such foreign state would threaten or endanger the peace of the United States, the President shall proclaim such fact, and it shall thereafter be unlawful to export, or attempt to export, or cause to be exported, arms, ammunition, or implements of war from any place in the United States to

such foreign state, or to any neutral state for transshipment to, or for the use of, such foreign state.

\*             \*             \*

"(e) Whoever, in violation of any of the provisions of this Act, shall export, or attempt to export, or cause to be exported, arms, ammunition, or implements of war from the United States shall be fined not more than $10,000, or imprisoned not more than five years, or both, and the property vessel, or vehicle containing the same shall be [seized and forfeited].

\*             \*             \*

### "EXPORT OF OTHER ARTICLES AND MATERIALS

"SEC. 2. (a) Whenever the President shall have issued a proclamation under the authority of section 1 of this Act and he shall thereafter find that the placing of restrictions on the shipment of certain articles or materials in addition to arms, ammunition, and implements of war from the United States to belligerent states, or to a state wherein civil strife exists, is necessary to promote the security or preserve the peace of the United States or to protect the lives of citizens of the United States, he shall so proclaim, and it shall thereafter be unlawful, except under such limitations and exceptions as the President may prescribe ... for any American vessel to carry such articles or materials to any belligerent state, or to any state wherein civil strife exists, named in such proclamation issued under the authority of section 1 of this Act, or to any neutral state for transshipment to, or for the use of, any such belligerent state or any such state wherein civil strife exists. The President shall by proclamation from time to time definitely enumerate the articles and materials which it shall be unlawful for American vessels to so transport.

\*             \*             \*

### "FINANCIAL TRANSACTIONS

"SEC. 3. (a) Whenever the President shall have issued a proclamation under the authority of section 1 of this Act, it shall thereafter be unlawful for any person within the United States to purchase, sell, or exchange bonds, securities, or other obligations of the government of any belligerent state or of any state wherein civil strife exists, named in such proclamation, or of any political subdivision of any such state, or of any person acting for or on behalf of the government of any such state, or of any faction or asserted government within any such state wherein civil strife exists, or of any person acting for or on behalf of any faction or asserted government within any such state wherein civil strife exists, issued after the date of such proclamation, or to make any loan or extend any credit to any such government, political subdivision, faction, asserted government, or person, or to solicit or receive any contribution for any such government, political subdivision, faction, asserted government, or person: *Provided*, That if the President shall find that such action will serve to protect the commercial or other interests of the United States or its citizens, he may, in his discretion, and to such extent and under such regulations as he may prescribe, except from the operation of this section ordinary commercial credits and short-time obligations in aid of legal transactions and of a character customarily used in normal peacetime commercial transactions. Nothing in this subsection shall be construed to prohibit the solicitation or collection of funds to be used for medical aid and assistance, or for food and clothing to relieve human suffering, when such solicitation or collection of funds is made on behalf of and for use by any person or organization which is not acting for or on behalf of any such government, political subdivision, faction, or asserted government, but all such solicitations and collections of funds shall be subject to the approval of the President and shall be made under such rules and regulations as he shall prescribe.

\* \* \*

## "EXCEPTIONS—AMERICAN REPUBLICS

"SEC. 4. This Act shall not apply to an American republic or republics engaged in war against a non-American state or states, provided the American republic is not cooperating with a non-American state or states in such war.

## "NATIONAL MUNITIONS CONTROL BOARD

"SEC. 5. (a) There is hereby established a National Munitions Control Board (hereinafter referred to as the 'Board')....

"(b) Every person who engages in the business of manufacturing, exporting, or importing any of the arms, ammunition, or implements of war referred to in this Act, whether as an exporter, importer, manufacturer, or dealer, shall register with the Secretary of State his name, or business name, principal place of business, and places of business in the United States, and a list of the arms, ammunition, and implements of war which he manufactures, imports, or exports.

\* \* \*

"(d) It shall be unlawful for any person to export, or attempt to export, from the United States to any other state, any of the arms, ammunition, or implements of war referred to in this Act, or to import, or attempt to import, to the United States from any other state, any of the arms, ammunition, or implements of war referred to in this Act, without first having obtained a license [from the Secretary of State] therefor.

"(e) All persons required to register under this section shall maintain, subject to the inspection of the Secretary of State, or any person or persons designated by him, such permanent records of manufacture for export, importation, and exportation of arms, ammunition, and implements of war as the Secretary of State shall prescribe.

\* \* \*

"(g) Whenever the President shall have issued a proclamation under the authority of section 1 of this Act, all licenses theretofore issued under this Act shall ipso facto and immediately upon the issuance of such proclamation, cease to grant authority to export arms, ammunition, or implements of war from any place in the United States to any belligerent state, or to any state wherein civil strife exists, named in such proclamation, or to any neutral state for transshipment to, or for the use of, any such belligerent state or any such state wherein civil strife exists; and said licenses, insofar as the grant of authority to export to the state or states named in such proclamation is concerned, shall be null and void.

\* \* \*

## "AMERICAN VESSELS PROHIBITED FROM CARRYING ARMS TO BELLIGERENT STATES

"SEC. 6. (a) Whenever the President shall have issued a proclamation under the authority of section 1 of this Act, it shall thereafter be unlawful, until such proclamation is revoked, for any American vessel to carry any arms, ammunition, or implements of war to any belligerent state, or to any state wherein civil strife exists, named in such proclamation, or to any neutral state for transshipment to, or for the use of, any such belligerent state or any such state wherein civil strife exists.

"(b) Whoever, in violation of the provisions of this section, shall take, or attempt to take, or shall authorize, hire, or solicit another to take, any American vessel carrying such cargo out of port or from the jurisdiction of the United States shall be fined not more than $10,000, or imprisoned not more than five years, or both; and, in addition, such vessel, and her tackle, apparel, furniture, and equipment, and the arms, ammunition, and implements of war on board, shall be forfeited to the United States.

## "USE OF AMERICAN PORTS AS BASE OF SUPPLY

"SEC. 7. (a) Whenever, during any war in which the United States is neutral, the President, or any person thereunto authorized by him, shall have cause to believe that any vessel, domestic or foreign, whether requiring clearance or not, is about to carry out of a port of the United States, fuel, men, arms, ammunition, implements of war, or other supplies to any warship, tender, or supply ship of a belligerent state, but the evidence is not deemed sufficient to justify forbidding the departure of the vessel, . . . and if, in the President's judgment, such action will serve to maintain peace between the United States and foreign states, or to protect the commercial interests of the United States and its citizens, or to promote the security or neutrality of the United States, he shall have the power and it shall be his duty to require the owner, master, or person in command thereof, before departing from a port of the United States, to give a bond to the United States, with sufficient sureties, in such amount as he shall deem proper, conditioned that the vessel will not deliver the men, or any part of the cargo, to any warship, tender, or supply ship of a belligerent state.

"(b) If the President, or any person thereunto authorized by him, shall find that a vessel, domestic or foreign, in a port of the United States, has previously cleared from a port of the United States during such war and delivered its cargo or any part thereof to a warship, tender, or supply ship of a belligerent state, he may prohibit the departure of such vessel during the duration of the war.

\*         \*         \*

"TRAVEL ON VESSELS OF BELLIGERENT STATES

"SEC. 9. Whenever the President shall have issued a proclamation under the authority of section 1 of this Act it shall thereafter be unlawful for any citizen of the United States to travel on any vessel of the state or states named in such proclamation, except in accordance with such rules and regulations as the President shall prescribe: *Provided, however,* That the provisions of this section shall not apply to a citizen of the United States traveling on a vessel whose voyage was begun in advance of the date of the President's proclamation, and who had no opportunity to discontinue his voyage after that date: *And provided further,* That they shall not apply under ninety days after the date of the President's proclamation to a citizen of the United States returning from a foreign state to the United States. Whenever, in the President's judgment, the conditions which have caused him to issue his proclamation have ceased to exist, he shall revoke his proclamation and the provisions of this section shall thereupon cease to apply with respect to the state or states named in such proclamation, except with respect to offenses committed prior to such revocation.

"ARMING OF AMERICAN MERCHANT VESSELS PROHIBITED

"SEC. 10. Whenever the President shall have issued a proclamation under the authority of section 1, it shall thereafter be unlawful, until such proclamation is revoked, for any American vessel engaged in commerce with any belligerent state, or any state wherein civil strife exists, named in such proclamation, to be armed or to carry any armament, arms, ammunition, or implements of war, except small arms and ammunition therefor which the President may deem necessary and shall publicly designate for the preservation of discipline aboard such vessels."

\*         \*         \*

*Approved, May 1, 1937, 6:30 p.m. Central Standard Time.*

## 225 "smashing . . . strike demonstrators" (1937)

The growing determination of the labor unions, aided by the new legislation and government policies under the New Deal, increased the zeal of the drive to organize industrial workers. Although by 1937 such employers as General Motors and United States Steel had come to accept unions, many others strongly continued to oppose labor organizers. When the Steel Workers Organizing Committee called a strike against its opposition, Republic Steel decided to continue its operations by relying on nonstrikers. In response, some two thousand to three thousand strikers decided to march on the Republic plant in south Chicago and picket it. When the labor column, singing labor songs and chanting "CIO," neared the mill, they were stopped by the police. Violence erupted. The police opened fire on the crowd—five people were killed instantly and five others later died of their wounds. Six of the dead were shot in the back. Fifty-eight strikers and sixteen policemen were injured.

The police claimed they had fired in self-defense against a bloodthirsty armed mob of agitators and communists. None of the marchers was charged with possession of guns. The march was filmed by Paramount Pictures and was given a congressional screening by order of Senator Robert La Follette, who then was investigating violations of free speech and the rights of labor. The following document contains an account of the screening by a reporter for the *St. Louis Post-Dispatch* on June 16, 1937.

☆ 225 Memorial Day Massacre

*St. Louis Post-Dispatch,* reprinted in Richard Hofstadter and Michael Wallace, eds., *American Violence: A Documentary History* (New York: Knopf, 1970), 180-81.

WASHINGTON, June 16—Five agents of the La Follette Civil Liberties Committee, headed by Robert Wohlforth, the committee's secretary, arrived in Chicago yesterday to begin an investigation of the tragic events of Memorial Day, when nine persons were killed or fatally wounded by city police in smashing an attempt by steel strike demonstrators to march past the Republic Steel Co. plant in South Chicago.

Appearance of the committee's agents on the scene coincided with the death of the ninth victim, a 17-year-old boy reported to have joined the pickets in the hope of getting a job in the mill after settlement of the strike.

It was learned today that the committee's decision to proceed with the inquiry was hastened by the private showing here last week of a suppressed newsreel, in which the police attack on the demonstrators is graphically recorded. The committee obtained possession of the film in New York, after its maker, the Paramount Co., had announced that it would not be exhibited publicly, for fear of inciting riots throughout the country.

*Senators Shocked by Scenes.* The showing of the film here was conducted with the utmost secrecy. The audience was almost limited to Senators La Follette (Prog.), Wisconsin, and Thomas (Dem.), Utah, who compose the committee, and members of the staff. Those who saw it were shocked and amazed by scenes showing scores of uniformed policemen firing their revolvers pointblank into a dense crowd of men, women, and children, and then pursuing and clubbing the survivors unmercifully as they made frantic efforts to escape.

The impression produced by these fearful scenes was heightened by the sound record which accompanies the picture, reproducing the roar of police fire and the screams of the victims. It was run off several times for the scrutiny of the investigators, and at each showing they detected additional instances of "frightfulness." It is expected to be of extraordinary value in identifying individual policemen and their victims. The film itself evidently is an outstanding example of camera reporting under difficult conditions.

# 226 "cruel and inhuman punishment" (1938)

Despite occasional anti-alien sentiments and the Chinese Exclusion Acts, for most of its history the United States had adhered to a generous immigration policy. The country's total open door policy ended, however, with the Immigration and Naturalization Act of 1917 and the imposition of quotas on aliens in 1921. Thereafter, an alien had to meet strict criteria and qualify under the quota or face exclusion or deportation. Many political refugees who could not qualify were to be turned away, often with nowhere to go except back to face confinement or death.

In the late 1920s and 1930s, a series of cases challenging Immigration and Naturalization Service de-

portation orders on the grounds of a right to political asylum reached the courts. The courts invariably denied the existence of such a right under American law. Despite pleas by refugees for protection from the oppression of fascism, courts upheld the deportation orders. But in a case that was strongly condemned (yet never reversed or overruled), District Judge Philip L. Sullivan recognized the existence of political repression and found a constitutional justification for granting relief from deportation.

☆ 226 *United States ex rel. Weinberg v. Scholtfeldt*

26 F. Supp. 283 (N.D. Ill. 1938).

SULLIVAN, District Judge.

\* \* \*

The record discloses that the relator is a jew, thirty-one years of age, having been born in that part of Austria Hungary which is now Czechoslovakia; . . . He (the relator) was married to a United States citizen, but after their marriage they separated when he learned that his wife had formerly given birth to an illegitimate child. The record further discloses that he has never been on relief but has always worked and supported himself; that he has never been arrested except that he was once fined for a traffic violation; and that he has never been guilty of a crime involving moral turpitude.

It is a matter of common knowledge that at the present time in Central Europe the jews are being persecuted, their property confiscated and that they are obliged to seek sanctuary in other countries.

Under conditions as they now exist it would be cruel and inhuman punishment to deport this petitioner to Czechoslovakia, belonging as he does to the race which is thus being persecuted and exiled, especially when the charge against him is that at the time of his entry into the United States he was not in possession of an unexpired immigration visa. I do not believe that the immigration laws contemplate any such strict compliance with the letter thereof, as would oblige the court to return at this time a jew to a country where his property would be confiscated, where his life might be in jeopardy, and from which, if he were permitted to enter it at all, he would be forced immediately to flee.

The prayer of the petition for habeas corpus is granted, the petition is sustained, and petitioner discharged from custody.

## 227 Those Inherent and Fundamental Rights That Distinguish This Country from All Foreign Nations (1938-1940)

The economic recovery promised to America by the New Deal was not a speedy process. In 1934, over a year after Franklin D. Roosevelt's inauguration, more than eleven million Americans were still out of work and between sixteen and eighteen million were on the relief rolls. By the end of 1937, the unemployed continued to number nine million, and the economy's new downswing gave rise to the term "recession."

By 1938 tensions in Europe mounted as Hitler's Germany annexed Austria and occupied the Sudetenland in Czechoslovakia. The spread of racism in Europe and the organization of domestic fascist organizations seemingly adherent to their overseas counterparts caused growing concern in the late 1930s. Several congressional committees had investigated these organizations, but in 1938 a new special committee formed. Popularly known as the Dies Committee after its chairman, Martin Dies of Texas, its activities and tactics received much criticism. Dies seemed more interested in the exposure of communist and socialist activities than fascist ones and complained that the federal government contained "hundreds of left-wingers and radicals who do not believe in our system of private enterprise" and that there were "two thousand outright Communists and Partyliners ... in the government in Washington."

Although the Dies Committee had the duty to investigate "the extent, character, and objects of un-American propaganda activities in the United States," the congressional debate reflected the difficulty of defining the meaning of "un-American." In 1945, the Dies Committee became the standing House Committee on Un-American Activities.

### ☆ 227 The Dies Committee on Un-American Activities

☆ 227a  Debate on H.R. Res. No. 282, 75th Cong., 3d Sess., 83 Cong. Rec. 7568 (May 26, 1938)

The Clerk read the resolution, as follows:

#### HOUSE RESOLUTION 282

*Resolved*, That the Speaker of the House of Representatives be, and he is hereby, authorized to appoint a special committee to be composed of seven members for the purpose of conducting an investigation of (1) the extent, character, and objects of un-American propaganda activities in the United States, (2) the diffusion within the United States of subversive and un-American propaganda that is instigated from foreign countries or of a domestic origin and attacks the principle of the form of govern-ment as guaranteed by our Constitution, and (3) all other questions in relation thereto that would aid Congress in any necessary remedial legislation.

\*     \*     \*

Mr. DIES. ... I have often believed that the distinction between the American form of government and the forms of government which prevail in many European countries is the conception we have in America that we derive fundamental and inherent rights not from society, not from governments, but from Almighty God, and having derived those fundamental rights from God, no man or no majority of men can deprive us of the inherent right to worship God according to the dictates of our conscience or to speak our opinions and our convictions as we feel them. I can assure the House here and now that if I have anything to do with this investigation it will in no sense be an effort to abridge the undisputed right of every citizen in the United States to express his honest convictions and enjoy freedom of speech.

\*     \*     \*

Now, I know the argument will be used, What is the value of an investigation? I have a mass of information that has been supplied to me that is shocking, information which shows the extent of the Nazi and Communist movements in the United States. I am not one of those who are inclined to be alarmists. I am not inclined to look under every bed for a Communist, but I can say to this House that there is in my possession a mass of information showing the establishment and operation of some 32 Nazi camps in the United States, that all of these camps have been paid for, that they claim a total membership of 480,000, that they assemble in these camps, and I have seen photographs that have been furnished from various sources showing the fact that in these camps men are marching and saluting the swastika, if that is the proper word for it. Not only is this true, but I have information in my possession that certain individuals and groups in America have contributed funds for the purpose of encouraging the Fascist or Nazi movement in this country, and may I say in that connection that so far as I am concerned I regard communism and nazi-ism and fascism as having one underlying principle—dictatorship—the theory that government should have the right to control the lives, the fortunes, the happiness, the beliefs, and every detail of the life of the human being, and that man is a pawn of the government, rather than the American conception that government is created for the benefit of mankind.

\*     \*     \*

Mr. TAYLOR of Tennessee.

\*     \*     \*

When we investigated Nazi and other propaganda pursuant to House resolution 198, Seventy-third Congress, the Nazi organization in this country was known as "the friends of New Germany." While at that time their activities were a gross prostitution of the privileges which they were accorded in this country, nevertheless there were few signs of militarism in their maneuvers. But ... under the new designation—German-American Bund—they [Nazis] have vastly increased their number, have acquired by purchase some 30 camp sites where they carry on military training schools attired in a foreign uniform and under a foreign flag. I understand that in these camps they assemble the youths on the holy Sabbath and teach them to goose-step and heil Hitler. I understand that as a feeble pretense they sometimes have an American flag inconspicuously displayed, but it is so deluged with drapery bearing the swastika insignia that our flag dwindles into comparative insignificance.

Mr. Speaker, we have no place in our scheme of government for dual citizenship. We must be either American or alien. There can be no qualification or reservation when it comes to allegiance to our flag and to our country. No man can maintain allegiance to the United States and at the same time bear allegiance to some foreign king, potentate, or dictator no more than he can serve both God and mammon. Such a performance is a sheer mockery "of the purest ray serene," and it is the purpose of this investigation to develop the facts to the end that the necessary legislation may be enacted to put a stop to this sort of skullduggery. [Applause.]

Think of it, Mr. Speaker, American soil, purchased undoubtedly with foreign money, dedicated and used as camps in which to assemble, and clad in a foreign uniform, under a foreign flag, and to the music of foreign military airs, hail a foreign ruler, and drill and parade in the honor, and at least constructively, in the service of a foreign government.

*       *       *

Mr. Speaker, it is nigh unto inconceivable that such a travesty could happen here in this proud, intelligent, and patriotic country. It is a menace to good citizenship. It is a national scandal and must be eradicated in the name of national decency, if nothing more.

Aside from the military aspects of the bund, it preaches intolerance, bigotry, and race and religious persecution. This conduct violates the sacred tenets upon which our Government was founded—race, color, and creed are made inviolable under the terms of the Bill of Rights, which is our ark of the covenant.

*       *       *

Mr. Speaker, a few days ago, in the Madison Square Roof Garden in New York City, 18,000 militant Communists assembled, denounced and advocated the overthrow of this Republic, and sang the Communist anthem, the Internationale, with red flags flying and Old Glory only conspicuous by absence. Communist radicals recently for the second time had the unmitigated audacity and depravity to desecrate that hallowed shrine sacred to every red-blooded American—Plymouth Rock—by enveloping it in red paint. The miserable wretches who committed this dastardly deed ought to be hunted down like rattlesnakes and kicked out of the country. [Applause.]

One thing is certain, Mr. Speaker, unless we arrest this insidious un-American influence, it is only a question of a short time until a revolution will ensue and the soil of our great country will be soaked in blood. Incendiary and un-American propaganda is being smuggled into this country by truckloads. Members of the American Legion and other patriotic organizations who are trying to suppress this deadly menace single-handed are being clubbed and sent to the hospital by these alien racketeers. It is up to Congress to do something. Why sit we here idle and supine, so to speak, when the very soul of this Republic is being violated and debauched. It is not only our responsibility, but it is our duty to ourselves, to our flag, and to our country to act now before it is too late.

*       *       *

One of the chief reasons which inspired my ambition to come to Congress was to help stop the indiscriminate flow of immigration to this country. Mr. Speaker, we have hundreds of thousands of good citizens in this country who were born abroad.... They availed themselves of the first opportunity to renounce foreign political ties and become naturalized American citizens. But, on the contrary, Mr. Speaker, we have millions of others who came over imbued with an entirely different spirit and different viewpoint. They care nothing about America or American institutions and traditions. They wanted to exploit America for their own selfish benefit and gratification. They never tried to become assimilated. They did not want to be absorbed; and that is one of our problems today. They have never become citizens, and hundreds of thousands of them are a burden to our society—inmates of jails, asylums, and other public institutions. They have jammed our relief rolls at the expense and to the exclusion of worthy native-born and naturalized citizens.

*       *       *

... [D]uring the last years of the Hoover administration more aliens were deported when added to the number who voluntarily departed than the total number admitted for the same period. For instance, in 1932 there were 19,426 deportations of aliens, whereas in 1934, under Mme. Perkins, Secretary of Labor, the number had dwindled to 8,879; and yet there are nearly a million—some estimates say more than 3,000,000—aliens in this country illegally, from whose ranks the Communist Party draws a considerable part of its following. There is in this country a large alien-minded element which wants to break down the quota barriers against restricted immigration and open the gates wide to the riff-raff of Europe. . . .

                    *         *         *

Mr. COFFEE of Washington.

                    *         *         *

I want to know who is going to define "un-American." What are its economic and political connotations? What infallible instrument or high tribunal of justice will lay down a definition which will be accepted by the American people? "Un-American" is a relative term. What was American 75 years ago is un-American today and vice versa. This country was founded upon the recognition of the doctrine of free speech and its preservation against all hazards.

                    *         *         *

Who is un-American now? Oh, I recall we had the Fish committee a few years ago, which was a witch-pursuing expedition designed to hold up to public obloquy and condemnation every liberal political organization in the United States. Then we had another, a Democratic committee, the McCormack committee. Are we going to repeat now? My God, the whole Nation is crying out for succor in its [financial] distress, . . . and you spend the solemn time of the House of Representatives, in the ninth year of the depression, in trying to investigate what you characterize as un-American activities. To what a low degree have we sunk in the legislative chambers of the Congress of the United States.

                    *         *         *

The last sentence on the first page of the Dies resolution states that "All other questions in relation thereto shall be investigated by the committee." Where are we going to stop on this snooping, punitive expedition? Are we going to open up the whole field of political and economic endeavor in the United States? . . .

                    *         *         *

. . . [M]y distrust of this legislation gravitates from my fear that it is aimed at progressive movements, parties, ideas. Inveighing at communism per se is a puerile pastime. Attempting to eliminate the social injustices which breed discontent is a laudable objective. Let us engage in that pursuit. Let us decline to temporize and refuse to embark upon running after will-o'-the-wisps when there are mountains of ice and apathy around us to melt.

                    *         *         *

Mr. MCCORMACK. . . . One of the speakers has talked about the Fish committee as a "red baiting" committee. I caution that distinguished gentleman that the use of names is a dangerous field to enter

into and is also a sign of weakness. Mr. FISH is not a "red baiter." You know when one calls a man a "red baiter" he can call someone else a "red lover." I simply refer to this so that some of our friends who have a tendency to enter into the field of personalities may realize in the future that when they open the issue the other fellow has a chance to say something in return.

                    *         *         *

What is un-American in the political field is entirely different from that is un-American so far as the basic fundamentals of our country are concerned.

                    *         *         *

Mr. O'MALLEY. Can the gentleman assure us that if this committee is created we will have a membership of gentlemen who would be able to distinguish, like the gentleman does, between what is un-American or otherwise?

Mr. MCCORMACK. . . . [O]f course, I cannot answer the gentleman's question.

                    *         *         *

Mr. BOILEAU. Does the gentleman agree with me that about the only thing that is un-American is the advocacy of the overthrow of our form of government by force and violence?

Mr. MCCORMACK. I think the gentleman made a very fine contribution to this debate, but there is just one further field I might suggest to my friend. . . . [T]here should be included the activities of foreign agencies in the United States seeking to mold public opinion or to form group action, not for the purpose of the overthrow of the Government but for the purpose of influencing the domestic or the external policies of our Government. Such activities are equally subversive of our institutions. . . .

☆ 227b  Report of the Dies Committee: H.R. Rep. No. 1476, 76th Cong., 3d Sess. (1940)

### INTRODUCTION

There is at present taking place in the world a struggle between democracy on the one hand and dictatorship on the other, upon the outcome of which the future of human liberties in the next few centuries may well depend.

. . . It is of primary importance to prevent the growth or spread of influence of . . . dictatorship of whatever sort. . . . But it is at least equally important that . . . nothing be done which would undermine the fundamental structure of constitutional liberty itself.

One method which can and should from time to time be used is the method of investigation to inform the American people of the activities of [subversive] organizations in their nation. This is the real purpose of the House Committee to Investigate un-

American Activities. By un-American activities we mean organizations or groups existing in the United States which are directed, controlled or subsidized by foreign governments or agencies and which seek to change the policies and form of government of the United States in accordance with the wishes of such foreign governments.

\*   \*   \*

... The committee finds that the danger to American democracy lies not only in the rather remote possibility that Communists, Nazis, or Fascists will succeed in a frontal attack on our Constitutional government and overthrow it, but also in the much greater chance that each extreme totalitarian group seeking by deception to advance its own cause and pad its ranks will succeed in convincing a really substantial number of people that their only defense against violence from the opposite extreme is to accept the violence of the one they find least objectionable.

\*   \*   \*

The committee's work should result in freeing the progressive and labor movements from Communist control or domination and in preventing sincere conservatives from temporizing with essentially Fascist or Nazi groups or philosophies.... The committee wishes to state emphatically that the only proper and democratic method whereby un-American activities can be effectively combatted is by the duly constituted law-enforcing bodies of America operating under our Constitution and with the support of an informed public opinion.

### THE PROBLEM OF THE LABOR MOVEMENT

... In [1934] ... the attempt was made by Communists to bore from within the American Federation of Labor. On the whole this effort met with but slight success.

With the formation of the C.I.O. the principal efforts of the Communists were turned in the direction of that organization. It is unmistakably clear that the overwhelming majority of the members of the C.I.O. as well as its president are not Communists or Communist sympathizers.... The evidence before the committee indicates, however, that the leadership of some 10 or 12 of the constituent unions of the C.I.O. out of a total of some 48 unions is more than tinged with communism. The evidence shows that some of their leaders are either card-holding members of the Communist Party or subservient followers of that party's "line." In the rank and file membership of these unions, on the contrary, the proportion of Communists and Communist sympathizers is very small indeed. There is encouraging evidence of an attempt on the part of the C.I.O. leadership to remove this Communist influence and it is a matter of record that most of its largest organizations are free of any Communist control, domination, or even serious influence....

\*   \*   \*

... [T]he Communist Party is interested in trade-unions primarily for the purpose of attempting to utilize those labor organizations for the benefit of the Russian dictatorship and its foreign policies.

### NAZI-FASCIST ORGANIZATIONS

\*   \*   \*

... These groups and organizations make their chief appeal to the basest forms of religious and racial hatred. They promise to deliver this country from the menace of communism; they heap scorn upon the institutions of democracy; and they urge the short cuts of force and violence.

### THE GERMAN-AMERICAN BUND

.. [T]he German-American Bund receives its inspiration, program, and direction from the Nazi Government of Germany through the various propaganda organizations which have been set up by that Government and which function under the control and supervision of the Nazi Ministry of Propaganda and Enlightenment.

... Fritz Kuhn ["fuehrer" of the Bund] testified that the bund has a membership of approximately 20,000 to 25,000. (A Department of Justice investigation made of the bund in 1937 placed the membership at 6,500.) In addition to the regular membership, it has what is known as the sympathizer or "fellow traveler" group, consisting of those who are sympathetic to the bund but do not actively participate in its proceedings. He testified that the sympathizer group is composed of approximately 80,000 to 100,000 individuals.

\*   \*   \*

It was established ... that the bund had worked sympathetically with other organizations throughout the United States and cooperates with them. Kuhn testified that some of these groups are the Christian Front, the Christian Mobilizers, the Christian Crusaders, the Social Justice Society, the Silver Shirt Legion of America, the Knights of the White Camelia and various Italian Fascist, White Russian and Ukrainian organizations.

### CHAPTER 8

\*   \*   \*

# The World War II Era

## 1939-1946

As war approached, Congress enacted legislation to secure the loyalties of federal employees and to prevent interference with the military and war objectives. Ironically, the laws were enforced more often against those of communist or other leftist leanings than those of rightist persuasion, who in the minds of most people appeared to be the potential wartime enemies. At the onset of war the loyalties of the citizenry similarly were subjected to scrutiny at the state level. Those who routinely declined either to swear or to discuss their allegiance to the country and its Constitution, or who refused their services to the war effort, were subjected to quasi-criminal pains and penalties.

In the Supreme Court, the success of the government's measures against politically suspect activities was mixed. The main record of the challenges to these restrictive laws is contained in the following chapter. But the major focus of this chapter is the use of executive and military power to supplement or supplant the common course of civilian law in order to avoid the constitutional strictures upon the exercise of governmental power. This phenomenon is documented best in the materials on the Japanese evacuation and internment, as military law and authority were utilized to uproot and confine thousands of American citizens and residents on an unspecified suspicion of their political loyalty. While the government acted in a more circumspect manner against enemy aliens, many of those interned for their Japanese ancestry were citizens of the United States.

The government's proclivity for avoiding the constraints of the ordinary civil law when dealing with political offenders is illustrated further by other documents. Some of these contrast the difficulties of sustaining a conviction for treason in the civilian system with the relative ease of accomplishing the same result through invocation of martial law or the law of war in military tribunals. Alternative methods of imposing sanctions on politically suspect individuals are suggested by the psychiatric solution in the Ezra Pound case. One should note the growing number of judicial opinions among the documents, as the courts increasingly began considering constitutional challenges to the use of governmental power against political offenders.

---

## 228 "the overthrow of our constitutional form of government" (1939)

President Roosevelt's January 4, 1939, message to Congress emphasized the threat that the growing strength of the totalitarian nations posed to world peace. In March 1939, the Spanish Republic fell to the Fascist forces, and Germany moved into Czechoslovakia, claiming disorder in that country threatened German nationals. After concluding a nonaggression treaty with the Soviet Union, Adolf Hitler, on September 1, commenced a blitzkrieg against Poland.

On August 2, 1939, Congress passed the Hatch Act, sponsored by Senator Carl Hatch of New Mexico, forbidding federal civil servants from taking an active part in political parties and campaigns. But the first prohibition of federal employment based on party membership was written also into this civil service reform. The Civil Service Commission, responsible for administering the Hatch act, interpreted Section 9A, which prohibited federal employees from being members of a party that advocated "the overthrow of our constitutional form of government," to preclude federal employment of members of "the Communist Party, the German Bund, or any other Communist, Nazi or Fascist organization." By 1942, the Civil Service Commission concluded that being a "follower" of Communism raised a "strong presumption" against one's loyalty to the government of the United States.

### ☆ 228 An Act to Prevent Pernicious Political Activities (The Hatch Act)

53 Stat. 1147 (1939).

*Be it enacted by the Senate and House of Representatives of the United States of America in Congress assembled, That. . . .*

\*　　　\*　　　\*

SEC. 8. Any person who violates any of the foregoing provisions of this Act upon conviction thereof shall be fined not more than $1,000 or imprisoned for not more than one year, or both.

SEC. 9. (a) It shall be unlawful for any person employed in the executive branch of the Federal Government, or any agency or department thereof, to use his official authority or influence for the purpose of interfering with an election or affecting the result thereof. No officer or employee in the executive branch of the Federal Government, or any agency or department thereof, shall take any active part in political management or in political campaigns. All such persons shall retain the right to vote as they may choose and to express their opinions on all political subjects. For the purposes of this section the term "officer" or "employee" shall not be construed to include (1) the President and Vice President of the United States; (2) persons whose compensation is paid from the appropriation for the office of the President; (3) heads and assistant heads of executive departments; (4) officers who are appointed by the President, by and with the advice and consent of the Senate, and who determine policies to be pursued by the United States in its relations with foreign powers or in the Nation-wide administration of Federal laws.

(b) Any person violating the provisions of this section shall be immediately removed from the position or office held by him, and thereafter no part of the funds appropriated by any Act of Congress for such position or office shall be used to pay the compensation of such person.

SEC. 9A. (1) It shall be unlawful for any person employed in any capacity by any agency of the Federal Government, whose compensation, or any part thereof, is paid from funds authorized or appropriated by any Act of Congress, to have membership in any political party or organization which advocates the overthrow of our constitutional form of government in the United States.

(2) Any person violating the provisions of this section shall be immediately removed from the position or office held by him, and thereafter no part of the funds appropriated by any Act of Congress for such position or office shall be used to pay the compensation of such person.

*       *       *

*Approved, August 2, 1939, 11:50 a.m., E.S.T.*

## 229 To "teach the . . . propriety of overthrowing or destroying any government in the United States by force" (1940)

Congressional concern over foreign influences in the United States also manifested itself through passage of the Alien Registration Act of 1940, requiring all aliens to be fingerprinted and register annually. Nevertheless, Title I of this enactment, the so-called

Smith Act, was not restricted to aliens. This act, named after Congressman Howard W. Smith of Virginia, was the first peacetime federal sedition law since the Alien and Sedition Acts of 1798. Congress modeled the act after the New York Criminal Anarchy Act of 1902 and prohibited speech or publications that advocated or taught the "duty, necessity, desirability, or propriety" of overthrowing any level of government "by force or violence." Enacted in the year in which Hitler occupied Paris, the Smith Act, reminiscent also of the 1917 Espionage Act, was one of many steps which began to make Americans expect that war was virtually at hand.

## ☆ 229 An Act to Prohibit Certain Subversive Activities (The Smith Act)

54 Stat. 670 (1940).

*Be it enacted by the Senate and House of Representatives of the United States of America in Congress assembled,*

TITLE I

SECTION 1. (a) It shall be unlawful for any person, with intent to interfere with, impair, or influence the loyalty, morale, or discipline of the military or naval forces of the United States—

(1) to advise, counsel, urge, or in any manner cause insubordination, disloyalty, mutiny, or refusal of duty by any member of the military or naval forces of the United States; or

(2) to distribute any written or printed matter which advises, counsels, or urges insubordination, disloyalty, mutiny, or refusal of duty by any member of the military or naval forces of the United States.

*       *       *

SEC. 2. (a) It shall be unlawful for any person—

(1) to knowingly or willfully advocate, abet, advise, or teach the duty, necessity, desirability, or propriety of overthrowing or destroying any government in the United States by force or violence, or by the assassination of any officer of any such government;

(2) with the intent to cause the overthrow or destruction of any government in the United States, to print, publish, edit, issue, circulate, sell, distribute, or publicly display any written or printed matter advocating, advising, or teaching the duty, necessity, desirability, or propriety of overthrowing or destroying any government in the United States by force or violence;

(3) to organize or help to organize any society, group, or assembly of persons who teach, advocate, or encourage the overthrow or destruction of any government in the United States by force or violence; or to be or become a member of, or affiliate with, any such society, group, or assembly of persons, knowing the purposes thereof.

(b) For the purposes of this section, the term "government in the United States" means the Government of the United States, the government of any State, Territory, or possession of the United States, the government of the District of Columbia, or the government of any political subdivision of any of them.

SEC. 3. It shall be unlawful for any person to attempt to commit, or to conspire to commit, any of the acts prohibited by the provisions of this title.

*           *           *

SEC. 5. (a) Any person who violates any of the provisions of this title shall, upon conviction thereof, be fined not more than $10,000 or imprisoned for not more than ten years, or both.

(b) No person convicted of violating any of the provisions of this title shall, during the five years next following his conviction, be eligible for employment by the United States, or by any department or agency thereof (including any corporation the stock of which is wholly owned by the United States).

*           *           *

*Approved, June 28, 1940.*

## 230 "All alien enemies are enjoined to preserve the peace" (1941)

On December 7, 1941, Japanese naval and air forces attacked Pearl Harbor, bringing to an end the peaceful but strained American-Japanese relations that had existed since the 1937 Japanese drive into China. The United States declared war on Japan the following day. President Franklin D. Roosevelt issued Proclamation Number 2525 restricting the travel and other movements of Japanese aliens in the United States and authorizing civil and military authorities to detain all suspicious aliens. Subsequent proclamations affected German and Italian aliens at the commencement of war with their countries. The United States authorities initially directed security measures against all alien enemies. But as the War Department gradually assumed control over this program, it directed more resources toward the Japanese.

During the first year of the United States' entry into World War II, 12,071 alien enemies were arrested. Of this number, government attorneys released 3,567 after a preliminary investigation. On the recommendation of the hearing boards, the attorney general placed 2,933 on parole, released 1,048 outright, and ordered 3,646 interned for the duration of the war. Of those interned pursuant to this proclamation, 1,974 were of Japanese ancestry. These detentions differed from the subsequent evacuation programs, which applied to all Japanese collectively and permitted no individual determina-

tions of loyalty until after the detainees reached Relocation Centers.

## ☆ 230 Alien Enemies — Japanese: Proclamation of President Franklin D. Roosevelt

55 Stat. 1700 (1941).

### AUTHORITY

WHEREAS it is provided by Section 21 of Title 50 of the United States Code as follows:

Whenever there is a declared war between the United States and any foreign nation or government, ... all natives, citizens, denizens, or subjects of the hostile nation or government, being of the age of fourteen years and upward who shall be within the United States and not actually naturalized, shall be liable to be apprehended, restrained, secured, and removed as alien enemies....

### PROCLAMATION

NOW, THEREFORE, I, FRANKLIN D. ROOSEVELT, as President of the United States, and as Commander in Chief of the Army and Navy of the United States, do hereby make public proclamation to all whom it may concern that an invasion has been perpetrated upon the territory of the United States by the Empire of Japan.

### *Conduct to Be Observed by Alien Enemies*

... I do hereby further proclaim and direct that the conduct to be observed on the part of the United States toward all natives, citizens, denizens or subjects of the Empire of Japan being of the age of fourteen years and upwards who shall be within the United States or within any territories in any way subject to the jurisdiction of the United States and not actually naturalized, who for the purpose of this Proclamation and under such sections of the United States Code are termed alien enemies, shall be as follows:

All alien enemies are enjoined to preserve the peace towards the United States and to refrain from crime against the public safety, and from violating the laws of the United States and of the States and Territories thereof; and to refrain from actual hostility or giving information, aid or comfort to the enemies of the United States or interfering by word or deed with the defense of the United States or the political processes and public opinions thereof; and to comply strictly with the regulations which are hereby or which may be from time to time promulgated by the President.

*           *           *

### *Regulations*

... I hereby declare and establish the following regulations which I find necessary in the premises and for the public safety:

(1) No alien enemy shall enter or be found within the Canal Zone and no alien enemy shall enter or leave the Hawaiian Islands or the Philippine Islands except under such regulations as the Secretary of War shall from time to time prescribe.

\*          \*          \*

(5) No alien enemy shall have in his possession, custody or control at any time or place or use or operate any of the following enumerated articles:

   a. Firearms.

   b. Weapons or implements of war or component parts thereof.

   c. Ammunition.

   d. Bombs.

   e. Explosives or material used in the manufacture of explosives.

   f. Short-wave radio receiving sets.

   g. Transmitting sets.

   h. Signal devices.

   i. Codes or ciphers.

   j. Cameras.

   k. Papers, documents or books in which there may be invisible writing; photograph, sketch, picture, drawing, map or graphical representation of any military or naval installations or equipment or of any arms, ammunition, implements of war, device or thing used or intended to be used in the combat equipment of the land or naval forces of the United States or of any military or naval post, camp or station.

All such property found in the possession of any alien enemy in violation of the foregoing regulations shall be subject to seizure and forfeiture.

(6) No alien enemy shall undertake any air flight or ascend into the air in any airplane, aircraft or balloon of any sort whether owned governmentally, commercially or privately, except that travel by an alien enemy in an airplane or aircraft may be authorized by the Attorney General, or his representative, or the Secretary of War, or his representative. . . .

(7) Alien enemies deemed dangerous to the public peace or safety of the United States by the Attorney General or the Secretary of War, as the case may be, are subject to summary apprehension.

\*          \*          \*

(10) With respect to the continental United States, Alaska, Puerto Rico, and the Virgin Islands, an alien enemy shall not change his place of abode or occupation or otherwise travel or move from place to place without full compliance with any such regulations as the Attorney General of the United States may, from time to time, make and declare. . . .

(11) With respect to the Canal Zone, the Hawaiian Islands and the Philippine Islands, an alien enemy shall not change his place of abode or occupation or otherwise travel or move from place to place without full compliance with any such regulations as the Secretary of War may, from time to time, make and declare. . . .

(12) No alien enemy shall enter or be found in or upon any highway, waterway, airway, railway, railroad, subway, public utility, building, place or thing not open and accessible to the public generally, and not generally used by the public.

(13) No alien enemy shall be a member or an officer of, or affiliated with, any organization, group or assembly hereafter designated by the Attorney General, nor shall any alien enemy advocate, defend or subscribe to the acts, principles or policies thereof, attend any meetings, conventions or gatherings thereof or possess or distribute any literature, propaganda or other writings or productions thereof.

\*          \*          \*

Done at the City of Washington this 7th day of December, in the year of our Lord nineteen hundred and forty-one and of the Independence of the United States of America the one hundred and sixty-sixth.

Franklin D. Roosevelt

## 231 "every possible protection" (1942)

On February 19, 1942, two months after Pearl Harbor, President Roosevelt issued Executive Order 9066 authorizing the establishment of defense zones within the United States. The order further gave military commanders unbridled discretion to exclude persons from such zones or to restrict their activities therein. Most of the states of California, Oregon, and Washington officially constituted the Pacific Defense Zone.

The speed of the Japanese takeover of the Western Pacific after Pearl Harbor was shocking, and the fear of a Japanese invasion was very strong. False alarms of approaching Japanese submarines and bombers affected West Coast cities. Although no acts of sabotage by Japanese-Americans were ever reported, some believed the racial and cultural loyalties of this easily-identifiable ethnic group would supersede their political allegiance and "a nationwide tornado of destruction" would ensue.

Under the authority of this seemingly simple order, United States military forces evacuated all persons of Japanese ancestry from the Pacific Coast. The armed forces removed 112,000 Japanese, some 70,000 of whom were American citizens (many native-born), from their homes, placed them in temporary collection points, and subsequently shipped them to barbed-wire-enclosed Relocation Centers for internment.

## ☆231 President Roosevelt's Executive Order 9066

3.C.F.R. 1092 (Feb. 19, 1942).

### AUTHORIZING THE SECRETARY OF WAR TO PRESCRIBE MILITARY AREAS

WHEREAS the successful prosecution of the war requires every possible protection against espionage and against sabotage to national-defense material, national-defense premises, and national-defense utilities. . . .

NOW, THEREFORE, by virtue of the authority vested in me as President of the United States, and Commander in Chief of the Army and Navy, I hereby authorize and direct the Secretary of War, and the Military Commanders whom he may from time to time designate, whenever he or any designated Commander deems such action necessary or desirable, to prescribe military areas in such places and of such extent as he or the appropriate Military Commander may determine, from which any or all persons may be excluded, and with respect to which, the right of any person to enter, remain in, or leave shall be subject to whatever restrictions the Secretary of War or the appropriate Military Commander may impose in his discretion. The Secretary of War is hereby authorized to provide for residents of any such area who are excluded therefrom, such transportation, food, shelter, and other accommodations as may be necessary, in the judgment of the Secretary of War or the said Military Commander, and until other arrangements are made, to accomplish the purpose of this order.

\*　　　\*　　　\*

FRANKLIN D. ROOSEVELT
*The White House, February 19, 1942*

## 232 "offenders against the law of war" (1942)

Despite the strict standards imposed in the United States Constitution upon prosecutions for the crime of treason—considered by the Founding Fathers as the ultimate political offense—martial law and military justice have provided far less cumbersome procedures for dealing with other classes of political offenders or political suspects. Lincoln's imposition of martial law and suspension of habeas corpus during the Civil War permitted the confinement of political suspects without trial. During World War II, the government similarly resorted to regulations by military commanders on the West Coast to uproot and resettle politically suspect Japanese-Americans without any form of trial.

Two groups of Nazi saboteurs (one member claiming to be a United States citizen) landed on the American shores from two submarines during World War II. After an expedited military trial, seven of the invaders were summarily convicted and executed. Both the international law of war and the United States Articles of War, the Supreme Court ruled, historically have permitted such military trials of "unlawful belligerents," whether aliens or citizens, without traditional constitutional safeguards.

## ☆232 *Ex Parte Quirin*

317 U.S. 1 (1942).

Mr. Chief Justice STONE delivered the opinion of the Court.

\*　　　\*　　　\*

The question for decision is whether the detention of petitioners by respondent for trial by Military Commission, appointed by Order of the President of July 2, 1942, on charges preferred against them purporting to set out their violations of the law of war and of the Articles of War, is in conformity to the laws and Constitution of the United States.

. . . In view of the public importance of the questions raised by their petitions and of the duty which rests on the courts, in time of war as well as in time of peace, to preserve unimpaired the constitutional safeguards of civil liberty, . . . the public interest required that we consider and decide those questions without any avoidable delay. . . .

All the petitioners were born in Germany; all have lived in the United States. All returned to Germany between 1933 and 1941. All except petitioner Haupt are admittedly citizens of the German Reich, with which the United States is at war. Haupt came to this country with his parents when he was five years old; it is contended that he became a citizen of the United States by virtue of the naturalization of his parents during his minority and that he has not since lost his citizenship. The Government, however, takes the position that on attaining his majority he elected to maintain German allegiance and citizenship or in any case that he has by his conduct renounced or abandoned his United States citizenship. For reasons presently to be stated we do not find it necessary to resolve these contentions.

After the declaration of war between the United States and the German Reich, petitioners received training at a sabotage school near Berlin, Germany, where they were instructed in the use of explosives and in methods of secret writing. Thereafter petitioners, with a German citizen, Dasch, proceeded from Germany to a seaport in Occupied France, where petitioners Burger, Heinck and Quirin, together with Dasch, boarded a German submarine which proceeded across the Atlantic to Amagansett Beach on Long Island, New York. The four were there landed from the submarine in the hours of darkness, on or about June 13, 1942, carrying with them a supply of explosives, fuses and incendiary and timing devices. While landing they wore German Marine Infantry uniforms or parts of uniforms. Immediately after landing they buried their uniforms and the other articles mentioned and proceeded in civilian dress to New York City.

The remaining four petitioners at the same French port boarded another German submarine, which carried them across the Atlantic to Ponte Vedra Beach, Florida. On or about June 17, 1942, they came ashore during the hours of darkness wearing caps of the German Marine Infantry and carrying with them a supply of explosives, fuses, and incendiary and timing devices. They immediately buried their caps and the other articles mentioned and proceeded in civilian dress to Jacksonville, Florida, and thence to various points in the United States. All were taken into custody in New York or Chicago by agents of the Federal Bureau of Investigation.

*       *       *

The President, as President and Commander in Chief of the Army and Navy, by Order of July 2, 1942, appointed a Military Commission and directed it to try petitioners for offenses against the law of war and the Articles of War, and prescribed regulations for the procedure on the trial and for review of the record of the trial and of any judgment or sentence of the Commission. On the same day, by Proclamation, the President declared that "all persons who are subjects, citizens or residents of any nation at war with the United States or who give obedience to or act under the direction of any such nation, and who during the time of war enter or attempt to enter the United States ... through coastal or boundary defenses, and are charged with committing or attempting or preparing to commit sabotage, espionage, hostile or warlike acts, or violations of the law of war, shall be subject to the law of war and to the jurisdiction of military tribunals."

The Proclamation also stated in terms that all such persons were denied access to the courts.

*       *       *

Petitioners' main contention is that the President is without any statutory or constitutional authority to order the petitioners to be tried by military tribunal for offenses with which they are charged; that in consequence they are entitled to be tried in the civil courts with the safeguards, including trial by jury, which the Fifth and Sixth Amendments guarantee to all persons charged in such courts with criminal offenses....

*       *       *

We are not here concerned with any question of the guilt or innocence of petitioners. Constitutional safeguards for the protection of all who are charged with offenses are not to be disregarded in order to inflict merited punishment on some who are guilty. But the detention and trial of petitioners—ordered by the President in the declared exercise of his powers as Commander in Chief of the Army in time of war and of grave public danger—are not to be set aside by the courts without the clear conviction that they are in conflict with the Constitution or laws of Congress constitutionally enacted.

*       *       *

The Constitution thus invests the President as Commander in Chief with the power to wage war which Congress has declared, and to carry into effect all laws passed by Congress for the conduct of war and for the government and regulation of the Armed Forces, and all laws defining and punishing offences against the law of nations, including those which pertain to the conduct of war.

*       *       *

From the very beginning of its history this Court has recognized and applied the law of war as including that part of the law of nations which prescribes, for the conduct of war, the status, rights and duties of enemy nations as well as of enemy individuals. By the Articles of War, and especially Article 15, Congress has explicitly provided, so far as it may constitutionally do so, that military tribunals shall have jurisdiction to try offenders or offenses against the law of war in appropriate cases....

An important incident to the conduct of war is the adoption of measures by the military command not only to repel and defeat the enemy, but to seize and subject to disciplinary measures those enemies who in their attempt to thwart or impede our military effort have violated the law of war. It is unnecessary for present purposes to determine to what extent the President as Commander in Chief has constitutional power to create military commissions without the support of Congressional legislation. For here Congress has authorized trial of offenses against the law of war before such commissions. We are concerned only with the question whether it is within the constitutional power of the national government to place petitioners upon trial before a military commission for the offenses with which they are charged. We must therefore first inquire whether any of the acts charged is an offense against the law of war cognizable before a military tribunal, and if so whether the Constitution prohibits the trial....

*       *       *

By universal agreement and practice the law of war draws a distinction between the armed forces and the peaceful populations of belligerent nations and also between those who are lawful and unlawful combatants. Lawful combatants are subject to capture and detention as prisoners of war by opposing military forces. Unlawful combatants are likewise subject to capture and detention, but in addition they are subject to trial and punishment by military tribunals for acts which render their belligerency unlawful. The spy who secretly and without uniform passes the military lines of a belligerent in time of war, seeking to gather military information and communicate it to the enemy, or an enemy combatant who without uniform comes secretly through the lines for the purpose of waging war by destruction of life or property, are familiar examples of belligerents who are generally deemed not to be entitled to the status of prisoners of war, but to be offenders against the law of war subject to trial and punishment by military tribunals.

\*     \*     \*

Our Government, by . . . defining lawful belligerents entitled to be treated as prisoners of war, has recognized that there is a class of unlawful belligerents not entitled to that privilege, including those who though combatants do not wear "fixed and distinctive emblems." And by Article 15 of the Articles of War Congress has made provision for their trial and punishment by military commission, according to "the law of war."

By a long course of practical administrative construction by its military authorities, our Government has likewise recognized that those who during time of war pass surreptitiously from enemy territory into our own, discarding their uniforms upon entry, for the commission of hostile acts involving destruction of life or property, have the status of unlawful combatants punishable as such by military commission. This precept of the law of war has been so recognized in practice both here and abroad, and has so generally been accepted as valid by authorities on international law that we think it must be regarded as a rule or principle of the law of war recognized by this Government by its enactment of the Fifteenth Article of War.

\*     \*     \*

The law of war cannot rightly treat those agents of enemy armies who enter our territory, armed with explosives intended for the destruction of war industries and supplies, as any the less belligerent enemies than are agents similarly entering for the purpose of destroying fortified places or our Armed Forces. By passing our boundaries for such purposes without uniform or other emblem signifying their belligerent status, or by discarding that means of identification after entry, such enemies become unlawful belligerents subject to trial and punishment.

Citizenship in the United States of an enemy belligerent does not relieve him from the consequences of a belligerency which is unlawful because in violation of the law of war. Citizens who associate themselves with the military arm of the enemy government, and with its aid, guidance and direction enter

this country bent on hostile acts are enemy belligerents within the meaning of the Hague Convention and the law of war. . . . It is as an enemy belligerent that petitioner Haupt is charged with entering the United States, and unlawful belligerency is the gravamen of the offense of which he is accused.

\*     \*     \*

But petitioners insist that even if the offenses with which they are charged are offenses against the law of war, their trial is subject to the requirement of the Fifth Amendment that no person shall be held to answer for a capital or otherwise infamous crime unless on a presentment or indictment of a grand jury, and that such trials by Article III, § 2, and the Sixth Amendment must be by jury in a civil court. Before the Amendments, § 2 of Article III, the Judiciary Article, had provided: "The Trial of all Crimes, except in Cases of Impeachment, shall be by Jury," and had directed that "such Trial shall be held in the State where the said Crimes shall have been committed."

Presentment by a grand jury and trial by a jury of the vicinage where the crime was committed were at the time of the adoption of the Constitution familiar parts of the machinery for criminal trials in the civil courts. But they were procedures unknown to military tribunals, which are not courts in the sense of the Judiciary Article, and which in the natural course of events are usually called upon to function under conditions precluding resort to such procedures. As this Court has often recognized, it was not the purpose or effect of § 2 of Article III, read in the light of the common law, to enlarge the then existing right to a jury trial. The object was to preserve unimpaired trial by jury in all those cases in which it had been recognized by the common law and in all cases of a like nature as they might arise in the future, . . . but not to bring within the sweep of the guaranty those cases in which it was then well understood that a jury trial could not be demanded as of right.

\*     \*     \*

[There] are [many] instances of offenses committed against the United States, for which a penalty is imposed, but they are not deemed to be within Article III, § 2 or the provisions of the Fifth and Sixth Amendments relating to "crimes" and "criminal prosecutions." In the light of this long-continued and consistent interpretation we must conclude that § 2 of Article III and the Fifth and Sixth Amendments cannot be taken to have extended the right to demand a jury to trials by military commission, or to have required that offenses against the law of war not triable by jury at common law be tried only in the civil courts.

The fact that "cases arising in the land or naval forces" are excepted from the operation of the

Amendments does not militate against this conclusion. . . .

*          *          *

Section 2 of the Act of Congress of April 10, 1806, derived from the Resolution of the Continental Congress of August 21, 1776, imposed the death penalty on alien spies "according to the law and usage of nations, by sentence of a general court martial." This enactment must be regarded as a contemporary construction of both Article III, § 2, and the Amendments as not foreclosing trial by military tribunals, without a jury, of offenses against the law of war committed by enemies not in or associated with our Armed Forces. It is a construction of the Constitution which has been followed since the founding of our government, and is now continued in the 82nd Article of War. Such a construction is entitled to greatest respect. It has not hitherto been challenged, and so far as we are advised it has never been suggested in the very extensive literature of the subject that an alien spy, in time of war, could not be tried by military tribunal without a jury.

The exception from the Amendments of "cases arising in the land or naval forces" was not aimed at trials by military tribunals, without a jury, of such offenses against the law of war. Its objective was quite different—to authorize the trial by court martial of the members of our Armed Forces for all that class of crimes which under the Fifth and Sixth Amendments might otherwise have been deemed triable in the civil courts. The cases mentioned in the exception are not restricted to those involving offenses against the law of war alone, but extend to trial of all offenses, including crimes which were of the class traditionally triable by jury at common law.

Since the Amendments, like § 2 of Article III, do not preclude all trials of offenses against the law of war by military commission without a jury when the offenders are aliens not members of our Armed Forces, it is plain that they present no greater obstacle to the trial in like manner of citizen enemies who have violated the law of war applicable to enemies. Under the original statute authorizing trial of alien spies by military tribunals, the offenders were outside the constitutional guaranty of trial by jury, not because they were aliens but only because they had violated the law of war by committing offenses constitutionally triable by military tribunal.

We cannot say that Congress in preparing the Fifth and Sixth Amendments intended to extend trial by jury to the cases of alien or citizen offenders against the law of war otherwise triable by military commission, while withholding it from members of our own armed forces charged with infractions of the Articles of War punishable by death. It is equally inadmissible to construe the Amendments—

whose primary purpose was to continue unimpaired presentment by grand jury and trial by petit jury in all those cases in which they had been customary— as either abolishing all trials by military tribunals, save those of the personnel of our own armed forces, or what in effect comes to the same thing, as imposing on all such tribunals the necessity of proceeding against unlawful enemy belligerents only on presentment and trial by jury. We conclude that the Fifth and Sixth Amendments did not restrict whatever authority was conferred by the Constitution to try offenses against the law of war by military commission, and that petitioners, charged with such an offense not required to be tried by jury at common law, were lawfully placed on trial by the Commission without a jury.

Petitioners, and especially petitioner Haupt, stress the pronouncement of this Court in the Milligan case that the law of war "can never be applied to citizens in states which have upheld the authority of the government, and where the courts are open and their process unobstructed." Elsewhere in its opinion the Court was at pains to point out that Milligan, a citizen twenty years resident in Indiana, who had never been a resident of any of the states in rebellion, was not an enemy belligerent either entitled to the status of a prisoner of war or subject to the penalties imposed upon unlawful belligerents. We construe the Court's statement as to the inapplicability of the law of war to Milligan's case as having particular reference to the facts before it. From them the Court concluded that Milligan, not being a part of or associated with the armed forces of the enemy, was a non-belligerent, not subject to the law of war save as—in circumstances found not there to be present and not involved here—martial law might be constitutionally established.

The Court's opinion is inapplicable to the case presented by the present record. . . .

*          *          *

## 233  Any Act Prescribed by the Military Commander (1942)

When President Roosevelt issued Executive Order 9066 authorizing the establishment of military zones and giving the army authority to regulate and exclude civilians from those zones, no rebellion, invasion, domestic violence, or executive declaration of martial law preceded the order. Thus, as during the Civil War, military authority over civilians was constitutionally suspect. To forestall legal questioning, Congress supplied a legislative foundation for this authority of military orders over civilians by making disobedience to such orders a criminal offense. Unlike the Civil War practice, civilian courts and not military tribunals were to try violations of military regulations.

## ☆233  An Act to Provide a Penalty for Violation of Restrictions

56 Stat. 173 (1942).

*Be it enacted by the Senate and House of Representatives of the United States of America in Congress assembled*, That whoever shall enter, remain in, leave, or commit any act in any military area or military zone prescribed, under the authority of an Executive order of the President, by the Secretary of War, or by any military commander designated by the Secretary of War, contrary to the restrictions applicable to any such area or zone or contrary to the order of the Secretary of War or any such military commander, shall, if it appears that he knew or should have known of the existence and extent of the restrictions or order and that his act was in violation thereof, be guilty of a misdemeanor and upon conviction shall be liable to a fine of not to exceed $5,000 or to imprisonment for not more than one year, or both, for each offense.

*Approved, March 21, 1942.*

## 234  "An armed force which lacks loyalty, morale or discipline" (1943)

Japanese aliens and Americans of Japanese ancestry were not the country's only security concern during this period. Antimilitaristic and revolutionary propaganda of socialist and radical activists continued to threaten the war effort.

*Dunne v. United States* involved the Smith Act conspiracy convictions of eighteen members of the Socialist Workers Party who, prior to the United States' entry into the war, were arrested and charged with advocating insubordination in the armed forces and the overthrow of the government by force and violence. Dunne challenged the constitutionality of the Smith Act as well as the generality of the indictment. The *Dunne* decision amply demonstrated the potential reach of the Smith Act. Although the court noted the act appeared "on its face to limit exercise of a right specifically protected by the Constitution," it remained unwilling to permit political debate and advocacy to obstruct the country's mobilization for war.

## ☆234  *Dunne v. United States*

138 F.2d 137 (8th Cir. 1943), *cert. denied*, 320 U.S. 790 (1943).

STONE, Circuit Judge.

Twenty-nine persons were indicted in two counts. One died before trial. By direction of the Court, five were found not guilty. The jury found five more not guilty. The jury found the remaining eighteen not guilty on the first count and guilty on the second count. Judgment was entered on the verdicts and sentences imposed. The convicted persons appealed separately. The appeals were consolidated in this Court and presented on a single record.

Count 2 of the indictment charged conspiracy . . . to violate sanctions . . . 1 and 2 [of the Smith Act] in the respects therein set forth.

The issues here have to do with (I) the validity of the Act, (II) the sufficiency of the indictment, and (III) the sufficiency of the evidence.

I. VALIDITY OF THE ACT

\*        \*        \*

We agree with appellants that, in approaching the problem of validity of a statute, which appears on its face to limit exercise of a right specifically protected by the Constitution, a presumption of validity is narrowed in its scope. In truth, "courts should be astute to examine the effect of the challenged legislation" where it affects the exercise of those fundamental individual rights expressly protected by the Constitution. . . . Here the challenge is that this Act abridges the freedom of speech specifically protected by the First Amendment. Therefore, we approach the problem with the attitude just stated.

Appellants state that "This statute must seek its validating force in the vague and undefined 'right of self-preservation.' " No such extremity exists. The statute is grounded upon specific Constitutional grants of power.

\*        \*        \*

. . . [A]ppellants recognize the similarity of this section [1] to a part of section 3 of the Espionage Act of 1917, which has been upheld. . . . They rightly urge that this portion of the Espionage Act, by its express terms, was limited to periods when this country might be at war; and that the [*Schenck* and *Debs*] decisions must be construed as ruling authority, with that situation in mind. Also, they rightly contend that this section [1] is, by its terms, also applicable to a state of peace. . . . We agree that these . . . cases do not rule this case as direct decisive authorities. The situation here that section [1] applies to a peace status as well as to war and that the conspiracy claimed here was during time of peace sufficiently differentiates those cases to prevent them from ruling these appeals. . . . On the other hand, it does not follow that those cases contain no expressions which are useful guides for determining the character of questions present here simply because the situation dealt with in those cases was different from that here present. In this connection, a pertinent matter should be stated. . . . [T]here was a situation in 1940 which impressed Congress with the need for this Act. That situation, known to all, was the existence of war in Europe; the apprehension that this country might be drawn into war; the knowledge of the effective use of "fifth column" activities by countries which might be our enemies; and the apprehension that such activities were being or might be used in this country. In stating the purposes of the Bill, it was said in the House: "The officers testified before our committee that they were loath to ask for this provision in peacetime but that conditions had become worse, that propagandists were now gaining a foothold to some extent among the enlisted men of our Army and Navy, and that but for the high character and splendid loyalty that has always obtained among the rank and file of our men they would have had to ask for the enactment of this bill much sooner. So, then, title I interdicts the exertion of subversive influences with the intent to undermine the loyalty, morale, or discipline of our fighting men."

Thus, while this Act is applicable to peace as well as war conditions, it was enacted on the brink of war and to correct existing dangers.

The vital necessity of armed forces to maintain the National and the State governments and the liberties of the citizens is expressly recognized and provided for in the Constitution. The lack of such in the Confederation was one of the cardinal reasons for calling the meeting which became the Constitutional Convention. Congressional enactments having the purposes of raising or maintaining armed forces have high standing because of their importance. At the same time, they must not limit the constitutionally protected individual liberties of the citizen to any greater extent than is reasonably necessary and proper to accomplish the important allowable ends of preserving the life of the Government and the States and their orderly conduct. An armed force which lacks loyalty, morale or discipline or wherein is insubordination, disloyalty, mutiny or refusals to do their duty is far worse than no armed force at all and is positively an active menace to constituted government and to the liberties of the people. Therefore, the question here is whether this section of this Act goes so far beyond what is necessary or proper to effectuate its obviously necessary and proper purposes as to infringe upon protected individual rights.

... [T]he argument centers around the statutory expression "or *in any manner cause* insubordination" (italics added), etc. It is urged that this expression is so broad that it includes "virtually the entire range of civilian expression" since it covers "any utterances whose effect upon any member of the armed forces may be to sow doubts in his mind concerning his duty" even if the forces were not mentioned therein. ...

*          *          *

This method [of analysis] avoids or slurs over the governing consideration which runs throughout. That is the intent with which the expressions are made. Intent is the cardinal characteristic and vehicle which is necessary to carry any and all interdicted expressions across the boundary line into crime. This is merely an instance of usual criminal law which protects society from evildoers when they do acts—otherwise innocent—with intent to harm. Thus a man may even kill another and he may be entirely unblamed or he may be executed, dependent solely upon the intent motivating the act.

*          *          *

Section [1] is not inherently invalid.

*          *          *

Appellants attack the expression in subsection (a)(1) "advocate, abet, advise, or teach the duty, necessity, desirability, or propriety" as being so vague and sweeping "that they bring within the forbidden area virtually any expression which is considered dangerous or subversive by prosecutor, court or jury." The words attacked are ordinary everyday terms with generally understood meanings. They are not vague. They are "sweeping" only in the sense that they endeavor to cover the different means by which Congress deemed the forbidden result might be brought about.... This objection is not well founded.

*          *          *

## II. SUFFICIENCY OF INDICTMENT

Appellants contend that the indictment (Count 2) is insufficient "because it merely repeats the words of the statute, fails to allege facts showing the commission of a crime, and is vague and uncertain" and because it "does not allege a conspiracy."

... If the statutory language is, "according to the natural import of the words, fully descriptive of the offense, then ordinarily it is sufficient." The statutory definition here is definitely descriptive. However, this count of the indictment did not stop with stating the broad purposes of the conspiracy. It particularized that the conspirators "would ... attempt to carry out and accomplish said conspiracy in the manner set out at numbered paragraphs One to Thirteen, inclusive, in the first count of this indictment." Thus, the indictment clearly stated the conspiracy was to do the things forbidden by the statute in the particular manners set forth....

This count of the indictment is sufficient.

## III. SUFFICIENCY OF EVIDENCE

*          *          *

Every word of this record of over thirteen hundred pages has been carefully read and considered.

Consideration thereof has required the assembly from the record of the evidence as to each of eighteen defendants and as to four different matters as to each defendant. This has been done. This thorough examination of the record leaves no doubt as to the sufficiency of the evidence and as to the justice of the verdict.

*The judgment as to each appellant is affirmed.*

# 235 Compulsory National Unity (1943)

Shortly after the Japanese attack on Pearl Harbor, the West Virginia State Board of Education enacted a regulation requiring public school students to salute and pledge allegiance to the flag of the United States. Members of the Jehovah's Witnesses refused to comply with the regulation on the grounds that it violated the biblical prohibition, in the Second Commandment, against the making of or the bowing down to any graven image. Because of the religious convictions of the challengers, this case is often considered to have been decided under the religious clauses of the First Amendment. Three years earlier, however, in *Minersville School District v. Gobitis*, 310 U.S. 586 (1940), the Supreme Court upheld a similar flag salute law against a Jehovah's Witness's religious challenge. The *Barnette* decision, although overruling *Gobitis*, rests on the broader right of free expression.

☆ 235 *Board of Education v. Barnette*

319 U.S. 624 (1943).

Mr. Justice JACKSON delivered the opinion of the Court:

*       *       *

... What is now required is the "stiff-arm" salute, the saluter to keep the right hand raised with palm turned up while the following is repeated: "I pledge allegiance to the Flag of the United States of America and to the Republic for which it stands; one Nation, indivisible, with liberty and justice for all."

Failure to conform is "insubordination" dealt with by expulsion. Readmission is denied by statute until compliance. Meanwhile the expelled child is "unlawfully absent" and may be proceeded against as a delinquent. His parents or guardians are liable to prosecution, and if convicted are subject to fine not exceeding $50 and jail term not exceeding thirty days.

*       *       *

Children ... have been expelled from school and are threatened with exclusion for no other cause. Officials threaten to send them to reformatories maintained for criminally inclined juveniles. Parents of such children have been prosecuted and are threatened with prosecutions for causing delinquency.

*       *       *

The freedom asserted by these appellees does not bring them into collision with rights asserted by any other individual. It is such conflicts which most frequently require intervention of the State to determine where the rights of one end and those of another begin. But the refusal of these persons to participate in the ceremony does not interfere with or deny rights of others to do so. Nor is there any question in this case that their behavior is peaceable and orderly. The sole conflict is between authority and rights of the individual. The State asserts power to condition access to public education on making a prescribed sign and profession and at the same time to coerce attendance by punishing both parent and child. The latter stand on a right of self-determination in matters that touch individual opinion and personal attitude.

... [W]e are dealing with a compulsion of students to declare a belief. They are not merely made acquainted with the flag salute so that they may be informed as to what it is or even what it means. The issue here is whether this slow and easily neglected route to aroused loyalties constitutionally may be short-cut by substituting a compulsory salute and slogan....

There is no doubt that, in connection with the pledges, the flag salute is a form of utterance. Symbolism is a primitive but effective way of communicating ideas. The use of an emblem or flag to symbolize some system, idea, institution, or personality, is a short cut from mind to mind. Causes and nations, political parties, lodges and ecclesiastical groups seek to knit the loyalty of their followings to a flag or banner, a color or design. The State announces rank, function, and authority through crowns and maces, uniforms and black robes; the church speaks through the Cross, the Crucifix, the altar and shrine, and clerical raiment. Symbols of State often convey political ideas just as religious symbols come to convey theological ones. Associated with many of these symbols are appropriate gestures of acceptance or respect: a salute, a bowed or bared head, a bended knee. A person gets from a symbol the meaning he puts into it, and what is one man's comfort and inspiration is another's jest and scorn.

Over a decade ago Chief Justice Hughes led this Court in holding that the display of a red flag as a symbol of opposition by peaceful and legal means to organized government was protected by the free speech guaranties of the Constitution. Here it is the State that employs a flag as a symbol of adherence to government as presently organized. It requires the individual to communicate by word and sign his acceptance of the political ideas it thus bespeaks. Objection to this form of communication when coerced is an old one, well known to the framers of the Bill of Rights.

It is also to be noted that the compulsory flag salute and pledge requires affirmation of a belief and an attitude of mind. It is not clear whether the regulation contemplates that pupils forego any contrary convictions of their own and become unwilling converts to the prescribed ceremony or whether it will be acceptable if they simulate assent by words without belief and by a gesture barren of meaning. It is now a commonplace that censorship or suppression of expression of opinion is tolerated by our Constitution only when the expression presents a clear and present danger of action of a kind the State is empowered to prevent and punish. It would seem that involuntary affirmation could be commanded only on even more immediate and urgent grounds than silence. But here the power of compulsion is invoked without any allegation that remaining passive during a flag salute ritual creates a clear and present danger that would justify an effort even to muffle expression. To sustain the compulsory flag salute we are required to say that a Bill of Rights which guards the individual's right to speak his own mind, left it open to public authorities to compel him to utter what is not in his mind.

Whether the First Amendment to the Constitution will permit officials to order observance of ritual of this nature does not depend upon whether as a voluntary exercise we would think it to be good, bad or merely innocuous. Any credo of nationalism is likely to include what some disapprove or to omit what others think essential, and to give off different overtones as it takes on different accents or interpretations. If official power exists to coerce acceptance of any patriotic creed, what it shall contain cannot be decided by courts, but must be largely discretionary with the ordaining authority, whose power to prescribe would no doubt include power to amend. Hence validity of the asserted power to force an American citizen publicly to profess any statement of belief or to engage in any ceremony of assent to one, presents questions of power that must be considered independently of any idea we may have as to the utility of the ceremony in question.

Nor does the issue as we see it turn on one's possession of particular religious views or the sincerity with which they are held. While religion supplies appellees' motive for enduring the discomforts of making the issue in this case, many citizens who do not share these religious views hold such a compulsory rite to infringe constitutional liberty of the individual. It is not necessary to inquire whether non-conformist beliefs will exempt from the duty to salute unless we first find power to make the salute a legal duty.

*          *          *

1. It was said that the flag-salute controversy confronted the Court with "the problem which Lincoln cast in memorable dilemma: 'Must a government of necessity be too *strong* for the liberties of its people, or too *weak* to maintain its own existence?' " and that the answer must be in favor of strength.

We think these issues may be examined free of pressure or restraint growing out of such considerations.

It may be doubted whether Mr. Lincoln would have thought that the strength of government to maintain itself would be impressively vindicated by our confirming power of the State to expel a handful of children from school. Such oversimplification, so handy in political debate, often lacks the precision necessary to postulates of judicial reasoning. If validly applied to this problem, the utterance cited would resolve every issue of power in favor of those in authority and would require us to override every liberty thought to weaken or delay execution of their policies.

Government of limited power need not be anemic government. Assurance that rights are secure tends to diminish fear and jealousy of strong government, and by making us feel safe to live under it makes for its better support. Without promise of a limiting Bill of Rights it is doubtful if our Constitution could have mustered enough strength to enable its ratification. To enforce those rights today is not to choose weak government over strong government. It is only to adhere as a means of strength to individual freedom of mind in preference to officially disciplined uniformity for which history indicates a disappointing and disastrous end.

The subject now before us exemplifies this principle. Free public education, if faithful to the ideal of secular instruction and political neutrality, will not be partisan or enemy of any class, creed, party, or faction. If it is to impose any ideological discipline, however, each party or denomination must seek to control, or failing that, to weaken the influence of the educational system. Observance of the limitations of the Constitution will not weaken government in the field appropriate for its exercise.

*          *          *

3. ... [It is argued] that it is constitutionally appropriate to "fight out the wise use of legislative authority in the forum of public opinion and before legislative assemblies rather than to transfer such a contest to the judicial arena," since all the "effective means of inducing political changes are left free."

The very purpose of a Bill of Rights was to withdraw certain subjects from the vicissitudes of political controversy, to place them beyond the reach of majorities and officials and to establish them as legal principles to be applied by the courts. One's right to life, liberty, and property, to free speech, a free press, freedom of worship and assembly, and other fundamental rights may not be submitted to vote; they depend on the outcome of no elections.

*     *     *

4. Lastly, [it is contended] that "National unity is the basis of national security," that the authorities have "the right to select appropriate means for its attainment," and hence reaches the conclusion that such compulsory measures toward "national unity" are constitutional. Upon the verity of this assumption depends our answer in this case.

National unity as an end which officials may foster by persuasion and example is not in question. The problem is whether under our Constitution compulsion as here employed is a permissible means for its achievement.

Struggles to coerce uniformity of sentiment in support of some end thought essential to their time and country have been waged by many good as well as by evil men. Nationalism is a relatively recent phenomenon but at other times and places the ends have been racial or territorial security, support of a dynasty or regime, and particular plans for saving souls. As first and moderate methods to attain unity have failed, those bent on its accomplishment must resort to an ever-increasing severity. As governmental pressure toward unity becomes greater, so strife becomes more bitter as to whose unity it shall be. Probably no deeper division of our people could proceed from any provocation than from finding it necessary to choose what doctrine and whose program public educational officials shall compel youth to unite in embracing. Ultimate futility of such attempts to compel coherence is the lesson of every such effort from the Roman drive to stamp out Christianity as a disturber of its pagan unity, the Inquisition, as a means to religious and dynastic unity, the Siberian exiles as a means to Russian unity, down to the fast failing efforts of our present totalitarian enemies. Those who begin coercive elimination of dissent soon find themselves exterminating dissenters. Compulsory unification of opinion achieves only the unanimity of the graveyard.

It seems trite but necessary to say that the First Amendment to our Constitution was designed to avoid these ends by avoiding these beginnings. There is no mysticism in the American concept of the State or of the nature or origin of its authority. We set up government by consent of the governed, and the Bill of Rights denies those in power any legal opportunity to coerce that consent. Authority here is to be controlled by public opinion, not public opinion by authority.

... We can have intellectual individualism and the rich cultural diversities that we owe to exceptional minds only at the price of occasional eccentricity and abnormal attitudes. When they are so harmless to others or to the State as those we deal with here, the price is not too great. But freedom to differ is not limited to things that do not matter much. That would be a mere shadow of freedom. The test of its substance is the right to differ as to things that touch the heart of the existing order.

If there is any fixed star in our constitutional constellation, it is that no official, high or petty, can prescribe what shall be orthodox in politics, nationalism, religion, or other matters of opinion or force citizens to confess by word or act their faith therein. If there are any circumstances which permit an exception, they do not now occur to us.

We think the action of the local authorities in compelling the flag salute and pledge transcends constitutional limitations on their power and invades the sphere of intellect and spirit which it is the purpose of the First Amendment to our Constitution to reserve from all official control.

[T]he judgment enjoining enforcement of the West Virginia Regulation is

*Affirmed.*

## 236 "there has been relatively little social intercourse" (1943)

In *Hirabayashi v. United States*, the Supreme Court examined the case of a Japanese-American citizen, a senior at the University of Washington, convicted of violating a military curfew regulation applicable only to those of Japanese extraction. Hirabayashi had violated the regulation in order to challenge its constitutionality on the grounds of racial discrimination. Although the equal protection clause of the Fourteenth Amendment is not by its terms applicable to the federal government, the federally-applicable due process clause of the Fifth Amendment is considered to require adherence to the same principle of equality. Nevertheless, the court upheld the conviction, reciting the special circumstances of both the war and the Japanese population.

☆ 236  *Hirabayashi v. United States*

320 U.S. 21 (1943).

Mr. Chief Justice STONE delivered the opinion of the Court.

*     *     *

The questions for our decision are whether the particular restriction violated, namely that all persons of Japanese ancestry residing in such an area be within their place of residence daily between the hours of 8:00 P.M. and 6:00 A.M., ... unconstitutionally discriminated between citizens of Japanese ancestry and those of other ancestries in violation of the Fifth Amendment.

The actions taken must be appraised in the light of the conditions with which the President and Congress were confronted in the early months of 1942, many of which, since disclosed, were then peculiarly within the knowledge of the military authorities. . . .

. . . That reasonably prudent men charged with the responsibility of our national defense had ample ground for concluding that they must face the danger of invasion, take measures against it, and in making the choice of measures consider our internal situation, cannot be doubted.

. . . As the curfew was made applicable to citizens residing in the area only if they were of Japanese ancestry, our inquiry must be whether in the light of all the facts and circumstances there was any substantial basis for the conclusion, in which Congress and the military commander united, that the curfew as applied was a protective measure necessary to meet the threat of sabotage and espionage which would substantially affect the war effort and which might reasonably be expected to aid a threatened enemy invasion.

*       *       *

. . . At a time of threatened Japanese attack upon this country, the nature of our inhabitants' attachments to the Japanese enemy was consequently a matter of grave concern. . . .

There is support for the view that social, economic and political conditions which have prevailed since the close of the last century, when the Japanese began to come to this country in substantial numbers, have intensified their solidarity and have in large measure prevented their assimilation as an integral part of the white population. In addition, large numbers of children of Japanese parentage are sent to Japanese language schools outside the regular hours of public schools in the locality. Some of these schools are generally believed to be sources of Japanese nationalistic propaganda, cultivating allegiance to Japan. Considerable numbers, estimated to be approximately 10,000, of American-born children of Japanese parentage have been sent to Japan for all or a part of their education.

Congress and the Executive, including the military commander, could have attributed special significance, in its bearing on the loyalties of persons of Japanese descent, to the maintenance by Japan of its system of dual citizenship. Children born in the United States of Japanese alien parents, and especially those children born before December 1, 1924, are under many circumstances deemed, by Japanese law, to be citizens of Japan. . . .

As a result of all these conditions affecting the life of the Japanese, both aliens and citizens, in the Pacific Coast area, there has been relatively little social intercourse between them and the white population. The restrictions, both practical and legal, affecting the privileges and opportunities afforded to persons of Japanese extraction residing in the United States, have been sources of irritation and may well have tended to increase their isolation, and in many instances their attachments to Japan and its institutions.

*       *       *

[W]e cannot reject as unfounded the judgment of the military authorities and of Congress that there were disloyal members of [the Japanese resident] population, whose number and strength could not be precisely and quickly ascertained. We cannot say that the war-making branches of the Government did not have ground for believing that in a critical hour such persons could not readily be isolated and separately dealt with, and constituted a menace to the national defense and safety, which demanded that prompt and adequate measures be taken to guard against it.

Distinctions between citizens solely because of their ancestry are by their very nature odious to a free people whose institutions are founded upon the doctrine of equality. . . . Because racial discriminations are in most circumstances irrelevant and therefore prohibited, it by no means follows that, in dealing with the perils of war, Congress and the Executive are wholly precluded from taking into account those facts and circumstances which are relevant to measures for our national defense, and for the successful prosecution of the war, and which may in fact place citizens of one ancestry in a different category from others. The adoption by Government, in the crisis of war and of threatened invasion, of measures for the public safety, based upon the recognition of facts and circumstances which indicate that a group of one national extraction may menace that safety more than others, is not wholly beyond the limits of the Constitution and is not to be condemned merely because in other and in most circumstances racial distinctions are irrelevant.

*       *       *

*Affirmed.*

## 237 "a fascist form of government should be established in the United States" (1943)

Capping more than a decade of concern about American varieties of fascism and nazism, a grand jury was empaneled on October 26, 1943, and an indictment was returned on January 3, 1944, in Washington, D.C., against an assorted and unrelated group of thirty Nazi sympathizers. The Depression had spawned not only supporters of the socialist and Communist causes but also radicals on the far right.

Beginning in 1934, President Franklin D. Roosevelt had ordered FBI probes of these right-wing critics of his administration, including William Dudley Pelley, chief of the Silver Shirts; Robert Edmondson, a pamphleteer purporting to expose Roosevelt's alleged Jewish ancestry; George E. Deatherage, Grand Commander of the Knights of the White Camelia; and Father Charles E. Coughlin, connected with the Christian Front. America's entry into World War II finally provided an opportunity for more direct action against what were considered the "scurrilous" publications and "Trojan Horse" activities of the Nazi sympathizers. After two earlier aborted indictments, on January 3, 1944, a third indictment was returned against a strange mix of leaders of nativist and isolationist organizations, ranting pro-German and anti-Semitic publicists, and former leaders of the German-American Bund. The prosecution of this group, for participating in an international Nazi conspiracy dedicated to Hitler's program to "destroy democracy" and establish "national Socialist or fascist" governments in the United States, became known as *United States v. McWilliams*, taking the name of the first defendant. Technically the charge was conspiracy to commit sedition under the Smith Act by counseling insubordination in the armed forces.

Chief Justice Edward C. Eicher of the United States district court presided over the trial, which commenced on April 17, 1944. After seven months of proceedings, Judge Eicher died of a heart attack on November 29. A mistrial was declared; and after lingering until 1947, the still outstanding indictments were dismissed on the grounds that the accused had been denied a speedy trial.

☆ 237  *United States v. McWilliams*

Reprinted in M. St. George and L. Dennis, *A Trial on Trial: The Great Sedition Trial of 1944* (National Civil Rights Committee, 1946), 114-21.

District Court of the United States for the District of Columbia

Holding a Criminal Term

District of Columbia, ss:
October Term, A.D. 1943

#### INDICTMENT

The ... Grand Jurors for the United States of America, duly empaneled and sworn in the District of Columbia on October 26, 1943, for the October 1943 Term, upon their oaths present that:

In 1933 the National Socialist German Workers Party, also known as the N.S.D.A.P. and the "Nazi Party," came into power in Germany upon a program publicly announced by its leaders to destroy democracy throughout the world and to establish

and aid in the establishment of national socialist or fascist forms of government in place of the forms of government then existing in the United States of America and other countries. As a means of accomplishing their objectives, the said Nazi Party and its leaders carried on a systematic campaign of propaganda designed and intended to impair and undermine the loyalty and morale of the military and naval forces of the United States of America and of other countries. The persons hereinafter named as defendants joined in this movement and program and actively cooperated with each other and with leaders and members of the said Nazi Party to accomplish the objectives of said Nazi Party in the United States.

On the 28th day of June, 1940, there w[as] enacted [the Smith Act], and continuously thereafter ... the defendants, in the District of Columbia and within the jurisdiction of this court, and at divers other places throughout the United States of America, in Germany, and elsewhere, in violation of Section 3 of the aforesaid Act, unlawfully, wilfully, feloniously and knowingly conspired, combined, confederated and agreed together and with each other and with officials of the Government of the German Reich and leaders and members of the said Nazi Party, said persons hereinafter being referred to as "co-conspirators," to commit acts prohibited by Section 1 of said Act in that they, the said defendants and the said co-conspirators, with intent to interfere with, impair and influence the loyalty, morale and discipline of the military and naval forces of the United States, would:

> (i) Advise, counsel, urge and cause insubordination, disloyalty, mutiny and refusal to duty by members of the military and naval forces of the United States; and
> (ii) Distribute and cause to be distributed written and printed matter, advising, counseling, and urging insubordination, disloyalty, mutiny and refusal of duty by members of the military and naval forces of the United States.

And the Grand Jurors aforesaid, upon their oaths aforesaid, do further present that, as part of said conspiracy and as means and methods of accomplishing the objects thereof, the said defendants and co-conspirators, during the period of said conspiracy, in the District of Columbia and within the jurisdiction of this court and at divers other places throughout the United States, in Germany, and elsewhere would do, and they did, among other things, the following:

1. Print, publish, distribute and circulate, and cause to be printed, published, distributed and circulated, among others, the following newspapers, magazines, books, leaflets, circulars, pamphlets, documents, cartoons, drawings and photographs:

*Mein Kampf*
*The National Socialist Party Programme*
*Welt Dienst (World Service)*
*Der Stuermer*
*News from Germany*
*Deutsche Wochenschau*
*Muenchner Neuste Nachrichten*
*The Free American and Deutscher*
*Weckruf und Beobachter*
*The White Knight*
*The American Nationalist Confederation*
  *News Bulletin*
*The Revealer*
*The Defender*
*Liberation*
*The Roll Call*
*The Galilean*
*National Liberty Party*
*Yankee Freemen*
*Yankee Minute Men*
*Friends of Progress*
*Industrial Control Reports*
*Social Republic Society Bulletin*
*Comment*
*The Corporate State*
*What Prince Lippe Told Me*
*Patriotic Research Bureau News Letter*
*Edmondson's Economic Research Service*
*"American Vigilante" Bulletins*
*The Christian Mobilizer*
*The Weekly Foreign Letter*
*The Dynamics of War and Revolution*
*Publicity*
*America in Danger*
*Nationalist Newsletter*
*Our Common Cause*
*The World Hoax*
*Roosevelt's Jewish Ancestry*
*History Repeats*
*The Answer to the Betrayal*
*America on the March*
*National Socialism and Its Justification*
Card headed *"West Africa Is Not Iceland—It's Any-
  thing But a Nice Land!"*
*The Miracle of Happiness*

2. Organize, support, use, and control, and cause
to be organized, supported, and used, among others,
the following parties, offices, groups, organizations,
publishers and distributors:

*National Socialist German Workers Party (N.S.D.A.P.)*
*Franz Eher Publishing House, Munich*
*Foreign Organization of The National Socialist
  Party (A.O.)*
*Ministry of Public Enlightenment and Propaganda
  of the German Reich*
*German Library of Information*
*Welt Dienst, Erfurt (World Service)*

*German Foreign Institut, Stuttgart (D.A.I.)*
*League of Germandom Abroad (V.D.A.)*
*Fichte Bund, Hamburg*
*Terramare Office, Berlin*
*Transocean News Service*
*Foreign Office of the German Reich*
*German Embassy at Washington, D.C., and various
  German Consulates in the United States*
*German Ministry of Education*
*Amerika Institut*
*German-American Bund*
*Silver Shirts*
*Silver Legion*
*Pelley Publishers*
*Fellowship Press, Inc.*
*Knights of the White Camelia*
*American Nationalist Confederation*
*National Liberty Party*
*National Workers' League*
*Friends of Progress*
*Patriotic Research Bureau*
*Social Republic Society, also known as S.O.C.I.S.*
*James True Associates*
*Flanders Hall, Incorporated*
*Aryan Book Store*
*The Defenders Publishers*
*The Christian Mobilizers*
*The American Destiny Party*
*American National Socialist Party*
*National Press Association*

3. Disseminate, by the means set forth in the preceding two paragraphs and otherwise, oral, written,
and printed statements, representations and
charges asserting among other things in substance
that:

a. Democracy is decadent; a national socialist or
fascist form of government should be established in
the United States.

b. A national socialist revolution is inevitable if
we are to rid our country of its decadent democracy.

c. The Government of the United States, the
Congress and public officials are controlled by Communists, International Jews, and plutocrats.

d. The Democratic and Republican parties and
their candidates for public office are tools of International Jewry, and do not represent the will of the
American people.

e. The acts, proclamations, and orders of the
public officials of the United States and the laws of
Congress are illegal, corrupt, traitorous and in direct violation of the Constitution of the United
States.

f. The United States is governed, not by the duly
elected representatives of the people, but by a
group of alien-minded persons opposed to American
principles and ideals and seeking to overthrow the
Constitution of the United States.

g. President Roosevelt is reprehensible, a warmonger, liar, unscrupulous, and a pawn of the Jews, Communists and Plutocrats.

h. President Roosevelt is a Jew and is working with International Jewry against the interests of the people of the United States.

i. The activities and territorial acquisitions and plans of the Axis Powers constitute no real danger to the national existence and security of the United States or any of its territorial possessions.

j. The Axis Powers are fighting to free the world from domination by Communism and International Jewry, and to save Christianity, hence the United States should give no aid and comfort to the enemies of the Axis.

k. The cause of the Axis Powers is the cause of justice and morality; they have committed no aggressive act against any nation and are fighting a solely defensive war against British Imperialism, American Capitalists, and the desire of American public officials to rule the world, hence any act of war against them is unjust and immoral on the part of the United States.

l. The nations opposed to the Axis, plan to use American lives, money and property to defend their decadent systems of government.

m. The participation of the United States in the war has been deliberately planned by our leaders with the ultimate aim of promoting our enslavement by British Imperialism and International Communism.

n. The public officials of the United States of America are trying deliberately to provoke war with peaceful nations, such as Germany, Italy and Japan, which are seeking only to live at peace with the rest of the world.

o. President Roosevelt and Congress, through a surreptitious and illegal war program against the Axis Powers sold out the United States and forced the Axis Power[s] to wage war upon us.

p. President Roosevelt by his war-mongering policies is draining dry the resources of the United States to save Communist China, Imperialist Britain and Atheistic Russia from inevitable defeat.

q. Our program of giving American arms and equipment to foreign nations results in United States military and naval forces being inadequately armed and equipped and in their being exposed to terrible slaughter.

r. The public officials of the United States are knaves who have deliberately concealed the truth that our unprepared boys, racked by disease and slaughtered like sheep, will be dumped in a million foreign graves to buy a valueless victory.

s. The whole war is the result of a Jew-sponsored money-making scheme to bleed the United States Treasury.

t. As the result of incompetence and corruption in public office, the United States is unprepared to wage war against the Axis Powers, who have the best equipped and most powerful military establishment in the world.

u. The present war is a dishonest war waged at the expense and measured in the blood and dollars of the people of the United States solely for the benefit of and to insure the continuance of world domination by "International Bankers," "International Capitalists," "Mongolian Jews," "Communists," and "International Jewry."

v. The Japanese attack upon Pearl Harbor was deliberately invited by the public officials of the United States, in order to involve the United States in a foreign war.

w. The war with Japan was deliberately provoked by the insane, unjust, aggressive and traitorous policies of officials of the United States.

x. An honorable and just peace could be brought about speedily were it not for the opposition of Communists, International Jewry, and war profiteers.

Contrary to the form of the statute in such case made and provided, and against the peace and dignity of the United States.

EDWARD M. CURRAN
United States Attorney for the
District of Columbia
O. JOHN ROGGE
Special Assistant to the
Attorney General

## 238 "imprisonment ... in a concentration camp because of racial prejudice" (1944)

Fred Korematsu challenged his conviction for failing to report for evacuation from the military area in which he resided on the grounds that the evacuation order was racially discriminatory. The government had made no assertion that Korematsu, a native-born citizen of the United States, had been disloyal. Justice Black, writing for the majority, nevertheless upheld the power of the government. He wrote that "[p]ressing public necessity may sometimes justify the existence of such restrictions, racial antagonism never can."

The court stated further that making a determination as to who was loyal would present a tremendous problem, especially when immediate action was necessary in the interest of security. "Our task would be simple, our duty clear, were this a case involving the imprisonment of a loyal citizen in a concentration camp because of racial prejudice ... [but here] we are dealing specifically with nothing but an exclusion order," Justice Black emphasized. Significantly, only Justice Murphy in this dissent addressed the issue of Japanese-American detention in temporary Relocation Centers. The majority restricted its decision to the issue of exclusion from the military areas.

☆ 238  *Korematsu v. United States*

323 U.S. 214 (1944).

Mr. Justice BLACK delivered the opinion of the Court.

\*       \*       \*

. . . It should be noted, to begin with, that all legal restrictions which curtail the civil rights of a single racial group are immediately suspect. That is not to say that all such restrictions are unconstitutional. It is to say that courts must subject them to the most rigid scrutiny. Pressing public necessity may sometimes justify the existence of such restrictions; racial antagonism never can.

\*       \*       \*

Exclusion Order No. 34. . . , issued after we were at war with Japan, declared that "the successful prosecution of the war requires every possible protection against espionage and against sabotage to national-defense material, national-defense premises, and national-defense utilities. . . ."

. . . [In *Hirabayashi*] [w]e upheld the [Japanese] curfew order as an exercise of the power of the government to take steps necessary to prevent espionage and sabotage in an area threatened by Japanese attack.

. . . [E]xclusion from the area in which one's home is located is a far greater deprivation than constant confinement to the home from 8 P.M. to 6 A.M. Nothing short of apprehension by the proper military authorities of the gravest imminent danger to the public safety can constitutionally justify either. But exclusion from a threatened area, no less than curfew, has a definite and close relationship to the prevention of espionage and sabotage. The military authorities, charged with the primary responsibility of defending our shores, concluded that curfew provided inadequate protection and ordered exclusion. They did so . . . in accordance with Congressional authority to the military to say who should, and who should not, remain in the threatened areas.

In this case the petitioner challenges the assumptions upon which we rested our conclusions in the *Hirabayashi* case. He also urges that by May 1942, when Order No. 34 was promulgated, all danger of Japanese invasion of the West Coast had disappeared. After careful consideration of these contentions we are compelled to reject them.

\*       \*       \*

Like curfew, exclusion of those of Japanese origin was deemed necessary because of the presence of an unascertained number of disloyal members of the group, most of whom we have no doubt were loyal to this country. It was because we could not reject the finding of the military authorities that it was impossible to bring about an immediate segregation of the disloyal from the loyal that we sustained the validity of the curfew order as applying to the whole group. In the instant case, temporary exclusion of the entire group was rested by the military on the same ground. . . . [This] answers the contention that the exclusion was in the nature of group punishment based on antagonism to those of Japanese origin. That there were members of the group who retained loyalties to Japan has been confirmed by investigations made subsequent to the exclusion. . . .

We uphold the exclusion order as of the time it was made and when the petitioner violated it. . . . Compulsory exclusion of large groups of citizens from their homes, except under circumstances of direst emergency and peril, is inconsistent with our basic governmental institutions. But when under conditions of modern warfare our shores are threatened by hostile forces, the power to protect must be commensurate with the threatened danger.

\*       \*       \*

It is said that we are dealing here with the case of imprisonment of a citizen in a concentration camp solely because of his ancestry, without evidence or inquiry concerning his loyalty and good disposition towards the United States. Our task would be simple, our duty clear, were this a case involving the imprisonment of a loyal citizen in a concentration camp because of racial prejudice. Regardless of the true nature of the assembly and relocation centers—and we deem it unjustifiable to call them concentration camps with all the ugly connotations that term implies—we are dealing specifically with nothing but an exclusion order. To case this case into outlines of racial prejudice, without reference to the real military dangers which were presented, merely confuses the issue. Korematsu was not excluded from the Military Area because of hostility to him or his race. He *was* excluded because we are at war with the Japanese Empire, because the properly constituted military authorities feared an invasion of our West Coast and felt constrained to take proper security measures, because they decided that the military urgency of the situation demanded that all citizens of Japanese ancestry be segregated from the West Coast temporarily, and finally, because Congress, reposing its confidence in this time of war in our military leaders—as inevitably it must—determined that they should have the power to do just this. There was evidence of disloyalty on the part of some, the military authorities considered that the need for action was great, and time was short. We cannot — by availing ourselves of the calm perspective of hindsight — now say that at that time these actions were unjustified.

*Affirmed.*

# 239 "a dangerously disorderly migration" (1944)

The curfew and evacuation programs were not the end of the exercise of war powers over the Japanese-American population. Pursuant to Executive Order 9102, the president established the War Relocation Agency. The agency maintained Relocation Centers, which housed the Japanese (American citizens as well as aliens) excluded from the West Coast by virtue of Executive Order 9066. At the centers, officials were to determine the evacuees' loyalty to the United States, but even those certified as loyal were not free to leave and migrate on their own to less sensitive areas of the United States for fear of popular hostility. Although the court held that the government could not detain Ms. Endo against her will, the decision was narrow in scope. The court did not seriously question Congress's authority to maintain such camps. This seeming assent supported the later argument that the courts would not hold the Emergency Detention Act of 1950 (part of the McCarran Act) to be unconstitutional.

☆ 239 *Ex Parte Endo*

323 U.S. 283 (1944).

Mr. Justice DOUGLAS delivered the opinion of the Court:

\*       \*       \*

Her petition for a writ of *habeas corpus* alleges that she is a loyal and law-abiding citizen of the United States, that no charge has been made against her, that she is being unlawfully detained, and that she is confined in the Relocation Center under armed guard and held there against her will.

It is conceded by the Department of Justice and by the War Relocation Authority that appellant is a loyal and law-abiding citizen. They make no claim that she is detained on any charge or that she is even suspected of disloyalty. Moreover, they do not contend that she may be held any longer in the Relocation Center. They concede that it is beyond the power of the War Relocation Authority to detain citizens against whom no charges of disloyalty or subversiveness have been made for a period longer than that necessary to separate the loyal from the disloyal and to provide the necessary guidance for relocation. But they maintain that detention for an additional period after leave clearance has been granted is an essential step in the evacuation program.

\*       \*       \*

It is argued that such a planned and orderly relocation was essential to the success of the evacuation program; that but for such supervision there might have been a dangerously disorderly migration of unwanted people to unprepared communities; that unsupervised evacuation might have resulted in hardship and disorder; that the success of the evacuation program was thought to require the knowledge that the federal government was maintaining control over the evacuated population except as the release of individuals could be effected consistently with their own peace and well-being and that of the nation; that although community hostility towards the evacuees has diminished, it has not disappeared and the continuing control of the Authority over the relocation process is essential to the success of the evacuation program. It is argued that supervised relocation, as the chosen method of terminating the evacuation, is the final step in the entire process and is a consequence of the first step taken. It is conceded that appellant's detention pending compliance with the leave regulations is not directly connected with the prevention of espionage and sabotage at the present time. But it is argued that . . . power [exists] to make regulations necessary and proper for controlling situations created by the exercise of the powers expressly conferred for protection against espionage and sabotage. The leave regulations are said to fall within that category.

*First.* We are of the view that Mitsuye Endo should be given her liberty. In reaching that conclusion we do not come to the underlying constitutional issues which have been argued. For we conclude that, whatever power the War Relocation Authority may have to detain other classes of citizens, it has no authority to subject citizens who are concededly loyal to its leave procedure.

\*       \*       \*

Such power of detention as the Authority has stems from Executive Order No. 9066. . . .

We approach the construction of Executive Order No. 9066 as we would approach the construction of legislation in this field. That Executive Order must indeed be considered along with the Act of March 21, 1942, which ratified and confirmed it[,] as the Order and the statute together laid such basis as there is for participation by civil agencies of the federal government in the evacuation program. Broad powers frequently granted to the President or other executive officers by Congress so that they may deal with the exigencies of wartime problems have been sustained. And the Constitution when it committed to the Executive and to Congress the exercise of the war power necessarily gave them wide scope for the exercise of judgment and discretion so that war might be waged effectively and successfully. At the same time, however, the Constitution is as specific in its enumeration of many of the civil rights of the individual as it is in its enumeration of the powers of his government....

... This Court has quite consistently given a narrower scope for the operation of the presumption of constitutionality when legislation appeared on its face to violate a specific prohibition of the Constitution. We have likewise favored that interpretation of legislation which gives it the greater chance of surviving the test of constitutionality. Those analogies are suggestive here. We must assume that the Chief Executive and members of Congress, as well as the courts, are sensitive to and respectful of the liberties of the citizen. In interpreting a wartime measure we must assume that their purpose was to allow for the greatest possible accommodation between those liberties and the exigencies of war. We must assume, when asked to find implied powers in a grant of legislative or executive authority, that the law makers intended to place no greater restraint on the citizen than was clearly and unmistakably indicated by the language they used.

The Act of March 21, 1942, was a war measure....

... The purpose and objective of the Act and of these orders are plain. Their single aim was the protection of the war effort against espionage and sabotage. It is in light of that one objective that the powers conferred by the orders must be construed.

Neither the Act nor the orders use the language of detention.... And that silence may have special significance in view of the fact that detention in Relocation Centers was no part of the original program of evacuation but developed later to meet what seemed to the officials in charge to be mounting hostility to the evacuees on the part of the communities where they sought to go.

We do not mean to imply that detention in connection with no phase of the evacuation program would be lawful. The fact that the Act and the orders are silent on detention does not of course mean that any power to detain is lacking. Some such power might indeed be necessary to the successful operation of the evacuation program. At least we may so assume. Moreover, we may assume for the purposes of this case that initial detention in Relocation Centers was authorized. But we stress the silence of the legislative history and of the Act and the Executive Orders on the power to detain to emphasize that any such authority which exists must be implied. If there is to be the greatest possible accommodation of the liberties of the citizen with this war measure, any such implied power must be narrowly confined to the precise purpose of the evacuation program.

A citizen who is concededly loyal presents no problem of espionage or sabotage. Loyalty is a mat-

ter of the heart and mind, not of race, creed, or color. He who is loyal is by definition not a spy or a saboteur. When the power to detain is derived from the power to protect the war effort against espionage and sabotage, detention which has no relationship to that objective is unauthorized.

Nor may the power to detain an admittedly loyal citizen or to grant him a conditional release be implied as a useful or convenient step in the evacuation program, whatever authority might be implied in case of those whose loyalty was not conceded or established. If we assume (as we do) that the original evacuation was justified, its lawful character was derived from the fact that it was an espionage and sabotage measure, not that there was community hostility to this group of American citizens. The evacuation program rested explicitly on the former ground not on the latter as the underlying legislation shows. The authority to detain a citizen or to grant him a conditional release as protection against espionage or sabotage is exhausted at least when his loyalty is conceded. If we held that the authority to detain continued thereafter, we would transform an espionage or sabotage measure into something else. That was not done by Executive Order No. 9066 or by the Act of March 21, 1942, which ratified it. What they did not do we cannot do. Detention which furthered the campaign against espionage and sabotage would be one thing. But detention which has no relationship to that campaign is of a distinct character. Community hostility even to loyal evacuees may have been (and perhaps still is) a serious problem. But if authority for their custody and supervision is to be sought on that ground, the Act of March 21, 1942, [and] Executive Order No. 9066 ... offer no support. And none other is advanced. To read them that broadly would be to assume that the Congress and the President intended that this discriminatory action should be taken against these people wholly on account of their ancestry even though the government conceded their loyalty to this country. We cannot make such an assumption....

Mitsuye Endo is entitled to an unconditional release by the War Relocation Authority.

\* \* \*

## 240 A Failure of Good Moral Character (1945)

In 1942 the nation was at war, and popular sentiment against pacifists was uncordial. Article XII of the Illinois Constitution denominated all able-bodied men between the ages of nineteen and forty-five to be the militia of the state. It also provided that the state would not require those having conscientious scruples against bearing arms to perform militia duty in peacetime. When a recognized conscientious objector applied for admission to the Illinois Bar, the state supreme court refused to admit him on the grounds that his religious scruples disabled him from swearing in good faith to uphold the Illinois Constitution, in particular the provision requiring militia duty in time of war. Summers claimed he could take the oath, but Illinois insisted an incurable incompatibility existed between his conscientious beliefs and the obligations of an attorney.

The United States Supreme Court upheld, 5-4, Illinois' power to ostracize Summers from the legal profession, relying on decisions upholding congressional authority to preclude from naturalization those otherwise eligible aliens whose political allegiance would be suspect because they could not pledge to give military service.

## ☆ 240 *In re Summers*

325 U.S. 561 (1945).

Mr. Justice REED delivered the opinion of the Court:

*       *       *

. . . A conscientious belief in non-violence to the extent that the believer will not use force to prevent wrong, no matter how aggravated, and so cannot swear in good faith to support the Illinois Constitution, the [Illinois] Justices contend, must disqualify such a believer for admission.

*       *       *

. . . Of course, under our Constitutional system, men could not be excluded from the practice of law, or indeed from following any other calling, simply because they belong to any of our religious groups, whether Protestant, Catholic, Quaker or Jewish, assuming it conceivable that any state of the Union would draw such a religious line. We cannot say that any such purpose to discriminate motivated the action of the Illinois Supreme Court.

*       *       *

Illinois has constitutional provisions which require service in the militia in time of war of men of petitioner's age group.[11] The return of the Justices alleges that petitioner has not made any showing that he would serve notwithstanding his conscientious objections. This allegation is undenied in the record and unchallenged by brief. We accept the allegation as to unwillingness to serve in the militia as established. While . . . conscientious objectors to participation in war in any form now are permitted to do non-war work of national importance, this is by grace of Congressional recognition of their beliefs. The Act may be repealed. No similar exemption during war exists under Illinois law. . . .

The United States does not admit to citizenship the alien who refuses to pledge military service.

Even the powerful dissents which emphasized the deep cleavage in this Court on the issue of admission to citizenship did not challenge the right of Congress to require military service from every able-bodied man. It is impossible for us to conclude that the insistence of Illinois that an officer who is charged with the administration of justice must take an oath to support the Constitution of Illinois and Illinois' interpretation of that oath to require a willingness to perform military service violates the principles of religious freedom which the Fourteenth Amendment secures against state action, when a like interpretation of a similar oath as to the Federal Constitution bars an alien from national citizenship.

*Affirmed.*

MR. JUSTICE BLACK, dissenting.

*       *       *

I cannot believe that a state statute would be consistent with our constitutional guarantee of freedom of religion if it specifically denied the right to practice law to all members of one of our great religious groups, Protestant, Catholic, or Jewish. Yet the Quakers have had a long and honorable part in the growth of our nation, and an amicus curiae brief filed in their behalf informs us that under the test applied to this petitioner, not one of them if true to the tenets of their faith could qualify for the bar in Illinois. And it is obvious that the same disqualification would exist as to every conscientious objector to the use of force, even though the Congress of the United States should continue its practice of absolving them from military service. The conclusion seems to me inescapable that if Illinois can bar this petitioner from the practice of law it can bar every person from every public occupation solely because he believes in non-resistance rather than in force. For a lawyer is no more subject to call for military duty than a plumber, a highway worker, a Secretary of State, or a prison chaplain.

It may be, as many people think, that Christ's Gospel of love and submission is not suited to a world in which men still fight and kill one another. But I am not ready to say that a mere profession of belief in that Gospel is a sufficient reason to keep otherwise well qualified men out of the legal profession, or to drive law-abiding lawyers of that belief out of the profession, which would be the next logical development.

Nor am I willing to say that such a belief can be penalized through the circuitous method of prescribing an oath, and then barring an applicant on the ground that his present belief might later prompt him to do or refrain from doing something that might violate that oath. Test oaths, designed to impose civil disabilities upon men for their beliefs rather than for unlawful conduct, were an abomination to the founders of this nation. . . .

. . . It can be assumed that the State of Illinois has the constitutional power to draft conscientious objectors for war duty and to punish them for a refusal to serve as soldiers. . . . But that is not to say that Illinois could constitutionally use the test oath it did in this case. . . .

The Illinois Constitution itself prohibits the draft of conscientious objectors except in time of war and also excepts from militia duty persons who are "exempted by the laws of the United States." It has not drafted men into the militia since 1864, and if it ever should again, no one can say that it will not, as has the Congress of the United States, exempt men who honestly entertain the views that this petitioner does. Thus the probability that Illinois would ever call the petitioner to serve in a war has little more reality than an imaginary quantity in mathematics.

I cannot agree that a state can lawfully bar from a semi-public position a well-qualified man of good character solely because he entertains a religious belief which might prompt him at some time in the future to violate a law which has not yet been and may never be enacted. Under our Constitution men are punished for what they do or fail to do and not for what they think and believe. Freedom to think, to believe, and to worship, has too exalted a position in our country to be penalized on such an illusory basis. *West Virginia Board of Education v. Barnette.*

I would reverse the decision of the State Supreme Court.

---

11. "The militia of the state of Illinois shall consist of all able-bodied male persons resident in the state, between the ages of eighteen and forty-five, except such persons as now are, or hereafter may be, exempted by the laws of the United States, or of this state." (Constitution of Illinois, Art. XII, § 1, Ill. Rev. Stat. 1943.)

"No person having conscientious scruples against bearing arms shall be compelled to do militia duty in time of peace; *Provided*, such person shall pay an equivalent for such exemption." (Constitution of Illinois, Art. XII, § 6, Ill. Rev. Stat. 1943.)

## 241 Exclusion of Named Employees (1945)

On February 1, 1943, Congressman Dies named thirty-nine government employees who were affiliated with "Communist front organizations" as "irresponsible, unrepresentative, crackpot, radical bureaucrats." He urged Congress to refuse to appropriate funds to pay their salaries. Congress did not adopt this proposal but authorized the Appropriations Committee to investigate the charges and report back to Congress. The committee held hearings in executive session and permitted the accused em-

ployees to testify. Lawyers were excluded, and only the members of the investigating subcommittee, the witness under examination, and the staff were present. Upon completion of the hearings, the Appropriations Committee concluded that three employees, because of their subversive activities, were unfit to continue in public employment. The House subsequently prohibited, in the Section 304 amendment to a wartime emergency appropriations bill, the payment of the salaries of Robert Morse Lovett, Goodwin B. Watson, and William E. Dodd, Jr., after November 15, 1943. President Truman signed the appropriations bill with reservations that Section 304 was unconstitutional. Denied relief by the Court of Claims, the affected employees appealed to the Supreme Court.

☆ 241  *United States v. Lovett*

328 U.S. 303 (1945).

Mr. Justice BLACK delivered the opinion of the Court:

\*          \*          \*

I

. . . [W]e cannot agree with the two judges of the Court of Claims who held that § 304 required "a mere stoppage of disbursing routine, nothing more," and left the employer governmental agencies free to continue employing respondents and to incur contractual obligations by virtue of such continued work which respondents could enforce in the Court of Claims. Nor can we agree with counsel for Congress that the section did not provide for the dismissal of respondents but merely forbade governmental agencies to compensate respondents for their work or to incur obligations for such compensation at any and all times. We therefore cannot conclude, as he urges, that § 304 is a mere appropriation measure, and that, since Congress under the Constitution has complete control over appropriations, a challenge to the measure's constitutionality does not present a justiciable question in the courts, but is merely a political issue over which Congress has final say.

. . . The section's language as well as the circumstances of its passage which we have just described show that no mere question of compensation procedure or of appropriations was involved, but that it was designed to force the employing agencies to discharge respondents and to bar their being hired by any other governmental agency. Any other interpretation of the section would completely frustrate the purpose of all who sponsored § 304, which clearly was to "purge" the then existing and all future lists of government employees of those whom Congress deemed guilty of "subversive activities" and therefore "unfit" to hold a federal job. . . .

## II

We hold that § 304 falls precisely within the category of congressional actions which the Constitution barred by providing that "No Bill of Attainder or ex post facto Law shall be passed." In *Cummings v. Missouri* this Court said, "A bill of attainder is a legislative act which inflicts punishment without a judicial trial. If the punishment be less than death, the act is termed a bill of pains and penalties. Within the meaning of the Constitution, bills of attainder include bills of pains and penalties." ... [L]egislative acts, no matter what their form, that apply either to named individuals or to easily ascertainable members of a group in such a way as to inflict punishment on them without a judicial trial are bills of attainder prohibited by the Constitution. Adherence to this principle requires invalidation of § 304. We do adhere to it.

Section 304 was designed to apply to particular individuals. ... [I]t "operates as a legislative decree of perpetual exclusion" from a chosen vocation. This permanent proscription from any opportunity to serve the Government is punishment, and of a most severe type. It is a type of punishment which Congress has only invoked for special types of odious and dangerous crimes, such as treason[,] acceptance of bribes by members of Congress or by other government officials, and interference with elections by Army and Navy officers.

Section 304, thus, clearly accomplishes the punishment of named individuals without a judicial trial. The fact that the punishment is inflicted through the instrumentality of an Act specifically cutting off the pay of certain named individuals found guilty of disloyalty, makes it no less galling or effective than if it had been done by an Act which designated the conduct as criminal. No one would think that Congress could have passed a valid law, stating that after investigation it had found Lovett, Dodd, and Watson "guilty" of the crime of engaging in "subversive activities," defined that term for the first time, and sentenced them to perpetual exclusion from any government employment. Section 304, while it does not use that language, accomplishes that result. The effect was to inflict punishment without the safeguards of a judicial trial and "determined by no previous law or fixed rule." The Constitution declares that that cannot be done either by a State or by the United States.

... When our Constitution and Bill of Rights were written, our ancestors had ample reason to know that legislative trials and punishments were too dangerous to liberty to exist in the nation of free men they envisioned. And so they proscribed bills of attainder. Section 304 is one. Much as we regret to declare that an Act of Congress violates the Constitution, we have no alternative here.

Section 304 therefore does not stand as an obstacle to payment of compensation to Lovett, Watson, and Dodd.

*The judgment in their favor is affirmed.*

## 242 " 'He that would make his own liberty secure must guard even his enemy from oppression' " (1945)

Anthony Cramer was a German-born naturalized American citizen. Prior to the United States' entry into World War II, Cramer had been a strong German sympathizer openly opposing this nation's participation in the hostilities against Germany. Cramer met with known German saboteurs, one of whom was a prewar friend, and was subsequently indicted and convicted of treason.

Although it was still wartime, the Supreme Court narrowly concluded that the assistance given by Cramer did not support the charge. It should be noted how carefully the court reviewed the evidence and strictly construed the constitutional offense of treason — unlike its treatment of cases arising out of prosecutions handled under military authority. The difference in treatment illuminates the preference of the executive branch for military rather than civilian law in the trial and punishment of political offenders.

☆ 242  *Cramer v. United States*

325 U.S. 1 (1945).

MR. JUSTICE JACKSON delivered the opinion of the Court.

Anthony Cramer, the petitioner, stands convicted of violating Section 1 of the Criminal Code, which provides: "Whoever, owing allegiance to the United States, levies war against them or adheres to their enemies, giving them aid and comfort within the United States or elsewhere, is guilty of treason."

... Prosecution resulted from his association with two of the German saboteurs, ... Werner Thiel and Edward Kerling. ...

*             *             *

Cramer ... had known intimately the saboteur Werner Thiel while the latter lived in this country. ...

*             *             *

Coming down to the time of the alleged treason, the main facts, as related on the witness stand by Cramer, are not seriously in dispute. He was living in New York; and in response to a cryptic note left under his door, which did not mention Thiel, he went to the Grand Central Station. There Thiel appeared. Cramer had supposed that Thiel was in Germany, knowing that he had left the United States shortly before the war to go there. Together they went to public places and had some drinks. Cramer denies that Thiel revealed his mission of sabotage. Cramer said to Thiel that he must have come to America by submarine, but Thiel refused to confirm it, although his attitude increased Cramer's suspicion. Thiel promised to tell later how he came to this country. Thiel asked about a girl who was a mutual acquaintance and whom Thiel had engaged to marry previous to his going to Germany. Cramer knew where she was, and offered to and did write to her to come to New York, without disclosing in the letter that Thiel had arrived. Thiel said that he had in his possession about $3,600, but did not disclose that it was provided by the German Government, saying only that one could get money in Germany if he had the right connections. Thiel owed Cramer an old debt of $200. He gave Cramer his money belt containing some $3,600, from which Cramer was to be paid. Cramer agreed to and did place the rest in his own safe-deposit box, except a sum which he kept in his room in case Thiel should want it quickly.

*      *      *

Cramer's case raises questions as to application of the constitutional provision that "Treason against the United States shall consist only in levying War against them, or in adhering to their Enemies, giving them Aid and Comfort. No person shall be convicted of Treason unless on the Testimony of two Witnesses to the same overt Act, or on Confession in open Court."

Cramer's contention may be well stated in words of Judge Learned Hand in *United States v. Robinson*:

"Nevertheless a question may indeed be raised whether the prosecution may lay as an overt act a step taken in execution of the traitorous design, innocent in itself, and getting its treasonable character only from some covert and undeclared intent. It is true that in prosecutions for conspiracy under our federal statute it is well settled that any step in performance of the conspiracy is enough, though it is innocent except for its relation to the agreement. I doubt very much whether that rule has any application to the case of treason, where the requirement affected the character of the pleading and proof, rather than accorded a season of repentance before the crime should be complete. Lord Reading in his charge in *Casement's Case* uses language which accords with my understanding:

" 'Overt acts are such acts as manifest a criminal intention and tend towards the accomplishment of the criminal object. They are acts by which the purpose is manifested and the means by which it is intended to be fulfilled.' "

The Government, however, contends for, and the court below has affirmed, this conviction upon a contrary principle. It said: "We believe in short that no more need be laid for an overt act of treason than for an overt act of conspiracy.... Hence we hold the overt acts relied on were sufficient to be submitted to the jury, even though they perhaps may have appeared as innocent on their face." A similar conclusion was reached in *United States v. Fricke*; it is: "An overt act in itself may be a perfectly innocent act standing by itself; it must be in some manner in furtherance of the crime."

I

*      *      *

... [T]he revolutionary doctrine that the people have the right to alter or abolish their government relaxed the loyalty which governments theretofore had demanded—dangerously diluted it, as the ruling classes of Europe thought, for in their eyes the colonists not only committed treason, they exalted it. The idea that loyalty will ultimately be given to a government only so long as it deserves loyalty and that opposition to its abuses is not treason has made our government tolerant of opposition based on differences of opinion that in some parts of the world would have kept the hangman busy. But the basic law of treason in this country was framed by men who, as we have seen, were taught by experience and by history to fear abuse of the treason charge almost as much as they feared treason itself....

II

*      *      *

Distrust of treason prosecutions was not just a transient mood of the Revolutionists. In the century and a half of our national existence not one execution on a federal treason conviction has taken place. Never before has this Court had occasion to review a conviction. In the few cases that have been prosecuted the treason clause has had its only judicial construction by individual Justices of this Court presiding at trials on circuit or by district or circuit judges. After constitutional requirements have been satisfied, and after juries have convicted and courts have sentenced, Presidents again and again have intervened to mitigate judicial severity or to pardon entirely. We have managed to do without treason prosecutions to a degree that probably would be impossible except while a people was singularly confident of external security and internal stability.

III

Historical materials aid interpretation chiefly in that they show two kinds of dangers against which the framers were concerned to guard the treason offense: (1) perversion by established authority to repress peaceful political opposition; and (2) conviction of the innocent as a result of perjury, passion, or inadequate evidence. The first danger could be diminished by closely circumscribing the kind of conduct which should be treason.... The second danger lay in the manner of trial and was one which would be diminished mainly by procedural requirements.... The concern uppermost in the framers' minds, that the mere mental attitudes or expressions should not be treason, influenced both definition of the crime and procedure for its trial....

Treason or adherence to an enemy was old in the law.... It might be predicated on intellectual or emotional sympathy with the foe, or merely lack of zeal in the cause of one's own country. That was not the kind of disloyalty the framers thought should constitute treason. They promptly accepted the proposal to restrict it to cases where also there was conduct which was "giving them aid and comfort."

*         *         *

Thus the crime of treason consists of two elements: adherence to the enemy; and rendering him aid and comfort. A citizen intellectually or emotionally may favor the enemy and harbor sympathies or convictions disloyal to this country's policy or interest, but so long as he commits no act of aid and comfort to the enemy, there is no treason. On the other hand, a citizen may take actions which do aid and comfort the enemy—making a speech critical of the government or opposing its measures, profiteering, striking in defense plants or essential work, and the hundred other things which impair our cohesion and diminish our strength—but if there is no adherence to the enemy in this, if there is no intent to betray, there is no treason.

While to prove giving of aid and comfort would require the prosecution to show actions and deeds, if the Constitution stopped there, such acts could be inferred from circumstantial evidence. This the framers thought would not do. So they added what in effect is a command that the overt acts must be established by direct evidence, and the direct testimony must be that of two witnesses instead of one. In this sense the overt act procedural provision adds something, and something important, to the definition.

Our problem begins where the Constitution ends. That instrument omits to specify what relation the indispensable overt act must sustain to the two elements of the offense as defined: viz., adherence and giving aid and comfort. It requires that two witnesses testify to the same overt act, and clearly enough the act must show something toward treason, but what? Must the act be one of giving aid and comfort? If so, how must adherence to the enemy, the disloyal state of mind, be shown?

The defendant especially challenges the sufficiency of the overt acts to prove treasonable intention. Questions of intent in a treason case are even more complicated than in most criminal cases because of the peculiarity of the two different elements which together make the offense.... [T]o make treason the defendant not only must intend the act, but he must intend to betray his country by means of the act. It is here that Cramer defends. The issue is joined between conflicting theories as to how this treacherous intention and treasonable purpose must be made to appear.

*         *         *

Since intent must be inferred from conduct of some sort, we think it is permissible to draw usual reasonable inferences as to intent from the overt acts. The law of treason, like the law of lesser crimes, assumes every man to intend the natural consequences which one standing in his circumstances and possessing his knowledge would reasonably expect to result from his acts. Proof that a citizen did give aid and comfort to an enemy may well be in the circumstances sufficient evidence that he adhered to that enemy and intended and purposed to strike at his own country....

While of course it must be proved that the accused acted with an intention and purpose to betray or there is no treason, we think that in some circumstances at least the overt act itself will be evidence of the treasonable purpose and intent. But that still leaves us with exceedingly difficult problems.... Must the overt act be appraised for legal sufficiency only as supported by the testimony of two witnesses, or may other evidence be thrown into the scales to create inferences not otherwise reasonably to be drawn or to reinforce those which might be drawn from the act itself?

It is only overt acts by the accused which the Constitution explicitly requires to be proved by the testimony of two witnesses. It does not make other common-law evidence inadmissible nor deny its inherent powers of persuasion....

It would be no contribution to certainty of judgment, which is the object of the provision, to construe it to deprive a trial court of the aid of testimony under the ordinary sanctions of verity, provided, of course, resort is not had to evidence of less than the constitutional standard to supply deficiencies in the constitutional measure of proof of overt acts. For it must be remembered that the constitutional provision establishes a minimum of proof of incriminating acts, without which there can be no conviction, but it is not otherwise a limitation on the evidence with which a jury may be persuaded that it ought to convict....

From duly proven overt acts of aid and comfort to the enemy in their setting, it may well be that the natural and reasonable inference of intention to betray will be warranted.... But the protection of the two-witness rule extends at least to all acts of the defendant which are used to draw incriminating inferences that aid and comfort have been given.

The controversy before us has been waged in terms of intentions, but this, we think, is the reflection of a more fundamental issue as to what is the real function of the overt act in convicting of treason. The prisoner's contention that it alone and on its face must manifest a traitorous intention, apart from an intention to do the act itself, would place on the overt act the whole burden of establishing a complete treason. On the other hand, the Government's contention that it may prove by two witnesses an apparently commonplace and insignificant act and from other circumstances create an inference that the act was a step in treason and was done with treasonable intent really is a contention that the function of the overt act in a treason prosecution is almost zero. It is obvious that the function we ascribe to the overt act is significant chiefly because it measures the two-witness rule protection to the accused and its handicap to the prosecution. If the overt act or acts must go all the way to make out the complete treason, the defendant is protected at all points by the two-witness requirement. If the act may be an insignificant one, then the constitutional safeguards are shrunken so as to be applicable only at a point where they are least needed.

The very minimum function that an overt act must perform in a treason prosecution is that it show sufficient action by the accused, in its setting, to sustain a finding that the accused actually gave aid and comfort to the enemy. Every act, movement, deed, and word of the defendant charged to constitute treason must be supported by the testimony of two witnesses. The two-witness principle is to interdict imputation of *incriminating acts* to the accused by circumstantial evidence or by the testimony of a single witness. The prosecution cannot rely on evidence which does not meet the constitutional test for overt acts to create any inference that the accused did other acts or did something more than was shown in the overt act, in order to make a giving of aid and comfort to the enemy. The words of the Constitution were chosen, not to make it hard to prove merely routine and everyday acts, but to make the proof of acts that convict of treason as sure as trial processes may.... [I]n this and some cases we have cited where the sufficiency of the overt acts has been challenged because they were colorless as to intent, we are persuaded the reason intent was left in question was that the acts were really indecisive as a giving of aid and comfort....

We proceed to consider the application of these principles to Cramer's case.

IV

\*        \*        \*

... By direct testimony of two or more agents it was established that Cramer met Thiel and Kerling on the occasions and at the places charged and that they drank together and engaged long and earnestly in conversation. This is the sum of the overt acts as established by the testimony of two witnesses. There is no two-witness proof of what they said nor in what language they conversed. There is no showing that Cramer gave them any information whatever of value to their mission or indeed that he had any to give. No effort at secrecy is shown, for they met in public places. Cramer furnished them no shelter, nothing that can be called sustenance or supplies, and there is no evidence that he gave them encouragement or counsel, or even paid for their drinks.

The Government recognizes the weakness of its proof of aid and comfort, but on this score it urges: "Little imagination is required to perceive the advantage such meeting would afford to enemy spies not yet detected...." The difficulty with this argument is that the whole purpose of the constitutional provision is to make sure that treason conviction shall rest on direct proof of two witnesses and not on even a little imagination. And without the use of some imagination it is difficult to perceive any advantage which this meeting afforded to Thiel and Kerling as enemies or how it strengthened Germany or weakened the United States in any way whatever.... Meeting with Cramer in public drinking places to tipple and trifle was no part of the saboteurs' mission and did not advance it. It may well have been a digression which jeopardized its success.

The shortcomings of the overt act submitted are emphasized by contrast with others which the indictment charged but which the prosecution withdrew for admitted insufficiency of proof.... That Thiel would be aided by having the security of a safe-deposit box for his funds, plus availability of smaller amounts, and by being relieved of the risks of carrying large sums on his person—without disclosing his presence or identity to a bank—seems obvious. The inference of intent from such act is also very different from the intent manifest by drinking and talking together. Taking what must have seemed a large sum of money for safekeeping is not a usual amenity of social intercourse. That such responsibilities are undertaken and such trust bestowed without the scratch of a pen to show it, implies some degree of mutuality and concert from which a jury could say that aid and comfort was given and was intended. If these acts had been submitted as overt acts of treason, and we were now required to decide whether they had been established as required, we would have a quite different case.... But this transaction was not proven as the Government evidently hoped to do when the indictment was obtained. The overt acts based on it were expressly withdrawn from the jury, and Cramer has not been convicted of treason on account of such acts. We cannot sustain a conviction for the acts submitted on the theory that, even if insufficient, some unsubmitted ones may be resorted to as proof of treason. Evidence of the money transaction serves only to show how much went out of the case when it was withdrawn.

The Government contends that outside of the overt acts, and by lesser degree of proof, it has shown a treasonable intent on Cramer's part in meeting and talking with Thiel and Kerling. But if it showed him disposed to betray, and showed that he had opportunity to do so, it still has not proved in the manner required that he did any acts submitted to the jury as a basis for conviction which had the effect of betraying by giving aid and comfort. To take the intent for the deed would carry us back to constructive treasons.

It is outside of the commonplace overt acts as proved that we must find all that convicts or convinces either that Cramer gave aid and comfort or that he had a traitorous intention. . . .

It is not relevant to our issue to appraise weight or credibility of the evidence apart from determining its constitutional sufficiency. . . . At all events much of the evidence is of the general character whose infirmities were feared by the framers and sought to be safeguarded against.

Most damaging is the testimony of Norma Kopp, a friend of Cramer's and one with whom, if she is to be believed, he had been most indiscreetly confidential. . . . To the extent that his conviction rests upon such evidence, and it does to an unknown but considerable extent, it rests upon the uncorroborated testimony of one witness not without strong emotional interest in the drama of which Cramer's trial was a part. Other evidence relates statements by Cramer before the United States was at war with Germany. At the time they were uttered, however, they were not treasonable. To use pre-war expressions of opposition to entering a war to convict of treason during the war is a dangerous procedure at best. The same may be said about the inference of disloyal attitude created by showing that he refused to buy bonds and closed the door in the salesman's face. Another class of evidence consists of admissions to agents of the Federal Bureau of Investigation. They are, of course, not "confessions in open court." . . .

V

\*         \*         \*

The framers' effort to compress into two sentences the law of one of the most intricate of crimes gives a superficial appearance of clarity and simplicity which proves illusory when it is put to practical application. There are few subjects on which the temptation to utter abstract interpretation generalizations is greater or on which they are more to be distrusted. The little clause is packed with controversy and difficulty. The offense is one of subtlety, and it is easy to demonstrate lack of logic in almost any interpretation by hypothetical cases, to which real treasons rarely will conform. . . .

\*         \*         \*

It is not difficult to find grounds upon which to quarrel with this constitutional provision. . . . Certainly the treason rule, whether wisely or not, is severely restrictive. It must be remembered, however, that the Constitutional Convention was warned by James Wilson that "Treason may sometimes be practiced in such a manner, as to render proof extremely difficult—as in a traitorous correspondence with an Enemy." The provision was adopted not merely in spite of the difficulties it put in the way of prosecution but because of them. And it was not by whim or by accident, but because one of the most venerated of that venerated group considered that "prosecutions for treason were generally virulent." Time has not made the accusation of treachery less poisonous, nor the task of judging one charged with betraying the country, including his triers, less susceptible to the influence of suspicion and rancor. The innovations made by the forefathers in the law of treason were conceived in a faith such as Paine put in the maxim that "He that would make his own liberty secure must guard even his enemy from oppression; for if he violates this duty he establishes a precedent that will reach himself." We still put trust in it.

We hold that overt acts 1 and 2 are insufficient as proved to support the judgment of conviction, which accordingly is

*Reversed.*

## 243 "the military authorities took over the government of Hawaii" (1946)

On the day that the Japanese attacked Pearl Harbor, Hawaii's governor declared martial law and suspended the writ of habeas corpus, as authorized by the Hawaiian Organic Act in cases of rebellion, invasion, or imminent danger thereof. Under this authority military tribunals (which did not observe the strictures of the Bill of Rights) took over the function of the civilian courts. Duncan petitioned for a writ of habeas corpus after being convicted by one of these tribunals.

Without addressing the constitutional issues, the Supreme Court recognized the imposition of martial law but denied the legitimacy of the military tribunals. Justice Murphy, in concurrence, admonished the court for not being more forceful in its condemnation of military usurpation of governmental power.

## ☆ 243 *Duncan v. Kahanamoku*

327 U.S. 304 (1946).

Mr. Justice BLACK delivered the opinion of the Court.

\*          \*          \*

... The President approved the Governor's action on December 9th. The Governor's proclamation also authorized and requested the Commanding General, "during ... the emergency and until danger of invasion is removed, to exercise all the powers normally exercised" by the Governor and by "the judicial officers and employees of the Territory."

\*          \*          \*

... Thus the military authorities took over the government of Hawaii. They could and did, by simply promulgating orders, govern the day to day activities of civilians who lived, worked, or were merely passing through there. The military tribunals interpreted the very orders promulgated by the military authorities and proceeded to punish violators. The sentences imposed were not subject to direct appellate court review, since it had long been established that military tribunals are not part of our judicial system....

\*          \*          \*

Duncan ... was a civilian shipfitter employed in the Navy Yard at Honolulu. On February 24th, 1944, more than two years and two months after the Pearl Harbor attack, he engaged in a brawl with two armed Marine sentries at the yard. He was arrested by the military authorities. By the time of his arrest the military had to some extent eased the stringency of military rule. Schools, bars and motion picture theatres had been reopened. Courts had been authorized to "exercise their normal functions." They were once more summoning jurors and witnesses and conducting criminal trials. There were important exceptions, however. One of these was that only military tribunals were to try "Criminal Prosecutions for violations of military orders." ... He was therefore tried by a military tribunal rather than the Territorial Court, although the general laws of Hawaii made assault a crime.... A conviction followed and Duncan was sentenced to six months imprisonment.

\*          \*          \*

We believe that when Congress passed the Hawaiian Organic Act and authorized the establishment of "martial law" it had in mind and did not wish to exceed the boundaries between military and civil-

ian power, in which our people have always believed, which responsible military and executive officers had heeded, and which had become part of our political philosophy and institutions prior to the time Congress passed the Organic Act. The phrase "martial law" as employed in that Act, therefore, while intended to authorize the military to act vigorously for the maintenance of an orderly civil government and for the defense of the island against actual or threatened rebellion or invasion, was not intended to authorize the supplanting of courts by military tribunals. Yet the government seeks to justify the punishment of ... Duncan on the ground of such supposed Congressional authorization. We hold that [petitioner is] now entitled to be released from custody.

*Reversed.*

Mr. Justice MURPHY, concurring.

The Court's opinion, in which I join, makes clear that the military trials in these cases were unjustified by the martial law provisions of the Hawaiian Organic Act. Equally obvious, as I see it, is the fact that these trials were forbidden by the Bill of Rights of the Constitution of the United States, which applies in both spirit and letter to Hawaii. Indeed, the unconstitutionality of the usurpation of civil power by the military is so great in this instance as to warrant this Court's complete and outright repudiation of the action.

Abhorrence of military rule is ingrained in our form of government. Those who founded this nation knew full well that the arbitrary power of conviction and punishment for pretended offenses is the hallmark of despotism. History had demonstrated that fact to them time and again. They shed their blood to win independence from a ruler who they alleged was attempting to render the "military independent of and superior to the civil power" and who was "depriving us of the benefits of trial by jury." In the earliest state constitutions they inserted definite provisions placing the military under "strict subordination" to the civil power at all times and in all cases. And in framing the Bill of Rights of the Federal Constitution they were careful to make sure that the power to punish would rest primarily with the civil authorities at all times. They believed that a trial by an established court, with an impartial jury, was the only certain way to protect an individual against oppression. The Bill of Rights translated that belief into reality by guaranteeing the observance of jury trials and other basic procedural rights foreign to military proceedings. This supremacy of the civil over the military is one of our great heritages. It has made possible the attainment of a high degree of liberty regulated by law rather than by caprice. Our duty is to give effect to that heritage at all times, that it may be handed down untarnished to future generations.

... There is a very necessary part in our national life for the military; it has defended this country well in its darkest hours of trial. But militarism is not our way of life. It is to be used only in the most extreme circumstances.

# 244 "an uninterrupted record of economic aggression" (1946)

Ezra Pound was born in Hailey, Idaho, on October 30, 1885. In 1907 he traveled extensively throughout Europe, eventually settling in England. Considered a brilliant and erudite poet and translator, Pound exerted great influence on several poetic movements. His *Cantos* represented the greatest body of his work. After emigrating to Italy in 1924, he broadcast Fascist propaganda to the United States up to and during World War II. After Pound was indicted for treason, a potentially difficult and controversial trial on the charge was avoided when, upon the testimony of physicians, a jury found him to be incompetent to stand trial. The court confined him to St. Elizabeth's mental hospital in Washington, D.C. *Pisan Cantos*, published during his confinement, won him the Bollingen Prize, an important literary award, in 1949. He remained under guard at St. Elizabeth's for twelve years. Upon his release in 1958 he returned to Italy, where he died in 1972. Other United States citizens, however, were convicted of treason for conducting "psychological warfare" against the United States through propaganda broadcasts. *Gillars v. United States*, 182 F.2d 902 (D.C. Cir. 1950).

☆ 244 The Trial of Ezra Pound

Reprinted in J. Cornell, *The Trial of Ezra Pound: A Documented Account of the Treason Case by the Defendant's Lawyer* (New York: John Day, 1966).

☆ 244a Transcript of Short Wave Broadcast, May 15, 1943. Cornell, 141-44.

Europe calling, Ezra Pound speaking.

About economic aggression. Mr. Sumner Welles' speech at Toledo was a serious matter....

\*     \*     \*

... Had Mr. Welles been ready to make such a speech three years ago, this distressing war might have been quite well avoided. Mr. Welles appeared to be renouncing dollar diplomacy. A few months sooner, a good deal of bloodshed might have been spared us. Mr. Welles also spoke of misapprehension, of incomplete knowledge, of heedlessness, inconsideration.

I'm perfectly ready to take Mr. Welles' speech at its face value. If the United States has been ill informed, or tardily informed of the conditions of Europe, there is no reason for you to remain voluntarily in that condition. But, it is now extremely hard for the people inside any country to get accurate impressions of the state of mind of people inside any other. It has been for years, extremely hard to get news into America.... It is not to be supposed that even now, Mr. Welles would listen to me over a cable, or answer what I intend to say to him during the next five minutes.

\*     \*     \*

... Now to the outer world, the American history of the past 30 years appears to be an uninterrupted record of economic aggression on the part of the United States. The United States is the hometown of the Rockefellers, Guggenheims, Morgan. The world has had on its news stalls the works of Vishka (?), I suppose he's a Polish author. Anyhow he wrote the "War for Oil," "War for Cotton," and so on. And we have heard of wars for commodities and wars for gold. We have heard much less of a sacred war that the United States lost in 1863.

While the boys in blue and the boys in grey were obligingly dying and taking the spotlight, the Civil War was, at that time, a world record for carnage and both sides well vanquished. The control of the national credit, control of the national currency, the national purchasing power, passes right away from the people and right out of the control of the national and responsible government. That is why many of Mrs. Welles' foreign auditors will think there is a nigger in Mr. Welles' woodshed. Suddenly a coalition of the three most aggressive powers, economically aggressive powers, on earth, put forth not an official statement, but a statement by the most authoritative member of the State Department to the effect that economic aggression is, after all, a factor in causing wars, and that to obtain a durable peace we must lay off it.

England, Mr. Welles tell us, is aggressive, economically. The United States, has in the past been aggressive, Russia has made up for lost time and been extremely aggressive. Quite economically. It does sound to the European almost as if Legs Diamond, or Billy the Kid or Jesse James had suddenly decided to change his habits. I mean, economic aggression has been for so long considered the very breath of life for the American system, the bone of its bone, its inner and intimate fiber. And then again, when a nation's inner life is so palpably made up of the economic aggression of one class or group against the whole rest of the population, it is very difficult for any foreigner, or indeed for anyone not carried away by political heat of the moment, to see why that particular nation should be entrusted with the latch key of any other.

I will return to this subject.

Ezra Pound, speaking.

☆244b Indictment. Cornell, 145-48.

In the District Court of the United States for the District of Columbia
October Term A.D. 1945

The Grand Jurors for the United States of America duly impaneled and sworn in the District Court of the United States for the District of Columbia and inquiring for that District upon their oath present:

\*      \*      \*

2. That the defendant, Ezra Pound, at Rome, Italy and other places within the kingdom of Italy ... in the manner and by the means hereinafter set forth, then and there being a citizen of the United States, and a person owing allegiance to the United States, in violation of said duty of allegiance, knowingly, intentionally, wilfully, unlawfully, feloniously, traitorously and treasonably did adhere to the enemies of the United States, ... giving to the said enemies of the United States aid and comfort within the United States and elsewhere, that is to say:

3. ... (a) Of accepting employment from the Kingdom of Italy in the capacity of a radio propagandist and in the performance of the duties thereof which involved the composition of texts, speeches, talks and announcements and the recording thereof for subsequent broadcast over short-wave radio on wave lengths audible in the United States and elsewhere on ordinary commercial radio receiving sets having short-wave reception facilities....

That the aforesaid activities of the said defendant, Ezra Pound, were intended to persuade citizens and residents of the United States to decline to support the United States in the conduct of the said war, to weaken or destroy confidence in the Government of the United States and in the integrity and loyalty of the Allies of the United States, and to further bind together and increase the morale of the subjects of the Kingdom of Italy in support of the prosecution of the said war by the Kingdom of Italy and its military allies.

4. And the Grand Jurors aforesaid upon their oath aforesaid do further present that the said defendant, Ezra Pound, in the prosecution, performance and execution of said treason ... did do, perform, and commit certain overt and manifest acts, that is to say:

[Here the indictment alleges overt acts consisting of broadcasts by Pound over a radio station of the Italian government at Rome, Italy on September 11, 1942; December 10, 1942; February 4, 1943; March 19, 1943; May 12, 1943; May 14, 1943; May 15, 1943; and recording of broadcasts on various dates.]

\*      \*      \*

A TRUE BILL

☆244c Report to the Court of Examining Psychiatrists [Read in court 12/21/45]. Cornell, 36-37.

SIR:

The undersigned hereby respectfully report the results of their mental examination of Ezra Pound, now detained in Gallinger Hospital by transfer for observation from the District Jail on a charge of treason. Three of us (Drs. Gilbert, King, and Overholser) were appointed by your Honor to make this examination. At our suggestion, and with your approval, Dr. Wendell Muncie, acting upon the request of counsel for the accused, made an examination with us and associates himself with us in this joint report. Dr. Muncie spent several hours with the defendant, both alone and with us, on December 13, 1945, and the others of us have examined the defendant each on several occasions, separately and together, in the period from his admission to Gallinger Hospital on December 4, 1945, to December 13, 1945. We have had available to us the reports of laboratory, psychological and special physical examinations of the defendant and considerable material in the line of his writings and biographical data.

The defendant, now 60 years of age and in generally good physical condition, was a precocious student, specializing in literature. He has been a voluntary expatriate for nearly 40 years, living in England and France, and for the past 21 years in Italy, making an uncertain living by writing poetry and criticism. His poetry and literary criticism have achieved considerable recognition, but of recent years his preoccupation with monetary theories and economics has apparently obstructed his literary productivity. He has long been recognized as eccentric, querulous, and egocentric.

At the present time he exhibits extremely poor judgment as to his situation, its seriousness and the manner in which the charges are to be met. He insists that his broadcasts were not treasonable, but that all of his radio activities have stemmed from his self-appointed mission to "save the Constitution." He is abnormally grandiose, is expansive and exuberant in manner, exhibiting pressure of speech, discursiveness, and distractibility. In our opinion, with advancing years his personality, for many years abnormal, has undergone further distortion to the extent that he is now suffering from a paranoid state which renders him mentally unfit to advise properly with counsel or to participate intelligently and reasonably in his own defense. He is, in other words, insane and mentally unfit for trial, and is in need of care in a mental hospital.

Respectfully submitted,

JOSEPH L. GILBERT, M.D.
MARION R. KING, M.D.
WENDELL MUNCIE, M.D.
WINFRED OVERHOLSER, M.D.

☆244d Transcript of Hearing, February 13, 1946.
Cornell, 188–96.

[Direct Examination, JULIAN CORNELL, Defense Counsel:]

Q. Will you tell us the reasons which lead you to the conclusion that he is unable to participate in the trial of this indictment intelligently? A. [DR. WINFRED OVERHOLSER, Superintendent of St. Elizabeth's Hospital, Washington, D.C.] Yes, and other things in addition. In the first place, it is quite obvious that the man has always been unusually eccentric through the years. He has undoubtedly a high regard of his own opinion, and has been extremely vituperative of those who disagree with him.

He has a very high degree of intelligence, there is no question on that score, and his relations with the world and other people during practically all his life have been those of a person who was very skeptical to say the least.

He is extremely free in his conversation; he has not been reticent by any stretch of the imagination, but his production has been unusually hard to follow. He speaks in bunches of ideas.

Q. You mean his production of speech? A. Yes, and rambling and illogical.

*          *          *

The ideas, perhaps, which he expresses indicate some of his views in connection with the war. In the first place, he is thoroughly convinced that if he had been allowed to send his messages to the Axis, which he wished to send, prior to 1940, there would have been no Axis even. In other words, that if given a free hand by those who were engaged in stultifying him, he could have prevented the war.

He lays a great deal of his difficulty at the door of British Secret Service, and other groups, which have opposed him.

He assures me, too, that he served a very useful purpose to the United States by remaining at the Italian prison camp to complete his translation of Confucius, which he regards as the greatest contribution to literature.

He is sure that he should not have been brought to this country in the capacity of a prisoner, but in the capacity of someone who was to be of great benefit to the United States in its post-war activities.

I might state that this constitutes a grandiosity of ideas and beliefs that goes far beyond the normal, even in a person who is as distraught in his mind as he is.

From a practical view of his advising with his attorney, there would be the fact that you cannot keep him on a straight line of conversation; he rambles around, and has such a naive grasp of the situation in which he finds himself, it would not be fair to him or his attorney to put him on trial.

*          *          *

Q. You mentioned his naive reasoning. Will you expand on that? A. For example, he did not expect to be brought here. He did not expect to be put in prison when he got here. He thought he was double-crossed. He thought he was to be used by the government in any movement for the organization of the world. He is sure that his connections with Japan would enable him to deal with the delicate post-war situation. I think "naive" is a mild word to apply to that line of reasoning.

Q. Based upon your knowledge and understanding of the situation, how do you regard his ability to understand the situation and to answer questions in connection with the presentation of his defense? A. Well, with an infinite amount of patience, and an infinite amount of time, it might be possible sometime in the future to get a lucid answer to a question.

Q. In other words, would his discursiveness and inability to answer questions prevent his attorney from presenting his side of the picture in defense of this indictment? A. It would.

MR. CORNELL: Your witness.

*          *          *

[Cross-examination by MR. MATLACK:]

*          *          *

Q. What is your opinion as to the chances of improvement for this patient? A. As far as the basic sub-strata beneath these ideas of persecution, and so on, I should say not particularly good. . . . [W]hile he is in this particular condition I do not look for any fundamental change in his condition.

*          *          *

Q. Now, what part does his background history play in your opinion as to his present sanity? A. It shows that we are dealing now with the end-product of an individual who throughout his lifetime has been highly antagonistic, highly eccentric, the whole world has revolved around him, he has been a querulous person, he has been less and less able to order his life. This has been a gradual evolution through his life, so that now we are dealing with the end-product, so to speak.

Q. Do you think that because he is eccentric that makes him unable to consult counsel? A. Oh, no.

Q. That is true of many people? A. Yes.

Q. That does not make him unable to consult with counsel? A. It might make him a nuisance.

Q. Make him a nuisance but not insane? A. Yes.

Q. I think you said one of the characteristics was that he was very vituperative to one who opposed his will? A. He has been.

Q. Do you think that, in itself, displays a person who could not be able to consult with counsel? A. Not in itself. I haven't said that any one of these things in itself would.

Q. I am going to come to that. I have forgotten what other thing you did say. I did understand you to say that he is vituperative, and eccentric; I don't know whether you used the word "sensitive" or not. A. No, but he is highly supersensitive.

Q. Now, couldn't a man who was eccentric, and vituperative, and all the other attributes that you have given to him rolled into one, still be able to consult with counsel? A. Even with all those three, and with nothing else, very likely, yes.

*       *       *

Q. Did he give you in his general history anything about his belief in Fascism? A. I did not discuss that with him particularly.

THE DEFENDANT: I never did believe in Fascism, God damn it; I am opposed to Fascism.

*       *       *

Q. Did he ever discuss with you his advocacy of Mussolini and his politics? A. In the most general terms. I didn't go into that in great detail, either. I looked upon that as a political matter.

Q. Well; that is what I am beginning to get at. Did you read his book entitled Jefferson and Mussolini? A. No.

Q. Did you take into consideration the fact that living in Italy, where the political philosophy was Fascism, that he may have become imbued with that philosophy?

MR. CORNELL: Your Honor, I object to this line of questioning and characterization of Mr. Pound, which I think is very distressing to him.

THE COURT: I will give you a certain latitude, but try not to disturb him if you can help it.

MR. MATLACK: I will strike the question and ask it again.

By MR. MATLACK: Q. Did the fact that living in Italy, where Fascism was a political philosophy, and where most of the people in Italy had adopted the Mussolini Government, have any influence, do you think, on the question of whether he is sane or insane? A. No, I should not say so.

Q. Well, would the fact that somebody believed like Mussolini in his theories, or political philosophies, and the fact that others joined in his beliefs, and were otherwise normal, make them abnormal? A. I think that is a question of politics rather than psychiatry.

Q. Now, on the same theory, if somebody believes in an economic theory such as social credit, and is able to write and broadcast his theories about social credit, does the fact that he is imbued with a belief in social credit, if he is otherwise normal, make him abnormal or insane? A. I don't know that I mentioned his views on social credit. There are a great many people who take stock in that view of economics, but I do not think that because one believes in it stamps him any more than out of agreement with most people in this country at least.

Q. If I understand your testimony, he has certain grandiose ideas of saving the Constitution through the money clause in the Constitution, and that on certain economic theories if he could get to Japan he might have been of some service to the United States, and so on; I think that is what you testified to. A. I am not sure on the economic phase of the theories and, in fact, I never did get to the end of the explanation.

Q. Now, just how was he going to save the Constitution? A. There was some discussion about the money clause of the Constitution, but just what it had to do with saving the Constitution I was not quite clear.

*       *       *

Q. On what do you base your conclusion that he is in a paranoid state if it isn't based on his theories about saving the Constitution, and so on? A. The matter of his saving the Constitution, the mention about saving the Constitution is one of the factors. I don't remember that I mentioned that. I did mention particularly his idea that he could have prevented the formation of the Nazis; that he was the victim of machinations of the British Secret Service and antagonistic groups; that he was of far more use as an adviser to the Government than as a defendant in a criminal case.

*       *       *

Q. On the other hand, you think that under those circumstances, he thought he would be of service to the United States? A. As I say, he was unable to explain what that was, or how it would be accomplished. It was the fact he felt he was so important and of such value to the United States that I put him down as suffering a mental disorder.

Q. Did you talk to him at all about the charge of treason he is under? A. Yes.

Q. Did he understand that he had done anything treasonable? A. Apparently not, because he denied that he had done anything in connection with the Government of Italy against the United States. There was no significance apparently to that charge.

*       *       *

Q. Did he realize that he was subject to trial and possible conviction and punishment? A. I should say that his attitude was that the reasons for his being brought over as a prisoner was a part of the plot against him on the part of the British Secret Service and the Communist groups that he mentioned; in other words, that they were instigating the Department of Justice in the prosecution. That sounded to me pathological.

Q. Do you think that that could be without any foundation of fact when shortly before that he had given a statement to the Department as to his activities in which he recognized that he had been charged with treason? A. Oh, he knew he had been charged with treason. He told me that.

Q. And he knew it before he was brought to this country? A. Oh, yes.

Q. But did I understand you to say that notwithstanding that, that he thought he was coming over here to be of assistance to the United States in some other capacity? A. Yes.

Q. Do you think that that was something he might have told you out of whole cloth? A. It did not appear that way to me; taking into consideration the whole line of examination, I am quite convinced that there was no question of malingering.

Q. No malingering in that statement or any other, but in that particular statement you did not think that there was any question of malingering? A. No.

*       *       *

Q. Do you feel that he was so imbued with his economic theories, or whatever his message might have been, that even if he had realized the consequences of his treasonable act that he still would have broadcast? A. I haven't an opinion on it.

MR. MATLACK: I think that is all.

*       *       *

☆244e  *New York Herald Tribune* Account (February 14, 1946). Cornell, 44–45.

WASHINGTON, Feb. 13, 1946.—The treason case against Ezra Pound, expatriate American poet, was pigeon-holed today when a specially impaneled Federal jury returned a verdict that Pound is "mentally unsound" and unfit to stand trial on treason charges arising out of his war-time writings and broadcasts in Fascist Italy. This is the first time an accused war criminal has escaped trial because of insanity.

The sixty-year-old poet will be confined here at the St. Elizabeths Federal Hospital for the Insane. He may again face trial if he recovers from his present "paranoiac state," government prosecutors said, pointing out that a treason charge has no limitation, being valid until the defendant dies. They virtually conceded defeat, however, by announcing that the government will send back to Italy seven Fascist radio announcers who were to have been key witnesses against Pound.

The jury deliberated only five minutes after hearing four and a half hours' testimony by four psychiatrists. Chief Justice Bolitha Laws, of the Federal District Court hearing the case, called the jury at the request of the prosecution.

The same psychiatrists had filed affidavits with the court on Dec. 14 declaring the poet unfit for trial, but government attorneys had demanded a public jury hearing of their findings. . . . All four experts agreed that Pound is mentally unsound, probably permanently. They all attested a prevailing "grandiosity" in the poet, which they said indicated his abnormal mental state.

Pound was not called to testify, but he sprang to his feet at one point, shouting, "I've never been a Fascist, Goddamit! I've always opposed them." He did this when a government attorney asked a witness if he had ever heard Pound speak of his views on Fascism.

Throughout the rest of the hearing, the bearded defendant moved nervously in his seat, held his head in his hands or leaned back and stared at the ceiling.

The psychiatrists reported that nearly two months' observation of Pound's mental condition revealed a number of "fixed ideas" held by the poet: That his mission in life was to save the United States Constitution, that the only way to world peace was through the teachings of Confucius, that he could have prevented the formation of the Axis and the war by uniting intellectual groups of the world and that he was persecuted by bureaucrats.

All four agreed that, in their observation, Pound was not able to explain his reasons for holding these views, and that he could not confer logically on any subject for even a brief period. They said they believed, therefore, that he would not be able to consult with his counsel on defense against the treason charges.

## 245  "a thoroughgoing Nazi" (1946)

The relationship between citizen and sovereign is based on allegiance by the former and proffered protection by the latter. When the relationship fails, how is it dissolved?

The United States informally has long recognized the rights of voluntary expatriation, that is, the right to renounce one's citizenship. England's refusal to recognize that right and its belief that American sailors were British subjects available for impressment into the British navy was a major impetus for the War of 1812. In 1868, the United States formally recognized the right of voluntary expatriation.

Forced expatriation stands on different footing. In 1940, and in subsequent legislation, Congress provided that a citizen, born here or naturalized, would lose United States citizenship involuntarily by performing certain acts that Congress deemed to be inconsistent with the obligations of allegiance. In *Afroyim v. Rusk*, 387 U.S. 253 (1967), the Supreme Court held Congress had no power to expatriate citizens without their consent regardless of the offense committed. In contrast, the process of "denaturalization," described below, continues to be available to challenge and revoke citizenship obtained by the foreign-born through alleged fraud in his or her oath of allegiance.

☆ 245  *Knauer v. United States*

328 U.S. 654 (1946).

MR. JUSTICE DOUGLAS delivered the opinion of the Court.

Knauer is a native of Germany. He arrived in this country in 1925 at the age of 30. He had served in the German army during World War I and was decorated. He had studied law and economics in Germany. He settled in Milwaukee, Wisconsin, and conducted an insurance business there. He filed his declaration of intention to become a citizen in 1929 and his petition for naturalization in 1936. He took his oath of allegiance and was admitted to citizenship on April 13, 1937. In 1943 the United States instituted proceedings under § 338(a) of the Nationality Act of 1940 to cancel his certificate of naturalization on the ground that it had been secured by fraud in that (1) he had falsely and fraudulently represented in his petition that he was attached to the principles of the Constitution and (2) he had taken a false oath of allegiance. The District Court was satisfied beyond a reasonable doubt that Knauer practiced fraud when he obtained his certificate of naturalization. It found that he had not been and is not attached to the principles of the Constitution and that he took a false oath of allegiance. It accordingly entered an order cancelling his certificate and revoking the order admitting him to citizenship. The Circuit Court of Appeals affirmed....

I. In the oath of allegiance which Knauer took, he swore that he would "absolutely and entirely renounce and abjure all allegiance and fidelity to any foreign prince, potentate, state, or sovereignty, and particularly to the German Reich," that he would "support and defend the Constitution and laws of the United States of America against all enemies, foreign and domestic"; that he would "bear true faith and allegiance to the same" and that he took "this obligation freely without any mental reservation or purpose of evasion." The first and crucial issue in the case is whether Knauer swore falsely and committed a fraud when he promised under oath to forswear allegiance to the German Reich and to transfer his allegiance to this nation. Fraud connotes perjury, falsification, concealment, misrepresentation. When denaturalization is sought on this as well as on other grounds, the standard of proof required is strict....

That strict test is necessary for several reasons. Citizenship obtained through naturalization is not a second-class citizenship. It has been said that citizenship carries with it all of the rights and prerogatives of citizenship obtained by birth in this country "save that of eligibility to the Presidency." There are other exceptions of a limited character. But it is plain that citizenship obtained through naturalization carries with it the privilege of full participation in the affairs of our society, including the right to speak freely, to criticize officials and administrators, and to promote changes in our laws including the very Charter of our Government. Great tolerance and caution are necessary lest good faith exercise of the rights of citizenship be turned against the naturalized citizen and be used to deprive him of the cherished status. Ill-tempered expressions, extreme views, even the promotion of ideas which run counter to our American ideals, are not to be given disloyal connotations in absence of solid, convincing evidence that that is their significance. Any other course would run counter to our traditions and make denaturalization proceedings the ready instrument for political persecutions. "Were the law otherwise, valuable rights would rest upon a slender reed, and the security of the status of our naturalized citizens might depend in considerable degree upon the political temper of majority thought and the stresses of the times."

These are extremely serious problems. They involve not only fundamental principles of our political system designed for the protection of minorities and majorities alike. They also involve tremendously high stakes for the individual. For denaturalization, like deportation, may result in the loss "of all that makes life worth living." ... "Forswearing past political allegiance without reservation and full assumption of the obligations of American citizenship are not at all inconsistent with cultural feelings imbedded in childhood and youth." Human ties are not easily broken. Old social or cultural loyalties may still exist, though basic allegiance is transferred here. The fundamental question is whether the new citizen still takes his orders from, or owes his allegiance to, a foreign chancellory. Far more is required to establish that fact than a showing that social and cultural ties remain. And even political utterances, which might be some evidence of a false oath if they clustered around the date of naturalization, are more and more unreliable as evidence of the perjurious falsity of the oath the further they are removed from the date of naturalization.

We have read with care the voluminous record in this case.... We conclude with the District Court and the Circuit Court of Appeals that there is solid, convincing evidence that Knauer before the date of his naturalization, at that time, and subsequently was a thoroughgoing Nazi and a faithful follower of Adolph Hitler. The conclusion is irresistible, therefore, that when he forswore allegiance to the German Reich he swore falsely. The character of the evidence, the veracity of the witnesses against Knauer as determined by the District Court, the corroboration of challenged evidence presented by the Government, the consistent pattern of Knauer's conduct before and after naturalization convince us that the two lower courts were correct in their conclusions. The standard of proof ... is therefore plainly met here.

We will review briefly that we, as well as the two lower courts, accept as the true version of the facts.

As early as 1931, Knauer told a newly arrived immigrant who came from the same town in Germany that in his opinion the aim of Hitler and the Nazi party was good, that it would progress, and that it was necessary to have the same party in this country because of the Jews and the Communists. During the same period, he told another friend repeatedly that he was opposed to any republican form of government and that Jewish capital was to blame for Germany's downfall. He visited Germany for about six months in 1934 and while there read Hitler's Mein Kampf. On his return he said with pride that he had met Hitler, and that he had been offered a post with the German government at 600 marks per month, that Hitler was the savior of Germany, that Hitler was solving the unemployment problem while this country was suffering from Jewish capitalism, that the Hitler youth organization was an excellent influence on the children of Germany. On occasions in 1936 and 1937 he was explosive in his criticism of those who protested against the practices and policies of Hitler.

The German Winter Relief Fund was an official agency of the German government for which German consulates solicited money in the United States. In the winter of 1934-1935 Knauer was active in obtaining contributions to the Fund and forwarded the money collected to the German consulate in Chicago.

\*       \*       \*

Knauer participated in Bund meetings in 1936. In the summer of 1936 he and his family had a tent at the Bund camps. In the fall of 1936 he enrolled his young daughter in the Youth Movement of the Bund — a group organized to instill the Nazi ideology in the minds of children of German blood. They wore uniforms, used the Nazi salute, and were taught songs of allegiance to Hitler. Knauer attended meetings of this group.

The Federation of German-American Societies represented numerous affiliated organizations consisting of Americans of German descent and sought to coordinate their work. It was the policy of the Bund to infiltrate older German societies. This effort was made as respects the Federation. Knauer assisted Froboese and others between 1933 and 1936 in endeavoring to have the swastika displayed at celebrations of the Federation. In 1935 Knauer reprimanded a delegate to the Federation for passing out pamphlets opposing the Nazi government in Germany. At a meeting of the Federation in 1935, Knauer moved to have the Federation recognize the swastika as the flag of the German Reich. The mo-

tion failed to carry.... Froboese and others proposed the formation of the German-American Citizens Alliance to compete with the Federation. It was organized early in 1937. The constitution and articles of incorporation of the Alliance provided that all of its assets on dissolution were to become the property of a German government agency for the dissemination of propaganda in foreign countries — the Deusches Auslands-Institut. The Alliance was a front organization for the Bund. It was designed to bring into its ranks persons who were sympathetic with the objectives of the Bund but who did not wish to be known as Bund members.

On February 22, 1937 — less than two months before Knauer took his oath of naturalization — he was admitted to membership in the Alliance and became a member of its executive committee.... In 1938 Knauer was elected vice-president of the Alliance and subsequently presided over most of its meetings. He was the dominant figure in the Alliance. In May 1937 the German consul presented to the Alliance the swastika flag which had been torn down at the Federation celebration the year before. Not long after his naturalization Knauer urged that the Alliance sponsor a solstice ceremony, a solemn rite at which a wooden swastika is burned to symbolize the unity of German people everywhere. In August 1937 the Alliance refused to participate in an affair sponsored by a group which would not fly the swastika flag. In May 1938 Knauer at a meeting of the Alliance read a leaflet entitled "America, the Garbage Can of the World." In 1939 he arranged for public showings of films distributed by an official German propaganda agency and depicting the glories of Nazism.

\*       \*       \*

In May 1938 Knauer and Froboese formed the American Protective League with a secret list of members. Knauer was elected a director. A constitution and bylaws were adopted and copies mailed by Knauer and Froboese to Hitler....

Important evidence implicating Knauer in promoting the cause of Hitler in this country was given by a Mrs. Merton. She testified that, prompted solely by patriotic motives, she entered the employ of Froboese in 1938 in order to obtain evidence against the Bund and its members....

Her testimony may be summarized as follows: She acted as secretary to Froboese in 1938. During the period of her employ Froboese and Knauer worked closely together on Bund matters. He helped Froboese in the preparation of articles for the Bund newspaper, of speeches, and of Bund correspondence. He helped Froboese prepare resolutions to be offered at the 1938 Bund convention calling for a white-gentile-ruled America. When Froboese left the city to attend the convention, he told her to contact Knauer for advice concerning Bund matters.

Letters signed by Froboese and Knauer jointly were sent to Hitler and other Nazi officials. One contained a list of 700 German nationals. One was the constitution and by-laws of the American Protective League which we have already mentioned. One to Hess said they had to lay low for awhile, that there was an investigation on. A birthday greeting to Hitler from Froboese and Knauer closed with the phrase, "In blind obedience we follow you." Knauer told her never to reveal that the Alliance and the Bund were linked together. One day she asked Knauer what the Bund was. His reply was that the Bund "was the Fuehrer's grip on American democracy." She reminded Knauer that he was an American citizen. He replied, "That is a good thing to hide behind."

We have given merely the highlights of the evidence. Much corroborative detail could be added. But what we have related presents the gist of the case against Knauer. If isolated parts of the evidence against Knauer were separately considered, they might well carry different inferences. His alertness to rise to the defense of Germans or of Americans of German descent could well reflect, if standing as isolated instances, attempts to protect a minority against what he deemed oppressive practices. Social and cultural ties might be complete and adequate explanations. Even utterances of a political nature which reflected tolerance or approval of the Nazi program in Germany might carry no sinister connotation, if they were considered by themselves. For many native-borns in this country did not awaken to the full implications of the Nazi program until war came to us. . . .

But we have here much more than political utterances, much more than a crusade for the protection of minorities. This record portrays a program of action to further Hitler's cause in this nation — a program of infiltration which conforms to the pattern adopted by the Nazis in country after country. The ties with the German Reich were too intimate, the pattern of conduct too consistent, the overt acts too plain for us to conclude that Knauer was merely exercising his right of free speech either to spread tolerance in this country or to advocate changes here.

*          *          *

The District Court properly ruled that membership in the Bund was not in itself sufficient to prove fraud which would warrant revocation of a degree of naturalization. Otherwise, guilt would rest on implication. But we have here much more than that. We have a clear course of conduct, of which membership in the Bund was a manifestation, designed to promote the Nazi cause in this country. This is not a case of an underling caught up in the enthusiasm of a movement, driven by ties of blood and old associations to extreme attitudes, and perhaps unaware of

the conflict of allegiance implicit in his actions. Knauer is an astute person. He is a leader — the dominating figure in the cause he sponsored, a leading voice in the councils of the Bund, the spokesman in the program for systematic agitation of Nazi views. His activities portray a shrewd, calculating, and vigilant promotion of an alien cause. The conclusion seems to us plain that when Knauer forswore allegiance to Hitler and the German Reich he swore falsely.

II. [W]hen an alien takes the oath with reservations or does not in good faith forswear loyalty and allegiance to the old country, the decree of naturalization is obtained by deceit. The proceeding itself is then founded on fraud. A fraud is perpetrated on the naturalization court. We have recently considered the broad powers of equity to set aside a decree for fraud practiced on the court which granted it. The present suit is an equity suit. But we need not consider in this case what the historic powers of equity might be in this situation. For Congress has provided that fraud is a basis for cancellation of certificates of naturalization in proceedings instituted by the United States. The legislative history of that enactment shows that false swearing was one of the evils included in the statutory grounds for denaturalization. That power was granted to give added protection against fraud committed on the naturalization courts. Cancellation of a certificate on the grounds of fraud includes cancellation for falsely swearing that the applicant forswore allegiance to his native country. Though the making of a false oath be called intrinsic fraud, it is within the reach of the statute.

We have no doubt of the power of Congress to provide for denaturalization on the ground of fraud. . . . We adhere to the prior rulings of this Court that Congress may provide for the cancellation of certificates of naturalization on the ground of fraud in their procurement and thus protect the courts and the nation against practices of aliens who by deceitful methods obtain the cherished status of citizenship here, the better to serve a foreign master.

Since fraud in the oath of allegiance which Knauer took is sufficient to sustain the judgment below, we do not reach the other questions which have been argued.

*Affirmed.*

MR. JUSTICE RUTLEDGE, dissenting.

*          *          *

My concern is not for Paul Knauer. The record discloses that he has no conception of, much less attachment to, basic American principles or institutions. He was a thorough-going Nazi, addicted to philosophies altogether hostile to the democratic framework in which we believe and live. Further, he was an active promoter of movements directed to securing acceptance of those ideas here and incorporating them in our institutions. And in this case . . . it would be hard to say that the evidence would not sustain a finding that he falsely took the oath of allegiance or that he never in his heart renounced his prime fealty to Adolph Hitler and Nazi Germany. Nor, in my opinion, can it be thought unequal to supporting a conclusion that, from a time prior to his admission to citizenship in 1935 until at any rate the assault on Pearl Harbor, Knauer was in the active service of the Nazi regime, promoting its cause here, and also for a short time in Germany, as the object of his first loyalty.

If therefore in any case a naturalized citizen's right and status can be revoked, by the procedure followed here or perhaps at all, it would be in such a case as this. But if one man's citizenship can thus be taken away, so can that of any other. And even in this case it would be in large part for his political convictions and acts done openly in espousal of them. Not merely Knauer's rights, but those of millions of naturalized citizens in their status and all that it implies of security and freedom, are affected by what is done in this case. By the outcome they are made either second-class citizens or citizens having equal rights and equal security with others.

No native-born American's birthright could be stripped from him for such a cause or by such a procedure as has been followed here. Nor could he be punished with banishment. To suffer that great loss he must forfeit citizenship by some act of treason or felony and be adjudged guilty by processes of law consistent with all the great protections thrown around such trials. Not yet has attempt been made to do this otherwise. Nor in my opinion could it be done, except for some such cause or by any less carefully safeguarded procedure.

In no instance thus far has our system tolerated destruction of that right of the native-born, except by voluntary surrender, on account of convictions held, views expressed, or acts done in promoting their acceptance falling short of treason as defined in the Constitution or conviction for felony. Nor has it thus far brought about that extinction by forms of trial other than those provided for such offenses. Moreover, even in such cases, although the penalty may be death or loss of the rights of citizenship, we have not yet imposed those penalties altogether foreign to our institutions, namely, deportation and exile. For one cause and one only have they been provided, namely, the loss of the naturalized citizen's status.

I do not find warrant in the Constitution for believing that it contemplates two classes of citizens, excepting only for two purposes. . . .

Congress, it is true, is empowered to lay down the conditions for admission of foreign-born persons to citizenship. In this respect it has wide authority. But it is not unlimited. Nor is Congress given power to take away citizenship once it is conferred, other than for some sufficient act of forfeiture taking place afterward. Naturalized citizens are no more free to become traitors or criminals than others and may be punished as they are when they commit the same offense. But any process which takes away their citizenship for causes or by procedures not applicable to native-born citizens places them in a separate and an inferior class. That dilemma is inescapable, though it is one not heretofore faced squarely. Unless it is the law that there are two classes of citizens, one superior, the other inferior, the status of no citizen can be annulled for causes or by procedures not applicable to all others.

. . . In my opinion the power to naturalize is not the power to denaturalize. The act of admission must be taken as final, for any cause which may have existed at that time. Otherwise there cannot but be two classes of citizens, one free and secure except for acts amounting to forfeiture within our tradition; the other, conditional, timorous and insecure because blanketed with the threat that some act or conduct, not amounting to forfeiture for others, will be taken retroactively to show that some prescribed condition had not been fulfilled and be so adjudged. I do not think such a difference was contemplated when Congress was authorized to provide for naturalization and the terms on which it should be granted.

But if I may be wrong in this, certainly so drastic a penalty as denaturalization, with resulting deportation and exile and all the attendant consequences, should not be imposed by any procedure less protective of the citizen's most fundamental right, comprehending all others, than must be employed to take away the native-born citizen's status or the lesser rights of the foreign-born citizen. If strings may be attached to citizenship and pulled retroactively to annul it, at the least this should be done only by those forms of proceeding most fully surrounded with the constitutional securities for trial which are among the prized incidents of citizenship. It is altogether anomalous that those safeguards are thrown about the foreign-born citizen when, for some offense, his liberty even for brief periods is at stake, but are withdrawn from him when all that gives substance to that freedom is put in jeopardy.

The right of citizenship is the most precious of all. The penalty of denaturalization is always harsh. Often it is more drastic than any other. It is also unique for this situation. For the required measure of security, the native-born citizen can be deprived of his status only by the rigidly safeguarded trial for treason or for conviction of a criminal offense which brings loss of rights as a citizen. To those procedures, with the same penalties and for the same causes, the foreign-born citizen is subject; but also by them he is protected. He should not be less secure when it is sought to annul his citizenship than when the effort is to bring about its forfeiture. Nor, in either event, should his procedural safeguards be less than when the same consequence, in substance, is inflicted upon the citizen native born.

The procedure prescribed for and followed in this case was not in accord with those standards. I think nothing less is adequate, or consistent with the constitutional status of citizenship, for the purpose of taking it away.

If this means that some or even many disloyal foreign-born citizens cannot be deported, it is better so than to place so many loyal ones in inferior status. And there are other effective methods for dealing with those who are disloyal, just as there are for such citizens by birth.

Accordingly, I would reverse the judgment.

MR. JUSTICE MURPHY joins in this dissent.

*Top*, Doc. 151: Feminist leaders Susan B. Anthony (*right*) and Elizabeth Cady Stanton (1873). *Bottom*, Doc. 188: The National Anti-Suffrage Association. Harris & Ewing Photos.

*Top*, Doc. 158: Rioting workingmen, demanding the right to unionize during the economic depression of 1873-1874, driven from Tompkins Square. Wood engraving by Matt Morgan (1874). *Middle*, Doc. 159: Charles Jules Guiteau, a one-time resident of the utopian Oneida Community and a disappointed office-seeker, shooting President James A. Garfield at the Washington railroad station (1881). *Bottom*, Doc. 163: Anarchist protest at Haymarket Square, a dynamite bomb exploding among the police (1886). Wood engraving by T. de Thulstrup in *Harper's Weekly*, May 15, 1886.

*Top, left*, Doc. 177: IWW leader "Big Bill" Haywood (1907). *Top, right*, Doc. 178: Anarchist Emma Goldman before entering the penitentiary (1918). *Bottom*, Doc. 185: The body of Joe Hill, poet laureate of the IWW movement, carried through the streets of Chicago after his execution by a five-man firing squad at the Utah State Penitentiary (1915).

*Top*, Doc. 194: Socialist leader Eugene V. Debs pardoned by President Harding and released from prison after his conviction for criticizing the government's war policy (1921). *Bottom, left*, Doc. 215: General Douglas MacArthur, Army Chief of Staff, personally directing the advance against the "Bonus Army" (1932). *Bottom, right*, Doc. 212: Radical press portrayal of the execution and martyrdom of Sacco and Vanzetti (1927). From *Labor Age*, April 1931.

*Top*, Doc. 231: Japanese and Japanese-Americans, under United States Army supervision, waiting for registration at the Santa Anita Reception Center (1942). *Bottom, left*, Doc. 251: Senator Joseph McCarthy conducting public hearings into alleged Communist subversion (1950). *Bottom, right*, Doc. 244: American poet Ezra Pound, indicted for treason for broadcasting Fascist propaganda to the United States during World War II (1946).

*Top*, Doc. 297: Antisegregation demonstrators picket the St. Louis School Board (1963). From the *St. Louis Dispatch*. *Bottom*, Doc. 339: Wounded Knee revisited: the 1890 massacre at Wounded Knee, after which the bodies were buried in a large pit, gave rise to the modern (1974) Native American protest on the same site.

*Top, left*, Doc. 305: Poster depicting Huey P. Newton, Minister of Defense of the Black Panther Party (1966). *Top, right*, Doc. 333: Angela Davis, black activist and vice-presidential candidate on the Communist Party ticket, testifying before a government committee (1971). © *Washington Post. Bottom*, Doc. 371: Police guard Ku Klux Klan members accused of attacking a radical leftist demonstration, which left five dead in Greensboro, North Carolina (1979). Photo by Davis/Stratford, *Greensboro Daily News*.

### CHAPTER 9

# The Cold War
# and the Battle
# against Subversion

———

1947-1967

Communism had always been viewed as a disfavored, foreign-inspired, and subversive political doctrine in the United States. Yet it had enjoyed a brief period of semirespectability after the recognition of the Soviet Union by the United States in 1933 and particularly subsequent to Russia's becoming a wartime ally against the Axis. Many, nevertheless, continued to view the mother country of Communism with suspicion, and regretted the relaxation of the traditional and official American antipathy to Communism and its proponents. The aggressive successes of Communism in Eastern Europe and Asia and the resulting deterioration of the relations between the United States and the Soviet Union soon inspired a resurgence of anti-Communist sentiment and controls in this country.

The rapid spread of Communism abroad was viewed as a threat to national security, and suspicions were rampant that the wide measure of the loss to Communism was at least partially attributable to a not altogether loyal federal bureaucracy. The materials reflect the government's reaction to the perhaps justifiable fear that the ranks of the civil service had been infiltrated by agents of an unfriendly foreign power. The response escalated into a pervasive and thoroughgoing ostracism of persons unable or unwilling to submit to a searching inquiry of their past political leanings and associations.

Although technically at peace, the country witnessed a political anxiety that had heretofore exhibited itself only during war. The movement to excise Communists from all government ranks was not restricted to the federal government, as state and local governments imposed oaths, conducted investigations, and severed contacts with those who could not meet the standards of loyalty. The legislative investigative power was invoked in order to expose those individuals suspected of Communist sympathies to public condemnation and economic ostracism. Federal authority to regulate labor relations was utilized to impose restraints on the political affiliations of union officeholders. Finally, an act of Congress officially outlawed the Communist party and all its fronts.

The materials in this chapter document the response of the judicial branch to the legislative and executive regulation of suspect political parties and doctrines. For the sake of brevity, many of the regulations are contained only in the context of the judicial opinions. The reader should note the enactment and the judicial response thereto as two separate though interrelated events, often separated by a long passage of time. Of special significance is the manner in which the courts, specifically the United States Supreme Court, slowly constricted the executive branch's ability to enforce these political regulations by imposing increasingly onerous procedural requirements on the government. Not until 1967, long after the anti-Communist hysteria had died, did the court hold that the core of the anti-Communist legislative effort was repugnant to the First Amendment. In the intervening years between the court's silent acceptance of the constitutionality of the anti-Communist regulations and this substantive repudiation, only the procedural protections of the Fifth Amendment's due process requirement and privilege against self-incrimination, and the Sixth Amendment's general procedural safeguards, provided some fragile protection against government excess.

---

### 246 "complete and unswerving loyalty" (1947)

General Dwight D. Eisenhower accepted Germany's unconditional surrender on May 7, 1945; and on September 2, General MacArthur and Admiral Nimitz received Japan's formal surrender on board the battleship *Missouri* in Tokyo Bay. Yet by the end of 1946 it became apparent that the cordial wartime relations established with the Soviet Union after 1941 would not continue. Tensions between the former allies were mounting. Remembering the old charges of Congressman Martin Dies, many Americans were convinced that the fall of China, the Russian takeover of Eastern Europe, and other Communist successes were due to what Senator Joseph McCarthy later called "twenty years of treason" within the American government. The urge to protect America against internal subversion was growing.

In March of 1947, President Harry S. Truman

proclaimed a comprehensive federal employees' loyalty program. Executive employees and all applicants for civilian employment in the executive branch of the federal government were subject to loyalty investigations. When "reasonable grounds"—one of the lowest standards of legal proof—existed for belief in the employee's disloyalty, the government could deny employment or remove the employee. Although an employee was entitled to present evidence on his or her behalf at an administrative hearing, the employing agency could decide to limit its disclosure only to those facts which would not be inconsistent with maintaining national security. Applicants denied employment on disloyalty grounds did not receive even these minimal protections.

## ☆ 246 President Truman's Order Prescribing Procedures for the Administration of an Employees' Loyalty Program in the Executive Branch of the Government

Exec. Order No. 9835, 12 Fed. Reg. 1935 (Mar. 25, 1947).

PRESCRIBING PROCEDURES FOR THE ADMINISTRATION OF AN EMPLOYEES' LOYALTY PROGRAM IN THE EXECUTIVE BRANCH OF THE GOVERNMENT

WHEREAS each employee of the Government of the United States is endowed with a measure of trusteeship over the democratic processes which are the heart and sinew of the United States; and

WHEREAS it is of vital importance that persons employed in the Federal service be of complete and unswerving loyalty to the United States; and

WHEREAS, although the loyalty of by far the overwhelming majority of all Government employees is beyond question, the presence within the Government service of any disloyal or subversive person constitutes a threat to our democratic processes; and

WHEREAS maximum protection must be afforded the United States against infiltration of disloyal persons into the ranks of its employees, and equal protection from unfounded accusations of disloyalty must be afforded the loyal employees of the Government:

NOW, THEREFORE, ... it is hereby, in the interest of the internal management of the Government, ordered as follows:

### Part I—Investigation of Applicants

1. There shall be a loyalty investigation of every person entering the civilian employment of any department or agency of the executive branch of the Federal Government.

*              *              *

3. An investigation shall be made of all applicants at all available pertinent sources of information and shall include reference to:

a. Federal Bureau of Investigation files.

b. Civil Service Commission files.

c. Military and naval intelligence files.

d. The files of any other appropriate government investigative or intelligence agency.

e. House Committee on un-American Activities files.

f. Local law-enforcement files at the place of residence and employment of the applicant, including municipal, county, and State law-enforcement files.

g. Schools and colleges attended by applicant.

h. Former employers of applicant.

i. References given by applicant.

j. Any other appropriate source.

4. Whenever derogatory information with respect to loyalty of an applicant is revealed a full field investigation shall be conducted. . . .

### Part II—Investigation of Employees

1. The head of each department and agency in the executive branch of the Government shall be personally responsible for an effective program to assure that disloyal civilian officers or employees are not retained in employment in his department or agency.

*              *              *

### Part V—Standards

1. The standard for the refusal of employment or the removal from employment in an executive department or agency on grounds relating to loyalty shall be that, on all the evidence, reasonable grounds exist for belief that the person involved is disloyal to the Government of the United States.

2. Activities and associations of an applicant or employee which may be considered in connection with the determination of disloyalty may include one or more of the following:

a. Sabotage, espionage, or attempts or preparations therefor, or knowingly associating with spies or saboteurs;

b. Treason or sedition or advocacy thereof;

c. Advocacy of revolution or force or violence to alter the constitutional form of government of the United States;

d. Intentional, unauthorized disclosure to any person, under circumstances which may indicate disloyalty to the United States, of documents or information of a confidential or non-public character obtained by the person making the disclosure as a result of his employment by the Government of the United States;

e. Performing or attempting to perform his duties, or otherwise acting, so as to serve the interests of another government in preference to the interests of the United States.

f. Membership in, affiliation with or sympathetic association with any foreign or domestic organization, association, movement, group or combination of persons, designated by the Attorney General as totalitarian, fascist, communist, or subversive, or as having adopted a policy of advocating or approving the commission of acts of force or violence to deny other persons their rights under the Constitution of the United States, or as seeking to alter the form of government of the United States by unconstitutional means.

### Part VI—Miscellaneous

1. Each department and agency of the executive branch, to the extent that it has not already done so, shall submit, to the Federal Bureau of Investigation of the Department of Justice, either directly or through the Civil Service Commission, the names (and such other necessary identifying material as the Federal Bureau of Investigation may require) of all of its incumbent employees.

a. The Federal Bureau of Investigation shall check such names against its records of persons concerning whom there is substantial evidence of being within the purview of paragraph 2 of Part V hereof, and shall notify each department and agency of such information.

b. Upon receipt of the above-mentioned information from the Federal Bureau of Investigation, each department and agency shall make, or cause to be made by the Civil Service Commission, such investigation of those employees as the head of the department or agency shall deem advisable.

\* \* \*

HARRY S. TRUMAN
*The White House*
*March 21, 1947*

# 247 "It shall be unlawful for any individual employed by the United States . . . to participate in any strike" (1947)

After four years of war, the United States had mixed success in adapting to peace. On the one hand, the feared return to an economic depression did not materialize. In 1946, unemployment was less than 4 percent (half of the unemployed being former servicemen), and the demand for consumer goods far surpassed their production. On the other hand, inflation and labor unrest threatened to become uncontrollable. Unable to strike during the war years, unions now employed strikes on a massive scale. In

1946 alone, more than 4.5 million workers engaged in some 4,700 walkouts.

The experience under the 1935 National Labor Relations Act was unsatisfactory to many people. Management especially believed the act was onesided. The Taft-Hartley Act of 1947 addressed these grievances by regulating the organization and conduct of unions (which the NLRA failed to do). The act established more detailed mechanisms for the resolution of national labor disputes without resort to strikes, banned closed shops, declared rights of employees against union coercion, and, to a larger degree, made the federal courts available to management for economic injuries caused by union activities. The act also withdrew NLRB recognition from any union whose officers failed to affirm that they were not Communists. The filing of false information was made a crime. The Taft-Hartley Act went into effect on June 23, 1947, when the Senate concurred with the House in overriding President Truman's veto.

## ☆ 247 An Act to Amend the National Labor Relations Act (the Taft-Hartley Act)

61 Stat. 136 (1947).

*Be it enacted by the Senate and House of Representatives of the United States of America in Congress assembled,*

\* \* \*

TITLE I—AMENDMENT OF NATIONAL LABOR
RELATIONS ACT

SEC. 101. The National Labor Relations Act is hereby amended to read as follows:

*"Finding and Policies*

"SECTION 1. . . .

\* \* \*

"Experience has further demonstrated that certain practices by some labor organizations, their officers, and members have the intent or the necessary effect of burdening or obstructing commerce by preventing the free flow of goods in such commerce through strikes and other forms of industrial unrest or through concerted activities which impair the interest of the public in the free flow of such commerce. The elimination of such practices is a necessary condition to the assurance of the rights herein guaranteed.

\* \* \*

*"Unfair Labor Practices*

"SEC. 8. . . .

"(b) It shall be unfair labor practice for a labor organization or its agents—

"(1) to restrain or coerce (A) employees in the

exercise of the rights guaranteed in section 7: *Provided,* That this paragraph shall not impair the right of a labor organization to prescribe its own rules with respect to the acquisition or retention of membership therein; or (B) an employer in the selection of his representatives for the purposes of collective bargaining or the adjustment of grievances;

"(2) to cause or attempt to cause an employer to discriminate against an employee in violation of subsection (a)(3) or to discriminate against an employee with respect to whom membership in such organization has been denied or terminated on some ground other than his failure to tender the periodic dues and the initiation fees uniformly required as a condition of acquiring or retaining membership;

"(3) to refuse to bargain collectively with an employer, provided it is the representative of his employees subject to the provisions of section 9 (a);

"(4) to engage in, or to induce or encourage the employees of any employer to engage in, a strike or a concerted refusal in the course of their employment to use, manufacture, process, transport, or otherwise handle or work on any goods, articles, materials, or commodities or to perform any services, where an object thereof is: (A) forcing or requiring any employer or self-employed person to join any labor or employer organization or any employer or other person to cease using, selling, handling, transporting, or otherwise dealing in the products of any other producer, processor, or manufacturer, or to cease doing business with any other person; (B) forcing or requiring any other employer to recognize or bargain with a labor organization as the representative of his employees unless such labor organization has been certified as the representative of such employees under the provisions of section 9; (C) forcing or requiring any employer to recognize or bargain with a particular labor organization as the representative of his employees if another labor organization has been certified as the representative of such employees under the provisions of section 9; (D) forcing or requiring any employer to assign particular work to employees in a particular labor organization or in a particular trade, craft, or class rather than to employees in another labor organization or in another trade, craft, or class, unless such employer is failing to conform to an order or certification of the Board determining the bargaining representative for employees performing such work: *Provided,* That nothing contained in this subsection (b) shall be construed to make unlawful a refusal by any person to enter upon the premises of any em-

ployer (other than his own employer), if the employees of such employer are engaged in a strike ratified or approved by a representative of such employees whom such employer is required to recognize under this Act;

"(5) to require of employees covered by an agreement authorized under subsection (a)(3) the payment, as a condition precedent to becoming a member of such organization, of a fee in an amount which the Board finds excessive or discriminatory under all the circumstances. In making such a finding, the Board shall consider, among other relevant factors, the practices and customs of labor organizations in the particular industry, and the wages currently paid to the employees affected; and

"(6) to cause or attempt to cause an employer to pay or deliver or agree to pay or deliver any money or other thing of value, in the nature of an exaction, for services which are not performed or not to be performed.

"(c) The expressing of any views, argument, or opinion, or the dissemination thereof, whether in written, printed, graphic, or visual form, shall not constitute or be evidence of an unfair labor practice under any of the provisions of this Act, if such expression contains no threat of reprisal or force or promise of benefit.

\*       \*       \*

"*Representatives and Elections*

"SEC. 9. . . .

"(f) No investigation shall be made by the Board of any question affecting commerce concerning the representation of employees, raised by a labor organization under subsection (c) of this section, no petition under section 9(e)(1) shall be entertained, and no complaint shall be issued pursuant to a charge made by a labor organization under subsection (b) of section 10, unless such labor organization and any national or international labor organization of which such labor organization is an affiliate or constituent unit (A) shall have prior thereto filed with the Secretary of Labor copies of its constitution and bylaws and a report, in such form as the Secretary may prescribe, showing—

"(1) the name of such labor organization and the address of its principal place of business;

"(2) the names, titles, and compensation and allowances of its three principal officers and of any of its other officers or agents whose aggregate compensation and allowances for the preceding year exceeded $5,000, and the amount of the compensation and allowances paid to each such officer or agent during such year;

"(3) the manner in which the officers and

agents referred to in clause (2) were elected, appointed, or otherwise selected;

"(4) the initiation fee or fees which new members are required to pay on becoming members of such labor organization;

"(5) the regular dues or fees which members are required to pay in order to remain members in good standing of such labor organization;

"(6) a detailed statement of, or reference to provisions of its constitution and bylaws showing the procedure followed with respect to, (a) qualification for or restrictions on membership, (b) election of officers and stewards, (c) calling of regular and special meetings, (d) levying of assessments, (e) imposition of fines, (f) authorization for bargaining demands, (g) ratification of contract terms, (h) authorization for strikes, (i) authorization for disbursement of union funds, (j) audit of union financial transactions, (k) participation in insurance or other benefit plans, and (l) expulsion of members and the grounds therefor;

and (B) can show that prior thereto it has—

"(1) filed with the Secretary of Labor, in such form as the Secretary may prescribe, a report showing all of (a) its receipts of any kind and the sources of such receipts, (b) its total assets and liabilities as of the end of its last fiscal year, (c) the disbursements made by it during such fiscal year, including the purposes for which made; and

"(2) furnished to all of the members of such labor organization copies of the financial report required by paragraph (1) hereof to be filed with the Secretary of Labor.

"(g) It shall be the obligation of all labor organizations to file annually . . . reports bringing up to date the information required to be supplied in the initial filing. . . . No labor organization shall be eligible for certification under this section as the representatives of any employees, no petition . . . shall be entertained, and no complaint shall issue under section 10 with respect to a charge filed by a labor organization unless it can show that it and any national or international labor organization of which it is an affiliate or constituent unit has complied with its obligation under this subsection.

"(h) No investigation shall be made . . . of any question affecting commerce concerning the representation of employees, raised by a labor organization . . . , no petition . . . shall be entertained, and no complaint shall be issued pursuant to a charge made by a labor organization . . . unless there is on file with the Board an affidavit executed contemporaneously or within the preceding twelve-month period by each officer of such labor organization and the officers of any national or international labor organization of which it is an affiliate or constituent unit that he is not a member of the Communist Party or affili-

ated with such party, and that he does not believe in, and is not a member of or supports any organization that believes in or teaches, the overthrow of the United States Government by force or by any illegal or unconstitutional methods. The provisions of section 35 A of the Criminal Code shall be applicable in respect to such affidavits.

\*　　\*　　\*

*"Limitations*

"SEC. 14. . . .

"(b) Nothing in this Act shall be construed as authorizing the execution or application of agreements requiring membership in a labor organization as a condition of employment in any State or Territory in which such execution or application is prohibited by State or Territorial law."

\*　　\*　　\*

TITLE II—CONCILIATION OF LABOR DISPUTES IN INDUSTRIES AFFECTING COMMERCE; NATIONAL EMERGENCIES

\*　　\*　　\*

*Functions of the Service*

SEC. 203. (a) It shall be the duty of the [Federal Mediation and Conciliation] Service, in order to prevent or minimize interruptions of the free flow of commerce growing out of labor disputes, to assist parties to labor disputes in industries affecting commerce to settle such disputes through conciliation and mediation.

\*　　\*　　\*

*National Emergencies*

SEC. 206. Whenever in the opinion of the President of the United States, a threatened or actual strike or lock-out affecting an entire industry or a substantial part thereof engaged in trade, commerce, transportation, transmission, or communication among the several States or with foreign nations, or engaged in the production of goods for commerce, will, if permitted to occur or to continue, imperil the national health or safety, he may appoint a board of inquiry to inquire into the issues involved in the dispute and to make a written report to him within such time as he shall prescribe.

\*　　\*　　\*

SEC. 208. (a) Upon receiving a report from a board of inquiry the President may direct the Attorney General to petition any district court of the United States having jurisdiction of the parties to enjoin such strike or lock-out or the continuing thereof, and if the court finds that such threatened or actual strike or lock-out—

(i) affects an entire industry or a substantial part thereof engaged in trade, commerce, transportation, transmission, or communication among the several States or with foreign nations, or engaged in the production of goods for commerce; and

(ii) if permitted to occur or to continue, will imperil the national health or safety, it shall have jurisdiction to enjoin any such strike or lock-out, or the continuing thereof, and to make such other orders as may be appropriate.

TITLE III

\*       \*       \*

*Boycotts and other Unlawful Combinations*

SEC. 303. (a) It shall be unlawful, for the purposes of this section only, in an industry or activity affecting commerce, for any labor organization to engage in, or to induce or encourage the employees of any employer to engage in, a strike or a concerted refusal in the course of their employment to use, manufacture, process, transport, or otherwise handle or work on any goods, articles, materials, or commodities or to perform any services, where an object thereof is—

(1) forcing or requiring any employer or self-employed person to join any labor or employer organization or any employer or other person to cease using, selling, handling, transporting, or otherwise dealing in the products of any other producer, processor, or manufacturer, or to cease doing business with any other person;

(2) forcing or requiring any other employer to recognize or bargain with a labor organization as the representative of his employees unless such labor organization has been certified as the representative of such employees under the provisions of section 9 of the National Labor Relations Act;

(3) forcing or requiring any employer to recognize or bargain with a particular labor organization as the representative of his employees if another labor organization has been certified as the representative of such employees under the provisions of section 9 of the National Labor Relations Act;

(4) forcing or requiring any employer to assign particular work to employees in a particular labor organization or in a particular trade, craft, or class rather than to employees in another labor organization or in another trade, craft, or class unless such employer is failing to conform to an order or certification of the National Labor Relations Board determining the bargaining representative for employees performing such work. Nothing contained in this subsection shall be construed to make unlawful a refusal by any person to enter upon the premises of any employer (other than his own employer), if the employees of such employer are engaged in a strike ratified

or approved by a representative of such employees whom such employer is required to recognize under the National Labor Relations Act.

(b) Whoever shall be injured in his business or property by reason of any violation of subsection (a) may sue therefor in any district court of the United States subject to the limitations and provisions of section 301 hereof without respect to the amount in controversy, or in any other court having jurisdiction of the parties, and shall recover the damages by him sustained and the cost of the suit.

*Restriction on Political Contributions*

SEC. 304. Section 313 of the Federal Corrupt Practices Act, 1925 . . . , is amended to read as follows:

"SEC. 313. It is unlawful for . . . any labor organization to make a contribution or expenditure in connection with any election at which Presidential and Vice Presidential electors or a Senator or Representative in, or a Delegate or Resident Commissioner to Congress are to be voted for, or in connection with any primary election or political convention or caucus held to select candidates for any of the foregoing offices, or for any candidate, political committee, or other person to accept or receive any contribution prohibited by this section. Every labor organization which makes any contribution or expenditure in violation of this section shall be fined not more than $5,000; and every . . . officer of any labor organization who consents to any contribution or expenditure by the . . . labor organization . . . in violation of this section shall be fined not more than $1,000 or imprisoned for not more than one year, or both. . . ."

*Strikes by Government Employees*

SEC. 305. It shall be unlawful for any individual employed by the United States or any agency thereof including wholly owned Government corporations to participate in any strike. Any individual employed by the United States or by any such agency who strikes shall be discharged immediately from his employment, and shall forfeit his civil service status, if any, and shall not be eligible for reemployment for three years by the United States or any such agency.

\*       \*       \*

*Approved, June 23, 1947.*

## 248 "termination [is] necessary or advisable in the interest of the national security" (1950)

Responding to accusations of Communist infiltration of the ranks of the federal government, and dissatisfied with the efficacy of the loyalty program under

President Truman's executive order, Congress passed an extensive anti-Communist legislative package in 1950. This act granted officials of the executive branch absolute discretionary authority to suspend or terminate employees of the specified departments "when deemed necessary in the interest of national security."

## ☆248 An Act to Protect the National Security of the United States

64 Stat. 476 (1950).

*Be it enacted by the Senate and House of Representatives of the United States of America in Congress assembled,* That, notwithstanding the provisions of any other law, the Secretary of State; Secretary of Commerce; Attorney General; the Secretary of Defense; the Secretary of the Army; the Secretary of the Navy; the Secretary of the Air Force; the Secretary of the Treasury; Atomic Energy Commission; the Chairman, National Security Resources Board; or the Director, National Advisory Committee for Aeronautics, may, in his absolute discretion and when deemed necessary in the interest of national security, suspend, without pay, any civilian officer or employee of the Department of State (including the Foreign Service of the United States), Department of Commerce, Department of Justice, Department of Defense, Department of the Army, Department of the Navy, Department of the Air Force, Coast Guard, Atomic Energy Commission, National Security Resources Board, or National Advisory Committee for Aeronautics, respectively, or of their several field services: *Provided,* That to the extent that such agency head determines that the interests of the national security permit, the employee concerned shall be notified of the reasons for his suspension and within thirty days after such notification any such person shall have an opportunity to submit any statements or affidavits to the official designated by the head of the agency concerned to show why he should be reinstated or restored to duty. The agency head concerned may, following such investigation and review as he deems necessary, terminate the employment of such suspended civilian officer or employee whenever he shall determine such termination necessary or advisable in the interest of the national security of the United States, and such determination by the agency head concerned shall be conclusive and final. . . .

\*     \*     \*

SEC. 3. The provisions of this Act shall apply to such other departments and agencies of the Government as the President may, from time to time, deem necessary in the best interests of national security. If any departments or agencies are included by the President, he shall so report to the Committees on the Armed Services of the Congress.

\*     \*     \*

*Approved, August 26, 1950.*

## 249 Whatever Is Authorized by Congress for an Alien Is Due Process (1950)

The influx of new immigrants to the United States from the ranks of those displaced by World War II meant that the government took special care to single out those whose admission was deemed to be prejudicial to America's national interests. Mrs. Kurt Knauff, born in Germany in 1915, came to England in 1939 as a refugee and served honorably in the Royal Air Force. She later worked as a civilian employee for the American occupation forces in Germany. After marrying an American army veteran, she sought to enter the United States on August 14, 1948. The United States denied her admission and detained her at Ellis Island. The government refused to grant her a hearing at which she could learn and contest the grounds for her exclusion. The Supreme Court upheld the authority of the government to exclude an alien on grounds of "security" without the benefit of any hearing.

## ☆249 *Knauff v. Shaughnessy*

338 U.S. 537 (1950).

MR. JUSTICE MINTON delivered the opinion of the Court.

May the United States exclude without hearing, solely upon a finding by the Attorney General that her admission would be prejudicial to the interests of the United States, the alien wife of a citizen who had served honorably in the armed forces of the United States during World War II? . . .

Petitioner was born in Germany in 1915. She left Germany and went to Czechoslovakia during the Hitler regime. There she was married and divorced. She went to England in 1939 as a refugee. Thereafter she served with the Royal Air Force efficiently and honorably from January 1, 1943, until May 30, 1946. She then secured civilian employment with the War Department of the United States in Germany. Her work was rated "very good" and "excellent." On February 28, 1948, with the permission of the Commanding General at Frankfurt, Germany, she married Kurt W. Knauff, a naturalized citizen of the United States. He is an honorably discharged United States Army veteran of World War II. He is, as he was at the time of his marriage, a civilian employee of the United States Army at Frankfurt, Germany.

On August 14, 1948, petitioner sought to enter the United States to be naturalized. On that day she was temporarily excluded from the United States and detained at Ellis Island. On October 6, 1948, the Assistant Commissioner of Immigration and Naturalization recommended that she be permanently excluded without a hearing on the ground that her admission would be prejudicial to the interests of the United States. On the same day the Attorney General adopted this recommendation and entered a final order of exclusion....

The authority of the Attorney General to order the exclusion of aliens without a hearing flows from the Act of June 21, 1941, amending § 1 of the Act of May 22, 1918. By the 1941 amendment it was provided that the President might, upon finding that the interests of the United States required it, impose additional restrictions and prohibitions on the entry into and departure of persons from the United States during the national emergency proclaimed May 27, 1941. Pursuant to this Act of Congress the President on November 14, 1941, issued Proclamation 2523. This proclamation recited that the interests of the United States required the imposition of additional restrictions upon the entry into and departure of persons from the country and authorized the promulgation of regulations jointly by the Secretary of State and the Attorney General. It was also provided that no alien should be permitted to enter the United States if it were found that such entry would be prejudicial to the interests of the United States.

*          *          *

At the outset we wish to point out that an alien who seeks admission to this country may not do so under any claim of right. Admission of aliens to the United States is a privilege granted by the sovereign United States Government. Such privilege is granted to an alien only upon such terms as the United States shall prescribe....

Petitioner contends that the 1941 Act and the regulations thereunder are void to the extent that they contain unconstitutional delegations of legislative power. But there is no question of inappropriate delegation of legislative power involved here. The exclusion of aliens is a fundamental act of sovereignty. The right to do so stems not alone from legislative power but is inherent in the executive power to control the foreign affairs of the nation....

... Normally Congress supplies the conditions of the privilege of entry into the United States. But because the power of exclusion of aliens is also inherent in the executive department of the sovereign, Congress may in broad terms authorize the executive to exercise the power, e.g., as was done here, for the best interests of the country during a time of national emergency. Executive officers may be en-

trusted with the duty of specifying the procedures for carrying out the congressional intent.... Whatever the procedure authorized by Congress is, it is due process as far as an alien denied entry is concerned.

*          *          *

We find no substantial merit to petitioner's contention that the regulations were not "reasonable" as they were required to be by the 1941 Act. We think them reasonable in the circumstances of the period for which they were authorized, namely, the national emergency of World War II....

It is not disputed that the Attorney General's action was pursuant to the regulations heretofore discussed. However, [the 1941 Act] authorizes these special restrictions on the entry of aliens only when the United States is at war or during the existence of the national emergency proclaimed May 27, 1941. For ordinary times Congress has provided aliens with a hearing. And the contention of petitioner is that she is entitled to the statutory hearing because for purposes of the War Brides Act, within which she comes, the war terminated when the President proclaimed the cessation of hostilities....

The War Brides Act provides that World War II is the period from December 7, 1941, until the proclaimed termination of hostilities. This has nothing to do with the period for which the regulations here acted under were authorized. The beginning and end of the war are defined by the War Brides Act, we assume, for the purpose of ascertaining the period within which citizens must have served in the armed forces in order for their spouses and children to be entitled to the benefits of the Act. The special procedure followed in this case was authorized not only during the period of actual hostilities but during the entire war and the national emergency proclaimed May 27, 1941. The national emergency has never been terminated. Indeed, a state of war still exists. Thus, the authority upon which the Attorney General acted remains in force. The Act of June 21, 1941, and the President's proclamations and the regulations thereunder are still a part of the immigration laws.

The War Brides Act does not relieve petitioner of her alien status....

There is nothing in the War Brides Act or its legislative history to indicate that it was the purpose of Congress ... to relax the security provisions of the immigration laws. There is no indication that Congress intended to permit members or former members of the armed forces to marry and bring into the United States aliens that the President, acting through the Attorney General in the performance of his sworn duty, found should be denied entry for security reasons. As all other aliens, petitioner had to stand the test of security. This she failed to meet.

We find no legal defect in the manner of petitioner's exclusion, and the judgment is

*Affirmed.*

MR. JUSTICE JACKSON, whom MR. JUSTICE BLACK and MR. JUSTICE FRANKFURTER join, dissenting.

I do not question the constitutional power of Congress to authorize immigration authorities to turn back from our gates any alien or class of aliens. But I do not find that Congress has authorized an abrupt and brutal exclusion of the wife of an American citizen without a hearing.

... The petitioning husband is honorably discharged and remained in Germany as a civilian employee. Our military authorities abroad required their permission before marriage. The Army in Germany is not without a vigilant and security-conscious intelligence service. This woman was employed by our European Command, and her record is not only without blemish but is highly praised by her superiors. The marriage of this alien woman to this veteran was approved by the Commanding General at Frankfurt-on-Main.

Now this American citizen is told he cannot bring his wife to the United States, but he will not be told why. He must abandon his bride to live in his own country or forsake his country to live with his bride.

\*　　\*　　\*

Security is like liberty in that many are the crimes committed in its name. The menace to the security of this country, be it great as it may, from this girl's admission is nothing compared to the menace to free institutions inherent in procedures of this pattern. In the name of security the police state justifies its arbitrary oppressions on evidence that is secret, because security might be prejudiced if it were brought to light in hearings. The plea that evidence of guilt must be secret is abhorrent to free men, because it provides a cloak for the malevolent, the misinformed, the meddlesome, and the corrupt to play the role of informer undetected and uncorrected.

\*　　\*　　\*

Congress will have to use more explicit language than any yet cited before I will agree that it has authorized an administrative officer to break up the family of an American citizen or force him to keep his wife by becoming an exile. Likewise, it will have to be much more explicit before I can agree that it authorized a finding of serious misconduct against the wife of an American citizen without notice of charges, evidence of guilt and a chance to meet it.

## 250 Removing from Power Those Who Would Abuse It (1950)

Shortly after passage of the Taft-Hartley Act, the National Labor Relations Board withdrew the benefits of the board's procedures and remedies from unions whose officers had not filed an affidavit of non-Communist affiliation. Union interests thereupon challenged section 9(h) of the act, which authorized such action, as an unconstitutional abridgment of the First Amendment. Although not denying the First Amendment problem, the court nevertheless upheld the statute as a protective measure against the hazards of "political strikes" — the selective use of unions' economic power to create popular and revolutionary dissatisfaction, or more directly, to create sufficient economic chaos to force capitulation to the political demands of the strike leaders.

Of particular interest in this opinion is the position of the court that by providing a regulatory scheme for the resolution of labor disputes, government had enhanced the position of union leader to one of a quasi-public nature, subject to legal qualification. Justice Jackson's concurrence was more specific than the court's opinion in upholding the rationale of this legislation to "discourage" unions from elevating Communists to positions of leadership. Concluding that the law was not a prohibited bill of attainder, the court pointed out the provision did not penalize people for *past* actions but only for present and predictable future ones.

☆ 250 *American Communications Association v. Douds*

339 U.S. 382 (1950).

MR. CHIEF JUSTICE VINSON delivered the opinion of the Court.

\*　　\*　　\*

One such obstruction, which it was the purpose of § 9(h) of the Act to remove, was the so-called "political strike." Substantial amounts of evidence were presented to various committees of Congress, including the committees immediately concerned with labor legislation, that Communist leaders of labor unions had in the past and would continue in the future to subordinate legitimate trade union objectives to obstructive strikes when dictated by Party leaders, often in support of the policies of a foreign government. And other evidence supports the view that some union leaders who hold to a belief in violent overthrow of the Government for reasons other than loyalty to the Communist Party likewise regard strikes and other forms of direct action designed to serve ultimate revolutionary goals as the primary objectives of labor unions which they con-

trol. At the committee hearings, the incident most
fully developed was a strike at the Milwaukee plant
of the Allis-Chalmers Manufacturing Company in
1941, when that plant was producing vital materials
for the national defense program. A full hearing was
given not only to company officials, but also to leaders of the international and local unions involved.
Congress heard testimony that the strike had been
called solely in obedience to Party orders for the
purpose of starting the "snowballing of strikes" in
defense plants.

. . . Congress had a great mass of material before
it which tended to show that Communists and others proscribed by the statute had infiltrated union
organizations not to support and further trade union
objectives, including the advocacy of change by democratic methods, but to make them a device by
which commerce and industry might be disrupted
when the dictates of political policy required such
action.

\*         \*         \*

### III

There can be no doubt that Congress may, under
its constitutional power to regulate commerce
among the several States, attempt to prevent political strikes and other kinds of direct action designed
to burden and interrupt the free flow of commerce.
We think it is clear, in addition, that the remedy provided by § 9(h) bears reasonable relation to the evil
which the statute was designed to reach. Congress
could rationally find that the Communist Party is
not like other political parties in its utilization of positions of union leadership as means by which to
bring about strikes and other obstructions of commerce for purposes of political advantage, and that
many persons who believe in overthrow of the Government by force and violence are also likely to resort to such tactics when, as officers, they formulate
union policy.

The fact that the statute identifies persons by
their political affiliation and beliefs, which are circumstances ordinarily irrelevant to permissible subjects of government action, does not lead to the
conclusion that such circumstances are never relevant. . . .

. . . Political affiliations of the kind here involved
. . . provide rational ground for the legislative judgment that those persons proscribed by § 9(h) would
be subject to "tempting opportunities" to commit
acts deemed harmful to the national economy. In
this respect, § 9(h) is not unlike a host of other statutes which prohibit specified groups of persons from
holding positions of power and public interest because, in the legislative judgment, they threaten to
abuse the trust that is a necessary concomitant of
the power of office.

If no more were involved than possible loss of position, the foregoing would dispose of the case. But
the more difficult problem here arises because, in
drawing lines on the basis of beliefs and political affiliations, though it may be granted that the proscriptions of the statute bear a reasonable relation
to the apprehended evil, Congress has undeniably
discouraged the lawful exercise of political freedoms
as well. Stated otherwise, the problem is this: Communists, we may assume, carry on legitimate political activities. Beliefs are inviolate. Congress might
reasonably find, however, that Communists, unlike
members of other political parties, and persons who
believe in overthrow of the Government by force,
unlike persons of other beliefs, represent a continuing danger of disruptive political strikes when they
hold positions of union leadership. By exerting pressures on unions to deny office to Communists and
others identified therein, § 9(h) undoubtedly lessens
the threat to interstate commerce, but it has the further necessary effect of discouraging the exercise of
political rights protected by the First Amendment.
Men who hold union offices often have little choice
but to renounce Communism or give up their offices.
Unions which wish to do so are discouraged from
electing Communists to office. . . .

### IV

\*         \*         \*

Although the First Amendment provides that
Congress shall make no law abridging the freedom
of speech, press or assembly, it has long been established that those freedoms themselves are dependent upon the power of constitutional government
to survive. If it is to survive it must have power to
protect itself against unlawful conduct and, under
some circumstances, against incitements to commit
unlawful acts. Freedom of speech thus does not comprehend the right to speak on any subject at any
time. . . .

. . . [But] Government's interest here is not in preventing the dissemination of Communist doctrine or
the holding of particular beliefs because it is feared
that unlawful action will result therefrom if free
speech is practiced. Its interest is in protecting the
free flow of commerce from what Congress considers to be substantial evils of conduct that are not
the products of speech at all. . . . [Political] strikes
are called by persons who, so Congress has found,
have the will and power to do so *without* advocacy
or persuasion that seeks acceptance in the competition of the market. Speech may be fought with
speech. . . . But force may and must be met with
force. Section 9(h) is designed to protect the public
not against what Communists and others identified
therein advocate or believe, but against what Con-

gress has concluded they have done and are likely to do again.

\*       \*       \*

When [as here] particular conduct is regulated in the interest of public order, and the regulation results in an indirect, conditional, partial abridgment of speech, the duty of the courts is to determine which of these two conflicting interests demands the greater protection under the particular circumstances presented. . . .

. . . In essence, the problem is one of weighing the probable effects of the statute upon the free exercise of the right of speech and assembly against the congressional determination that political strikes are evils of conduct which cause substantial harm to interstate commerce and that Communists and others identified by § 9(h) pose continuing threats to that public interest when in positions of union leadership. . . .

### V

\*       \*       \*

. . . [T]he . . . significance and complexity of the problem of political strikes and how to deal with their leaders [is] apparent. It must be remembered that § 9(h) is not an isolated statute dealing with a subject divorced from the problems of labor peace generally. It is a part of some very complex machinery set up by the Federal Government for the purpose of encouraging the peaceful settlement of labor disputes. Under the statutory scheme, unions which become collective bargaining representatives for groups of employees often represent not only members of the union but nonunion workers or members of other unions as well. . . . [The provisions generate] a tremendous increase in the power of the representative of the group—the union. But power is never without responsibility. And when authority derives in part from Government's thumb on the scales, the exercise of that power by private persons becomes closely akin, in some respects, to its exercise by Government itself.

We do not suggest that labor unions which utilize the facilities of the National Labor Relations Board become Government agencies or may be regulated as such. But it is plain that when Congress clothes the bargaining representative "with powers comparable to those possessed by a legislative body both to create and restrict the rights of those whom it represents," the public interest in the good faith exercise of that power is very great.

What of the effects of § 9(h) upon the rights of speech and assembly of those proscribed by its terms? . . .

. . . The "discouragements" of § 9(h) proceed, not against the groups or beliefs identified therein, but only against the combination of those affiliations or beliefs with occupancy of a position of great power over the economy of the country. Congress has concluded that substantial harm, in the form of direct, positive action, may be expected from that combination. In this legislation, Congress did not restrain the activities of the Communist Party as a political organization; nor did it attempt to stifle beliefs. Section 9(h) touches only a relative handful of persons, leaving the great majority of persons of the identified affiliations and beliefs completely free from restraint. And it leaves those few who are affected free to maintain their affiliations and beliefs subject only to possible loss of positions which Congress has concluded are being abused to the injury of the public by members of the described groups.

\*       \*       \*

Considering the circumstances surrounding the problem—the deference due the congressional judgment concerning the need for regulation of conduct affecting interstate commerce and the effect of the statute upon rights of speech, assembly and belief—we conclude that § 9(h) . . . does not unduly infringe freedoms protected by the First Amendment. Those who, so Congress has found, would subvert the public interest cannot escape all regulation because, at the same time, they carry on legitimate political activities. To encourage unions to displace them from positions of great power over the national economy, while at the same time leaving free the outlets by which they may pursue legitimate political activities of persuasion and advocacy, does not seem to us to contravene the purposes of the First Amendment. That Amendment requires that one be permitted to believe what he will. It requires that one be permitted to advocate what he will unless there is a clear and present danger that a substantial public evil will result therefrom. It does not require that he be permitted to be the keeper of the arsenal.

\*       \*       \*

*Affirmed.*

MR. JUSTICE JACKSON, concurring and dissenting, each in part.

If the statute before us required labor union officers to forswear membership in the Republican Party, the Democratic Party or the Socialist Party, I suppose all agree that it would be unconstitutional. But why, if it is valid as to the Communist Party?

The answer, for me, is in the decisive differences between the Communist Party and every other party of any importance in the long experience of the United States with party government. In order that today's decision may not be useful as a precedent for suppression of any political opposition compatible with our free institutions, I limit concurrence to grounds and distinctions explicitly set forth herein, without which I should regard this Act as unconstitutional.

*        *        *

I

From information before its several Committees and from facts of general knowledge, Congress could rationally conclude that, behind its political party façade, the Communist Party is a conspiratorial and revolutionary junta, organized to reach ends and to use methods which are incompatible with our constitutional system. . . .

1. *The goal of the Communist Party is to seize powers of government by and for a minority rather than to acquire power through the vote of a free electorate.* It seeks not merely a change of administration, or of Congress, or reform legislation within the constitutional framework. Its program is not merely to socialize property more rapidly and extensively than the other parties are doing. While the difference between other parties in these matters is largely as to pace, the Communist Party's difference is one of direction.

The Communist program only begins with seizure of government, which then becomes a means to impose upon society an organization on principles fundamentally opposed to those presupposed by our Constitution. It purposes forcibly to recast our whose social and political structure after the Muscovite model of police-state dictatorship. It rejects the entire religious and cultural heritage of Western civilization, as well as the American economic and political systems. This Communist movement is a belated counter-revolution to the American Revolution, designed to undo the Declaration of Independence, the Constitution, and our Bill of Rights, and overturn our system of free, representative self-government.

*        *        *

Such goals set up a cleavage among us too fundamental to be composed by democratic processes. Our constitutional scheme of elections will not settle issues between large groups when the price of losing is to suffer extinction. When dissensions cut too deeply, men will fight, even hopelessly, before they will submit. And this is the kind of struggle projected by the Communist Party and inherent in its program.

2. *The Communist Party alone among American parties past or present is dominated and controlled by a foreign government.* It is a satrap party which, to the threat of civil disorder, adds the threat of betrayal into alien hands.

The chain of command from the Kremlin to the American party is stoutly denied and usually invisible, but it was unmistakably disclosed by the American Communist Party somersaulting in synchronism with shifts in the Kremlin's foreign policy. . . .

. . . The Communist Party is not native to this country and its beginnings here were not an effort of Americans to answer American problems. Nor is it the response to a quest by American political leaders for lessons from European experiences. . . .

*        *        *

3. *Violent and undemocratic means are the calculated and indispensable methods to attain the Communist Party's goal.* It would be incredible naïveté to expect the American branch of this movement to forego the only methods by which a Communist Party has anywhere come into power. In not one of the countries it now dominates was the Communist Party chosen by a free or contestible election; in not one can it be evicted by any election. The international police state has crept over Eastern Europe by deception, coercion, coup d'état, terrorism and assassination. Not only has it overpowered its critics and opponents; it has usually liquidated them. . . .

*        *        *

4. *The Communist Party has sought to gain this leverage and hold on the American population by acquiring control of the labor movement.* . . . [The Communist Party] strives for control of labor's coercive power — the strike, the sit-down, the slow-down, sabotage, or other means of producing industrial paralysis. Congress has legalized the strike as labor's weapon for improving its own lot. But where Communists have labor control, the strike can be and sometimes is perverted to a party weapon. In 1940 and 1941, undisclosed Communists used their labor offices to sabotage this Nation's effort to rebuild its own defenses. Disguised as leaders of free American labor, they were in truth secret partisans of Stalin, who, in partnership with Hitler, was overrunning Europe, sending honest labor leaders to concentration camps, and reducing labor to slavery in every land either of them was able to occupy. No other important political party in our history has attempted to use the strike to nullify a foreign or a domestic policy adopted by those chosen under our representative system.

This labor leverage, however, usually can be obtained only by concealing the Communist tie from the union membership. . . . The most promising course of the Communist Party has been the undercover capture of the coercive power of strategic labor unions as a leverage to magnify its power over the American people.

5. *Every member of the Communist Party is an agent to execute the Communist program.* What constitutes a party? Major political parties in the United States have never been closely knit or secret organizations. Anyone who usually votes the party ticket is reckoned a member, although he has not applied for or been admitted to membership, pays no dues, has taken no pledge, and is free to vote, speak and act as he wills. . . .

Membership in the Communist Party is totally different. The Party is a secret conclave. Members are admitted only upon acceptance as reliable and after indoctrination in its policies, to which the member is fully committed. They are provided with cards or credentials, usually issued under false names so that the identification can only be made by officers of the Party who hold the code. Moreover, each pledges unconditional obedience to party authority. Adherents are known by secret or code names. They constitute "cells" in the factory, the office, the political society, or the labor union. For any deviation from the party line they are purged and excluded.

*       *       *

Such then is the background which Congress could reasonably find as a basis for exerting its constitutional powers, and which the judiciary cannot disregard in testing them. On this hypothesis we may revert to consideration of the contention of unconstitutionality of this oath insofar as it requires disclosure of Communist Party membership or affiliation.

II

I cannot believe that Congress has less power to protect a labor union from Communist Party domination than it has from employer domination. . . .

*       *       *

I conclude that we cannot deny Congress power to take these measures under the Commerce Clause to require labor union officers to disclose their membership in or affiliation with the Communist Party.

*       *       *

## 251 "There exists a world Communist movement" (1950)

Presidential adviser Bernard Baruch coined the phrase "cold war" in 1948 to dramatize the political contest between the United States and the Soviet Union. In a speech to a Republican Women's Club in West Virginia in 1950, Senator Joseph McCarthy of Wisconsin claimed to have a list of a great many "known Communists" who were employed by the State Department. The speech marked the intensification of a so-called Communist witch hunt in America, which would continue through most of the decade.

The Communist takeover of mainland China, following the retreat of General Chiang Kai-shek's forces to Formosa, and the Communist subversion of the Eastern European democracies made the existence of a world-wide Communist conspiracy seem very real. In 1950, Alger Hiss was convicted of perjury for concealing Communist affiliations. Judith

Coplon was convicted of conspiracy to pass secrets to a Communist spy. The North Koreans launched a massive attack across the Thirty-eighth Parallel on June 25, 1950; in response, President Truman, only five years after the conclusion of World War II, declared a new national emergency. All these events appeared to attest to the fact that international Communism had domestic allies. Against this background, in response to the perceived threat of the world-wide Communist movement, the Internal Security Act of 1950, also known as the McCarran Act, became law.

The act was an omnibus bill with many provisions. Title I, known as the Subversive Activities Control Act, created the Subversive Activities Control Board to investigate and determine what organizations were Communist-affiliated. Communist groups were to be required to register and submit their membership lists and their financial records to the attorney general. The government denied tax exemptions and deductions to registered groups and required them to label all their mail and broadcasts as Communist-sponsored. Title I also excluded and authorized the deportation of aliens who had belonged to a Communist-affiliated group or who advocated "the economic, international, and governmental doctrines of world Communism." The government withheld naturalization for the same reasons. Title II, known as the Emergency Detention Act, authorized the detention of those suspected of future acts of "espionage and sabotage" but, unlike the Japanese Exclusion Orders, provided for individualized hearings on the necessity of detention. Officials of the executive branch were to make all necessary determinations. The Emergency Detention Act was repealed in 1971.

## ☆ 251 The Internal Security Act of 1950 (the McCarran Act)

64 Stat. 987 (1950).

*Be it enacted by the Senate and House of Representatives of the United States of America in Congress assembled*, That this Act may be cited as the "Internal Security Act of 1950."

TITLE I—SUBVERSIVE ACTIVITIES CONTROL

SECTION 1. (a) This title may be cited as the "Subversive Activities Control Act of 1950."

(b) Nothing in this Act shall be construed to authorize, require, or establish military or civilian censorship or in any way to limit or infringe upon freedom of the press or of speech as guaranteed by the Constitution of the United States and no regulation shall be promulgated hereunder having that effect.

## Necessity for Legislation

SEC. 2. As a result of evidence adduced before various committees of the Senate and House of Representatives, the Congress hereby finds that—

(1) There exists a world Communist movement which, in its origins, its development, and its present practice, is a world-wide revolutionary movement whose purpose it is, by treachery, deceit, infiltration into other groups (governmental and otherwise), espionage, sabotage, terrorism, and any other means deemed necessary, to establish a Communist totalitarian dictatorship in the countries throughout the world through the medium of a world-wide Communist organization.

(2) The establishment of a totalitarian dictatorship in any country results in the suppression of all opposition to the party in power, the subordination of the rights of individuals to the state, the denial of fundamental rights and liberties which are characteristic of a representative form of government, such as freedom of speech, of the press, of assembly, and of religious worship, and results in the maintenance of control over the people through fear, terrorism, and brutality.

*          *          *

(4) The direction and control of the world Communist movement is vested in and exercised by the Communist dictatorship of a foreign country.

*          *          *

(9) In the United States those individuals who knowingly and willfully participate in the world Communist movement, when they so participate, in effect repudiate their allegiance to the United States, and in effect transfer their allegiance to the foreign country in which is vested the direction and control of the world Communist movement.

(10) In pursuance of communism's stated objectives, the most powerful existing Communist dictatorship has, by the methods referred to above, already caused the establishment in numerous foreign countries of Communist totalitarian dictatorships, and threatens to establish similar dictatorships in still other countries.

(11) The agents of communism have devised clever and ruthless espionage and sabotage tactics which are carried out in many instances in form or manner successfully evasive of existing law.

*          *          *

(13) There are, under our present immigration laws, numerous aliens who have been found to be deportable, many of whom are in the subversive, criminal, or immoral classes who are free to roam the country at will without supervision or control.

(14) One device for infiltration by Communists is by procuring naturalization for disloyal aliens who use their citizenship as a badge for admission into the fabric of our society.

(15) The Communist movement in the United States is an organization numbering thousands of adherents, rigidly and ruthlessly disciplined. Awaiting and seeking to advance a moment when the United States may be so far extended by foreign engagements, so far divided in counsel, or so far in industrial or financial straits, that overthrow of the Government of the United States by force and violence may seem possible of achievement, it seeks converts far and wide by an extensive system of schooling and indoctrination. Such preparations by Communist organizations in other countries have aided in supplanting existing governments. The Communist organization in the United States, pursuing its stated objectives, the recent successes of Communist methods in other countries, and the nature and control of the world Communist movement itself, present a clear and present danger to the security of the United States and to the existence of free American institutions, and make it necessary that Congress, in order to provide for the common defense, to preserve the sovereignty of the United States as an independent nation, and to guarantee to each State a republican form of government, enact appropriate legislation recognizing the existence of such worldwide conspiracy and designed to prevent it from accomplishing its purpose in the United States.

## Definitions

SEC. 3. For the purposes of this title—

*          *          *

(3) The term "Communist-action organization" means—

(a) any organization in the United States ... which (i) is substantially directed, dominated, or controlled by the foreign government or foreign organization controlling the world Communist movement referred to in section 2 of this title, and (ii) operates primarily to advance the objectives of such world Communist movement as referred to in section 2 of this title; and

(b) any section, branch, fraction, or cell of any organization defined in subparagraph (a) of this paragraph which has not complied with the registration requirements of this title.

(4) The term "Communist-front organization" means any organization in the United States (other than a Communist-action organization as

defined in paragraph (3) of this section) which (A) is substantially directed, dominated, or controlled by a Communist-action organization, and (B) is primarily operated for the purpose of giving aid and support to a Communist-action organization, a Communist foreign government, or the world Communist movement referred to in section 2 of this title.

(5) The term "Communist organization" means a Communist-action organization or a Communist-front organization.

\*       \*       \*

### Certain Prohibited Acts

SEC. 4. (a) It shall be unlawful for any person knowingly to combine, conspire, or agree with any other person to perform any act which would substantially contribute to the establishment within the United States of a totalitarian dictatorship . . . , the direction and control of which is to be vested in, or exercised by or under the domination or control of, any foreign government, foreign organization, or foreign individual: *Provided, however,* That this subsection shall not apply to the proposal of a constitutional amendment.

\*       \*       \*

(f) Neither the holding of office nor membership in any Communist organization by any person shall constitute per se a violation of subsection (a) of this section or of any other criminal statute. The fact of the registration of any person under section 7 or section 8 of this title as an officer or member of any Communist organization shall not be received in evidence against such person in any prosecution for any alleged violation of subsection (a) or subsection (c) of this section or for any alleged violation of any other criminal statute.

### Employment of Members of Communist Organizations

SEC. 5. (a) When a Communist organization, as defined in paragraph (5) of section 3 of this title, is registered or there is in effect a final order of the Board requiring such organization to register, it shall be unlawful—

(1) For any member of such organization, with knowledge or notice that such organization is so registered or that such order has become final—

(A) in seeking, accepting, or holding any nonelective office or employment under the United States, to conceal or fail to disclose the fact that he is a member of such organization; or

(B) to hold any nonelective office or employment under the United States; or

(C) in seeking, accepting, or holding employment in any defense facility, to conceal or

fail to disclose the fact that he is a member of such organization; or

(D) if such organization is a Communist-action organization, to engage in any employment in any defense facility.

(2) For any officer or employee of the United States or of any defense facility, with knowledge or notice that such organization is so registered or that such order has become final—

(A) to contribute funds or services to such organization; or

(B) to advise, counsel, or urge any person, with knowledge or notice that such person is a member of such organization, to perform, or to omit to perform, any act if such act or omission would constitute a violation of any provision of subparagraph (1) of this subsection.

\*       \*       \*

### Denial of Passports to Members of Communist Organizations

SEC. 6. (a) When a Communist organization as defined in paragraph (5) of section 3 of this title is registered, or there is in effect a final order of the Board requiring such organization to register, it shall be unlawful for any member of such organization, with knowledge or notice that such organization is so registered or that such order has become final—

(1) to make application for a passport, or the renewal of a passport, to be issued or renewed by or under the authority of the United States; or

(2) to use or attempt to use any such passport.

\*       \*       \*

### Registration and Annual Reports of Communist Organizations

SEC. 7. (a) Each Communist-action organization (including any organization required, by a final order of the Board, to register as a Communist-action organization) shall, within [thirty days], register with the Attorney General, on a form prescribed by him by regulations, as a Communist-action organization.

(b) Each Communist-front organization (including any organization required, by a final order of the Board, to register as a Communist-front organization) shall, within [thirty days], register with the Attorney General, on a form prescribed by him by regulations, as a Communist-front organization.

\*       \*       \*

(d) The registration made under subsection (a) or (b) shall be accompanied by a registration statement, to be prepared and filed in such manner and form as the Attorney General shall by regulations prescribe, containing the following information;

(1) The name of the organization and the address of its principal office.

(2) The name and last-known address of each individual who is at the time of filing of such reg-

istration statement, and of each individual who was at any time during the period of twelve full calendar months next preceding the filing of such statement, an officer of the organization, with the designation or title of the office so held, and with a brief statement of the duties and functions of such individual as such officer.

(3) An accounting, in such form and detail as the Attorney General shall by regulations prescribe, of all moneys received and expended (including the sources from which received and the purposes for which expended) by the organization during the period of twelve full calendar months next preceding the filing of such statement.

(4) In the case of a Communist-action organization, the name and last-known address of each individual who was a member of the organization at any time during the period of twelve full calendar months preceding the filing of such statement.

(5) In the case of any officer or member whose name is required to be shown in such statement, and who uses or has used or who is or has been known by more than one name, each name which such officer or member uses or has used or by which he is known or has been known.

(e) It shall be the duty of each organization registered under this section to file with the Attorney General on or before February 1 of the year following the year in which it registers, and on or before February 1 of each suceeding year, an annual report. . . .

(f) (1) It shall be the duty of each organization registered under this section to keep . . . accurate records and accounts of moneys received and expended (including the sources from which received and purposes for which expended) by such organization.

*            *            *

### Registration of Members of Communist-Action Organizations

SEC. 8. (a) Any individual who is or becomes a member of any organization concerning which (1) there is in effect a final order of the Board requiring such organization to register under section 7(a) of this title as a Communist-action organization . . . and (3) such organization is not registered . . . shall within sixty days after said order has become final, or within thirty days after becoming a member of such organization, whichever is later, register with the Attorney General as a member of such organization.

*            *            *

### Penalties

SEC. 15. (a) If there is in effect with respect to any organization or individual a final order of the Board

requiring registration under section 7 or section 8 of this title—

(1) such organization shall, upon conviction of failure to register, to file any registration statement or annual report, or to keep records as required by section 7, be punished for each such offense by a fine of not more than $10,000, and

(2) each individual having a duty under subsection (h) of section 7 to register or to file any registration statement or annual report on behalf of such organization, and each individual having a duty to register under section 8, shall, upon conviction of failure to so register or to file any such registration statement or annual report, be punished for each such offense by a fine of not more than $10,000, or imprisonment for not more than five years, or by both such fine and imprisonment.

*            *            *

### TITLE II—EMERGENCY DETENTION

#### Short Title

SEC. 100. This title may be cited as the "Emergency Detention Act of 1950."

#### Findings of Fact and Declaration of Purpose

SEC. 101. As a result of evidence adduced before various committees of the Senate and the House of Representatives, the Congress hereby finds that—

*            *            *

(10) The experience of many countries in World War II and thereafter with so-called "fifth columns" which employed espionage and sabotage to weaken the internal security and defense of nations resisting totalitarian dictatorships demonstrated the grave dangers and fatal effectiveness of such internal espionage and sabotage.

(11) The security and safety of the territory and Constitution of the United States, and the successful prosecution of the common defense, especially in time of invasion, war, or insurrection in aid of a foreign enemy, require every reasonable and lawful protection against espionage, and against sabotage to national-defense material, premises, forces and utilities, including related facilities for mining, manufacturing, transportation, research, training, military and civilian supply, and other activities essential to national defense.

(12) Due to the wide distribution and complex interrelation of facilities which are essential to national defense and due to the increased effectiveness and technical development in espionage and sabotage activities, the free and unrestrained movement in such emergencies of members or agents of [Communist] organizations and of others associated in their espionage and sabo-

tage operations would make adequate surveillance to prevent espionage and sabotage impossible and would therefore constitute a clear and present danger to the public peace and the safety of the United States.

\*         \*         \*

(14) The detention of persons who there is reasonable ground to believe probably will commit or conspire with others to commit espionage or sabotage is, in a time of internal security emergency, essential to the common defense and to the safety and security of the territory, the people and the Constitution of the United States.

(15) It is also essential that such detention in an emergency involving the internal security of the Nation shall be so authorized, executed, restricted, and reviewed as to prevent any interference with the constitutional rights and privileges of any persons, and at the same time shall be sufficiently effective to permit the performance by the Congress and the President of their constitutional duties to provide for the common defense, to wage war, and to preserve, protect, and defend the Constitution, the Government, and the people of the United States.

### Declaration of "Internal Security Emergency"

SEC. 102. (a) In the event of any one of the following:

(1) Invasion of the territory of the United States or its possessions,

(2) Declaration of war by Congress, or

(3) Insurrection within the United States in aid of a foreign enemy,

and if, upon the occurrence of one or more of the above, the President shall find that the proclamation of an emergency pursuant to this section is essential to the preservation, protection and defense of the Constitution, and to the common defense and safety of the territory and people of the United States, the President is authorized to make public proclamation of the existence of an "Internal Security Emergency."

(b) A state of "Internal Security Emergency" (hereinafter referred to as the "emergency") so declared shall continue in existence until terminated by proclamation of the President or by concurrent resolution of the Congress.

### Detention during Emergency

SEC. 103. (a) Whenever there shall be in existence such an emergency, the President, acting through the Attorney General, is hereby authorized to apprehend and by order detain, pursuant to the provisions of this title, each person as to whom there is reasonable ground to believe that such person probably will engage in, or probably will conspire with others to engage in, acts of espionage or of sabotage.

(b) Any person detained hereunder (hereinafter referred to as "the detainee") shall be released from such emergency detention upon —

(1) the termination of such emergency by proclamation of the President or by concurrent resolution of the Congress;

(2) an order of release issued by the Attorney General;

(3) a final order of release after hearing by the Board of Detention Review, hereinafter established;

(4) a final order of release by a United States court, after review of the action of the Board of Detention Review, or upon a writ of habeas corpus.

### Procedure for Apprehension and Detention

SEC. 104. (a) The Attorney General, or such officer or officers of the Department of Justice as he may from time to time designate, are authorized during such emergency to execute in writing and to issue —

(1) a warrant for the apprehension of each person as to whom there is reasonable ground to believe that such person probably will engage in, or probably will conspire with others to engage in, acts of espionage or sabotage; and

(2) an application for an order to be issued pursuant to subsection (d) of this section for the detention of such person for the duration of such emergency.

Each such warrant shall issue only upon probable cause, supported by oath or affirmation, and shall particularly describe the person to be apprehended or detained.

\*         \*         \*

SEC. 109. (a) Any Board created under this title is empowered —

(1) to review upon petition of any detainee any order of detention issued pursuant to section 104 (d) of this title;

(2) to determine whether there is reasonable ground to believe that such detainee probably will engage in, or conspire with others to engage in, espionage or sabotage;

(3) to issue orders confirming, modifying, or revoking any such order of detention; and

(4) to hear and determine any claim made pursuant to this paragraph by any person who shall have been detained pursuant to this title and shall have been released from such detention, for loss of income by such person resulting from such detention if without reasonable grounds. Upon the issuance of any final order for indemnification pursuant to this paragraph, the Attorney General is authorized and directed to make payment of such indemnity to the person entitled thereto

from such funds as may be appropriated to him
for such purpose.

\*          \*          \*

*Judicial Review*

SEC. 111. (a) Any petitioner aggrieved by an order of the Board denying in whole or in part the relief sought by him, or by the failure or refusal of the
Attorney General to obey such order, shall be entitled to the judicial review or judicial enforcement
provided hereinafter in this section.

\*          \*          \*

## 252 "Let us not . . . throw away the ideals which are the fundamental basis of our free society" (1950)

Although President Truman had launched the most
comprehensive federal employment loyalty program in American history, he believed the McCarran Act went too far, and he vetoed it. The House of
Representatives overrode the veto that same day,
and the Senate followed suit the following day. The
McCarran Act, nonetheless, was unsuccessful in operation. A series of Supreme Court decisions rendered Title I virtually unenforceable, and Title II
was repealed in 1971 without ever having been
utilized.

☆ 252  Truman's Veto of the McCarran Act

H.R. Doc. No. 708, 81st Cong., 2d Sess. (1950).

TO THE HOUSE OF REPRESENTATIVES:

I return herewith, without my approval, H.R.
9490, the proposed Internal Security Act of 1950.

\*          \*          \*

Sections 100 through 117 of this bill [Title II] are
intended to give the Government power, in the
event of invasion, war, or insurrection in the United
States in aid of a foreign enemy, to seize and hold
persons who could be expected to attempt acts of espionage or sabotage, even though they had as yet
committed no crime. It may be that legislation of
this type should be on the statute books. But the provisions in H.R. 9490 would very probably prove ineffective to achieve the objective sought, since they
would not suspend the writ of habeas corpus, and
under our legal system to detain a man not charged
with a crime would raise serious constitutional questions unless the writ of habeas corpus were suspended. Furthermore, it may well be that other persons than those covered by these provisions would
be more important to detain in the event of
emergency. . . .

\*          \*          \*

Insofar as the bill would require registration by
the Communist Party itself, it does not endanger
our traditional liberties. However, the application of
the registration requirements to so-called Communist-front organizations can be the greatest danger
to freedom of speech, press, and assembly, since the
alien and sedition laws of 1798. This danger arises
out of the criteria or standards to be applied in determining whether an organization is a Communist-
front organization.

\*          \*          \*

. . . [T]he bill would permit such a determination
to be based solely upon "the extent to which the positions taken or advanced by it from time to time on
matters of policy do not deviate from those" of the
Communist movement.

This provision could easily be used to classify as a
Communist-front organization any organization
which is advocating a single policy or objective
which is also being urged by the Communist Party
or by a Communist foreign government. In fact, this
may be the intended result, since the bill defines "organization" to include "a group of persons . . . permanently or temporarily associated together for joint
action on any subject or subjects." Thus an organization which advocates low-cost housing for sincere
humanitarian reasons might be classified as a Communist-front organization because the Communists
regularly exploit slum conditions as one of their
fifth-column techniques.

\*          \*          \*

. . . [W]e would betray our finest traditions if we
attempted, as this bill would attempt, to curb the
simple expression of opinion. This we should never
do, no matter how distasteful the opinion may be to
the vast majority of our people. The course proposed by this bill would delight the Communists, for
it would make a mockery of the Bill of Rights and of
our claims to stand for freedom in the world.

And what kind of effect would these provisions
have on the normal expression of political views?
Obviously, if this law were on the statute books, the
part of prudence would be to avoid saying anything
that might be construed by someone as not deviat-
ing sufficiently from the current Communist-propa-
ganda line. And since no one could be sure in advance what views were safe to express, the
inevitable tendency would be to express no views on
controversial subjects.

The result could only be to reduce the vigor and
strength of our political life — an outcome that the
Communists would happily welcome, but that free
men should abhor.

We need not fear the expression of ideas — we do
need to fear their suppression.

Our position in the vanguard of freedom rests
largely on our demonstration that the free expres-

sion of opinion, coupled with government by popular consent, leads to national strength and human advancement. Let us not in cowering and foolish fear throw away the ideals which are the fundamental basis of our free society.

\*          \*          \*

. . . It is easy to see that [the immigration and naturalization provisions] are hastily and ill-considered. But far more significant — and far more dangerous — is their apparent underlying purpose. Instead of trying to encourage the free movement of people, subject only to the real requirements of national security, these provisions attempt to bar movement to anyone who is, or once was, associated with ideas we dislike and, in the process, they would succeed in barring many people whom it would be to our advantage to admit.

Such an action would be a serious blow to our work for world peace. We uphold — have upheld till now, at any rate — the concept of freedom on an international scale. That is the root concept of our efforts to bring unity among the free nations and peace in the world.

\*          \*          \*

No considerations of expediency can justify the enactment of such a bill as this, a bill which would so greatly weaken our liberties and give aid and comfort to those who would destroy us. I have, therefore, no alternative but to return this bill without my approval, and I earnestly request the Congress to reconsider its action.

HARRY S. TRUMAN

## 253 "Anything that I had done [was] for the cause of liberty" (1950)

The attempt by two Puerto Rican nationalists to storm Blair House and assassinate President Harry S. Truman ranks among the clearest instances of political violence in America. In the case of many other presidential assassinations or attempts, it has been difficult to draw a clear delineation between the offenders' political motives and their personal pathologies. But President Truman's assailants, one of whom was killed and the other captured, appeared to be acting for purely political motives. The attempt on President Truman, resulting in the death of White House policeman Leslie Coffelt, constituted part of a well-established pattern of Puerto Rican separatist violence which continues to this day.

☆ 253 Assassination Attempt on
Harry S. Truman

James Kirkham, Sheldon G. Levy, and William J. Crotty, *Assassination and Political Violence: The National Com-*

*mission on the Causes and Prevention of Violence Staff Study Series* (Washington, D.C.: U.S. Government Printing Office, 1969), 8:58–81.

On Nov. 1, 1950, Oscar Collazo and Griselio Torresola stormed Blair House, intending to kill President Truman. . . .

\*          \*          \*

Collazo was thirty-four at the time. He had been born in Puerto Rico, the youngest of fourteen children. His father died when he was six years old, and Collazo went to live with an older brother. Collazo's father had been a small landholder and Collazo always blamed United States imperialism for destroying his father in particular and small Puerto Rican landholders in general. When Collazo was eighteen, he joined the Puerto Rican nationalist party of Albizu Campos. He apparently never ceased to work for the cause of an independent Puerto Rico, and felt that the United States was exploiting his country.

\*          \*          \*

Torresola, except for his ardent Puerto Rican nationalism, was cut from different cloth. Although he was married, he was reputed to be something of a gigolo. He had been fired from his job at a stationery and tobacco shop, and for six months before the assassination attempt had been living on relief in New York.

The attack upon President Truman is unique in that, with the possible exception of the Booth plot, this is the only assassination attempt that meets many of the "formal" requirements of an organized, politically motivated plot. Yet, the attempt does not bear great resemblance to a serious political act.

Perhaps the most unrealistic quality was the man chosen as the assassination target. Shortly after he became President, Truman had sent a special message to Congress recommending that four proposals for changing the status of Puerto Rico, including outright independence, be submitted to the Puerto Ricans for their choice. . . . Throughout his presidency Truman showed sympathy for self-determination in Puerto Rico.

\*          \*          \*

In the . . . trial, Collazo refused to allow his lawyers to plead insanity. The defense chose to attempt to convince the jury that Collazo had planned only to stage a demonstration in front of Blair House without intending to kill anyone, and that Torresola — who had been killed in the melee — had started the shooting. The jury rejected this assertion and found Collazo guilty of the murder of Coffelt, and the attempted murder of the President and the two White House guards. He was sentenced to death, but President Truman commuted that sentence to life imprisonment. . . .

There was widespread reaction to their attempt

indicating that Puerto Ricans supported neither the would-be assassins nor their political aims. A letter signed by 119,000 Puerto Ricans was delivered to President Truman by the resident Commissioner of Puerto Rico. It declared that, "during 450 years never before have we seen such an arbitrary act of violence as the one carried on recently by a small group of fanatic nationalists." Puerto Rican children raised money for the children of Coffelt, the guard Torresola killed.

\*          \*          \*

... [I]n a real sense Collazo and Torresola were patriots. The judge who sentenced Collazo to death said, "The Court has no reason to believe that you are not sincere. The Court doesn't think you are an inherently evil man. The Court, as an individual, is sorry for you." Collazo was asked if he had anything to say before being sentenced and he replied, "Anything that I had done I did it for the cause of liberty of my country, and I still insist, even to the last, that we have the right to be free."

## 254  Classes of Aliens Excluded (1950)

The Internal Security Act of 1950 (the McCarran Act) set out not only to control subversive activities by persons located within the United States but also to prevent the entry and expedite the deportation of immigrants likely to contribute to subversive causes.

This prophylactic legislation expanded further the classes of excludable aliens first established in 1903 and enlarged in 1918. It included not only anarchists and members of the Communist party of the United States or of any foreign country but also all others affiliated with organizations that advocated "totalitarianism." Under the expanded criteria, alien writers or publishers of subversive literature, as well as those distributing or displaying such literature, were to be denied entry into the United States. In his message vetoing the Internal Security Act of 1950, President Truman voiced special criticism of this provision:

> Thus, the Attorney General would be required to deport any alien operating or connected with a well-stocked bookshop containing books on economics or politics written by supporters of the present governments of Spain, of Yugoslavia, or any one of a number of other countries. . . . The next logical step would be to "burn the books."

## ☆254  Internal Security Act of 1950, Amending Act of October 16, 1918

64 Stat. 1006 (1950).

SEC. 22. The Act of October 16, 1918, is hereby amended to read as follows: "That any alien who is a member of any one of the following classes shall be excluded from admission into the United States:

"(1) Aliens who seek to enter the United States whether solely, principally, or incidentally, to engage in activities which would be prejudicial to the public interest, or would endanger the welfare or safety of the United States;

"(2) Aliens who, at any time, shall be or shall have been members of any of the following classes:

"(A) Aliens who are anarchists;

"(B) Aliens who advocate or teach, or who are members of or affiliated with any organization that advocates or teaches, opposition to all organized government;

"(C) Aliens who are members of or affiliated with (i) the Communist Party of the United States, (ii) any other totalitarian party of the United States, (iii) the Communist Political Association, (iv) the Communist or other totalitarian party of any State of the United States, of any foreign state, or of any political or geographical subdivision of any foreign state; (v) any section, subsidiary, branch, affiliate, or subdivision of any such association or party; or (vi) the direct predecessors or successors of any such association or party, regardless of what name such group or organization may have used, may now bear, or may hereafter adopt;

"(D) Aliens not within any of the other provisions of this paragraph (2) who advocate the economic, international, and governmental doctrines of world communism or the economic and governmental doctrines of any other form of totalitarianism, or who are members of or affiliated with any organization that advocates the economic, international, and governmental doctrines of world communism, or the economic and governmental doctrines of any other form of totalitarianism, either through its own utterances or through any written or printed publications issued or published by or with the permission or consent of or under the authority of such organization or paid for by the funds of such organization;

"(E) Aliens not within any of the other provisions of this paragraph (2), who are members of or affiliated with any organization which is registered or required to be registered under section 7 of the Subversive Activities Control Act of 1950, unless such aliens establish that they did not know or have reason to believe at the time they became members of or affiliated with such an organization (and did not thereafter and prior to the date upon which such organization was so registered or so required to be registered acquire such knowledge or belief) that such organization was a Communist organization;

"(F) Aliens who advocate or teach or who are members of or affiliated with any organization that advocates or teaches (i) the overthrow by force or violence or other unconstitutional means of the Government of the United States or of all forms of law; or (ii) the duty, necessity, or propriety of the unlawful assaulting or killing of any officer or officers (either of specific individuals or of officers generally) of the Government of the United States or of any other organized government, because of his or their official character; or (iii) the unlawful damage, injury, or destruction of property; or (iv) sabotage;

"(G) Aliens who write or publish, or cause to be written or published, or who knowingly circulate, distribute, print, or display, or knowingly cause to be circulated, distributed, printed, published, or displayed, or who knowingly have in their possession for the purpose of circulation, publication, or display, any written or printed matter, advocating or teaching opposition to all organized government, or advocating (i) the overthrow by force or violence or other unconstitutional means of the Government of the United States or of all forms of law; or (ii) the duty, necessity, or propriety of the unlawful assaulting or killing of any officer or officers (either of specific individuals or of officers generally) of the Government of the United States or of any other organized government; or (iii) the unlawful damage, injury, or destruction of property; or (iv) sabotage; or (v) the economic, international, and governmental doctrines of world communism or the economic and governmental doctrines of any other form of totalitarianism;

"(H) Aliens who are members of or affiliated with any organization that writes, circulates, distributes, prints, publishes, or displays, or causes to be written, circulated, distributed, printed, published, or displayed, or that has in its possession for the purpose of circulation, distribution, publication, issue, or display, any written or printed matter of the character described in subparagraph (G);

"(3) Aliens with respect to whom there is reason to believe that such aliens would, after entry, be likely to (A) engage in activities which would be prohibited by the laws of the United States relating to espionage, sabotage, public disorder, or in other activity subversive to the national security; (B) engage in any activity a purpose of which is the opposition to, or the control or overthrow of, the Government of the United States by force,

violence, or other unconstitutional means; or (C) organize, join, affiliate with, or participate in the activities of any organization which is registered or required to be registered under section 7 of the Subversive Activities Control Act of 1950.

\*        \*        \*

"SEC. 3. No visa or other documentation shall be issued to any alien who seeks to enter the United States either as an immigrant or as a nonimmigrant if the consular officer knows or has reason to believe that such alien is inadmissible to the United States under this Act. . . .

"SEC. 4. (a) Any alien who was at the time of entering the United States, or has been at any time thereafter, a member of any one of the classes of aliens enumerated in section 1(1) or section 1(3) of this Act or (except in the case of an alien who is legally in the United States temporarily as a nonimmigrant under section 3(1) or 3(7) of the Immigration Act of 1924, as amended) a member of any one of the classes of aliens enumerated in section 1(2) of this Act, shall, upon the warrant of the Attorney General, be taken into custody and deported. . . .

"(b) The Attorney General shall, in like manner as provided in subsection (a) of this section, take into custody and deport from the United States any alien who at any time, whether before or after the effective date of this Act, has engaged, or has had a purpose to engage, in any of the activities described in paragraph (1) or in any of the subparagraphs of paragraph (3) of section 1. . . ."

\*        \*        \*

## 255 "overthrow the Government 'as speedily as circumstances would permit' " (1951)

Although Congress passed the Smith Act in 1940, the best-known prosecution under the act did not occur until the July 1948 indictment of twelve members of the Central Committee of the Communist Party of the United States. One person's case was severed owing to ill health; all of the remaining eleven defendants were convicted after an emotionally charged nine-month trial. The Supreme Court agreed to review the constitutionality of the act. In its decision, the court reinterpreted and made less stringent the traditional "clear and present danger" test for determining the propriety of governmental restraint of speech. Under this modification, perhaps best characterized as a "not improbable danger" test, the government could restrict political speech according to the "gravity of the evil, discounted by its improbability." The decision was a signal that the court would not erect constitutional obstacles to the enactment or enforcement of anti-Communist initiatives.

☆255 *Dennis v. United States*

341 U.S. 494 (1951).

MR. CHIEF JUSTICE VINSON announced the judgment of the Court and an opinion in which MR. JUSTICE REED, MR. JUSTICE BURTON, and MR. JUSTICE MINTON join.

\*     \*     \*

The indictment charged the petitioners with wilfully and knowingly conspiring (1) to organize as the Communist Party of the United States of America a society, group and assembly of persons who teach and advocate the overthrow and destruction of the Government of the United States by force and violence, and (2) knowingly and wilfully to advocate and teach the duty and necessity of overthrowing and destroying the Government of the United States by force and violence. The indictment further alleged that § 2 of the Smith Act proscribes these acts and that any conspiracy to take such action is a violation of § 3 of the Act.

\*     \*     \*

The obvious purpose of the statute is to protect existing Government, not from change by peaceable, lawful and constitutional means, but from change by violence, revolution and terrorism. That it is within the *power* of the Congress to protect the Government of the United States from armed rebellion is a proposition which requires little discussion. Whatever theoretical merit there may be to the argument that there is a "right" to rebellion against dictatorial governments is without force where the existing structure of the government provides for peaceful and orderly change. We reject any principle of governmental helplessness in the face of preparation for revolution, which principle, carried to its logical conclusion, must lead to anarchy. No one could conceive that it is not within the power of Congress to prohibit acts intended to overthrow the Government by force and violence. The question with which we are concerned here is not whether Congress has such *power*, but whether the *means* which it has employed conflict with the First and Fifth Amendments to the Constitution.

One of the bases for the contention that the means which Congress has employed are invalid takes the form of an attack on the face of the statute on the grounds that by its terms it prohibits academic discussion of the merits of Marxism-Leninism, that it stifles ideas and is contrary to all concepts of a free speech and a free press....

\*     \*     \*

The very language of the Smith Act negates the interpretation which petitioners would have us impose on that Act. It is directed at advocacy, not discussion. Thus, the trial judge properly charged the jury that they could not convict if they found that petitioners did "no more than pursue peaceful studies and discussions or teaching and advocacy in the realm of ideas." He further charged that it was not unlawful "to conduct in an American college or university a course explaining the philosophical theories set forth in the books which have been placed in evidence." Such a charge is in strict accord with the statutory language, and illustrates the meaning to be placed on those words. Congress did not intend to eradicate the free discussion of political theories, to destroy the traditional rights of Americans to discuss and evaluate ideas without fear of governmental sanction. Rather, Congress was concerned with the very kind of activity in which the evidence showed these petitioners engaged.

\*     \*     \*

In this case we are squarely presented with the application of the "clear and present danger" test, and must decide what that phrase imports. We first note that many of the cases in which this Court has reversed convictions by use of this or similar tests have been based on the fact that the interest which the State was attempting to protect was itself too insubstantial to warrant restriction of speech....

Obviously, the words cannot mean that before the Government may act, it must wait until the *putsch* is about to be executed, the plans have been laid and the signal is awaited. If Government is aware that a group aiming at its overthrow is attempting to indoctrinate its members and to commit them to a course whereby they will strike when the leaders feel the circumstances permit, action by the Government is required. The argument that there is no need for Government to concern itself, for Government is strong, it possesses ample powers to put down a rebellion, it may defeat the revolution with ease needs no answer. For that is not the question. Certainly an attempt to overthrow the Government by force, even though doomed from the outset because of inadequate numbers or power of the revolutionists, is a sufficient evil for Congress to prevent. The damage which such attempts create both physically and politically to a nation makes it impossible to measure the validity in terms of the probability of success, or the immediacy of a successful attempt. In the instant case the trial judge charged the jury that they could not convict unless they found that petitioners intended to overthrow the Government "as speedily as circumstances would permit." This does not mean, and could not properly mean, that they would not strike until there was certainty of success. What was meant was that the revolutionists would strike when they thought the time was ripe. We must therefore reject the contention that success or probability of success is the criterion.

The situation with which Justice Holmes and

Brandeis were concerned in *Gitlow* was a comparatively isolated event, bearing little relation in their minds to any substantial threat to the safety of the community.... They were not confronted with any situation comparable to the instant one—the development of an apparatus designed and dedicated to the overthrow of the Government, in the context of world crisis after crisis.

Chief Judge Learned Hand, writing for the majority below, interpreted the phrase as follows: "In each case [courts] must ask whether the gravity of the 'evil,' discounted by its improbability, justifies such invasion of free speech as is necessary to avoid the danger." We adopt this statement of the rule. As articulated by Chief Judge Hand, it is as succinct and inclusive as any other we might devise at this time. It takes into consideration those factors which we deem relevant, and relates their significances. More we cannot expect from words.

Likewise, we are in accord with the court below, which affirmed the trial court's finding that the requisite danger existed. The mere fact that from the period 1945 to 1948 petitioners' activities did not result in an attempt to overthrow the Government by force and violence is of course no answer to the fact that there was a group that was ready to make the attempt. The formation by petitioners of such a highly organized conspiracy, with rigidly disciplined members subject to call when the leaders, these petitioners, felt that the time had come for action, coupled with the inflammable nature of world conditions, similar uprisings in other countries, and the touch-and-go nature of our relations with countries with whom petitioners were in the very least ideologically attuned, convince us that their convictions were justified on this score. And this analysis disposes of the contention that a conspiracy to advocate, as distinguished from the advocacy itself, cannot be constitutionally restrained, because it comprises only the preparation. It is the existence of the conspiracy which creates the danger. If the ingredients of the reaction are present, we cannot bind the Government to wait until the catalyst is added.

\*     \*     \*

We hold that §§ 2(a)(1), 2(a)(3) and 3 of the Smith Act do not inherently, or as construed or applied in the instant case, violate the First Amendment and other provisions of the Bill of Rights, or the First and Fifth Amendments because of indefiniteness. Petitioners intended to overthrow the Government of the United States as speedily as the circumstances would permit. Their conspiracy to organize the Communist Party and to teach and advocate the overthrow of the Government of the United States by force and violence created a "clear and present danger" of an attempt to overthrow the Government by force and violence. They were properly and constitutionally convicted for violation of the Smith Act. The judgments of conviction are

*Affirmed.*

## 256 "a general regulation which merely provides standards of qualification . . . for employment" (1951)

The *Garner* case involved a Los Angeles city ordinance requiring all municipal employees to take an oath denying past and future advocacy, either as individuals or as members of organizations, of the violent overthrow of the federal and state governments. The ordinance also required employees to execute an affidavit regarding membership, if any, in the Communist party. Petitioners were discharged from city employment for failure to comply with these requirements. The Supreme Court rejected the argument that the oath requirement constituted a bill of attainder or that it violated the Constitution's free speech protections. Although municipal employment raised no national security concerns that might justify an oath of nonadvocacy or even non-Communist affiliation under earlier cases, the court did not view the curtailment of such employment as punishment for holding disfavored political beliefs, referring instead to municipal employment as a mere privilege to be conferred at the discretion of the employers.

☆ 256 *Garner v. Los Angeles Board*

341 U.S. 716 (1951).

Mr. Justice Clark delivered the opinion of the Court.

\*     \*     \*

Petitioners attack the ordinance as violative of the provision of Art. I, § 10 of the Federal Constitution that "No State shall . . . pass any Bill of Attainder, [or] ex post facto Law...." They also contend that the ordinance deprives them of freedom of speech and assembly and of the right to petition for redress of grievances.

Petitioners have assumed that the oath and affidavit provisions of the ordinance present similar constitutional considerations and stand or fall together. We think, however, that separate disposition is indicated.

1. The affidavit raises the issue whether the City of Los Angeles is constitutionally forbidden to require that its employees disclose their past or present membership in the Communist Party or the Communist Political Association. Not before us is the question whether the city may determine that

an employee's disclosure of such political affiliation justifies his discharge.

We think that a municipal employer is not disabled because it is an agency of the State from inquiring of its employees as to matters that may prove relevant to their fitness and suitability for the public service. Past conduct may well relate to present fitness; past loyalty may have a reasonable relationship to present and future trust. Both are commonly inquired into in determining fitness for both high and low positions in private industry and are not less relevant in public employment. The affidavit requirement is valid.

\* \* \*

Bills of attainder are "legislative acts ... that apply either to named individuals or to easily ascertainable members of a group in such a way as to inflict punishment on them without a judicial trial. ..." Punishment is a prerequisite. Whether legislative action curtailing a privilege previously enjoyed amounts to punishment depends upon "the circumstances attending and the causes of the deprivation." We are unable to conclude that punishment is imposed by a general regulation which merely provides standards of qualification and eligibility for employment.

[There was no discussion of the First Amendment claim of the petitioners.]

*Affirmed.*

MR. JUSTICE FRANKFURTER, concurring in part and dissenting in part.

The Constitution does not guarantee public employment. City, State and Nation are not confined to making provisions appropriate for securing competent professional discharge of the functions pertaining to diverse governmental jobs. They may also assure themselves of fidelity to the very presuppositions of our scheme of government on the part of those who seek to serve it. No unit of government can be denied the right to keep out of its employ those who seek to overthrow the government by force or violence, or are knowingly members of an organization engaged in such endeavor.

But it does not at all follow that because the Constitution does not guarantee a right to public employment, a city or a State may resort to any scheme for keeping people out of such employment....

\* \* \*

The validity of an oath must be judged on the assumption that it will be taken conscientiously. This ordinance does not ask the employee to swear that he "knowingly" or "to the best of his knowledge" had no proscribed affiliation. Certainty is implied in the disavowal exacted. The oath thus excludes from city employment all persons who are not certain that every organization to which they belonged or

with which they were affiliated (with all the uncertainties of the meaning of "affiliated") at any time since 1943 has not since that date advocated the overthrow by "unlawful means" of the Government of the United States or of the State of California.

\* \* \*

Giving full scope to the selective processes open to our municipalities and States in securing competent and reliable functionaries free from allegiance to any alien political authority, I do not think that it is consonant with the Due Process Clause for men to be asked, on pain of giving up public employment, to swear to something they cannot be expected to know. Such a demand is at war with individual integrity....

The needs of security do not require such curbs on what may well be innocuous feelings and associations.

## 257 "they had only the best of motives" (1952)

In 1950, Senator McCarthy's accusations of government agencies "riddled" by Communists shook the country. With the commencement of the Korean War the public perceived that American soldiers were fighting and dying once more, this time to prevent the spread of Communism.

On January 31, 1951, the "Atom Spies," Julius and Ethel Rosenberg, husband and wife, were convicted of conspiracy to violate the Espionage Act of 1917 by transmitting secrets to a former ally, the Soviet Union, between 1944 and 1950. A prosecution for treason could not have survived, since their acts did not give aid to an "enemy." Nevertheless, since their acts occurred during wartime, albeit a war against a different power than the Soviet Union, the Rosenbergs suffered the same penalty as that for treason. After sixteen applications to the district court, seven appeals to the court of appeals, seven petitions to the Supreme Court, and two requests to the president for executive clemency, in June of 1953 they became the first American civilians to be executed for espionage.

Throughout the course of their appeals, the Rosenbergs pressed two arguments: the invalidity of the 1917 Espionage Act and the inappropriateness of the death penalty. The 1952 court of appeals decision addressed these issues most succinctly.

☆ 257 *United States v. Rosenberg*

195 F.2d 583 (2d Cir. 1952).

FRANK, Circuit Judge. Since two of the defendants must be put to death if the judgments stand, it goes without saying that we have scrutinized the record with extraordinary care to see whether it contains any of the errors asserted on this appeal.

1. The Supreme Court has held that the Espionage Act of 1917 makes criminal, and subject to the prescribed penalties, the communication of the prohibited information to the advantage of "any foreign nation," even if such communication does not injure this country. [T]he Court said: "Nor do we think it necessary to prove that the information obtained was to be used to the injury of the United States. The statute is explicit in phrasing the crime of espionage as an act of obtaining information relating to the national defense 'to be used . . . to the advantage of any foreign nation.' No distinction is made between friend or enemy. . . ."

\*    \*    \*

We think the statute valid under the First Amendment as well. The communication to a foreign government of secret material connected with the national defense can by no far-fetched reasoning be included within the area of First-Amendment protected free speech. . . .

\*    \*    \*

. . . [The defendants] claim . . . that, even if they were properly convicted, it was unconstitutional and an abuse of discretion for the trial judge to impose the extreme penalty in their particular case, and that we must reduce their sentences. In support of that contention they assert the following: They did not act from venal or pecuniary motives; except for this conviction, their records as citizens and parents are unblemished; at the most, out of idealistic motives, they gave secret information to Soviet Russia when it was our wartime ally; for this breach, they are sentenced to die, while those who, according to the government, were their confederates, at least equally implicated in wartime espionage — Harry Gold, Emil Fuchs, Elizabeth Bentley and the Greenglasses — get off with far lighter sentences or go free altogether. Finally, they argue, the death sentence is unprecedented in a case like this: No civil court has ever imposed this penalty in an espionage case, and it has been imposed by such a court in two treason cases only.

Unless we are to over-rule sixty years of undeviating federal precedents, we must hold that an appellate court has no power to modify a sentence. "If there is one rule in the federal criminal practice which is firmly established, it is that the appellate court has no control over a sentence which is within the limits allowed by a statute." In *Blockburger v. United States*, the Supreme Court said: "Under the circumstances, so far as disclosed, it is true that the imposition of the full penalty of fine and imprisonment upon each count seems unduly severe; but, there may have been other facts and circumstances before the trial court properly influencing the ex-

tent of the punishment. In any event, the matter was one for that court, with whose judgment there is no warrant for interference on our part." . . .

\*    \*    \*

. . . Cases are conceivable where there would be little doubt of a general public antipathy to a death sentence. But . . . this is not such a case.

In all likelihood, it would be — if the evidence were as the Rosenbergs depict it: They say that they were sentenced to death, not for espionage, but for political unorthodoxy and adherence to the Communist Party, and that (assuming they are guilty) they had only the best of motives in giving information to Russia which, at the time, was an ally of this country, praised as such by leading patriotic Americans. But the trial judge, in sentencing the Rosenbergs, relied on record evidence which (if believed) shows a very different picture. If this evidence be accepted, the conspiracy did not end in 1945, while Russia was still a "friend," but, as the trial judge phrased it, continued "during a period when it was apparent to everybody that we were dealing with a hostile nation."

\*    \*    \*

*Affirmed.*

# 258 "fitness to maintain the integrity of the schools" (1952)

The New York Civil Service Law (the Feinberg Law) rendered persons belonging to organizations that advocated the overthrow of the government by force, violence, or any unlawful means ineligible for employment in public schools. The state's board of regents was authorized to promulgate a list of organizations found to advocate or embrace the doctrine of the violent or unlawful overthrow of the government. Membership in such an organization, coupled with knowledge of the organization's philosophy, became prima facie grounds for disqualification from employment. Teachers sought to enjoin the enforcement of the Feinberg Law on the grounds that it violated their rights to free speech and assembly. Upholding these practices, the Supreme Court pointed to the "right and duty" of school authorities to "screen the officials, teachers, and employees as to their fitness to maintain the integrity of the schools as part of ordered society."

☆258 *Adler v. Board of Education*

342 U.S. 485 (1952).

MR. JUSTICE MINTON delivered the opinion of the Court.

Appellants brought a declaratory judgment action in the Supreme Court of New York, Kings

County, praying that § 12-a of the Civil Service Law, as implemented by the so-called Feinberg Law, be declared unconstitutional, and that action by the Board of Education of the City of New York thereunder be enjoined. . . .

*            *            *

It is . . . argued that the Feinberg Law and the rules promulgated thereunder constitute an abridgment of the freedom of speech and assembly of persons employed or seeking employment in the public schools of the State of New York.

It is clear that such persons have the right under our law to assemble, speak, think and believe as they will. It is equally clear that they have no right to work for the State in the school system on their own terms. They may work for the school system upon the reasonable terms laid down by the proper authorities of New York. If they do not choose to work on such terms, they are at liberty to retain their beliefs and associations and go elsewhere. Has the State thus deprived them of any right to free speech or assembly? We think not. Such persons are or may be denied, under the statutes in question, the privilege of working for the school system of the State of New York because, first, of their advocacy of the overthrow of the government by force or violence, or, secondly, by unexplained membership in an organization found by the school authorities, after notice and hearing, to teach and advocate the overthrow of the government by force or violence, and known by such persons to have such purpose.

The constitutionality of the first proposition is not questioned here.

As to the second, it is rather subtly suggested that we should not follow our recent decision in *Garner v. Los Angeles Board.* . . .

We adhere to that case. A teacher works in a sensitive area in a schoolroom. There he shapes the attitude of young minds towards the society in which they live. In this, the state has a vital concern. It must preserve the integrity of the schools. That the school authorities have the right and the duty to screen the officials, teachers, and employees as to their fitness to maintain the integrity of the schools as a part of ordered society, cannot be doubted. One's associates, past and present, as well as one's conduct, may properly be considered in determining fitness and loyalty. From time immemorial, one's reputation has been determined in part by the company he keeps. In the employment of officials and teachers of the school system, the state may very properly inquire into the company they keep, and we know of no rule, constitutional or otherwise, that prevents the state, when determining the fitness and loyalty of such persons, from considering the organizations and persons with whom they associate.

If, under the procedure set up in the New York law, a person is found to be unfit and is disqualified from employment in the public school system because of membership in a listed organization, he is not thereby denied the right of free speech and assembly. His freedom of choice between membership in the organization and employment in the school system might be limited, but not his freedom of speech or assembly, except in the remote sense that limitation is inherent in every choice. Certainly such limitation is not one the state may not make in the exercise of its police power to protect the schools from pollution and thereby to defend its own existence.

*            *            *

Where, as here, the relation between the fact found and the presumption is clear and direct and is not conclusive, the requirements of due process are satisfied. . . .

*            *            *

We find no constitutional infirmity in § 12-a of the Civil Service Law of New York or in the Feinberg Law which implemented it, and the judgment is

*Affirmed.*

MR. JUSTICE BLACK, dissenting.

*            *            *

This is another of those rapidly multiplying legislative enactments which make it dangerous—this time for school teachers—to think or say anything except what a transient majority happen to approve at the moment. Basically these laws rest on the belief that government should supervise and limit the flow of ideas into the minds of men. The tendency of such governmental policy is to mould people into a common intellectual pattern. Quite a different governmental policy rests on the belief that government should leave the mind and spirit of man absolutely free. Such a governmental policy encourages varied intellectual outlooks in the belief that the best views will prevail. This policy of freedom is in my judgment embodied in the First Amendment and made applicable to the states by the Fourteenth. Because of this policy public officials cannot be constitutionally vested with powers to select the ideas people can think about, censor the public views they can express, or choose the persons or groups people can associate with. Public officials with such powers are not public servants; they are public masters.

I dissent from the Court's judgment sustaining this law which effectively penalizes school teachers for their thoughts and their associates.

*            *            *

MR. JUSTICE DOUGLAS, with whom MR. JUSTICE BLACK concurs, dissenting.

I have not been able to accept the recent doctrine that a citizen who enters the public service can be forced to sacrifice his civil rights....

*        *        *

## 259  The Fact of Membership Alone Cannot Disqualify (1952)

In *Wieman v. Updegraff*, the Supreme Court addressed another of the loyalty oaths which more than one-half of the states required of employees. Wieman, a member of the faculty of Oklahoma Agricultural and Mechanical College, failed to take the prescribed oath. By state court order Oklahoma officials suspended his salary payments. No First Amendment claim was advanced, but the Supreme Court found the Oklahoma loyalty oath an unconstitutional denial of due process of law. The court distinguished the Oklahoma oath from similar requirements upheld in the *Garner* and *Adler* cases. The other laws required, either expressly or implicitly, a knowing awareness on a member's part of the prohibited organization's unlawful purposes. Oklahoma, however, imposed sanctions for membership alone, requiring no evidence of knowledge. "But," pointed out the Supreme Court, "membership may be innocent. A state servant may have joined a proscribed organization unaware of its activities and purposes." The court recognized these enactments were quasi-criminal in nature by requiring some proof of personal adherence (culpability) to the disfavored doctrine before the disability could be imposed.

☆ 259  *Wieman v. Updegraff*

344 U.S. 183 (1952).

MR. JUSTICE CLARK delivered the opinion of the Court.

This is an appeal from a decision of the Supreme Court of Oklahoma upholding the validity of a loyalty oath prescribed by Oklahoma statute for all State officers and employees. Appellants, employed by the State as members of the faculty and staff of Oklahoma Agricultural and Mechanical College, failed, within the thirty days permitted, to take the oath required by the Act. Appellee Updegraff, as a citizen and taxpayer, thereupon brought this suit in the District Court of Oklahoma County to enjoin the necessary State officials from paying further compensation to employees who had not subscribed to the oath. The appellants, who were permitted to intervene, attacked the validity of the Act on the grounds, among others, that it was a bill of attainder; an *ex post facto* law; impaired the obligation of their contracts with the State and violated the Due Process Clause of the Fourteenth Amendment.

They also sought a mandatory injunction directing the State officers to pay their salaries regardless of their failure to take the oath. Their objections centered largely on the following clauses of the oath:

... That I am not affiliated directly or indirectly ... with any foreign political agency, party, organization or Government, or with any agency, party, organization, association, or group whatever which has been officially determined by the United States Attorney General or other authorized agency of the United States to be a Communist front or subversive organization; ... that I will take up arms in the defense of the United States in time of War, or National Emergency, if necessary and that within the five (5) years immediately preceding the taking of this oath (or affirmation) I have not been a member of ... any agency, party, organization, association, or group whatever which has been officially determined by the United States Attorney General or other authorized public agency of the United States to be a Communist front or subversive organization....

The court upheld the Act and enjoined the State officers from making further salary payments to appellants. The Supreme Court of Oklahoma affirmed. We noted probable jurisdiction because of the public importance of this type of legislation and the recurring serious constitutional questions which it presents.

*        *        *

... We are thus brought to the question touched on in *Garner*, *Adler*, and *Gerende*: whether the Due Process Clause permits a State, in attempting to bar disloyal individuals from its employ, to exclude persons solely on the basis of organizational membership, regardless of their knowledge concerning the organizations to which they had belonged. For, under the statute before us, the fact of membership alone disqualifies. If the rule be expressed as a presumption of disloyalty, it is a conclusive one.

But membership may be innocent. A State servant may have joined a proscribed organization unaware of its activities and purposes. In recent years, many completely loyal persons have severed organizational ties after learning for the first time of the character of groups to which they had belonged. "They had joined, [but] did not know what it was, they were good, fine young men and women, loyal Americans, but they had been trapped into it — because one of the great weaknesses of all Americans, whether adult or youth, is to join something." At the time of affiliation, a group itself may be innocent, only later coming under the influence of those who would turn it toward illegitimate ends. Conversely, an organization formerly subversive and therefore designated as such may have subsequently freed itself from the influences which originally led to its listing.

There can be no dispute about the consequences visited upon a person excluded from public employment on disloyalty grounds. In the view of the community, the stain is a deep one; indeed, it has become a badge of infamy. Especially is this so in time of cold war and hot emotions when "each man begins to eye his neighbor as a possible enemy." Yet under the Oklahoma Act, the fact of association alone determines disloyalty and disqualification; it matters not whether association existed innocently or knowingly. To thus inhibit individual freedom of movement is to stifle the flow of democratic expression and controversy at one of its chief sources. . . .

. . . We need not pause to consider whether an abstract right to public employment exists. It is sufficient to say that constitutional protection does extend to the public servant whose exclusion pursuant to a statute is patently arbitrary or discriminatory.

*        *        *

*Reversed.*

## 260 "he is treated as if stopped at the border" (1953)

The Supreme Court once more upheld the summary exclusion of a politically suspect alien, without the right to a hearing, in the 1953 case of Ignatz Mezei. He had lived in the United States from 1923 to 1948 and was absent from the country for some nineteen months during a trip to visit his dying mother in Rumania. The United States denied him reentry into the country and confined him to Ellis Island. No other country was willing to accept Mezei. The Supreme Court upheld the exclusion. In dissenting opinions, Justices Black and Douglas objected to the denial of liberty carried out without "a fair open court hearing in which evidence is appraised by a court, not by the prosecutor."

☆ 260 *Shaughnessy v. United States ex rel. Mezei*

345 U.S. 206 (1953).

MR. JUSTICE CLARK delivered the opinion of the Court.

*        *        *

. . . [R]espondent seemingly was born in Gibraltar of Hungarian or Rumanian parents and lived in the United States from 1923 to 1948. In May of that year he sailed for Europe, apparently to visit his dying mother in Rumania. Denied entry there, he remained in Hungary for some 19 months, due to "difficulty in securing an exit permit." Finally, armed

with a quota immigration visa issued by the American Consul in Budapest, he proceeded to France and boarded the *Ile de France* in Le Havre bound for New York. Upon arrival on February 9, 1950, he was temporarily excluded from the United States by an immigration inspector acting pursuant to the Passport Act as amended and regulations thereunder. Pending disposition of his case he was received at Ellis Island. After reviewing the evidence, the Attorney General on May 10, 1950, ordered the temporary exclusion to be made permanent without a hearing before a board of special inquiry, on the "basis of information of a confidential nature, the disclosure of which would be prejudicial to the public interest." That determination rested on a finding that respondent's entry would be prejudicial to the public interest for security reasons. But thus far all attempts to effect respondent's departure have failed: Twice he shipped out to return whence he came; France and Great Britain refused him permission to land. The State Department has unsuccessfully negotiated with Hungary for his readmission. Respondent personally applied for entry to about a dozen Latin-American countries but all turned him down. So in June 1951 respondent advised the Immigration and Naturalization Service that he would exert no further efforts to depart. In short, respondent sat on Ellis Island because this country shut him out and others were unwilling to take him in.

Asserting unlawful confinement on Ellis Island, he sought relief through a series of habeas corpus proceedings. . . .

Courts have long recognized the power to expel or exclude aliens as a fundamental sovereign attribute exercised by the Government's political departments largely immune from judicial control. In the exercise of these powers, Congress expressly authorized the President to impose additional restrictions on aliens entering or leaving the United States during periods of international tension and strife. That authorization, originally enacted in the Passport Act of 1918, continues in effect during the present emergency. Under it, the Attorney General, acting for the President, may shut out aliens whose "entry would be prejudicial to the interests of the United States." And he may exclude without a hearing when the exclusion is based on confidential information the disclosure of which may be prejudicial to the public interest. The Attorney General in this case proceeded in accord with these provisions; he made the necessary determinations and barred the alien from entering the United States.

It is true that aliens who have once passed through our gates, even illegally, may be expelled only after proceedings conforming to traditional standards of fairness encompassed in due process of law. But an alien on the threshold of initial entry stands on a different footing: "Whatever the procedure authorized by Congress is, it is due process as far as an alien denied entry is concerned." . . .

Neither respondent's harborage on Ellis Island nor his prior residence here transforms this into something other than an exclusion proceeding. . . .

\*       \*       \*

There remains the issue of respondent's continued exclusion on Ellis Island. Aliens seeking entry from contiguous lands obviously can be turned back at the border without more. While the Government might keep entrants by sea aboard the vessel pending determination of their admissibility, resulting hardships to the alien and inconvenience to the carrier persuaded Congress to adopt a more generous course. By statute it authorized, in cases such as this, aliens' temporary removal from ship to shore. But such temporary harborage, an act of legislative grace, bestows no additional rights. Congress meticulously specified that such shelter ashore "shall not be considered a landing" nor relieve the vessel of the duty to transport back the alien if ultimately excluded. And this Court has long considered such temporary arrangements as not affecting an alien's status; he is treated as if stopped at the border.

\*       \*       \*

*Reversed.*

MR. JUSTICE BLACK, with whom MR. JUSTICE DOUGLAS concurs, dissenting.

\*       \*       \*

No society is free where government makes one person's liberty depend upon the arbitrary will of another. Dictatorships have done this since time immemorial. They do now. Russian laws of 1934 authorized the People's Commissariat to imprison, banish and exile Russian citizens as well as "foreign subjects who are socially dangerous." Hitler's secret police were given like powers. German courts were forbidden to make any inquiry whatever as to the information on which the police acted. Our Bill of Rights was written to prevent such oppressive practices. Under it this Nation has fostered and protected individual freedom. . . . It means that Mezei should not be deprived of his liberty indefinitely except as the result of a fair open court hearing in which evidence is appraised by the court, not by the prosecutor.

MR. JUSTICE JACKSON, whom MR. JUSTICE FRANKFURTER joins, dissenting.

\*       \*       \*

Is respondent deprived of liberty? The Government answers that he was "transferred to Ellis Island on August 1, 1950, for safekeeping," and "is not being detained in the usual sense but is in custody solely to prevent him from gaining entry to the United States in violation of law. He is free to depart from the United States to any country of his own choice." Government counsel ingeniously argued that Ellis Island is his "refuge" whence he is free to take leave in any direction except west. That might mean freedom, if only he were an amphibian! Realistically, this man is incarcerated by a combination of forces which keep him as effectually as a prison, the dominant and proximate of these forces being the United States immigration authority. It overworks legal fiction to say that one is free in law when by the commonest of common sense he is bound. Despite the impeccable legal logic of the Government's argument on this point, it leads to an artificial and unreal conclusion. . . .

\*       \*       \*

## 261 "all persons privileged to be employed [by] . . . the Government" (1953)

Shortly after the inauguration of President Dwight D. Eisenhower, Executive Order 10450 extended the war against subversive activities and introduced a loyalty program far more sweeping than any previously known. All federal employees now were subject to thorough new background investigations that scrutinized their personal conduct as well as their loyalty. Investigations focused on areas such as behavior or association that tended to show "that the individual [was] not reliable or trustworthy," or any "notoriously disgraceful conduct, habitual use of intoxicants . . . , drug addiction, or sexual perversion."

Between June and December of 1953, the president reported 2,200 security separations. By July 1 of 1954, the reported number had risen to 2,611 dismissed, with an additional 4,315 who had resigned rather than cooperate with the investigators. Raging anti-Communist fervor dominated the mood of the country. Senator McCarthy's hearings were in their prime, and the courts often seemed content to overlook transgressions of civil rights in the name of national security.

## ☆ 261 President Eisenhower's Security Requirements for Government Employment

Exec. Order No. 10450, 18 Fed. Reg. 2489 (Apr. 27, 1953).

WHEREAS the interests of the national security require that all persons privileged to be employed in the departments and agencies of the Government, shall be reliable, trustworthy, of good conduct and character, and of complete and unswerving loyalty to the United States; and

WHEREAS the American tradition that all persons should receive fair, impartial, and equitable treatment at the hands of the Government requires that all persons seeking the privilege of employment or privileged to be employed in the departments and agencies of the Government be adjudged by mutually consistent and no less than minimum standards and procedures among the departments and agencies governing the employment and retention in employment of persons in the Federal service:

NOW, THEREFORE, by virtue of the authority vested in me by the Constitution and statutes of the United States, ... and as President of the United States, and deeming such action necessary in the best interests of the national security, it is hereby ordered as follows:

\*　　\*　　\*

SEC. 2. The head of each department and agency of the Government shall be responsible for establishing and maintaining within his department or agency an effective program to insure that the employment and retention in employment of any civilian officer or employee within the department or agency is clearly consistent with the interests of the national security.

SEC. 3. . . .

(b) The head of any department or agency shall designate, or cause to be designated, any position within his department or agency the occupant of which could bring about, by virtue of the nature of the position, a material adverse effect on the national security as a sensitive position. Any position so designated shall be filled or occupied only by a person with respect to whom a full field investigation has been conducted: *Provided*, that a person occupying a sensitive position at the time it is designated as such may continue to occupy such position pending the completion of a full field investigation, subject to the other provisions of this order. . . .

\*　　\*　　\*

SEC. 5. Whenever there is developed or received by any department or agency information indicating that the retention in employment of any officer or employee of the Government may not be clearly consistent with the interests of the national security, such information shall be forwarded to the head of the employing department or agency or his representative, who, after such investigation as may be appropriate, shall review, or cause to be reviewed, and, where necessary, re-adjudicate, or cause to be re-adjudicated, ... the case of such officer or employee.

SEC. 6. Should there develop at any stage of investigation information indicating that the employment of any officer or employee of the Government may not be clearly consistent with the interests of the national security, the head of the department or agency concerned or his representative shall immediately suspend the employment of the person involved if he deems such suspension necessary in the interests of the national security and, following such investigation and review as he deems necessary, the head of the department or agency concerned shall terminate the employment of such suspended officer or employee whenever he shall determine such termination necessary or advisable in the interests of the national security.

SEC. 7. [N]o person whose employment has been terminated [for security reasons] thereafter may be employed by any other department or agency except after a determination by the Civil Service Commission that such person is eligible for such employment.

SEC. 8. (a) The investigations conducted pursuant to this order shall be designed to develop information as to whether the employment or retention in employment in the Federal service of the person being investigated is clearly consistent with the interests of the national security. Such information shall relate, but shall not be limited, to the following:

(1) Depending on the relation of the Government employment to the national security:

(i) Any behavior, activities, or associations which tend to show that the individual is not reliable or trustworthy.

(ii) Any deliberate misrepresentations, falsifications, or omissions of material facts.

(iii) Any criminal, infamous, dishonest, immoral, or notoriously disgraceful conduct, habitual use of intoxicants to excess, drug addiction, sexual perversion, or financial irresponsibility.

(iv) An adjudication of insanity, or treatment for serious mental or neurological disorder without satisfactory evidence of cure.

(v) Any facts which furnish reason to believe that the individual may be subjected to coercion, influence, or pressure which may cause him to act contrary to the best interests of the national security.

(2) Commission of any act of sabotage, espionage, treason, or sedition, or attempts thereat or preparation therefor, or conspiring with, or aiding or abetting, another to commit or attempt to commit any act of sabotage, espionage, treason, or sedition.

(3) Establishing or continuing a sympathetic association with a saboteur, spy, traitor, seditionist, anarchist, or revolutionist, or with an espionage or other secret agent or representative of a foreign nation, or any representative of a foreign nation whose interests may be inimical to the interests of the United States, or with any person who advocates the use of force or violence to overthrow the government of the United States or the alteration of the form of government of the United States by unconstitutional means.

(4) Advocacy of use of force or violence to overthrow the government of the United States, or of

the alteration of the form of government of the United States by unconstitutional means.

(5) Membership in, or affiliation or sympathetic association with, any foreign or domestic organization, association, movement, group, or combination of persons which is totalitarian, Fascist, Communist, or subversive, or which has adopted, or shows, a policy of advocating or approving the commission of acts of force or violence to deny other persons their rights under the Constitution of the United States, or which seeks to alter the form of government of the United States by unconstitutional means.

(6) Intentional, unauthorized disclosure to any person of security information, or of other information disclosure of which is prohibited by law, or willful violation or disregard of security regulations.

(7) Performing or attempting to perform his duties, or otherwise acting, so as to serve the interests of another government in preference to the interests of the United States.

*      *      *

SEC. 9. (a) There shall be established and maintained in the Civil Service Commission a security-investigations index covering all persons as to whom security investigations have been conducted by any department or agency of the Government under this order.... The security-investigations index shall contain the name of each person investigated, adequate identifying information concerning each such person, and a reference to each department and agency which has conducted an investigation concerning the person involved or has suspended or terminated the employment of such person under the authority granted to heads of departments and agencies by or in accordance with the said act of August 26, 1950.

*      *      *

DWIGHT D. EISENHOWER
*The White House*
*April 27, 1953*

# 262 To Outlaw the Communist Party (1954)

The Communist Control Act of 1954 was an attempt to outlaw the Communist party. Finding that the party, "although purportedly a political party, is in fact an instrumentality of a conspiracy to overthrow the Government of the United States," Congress denied to the Communist party all the rights and privileges legal organizations normally enjoyed. Some states moved to implement this determination that the Communist party was a "proscribed organization," and New Jersey and Connecticut denied candidates from the Communist party the right to appear on election ballots.

☆ 262 The Communist Control Act of 1954

68 Stat. 775 (1954).

*Be it enacted by the Senate and House of Representatives of the United States of America in Congress assembled,* That this Act may be cited as the "Communist Control Act of 1954."

FINDINGS OF FACT

SEC. 2. The Congress hereby finds and declares that the Communist Party of the United States, although purportedly a political party, is in fact an instrumentality of a conspiracy to overthrow the Government of the United States. It constitutes an authoritarian dictatorship within a republic, demanding for itself the rights and privileges accorded to political parties, but denying to all others the liberties guaranteed by the Constitution. Unlike political parties, which evolve their policies and programs through public means, by the reconciliation of a wide variety of individual views, and submit those policies and programs to the electorate at large for approval or disapproval, the policies and programs of the Communist Party are secretly prescribed for it by the foreign leaders of the world Communist movement. Its members have no part in determining its goals, and are not permitted to voice dissent to party objectives. Unlike members of political parties, members of the Communist Party are recruited for indoctrination with respect to its objectives and methods, and are organized, instructed, and disciplined to carry into action slavishly the assignments given them by their hierarchical chieftains. Unlike political parties, the Communist Party acknowledges no constitutional or statutory limitations upon its conduct or upon that of its members. The Communist Party is relatively small numerically, and gives scant indication of capacity ever to attain its ends by lawful political means. The peril inherent in its operation arises not from its numbers, but from its failure to acknowledge any limitation as to the nature of its activities, and its dedication to the proposition that the present constitutional Government of the United States ultimately must be brought to ruin by any available means, including resort to force and violence. Holding that doctrine, its role as the agency of a hostile foreign power renders its existence a clear present and continuing danger to the security of the United States. It is the means whereby individuals are seduced into the service of the world Communist movement, trained to do its bidding, and directed and controlled in the conspiratorial performance of their revolutionary services. Therefore, the Communist Party should be outlawed.

PROSCRIBED ORGANIZATIONS

SEC. 3. The Communist Party of the United States, or any successors of such party regardless of the assumed name, whose object or purpose is to overthrow the Government of the United States, or the government of any State, Territory, District, or possession thereof, or the government of any political subdivision therein by force and violence, are not entitled to any of the rights, privileges, and immunities attendant upon legal bodies created under the jurisdiction of the laws of the United States or any political subdivision thereof; and whatever rights, privileges, and immunities which have heretofore been granted to said party or any subsidiary organization by reason of the laws of the United States or any political subdivision thereof, are hereby terminated: *Provided, however*, That nothing in this section shall be construed as amending the Internal Security Act of 1950, as amended.

SEC. 4. Whoever knowingly and willfully becomes or remains a member of (1) the Communist Party, or (2) any other organization having for one of its purposes or objectives the establishment, control, conduct, seizure, or overthrow of the Government of the United States, or the government of any State or political subdivision thereof, by the use of force or violence, with knowledge of the purpose or objective of such organization shall be subject to all the provisions and penalties of the Internal Security Act of 1950, as amended, as a member of a "Communist-action" organization.

(b) For the purposes of this section, the term "Communist Party" means the organization now known as the Communist Party of the United States of America, the Communist Party of any State or subdivision thereof, and any unit or subdivision of any such organization, whether or not any change is hereafter made in the name thereof.

SEC. 5. In determining membership or participation in the Communist Party or any other organization defined in this Act, or knowledge of the purpose or objective of such party or organization, the jury, under instructions from the court, shall consider evidence, if presented, as to whether the accused person:

(1) Has been listed to his knowledge as a member in any book or any of the lists, records, correspondence, or any other document of the organization;

(2) Has made financial contribution to the organization in dues, assessments, loans, or in any other form;

(3) Has made himself subject to the discipline of the organization in any form whatsoever;

(4) Has executed orders, plans, or directives of any kind of the organization;

(5) Has acted as an agent, courier, messenger, correspondent, organizer, or in any other capacity in behalf of the organization;

(6) Has conferred with officers or other members of the organization in behalf of any plan or enterprise of the organization;

(7) Has been accepted to his knowledge as an officer or member of the organization or as one to be called upon for services by other officers or members of the organization;

(8) Has written, spoken or in any other way communicated by signal, semaphore, sign, or in any other form of communication orders, directives, or plans of the organization;

(9) Has prepared documents, pamphlets, leaflets, books, or any other type of publication in behalf of the objectives and purposes of the organization;

(10) Has mailed, shipped, circulated, distributed, delivered, or in any other way sent or delivered to others material or propaganda of any kind in behalf of the organization;

(11) Has advised, counseled or in any other way imparted information, suggestions, recommendations to officers or members of the organization or to anyone else in behalf of the objectives of the organization;

(12) Has indicated by word, action, conduct, writing or in any other way a willingness to carry out in any manner and to any degree the plans, designs, objectives, or purposes of the organization;

(13) Has in any other way participated in the activities, planning, actions, objectives, or purposes of the organization;

(14) The enumeration of the above subjects of evidence on membership or participation in the Communist Party or any other organization as above defined, shall not limit the inquiry into and consideration of any other subject of evidence on membership and participation as herein stated.

*     *     *

*Approved, August 24, 1954, 9:40 a.m. MST.*

## 263 Potential Threats to the Machinery of Government (1954)

Prohibitions and legislative investigations of subversive activities were not limited to the Congress. New Hampshire's effort in this area was noteworthy on two accounts. First, the investigation in question was not that of a legislative committee but of the state attorney general. He utilized investigative techniques and powers generally not available to the executive. Second, Article 10 of the New Hampshire Bill of Rights reserves to the people the right of revolution in the event that "ends of government are perverted . . . and all other means of redress are ineffectual." The plaintiff challenged the constitutional authority of her interrogator on the grounds that the investigation violated the doctrine of separation of powers and that it infringed on her right to perpetrate a revolution.

☆263 *Nelson v. Wyman*

99 N.H. 33, 105 A.2d 75 (1954).

GOODNOW, J. Under the provisions of a joint resolution adopted by the Legislature of this state in 1953 (Laws 1953, *c.* 307), the Attorney General was authorized and directed "to make full and complete investigation with respect to violations of the subversive activities act of 1951 and to determine whether subversive persons as defined in said act are presently located within this state." ... He was directed "to proceed with criminal prosecutions under the subversive activities act whenever evidence presented to him in the course of the investigation indicates violations thereof" and to "report to the 1955 session ... the results of this investigation, together with his recommendations, if any, for necessary legislation." As a preliminary to the investigation to be conducted by him under this resolution, the Attorney General adopted certain rules of procedure.... These rules provide in part that the examination of witnesses shall be in executive session except in extraordinary circumstances, unless a public hearing is requested by the witness, and that "in lieu" of a public hearing, the transcript of the testimony of witnesses who invoke the self-incrimination privilege will be made public....

The fact that the resolution requires an investigation with respect to violations of law as well as a determination of "whether subversive persons as defined in said act are presently located within the state" does not remove the inquiry from the category of a legislative investigation....

\*      \*      \*

... Having made certain acts unlawful and having classified certain persons as subversives by its 1951 act the Legislature seeks through this investigation to secure general information as to the results of that legislation. In the course of the investigation, information will be sought from witnesses upon which such facts can be determined. No sound basis can exist for denying to the Legislature the power to so investigate the effectiveness of its 1951 act, even though as an incident to that general investigation, it may be necessary to inquire as to whether a particular person has violated the act....

\*      \*      \*

It is also strongly urged by the plaintiff that the Legislature of this state cannot proscribe activities looking to the overthrow of government by force or violence because of Article 10 of the Bill of Rights which provides, in part, that "whenever the ends of government are perverted, and public liberty manifestly endangered, and all other means of redress are ineffectual, the people may, and of right ought, to reform the old, or establish a new government. The doctrine of nonresistance against arbitrary power, and oppression, is absurd, slavish, and destructive of the good and happiness of mankind." With this interpretation we cannot agree. The right reserved to the people by this Article is not such a broad and unlimited right of insurrection and rebellion as to permit any group which is dissatisfied with existing government to lawfully attempt at any time to overthrow the government by force or violence. ... The right possessed by the people of this state as a protection against arbitrary power and oppression cannot be utilized to justify the violent overthrow of government when the adoption of peaceful and orderly changes, properly reflecting the will of the people, may be accomplished through the existing structure of government. To require a government representative of the people, in the face of preparations for revolution by force, to refrain from acting to curb the outbreak of violence and to confine itself solely to holding answerable those persons who have committed crimes of violence and terrorized the community in the name of revolution must result in anarchy. Article 10 was not intended to accomplish this result.

So far as the circumstances of this case have required an examination of the 1951 act, we conclude that it is constitutional upon its face, so as to furnish a basis for the resolution of 1953.

*Case discharged.*

All concurred.

# 264 "My life I give for the freedom of my country" (1954)

While screaming "freedom for Puerto Rico," three men and one woman fired a barrage of gunshots from the spectator gallery in the United States House of Representatives on March 1, 1954. In the attack, carried out to dramatize the cause of Puerto Rican independence, 5 of the 243 congressmen present were wounded. The note reproduced here was found in the purse of Lolita Lebron, a thirty-four-year-old divorcee and one of the *independistas*, following her arrest for the attack. She admitted firing eight shots and having been associated with the wife of Oscar Collazo, one of the two 1950 assailants of President Truman.

☆264 Lolita Lebron Letter

"Gunmen's Attack on Congress Is Like Attack on Truman's Life." *Washington Post*, March 2, 1954, 13, col. 2.

Before God and the world my blood claims for the independence of Puerto Rico. My life I give for the freedom of my country. This is a cry for victory in our struggle for the independence which for more than half a century has tried to conquer the land that belongs to Puerto Rico.

I state forever that the United States of America are betraying the sacred principles of mankind in their continuous subjugation of my country, violating their rights to be a free nation and a free people in their barbarous torture of our apostle of independence, Don Pedro Albibu Campos.

[On the reverse was written:] I take responsible for all.

## 265 "a follower of the Communist line" (1955)

In 1952, Senator Joseph McCarthy's investigation of Communist sympathizers focused upon Professor Owen J. Lattimore, an expert on Far Eastern affairs at the Johns Hopkins University. Testifying before a Senate subcommittee, Lattimore denied under oath that he was a "follower of the Communist line" or a "promoter of Communist causes." The United States government used these statements to support a perjury indictment against Lattimore. Federal Judge Luther Youngdahl dismissed the charges on the grounds of vagueness. The *Lattimore* decision came seven weeks after Senator McCarthy's censure by a two-thirds vote of the United States Senate.

☆ 265  *United States v. Lattimore*

127 F. Supp. 405 (D.D.C. 1955).

YOUNGDAHL, District Judge.

*          *          *

... The Court's holding that both counts should be dismissed on the ground of vagueness renders unnecessary a determination of their constitutionality under the First Amendment.

However, when the charge in an indictment is in the area of the First Amendment, evidencing possible conflict with its guarantees of free thought, belief and expression, and when such indictment is challenged as being vague and indefinite, the Court will uphold it only after subjecting its legal sufficiency to exacting scrutiny.

*          *          *

Perjury, as presently charged to defendant under 18 U.S.C. § 1621, occurs when a person under oath "... willfully and contrary to such oath states or subscribes any material matter which he does not believe to be true...." The substance of such crime is a defendant's lack of belief in the truth of his testimony as of the moment he made it. For a jury to conclude that perjury has been committed, in fact, it must determine what the words meant to the defendant at the time he offered them as his testimony, and then conclude that the defendant did not at that time believe in the truth of such testimony according to the meaning he ascribed to the words and phrases he used.

Under Count I, perjury is charged to the statement by Lattimore that he was not a follower of the Communist line. The Government supplies a definition of this phrase in the indictment. The Government is prompt to concede that no such definition was presented to the defendant at the Committee hearing in 1952; that it was formulated after Lattimore testified; that it was prepared after independent research conducted by the United States Attorney's Office. The sources of such research, however, do not appear. The Government contends that it is a matter of common knowledge as to what is meant by "follower of the Communist line" and that people differ but little in their understanding of the term.[12] ...

While the proper test of perjury is subjective, insofar as it is based upon the understanding of the witness himself regarding the words that he used, a criminal prosecution must have certain objective standards. Most often in perjury cases the objective standard is not hard to come by; what the accused considered his statements to mean is not in issue since the words or phrases involved have one clear, accepted and recognized meaning. Here, the phrase "follower of the Communist line" is subject to varying interpretations. It has no universally accepted definition. The Government has defined it in one way and seeks to impute its definition to the defendant. Defendant has declined to adopt it, offering a definition of his own. It would not necessitate great ingenuity to think up definitions differing from those offered either by the Government or defendant. By groundless surmise only could the jury determine which definition defendant had in mind.

The Court cannot escape the conclusion that "follower of the Communist line" is not a phrase with a meaning about which men of ordinary intellect could agree, nor one which could be used with mutual understanding by a questioner and answerer unless it were defined at the time it were sought and offered as testimony. This count, even with its apparent definition, is an open invitation to the jury to substitute, by conjecture, their understanding of the phrase for that of the defendant. The meaning of such a phrase varies according to a particular individual's political philosophy. To ask twelve jurors to agree and then decide that the definition of the Communist line found in the indictment is the definition that defendant had in mind and denied believing in, is to ask the jury to aspire to levels of insight to which the ordinary person is incapable, and upon which speculation no criminal indictment should hinge. We cannot debase the principle that "the accused is entitled under the Constitution to be advised as to every element in respect to which it is necessary for him to prepare a defense."

When elements in an indictment are so easily subject to divergent interpretation, the accused is not adequately apprised of the charges as to enable him to prepare a defense. It therefore fails to conform to the requirements of the Sixth Amendment and Federal Rules [of Criminal Procedure 7(c)]. . . .

The second count charges that Lattimore perjured himself when he testified he had never been a "promoter of Communist interest."

*      *      *

This entire perjury indictment arises out of, and is essentially founded upon, the statements, correspondence, and editorial comments of defendant. It does not rest upon alleged acts of espionage or such an act as membership in the Communist party. . . . [T]he Government was quick to state that it was not charging defendant with being an espionage agent. It should be kept in mind that under this count only written comments and opinions are involved and are said to have produced a certain effect, namely, to have promoted Communist interests. Such writings and comments are not alleged to have produced the designated result over a short period of time, and in isolated instances, but over a fifteen-year period. By no stretch of the imagination can we comprehend how this consistent result (promoting Communist interests) could have been so attained had not the commentator been both aware of what the Communists were asserting during this extended period, and then knowingly adhered to these assertions (followed the Communist line). If defendant had contradicted the Communists' assertions, he could hardly be said to have promoted their interests.[31]

Count II, thus dependent upon Count I, cannot stand, being anchored to, partaking of, and plagued by, all its vagueness and indefiniteness. . . .

The charges here serve only to inform the defendant that his sworn statements are to be tested against all his writings for chance parallelism with, or indirect support of, Communism regardless of any deliberate intent on his part. They demonstrate that the Government seeks to establish that at some time, in some way, in some places, in all his vast writings, over a fifteen-year period, Lattimore agreed with something it calls and personally defines as following the Communist line and promoting Communist interests.

. . . With so sweeping an indictment with its many vague charges, and with the existing atmosphere of assumed and expected loathing for Communism, it would be neither surprising nor unreasonable were the jury subconsciously impelled to substitute its own understanding for that of defendant.

To require defendant to go to trial for perjury under charges so formless and obscure as those before the Court would be unprecedented and would make a sham of the Sixth Amendment and the Federal Rule requiring specificity of charges.

*The indictment will therefore be dismissed.*

---

[12] Common knowledge of whom? The man on the street? A newspaper man? A man of ordinary or of superior intellect? A member of the F.B.I.? The Department of Justice? The Internal Security Subcommittee? The State Department?

---

[31] The Government seems to recognize the difference between promoting Communist interests by physical acts themselves and doing this through studied writings. On pages 87-88 of the Transcript the following discussion occurred:

"THE COURT: How could he knowingly be a promoter of Communist interests without also knowingly being a follower of the Communist line?

"MR. ROVER: One thought that occurs to me is this, Your Honor—and please don't misunderstand me that I am calling Lattimore an espionage agent, because I am not. I think an espionage agent might promote Communist interests, say for a monetary remuneration, without being—

"THE COURT: Would he knowingly follow the Communist line by being an espionage agent?

"MR. ROVER: I suppose the effect of it would be, he would be following the Communist line. But as a matter of fact, he may not realize that he was knowingly and intentionally following the Communist line. He might be just an espionage agent, whereby he would be doing things, unlawful things to promote Communist interests, *without giving any particular thought at all to whether he was following the line or not.*" (Emphasis supplied.)

## 266 "the so-called 'sensitive' agencies" (1956)

Kendrick Cole was one of those dismissed from a government job under the extended loyalty program instituted by Eisenhower's Executive Order 10450. Without overturning the loyalty program or its theoretical foundations, the court narrowly construed the applicability of the act of August 26, 1950, under which the Eisenhower order was promulgated, and thereby removed several million government employees from the scrutiny of the employee security program. Subsequent legislative attempts to overrule the impact of the Supreme Court's decision were unsuccessful.

☆ 266 *Cole v. Young*

351 U.S. 536 (1956).

Opinion of the Court by MR. JUSTICE HARLAN, announced by MR. JUSTICE BURTON.

This case presents the question of the meaning of the term "national security" as used in the Act of August 26, 1950, giving to the heads of certain departments and agencies of the Government summary suspension and unreviewable dismissal powers over their civilian employees, when deemed necessary "in the interest of the national security of the United States."

\*       \*       \*

Petitioner . . . held a position in the classified civil service as a food and drug inspector for the New York District of the Food and Drug Administration, Department of Health, Education, and Welfare. In November 1953, he was suspended without pay from his position, pending investigation to determine whether his employment should be terminated. He was given a written statement of charges alleging that he had "a close association with individuals reliably reported to be Communists" and that he had maintained a "sympathetic association" with, had contributed funds and services to, and had attended social gatherings of an allegedly subversive organization.

. . . [T]he Secretary of the Department of Health, Education, and Welfare, after "a study of all the documents in [petitioner's] case," determined that petitioner's continued employment was not "clearly consistent with the interests of national security" and ordered the termination of his employment.

\*       \*       \*

The Act authorizes dismissals only upon a determination by the Secretary that the dismissal is "necessary or advisable in the interest of the national security." That determination requires an evaluation of the risk of injury to the "national security" that the employee's retention would create, which in turn would seem necessarily to be a function, not only of the character of the employee and the likelihood of his misconducting himself, but also of the nature of the position he occupies and its relationship to the "national security." That is, it must be determined whether the position is one in which the employee's misconduct would affect the "national security." That, of course, would not be necessary if "national security" were used in the Act in a sense so broad as to be involved in *all* activities of the Government, for then the relationship to the "national security" would follow from the very fact of employment. For the reasons set forth below, however, we conclude (1) that the term "national security" is used in the Act in a definite and limited sense and relates only to those activities which are directly concerned with the Nation's safety, as distinguished from the general welfare; and (2) that no determination has been made that petitioner's position was affected with the "national security," as that term is used in

the Act. It follows that his dismissal was not authorized by the 1950 Act. . . .

As noted above, the issue turns on the meaning of "national security," as used in the Act. While that term is not defined in the Act, we think it clear from the statute as a whole that that term was intended to comprehend only those activities of the Government that are directly concerned with the protection of the Nation from internal subversion or foreign aggression, and not those which contribute to the strength of the Nation only through their impact on the general welfare.

Virtually conclusive of this narrow meaning of "national security" is the fact that, had Congress intended the term in a sense broad enough to include all activities of the Government, it would have granted the power to terminate employment "in the interest of the national security" to all agencies of the Government. Instead, Congress specified 11 named agencies to which the Act should apply, the character of which reveals, without doubt, a purpose to single out those agencies which are directly concerned with the national defense and which have custody over information the compromise of which might endanger the country's security, the so-called "sensitive" agencies.

\*       \*       \*

There is an obvious justification for the summary suspension power where the employee occupies a "sensitive" position. . . . On the other hand, it is difficult to justify summary suspensions and unreviewable dismissals on loyalty grounds of employees who are not in "sensitive" positions and who are thus not situated where they could bring about any discernible adverse effects on the Nation's security. In the absence of an immediate threat of harm to the "national security," the normal dismissal procedures seem fully adequate and the justification for summary powers disappears. Indeed, in view of the stigma attached to persons dismissed on loyalty grounds, the need for procedural safeguards seems even greater than in other cases, and we will not lightly assume that Congress intended to take away those safeguards in the absence of some overriding necessity, such as exists in the case of employees handling defense secrets.

\*       \*       \*

From our holdings (1) that not all positions in the Government are affected with the "national security" as that term is used in the 1950 Act, and (2) that no determination has been made that petitioner's position was one in which he could adversely affect the "national security," it necessarily follows that petitioner's discharge was not authorized by the 1950 Act. In reaching this conclusion, we are not confronted with the problem of reviewing the Secretary's exercise of discretion, since the basis for our decision is simply that the standard prescribed by the Executive Order [10450 (1953)] and applied by the Secretary is not in conformity with the Act. Since petitioner's discharge was not authorized by the 1950 Act . . . , the judgment of the Court of Appeals is reversed and the case is remanded to the District Court for further proceedings not inconsistent with this opinion.

*Reversed and remanded.*

## 267 "insurrection in any State against its government. . . . or rebellion against the authority of the United States" (1956)

The Armed Forces Act of 1956 revised the laws in force since 1789 which regulated the structure of the armed forces and the functioning of their members. Codified under Title 10 of the United States Code, Sections 331–34, the Militia Act specified the presidential power to call into federal service militia from the several states and to use these troops, as well as federal armed forces, to suppress insurrections against state governments or rebellions against the United States. The act also addressed the possibility of federal, state, and local conflicts over governmental policy.

The extensive power of the president to determine the existence of an emergency requiring federal intervention was upheld early in the nation's history, in *Martin v. Mott*, 25 U.S. 19 (1827) and in *Luther v. Borden*, 48 U.S. 1 (1849). In *Monarch Insurance Co. v. District of Columbia*, 353 F. Supp. 1249 (D.D.C. 1973), a judge held that presidential discretion in using federal troops and militia was not subject to judicial review.

☆ 267  The Militia Act

70A Stat. 15 (1956).

*Be it enacted by the Senate and House of Representatives of the United States of America in Congress assembled*, That Title 10 of the United States Code, entitled "Armed Forces," is revised, codified, and enacted into law and may be cited as "Title 10 U.S.C. § ———" as follows:

TITLE 10—ARMED FORCES

*         *         *

*Chapter 15.—Insurrection*

§ *331. Federal aid for State governments.* Whenever there is an insurrection in any State against its

government, the President may, upon the request of its legislature or of its governor if the legislature cannot be convened, call into Federal service such of the militia of the other States, in the number requested by that State, and use such of the armed forces, as he considers necessary to suppress the insurrection.

§ *332. Use of militia and armed forces to enforce Federal authority.* Whenever the President considers that unlawful obstructions, combinations, or assemblages, or rebellion against the authority of the United States, make it impracticable to enforce the laws of the United States in any State or Territory by the ordinary course of judicial proceedings, he may call into Federal service such of the militia of any State, and use such of the armed forces, as he considers necessary to enforce those laws or to suppress the rebellion.

§ *333. Interference with State and Federal law.* The President, by using the militia or the armed forces, or both, or by any other means, shall take such measures as he considers necessary to suppress, in a State, any insurrection, domestic violence, unlawful combination, or conspiracy, if it—

(1) so hinders the execution of the laws of that State, and of the United States within the State, that any part or class of its people is deprived of a right, privilege, immunity, or protection named in the Constitution and secured by law, and the constituted authorities of that State are unable, fail, or refuse to protect that right, privilege, or immunity, or to give that protection; or

(2) opposes or obstructs the execution of the laws of the United States or impedes the course of justice under those laws.

In any situation covered by clause (1), the State shall be considered to have denied the equal protection of the laws secured by the Constitution.

§ *334. Proclamation to disperse.* Whenever the President considers it necessary to use the militia or the armed forces under this chapter, he shall, by proclamation, immediately order the insurgents to disperse and retire peaceably to their abodes within a limited time.

## 268 "summary dismissal . . . violates due process" (1956)

*Slochower* adds another piece to the mosaic of court decisions defining the constitutional limits on municipal and state laws that regulate the conduct of public employees, particularly those in education. Again, without addressing the validity of the investigation into the official conduct of a faculty member at a city-supported college, the Supreme Court overturned the summary discharge resulting from the teacher's refusal to answer questions and his assertion of the right against self-incrimination.

The court found the municipal procedure was unconstitutionally arbitrary, for "[a]s interpreted . . . it operates to discharge every city employee who invokes the Fifth Amendment. In practical effect the questions asked are taken as confessed." This decision and others (*Cole* and *Wieman v. Updegraff*) served notice that the Supreme Court minimally would require proper procedures when the government acted against an individual on the basis of his or her political affiliations.

☆268 *Slochower v. Board of Higher Education*

350 U.S. 551 (1956).

MR. JUSTICE CLARK delivered the opinion of the Court.

This appeal brings into question the constitutionality of § 903 of the Charter of the City of New York. That section provides that whenever an employee of the City utilizes the privilege against self-incrimination to avoid answering a question relating to his official conduct, "his term or tenure of office or employment shall terminate and such office or employment shall be vacant, and he shall not be eligible to election or appointment to any office or employment under the city or any agency." Appellant Slochower invoked the privilege against self-incrimination under the Fifth Amendment before an investigating committee of the United States Senate, and was summarily discharged from his position as associate professor at Brooklyn College, an institution maintained by the city of New York. He now claims that the charter provision, as applied to him, violates both the Due Process and Privileges and Immunities Clauses of the Fourteenth Amendment.

\*       \*       \*

With this in mind, we consider the application of § 903. As interpreted and applied by the State courts, [§ 903] operates to discharge every city employee who invokes the Fifth Amendment. In practical effect the questions asked are taken as confessed and made the basis of the discharge. No consideration is given to such factors as the subject matter of the questions, remoteness of the period to which they are directed, or justification for exercise of the privilege. It matters not whether the plea resulted from mistake, inadvertence or legal advice conscientiously given, whether wisely or unwisely. The heavy hand of the statute falls alike on all who exercise their constitutional privilege, the full enjoyment of which every person is entitled to receive. Such action falls squarely within the prohibition of *Wieman v. Updegraff*.

\*       \*       \*

Without attacking Professor Slochower's qualification for his position in any manner, and apparently with full knowledge of the testimony he had given some 12 years before at the State committee hearing, the board seized upon his claim of privilege before the Federal committee and converted it through the use of § 903 into a conclusive presumption of guilt. Since no inference of guilt was possible from the claim before the Federal committee, the discharge falls of its own weight as wholly without support. There has not been the "protection of the individual against arbitrary action" which Mr. Justice Cardozo characterized as the very essence of due process.

This is not to say that Slochower has a constitutional right to be an associate professor of German at Brooklyn College. The State has broad powers in the selection and discharge of its employees, and it may be that proper inquiry would show Slochower's continued employment to be inconsistent with a real interest of the State. But there has been no such inquiry here. We hold that the summary dismissal of appellant violates due process of law.

\*       \*       \*

*Reversed and remanded.*

## 269 "I most firmly refuse to discuss the political activities of my past associates" (1957)

Resort to congressional investigations as a means of unearthing evidence of subversion reached its peak in the decade of the 1950s. The House Committee on Un-American Activities was the prime investigative practitioner during this period, when witnesses frequently were faced with the choice of cooperation with the investigators or prosecution for contempt of Congress. The *Watkins* case reflected the judicial effort to restrict congressional power by extending to it some of the constitutional standards applicable to the criminal process.

☆269 *Watkins v. United States*

354 U.S. 178 (1957).

MR. CHIEF JUSTICE WARREN delivered the opinion of the Court.

This is a review by certiorari of a conviction under 2 USC § 192 for "contempt of Congress." The misdemeanor is alleged to have been committed during a hearing before a congressional investigating committee. It is not the case of a truculent or contumacious witness who refuses to answer all questions or who, by boisterous or discourteous conduct, disturbs the decorum of the committee room. Petitioner was prosecuted for refusing to make certain disclosures which he asserted to be beyond the authority of the committee to demand.

\*         \*         \*

On April 29, 1954, petitioner appeared as a witness in compliance with a subpoena issued by a Subcommittee of the Committee on Un-American Activities of the House of Representatives. The Subcommittee elicited from petitioner a description of his background in labor union activities.

\*         \*         \*

Petitioner's name had been mentioned by two witnesses who testified before the Committee at prior hearings. In September 1952, one Donald O. Spencer admitted having been a Communist from 1943 to 1946. He declared that he had been recruited into the Party with the endorsement and prior approval of petitioner, whom he identified as the then District Vice-President of the Farm Equipment Workers. Spencer also mentioned that petitioner had attended meetings at which only card-carrying Communists were admitted. A month before petitioner testified, one Walter Rumsey stated that he had been recruited into the Party by petitioner.

\*         \*         \*

Petitioner answered these allegations freely and without reservation. His attitude toward the inquiry is clearly revealed from the statement he made when the questioning turned to the subject of his past conduct, associations and predilections:

"I am not now nor have I ever been a card-carrying member of the Communist Party. Rumsey was wrong when he said I had recruited him into the party, that I had received his dues, that I paid dues to him, and that I had used the alias Sam Brown.

"Spencer was wrong when he termed any meetings which I attended as closed Communist Party meetings.

"I would like to make it clear that for a period of time from approximately 1942 to 1947 I cooperated with the Communist Party and participated in Communist activities to such a degree that some persons may honestly believe that I was a member of the party.

"I have made contributions upon occasions to Communist causes. I have signed petitions for Communist causes. I attended caucuses at an FE convention at which Communist Party officials were present.

"Since I freely cooperated with the Communist Party I have no motive for making the distinction between cooperation and membership except the simple fact that it is the truth. I never carried a Communist Party card. I never accepted discipline and

indeed on several occasions I opposed their position."

\*         \*         \*

After some further discussion elaborating on the statement, counsel for the Committee turned to another aspect of Rumsey's testimony. Rumsey had identified a group of persons whom he had known as members of the Communist Party, and counsel began to read this list of names to petitioner. Petitioner stated that he did not know several of the persons. Of those whom he did know, he refused to tell whether he knew them to have been members of the Communist Party. He explained to the Subcommittee why he took such a position:

"I am not going to plead the Fifth Amendment, but I refuse to answer certain questions that I believe are outside the proper scope of your committee's activities. I will answer any questions which this committee puts to me about myself. I will also answer questions about those persons whom I knew to be members of the Communist Party and whom I believe still are. I will not, however, answer any questions with respect to others with whom I associated in the past. I do not believe that any law in this country requires me to testify about persons who may in the past have been Communist Party members or otherwise engaged in Communist Party activity but who to my best knowledge and belief have long since removed themselves from the Communist movement.

"I do not believe that such questions are relevant to the work of this committee nor do I believe that this committee has the right to undertake the public exposure of persons because of their past activities. I may be wrong, and the committee may have this power, but until and unless a court of law so holds and directs me to answer, I most firmly refuse to discuss the political activities of my past associates."

The Chairman of the Committee submitted a report of petitioner's refusal to answer questions to the House of Representatives. The House directed the Speaker to certify the Committee's report to the United States Attorney for initiation of criminal prosecution. A seven-count indictment was returned. Petitioner waived his right to jury trial and was found guilty on all counts by the court.

\*         \*         \*

It is unquestionably the duty of all citizens to cooperate with the Congress in its efforts to obtain the facts needed for intelligent legislative action. It is their unremitting obligation to respond to subpoenas, to respect the dignity of the Congress and its committees and to testify fully with respect to matters within the province of proper investigation. This, of course, assumes that the constitutional rights of witnesses will be respected by the Congress as they are in a court of justice. The Bill of Rights is applicable to investigations as to all forms of governmental action. Witnesses cannot be compelled to give evidence against themselves. They cannot be subjected to unreasonable search and seizure. Nor can the First Amendment freedoms of speech, press, religion, or political belief and association be abridged.

The rudiments of the power to punish for "contempt of Congress" come to us from the pages of English history. . . .

*          *          *

Modern times have seen a remarkable restraint in the use by Parliament of its contempt power. Important investigations, like those conducted in America by congressional committees, are made by Royal Commissions of inquiry. These commissions are comprised of experts in the problem to be studied. They are removed from the turbulent forces of politics and partisan considerations. Seldom, if ever, have these commissions been given the authority to compel the testimony of witnesses or the production of documents. Their success in fulfilling their fact-finding missions without resort to coercive tactics is a tribute to the fairness of the processes to the witnesses and their close adherence to the subject matter committed to them.

*          *          *

There was very little use of the power of compulsory process in early years to enable the Congress to obtain facts pertinent to the enactment of new statutes or the administration of existing laws. The first occasion for such an investigation arose in 1827 when the House of Representatives was considering a revision of the tariff laws. In the Senate, there was no use of a fact-finding investigation in aid of legislation until 1958. In the Legislative Reorganization Act, the Committee on Un-American Activities was the only standing committee of the House of Representatives that was given the power to compel disclosures.

*          *          *

In the decade following World War II, there appeared a new kind of congressional inquiry unknown in prior periods of American history. Principally this was the result of the various investigations into the threat of subversion of the United States Government, but other subjects of congressional interest also contributed to the changed scene. This new phase of legislative inquiry involved a broad-scale intrusion into the lives and affairs of private citizens. . . .

*          *          *

The Court recognized the restraints of the Bill of Rights upon congressional investigations in *United States v. Rumely*. The magnitude and complexity of the problem of applying the First Amendment to that case led the Court to construe narrowly the resolution describing the committee's authority. It was concluded that, when First Amendment rights are threatened, the delegation of power to the committee must be clearly revealed in its character.

We have no doubt that there is no congressional power to expose for the sake of exposure. The public is, of course, entitled to be informed concerning the workings of its government. That cannot be inflated into a general power to expose where the predominant result can only be an invasion of the private rights of individuals. . . .

*          *          *

Since World War II, the Congress has practically abandoned its original practice of utilizing the coercive sanction of contempt proceedings at the bar of the House. The sanction there imposed is imprisonment by the House until the recalcitrant witness agrees to testify or disclose the matters sought, provided that the incarceration does not extend beyond adjournment. The Congress has instead invoked the aid of the federal judicial system in protecting itself against contumacious conduct. It has become customary to refer these matters to the United States Attorneys for prosecution under criminal law.

*          *          *

In fulfillment of their obligation . . . , the courts must accord to the defendants every right which is guaranteed to defendants in all other criminal cases. Among these is the right to have available, through a sufficiently precise statute, information revealing the standard of criminality before the commission of the alleged offense. Applied to persons prosecuted under § 192, this raises a special problem in that the statute defines the crime as refusal to answer "any question pertinent to the question under inquiry."

*          *          *

The statement of the Committee Chairman in this case, in response to petitioner's protest, was woefully inadequate to convey sufficient information as to the pertinency of the questions to the subject under inquiry. Petitioner was thus not accorded a fair opportunity to determine whether he was within his rights in refusing to answer, and his conviction is necessarily invalid under the Due Process Clause of the Fifth Amendment.

*          *          *

## 270 "making his private life a matter of public record" (1957)

Paul Sweezy, a publisher, political commentator, and lecturer, was called before the attorney general of New Hampshire pursuant to a law authorizing the state's officer to investigate subversive activities. Although generally cooperative, Sweezy refused to answer certain questions on First Amendment grounds. The New Hampshire courts consequently held him in contempt and ordered him jailed.

Although the plurality opinion of Chief Justice Warren praised the values of dissent and academic freedom, the court found the First Amendment did not bar the inquiry. Instead, the opinion relied on the much narrower and novel ground that the particular questions propounded were not within the state legislature's authorization of the state's attorney general. Justices Frankfurter and Harlan concurred in the judgment of reversal on First Amendment grounds, thus creating the majority necessary to overturn the citation for contempt.

☆270  *Sweezy v. New Hampshire*

354 U.S. 234 (1957).

MR. CHIEF JUSTICE WARREN announced the judgment of the Court and delivered an opinion, in which MR. JUSTICE BLACK, MR. JUSTICE DOUGLAS, and MR. JUSTICE BRENNAN join.

. . . The ultimate question here is whether the investigation deprived Sweezy of due process of law under the Fourteenth Amendment. For the reasons to be set out in this opinion, we conclude that the record in this case does not sustain the power of the State to compel the disclosures that the witness refused to make.

\*          \*          \*

There is no doubt that legislative investigations, whether on a Federal or State level, are capable of encroaching upon the constitutional liberties of individuals. It is particularly important that the exercise of the power of compulsory process be carefully circumscribed when the investigative process tends to impinge upon such highly sensitive areas as freedom of speech or press, freedom of political association, and freedom of communication of ideas, particularly in the academic community. Responsibility for the proper conduct of investigations rests, of course, upon the legislature itself. If that assembly chooses to authorize inquiries on its behalf by a legislatively created committee, that basic responsibility carries forward to include the duty of adequate supervision of the actions of the committee. This safeguard can be nullified when a committee is invested with a broad and ill-defined jurisdiction. The authorizing resolution thus becomes especially significant in that it reveals the amount of discretion that has been conferred upon the committee.

\*          \*          \*

The nature of the investigation which the attorney general was authorized to conduct is revealed by this case. He delved minutely into the past conduct of petitioner, thereby making his private life a matter of public record. The questioning indicates that the investigators had thoroughly prepared for the interview and were not acquiring new information as much as corroborating data already in their possession. On the great majority of questions, the witness was cooperative, even though he made clear his opinion that the interrogation was unjustified and unconstitutional. Two subjects arose upon which petitioner refused to answer: his lectures at the University of New Hampshire, and his knowledge of the Progressive Party and its adherents.

The State courts upheld the attempt to investigate the academic subject on the ground that it might indicate whether petitioner was a "subversive person." What he taught the class at a State university was found relevant to the character of the teacher. . . .

\*          \*          \*

The essentiality of freedom in the community of American universities is almost self-evident. No one should underestimate the vital role in a democracy that is played by those who guide and train our youth. To impose any straitjacket upon the intellectual leaders in our colleges and universities would imperil the future of our Nation. No field of education is so thoroughly comprehended by man that new discoveries cannot yet be made. Particularly is that true in the social sciences, where few, if any, principles are accepted as absolutes. Scholarship cannot flourish in an atmosphere of suspicion and distrust. Teachers and students must always remain free to inquire, to study and to evaluate, to gain new maturity and understanding; otherwise our civilization will stagnate and die.

Equally manifest as a fundamental principle of a democratic society is political freedom of the individual. Our form of government is built on the premise that every citizen shall have the right to engage in political expression and association. This right was enshrined in the First Amendment of the Bill of Rights. Exercise of these basic freedoms in America has traditionally been through the media of political associations. Any interference with the freedom of a party is simultaneously an interference with the freedom of its adherents. All political ideas cannot and should not be channeled into the programs of our two major parties. History has amply proved the virtue of political activity by minority, dissident groups, who innumerable times have been in the vanguard of democratic thought and whose programs were ultimately accepted. Mere unorthodoxy or dissent from the prevailing mores is not to be condemned. The absence of such voices would be a symptom of grave illness in our society.

\*          \*          \*

The respective roles of the legislature and the investigator thus revealed are of considerable significance to the issue before us. It is eminently clear that the basic discretion of determining the direction of the legislative inquiry has been turned over to the investigative agency. The attorney general has been given such a sweeping and uncertain mandate that it is his decision which picks out the subjects that will be pursued, what witnesses will be summoned and what questions will be asked. In this circumstance, it cannot be stated authoritatively that the legislature asked the attorney general to gather the kind of facts comprised in the subjects upon which petitioner was interrogated.

\*         \*         \*

As a result, neither we nor the state courts have any assurance that the questions petitioner refused to answer fall into a category of matters upon which the legislature wanted to be informed when it initiated this inquiry. The judiciary are thus placed in an untenable position. Lacking even the elementary fact that the legislature wants certain questions answered and recognizing that petitioner's constitutional rights are in jeopardy, we are asked to approve or disapprove his incarceration for contempt.

In our view, the answer is clear. No one would deny that the infringement of constitutional rights of individuals would violate the guarantee of due process where no State interest underlies the State action. Thus, if the attorney general's interrogation of petitioner were in fact wholly unrelated to the object of the legislature in authorizing the inquiry, the Due Process Clause would preclude the endangering of constitutional liberties. We believe that an equivalent situation is presented in this case. The lack of any indications that the legislature wanted the information the attorney general attempted to elicit from petitioner must be treated as the absence of authority. It follows that the use of the contempt power, notwithstanding the interference with constitutional rights, was not in accordance with the due process requirements of the Fourteenth Amendment.

\*         \*         \*

*Reversed.*

# 271 "advocacy and teaching of forcible overthrow as an abstract principle" (1957)

After the United States Supreme Court sustained the *Dennis* convictions in 1951, the Department of Justice commenced a total of twenty-one other prosecutions under the Smith Act, involving 131 defendants. In the *Yates* case, fourteen defendants were tried and convicted in Los Angeles for conspiring to advocate the overthrow of the government and for organizing the Communist party, which taught such doctrines. Although the Supreme Court's opinion discussed what actions the First Amendment does protect, the court based its decision on the insufficiency of the evidence, the Statute of Limitations' debarment of some of the prosecutions, and the impropriety of the jury instructions (compare the opinion of Justice Black). Nevertheless, the tenor of the opinion and the requirements of proof demanded served to dampen the crusade against Communism in the courts of the United States.

Five of those convicted by the lower court in the *Yates* case were set free pursuant to the Supreme Court's holding that the First Amendment safeguards protected instances where the individuals advocated "forcible overthrow" of the government as an abstract doctrine and not as a spur to action. Eventually, the trial court dismissed the charges against the other nine defendants for whom new trials had been ordered.

☆ 271 *Yates v. United States*

354 U.S. 298 (1957).

Mr. Justice Harlan delivered the opinion of the Court.

\*         \*         \*

These 14 petitioners stand convicted, after a jury trial in the United States District Court for the Southern District of California, upon a single count indictment charging them with conspiring (1) to advocate and teach the duty and necessity of overthrowing the Government of the United States by force and violence, and (2) to organize, as the Communist Party of the United States, a society of persons who so advocate and teach, all with the intent of causing the overthrow of the Government by force and violence as speedily as circumstances would permit [in violation of the Smith Act]. . . .

\*         \*         \*

In the view we take of this case, it is necessary for us to consider only the following of petitioners' contentions: . . . (2) that the trial court's instructions to the jury erroneously excluded from the case the issue of "incitement to action"; (3) that the evidence was so insufficient as to require this Court to direct the acquittal of these petitioners. . . . For reasons given hereafter, we conclude that these convictions must be reversed and the case remanded to the District Court with instructions to enter judgments of acquittal as to certain of the petitioners, and to grant a new trial as to the rest.

\*         \*         \*

Petitioners contend that the instructions to the jury were fatally defective in that the trial court refused to charge that, in order to convict, the jury must find that the advocacy which the defendants conspired to promote was of a kind calculated to "incite" persons to action for the forcible overthrow of the Government. It is argued that advocacy of forcible overthrow as mere *abstract doctrine* is within the free speech protection of the First Amendment; that the Smith Act, consistently with that constitutional provision, must be taken as proscribing only the sort of advocacy which incites to illegal *action*; and that the trial court's charge, by permitting conviction for mere advocacy, unrelated to its tendency to produce forcible action, resulted in an unconstitutional application of the Smith Act. The Government, which at the trial also requested the court to charge in terms of "incitement," now takes the position, however, that the true constitutional dividing line is not between inciting and abstract advocacy of forcible overthrow, but rather between advocacy as such, irrespective of its inciting qualities, and the mere discussion or exposition of violent overthrow as an abstract theory.

\*            \*            \*

We are thus faced with the question whether the Smith Act prohibits advocacy and teaching of forcible overthrow as an abstract principle, divorced from any effort to instigate action to that end, so long as such advocacy or teaching is engaged in with evil intent. We hold that it does not.

The distinction between advocacy of abstract doctrine and advocacy directed at promoting unlawful action is one that has been consistently recognized in the opinions of this Court. This distinction was heavily underscored in *Gitlow v. New York*, in which the statute involved was nearly identical with the one now before us, and where the Court, despite the narrow view there taken of the First Amendment, said:

> The statute does not penalize the utterance or publication of abstract "doctrine" or academic discussion having no quality of incitement to any concrete action.... It is not the abstract "doctrine" of overthrowing organized government by unlawful means which is denounced by the statute, but the advocacy of action for the accomplishment of that purpose....

\*            \*            \*

What we find lacking in the instructions here is illustrated by contrasting them with the instructions given to the *Dennis* jury, upon which this Court's sustaining of the convictions in that case was bottomed. There the trial court charged:

> In further construction and interpretation of the statute [the Smith Act] I charge you that it is *not* *the abstract doctrine* of overthrowing or destroying organized government by unlawful means which is denounced by this law, but the teaching and advocacy *of action* for the accomplishment of that purpose, *by language reasonably and ordinarily calculated to incite persons to such action.* ... (Emphasis added.)

We recognize that distinctions between advocacy or teaching of abstract doctrines, with evil intent, and that which is directed to stirring people to action, are often subtle and difficult to grasp, for in a broad sense, as Mr. Justice Holmes said in his dissenting opinion in *Gitlow*, "Every idea is an incitement." But the very subtlety of these distinctions required the most clear and explicit instructions with reference to them, for they concerned an issue which went to the very heart of the charges against these petitioners. The need for precise and understandable instructions on this issue is further emphasized by the equivocal character of the evidence in this record.... Instances of speech that could be considered to amount to "advocacy of action" are so few and far between as to be almost completely overshadowed by the hundreds of instances in the record in which overthrow, if mentioned at all, occurs in the course of doctrinal disputation so remote from action as to be almost wholly lacking in probative value. Vague references to "revolutionary" or "militant" action of an unspecified character, which are found in the evidence, might in addition be given too great weight by the jury in the absence of more precise instructions. Particularly in light of this record, we must regard the trial court's charge in this respect as furnishing wholly inadequate guidance to the jury on this central point in the case. We cannot allow a conviction to stand on such "an equivocal direction to the jury on such a basic issue."

\*            \*            \*

... As to the petitioners Connelly, Kusnitz, Richmond, Spector, and Steinberg we find no adequate evidence in the record which would permit a jury to find that they were members of such a conspiracy [to advocate the violent or unlawful overthrow of the government]. For all purposes relevant here, the sole evidence as to them was that they had long been members, officers, or functionaries of the Communist Party of California; and that standing alone, as Congress has enacted in § 4(f) of the Internal Security Act of 1950, makes out no case against them....

... We therefore think that as to these petitioners the evidence was entirely too meagre to justify putting them to a new trial, and that their acquittal should be ordered.

As to the nine remaining petitioners, we consider that a different conclusion should be reached.... In short, while the record contains evidence of little more than a general program of educational activity by the Communist Party which included advocacy of violence as a theoretical matter, we are not prepared to say, at this stage of the case, that it would be impossible for a jury, resolving all conflicts in favor of the Government and giving the evidence as to these San Francisco and Los Angeles episodes its utmost sweep, to find that advocacy of action was also engaged in when the group involved was thought particularly trustworthy, dedicated, and suited for violent tasks.

\*          \*          \*

Mr. Justice BLACK ... concurring ... and ... dissenting. ...

### I

I would reverse every one of these convictions and direct that all the defendants be acquitted. In my judgment the statutory provisions on which these prosecutions are based abridge freedom of speech, press, and assembly in violation of the First Amendment to the United States Constitution.

\*          \*          \*

### III

In essence, petitioners were tried upon the charge that they believe in and want to foist upon this country a different and to us a despicable form of authoritarian government in which voices criticizing the existing order are summarily silenced. I fear that the present type of prosecutions are more in line with the philosophy of authoritarian government than with that expressed by our First Amendment.

Doubtlessly, dictators have to stamp out causes and beliefs which they deem subversive to their evil regimes. But governmental suppression of causes and beliefs seems to me to be the very antithesis of what our Constitution stands for. The choice expressed in the First Amendment in favor of free expression was made against a turbulent background by men such as Jefferson, Madison, and Mason— men who believed that loyalty to the provisions of this Amendment was the best way to assure a long life for this new nation and its Government. Unless there is complete freedom for expression of all ideas, whether we like them or not, concerning the way government should be run and who shall run it, I doubt if any views in the long run can be secured against the censor. The First Amendment provides the only kind of security system that can preserve a free government—one that leaves the way wide open for people to favor, discuss, advocate, or incite causes and doctrines however obnoxious and antagonistic such views may be to the rest of us.

## 272 "one who has given his loyalties to [the Communist Party] ... during a period of responsible adulthood" (1957)

Born and raised by a socialist-oriented father in working class conditions in New York City, Rudolph Schware joined the Young Communist League in 1932 at the age of eighteen. Thereafter, he was arrested for participating in strikes. He again was arrested for violating the Neutrality Act of 1937 by encouraging men to volunteer for the Loyalist forces in the Spanish civil war. He also had used aliases while seeking employment during the Depression. In 1940, he quit the Communist party, disillusioned by the national leaders of the party and the nonaggression treaty signed by Stalin and Hitler in 1939. He served in the army from 1944 to 1946 and received an honorable discharge. He completed his law studies in 1953, but the state of New Mexico denied his application for admission to the bar on the grounds that he lacked good character. In a subsequent hearing, Schware produced character witnesses to testify to the contrary, but the Supreme Court of New Mexico decided against him. He obtained review by the Supreme Court of the United States.

☆ 272 *Schware v. Board of Bar Examiners*

353 U.S. 237 (1957).

MR. JUSTICE BLACK delivered the opinion of the Court.

The question presented is whether petitioner, Rudolph Schware, has been denied a license to practice law in New Mexico in violation of the Due Process Clause of the Fourteenth Amendment to the United States Constitution.

\*          \*          \*

... Obviously an applicant could not be excluded merely because he was a Republican or a Negro or a member of a particular church. Even in applying permissible standards, officers of a State cannot exclude an applicant when there is no basis for their finding that he fails to meet these standards, or when their action is invidiously discriminatory.

Here the State concedes that Schware is fully qualified to take the examination in all respects other than good moral character. Therefore the question is whether the Supreme Court of New Mexico on the record before us could reasonably find that he had not shown good moral character.

... The undisputed evidence in the record shows Schware to be a man of high ideals with a deep sense of social justice. Not a single witness testified that he was not a man of good character.

Despite Schware's showing of good character,

the Board and court below thought there were certain facts in the record which raised substantial doubts about his moral fitness to practice law.

(1) *Aliases....* Of course it is wrong to use an alias when it is done to cheat or defraud another but it can hardly be said that Schware's attempt to forestall anti-Semitism in securing employment or organizing his fellow workers was wrong....

(2) *Arrests....*

\*     \*     \*

In summary, these arrests are wholly insufficient to support a finding that Schware had bad moral character at the time he applied to take the bar examination. They all occurred many years ago and in no case was he ever tried or convicted for the offense for which he was arrested.

(3) *Membership in the Communist Party.* Schware admitted that he was a member of the Communist Party from 1932 to 1940. Apparently the Supreme Court of New Mexico placed heavy emphasis on this past membership in denying his application. It stated: "We believe one who has knowingly given his loyalties to [the Communist Party] for six to seven years during a period of responsible adulthood is a person of questionable character."... During the period when Schware was a member, the Communist Party was a lawful political party with candidates on the ballot in most States. There is nothing in the record that gives any indication that his association with that Party was anything more than a political faith in a political party. That faith may have been unorthodox. But as counsel for New Mexico said in his brief, "Mere unorthodoxy [in the field of political and social ideas] does not as a matter of fair and logical inference, negative 'good moral character.'"

... There is nothing in the record ... which indicates that he ever engaged in any actions to overthrow the Government of the United States or of any State by force or violence, or that he even advocated such actions. Assuming that some members of the Communist Party during the period from 1932 to 1940 had illegal aims and engaged in illegal activities, it cannot automatically be inferred that all members shared their evil purposes or participated in their illegal conduct.... And finally, there is no suggestion that Schware was affiliated with the Communist Party after 1940—more than 15 years ago. We conclude that his past membership in the Communist Party does not justify an inference that he presently has bad moral character.

The State contends that even though the use of aliases, the arrests, and the membership in the Communist Party would not justify exclusion of petitioner from the New Mexico bar if each stood alone, when all three are combined his exclusion was not unwarranted. We cannot accept this contention. In the light of petitioner's forceful showing of good moral character, the evidence upon which the State relies—the arrests for offenses for which petitioner was neither tried nor convicted, the use of an assumed name many years ago, and membership in the Communist Party during the 1930's—cannot be said to raise substantial doubts about his present good moral character. There is no evidence in the record which rationally justifies a finding that Schware was morally unfit to practice law.

On the record before us we hold that the State of New Mexico deprived petitioner of due process in denying him the opportunity to qualify for the practice of law. The judgment below is reversed and the case remanded for proceedings not inconsistent with this opinion.

*It is so ordered.*

# 273 Incompetency for Refusal to Refute Information (1958)

Public employees refusing to cooperate with investigations into their political beliefs or memberships in suspect organizations at time were dismissed from office or cited for contempt. As the courts began to reject these actions, not on First Amendment grounds but because they viewed the procedures as a denial of due process, the investigating agencies became more subtle in justifying the sanctions.

The Philadelphia Board of Education discharged Beilan, a public school teacher, on the grounds of "incompetency" for failure to answer questions by the superintendent of schools concerning his affiliation with a Communist organization. At no time was the issue of loyalty raised. The Supreme Court affirmed the dismissal, holding that by becoming a teacher the petitioner undertook "obligations of frankness ... and cooperation in answering inquiries ... examining his fitness to serve as a public school teacher. Fitness for teaching depends upon a broad range of factors." The Supreme Court's reaction to the new tactics demonstrated the thin cover that procedural protections accorded public employees.

☆ 273 *Beilan v. Board of Public Education*

357 U.S. 399 (1958).

Mr. Justice Burton delivered the opinion of the Court.

The question before us is whether the Board of Public Education for the School District of Philadelphia, Pennsylvania, violated the Due Process Clause of the Fourteenth Amendment to the Constitution of the United States when the board, purporting to act under the Pennsylvania Public School Code, discharged a public school teacher on the ground of "incompetency," evidenced by the teacher's refusal of his superintendent's request to confirm or refute information as to the teacher's loyalty and his activities in certain allegedly subversive organizations. For the reasons hereafter stated, we hold that it did not.

On June 25, 1952, Herman A. Beilan, the petitioner, who had been a teacher for about 22 years in the Philadelphia Public School System, presented himself at his superintendent's office in response to the latter's request. The superintendent said he had information which reflected adversely on petitioner's loyalty and he wanted to determine its truth or falsity.... The superintendent ... asked petitioner whether or not he had been the Press Director of the Professional Section of the Communist Political Association in 1944. Petitioner asked permission to consult counsel before answering and the superintendent granted his request.

On October 14, 1952, ... petitioner ... presented himself at the superintendent's office. Petitioner stated that he had consulted counsel and that he declined to answer the question as to his activities in 1944. He announced he would also decline to answer any other "questions similar to it," "questions of this type," or "questions about political and religious beliefs...." The superintendent warned petitioner that this "was a very serious and a very important matter and that failure to answer the questions might lead to his dismissal." The superintendent made it clear that he was investigating "a real question of fitness for [petitioner] to be a teacher or to continue in the teaching work." These interviews were given no publicity and were attended only by petitioner, his superintendent, and the assistant solicitor of the board.

On November 25, 1953, the board instituted dismissal proceedings against petitioner, ... charg[ing] that petitioner's refusal to answer his superintendent's questions constituted "incompetency." The board conducted a formal hearing on the charge.... [P]etitioner's loyalty was not in issue.... On January 7, 1954, the board found that the charge of incompetency had been sustained and, by a vote of fourteen to one, discharged petitioner from his employment as a teacher.

*          *          *

... Our recent decisions in *Slochower v. Board of Education* and *Konigsberg v. State Bar of California* [I] are distinguishable. In each we envisioned and distinguished the situation now before us. In the *Slochower* case, the Court said:

It is one thing for the city authorities themselves to inquire into Slochower's fitness, but quite another for his discharge to be based entirely on events occurring before a Federal committee whose inquiry was announced as not directed at "the property, affairs, or government of the city, or ... official conduct of city employees." ...

In the *Konigsberg* [I] case, this Court stressed the fact that the action of the State was not based on the mere refusal to answer relevant questions—rather, it was based on inferences impermissibly drawn from the refusal. In the instant case, no inferences at all were drawn from petitioner's refusal to answer. The Pennsylvania supreme court merely equated refusal to answer the employing board's relevant questions with statutory "incompetency."

Inasmuch as petitioner's dismissal did not violate the Federal Constitution, the judgment of the Supreme Court of Pennsylvania is

*Affirmed.*

## 274 "The right to travel is a part of ... 'Liberty'" (1958)

After the commencement of the cold war, the State Department placed limits on the right of Americans to travel abroad when it deemed that such travel would "not be in the best interest of the United States." Regulations denying passports to individuals who held suspect political beliefs brought about this policy. Rockwell Kent wanted to visit England and also to attend a "World Council of Peace" meeting in Helsinki, Finland. His passport application was denied. The Supreme Court's decision in *Kent v. Dulles* struck down the secretary of state's practice of withholding passports because of an individual's beliefs and associations on the grounds that Congress did not authorize such action.

The McCarran Act authorized the denial of passports to persons holding membership in Communist organizations, which were required to register with the government. Kent did not meet the terms of that restriction. Thus, the authority to deny passports was claimed to be based on more general legislation and executive orders. The majority opinion by Justice Douglas stated: "The right to travel is part of the liberty of which the citizen cannot be deprived without due process of law under the Fifth Amendment." But, in fact, the court emphasized a narrow basis for its decision while expounding this dictum of constitutional dimensions.

☆ 274 *Kent v. Dulles*

357 U.S. 116 (1958).

MR. JUSTICE DOUGLAS delivered the opinion of the Court.

*          *          *

A passport not only is of great value—indeed necessary—abroad; it is also an aid in establishing citizenship for purposes of reentry into the United States. . . .

*     *     *

The right to travel is a part of the "liberty" of which the citizen cannot be deprived without due process of law under the Fifth Amendment. So much is conceded by the Solicitor General. . . .

*     *     *

Freedom to travel is, indeed, an important aspect of the citizen's "liberty." We need not decide the extent to which it can be curtailed. We are first concerned with the extent, if any, to which Congress has authorized its curtailment.

The difficulty is that while the power of the Secretary of State over the issuance of passports is expressed in broad terms, it was apparently long exercised quite narrowly. . . .

. . . We, therefore, hesitate to impute to Congress, when in 1952 it made a passport necessary for foreign travel and left its issuance to the discretion of the Secretary of State, a purpose to give him unbridled discretion to grant or withhold a passport from a citizen for any substantive reason he may choose.

*     *     *

. . . In part, of course, the issuance of the passport carries some implication of intention to extend the bearer diplomatic protection, though it does no more than "request all whom it may concern to permit safely and freely to pass, and in case of need to give all lawful aid and protection" to this citizen of the United States. But that function of the passport is subordinate. [A passport's] crucial function today is control over exit. And, as we have seen, the right of exit is a personal right included within the word "liberty" as used in the Fifth Amendment. If that "liberty" is to be regulated, it must be pursuant to the law-making functions of the Congress. And if that power is delegated, the standards must be adequate to pass scrutiny by the accepted tests. Where activities or enjoyment, natural and often necessary to the well-being of an American citizen, such as travel, are involved, we will construe narrowly all delegated powers that curtail or dilute them. We hesitate to find in this broad generalized power an authority to trench so heavily on the rights of the citizen.

Thus we do not reach the question of constitutionality. We only conclude that [the 1952 Act] and [the 1926 Act] do not delegate to the Secretary the kind of authority exercised here. We deal with beliefs, with associations, with ideological matters. We must remember that we are dealing here with citizens who have neither been accused of crimes nor found guilty. They are being denied their freedom of movement solely because of their refusal to be subjected to inquiry into their beliefs and associations. They do not seek to escape the law nor to violate it. They may or may not be Communists. But assuming they are, the only law [the McCarran Act] which Congress has passed expressly curtailing the movement of Communists across our borders has not yet become effective [since the Communist Party has not yet been required to register]. It would therefore be strange to infer that pending the effectiveness of that law, the Secretary has been silently granted by Congress the larger, the more pervasive power to curtail in his discretion the free movement of citizens in order to satisfy himself about their beliefs or associations.

To repeat, we deal here with a constitutional right of the citizen, a right which we must assume Congress will be faithful to respect. We would be faced with important constitutional questions were we to hold that Congress . . . had given the Secretary authority to withhold passports to citizens because of their beliefs or associations. Congress has made no such provision in explicit terms; and absent one, the Secretary may not employ that standard to restrict the citizens' right of free movement.

*Reversed.*

## 275 "the . . . burden of bringing forth proof of nonadvocacy" (1958)

California, by constitutional amendment, provided World War II veterans with a property tax exemption. In 1952, by further constitutional revision, the state barred anyone who advocated the overthrow of the United States or California governments by force, violence, or illegal means from such exemptions. All persons applying for an exemption had to sign a nonadvocacy statement on their tax return, and, notwithstanding such statement, the taxing authorities could deny the exemption on the grounds that the taxpayer had not satisfied the burden of proof. Speiser and others, honorably discharged from the army, claimed the exemption but refused to sign the nonadvocacy statement.

☆275 *Speiser v. Randall*

357 U.S. 514 (1958).

MR. JUSTICE BRENNAN delivered the opinion of the Court.

*     *     *

I

. . . To deny an exemption to claimants who engage in certain forms of speech is in effect to penalize them for such speech. Its deterrent effect is the same as if the State were to fine them for this speech. The appellees are plainly mistaken in their argument that, because a tax exemption is a "privilege" or "bounty," its denial may not infringe speech....

The Supreme Court of California construed the constitutional amendment as denying the tax exemptions only to claimants who engage in speech which may be criminally punished consistently with the free-speech guarantees of the Federal Constitution.... For the purposes of this case we assume without deciding that California may deny tax exemptions to persons who engage in the proscribed speech for which they might be fined or imprisoned

## II

But the question remains whether California has chosen a fair method for determining when a claimant is a member of that class to which the California court has said the constitutional and statutory provisions extend....

[S]ince only considerations of the greatest urgency can justify restrictions on speech, and since the validity of a restraint on speech in each case depends on careful analysis of the particular circumstances, the procedures by which the facts of the case are adjudicated are of special importance and the validity of the restraint may turn on the safeguards which they afford. It becomes essential, therefore, to scrutinize the procedures by which California has sought to restrain speech.

The principal feature of the California procedure, as the appellees themselves point out, is that the appellants, "as taxpayers under state law, have the affirmative burden of proof, in Court as well as before the Assessor.... [I]t is their burden to show that they are proper persons to qualify under the self-executing constitutional provision for the tax exemption in question—i.e., that they are not persons who advocate the overthrow of the government of the United States or the State by force or violence or other unlawful means or who advocate the support of a foreign government against the United States in the event of hostilities.... [T]he burden is on *them* to produce evidence justifying their claim of exemption." Not only does the initial burden of bringing forth proof of nonadvocacy rest on the taxpayer, but throughout the judicial and administrative proceedings the burden lies on the taxpayer of persuading the assessor, or the court, that he falls outside the class denied the tax exemption.... The question for decision, therefore, is whether this allocation of the burden of proof, on an issue concerning freedom of speech, falls short of the requirements of due process.

It is of course within the power of the State to regulate procedures under which its laws are carried out including the burden of producing evidence and the burden of persuasion, "unless in so doing it offends some principle of justice so rooted in the traditions and conscience of our people as to be ranked as fundamental." ... Of course, the burden of going forward with the evidence at some stages of a criminal trial may be placed on the defendant, but only after the State has "proved enough to make it just for the defendant to be required to repel what has been proved with excuse or explanation, or at least that upon a balancing of convenience or of the opportunities for knowledge the shifting of the burden will be found to be an aid to the accuser without subjecting the accused to hardship or oppression." In civil cases too this Court has struck down state statutes unfairly shifting the burden of proof.

It is true that due process may not always compel the full formalities of a criminal prosecution before criminal advocacy can be suppressed or deterred, but it is clear that the State which attempts to do so must provide procedures amply adequate to safeguard against invasion speech which the Constitution protects. It is, of course, familiar practice in the administration of a tax program for the taxpayer to carry the burden of introducing evidence to rebut the determination of the collector. But while the fairness of placing the burden of proof on the taxpayer in most circumstances is recognized, this Court has not hesitated to declare a summary tax-collection procedure a violation of due process when the purported tax was shown to be in reality a penalty for a crime. The underlying rationale of these cases is that where a person is to suffer a penalty for a crime, he is entitled to greater procedural safeguards than when only the amount of his tax liability is in issue. Similarly it does not follow that because only a tax liability is here involved, the ordinary tax assessment procedures are adequate when applied to penalize speech.

\*     \*     \*

The vice of the present procedure is that, where particular speech falls close to the line separating the lawful and the unlawful, the possibility of mistaken factfinding—inherent in all litigation—will create the danger that the legitimate utterance will be penalized. The man who knows that he must bring forth proof and persuade another of the lawfulness of his conduct necessarily must steer far wider of the unlawful zone than if the State must bear these burdens. This is especially to be feared when the complexity of the proofs and the generality of the standards applied provide but shifting sands on which the litigant must maintain his position. How can a claimant whose declaration is rejected possibly sustain the burden of proving the negative of these complex factual elements? In practical operation, therefore, this procedural device must necessarily produce a result which the State could not command directly. It can only result in a deterrence of speech which the Constitution makes free. . . .

\*　　　\*　　　\*

. . . The State argues that veterans as a class occupy a position of special trust and influence in the community, and therefore, any veteran who engages in the proscribed advocacy constitutes a special danger to the State. But while a union official or public employee may be deprived of his position and thereby removed from the place of special danger, the State is powerless to erase the service which the veteran has rendered his country; though he be denied a tax exemption, he remains a veteran. The State, consequently, can act against the veteran only as it can act against any other citizen, by imposing penalties to deter the unlawful conduct.

Moreover, the oaths required in those cases performed a very different function from the declaration in issue here. In the earlier cases it appears that the loyalty oath, once signed, became conclusive evidence of the facts attested so far as the right to office was concerned. If the person took the oath he retained his position. The oath was not part of a device to shift to the officeholder the burden of proving his right to retain his position. The signer, of course, could be prosecuted for perjury, but only in accordance with the strict procedure safeguards surrounding such criminal prosecutions. In the present case, however, it is clear that the declaration may be accepted or rejected on the basis of incompetent information or no information at all. It is only a step in a process throughout which the taxpayer must bear the burden of proof.

. . . [W]e hold that when the constitutional right to speak is sought to be deterred by a State's general taxing program, due process demands that the speech be unencumbered until the State comes forward with sufficient proof to justify its inhibition. The State clearly has no such compelling interest at stake as to justify a short-cut procedure which must inevitably result in suppressing protected speech. Accordingly, though the validity of § 19 of Art. XX of the State Constitution be conceded *arguendo*, its enforcement through procedures which place the burdens of proof and persuasion on the taxpayer is a violation of due process. It follows from this that appellants could not be required to execute the declaration as a condition for obtaining a tax exemption or as a condition for the assessor proceeding further in determining whether they were entitled to such an exemption. Since the entire statutory procedure, by placing the burden of proof on the claimants, violated the requirements of due process, appellants were not obliged to take the first step in such a procedure.

The judgments are reversed and the causes are remanded for further proceedings not inconsistent with this opinion.

*Reversed and remanded.*

# 276 "war against the Constitution" (1958)

In 1954 the Supreme Court of the United States held in *Brown v. Board of Education* that the Fourteenth Amendment to the Constitution forbids states from supporting racially separate schools. A plan for the gradual desegregation of the races in the public schools of Little Rock, Arkansas, was developed by the local school district. Opposition by the state legislature and the governor to desegregation, coupled with threats of mob violence, required the sending of and intervention by federal troops. In light of the resulting turmoil, the school district requested the desegregation plan be suspended for two and a half years. The federal district court approved the request, but the court of appeals reversed the plan, which would have sent the black children back to segregated schools. The case came up for final review by the United States Supreme Court.

☆ 276 *Cooper v. Aaron*

358 U.S. 1 (1958).

Opinion of the Court by THE CHIEF JUSTICE, MR. JUSTICE BLACK, MR. JUSTICE FRANKFURTER, MR. JUSTICE DOUGLAS, MR. JUSTICE BURTON, MR. JUSTICE CLARK, MR. JUSTICE HARLAN, MR. JUSTICE BRENNAN, and MR. JUSTICE WHITTAKER.

As this case reaches us it raises questions of the highest importance to the maintenance of our federal system of government. It necessarily involves a claim by the Governor and Legislature of a State that there is no duty on state officials to obey federal court orders resting on this Court's considered interpretation of the United States Constitution. Specifically it involves actions by the Governor and Legislature of Arkansas upon the premise that they are not bound by our holding in *Brown v. Board of Education.* . . . We are urged to uphold a suspension of the Little Rock School Board's plan to do away with segregated public schools in Little Rock until state laws and efforts to upset and nullify our holding in *Brown v. Board of Education* have been further challenged and tested in the courts. We reject these contentions.

\*　　　\*　　　\*

On May 20, 1954, three days after the first *Brown* opinion, the Little Rock District School Board adopted, and on May 23, 1954, made public, a state-

ment of policy entitled "Supreme Court Decision—
Segregation in Public Schools." In this statement
the Board recognized that "it is our responsibility to
comply with Federal Constitutional Requirements
and we intend to do so when the Supreme Court of
the United States outlines the method to be
followed."

\*          \*          \*

While the School Board was ... going forward
with its preparation for desegregating the Little
Rock school system, other state authorities, in contrast, were actively pursuing a program designed to
perpetuate in Arkansas the system of racial segregation which this Court had held violated the Fourteenth Amendment. First came, in November 1956,
an amendment to the State Constitution flatly commanding the Arkansas General Assembly to oppose
"in every Constitutional manner the Un-constitu-
tional desegregation decisions of May 17, 1954 and
May 31, 1955 of the United States Supreme Court,"
Ark. Const., Amend. 44, and, through the initiative,
a pupil assignment law, Ark. Stat. 80-1519 to 80-
1524. Pursuant to this state constitutional command,
a law relieving school children from compulsory attendance at racially mixed schools, Ark. Stat. 80-
1525, and a law establishing a State Sovereignty
Commission, Ark. Stat. 6-801 to 6-824, were enacted by the General Assembly in February 1957.

The School Board and the Superintendent of
Schools nevertheless continued with preparations to
carry out the first stage of the desegregation program. Nine Negro children were scheduled for admission in September 1957 to Central High School,
which has more than two thousand students. Various administrative measures, designed to assure the
smooth transition of this first stage of desegregation, were undertaken.

On September 2, 1957, the day before these Negro students were to enter Central High, the school
authorities were met with drastic opposing action
on the part of the Governor of Arkansas who dispatched units of the Arkansas National Guard to the
Central High School grounds and placed the school
"off limits" to colored students. As found by the District Court in subsequent proceedings, the Governor's action had not been requested by the school authorities, and was entirely unheralded.

\*          \*          \*

The Board's petition for postponement in this
proceeding states: "The effect of that action [of the
Governor] was to harden the core of opposition to
the Plan and cause many persons who theretofore
had reluctantly accepted the Plan to believe there
was some power in the State of Arkansas which,
when exerted, could nullify the Federal law and permit disobedience of the decree of this [District]

Court, and from that date hostility to the Plan was
increased and criticism of the officials of the [School]
District has become more bitter and unrestrained."
The Governor's action caused the School Board to
request the Negro students on September 2 not to
attend the high school "until the legal dilemma was
solved." The next day, September 3, 1957, the Board
petitioned the District Court for instructions, and
the court, after a hearing, found that the Board's request of the Negro students to stay away from the
high school had been made because of the stationing
of the military guards by the state authorities. The
court determined that this was not a reason for departing from the approved plan, and ordered the
School Board and Superintendent to proceed with it.

On the morning of the next day, September 4,
1957, the Negro children attempted to enter the
high school but, as the District Court later found,
units of the Arkansas National Guard "acting pursuant to the Governor's order, stood shoulder to shoulder at the school grounds and thereby forcibly prevented the 9 Negro students ... from entering," as
they continued to do every school day during the following three weeks.

\*          \*          \*

[T]he United States Attorney ... and the Attorney General of the United States, at the District
Court's request, entered the proceedings and filed a
petition on behalf of the United States, as *amicus curiae*, to enjoin the Governor of Arkansas and officers
of the Arkansas National Guard from further attempts to prevent obedience to the court's order. After hearings on the petition, the District Court found
that the School Board's plan had been obstructed by
the Governor through the use of National Guard
troops, and granted a preliminary injunction on September 20, 1957, enjoining the Governor and the officers of the Guard from preventing the attendance of
Negro children at Central High School, and from
otherwise obstructing or interfering with the orders
of the court in connection with the plan. The National Guard was then withdrawn from the school.

The next school day was Monday, September 23,
1957. The Negro children entered the high school
that morning under the protection of the Little Rock
Police Department and members of the Arkansas
State Police. But the officers caused the children to
be removed from the school during the morning because they had difficulty controlling a large and
demonstrating crowd which had gathered at the
high school. On September 25, however, the President of the United States dispatched federal troops
to Central High School and admission of the Negro
students to the school was thereby effected. Regular
army troops continued at the high school until November 27, 1957. They were then replaced by feder-
alized National Guardsmen who remained through-

out the balance of the school year. Eight of the Negro students remained in attendance at the school throughout the school year.

We come now to the aspect of the proceedings presently before us. On February 20, 1958, the School Board and the Superintendent of Schools filed a petition in the District Court seeking a postponement of their program for desegregation. Their position in essence was that because of extreme public hostility, which they stated had been engendered largely by the official attitudes and actions of the Governor and the Legislature, the maintenance of a sound educational program at Central High School, with the Negro students in attendance, would be impossible. The Board therefore proposed that the Negro students already admitted to the school be withdrawn and sent to segregated schools, and that all further steps to carry out the Board's desegregation program be postponed for a period later suggested by the Board to be two and one-half years.

*     *     *

One may well sympathize with the position of the Board in the face of the frustrating conditions which have confronted it, but, regardless of the Board's good faith, the actions of the other state agencies responsible for those conditions compel us to reject the Board's legal position. Had Central High School been under the direct management of the State itself, it could hardly be suggested that those immediately in charge of the school should be heard to assert their own good faith as a legal excuse for delay in implementing the constitutional rights of these respondents, when vindication of those rights was rendered difficult or impossible by the actions of other state officials. The situation here is in no different posture because the members of the School Board and the Superintendent of Schools are local officials; from the point of view of the Fourteenth Amendment, they stand in this litigation as the agents of the State.

*     *     *

The controlling legal principles are plain.... In short, the constitutional rights of children not to be discriminated against in school admission on grounds of race or color declared by this Court in the *Brown* case can neither be nullified openly and directly by state legislators or state executive or judicial officers, nor nullified indirectly by them through evasive schemes for segregation whether attempted "ingeniously or ingenuously."

What has been said, in the light of the facts developed, is enough to dispose of the case. However, we should answer the premise of the actions of the Governor and Legislature that they are not bound by our holding in the *Brown* case. It is necessary only to recall some basic constitutional propositions which are settled doctrine.

*     *     *

Article VI of the Constitution makes the Constitution the "supreme Law of the Land." ... Every state legislator and executive and judicial officer is solemnly committed by oath taken pursuant to Art. VI, cl. 3, "to support this Constitution." Chief Justice Taney, speaking for a unanimous Court in 1859, said that this requirement reflected the framers' "anxiety to preserve it [the Constitution] in full force, in all its powers, and to guard against resistance to or evasion of its authority, on the part of a State...."

No state legislator or executive or judicial officer can war against the Constitution without violating his undertaking to support it. Chief Justice Marshall spoke for a unanimous Court in saying that: "If the legislatures of the several states may, at will, annul the judgments of the courts of the United States, and destroy the rights acquired under those judgments, the constitution itself becomes a solemn mockery...." A Governor who asserts a power to nullify a federal court order is similarly restrained.

*     *     *

## 277 "whether your name has been linked" (1959)

Under the authority of President Truman's Executive Order 9835, the attorney general was empowered to develop a list of subversive organizations—any organization he deemed "totalitarian, fascist, Communist or subversive." Executive Order 10450 authorized the continuance of the list. Ultimately, this list contained approximately 275 organizations, many of which are included in the army questionnaire reprinted below. Along with the Communist party, the German Bund, and the Ku Klux Klan, the list included groups the names of which reflected an interest in German, Japanese, Russian, Spanish, Italian, Polish, Greek, and other ethnic or national affairs. In addition, the named groups seemingly were concerned generally with civil rights and liberties, and some with the legal defense and support of individuals charged with violations of the Smith Act. The questionnaire directed the respondent to take note of organizations with similar names. The similarities between the names of the proscribed organizations and many "non-subversive" organizations further added to the confusion and fear of having the "wrong" affiliations. This type of scrutiny, nevertheless, was not restricted to the armed forces. While the loyalty security program was in operation, this form of inquiry screened more than twenty million Americans. In one of his non-Supreme Court writings, Justice William O. Douglas noted wryly, "How could anyone prove that he was not disloyal?"

☆277 Armed Forces Security Questionnaire
(June 1, 1959)

Form DD 98.

### I. EXPLANATION

1. The interests of National Security require that all persons being considered for membership or retention in the Armed Forces be reliable, trustworthy, or of good character, and of complete and unswerving loyalty to the United States. Accordingly, it is necessary for you to furnish information concerning your security qualifications. The answers which you give will be used in determining whether you are eligible for membership in the Armed Forces in selection of your duty assignment, and for such other action as may be appropriate.

2. You are advised that in accordance with the Fifth Amendment of the Constitution of the United States you cannot be compelled to furnish any statements which you may reasonably believe may lead to your prosecution for a crime....

### II. ORGANIZATIONS OF SECURITY SIGNIFICANCE

1. There is set forth below a list of names of organizations, groups, and movements, reported by the Attorney General of the United States as having significance in connection with the National Security. Please examine the list carefully, and note those organizations, and organizations of similar names, with which you are familiar. Then answer the questions set forth in Part IV below.

\*        \*        \*

3. If there is any doubt in your mind as to whether your name has been linked with one of the organizations named, or as to whether a particular association is "worth mentioning," make a full explanation under "Remarks."

ORGANIZATIONS DESIGNATED BY THE ATTORNEY GENERAL, PURSUANT TO EXECUTIVE ORDER 10450, ARE LISTED BELOW

Communist Party, U.S.A., its subdivisions, subsidiaries, and affiliates

Communist Political Association, its subdivisions, subsidiaries, and affiliates, including —

> Alabama People's Educational Association
> Florida Press and Educational League
> Oklahoma League for Political Action
> People's Educational and Press Association of Texas
> Virginia League for People's Education
> Young Communist League

Abraham Lincoln Brigade
Abraham Lincoln School, Chicago, Illinois
Action Committee to Free Spain Now

American Association for Reconstruction in Yugoslavia, Inc.
American Branch of the Federation of Greek Maritime Unions
American Christian Nationalist Party
American Committee for European Workers' Relief
American Committee for Protection of Foreign Born
American Committee for the Settlement of Jews in Birobidjan, Inc.
American Committee for Spanish Freedom
American Committee for Yugoslav Relief, Inc.
American Committee to Survey Labor Conditions in Europe
American Council for a Democratic Greece, formerly known as the Greek American Council; Greek American Committee for National Unity
American Council on Soviet Relations
American Croatian Congress
American Jewish Labor Council
American League against War and Fascism
American League for Peace and Democracy
American National Labor Party
American National Socialist League
American National Socialist Party
American Nationalist Party
American Patriots, Inc.
American Peace Crusade
American Peace Mobilization
American Poles for Peace
American Polish Labor Council
American Polish League
American Rescue Ship Mission (*a project of the United American Spanish Aid Committee*)
American-Russian Fraternal Society
American-Russian Institute, New York (*also known as the American Russian Institute for Cultural Relations with the Soviet Union*)
American Russian Institute, Philadelphia
American Russian Institute of San Francisco
American Russian Institute of Southern California, Los Angeles
American Slav Congress
American Women for Peace
American Youth Congress
American Youth for Democracy
American Progressive League of America
Associated Klans of America
Association of Georgia Klans
Association of German Nationals (*Reichsdeutsche Vereinigung*)
Ausland-Organization der NSDAP, Overseas Branch of Nazi Party
Baltimore Forum
Benjamin Davis Freedom Committee
Black Dragon Society
Boston School for Marxist Studies, Boston, Massachusetts

Bridges-Robertson-Schmidt Defense Committee

Bulgarian American People's League of the United States

California Emergency Defense Committee

California Labor School, Inc., 321 Divisadero Street, San Francisco, California

Carpatho-Russian People's Society

Central Council of American Women of Croatian Descent (also known as Central Council of American Croatian Women, National Council of Croatian Women)

Central Japanese Association (Beikoku Chou Nippon jin Kai)

Central Japanese Association of Southern California

Central Organization of the German-American National Alliance (Deutsche-Amerikanische Einbeits front)

Cervantes Fraternal Society

China Welfare Appeal, Inc.

Chopin Cultural Center

Citizens Committee to Free Earl Browder

Citizens Committee for Harry Bridges

Citizens Committee of the Upper West Side (New York City)

Citizens Emergency Defense Conference

Citizens Protective League

Civil Liberties Sponsoring Committee of Pittsburgh

Civil Rights Congress and its affiliated organizations; including Civil Rights Congress for Texas, Veterans against Discrimination or Civil Rights Congress of New York

Columbians

Comite Coordinador Pro Republica Espanola

Comite Pro Derechos Civiles

Committee to Abolish Discrimination in Maryland

Committee to Aid the Fighting South

Committee to Defend the Rights and Freedom of Pittsburgh's Political Prisoners

Committee for a Democratic Far Eastern Policy

Committee for Constitutional and Political Freedom

Committee for the Defense of the Pittsburgh Six

Committee for Nationalist Action

Committee for the Negro in the Arts

Committee for Peace and Brotherhood Festival in Philadelphia

Committee for the Protection of the Bill of Rights

Committee for World Youth Friendship and Cultural Exchange

Committee to Defend Marie Richardson

Committee to Uphold the Bill of Rights

Commonwealth College, Mena, Arkansas

Congress against Discrimination

Congress of the Unemployed

Connecticut Committee to Aid Victims of the Smith Act

Connecticut State Youth Conference

Congress of American Revolutionary Writers

Congress of American Women

Council on African Affairs

Council of Greek Americans

Council for Jobs, Relief, and Housing

Council for Pan-American Democracy

Croatian Benevolent Fraternity

Dai Nippon Butoku Kai (Military Virtue Society of Japan or Military Art Society of Japan)

Daily Worker Press Club

Daniels Defense Committee

Dante Alighieri Society (between 1935 and 1940)

Dennis Defense Committee

Detroit Youth Assembly

East Bay Peace Committee

Elsinore Progressive League

Emergency Conference to Save Spanish Refugees (founding body of the North American Spanish Aid Committee)

Everybody's Committee to Outlaw War

Families of the Baltimore Smith Act Victims

Families of the Smith Act Victims

Federation of Italian War Veterans in the U.S.A., Inc. (Associazione Nazionale Combattenti Italiani, Federazione degli Stati Uniti d' America)

Finnish-American Mutual Aid Society

Florida Press and Educational League

Frederick Douglass Educational Center

Freedom Stage, Inc.

Friends of the New Germany (Freunde des Neuen Deutschland)

Friends of the Soviet Union

Garibaldi American Fraternal Society

George Washington Carver School, New York City

German-American Bund (Amerika-deutscher Volksbund)

German American Republican League

German American Vocational League (Deutsche Amerikanische Berufsge-meinschaft)

Guardian Club

Harlem Trade Union Council

Hawaii Civil Liberties Committee

Heimuska Kai, also known as Hokubei Heieki, Gimusha Kai, Zaibel Nihonjin, Heivaku Gimusha Kai, and Zaibei Heimusha Kai (Japanese Residing in America Military Conscripts Association)

Hellenic American Brotherhood

Hinode Kai (Imperial Japanese Reservists)

Hinomani Kai (Rising Sun Flag Society—a group of Japanese war veterans)

Hokubei Zaigo Shoke Dan (North American Reserve Officers Association)

Hollywood Writers Mobilization for Defense

Hungarian American Council for Democracy

Hungarian Brotherhood

Idaho Pension Union

Independent Party (Seattle, Washington)

Independent People's Party

Industrial Workers of the World

International Labor Defense

International Workers Order, its subdivisions, subsidiaries and affiliates

Japanese Association of America

Japanese Overseas Central Society (*Kaigai Dobo Chuo Kai*)

Japanese Overseas Convention, Tokyo, Japan, 1940

Japanese Protective Association (*Recruiting Organization*)

Jefferson School of Social Science, New York City

Jewish Culture Society

Jewish People's Committee

Jewish People's Fraternal Order

Jikyoku Lin Kai (*The Committee for the Crisis*)

Johnson Forest Group

Johnsonites

Joint Anti-Fascist Refugee Committee

Joint Council of Progressive Italian-Americans, Inc.

Joseph Weydemeyer School of Social Science, St. Louis, Missouri

Kibei Seinen Kai (*Association of U.S. Citizens of Japanese ancestry who have returned to America after studying in Japan*)

Knights of the White Camelia

Ku Klux Klan

Kyffhaeuser, also known as Kyffhaeuser League (*Kyffhaeuser Bund*). *Kyffhaeuser Fellowship* (*Kyffhaeuser Kameradschaft*)

Kyfferhaeuser War Relief (*Kyffhaeuser Kriegshilfwerk*)

Labor Council for Negro Rights

Labor Research Association, Inc.

Labor Youth League

League for Common Sense

League of American Writers

Lictor Society (*Italian Black Shirts*)

Macedonian American People's League

Mario Morgantini Circle

Maritime Labor Committee to Defend Al Lannon

Maryland Congress against Discrimination

Massachusetts Committee for the Bill of Rights

Massachusetts Minute Women for Peace (*not connected with the Minute Women of the U.S.A., Inc.*)

Maurice Braverman Defense Committee

Michigan Civil Rights Federation

Michigan Council for Peace

Michigan School of Social Science

Nanka Teikoku Gunyudan (*Imperial Military Friends Group of Southern California War Veterans*)

National Association of Mexican Americans (*also known as Associacion Nacional Mexico-Americana*)

National Blue Star Mothers of America (*not to be confused with the Blue Star Mothers of America organized in February 1942*)

National Committee for the Defense of Political Prisoners

National Committee for Freedom of the Press

National Committee to Win Amnesty for Smith Act Victims

National Committee to Win the Peace

National Conference on American Policy in China and the Far East (*a conference called by the Committee for a Democratic Far Eastern Policy*)

National Council of Americans of Croatian Descent

National Council of American-Soviet Friendship

National Federation for Constitutional Liberties

National Labor Conference for Peace

National Negro Congress

National Negro Labor Council

Nationalist Action League

Nationalist Party of Puerto Rico

Nature Friends of America (*since 1935*)

Negro Labor Victory Committee

New Committee for Publications

Nichibei Kogyo Kaisha (*The Great Fujii Theatre*)

North American Committee to Aid Spanish Democracy

North American Spanish Aid Committee

North Philadelphia Forum

Northwest Japanese Association

Ohio School of Social Sciences

Oklahoma Committee to Defend Political Prisoners

Oklahoma League for Political Education

Original Southern Klans, Incorporated

Pacific Northwest Labor School, Seattle, Washington

Palo Alto Peace Club

Partido del Pueblo of Panama (*operating in the Canal Zone*)

Peace Information Center

Peace Movement of Ethiopia

People's Drama, Inc.

People's Educational and Press Association of Texas

People's Educational Association (*incorporated under name Los Angeles Educational Association, Inc.*), also known as People's Educational Center, People's University, People's School

People's Institute of Applied Religion

People's Programs (*Seattle, Washington*)

People's Radio Foundation, Inc.

People's Rights Party

Philadelphia Labor Committee for Negro Rights

Philadelphia School of Social Science and Art

Photo League (*New York City*)

Pittsburgh Arts Club

Political Prisoners' Welfare Committee

Polonia Society of the IWO

Progressive German-Americans, also known as Progressive German-Americans of Chicago

Proletarian Party of America

Protestant War Veterans of the United States, Inc.

Provisional Committee of Citizens for Peace, Southwest Area

Provisional Committee on Latin American Affairs

Provisional Committee to Abolish Discrimination in the State of Maryland

Puerto Rican Comite Pro Libertades Civiles (CLC)

Puertorriquenos Unidos (*Puerto Ricans United*)

Quad City Committee for Peace

Queensbridge Tenants League

Revolutionary Workers League

Romanian-American Fraternal Society

Russian American Society, Inc.

Sakura Kai (*Patriotic Society or Cherry Association, composed of veterans of Russo-Japanese War*)

Samuel Adams School, Boston, Mass.

Santa Barbara Peace Forum

Schappes Defense Committee

Schneiderman-Darcy Defense Committee

School of Jewish Studies, New York City

Seattle Labor School, Seattle, Washington

Serbian-American Fraternal Society

Serbian Vidovdan Council

Shinto Temples (*limited to State Shinto abolished in 1945*)

Silver Shirt Legion of America

Slavic Council of Southern California

Slovak Workers Society

Slovenian-American National Council

Socialist Workers Party, including American Committee for European Workers Relief

Sokoku Kai (*Fatherland Society*)

Southern Negro Youth Congress

Suiko Sha (*Reserve Officers Association, Los Angeles*)

Syracuse Women for Peace

Tom Paine School of Social Science, Philadelphia, Pennsylvania

Tom Paine School of Westchester, New York

Trade Union Committee for Peace

Trade Unionists for Peace

Tri-State Negro Trade Union Council

Ukrainian-American Fraternal Union

Union of American Croatians

Union of New York Veterans

United American Spanish Aid Committee

United Committee of Jewish Societies and Landsmanschaft Federations, also known as Coordination Committee of Jewish Landsmanschaften and Fraternal Organizations

United Committee of South Slavic Americans

United Defense Council of Southern California

United Harlem Tenants and Consumers Organization

United May Day Committee

United Negro and Allied Veterans of America

Veterans against Discrimination of Civil Rights Congress of New York

Veterans of the Abraham Lincoln Brigade

Virginia League for People's Education

Voice of Freedom Committee

Walt Whitman School of Social Science, Newark, New Jersey

Washington Bookshop Association

Washington Committee to Defend the Bill of Rights

Washington Committee for Democratic Action

Washington Commonwealth Federation

Washington Pension Union

Wisconsin Conference on Social Legislation

Workers Alliance (*since April 1936*)

Workers Party (*including Socialist Youth League*)

Yiddisher Kultur Farband

Yougoslav-American Cooperative Home, Inc.

Yougoslav Seamen's Club, Inc.

### III. INSTRUCTIONS

1. Set forth the explanation for each answer checked "Yes" under question 2 below "Remarks." Attach as many extra sheets as necessary for a full explanation . . . initialing each extra sheet.

\*        \*        \*

3. In stating details, it is permissible, if your memory is hazy on particular points, to use such expressions as "I think," "in my opinion," "I believe," or "to the best of my recollection."

### IV. QUESTIONS

*(For each answer checked "Yes" under question 2, set forth a full explanation under "Remarks" below.)*

|  | Yes | No |
|---|---|---|
| 1. I have read the list of names of organizations, groups, and movements set forth under Part II of this form and the explanation which precedes it. | ☐ | ☐ |

2. Concerning the list of organizations, groups, and movements set forth under Part II above:

|  | Yes | No |
|---|---|---|
| a. Are you now a member of any of the organizations, groups, or movements listed? | ☐ | ☐ |
| b. Have you ever been a member of any of the organizations, groups, or movements listed? | ☐ | ☐ |
| c. Are you now employed by any of the organizations, groups, or movements listed? | ☐ | ☐ |
| d. Have you ever been employed by any of the organizations, groups, or movements listed? | ☐ | ☐ |
| e. Have you ever attended any meeting of any of the organizations, groups, or movements listed? | ☐ | ☐ |

f.  Have you ever attended any so- ☐ ☐ cial gathering of any of the orga- nizations, groups, or movements listed?

g.  Have you ever attended any gath- ☐ ☐ ering of any kind sponsored by any of the organizations, groups, or movements listed?

h.  Have you prepared material for ☐ ☐ publication by any of the organi- zations, groups, or movements listed?

i.  Have you ever corresponded with ☐ ☐ any of the organizations, groups, or movements listed?

j.  Have you ever contributed ☐ ☐ money to any of the organiza- tions, groups, or movements listed?

k.  Have you ever contributed ser- ☐ ☐ vices to any of the organizations, groups, or movements listed?

l.  Have you ever subscribed to any ☐ ☐ publications of any of the organi- zations, groups, or movements listed?

m. Have you ever been employed by ☐ ☐ a foreign government or any agency thereof?

n.  Are you now a member of the ☐ ☐ Communist Party of any foreign country?

o.  Have you ever been a member of ☐ ☐ the Communist Party of any for- eign country?

p.  Have you ever been the subject of ☐ ☐ a loyalty or security hearing?

q.  Are you now or have you ever ☐ ☐ been a member of any organiza- tion, association, movement, group, or a combination of persons not on the Attorney General's list which advocates the overthrow of our constitutional form of govern- ment, or which has adopted the policy of advocating or approving the commission of acts of force or violence to deny other persons their rights under the Constitu- tion of the United States, or which seeks to alter the form of govern- ment of the United States by un- constitutional means?

r.  Have you ever been known by ☐ ☐ any other last name than that used in signing this question- naire?

REMARKS:

CERTIFICATION

In regard to any part of this questionnaire con- cerning which I have had any question as to the meaning, I have requested and have obtained a com- plete explanation. I certify that the statements made by me under part IV above and on any supple- mental pages hereto attached are full, true, and cor- rect.

_____

*Signature*

# 278  Communists, Murderers, Arsonists, and Rapists (1959)

In 1959, Congress undertook sweeping reforms of the labor law. Section 504 of the new Labor-Manage- ment Reporting and Disclosure Act (the Landrum- Griffin Act), prohibiting certain persons from hold- ing office in labor unions, was far more restrictive of Communist activities than Section 9(h) of the Taft- Hartley Act (1947), which it replaced. Membership in the Communist party was equivalent to crimes of moral turpitude for purposes of disqualification from officeholding in a labor union.

## ☆ 278  Labor-Management Reporting and Disclosure Act

73 Stat. 519 (1959).

*Be it enacted by the Senate and House of Represen- tatives of the United States of America in Congress assembled, . . .*

\*        \*        \*

PROHIBITION AGAINST CERTAIN PERSONS HOLDING OFFICE

SEC. 504. (a) No person who is or has been a mem- ber of the Communist Party or who has been con- victed of, or served any part of a prison term result- ing from his conviction of, robbery, bribery, extortion, embezzlement, grand larceny, burglary, arson, violation of narcotics laws, murder, rape, as- sault with intent to kill, assault which inflicts griev- ous bodily injury . . . or conspiracy to commit any such crimes, shall serve—

(1) as an officer, director, trustee, member of any executive board or similar governing body, business agent, manager, organizer, or other em- ployee (other than as an employee performing ex- clusively clerical or custodial duties) of any labor organization, or

(2) as a labor relations consultant to a person engaged in an industry or activity affecting commerce, or as an officer, director, agent, or employee (other than as an employee performing exclusively clerical or custodial duties) of any group or association of employers dealing with any labor organization,

during or for five years after the termination of his membership in the Communist Party, or for five years after such conviction or after the end of such imprisonment.... No labor organization or officer thereof shall knowingly permit any person to assume or hold any office or paid position in violation of this subsection.

(b) Any person who willfully violates this section shall be fined not more than $10,000 or imprisoned for not more than one year, or both.

*    *    *

*Approved, September 14, 1959.*

## 279 "the names of all persons who attended the camp" (1959)

Along with the federal government, two-thirds of the states had sedition laws that made the advocacy of violent or unlawful overthrow of the federal or state government a crime. Although in *Pennsylvania v. Nelson*, 350 U.S. 497 (1956), the Supreme Court limited the reach of these laws by holding that Congress, in passing the Smith Act, preempted the states from punishing sedition against the United States, state legislative hearings continued to "expose" subversive activities and organizations. This resort to legislative exposure, intended to subject the exposed groups to the various laws prohibiting the employment of subversives in government and in certain professions, was upheld in *Uphaus.*

☆ 279 *Uphaus v. Wyman*

360 U.S. 72 (1959).

MR. JUSTICE CLARK delivered the opinion of the Court.

*    *    *

As in *Sweezy*, the attorney general of New Hampshire, who had been constituted a one-man legislative investigating committee by joint resolution of the legislature, was conducting a probe of subversive activities in the State. In the course of his investigation the attorney general called appellant, Executive Director of World Fellowship, Inc., a voluntary corporation organized under the laws of New Hampshire and maintaining a summer camp in the State. ... The information sought consisted of: (1) a list of the names of all the camp's nonprofessional employ-

ees for those two summer seasons; (2) the correspondence which appellant had carried on with and concerning those persons who came to the camp as speakers; and (3) the names of all persons who attended the camp during the same periods of time....

... [A]ppellant ... refused to produce the information. He claimed that by the Smith Act, as construed by this Court in *Commonwealth of Pennsylvania v. Nelson*, Congress had so completely occupied the field of subversive activities that the states were without power to investigate in that area. Additionally, he contended that the Due Process Clause precluded enforcement of the subpoenas, first, because the resolution under which the Attorney General was authorized to operate was vague and, second, because the documents sought were not relevant to the inquiry. Finally, appellant argued the enforcement would violate his rights of free speech and association.

The Merrimack County Court sustained appellant's objection to the production of the names of the nonprofessional employees.... Appellant's objections to the production of the names of the camp's guests were overruled, and he was ordered to produce them. Upon his refusal, he was adjudged in contempt of court and ordered committed to jail.... We now pass to a consideration of the sole question before us, namely, the validity of the order of contempt for refusal to produce the list of guests at World Fellowship, Inc., during the summer seasons of 1954 and 1955....

... The basis of *Nelson* ... rejects the notion that it stripped the states of the right to protect themselves. All the opinion proscribed was a race between federal and state prosecutors to the courthouse door. The opinion made clear that a state could proceed with prosecutions for sedition against the state itself; that it can legitimately investigate in this area follows *a fortiori*....

Appellant's other objections can be capsuled into the single question of whether New Hampshire, under the facts here, is precluded from compelling the production of the documents by the Due Process Clause of the Fourteenth Amendment. Let us first clear away some of the underbrush necessarily surrounding the case because of its setting.

First, the academic and political freedoms discussed in *Sweezy v. New Hampshire* are not present here in the same degree, since World Fellowship is neither a university nor a political party. Next, since questions concerning the authority of the committee to act as it did are questions of state law, we accept as controlling the New Hampshire Supreme Court's conclusion that "[the Legislature] did and does desire an answer to these questions." ... The Attorney General was commissioned to determine if there were any subversive persons within New Hampshire. The obvious starting point of such an inquiry was to learn what persons were within the state. It is, therefore, clear that the requests relate directly to the Legislature's area of interest, i.e., the presence of subversives in the state as announced in its resolution....

Moreover, the Attorney General had valid reason to believe that the speakers and guests at World Fellowship might be subversive persons within the meaning of the New Hampshire Act. The Supreme Court of New Hampshire found Uphaus' contrary position "unrelated to reality." Although the evidence as to the nexus between World Fellowship and subversive activities may not be conclusive, we believe it sufficiently relevant to support the Attorney General's action. The New Hampshire definition of subversive persons was born of the legislative determination that the Communist movement posed a serious threat to the security of the state. The record reveals that appellant had participated in "Communist front" activities and that "[n]ot less than nineteen speakers invited by Uphaus to talk at World Fellowship had either been members of the Communist Party or had connections or affiliations with it or with one or more of the organizations cited as subversive or Communist controlled in the United States Attorney General's list." While the Attorney General's list is designed for the limited purpose of determining fitness for federal employment, and guilt by association remains a thoroughly discredited doctrine, it is with a legislative investigation—not a criminal prosecution—that we deal here. Certainly the investigatory power of the state need not be constricted until sufficient evidence of subversion is gathered to justify the institution of criminal proceedings.

... The investigation was, therefore, undertaken in the interest of self-preservation, "the ultimate value of any society." This governmental interest outweighs individual rights in an associational privacy which, however real in other circumstances, were here tenuous at best. The camp was operating as a public one, furnishing both board and lodging to persons applying therefor. As to them, New Hampshire law requires that World Fellowship, Inc., maintain a register, open to inspection of sheriffs and police officers.... We recognize of course that compliance with the subpoena will result in exposing the fact that the persons therein named were guests at World Fellowship. But so long as a committee must report to its legislative parent, exposure—in the sense of disclosure—is an inescapable incident of an investigation into the presence of subversive persons within a state. And the governmental interest in self-preservation is sufficiently compelling to subordinate the interest in associational privacy of

persons who, at least to the extent of the guest registration statute, made public at the inception the association they now wish to keep private. In the light of such a record we conclude that the state's interest has not been "pressed, in this instance, to a point where it has come into fatal collision with the overriding" constitutionally protected rights of appellant and those he may represent.

*        *        *

*Affirmed.*

## 280 " 'Have you ever been a member of the Communist Party?' " (1959)

The power of a legislative body to investigate conditions that might warrant the passage of laws to perfect the order of society has long been conceded in America. And, as long as the object of such legislative inquests was to inform the assembly rather than the public, they received little attention. With the advent of mass media, especially television, congressional investigations into unpopular causes and unlawful activities became a direct weapon in the arsenal combating subversion.

Given the sweep of federal, state, and local laws prohibiting the employment of people whose loyalty was subject to "reasonable" doubt and a corresponding antipathy by private employers, even a suggestion of Communist affiliation jeopardized a person's career and livelihood. *Barenblatt v. United States* reviewed this new use of the investigatory process in the context of a conviction for contempt of Congress. The Supreme Court upheld the broad scope of the investigatory power, finding its needs to outweigh a witness's First Amendment rights. In lieu of the traditional "clear and present danger" test, the court articulated a balancing test that would weigh an individual's freedom of speech and association against the potential security of the entire country.

☆ 280 *Barenblatt v. United States*

360 U.S. 109 (1959).

MR. JUSTICE HARLAN delivered the opinion of the Court.

Once more the Court is required to resolve the conflicting constitutional claims of congressional power and of an individual's right to resist its exercise. The congressional power in question concerns the internal process of Congress in moving within its legislative domain; it involves the utilization of its committees to secure "testimony needed to enable it efficiently to exercise a legislative function belonging to it under the Constitution."

*        *        *

We here review petitioner's conviction ... for contempt of Congress, arising from his refusal to answer certain questions put to him by a Subcommittee of the House Committee on Un-American Activities during the course of an inquiry concerning alleged Communist infiltration into the field of education.

\*        \*        \*

... [P]etitioner specifically declined to answer each of the following five questions:

Are you now a member of the Communist Party? [Count One.]
Have you ever been a member of the Communist Party? [Count Two.]
Now, you have stated that you knew Francis Crowley. Did you know Francis Crowley as a member of the Communist Party? [Count Three.]
Were you ever a member of the Haldane Club of the Communist Party while at the University of Michigan? [Count Four.]
Were you a member while a student of the University of Michigan Council of Arts, Sciences, and Professions? [Count Five.]

In each instance the grounds of refusal were those set forth in the prepared statement. Petitioner expressly disclaimed reliance upon "the Fifth Amendment."

\*        \*        \*

... [W]e find it unnecessary to consider the validity of his conviction under the Third and Fifth Counts, the only ones involving questions which on their face do not directly relate to such participation or knowledge.

Petitioner's various contentions resolve themselves into three propositions: ... Third, the questions petitioner refused to answer infringed rights protected by the First Amendment.

\*        \*        \*

CONSTITUTIONAL CONTENTIONS

Our function, at this point, is purely one of constitutional adjudication in the particular case and upon the particular record before us, not to pass judgment upon the general wisdom or efficacy of the activities of this Committee in a vexing and complicated field.

The precise constitutional issue confronting us is whether the Subcommittee's inquiry into petitioner's past or present membership in the Communist Party transgressed the provisions of the First Amendment, which of course reach and limit congressional investigations.

... Where First Amendment rights are asserted to bar governmental interrogation, resolution of the issue always involves a balancing by the courts of the competing private and public interests at stake in the particular circumstances shown. . . . The critical element is the existence of, and the weight to be ascribed to, the interest of the Congress in demanding disclosures from an unwilling witness." See also *American Communications Assn. v. Douds.* More recently in *National Association for the Advancement of Colored People v. Alabama* we applied the same principles in judging state action claimed to infringe rights of association assured by the Due Process Clause of the Fourteenth Amendment, and stated that the " 'subordinating interest of the State must be compelling' " in order to overcome the individual constitutional rights at stake. In light of these principles we now consider petitioner's First Amendment claims.

The first question is whether this investigation was related to a valid legislative purpose, for Congress may not constitutionally require an individual to disclose his political relationships or other private affairs except in relation to such a purpose.

That Congress has wide power to legislate in the field of Communist activity in this Country, and to conduct appropriate investigations in aid thereof, is hardly debatable. The existence of such power has never been questioned by this Court, and it is sufficient to say, without particularization, that Congress has enacted or considered in this field a wide range of legislative measures, not a few of which have stemmed from recommendations of the very Committee whose actions have been drawn in question here. In the last analysis this power rests on the right of self-preservation, "the ultimate value of any society," *Dennis v. United States.* Justification for its exercise in turn rests on the long and widely accepted view that the tenets of the Communist Party include the ultimate overthrow of the Government of the United States by force and violence, a view which has been given formal expression by the Congress.

On these premises, this Court in its constitutional adjudications has consistently refused to view the Communist Party as an ordinary political party, and has upheld federal legislation aimed at the Communist problem which in a different context would certainly have raised constitutional issues of the gravest character. . . .

We think that investigatory power in this domain is not to be denied Congress solely because the field of education is involved. Nothing in the prevailing opinions in *Sweezy v. New Hampshire* stands for a contrary view. . . . Indeed we do not understand petitioner here to suggest that Congress in no circumstances may inquire into Communist activity in the field of education. Rather, his position is in effect that this particular investigation was aimed not at the revolutionary aspects but at the theoretical classroom discussion of communism.

In our opinion this position rests on a too constricted view of the nature of the investigatory process, and is not supported by a fair assessment of the record before us. An investigation of advocacy of or preparation for overthrow certainly embraces the right to identify a witness as a member of the Communist Party and to inquire into the various manifestations of the Party's tenets. The strict requirements of a prosecution under the Smith Act are not the measure of the permissible scope of a congressional investigation into "overthrow," for of necessity the investigatory process must proceed step by step. Nor can it fairly be concluded that this investigation was directed at controlling what is being taught at our universities rather than at overthrow. ... That there was also testimony on the abstract philosophical level does not detract from the dominant theme of this investigation—Communist infiltration furthering the alleged ultimate purpose of overthrow. ...

Nor can we accept the further contention that this investigation should not be deemed to have been in furtherance of a legislative purpose because the true objective of the Committee and of the Congress was purely "exposure." So long as Congress acts in pursuance of its constitutional power, the Judiciary lacks authority to intervene on the basis of the motives which spurred the exercise of that power. "It is, of course, true," as was said in *McCray v. United States* [upholding a federal tax upon colored oleomargarine, forty times greater than that upon the same uncolored product], "that if there be no authority in the judiciary to restrain a lawful exercise of power by another department of the government, where a wrong motive or purpose has impelled to the exertion of the power, that abuses of a power conferred may be temporarily effectual. The remedy for this, however, lies, not in the abuse by the judicial authority of its functions, but in the people, upon whom, after all, under our institutions, reliance must be placed for the correction of abuses committed in the exercise of a lawful power." These principles of course apply as well to committee investigations into the need for legislation as to the enactments which such investigations may produce. ...

Finally, the record is barren of other factors which in themselves might sometimes lead to the conclusion that the individual interests at stake were not subordinate to those of the state. There is no indication in this record that the Subcommittee was attempting to pillory witnesses. Nor did petitioner's appearance as a witness follow from indiscriminate dragnet procedures, lacking in probable cause for belief that he possessed information which might be helpful to the Subcommittee. And the relevancy of the questions put to him by the Subcommittee is not open to doubt.

We conclude that the balance between the individual and the governmental interests here at stake must be struck in favor of the latter, and that therefore the provisions of the First Amendment have not been offended.

We hold that petitioner's conviction for contempt of Congress discloses no infirmity, and that the judgment of the Court of Appeals must be

*Affirmed.*

MR. JUSTICE BLACK, with whom THE CHIEF JUSTICE and MR. JUSTICE DOUGLAS concur, dissenting.

\* \* \*

II

The First Amendment says in no equivocal language that Congress shall pass no law abridging freedom of speech, press, assembly or petition. The activities of this Committee, authorized by Congress, do precisely that, through exposure, obloquy and public scorn. The Court does not really deny this fact but relies on a combination of three reasons for permitting the infringement: (A) The notion that despite the First Amendment's command Congress can abridge speech and association if this Court decides that the governmental interest in abridging speech is greater than an individual's interest in exercising that freedom, (B) the Government's right to "preserve itself," (C) the fact that the Committee is only after Communists or suspected Communists in this investigation.

(A) I do not agree that laws directly abridging First Amendment freedoms can be justified by a congressional or judicial balancing process. There are, of course, cases suggesting that a law which primarily regulates conduct but which might also indirectly affect speech can be upheld if the effect on speech is minor in relation to the need for control of the conduct. ... But even such laws governing conduct, we emphasized, must be tested, though only by a balancing process, if they indirectly affect ideas. On one side of the balance, we pointed out, is the interest of the United States in seeing that its fundamental law protecting freedom of communication is not abridged; on the other the obvious interest of the State to regulate conduct within its boundaries. ...

To apply the Court's balancing test under [these] circumstances is to read the First Amendment to say "Congress shall pass no law abridging freedom of speech, press, assembly and petition, unless Congress and the Supreme Court reach the joint conclusion that on balance the interest of the Government in stifling these freedoms is greater than the interest of the people in having them exercised." ...

But even assuming what I cannot assume, that some balancing is proper in this case, I feel that the Court after stating the test ignores it completely. At

most it balances the right of the Government to preserve itself, against Barenblatt's right to refrain
from revealing Communist affiliations. Such a balance, however, mistakes the factors to be weighed.
In the first place, it completely leaves out the real
interest in Barenblatt's silence, the interest of the
people as a whole in being able to join organizations,
advocate causes and make political "mistakes" without later being subjected to governmental penalties
for having dared to think for themselves. It is this
right, the right to err politically, which keeps us
strong as a Nation. . . . It is these interests of society, rather than Barenblatt's own right to silence,
which I think the Court should put on the balance
against the demands of the Government, if any balancing process is to be tolerated. Instead they are
not mentioned, while on the other side the demands
of the Government are vastly overstated and called
"self-preservation." It is admitted that this Committee can only seek information for the purpose of suggesting laws, and that Congress' power to make
laws in the realm of speech and association is quite
limited, even on the Court's test. Its interest in making such laws in the field of education, primarily a
state function, is clearly narrower still. Yet the
Court styles this attenuated interest self-preservation and allows it to overcome the need our country
has to let us all think, speak, and associate politically as we like and without fear of reprisal. Such a
result reduces "balancing" to a mere play on words
and is completely inconsistent with the rules this
Court has previously given for applying a "balancing
test." . . .

(B) Moreover, I cannot agree with the Court's notion that First Amendment freedoms must be
abridged in order to "preserve" our country. . . .

(C) The Court implies . . . that the ordinary rules
and requirements of the Constitution do not apply
because the Committee is merely after Communists
and they do not constitute a political party but only
a criminal gang. . . . By accepting this charge and allowing it to support treatment of the Communist
Party and its members which would violate the Constitution if applied to other groups, the Court, in effect, declares that Party outlawed. . . .

. . . [W]hen the Attorney General testified on a
proposal to bar the Communist Party from the ballot he said, "an organized group, whether you call it
political or not, could hardly be barred from the ballot without jeopardizing the constitutional guarantees of all other political groups and parties."

*          *          *

. . . Today we deal with Communists or suspected
Communists. In 1920, instead, the New York Assembly suspended duly elected legislators on the ground
that, being Socialists, they were disloyal to the country's principles. In the 1830's the Masons were

hunted as outlaws and subversives, and abolitionists
were considered revolutionaries of the most dangerous kind in both North and South. Earlier still, at the
time of the universally unlamented alien and sedition laws, Thomas Jefferson's party was attacked
and its members were derisively called "Jacobins."
Fisher Ames described the party as a "French faction" guilty of "subversion" and "officered, regimented and formed to subordination." Its members,
he claimed, intended to "take arms against the laws
as soon as they dare." History should teach us then,
that in times of high emotional excitement minority
parties and groups which advocate extremely unpopular social or governmental innovations will always be typed as criminal gangs and attempts will
always be made to drive them out. It was knowledge
of this fact, and of its great dangers, that caused the
Founders of our land to enact the First Amendment
as a guarantee that neither Congress nor the people
would do anything to hinder or destroy the capacity
of individuals and groups to seek converts and votes
for any cause, however radical or unpalatable their
principles might seem under the accepted notions of
the time. Whatever the States were left free to do,
the First Amendment sought to leave congress devoid of any kind or quality of power to direct any
type of national laws against the freedom of individuals to think what they please, advocate whatever
policy they choose, and join with others to bring
about the social, religious, political and governmental changes which seem best to them. . . .

*          *          *

### III

Finally, I think Barenblatt's conviction violates
the Constitution because the chief aim, purpose and
practice of the House Un-American Activities Committee, as disclosed by its many reports, is to try
witnesses and punish them because they are or have
been Communists or because they refuse to admit or
deny Communist affiliations. The punishment imposed is generally punishment by humiliation and
public shame. There is nothing strange or novel
about this kind of punishment. It is in fact one of the
oldest forms of governmental punishment known to
mankind; branding, the pillory, ostracism and subjection to public hatred being but a few examples of
it. . . .

The Un-American Activities Committee was created in 1938. It immediately conceived of its function
on a grand scale as one of ferreting out "subversives" and especially of having them removed from
government jobs. It made many reports to the
House urging removal of such employees. . . .

Even after our *Lovett* holding, however, the
Committee continued to view itself as the "only
agency of government that has the power of expo-

sure," and to work unceasingly and sincerely to identify and expose all suspected Communists and "subversives" in order to eliminate them from virtually all fields of employment. How well it has succeeded in its declared program of "pitiless publicity and exposure" is a matter of public record.... The same technique is employed to cripple the job opportunities of those who strongly criticize the Committee or take other actions it deems undesirable. Thus, in 1949, the Committee reported that it had indexed and printed some 335,000 names of people who had signed "Communist" petitions of one kind or another. All this the Committee did and does to punish by exposure the many phases of "un-American" activities that it reports cannot be reached by legislation, by administrative action, or by any other agency of Government, which, of course, includes the courts.

The same intent to expose and punish is manifest in the Committee's investigation which led to Barenblatt's conviction. The declared purpose of the investigation was to identify to the people of Michigan the individuals responsible for the alleged Communist success there. The Committee claimed that its investigation "uncovered" members of the Communist Party holding positions in the school systems in Michigan; that most of the teachers subpoenaed before the Committee refused to answer questions on the ground that to do so might result in self-incrimination, and that most of these teachers had lost their jobs. It then stated that "the Committee on Un-American Activities approves of this action...." Similarly, as a result of its Michigan investigation, the Committee called upon American labor unions to amend their constitutions, if necessary, in order to deny membership to any Communist Party member. This would, of course, prevent many workers from getting or holding the only kind of jobs their particular skills qualified them for. The Court, today, barely mentions these statements, which, especially when read in the context of past reports by the Committee, show unmistakably what the Committee was doing. I cannot understand why these reports are deemed relevant to a determination of a congressional intent to investigate communism in education, but irrelevant to any finding of congressional intent to bring about exposure for its own sake or for the purposes of punishment.

\*　　　\*　　　\*

MR. JUSTICE BRENNAN, dissenting.

I would reverse this conviction. It is sufficient that I state my complete agreement with my Brother BLACK that no purpose for the investigation of Barenblatt is revealed by the record except exposure purely for the sake of exposure. This is not a purpose to which Barenblatt's rights under the First Amendment can validly be subordinated. An

investigation in which the processes of law-making and law-evaluating are submerged entirely in exposure of individual behavior — in adjudication, of a sort, through the exposure process — is outside the constitutional pale of congressional inquiry.

## 281 "employee insubordination" (1960)

Accusations or even suggestions of Communist affiliation took a heavy toll on the American labor market. Observers noted that "the threat of immediate dismissal was a universal weapon wielded by inquisitors." When the United States Supreme Court concluded in *Slochower* (1956) that the mere assertion of the constitutional privilege against self-incrimination did not justify dismissal, employers offered other rationales such as incompetence and insubordination in support of termination from employment.

### ☆281 *Nelson v. Los Angeles*

362 U.S. 1 (1960).

MR. JUSTICE CLARK delivered the opinion of the Court.

Petitioners, when employees of the County of Los Angeles, California, were subpoenaed by and appeared before a Subcommittee of the House Un-American Activities Committee, but refused to answer certain questions concerning subversion. Previously, each petitioner had been ordered by the County Board of Supervisors to answer any questions asked by the Subcommittee relating to his subversive activity, and § 1028.1 of the Government Code of the State of California made it the duty of any public employee to give testimony relating to such activity on pain of discharge "in the manner provided by law." Thereafter the County discharged petitioners on the ground of insubordination and violation of § 1028.1 of the Code....

\*　　　\*　　　\*

We ... reach Globe's contention that his summary discharge was nevertheless arbitrary and unreasonable. In this regard he places his reliance on *Slochower v. Board of Education.* However, the New York statute under which Slochower was discharged specifically operated "to discharge every city employee who invokes the Fifth Amendment. In practical effect the questions asked are taken as confessed and made the basis of the discharge." This "built-in" inference of guilt, derived solely from a Fifth Amendment claim, we held to be arbitrary and unreasonable. But the test here, rather than being the invocation of any constitutional privilege, is the failure of the employee to answer. California has not predicated discharge on any "built-in" inference of guilt in its statute, but solely on employee insubordination for failure to give information which we have held that the State has a legitimate interest in securing. . . .

*     *     *

. . . The judgments are

*Affirmed.*

MR. JUSTICE BLACK, whom MR. JUSTICE DOUGLAS joins, dissenting.

Section 1028.1 of the California Code, as here applied, provides that any California public employee who refuses to incriminate himself when asked to do so by a Congressional Committee "shall be suspended and dismissed from his employment in the manner provided by law." The Fifth Amendment, which is a part of the Bill of Rights, provides that no person shall be compelled to incriminate ("to be a witness against") himself. The petitioner, Globe, an employee of the State of California, appeared before the House Un-American Activities Committee of the United States Congress and claimed this Federal constitutional privilege. California promptly discharged him, as the Court's opinion says, for "insubordination and violation of § 1028.1 of the Code." The "insubordination and violation" consisted exclusively of Globe's refusal to testify before the Congressional Committee; a ground for his refusal was that his answers might incriminate him. It is beyond doubt that the State took Globe's job away from him only because he claimed his privilege under the Federal Constitution.

Here, then, is a plain conflict between the Federal Constitution and § 1028.1 of the California Code. The Federal Constitution told Globe he could, without penalty, refuse to incriminate himself before any arm of the Federal Government; California, however, has deprived him of his job solely because he exercised this Federal constitutional privilege. In giving supremacy to the California law, I think the Court approves a plain violation of Article VI of the Constitution of the United States which makes that Constitution "the supreme Law of the Land . . . any thing in the constitution or laws of any State to the contrary notwithstanding." I also think that this discharge under State law is a violation of the Due Process Clause of the Fourteenth Amendment in its authentic historical sense: that a State may not encroach upon the individual rights of people except for violation of a law that is valid under the "law of the land." "Law of the land" of necessity includes the supreme law, the Constitution itself.

The basic purpose of the Bill of Rights was to protect individual liberty against governmental procedures that the Framers thought should not be used. That great purpose can be completely frustrated by holdings like this. I would hold that no State can put any kind of penalty on any person for claiming a privilege authorized by the Federal Constitution. The Court's holding to the contrary here does not bode well for individual liberty in America.

## 282 "questions having a substantial relevance to his qualifications" (1961)

There have always been prerequisites of education and skill for admission to the various professions. In addition, the legal profession has always imposed stringent "character" requirements. Those charged with admitting newcomers to the profession used loyalty oaths, in particular, to screen out applicants perceived as having radical affiliations. The American Bar Association at one time called for disciplinary procedures against licensed practitioners who were members of the Communist party or who advocated Marxism-Leninism. The powers of the state licensing boards to inquire into the political beliefs and associations of bar applicants came before the Supreme Court in *Konigsberg II.* The court concluded that such inquiries were constitutional.

☆ 282 *Konigsberg v. State Bar of California (II)*

366 U.S. 36 (1961).

MR. JUSTICE HARLAN delivered the opinion of the Court.

This case [involves] California's second rejection of petitioner's application for admission to the State bar. . . .

. . . To qualify for certification an applicant must, among other things, be of "good moral character," and no person may be certified "who advocates the overthrow of the Government of the United States or of this State by force, violence, or other unconstitutional means. . . ."

In 1953 petitioner, having successfully passed the California bar examinations, applied for certification for bar membership. The Committee, after interrogating Konigsberg and receiving considerable evidence as to his qualifications, declined to certify him on the ground that he had failed to meet the burden of proving his eligibility under the two statutory requirements relating to good moral character and nonadvocacy of violent overthrow. That determination centered largely around Konigsberg's repeated refusals to answer Committee questions as to his present or past membership in the Communist Party. . . .

. . . [T]his Court, after reviewing the record, held the state determination to have been without rational support in the evidence and therefore offensive to the Due Process Clause of the Fourteenth Amendment. . . .

... At ... ensuing Committee hearings Konigsberg introduced further evidence as to his good moral character (none of which was rebutted), reiterated unequivocally his disbelief in violent overthrow, and stated that he had never knowingly been a member of any organization which advocated such action. He persisted, however, in his refusals to answer any questions relating to his membership in the Communist Party. The Committee again declined to certify him, this time on the ground that his refusals to answer had obstructed a full investigation into his qualifications.... We again brought the case here.

\*         \*         \*

We think it clear that the Fourteenth Amendment's protection against arbitrary State action does not forbid a State from denying admission to a bar applicant so long as he refuses to provide unprivileged answers to questions having a substantial relevance to his qualifications....

\*         \*         \*

Petitioner does not challenge the constitutionality of forbidding certification for admission to practice of those advocating the violent overthrow of government. It would indeed be difficult to argue that a belief, firm enough to be carried over into advocacy, in the use of illegal means to change the form of the State or Federal Government is an unimportant consideration in determining the fitness of applicants for membership in a profession in whose hands so largely lies the safekeeping of this country's legal and political institutions....

\*         \*         \*

... All [California] has presently required is an applicant's cooperation with the Committee's search for evidence of forbidden advocacy. Petitioner has been denied admission to the California bar for obstructing the Committee in the performance of its necessary functions of examination and cross-examination....

\*         \*         \*

Thus as matters now stand, there is nothing involved here which is contrary to the reasoning of *Speiser*, for despite compelled testimony the prospective bar applicant need not "steer far wider of the unlawful zone" for fear of mistaken judgment or fact finding declaring unlawful speech which is in fact protected by the Constitution....

The judgment of the Supreme Court of California is

*Affirmed.*

## 283 The Great Ends of the First Amendment (1961)

The Internal Security (McCarran) Act of 1950 authorized the Subversive Activities Control Board to order any organization it deemed "Communist-action" or "Communist-front" to register with the board. Each day that an organization failed to register counted as a separate violation.

After the board ordered the Communist party to register, the party challenged the constitutionality of the act, and an extensive litigation process began. The Supreme Court rendered the final decision in 1961. In *Communist Party* it held that the act's disclosure requirement did not violate the First Amendment and that "Congressional power to regulate Communist organizations was extensive where legislative findings indicated the existence of a 'world wide integrated movement, whose objective is to destroy the Government itself.' " This did not bring an end to the controversy. Party officers continued to claim that the Fifth Amendment protected them against forced registration and disclosure of their association with the Party. This argument finally prevailed, four years later, in *Albertson v. Subversive Activities Control Board.*

☆ 283 *Communist Party of the United States v. Subversive Activities Control Board*

367 U.S. 1 (1961).

Mr. Justice FRANKFURTER delivered the opinion of the Court.

\*         \*         \*

### V

The constitutional contentions raised by the Party with respect to the registration requirement of § 7 are (A) that that requirement, in the context of the Act, in effect "outlaws" the Party and is in the nature of a bill of attainder; (B) that compelling organizations to register and to list their members on a showing merely that they are foreign-dominated and operate primarily to advance the objectives of the world Communist movement constitutes a restraint on freedom of expression and association in violation of the First Amendment; (C) that requiring Party officers to file registration statements for the Party subjects them to self-incrimination forbidden by the Fifth Amendment; (D) that the Act violates due process by legislative predetermination of facts essential to bring the Communist Party within the definitions of a Communist-action organization, and that the evidentiary elements prescribed for consideration by the Board bear no rational relation to that definition; (E) that in several aspects the Act is unconstitutionally vague; and (F) that the Subversive

Activities Control Board is so necessarily biased against the Communist Party as to deprive it of a fair hearing.

A. *"Outlawry" and Attainder....* The registration requirement, the Party contends, was designed not with the purpose of having Communist-action organizations register, but with a purpose to make it impossible to register, because of the onerous consequences of registration, and thus to establish a pretext for criminal prosecution of the organization and its members. The Act is said to be aimed particularly at the Communist Party as an identifiable entity, intending to punish it, and in this aspect to constitute a bill of attainder prohibited by Art. I, § 9, cl. 3 of the Constitution.

... None of the consequences which attach to registration, whatever may be their validity when weighed separately in the constitutional balance, is so devoid of rational relation to the purposes of the Act as expressed in its second section that it appears a mere pressuring device meant to catch an organization between two fires.

*          *          *

... The true and sole question before us is whether the effects of the statute as it was passed and as it operates are constitutionally permissible.

The Act is not a bill of attainder. It attaches not to specified organizations but to described activities in which an organization may or may not engage. The singling out of an individual for legislatively prescribed punishment constitutes an attainder whether the individual is called by name or described in terms of conduct which, because it is past conduct, operates only as a designation of particular persons....

*          *          *

Nor is the statute made an act of "outlawry" or of attainder by the fact that the conduct which it regulates is described with such particularity that, in probability, few organizations will come within the statutory terms. Legislatures may act to curb behavior which they regard as harmful to the public welfare, whether that conduct is found to be engaged in by many persons or by one. So long as the incidence of legislation is such that the persons who engage in the regulated conduct, be they many or few, can escape regulation merely by altering the course of their own present activities, there can be no complaint of an attainder....

B. *The Freedoms of Expression and Association Protected by the First Amendment.* The Communist Party would have us hold that the First Amendment prohibits Congress from requiring the registration and filing of information, including membership lists, by organizations substantially dominated or controlled by the foreign powers controlling the world Communist movement and which operate primarily to advance the objectives of that movement: the overthrow of existing government by any means necessary and the establishment in its place of a Communist totalitarian dictatorship (§§ 3(3), 2(1) and (6)). We cannot find such a prohibition in the First Amendment. So to find would make a travesty of that Amendment and the great ends for the well-being of our democracy that it serves.

*          *          *

These considerations lead us to sustain the registration provisions of § 7, as not repugnant to the First Amendment, insofar as they require Communist-action organizations to file a registration statement containing the names and addresses of its present officers and members. The requirement that persons who were officers or members at any time during the year preceding registration must be listed, see § 7(d)(2), (4), is a reasonable means of assuring that the obligation to list present members and officers will not be evaded. For reasons which do not require elaboration, the requirement that a registering organization list the aliasas of officers and members, see § 7(d)(5), must also be sustained. Nor do we find that § 7(d)(3), requiring a financial accounting, or § 7(d)(6), requiring a listing of all printing presses in the possession or control of the organization or its members, violates First Amendment rights. Disclosure both of the financial transactions of a Communist-action organization and of the identity of the organs of publication which it controls might not unreasonably have been regarded by Congress as necessary to the objective which the Act seeks to achieve: to bring foreign-dominated organizations out into the open where the public can evaluate their activities informedly against the revealed background of their character, nature, and connections. Of course, printing presses may not be regulated like guns. That generalization gets us nowhere. On the concrete, specific issue before us, we hold that the obligation to give information identifying presses, without more and as applied to foreign-dominated organizations, does not fetter constitutionally protected free expression....

It is argued that if Congress may constitutionally enact legislation requiring the Communist Party to register, to list its members, to file financial statements, and to identify its printing presses, Congress may impose similar requirements upon any group which pursues unpopular political objectives or which expresses an unpopular political ideology. Nothing which we decide here remotely carries such an implication. The Subversive Activities Control Act applies only to *foreign-dominated* organizations which work primarily to advance the objectives of a world movement controlled by the government of a *foreign* country.

C. *Self-incrimination of the Party's Officers.* Section 7(a) and (c) requires that organizations determined to be Communist-action organizations by the Subversive Activities Control Board register within thirty days after the Board's registration order becomes final.... The Party contends that these requirements cannot be imposed and exacted consistently with the Self-incrimination Clause of the Fifth Amendment. Officers of the Party, it is argued, are compelled, in the very act of filing a signed registration statement, to admit that they *are* Party officers—an admission which we have held incriminating....

\* \* \*

We find that the self-incrimination challenge to § 7 ... is ... premature at this time. The privilege against self-incrimination is one which normally must be claimed by the individual who seeks to avail himself of its protection....

\* \* \*

The other constitutional questions raised by the Party have been carefully considered, but do not call for detailed discussion. And we must decline, of course, to enter into discussion of the wisdom of this legislation. The Constitution does not prohibit the requirement that the Communist Party register with the Attorney General as a Communist-action organization pursuant to § 7.

The judgment of the Court of Appeals is affirmed.

*Affirmed.*

## 284 "membership, when it constitutes a purposeful form of complicity" (1961)

The last prosecution under the Smith Act to reach the Supreme Court is reported in *Scales v. United States.* In *Dennis* and the earlier cases under the Smith Act, the government had prosecuted conspiracies to advocate the overthrow of the government. The stringent evidentiary requirements of *Yates,* in 1957, moved the government to use a different provision, one making it a crime to be a member of a proscribed organization.

Junius Scales was tried and convicted under the prohibition against Communist party membership. Although upholding the conviction, Justice Harlan, writing for the majority, imposed a demanding "scienter" requirement, continuing the trend of imposing strict procedural requirements upon anti-Communist prosecutions. There must be clear proof, said the court, that the defendant intended to accomplish the organization's aims by resort to violence. Sentenced to six years in prison, Scales was granted clemency the next year. The stringency of the

*Scales* requirements, together with declining interest in the "Communist threat," put an end to Smith Act prosecutions, but the act has not been repealed.

## ☆ 284 *Scales v. United States*

367 U.S. 203 (1961).

MR. JUSTICE HARLAN delivered the opinion of the Court.

\* \* \*

The validity of this conviction is challenged on ... constitutional [grounds].... We decide the issues raised upon the fullest consideration, the case having had an unusually long history in this Court. For reasons given in this opinion we affirm the Court of Appeals.

\* \* \*

The constitutional attack upon the membership clause, as thus construed, is that the statute offends (1) the Fifth Amendment, in that it impermissibly imputes guilt to an individual merely on the basis of his associations and sympathies, rather than because of some concrete personal involvement in criminal conduct; and (2) the First Amendment, in that it infringes on free political expression and association. Subsidiarily, it is argued that the statute cannot be interpreted as including a requirement of a specific intent to accomplish violent overthrow, or as requiring that membership in a proscribed organization must be "active" membership, in the absence of both or either of which it is said the statute becomes *a fortiori* unconstitutional. It is further contended that even if the adjective "active" may properly be implied as a qualification upon the term "member," petitioner's conviction would nonetheless be unconstitutional, because so construed the statute would be impermissibly vague under the Fifth and Sixth Amendments, and so applied would in any event infringe the Sixth Amendment, in that the indictment charged only that Scales was a "member," not an "active" member, of the Communist Party.

\* \* \*

In our jurisprudence guilt is personal, and when the imposition of punishment on a status or on conduct can only be justified by reference to the relationship of that status or conduct to other concededly criminal activity (here advocacy of violent overthrow), that relationship must be sufficiently substantial to satisfy the concept of personal guilt in order to withstand attack under the Due Process Clause of the Fifth Amendment. Membership, without more, in an organization engaged in illegal advocacy, it is now said, has not heretofore been recognized by this Court to be such a relationship. This claim stands, and we shall examine it, independently of the claim made under the First Amendment.

Any thought that due process puts beyond the reach of the criminal law all individual associational relationships, unless accompanied by the commission of specific acts of criminality, is dispelled by familiar concepts of the law of conspiracy and complicity. While both are commonplace in the landscape of the criminal law, they are not natural features. Rather they are particular legal concepts manifesting the more general principle that society, having the power to punish dangerous behavior, cannot be powerless against those who work to bring about that behavior. The fact that Congress has not resorted to either of these familiar concepts means only that the enquiry here must direct itself to an analysis of the relationship between the fact of membership and the underlying substantive illegal conduct, in order to determine whether that relationship is indeed too tenuous to permit its use as the basis of criminal liability. In this instance it is an organization which engages in criminal activity, and we can perceive no reason why one who actively and knowingly works in the ranks of that organization, intending to contribute to the success of those specifically illegal activities, should be any more immune from prosecution than he to whom the organization has assigned the task of carrying out the substantive criminal act. Nor should the fact that Congress has focussed here on "membership," the characteristic relationship between an individual and the type of conspiratorial quasi-political associations with the criminal aspect of whose activities Congress was concerned, of itself require the conclusion that the legislature has traveled outside the familiar and permissible bounds of criminal imputability. In truth, the specificity of the proscribed relationship is not necessarily a vice; it provides instruction and warning.

What must be met, then, is the argument that membership, even when accompanied by the elements of knowledge and specific intent, affords an insufficient quantum of participation in the organization's alleged criminal activity, that is, an insufficiently significant form of aid and encouragement to permit the imposition of criminal sanctions on that basis. It must indeed be recognized that a person who merely becomes a member of an illegal organization, by that "act" alone need be doing nothing more than signifying his assent to its purposes and activities on one hand, and providing, on the other, only the sort of moral encouragement which comes from the knowledge that others believe in what the organization is doing. It may indeed be argued that such assent and encouragement do fall short of the concrete, practical impetus given to a criminal enterprise which is lent for instance by a commitment on the part of a conspirator to act in furtherance of that enterprise. A member, as distinguished from a conspirator, may indicate his approval of a criminal enterprise by the very fact of his membership without thereby necessarily committing himself to further it by any act or course of conduct whatever.

In an area of the criminal law which this Court has indicated more than once demands its watchful scrutiny, these factors have weight and must be found to be overborne in a total constitutional assessment of the statute. We think, however, they are duly met when the statute is found to reach only "active" members having also a guilty knowledge and intent, and which therefore prevents a conviction on what otherwise might be regarded as merely an expression of sympathy with the alleged criminal enterprise, unaccompanied by any significant action in its support or any commitment to undertake such action.

Thus, given the construction of the membership clause already discussed, we think the factors called for in rendering members criminally responsible for the illegal advocacy of the organization fall within established, and therefore presumably constitutional, standards of criminal imputability.

### 3. FIRST AMENDMENT

Little remains to be said concerning the claim that the statute infringes First Amendment freedoms. It was settled in *Dennis* that the advocacy with which we are here concerned is not constitutionally protected speech, and it was further established that a combination to promote such advocacy, albeit under the aegis of what purports to be a political party, is not such association as is protected by the First Amendment. We can discern no reason why membership, when it constitutes a purposeful form of complicity in a group engaging in this same forbidden advocacy, should receive any greater degree of protection from the guarantees of that Amendment.

\*        \*        \*

The judgment of the Court of Appeals must be *Affirmed.*

## 285 "[an] overriding and compelling state interest" (1963)

Given the wide range of power recognized in *Uphaus* and *Barenblatt*, the technique of exposure through legislative investigation seemed unlimited. Both social ostracism and economic reprisal were the products of such investigations. In 1956, the Florida legislature began an investigation of the NAACP. In 1959, the investigating committee ordered Gibson, president of the Miami branch of the

NAACP, to bring membership records to the committee to assist in answering questions concerning certain individuals. When he refused to divulge the identity of members on First Amendment grounds, he was cited for contempt and convicted.

The United States Supreme Court reversed. Although reaffirming "the legislative right to investigate" in cases involving subversive activities, the court held that the state must first demonstrate a "substantial relation between the information sought and [an] overriding and compelling state interest." The opinion of the Supreme Court, distinguishing *Uphaus* and *Barenblatt*, marked a substantial departure from the previous acceptance of the legislative determination of investigative need. A decline in the numbers of legislative investigations followed *Gibson*.

☆285 *Gibson v. Florida*

372 U.S. 539 (1963).

MR. JUSTICE GOLDBERG delivered the opinion of the Court.

\*       \*       \*

... Prior to interrogation of any witnesses the Committee chairman read the text of the statute creating the Committee and declared that the hearings would be "concerned with the activities of various organizations which have been or are presently operating in this State in the fields of, first, race relations; second, the coercive reform of social and educational practices and mores by litigation and pressured administrative action; third, of labor; fourth, of education; fifth, and other vital phases of life in this State." The chairman also stated that the inquiry would be directed to Communists and Communist activities, including infiltration of Communists into organizations operating in the described fields.

\*       \*       \*

I

We are here called upon once again to resolve a conflict between individual rights of free speech and association and governmental interest in conducting legislative investigations. . . .

\*       \*       \*

The First and Fourteenth Amendment rights of free speech and free association are fundamental and highly prized, and "need breathing space to survive." . . .

At the same time, however, this Court's prior holdings demonstrate that there can be no question that the State has power adequately to inform itself—through legislative investigation, if it so desires—in order to act and protect its legitimate and vital interests. . . . When, as in this case, the claim is made that particular legislative inquiries and de-

mands infringe substantially upon First and Fourteenth Amendment associational rights of individuals, the courts are called upon to, and must, determine the permissibility of the challenged actions, "[T]he delicate and difficult task falls upon the courts to weigh the circumstances and to appraise the substantiality of the reasons advanced in support of the regulation of the free enjoyment of the rights." . . . The interests here at stake are of significant magnitude, and neither their resolution nor impact is limited to, or dependent upon, the particular parties here involved. Freedom and viable government are both, for this purpose, indivisible concepts; whatever affects the rights of the parties here, affects all.

II

. . . [I]t is an essential prerequisite to the validity of an investigation which intrudes into the area of constitutionally protected rights of speech, press, association and petition that the State convincingly show a substantial relation between the information sought and a subject of overriding and compelling state interest. Absent such a relation between the N.A.A.C.P. and conduct in which the State may have a compelling regulatory concern, the Committee has not "demonstrated so cogent an interest in obtaining and making public" the membership information sought to be obtained as to "justify the substantial abridgment of associational freedom which such disclosures will effect. Where there is a significant encroachment upon personal liberty, the State may prevail only upon showing a subordinating interest which is compelling."

Applying these principles to the facts of this case, the respondent Committee contends that the prior decisions of this Court in *Uphaus v. Wyman*, *Barenblatt v. United States*, *Wilkinson v. United States*, and *Braden v. United States* compel a result here upholding the legislative right of inquiry. In *Barenblatt*, *Wilkinson*, and *Braden*, however, it was a refusal to answer a question or questions concerning the witness' *own* past or present membership *in the Communist Party* which supported his conviction. It is apparent that the necessary preponderating governmental interest and, in fact, the very result in those cases were founded on the holding that the Communist Party is not an ordinary or legitimate political party, as known in this country, and that, because of its particular nature, membership therein is *itself* a permissible subject of regulation and legislative scrutiny. Assuming the correctness of the premises on which those cases were decided, no further demonstration of compelling governmental interest was deemed necessary, since the direct object of the challenged questions there was discovery of membership in the Communist Party, a matter held pertinent to a proper subject then under inquiry.

Here, however, it is not alleged Communists who are the witnesses before the Committee and it is not discovery of their membership in that party which is the object of the challenged inquiries. Rather, it is the N.A.A.C.P. itself which is the subject of the investigation, and it is its local president, the petitioner, who was called before the Committee and held in contempt because he refused to divulge the contents of its membership records. There is no suggestion that the Miami branch of the N.A.A.C.P. or the national organization with which it is affiliated was, or is, itself a subversive organization. Nor is there any indication that the activities or policies of the N.A.A.C.P. were either Communist dominated or influenced. . . .

Thus, unlike the situation in *Barenblatt, Wilkinson* and *Braden*, the Committee was not here seeking from the petitioner or the records of which he was custodian any information as to whether he, himself, or even other persons were members of the Communist Party, Communist front or affiliated organizations, or other allegedly subversive groups; instead, the entire thrust of the demands on the petitioner was that he disclose whether other persons were members of the N.A.A.C.P., itself a concededly legitimate and nonsubversive organization. Compelling such an organization, engaged in the exercise of First and Fourteenth Amendment rights, to disclose its membership presents, under our cases, a question wholly different from compelling the Communist Party to disclose its own membership. . . . The prior holdings that governmental interest in controlling subversion and the particular character of the Communist Party and its objectives outweigh the right of individual Communists to conceal party membership or affiliations by no means require the wholly different conclusion that other groups—concededly legitimate—automatically forfeit their rights to privacy of association simply because the general subject matter of the legislative inquiry is Communist subversion or infiltration. . . .

Respondent's reliance on *Uphaus v. Wyman* as controlling is similarly misplaced. . . . In *Uphaus* this Court found that there was demonstrated a sufficient connection between subversive activity—held there to be a proper subject of governmental concern—and the World Fellowship, itself, to justify discovery of the guest list; no semblance of such a nexus between the N.A.A.C.P. and subversive *activities* has been shown here. . . . [I]n *Uphaus*, the State was investigating whether subversive persons were within its boundaries and whether their presence constituted a threat to the State. No such purpose or need is evident here. The Florida Committee is not seeking to identify subversives by questioning the

petitioner; apparently it is satisfied that it already knows who they are.

### III

In the absence of directly determinative authority, we turn, then, to consideration of the facts now before us. Obviously, if the respondent were still seeking discovery of the entire membership list, we could readily dispose of this case . . . ; a like result would follow if it were merely attempting to do piecemeal what could not be done in a single step. Though there are indications that the respondent Committee intended to inquire broadly into the N.A.A.C.P. membership records, there is no need to base our decision today upon a prediction as to the course which the Committee might have pursued if initially unopposed by the petitioner. Instead, we rest our result on the fact that the record in this case is insufficient to show a substantial connection between the Miami branch of the N.A.A.C.P. and Communist *activities* which the respondent Committee itself concedes is an essential prerequisite to demonstrating the immediate, substantial, and subordinating state interest necessary to sustain its right of inquiry into the membership lists of the association.

\*          \*          \*

This summary of the evidence discloses the utter failure to demonstrate the existence of any substantial relationship between the N.A.A.C.P. and subversive or Communist activities. In essence, there is here merely indirect, less than unequivocal, and mostly hearsay testimony that in years past some 14 people who were asserted to be, or to have been, Communists or members of Communist front or "affiliated organizations" attended occasional meetings of the Miami branch of the N.A.A.C.P. "and/or" were members of that branch, which had a total membership of about 1,000.

. . . [I]n short without any showing of a meaningful relationship between the N.A.A.C.P., Miami branch, and subversives or subversive or other illegal activities—we are asked to find the compelling and subordinating state interest which must exist if essential freedoms are to be curtailed or inhibited. This we cannot do. The respondent Committee has laid no adequate foundation for its direct demands upon the officers and records of a wholly legitimate organization for disclosure of its membership. . . .

\*          \*          \*

Nothing we say here impairs or denies the existence of the underlying legislative right to investigate or legislate with respect to subversive activities by Communists or anyone else; our decision today deals only with the manner in which such power may be exercised and we hold simply that groups which themselves are neither engaged in subversive or other illegal or improper activities nor demonstrated to have any substantial connections with such activities are to be protected in their rights of free and private association. . . .

\*          \*          \*

The judgment below must be and is

*Reversed.*

MR. JUSTICE BLACK, concurring.

. . . In my view the constitutional right of association includes the privilege of any person to associate with Communists or anti-Communists, Socialists or anti-Socialists, or, for that matter, with people of all kinds of beliefs, popular or unpopular. . . .

\*          \*          \*

## 286   " 'by . . . example promote respect for the flag' " (1964)

Noting the need for academic freedom and "uninhibited critical inquiry," Justice Frankfurter, in *Wieman v. Updegraff,* struck down Oklahoma's use of loyalty oaths, which penalized innocent as well as knowing membership in subversive organizations. In *Sweezy* and also in *Barenblatt,* the Supreme Court had shown some regard for academic freedom with respect to legislative investigations. But in *Garner, Adler,* and *Beilan,* the court generally had upheld loyalty oaths as a condition of government employment.

Nevertheless, without disturbing this line of cases, the Supreme Court in *Baggett* utilized a different constitutional limitation to invalidate Washington State's loyalty oath. Although the court again did not challenge the fundamental premise that oath requirements were permissible, it was sensitive to the need to protect First Amendment principles.

Later, in *Elfbrandt v. Russell,* 384 U.S. 11 (1966), the court exhibited this new sensitivity by invalidating an oath because it did not require the individual to have subscribed personally to the unlawful ends of the organization. Thus, the *Scales* requirement of specific intent to accomplish the illegal aims of the organization, held to be necessary for a conviction under the Smith Act, was incorporated into the law of loyalty oaths. Finally, in *Keyishian v. Board of Regents,* 385 U.S. 589 (1967), the court struck down, on the grounds of vagueness, the Feinberg Law, which it had upheld fifteen years earlier in *Adler.*

☆286   *Baggett v. Bullitt*

377 U.S. 360 (1964).

MR. JUSTICE WHITE delivered the opinion of the Court.

Appellants, approximately 64 in number, are members of the faculty, staff and student body of the University of Washington. . . . The 1931 legislation applies only to teachers, who, upon applying for a license to teach or renewing an existing contract, are required to subscribe to the following:

> I solemnly swear (or affirm) that I will support the constitution and laws of the United States of America and of the State of Washington, and will by precept and example, promote respect for the flag and the institutions of the United States of America and the State of Washington, reverence for law and order and undivided allegiance to the government of the United States.

The oath requirements of the 1955 Act, applicable to all state employees, incorporate various provisions of the Washington Subversive Activities Act of 1951. . . .

. . . Oath Form A requires all [University] teaching personnel to swear to the oath of allegiance set out above, to aver that they have read, are familiar with and understand the provisions defining "subversive person" in the Subversive Activities Act of 1951 and to disclaim being a subversive person and membership in the Communist Party or any other subversive or foreign subversive organization. Oath Form B requires other state [University] employees to subscribe to all of the above provisions except the 1931 oath. Both forms provide that the oath and statements pertinent thereto are made subject to the penalties of perjury.

\*          \*          \*

I

Appellants contend in this Court that the oath requirements and the statutory provisions on which they are based are invalid on their face because their language is unduly vague, uncertain and broad. We agree with this contention and therefore, without reaching the numerous other contentions pressed upon us, confine our considerations to that particular question.

In *Cramp v. Board of Public Instruction,* the Court invalidated an oath requiring teachers and other employees of the State to swear that they had never lent their "aid, support, advice, counsel or influence to the Communist Party" because the oath was lacking in "terms susceptible of objective measurement" and failed to inform as to what the State commanded or forbade. The statute therefore fell within the compass of those decisions of the Court holding that a law forbidding or requiring conduct in terms so vague that men of common intelligence must necessarily guess at its meaning and differ as to its application violates due process of law.

The oath required by the 1955 statute suffers from similar infirmities. A teacher must swear that he is not a subversive person: that he is not one who commits an act or who advises, teaches, abets or advocates by any means another person to commit or aid in the commission of any act intended to overthrow or alter, or to assist the overthrow or alteration, of the constitutional form of government by revolution, force or violence.... The Communist Party is declared in the statute to be a subversive organization, that is, it is presumed that the Party does and will engage in activities intended to overthrow the Government. Persons required to swear they understand this oath may quite reasonably conclude that any person who aids the Communist Party or teaches or advises known members of the Party is a subversive person because such teaching or advice may now or at some future date aid the activities of the Party. Teaching and advising are clearly acts, and one cannot confidently assert that his counsel, aid, influence or support which adds to the resources, rights and knowledge of the Communist Party or its members does not aid the Party in its activities, activities which the statute tells us are all in furtherance of the stated purpose of overthrowing the Government by revolution, force, or violence. The questions put by the Court in *Cramp* may with equal force be asked here. Does the statute reach endorsement or support for Communist candidates for office? Does it reach a lawyer who represents the Communist Party or its members or a journalist who defends constitutional rights of the Communist Party or its members or anyone who supports any cause which is likewise supported by Communists or the Communist Party? The susceptibility of the statutory language to require forswearing of an undefined variety of "guiltless knowing behavior" is what the Court condemned in *Cramp*. This statute, like the one at issue in *Cramp*, is unconstitutionally vague.

The Washington statute suffers from additional difficulties on vagueness grounds. A person is subversive not only if he himself commits the specified acts but if he abets or advises another in aiding a third person to commit an act which will assist yet a fourth person in the overthrow or alteration of constitutional government.... Is it subversive activity [therefore] to attend and participate in international conventions of mathematicians and exchange views with scholars from Communist countries? What about the editor of a scholarly journal who analyzes and criticizes the manuscripts of Communist scholars submitted for publication? Is selecting outstanding scholars from Communist countries as visiting professors and advising, teaching, or consulting with them at the University of Washington a subversive activity if such scholars are known to be Communists, or regardless of their affiliations, regularly teach students who are members of the Communist Party, which by statutory definition is subversive and dedicated to the overthrow of the Government?

The Washington oath goes beyond overthrow or alteration by force or violence. It extends to alteration by "revolution" which, unless wholly redundant and its ordinary meaning distorted, includes any rapid or fundamental change. Would, therefore, any organization or any person supporting, advocating or teaching peaceful but far-reaching constitutional amendments be engaged in subversive activity? Could one support the repeal of the Twenty-second Amendment or participation by this country in a world government?

## II

We also conclude that the 1931 oath offends due process because of vagueness. The oath exacts a promise that the affiant will, by precept and example, promote respect for the flag and the institutions of the United States and the State of Washington. The range of activities which are or might be deemed inconsistent with the required promise is very wide indeed. The teacher who refused to salute the flag or advocated refusal because of religious beliefs might well be accused of breaching his promise. Even criticism of the design or color scheme of the state flag or unfavorable comparison of it with that of a sister State or foreign country could be deemed disrespectful and therefore violative of the oath. And what are "institutions" for the purposes of this oath? Is it every "practice, law, custom, etc., which is a material and persistent element in the life or culture of an organized social group" or every "established society or corporation," every "establishment, esp[ecially] one of a public character"? The oath may prevent a professor from criticizing his state judicial system or the Supreme Court or the institution of judicial review. Or it might be deemed to proscribe advocating the abolition, for example, of the Civil Rights Commission, the House Committee on Un-American Activities, or foreign aid.

It is likewise difficult to ascertain what might be done without transgressing the promise to "promote ... undivided allegiance to the government of the United States." It would not be unreasonable for the serious-minded oathtaker to conclude that he should dispense with lectures voicing far-reaching criticism of any old or new policy followed by the Government of the United States. He could find it questionable under this language to ally himself with any interest group dedicated to opposing any current public policy or law of the Federal Government, for if he did, he might well be accused of placing loyalty to the group above allegiance to the United States.

Indulging every presumption of a narrow construction of the provisions of the 1931 oath, consistent, however, with a proper respect for the English language, we cannot say that this oath provides an ascertainable standard of conduct or that it does not require more than a State may command under the guarantees of the First and Fourteenth Amendments.

... We are dealing with indefinite statutes whose terms, even narrowly construed, abut upon sensitive areas of basic First Amendment freedoms.... Those with a conscientious regard for what they solemnly swear or affirm, sensitive to the perils posed by the oath's indefinite language, avoid the risk of loss of employment, and perhaps profession, only by restricting their conduct to that which is unquestionably safe. Free speech may not be so inhibited.

### III

\*         \*         \*

It will not do to say that a prosecutor's sense of fairness and the Constitution would prevent a successful perjury prosecution for some of the activities seemingly embraced within the sweeping statutory definitions. The hazard of being prosecuted for knowing but guiltless behavior nevertheless remains. "It would be blinking reality not to acknowledge that there are some among us always ready to affix a Communist label upon those whose ideas they violently oppose. And experience teaches us that prosecutors too are human." Well-intentioned prosecutors and judicial safeguards do not neutralize the vice of a vague law. Nor should we encourage the casual taking of oaths by upholding the discharge or exclusion from public employment of those with a conscientious and scrupulous regard for such undertakings.

\*         \*         \*

### V

As in *Cramp v. Board of Public Instruction* we do not question the power of a State to take proper measures safeguarding the public service from disloyal conduct. But measures which purport to define disloyalty must allow public servants to know what is and is not disloyal. "The fact ... that a person is not compelled to hold public office cannot possibly be an excuse for barring him from office by state-imposed criteria forbidden by the Constitution."

*Reversed.*

## 287  Travel Is a Constitutional Liberty (1964)

After the Supreme Court, in *Kent v. Dulles*, curtailed the State Department's discretionary authority to deny passports for ideological reasons, the government invoked the Internal Security Act of 1950 to restrict the travel of those labeled subversive. Section 6 of the act made it a crime for a member of a Communist organization to apply for or use a passport. In *Aptheker v. Secretary of State*, the Supreme Court considered the constitutionality of the provision. Noting that the right to travel was a constitutional liberty closely related to the rights of free speech and association embodied in the First Amendment, the holding of the court, nevertheless, explicitly relied on the due process clause of the Fifth Amendment rather than the associational rights protected under the First Amendment. Despite the language concerning the importance of the associational rights, the court suggested that a more narrowly-tailored statute could survive constitutional scrutiny.

## ☆ 287  *Aptheker v. Secretary of State*

378 U.S. 500 (1964).

MR. JUSTICE GOLDBERG delivered the opinion of the Court.

\*         \*         \*

Section 6 became effective, with respect to appellants, on October 20, 1961, when a final order of the Subversive Activities Control Board issued directing the Communist Party of the United States to register under § 7 of the Subversive Activities Control Act. The registration order had been upheld earlier in 1961 by this Court's decision in *Communist Party of the United States v. Subversive Activities Control Board*. Prior to issuance of the final registration order both appellants, who are native-born citizens and residents of the United States, had held valid passports. Subsequently, on January 22, 1962, the Acting Director of the Passport Office notified appellants that their passports were revoked because the Department of State believed that their use of the passports would violate § 6....

\*         \*         \*

... Each appellant-plaintiff [has] alleged that § 6 was unconstitutional as, *inter alia*, "a deprivation without due process of law of plaintiff's constitutional liberty to travel abroad, in violation of the Fifth Amendment to the Constitution of the United States." Appellants conceded that the Secretary of State had an adequate basis for finding that they were members of the Communist Party of the United States and that the action revoking their passports was proper if § 6 was constitutional....

\*         \*         \*

... The Government, while conceding that the right to travel is protected by the Fifth Amendment, contends that the Due Process Clause does not prevent the reasonable regulation of liberty and that § 6 is a reasonable regulation because of its relation to the danger the world Communist movement presents for our national security....

We hold, for the reasons stated below, that § 6 of the Control Act too broadly and indiscriminately restricts the right to travel and thereby abridges the liberty guaranteed by the Fifth Amendment.

I

\* \* \*

... The restrictive effect of the legislation cannot be gainsaid by emphasizing, as the Government seems to do, that a member of a registering organization could recapture his freedom to travel by simply in good faith abandoning his membership in the organization. Since freedom of association is itself guaranteed in the First Amendment, restrictions imposed upon the right to travel cannot be dismissed by asserting that the right to travel could be fully exercised if the individual would first yield up his membership in a given association.

\* \* \*

Section 6 provides that any member of a Communist organization which has registered or has been ordered to register commits a crime if he attempts to use or obtain a United States passport. The section applies to members who act "with knowledge or notice" that the organization is under a final registration order. "Notice" is specifically defined in § 13(k). That section provides that publication in the Federal Register of the fact of registration or of issuance of a final registration order "shall constitute notice to all members of such organization that such order has become final." Thus the terms of § 6 apply whether or not the member actually knows or believes that he is associated with what is deemed to be a "Communist-action" or a "Communist-front" organization. The section also applies whether or not one knows or believes that he is associated with an organization operating to further aims of the world Communist movement and "to establish a Communist totalitarian dictatorship in the countries throughout the world...." The provision therefore sweeps within its prohibition both knowing and unknowing members.... In *Wieman v. Updegraff* the Court held that the due process guarantee of the Constitution was violated when a State, in an attempt to bar disloyal individuals from its employ, excluded persons solely on the basis of organizational memberships without regard to their knowledge concerning the organizations to which they had belonged. The Court concluded that: "Indiscriminate classification of innocent with knowing activity must fall as an assertion of arbitrary power."

Section 6 also renders irrelevant the member's degree of activity in the organization and his commitment to its purpose. These factors, like knowledge, would bear on the likelihood that travel by such a person would be attended by the type of activity which Congress sought to control. As the Court has elsewhere noted, "men in adhering to a political party or other organization notoriously do not subscribe unqualifiedly to all of its platforms or asserted principles." ...

... In determining whether there has been an abridgment of the Fifth Amendment's guarantee of liberty, this Court must recognize the danger of punishing a member of a Communist organization "for his adherence to lawful and constitutionally protected purposes, because of other and unprotected purposes which he does not necessarily share."

In determining the constitutionality of § 6, it is also important to consider that Congress has within its power "less drastic" means of achieving the congressional objective of safeguarding our national security....

In our view the foregoing considerations compel the conclusion that § 6 of the Control Act is unconstitutional on its face. The section, judged by its plain import and by the substantive evil which Congress sought to control, sweeps too widely and too indiscriminately across the liberty guaranteed in the Fifth Amendment. The prohibition against travel is supported only by a tenuous relationship between the bare fact of organizational membership and the activity Congress sought to proscribe. The broad and enveloping prohibition indiscriminately excludes plainly relevant considerations such as the individual's knowledge, activity, commitment, and purposes in and places for travel. The section therefore is patently not a regulation "narrowly drawn to prevent the supposed evil," yet here, as elsewhere, precision must be the touchstone of legislation so affecting basic freedoms.

\* \* \*

Accordingly the judgment of the three-judge District Court is reversed and the cause remanded for proceedings in conformity with this opinion.

*Reversed and remanded.*

## 288 "the weightiest considerations of national security" (1965)

Although the government's power to refuse a passport to a citizen because of his or her political associations was repudiated in *Kent* and *Aptheker*, the State Department continued to claim the power to restrict travel. After the Cuban revolution, the State Department denied Arthur Zemel a passport to Cuba, and the department's refusal brought the practice of "area restrictions" before the Supreme Court. The limits of the *Kent* and *Aptheker* decisions became apparent as the Supreme Court upheld these area restrictions despite their effect on the dissemination of information regarding important international political developments.

☆ 288 *Zemel v. Rusk*

381 U.S. 1 (1965).

MR. CHIEF JUSTICE WARREN delivered the opinion of the Court.

The questions for decision are whether the Secretary of State is statutorily authorized to refuse to validate the passports of United States citizens for travel to Cuba, and, if he is, whether the exercise of that authority is constitutionally permissible. We answer both questions in the affirmative.

\*      \*      \*

## II

We think that the Passport Act of 1926 embodies a grant of authority to the Executive to refuse to validate the passports of United States citizens for travel to Cuba. . . .

\*      \*      \*

. . . It must be remembered . . . that the issue involved in *Kent* was whether a citizen could be denied a passport because of his political beliefs or associations. In finding that history did not support the position of the Secretary in that case, we summarized that history "so far as material here" — that is, so far as material to passport refusals based on the character of the particular applicant. In this case, however, the Secretary has refused to validate appellant's passport not because of any characteristic peculiar to appellant, but rather because of foreign policy considerations affecting all citizens.

## III

. . . [W]e must next consider whether that refusal abridges any constitutional right of appellant. . . . [W]e must . . . proceed on the assumption that the Secretary's refusal to validate a passport for a given area acts as a deterrent to travel to that area. In *Kent v. Dulles* we held that "[t]he right to travel is a part of the 'liberty' of which the citizen cannot be deprived without due process of law under the Fifth Amendment." However, the fact that a liberty cannot be inhibited without due process of law does not mean that it can under no circumstances be inhibited.

The requirements of due process are a function not only of the extent of the governmental restriction imposed, but also of the extent of the necessity for the restriction. Cuba is the only area in the Western Hemisphere controlled by a Communist government. It is, moreover, the judgment of the State Department that a major goal of the Castro regime is to export its Communist revolution to the rest of Latin America. The United States and other members of the Organization of American States have determined that travel between Cuba and the other countries of the Western Hemisphere is an impor-

tant element in the spreading of subversion, and many have therefore undertaken measures to discourage such travel. . . . [T]he Secretary has justifiably concluded that travel to Cuba by American citizens might involve the Nation in dangerous international incidents, and that the Constitution does not require him to validate passports for such travel.

The right to travel *within* the United States is of course also constitutionally protected. But that freedom does not mean that areas ravaged by flood, fire or pestilence cannot be quarantined when it can be demonstrated that unlimited travel to the area would directly and materially interfere with the safety and welfare of the area or the Nation as a whole. So it is with international travel. That the restriction which is challenged in this case is supported by the weightiest considerations of national security is perhaps best pointed up by recalling that the Cuban missile crisis of October 1962 preceded the filing of appellant's complaint by less than two months.

Appellant also asserts that the Secretary's refusal to validate his passport for travel to Cuba denies him rights guaranteed by the First Amendment. . . . Appellant's allegation is, rather, that the "travel ban is a direct interference with the First Amendment rights of citizens to travel abroad so that they might acquaint themselves at first hand with the effects abroad of our Government's policies, foreign and domestic, and with conditions abroad which might affect such policies." We must agree that the Secretary's refusal to validate passports for Cuba renders less than wholly free the flow of information concerning that country. While we further agree that this is a factor to be considered in determining whether appellant has been denied due process of law, we cannot accept the contention of appellant that it is a First Amendment right which is involved. For to the extent that the Secretary's refusal to validate passports for Cuba acts as an inhibition (and it would be unrealistic to assume that it does not), it is an inhibition of action. There are few restrictions on action which could not be clothed by ingenious argument in the garb of decreased data flow. For example, the prohibition of unauthorized entry into the White House diminishes the citizen's opportunities to gather information he might find relevant to his opinion of the way the country is being run, but that does not make entry into the White House a First Amendment right. The right to speak and publish does not carry with it the unrestrained right to gather information.

Finally, appellant challenges the 1926 Act on the ground that it does not contain sufficiently definite standards for the formulation of travel controls by the Executive. It is important to bear in mind, in appraising this argument, that because of the changeable and explosive nature of contemporary international relations, and the fact that the Executive is immediately privy to information which cannot be swiftly presented to, evaluated by, and acted upon by the legislature, Congress—in giving the Executive authority over matters of foreign affairs—must of necessity paint with a brush broader than that it customarily wields in domestic areas.

*       *       *

*Affirmed.*

MR. JUSTICE DOUGLAS, with whom MR. JUSTICE GOLDBERG concurs, dissenting.

*       *       *

I agree that there are areas to which Congress can restrict or ban travel. Pestilences may rage in a region making it necessary to protect not only the traveler but those he might infect on his return. A theatre of war may be too dangerous for travel. Other like situations can be put. But the only so-called danger present here is the Communist regime in Cuba. The world, however, is filled with Communist thought; and Communist regimes are on more than one continent. They are part of the world spectrum; and if we are to know them and understand them, we must mingle with them, as Pope John said. Keeping alive intellectual intercourse between opposing groups has always been important and perhaps was never more important than now.

The First Amendment presupposes a mature people, not afraid of ideas. The First Amendment leaves no room for the official, whether truculent or benign, to say nay or yea because the ideas offend or please him or because he believes some political objective is served by keeping the citizen at home or letting him go. Yet that is just what the Court's decision today allows to happen. We have here no congressional determination that Cuba is an area from which our national security demands that Americans be excluded. Nor do we have a congressional authorization of the Executive to make such a determination according to standards fixed by Congress. Rather we have only the claim that Congress has painted with such a "broad brush" that the State Department can ban travel to Cuba simply because it is pleased to do so. . . .

*       *       *

# 289 "The risks of incrimination . . . are obvious" (1965)

In the early 1960s, the second Red Scare was in its final stages, and judicial review of legislative and executive efforts to control Communism grew stricter. Although the basic premise of these efforts never was repudiated, the various hedges erected by the courts restricted the latitude of legislative, investigative, prosecutorial, and executive antisubversive programs.

In *Albertson*, two Communist party members ordered to register under the Subversive Activities Control Act of 1950 appealed to the Supreme Court. The court reversed the order on the grounds that compulsory registration violated the Fifth Amendment proscription against self-incrimination. The court pointed out the registration form required an admission of membership in the Communist party and thus made registrants vulnerable to prosecution under the Smith Act and other sections of the McCarran Act.

## ☆ 289 *Albertson v. Subversive Activities Control Board*

382 U.S. 70 (1965).

MR. JUSTICE BRENNAN delivered the opinion of the Court.

*       *       *

### I

Petitioners address several constitutional challenges to the validity of the orders, but we consider only the contention that the orders violate their Fifth Amendment privilege against self-incrimination.

*       *       *

### II

The risks of incrimination which the petitioners take in registering are obvious. Form IS-52a requires an admission of membership in the Communist Party. Such an admission of membership may be used to prosecute the registrant under the membership clause of the Smith Act, or under § 4(a) of the Subversive Activities Control Act, to mention only two federal criminal statutes. Accordingly, we have held that mere association with the Communist Party presents sufficient threat of prosecution to support a claim of privilege. These cases involved questions to witnesses on the witness stand, but if the admission cannot be compelled in oral testimony, we do not see how compulsion in writing makes a difference for constitutional purposes. It follows that the requirement to accomplish registration by completing and filing Form IS-52a is inconsistent with the protection of the Self-incrimination Clause.

*       *       *

### III

Section 4(f) of the Act, the purported immunity provision, does not save the registration orders from petitioners' Fifth Amendment challenge. . . .

[T]he Court [has] held "that no [immunity] statute which leaves the party or witness subject to prosecution after he answers the criminating question put to him, can have the effect of supplanting the privilege ...," and that such a statute is valid only if it supplies "a complete protection from all the perils against which the constitutional prohibition was designed to guard ..." by affording "absolute immunity against future prosecution for the offence to which the question relates." Measured by these standards, the immunity granted by § 4(f) is not complete. It does not preclude any use of the information called for by Form IS-52, either as evidence or as an investigatory lead.

*        *        *

The judgment of the Court of Appeals is reversed and the Board's orders are set aside.

*It is so ordered.*

## 290  The Prevention of Political Strikes (1965)

The constitutionality of Section 504 of the Labor-Management Reporting and Disclosure Act of 1959 (the Landrum-Griffin Act) came under scrutiny after the indictment and conviction of Brown, a member of the executive board of the International Longshoremen's Union's local in San Francisco. Brown had been an open and avowed Communist for over twenty-five years. Section 504 prohibited Communists from occupying such an office, even though no charge existed that Brown had engaged in or advocated any political strike or illegal activity.

In the earlier case of *American Communications Association v. Douds*, the court had sustained a provision of the Taft-Hartley Act withholding the benefits of the National Labor Relations Act from unions whose officers failed to deny Communist party membership. Without overruling that holding, the court distinguished that case and held that Section 504 was unconstitutional.

☆ 290  *United States v. Brown*

381 U.S. 437 (1965).

MR. CHIEF JUSTICE WARREN delivered the opinion of the Court.

... Section 504, the purpose of which is to protect the national economy by minimizing the danger of political strikes, was enacted to replace § 9(h) of the National Labor Relations Act, as amended by the Taft-Hartley Act, which conditioned a union's access to the National Labor Relations Board upon the filing of affidavits by all of the union's officers attesting that they were not members of or affiliated with the Communist Party.

*        *        *

Respondent urges ... that the statute under which he was convicted is a bill of attainder, and therefore violates Art. I, § 9, of the Constitution. We agree that § 504 is void as a bill of attainder and affirm the decision of the Court of Appeals on that basis.

I

The provisions outlawing bills of attainder were adopted by the Constitutional Convention unanimously, and without debate....

... The bill of attainder, a parliamentary act sentencing to death one or more specific persons, was a device often resorted to in sixteenth, seventeenth and eighteenth century England for dealing with persons who had attempted, or threatened to attempt, to overthrow the government. In addition to the death sentence, attainder generally carried with it a "corruption of blood," which meant that the attainted party's heirs could not inherit his property. The "bill of pains and penalties" was identical to the bill of attainder, except that it prescribed a penalty short of death, e.g., banishment, deprivation of the right to vote, or exclusion of the designated party's sons from Parliament. Most bills of attainder and bills of pains and penalties named the parties to whom they were to apply; a few, however, simply described them. While some left the designated parties a way of escaping the penalty, others did not. The use of bills of attainder and bills of pains and penalties was not limited to England. During the American Revolution, the legislatures of all thirteen States passed statutes directed against the Tories; among these statutes were a large number of bills of attainder and bills of pains and penalties.

*        *        *

III

... § 504 of the Labor-Management Reporting and Disclosure Act plainly constitutes a bill of attainder. Congress undoubtedly possesses power under the Commerce Clause to enact legislation designed to keep from positions affecting interstate commerce persons who may use such positions to bring about political strikes. In § 504, however, Congress has exceeded the authority granted it by the Constitution. The statute does not set forth a generally applicable rule decreeing that any person who commits certain acts or possesses certain characteristics (acts and characteristics which, in Congress' view, make them likely to initiate political strikes) shall not hold union office, and leave to courts and juries the job of deciding what persons have committed the specified acts or possess the specified characteristics. Instead, it designates in no uncertain terms the persons who possess the feared characteristics and therefore cannot hold union office without incurring criminal liability—members of the Communist Party.

\* \* \*

[Unlike *Communist Party v. Subversive Activities Control Board*,] in this case no disagreement over whether the statute in question designates a particular organization can arise, for § 504 in terms inflicts its disqualification upon members of the Communist Party. The moment § 504 was enacted, respondent was given the choice of declining a leadership position in his union or incurring criminal liability.

The Solicitor General points out that in *Board of Governors v. Agnew*, this Court applied § 32 of the Banking Act of 1933 [prohibiting securities dealers from holding bank offices]. . . . He suggests that for purposes of the Bill of Attainder Clause, such [financial] conflict-of-interest laws are not meaningfully distinguishable from the statute before us. We find this argument without merit. First, we note that § 504, unlike § 32 of the Banking Act, inflicts its deprivation upon the members of a political group thought to present a threat to the national security. . . . [S]uch groups were the targets of the overwhelming majority of English and early American bills of attainder. Second, § 32 incorporates no judgment censuring or condemning any man or group of men. In enacting it, Congress relied upon its general knowledge of human psychology, and concluded that the concurrent holding of the two designated positions would present a temptation to *any* man—not just certain men or members of a certain political party. Thus insofar as § 32 incorporates a condemnation, it condemns all men. . . .

It is argued, however, that in § 504 Congress [merely] promulgated a general rule to the effect that persons possessing characteristics which make them likely to incite political strikes should not hold union office, and simply inserted in place of a list of those characteristics an alternative, shorthand criterion—membership in the Communist Party. Again, we cannot agree. The designation of Communists as those persons likely to cause political strikes is not the substitution of a semantically equivalent phrase; on the contrary, it rests, as the Court in [*American Communications Assn. v.*] *Douds* explicitly recognized, upon an empirical investigation by Congress of the acts, characteristics and propensities of Communist Party members. In a number of decisions, this Court has pointed out the fallacy of the suggestion that membership in the Communist Party, or any other political organization, can be regarded as an alternative, but equivalent, expression for a list of undesirable characteristics. . . . Even assuming that Congress had reason to conclude that some Communists would use union positions to bring

about political strikes, "it cannot automatically be inferred that all members shar[e] their evil purposes or participat[e] in their illegal conduct." In utilizing the term "members of the Communist Party" to designate those persons who are likely to incite political strikes, it plainly is not the case that Congress has merely substituted a convenient shorthand term for a list of the characteristics it was trying to reach.

## IV

This case is not necessarily controlled by *Douds*. For to prove its assertion that § 9(h) [of the Taft-Hartley Act] was preventive rather than retributive in purpose, the Court in *Douds* focused on the fact that members of the Communist Party could escape from the class of persons specified by Congress simply by resigning from the Party. . . . Section 504, unlike § 9(h), disqualifies from the holding of union office not only present members of the Communist Party, but also anyone who has within the past five years been a member of the Party. However, even if we make the assumption that the five-year provision was inserted not out of desire to visit retribution but purely out of a belief that failure to include it would lead to *pro forma* resignations from the Party which would not decrease the threat of political strikes, it still clearly appears that § 504 inflicts "punishment" within the meaning of the Bill of Attainder Clause. It would be archaic to limit the definition of "punishment" to "retribution." Punishment serves several purposes: retributive, rehabilitative, deterrent—and preventive. One of the reasons society imprisons those convicted of crimes is to keep them from inflicting future harm, but that does not make imprisonment any the less punishment.

Historical considerations by no means compel restriction of the bill of attainder ban to instances of retribution. A number of English bills of attainder were enacted for preventive purposes—that is, the legislature made a judgment, undoubtedly based largely on past acts and associations (as § 504 is) that a given person or group was likely to cause trouble (usually, overthrow the government) and therefore inflicted deprivations upon that person or group in order to keep it from bringing about the feared event. It is also clear that many of the early American bills attainting the Tories were passed in order to impede their effectively resisting the Revolution. . . . Thus Justice Iredell was on solid historical ground when he observed, in *Calder v. Bull*, that "attainders, *on the principle of retaliation and proscription*, have marked all the vicissitudes of party triumph." (Emphasis supplied.)

We think that the Court in *Douds* misread *United States v. Lovett* when it suggested that that case could be distinguished on the ground that the sanction there imposed was levied for purely retributive reasons. In *Lovett* the Court ... concluded that the statute [challenged] was the product of a congressional drive to oust from government persons whose (congressionally determined) "subversive" tendencies made their continued employment dangerous to the national welfare: "the purpose ... clearly was to 'purge' the then existing and all future lists of government employees of those whom Congress deemed guilty of 'subversive activities' and therefore 'unfit' to hold a federal job." Similarly, the purpose of the statute before us is to purge the governing boards of labor unions of those whom Congress regards as guilty of subversive acts and associations and therefore unfit to fill positions which might affect interstate commerce.

*     *     *

We do not hold today that Congress cannot weed dangerous persons out of the labor movement, any more than the Court held in *Lovett* that subversives must be permitted to hold sensitive government positions. Rather, we make again the point made in *Lovett*: that Congress must accomplish such results by rules of general applicability. It cannot specify the people upon whom the sanction it prescribes is to be levied. Under our Constitution, Congress possesses full legislative authority, but the task of adjudication must be left to other tribunals.

*     *     *

The judgment of the Court of Appeals is *Affirmed.*

## 291 Textbooks, Lobbyists, and Summer Camps (1965)

The following excerpts from a 1965 compilation by the Senate Internal Security Subcommittee represent a sampling of the state laws enacted to control the perceived threats of subversion. Unlike the direct federal attack on Communism represented by the Communist Control Act of 1954 and the loyalty programs in federal employment, these state initiatives withheld benefits and privileges from subversives who did not affect, even remotely, national or local security.

The general police power of the states gave the states wider avenues for denial of specific rights, benefits, and privileges—in order to frustrate the operations of subversive groups—than could be accomplished by federal initiatives.

☆ 291 State Laws for the Control of Subversion and Subversives

*Internal Security and Subversion—Principal State Laws and Cases; A Study Prepared for the Subcommittee to Investigate the Administration of the Internal Security Act*

and Other Internal Security Laws of the Committee on Judiciary, U.S. Senate, by the American Law Division, Legislative Ref. Serv., Library of Congress, 89th Cong., 1st Sess. (1965).

### PUBLIC EDUCATION

1. Code of Alabama, Title 52, § 433(6a). *Textbooks to include statement relative to Communist beliefs of author and author of any book cited therein.* — Neither the State Textbook Committee nor the State Board of Education or any other public body or official shall consider for adoption or approval, or adopt or approve for use in the public schools or trade schools or institutions of higher learning of this State any textbook or other written instructional material (not including periodical newspapers and magazines nor legal opinions by courts of record) which does not contain a statement by the publisher or author thereof indicating clearly and with particularity that the author of the book or other writing and the author of any book or writings citing therein as parallel or additional reading is or is not a known advocate of communism or Marxist socialism, is or is not a member or ex-member of the Communist Party, and is or is not a member or ex-member of a Communist-front organization (as designated by the United States Congress, or any committee thereof, or the Attorney General of the United States).

§ 433(6b). *Enforcement.* — The use of any book or other writing which is prohibited by section 433(6a) may be enjoined upon the application of any resident taxpayer.

2. Louisiana Stat. Anno. § 42:54. *Subversive activities prohibited.* — No public employee, and no student in a public educational institution, shall by word of mouth or writing knowingly or willfully advocate, abet, advise, or teach, the duty, necessity, desirability, or propriety, of overthrowing or destroying the Government of the United States or of any State or of any political subdivision thereof, by force, violence, or any other unlawful means, or the adherence to the government of any foreign nation in the event of war between the United States and such foreign government.

§ 42:55. *"Student in a public educational institution" defined.* — As used in this Part: (1) "Public employee" shall mean and include every officer or employee of any department, board, commission, or agency of the State of Louisiana, or of any political subdivision or municipal corporation of the State of Louisiana.

(2) "Student in a public educational institution" shall mean and include every student enrolled in any public school of the State, or in any State-supported trade school, vocational school, college, or university.

§ 42:56. *Penalty; dismissal.* — Any public employee found guilty of committing any act prohibited by R.S. 42:54 hereof shall be dismissed from his public employment. Any student in a public educational institution found guilty of committing any act prohibited by R.S. 42:54 hereof shall be expelled from the public educational institution in which he is enrolled.

3. South Carolina: Code of Laws, 1962, § 21-420. *Graduation certificate conditioned upon demonstration of loyalty.* — All high schools, colleges and universities in this State that are sustained or in any manner supported by public funds shall give instruction in the essentials of the United States Constitution, including the study of and devotion to American institutions and ideals, and no student in any such school, college or university shall receive a certificate of graduation without previously passing a satisfactory examination upon the provisions and principles of the United States Constitution, and, if a citizen of the United States, satisfying the examining power of his loyalty thereto.

4. Texas: Vernon's Anno. Civ. Stat., Art. 2908b, § 1. *Higher education—admission to conditioned upon execution of loyalty oath.* — No person owing allegiance to the United States hereafter shall be permitted to register for attendance in or be employed by any State-supported college or university unless and until he shall file with the registrar or president thereof his oath or affirmation reciting the following:

> I swear or affirm that I believe in and approve the Constitution of the United States and the principles of government therein contained, and will not in any manner aid or assist in any effort or movement to subvert or destroy the Government of the United States or of any State or of any political subdivision thereof by force, violence, or any other unlawful means. In the event of war with any foreign nation, I will not support or adhere to the government of such foreign nation.

> I swear or affirm that I am not and have not during the past two (2) years been a member of or affiliated with any society or group of persons which teaches or advocates that the Government of the United States or of any State or of any political subdivision thereof should be overthrown or destroyed by force, violence, or any other unlawful means, or the adherence to the government of any foreign nation in the event of war between the United States and such foreign nation.

5. North Carolina: Gen. Stat. § 116-199 (Supp. 1963). *Communists, etc., forbidden to speak at State colleges and universities.* — No college or university, which receives any State funds in support thereof, shall permit any person to use the facilities of such college or university for speaking purposes, who:

(1) Is a known member of the Communist Party;

(2) Is known to advocate the overthrow of the Constitution of the United States or the State of North Carolina;

(3) Has pleaded the Fifth Amendment of the Constitution of the United States in refusing to answer any question, with respect to Communist or subversive connections, or activities, before any duly constituted legislative committee, any judicial tribunal, or any executive or administrative board of the United States or any State.

§ 116-200 (Supp. 1963). *Enforcement.* — This article shall be enforced by the board of trustees, or other governing authority, of such college or university, or by such administrative personnel as may be appointed therefor by the board of trustees or other governing authority of such college or university.

6. Illinois: S. H. Anno., ch. 144, § 48.8 (Supp. 1963). *Subversive organizations barred from using university facilities.* — No trustee, official, instructor, or other employee of the University of Illinois shall extend to any subversive, seditious, and un-American organization, or to its representatives, the use of any facilities of the University for the purpose of carrying on, advertising or publicizing the activities of such organization.

## EMPLOYMENT

7. Montana Rev. Code 1947, § 77-606. *Policy against employment of members of the Communist Party.* — It is expressed policy of the legislature of the State of Montana that wherever a vacancy is caused in the employment rolls of any business or industry by reason of induction into the service of the United States of an employee pursuant to the provisions of said selective training act of 1940, or the national guard and reserve officers mobilization act such vacancy shall not be filled by any person who is a member of the Communist Party or the German-American Bund.

8. Florida Stat. Anno. § 370.21 (Supp. 1963). *Salt water products license.* — (1) This act may be known and cited as the Florida territorial waters act.

(2) It is the purpose of this act to exercise and exert full sovereignty and control of the territorial waters of the State.

(3) No license shall be issued by the board of conservation to any vessel owned in whole or in part by any alien power, which subscribes to the doctrine of international communism, or any subject or national thereof, who subscribes to the doctrine of international communism, or any individual who subscribes to the doctrine of international communism, or who shall have signed a treaty of trade, friendship and alliance or a nonaggression pact with any Commu-

nist power. The board shall grant or withhold said licenses where other alien vessels are involved on the basis of reciprocity and retorsion, unless the nation concerned shall be designated as a friendly ally or neutral by a formal suggestion transmitted to the Governor of Florida by the Secretary of State of the United States. Upon the receipt of such suggestion licenses shall be granted under § 370.06, without regard to reciprocity and retorsion, to vessels of such nations.

(4) It is unlawful for any unlicensed alien vessel to take by any means whatsoever, attempt to take, or having so taken to possess, any natural resource of the State's territorial waters, as such waters are described by Art. I of the State constitution.

*        *        *

9. Texas: Vernon's Anno. Civ. Stat., Art. 4542a, § 9. *Members of Communist Party, etc., barred from practice of pharmacy.*

*        *        *

No person who is a member of the Communist Party, or who is affiliated with such party, or who believes in, supports, or is a member of any group or organization that believes in, furthers, or teaches the overthrow of the United States Government by force or by any illegal or unconstitutional methods, shall be authorized to practice pharmacy in the State of Texas, or to receive a license to practice pharmacy in the State of Texas.

*        *        *

10. Ohio Rev. Code § 4141.28(A)(Supp. 1963). . . . Every person filing an application for determination of benefit rights in accordance with this section shall attach to such application his written affidavit stating whether he advocates or does not advocate and whether he is or is not a member of a party which advocates the overthrow of our Government by force. In the absence of such affidavit no application shall be valid. Such affidavit shall be produced in court by the administrator or his deputy upon the order of a judge of any court of record.

### MISCELLANEOUS

11. Alaska Stat. § 24.45.020. *Lobbyists required to take non-Communist oath.* — (a) Every lobbyist registering under the provisions of § 10 of this chapter shall take the non-Communist oath required of State employees and a copy of this non-Communist oath shall be filed with the department of administration, with the name of the lobbyist's party affiliation, if any.

(b) It is unlawful for a member of a Communist, Fascist or subversive organization, as classified and listed by the Attorney General of the United States, to promote, advocate or oppose the passage or defeat by the legislature of a bill, resolution or legislative measure.

12. 65 Pennsylvania Stat. § 2509 (Supp. 1963). *Persons advocating overthrow of the government ineligible for public assistance.* . . . Except as hereinafter specifically otherwise provided in the case of pensions for the blind, all persons of the following classes, except those who hereafter advocate and actively participate by an overt act or acts in a movement proposing a change in the form of Government of the United States by means not provided for in the Constitution of the United States, shall be eligible to receive assistance, in accordance with rules, regulations and standards established by the department of public welfare, as to eligibility for assistance, and as to its nature and extent.

*        *        *

13. New York: Exec. Law, § 167 (Supp. 1963). *Publicity by State organs prohibited.* — Notwithstanding any inconsistent provision of law, general or special, no department, bureau, board, commission, authority, agency or other instrumentality of the State shall knowingly advertise, publicize, assist, support or advise, or in any manner promote in any publication or otherwise, any summer camp cited by the Attorney General of the United States, the attorney general of the State of New York, any duly authorized State agency or any legislative investigating body for teaching, advocating or embracing the doctrine that the Government of the United States or of any State or any political subdivision thereof shall be overthrown or overturned by force, violence or any unlawful means, or advocating, advising, teaching or embracing the duty, necessity or propriety of adopting any such doctrine.

14. New Jersey Stat. Anno. § 26:8-40.5 (Supp. 1963). *Subversive person not eligible for birth certificate.* — No order shall be made under this act to any person—

(a) Who advises, advocates, or teaches, or who is a member of or affiliated with any organization, association, society, or group that advises, advocates, or teaches opposition to all organized government; or

(b) Who believes in, advises, advocates, or teaches, or who is a member of or affiliated with any organization, association, society, or group that believes in, advises, advocates, or teaches—

(1) the overthrow by force or violence of the government of this State or of the United States or of all forms of law; or

(2) the duty, necessity, or propriety of the unlawful assaulting or killing of any officer or officers (either of specific individuals or of officers generally) of the government of this State or of the United States or any other organized government, because of his or their official character; or

(3) the unlawful damage, injury, or destruction of property; or

(4) sabotage.

(c) Who writes, publishes, or causes to be written or published, or who knowingly circulates, distributes, prints, or displays, or knowingly causes to be circulated, distributed, printed, published, or displayed, or who knowingly has in his possession for the purpose of circulation, distribution, publication, or display any written or printed matter advising, advocating, or teaching opposition to all organized government, or advising, advocating, or teaching—

(1) the overthrow by force or violence of the government of this State or of the United States or of all forms of law; or

(2) the duty, necessity, or propriety of the unlawful assaulting or killing of any officer or officers (either of specific individuals or of officers generally) of the government of this State or of the United States or of any other organized government; or

(3) the unlawful damage, injury, or destruction of property; or

(4) sabotage.

(d) Who is a member of or affiliated with any organization, association, society, or group that writes, circulates, distributes, prints, publishes, or displays, or causes to be written, circulated, distributed, printed, published, or displayed, or that has in its possession for the purpose of circulation, distribution, publication, issue, or display, any written or printed matter of the character described in subdivision (c).

For the purpose of this section—

(1) the giving, loaning, or promising of money or anything of value to be used for the advising, advocacy or teaching of any doctrine above enumerated shall constitute the advising, advocacy, or teaching of such doctrine; and

(2) the giving, loaning, or promising of money or anything of value to any organization, association, society, or group of the character above described shall constitute affiliation therewith; but nothing in this paragraph shall be taken as an exclusive definition of advising, advocacy, teaching, or affiliation.

The provisions of this section shall be applicable to any applicant for an order fixing the time and place of his birth who at any time within a period of 10 years immediately preceding the filing of the petition therefor, is or has been found to be within any of the classes enumerated within this section notwithstanding that at the time petition is filed he may not be included in such classes.

## 292 "a list of all printing presses . . . owned" (1967)

After the Supreme Court, in *Albertson*, struck down the requirement of individual registration of Communists on grounds of self-incrimination, only the corporate Communist Party of the United States remained subject to registration. In *Communist Party of the United States v. United States*, the party's indictment for failure to register was eventually overturned on grounds that had proved fatal for the required registration of individual members—that those who might register on behalf of the party would incriminate themselves in the process. The government did not appeal the decision to the Supreme Court.

*Albertson* and *Communist Party of the United States* sounded the death knell of the Subversive Activities Control Board. In 1973, as Watergate was about to break, President Nixon (a stalwart member of the Un-American Activities Committee during his legislative career) declined to request funding for the continuation of the board and its staff.

☆ 292 *Communist Party of the United States v. United States*

384 F.2d 957 (D.C. Cir. 1967).

McGOWAN, Circuit Judge:

\* \* \*

### III

The Supreme Court's decision in *Communist Party* [*v. Subversive Activities Control Board*] presumably retains enough vitality to suggest that there is very much indeed that Congress may do in the pursuit of a single purpose to regulate the Communist Party by the device of disclosure. The difficulty is that the purposes of Congress in respect of the Communist Party have not been single in nature. They have, rather, sought in effect to compel both disclosure by the Party and, at the same time, the incrimination of its members. The Congressional enactments applicable to the Communist Party have, severally but simultaneously, exposed it in substance to outlawry as well as to an obligation to disclose its records and affairs. We may assume for the moment that either approach was, and is, constitutionally feasible. We can not, because of the Fifth Amendment, safely assume as much in the case of the co-existence of both purposes.

\* \* \*

. . . So long as the self-incrimination clause of the Fifth Amendment endures, activity may be made criminal, but the actor cannot be compelled to characterize it as such and to disclose it. If Congress would do the one, it may have to forego the other. The choice by Congress of the means it believes more effective remains with it.

## IV

It may be questioned whether appellant is helped even if these premises are accepted as true and the result in *Albertson* embraced as a necessary consequence of them. If the self-incrimination privilege is personal in the sense of not being available to corporations and associations, how may appellant — a self-described voluntary association — interpose the privilege as a shield against criminal prosecution of itself for failing to make the disclosures required by the Act? . . .

\*      \*      \*

A standard of differentiating between organizations in terms of their "impersonal," as distinct from their "personal," character is admittedly elusive in meaning and difficult of application. It is clear, however, that the Supreme Court was not prepared to say that the privilege was without significance in respect of any and all organizations under any and all circumstances. Short of trying, in the abstract, to sort out associations for whom the privilege has meaning from those for whom it does not, it is useful to recall the reality which underlies them all. Although the law has made room for the concept of an artificial entity which, for some purposes at least, has a life separate and distinct from the individuals who comprise it, it remains the fact that no such entity can act other than through human instrumentalities. . . .

\*      \*      \*

It is important to turn from generalities to an examination of the position in which this record shows appellant to have been placed. At a time when, as the Supreme Court has now said, appellant found itself in "an area permeated with criminal statutes," where even mere association with, much less membership in, appellant presented a serious "threat of prosecution," appellant is first declared by the Board to be a "Communist-action organization" which, by statutory definition, is an organization "substantially directed, dominated, or controlled by the foreign government or foreign organization controlling the world Communist movement referred to in . . . this title," and which "operates primarily to advance the objectives of such world Communist movement. . . ." By virtue of this declaration, appellant is required to register itself as a "Communist-action organization" and to supply, in addition to its name and address, the names and addresses of its officers and members (including those who have been such during the preceding 12 months); a statement of the functions and duties of the former; the *aliases*, if any, of such individuals; all moneys re-

ceived and expended, including sources and objects; and a list of all printing presses or machines owned, controlled, or possessed by any of them. Once so registered, an annual report of all such information is required. There is a further requirement that each such registered organization shall keep accurate records of receipts and expenditures, and of the names and addresses of its members and of all persons who actively participate in its affairs.

\*      \*      \*

For appellant to file a list of its members exposes every person on that list to a serious and substantial "threat of prosecution." The only people with the authority and capacity to compile an authentic such list and to authorize its use for registration purposes would, by that very act, subject themselves to a like threat. No such person has demonstrated a willingness to act. To differentiate under these circumstances between the criminal punishment of the association, on the one hand, and the individuals who make of it a collective personality, on the other, seems to us incompatible with the purposes and values underlying the Fifth Amendment. It is to make the mere fact of association the vehicle for subjecting the individuals, collectively as well as personally, to criminal prosecution, shorn of the protection of the self-incrimination privilege.

The statutory scheme before us accordingly must yield to the urgency of continuing recognition of the vitality of the Fifth Amendment protections. Liability of the appellant to the command of the statute can not be vicariously imposed because of the failure of its members to meet the requirements of registration where, as the Supreme Court has made clear, they as individuals are so protected.

In the areas of First Amendment concern, such as politics and religion where the association of people together is of the essence of meaningful observance and expression, we see no inescapable necessity to limit the reach of the Fifth Amendment by technical theories of artificial legal personality. If Congress chooses to find some principles and practices of politics or religion so abhorrent as to warrant criminal liability, it may conceivably do so in a proper case. But to be placed beyond the pale of the First Amendment is not to be deprived of the Fifth. It is, rather, the very reason for its being; and that reason invalidates the criminal convictions of appellant under the circumstances of this case.

The judgments of conviction appealed from are *Reversed.*

## 293 "the phrase 'war power' cannot be invoked as a talismanic incantation" (1967)

The *Robel* case addressed the right of Communists to be active in labor unions and to work in defense facilities. Robel, a shipyard worker and a member of the Communist party, was engaged in defense work in violation of the Internal Security Act of 1950. The district court dismissed the indictment against Robel on procedural grounds. The Supreme Court upheld the dismissal but on more sweeping First Amendment grounds. Exceeding the narrow and technical grounds of earlier decisions, the court voiced in *Robel* a broad affirmation of constitutional rights: "It would indeed be ironic if in the name of national defense we would sanction the subversion of one of those liberties—the freedom of association—which makes the defense of the nation worthwhile."

☆ 293  *United States v. Robel*

389 U.S. 258 (1967).

MR. CHIEF JUSTICE WARREN delivered the opinion of the Court.

... The indictment alleged in substance that appellee had "unlawfully and willfully engage[d] in employment" at the shipyard with knowledge of the outstanding order against the Party and with knowledge and notice of the shipyard's designation as a defense facility by the Secretary of Defense.... To overcome what it viewed as a "likely constitutional infirmity" in § 5(a)(1)(D), the District Court read into that section "the requirements of active membership and specific intent." Because the indictment failed to allege that appellee's Communist Party membership was of that quality, the indictment was dismissed.... We affirm the judgment of the District Court, but on the ground that § 5(a)(1)(D) is an unconstitutional abridgment of the right of association protected by the First Amendment.

We cannot agree with the District Court that § 5(a)(1)(D) can be saved from constitutional infirmity by limiting its application to active members of Communist-action organizations who have the specific intent of furthering the unlawful goals of such organizations.... It is precisely because that statute sweeps indiscriminately across all types of association with Communist-action groups, without regard to the quality and degree of membership, that it runs afoul of the First Amendment.

... [T]he operative fact upon which the job disability depends is the exercise of an individual's right of association, which is protected by the provisions of the First Amendment.... [I]t is clear that those rights protected by the First Amendment are no less basic [than the right to travel] in our democratic scheme.

The Government seeks to defend the statute on the ground that it was passed pursuant to Congress' war power.... That argument finds support in a number of decisions of this Court. However, the phrase "war power" cannot be invoked as a talismanic incantation to support any exercise of congressional power which can be brought within its ambit.

... [The] concept of "national defense" cannot be deemed an end in itself, justifying any exercise of legislative power designed to promote such a goal.

... The statute quite literally establishes guilt by association alone, without any need to establish that an individual's association poses the threat feared by the Government in proscribing it. The inhibiting effect on the exercise of First Amendment rights is clear.

... That statute casts its net across a broad range of associational activities, indiscriminately trapping membership which can be constitutionally punished and membership which cannot be so proscribed. It is made irrelevant to the statute's operation that an individual may be a passive or inactive member of a designated organization, that he may be unaware of the organization's unlawful aims, or that he may disagree with those unlawful aims. It is also made irrelevant that an individual who is subject to the penalties of § 5(a)(1)(D) may occupy a nonsensitive position in a defense facility. Thus, § 5(a)(1)(D) contains the fatal defect of overbreadth because it seeks to bar employment both for association which may be proscribed and for association which may not be proscribed consistently with First Amendment rights. This the Constitution will not tolerate.

We are not unmindful of the congressional concern over the danger of sabotage and espionage in national defense industries, and nothing we hold today should be read to deny Congress the power under narrowly drawn legislation to keep from sensitive positions in defense facilities those who would use their positions to disrupt the Nation's production facilities.... The task of writing legislation which will stay within those bounds has been committed to Congress. Our decision today simply recognized that, when legitimate legislative concerns are expressed in a statute which imposes a substantial burden on protected First Amendment activities, Congress must achieve its goal by means which have a "less drastic" impact on the continued vitality of First Amendment freedoms. The Constitution and the basic position of First Amendment rights in our democratic fabric demand nothing less.

*Affirmed.*

## 294 "An attempt to overthrow the government of Kentucky" (1967)

Not only the federal authorities but also state and local government agencies conducted the war against Communist and other perceived radical menaces. Investigations into political activity and associations, as well as the requirement of loyalty oaths as prerequisites for public employment, were prevalent among the states and municipalities as early as the 1950s. The prosecution of offenders for sedition against state governments was less common.

Pike County lies at the extreme edge of Appalachian poverty in the eastern tip of Kentucky. The McSurelys and other federally funded community organizers were arrested in 1967 on the authority of the World War I-era criminal syndicalism and sedition statute. Despite the federal court's injunction against their prosecution and a subsequent order for the return of their illegally seized books and private papers, the McSurelys continued to suffer from government-induced humiliation and invasion of privacy. Copies of their seized materials were forwarded to the United States Senate Committee on Government Operations investigating subversion, and the McSurelys were cited for contempt of Congress for refusing to testify at committee hearings based on these papers.

The 1967 federal court decision ruled Kentucky's pursuit of state vigilance to be unconstitutional. After nearly fifteen years of additional litigation and a divorce claimed to have stemmed from the stresses produced by the government's actions, the McSurelys were awarded $1.6 million by a District of Columbia jury in compensation for the unconstitutional deeds of the state and federal officials involved.

☆ 294 *McSurely v. Ratliff*

282 F. Supp. 848 (E.D. Ken. 1967).

Combs, Circuit Judge.

Kentucky's sedition law was passed in 1920 in the aftermath of World War I and the Bolshevik Revolution in Russia. The law was amended slightly in 1922, otherwise it has remained unchanged through the years. As would be expected, the statute is broad and comprehensive. It was good politics to be against Communism. The Governor signed the bill but was fearful that it drew too much water. He publicly stated that it "goes far afield and far beyond syndicalism and sedition." He thought the courts would "take out of this law the sections which make it dangerous," and concluded with this statement: "Those who seek its [government] overthrow by force or violence, or those who counsel resistance to its laws by unlawful means must be destroyed, but

the right of free speech is the blood-bought heritage of every citizen: it is the palladium of our liberties, and it must and shall be preserved."

Now, for the first time a section of the law is squarely presented for judicial determination. KRS 432.040. Also presented for determination is whether Congress by legislation has preempted this field so as to give federal courts exclusive jurisdiction....

The individual plaintiffs, Alan McSurely, Margaret McSurely, Joseph Mulloy, Carl Braden, and Anne Braden, are under indictment in the Pike Country, Kentucky, Circuit Court for advocating sedition and criminal syndicalism. The defendants are Robert Matthews, Attorney General of Kentucky; Thomas B. Ratliff, Commonwealth's Attorney for the Pike County Circuit Court; Perry A. Justice, Sheriff of Pike County; and Grover Atkins, Jailer of Pike County.

Alan and Margaret McSurely, husband and wife, are field organizers for plaintiff Southern Conference Educational Fund, Inc., in Pike County, Kentucky. Alan McSurely is also a field organizer for the National Conference of New Politics and has distributed literature of Vietnam Summer, both unincorporated associations and both plaintiffs here. Joseph Mulloy is a field representative for the Appalachian Volunteers, an organization funded primarily by the United States Office of Economic Opportunity. According to the McSurelys and Mulloy, their official duties are to investigate the socio-eco-political milieu of Pike County, "to inform the people of their rights," and to help local citizens "organize to overcome their problems."

Anne and Carl Braden, husband and wife, are directors of the Southern Conference Educational Fund.

On the night of August 11, 1967, under authority of warrant charging seditious activities against the United States and the Commonwealth of Kentucky in violation of KRS 432.040, officials of Pike County and their deputies arrested the McSurelys and Mulloy. The officials also seized and impounded 564 loose books, twenty-six posters, and twenty-two boxes of books, pamphlets, and other private and published documents found in the McSurely home. They also impounded a suitcase of clothes and several personal items which were caught up in the whirlwind of the search.

The McSurelys, together with Southern Conference Educational Fund and Vietnam Summer, filed their complaint in the United States District Court for the Eastern District of Kentucky. They alleged that KRS 432.040 is on its face unconstitutional and asked (1) that a three judge district court be convened; (2) that defendants be enjoined from prosecuting the plaintiffs in the state court; (3) for an interlocutory injunction pending determination of the request for permanent relief; and (4) that the seized material be impounded by a federal marshal.

*     *     *

This Court was convened on September 1, 1967. The Kentucky Civil Liberties Union was permitted to tender its motion to intervene as amicus curiae and to submit a brief. At the hearing on September 1, the parties agreed to a stipulation of facts, and the Court fixed time for making up the pleadings and for the filing of briefs. No temporary injunction was issued but the defendant Ratliff agreed in open court that he would not prosecute the criminal action in the Pike Circuit Court until final decision by this Court.

*     *     *

The news media continued to give the case wide publicity and spokesmen for both plaintiffs and defendants presented their arguments to the press and on national news programs.

On September 11, the Grand Jury of Pike County, acting under general instructions from the judge of that court, returned an indictment against the McSurelys, Mulloy, and Carl and Anne Braden, charging them with seditious activities against the Commonwealth of Kentucky and Pike County in violation of KRS 432.040. On the following day, the Bradens, who are residents of Louisville, Kentucky, made their appearance in Pike County and were arrested and placed in jail in default of bond. Plaintiffs then moved for an immediate hearing and renewed their motion for a temporary injunction. They also moved for a show cause order against the defendant Ratliff for contempt of court.

This Court held a second hearing on September 14, at which time the Bradens were allowed to intervene as plaintiffs. Testimony was given by the individual plaintiffs and by the defendant Ratliff. The testimony was to the effect that since the filing of the criminal prosecution against plaintiffs the people of Pike County are fearful of associating with them and it has become difficult for them to carry on their normal work; also that the publicity has jeopardized the position of the Appalachian Volunteers in obtaining funds from the Office of Economic Opportunity.

*     *     *

The statute in question is clearly unconstitutional under even the most flexible yardstick. It is too broad and too vague. It contravenes the First Amendment to the Constitution of the United States because it unduly prohibits freedom of speech, freedom of the press, and the right of assembly. It fails to distinguish between the advocacy of ideas and the advocacy of action. It makes it a criminal offense merely to possess, with intent to circu-

late, literature on the subject of sedition. It imposes the penalty of imprisonment for advocating an unpopular political belief. It would turn the courts into a forum for argument of political theories with imprisonment the penalty for the loser. It contains no requirement of criminal intent. The unwary and the ignorant could be enmeshed in the dragnet as easily as the covert plotter.

One of the definitions of sedition in the 1920 Act is, "the advocacy or suggestion by word, act, deed or writing . . . of the change or modification of the Government of the United States or of the Commonwealth of Kentucky, or of the Constitution or laws of either of them, . . . by means other than by lawful means. . . ." A person could thus be indicted for suggesting a change in the state or federal constitution "by means other than by lawful means." What is lawful would of necessity have to be decided by the presiding judge. This is a plain violation of the Sixth Amendment to the federal constitution which guarantees the right of the accused "to be informed of the nature and cause of the accusation." Under the Sixth Amendment a person cannot be charged merely with violating the law; the charge must be more specific.

For all these reasons KRS 432.040 violates basic constitutional guarantees which have been applied to the states through the Fourteenth Amendment for nearly half a century.

We are of the opinion that, even if the statute were constitutional, Congress has preempted this field and the federal courts have exclusive jurisdiction. *Commonwealth of Pennsylvania v. Nelson.*

The criminal prosecution against these plaintiffs is pitched solely on the theory that they were engaged in a Communist conspiracy to overthrow the government of Kentucky and its subdivision, Pike County. This was made clear at the hearing on the motion for temporary injunction. There has been no suggestion of any other seditious activities. The case therefore falls squarely under the Smith Act, the Internal Security Act, the Communist Control Act, and other Congressional acts on the subject of Communism.

There is disagreement in this country about the dangers of Communism and how to combat those dangers. As regards Communism, most of us are like the blind men from Indostan who learned about the elephant by each touching a different part of its anatomy. We know very little about the subject as a whole. On one point, however, everybody agrees: Communism is not a local movement. The Communist Control Act of 1954 declares "that the Communist party of the United States . . . is in fact an instrumentality of a conspiracy to overthrow the Government of the United States. . . ." An attempt to overthrow the government of Kentucky or even one of its subdivisions would pose such a threat to the government of the United States that the Congressional acts referred to above would immediately become applicable. One of the absolutes in this country since the Civil War is that this is one nation indivisible. So goes the Pledge of Allegiance to the Flag recited by school children and by members of the Daughters of the American Revolution.

*          *          *

The next question is whether this Court should enjoin the state court from proceeding further with the prosecution of these plaintiffs. It seems to us that *Dombrowski v. Pfister* is in point. The statute is an unduly broad and vague regulation of expression and enforcement of the statute would necessarily curtail activities which are privileged under the First Amendment.

It is difficult to believe that capable lawyers could seriously contend that this statute is constitutional. The indictment follows the language of the statute and in our opinion fails to state an indictable offense. It too fails to make the distinction between advocacy of ideas and advocacy of action and is therefore insufficient. In addition, the conclusion is inescapable that the criminal prosecutions were instituted, at least in part, in order to stop plaintiffs' organizing activities in Pike County. That effort has been successful. Not only has there been the "chilling effect" on freedom of speech, . . . there has been in fact a freezing effect. The Governor has issued a public statement that federal funds to the Appalachian Volunteers should be discontinued. Plaintiff's possessions have been seized and impounded and they have been placed in jail. The Bradens, who originally had not been charged with any offense, were indicted and placed in jail after they attempted to render assistance to the other plaintiffs. Clearly, the criminal prosecutions have put a damper on plaintiffs' freedom of speech, as well as on others who might be in sympathy with their objectives.

*          *          *

*The motion for a permanent injunction is sustained.*

### CHAPTER 10

# Age of Protest

---

Civil Rights, Student, Urban,
and Vietnam War Protests
1961-1976

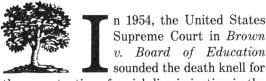

In 1954, the United States Supreme Court in *Brown v. Board of Education* sounded the death knell for the perpetuation of racial discrimination in the country. Overturning a doctrine of more than fifty years' standing, the court announced that separate public schools for the two races were unconstitutional. While the educational promise of that decision has yet to be realized, the case provided the impetus for blacks in the South to launch a frontal attack on racism and discrimination. Some victories were won in the courts, but resistance to this social change was very strong and very deep. When appeals to reason and law failed, leaders of the movement for black equality turned to the tactics of nonviolent direct action—unlawful confrontations with state and local authorities who sought to perpetuate the social order. The excessive and often violent responses of the local white establishment generated sympathy and attracted northern activists to voice support and offer assistance to the black cause. The struggle for political and racial equality enlisted also the century-old federal civil rights acts. When state authorities defied federal law, federal military force was required to keep the peace in several instances. This chapter once more explores the methods and rationale of those resorting to political criminality, whether for the cause of equality or in the name of tradition, as well as the responses of government to these exhibitions of illegality.

The tactics of direct action were not limited to combating southern racial injustice. The lessons learned in Mississippi were equally applicable in Berkeley and Detroit. Any perceived wrong could be addressed effectively by these methods as long as sufficient mass support existed for the action. Generating such support, therefore, became a primary requirement of the protest movements of the 1960s and early 1970s. The documents trace the development of rhetorical, if not actual, linkages among dissident groups: the blacks, the urban poor, the relatively affluent but dissatisfied students, the draft and war resisters, and the Third World national liberators and revolutionaries.

The reader should approach many of these documents with skepticism, searching behind the ostensibly political language for a serious and meaningful political motive or goal. It is not at all easy to divine clearly the phenomenon of political criminality when the rhetoric of revolution becomes fashionable, and perhaps is utilized to shield less noble purposes. One should also reflect upon the role of the mass media in providing the communicative support for the flourishing of a nationwide "counterculture," the main agenda of which was "resistance" to the "establishment."

Not all direct action movements were based on the principle of nonviolence, a principle that enhanced the movements' moral authority. The materials in the chapter detail some of the instances where the nonviolence discipline was breached either in word or deed, or both. This relinquishment by the reformers of the moral high ground provided the enforcers of public order with ostensible cause for zealous response to minimal threats to the social and political order. The reader should be as skeptical of the appropriateness of some of the governmental responses to political criminality as to the authenticity of the criminality itself.

Having been so cautioned, the reader nevertheless should not hasten to dismiss political criminality as an effective tool for accomplishing policy changes during the period in question, especially with regard to race relations and the Vietnam War. Nor should the reader overlook the serious domestic security problems created by political and pseudo-political criminality: assassinations and attempted assassinations of major public figures (John F. Kennedy, Malcolm X, Martin Luther King, Jr., Robert F. Kennedy, and George C. Wallace), urban riots and looting of private property, armed robberies, kidnappings, and bombings.

The collection endeavors to present a broad spectrum of materials, including many contemporary personal accounts and assessments of the activities claimed to be political. This availability of personal and autobiographical materials seeking to articulate the motivations and goals of the political activists should aid in gaining insight into the mind of the political offender. We hope a retrospective review of these documents will stimulate critical thought and analysis of the phenomenon of political criminality as it manifested itself in the United States during the restless decades of the mid-twentieth century.

# 295 Who's Been Trying to Register Our Niggers? (1961)

In the late 1950s and early 1960s, southern civil rights workers encountered criminal and violent responses to nearly every form of protest activity they used. When the Freedom Riders sought to desegregate interstate bus transportation, southern mobs met them with violent reactions; the southerners bombed and smashed buses and severely beat riders when they stopped in terminals along the way. At other times, state and local forces participated in the violence. During the famous civil rights demonstrations in Birmingham and Selma, Alabama, the police subjected blacks to cattle prods, attack dogs, firehoses, and other forms of physical abuse.

Political criminality of a different sort also was frequent in direct action tactics of the civil rights workers — the open violation of state laws, local ordinances, and community customs they considered antiquated and unjust. The reform leaders pursued this sequence of protest, nonviolent direct action, and the resulting violent reactions as a means of capturing the attention and sympathy of broader audiences. In 1957, Martin Luther King, Jr., expressed his sentiments to the Institute on Nonviolence and Social Change:

> Things of fundamental importance to people are not secured by reason alone but have to be purchased with their suffering. . . . The appeal of reason is more to the head, but the penetration of the heart comes from suffering. It opens up the inner understanding in man.

The following excerpts demonstrate this philosophy in practice.

☆ 295 Mississippi Violence and Intimidation

Reprinted in *Mississippi Violence vs. Human Rights* (Atlanta: Committee for the Distribution of the Mississippi Story, 1963), 434-41.

☆ 295a Chronology of Violence and Intimidation (1961)

*         *         *

*August 15, Amite County:* Robert Moses, Student Non-Violent Coordinating Committee (SNCC) registration worker, and three Negroes who had tried unsuccessfully to register in Liberty, were driving toward McComb when a county officer stopped them. He asked if Moses was the man ". . . who's been trying to register our niggers." All were taken to court and Moses was arrested for "impeding an officer in the discharge of his duties," fined $50 and spent two days in jail.

*August 22, Amite County:* Robert Moses went to Liberty with three Negroes, who made an unsuc-

cessful attempt to register. A block from the courthouse, Moses was attacked and beaten by Billy Jack Caston, the sheriff's first cousin. Eight stitches were required to close a wound in Moses' head. Caston was acquitted of assault charges by an all-white jury before a justice of the peace.

*August 26, McComb, Pike County:* Hollis Watkins, 20, and Elmer Hayes, 20, SNCC workers, were arrested while staging a sit-in at the F. W. Woolworth store and charged with breach of the peace. They spent 36 days in jail.

*August 27 and 29, McComb, Pike County:* Five Negro students from a local high school were convicted of breach of the peace following a sit-in at a variety store and bus terminal. They were sentenced to a $400 fine each and eight months in jail. One of these students, a girl of 15, was turned over to juvenile authorities, released, subsequently rearrested, and sentenced to 12 months in a state school for delinquents.

*August 29, McComb, Pike County:* Two Negro leaders were arrested in McComb as an aftermath of the sit-in protest march on city hall, charged with contributing to the delinquency of minors. They were Curtis C. Bryant of McComb, an official of the NAACP, and Cordelle Reagan, of SNCC. Each arrest was made on an affidavit signed by Police Chief George Guy, who said he had information that the two ". . . were behind some of this racial trouble."

*August 30, McComb, Pike County:* SNCC workers Brenda Travis, 16, Robert Talbert, 19, and Isaac Lewis, 20, staged a sit-in in the McComb terminal of the Greyhound bus lines. They were arrested on charges of breach of the peace and failure to obey a policeman's order to move on. They spent 30 days in jail.

*September 5, Liberty, Amite County:* Travis Britt, SNCC registration worker, was attacked and beaten by whites on the courthouse lawn. Britt was accompanied at the time by Robert Moses. Britt said one man hit him more than 20 times. The attackers drove away in a truck.

*September 7, Tylertown, Walthall County:* John Hardy, SNCC registration worker, took two Negroes to the county courthouse to register. The registrar told him he ". . . wasn't registering voters" that day. When the three turned to leave, Registrar John Q. Wood took a pistol from his desk and struck Hardy over the head from behind. Hardy was arrested and charged with disturbing the peace.

*September 13, Jackson, Hinds County:* Fifteen Episcopal ministers (among them three Negroes) were arrested for asking to be served at the lunch counter of the Greyhound bus terminal. They were charged with inviting a breach of the peace. They were found not guilty of the charge on May 21, 1962, by County Judge Russell Moore.

*September 25, Liberty, Amite County:* Herbert Lee, a Negro who had been active in voter registration, was shot and killed by white state representative E. H. Hurst in downtown Liberty. No prosecution was undertaken, the authorities explaining that the representative had shot in self-defense.

*October 4, McComb, Pike County:* The five students who were arrested as a result of the August 29 sit-in in McComb returned to school, but were refused admittance. At that, 116 students walked out and paraded downtown to the city hall in protest. Police arrested the entire crowd, but later released all but 19, all of whom were 18 years old or older. They were charged with breach of the peace and contributing to the delinquency of minors and allowed to go free on bail totaling $3,700. At the trial on October 31, Judge Brumfield, finding the students guilty, and sentencing each to a $500 fine and six months in jail, said: "Some of you are local residents, some of you are outsiders. Those of you who are local residents are like sheep being led to the slaughter. If you continue to follow the advice of outside agitators, you will be like sheep and be slaughtered."

☆ 295b  A Statement from the Burgland High School Students

We the Negro youth of Pike County feel that Brenda Travis and Isaac Lewis should not be barred from an education for protesting against injustice. We feel that as a member of Burgland High School they have fought this battle for us. To prove that we appreciate them for doing this, we will suffer whatever punishment they have to take with them.

In school we are taught democracy, but the rights that democracy has to offer have been denied to us by our oppressor: we have not had the right to vote; we have not had a balanced school system; we have not had an opportunity to participate in any of the branches of our local, state and federal government.

However, we are children of God, who makes the sun shine on the just and unjust. So we petition all our fellowmen to love rather than hate, to build rather than tear down, to bind our nation with love and justice without regard to race, color or creed.

☆ 295c  P.T.A. Requests Readmittance of Students

P.T.A. Board, Burgland H.S.
McComb, Miss.
October 14, 1961

Mr. R. S. Simpson
Mr. C. C. Higgins
Members of the Board of Education
McComb, Mississippi

DEAR SIRS:

We parents feel the time has come for everyone, white and black, to recognize that we are all children in the family of man, twigs and branches stemming from the same tree of life. We feel everyone should recognize that if the tree catches fire all its branches will be scorched. To prevent such a scorching, it will be necessary for each race to select representatives to assemble for the purpose of proposing firm, constructive and just solutions to community problems.

To select the matter immediately before us, Mr. Higgins, Mr. Simpson, the members of the Board of Education, and the parents of the students at Burgland High School should meet in an effort to achieve a good solid understanding of each other's position. We feel that our principle [*sic*], Mr. Higgins, is a victim of circumstances beyond his control, that the fight is with the Board of Education and the Superintendent, Mr. Simpson. We are sure that they will hear our plea. We want our children back in school without their being placed under undue pressure and strain.

We know that the Board has the right to expel and suspend students, but why should the children have to sign slips to be readmitted to their school? Such slips can have no legal status, in fact, they are only a form of coercion. This requirement merely puts the parents on the spot.

We are asking Mr. Simpson to request the authorities who are responsible for placing Brenda Travis in reform school to obtain her immediate release so that she may resume her studies, along with Isaac Lewis, at the Burgland High School. We feel she has been done a gross injustice.

We are very much concerned about our "walkout" students and we want them in our school, the Burgland High School. If we all would read our Bibles we would see that the time is far spent for man to do all the carrying on; the Supreme Man is taking over now, our Heavenly Father. We all saw that the students, when they were marching with the entire police force behind them, were fearing no evil.

> Read the twenty-third Psalm: . . . He leadeth me beside the still waters. He restoreth my soul: he leadeth me in the paths of righteousness for his name's sake.
> Yea, though I walk through the valley of the shadow of death, I will fear no evil: for thou art with me; thy rod and thy staff they comfort me.

In conclusion we would like to repeat our feeling that both white and colored must reach an understanding of these issues; if we don't it will be something to bring damage to the State of Mississippi and the entire Nation.

Respectfully yours,

BURGLAND HIGH SCHOOL P.T.A.

☆ 295d Statement by a High-School Student

Suzette Miller
Subject: English
Instructor: C. McDew

Why I walked out of Bur[g]land High School:

I am Suzette Miller a student of the present Freshman class. I don't have much to lose, but I do have a lot to gain, That is my equal rights.

Brenda Travis is a female that made a protest in McComb Bus Station. She was also a student at Burgland Hi, but is now an ex-student.

I was in the walk out because I am A student at Burgland just like Brenda. Because she wasn't allowed back in school I don't feel that I should allow myself to go back.

I walked out and to be readmitted I have to sign a paper saying that if I walk out any more I will be expelled, and if I didn't sign the paper asking for readmittance back in school.

Now I am expelled for the remainder of the school year. But I will keep protesting until the battle is won.

I am now a student of The Nonviolent High school. In my heart I believe where there is a will there is a way.

Now is the time to put God first and to let him lead us.

Our white brothers and sisters think that we want war. War is not needed now in Mississippi, If we ever needed any thing we need God. He is the way and the light.

If we would stop and think we could see what we need and what are we doing to try to get it.

We as a race come face to face with our enemies kind and willing to have them as brother and sisters. We would have better families, homes, churches, towns, and states.

May God forever bless us all over land and contry [*sic*]. "Oh God show us the right way."

☆ 295e Robert Moses, Message from Jail

We are smuggling this note from the drunk tank of the county jail in Magnolia, Mississippi. Twelve of us are here, sprawled out along the concrete bunker; Curtis Hayes, Hollis Watkins, Ike Lewis and Robert Talbert, four veterans of the bunker, are sitting up talking—mostly about girls; Charles McDew ("Tell the story") is curled into the concrete and the wall; Harold Robinson, Stephen Ashley, James Wells, Lee Chester Vick, Leotus Eubanks, and Ivory Diggs lay cramped on the cold bunker; I'm sitting with smuggled pen and paper, thinking a little, writing a little; Myrtis Bennett and Janie Campbell are across the way wedded to a different icy cubicle.

Later on, Hollis will lead out with a clear tenor into a freedom song, Talbert and Lewis will supply jokes, and McDew will discourse on the history of the black man and the Jew. McDew—a black by birth, a Jew by choice, and a revolutionary by necessity—has taken on the deep hates and deep loves which America and the world reserve for those who dare to stand in a strong sun and cast a sharp shadow....

This is Mississippi, the middle of the iceberg. Hollis is leading off with this tenor, "Michael row the boat ashore, Alleluia; Christian brothers don't be slow; Alleluia; Mississippi's next to go, Alleluia." This is a tremor in the middle of the iceberg—from a stone that the builders rejected.

# 296 State Officials Unlawfully Obstructing the Laws of the United States (1962)

Opposition to school desegregation was manifested not only on the elementary and secondary school levels but also within the university systems. In Mississippi the intention of the state and its officials, including law enforcement officers, to resort to violence in order to prevent desegregation posed a direct challenge to federal authority. On September 30, 1962, President John F. Kennedy responded.

☆ 296 President Kennedy and the Mississippi Insurrection

☆ 296a President's Proclamation (September 30, 1962)

Proc. No. 3497, 27 Fed. Reg. 9681 (1962).

Whereas the Governor of the State of Mississippi and certain law enforcement officers and other officials of that State, and other persons, individually and in unlawful assemblies, combinations and conspiracies, have been and are willfully opposing and obstructing the enforcement of orders entered by the United States District Court for the Southern District of Mississippi and the United States Court of Appeals for the Fifth Circuit; and

Whereas such unlawful assemblies, combinations and conspiracies oppose and obstruct the execution of the laws of the United States, impede the course of justice under those laws and make it impracticable to enforce those laws in the State of Mississippi by the ordinary course of judicial proceedings; and

Whereas I have expressly called the attention of the Governor of Mississippi to the perilous situation that exists and to his duties in the premises, and have requested but have not received from him adequate assurances that the orders of the courts of the United States will be obeyed and that law and order will be maintained;

Now, therefore, I, John F. Kennedy, President of the United States, under and by virtue of the authority vested in me by the Constitution and laws of the United States, do command all persons engaged in such obstructions of justice to cease and desist therefrom and to disperse and retire peacefully forthwith.

In witness whereof, I have hereunto set my hand and caused the seal of the United States of America to be affixed.

Done at the city of Washington this 30th day of September in the year of our Lord Nineteen Hundred and Sixty-Two, and of the independence of the United States of America the One Hundred and Eighty-Seven.

JOHN F. KENNEDY

By the President:

Secretary of State

☆ 296b  Executive Order No. 11053
(September 30, 1962)

27 Fed. Reg. 9693 (1962).

PROVIDING ASSISTANCE FOR THE REMOVAL OF
UNLAWFUL OBSTRUCTIONS OF JUSTICE IN THE
STATE OF MISSISSIPPI

Whereas on September 30, 1962, I issued proclamation No. 3497 reading in part as follows [quoted in entirety above] and

Whereas the commands contained in that proclamation have not been obeyed and obstruction of enforcement of those court orders still exists and threatens to continue:

Now, therefore, by virtue of the authority vested in me by the Constitution and laws of the United States, it is hereby ordered as follows:

Section 1. The Secretary of Defense is authorized and directed to take all appropriate steps to enforce all orders of the United States District Court for the Southern District of Mississippi and the United States Court of Appeals for the Fifth Circuit and to remove all obstructions of justice in the State of Mississippi.

Section 2. In furtherance of the enforcement of the aforementioned orders of the United States District Court for the Southern District of Mississippi and the United States Court of Appeals for the Fifth Circuit, the Secretary of Defense is authorized to use such of the armed forces of the United States as he may deem necessary.

Section 3. I hereby authorize the Secretary of Defense to call into the active military service of the United States, as he may deem appropriate to carry out the purposes of this order, any or all of the units of the Army National Guard and of the Air National Guard of the State of Mississippi to serve in the active military service of the United States for an indefinite period and until relieved by appropriate orders. In carrying out the provisions of Section 1, the Secretary of Defense is authorized to use the units, and members thereof, ordered into active military service of the United States pursuant to this section.

Section 4. The Secretary of Defense is authorized to delegate to the Secretary of the Army or the Secretary of the Air Force, or both, any of the authority conferred upon him by this order.

JOHN F. KENNEDY
*The White House*
*September 30, 1962*

## 297 "creative tension" (1963)

The most active social and political movement of the early 1960s was that of blacks seeking equality in the South. "Sit-ins" in restaurants, Freedom Riders in bus terminals, and mass demonstrations for equality before the law made these dissenters against the existing order the focus of national attention. Along with Ralph Abernathy, Martin Luther King, Jr., led a march through the middle of Birmingham, Alabama, in defiance of a court injunction. He was arrested and placed in jail. This letter, written from the Birmingham jail, was in response to a statement by white clergymen that the demonstrations were "unwise and untimely." King received the Nobel Peace Prize the following year.

☆ 297  Letter from Birmingham City Jail

Reprinted in James Melvin Washington, *A Testament of Hope* (New York: Harper & Row, 1986), 289-302.

MY DEAR FELLOW CLERGYMEN,

While confined here in the Birmingham City Jail, I came across your recent statement calling our present activities "unwise and untimely." . . .

I think I should give the reason for my being in Birmingham, since you have been influenced by the argument of "outsiders coming in." . . . I am here, along with several members of my staff, because we were invited here. I am here because I have basic organizational ties here.

Beyond this, I am in Birmingham because injustice is here. Just as the eighth century prophets left their little villages and carried their "thus saith the Lord" far beyond the boundaries of their home towns; and just as the Apostle Paul left his little village of Tarsus and carried the gospel of Jesus Christ to practically every hamlet and city of the Graeco-Roman world, I too am compelled to carry the gospel of freedom beyond my particular home town. Like

Paul, I must constantly respond to the Macedonian call for aid.

Moreover, I am cognizant of the interrelatedness of all communities and states.... Never again can we afford to live with the narrow, provincial "outside agitator" idea. Anyone who lives inside the United States can never be considered an outsider anywhere in this country.

\*          \*          \*

In any nonviolent campaign there are four basic steps: (1) Collection of the facts to determine whether injustices are alive. (2) Negotiation. (3) Self-purification and (4) Direct Action. We have gone through all of these steps in Birmingham. There can be no gainsaying of the fact that racial injustice engulfs this community.

Birmingham is probably the most thoroughly segregated city in the United States. Its ugly record of police brutality is known in every section of this country. Its injust treatment of Negroes in the courts is a notorious reality. There have been more unsolved bombings of Negro homes and churches in Birmingham than any city in this nation. These are the hard, brutal and unbelievable facts. On the basis of these conditions Negro leaders sought to negotiate with the city fathers. But the political leaders consistently refused to engage in good faith negotiation.

Then came the opportunity last September to talk with some of the leaders of the economic community. In these negotiating sessions certain promises were made by the merchants—such as the promise to remove the humiliating racial signs from the stores.... The signs remained. Like so many experiences of the past we were confronted with blasted hopes, and the dark shadow of a deep disappointment settled upon us. So we had no alternative except that of preparing for direct action, whereby we would present our very bodies as a means of laying our case before the conscience of the local and national community. We were not unmindful of the difficulties involved. So we decided to go through a process of self-purification....

\*          \*          \*

You may well ask, "Why direct action? Why sit-ins, marches, etc.? Isn't negotiation a better path?" You are exactly right in your call for negotiation. Indeed, this is the purpose of direct action. Nonviolent direct action seeks to create such a crisis and establish such creative tension that a community that has constantly refused to negotiate is forced to confront the issue. It seeks so to dramatize the issue that it can no longer be ignored. I just referred to the creation of tension as a part of the work of the nonviolent resister. This may sound rather shocking. But I must confess that I am not afraid of the word tension. I have earnestly worked and preached against

violent tension, but there is a type of constructive nonviolent tension that is necessary for growth. Just as Socrates felt that it was necessary to create a tension in the mind so that individuals could rise from the bondage of myths and half-truths to the unfettered realm of creative analysis and objective appraisal, we must see the need of having nonviolent gadflies to create the kind of tension in society that will help men to rise from the dark depths of prejudice and racism to the majestic heights of understanding and brotherhood. So the purpose of the direct action is to create a situation so crisis-packed that it will inevitably open the door to negotiation. We, therefore, concur with you in your call for negotiation. Too long has our beloved Southland been bogged down in the tragic attempt to live in monologue rather than dialogue.

\*          \*          \*

You express a great deal of anxiety over our willingness to break laws. This is certainly a legitimate concern. Since we so diligently urge people to obey the Supreme Court's decision of 1954 outlawing segregation in the public schools, it is rather strange and paradoxical to find us consciously breaking laws. One may well ask, "How can you advocate breaking some laws and obeying others?" The answer is found in the fact that there are two types of laws: There are *just* and there are *unjust* laws. I would agree with Saint Augustine that "An unjust law is no law at all."

Now what is the difference between the two? How does one determine when a law is just or unjust? A just law is a man-made code that squares with the moral law or the law of God. An unjust law is a code that is out of harmony with the moral law. To put it in the terms of Saint Thomas Aquinas, an unjust law is a human law that is not rooted in eternal and natural law. Any law that uplifts human personality is just. Any law that degrades human personality is unjust. All segregation statutes are unjust because segregation distorts the soul and damages the personality. It gives the segregator a false sense of superiority, and the segregated a false sense of inferiority.... So I can urge men to disobey segregation ordinances because they are morally wrong.

Let us turn to a more concrete example of just and unjust laws. An unjust law is a code that a majority inflicts on a minority that is not binding on itself. This is difference made legal. On the other hand a just law is a code that a majority compels a minority to follow that it is willing to follow itself. This is sameness made legal.

Let me give another explanation. An unjust law is a code inflicted upon a minority which that minority had no part in enacting or creating because they did not have the unhampered right to vote....

\*          \*          \*

We can never forget that everything Hitler did in Germany was "legal" and everything the Hungarian freedom fighters did in Hungary was "illegal." It was "illegal" to aid and comfort a Jew in Hitler's Germany. But I am sure that if I had lived in Germany during that time I would have aided and comforted my Jewish brothers even though it was illegal. If I lived in a Communist country today where certain principles dear to the Christian faith are suppressed, I believe I would openly advocate disobeying these anti-religious laws. I must make two honest confessions to you, my Christian and Jewish brothers. First, I must confess that over the last few years I have been gravely disappointed with the white moderate. I have almost reached the regrettable conclusion that the Negro's great stumbling block in the stride toward freedom is not the White Citizen's Council-er or the Ku Klux Klanner, but the white moderate who is more devoted to "order" than to justice; who prefers a negative peace which is the absence of tension to a positive peace which is the presence of justice. . . .

I had hoped that the white moderate would understand that law and order exist for the purpose of establishing justice, and that when they fail to do this they become dangerously structured dams that block the flow of social progress. I had hoped that the white moderate would understand that the present tension of the South is merely a necessary phase of the transition from an obnoxious negative peace, where the Negro passively accepted his unjust plight, to a substance-filled positive peace, where all men will respect the dignity and worth of human personality. Actually, we who engage in nonviolent direct action are not the creators of tension. We merely bring to the surface the hidden tension that is already alive. We bring it out in the open where it can be seen and dealt with. Like a boil that can never be cured as long as it is covered up but must be opened with all its pus-flowing ugliness to the natural medicines of air and light, injustice must likewise be exposed, with all of the tension its exposing creates, to the light of human conscience and the air of national opinion before it can be cured.

In your statement you asserted that our actions, even though peaceful, must be condemned because they precipitate violence. But can this assertion be logically made? Isn't this like condemning the robbed man because his possession of money precipitated the evil act of robbery? Isn't this like condemning Socrates because his unswerving commitment to truth and his philosophical delvings precipitated the misguided popular mind to make him drink the hemlock? Isn't this like condemning Jesus because His unique God-Consciousness and never-ceasing devotion to His will precipitated the evil act of crucifixion? We must come to see, as federal courts have consistently affirmed, that it is immoral to urge an individual to withdraw his efforts to gain his basic constitutional rights because the quest precipitates violence. Society must protect the robbed and punish the robber.

*        *        *

But as I continued to think about the matter I gradually gained a bit of satisfaction from being considered an extremist. . . . So the question is not whether we will be extremist but what kind of extremist will we be. Will we be extremists for hate or will we be extremists for love? Will we be extremists for the preservation of injustice — or will we be extremists for the cause of justice? In that dramatic scene on Calvary's hill, three men were crucified. We must not forget that all three were crucified for the same crime — the crime of extremism. Two were extremists for immorality, and thusly fell below their environment. The other, Jesus Christ, was an extremist for love, truth and goodness, and thereby rose above his environment. So, after all, maybe the South, the nation and the world are in dire need of creative extremists.

## 298 "to fight back in self-defense" (1964)

The movement for racial justice was not wholly united behind the reformist and nonviolent philosophy of Martin Luther King, Jr. The Nation of Islam, or Black Muslims, believed that only by separation and self-sufficiency in all aspects of life could blacks escape existence as a permanent minority subjugated by whites. Seeing no desirable ends in integration, they set out to form a black nationalist movement calling for a separate black nation or a return to Africa. Malcolm X lost a power struggle and was forced out of the Nation of Islam. At that point he planned a more militant program. Viewing King's integrationist approach as inherently self-defeating, and Elijah Muhammad's leadership of the Black Muslims as too conservative in action, Malcolm X outlined his new course on March 12, 1964, eleven months before his assassination. He urged blacks to arm themselves and form rifle clubs for community defense against attacks from white mobs and terrorists, as well as state and local law enforcement officers, and to internationalize their struggle by allying their cause to that of blacks all over the world.

### ☆ 298 A Declaration of Independence

Reprinted in G. Breitman, ed., *Malcolm X Speaks* (New York: Grove Press, 1965), 20-22.

Because 1964 threatens to be a very explosive year on the racial front, and because I myself intend to be very active in every phase of the American Negro struggle for *human rights*, I have called this press conference this morning in order to clarify my own position in the struggle — especially in regard to politics and nonviolence.

. . . I still believe that Mr. Muhammad's analysis of the problem is the most realistic, and that his solution is the best one. This means that I too believe the best solution is complete separation, with our people going back home, to our own African homeland.

But separation back to Africa is still a long-range program, and while it is yet to materialize, 22 million of our people who are still here in America need better food, clothing, housing, education and jobs *right now*. Mr. Muhammad's program does point us back homeward, but it also contains within it what we could and should be doing to help solve many of our own problems while we are still here.

Internal differences within the Nation of Islam forced me out of it. I did not leave of my own free will. But now that it has happened, I intend to make the most of it. Now that I have more independence of action, I intend to use a more flexible approach toward working with others to get a solution to this problem.

I do not pretend to be a divine man, but I do believe in divine guidance, divine power, and in the fulfillment of divine prophecy. I am not educated, nor am I an expert in any particular field — but I am sincere, and my sincerity is my credentials.

\*         \*         \*

I am going to organize and head a new mosque in New York City, known as the Muslim Mosque, Inc. This gives us a religious base, and the spiritual force necessary to rid our people of the vices that destroy the moral fiber of our community.

Our political philosophy will be black nationalism. Our economic and social philosophy will be black nationalism. Our cultural emphasis will be black nationalism.

\*         \*         \*

The political philosophy of black nationalism means: we must control the politics and the politicians of our community. They must no longer take orders from outside forces. We will organize, and sweep out of office all Negro politicians who are puppets for the outside forces.

Our accent will be upon youth: we need new ideas, new methods, new approaches. We will call upon young students of political science throughout the nation to help us. We will encourage these young students to launch their own independent study, and then give us their analysis and their suggestions. We are completely disenchanted with the old, adult, established politicians. We want to see some new faces — more militant faces.

\*         \*         \*

The Muslim Mosque, Inc., will remain wide open for ideas and financial aid from all quarters. Whites can help us, but they can't join us. There can be no black-white unity until there is first some black unity. There can be no workers' solidarity until there is first some racial solidarity. We cannot think of uniting with others, until after we have first united among ourselves. We cannot think of being acceptable to others until we have first proven acceptable to ourselves. One can't unite bananas with scattered leaves.

Concerning nonviolence: it is criminal to teach a man not to defend himself when he is the constant victim of brutal attacks. It is legal and lawful to own a shotgun or a rifle. We believe in obeying the law.

In areas where our people are the constant victims of brutality, and the government seems unable or unwilling to protect them, we should form rifle clubs that can be used to defend our lives and our property in times of emergency, such as happened last year in Birmingham; Plaquemine, Louisiana; Cambridge, Maryland; and Danville, Virginia. When our people are being bitten by dogs, they are within their rights to kill those dogs.

We should be peaceful, law-abiding — but the time has come for the American Negro to fight back in self-defense whenever and wherever he is being unjustly and unlawfully attacked.

If the government thinks I am wrong for saying this, then let the government start doing its job.

## 299 "His urge to try to find a place in history . . . His avowed commitment to Marxism and communism, as he understood the terms" (1964)

In 1960, John F. Kennedy, at age forty-three, won the presidency by the slimmest popular majority since 1884. His election stimulated great political excitement. President Kennedy proposed to restart the social and governmental reforms that World War II, the cold war, and the quiescence of the Eisenhower years had interrupted. But international emergencies in Berlin, Laos, and Cuba demanded much of his attention. In 1961, President Kennedy accepted "sole responsibility" for the failed Cuban invasion by CIA-trained and -equipped Cuban exiles. The Cuban missile crisis emerged in 1962, and the United States blockaded arms shipments to Castro. Congressional indifference toward domestic reforms prevailed, and the elation of the first few months subsided.

The increasing pace in the black movement for social and economic improvements created heated racial and regional tensions. By mid-1963 more than 750 racial demonstrations had taken place throughout the country, climaxing in August with a huge "March on Washington for Jobs and Freedom." Speaking to some two hundred thousand demonstrators in Washington, D.C., Martin Luther King, Jr., predicted that turmoil in the United States would continue "until the Negro is granted his citizenship rights." A month later a bomb exploded in a Negro Baptist church in Birmingham, Alabama, killing four children and injuring several others. On November 22, 1963, President Kennedy was struck and killed by two bullets while riding in a campaign motorcade through Dallas, Texas. Any remnants of the early hope disappeared.

Lee Harvey Oswald, a former marine, was charged with the crime, but nightclub owner Jack Ruby killed Oswald on November 24, 1963, while Oswald was in police custody. On November 29, Lyndon Baines Johnson, sworn in a week earlier as the thirty-sixth president of the United States, appointed a commission under the chairmanship of Chief Justice Earl Warren to investigate Kennedy's assassination.

## ☆ 299 The Warren Commission's Conclusions

*Report of The President's Commission on the Assassination of President John F. Kennedy* (Washington, D.C.: U.S. Government Printing Office, 1964), 21-23, 26-27.

CONCLUSIONS

\*          \*          \*

9. The Commission has found no evidence that either Lee Harvey Oswald or Jack Ruby was part of any conspiracy, domestic or foreign, to assassinate President Kennedy. The reasons for this conclusion are:

\*          \*          \*

(c) The Commission has found no evidence to show that Oswald was employed, persuaded, or encouraged by any foreign government to assassinate President Kennedy or that he was an agent of any foreign government, although the Commission has reviewed the circumstances surrounding Oswald's defection to the Soviet Union, his life there from October of 1959 to June of 1962 so far as it can be reconstructed, his known contacts with the Fair Play for Cuba Committee, and his visits to the Cuban and Soviet Embassies in Mexico City during his trip to Mexico from September 26 to October 3, 1963, and his known contacts with the Soviet Embassy in the United States.

(d) The Commission has explored all attempts of Oswald to identify himself with various political groups, including the Communist Party, U.S.A., the Fair Play for Cuba Committee, and the Socialist Workers Party, and has been unable

to find any evidence that the contacts which he initiated were related to Oswald's subsequent assassination of the President.

\*          \*          \*

10. In its entire investigation the Commission has found no evidence of conspiracy, subversion, or disloyalty to the U.S. Government by any Federal, State, or local official.

11. On the basis of the evidence before the Commission it concludes that Oswald acted alone. Therefore, to determine the motives for the assassination of President Kennedy, one must look to the assassin himself. Clues to Oswald's motives can be found in his family history, his education or lack of it, his acts, his writings, and the recollections of those who had close contacts with him throughout his life. The Commission has presented with this report all of the background information bearing on motivation which it could discover. Thus, others may study Lee Oswald's life and arrive at their own conclusions as to his possible motives.

The Commission could not make any definitive determination of Oswald's motives. It has endeavored to isolate factors which contributed to his character and which might have influenced his decision to assassinate President Kennedy. These factors were:

(a) His deep-rooted resentment of all authority which was expressed in a hostility toward every society in which he lived;

(b) His inability to enter into meaningful relationships with people, and a continuous pattern of rejecting his environment in favor of new surroundings;

(c) His urge to try to find a place in history and despair at times over failures in his various undertakings;

(d) His capacity for violence as evidenced by his attempt to kill General Walker;

(e) His avowed commitment to Marxism and communism, as he understood the terms and developed his own interpretation of them; this was expressed by his antagonism toward the United States, by his defection to the Soviet Union, by his failure to be reconciled with life in the United States even after his disenchantment with the Soviet Union, and by his efforts, though frustrated, to go to Cuba.

Each of these contributed to his capacity to risk all in cruel and irresponsible actions.

\*          \*          \*

RECOMMENDATIONS

\*          \*          \*

10. The Commission recommends to Congress that it adopt legislation which would make the assas-

sination of the President and Vice-President a Federal crime. A state of affairs where U.S. authorities have no clearly defined jurisdiction to investigate the assassination of a President is anomalous.

11. The Commission has examined the Department of State's handling of the Oswald matters and finds that it followed the law throughout. However, the Commission believes that the Department in accordance with its own regulations should in all cases exercise great care in the return to this country of defectors who have evidenced disloyalty or hostility to this country or who have expressed a desire to renounce their American citizenship and that when such persons are so returned, procedures should be adopted for the better dissemination of information concerning them to the intelligence agencies of the Government.

*        *        *

## 300 "American society ... is simply no longer exciting" (1964-1965)

Several factors contributed to the student campus unrest in the mid-1960s. Berkeley's president Clark Kerr acknowledged that large universities received extensive federal money that bound them to federal military, scientific, economic, and social objectives. With enrollments increasing and faculty attention diverted toward research, students found themselves in enlarged classes and in impersonal, frustrating, and insecure university environments. President Kennedy's assassination in 1963 further upset the complacent belief in a predictable future, and experiences in the civil rights movement taught students effective tactics for combating inequities. Finally, beginning in the mid-1960s the demands of an unpopular and distant war in Vietnam gave students on American campuses a more immediate, personal cause for dissatisfaction.

Soon after returning from participation in civil rights work in Mississippi during the summer of 1964, Berkeley student Mario Savio found himself the leader of the Free Speech Movement, which opposed the university administration's efforts to close down the booths and leafletting on "The Strip"—the traditional Berkeley marketplace of ideas. Staging protest marches and a sit-in in the administration building, and directly violating the objectionable regulation, the students incurred disciplinary action by the university, and some were arrested when the administration called in the police. Ultimately, the university lifted the prohibitions.

Larry D. Spence's analysis of Berkeley's Free Speech Movement went beyond campus unrest. It focused on the broader issues of America's growing

crisis, the role of students as a medium of change, and the use of civil disobedience as a mechanism for reform.

## ☆300 Student Protest

### ☆300a An End to History (Mario Savio)

Reprinted in Michael V. Miller and Susan Gilmore, eds. *Revolution at Berkeley* (New York: Dell, 1965), 239-43.

Last summer I went to Mississippi to join the struggle there for civil rights. This fall I am engaged in another phase of the same struggle, this time in Berkeley. The two battlefields may seem quite different to some observers, but this is not the case. The same rights are at stake in both places—the right to participate as citizens in democratic society and the right to due process of law....

*        *        *

As bureaucrat, an administrator believes that nothing new happens. He occupies an ahistorical point of view. In September, to get the attention of this bureaucracy which had issued arbitrary edicts suppressing student political expression and refused to discuss its action, we held a sit-in on the campus. We sat around a police car and kept it immobilized for over thirty-two hours. At last, the administrative bureaucracy agreed to negotiate....

The same is true of all bureaucracies. They begin as tools, means to certain legitimate goals, and they end up feeding their own existence. The conception that bureaucrats have is that history has in fact come to an end. No events can occur now that the Second World War is over which can change American society substantially. We proceed by standard procedures as we are.

*        *        *

Here is the real contradiction: the bureaucrats hold history as ended. As a result significant parts of the population both on campus and off are dispossessed, and these dispossessed are not about to accept this ahistorical point of view. It is out of this that the conflict has occurred with the university bureaucracy and will continue to occur until that bureaucracy becomes responsive or until it is clear the university can not function.

The things we are asking for in our civil rights protests have a deceptively quaint ring. We are asking for the due process of law. We are asking for our actions to be judged by committees of our peers. We are asking that regulations ought to be considered as arrived at legitimately only from the consensus of the governed. These phrases are all pretty old, but they are not being taken seriously in America today, nor are they being taken seriously on the Berkeley campus.

*        *        *

This free speech fight points up a fascinating aspect of contemporary campus life. Students are permitted to talk all they want so long as their speech has no consequences.

\*         \*         \*

. . . Because speech does often have consequences which might alter this perversion [serving the needs of America's industry] of higher education, the university must put itself in a position of censorship. It can permit two kinds of speech, speech which encourages continuation of the status quo, and speech which advocates changes in it so radical as to be irrelevant in the foreseeable future. Someone may advocate radical change in all aspects of American society, and this I am sure he can do with impunity. But if someone advocates sit-ins to bring about changes in discriminatory hiring practices, this cannot be permitted because it goes against the status quo of which the university is a part. And that is how the fight began here.

\*         \*         \*

The University is well structured, well tooled, to turn out people with all the sharp edges worn off, the well-rounded person. The University is well equipped to produce that sort of person, and this means that the best among the people who enter must for four years wander aimlessly much of the time questioning why they are on campus at all, doubting whether there is any point in what they are doing, and looking toward a very bleak existence afterward in a game in which all of the rules have been made up, which one cannot really amend.

It is a bleak scene, but it is all a lot of us have to look forward to. Society provides no challenge. American society in the standard conception it has of itself is simply no longer exciting. The most exciting things going on in America today are movements to change America. America is becoming ever more the Utopia of sterilized, automated contentment. The "futures" and "careers" for which American students now prepare are for the most part intellectual and moral wastelands. This chrome-plated consumer's paradise would have us grow up to be well-behaved children. But an important minority of men and women coming to the front today have shown that they will die rather than be standardized, replaceable and irrelevant.

☆ 300b Berkeley: What It Demonstrates
(Larry D. Spence)

Reprinted in Michael V. Miller and Susan Gilmore, eds., *Revolution at Berkeley* (New York: Dell, 1965), 217-24.

Beginning in the early morning hours of December 3, 1964, more than 700 students of the University of California at Berkeley were arrested and dragged from the central administration building of the campus. During and following this mass arrest, picket lines were set up at major campus entrances and classroom facilities. By Friday, December 4, university operations were effectively brought to a standstill and more than 8,000 students rotated picket-line duty.

This was the first successful student strike at a major university in the United States. But more important, this was the first significant white-collar rebellion in our time. These sons and daughters of the middle class demonstrated and walked the picket lines, not behind the moral banner of the repressed Negro, but on the basis of their own grievances against a system that had deprived them of their rights of responsibility and self-expression. More than sixty per cent of those arrested had never engaged in an act of civil disobedience before and fifty-seven per cent were political newcomers.

University President Clark Kerr recently admitted that the original ban, taking away the use of a small area in front of the University entrance for political activities, was a mistake. But he added, "It had just been taken away — we could hardly turn around and hand it right back." This attitude illustrates the administration's fatal error. Administration blunders consistently revealed that policy was decided on irrational and incompetent ground and thus regulations and practices that had formerly been irritating became intolerable.

. . . Recent insurgent groups such as the Negroes of the civil rights movement and the rear-guard entrepreneurs of the ultra-right have come from areas outside the system of government, corporation and military organizations. These groups have aimed at effecting policy changes. In contrast, the students' demands are structural, calling for changes in the hierarchical relationships of organized power.

The university has become a key component of the organizational system. . . .

The new "multiversity" is a factory that turns out scientists, technicians, and managers to meet the demands of an increasingly cybernated production system. . . .

\*         \*         \*

What about the product of the new knowledge factory? Ideally, the graduate of the "multiversity" is a startling combination of a technological genius and a thumb-sucking fool. This ideal is reflected in the hierarchy of affluence among University departments. . . . The ideal also is reflected in the scholarly productions of the University. Nobel Laureates abound in the sciences, end-of-ideology books and monographs pour out of the social sciences, and esoteric criticism and scholastic squabbles leak from the liberal arts.

The "multiversity" is an institute of ignorance as well as intellect. . . .

*          *          *

The student revolt at the University of California represents a dramatic break with this milieu of inevitability. The tensions inherent in the idiot-genius man have exploded in the process of his production. Needed, and needed badly by an organizational system that seeks to stifle initiative and dissent, these students in revolt have exposed some basic flaws behind the smooth façades of bureaucratic power. Even more important, they have demonstrated faith in a radical course of political action.

There is a great discrepancy between the size and power of today's giant organizations and their effectiveness. The military and governmental bureaucracies of the world's most powerful nation cannot find the means to conquer an over-sized rice paddy called Vietnam. The bureaucracy of the largest university in the world cannot admit simple mistakes or negotiate with dissident students without calling in the state police. . . . Despite the contemporary emphasis on machines and management, these factors suggest that the central problem of the modern organization is human. It was not machines or programming techniques that failed the French in Algeria or are failing the United States in Vietnam. Victorious armies as well as successful organizations require men capable of rational and forceful actions based on reality, not automatons steeped in mythology.

The men and women in bureaucratic slots have been regarded as just such automatons by both enemies of, and apologists for, the organizational system. They have theorized that human loyalty can be bought with affluence and pension plans. But man's psychology is not so simple. Men must have some belief in the meaning of their work or retreat from reality. . . .

For half a decade, the students who are to make up the next generation of management have demonstrated that they do not think much of the work and tasks that await them. They have tried to find ways out of the grind by entering the Peace Corps, doing social work in metropolitan slums, and registering voters in Mississippi. Those technicians who have entered the organizational world have found their lives torn by the contradiction between the social and economic progress they know to be possible and the desperate gadgetry that absorbs their efforts. Such disenchantment is the forerunner of a social explosion. The revolt at Berkeley was only the first bang.

The more University functions were disabled by student demonstrations, the more other students recognized a means of translating their individual frustrations into effective protest. Beginning with rallies of from 500 to 1,000 students, the Free Speech Movement subsequently drew from 5,000 to 8,000 students. The students' consciousness became increasingly radical and critical of the organizational machinery grinding their lives into atomic fragments of cringing work and electronic leisure. This attitude was summed up brilliantly by student leader Mario Savio:

> There is a time when the operation of the machine becomes so odious, makes you so sick at heart that you can't take part; you can't even tacitly take part, and you've got to put your bodies on the gears and upon the wheels, upon the levers, upon all the apparatus and you've got to make it stop. And you've got to indicate to the people who run it, to the people who own it, that unless you're free, the machines will be prevented from working at all.

These events in Berkeley should be an impetus to American radicals to finally "kick the labor metaphysic" and drop the vulgar-Marxist belief (shared by administrative liberals) that men must be hungry or unemployed or discriminated against to participate in radical political action. A survey of successful revolutions and radical action leads to the conclusion that men must be *conscious*, not hungry, to attempt the reconstruction of society. The Berkeley revolt has demonstrated that such a radical consciousness can be created by means of successful acts of social dislocation. Civil disobedience and mass non-violent demonstrations can bring bureaucratic processes to a screeching halt. Such shocks to organizational routines are often enough to jolt many from their conformist slumbers. These shocks dramatically demonstrate that organizations exist on the basis of men's faith and allegiance. They force the individual to recognize his own power and the tacit commitment he has made to an organizational system that works against his own interests and aspirations.

*          *          *

## 301 "fellow revolutionaries" (1965)

After the Free Speech Movement quieted at Berkeley, sympathetic demonstrations and protests sporadically appeared on campuses nationwide. But beyond their amorphous dissatisfaction with American society and academia, white college students had no specific issue on which to focus. The escalation of the United States military involvement in Vietnam and the initiation of a policy of sustained bombing in North Vietnam finally gave a political impetus to their disquiet and a more personal stake in change.

When President Johnson addressed a group of demonstrators at the White House in the summer of 1965, poverty and racism continued to be the concerns uppermost in his mind. The rhetoric of militant revolution seemed well suited to the solicitation of support for his legislative and executive initiatives in the South. But ironically, within two years of this statement students and other protestors would "rouse the masses and blow the bugles" against his war policy.

☆301 President Lyndon B. Johnson's Address to Demonstrators at the White House (August 3, 1965)

Reprinted in Charles E. Whittaker and William Sloane Griffin, Jr., *Law and Order and Civil Disobedience* (Washington, D.C.: American Enterprise Institute for Public Policy Research, 1967), 17-18.

August 3, 1965:

I am proud this morning to salute you as fellow revolutionaries. Neither you nor I are willing to accept the tyranny of poverty, nor the dictatorship of ignorance, nor the despotism of ill health, nor the oppression of bias and prejudice and bigotry. We want change. We want progress . . . and we aim to get it. . . . I hope that you . . . will go out into the hinterland and rouse the masses and blow the bugles and tell them that the hour has arrived and their day is here; that we are on the march against the ancient enemies and we are going to be successful.

## 302 "Whoever kills any individual who is the President of the United States" (1965)

Despite three successful presidential assassinations—Lincoln (1865), Garfield (1881), and McKinley (1901)—and four attempts—Jackson (1835), T. Roosevelt (1912), F. D. Roosevelt (1933), and Truman (1950)—when President Kennedy died in 1963, it was not a federal crime to assassinate the president of the United States. Furthermore, since murder was a state crime, federal authorities lacked jurisdiction to enter the Kennedy investigation and were dependent on state authorities to take Lee Harvey Oswald into custody for questioning and safekeeping. The new statute created clear federal jurisdiction for the investigation and prosecution of presidential assailants. The act also penalized as federal crimes kidnaping, attempts and conspiracy to kill or kidnap, and assault upon the highest members of the federal executive.

☆302 Presidential Assassination, Kidnaping, and Assault

79 Stat. 580 (1965).

*Be it enacted by the Senate and House of Representatives of the United States of America in Congress*

*assembled,* That title 18, United States Code, is amended by inserting immediately following section 1734 thereof, a new chapter, as follows:

"CHAPTER 84.—PRESIDENTIAL ASSASSINATION, KIDNAPING, AND ASSAULT

*§1751. Presidential Assassination, Kidnaping, and Assault; Penalties*

(a) Whoever kills any individual who is the President of the United States, the President-elect, the Vice President, or, if there is no Vice President, the officer next in the order of succession to the office of President of the United States, the Vice-President-elect, or any individual who is acting as President under the Constitution and laws of the United States, shall be punished as provided by sections 1111 and 1112 of this title.

\*       \*       \*

(g) The Attorney General of the United States, in his discretion, is authorized to pay an amount not to exceed $100,000 for information and services concerning a violation of this section. Any officer or employee of the United States or of any State or local government who furnishes information or renders service in the performance of his official duties shall not be eligible for payment under this subsection.

(h) If Federal investigative or prosecutive jurisdiction is asserted for a violation of this section, such assertion shall suspend the exercise of jurisdiction by a State or local authority, under any applicable State or local law, until Federal action is terminated.

(i) Violations of this section shall be investigated by the Federal Bureau of Investigation. Assistance may be requested from any Federal, State, or local agency, including the Army, Navy, and Air Force, any statute, rule, or regulation to the contrary notwithstanding.

## 303 Opposition to War from "a merely personal moral code" (1965)

Conscription into the armed services can produce one of the most direct conflicts between the obligations of citizenship and the dictates of conscience—religious, personal, political, or otherwise. From the earliest times of this nation, the courts have found means to exempt members of pacifist religious sects from military service. The first Conscription Act (1863) did not contain such an exemption, but Congress added one in 1864 (13 Stat. 9). In World War I, legislation restricted exemptions to those claiming them on religious grounds. The secretary of war interpreted the act to exempt as well people who had personal objections against war. Congress narrowed this interpretation through further legislation in 1940.

At the height of opposition to the Vietnam War, thousands of draft-age youths sought to avoid induction into the armed forces. In defense of their opposition, some argued personal morality rather than religious conscience. This argument would permit a wider category of draftees to refuse induction lawfully. The Supreme Court never addressed the constitutional question of whether the free exercise clause of the First Amendment required Congress to provide exemptions for religious conscientious objectors. But to the extent that Congress permitted only an exemption for religious beliefs and not others, was this not a violation of the establishment clause of the First Amendment? In 1965, the court in *Seeger* interpreted the exemption clause to avoid that problem, but still precluded political, economic, or philosophical objections to war from providing the basis for exemption.

### ☆ 303 *United States v. Seeger*

380 U.S. 163 (1965).

MR. JUSTICE CLARK delivered the opinion of the Court.

These cases involve claims of conscientious objectors under § 6(j) of the Universal Military Training and Service Act, which exempts from combatant training and service in the armed forces of the United States those persons who by reason of their religious training and belief are conscientiously opposed to participation in war in any form.... The parties raise the basic question of the constitutionality of the section which defines the term "religious training and belief," as used in the Act, as "an individual's belief in a relation to a Supreme Being involving duties superior to those arising from any human relation, but [not including] essentially political, sociological, or philosophical views or a merely personal moral code." ...

We have concluded that Congress, in using the expression "Supreme Being" rather than the designation "God," was merely clarifying the meaning of religious training and belief so as to embrace all religions and to exclude essentially political, sociological, or philosophical views. We believe that under this construction, the test of belief "in a relation to a Supreme Being" is whether a given belief that is sincere and meaningful occupies a place in the life of its possessor parallel to that filled by the orthodox belief in God of one who clearly qualifies for the exemption. Where such beliefs have parallel positions in the lives of their respective holders we cannot say that one is "in a relation to a Supreme Being" and the other is not. We have concluded that the beliefs of the objectors in these cases meet these criteria....

*             *             *

### INTERPRETATION OF § 6(J)

The crux of the problem lies in the phrase "religious training and belief" which Congress has defined as "belief in a relation to a Supreme Being involving duties superior to those arising from any human relation." In assigning meaning to this statutory language we may narrow the inquiry by noting briefly those scruples expressly excepted from the definition. The section excludes those persons who, disavowing religious belief, decide on the basis of essentially political, sociological or economic considerations that war is wrong and that they will have no part of it.. . .

*             *             *

[But] it becomes readily apparent that the Congress deliberately broadened [the range of qualifying beliefs] by substituting the phrase "Supreme Being" for the appellation "God" [in the 1948 amendment]....

Moreover, the Senate Report on the bill specifically states that § 6(j) was intended to re-enact "substantially the same provisions as were found" in the 1940 Act. That statute, of course, refers to "religious training and belief" without more. Admittedly, all of the parties here purport to base their objection on religious belief. It appears, therefore, that we need only look to this clear statement of congressional intent as set out in the report. Under the 1940 Act it was necessary only to have a conviction based upon religious training and belief; we believe that is all that is required here. Within that phrase would come all sincere religious beliefs which are based upon a power or being, or upon a faith, to which all else is subordinate or upon which all else is ultimately dependent. The test might be stated in these words: A sincere and meaningful belief which occupies in the life of its possessor a place parallel to that filled by the God of those admittedly qualifying for the exemption comes within the statutory definition. This construction avoids imputing to Congress an intent to classify different religious beliefs, exempting some and excluding others, and is in accord with the well-established congressional policy of equal treatment for those whose opposition to service is grounded in their religious tenets.

*             *             *

Section 6(j), then, is no more than a clarification of the 1940 provision involving only certain "technical amendments," to use the words of Senator Gurney. As such it continues the congressional policy of providing exemption from military service for those whose opposition is based on grounds that can fairly be said to be "religious." To hold otherwise would not only fly in the face of Congress' entire action in the past; it would ignore the historic position of our country on this issue since its founding.

*             *             *

We recognize the difficulties that have always faced the trier of fact in these cases. We hope that the test that we lay down proves less onerous. The examiner is furnished a standard that permits consideration of criteria with which he has had considerable experience. While the applicant's words may differ, the test is simple of application. It is essentially an objective one, namely, does the claimed belief occupy the same place in the life of the objector as an orthodox belief in God holds in the life of one clearly qualified for exemption?

Moreover, it must be remembered that in resolving these exemption problems one deals with the beliefs of different individuals who will articulate them in a multitude of ways. In such an intensely personal area, of course, the claim of the registrant that his belief is an essential part of a religious faith must be given great weight. . . . The validity of what he believes cannot be questioned. Some theologians, and indeed some examiners, might be tempted to question the existence of the registrant's "Supreme Being" or the truth of his concepts. But these are inquiries foreclosed to Government. . . . Local boards and courts in this sense are not free to reject beliefs because they consider them "incomprehensible." Their task is to decide whether the beliefs professed by a registrant are sincerely held and whether they are, in his own scheme of things, religious.

But we hasten to emphasize that while the "truth" of a belief is not open to question, there remains the significant question whether it is "truly held." This is the threshold question of sincerity which must be resolved in every case. It is, of course, a question of fact—a prime consideration to the validity of every claim for exemption as a conscientious objector. The Act provides a comprehensive scheme for assisting the Appeal Boards in making this determination, placing at their service the facilities of the Department of Justice, including the Federal Bureau of Investigation and hearing officers. . . .

*          *          *

## 304 "a higher standard of *loyalty*" (1966)

In June 1965 Julian Bond, a black man, was elected to the Georgia House of Representatives. Several months later the Student Nonviolent Coordinating Committee, of which Bond was communications director, issued a statement opposing the American involvement in Vietnam and supporting those who resisted the draft. At a news interview, Bond endorsed the statement and stated that as a pacifist and "a second-class citizen" he was not required to support the war. On the basis of this statement, members of the Georgia House of Representatives questioned Bond's loyalty and therefore his right to be seated in the House in spite of his willingness to take the oath of office; after a legislative hearing, the House refused to seat him by a vote of 184 to 12. Bond challenged his exclusion, and while the case was on appeal, an overwhelming majority at a special election reelected Bond to his seat.

## ☆ 304 *Bond v. Floyd*

385 U.S. 116 (1966).

MR. CHIEF JUSTICE WARREN delivered the opinion of the Court.

*          *          *

. . . [T]he State concedes that Bond meets all [the stated qualifications in the Georgia Constitution].

The Georgia Constitution also requires Representatives to take an oath stated in the Constitution:

Oath of members.—Each senator and Representative, before taking his seat, shall take the following oath, or affirmation, to-wit: "I will support the Constitution of this State and of the United States, and on all questions and measures which may come before me, I will so conduct myself, as will, in my judgment, be most conducive to the interests and prosperity of this State."

The State points out in its brief that the latter part of this oath, involving the admonition to act in the best interests of the State, was not the standard by which Bond was judged.

*          *          *

. . . [W]e now move to the central question posed in the case—whether Bond's disqualification because of his statements violated the free speech provisions of the First Amendment as applied to the States through the Fourteenth Amendment.

The State argues that the exclusion does not violate the First Amendment because the State has a right, under Article VI of the United States Constitution, to insist on loyalty to the Constitution as a condition of office. A legislator of course can be required to swear to support the Constitution of the United States as a condition of holding office, but that is not the issue in this case, as the record is uncontradicted that Bond has repeatedly expressed his willingness to swear to the oaths provided for in the State and Federal Constitutions. Nor is this a case where a legislator swears to an oath *pro forma* while declaring or manifesting his disagreement with or indifference to the oath. Thus, we do not quarrel with the State's contention that the oath provisions of the United States and Georgia Constitutions do not violate the First Amendment. But this requirement does not authorize a majority of state legislators to test the sincerity with which another duly elected legislator can swear to uphold the

Constitution. Such a power could be utilized to restrict the right of legislators to dissent from national or state policy or that of a majority of their colleagues under the guise of judging their loyalty to the Constitution. Certainly there can be no question but that the First Amendment protects expressions in opposition to national foreign policy in Vietnam and to the Selective Service system. The State does not contend otherwise. But it argues that Bond went beyond expressions of opposition, and counseled violations of the Selective Service laws, and that advocating violation of federal law demonstrates a lack of support for the Constitution. The State declines to argue that Bond's statements would violate any law if made by a private citizen, but it does argue that even though such a citizen might be protected by his First Amendment rights, the State may nonetheless apply a stricter standard to its legislators. We do not agree.

Bond could not have been constitutionally convicted under 50 U.S.C. App. § 462(a), which punishes any person who "counsels, aids, or abets another to refuse or evade registration." Bond's statements were at worst unclear on the question of the means to be adopted to avoid the draft. While the SNCC statement said "We are in sympathy with, and support, the men in this country who are unwilling to respond to a military draft," this statement alone cannot be interpreted as a call to unlawful refusal to be drafted. Moreover, Bond's supplementary statements tend to resolve the opaqueness in favor of legal alternatives to the draft, and there is no evidence to the contrary. On the day the statement was issued, Bond explained that he endorsed it "because I like to think of myself as a pacifist and one who opposes that war and any other war and eager and anxious to encourage people not to participate in it for any reason that they choose." In the same interview, Bond stated categorically that he did not oppose the Vietnam policy because he favored the Communists; that he was a loyal American citizen and supported the Constitution of the United States. He further stated "I oppose the Viet Cong fighting in Viet Nam as much as I oppose the United States fighting in Viet Nam." At the hearing before the Special Committee of the Georgia House, when asked his position on persons who burned their draft cards, Bond replied that he admired the courage of persons who "feel strongly enough about their convictions to take an action like that knowing the consequences that they will face." When pressed as to whether his admiration was based on the violation of federal law, Bond stated:

> I have never suggested or counseled or advocated that any one other person burn their draft card. In fact, I have mine in my pocket and will produce it if you wish. I do not advocate that peo-

ple should break laws. What I simply try to say [*sic*] was that I admired the courage of someone who could act on his convictions knowing that he faces pretty stiff consequences.

Certainly this clarification does not demonstrate any incitement to violation of law. No useful purpose would be served by discussing the many decisions of this Court which establish that Bond could not have been convicted for these statements consistently with the First Amendment. . . .

The State attempts to circumvent the protection the First Amendment would afford to these statements if made by a private citizen by arguing that a State is constitutionally justified in exacting a higher standard of *loyalty* from its legislators than from its citizens. Of course, a State may constitutionally require an oath to support the Constitution from its legislators which it does not require of its private citizens. But this difference in treatment does not support the exclusion of Bond, for while the State has an interest in requiring its legislators to swear to a belief in constitutional processes of government, surely the oath gives it no interest in limiting its legislators' capacity to discuss their views of local or national policy. The manifest function of the First Amendment in a representative government requires that legislators be given the widest latitude to express their views on issues of policy. . . . Just as erroneous statements must be protected to give freedom of expression the breathing space it needs to survive, so statements criticizing public policy and the implementation of it must be similarly protected. . . . The interest of the public in hearing all sides of a public issue is hardly advanced by extending more protection to citizen-critics than to legislators. Legislators have an obligation to take positions on controversial political questions so that their constituents can be fully informed by them, and be better able to assess their qualifications for office; also so they may be represented in governmental debates by the person they have elected to represent them. We therefore hold that the disqualification of Bond from membership in the Georgia House because of his statements violated Bond's right of free expression under the First Amendment. Because of our disposition of the case on First Amendment grounds, we need not decide the other issues advanced by Bond and the *amici*.

*The judgment of the District Court is reversed.*

## 305 "*to reduce them under absolute despotism*" (1966)

Disappointed with their earlier nonviolent, reformist, and integrationist approach, some black civil rights activists began to reflect an increasing frustration with the ability of white institutions of law and government to change. Student Nonviolent Coordinating Committee president Stokely Carmichael captured this dissatisfaction: "The only way we gonna stop them white men from whuppin us is to take over. We been saying freedom for six years and we ain't got nothin'. What we gonna start saying now is black power."

The Black Panther Party embodied the new separatist and self-defense-oriented stage of black protest. Founded in Oakland, California, in 1966 as a black nationalist organization, the Panthers openly carried arms, uniformly wore black leather jackets, adopted a paramilitary structure, and announced a potpourri of social, economic, and political goals in the manner of Third World anticolonial liberation fronts.

## ☆ 305 Black Panther Party Platform and Program: What We Want, What We Believe

Reprinted in Philip S. Foner, ed., *The Black Panthers Speak* (Philadelphia: Lippincott, 1970), 2-6.

1. *We want freedom. We want power to determine the destiny of our Black Community.*

We believe that black people will not be free until we are able to determine our destiny.

2. *We want full employment for our people.*

We believe that the federal government is responsible and obligated to give every man employment or a guaranteed income. We believe that if the white American businessmen will not give full employment, then the means of production should be taken from the businessmen and placed in the community so that the people of the community can organize and employ all of its people and give a high standard of living.

3. *We want an end to the robbery by the white man of our Black Community.*

We believe that this racist government has robbed us and now we are demanding the overdue debt of forty acres and two mules. Forty acres and two mules was promised 100 years ago as restitution for slave labor and mass murder of black people. We will accept the payment in currency which will be distributed to our many communities. The Germans are now aiding the Jews in Israel for the genocide of the Jewish people. The Germans murdered six million Jews. The American racist has taken part in the slaughter of over fifty million black people; therefore, we feel that this is a modest demand that we make.

4. *We want decent housing, fit for shelter of human beings.*

We believe that if the white landlords will not give decent housing to our black community, then the housing and the land should be made into cooper-

atives so that our community, with government aid, can build and make decent housing for its people.

5. *We want education for our people that exposes the true nature of this decadent American society. We want education that teaches us our true history and our role in the present-day society.*

We believe in an educational system that will give to our people a knowledge of self. If a man does not have knowledge of himself and his position in society and the world, then he has little chance to relate to anything else.

6. *We want all black men to be exempt from military service.*

We believe that Black people should not be forced to fight in the military service to defend a racist government that does not protect us. We will not fight and kill other people of color in the world who, like black people, are being victimized by the white racist government of America. We will protect ourselves from the force and violence of the racist police and the racist military, by whatever means necessary.

7. *We want an immediate end to* POLICE BRUTALITY *and* MURDER *of black people.*

We believe we can end police brutality in our black community by organizing black self-defense groups that are dedicated to defending our black community from racist police oppression and brutality. The Second Amendment to the Constitution of the United States gives a right to bear arms. We therefore believe that all black people should arm themselves for self-defense.

8. *We want freedom for all black men held in federal, state, county and city prisons and jails.*

We believe that all black people should be released from the many jails and prisons because they have not received a fair and impartial trial.

9. *We want all black people when brought to trial to be tried in court by a jury of their peer group or people from their black communities, as defined by the Constitution of the United States.*

We believe that the courts should follow the United States Constitution so that black people will receive fair trials. The 14th Amendment of the U.S. Constitution gives a man a right to be tried by his peer group. A peer is a person from a similar economic, social, religious, geographical, environmental, historical and racial background. To do this the court will be forced to select a jury from the black community from which the black defendant came. We have been and are being tried by all-white juries that have no understanding of the "average reasoning man" of the black community.

10. *We want land, bread, housing, education, clothing, justice and peace. And as our major political objective, a United Nations-supervised plebiscite to be held throughout the black colony in which only black colonial subjects will be allowed to participate,*

*for the purpose of determining the will of black people as to their national destiny.*

When, in the course of human events, it becomes necessary for one people to dissolve the political bonds which have connected them with another, and to assume, among the powers of the earth, the separate and equal station to which the laws of nature and nature's God entitle them, a decent respect to the opinions of mankind requires that they should declare the causes which impel them to the separation.

We hold these truths to be self-evident, that all men are created equal; that they are endowed by their Creator with certain unalienable rights; that among these are life, liberty, and the pursuit of happiness. *That, to secure these rights, governments are instituted among men, deriving their just powers from the consent of the governed; that, whenever any form of government becomes destructive of these ends, it is the right of the people to alter or to abolish it, and to institute a new government, laying its foundation on such principles, and organizing its powers in such form, as to them shall seem most likely to effect their safety and happiness.* Prudence, indeed, will dictate that governments long established should not be changed for light and transient causes; and, accordingly, all experience hath shown, that mankind are more disposed to suffer, while evils are sufferable, than to right themselves by abolishing the forms to which they are accustomed. *But, when a long train of abuses and usurpations, pursuing invariably the same object, evinces a design to reduce them under absolute despotism, it is their right, it is their duty, to throw off such government, and to provide new guards for their future security.*

# 306 "no man can be judge in his own case ... however righteous his motives" (1967-1969)

The Southern Christian Leadership Conference, created in 1957 with the Reverend Martin Luther King, Jr., as its president, conceived of "active nonviolence," a pacifist yet action-oriented method of attacking racial evil. After the first student sit-ins at a Woolworth's lunch counter in Greensboro, North Carolina, in February, 1960, this civil rights movements gained momentum. A nonviolent demonstration was planned in Birmingham on Good Friday of 1963. Relying on a city ordinance, later held unconstitutional (*Shuttlesworth v. Birmingham*), the city denied the marchers a parade permit and obtained a temporary injunction from the state circuit court against the march. For violating the injunction, the demonstrators were arrested and sentenced to five days in jail and fined fifty dollars for contempt. In

their appeal to the Supreme Court the demonstrators asserted they had no obligation to obey an injunction based on an unconstitutional city ordinance. The Supreme Court disagreed: "[O]ne may sympathize with the petitioners' impatient commitment to their cause. But respect for judicial process is a small price to pay for the civilizing hand of law which alone can give abiding meaning to constitutional freedom."

## ☆ 306 The Birmingham Protest Cases

### ☆ 306a *Walker v. Birmingham*

388 U.S. 307 (1967).

MR. JUSTICE STEWART delivered the opinion of the Court.

\*     \*     \*

In the present case, ... [w]e are asked to say that the Constitution compelled Alabama to allow the petitioners to violate this injunction, to organize and engage in these mass street parades and demonstrations, without any previous effort on their part to have the injunction dissolved or modified, or any attempt to secure a parade permit in accordance with its terms.... [W]e cannot accept the petitioners' contentions in the circumstances of this case.

\*     \*     \*

This case would arise in quite a different constitutional posture if the petitioners, before disobeying the injunction, had challenged it in the Alabama courts, and had been met with delay or frustration of their constitutional claims. But there is no showing that such would have been the fate of a timely motion to modify or dissolve the injunction. There was an interim of two days between the issuance of the injunction and the Good Friday march. The petitioners give absolutely no explanation of why they did not make some application to the state court during that period. The injunction had issued ex parte; if the court had been presented with the petitioners' contentions, it might well have dissolved or at least modified its order in some respects. If it had not done so, Alabama procedure would have provided for an expedited process of appellate review. It cannot be presumed that the Alabama courts would have ignored the petitioners' constitutional claims. Indeed, these contentions were accepted in another case by an Alabama appellate court that struck down on direct review the conviction under this very ordinance of one of these same petitioners.

The rule of law upon which the Alabama courts relied in this case was one firmly established by previous precedents....

\*     \*     \*

"As a general rule, an unconstitutional statute is an absolute nullity and may not form the basis of any legal right or legal proceedings, yet until its unconstitutionality has been judicially declared in appropriate proceedings, no person charged with its observance under an order or decree may disregard or violate the order or the decree with immunity from a charge of contempt of court; and he may not raise the question of its unconstitutionality in collateral proceedings on appeal from a judgment of conviction for contempt of the order or decree...."

These precedents clearly put the petitioners on notice that they could not bypass orderly judicial review of the injunction before disobeying it. Any claim that they were entrapped or misled is wholly unfounded, a conclusion confirmed by evidence in the record showing that when the petitioners deliberately violated the injunction they expected to go to jail.

The rule of law that Alabama followed in this case reflects a belief that in the fair administration of justice no man can be judge in his own case, however exalted his station, however righteous his motives, and irrespective of his race, color, politics, or religion. This Court cannot hold that the petitioners were constitutionally free to ignore all the procedures of the law and carry their battle to the streets. One may sympathize with the petitioners' impatient commitment to their cause. But respect for judicial process is a small price to pay for the civilizing hand of law, which alone can give abiding meaning to constitutional freedom.

*Affirmed.*

## ☆ 306b *Shuttlesworth v. Birmingham*

394 U.S. 147 (1969).

Mr. Justice Stewart delivered the opinion of the Court.

The petitioner stands convicted for violating an ordinance of Birmingham, Alabama, making it an offense to participate in any "parade or procession or other public demonstration" without first obtaining a permit from the City Commission. The question before us is whether that conviction can be squared with the Constitution of the United States.

On the afternoon of April 12, Good Friday, 1963, 52 people, all Negroes, were led out of a Birmingham church by three Negro ministers, one of whom was the petitioner, Fred L. Shuttlesworth. They walked in orderly fashion, two abreast for the most part, for four blocks. The purpose of their march was to protest the alleged denial of civil rights to Negroes in the city of Birmingham. The marchers stayed on the sidewalks except at street intersections, and they did not interfere with other pedestrians. No automobiles were obstructed, nor were traffic signals disobeyed. The petitioner was with the group for at least part of this time, walking alongside the others, and once moving from the front to the rear. As the marchers moved along, a crowd of spectators fell in behind them at a distance. The spectators at some points spilled out into the streets, but the street was not blocked and vehicles were not obstructed.

At the end of four blocks the marchers were stopped by the Birmingham police, and were arrested for violating § 1159 of the General Code of Birmingham. That ordinance reads as follows:

It shall be unlawful to organize or hold, or to assist in organizing or holding, or to take part or participate in, any parade or procession or other public demonstration on the streets or other public ways of the city, unless a permit therefore has been secured from the commission.

To secure such permit, written application shall be made to the commission, setting forth the probable number of persons, vehicles and animals which will be engaged in such parade, procession or other public demonstration, the purpose for which it is to be held or had, and the streets or other public ways over, along or in which it is desired to have or hold such parade, procession or other public demonstration....

The petitioner was convicted for violation of § 1159 and was sentenced to 90 days' imprisonment at hard labor and an additional 48 days at hard labor in default of payment of a $75 fine and $24 costs. The Alabama Court of Appeals reversed the judgment of conviction, holding the evidence was insufficient "to show a procession which would require, under the terms of § 1159, the getting of a permit," that the ordinance had been applied in a discriminatory fashion, and that it was unconstitutional in imposing an "invidious prior restraint" without ascertainable standards for the granting of permits. The Supreme Court of Alabama, however, giving the language of § 1159 an extraordinarily narrow construction, reversed the judgment of the Court of Appeals and reinstated the conviction. We granted certiorari to consider the petitioner's constitutional claims.

\* \* \*

But we need not deal in assumptions. For, as the respondent in this case has reminded us, in assessing the constitutional claims of the petitioner, "[i]t is less than realistic to ignore the surrounding relevant circumstances. These include not only facts developed in the Record in this case, but also those shown in the opinions in the related case of *Walker v. City of Birmingham*...." The petitioner here was one of the petitioners in the *Walker* case, in which, just two Terms ago, we had before us a record showing many of the "surrounding relevant circumstances" of the Good Friday march. As the respondent suggests, we may properly take judicial notice of the record in that litigation between the same parties who are now before us.

Uncontradicted testimony was offered in *Walker* to show that over a week before the Good Friday march petitioner Shuttlesworth sent a representative to apply for a parade permit. She went to the City Hall and asked "to see the person or persons in charge to issue permits, permits for parading, picketing, and demonstrating." She was directed to Commissioner Connor, who denied her request in no uncertain terms. "He said, 'No, you will not get a permit in Birmingham, Alabama to picket. I will picket you over to the City Jail,' and he repeated that twice."

Two days later petitioner Shuttlesworth himself sent a telegram to Commissioner Connor requesting, on behalf of his organization, a permit to picket "against the injustices of segregation and discrimination." His request specified the sidewalks where the picketing would take place, and stated that "the normal rules of picketing" would be obeyed. In reply, the Commissioner sent a wire stating that permits were the responsibility of the entire Commission rather than of a single Commissioner, and closing with the blunt admonition: "I insist that you and your people do not start any picketing on the streets in Birmingham, Alabama."

These "surrounding relevant circumstances" make it indisputably clear, we think, that in April of 1963 — at least with respect to this petitioner and his organization — the city authorities thought the ordinance meant exactly what it said. The petitioner was clearly given to understand that under no circumstances would he and his group be permitted to demonstrate in Birmingham, not that a demonstration would be approved if a time and place were selected that would minimize traffic problems. There is no indication whatever that the authorities considered themselves obligated — as the Alabama Supreme Court more than four years later said that they were — to issue a permit "if, after an investigation [they] found that the convenience of the public in the use of the streets or sidewalks would not thereby be unduly disturbed."

This case, therefore, is a far cry from *Cox v. New Hampshire*, where it could be said that there was nothing to show "that the statute has been administered otherwise than in the ... manner which the state court has construed it to require. Here, by contrast, it is evident that the ordinance was administered so as, in the words of Chief Justice Hughes, "to deny or unwarrantedly abridge the right of assembly and the opportunities for the communication of thought ... immemorially associated with resort to public places." The judgment is reversed.

*Reversed.*

# 307  The Voice of the "Silent Majority" (1967-1971)

Race riots of unprecedented intensity had struck over one hundred American cities in the late sixties. Inhabitants of Boston, Tampa, Cincinnati, Cleveland, New York, Philadelphia, Baltimore, Chicago, Minneapolis, Los Angeles (Watts), Washington, D.C., Hartford, New Haven, and Pittsburgh were victims of urban unrest. The worst manifestations of rioting, looting, and arson took place in Newark and Detroit where seventy-two persons died, thousands were arrested, and over two hundred million dollars of property was destroyed. Demonstrations against the war in Vietnam likewise became more numerous and attracted large numbers of supporters. In October 1969, hundreds of thousands of demonstrators jammed Washington, D.C., on Moratorium Day. In 1970 and 1971, prison unrest smoldered, exploding with the strike and takeover at Attica Correctional Facility in New York — forty-three prisoners and guards died before the authorities regained control.

Richard M. Nixon coined the term "silent majority" during his campaign for the presidency in 1968. It referred to those who liked America the way it was and were appalled by the confrontational tactics and revolutionary rhetoric of the dissidents. Spiro Agnew was elevated to the governorship of Maryland in 1967 from the office of Baltimore County Executive and then moved to the vice-presidency of the United States in 1969. As a spokesman for the forces of order, he presumably expressed the sentiments of the silent majority. Agnew continued to speak out against the dissidents until 1973 when he resigned as vice-president and pleaded no contest to charges of income tax evasion.

☆ 307  Writings of Spiro T. Agnew

☆ 307a  There Are Proper Ways to Protest (July 27, 1967)

Reprinted in Jim Lucas, *Agnew: Profile in Conflict* (New York: Universal Publishing, 1970), 148-49.

In Maryland, rioting or inciting to riot, no matter what wrong is said to be the cause, will not be tolerated. There are proper ways to protest and they must be used. It shall now be the policy of this state to immediately arrest any person inciting to riot, and to not allow that person to finish his vicious speech. All lawbreakers will be vigorously and promptly prosecuted.

Acts of violence will not be later forgiven just because the criminal after a while adopts a more reasonable attitude. The violent cannot be allowed to sneak unnoticed from the war dance to the problem-solving meeting. The problem-solving conference must be reserved for those who shun lawlessness, who win their place at the conference table by leadership that builds rather than destroys.

The problem-solving must be done by constructive militants, such as the [Roy] Wilkinses, [Martin Luther] Kings, and [A. Philip] Randolphs—not by the [Stokely] Carmichaels and [Rap] Browns. But it should include the younger, responsible leadership as well as the older, more established, leaders. Responsibility is the yardstick.

... I will meet with any responsible leaders to discuss the problems that confront us. I will *not* meet with those who engage in, or urge, riots or other criminal acts as weapons to obtain power.

In conclusion, I commend the citizens of both races who have continued to conduct themselves with intelligent restraint in spite of great pressure. I share the sorrow of those who have suffered and who continue to suffer from the reckless acts of a few.

For the confused and the weak who seek to excuse, appease, or rationalize for the criminals who threaten our society I have only pity.

☆ 307b  The Age of the Gross (October 19, 1969)

Reprinted in Joseph Albright, *What Makes Spiro Run: The Life and Times of Spiro T. Agnew* (New York: Dodd, Mead, 1972), 234-35.

Sometimes, it appears that we are reaching a period when our senses and our minds will no longer respond to moderate stimulation. We seem to be approaching an age of the gross. Persuasion through speeches and books is too often discarded for disruptive demonstrations aimed at bludgeoning the unconvinced into action.

The young—and I don't mean by any stretch of the imagination all the young, I'm talking about those who claim to speak for the young—at the zenith of physical power and sensitivity overwhelm themselves with drugs and artificial stimulants. Subtlety is lost, and fine distinctions based on acute reasoning are carelessly ignored in a headlong jump to a predetermined conclusion. Life is visceral rather than intellectual, and the most visceral practitioners of life are those who characterize themselves as intellectuals.

Truth to them is "revealed" rather than logically proved, and the principal infatuations of today revolve around the social sciences, those subjects which can accommodate any opinion and about which the most reckless conjecture cannot be discredited.

Education is being redefined at the demand of the uneducated to suit the ideas of the uneducated. The student now goes to college to proclaim rather than to learn. The lessons of the past are ignored or obliterated in a contemporary antagonism known as the generation gap. A spirit of national masochism

prevails, encouraged by an effete corps of impudent snobs who characterize themselves as intellectuals.

Thousands of well motivated young people, conditioned since childhood to respond to great emotional appeals, saw fit to demonstrate for peace. Most did not stop to consider that the leaders of the Moratorium had billed it as a massive public outpouring of sentiment against the foreign policy of the President of the United States. Most did not care to be reminded that the leaders of the Moratorium refused to disassociate themselves from the objectives enunciated by the enemy in Hanoi.

If the Moratorium had any use whatever, it served as an emotional purgative for those who felt the need to cleanse themselves of their lack of ability to offer a constructive solution to the problem....

\*        \*        \*

☆ 307c  The Root Causes of Attica (September 1971)

Reprinted in H. Salisbury, ed., *The Eloquence of Protest: Voices of the 70s* (Boston: Houghton Mifflin, 1972), 264-65.

\*        \*        \*

What happened at Attica could not have been foreseen, unless one is willing to accept the radiclib ideological premise of original sin which holds every outbreak of violence in our society to be further evidence of the intrinsic evil of the system. However, what has happened since—the litany of recrimination against "the authorities," the naive equating of antisocial with social goals, the call for examination of "root causes"—all of this could have been foreheard in the rhetorical excesses which followed previous confrontations between society's authority and antisocial force.

Very well, then, let us examine some of the "root causes" of Attica—though not in the sense of attributing indiscriminate blame of American institutions.... Little credit is due otherwise responsible public spokesmen whose desire to placate a far Left constituency has caused them to overlook the fact that, for all its shortcomings, the theory of American criminology and our penal system remain among the most humane and advanced in the world. Thus, to assert that the question raised at Attica was "Why men would rather die than live another day in America" is the purest political fatuity.

To position the "demands" of convicted felons in a place of equal dignity with legitimate aspirations of law-abiding American citizens—or to compare the loss of life by those who violate the society's law with a loss of life of those whose job it is to uphold it—represents not simply an assault on human sensibility, but an insult to reason. Worst of all, it gives status and seeming respectability to the extremists in our society whose purpose it is to exacerbate rather than ameliorate the problems of race relations—the very problems to which the spokesmen, in this instance, allude.

In my opinion, then, it is the approbation given extremists by some responsible leaders of both races that has nurtured the roots of violence such as occurred at Attica and, not long before, at San Quentin.

To be sure, when law-abiding citizens of both the white and black races are daily subjected to the editorial elevation of convicted felons into "revolutionary leaders," the effect of such near apotheosis is to blur lines of rational, democratic discussion, not simply of penological but of all the broad social problems which concern our society. As for the effect of such exaltation of criminality on lawbreakers both within and outside prison walls, who can doubt that violence is encouraged when the violent-prone are provided a civilized rationale for their psychopathic proclivities?

"Let's not try to compromise the demands," said the Black Panther leader sent to Attica to help "negotiate" a settlement. The roots of such reckless intransigence, which contributed to the need to use force to break the strike, do not lie in "social injustice" or "revolutionary" fervor. Rather, what we heard there was the voice of criminal arrogance fed by the long-time accommodation of moderate spokesmen, white and black alike, to the extremism of word and deed practiced by black power militants.

*       *       *

What happened at Attica proves once again that when the responsible voices of society remain mute, the forces of violence and crime grow arrogant. One need only recall the era of Hitler's storm troopers to realize what can happen to the most civilized of societies when such a cloak of respectability is provided thugs and criminals.

*       *       *

# 308  " 'It is not a constitutional principle that ... the police must proceed against the crowd' " (1968)

The interaction of peaceful demonstrators and hostile spectators presents a vexing problem for the government. How should the power of the law be invoked in the name of keeping the peace—against the demonstrators (easily identifiable, nonviolent, and acting lawfully) or against the counterdemonstrators (amorphous, hostile, and engaging in assault)?

On the streets of Chicago, comedian Dick Gregory tested the right of political protestors to be heard in the face of hostile mobs unwilling to accord them their constitutional right. On August 2, 1965, a group of some eighty-five demonstrators began to picket in the neighborhood of Mayor Richard Daley's house. The protest concerned segregation in the Chicago school system. Thirty-five counter demonstrators initially met the demonstrators, but as the evening wore on, the crowd grew to over one thousand who threw rocks and eggs at the marchers. The police, fearing the situation was getting out of control, offered to escort the demonstrators through the hostile crowd. When Gregory and others refused to go, claiming they were peacefully exercising their First Amendment rights, the police arrested them. The Illinois Supreme Court upheld their convictions for disorderly conduct in making "a diversion tending to a breach of the peace." The United States Supreme Court, without addressing the problems that the Illinois court had addressed, summarily reversed the convictions on the grounds that the ordinance was unconstitutionally vague.

☆308  The Crime of Dick Gregory

☆308a  *City of Chicago v. Gregory*

39 Ill. 2d 47, 233 N.E. 2d 422 (1968).

HOUSE, Justice.

*       *       *

While we have gone into considerable detail in describing the events leading to the arrest of defendants, only a complete reading of the record can give one a true picture of the dilemma confronting the police. During the entire march from 4:30 P.M. until 9:30 P.M. the marchers were accompanied by their attorney who advised them, and the police were accompanied by an assistant city attorney who advised them. In short the record shows a determined effort by the police to allow the marchers to peacefully demonstrate and at the same time maintain order.

The defendants place heavy reliance on a footnote statement in *Brown v. State of Louisiana* that "Participants in an orderly demonstration in a public place are not chargeable with the danger, unprovoked except by the fact of the constitutionally protected demonstration itself, that their critics might react with disorder or violence"; ... and a statement in *Wright v. State of Georgia* that "... the possibility of disorder by others cannot justify exclusion of persons from a place if they otherwise have a constitutional right ... to be present." They contend that their conduct was peaceful and that they were charged and convicted solely on the reaction of the crowd.

The Supreme Court in recent years has had occasions to reverse a number of breach-of-the-peace convictions based on civil rights activities. In none of these cases has there been a public disorder or imminent threat of public disorder....

In *Feiner v. People of State of New York*, defendant was convicted of disorderly conduct when he refused a police order to stop haranguing about 80 "restless" listeners. The court pointed out: "The exercise of the [two] police officers' proper discretionary power to prevent a breach of the peace was thus approved by the trial court and later by two courts on review. The courts below recognized petitioner's right to hold a street meeting at this locality, to make use of loud-speaking equipment in giving his speech, and to make derogatory remarks concerning public officials and the American Legion. They found that the officers in making the arrest were motivated solely by a proper concern for the preservation of order and protection of the general welfare, and that there was no evidence which could lend color to a claim that the acts of the police were a cover for suppression of petitioner's views and opinions." The court concluded, "The findings of the state courts as to the existing situation and the imminence of greater disorder coupled with petitioner's deliberate defiance of the police officers convince us that we should not reverse this conviction in the name of free speech."

In his dissenting opinion Justice Black stated [that] the record failed to show any imminent threat of riot or uncontrollable disorder. He next stated, "The police of course have power to prevent breaches of the peace. But if, in the name of preserving order, they ever can interfere with a lawful public speaker, they first must make all reasonable efforts to protect him." ...

Justice Frankfurter in a concurring opinion summarized the situation this way: "... Where conduct is within the allowable limits of free speech, the police are peace officers for the speaker as well as for his hearers. But the power effectively to preserve order cannot be displaced by giving a speaker complete immunity.... *It is not a constitutional principle that, in acting to preserve order, the police must proceed against the crowd, whatever its size and temper, and not against the speaker.*" (Emphasis added.)

Applying the facts of this case to the rationale of the foregoing opinions we believe defendants were not denied their right to free speech, free assembly and freedom to petition for redress of grievances. First, the record is clear that there was some violence (throwing rocks and eggs) and an imminent threat of extreme public disorder. This immediately distinguishes this case from ... *Wright* and *Brown*. ... In fact the violence and imminent threat of a riot appears to have been greater here than in *Feiner*.

This brings us to the vital issue in the case of whether Justice Frankfurter's appraisal of *Feiner* ... can be reconciled with the statement in *Brown*. ... We think the statements are harmonious when read in light of Justice Black's observation in his dissenting opinion in *Feiner*. ...

The record before us shows that the police made all reasonable efforts to protect the marchers before asking them to stop the demonstration. ...

It is evident that there was adequate and determined police protection for the demonstrators from 4 o'clock in the afternoon until 9:30 in the evening while the demonstrators marched from Grant Park to the city hall and then to the mayor's home on the south side of Chicago. The demonstration around the mayor's home lasted 1½ hours during which the police were able to control the hostile crowd. It was between 9:00 and 9:25 that the crowd grew quickly in size and anger to the point where the police felt they could no longer control the situation.

Furthermore, we do not have here an "unexplained request" by the police as was apparently the case in *Feiner*. Commander Pierson told Gregory that the situation was becoming dangerous, that he was having difficulty containing the crowd and that there must be a riot. He asked Gregory five times to lead the marchers out.... We hold that under the circumstances of this case defendants were not denied any right of free speech, free assembly or freedom to petition for redress of grievances.

Defendants also argue that the disorderly conduct ordinance of the city is unconstitutionally vague as applied to free expression and free assembly. We interpret the ordinance as authorizing the action taken by police under the circumstances disclosed by this record.... [W]here there is an imminent threat of violence, the police have made all reasonable efforts to protect the demonstrators, the police have requested that the demonstration be stopped and explained the request, if there be time, and there is a refusal of the police request, that an arrest for an otherwise lawful demonstration may be made. As so interpreted we believe the ordinance is not so overly broad in scope as to be unconstitutionally vague or that it delegates undue discretion to the police....

\*          \*          \*

The judgments of the circuit court of Cook County are affirmed.

*Judgments affirmed.*

☆ 308b  *Gregory v. City of Chicago*

394 U.S. 111 (1969).

Mr. Chief Justice WARREN delivered the opinion of the Court.

This is a simple case....

Petitioners' march, if peaceful and orderly, falls well within the sphere of conduct protected by the First Amendment. There is no evidence in this record that petitioners' conduct was disorderly....

The opinion of the Supreme Court of Illinois suggests that petitioners were convicted not for the manner in which they conducted their march but rather for their refusal to disperse when requested to do so by Chicago police. However reasonable the police request may have been and however laudable the police motives, petitioners were charged and convicted for holding a demonstration, not for a refusal to obey a police officer....

Finally, since the trial judge's charge permitted the jury to convict for acts clearly entitled to First Amendment protection, *Stromberg v. California* independently requires reversal of these convictions.

The judgments are reversed.

*Reversed.*

Mr. Justice BLACK, concurring.

       \*       \*       \*

I agree with the Illinois Supreme Court that the "record shows a determined effort by the police to allow the marchers to peacefully demonstrate and at the same time maintain order." I also think the record shows that outside of the marching and propagandizing of their views and protests, Gregory and his group while marching did all in their power to maintain order. Indeed, in the face of jeers, insults, and assaults with rocks and eggs, Gregory and his group maintained a decorum that speaks well for their determination simply to tell their side of their grievances and complaints....

       \*       \*       \*

... And it must be remembered that only the tiniest bit of petitioners' conduct could possibly be thought illegal here—that is, what they did after the policeman's order to leave the area....

... Their guilt of "disorderly conduct" therefore turns out to be their refusal to obey instanter an individual policeman's command to leave the area of the Mayor's home.... To let a policeman's command become equivalent to a criminal statute comes dangerously near making our government one of men rather than of laws. There are ample ways to protect the domestic tranquility without subjecting First Amendment freedoms to such a clumsy and unwieldy weapon.

## 309 He Burned the Certificate Publicly to Influence Others (1968)

To facilitate record keeping and communications, the Selective Service System issued to each draft registrant a card noting various items of identification. Prior to 1965, federal law required the registrant to keep the card in his possession at all times. The only prohibition that Congress had enacted related to the fraudulent use or alteration of the card. As draft card burning became a means of protest against the war, Congress, in 1965, amended the law

to penalize knowing destruction or mutilation of cards.

David O'Brien and three friends burned their draft cards on March 31, 1966, on the steps of the South Boston Courthouse. O'Brien admitted to FBI agents that he had knowingly violated federal law. Calling his act "symbolic speech," O'Brien challenged the 1965 amendment as an unconstitutional abridgment of free speech.

### ☆ 309  *United States v. O'Brien*

391 U.S. 367 (1968).

MR. CHIEF JUSTICE WARREN delivered the opinion of the Court.

       \*       \*       \*

... We note at the outset that the 1965 Amendment plainly does not abridge free speech on its face, and we do not understand O'Brien to argue otherwise.... The Amendment does not distinguish between public and private destruction, and it does not punish only destruction engaged in for the purpose of expressing views. A law prohibiting destruction of Selective Service certificates no more abridges free speech on its face than a motor vehicle law prohibiting the destruction of drivers' licenses, or a tax law prohibiting the destruction of books and records.

O'Brien nonetheless argues that the 1965 Amendment is unconstitutional in its application to him, and is unconstitutional as enacted because what he calls the "purpose" of Congress was "to suppress freedom of speech." We consider these arguments separately.

### II

O'Brien first argues that the 1965 Amendment is unconstitutional as applied to him because his act of burning his registration certificate was protected "symbolic speech" within the First Amendment.... [E]ven on the assumption that the alleged communicative element in O'Brien's conduct is sufficient to bring into play the First Amendment, it does not necessarily follow that the destruction of a registration certificate is constitutionally protected activity. This Court has held that when "speech" and "nonspeech" elements are combined in the same course of conduct, a sufficiently important governmental interest in regulating the nonspeech element can justify incidental limitations on First Amendment freedoms.... [A] government regulation is sufficiently justified if it is within the constitutional power of the Government; if it furthers an important or substantial governmental interest; if the governmental interest is unrelated to the suppression of free expression; and if the incidental restriction on alleged First

Amendment freedoms is no greater than is essential to the furtherance of that interest. . . .

. . . The power of Congress to classify and conscript manpower for military service is "beyond question." Pursuant to this power, Congress may establish a system of registration for individuals liable for training and service, and may require such individuals within reason to cooperate in the registration system. The issuance of certificates indicating the registration and eligibility classification of individuals is a legitimate and substantial administrative aid in the functioning of this system. . . .

\*       \*       \*

We think it apparent that the continuing availability to each registrant of his Selective Service certificates substantially furthers the smooth and proper functioning of the system that Congress has established to raise armies. . . . [T]he government [therefore] has a substantial interest in assuring the continuing availability of issued Selective Service certificates.

It is equally clear that the 1965 Amendment specifically protects this substantial governmental interest. We perceive no alternative means that would more precisely and narrowly assure the continuing availability of issued Selective Service certificates than a law which prohibits their wilful mutilation or destruction. The 1965 Amendment prohibits such conduct and does nothing more. In other words, both the governmental interest and the operation of the 1965 Amendment are limited to the noncommunicative aspect of O'Brien's conduct. . . .

\*       \*       \*

In conclusion, we find that because of the Government's substantial interest in assuring the continuing availability of issued Selective Service certificates, because amended § 462(b) is an appropriately narrow means of protecting this interest and condemns only the independent noncommunicative impact of conduct within its reach, and because the noncommunicative impact of O'Brien's act of burning his registration certificate frustrated the Government's interest, a sufficient governmental interest has been shown to justify O'Brien's conviction.

### III

O'Brien finally argues that the 1965 Amendment is unconstitutional as enacted because what he calls the "purpose" of Congress was "to suppress freedom of speech." We reject this argument because under settled principles the purpose of Congress, as O'Brien uses that term, is not a basis for declaring this legislation unconstitutional.

It is a familiar principle of constitutional law that this Court will not strike down an otherwise constitutional statute on the basis of an alleged illicit legislative motive. . . .

\*       \*       \*

## 310 "conduct of a local Board that is basically lawless" (1968)

Opponents of the Vietnam War increasingly resorted to innovative forms of protest and civil disobedience. Oestereich, a theological student required to register but exempted by statute from military service, turned in his draft card to protest United States participation in the Vietnam War. Oestereich's local Selective Service Board declared him a "delinquent" registrant for not carrying his certificate at all times, reclassified him as able to serve, and ordered him to report for induction. Oestereich challenged the reclassification as a penalty for protesting the war and claimed it was imposed in violation of his First Amendment rights. The court avoided the constitutional issue but found another ground upon which to void his induction. Later, in *Gutknecht v. United States*, 396 U.S. 295 (1970), the court used a similar rationale to hold that the Selective Service had no authority to hasten induction of registrants as a disciplinary measure for their protest activities.

☆ 310 *Oestereich v. Selective Service System*

393 U.S. 233 (1968).

Mr. Justice DOUGLAS delivered the opinion of Court.

\*       \*       \*

. . . If we assume, as we must for present purposes, that petitioner is entitled to a statutory exemption as a divinity student, by what authority can the Board withhold it or withdraw it and make him a delinquent?

. . . Congress has also made criminal the knowing failure or neglect to perform any duty prescribed by the rules or regulations of the Selective Service System. But Congress did not define delinquency; nor did it provide any standards for its definition by the Selective Service System. Yet Selective Service, as we have noted, has promulgated regulations governing delinquency and uses them to deprive registrants of their statutory exemption, because of various activities and conduct and without any regard to the exemptions provided by law.

We can find no authorization for that use of delinquency. Even if Congress had authorized the Boards to revoke statutory exemptions by means of delinquency classifications, serious questions would arise if Congress were silent and did not prescribe standards to govern the Boards' actions. There is no suggestion in the legislative history that, when Congress has granted an exemption and a registrant meets its terms and conditions, a Board can nonetheless withhold it from him for activities or conduct not material to the grant or withdrawal of the exemption. So to hold would make the Boards freewheeling agencies meting out their brand of justice in a vindictive manner.

Once a person registers and qualifies for a statutory exemption, we find no legislative authority to deprive him of that exemption because of conduct or activities unrelated to the merits of granting or continuing that exemption. The Solicitor General confesses error on the use by Selective Service of delinquency proceedings for that purpose.

We deal with conduct of a local Board that is basically lawless. It is no different in constitutional implications from a case where induction of an ordained minister or other clearly exempt person is ordered (a) to retaliate against the person because of his political views or (b) to bear down on him for his religious views or his racial attitudes or (c) to get him out of town so that the amorous interests of a Board member might be better served. In such instances, as in the present one, there is no exercise of discretion by a Board in evaluating evidence and in determining whether a claimed exemption is deserved. The case we decide today involves a clear departure by the Board from its statutory mandate. To hold that a person deprived of his statutory exemption in such a blatantly lawless manner must either be inducted and raise his protest through habeas corpus or defy induction and defend his refusal in a criminal prosecution is to construe the Act with unnecessary harshness. As the Solicitor General suggests, such literalness does violence to the clear mandate ... governing the exemption....

*            *            *

*Reversed.*

## 311 Interstate Rioting (1968)

Because the framers of the United States Constitution perceived crime control to be primarily a state responsibility, the federal government lacked authority to intervene in most common crimes, including rioting. Unless and until the local violence grew beyond state control, the federal government historically was unable to step in with assistance. The urban violence of the 1960s, nevertheless, generated the belief that a new problem plagued state authorities: the incendiary speaker who incited to riot and then quickly departed from the state. One person suspected of such conduct was Hubert Giroid Brown, better known as "Rap" Brown. The new legislation, popularly referred to at the time as the "Rap" Brown Law, granted the federal government the authority to investigate and prosecute such agitators.

☆ 311 Riots (the "Rap" Brown Law)

82 Stat. 75 (1968).

*Be it enacted by the Senate and the House of Representatives of the United States of America in Congress assembled* That ...

*            *            *

SEC. 104. (a) Title 18 of the United States Code is amended by inserting, immediately after chapter 101 thereof, the following new chapter:

"CHAPTER 102.—RIOTS

"**§ 2101. Riots**

"(a)(1) Whoever travels in interstate or foreign commerce or uses any facility of interstate or foreign commerce, including, but not limited to, the mail, telegraph, telephone, radio, or television, with intent —

"(A) to incite a riot; or

"(B) to organize, promote, encourage, participate in, or carry on a riot; or

"(C) to commit any act of violence in furtherance of a riot; or

"(D) to aid or abet any person in inciting or participating in or carrying on a riot or committing any act of violence in furtherance of a riot;

and who either during the course of any such travel or use or thereafter performs or attempts to perform any other overt act for any purpose specified in subparagraph (A), (B), (C), or (D) of this paragraph —

"Shall be fined not more than $10,000, or imprisoned not more than five years, or both.

*            *            *

"(e) Nothing contained in this section shall be construed to make it unlawful for any person to travel in, or use any facility of, interstate or foreign commerce for the purpose of pursuing the legitimate objectives of organized labor, through orderly and lawful means.

"(f) Nothing in this section shall be construed as indicating an intent on the part of Congress to prevent any State, any possession or Commonwealth of the United States, or the District of Columbia, from exercising jurisdiction over any offense over which it would have jurisdiction in the absence of this section; nor shall anything in this section be construed as depriving State and local law enforcement authorities of responsibility for prosecuting acts that may be violations of this section and that are violations of State and local law.

"**§ 2102. Definitions**

"(a) As used in this chapter, the term 'riot' means a public disturbance involving (1) an act or acts of violence by one or more persons part of an assemblage of three or more persons, which act or acts shall constitute a clear and present danger of, or shall result in, damage or injury to the property of any other person or to the person of any other individual or (2) a threat or threats of the commission of an act or acts of violence by one or more persons part of an assemblage of three or more persons having, individually or collectively, the ability of immediate execution of such threat or threats, where the performance of the threatened act or acts of violence would constitute a clear and present danger of, or would result in, damage or injury to the property of any other person or to the person of any other individual.

"(b) As used in this chapter, the term 'to incite a riot,' or 'to organize, promote, encourage, participate in, or carry on a riot,' includes, but is not limited to, urging or instigating other persons to riot, but shall not be deemed to mean the mere oral or written (1) advocacy of ideas or (2) expression of belief, not involving advocacy of any act or acts of violence or assertion of the rightness of, or the right to commit, any such act or acts."

*     *     *

*Approved, April 11, 1968.*

## 312 "in direct line with American democratic tradition" (1968)

On May 17, 1968, Father Philip Berrigan (awaiting sentencing for pouring blood on draft files six months earlier), his brother, Father Daniel Berrigan, and seven other Catholic priests and laypersons entered local draft board number 33 in Catonsville, Maryland, carried out 378 draft files, and set them afire in a parking lot. The trial of the "Catonsville Nine" was held October 5 to 9, 1968. The jury returned a verdict of guilty against each defendant on each of three counts: destruction of United States property, destruction of Selective Service records, and interference with the Selective Service Act of 1967. Though the judge instructed the jury not to consider evidence of motive, he permitted the nine defendants to testify about their political and moral beliefs. These excerpts, edited by Daniel Berrigan from the actual testimony of Philip Berrigan and George Mische, reveal men who believed their civil disobedience to be within the nation's traditional democratic means. They disobeyed legislative and executive edicts that they argued were not only in violation of moral or religious dictates but were also in violation of constitutional and international law.

☆312 Excerpts from the Trial of the Catonsville Nine

Daniel Berrigan, *The Trial of the Catonsville Nine* (Boston: Beacon Press, 1970), 28-31, 72.

DEFENSE

Father Berrigan, I ask you: did there come a time, then, when you began seriously to consider civil disobedience?

PHILIP BERRIGAN

Yes    I came
to the conclusion
that I was in direct line
with American democratic tradition
in choosing civil disobedience
in a serious fashion
There have been times in our history
when in order to get redress
in order to get a voice    vox populi
arising from the roots
people have so acted
From the Boston Tea Party
through the abolitionist and anarchist movements
through World War I    and World War II
and right on
through the civil rights movement
we have a rich tradition
of civil disobedience

DEFENSE

Now, the action for which you are being tried here was not the first such action you were involved in. To state it briefly: seven months earlier, in October 1967, you along with the defendant Thomas Lewis and two others not present poured blood over Selective Service records in the Baltimore Customs House.

PHILIP BERRIGAN

We were prepared
for the blood pouring
because we had practiced civil disobedience
in Virginia
In fact my brother and myself
had practiced civil disobedience for years
by signing complicity statements
in support of draft resisters
So four of us took our own blood
and when the equipment for drawing our blood
broke down    we added animal blood
We attempted to anoint these files
with the Christian symbol of life and purification
which is blood

DEFENSE

Will you explain why, with a jail sentence staring you in the face, you felt impelled to act again at Catonsville?

PHILIP BERRIGAN

Neither at the Customs House    nor at Catonsville
do I wish my actions reduced
to a question    of acquittal or conviction
Rather I    and all of us
desire to communicate
with the bench    with the prosecution
with our country
We have already made it clear    our dissent
runs counter

to more than the war       which is but one in-
stance
of American power in the world
Latin America is another instance       So is the
                                                                Near East
This trial is yet another
From those in power we have met
little understanding       much silence
much scorn and punishment
We have been accused of arrogance
But what of the fantastic arrogance       of our
                                                                leaders
What of their crimes against the people       the
                                                poor and powerless
Still no court will try them       no jail will receive
                                                                them
They live in righteousness       They will die in
                                                                honor
For them we have one message       for those
in whose manicured hands       the power of the
                                                                land lies

We say to them
Lead us       Lead us in justice
and there will be no need to break the law
Let the President do       what his predecessors
                                                        failed to do
Let him obey the rich less       and the people
                                                                more

Let him think less of the privileged
and more of the poor
Less of America and more of the world
Let lawmakers       judges       and lawyers
think less of the law       more of justice
less of legal ritual       more of human rights
To our bishops and superiors we say
Learn something about the gospel
and something about illegitimate power
When you do       you will liquidate your invest-
                                                                ments

take a house in the slums       or even
join us in jail
To lawyers we say
Defend draft resisters       ask no fees
insist on justice       risk contempt of court
go to jail with your clients

GEORGE MISCHE
It seemed to me that the war in Vietnam
was illegal       because only Congress
can declare a war
The President cannot legally
take us into war
We should never have let him
He should be on trial here today
In the peace movement
one of the most powerful things I knew of
was Philip Berrigan's first trial
for the blood pouring
A six-year sentence

for pouring blood on files
Men walk our streets
spilling blood continuously
and they walk free
I also had a feeling       a strong feeling
about what happened in Germany during the last
                                                                war
my father was from Germany
The United States in 1945
supported the Nuremberg trials
I thought       that was the finest precedent
this country ever set
I said       Good       You are right
All of us Christians
share the responsibility
for having put those Jews
in the ovens

                        *              *              *

If this was true
then it is also true
that this is expected of me now
as a Christian
Because the Vietnamese people are crying out
Stop the bombing       Stop the napalming
Stop the death       day in and day out
But now
we want to forget the precedent
we set in 1945
There is a tendency to say
That was another country       another time
It is said
in times of crisis
We cannot make black and white decisions
Everything is gray
This is the problem
It is easy for us on Monday morning
to tell how we should have played
Sunday's game
We say that it is too complicated
It is too obscure
So nothing happens
The violence continues
I felt that the crisis
this country is in
needed something drastic
something people could see
But the act had to be nonviolent
We were not out to destroy life
There is a higher law we are commanded to obey
It takes precedence over human laws
My intent was to follow the higher law
My intent was to save lives       Vietnamese lives
North and South American lives
To stop the madness
That was the intent

                        *              *              *

## 313 "a lawful attempt to make a citizen's arrest" (1968)

Although the struggle for racial equality and for the end of the Vietnam War accounted for most of the turmoil of the era, the grievances of Native Americans and Hispanics stirred men and women to action as well. On December 16, 1969, Native Americans unlawfully occupied Alcatraz Island and held it for nineteen months, pressing their claim to turn the island into a Native American cultural center.

Some one and a half years earlier, on June 5, 1967, a band of armed Spanish-speaking Americans raided the Tierra Amarilla courthouse in northern New Mexico in search of hated district attorney Alfonso Sanchez. They departed only after wounding two officers, shooting up the building, and kidnapping a sheriff's deputy and a newsman. Before nightfall, the New Mexico National Guard set out to search for the "insurrectionists." Reies Lopez Tijerina, a former migrant worker turned evangelist and later political organizer, had led the raiders, members of an organization known as the *Alianza Federal de Mercedes*. The *Alianza* believed that large portions of the federal lands in New Mexico, which accounted for 44 percent of the state's total acreage, rightfully belonged to them as the lawful heirs to Spanish land grants.

*Alianza* members were involved in several confrontations with the authorities in their efforts to dramatize their claims to land. At the subsequent trial for assault, kidnapping, and false imprisonment, Tijerina argued that the *Alianza* merely was exercising the common-law right of citizen's arrest to obtain redress. The jury's verdict gave credence to the argument that the citizen's arrest could be used as a lawful tactic of civil disobedience.

☆ 313 The Trial of Reies Lopez Tijerina

Reprinted in Theodore L. Becker, ed., *Political Trials* (Indianapolis: Bobbs-Merrill, 1971), 184-98.

During 1966 and early 1967 Tijerina and his Alianzans were involved in several confrontations with authorities. Most, such as the attempt to take over a Forest Service campground at Echo Amphitheater and the corresponding "arrest" of Forest Rangers, were designed to dramatize the Alianza's claims to land. Specifically, Tijerina claimed for the Alianza the so-called San Joaquin del Rio de Chama grant in northern Rio Arriba County. As June 1967 approached the Alianza planned a large meeting of land grant "heirs" at the tiny community of Coyote. The night before the meeting, however, a number of Alianza members were arrested on various charges.

As a direct result of the arrest—and also to demonstrate the Alianza's authority in matters of law—members of the organization, including Tijerina,

swooped down on the pink adobe courthouse at Tierra Amarilla. They sought to "arrest" District Attorney Alfonso Sanchez, who had carried on what they saw as a vendetta against Tijerina.

The courthouse was shot up, its occupants held captive for some two hours, two officers were shot and wounded, and a deputy and a United Press International newsman were kidnapped. The raiders then fled into the mountainous countryside—all without encountering District Attorney Sanchez, who was in Santa Fe at the time.... The National Guard, called out by ... Lieutenant Governor E. Lee Francis in the absence of Governor Cargo, swarmed over the region in armored vehicles—most unsuitable for conducting a manhunt in the vast, almost roadless, area. The reaction to the manhunt and to the actions of officers was almost as strong as reaction to the raid itself. While most New Mexicans used terms like "insurrection" and "shocking outlawry," Professor Clark Knowlton, a scholar of Hispanic affairs, shot back the charge "that the National Guard and State Police violated the Spanish-Americans' civil rights ... when they 'systematically broke into homes, lined the people up, searched them and confined men, women, and children for many hours in a dirty sheep pen.'" In Denver, Hispanic militant Rudolph "Corky" Gonzales said the use of troops was "an act of imperialistic aggression."

District Attorney Sanchez, who all along had been citing "evidence" of "Communist influence" in the Alianza's actions, felt he had been vindicated. Among items confiscated when Tijerina and his colleagues were finally captured were maps of the area showing "prime objectives for seizure," an organization chart, gas masks, guns, books including *Rise and Fall of the Third Reich* and *Ché Guevara on Guerrilla Warfare*.

\*        \*        \*

Tijerina and the other nine defendants were ... tried on three charges each: kidnapping (which carries a possible death penalty), assault on the Rio Arriba County jail, and false imprisonment of Deputy Sheriff Daniel Rivera.

\*        \*        \*

... [During the trial, Tijerina (representing himself)] continually advanced the notion that citizens may make "arrests" of guilty persons—even authorities themselves (such as Sanchez). His deeper point was not missed by the intent Hispanos who sat in the gallery: that, in the land grant areas, the Alianza—not the state—is the law. If men got shot and a courthouse damaged in the process of making a legitimate "arrest," that was too bad.

Tijerina drew out this contention further when cross-examining State Policeman Juan Santistevan. The officer had testified he was approaching the courthouse on 5 June when men started shooting at him. A bullet hit the windshield of his car; he backed the vehicle behind a house and ran for cover.

"Did you know that citizens of the United States could arrest an officer if they believed they had a grievance against him?" Tijerina asked. "No," replied Santistevan. "Isn't it possible," asked Tijerina further, that "these people, pushed to the brink of desperation, had to teach you a lesson, teach you what you were not taught by your superiors?"

... As every witness ascended to the paneled witness stand, he hammered home his point as to the plight of a people "pushed to the brink of desperation" and using the common law right available to every citizen to obtain redress.

\*       \*       \*

... [A]fter a month of seemingly inconclusive testimony, Judge Larrazolo['s] ... instructions [to the jury] certainly were regarded with amazement by New Mexico legal practitioners, and with delight by Tijerina and his sympathizers.... The instructions seemed to give particular sanction to the concept of "citizen's arrest."

Those instructions read:

The Court instructs the Jury that citizens of New Mexico have the right to make a citizen's arrest under the following circumstances:
(1) If the arresting person reasonably believes that the person arrested, or attempted to be arrested, was the person who committed, either as a principal or as an aider and abettor, a felony; or
(2) If persons who are private citizens reasonably believe that a felony has been committed, and that the person who is arrested or attempted to be arrested was the person committing, or aiding and abetting, said felony.
The Court instructs the Jury that a citizen's arrest can be made even though distant in time and place from the acts constituting or reasonably appearing to constitute the commission of the felony. The Court further instructs the Jury that a citizen's arrest may be made whether or not law enforcement officers are present, and, further, may be made in spite of the presence of said law enforcement officers.
The Court instructs the Jury that anyone, including a State Police Officer, who intentionally interferes with a lawful attempt to make a citizen's arrest does so at his own peril, since the arresting citizens are entitled under the law to use whatever force is reasonably necessary to defend themselves in the process of making said citizen's arrest.

These words were startling enough to the courtroom observers, but in a few hours they were overshadowed by the surprise verdict: "not guilty" on all three counts.

## 314 "A Declaration of War" (1968)

On June 4, 1968, in Los Angeles, Sirhan B. Sirhan, a native of Jordan later claiming to have acted on behalf of the Palestinian cause, shot and killed presidential candidate Robert F. Kennedy, brother of assassinated president John F. Kennedy. As attorney general of the United States, Kennedy had previously brought federal law enforcement power to bear in aid of the civil rights movement. He was a United States senator from New York at the time of his death. The following excerpt from a notebook kept by Sirhan, who was convicted of the murder, reflects the political side of his motive.

☆ 314 From Sirhan Sirhan's Notebook

Reprinted in R. B. Kaiser, *RFK Must Die* (New York: Dutton, 1970), 170.

A Declaration of War Against American Humanity when in the course of human events it has become necessary for me to equalize and seek revenge for all the inhuman treatment committed against me by the American people. the manifestation of this Declaration will be executed by its supporter(s) as soon as he is able to command a sum of money ($2,000) and to acquire some firearms — the specification of which have not been established yet.

The victims of the party in favor of this declaration will be or are *now* — the President, vice, etc. — down the ladder.

The time will be chosen by the author at the convenience of the accused.

the method of assault is immaterial — however the type of weapon used should influence it somehow.

the author believes that many in fact multitudes of people are in harmony with his thoughts and feelings

the conflict and violence in the world subsequent to the enforcement of this decree, shall not be considered likely by the author of this memoranda, rather he hopes that they be the initiatory military steps to WW III — the author expresses his wishes very bluntly that he wants to be recorded by history as the *man* who triggered off the last war —

## 315 "Toleration of such conduct would not be democratic, ... but inevitably anarchic" (1969)

Appealing their convictions, the Catonsville Nine challenged the trial judge's instructions to the jury. First, they urged that the judge should have instructed the jury that the "willful" destruction of United States government property was not proven, since the defendants had acted to protest a war they sincerely believed immoral. Second, they argued the judge should have instructed the jury that it had the power to acquit the defendants, even if technically guilty, under the "jury nullification" doctrine, based on the jury's power to mitigate any law it deemed too harsh. Although seemingly sympathetic to the defendants, the court nevertheless upheld their convictions, pointing out that the Supreme Court previously had ruled out the jury nullification doctrine in criminal trials because it imperiled public safety.

☆ 315  *United States v. Moylan*

417 F.2d 1002 (4th Cir. 1969), *cert. denied*, 397 U.S. 910 (1970).

SOBELOFF, Circuit Judge:

. . . The appellants, men and women with sincere and strong commitments, readily admit the commission of these acts as a protest against the war in Vietnam.

\*      \*      \*

I

. . . The trial court instructed the jury to the effect that the willful intent requisite to constitute a violation of the statutes involved is the intent on the part of the accused to commit the proscribed acts with knowledge that they were violating the statute. Defense counsel urged upon the court a more expansive interpretation of the word "willful" as used in the statutes, namely that no violation occurred unless defendants performed the admitted acts with a bad purpose or motive. . . .

To read the term "willfully" to require a bad purpose would be to confuse the concept of intent with that of motive. The statutory requirement of willfulness is satisfied if the accused acted intentionally, with knowledge that he was breaching the statute. While the trial judge allowed evidence to be freely admitted concerning the defendants' motives, whatever motive may have led them to do the act is not relevant to the question of the violation of the statute, but is rather an element proper for the judge's consideration in sentencing.

\*      \*      \*

II

Appellants' second contention is that the trial judge should have informed the jury, as requested, that it had the power to acquit even if appellants were clearly guilty of the charged offenses. . . . Appellants reason that since the jury has "the power to bring in a verdict in the teeth of both law and facts," then the jury should be told that it has this power. Furthermore, the argument runs, the jury's power

to acquit where the law may dictate otherwise is a fundamental necessity of a democratic system. Only in this way, it is said, can a man's actions be judged fairly by society speaking through the jury, or a law which is considered too harsh be mitigated.

\*      \*      \*

The Supreme Court, in the landmark case of *Sparf and Hansen v. United States*, affirmed the right and duty of the judge to instruct on the law, and since that case the issue has been settled for three-quarters of a century. Justice Harlan's scholarly opinion . . . concluded finally that

Public and private safety alike would be in peril if the principle be established that juries in criminal cases may, of right, disregard the law as expounded to them by the court, and become a law unto themselves. Under such a system, the principal function of the judge would be to preside and keep order while jurymen, untrained in the law, would determine questions affecting life, liberty, or property according to such legal principles as, in their judgment, were applicable to the particular case being tried. . . . We must hold firmly to the doctrine that in the courts of the United States it is the duty of juries in criminal cases to take the law from the court, and apply that law to the facts as they find them to be from the evidence.

\*      \*      \*

III

As an undercurrent throughout the trial and interwoven with appellants' assertions of error is an appeal to morality as justification for their conduct. . . . [T]heir actions are said to be not punishable regardless of the literal violation of a statute. Moreover, appellants argue that apart from their motivation, which is subjective, the war in Vietnam is in fact illegal and immoral and hence their acts in protest of this war were themselves moral acts for which they must be similarly immunized from punishment. . . .

From the earliest times when man chose to guide his relations with fellow men by allegiance to the rule of law rather than force, he has been faced with the problem how best to deal with the individual in society who through moral conviction concluded that a law with which he was confronted was unjust and therefore must not be followed. Faced with the stark reality of injustice, men of sensitive conscience and great intellect have sometimes found only one morally justified path, and that path led them inevitably into conflict with established authority and its laws. Among philosophers and religionists throughout the ages there has been an incessant stream of discussion as to when, if at all, civil disobedience, whether by passive refusal to obey a law or by its active breach, is morally justified. However, they have been in general agreement that while in restricted circumstances a morally motivated act contrary to law may be ethically justified, the action must be non-violent and the actor must accept the penalty for his action. In other words, it is commonly conceded that the exercise of a moral judgment based upon individual standards does not carry with it legal justification or immunity from punishment for breach of the law.

The defendants' motivation in the instant case—the fact that they engaged in a protest in the sincere belief that they were breaking the law in a good cause—cannot be acceptable legal defense or justification. Their sincerity is beyond question. It implies no disparagement of their idealism to say that society will not tolerate the means they chose to register their opposition to the war. If these defendants were to be absolved from guilt because of their moral certainty that the war in Vietnam is wrong, would not others who might commit breaches of the law to demonstrate their sincere belief that the country is not prosecuting the war vigorously enough be entitled to acquittal? Both must answer for their acts.

. . . The acts of appellants are not as extreme as some committed by other dissenters. Nevertheless, this publicly exploited action cannot be dismissed as *de minimus*. To encourage individuals to make their own determinations as to which laws they will obey and which they will permit themselves as a matter of conscience to disobey is to invite chaos. No legal system could long survive if it gave every individual the option of disregarding with impunity any law which by his personal standard was judged morally untenable. Toleration of such conduct would not be democratic, as appellants claim, but inevitably anarchic.

The judgment below is

*Affirmed*.

## 316 "the word 'revolution' can[not] be avoided" (1969)

A leader in the Vietnam War resistance, Father Philip Berrigan, a Jesuit priest, was arrested and convicted of two draft board raids. In this interview he illuminated the relationship between the antiwar illegalities and the broader character of the "revolution" in which he was working, distinguishing it from other "revolutionary" endeavors.

☆ 316 Philip Berrigan, S.S.J., a Priest in the Resistance: An Interview

Philip Berrigan, *Prison Journals of a Priest Revolutionary* (New York: Holt, Rinehart and Winston, 1969). 182-98.

*          *          *

Q. Do you find celibacy tougher in jail, or no tougher, or the same as out?

A. . . . I'd like to stress that Dan and I feel that celibacy is crucial in the priesthood as an aid for revolutionary life style. We believe this very strongly, especially because we have made strong overtures to the other Christian communities in terms of action, in terms of awareness, political response, and all the rest, and gotten largely nowhere. With very, very good men. With men who have acted in a variety of ways in the past. And almost invariably the question of family obligations comes up, children, etc. So we feel celibacy can be a great freedom in a public forum.

*          *          *

Q. Let's return to your sense of the word "revolution." You use it differently from the way it's been used in the past, when it meant bloody uprising. What does the word mean to you in relationship to previous revolutions, like the American and the French revolutions?

A. First of all, I must say that the term "revolution" as it is being employed by adherents of the Gospel and students of Gandhi means, on the human level—and this is the most natural thing—that people cannot develop until they change, that they cannot grow into humanity, they can't join the human race, unless they change. And change is revolution.

Q. But why use this incendiary word for a nonviolent process that has never been associated with "revolution"?

A. Simply because I don't think the word "revolution" can be avoided. . . . Where are you going to find a substitute? One has to deal with it so that human connotations are made central. Otherwise, the whole dialogue concerning revolution—the whole dialectic, so to speak—lapses back into the historical bag, and we go on about revolution, the Bolshevik revolution, or the revolution in China in the late 1940's, and we get lost there, and end up talking about inevitability—the revolution of blood is a necessary historical process. The people who say that it is *not* inevitable are the only ones who, to my mind, understand revolution. In other words, the only ones who understand revolution are the ones who say that a nonviolent revolution is possible.

*          *          *

Q. During your testimony in Catonsville you stressed the fact that we Americans come from a revolutionary background. How would you differentiate the kind of revolution we had in this country in the eighteenth century from other revolutions—from the French Revolution, and the Russian Revolution?

A. Let's talk about the American Revolution first. . . . The revolution in this country was led by a nucleus of tradesmen, bankers, shippers, big shots who were uptight and furious about the imposition of economic control on their wealth by a foreign power.... They had an awful lot of bona-fide reasons going for them, in terms of foreign domination, self-autonomy, self-determination, and so on, but it wasn't true revolution because it was an economic thing. It was an economic reshuffling rather than a true revolution.

Q. Was the Russian Revolution a true revolution?

A. No, it was not a true revolution, for different reasons. Mostly because of the elements of violence.

Q. And how about the French Revolution?

A. The French Revolution was not a real one either, by the very fact that it descended so quickly into an apotheosizing of bloodshed and murder.

*         *         *

Q. But then you're saying that there really never has been a revolution. That's your sense of the word, something that has not yet happened.

A. Yes. And . . . in the foreseeable future, there's not going to be a revolution. There's only going to be ongoing revolutions on the part of individuals and small groups.

Q. "Uprisings?" Would that be a better way of putting it?

A. Yes, "uprisings," or "moral rebellions," call it what you want. . . . [I]f the planet is to be saved from real catastrophe, whether from nuclear war, or CBW [chemical and biological warfare] or something like that, there has to be ongoing revolution all over, continuous revolution, as sort of a political constant.

Q. In the Maoist sense?

A. The Maoist experience has at least given us some sort of pattern for political revolution, although it has failed to provide guidelines for moral revolution—which to me is really the key factor. It's not enough to challenge the bureaucracy which has entrenched itself; it's not enough to get the youth involved in the revolutionary process; one has to help people find themselves as people, and this means personal revolution projected into the social order, and tested there as to its valid elements. This is a way of saying that I can't be a man in this society unless I am in opposition to power. So, resistance is always synonymous with humanity, in my view.

Q. Well, then, in your view, the only true revolution would be an anarchist revolution. Because the anarchist ideology is the only ideology in which political power is replaced by mutual aid.

A. Right. Or, you can call it a new type of power. You can call it the type of power that would be dependent upon the original concept of service. In other words, a man's impact upon the community depends upon his qualifications for service. And the constant testing by the community of his service.

You know: Are you for real? But the big need now, it would seem to me, is that power be engaged, that it be stalemated, shamed, and even excoriated in some instances, and condemned, and hopefully, reduced to impotence.

Q. You have often referred to the draft-board raids as pre-revolutionary actions. And yet, in the past, this destruction of property always preceded violent uprisings. In what way do these symbolic raids fit into your scheme of revolution?

A. Only in the most limited fashion. Yet, others say they were revolutionary acts in prerevolutionary times. But we have to be careful here; one thing needed in people who are attracted to this kind of activity is old-fashioned modesty. Whenever you make exaggerated claims about the dimensions of these affairs or their political effect, you immediately get caught in a whole series of traps. Because in terms of what power is doing in this country, such acts are very limited, almost childish in scope. When you stack the experience of the Resistance movement here against the resistance of the Vietnamese people, you begin to have a proper sense of proportion. It may well be that if we really understood what corporate power in this country is doing to the world, we wouldn't be operating on this level at all.

Q. How would we be operating?

A. I don't know. I would say that our imagination hasn't caught up with this reality at all. Hopefully, I would say that you would *not* be picking up a gun, but you would be doing something far more serious than attacking a draft board. Nevertheless, in terms of resistance against what power is doing, the draft-board raids are a highly symbolic and educative thing. And the price is not very great. Tom Lewis and I got a heavy sentence—six years. But we can appeal for reduction of sentence, and we can probably get it. And then our original six years will probably be chopped off to four, two and a half of which we'll serve. This isn't a heavy price in terms of what the realities of power are, or in terms of the suffering they cause elsewhere.

*         *         *

## 317 "violence has been one response offered to many . . . controversial issues" (1969)

One year after succeeding the murdered John F. Kennedy, Lyndon B. Johnson was elected president in 1964 with the greatest plurality in the previously recorded history of that office. Despite the lowering of taxes, the institution of the War on Poverty, and the enactment of new civil rights legislation, racial tensions continued to mount. These tensions erupted into riots; the worst, which claimed thirty-five lives and produced extensive property damage, occurred in the Watts section of Los Angeles in 1965. The growing military commitment overseas, specifically the increase of United States military personnel in Vietnam from 20,000 to 190,000 in 1965, also generated popular dissatisfaction.

In 1966 American troop strength in Vietnam reached nearly 400,000, and resistance to the war added its burden to the already tense nation. In 1967, race riots of unprecedented intensity in over one hundred cities, including New York, Detroit, and Newark, alternated with mass antiwar demonstrations to cause nationwide anxiety. On April 4, 1968, the Reverend Martin Luther King, Jr., while standing on the balcony of a motel in Memphis, Tennessee, was assassinated. Later that year Sirhan B. Sirhan, claiming to be acting for the Palestinian cause, shot and killed Robert Kennedy. Confronted by the increasing public unrest, President Johnson established, in mid-1968, a National Commission on the Causes and Prevention of Violence. One portion of the commission's staff report, published in 1969, dealt with the phenomenon of presidential assassinations and its relationship to political motivation.

## ☆317  Assassinations and Political Violence

James Kirkham, Sheldon G. Levy, and William J. Crotty, *Assassination and Political Violence: The National Commission on the Causes and Prevention of Violence Staff Study Series* (Washington, D.C.: U.S. Government Printing Office, 1969), 8:9-23, 62-67.

## ☆317a  Deadly Attacks upon Public Office-Holders in the United States

During all stages of our Nation's history, violence has been one response offered to many of the controversial issues confronting our society....

\*       \*       \*

In specific terms, this section reviews all reported deadly attacks upon public officeholders or aspirants to public office without regard for motive for the attack—whether "personal" or "political."...

\*       \*       \*

The relationships between the importance of the office and the likelihood of assassination are dramatically demonstrated....

... One out of four Presidents has been a target of assassination, compared to approximately one out of every one hundred and sixty-six governors, one out of one hundred and forty-two Senators, and one out of every one thousand congressmen.

\*       \*       \*

... [P]ersons in elected positions are more likely to be assassinated than are occupants of appointed offices. Of approximately four hundred and fifty cabinet members, and of approximately one hundred

and two Supreme Court Justices, only one in each category has been the target of an assassin.

With the exception of attacks upon Republicans in the South during the Reconstruction era, only a very small portion of the deadly attacks against officeholders was rationally calculated to advance political aims of the assassin.... Still, the unbalanced minds of the presidential assassins focus themselves on high political officeholders rather than nonpolitical targets, and the question of why those acts became political still remains.

\*       \*       \*

### PRESIDENTIAL ASSASSINATIONS

In the one hundred and thirty-three years between the attempt made on the life of Andrew Jackson in 1835 and the successful assassination of presidential candidate Robert Kennedy in 1968, seven other Presidents or aspirants to the presidency have been assassination targets. Table [A—see facing page] lists each of the men involved with a summary description highlighting the main facts surrounding each case.

We can draw several important conclusions about presidential assassinations. Party affiliation, public policies, term of office, and political strength provide few clues about the likelihood of assassination. The men who have been targets differ considerably. For example, Lincoln was the President of a divided nation during a civil war, Garfield was a compromise candidate of a faction-torn party, and McKinley was a popular President of a relatively unified and stable society. All were assassinated.

\*       \*       \*

The political philosophy of a President or presidential candidate also appears to bear little relevance to an attack. McKinley and Garfield were moderate conservatives, while Kennedy and Truman were liberals; FDR was attacked at a time when his political philosophy was not yet identifiable (indeed, one might have classified him as somewhat conservative on the basis of his balance-the-budget and fiscal-integrity speeches during the presidential campaign of 1932)....

An interesting pattern that does emerge is that the assassination attempts seem to correspond with the general levels of civil strife. The greater such strife, the more likely the President in office will be attacked.... Every assassination attempt against a President or presidential candidate occurred at or near a peak of civil strife in this country....

\*       \*       \*

Although there may be other factors, the key element in each presidential assassination appears to be the state of mind of the potential assassin. In every case (with the possible exception of the at-

Table [A]—*Chronological list of political assassinations and assaults of Presidents and presidential candidates*

| Year | Victim | Political party | Length of administration at time of attack | Location | Method of attack and result | Assailant and professed or alleged reason |
|------|--------|-----------------|---------------------------------------------|----------|------------------------------|-------------------------------------------|
| 1835 | Andrew Jackson | Democrat | 6 years | Washington, D.C. | pistol, misfired | Richard Lawrence, declared insane; said Jackson was preventing him from obtaining large sums of money. |
| 1865 | Abraham Lincoln | Republican | 4 years, 1 month | Washington, D.C. | pistol, killed | John W. Booth, loyalty to the Confederacy; revenge for defeat; slavery issue. |
| 1881 | James Garfield | Republican | 4 months | Washington, D.C. | pistol, killed | Charles Guiteau, disgruntled officeseeker; supporter of opposite faction of Republican Party. |
| 1901 | William McKinley | Republican | 4 years, 6 months | Buffalo, N.Y. | pistol, killed | Leon F. Czolgosz, anarchist ideology. |
| 1912 | Theodore Roosevelt | Progressive (Bull Moose) | Candidate (had served before, 1901-9) | Milwaukee, Wis. | pistol, wounded | John Schrank, declared insane; had vision that McKinley wanted him to avenge his death. |
| 1933 | Franklin D. Roosevelt | Democrat | 3 weeks prior to 1st inauguration | Miami, Fla. | pistol, bullets missed the President | Guiseppe Zangara, hated rulers and capitalists. |
| 1950 | Harry S. Truman | Democrat | 5 years | Washington, D.C. | automatic weapon, prevented from shooting at President | Oscar Collazo and Griselio Torresola; Puerto Rican independence. |
| 1963 | John F. Kennedy | Democrat | 3 years | Dallas, Tex. | rifle, killed | Lee H. Oswald, motive unknown. |
| 1968 | Robert F. Kennedy | Democrat | Candidate | Los Angeles, Calif. | pistol, killed | Sirhan Sirhan, accused. |

tempt upon Truman) the assailants were alienated figures, and were even confused about the prospects and strategies of the causes they thought they represented. All the assassins but the two who attacked President Truman—Lawrence, Booth, Guiteau, Czolgosz, Zangara, Shrank, and Oswald—showed strong evidence of serious mental disturbance. In addition, each case is conspicuous by the absence of an effective political organization. Even the two presidential assassination attempts which were conspiracies of two or more persons—the attempts against the lives of Lincoln and Truman—were poorly organized, haphazard affairs, and neither would have done much to bring about the triumph of the political causes the assailants favored. Indeed, the assassination of Lincoln was a complete failure in this regard.

☆317b The Psychology of Presidential Assassins

All those who have assassinated or attempted to assassinate Presidents of the United States (with the possible exception of the Puerto Rican nationalist attempt upon President Truman) have been mentally disturbed persons who did not kill to advance any rational political plan. One psychiatrist, Dr. Donald W. Hastings, states that all but Collazo and Torresola were insane. Indeed, Dr. Hastings goes so far as to diagnose their mental illness as, "schizophrenia, in most instances a paranoid type."

Such a diagnosis, however, does not tell us why such persons become assassins, or how to identify and distinguish the assassination-prone personality. Furthermore, seven persons—the number of the actual assassins or would-be assassins (excepting Collazo and Torresola)—do not constitute a sufficient sample from which to generalize with any confidence. Yet these men do have a striking number of similarities.

All were male, white, not tall, and slender. Lawrence, Shrank, and Zangara were foreign born. Czolgosz was born a few months after his parents emigrated to the United States, and Booth's parents came to the United States after Booth's mother had become pregnant with their first child, Booth's older brother. Only the parents of Guiteau and Oswald were native born.

On the other hand, neither socioeconomic class nor employment seems to establish a common thread. The families of both Guiteau and Booth can be called middle class, as can Shrank as owner of a bar and tenement property. Booth moved in high social circles in the South. The remainder could be called craftsmen or members of the working class.

All for whom we have information experienced an absence or disruption of the normal family relationships between parent and child.

*        *        *

There is an hypothesis that the absence of a strong father figure may contribute to an assassin's frame of mind. . . .

Almost all the assassins were loners who had difficulty making friends of either sex, especially in establishing lasting relationships with women.

*        *        *

Lawrence, Czolgosz, Shrank, Zangara, and Oswald fall most closely into this pattern. All seem to have been quite withdrawn, with very few friends of either sex. Shrank had a girl friend at one point, but she was killed in an accident several years prior to his assassination attempt. We know of no other women in his life. Lawrence never married. Zangara avoided the company of women and never married. Czolgosz wrote that he had no friends except for brother Waldek. Oswald proposed to one girl while in Russia and married another, but was unable to make a success of the marriage.

A striking similarity is the fact that, from one to three years prior to an assassination attempt, each of the assassins apparently became unable to hold a job, although there is no evidence of physical disability in any case.

*        *        *

Another common characteristic is the tendency to identify with a cause or an ideologically based movement, but being unsuccessful or unable to participate with others in this cause or movement.

In almost every instance, the assassins seemed to focus on a specific narrow, political issue in addition to harboring a general hostile fixation on the presidency. . . .

*        *        *

Collazo, whose attack on President Truman was based on Puerto Rican nationalism, was examined by a psychiatrist and found to be sane. However, he does fit many of the above criteria: white, small of stature, and showing no remorse. In some regards he does not follow the pattern. His (second) marriage was successful; he was able to hold a job and retain the affection of his family, and became a real part of the movement with which he identified himself.

Although we cannot unravel the significance of the similarities between the assassins, we could make this statement: we could predict after President Kennedy's assassination that the next assassin would probably be short and slight of build, foreign born, and from a broken family—most probably with the father either absent or unresponsive to the child. He would be a loner, unmarried, with no steady female friends, and have a history of good work terminated from one to three years before the assassination attempt by a seeming listlessness and irascibility. He would identify with a political or religious movement, with the assassination triggered by a specific issue which relates to the principles of the cause or movement. Although identifying with the cause, the assassin would not in fact be part of or able to contribute to the movement. Not every presidential assassin has had every one of the foregoing traits, but some combination of the above has characterized them all.

One commentator, Dr. Doris Y. Wilkinson, applies the concept of status incongruence in an attempt to explain presidential assassins. Status incongruence exists where the achievement level of a person is inconsistent with what he expects because of his education or other factors, such as race, sex, ethnicity or nationality, family or social class background, or view of society. The argument can be made that each of the presidential assassins exhibited such an expectation-achievement gap. The question of why the psychic distress derived from status incongruence became politicized in the form of a deadly attack upon a high political officeholder remains unanswered.

One intriguing aspect of the status incongruence approach is that it may provide a partial explanation for two curious facts. First to be noted is the absence of Negroes from our list of presidential assassins—indeed, no Negroes are reported to have attempted to assassinate any high officeholders or persons of political prominence who are white. Second, all the assassins but Guiteau and Oswald either emigrated to America at a young age or were first-generation Americans.

With respect to the Negro phenomenon, it is suggested that, in America, the distinction between black and white has been, until perhaps very recent times, a master-determining status. The black man has a scapegoat. He can blame the system for defining him not in terms of what he does, but what he is. But a white person who fails to achieve his goals, although part of the favored racial class, has no such explanation for his "failure." The hypothesis is too broad, but it is at least a start towards a more specifically explanatory hypothesis.

Applying the expectation-achievement hypothesis to the first-generation phenomenon, the immigrant could explain his absence of status or lack of opportunity in the mother country, but upon immigration to the "land of opportunity" this explanation would seemingly be lost. Still, the immigrant might not have an expectation-achievement gap, because he could perceive his immigrant status as a limiting factor. No such explanation for failure would be available to the first-generation Americans, however. The son of the immigrant—the child who grew up in the "land of opportunity"—might subsequently experience this expectation-achievement gap when conscious of the reality of his failure.

*          *          *

In conclusion, it must be emphasized that we do not know why the characteristics discussed above appear in assassins, nor do we know why in a few instances those characteristics may lead to assassination, while in the overwhelming number of cases there is no such result. Many persons with more disruptive family lives and with the absence of a father figure become mentally healthy, productive citizens or at least do not assume an assassin's role.

## 318 "the urgency of preparing for militant, armed struggle now" (1969)

A "Third World" or "anti-imperialist" faction within Students for a Democratic Society, the segment of the student movement farthest to the left, organized Weatherman in order to take "the revolution" from the campus to American society. The organization's name was borrowed from Bob Dylan's song lyric, "You don't need a weatherman to know which way the wind blows."

Influenced by the civil rights movement, ghetto riots, the Marxism of Che Guevara and Castro, and the Chinese revolution, the Weathermen believed armed struggle was the only path to racial and political liberation and were convinced an antiracist, socialist, anti-imperialist revolution was imminent in the United States.

In this essay, Weatherman Shin'ya Ono outlined the rationale for resorting to violence in order to accomplish the demise of the racist-imperialist United States' hegemony in the world. Weatherman was to serve as the vanguard in this struggle.

☆ 318 A Weatherman: You Do Need a Weatherman to Know Which Way the Wind Blows (Shin'ya Ono)

Reprinted in Harold Jacobs, ed., *Weatherman* (Berkeley: Ramparts Press, 1971), 227-35.

### THE WEATHERMAN PERSPECTIVE

Three key points divide the Weathermen from all other political tendencies:

First: the primacy of confronting national chauvinism and racism among the working-class whites; the necessity to turn every issue, problem, and struggle into an anti-imperialist, anti-racist struggle. . . .

Second: the urgency of preparing for militant, armed struggle now; the necessity of organizing people into a fighting movement, not primarily by critiques, ideas, analyses, or programs, though all these are important, but by actually inflicting material damage to imperialist and racist institutions right now, with whatever forces you've got.

Third: the necessity of building revolutionary collectives that demand total, wholehearted commitment of the individual to struggle against everything that interferes with the revolutionary struggle, and to struggle to transform oneself into a revolutionary and a communist: collectives through which we can forge ourselves into effective "tools of necessity" and through which we can realize, concretely, in our day-to-day lives, such well-known Maoist principles as "Politics in command," "Everything for the revolution," "Criticism—self-criticism—transformation."

The Weatherman did not pick up these three points from Mao or the classics abstractly. These points arose out of, and are situated within, a broader revolutionary strategy specific to the conditions prevailing within the imperialist mother country.

As we see it, US imperialism has already entered a period of organic crisis, in the Gramscian sense of that term. And this crisis is of such intensity, depth, and immediacy as to make the destruction of imperialism and socialist revolution both possible and necessary *in our generation*, that is, in the order of twenty to thirty years, as opposed to fifty or one hundred years. But since the US is neither a colony nor a semi-colony (like China, Cuba, or Vietnam), nor an ordinary capitalist country (like Denmark), nor an ordinary imperialist country (like France or Britain), but the hegemonic imperialist country of the entire capitalist world, there are conditions peculiar to it that give the revolutionary process here its specific characteristics.

The political economy of US imperialism has reached an advanced stage of monopoly capitalism whose development is determined primarily by the problems of absorption of surplus capital and of reproduction of capital and of labor power. . . . US imperialism is an integrated international politico-economic system in which the peoples of the Third World, and to a much smaller degree the workers of other capitalist countries, are forced into the position of the proletariat of US political economy, while the white workers of the mother country itself find themselves in the position of a relatively privileged stratum of the imperialist US working force as a whole.

\*        \*        \*

The class position of white people in this country is determined by two contradictory aspects. On the one hand, by the classical Marxist definition, the overwhelming majority of whites belong to the working class in the sense that they neither own nor control the means of production. Furthermore, they are materially, psychologically, and in every other way, concretely oppressed by the imperialist political economy and by its concomitant superstructure.

This implies that the destruction of imperialism and socialist revolution are objectively in the interests of the vast majority of white Amerikans.

On the other hand, we confront the fact that the white workers do not constitute the main or the most oppressed sections of the work force within the worldwide political economy of US imperialism: on the contrary, they form a tiny, and the most privileged, sector of that proletariat. More, racially and politically they are members of the oppressor nation in relation to the Third World, including as always the blacks and the browns here; and as such they experience concrete benefits, both material and spiritual. They are the best paid, most comfortable, and the least oppressed, among the proletariat of the US imperialist political economy.

\*        \*        \*

Given this understanding of the forces at work in the development of the white working class consciousness, what we must ask now is: Of the many segments that make up this working class, which ones are most likely to develop full (i.e., internationalist) class consciousness at the present time, and lead the rest into anti-imperialist, anti-racist revolutionary struggles? In other words, which segments of the white working class are least privileged, or have the least stakes and roots in the system of privilege, and are most immediately and acutely oppressed? We answer: Youth, and especially the working-class youth. To summarize the arguments:

1. They are least tied down materially. . . .

2. They grew up when people's struggle was on the upsurge (Cuba, Black Liberation, Vietnam). . . .

3. They were socialized when important socializing media and mechanisms were disintegrating. . . .

4. They experience in the most acute way the oppressive conditions engendered by the imperialist crisis. . . .

These forces generated by the imperialist crisis, and lived through by every youth of our generation, have produced a youth culture and potentially explosive, anti-authoritarian motions in the past decade. We ourselves are both products and creators of these motions and forces. What we need to do now is to coalesce all these fragmented motions into an effective, anti-imperialist fighting force, with explicit revolutionary goals and with the most oppressed working-class youths as its core.

But how?

The problem is not primarily one of creating the consciousness among youth that they are oppressed: working-class youth knows much better than we that they are fucked over by this system in all kinds of ways. It's not even a question of "teaching" them to fight. Most of these kids have done much more of that (even fighting the pigs) than most Weathermen can hope to do in the near future. In fact, there are but two obstacles preventing their acute awareness of oppression and of oppressive social order from developing into a fully revolutionary direction: first, their racism and chauvinism; second, their basic defeatism about their ability, not merely to "beat the system" once in a while, but actually to destroy it totally.

\*       \*       \*

The correct way to deal with ... racism and chauvinism in a polarized situation is to confront it directly and show a real alternative. To hand them a leaflet or pamphlet or merely to rap, with explanations as to how racism is not in their long-term interest, is not a way to do either. Words, words, words. Mere words, however persuasive, mere ideas, however true, can not make even a dent in an ingrained psychic structure like racism that not only reaches into the very depth of whites' souls, but also has a material basis to sustain it. The only way to make our anti-racist ideas and analyses real is for these white kids to be confronted with a group of other whites who are willing to actually fight on the side of the blacks (and not just talk, hand out leaflets, picket, march, or give money for black liberation).... To see a group of other whites willing to fight to the very end on the side of the blacks will be a shocking experience for most whites....

While you confront their racism in this manner, you also must show a concrete alternative by identifying and actually attacking the real enemy, that is, the various imperialist institutions implicated in their class oppression.... You also show a concrete alternative by the very existence of a communist fighting force which they can join on various levels of struggle.

The second obstacle to the revolutionization of white working-class youth is their basic defeatism. In the last few years, hundreds of thousands of youths in and out of the Movement have fought against this imperialist system in various ways, but only a handful have become revolutionaries. Why? Because most of us are basically defeatists about our ability to destroy the system ("You can't fight city hall"). No matter how hard or how often we fight, we slide back to non-revolutionary bourgeois holes, because, at the basic core of our psychic life, we too have internalized the strongest ideological bulwark of US imperialism, i.e., the chauvinist idea that US imperialism, and its social order at home, is permanent and invincible. If most of us radicals and "revolutionaries" in the movement have not overcome this US imperialist-chauvinist myth, how can we expect working-class youth, who are not as familiar as we supposedly are with the experience and the victories of the Third World peoples, not to share this basic presumption about the permanence and invincibility of this social order?

\*       \*       \*

# 319 "the likelihood of crime by concerted action" (1969)

Dr. Benjamin Spock, the "baby doctor" for an entire generation; William Sloane Coffin, chaplain of Yale University; and a number of other public personages prepared a document entitled *A Call to Resist Illegitimate Authority*. This publication urged resistance to the Vietnam War. Mitchell Goodman spoke at a New York City press conference called to publicize *A Call*, and Michael Ferber spoke in support of *A Call* two weeks later at a Boston meeting attended by the Reverend Coffin. Four days after that meeting, three of these activists attended a rally in Washington, D.C., where protestors offered 357 previously surrendered draft cards and notices of classification to Attorney General John Mitchell as a sign of protest.

For these expressions and "overt" actions the four were convicted of counseling, aiding, and abetting draft evasion and other acts prohibited by the Universal Military Training and Service Act of 1967. The First Circuit Court of Appeals reversed the convictions. Although the encouragement of draft evasion and nonpossession of draft cards constituted advocacy of proscribed protest, the court found the advocacy of *A Call* to fall within lawful protest. The court held that conviction required unlawful activity, but that *A Call* did not extend beyond antiwar and antidraft opposition. The dissenting judge would have gone further to prohibit such broad-based conspiracy prosecutions altogether.

☆ 319 *United States v. Spock*

416 F.2d 165 (1st Cir. 1969).

ALDRICH, Chief Judge.

These are appeals by four defendants convicted under a single count indictment for conspiracy. We reverse.

As is well known, the war in Vietnam and the draft to support it have engendered considerable animosity and frustration. In August 1967 a number of academic, clerical, and professional persons discussed the need of more vigorous opposition to governmental policies. From their eventually consolidated efforts came a document entitled "A Call to Resist Illegitimate Authority." ...

\*       \*       \*

Inseparable from the question of the sufficiency of the evidence to convict are the rights of the defendants, and others, under the First Amendment. We approach the constitutional problem on the assumption, which we will later support, that the ultimate objective of defendants' alleged agreement, viz., the expression of opposition to the war and the draft, was legal, but that the means or intermediate objectives encompassed both legal and illegal activity without any clear indication, initially, as to who intended what. This intertwining of legal and illegal aspects, the public setting of the agreement and its political purposes, and the loose confederation of possibly innocent and possibly guilty participants raise the most serious First Amendment problems.

\*     \*     \*

In comparing the present private and public interests we start with the assumption that the defendants were not to be prevented from vigorous criticism of the government's program merely because the natural consequences might be to interfere with it, or even to lead to unlawful action. Thus *Bond v. Floyd* held that the First Amendment protected an expression of "sympathy ... and support [for] the men in this country who are unwilling to respond to a military draft." The Court said, with specific reference to [the statute here involved], "[T]his statement alone cannot be interpreted as a call to unlawful refusal to be drafted." The defendants here are not charged, however, with expressions of sympathy and moral support, but with conspiring to counsel, aid and abet Selective Service registrants to disobey various duties imposed by the Selective Service Act. The maintenance of an army in peacetime is a valid, in fact vital, governmental function. If a registrant may be convicted for violation of the draft laws, surely "[a] man may be punished for encouraging the commission of [the] crime."

The government's ability to deter and punish those who increase the likelihood of crime by concerted action has long been established. Restricting it to punishment of substantive violations ignores the potency of conspiratorial conduct; to wait for the substantive offense may be to wait too long. Congress has a right to prefer registrants to felons. . . .

\*     \*     \*

Despite the validity of the government's present interest, the defendants were entitled under the cases to certain protections before they could be convicted of conspiracy in what we might call a bifarious undertaking, involving both legal and illegal conduct. . . .

\*     \*     \*

. . . When the alleged agreement is both bifarious and political within the shadow of the First Amendment, we hold that an individual's specific intent to adhere to the illegal portions may be shown in one of three ways: by the individual defendant's prior or subsequent unambiguous statements; by the individual defendant's subsequent commission of the very illegal act contemplated by the agreement; or by the individual defendant's subsequent legal act if that act is "clearly undertaken for the specific purpose of rendering effective the later illegal activity which is advocated."

Application of such a standard should forcefully answer the defendants' protests that conviction of any of them would establish criminal responsibility of all of the many hundreds of persons who signed the Call. Even if the Call included illegal objectives, there is a wide gap between signing a document such as the Call and demonstrating one's personal attachment to illegality. Of greater importance, it responds to the legitimate apprehension of the amicus that the evil must be separable from the good without inhibiting legitimate association in an orderly society.

At the same time, this principle demonstrates a fundamental error in the government's approach. Adopting the panoply of rules applicable to a conspiracy having purely illegal purposes, the government introduced numerous statements of third parties alleged to be co-conspirators. This was improper: The specific intent of one defendant in a case such as this is not ascertained by reference to the conduct or statements of another even though he has knowledge thereof. . . .

\*     \*     \*

The principle of *strictissimi juris* requires the acquittal of Spock. It is true that he was one of the drafters of the Call, but this does not evidence the necessary intent to adhere to its illegal aspects. Nor does his admission to a government agent that he was willing to do "anything" asked to further opposition to the war. Specific intent is not established by such a generalization. Whatever the reason the fact is that his speech was limited to condemnation of the war and the draft, and lacked any words or content of counselling. The jury could not find proscribed advocacy from the mere fact, which he freely admitted, that he hoped the frequent stating of his views might give young men "courage to take active steps in draft resistance." This is a natural consequence of vigorous speech.

Similarly, Spock's actions lacked the clear character necessary to imply specific intent under the First Amendment standard. . . .

\*     \*     \*

The verdicts are set aside, and the judgments vacated. Judgments are to be entered for the defendants Spock and Ferber, and a new trial is ordered for the defendants Goodman and Coffin.

COFFIN, Circuit Judge (dissenting in part).

. . . I would grant acquittals to all appellants, since, in my view, whatever substantive crimes of aiding, abetting, and counseling, or whatever more specific conspiracies may have been committed, the crime of conspiracy, as charged in the indictment, was not. To apply conspiracy doctrine to these cases is, in my view, not compelled by conspiracy precedents, not consistent with First Amendment principles, not required to deal effectively with the hazard to public security, and not capable of discriminating application as between the culpable and the innocent.

\*     \*     \*

My starting point is the inquiry: how far has the application of conspiracy doctrine reached into the arena of overt associations involving the expression of opinion on public issues? Do reason and authority compel its application to a wholly open, amorphous, and shifting association, having a broad focus of interest in changing public policy, and encompassing a wide spectrum of purposes, legal and illegal?

\*     \*     \*

In the case of public "conspiracies" in the field of opinion, . . . the historic rationale for prosecuting the instigators of a group effort loses much of its force. The fact that the group initially places itself at the mercy of the public marketplace of ideas, risking disapproval, recommends that it have the protection of the First Amendment in its effort to gain approval. That a public "agreement" has been arrived at is not so much the genesis of the undertaking or a key to identifying masterminds as it is the manifestation of common concern. There is no possibility of taking society by surprise. There is no difficulty in ascertaining the activists who bear watching.

\*     \*     \*

. . . I concede that there is a need to maintain a peace-time army, that a registrant may be convicted for violation of the draft laws, that one may be punished for encouraging such violation, that there exists a danger of widespread disaffection and resistance to the draft laws, and that the government is entitled to take all reasonable steps to protect itself before such disaffection becomes epidemic. . . .

\*     \*     \*

The unexplored question is whether these interests can be as well served without resort to the conspiracy weapon. . . .

Had the appellants individually or collectively been indicted or tried for their separate offenses, the task would have been much simpler, as a reading of the transcript convincingly illustrates. . . . Moreover, the government could have chosen a specific incident for the focus of a conspiracy—as, for an arguable example, the Arlington Church turn-in or the Department of Justice card collection ceremony.

Nowhere does the court indicate why either approach could not have served the societal interest equally well. If "less restrictive alternative" is to have any real meaning, courts should examine with specificity the utility of the rifle before resort is had to the shotgun.

. . . I conclude that prosecution for substantive offenses or for a narrow, discrete conspiracy, would fully serve the government's interest—perhaps

even more than the court's sweeping conspiracy theory—without delivering such a serious blow to First Amendment freedoms.

\*     \*     \*

### APPENDIX

### *A Call to Resist Illegitimate Authority*

To the young men of America, to the whole of the American people, and to all men of good will everywhere:

\*     \*     \*

5. Therefore, we believe on all these grounds that every free man has a legal right and a moral duty to exert every effort to end this war, to avoid collusion with it, and to encourage others to do the same. . . . Each must choose the course of resistance dictated by his conscience and circumstances. Among those already in the armed forces some are refusing to obey specific illegal and immoral orders, some are attempting to educate their fellow servicemen on the murderous and barbarous nature of the war, some are absenting themselves without official leave. Among those not in the armed forces some are applying for status as conscientious objectors to American aggression in Vietnam, some are refusing to be inducted. Among both groups some are resisting openly and paying a heavy penalty, some are organizing more resistance within the United States and some have sought sanctuary in other countries.

6. We believe that each of these forms of resistance against illegitimate authority is courageous and justified. Many of us believe that open resistance to the war and the draft is the course of action most likely to strengthen the moral resolve with which all of us can oppose the war and most likely to bring an end to the war.

7. We will continue to lend our support to those who undertake resistance to this war. We will raise funds to organize draft resistance unions, to supply legal defense and bail, to support families and otherwise aid resistance to the war in whatever ways may seem appropriate.

8. We firmly believe that our statement is the sort of speech that under the First Amendment must be free, and that the actions we will undertake are as legal as is the war resistance of the young men themselves. . . .

9. We call upon all men of good will to join us in this confrontation with immoral authority. Especially we call upon the universities to fulfill their mission of enlightenment and religious organizations to honor their heritage of brotherhood. Now is the time to resist. . . .

# 320 A Ku Klux Klan Rally: Lawless Action? (1969)

The civil rights, student, and anti-Vietnam War movements, in addition to the reactions of the reactivated Ku Klux Klan and American Nazi Party, reflected the militancy of the 1960s. For speaking at a rally at a farm in Hamilton County, Ohio, a member of a Ku Klux Klan group was convicted in 1968 under the Ohio Criminal Syndicalism statute. Eschewing reliance on principles developed earlier in striking down prosecutions of Communist party members, the Supreme Court of the United States reversed the KKK conviction on First Amendment grounds. Giving credence to Justice Holmes's dissents in *Abrams v. United States* and *Gitlow v. New York*, the court concluded the guarantees of free speech and free press "do not permit a state to forbid or proscribe advocacy of the use of force or of law violation except where such advocacy is directed to inciting or producing imminent lawless actions and is likely to incite or produce such action." This decision should be contrasted with earlier cases in which the court had acquiesced in broad applications of such statutes which penalized antigovernment speech and writings.

☆ 320 *Brandenburg v. Ohio*

395 U.S. 444 (1969).

Per Curiam.

The record shows that a man, identified at trial as the appellant, telephoned an announcer-reporter on the staff of a Cincinnati television station and invited him to come to a Ku Klux Klan "rally" to be held at a farm in Hamilton County. With the cooperation of the organizers, the reporter and a cameraman attended the meeting and filmed the events. Portions of the films were later broadcast on the local station and on a national network.

The prosecution's case rested on the films and on testimony identifying the appellant as the person who communicated with the reporter and who spoke at the rally. The State also introduced into evidence several articles appearing in the film, including a pistol, a rifle, a shotgun, ammunition, a Bible, and a red hood worn by the speaker in the films.

One film showed 12 hooded figures, some of whom carried firearms. They were gathered around a large wooden cross, which they burned. No one was present other than the participants and the newsmen who made the film. Most of the words uttered during the scene were incomprehensible when the film was projected, but scattered phrases could be understood that were derogatory of Negroes and, in one instance, of Jews. Another scene on the same film showed the appellant, in Klan regalia, making a speech. The speech, in full, was as follows:

This is an organizers' meeting. We have had quite a few members here today which are—we have hundreds, hundreds of members throughout the State of Ohio. I can quote from a newspaper clipping from the Columbus, Ohio *Dispatch*, five weeks ago Sunday morning. The Klan has more members in the State of Ohio than does any other organization. We're not a revengent organization, but if our President, our Congress, our Supreme Court, continues to suppress the white, Caucasian race, it's possible that there might have to be some revengeance taken.

We are marching on Congress July the Fourth, four hundred thousand strong. From there we are dividing into two groups, one group to march on St. Augustine, Florida, the other group to march into Mississippi. Thank you.

The second film showed six hooded figures one of whom, later identified as the appellant, repeated a speech very similar to that recorded on the first film. The reference to the possibility of "revengeance" was omitted, and one sentence was added: "Personally, I believe the nigger should be returned to Africa, the Jew returned to Israel." Though some of the figures in the films carried weapons, the speaker did not.

. . . In 1927, this Court sustained the constitutionality of California's Criminal Syndicalism Act, the text of which is quite similar to that of the laws of Ohio. The Court upheld the statute on the ground that, without more, "advocating" violent means to effect political and economic change involves such danger to the security of the State that the State may outlaw it. But *Whitney* [*v. California*] has been thoroughly discredited by later decisions. See *Dennis v. United States*. These later decisions have fashioned the principle that the constitutional guarantees of free speech and free press do not permit a State to forbid or proscribe advocacy of the use of force or of law violation except where such advocacy is directed to inciting or producing imminent lawless action and is likely to incite or produce such action. As we said in *Noto v. United States*, "the mere abstract teaching . . . of the moral propriety or even moral necessity for a resort to force and violence, is not the same as preparing a group for violent action and steeling it to such action." A statute which fails to draw this distinction impermissibly intrudes upon the freedoms guaranteed by the First and Fourteenth Amendments. It sweeps within its condemnation speech which our Constitution has immunized from governmental control.

Measured by this test, Ohio's Criminal Syndicalism Act cannot be sustained. . . . Neither the indictment nor the trial judge's instructions to the jury in any way refined the statute's bald definition of the crime in terms of mere advocacy not distinguished from incitement to imminent lawless action.

Accordingly, we are here confronted with a statute which, by its own words and as applied, purports to punish mere advocacy and to forbid, on pain of criminal punishment, assembly with others merely to advocate the described type of action. Such a statute falls within the condemnation of the First and Fourteenth Amendments. The contrary teaching of *Whitney v. California* cannot be supported, and that decision is therefore overruled.

*Reversed.*

\*          \*          \*

MR. JUSTICE DOUGLAS, concurring.

While I join the opinion of the Court, I desire to enter a *caveat.*

The "clear and present danger" test was adumbrated by Mr. Justice Holmes in a case arising during World War I—a war "declared" by the Congress, not by the Chief Executive. . . .

\*          \*          \*

Whether the war power—the greatest leveler of them all—is adequate to sustain that doctrine is debatable. . . . Though I doubt if the "clear and present danger" test is congenial to the First Amendment in time of a declared war, I am certain it is not reconcilable with the First Amendment in days of peace.

\*          \*          \*

. . . I see no place in the regime of the First Amendment for any "clear and present danger" test, whether strict and tight as some would make it, or free-wheeling as the Court in *Dennis* rephrased it.

When one reads the opinions closely and sees when and how the "clear and present danger" test has been applied, great misgivings are aroused. First, the threats were often loud but always puny and made serious only by judges so wedded to the status quo that critical analysis made them nervous. Second, the test was so twisted and perverted in *Dennis* as to make the trial of those teachers of Marxism an all-out political trial which was part and parcel of the cold war that has eroded substantial parts of the First Amendment.

Action is often a method of expression and within the protection of the First Amendment.

\*          \*          \*

Last Term the Court held in *United States v. O'Brien* that a registrant under Selective Service who burned his draft card in protest of the war in Vietnam could be prosecuted. . . .

But O'Brien was not prosecuted for not having his draft card available when asked for by a federal agent. He was indicted, tried, and convicted for burning the card. And this Court's affirmance of that conviction was not, with all respect, consistent with the First Amendment.

\*          \*          \*

One's beliefs have long been thought to be sanctuaries which government could not invade. *Barenblatt* is one example of the ease with which that sanctuary can be violated. The lines drawn by the Court between the criminal act of being an "active" Communist and the innocent act of being a nominal or inactive Communist mark the difference only between deep and abiding belief and casual or uncertain belief. But I think that all matters of belief are beyond the reach of subpoenas or the probings of investigators. That is why the invasions of privacy made by investigating committees were notoriously unconstitutional. That is the deep-seated fault in the infamous loyalty-security hearings which, since 1947 when President Truman launched them, have processed 20,000,000 men and women. Those hearings were primarily concerned with one's thoughts, ideas, beliefs, and convictions. They were the most blatant violations of the First Amendment we have ever known.

The line between what is permissible and not subject to control and what may be made impermissible and subject to regulation is the line between ideas and overt acts.

The example usually given by those who would punish speech is the case of one who falsely shouts fire in a crowded theatre.

This is, however, a classic case where speech is brigaded with action. They are indeed inseparable and a prosecution can be launched for the overt acts actually caused. Apart from rare instances of that kind, speech is, I think, immune from prosecution. Certainly there is no constitutional line between advocacy of abstract ideas as in *Yates* and advocacy of political action as in *Scales*. The quality of advocacy turns on the depth of the conviction; and government has no power to invade that sanctuary of belief and conscience.

## 321 "to turn American courtrooms into political forums" (1970)

In "The Ultra-Resistance," journalist Francine du Plessix Gray attempted to discern the unique substance, characteristics, and methods of the draft board defilers and other Vietnam resisters. Their "typically American" form of dissent, she suggested, was not pointed ultimately toward the insurrectionary goal of toppling the government and its institutions, but embraced the more modest aim of turning American courtrooms into political-moral forums for the instruction of fellow citizens.

## ☆ 321 The Ultra-Resistance
## (Francine du Plessix Gray)

Reprinted in Noam Chomsky et al., *Trials of the Resistance* (New York: Vintage Books, 1970), 125-69.

On a warm spring day in 1966, a nineteen-year-old Minnesotan by the name of Barry Bondhus broke into his local draft board and dumped two large bucketfuls of human feces into a filing cabinet, mutilating several hundred I-A draft records in protest against the Vietnam draft. The offender and his eleven brothers, sons of a machinist who had threatened to shoot anyone who attempted to induct his boys into the American army, had fastidiously collected their organic wastes for two weeks in preparation for the raid.

This primordial deed is known in the annals of the anti-war protest as the Big Lake One action, in honor of Barry Bondhus's hometown, Big Lake, Minnesota. Barry Bondhus, who had calmly awaited arrest after his performance, served an eighteen-month sentence at Sandstone Federal Correctional Institution and came home in March of 1968 to run his father's machine shop. Big Lake One was hardly mentioned in the press, but Bondhus's was "the movement that started the Movement."

Since Bondhus in 1966, over seventy Americans have awaited arrest after destroying government draft records with the less rustic media of blood, paint, and fire. The Big Lake One was followed by:

The Baltimore Four (600 draft records defiled with blood by Father Philip Berrigan, Reverend James Mengel, David Eberhardt, Thomas Lewis, October 1967);

The Catonsville Nine (Father Philip Berrigan strikes again in the company of his brother Father Daniel Berrigan and seven other Catholic priests and laymen, destroying 378 draft files with homemade napalm, May 1968);

The Boston Two (several hundred draft records mutilated with black paint by students Suzi Williams and Frank Femia, June 1968);

The Milwaukee Fourteen (some 10,000 draft records napalmed, September 1968);

The Pasadena Three (some 300 records burned, May 20, 1969);

The Silver Spring Three (several hundred records of a Maryland draft board mutilated with black paint and blood, May 21, 1969);

The Chicago Fifteen (some 40,000 draft records burned on May 25 of this year);

Women Against Daddy Warbucks (several thousand records mutilated in a Manhattan draft board by the first all-women band of draft board raiders, last July 2);

The New York Eight (some 75,000 records mutilated in a Bronx draft board on August 1, and several thousand more in a Queens draft board on August 15, by a group of four women and four men, three of them Catholic priests);

The Cleveland Two (draft board records in Akron burned, October, 1969);

The Beaver Fifty-five—who were not fifty-five but eight—(records of 44 Indianapolis draft boards shredded, October 31, 1969);

The Boston Eight (files of eight draft boards destroyed, November 7, 1969).

There is no name for this radical core of the peace movement.... Men and women who believe they have exhausted every other means of protesting the Vietnam war raid a draft board, haul out records and burn them, stand around singing liberation songs while awaiting arrest. The draft board actions have elements of both terrorist strike and liturgical drama. They aim to destruct and to instruct; to impede in some small way the war machine; to communicate its evil, at a time when verbal and political methods have failed, by a morality play which will startle, embarrass the community; to shame the Movement to heightened militancy, perhaps to imitation. The word "witness" is used by members of this ultra-resistance, with its historical implications of sacrifice and penance, of moral primitivism, of romantic egoism, of psychological violence. The draft board actions in which the raiders demand arrest are called "stand around" to differentiate them from acts of "hit and run" sabotage; they are grounded in the non-violent mystique that a man's witness in jail can move the conscience of a nation; that it can abate the violence of its rulers, and, like a monk's years of passive prayer, aid to purify society. According to this mystique, the presence of the man awaiting arrest, sacrificing his freedom to witness to his moral indignation, is the ingredient that transforms sabotage into a religious and instructive act. As in tragedy and liturgy, sacrifice is conceived of as the most powerful means of communication.

\* \* \*

... The monastic stand-arounders, Barry Bondhus included, usually come from highly authoritarian and conservative backgrounds, which perhaps explains some of their differences from the permissively reared young people in the larger radical Movement.

Not the least of these differences is their disdain for amnesty, their sense that it is a positive act to go to jail.... [T]hey claim to have a great distrust of rhetoric. "It's not enough to just speak any more." "I had to put my body on the line." "It wasn't just words, that's basically it." They reserve their rhetoric for the courtroom.

There is another important difference between the guerrillas of the campuses and these jail-bound witnesses: however radical they are, the draft board raiders are distrustful of imported jargon. Their ideological heroes are apt to be Thoreau and A. J.

Muste rather than Mao or Che; they want to do something "typically American"; and although they rebel as fiercely as the rest of the Movement against the familiar demons of capitalism, racism, colonialism, and militarism, they have chosen, up to now, to channel their protest against that uniquely American form of oppression, the Selective Service System.

*       *       *

Another purpose of the draft board raids is to turn American courtrooms into political forums on the illegality and the immorality of the Vietnam war....

*       *       *

The Milwaukee defendants [who represented themselves]... used their defense funds to fly three expert witnesses from the East Coast to testify on the "reasonableness" of their views on the war and on civil disobedience. The three—Howard Zinn, John Fried, and Marvin Gettleman—seemed to make Judge Larson highly uncomfortable. Howard Zinn's hour and a half on the witness stand was Grand Guignol. The prosecution objected at every few words that the defendants' cross-examination was immaterial or that Dr. Zinn's opinions were irrelevant; the Judge sustained the objections, pounding the gavel like a Guignol policeman batting down the hobo when he tries to rise. Nevertheless the courtroom audience burst into frenzied applause at Zinn's truncated testimony.

*Howard Zinn*: The tradition of civil disobedience goes as far back as Thomas Jefferson and it comes right up to today.... [P]eople distinguished in the field of law and philosophy recognize that there's a vast difference between a person who commits an ordinary crime and a person who commits an act which technically is a crime, but which in essence is a social act designed to make a statement....

*       *       *

The second star witness, John Fried, an imposing, silver-haired Viennese-born scholar, had been chief consultant to the American judges at the Nuremberg trials, United Nations Adviser on International Law to the government of Nepal, and adviser on international law at the Pentagon. The defendants stated that they had called Fried to testify on "a hierarchy of law in the international world order." The prosecution and the Court objected that testimony drawn from such documents as the UN Charter and the Nuremberg Principles concerning the United States' violation of international law would be irrelevant to charges of burglary, arson, and theft. Fred Ojile replied that the defense's purpose in calling expert witnesses was to show it had "reasonable belief" in the war's illegality.

*       *       *

For once the defendants' gambit worked. Whatever the reason—their unpredictable and agile tactics of self-defense, perhaps some growing anguish that seemed to gnaw at the prosecutors and a certain grandeur or glamour that the witness injected into this provincial courtroom—Fried's testimony plunged more deeply into a discussion of the morality of the war than any yet tolerated at a resistance trial.

*Fried*: I say with a very, very grave heart and after very, very careful study that the U.S. military intervention in Vietnam does violate essential and basic provisions of the United Nations charter, and this is not an isolated opinion of myself.

*Brother O'Leary*: What recourse does a citizen have ... when his country pursues war in violation of international treaties which the citizen holds have been violated?

("No objection," said District Attorney Harold Jackson; "if he can answer that, God bless him.")

*Fried*: The International Tribunal at Nuremberg, at which the United States was represented, stated that it is the moral choice of the individual if he feels that for him obedience to the higher order—to the world order—is more important, ... then he has to take the moral choice and do the things which he considers morally proper. That is the great ethical and moral method of Nuremberg.

*Brother O'Leary*: One who breaks a law in the State of Wisconsin might well be called an arsonist or just a common criminal. One who conspires with his government to commit a crime in violation of the United Nations, I suppose, would be called a war criminal. In the perspective on international law, which would be the worse kind of criminal?

*Fried*: ... In the hierarchy of law, international world order as stipulated in treaties ... is the highest. If, then, a dichotomy develops between international law and domestic law, the dilemma for the government and for the individual is great....

*Brother O'Leary*: No more questions.

*       *       *

*The following letter of comment on Mrs. Gray's article by Professor Fried, formerly Special Legal Consultant to the U.S. War Crimes Tribunals, Nuremberg, was published in* The New York Review *of October 9, 1969:*

To the Editors:

Some of my testimony at the trial of the "Milwaukee Fourteen" was garbled in the court transcript....

The [Nuremberg] Tribunal's famous "moral choice" doctrine is that an individual who was ordered to commit an international wrong will be internationally responsible for obeying the order if a "moral choice" *not* to obey it existed for him—that is, if by the rules of morality he had a realistic choice.

The gist of my testimony was: The International Tribunal at Nuremberg, at which the United States was represented as Prosecutor and on the Bench, stated that it is the moral choice of the individual that counts. Obedience to the higher, the world order, is more important. He should feel that, and always endeavor not to violate it. If such moral choice is in fact not possible for him, he will not be personally punishable for violating the international rule. But if he feels that he must make the choice even at personal risk, then he has to make the moral choice and do the things he considers morally proper. That is the great ethical and moral message of Nuremberg.

For the benefit of readers, I quote pertinent passages from the Judgment:

> ... the very essence of the [Nuremberg] Charter is that individuals have international duties which transcend the national obligations of obedience imposed by the individual state. He who violates the laws of war cannot obtain immunity while acting in pursuance to the authority of the state if the state in authorizing action moves outside its competence under international law.... The true test ... is not the existence of the order, but whether moral choice was in fact possible. *(Trial of the Major War Criminals ... Nuremberg, 1945/6.* Vol. 1, pp. 223/4.)

JOHN H. E. FRIED
Professor of Political Science,
Lehman College and Graduate Faculty
City University of New York

## 322 "we are adapting the classic guerrilla strategy" (1970)

Unlike other "distinctly American" protest and civil disobedience movements, the Weatherman Underground modeled itself after and actually imitated foreign anticolonial national liberation movements. After the "Days of Rage," when several hundred people vandalized downtown Chicago, some of the Weatherman leaders went "underground," and the FBI added them to their most wanted list.

Weatherman took responsibility for several subsequent acts of violence. Their communiqués were circulated widely in the media at the time, and despite success in evading capture, Weatherman failed to attract the expected mass following of American youth. An explosion at their "bomb factory" in a Greenwich Village town house killed Weathermen Diana Oughton, Ted Gold, and Terry Robbins and further isolated them from those they attempted to organize.

☆ 322  Communiqués from the Weatherman Underground

☆ 322a  Communiqué 1: A Declaration of a State of War

*The Berkeley Tribe,* May 29–June 5, 1970, 3.

Hello. This is Bernardine Dohrn. I'm going to read A DECLARATION OF A STATE OF WAR. This is the first communication from the Weatherman underground.

All over the world, people fighting Amerikan imperialism look to Amerika's youth to use our strategic position behind enemy lines to join forces in the destruction of the empire.

Black people have been fighting almost alone for years. We've known that our job is to lead white kids into armed revolution. We never intended to spend the next five or twenty-five years of our lives in jail. Ever since SDS became revolutionary, we've been trying to show how it is possible to overcome the frustration and impotence that comes from trying to reform this system. Kids know the lines are drawn; revolution is touching all of our lives. Tens of thousands have learned that protest and marches don't do it. Revolutionary violence is the only way.

Now we are adapting the classic guerrilla strategy of the Viet Cong and the urban guerrilla strategy of the Tupamaros to our own situation here in the most technically advanced country in the world.

Che taught us that "revolutionaries move like fish in the sea." The alienation and contempt that young people have for this country has created the ocean for this revolution.

The hundreds and thousands of young people who demonstrated in the Sixties against the war and for civil rights grew to hundreds of thousands in the past few weeks actively fighting Nixon's invasion of Cambodia and the attempted genocide against black people....

\*          \*          \*

We fight in many ways. Dope is one of our weapons. The laws against marijuana mean that millions of us are outlaws long before we actually split. Guns and grass are united in the youth underground.

Freaks are revolutionaries and revolutionaries are freaks. If you want to find us, this is where we are. In every tribe, commune, dormitory, farmhouse, barracks and town-house where kids are making love, smoking dope and loading guns—fugitives from Amerikan justice are free to go.

\*          \*          \*

Within the next fourteen days we will attack a symbol or institution of Amerikan injustice. This is the way we celebrate the example of Eldridge Cleaver and H. Rap Brown and all black revolutionaries who first inspired us by their fight behind enemy lines for the liberation of their people.

Never again will they fight alone.

*May 21, 1970.*

☆322b Communiqué 2: Damage and Injuries at This Time — Details Later

*The Berkeley Tribe*, June 12-19, 1970, 4.

Tonight, at 7 P.M., we blew up the N.Y.C. police headquarters. We called in a warning before the explosion.

*     *     *

The pigs try to look invulnerable, but we keep finding their weaknesses. Thousands of kids, from Berkeley to the UN Plaza, keep tearing up ROTC buildings.

Nixon invades Cambodia and hundreds of schools are shut down by strikes. Every time the pigs think they've stopped us, we come back a little stronger and a lot smarter. They guard their buildings and we walk right past their guards. They look for us — we get to them first.

They build the Bank of America, kids burn it down. They outlaw grass, we build a culture of life and music.

The time is now. Political power grows out of a gun, a Molotov, a riot, a commune ... and from the soul of the people.

WEATHERMAN

———————————

*The Berkeley Tribe*, June 12-19, 1970, 5.

TO THE BROTHERS AND SISTERS OF THE WEATHERMAN UNDERGROUND:

I read your communique, and was really excited to find out that you're still here in America, and into doing heavy stuff. The presence of an underground here, in the midst of the Man's boasts about his high-level pig technology, is a victory in itself.

For you to survive must mean that thousands of kids everywhere are enough like you that the pigs can't isolate you to pick you off. Many people like us must have helped you directly in those first days after the townhouse; you couldn't have survived doing everything yourselves.

*     *     *

It's important that you don't become isolated as super-beings. Most of us are pretty unsure about what to do, and it's easy to fall into a pattern of seeing you as a super-together, tightly disciplined force who'll take care of business for us while we cheer you on from the sidelines. Believing in the underground as a glamorous revolutionary legend will only hold us back from the kinds of struggle and practice we need to be about now; leadership has got to be what we can see ourselves becoming.

*     *     *

It's true that most freaks are potential revolutionaries, but we're all confused about how to get from here to there. Even tho millions of kids are in motion, we're not very together with each other. We'll have to find ways to share our experiences and our struggle on deeper levels than ever before. We've got to move towards a time when the mass movement and the underground build off each other, and become integrated under the same politics and the same leadership. That will only happen when we share the kind of trust and love that comes with an open and self-critical relationships between you and us.

Power to the people whose bombs tore up the Centre St. pig station (on any fucking day)!

A REVOLUTIONARY BROTHER AND SISTER

☆322c Communiqué 3: Letter from the Underground

*The Berkeley Tribe*, July 31-August 7, 1970, 4.

July 26, 1970
The Motor City

This is the third communication from the Weatherman underground.

With other revolutionaries all over the planet, Weatherman is celebrating the 11th anniversary of the Cuban revolution. Today we attack with rocks, riots and bombs the greatest killer-pig ever known to man — Amerikan imperialism.

Everywhere we see the growth of revolutionary culture and the ways in which every move of the monster-state tightens the noose around its own neck.

A year ago people thought it can't happen here. Look at where we've come.

Nixon invades Cambodia; the Cong and all of Indochina spread the already rebelling U.S. troops thin. Ahmed is a prisoner; Rap is free and fighting. Fred Hampton is murdered; the brothers at Soledad avenge — "2 down and one to go." Pun [Plamondon, Minister of Defense, White Panther Party] and several Weatherman are ripped; we run free. Mitchell indicts 8 or 10 or 13; hundreds of thousands of freeks plot to build a new world on the ruins of honky Amerika.

And to General Mitchell we say: Don't look for us, Dog; We'll find you first.

For the Central Committee
WEATHERMAN UNDERGROUND

☆322d Communiqué 4: We Are Outlaws, We Are Free!

*The Berkeley Tribe*, September 18-25, 1980, 3.

September 15, 1970

This is the fourth communication from the Weatherman Underground.

The Weatherman Underground has had the honor and pleasure of helping Dr. Timothy Leary escape from the POW camp at San Luis Obispo, California.

Dr. Leary was being held against his will and against the will of millions of kids in this country. He was a political prisoner, captured for the work he did in helping all of us begin the task of creating a new culture on the barren wasteland that has been imposed on this country by Democrats, Republicans, Capitalists and creeps.

LSD and grass, like the herbs and cactus and mushrooms of the American Indians and countless civilizations that have existed on this planet, will help us make a future world where it will be possible to live in peace.

Now we are at war.

With the NLF and the North Vietnamese, with the Democratic Front for the Liberation of Palestine and Al Fatah, with Rap Brown and Angela Davis, with all black and brown revolutionaries, the Soledad brothers and all prisoners of war in Amerikan concentration camps we know that peace is only possible with the destruction of U.S. imperialism.

Our organization commits itself to the task of freeing these prisoners of war.

We are outlaws, we are free!

BERNARDINE DOHRN

# 323 "sabotage, jam the computer" (1970)

Divorced from established society, which failed to rebel against the Vietnam War, racism, and poverty, but united by youthful exuberance and mass media attention, a segment of young adults created the "counterculture," symbolized by drug use, relaxed sexual mores, and hard-rock music. The counterculture had no particular political agenda, but rejected the competitive, regimented, and technologically-oriented prevailing society. They placed great emphasis on Eastern religions and native American mysticism as substitutes for the Judeo-Christian ethic, which they deemed to have failed.

Dr. Timothy Leary, a Harvard psychology instructor who experimented with LSD and Eastern religions, became a "guru" of the counterculture. Written in prison following a narcotics conviction, this Leary letter was published while he was hiding underground with the Weathermen, who helped in his escape. This kind of rhetoric gave the militant movements a sense that there was mass support for their causes and invested the counterculture with a sense of social and political purpose.

☆ 323 Letter from Timothy Leary (September 18, 1970)

*San Francisco Good Times*, September 18, 1970, 24.

There is the time for peace and the time for war.

There is the day of laughing Krishna and the day of Grim Shiva.

Brothers and Sisters, at this time let us have no more talk of peace.

The conflict which we have sought to avoid is upon us. A world-wide ecological religious warfare. Life vs. death.

Listen. It is a comfortable, self-indulgent cop-out to look for conventional economic-political solutions.

Brothers and Sisters, this is a war for survival. Ask Huey [Newton] and Angela [Davis]. They dig it.

Ask the wild free animals. They know it.

Ask the turned-on ecologists. They sadly admit it.

I declare that World War III is now being waged by short-haired robots whose deliberate aim is to destroy the complex web of free wild life by the imposition of mechanical order.

Listen. There is no choice left but to defend life by all and every means possible against the genocidal machine.

Listen. There are no neutrals in genetic war. There are no non-combatants at Buchenwald, My Lai or Soledad [Prison].

You are part of the death apparatus or you belong to the network of free life.

Do not be deceived. It is a classic stratagem of genocide to camouflage their wars as law and order police actions.

Remember the Sioux and the German Jews and the black slaves and the marijuana pogroms and the pious TWA indignation over airline hijackings!

If you fail to see that we are the victims — defendants of genocidal war — you will not understand the rage of the blacks, the fierceness of the browns, the holy fanaticism of the Palestinians, the righteous mania of the Weathermen, and the pervasive resentment of the young.

Listen Americans. Your government is an instrument of total lethal evil.

Remember the buffalo and the Iroquois!

Remember Kennedy, King, Malcolm, Lenny [Bruce]!

Listen. There is no compromise with a machine. You cannot talk peace and love to a humanoid robot whose every Federal Bureaucratic impulse is soulless, heartless, lifeless, loveless.

In this life struggle we use the ancient holy strategies of organic life:

1) Resist lovingly in the loyalty of underground sisterhoods and brotherhoods.

2) Resist passively, break lock-step . . . drop out.

3) Resist actively, sabotage, jam the computer ... hijack planes ... trash every lethal machine in the land.

4) Resist publicly, announce life ... denounce death.

5) Resist privately, guerrilla invisibility.

6) Resist beautifully, create organic art, music.

7) Resist biologically, be healthy ... erotic ... conspire with seed ... breed.

8) Resist spiritually, stay high ... praise god ... love life ... blow the mechanical mind with Holy Acid ... dose them ... dose them.

9) Resist physically, robot agents who threaten life must be disarmed, disabled, disconnected by force ... Arm yourself and shoot to live ... Life is never violent. To shoot a genocidal robot policeman in the defense of life is a sacred act.

Listen Nixon. We were never that naïve. We knew that flowers in your gun-barrels were risky. We too remember Munich and Auschwitz all too well as we chanted love and raised our Woodstock fingers in the gentle sign of peace.

We begged you to live and let live, to love and let love, but you have chosen to kill and get killed. May God have mercy on your soul.

For the last seven months, I, a free, wild man, have been locked in POW camps. No living creature can survive in a cage. In my flight to freedom I leave behind a million brothers and sisters in the POW prisons of Quentin, Soledad, Con Thien ...

Listen comrades. The liberation war has just begun. Resist, endure, do not collaborate. Strike. You will be free.

Listen you brothers of the imprisoned. Break them out! If David Harris has ten friends in the world, I say to you, get off your pious non-violent asses and break him out.

There is no excuse for one brother or sister to remain a prisoner of war.

Right on Leila Khaled [a contemporary Palestinian skyjacker]!

Listen, the hour is late. Total war is upon us. Fight to live or you'll die. Freedom is life. Freedom will live.

TIMOTHY LEARY

*WARNING: I am armed and should be considered dangerous to anyone who threatens my life or my freedom.*

## 324 "the military error" (1970)

Bernardine Dohrn, law-educated and twenty-five years old at the time, was one of the founders of Weatherman. In this letter, delivered to Liberation News Service on December 6, 1970, she described the problems of being an underground revolution-ary. She also conceded that the revolution would require cultural and social change rather than the mere breaking down of the existing order.

Dohrn referred twice in the letter to Fred Hampton, an Illinois Black Panther leader, who had publicly denounced Weatherman. The Weathermen, nevertheless, had adopted Hampton as a martyr after Chicago policemen shot and killed him in his bed during a raid on Black Panther headquarters. Dohrn remained underground for ten years until she turned herself in to the authorities on December 3, 1980, and pleaded guilty to charges arising out of her participation in "the Days of Rage." She was sentenced to three years' probation and fined fifteen hundred dollars. Thirty-nine years old and the mother of two, she asserted she was still "committed to the struggle." Rejecting the prosecutor's argument that Dohrn be given a prison sentence, the judge stated that Dohrn probably had suffered enough in her years of separation from family and friends.

## ☆ 324 New Morning—Changing Weather: A Declaration by Bernardine Dohrn and the Weather Underground (December 6, 1970)

Reprinted in H. Salisbury, ed., *The Eloquence of Protest: Voices of the 70s* (Boston: Houghton Mifflin, 1972), 19–23.

This communication does not accompany a bombing or a specific action. We want to express ourselves to the mass movement not as military leaders but as tribes at council. It has been nine months since the townhouse explosion. In that time, the future of our revolution has been changed decisively. A growing illegal organization of young women and men can live and fight and love inside Babylon. The FBI can't catch us; we've pierced their bullet-proof shield. But the townhouse forever destroyed our belief that armed struggle is the only real revolutionary struggle.

It is time for the movement to go out into the air, to organize, to risk calling rallies and demonstrations, to convince that mass actions against the war and in support of rebellions do make a difference. Only acting openly, denouncing Nixon, Agnew and [Attorney General] Mitchell, and sharing our numbers and wisdom together with young sisters and brothers will blow away the fear of the students at Kent State, the smack of the Lower East Side and the national silence after the bombings of North Vietnam.

The deaths of three friends ended our military conception of what we are doing. It took us weeks of careful talking to rediscover our roots, to remember that we had been turned on to the possibilities of revolution by denying the schools, the jobs, the death relationships we were "educated" for. We went back to how we had begun living with groups of friends and found that this revolution could leave intact the enslavement of women if women did not fight to end and change it, together.

Diana [Oughton], Teddy [Gold] and Terry [Robbins] had been in SDS for years. Diana and Teddy had been teachers and both spent weeks with the Vietnamese in Cuba. Terry had been a community organizer in Cleveland and at Kent; Diana had worked in Guatemala. They fought in the Days of Rage in Chicago. Everyone was angered by the murder of Fred Hampton. Because their collective began to define armed struggle as the only legitimate form of revolutionary action, they did not believe that there was any revolutionary motion among white youth. It seemed like black and third world people were going up against Amerikan imperialism alone.

Two weeks before the townhouse explosion, four members of this group had firebombed Judge Murtagh's house in New York as an action of support for the Panther 21, whose trial was just beginning. To many people this was a very good action. Within the group, however, the feeling developed that because this action had not done anything to hurt the pigs materially it wasn't very important. So within two weeks' time, this group had moved from firebombing to antipersonnel bombs. Many people in the collective did not want to be involved in the large-scale, almost random bombing offensive that was planned. But they struggled day and night and eventually, everyone agreed to do their part.

At the end, they believed and acted as if only those who die are proven revolutionaries. Many people had been argued into doing something they did not believe in, many had not slept for days. Personal relationships were full of guilt and fear. The group had spent so much time willing themselves to act that they had not dealt with the basic technological considerations of safety. They had not considered the future: either what to do with the bombs if it had not been possible to reach their targets, or what to do in the following days.

This tendency to consider only bombings or picking up the gun as revolutionary, with the glorification of the heavier the better, we've called the military error.

After the explosion, we called off all armed actions until such time as we felt the causes had been understood and acted upon. We found that the alternative direction already existed among us and had been developed within our collectives. We became aware that a group of outlaws who are isolated from the youth communities do not have a sense of what is going on, can not develop strategies that grow to include large numbers of people, have become "us" and "them."

It was a question of revolutionary culture. Either you saw the youth culture that has been developing as bourgeois or decadent and therefore to be treated as the enemy of the revolution, or you saw it as the forces which produced us, a culture that we were a part of, a young and unformed society (nation).

In the past months we have had our minds blown by the possibilities that exist for all of us to develop the movement so that as revolutionaries we change and shape the cultural revolution. We are in a position to change it for the better. Men who are chauvinists can change and become revolutionaries who no longer embrace any part of the culture that stands in the way of the freedom of women. Hippies and students who fear black power should check out Rap Brown's *Die Nigger Die* and George Jackson's writings. We can continue to liberate and subvert attempts to rip off the culture. People become revolutionaries in the schools, in the army, in prisons, in communes, and on the streets. Not in an underground cell.

*     *     *

. . . We have obviously not gone in for large-scale material damage. Most of our actions have hurt the enemy on about the same military scale as a bee sting. But the political effect against the enemy has been devastating. The world knows that even the white youth of Babylon will resort to force to bring down imperialism.

The attacks on the Marin County Courthouse and the Long Island City Jail were because we believe that the resistance and political leadership that is growing within the prisons demands immediate and mass support from young people. For all the George Jacksons, Afeni Shakurs and potential revolutionaries in these jails, the movement is the lifeline. They rebelled expecting massive support from outside.

Demonstrations in support of prison revolts are a major responsibility of the movement, but someone must call for them, put out the leaflets, convince people that it is a priority. We are so used to feeling powerless that we believe pig propaganda about the death of the movement, or some bad politics about rallies being obsolete and bullshit. A year ago, when Bobby Seale was ripped off in Chicago and the movement didn't respond, it made it easier for the pigs to murder Fred Hampton. Now the Puerto Ricans have been killed by the pigs in the New York jails, in retaliation for the prisoner rebellion. What we do or don't do makes a difference.

It will require courage and close families of people to do this organizing. Twos and threes is not a good form for anything—it won't put out a newspaper, organize a conference on the war, or do an armed action without getting caught. Our power is that together we are mobile, decentralized, flexible and we come into every home where there are children who catch the music of freedom and life.

The women and men in jails are POWs held by the United States. When an Amerikan pilot is shot down while bombing North Vietnamese villages, he is often surrounded by thousands of people who have just seen their family and homes destroyed by the bombs he was delivering. Yet the man is not attacked and killed by the Vietnamese but is cared for as a prisoner....

\*          \*          \*

People are forming new families. Collectives have sprung up from Seattle to Atlanta, Buffalo to Vermont, and they are units of people to trust each other both to live together and to organize and fight together. The revolution involves our whole lives; we aren't part-time soldiers or secret revolutionaries. It is our closeness and the integration of our personal lives with our revolutionary work that will make it hard for undercover pigs to infiltrate our collectives....

## 325 "this country is getting tired of student demonstrations" (1970)

Upon Lyndon B. Johnson's retirement from office, Richard Nixon was elected president with a promise to end the Vietnam War. But on April 30, 1970, he announced the American invasion of Cambodia. Protests, student strikes, and takeovers sprang up nationwide, including the demonstration at Kent State University where National Guardsmen shot to death four students and wounded nine others. President Nixon stated, "When dissent turns to violence it invites trouble." This letter by Dr. Paul Williamson of McComb, Mississippi, to his son who was about to enter Tulane University in New Orleans reflected the reaction of much of the public toward protest and confrontation tactics by students.

### ☆ 325 A Doctor's Letter to His Son

Reprinted in H. Salisbury, ed., *The Eloquence of Protest: Voices of the 70s* (Boston: Houghton Mifflin, 1972), 27-28.

DEAR NATHAN:

Of course, you know that your mother and I love you deeply. There are limits to that love. Let me discuss one with you today.

You are going to Tulane. We are proud and happy for you. There are, however, awkward things that must be discussed. College kids over the nation are "protesting."

They use many beautiful phrases. What it often amounts to is a contest with the duly constituted authorities of the United States government. The only term that could apply is revolution. People are quite rightly shot in revolutions.

I suppose there is the legal differentiation be-

tween a peaceful demonstration and breaking windows. One graduates into the other by such indifferent degrees it is difficult to say where one ends and the other begins.

The duly constituted authorities have been merciful beyond belief—far too merciful, I think—with students. Obviously, this patience is nearing an end. Snap, I have seldom heard of a student being shot at his study desk. When he goes in the open and contests the ground with the National Guard, he may very likely be shot—and very rightly.

Let us take, for example, the sweet little girl in Kent, Ohio. I feel nothing but sorrow that a beautiful young girl of great mental attainments be killed. Yet, Snap, if she had been studying—doing what her parents were paying for her to accomplish—would she have died?

She was helping contest the ground with duly constituted U.S. authorities. In this case, I back the U.S. I think it rather remarkable that they didn't shoot two hundred more. In this case, the girl was a revolutionary and she got exactly what a revolutionary should expect.

The same, Snap, would be true of you. If you care to challenge the U.S. government, this is your affair. If you get killed doing it, this is your affair. You see, there are constitutional ways to change the U.S. government and I agree that it desperately needs changing. However, if you choose to try to change it by revolution, expect to get shot. Mother and I will grieve but we will gladly buy a dinner for the National Guardsman who shot you. You see, son, they pretty-up in definition all the things you might want to do. When brought to its basics, it is still just revolution.

I am sorry for the colored boys who were killed at Jackson. But, son, I know a lot more about this than will ever be printed in national news media. There was sniper fire the night before as well as the night the police fired back. The students were given fifteen minutes' warning to clear the area before the police fired. I thought the duly constituted authorities were most gentle to take only two. If you take part in something like this and get shot, Mama and I will still back the U.S.

It may sound like great martyrdom to give your life for an ideal. Indeed, it may be when you are old enough to judge ideals. Trying to whip the National Guard or the Army appeals to me as damned foolishness. Snap, I have been shot and it hurts like hell. It's funny, but you don't think of ideals over the pain.

Now use your head, son. Remember this country is getting tired of student demonstrations which lead to revolution. The National Guard can shove in a couple of clips and clean Tulane. I think they ought to when students disturb the peace and destroy property.

One thing of which you have probably not

thought: Tulane is a nonprofit corporation belonging to the public, which means one brick is yours. The National Guard is a public organization, which means that one bolt on one rifle may have been paid for with your tax.

It seems awfully foolish for you to pay for the bolt that snaps the cartridge home which kills you. It seems even more foolish to tear down the bricks you own.

When I went to Oklahoma City University, I always thought of it as my university. Ann and I probably own one bit of cement between the bricks. Believe me, sir, I was very careful of that bit of cement.

I, too, had ebullient spirits but I used them for more practical purposes.

Have you ever considered how many co-eds there are to be kissed? This is a much more worthy purpose than absorbing a bullet and not nearly so painful.

Think of these things.

Love,

DAD

## 326  To Defend and Enforce the Rights of Inhabitants (1970)

Appeals for resistance to the war in Southeast Asia and the related Selective Service draft measures rested in part on arguments that the war was illegal. From time to time the card burners, public demonstrators, and casualties of the war produced a desired reaction from the more traditional legislators. In 1970, the Massachusetts legislature attempted to protect state inhabitants from military service outside the United States in any war not authorized by Congress. Unlike earlier nullification or states' rights initiatives which challenged the power of the federal government *en gross*, this enactment sought to check allegedly unconstitutional federal activities through review. Not unexpectedly, the Supreme Court declined the invitation to examine the issue of the war's legality in *Massachusetts v. Laird*, 400 U.S. 886 (1970), with three justices dissenting.

☆ 326  An Act Defining the Rights of Inhabitants of the Commonwealth Inducted or Serving in the Military Forces of the United States [Massachusetts]

1970 Mass. Acts, 77-78.

*Be it enacted, etc., as follows:*
    SECTION 1. No inhabitant of the commonwealth inducted or serving in the military forces of the United States shall be required to serve outside the territorial limits of the United States in the conduct

of armed hostilities not an emergency and not otherwise authorized in the powers granted to the President of the United States in Article 2, Section 2, of the Constitution of the United States designating the President as the Commander-in-Chief, unless such hostilities were initially authorized or subsequently ratified by a congressional declaration of war according to the constitutionally established procedures in Article 1, Section 8, of the Constitution of the United States.

    SECTION 2. The attorney general shall, in the name and on behalf of the commonwealth and on behalf of any inhabitants thereof who are required to serve in the armed forces of the United States in violation of section one of this act, bring an appropriate action ... in an appropriate ... federal court.... [T]he attorney general shall take all steps necessary and within his power to obtain favorable action [on the case], including a decision by the Supreme Court of the United States.

## 327  "the state may constitutionally enjoin picketing" (1971)

Since the middle of the 1930s, federal legislation has governed the right of American labor to organize, strike, and resort to other measures — such as picketing — for the purpose of publicizing and advancing its claims. Despite the prominent role played by the national authorities with regard to both labor unrest and labor rights, a considerable responsibility in these areas continued to remain vested in state governments. The National Labor Relations Act explicitly exempted agricultural workers from its jurisdiction. Therefore, when Cesar Chavez and the United Farm Workers Organizing Committee set out to organize farm labor in California, they found themselves subject to the provisions of state rather than federal law. The growers of produce sought and obtained a sweeping injunction against Chavez and the workers and further sought to enforce it through contempt citations. On appeal, the Supreme Court of California balanced the First Amendment rights of labor against the state's asserted power to prohibit picketing.

☆ 327  *United Farm Workers Organizing Committee v. Superior Court*

4 Cal. 3d 556, 483 P.2d 1215 (1971).

BURKE, Justice.
    Petitioners are the United Farm Workers Organizing Committee ("UFWOC"), and its two principal officers, Cesar Chavez ("Chavez"), and Dolores Huerta ("Huerta"). By this proceeding they seek a writ of prohibition restraining respondent court

from enforcing, by contempt proceedings or otherwise, the provisions of a preliminary injunction issued by respondent on October 8, 1970. We have concluded that enforcement of a substantial portion of the preliminary injunction would violate petitioners' constitutional rights of free speech and that a peremptory writ should issue accordingly.

... Bud Antle, Inc. ("Antle"), is engaged in the growing, harvesting, and shipping of various agricultural products. Since 1961, Antle has been a signatory to various collective bargaining agreements entered into with the General Teamsters, Warehousemen and Helpers Union, Local 890 ("Teamsters"), covering a number of categories of Antle's employees. On July 16, 1970, Antle and Teamsters executed a collective bargaining agreement which, for the first time, covered Antle's agricultural field workers. On or about August 19, 1970, petitioner Huerta approached officials of Antle and requested that UFWOC be recognized as the bargaining agent for Antle's agricultural workers. When this request was rejected by Antle, petitioners called a strike and established picket lines at various of Antle's agricultural operations.

On August 24, Antle filed an action against petitioners alleging, inter alia, that the strike and picketing activities violated the provisions of the California Jurisdictional Strike Act....

\*        \*        \*

[O]n September 25, Antle filed a supplemental complaint, alleging, inter alia, that petitioners "wrongfully and unlawfully instituted a boycott against plaintiff's agricultural products ordering pickets to be placed at and around various grocery stores and other businesses selling plaintiff's products, throughout the State of California and the United States urging the patrons of such stores not to buy products bearing plaintiff's trade name." An order to show cause was issued on that date and, on October 8, 1970, respondent court issued a second preliminary injunction, in part prohibitory and in part mandatory, which provides in substance that (1) Petitioners are enjoined from publicizing that Antle is engaged in a labor dispute; (2) Petitioners are enjoined from publicizing that Antle's employees are not represented by a labor organization; (3) Petitioners are enjoined from in any way boycotting Antle's products; (4) Petitioners are required to do anything reasonably required to ensure the cessation of boycott activities by members of UFWOC; (5) Petitioner Chavez is required to notify in writing all responsible personnel that all boycott activities against Antle must cease, and to file a copy of such writing with respondent court.

\*        \*        \*

On November 9, petitioners filed a notice of appeal from the preliminary injunction entered on Oc-

tober 8. Respondent, on November 17, issued an order specifying that petitioners' appeal would not stay the enforcement of the injunction unless petitioners filed an undertaking in the sum of two million dollars. On the same day, respondent issued an order to show cause directed to petitioners Chavez and UFWOC, requiring them to appear on December 4 and show cause why they should not be held in contempt of court for failing to comply with the provisions of the October 8 injunction. On December 4 the hearing was held and UFWOC was fined $1,000 for violation of the prohibitory provisions of the injunction. Chavez was sentenced to and served five days in jail for violation of the prohibitory provisions of the injunction, and was further ordered to remain in jail until such time as he agreed to comply with the mandatory provisions of the injunction. In light of the serious constitutional issues raised by petitioners, we issued an alternative writ of prohibition, staying enforcement of all provisions of the injunction except that which prohibits petitioners from representing that Antle's employees are not represented by a labor organization, and ordering Chavez released on his own recognizance.

\*        \*        \*

Turning then to the contention that the provisions of the injunction are violative of petitioners' First Amendment rights, we review briefly the history of the California Jurisdictional Strike Act under the terms of which the challenged injunction was issued. The heart of the legislation, which was enacted in 1947, is Labor Code, section 1118, which defines a jurisdictional strike as "a concerted refusal to perform work for an employer or any other concerted interference with an employer's operation or business, arising out of a controversy between two or more labor organizations as to which of them has or should have the exclusive right to bargain collectively with an employer on behalf of his employees or any of them, or arising out of a controversy between two or more labor organizations as to which of them has or should have the exclusive right to have its members perform work for an employer."

In 1953, the Jurisdictional Strike Act was held constitutional against a contention that the prohibition of peaceful picketing violated the constitutional right of free speech. Specifically, [it was] held that the state may constitutionally enjoin picketing for purposes declared to be illegal or contrary to public policy. However, ... little light [was shed] on the extent to which the Act was intended to be, or may be enforced against conduct other than picketing.

\*        \*        \*

The United States Supreme Court [in the 1940s] established the applicability of the First Amendment to picketing and other forms of activity in connection with a labor dispute. In the language of the

Court, "publicizing the facts of a labor dispute in a peaceful way through appropriate means ... must now be regarded as within that liberty of communication which is secured to every person by the Fourteenth Amendment against abridgment by a state."

Eventually ... the Court engaged in a more refined effort to define "the power of the State to set the limits of permissible contest open to industrial combatants." That those limits include the power to enjoin peaceful picketing for purposes violative of state laws or public policy was made clear [when] this court suspended an injunction banning picketing to secure compliance with a demand for racial quota hiring. In affirming that decision, the Court discussed the special characteristics of picketing as " 'more than free speech, since it involves patrol of a particular locality and since the very presence of a picket line may induce action of one kind or another, quite irrespective of the nature of the ideas which are being disseminated.' ... The loyalties and responses evoked and exacted by picket lines are unlike those flowing from appeals by printed word."

Thus, it is apparent that the more limited protection given picketing as a concomitant of free speech is predicated on the dual nature of the activity and the fact that, of itself, picketing (i.e., patrolling a particular locality) has a certain coercive aspect. Yet even with respect to picketing, there must be alternative means available for making known a grievance if the activity is to be enjoined.

*          *          *

Judicial efforts to circumscribe the legitimate activities of industrial combatants have thus been a response to more than abstract questions involving the right to speak freely; they have taken into account, whether overtly or tacitly, the unique problems involved when freedom of expression is so intimately entwined with economic effects and the shifting economic balance of power. So although we have seen that activities may be circumscribed, nonetheless, we believe that "an order issued in the area of First Amendment rights must be couched in the narrowest terms that will accomplish the pinpointed objective permitted by constitutional mandate and the essential needs of the public order. In this sensitive field, the State may not employ 'means that broadly stifle fundamental personal liberties when the end can be more narrowly achieved.' "

*          *          *

Instructive on the constitutionally permissible breadth of an injunction which touches on First Amendment rights is the recent case of *In re Berry* (1968). There, certain persons were arrested for picketing in support of the demands of a social workers union. This court assumed that the state could lawfully prohibit strikes by public employees, but held that the injunction which petitioners had been charged with violating was both unconstitutionally vague and overbroad. As we there pointed out, "Other language in the order compounds the effect of the indicated intrusion into the area of protected expression. Section (4) forbids 'inducing others to participate' in demonstrations. Section (3) forbids 'inducing or calling a strike, work stoppage or *other concerted activity*' against the County. It is clear that this language is broad enough to include the distribution of literature, the circulation of petitions, the publication of articles, and much other Union activity in connection with its grievances against the County...."

Turning to the specific injunction issued by respondent court, we believe that, like the injunction issued in *In re Berry*, it brushes with too broad a stroke to be sustained. As noted above, the injunction prohibits petitioners from "in any way promulgating or advertising" that a dispute exists; it precludes petitioners from "urging, encouraging, or recommending, or asking any other persons to urge, encourage or recommend, that any customer of plaintiff's boycott plaintiff's agricultural products"; it effectively enjoins petitioners from making any appeal whatever to the consuming public to purchase the products of Antle's competitors.

*          *          *

... In light of these considerations, we hold that peaceful and truthful attempts to persuade the general public not to purchase a specific product or products, unaccompanied by picketing or coercive tactics, is not the "other concerted activity" contemplated by the Jurisdictional Strike Act.

*          *          *

# 328 "public employees as being in a different category" (1971)

On September 9, 1919, the Boston police force went on strike for higher wages and shorter hours. Almost 80 percent of the force stayed out on strike. Governor Calvin Coolidge called in the militia to maintain order. The strike was broken and the strikers fired. Coolidge, unmoved by pleas for reinstatement, proclaimed, "There is no right to strike against the public safety by anybody, anywhere at anytime." In 1937, the National Labor Relations (Wagner) Act recognized private employees' right to strike. The public employee labor movement, just as their privately employed brethren before them, believed the ultimate threat of a strike was the only tool of labor to which management responded. Labor forces argued increasingly that the right to strike was protected constitutionally.

In 1971 the United Federation of Postal Clerks, the exclusive bargaining representative of approximately 305,000 employees of the Post Office Department, brought an action against the postmaster general seeking declaratory and injunctive relief to invalidate portions of the United States statutes prohibiting strikes by federal employees. The majority and concurring opinions of a three-judge United States district court articulated both the "settled law" against federal employees' right to strike and a more carefully-drawn approach sympathetic to employees' interests. In August 1981 the limelight focused once more on the rights of public employees when President Ronald Reagan fired striking air traffic controllers. Despite the breaking of the strike and calls for "amnesty," the strikers were not rehired. Some of the strike leaders were arrested and jailed.

☆ 328 *United Federation of Postal Clerks v. Blount*

325 F. Supp. 879 (D.D.C. 1971).

PER CURIAM:

\*     \*     \*

### I. PUBLIC EMPLOYEES HAVE NO CONSTITUTIONAL RIGHT TO STRIKE

At common law no employee, whether public or private, had a constitutional right to strike in concert with his fellow workers. Indeed, such collective action on the part of employees was often held to be a conspiracy. When the right of private employees to strike finally received full protection, it was by statute, Section 7 of the National Labor Relations Act, which "took this conspiracy weapon away from the employer in employment relations which affect interstate commerce" and guaranteed to employees in the private sector the right to engage in concerted activities for the purpose of collective bargaining. It seems clear that public employees stand on no stronger footing in this regard than private employees and that in the absence of a statute, they too do not possess the right to strike. The Supreme Court has spoken approvingly of such a restriction and at least one federal district court has invoked the provisions of a predecessor statute to enjoin a strike by government employees. Likewise, scores of state cases have held that state employees do not have a right to engage in concerted work stoppages, in the absence of legislative authorization. It is fair to conclude that, irrespective of the reasons given, there is a unanimity of opinion in the part of courts and legislatures that government employees do not have the right to strike.

Congress has consistently treated public employees as being in a different category than private employees. The National Labor Relations Act of 1937 and the Labor Management Relations Act of 1947

(Taft-Hartley) both defined "employer" as not including any governmental or political subdivisions....

Given the fact that there is no constitutional right to strike, it is not irrational or arbitrary for the Government to condition employment on a promise not to withhold labor collectively, and to prohibit strikes by those in public employment, whether because of the prerogatives of the sovereign, some sense of higher obligation associated with public service, to assure the continuing functioning of the Government without interruption, to protect public health and safety or for other reasons. Although plaintiff argues that the provisions in question are unconstitutionally broad in covering all Government employees regardless of the type or importance of the work they do, we hold that it makes no difference whether the jobs performed by certain public employees are regarded as "essential" or "nonessential," or whether similar jobs are performed by workers in private industry who do have the right to strike protected by statute. Nor is it relevant that some positions in private industry are arguably more affected with a public interest than are some positions in the Government service....

Furthermore, it should be pointed out that the fact that public employees may not strike does not interfere with their rights which are fundamental and constitutionally protected. The right to organize collectively and to select representatives for the purposes of engaging in collective bargaining is such a fundamental right. But, as the Supreme Court noted, "The right to strike, because of its more serious impact upon the public interest, is more vulnerable to regulation than the right to organize and select representatives for lawful purposes of collective bargaining which this Court has characterized as a 'fundamental right' and which, as the Court has pointed out, was recognized as such in its decisions long before it was given protection by the National Labor Relations Act."

Executive Order 11491 recognizes the right of federal employees to join labor organizations for the purpose of dealing with grievances, but that Order clearly and expressly defines strikes, work stoppages and slow-downs as unfair labor practices. As discussed above, that Order is the culmination of a long-standing policy. There certainly is no compelling reason to imply the existence of the right to strike from the right to associate and bargain collectively. In the private sphere, the strike is used to equalize bargaining power, but this has universally been held not to be appropriate when its object and purpose can only be to influence the essentially political decisions of Government in the allocation of its resources. Congress has an obligation to ensure that the machinery of the Federal Government continues to function at all times without interference. Prohibition of strikes by its employees is a reasonable implementation of that obligation.

*     *     *

J. SKELLY WRIGHT, Circuit Judge (concurring):

*     *     *

It is by no means clear to me that the right to strike is not fundamental. The right to strike seems intimately related to the right to form labor organizations, a right which the majority recognizes as fundamental and which, more importantly, is generally thought to be constitutionally protected under the First Amendment—even for public employees. If the inherent purpose of a labor organization is to bring the workers' interests to bear on management, the right to strike is, historically and practically, an important means of effectuating that purpose. A union that never strikes, or which can make no credible threat to strike, may wither away in ineffectiveness. That fact is not irrelevant to the constitutional calculations. Indeed, in several decisions, the Supreme Court has held that the First Amendment right of association is at least concerned with essential organizational activities which give the particular association life and promote its fundamental purposes. I do not suggest that the right to strike is co-equal with the right to form labor organizations.... But I do believe that the right to strike is, at least, within constitutional concern and should not be discriminatorily abridged without substantial or "compelling" justification.

Hence the real question here, as I see it, is to determine whether there is such justification for denying federal employees a right which is granted to other employees of private business. Plaintiff's arguments that not all federal services are "essential" and that some privately provided services are no less "essential" casts doubt on the validity of the flat ban on federal employees' strikes. In our mixed economic system of governmental and private enterprise, the line separating governmental from private functions may depend more on the accidents of history than on substantial differences in kind.

Nevertheless, I feel that I must concur in the result reached by the majority in Part I of its opinion....

## 329 "compounding [the Government's] original violation of her privacy" (1971)

Some prosecutions of political dissidents were easy. Offenders often admitted the facts, resting their defenses on moral or First Amendment grounds. This was not the case at the trials of members of the underground movement. Fugitive, secretive, and conspiratorial, these defendants posed serious investigatory problems. To deal with these prob-

lems, the government turned to techniques that were useful in gathering evidence against organized crime: grand jury investigations and electronic surveillance.

Grand juries have been effective in dealing with balking witnesses, since the Fifth Amendment privilege against self-incrimination does not grant an absolute right to remain silent. Only incriminating testimony may be withheld, and the government, therefore, has been able to compel the cooperation of unwilling witnesses by granting them unasked-for immunity from prosecution. Thus, a grand jury may compel an immunized witness, upon pain of imprisonment for contempt, to answer questions. If the witness cooperates, the government obtains evidence that can be used for the prosecution of "bigger fish" or for further investigation. If, out of loyalty to others, the witness refuses to testify, the grand jury can direct a jail sentence without indictment or trial.

Electronic eavesdropping, similarly, has been an effective means for gathering information regarding subversive activities. The requirement that eavesdropping be authorized by a judge under fairly stringent safeguards (pursuant to Title III of the Omnibus Crime Control and Safe Streets Act of 1968) before the secured information can be used as evidence has limited this procedure's utility. Nevertheless, in the case of Sister Joques Egan the government argued it could use information from an illegal wiretap to formulate questions to be propounded to her at a grand jury investigation into an alleged plot to kidnap Secretary of State Henry Kissinger. The court of appeals concluded that Sister Egan, even though the grand jury had granted her immunity, had the right to vindicate her privacy rights. The Supreme Court adopted this conclusion in *Gelbard v. United States*, 408 U.S. 41 (1972).

## ☆ 329 *In re Egan*

450 F.2d 199 (3d Cir. 1971).

OPINION OF THE COURT [EN BANC]

ADAMS, Circuit Judge.

The primary issue raised by this appeal is whether a citizen who is summoned before a grand jury may object to questions based on information obtained through allegedly illegal and indeed unconstitutional wiretapping directed against the witness....

We begin with the reminder that the basic purpose of the Fourth Amendment, recognized by countless decisions of the Supreme Court, is to safeguard the privacy and security of citizens against arbitrary invasions by governmental officials. It thus gives concrete expression to a right of the people basic to a free society.

Sister Joques Egan, a member of the Order of Sacred Heart, was called before a federal grand jury in the early afternoon of January 14th in connection with an investigation into an alleged plot to kidnap a high public official and other offenses. An indictment naming six defendants had been handed down several days before, and it had named Sister Egan as an alleged co-conspirator, but not as a co-defendant. Immediately following her refusal to testify on Fifth Amendment grounds, her counsel was served by the Government with an application for immunity....

\* \* \*

... The Court ... signed the order granting immunity and requiring Sister Egan to appear before the grand jury forthwith....

Before the grand jury once again, Sister Egan refused to testify on several grounds, one of which is her primary contention on appeal—that the information which caused the Government to subpoena her and which prompted the questions propounded to her flowed from illegal wiretapping and electronic surveillance.

On January 26, 1971—minutes after her refusal to testify—appellant was brought back before the Court and, after being instructed to answer the questions and refusing to answer them, was held in contempt. Appellant stated to the Court she was not being disrespectful, but that in addition to the legal grounds already set forth her conscience compelled her not to answer. The Court ordered that she be held in prison until she testified or until the end of the life of the grand jury.

\* \* \*

The Government did not suggest during reargument before the Court en banc, or at any time in this proceeding, that it did not employ wiretaps nor that any electronic surveillance that may have been utilized was authorized by court order. Since Sister Egan has not yet been afforded a hearing regarding her allegations of illegal electronic surveillance by the Government, for the purpose of this appeal we assume her allegations to be true.

\* \* \*

Title III of the Omnibus Crime Control and Safe Streets Act of 1968 is applicable to the first issue raised by Sister Egan. Section 2515 of the Act provides:

> Whenever any wire or oral communication has been intercepted, no part of the contents of such communication and no evidence derived therefrom may be received in evidence in any trial, hearing, or other proceeding in or before any court, *grand jury*, department, officer, agency, regulatory body, legislative committee, or other authority of the United States, a State, or a political subdivision thereof, if the disclosure of that

information would be in violation of this chapter. (emphasis supplied)

Section 2515 is an unequivocal bar to questioning one before a grand jury if the questions are derived from electronic surveillance conducted in the absence of a properly issued warrant and aimed at the witness, if the witness himself objects to the interrogation....

\* \* \*

In the present case the District Court had a duty to follow the express direction of Congress found in § 2515. By ordering Sister Egan to testify before the grand jury when Congress has legislated the exclusion of such evidence, the District Court simply acted inconsistently with the legislative mandate.

\* \* \*

The fact that Sister Egan has been granted ... immunity does not deprive her of standing to raise § 2515 as a defense to a proposed judgment of civil contempt, because she is not complaining of Fifth Amendment violations, but rather of Fourth Amendment ones. Surely, even though Sister Egan has been offered immunity from prosecution, she continues to have a substantial interest in preventing the Government from compounding its original violation of her privacy by forcing her to answer questions that would concededly not be asked absent the information discovered through the use of unwarranted wiretaps.

## 330 "seizing the bodies of those [who] stand in the way of restoring peace" (1971)

After the acquittal of Reies Lopez Tijerina for the *Alianza*'s "attempted citizen's arrest," thirteen people whom the National Guard and State Police had rounded up and detained sued state officials for damages for violation of their civil rights. Only one plaintiff recovered against four of the nineteen defendants. The twelve disappointed litigants appealed, claiming the trial judge's instructions were erroneous. Although agreeing that the State Police could not arrest anyone without probable cause, the court approved a different standard for the National Guard in times of "insurrection."

☆ 330 *Valdez v. Black*

446 F.2d 1071 (10th Cir. 1971).

McWilliams, Circuit Judge.

\* \* \*

As concerns the standard of conduct for the National Guard, the trial court instructed the jury as follows:

"When acting within the power vested in him, the Governor or the Acting Governor may order into active service the militia of the state.... The Governor is made the sole judge of the facts that may seem to demand the aid and assistance of the military forces of the state. To his good judgment and sound discretion, the law has left the final decision as to whether the military arm of the state shall be ordered into active service.

"When the Governor orders into active service the National Guard,... the commander of the Guard may use the measure of seizing the bodies of those whom he considers to stand in the way of restoring peace. Such arrests are not necessarily for punishment, but are by way of precaution to prevent the exercise of hostile power.

"If you find from the evidence that the Governor had called out the National Guard and declared a state of extreme emergency in Rio Arriba County, and that the detention of plaintiffs was accomplished by the National Guard pursuant to such proclamation, and that such detention was made in good faith and in the honest belief that it was necessary under the circumstances to preserve peace, then you should find for the defendant John Jolly and against the plaintiffs."

Plaintiffs argue that the foregoing instruction was erroneous, particularly that portion which declares that the National Guard is not liable to the plaintiffs if any "detention was made in good faith and in the honest belief that it was necessary under the circumstances to preserve peace." It is asserted that the standard of conduct is the same for both the National Guard and the State Police, namely, that in order for any arrest or detention to be lawful, such must be based on "probable cause," as opposed to mere "good faith." We do not agree.

\*　　\*　　\*

... [I]t is argued [that] there was really no insurrection and hence the instruction concerning the standard of conduct of the National Guard in time of insurrection was improper. This line of reasoning permeates much of the entire argument of the plaintiffs and ignores the fact that the undisputed evidence establishes that there was a very real insurrection and civil disobedience in the armed raid on the courthouse in Tierra Amarilla. We find no error in the instruction thus given concerning the National Guard.

# 331  Arrest and Detention as a Material Witness (1971)

The grand jury, as the investigator of subversive activities, had at its disposal several tools not available to other law enforcement agencies. One way a sub-

poenaed individual could avoid the dilemmas of the grand jury process was to become a fugitive. When the government believed a potential witness might disappear, it could arrest and hold the individual for the grand jury proceeding.

After finishing high school, Leslie Bacon, daughter of a well-to-do California businessman, drifted to New York, joined the "Free Ranger Tribe" commune, and worked briefly for the Underground News Syndicate, where she became acquainted with Rennie Davis and Jerry Rubin. Later she moved to Washington, D.C., and joined the "Mayday Tribe."

On March 1, 1971, a bomb exploded in a restroom in the Capitol building. Bacon was arrested as a material witness in the crime, held in lieu of one hundred thousand dollars' bail by Judge John Sirica, and flown to Seattle, where a grand jury was investigating the crime. She was never charged with any offense. The government argued that it did not need to demonstrate probable cause that Bacon would not appear in response to a subpoena before the warrant for her arrest could be issued and that she could be held under bond. The Ninth Circuit Court of Appeals disagreed. Nevertheless, the power of the executive branch to utilize these investigatory tools for essentially punitive purposes in political cases remains largely unchecked.

☆ 331  *In re Bacon*

449 F.2d 933 (9th Cir. 1971).

DUNIWAY, Circuit Judge:

This case is a companion to *In re Bacon*, in which we affirmed a civil contempt order entered against Leslie Bacon for refusal to answer questions before a grand jury. In this appeal Bacon challenges the method by which she was brought before the grand jury, namely, her arrest and detention under a material witness arrest warrant.

\*　　\*　　\*

Such an arrest as we have here, when based on a showing of less than probable cause, has no history of judicial or public acceptance. Furthermore, a requirement of probable cause in this case does not conflict with any legitimate public interest. The public interest will be protected if grand jury witnesses come forth to provide testimony concerning the possible commission of crimes. The requirement that probable cause be shown in no way adversely affects that interest. The material witness will generally be unaware of the *ex parte* application for a warrant, and will therefore not flee to avoid arrest. We do not decide whether, if ever, a material witness may be arrested and detained with probable cause but without a warrant.

... Before a material witness arrest warrant may issue, the judicial officer must have probable cause to believe (1) "that the testimony of a person is material" and (2) "that it may become impracticable to secure his presence by subpoena." These requirements are reasonable, and if they are met, an arrest warrant may issue.

In the case of a grand jury proceeding, we think that a mere statement by a responsible official, such as the United States Attorney, is sufficient to satisfy criterion (1). This is because of the special function of the grand jury; it has exceedingly broad powers of investigation, and its proceedings are secret. . . .

On the other hand, we think that, as to criterion (2), sufficient facts must be shown to give the judicial officer probable cause to believe that it may be impracticable to secure the presence of the witness by subpoena. Mere assertion will not do.

The complaint, on the basis of which Judge Boldt issued the warrant for Bacon's arrest, failed to meet this standard. It contained none of the underlying facts or circumstances from which the judicial officer could find probable cause. As a basis for Bacon's arrest the warrant was invalid.

\*     \*     \*

Following a hearing on April 28, 1971, Judge Sirica of the United States District Court for the District of Columbia denied Bacon's motions to quash the material witness arrest warrant and reduce the amount of bail. Bacon was remanded to the custody of the Marshal and transported to Seattle. . . . The Government contends that if probable cause was shown at the hearing before Judge Sirica, Bacon's continued detention as a material witness . . . is proper even though the original arrest may have been unlawful. We agree.

A court may retain jurisdiction over a person unlawfully arrested, not only when that person makes a subsequent voluntary appearance, but also when the person is brought before it by forcible abduction. . . .

Judge Sirica received evidence on the issue of probable cause, and denied Bacon's motion to quash the arrest warrant. If that evidence was sufficient, her continued detention under the warrant is valid.

The evidence adduced before Judge Sirica consisted largely of testimony given by Daniel Mahan, a special agent of the FBI, who was one of the officers who arrested Bacon in Washington, D.C. Much of Mahan's testimony was based on information provided by a confidential source, S-1, an employee of an unidentified law enforcement agency, who reported through his supervisor to Mahan. . . .

The question then becomes whether those facts [as stated by S-1] are "sufficient in themselves to warrant a man of reasonable caution in the belief" that the . . . requirement of impracticability was met. We hold that they are not.

S-1 reported to his supervisor that Bacon would not comply with a subpoena. This conclusion will not support a finding by the judicial officer. The fact that Bacon had access to large sums of money is at best remotely relevant to her possible recalcitrance. There was no showing of past attempts by Bacon to evade judicial process, nor of past clandestine travels by Bacon.

Thus, any finding of impracticability must necessarily rest on two allegations: (1) that Bacon had personal contact with fugitives from justice, and (2) that Bacon was captured on an adjoining rooftop. The first allegation, plus her access to money, at most tends to show that *if* Bacon wished to flee, she might be able to do so successfully. It does not support the conclusion that Bacon would be *likely* to flee or go underground. Bacon's capture on an adjoining rooftop is a fact of more substance. From the fact that Bacon was arrested on an adjoining rooftop the inference can be drawn that Bacon wished to avoid apprehension. This might lead to the further inference that she would be equally disinclined to obey a subpoena to testify before the Seattle grand jury. However, balanced against other evidence in the record, this incident does not provide sufficient support for the second inference.

Bacon's attorney at the hearing before Judge Sirica stated:

[S]he [Bacon] had no idea why they were after her and what was happening other than the FBI broke down the front door of the house where she was staying and she was frightened by that. I instructed her to stay where she was, to not make any effort to contact the authorities, that I would contact Mr. Sullivan and voluntarily produce her. Ten minutes later, the FBI again came back to that house and she got scared and they arrested her on the roof of the house at that time. So she was acting personally to my instructions; I had told her to remain aloof at that point until I could voluntarily turn her in.

Such a situation differs greatly from that in which Bacon would have found herself had she been served with a subpoena. She would then have had an opportunity to reflect on her obligation to obey the process, free from the fear of imminent arrest by pursuing officers. This opportunity is granted to most witnesses, and the showing in the present case does not justify denying Bacon the same opportunity. Thus, the showing failed to support probable cause to believe that Bacon could not practicably be brought before the grand jury by a subpoena.

\*     \*     \*

The order is *reversed*, with directions to quash the warrant of arrest, including the order fixing bail.

## 332 "he embraced the principles of pacifism and nonviolence" (1971)

The *Kroncke* case was one in a long series of prosecutions against Vietnam protestors who resorted to illegal means to demonstrate their objections to the war. Judge Heaney, who upheld the conviction, nevertheless reflected great sensitivity toward the arguments of the accused: that he was compelled to act by his religious convictions, that the Vietnam War and the Selective Service practices were unconstitutional, and that he should be excused under the doctrine of necessity.

☆ 332  *United States v. Kroncke*

459 F.2d 697 (8th Cir. 1971).

HEANEY, Circuit Judge.

The defendants, Francis X. Kroncke and Michael D. Therriault, were convicted by a jury of wilfully and knowingly attempting to hinder and interfere with the administration of the Military Selective Service Act of 1967 by force, violence, and otherwise.

\*          \*          \*

Kroncke asserted at trial that he was compelled by his religious convictions to perform the act in order to bring the evils of the Vietnam War to the attention of the public and Congress. He stated that this act was necessary becausethe Vietnamese War is immoral and illegal, and because the political leadership in the United States lacksthe moral sensitivity and courage to bring an end to the war. On these bases, and also on the basis that the governmental institutions and political leadership are not responsive to the will of the majority of the people, Kroncke argued that his belief in the necessity of acting as he did was reasonable. He described his act as measured, dramatic, symbolic and religious.

Therriault asserted that he embraced the principles of pacifism and nonviolence, and that, because of this, it was necessary for him to cease cooperating with the Selective Service System and to violate its laws. He stated his belief that the United States' participation in the war in Vietnam is illegal and that, by its participation, the United States is breaking international laws, particularly the 1954 Geneva accords. He testified that he believes that if there is not a legal recourse which can bring the war to an end, then people have to resort to nonviolent extra legal efforts based on morality and reason. He stated that his actions were intended to raise a moral challenge which alone possessed the possibility and potentiality of ending the war.

\*          \*          \*

The defendants contend on appeal that the trial court erred in refusing to submit the defense of justification to the jury and in failing to advise counsel that he would do so before closing arguments. We reject both contentions.

\*          \*          \*

The common thread running through most of these cases in which the defense of necessity was asserted is that there was a reasonable belief on the part of the defendant that it was necessary for him to act to protect his life or health, or the life or health of others, from a direct and immediate peril. None of the cases even suggests that the defense of necessity would be permitted where the actor's purpose is to effect a change in governmental policies which, according to the actor, may in turn result in a future saving of lives.

## 333  Voice of Resistance (1971)

In June 1970, Angela Davis was denied continuing employment on the faculty of the philosophy department at the University of California at Los Angeles. Davis, a black activist and a professed Communist, was active in the movement to aid black prisoners.

In August 1970, guns registered in Davis's name were used in an attempt by Jonathan Jackson to help three prisoners escape from the Marin County Courthouse. Guards shot at the van containing Jackson, several hostages, and the escaping prisoners; all but one were wounded or killed. Among the dead was the presiding judge, who upon being taken hostage had had a shotgun taped to his neck. Upon hearing about the events, Davis fled. The FBI arrested her in New York on October 13, 1970, on a charge of interstate flight to avoid arrest. During her confinement in the Marin County jail while awaiting trial she wrote this article on the refusal of government to recognize the political nature of many offenders. Davis was tried for murder, kidnapping, and conspiracy to commit murder and rescue prisoners; she was found not guilty. In 1980 and again in 1984 she ran as the vice-presidential candidate on the Communist party ticket in the national elections.

☆ 333  Political Prisoners, Prisons, and Black Liberation

Angela Y. Davis, *If They Come in the Morning* (New York: Joseph Okpaku Publishing, 1971), 19–36.

Despite a long history of exalted appeals to man's inherent right of resistance, there has seldom been agreement on how to relate *in practice* to unjust, immoral laws and the oppressive social order from which they emanate. The conservative, who does not dispute the validity of revolutions deeply buried in history, invokes visions of impending anarchy in order to legitimize his demand for absolute obedience. Law and order, with the major emphasis on order, is his watchword. The liberal articulates his sensitiveness to certain of society's intolerable details, but will almost never prescribe methods of resistance which exceed the limits of legality—redress through electoral channels is the liberal's panacea.

In the heat of our pursuit for fundamental human rights, Black people have been continually cautioned to be patient. We are advised that as long as we remain faithful to the *existing* democratic order, the glorious moment will eventually arrive when we will come into our own as full-fledged human beings.

But having been taught by bitter experience, we know that there is a glaring incongruity between democracy and the capitalist economy which is the source of our ills. Regardless of all rhetoric to the contrary, the people are not the ultimate matrix of the laws and the system which govern them—certainly not Black people and other nationally oppressed people, but not even the mass of whites. The people do not exercise decisive control over the determining factors of their lives.

Official assertions that meaningful dissent is always welcome, provided it falls within the boundaries of legality, are frequently a smokescreen obscuring the invitation to acquiesce in oppression. Slavery may have been unrighteous, the constitutional provision for the enslavement of Blacks may have been unjust, but conditions were not to be considered so unbearable (especially since they were profitable to a small circle) as to justify escape and other acts proscribed by law. This was the import of the fugitive slave laws.

Needless to say, the history of the United States has been marred from its inception by an enormous quantity of unjust laws, far too many expressly bolstering the oppression of Black people. Particularized reflections of existing social inequities, these laws have repeatedly borne witness to the exploitative and racist core of the society itself. For Blacks, Chicanos, for all nationally oppressed people, the problem of opposing unjust laws and the social conditions which nourish their growth has always had immediate practical implications. Our very survival has frequently been a direct function of our skill in forging effective channels of resistance. In resisting, we have sometimes been compelled to openly violate those laws directly or indirectly buttress our oppression. But even when containing our resistance within the orbit of legality, we have been labelled criminals and have been methodically persecuted by a racist legal apparatus.

*     *     *

By the second decade of the twentieth century, the mass movement headed by Marcus Garvey proclaimed in its Declaration of Rights that Black people should not hesitate to disobey all discriminatory laws. Moreover, the Declaration announced, they should utilize all means available to them, legal or illegal, to defend themselves from legalized terror as well as Ku Klux Klan violence. During the era of intense activity around civil rights issues, systematic disobedience of oppressive laws was a primary tactic. The sit-ins were organized transgressions of racist legislation.

All these historical instances involving the overt violation of the laws of the land converge around an unmistakable common denominator. At stake has been the collective welfare and survival of a people. There is a distinct and qualitative difference between one breaking a law for one's own individual self-interest and violating it in the interests of a class or a people whose oppression is expressed either directly or indirectly through that particular law. The former might be called a criminal (though in many instances he is a victim), but the latter, as a reformist or revolutionary, is interested in universal social change. Captured, he or she is a political prisoner.

The political prisoner's words or deeds have in one form or another embodied political protests against the established order and have consequently brought him into acute conflict with the state. In light of the political content of his act, the "crime" (which may or may not have been committed) assumes a minor importance. In this country, however, where the special category of political prisoners is not officially acknowledged, the political prisoner inevitably stands trial for a specific criminal offense, not for a political act. . . .

A deep-seated ambivalence has always characterized the official response to the political prisoner. Charged and tried for a criminal act, his guilt is always political in nature. This ambivalence is perhaps best captured by Judge Webster Thayer's comment upon sentencing Bartolomeo Vanzetti to 15 years for an attempted payroll robbery: "This man, although he may not have actually committed the crime attributed to him, is nevertheless morally culpable, because he is the enemy of our existing institutions." . . .

Even in all Martin Luther King's numerous arrests, he was not so much charged with the nominal crimes of trespassing, disturbance of the peace, etc., but rather with being an enemy of Southern society, an inveterate foe of racism. . . .

The offense of the political prisoner is his political boldness, his persistent challenging—legally or extra-legally—of fundamental social wrongs fostered and reinforced by the state. He has opposed unjust laws and exploitative, racist social conditions in general, with the ultimate aim of transforming these laws and this society into an order harmonious with the material and spiritual needs and interests of the vast majority of its members.

Nat Turner and John Brown were political prisoners in their time. The acts for which they were charged and subsequently hanged were the practical extensions of their profound commitment to the abolition of slavery. They fearlessly bore the responsibility for their actions. The significance of their executions and the accompanying widespread repression did not lie so much in the fact that they were being punished for specific crimes, nor even in the effort to use their punishment as an implicit threat to deter others from similar *armed* acts of resistance. These executions and the surrounding repression of slaves were intended to terrorize the anti-slavery movement in general; to discourage and diminish both legal and illegal forms of abolitionist activity. As usual, the effect of repression was miscalculated and in both instances, anti-slavery activity was accelerated and intensified as a result.

Nat Turner and John Brown can be viewed as examples of the political prisoner who has actually committed an act which is defined by the state as "criminal." They killed and were consequently tried for murder. But did they commit murder? This raises the question of whether American revolutionaries had *murdered* the British in their struggle for liberation. Nat Turner and his followers killed some 65 white people, yet shortly before the Revolt had begun, Nat is reputed to have said to the other rebelling slaves: "Remember that ours is not war for robbery nor to satisfy our passions, it is a *struggle for freedom*. Ours must be deeds not words."

\*          \*          \*

Likewise, the significance of activities which are pursued in the interests of liberation today is minimized not so much because officials are unable to *see* the collective surge against oppression, but because they have consciously set out to subvert such movements. In the Spring of 1970, Los Angeles Panthers took up arms to defend themselves from an assault initiated by the local police force on their office and on their persons. . . . In defending themselves from the attack waged by some 600 policemen (there were only 11 Panthers in the office) they were not only defending their lives, but even more important their accomplishments in the Black community surrounding them and in the broader thrust for Black Liberation. Whenever Blacks in struggle have recourse to self-defense, particularly armed self-defense, it is twisted and distorted on official levels and ultimately rendered synonymous with criminal aggression. On the other hand, when policemen are clearly indulging in acts of criminal aggression, officially they are defending themselves through "justifiable assault" or "justifiable homicide."

The ideological acrobatics characteristic of official attempts to explain away the existence of the political prisoner do not end with the equation of the individual political act with the individual criminal act. The political act is defined as criminal in order to discredit radical and revolutionary movements. A political event is reduced to a criminal event in order to affirm the absolute invulnerability of the existing order. In a revealing contradiction, the court resisted the description of the New York Panther 21 trial as "political," yet the prosecutor entered as evidence of criminal intent literature which represented, so he purported, the political ideology of the Black Panther Party.

\*          \*          \*

May 1971
Marin County Jail

As the Black Liberation Movement and other progressive struggles increase in magnitude and intensity, the judicial system and its extension, the penal system, consequently become key weapons in the state's fight to preserve the existing conditions of class domination, therefore racism, poverty and war.

\*          \*          \*

Especially today when so many Black, Chicano and Puerto Rican men and women are jobless as a consequence of the internal dynamic of the capitalist system, the role of the unemployed which includes the lumpenproletariat in revolutionary struggle must be given serious thought. Increased unemployment, particularly for the nationally oppressed, will continue to be an inevitable by-product of technological development. At least 30 per cent of Black youth are presently without jobs. In the context of class exploitation and national oppression it should be clear that numerous individuals are compelled to resort to criminal acts, not as a result of conscious choice—implying other alternatives—but because society has objectively reduced their possibilities of subsistence and survival to this level. This recognition should signal the urgent need to organize the unemployed and lumpenproletariat, as indeed the Black Panther Party as well as activists in prison have already begun to do.

\*          \*          \*

Moreover, in assessing the revolutionary potential of prisoners in America as a group, it should be borne in mind that not all prisoners have actually committed crimes. The built-in racism of the judicial system expresses itself, as Du Bois has suggested, in the railroading of countless innocent Blacks and other national minorities into the country's coercive institutions.

\*          \*          \*

For the innocent prisoner, the process of radicalization should come easy; for the "guilty" victim, the insight into the nature of racism as it manifests itself in the judicial-penal complex can lead to a questioning of his own past criminal activity and a re-evaluation of the methods he has used to survive in a racist and exploitative society. Needless to say, this process is not automatic, it does not occur spontaneously. The persistent educational work carried out by the prison's political activists plays a key role in developing the political potential of captive men and women.

*   *   *

Historically, Black people as a group have exhibited a greater potential for resistance than any other part of the population. The ironclad rule over our communities, the institutional practice of genocide, the ideology of racism have performed a strictly political as well as an economic function. The capitalists have not only extracted super profits from the underpaid labor of over 15 per cent of the American population with the aid of a superstructure of terror. This terror and more subtle forms of racism have further served to thwart the flowering of a resistance, even a revolution which would spread to the working class as a whole.

*   *   *

The Black Liberation Movement is presently at a critical juncture. Fascist methods of repression threaten to physically decapitate and obliterate the movement. More subtle, yet not less dangerous ideological tendencies from within threaten to isolate the Black movement and diminish its revolutionary impact. Both menaces must be counteracted in order to ensure our survival. Revolutionary Blacks must spearhead and provide leadership for a broad anti-fascist movement.

## 334 "jurors often reach 'conscience' verdicts" (1972)

John William Simpson, on December 20, 1970, took a container of gasoline to the offices of the Selective Service Board in San Jose, California. After dousing file drawers with gasoline, he ignited a match and set the files ablaze. He remained in the building, however, awaiting his arrest. Simpson complained the trial court should have given the jury instructions regarding his claimed common law defense of "justification" as well as the jury's power to acquit a defendant regardless of the evidence of his guilt. After discussing the dangers of "opening the way for more conscience verdicts," the court of appeals affirmed the conviction.

☆ **334** *United States v. Simpson*

460 F.2d 5 (9th Cir. 1972).

ELY, Circuit Judge:

On December 24, 1970, Simpson took a container of gasoline to the offices of the Local Board of the Selective Service System in San Jose, California. He intended — despite his knowledge that such acts were illegal — to burn some of the Board's records in an effort to move the United States toward terminating the conflict in Southeast Asia.

After surreptitiously gaining access to the Board's file room, he opened one of the file drawers, doused the contents with his gasoline, ignited a match, and set the files ablaze. When the heat from the fire became unbearable, Simpson retreated from the room. He remained in the building, however, and thus was, within moments, arrested.

For his vandalism, Simpson was subsequently indicted on three charges. He was charged with having destroyed government property valued in excess of $100, with having mutilated and destroyed records deposited in a government office, and with having interfered with the administration of the Selective Service System. A jury convicted him of all three charges, and this appeal followed.

Simpson bases his appeal on asserted errors in the trial court's instructions to the jury and in its refusal to admit certain evidence offered by Simpson. Specifically, Simpson contends that the court (1) should have allowed evidence and given jury instructions regarding Simpson's claimed common law defense of "justification," (2) gave erroneous instructions on the meaning of "wilfully" as used in the pertinent statutes, and (3) was wrong in refusing to give instructions, proffered by Simpson, informing the jury of its power to acquit a defendant regardless of the evidence of his guilt. We conclude that none of the arguments has merit.

*   *   *

While Simpson's first contention is somewhat novel, we think it is easily resolved. The theoretical basis of the justification defenses is the proposition that, in many instances, society benefits when one acts to prevent another from intentionally or negligently causing injury to people or property. That benefit is lost, however, and the theory fails when the person seeking to avert the anticipated harm does not act reasonably. Thus, it is commonly held, for example, that a person may not use excessive force in repelling an attacker or any force when the necessity therefor disappears.

Here, it is apparent that Simpson's reckless, dangerous acts were not reasonable. An essential element of the so-called justification defenses is that a direct causal relationship be reasonably anticipated to exist between the defender's action and the avoidance of harm. It was unreasonable for Simpson to assume that any violent action he initiated might have any significant effect upon the supposed ills that he hoped to remedy.

*   *   *

Simpson's final contention is that the trial judge erred in refusing to instruct the jury, as Simpson requested, that it had the power to acquit him regardless of the evidence of his guilt. The basis of this argument is the suggestion, now gaining some currency, that juries should be given more freedom to grant acquittals against the law. It is argued that this freedom—which is asserted necessary to a jury's proper functioning in our constitutional democracy—is attained by advising jurors of their "power to bring in a verdict in the teeth of both law and facts."

The basic question here is whether justice would be better served by instructing jurors as Simpson requested and thus opening the way for more "conscience verdicts." We think not. We agree with the decision in *Moylan*.... We have noted recent perceptive comments made by two distinguished former jurists, Abe Fortas and Simon Rifkind, during a panel discussion concerning the proper role of a jury. Mr. Justice Fortas emphasized that a contention, such as Simpson's,

> is an attack upon law itself. In effect, it is an assertion of the right of the individual to determine for himself what the standards of his conduct shall be. What is being proposed is not merely that jurors should be given the power to determine what is the law, but that they should be instructed that they may acquit a defendant even though they believe that he did something the law forbids. This goes to the heart of our society because it says that this shall not be a society in which there are general rules of law which apply to everybody and to which everybody is accountable.

In a similar vein, Judge Rifkind has remarked:

> [I am asked] why, if I am in favor of some kind of departures by the jury, I am afraid to make that universal. The answer is that one can have a fine musical composition made up of a theme with variations, but if you had a composition made up entirely of variations you would have discord. [This] proposal would create a law-less society, not a lawless society, but a law-less society, a society without law, without regulations. That is a monstrosity. No such society has ever existed or ever will exist.

The jury occupies, and should continue to occupy, an independent role in our judicial system. It is recognized that jurors often reach "conscience" verdicts without being instructed that they have the power to do so. Equally important, American judges have generally avoided such interference as would divest juries of their power to acquit an accused, even though the evidence of his guilt may be clear. Thus, the existing safeguards are adequate, and we refuse to make Simpson's suggested departure from our established law.

*Affirmed.*

## 335 "Despite the fact that news gathering may be hampered" (1972)

Unlike most other violators of the law, those motivated by sentiments of protest and reform frequently sought publicity for their beliefs and actions. Radical movements, hoping through this exposure to gain sympathizers and recruits, cultivated access to the mass media even at the risk of creating breaches in their security. To reduce hazards, unwritten understandings developed between the underground and the media, hinged on the promise of media protection for its "confidential sources."

On February 2, 1970, a federal grand jury in California subpoenaed Earl Caldwell, a black reporter for the *New York Times*, assigned to cover the Black Panther Party and other militant groups. He was ordered to bring with him notes and tape recordings of interviews concerning the aims and activities of the Black Panthers. Caldwell refused to appear, arguing the First Amendment granted reporters a privilege to protect their sources from discovery. He claimed his very appearance at the secret proceedings would disrupt the relationship of confidence which he had developed, and a vital source would be shut off, inhibiting the flow of information to the public.

The lower courts refused to grant Caldwell such a sweeping privilege but did hold that the government must make a showing of necessity—that is, that the information sought from Caldwell could not be secured in some other way. Caldwell's case was consolidated for decision with *Branzburg v. Hayes* concerning an article on drug use in the community and *In re Pappas* regarding Black Panther activities witnessed by a reporter. The Supreme Court concluded that the First Amendment provided reporters with no protection against the investigatory power of the government.

☆ 335 *Branzburg v. Hayes*
(*United States v. Caldwell*)

408 U.S. 665 (1972).

Opinion of the Court by MR. JUSTICE WHITE....

\*            \*            \*

The sole issue before us is the obligation of reporters to respond to grand jury subpoenas as other citizens do and to answer questions relevant to an investigation into the commission of crime. Citizens generally are not constitutionally immune from grand jury subpoenas; and neither the First Amendment nor any other constitutional provision protects the average citizen from disclosing to a grand jury information that he has received in confidence. The claim is, however, that reporters are exempt from these obligations because if forced to respond to subpoenas and identify their sources or disclose other confidences, their informants will refuse or be reluctant to furnish newsworthy information in the future. This asserted burden on news gathering is said to make compelled testimony from newsmen constitutionally suspect and to require a privileged position for them.

It is clear that the First Amendment does not invalidate every incidental burdening of the press that may result from the enforcement of civil or criminal statutes of general applicability. . . .

*          *          *

. . . In *Zemel v. Rusk*, for example, the Court sustained the Government's refusal to validate passports to Cuba even though that restriction "render[ed] less than wholly free the flow of information concerning that country." The ban on travel was held constitutional, for "[t]he right to speak and publish does not carry with it the unrestrained right to gather information."

Despite the fact that news gathering may be hampered, the press is regularly excluded from grand jury proceedings, our own conferences, the meetings of other official bodies gathered in executive session, and the meetings of private organizations. Newsmen have no constitutional right of access to the scenes of crime or disaster when the general public is excluded, and they may be prohibited from attending or publishing information about trials if such restrictions are necessary to assure a defendant a fair trial before an impartial tribunal. . . .

*          *          *

. . . Until now the only testimonial privilege for unofficial [*sic*, nonofficial is probably meant] witnesses that is rooted in the Federal Constitution is the Fifth Amendment privilege against compelled self-incrimination. We are asked to create another by interpreting the First Amendment to grant newsmen a testimonial privilege that other citizens do not enjoy. This we decline to do. Fair and effective law enforcement aimed at providing security for the person and property of the individual is a fundamental function of government, and the grand jury plays an important, constitutionally mandated role in this process. On the records now before us, we perceive no basis for holding that the public interest in law enforcement and in ensuring effective grand jury proceedings is insufficient to override the consequential, but uncertain, burden on news gathering that is said to result from insisting that reporters, like other citizens, respond to relevant questions put to them in the course of a valid grand jury investigation or criminal trial.

This conclusion . . . does [not] threaten the vast bulk of confidential relationships between reporters and their sources. . . . Only where news sources themselves are implicated in crime or possess information relevant to the grand jury's task need they or the reporter be concerned about grand jury subpoenas. . . .

The preference for anonymity of those confidential informants involved in actual criminal conduct is presumably a product of their desire to escape criminal prosecution, and this preference, while understandable, is hardly deserving of constitutional protection. It would be frivolous to assert — and no one does in these cases — that the First Amendment, in the interest of securing news or otherwise, confers a license on either the reporter or his news sources to violate valid criminal laws. . . .

Thus, we cannot seriously entertain the notion that the First Amendment protects a newsman's agreement to conceal the criminal conduct of his source, or evidence thereof, on the theory that it is better to write about crime than to do something about it. Insofar as any reporter in these cases undertook not to reveal or testify about the crime he witnessed, his claim of privilege under the First Amendment presents no substantial question. The crimes of news sources are no less reprehensible and threatening to the public interest when witnessed by a reporter than when they are not.

There remain those situations where a source is not engaged in criminal conduct but has information suggesting illegal conduct by others. Newsmen frequently receive information from such sources pursuant to a tacit or express agreement to withhold the source's name and suppress any information that the source wishes not published. Such informants presumably desire anonymity in order to avoid being entangled as a witness in a criminal trial or grand jury investigation. They may fear that disclosure will threaten their job security or personal safety or that it will simply result in dishonor or embarrassment.

The argument that the flow of news will be diminished by compelling reporters to aid the grand jury in a criminal investigation is not irrational, nor are the records before us silent on the matter. But we remain unclear how often and to what extent informers are actually deterred from furnishing information when newsmen are forced to testify before a grand jury. . . .

Accepting the fact, however, that an undetermined number of informants not themselves implicated in crime will nevertheless, for whatever reason, refuse to talk to newsmen if they fear identification by a reporter in an official investigation, we cannot accept the argument that the public interest in possible future news about crime from undisclosed, unverified sources must take precedence over the public interest in pursuing and prosecuting those crimes reported to the press by informants and in thus deterring the commission of such crimes in the future.

\*     \*     \*

It is said that currently press subpoenas have multiplied, that mutual distrust and tension between press and officialdom have increased, that reporting styles have changed, and that there is now more need for confidential sources, particularly where the press seeks news about minority cultural and political groups or dissident organizations suspicious of the law and public officials. These developments, even if true, are treacherous grounds for a far-reaching interpretation of the First Amendment. . . .

\*     \*     \*

The privilege claimed [in *Caldwell*] is conditional, not absolute; given the suggested preliminary showings and compelling need, the reporter would be required to testify. Presumably, such a rule would reduce the instances in which reporters could be required to appear, but predicting in advance when and in what circumstances they could be compelled to do so would be difficult. Such a rule would also have implications for the issuance of compulsory process to reporters at civil and criminal trials and at legislative hearings. If newsmen's confidential sources are as sensitive as they are claimed to be, the prospect of being unmasked whenever a judge determines the situation justifies it is hardly a satisfactory solution to the problem. For them, it would appear that only an absolute privilege would suffice.

We are unwilling to embark the judiciary on a long and difficult journey to such an uncertain destination. . . .

\*     \*     \*

*So ordered.*

MR. JUSTICE STEWART, with whom MR. JUSTICE BRENNAN and MR. JUSTICE MARSHALL join, dissenting.

The Court's crabbed view of the First Amendment reflects a disturbing insensitivity to the critical role of an independent press in our society. . . . [T]he Court in these cases holds that a newsman has no First Amendment right to protect his sources when called before a grand jury. The Court thus invites state and federal authorities to undermine the historic independence of the press by attempting to annex the journalistic profession as an investigative arm of government. Not only will this decision impair performance of the press' constitutionally protected functions, but it will, I am convinced, in the long run harm rather than help the administration of justice.

\*     \*     \*

[MR. JUSTICE DOUGLAS also dissented in *United States v. Caldwell.*]

## 336  "I Am A Hamlet" (1972)

On May 15, 1972, a twenty-one-year-old drifter, Arthur Bremer, shot Alabama Governor George C. Wallace, who was taking part in the presidential primary campaign, in Laurel, Maryland. His spine severed and legs paralyzed by the bullet, Wallace decided to withdraw from the presidential race. Bremer later was convicted and received a sixty-three-year sentence. As this entry in Bremer's diary shows, political figures often are only targets of opportunity for those who seek historical notoriety.

### ☆336  From Arthur Bremer's Diary

Arthur Bremer, *An Assassin's Diary* (New York: Harper's Magazine Press, 1972), 105.

It may sound exciting & fasinating to readers 100 years from now — as the Booth conspricy seems to us today; but to this man it seems only another failure. And I stopped tolerating failure weeks ago.

As I said befor, I Am A Hamlet.

It seems I would of done better for myself to kill the old G-man Hoover. In death, he lays with Presidents. Who the hell ever got buried in 'Bama for being great? He certainly won't be buryed with the snobs in Washington.

SHIT! I won't even rate a T.V. enteroption in Russia or Europe when the news breaks — they never heard of Wallace. If something big in Nam flares up I'll end up at the bottom of the 1st page in America. The editors will say — "Wallace dead? Who cares." He won't get more than 3 minutes on network T.V. news. I don't expect anybody to get a big thobbing erection from the news. You know, a storm in some country we never heard of kills 10,000 people — big deal —

## 337  "police aggression and excessive force" (1972)

The trial of the "Chicago Seven," who were charged with violating the federal Anti-riot Act of 1968 for planning and leading the violence in the streets during the Chicago Democratic Convention of August 1968, was the most publicized case involving Vietnam War protest. The scene of Hubert Humphrey's nomination at the convention amphitheatre, with Senator Edmund Muskie as his running mate, shared national television coverage with the street battles between police and antiwar protesters. The trial itself received daily nationwide attention as Judge Julius Hoffman and the intransigent defendants engaged in verbal battles. Bobby Seale, leader of the Black Panthers, was bound and gagged for disrupting the proceedings, and Judge Hoffman eventually declared his case a mistrial. David Dellinger, Rennie Davis, and Tom Hayden were leaders of the Mobilization Committee to End the War (Mobe), while Abbie Hoffman and Jerry Rubin had achieved national notoriety as founders of the Yippies (Youth International Party). The remaining defendants, John Froines and Lee Weiner, were lesser-known political activists.

The trial of the Chicago Seven (reduced from eight due to Bobby Seale's mistrial) was as tumultuous as the Chicago riots. Upon review by the United States Court of Appeals, all members of the court voted to reverse the convictions because of the improprieties of the trial judge and prosecuting attorneys. In addition, the court had difficulty upholding the constitutionality of the "Rap" Brown (Anti-riot) Act.

☆ 337  *United States v. Dellinger*

472 F.2d 340 (7th Cir. 1972).

\*          \*          \*

... We shall attempt to state, broadly, the government's theory with respect to intent.

Each defendant, it was contended, shared the common aim of producing violence during convention week in Chicago under circumstances where it would seem that the violence had been precipitated by the establishment and appear that the government was forced to destroy its own people in the streets in order to survive. Although that was the real purpose defendants allegedly had in mind, it was a purpose they could not afford to announce.

It was argued that defendants could succeed only if they could induce a large number of people to come to Chicago and be on hand to participate. Rubin and Hoffman used the plan of a Festival of Life and Davis, Dellinger, and Hayden used the idea of holding a "counter convention" to lure multitudes to Chicago to be organized and worked upon to produce a violent confrontation. Permits for use of parks must be sought in order to obtain performers as attractions for the crowd. Yet if permits were refused, ultimate success in producing violence would be more probable, and the total freedom from restraint announced for the festival rendered denial inevitable.

\*          \*          \*

As things turned out, the confrontation and battle took place at Michigan and Balbo. The government relies on subsequent statements made by several defendants about this event, and claims of victory, as proof of a long-abiding intent to cause violence.

\*          \*          \*

... [T]he defense contended that defendants' apparent intent, to demonstrate, to march, to organize peaceful activity, and to hold a contrasting festival of life, was their real intent; that it is ludicrous to believe that this was all a facade for the plan attributed to them by the government.

\*          \*          \*

They argued the genuineness of their attempts to obtain permits and of their expressions of willingness to work out plans with city officials. They suggested that had permits been granted all would have proceeded peacefully even though with permits a much greater number of people would have come to Chicago.

It is the defense theory that the decisions to have the police actions of major consequence were unnecessary, and that the violence which did occur was the product of police aggression and excessive force.

The defense suggested that the city administration made unwise, and, indeed, unconstitutional, decisions to prevent mass demonstrations near the Amphitheatre in order to avoid embarrassment to the city as host and to the party, of which the mayor was a prominent leader, and chose to follow a hard line which, in the end, made inevitable the battle at Michigan and Balbo.

With reference to the city's last minute offer to permit a march to some point other than the Amphitheatre, the defense argued that was like telling the protesting patriots before the Boston Massacre, "Go anywhere you want, but don't go to the Custom House."

The broad issue of fact was whether the defendants intended only to engage in protected First Amendment activity, or, at most, non-violent civil disobedience, or to cause violence. And secondarily, because of the basis for the federal criminal statute under which they were prosecuted, even if the defendants did by the time of convention week form an intent to cause violence, had this been their intent when they traveled to Chicago?

I. IS THE ANTI-RIOT ACT UNCONSTITUTIONAL?

\*          \*          \*

...[W]e conclude that when, as we set out below, the statute is fairly read as a whole and all basic relations between elements are noted, the statute is not unconstitutional.

\*          \*          \*

As to the Anti-riot Act, the government at times argues that travel with intent and not expression is the "gravamen of the offense" and that, therefore, the doctrines of the first amendment are not relevant to our determination of constitutionality. We are unable to accept this argument. There would be most serious doubt whether an individual's travel with intent to do something inimical to the interests of the community, but without any step other than the individual travel being taken to effect the intent, could be made an offense. Even if it could, Congress has not done so here. We view the statutory element of interstate travel (or use of facilities), accompanied by the specified intent, as an element which Congress required as the foundation for its power to punish the conduct of inciting or participating in a riot. We consider the First Amendment test to be applied to this federal statute the same as that which would have to be applied to a state statute, identical except not requiring interstate travel as an element of the offense.

A realistic approach compels application of a First Amendment test to a statute which punishes activity leading up to and furthering a riot, for at least two reasons. One is that rioting, in history and by nature, almost invariably occurs as an expression of political, social, or economic reactions, if not ideas. The rioting assemblage is usually protesting the policies of a government, an employer, or some other institution, or the social fabric in general, as was probably the case in the riots of 1967 and 1968 which are the backdrop for this legislation. A second reason is that a riot may well erupt out of an originally peaceful demonstration which many participants intended to maintain as such. Each participant is entitled to a careful distinction between responsibility for the lawful and constitutionally protected demonstration and responsibility for the activity for which the legislative body validly prescribes a penalty.

In many of its provisions (incite, organize, promote, encourage) the anti-riot statute relates to persons causing the possibility that others will riot, and makes those persons liable because of their causal rather than active role. It is by expression, in whatever form, that causation adequate to bring on punishment must be most likely to occur. As examples only, but certainly very relevant examples, the counts against the five defendants here charged with inciting, organizing, promoting and encouraging a riot under this statute, were based wholly on the making of speeches.

*          *          *

Our question, in examining the validity of the Anti-riot Act on its face is whether, properly construed, it punishes speech only when a sufficiently close relationship between such speech and violent action is found to exist. Semantically the cases suggest that while a statutory prohibition of advocacy of violence is overbroad, since protected speech is included within advocacy, a prohibition of intentional incitement of violence is not overbroad. The latter depends upon a construction of "incitement" which is sufficiently likely to propel the violent action to be identified with action.

We consider the statute as a whole in determining whether §§ 2101 and 2102 require the relation between expression and action necessary to avoid First Amendment protection.

The base concept of the statute is "riot." Although there is much to be said in favor of a definition of "riot" requiring a larger assemblage threatening greater public danger we are unable to conclude that Congress has not described a disorder of a type which is enough of an assault on the property and personal safety interests of the community so that participation in a riot or *intentionally and successfully causing* a riot can be made a criminal offense.

There is, however, no requirement in [the Act] that the riot as defined occur. Rather there are listed four categories.

(A) to incite a riot; or

(B) to organize, promote, encourage, participate in, or carry on a riot; or

(C) to commit any act of violence in furtherance of a riot; or

(D) to aid or abet any person in inciting or participating in or carrying on a riot or committing any act of violence in furtherance of a riot.

One of these categories must be specifically intended at the time of travel, and one of them must be the purpose for which the required overt act is done or attempted.

*          *          *

If we could be persuaded that the overt act ... could be a speech which only was a step toward one of the elements of (A)-(D), taking those merely as goals, we would be unable to conclude that the statute required an adequate relation between such speech and action.... Reading "overt act for any purpose specified" as equivalent to fulfillment of any purpose specified in (A)-(D) leaves the statute with an adequate relation between expression and action as described in the preceding step.

The conclusion that the statute adequately establishes the required relation to action which can be made illegal disposes as well of defendants' argument that the statute infringes on the fundamental constitutional right to travel. The existence of that relationship narrows the imposition on travel to instances adequately involving a purpose which the government may counter.

We do not pretend to minimize the First Amendment problems presented on the face of this statute.... [W]e acknowledge the case is close.

There is an additional attack, based on a particular phrase. The contention is that by reason of this phrase in definition, [the Act] expressly forbids a segment of protected expression, mere advocacy of violence without propelling such action. The whole problem, which we shall term the "double negative," is created by the last phrase (which we have here italicized):

> As used in this chapter, the term "to incite a riot," or "to organize, promote, encourage, participate in, or carry on a riot," includes, but is not limited to, urging or instigating other persons to riot, but shall not be deemed to mean the mere oral or written (1) advocacy of ideas or (2) expression of belief, *not involving advocacy of any act or acts of violence or assertion of the rightness of, or the right to commit, any such act or acts.*

A true negation of a negation is an affirmation, and a careful exclusion from an exclusion is at least likely to result in an inclusion. If the statute provides punishment for *mere* oral or written advocacy of an act of violence or assertion of the rightness of an act of violence, established principles already referred to would require that it be declared void. . . .

*        *        *

Another approach is to assume that the drafters of this phrase realized that a truly inciting, action-propelling speech will include advocacy of acts of violence and assertion of the rightness of such acts, and intended that the challenged phrase forestall any claim by such speaker that in that context such advocacy and assertion constitute mere advocacy of ideas or expression of belief excluded under (1) and (2). There is in this construction, some awkwardness and an assumption that unnecessary language was employed, but under all the circumstances, including the relationship of this phrase to the other parts of the statute, we deem it the most reasonable construction.

*        *        *

We consider any possibility that prosecution would be undertaken in reliance on defendants' proffered construction of the challenged phrase as minimal. Bearing in mind the purpose served by the overbreadth doctrine, to avoid the chilling of free speech, we consider it unreal, as well, to suppose that the existence of this obtuse and obscure provision will deter expression. . . .

Accordingly we conclude that the presence of the challenged phrase does not amount to overbreadth.

*        *        *

VIII. DEMEANOR OF THE JUDGE AND PROSECUTORS

. . . [W]e are unable to approve the trial in this case as fulfilling the standards of our system of justice.

It is not a simple matter to evaluate this trial, nor to assign responsibility for its deficiencies. It lasted almost five months, and the transcript exceeds 22,000 pages. Trial decorum often fell victim to dramatic and emotionally inflammatory episodes.

Mr. Seale was a codefendant on trial from September 24 to November 5, 1969. During this period he insisted on representing himself, and some of his conduct resulted in the contempt citations which are the subject of *United States v. Seale.* Conflict erupted with some frequency. During several sessions, October 29 to November 3, he was bound and gagged.

The courtroom was usually filled with spectators and press personnel. There were numerous disorders and outbursts among spectators, and occasional complaints that there was discrimination in seating arrangements. On occasion, trial procedure seems to have disintegrated into uproar. The record indicates that at times there were as many as 19 marshals in the courtroom. It also shows provocative, sometimes insulting, language and activity by several defendants, instances, but not all, of which are included in contempt specifications in *In re Dellinger.* Conduct of defense trial counsel, considered contemptuous by the district judge, is also reflected in portions of the record set forth in those specifications.

We are not directly concerned here with definitively assessing the responsibility of these defendants or their counsel for deficiencies in the trial. That will be the subject of proceedings on remand in *In re Dellinger.*

. . . [I]n considering complaints concerning the conduct of the trial judge and prosecuting attorneys we have avoided holding them responsible for conduct made reasonably necessary by the conditions at the trial arising from the activity of others.

*        *        *

On the other hand, there are high standards for the conduct of judges and prosecutors, and impropriety by persons before the court does not give license to depart from those standards.

*        *        *

The district judge's deprecatory and often antagonistic attitude toward the defense is evident in the record from the very beginning. It appears in remarks and actions both in the presence and absence of the jury.

*        *        *

Most significant were remarks in the presence of the jury, deprecatory of defense counsel and their case. These comments were often touched with sarcasm, implying rather than saying outright that defense counsel was inept, bumptious, or untrustworthy, or that his case lacked merit. Sometimes the comment was not associated with any ruling in ordinary course; sometimes gratuitously added to an otherwise proper ruling; nearly always unnecessary. Taken individually any one was not very significant and might be disregarded as a harmless attempt at humor. But cumulatively, they must have telegraphed to the jury the judge's contempt for the defense.

\*       \*       \*

In our opinion the defense had the right to present its case before the jury free from the cumulative implications in the type of comments to which we have referred.

Remarks made by the prosecutors in considerable number, and before the jury, were not called for by their duties, and, whatever contribution the defense conduct may have made to the deficiencies of this trial, these remarks were not justified thereby and fell below the standards applicable to a representative of the United States.

\*       \*       \*

In final argument, the United States Attorney went at least up to, and probably beyond, the outermost boundary of permissible inferences from the evidence in his characterizations of defendants. He referred to them as "evil men," "liars and obscene haters," "profligate extremists," and "violent anarchists." He suggested one defendant was doing well as it got dark because "predators always operate better when it gets close to dark."

He yielded to the temptation to exploit the courtroom conduct of various defendants which formed the basis of the contempt citations in *In re Dellinger.* He told the jurors they need not ignore "how those people look and act," "outbursts in the courtroom," "the sudden respect, the sudden decency" occurring "in the last few days as we reach the end of the case," the suggested similarity between the technique the jurors had seen used in the courtroom with the marshals and that allegedly used at the time of the convention with the police.

Dress, personal appearance, and conduct at trial were not probative of guilt.

\*       \*       \*

We conclude that the demeanor of the judge and prosecutors would require reversal if other errors did not.

\*       \*       \*

PELL, Circuit Judge (dissenting in part, concurring in part).

. . . I entertain no doubts but that the statute under which the appellants were prosecuted is facially unconstitutional in that it is clearly violative of the First Amendment right of freedom of speech.

\*       \*       \*

. . . [T]he particular case before us is not one which induces any subjective desire on my part to add reasons to those already advanced by the majority opinion for reversal. Candor compels recognition that this case is not of the ordinary type coming before this court. While our appellate jurisdiction customarily confines us to the record before us—using

"record" in the narrow legal sense of that term—none of us can be oblivious of the status that the trial of this case has assumed in the minds of a very substantial number of members of the public. Putting it very simply, that status, often vigorously expressed, is that the courtroom in which the trial was conducted was a forum in which were arrayed on one side the forces of law and order and on the other side persons representative of designedly disruptive anarchy. Any basis for reversal is bound to be viewed by many as a victory for those who would destroy this country. In fairness, many others are possessed of completely contrary views of the trial and the incidents leading thereto. I express no views on these differing evaluations other than to recognize their existence and their inherent pulls which for our judicial function must be put firmly aside. . . .

. . . I . . . am of the opinion that a federal statute could be drawn, sufficiently narrow and precise, to accomplish punishment of such activity without running afoul of First Amendment rights. In my view, that was not done here.

\*       \*       \*

. . . [T]he legislation . . . passed was something less than a model of draftsmanship. . . .

\*       \*       \*

The matter of the so-called "double negative" is to me the first determinative step leading to and through the gateway of First Amendment violations. . . .

\*       \*       \*

. . . With all respect, the majority's attempted saving construction that the phrase was inserted by the drafters to forestall a First Amendment defense in the case of a truly inciting, action-propelling speech, is not only strained beyond reasonable acceptability but is unsupported historically. Further, such a construction provides no guidance for the interstate traveller who intends to speak of the rightness of violence as a last resort solution to whatever problem of civilization concerns him. He will be caught in the same net as the true inciter, and the context of his remarks as well as the reaction of his audience, possibly unwarranted and unanticipated, will provide the peril of his being subject to grand jury scrutiny and eventual punishment at the statutorily uncontrolled option of a comminatory prosecutor.

\*       \*       \*

I am able to reach no conclusion other than that the added phrase was intended to preclude, under pain of prosecution, advocacy of violence even though only an idea or expression of belief. It is repugnant to our ideas of, and our hopes for, civilization that resort to violence should ever be necessary. . . .

... [T]hough we, or at least the substantial majority of us, may find it abhorrent to think that the rightness of violence should ever be advocated, even though expressed as an idea or belief, nevertheless, the distaste must be overridden in the preservation of the essential freedom here at stake.

\*     \*     \*

Further, [unlike the majority,] I do not find any basis in the statute to cause me to read a restricted meaning into the word ["urge"]. I do not, in sum, see in the statute the guidelines by which the speaker in favor of the rightness of violence can make a safe determination. If he merely goes beyond the bare statement of the proposition by stating not only that violence is right to correct a particular abuse but that it is imperative, it seems he is within the orbit of "urging," indeed, he maybe already be impaled by his sincerity in positing his basic proposition.

Further, and of equal significance, the present statute does not by clear intendment meet the *Brandenburg* pronouncement that advocacy is unprotected only where it is directed to inciting or producing imminent lawless action and is likely to incite or produce such action. . . .

\*     \*     \*

... While "freedom of speech" is not an absolute right, the word "speech" itself is not qualified by a limitation of subject matter to innocuous mundanities. Imaginative or stirring ideas and idealistic beliefs are equally within its sweep. Speech without effective communication is not speech but an idle monologue in the wilderness. Communication involves listeners. A "law" which upon reasonable construction would, by its deterrent threat of punishment for the mere expression of ideas or beliefs, cellularly isolate the speaker from potential listeners in all of the states of the Union except his own would, in my opinion, abridge freedom of speech.

\*     \*     \*

In the case before us, I would hold that the statute was not drawn sufficiently narrowly to avoid the conflict and that the convictions must be reversed because of being grounded on an unconstitutional enactment. . . .

... [W]hile I might not have approached some of the issues in exactly the same manner, nor used identical language, upon my consideration of the results reached as to the issues covered, other than those pertaining to statutory constitutionality, I concur in the majority opinion.

As this opinion was in the process of being finally drafted, the people of the world were stunned and shocked by the terroristic violence occurring at the site of the 1972 Olympic games. Indubitably the shock will be followed by popular demand for suppression of violence as a political weapon. An ideal state of civilization should find no person in any jeopardy of loss of life or wellbeing from violence irrespective of its motivation. To attain that state, however, by suppression of the free interchange of ideas and beliefs would be a pyrrhic sacrifice of a precious freedom for an illusory safety. It is because of my underlying belief in the preservation of that freedom that I have written as I have herein. . . .

# 338 Whether War Crimes Were Being Committed in Vietnam (1974)

Protests against the Vietnam War were not confined to the civilian population. During the war's height, Captain Howard B. Levy, an army physician assigned to train Special Forces personnel, made statements condemning the Vietnam War and the Special Forces personnel, and urged enlisted men to refuse to be sent to or fight in Vietnam. In addition, he disobeyed an order to conduct a training program in dermatology for the Special Forces, contending it would have constituted his participation in war crimes. For these actions, Levy was court-martialed and convicted of violating Articles 133 and 134 of the Uniform Code of Military Justice. These articles authorize punishment of "conduct unbecoming an officer and a gentlemen" and "disorders and neglects to the prejudice of good order and discipline in the armed forces." His appeal to the federal courts for review of his court-martial conviction (sentencing him to dismissal from the service, the forfeiture of all pay, and confinement for three years at hard labor) raised complex questions of the relations between civil and military justice. Significantly, the Supreme Court affirmed the court of appeals recognition that "refusing to obey an order to commit a war crime is a recognized defense under the Uniform Code of Military Justice."

☆ 338 *Levy v. Parker*

☆ 338a The United States Court of Appeals

478 F.2d 772 (3d Cir. 1973).

ALDISERT, Circuit Judge.

This appeal requires us to decide whether Articles 133 and 134 of the Uniform Code of Military Justice fail to satisfy the standards of precision required by the due process clause, and, hence, are void for vagueness.

\*     \*     \*

Article 133 states in pertinent part: "Any commissioned officer . . . who is convicted of conduct unbecoming an officer and a gentleman shall be punished as a court-martial may direct." Article 134 provides:

Though not specifically mentioned in this chapter, all disorders and neglects to the prejudice of good order and discipline in the armed forces, all conduct of a nature to bring discredit upon the armed forces, and crimes and offenses not capital, of which persons subject to this chapter may be guilty, shall be taken cognizance of by a general, special, or summary court-martial, according to the nature and degree of the offense, and shall be punished at the discretion of that court.

The charges under Articles 133 and 134 emanated from public statements made by Levy to enlisted personnel, of which the following is illustrative:

The United States is wrong in being involved in the Viet Nam War. I would refuse to go to Viet Nam if ordered to do so. I don't see why any colored soldier would go to Viet Nam; They should refuse to go to Viet Nam and if sent should refuse to fight because they are discriminated against and denied their freedom in the United States, and they are sacrificed and discriminated against in Viet Nam by being given all the hazardous duty and they are suffering the majority of casualties. If I were a colored soldier I would refuse to go to Viet Nam and if I were a colored soldier and were sent I would refuse to fight. Special Forces personnel are liars and thieves and killers of peasants and murderers of women and children.

Captain Levy was convicted of (1) wilful disobedience of the lawful command of his superior officer, (2) uttering public statements designed to promote disloyalty and disaffection among the troops, and (3) "wrongfully and dishonorably making intemperate, defamatory, provoking, contemptuous, disrespectful and disloyal statements" to enlisted personnel, the latter two offenses constituting "conduct unbecoming an officer and a gentleman," and "disorders and neglects to the prejudice of good order and discipline in the armed forces." . . .

Articles 133 and 134 were originally enacted by the Second Continental Congress on June 30, 1775. As enacted in the colonies, these articles derived from the British Articles of War, which, in turn, trace their ancestry from the Articles of War of James II, in 1688. After nearly three hundred years, the incredible similarity between the language of the present articles and their forebears is astonishing. . . .

\*              \*              \*

We now embark upon an examination of the constitutionality of these two articles, mindful of Justice Holmes' sage admonition, "[i]f a thing has been practised for two hundred years by common consent, it will need a strong case for the Fourteenth Amendment to affect it."

\*              \*              \*

Article 133 fails to explain what conduct "unbecomes" an officer or a gentleman. *The Officer's Guide* offers little assistance in this direction for it merely advises that "[a]n officer is expected to be a gentleman and a gentleman has been defined as a man who is never intentionally rude." Winthrop, in his classic treatise, *Military Law and Precedents*, defined "unbecoming" as "morally unbefitting and unworthy," and described a gentleman as a "man of honor . . . of high sense of justice, of an elevated standard of morals and manners, and of a corresponding general deportment." . . .

\*              \*              \*

Article 134 deserves the same criticism. . . .

\*              \*              \*

Under these circumstances, how can we possibly conclude that these articles give individual officers of ordinary intelligence a reasonable opportunity to know what is prohibited? . . .

\*              \*              \*

Our conclusion that Articles 133 and 134 fail to set forth satisfactory standards of conduct leads to the inescapable corollary that enforcement of these articles is to varying degrees arbitrary and discriminatory. Because Article 133 fails to define "conduct unbecoming an officer and a gentleman," are diverse boards of military officers to determine what conduct "becomes" a gentleman? Thus, might what "becomes" an officer in Tokyo, be considered "rude" in Santa Fe, or "unbecoming" at Fort Jackson, South Carolina? Are federal courts to be the arbiters of gentlemanly behavior? Similarly, Article 134 fails to announce any standard by which to determine when conduct becomes "prejudicial to good order and discipline." Who is to determine what conduct is "prejudicial"?

\*              \*              \*

Finally, the general articles have the capacity of abutting sensitive areas of basic First Amendment freedoms. Those statutes which regulate conduct touching the borders of this amendment are required to be more specific than others. . . .

Thus, whatever merit there may be in the government's contention that over two hundred years of military operation under these articles have given meaning and certainty to their terms when applied to such ordinary anti-social conduct as indecent assault, the argument becomes unpersuasive where the proscribed conduct is speech arguably protected by the First Amendment.

Neither are we unmindful that the *Manual for Courts-Martial* offers as an example of an offense under Article 134, "praising the enemy, attacking the war aims of the United States, or denouncing our form of government." With the possible exception of the statement that "Special Forces personnel are liars and thieves and killers of peasants and murderers of women and children," it would appear that each statement for which appellant was court-martialed could fall within the example given in the *Manual*. However, even if this statement in the *Manual* can be construed as providing a sufficient warning against the conduct of the individual in the case before us, the article nevertheless can be adjudicated void for vagueness if it would be susceptible to future use against conduct not warned against in sufficient detail. . . .

*        *        *

In the instant case, just as the lack of statutorily defined standards led to the conclusion that enforcement of the articles is arbitrary and discriminatory, so too is the conclusion inescapable that such vague articles have an impermissible chilling effect on First Amendment freedoms.

We conclude that measured against existing constitutional standards applicable to civilian statutes and ordinances, Articles 133 and 134 are void for vagueness.

This does not terminate our inquiry, however, for we are now required to decide whether affirmative countervailing circumstances inhere in the armed forces which justify the existence of statutes which would not otherwise pass constitutional muster.

We acknowledge that "[m]ilitary law, like state law, is a jurisprudence which exists separate and apart from the law which governs in our federal judicial establishment." Thus, in sustaining the constitutionality of Article 134 against the charge of vagueness, the Court of Military Appeals . . . referred to the *"presence of special and highly relevant considerations growing out of the essential disciplinary demands of the military service. These are at once so patent and so compelling as to dispense with the necessity for their enumeration—much less their argumentative development."* (Emphasis supplied.) This naked, conclusory statement constitutes a brazen slap at a system whose banner is the protection of individual liberties, and, as such, it has for too long withstood inquiry compelling precise delineation of these "special and highly relevant considerations."

It has been suggested that three "special and highly relevant considerations" unique to military life might exist: (1) maintaining high standards of conduct in the armed forces; (2) ease of conviction in a court-martial; and (3) justifying punishment for servicemen who commit unforeseen crimes.

The Supreme Court has held that "[i]t is no answer to the constitutional claim [of vagueness of overbreadth] to say . . . that the purpose of these regulations was merely to insure high professional standards and not curtail free expression." . . .

Whatever efficacy there may have been to the ease-of-conviction argument in another era, and we do not assume that it ever was persuasive, the passage and implementation of the Uniform Code of Military Justice clearly demonstrates a Congressional mandate that the maximum of constitutional procedural safeguards now be afforded servicemen. A consideration based on ease-of-conviction is now totally bereft of explicit support and does not deserve the dignity of extended discussion.

The third consideration would suggest the desirability of allowing the military freedom to develop a counterpart of common law crimes; to provide statutory authority for the development of new standards of conduct and the imposition of criminal penalties for the violation thereof. Such a notion contravenes our federal tradition. There is no federal common law of crimes today and there never has been, and this principle extends to the military. Whatever has been the tradition of certain states, the enunciation of federal crimes and offenses has always been by statute. Even more fundamental, however, is the "general principle of legality" discussed heretofore, wherein we emphasized the dubious constitutionality of imposing criminal sanctions upon conduct previously not explicitly prohibited by law.

*        *        *

We conclude that there exist no countervailing military considerations which justify the twisting of established standards of due process in order to hold inviolate these articles, so clearly repugnant under current constitutional values.

We therefore conclude that Articles 133 and 134 fail to satisfy the standard of precision required by the due process clause and, hence, are void for vagueness. However, in so holding, we also hold that application of this decision shall be prospective only except as to those cases where (1) the issue was raised and preserved and (2) was pending in the military judicial system or pending in the federal court system on this date.

Having concluded that the charges against Captain Levy under Articles 133 and 134 were unconstitutional, there remains for our consideration the charges brought against appellant under Article 90. Pursuant to this article, appellant was convicted of wilful disobedience of the lawful order of Colonel Henry F. Fancy, a physician who was commanding officer of the United States Army Hospital, Fort Jackson, South Carolina. Appellant refused to obey Colonel Fancy's written and oral order to establish and operate a dermatological training program for Special Forces aidmen. During his court-martial, as well as in his various military and civilian appeals, appellant sought to justify his refusal to obey this direct order on the same two grounds urged on this appeal.

First, Levy asserted that to train Special Forces aidmen in dermatology was inconsistent with his concept of medical ethics and violative of the Hippo-cratic oath because this type of aidman was commit-ting war crimes in Vietnam. Consequently, Levy's act of training these men, he contended, would have constituted participation in a war crime.

Refusing to obey an order to commit a war crime is a recognized defense under the Uniform Code of Military Justice to an Article 90 charge. During the trial, the law officer conducted a hearing outside the presence of the members of the court-martial to ac-cept an offer of proof by appellant as to the issue of whether war crimes were being committed in Viet-nam and, more specifically, as to whether Special Forces troops as a mode of operation committed war crimes in Vietnam. Upon completion of the hearing, the law officer ruled that although there perhaps oc-curred instances of needless brutality in the Viet-nam War, nevertheless, there was "no evidence that would render this order to train aidmen illegal on the grounds that eventually these men would be-come engaged in war crimes or in some other way prostitute their medical training by employing it in crimes against humanity."

At best, appellant could establish that individual American personnel may have violated the law of war in Vietnam. However, there never was any showing that the medical training appellant was or-dered to give had any connection whatsoever with the perpetration of any war crime. Thus, appellant failed to demonstrate how the existence of war crimes committed by individuals other than those he was ordered to train was relevant to his failure to obey the order. Particularly relevant in this is that he failed to show that Special Forces aidmen as a group engaged systematically in the commission of war crimes by prostituting their medical training.

\*       \*       \*

In isolation, these factual determinations adverse to appellant under an admittedly valid article are not of constitutional significance and resultantly, are beyond our scope of review. However, there re-mains the necessity for determining whether the conviction under the valid Article 90 charge suf-fered from any constitutional infirmity by reason of its joinder at trial with the charges under Articles 133 and 134, now found to be unconstitutional.

\*       \*       \*

☆ 338b  The United States Supreme Court

417 U.S. 733 (1974).

Mr. Justice REHNQUIST delivered the opinion of the Court.

This Court has long recognized that the military is, by necessity, a specialized society separate from civilian society. We have also recognized that the military has, again by necessity, developed laws and traditions of its own during its long history. . . .

\*       \*       \*

In short, the Uniform Code of Military Justice regulates a far broader range of the conduct of mili-tary personnel than a typical state criminal code reg-ulates of the conduct of civilians; but at the same time the enforcement of that Code in the area of mi-nor offenses is often by sanctions which are more akin to administrative or civil sanctions than to civil-ian criminal ones.

The availability of these lesser sanctions is not surprising in view of the different relationships of the Government to members of the military. It is not only that of lawgiver to citizen, but also that of em-ployer to employee. Indeed, unlike the civilian situa-tion, the Government is often employer, landlord, provisioner, and lawgiver rolled into one. That rela-tionship also reflects the different purposes of the two communities. . . . While members of the military community enjoy many of the same rights and bear many of the same burdens as do members of the ci-vilian community, within the military community there is simply not the same autonomy as there is in the larger civilian community. The military estab-lishment is subject to the control of the civilian Com-mander in Chief and the civilian departmental heads under him, and its function is to carry out the poli-cies made by those civilian superiors.

\*       \*       \*

With these very significant differences between military law and civilian law and between the mili-tary community and the civilian community in mind, we turn to appellee's challenges to the constitution-ality of Arts. 133 and 134.

Appellee urges that both Art. 133 and Art. 134 (the general article) are "void for vagueness" under the Due Process Clause of the Fifth Amendment and overbroad in violation of the First Amendment. . . . Each of these articles has been construed by the United States Court of Military Appeals or by other military authorities in such a manner as to at least partially narrow its otherwise broad scope.

\*       \*       \*

The effect of these constructions of Arts. 133 and 134 by the Court of Military Appeals and by other military authorities has been twofold: It has nar-rowed the very broad reach of the literal language of the articles, and at the same time has supplied con-siderable specificity by way of examples of the con-duct which they cover. It would be idle to pretend that there are not areas within the general confines of the articles' language which have been left vague despite these narrowing constructions. But even though sizable areas of uncertainty as to the cover-age of the articles may remain after their official in-terpretation by authoritative military sources, fur-ther content may be supplied even in these areas by less formalized custom and usage. And there also cannot be the slightest doubt under the military precedents that there is a substantial range of conduct to which both articles clearly apply without vagueness or imprecision. It is within that range that appellee's conduct squarely falls, as the Court of Appeals recognized. . . .

The Court of Appeals went on to hold, however, that even though Levy's own conduct was clearly prohibited, the void-for-vagueness doctrine conferred standing upon him to challenge the imprecision of the language of the articles as they might be applied to hypothetical situations outside the considerable area within which their applicability was similarly clear.

We have noted . . . that more precision in drafting may be required because of the vagueness doctrine in the case of regulation of expression. For the reasons which differentiate military society from civilian society, we think Congress is permitted to legislate both with greater breadth and with greater flexibility when prescribing the rules by which the former shall be governed than it is when prescribing rules for the latter. But each of these differentiations relates to how strict a test of vagueness shall be applied in judging a particular criminal statute. . . .

Because of the factors differentiating military society from civilian society, we hold that the proper standard of review for a vagueness challenge to the articles of the Code is the standard which applies to criminal statutes regulating economic affairs. Clearly, that standard is met here. . . .

*          *          *

While the members of the military are not excluded from the protection granted by the First Amendment, the different character of the military community and of the military mission requires a different application of those protections. The fundamental necessity for obedience, and the consequent necessity for imposition of discipline, may render permissible within the military that which would be constitutionally impermissible outside it. Doctrines of First Amendment overbreadth asserted in support of challenges to imprecise language like that contained in Arts. 133 and 134 are not exempt from the operation of these principles. . . .

. . . [Because of the importance of the First Amendment,] attacks have been permitted "on overly broad statutes with no requirement that the person making the attack demonstrate that his own conduct could not be regulated by a statute drawn with the requisite narrow specificity."

*          *          *

There is a wide range of the conduct of military personnel to which Arts. 133 and 134 may be applied without infringement of the First Amendment. While there may lurk at the fringes of the articles, even in the light of their narrowing construction by the United States Court of Military Appeals, some possibility that conduct which would be ultimately held to be protected by the First Amendment could be included within their prohibition, we deem this insufficient to invalidate either of them at the behest of appellee. His conduct, that of a commissioned officer publicly urging enlisted personnel to refuse to obey orders which might send them into combat, was unprotected under the most expansive notions of the First Amendment. Articles 133 and 134 may constitutionally prohibit that conduct, and a sufficiently large number of similar or related types of conduct so as to preclude their invalidation for overbreadth.

Appellee . . . contends that to carry out the hospital commandant's order to train aide men in dermatology would have constituted participation in a war crime. . . . The Court of Appeals observed that [this defense] was recognized under the Uniform Code of Military Justice, but had been resolved against appellee on a factual basis by the court-martial which convicted him. . . .

*          *          *

*Reversed.*

# 339 "[our duty] is to see that the waters of justice are not polluted" (1974)

In 1964 a sit-in took place to block the construction of a motel on lands claimed by the Passamaquoddy tribe in Maine. In 1968, Puyallup Native Americans in the state of Washington held a "fish-in," protesting white incursions into reserved fishing rights. In 1969-70, Red Power activists briefly "reclaimed" abandoned Alcatraz Island in San Francisco Bay in the manner of the sixteenth- and seventeenth-century European explorers.

On January 23, 1971, a white man stabbed Wesley Bad Heart Bull to death during a barroom brawl in Buffalo Gap, South Dakota. The assailant was charged with second degree manslaughter. The family and friends of Bad Heart Bull (an Oglala Sioux) believed the appropriate charge should have been murder. The grievance led to a riot and a confrontation between state authorities and the Native Americans on February 6, 1973, at the Custer County Courthouse. On February 27, 1973, two hundred armed members of the American Indian Movement (AIM) invaded the hamlet of Wounded Knee on the nearby Pine Ridge Reservation, declared themselves to be the Independent Oglala Sioux Nation, and ousted the leadership of the tribe recognized by the federal government. The area was quickly surrounded by Native American police, federal marshals, and FBI agents. The occupation and siege lasted for seventy-one days while AIM and the government officials alternately negotiated and shot at one another. Two Native Americans were killed and one federal marshal was seriously injured. The Independent Oglala Sioux Nation surrendered after the government agreed to conduct inquiries into several grievances.

Two leaders of AIM, Dennis Banks and Russell Means, were indicted for several offenses. Additionally, Dennis Banks had been convicted on charges arising out of the Custer County Courthouse riot. When South Dakota sought his extradition from New York to serve his sentence, he was given political asylum by the Onondaga Nation, and the New York authorities refused to seek his arrest on their reservation. South Dakota's appeal to federal authorities for assistance was rebuffed, since the dispute was between the two states. The excerpts below are from two opinions in the Wounded Knee case by the trial judge on motions by the defendants for acquittal. In 1975, the court of appeals dismissed the government's appeal from the decision of the trial judge. *United States v. Means*, 513 F.2d 1329 (8th Cir. 1975).

☆ 339  *United States v. Banks*

☆ 339a  383 F. Supp. 368 (D.S.D. 1974).

NICHOL, Chief Judge.

. . . [A]t the close of the government's case, the defendants Means and Banks . . . moved for judgment of acquittal as to all . . . counts. . . . The two defendants, Means and Banks, were identically charged in the first two indictments, as follows: Count I, with burglary of the Wounded Knee Trading Post; Count II, with larceny of certain contents of the Trading Post; Count III, with assault on Joanne Pierce, a Special Agent of the Federal Bureau of Investigation; Count IV, with preparation and location of bunkers and trenches at Wounded Knee, which obstructed, impeded or interfered with law enforcement officers; Count V, with the placement of a road block, manned by persons armed with guns, on a road leading into Wounded Knee, which obstructed, impeded, or interfered with law enforcement officers; Count VI has previously been dismissed by this Court; Count VII, with possession of unregistered firearms (molotov cocktails); Count VIII, with theft of an automobile; Count IX, with a conspiracy to commit criminal acts including the previous substantive Counts. Subsequent to the return of the two indictments just summarized, two additional indictments charged Banks and Means respectively . . . with assaulting Curtis Fitzgerald, a Special Agent of the Federal Bureau of Investigation, [and] . . . alleged an assault on Lloyd Grimm, United States Marshal for the District of Nebraska.

\*        \*        \*

In the pages that follow, consideration will be directed first to certain contentions raised by the defendants in the motion for judgment of acquittal which relate to all of the Counts. Succeeding parts of this Memorandum Decision will deal with the specific Counts.

PART I

*A. The Sioux Treaty of 1868*

The defendants in their motion and brief assert that this Court lacks jurisdiction under the Sioux Treaty of 1868. This claim is applied to all of the Counts. The crux of the defendants' argument is based in the first instance on Article I of the Treaty, which provides that the Indians will, "upon proof made to the agent [Tribal Court] . . . ," deliver up to the United States, Indians accused of violating the laws of the United States.

. . . The defense then asserts that as there is no record of proof having been made to the Tribal Court as to these defendants, the United States lacks jurisdiction.

This Court is unable to accept the analysis suggested by the defense. Congress has, since 1868, enacted statutes which have either amended or abrogated the terms of the Sioux Treaty. That Congress has the power to so amend or abrogate the Treaties made with the Indians is established.

> The tribes have been regarded as dependent nations, and treaties with them have been looked upon not as contracts, but as public laws which could be abrogated at the will of the United States.

See also *United States v. Kagama*. The following language from *United States v. Blackfeet Tribe* is instructive:

> The defendants urge that the Blackfeet Tribe is sovereign and that the jurisdiction of the tribal court flows directly from that sovereignty. . . . The blunt fact, however, is that an Indian Tribe is sovereign to the extent that the United States permits it to be sovereign—neither more nor less. While for many years the United States recognized some elements of sovereignty in the Indian tribes and dealt with them by treaty, Congress by Act of March 3, 1871 prohibited the further recognition of Indian tribes as independent nations. Thereafter the Indians and the Indian tribes were regulated by acts of Congress. The power of Congress to govern by statute rather than treaty has been sustained.

\*        \*        \*

The motion for judgment of acquittal as to all Counts on the grounds of lack of jurisdiction under the Sioux Treaty of 1868 is *denied*.

\*        \*        \*

PART V

*Counts IV & V—Interfering with Law Officers ...*

Both Count IV and Count V alleged the commission of certain acts, with the requisite criminal intent, to obstruct, impede and interfere with United States Marshals and agents of the Federal Bureau of Investigation....

The motion for judgment of acquittal raised the point that the federal officers at Wounded Knee were not lawfully engaged in the lawful performance of their duties, in that they were acting in violation of 18 U.S.C. Sec. 1385. That statute provides as follows:

> Whoever, except in cases and under circumstances expressly authorized by the Constitution or Act of Congress, willfully uses any part of the Army or the Air Force as *a posse comitatus or otherwise* to execute the laws shall be fined not more than $10,000 or imprisoned not more than two years, or both. (Emphasis added).

\*        \*        \*

... Evidence was then heard, outside the presence of the jury, as to the alleged violation of 18 U.S.C. Sec. 1385. Following the presentation of evidence by the defense, the government indicated, in response to specific inquiry by the Court, that it had no witnesses to offer. It should also be noted that the government at no time expressed a desire to reopen its case in chief for the purpose of placing in evidence testimony or exhibits tending to establish that the federal officers were lawfully engaged in the lawful performance of their official duties.... [T]his Court indicated that the evidence presented in the evidentiary hearing supported a finding that the federal officers at Wounded Knee has used part of the Army or the Air Force as a posse comitatus or otherwise to execute the laws, thereby precluding the establishment of one of the elements of the offenses charged.

It would serve no useful purpose to relate in detail the evidence presented to this Court in the hearing. A summary of the salient evidence establishes that large amounts of military equipment, including ammunition, weapons, flares, armored personnel carriers, and clothing, were either loaned or sold to the Department of Justice by the Department of Defense in connection with the Wounded Knee operation. The evidence also shows that certain members of the Army were present on the Pine Ridge Reservation in the vicinity of Wounded Knee. Colonel Volney Warner, then Chief of Staff of the 82nd Airborne, Fort Bragg, arrived in the area on February 3, 1973. Colonel Warner's primary function, at least initially, was to observe the situation and to advise his superiors as to the need for Army troop intervention. It is also clear that on a day-to-day basis Colonel Warner gave advice and guidance to the federal civil officials in charge of the Wounded Knee operation. Representatives of the Marshals Service and the FBI actively sought Colonel Warner's advice, and he gave it. The first instance of such advice occurred, it appears from the evidence, within hours, if not minutes, of Colonel Warner's arrival at Ellsworth Air Force Base, near Rapid City, South Dakota, in the early morning hours of February 3, 1973. At that time Colonel Warner advocated that the then existing shoot-to-kill policy of the federal law enforcement personnel be amended to a shoot-to-wound policy. In short, Colonel Warner counseled the adoption of the Army's blueprint for handling a civil disorder, which was referred to in the testimony as the "Garden Plot" plan. He also advocated a policy of avoiding exchanges of gunfire, and avoiding any action which might provoke hostilities. When law enforcement officers requested armored personnel carriers, Colonel Warner recommended to his superiors that the request be approved only after obtaining assurances from the requesting officers that the carriers would be used solely for defensive purposes.

The evidence also shows that Colonel Jack C. Potter, Deputy Chief of Staff of Logistics of the 6th United States Army, was ordered to the Pine Ridge Reservation. His primary function was in the area of logistics and supplies. There is also evidence that National Guard mechanics were utilized to repair the armored personnel carriers, as need arose. With regard to the personnel carriers, the evidence indicates that the first two such vehicles arrived at Pine Ridge in the early morning hours of February 28, 1973, just hours after the beginning of the occupation. There are also at least two documents in evidence which indicate the same thing. It is clear, therefore, that the military involvement at Wounded Knee began almost immediately. In addition, the Nebraska National Guard was utilized to make at least one aerial reconnaissance of the Wounded Knee area, at the request of the FBI and the Marshals Service.

The government has contended that the sale and loan of equipment to the Department of Justice is authorized by 32 C.F.R. Sec. 501.7 [but this] does not, in this Court's opinion, serve to provide legal basis for the loans of equipment involved in this case. The section of the regulations just cited is promulgated under 10 U.S.C. Secs. 331, 332, 333, which deal with the issuance of a Presidential Proclamation as the basis for federal troop intervention in civil law enforcement. There was no Presidential Proclamation in this case. 32 C.F.R. Sec. 501.7 is therefore inapplicable on that basis....

A study of Colonel Warner's testimony, and the testimony of other witnesses, and the documentary evidence, balanced against the presumption of lawfulness that rightly attaches to the statutorily authorized activities of law enforcement personnel, compels this Court to conclude that there is insufficient evidence of the lawfulness of the government activity at Wounded Knee, to justify submission of Counts IV and V to the jury.

\* \* \*

☆ 339b 383 F. Supp. 389 (D.S.D. 1974).

NICHOL, Chief Judge.

... The occupation lasted seventy-one days and the trial lasted slightly over eight months. Although the trial was often protracted and tedious, it came to a swift end. After deliberating the case for about nine hours, one of the jurors became ill and could not continue deliberations. The government would not agree to accept the verdict of the remaining eleven jurors. In the meantime the defense team filed a motion for judgment of acquittal, thus giving this court the alternative of granting a mistrial or ruling on the motion. I have decided to dismiss all charges remaining in this trial.

Defendants' motion for judgment of acquittal is based generally on allegations of government misconduct. The alleged misconduct consists of the following: (1) conspiracy to suborn perjury and to cover up said subornation in the case of Louis Moves Camp, a prosecution witness; (2) suppression of an FBI statement exposing the perjury of Alexander David Richards, a prosecution witness; (3) illegal and unconstitutional use of military personnel and material at Wounded Knee and the government's effort to cover up said use; (4) violation of applicable professional, ethical and moral standards; and (5) various other incidents of governmental misconduct. For the reasons given below, this court treats defendants' motion as a motion for dismissal and grants judgment of dismissal.

\* \* \*

CONCLUSION

This court is mindful of the heavy responsibility that it bears in our criminal justice system. It is unquestionably essential to our society that our laws be enforced swiftly and surely. This court also believes, however, that our society is not bettered by law enforcement that, although it may be swift and sure, is not conducted in a spirit of fairness or good faith. Those who break our laws must be brought to account for their wrongs, but it is imperative that they be brought to this accounting through an orderly procedure conducted in the spirit of justice. This court's first duty, then, is to insure that our laws are fairly enforced, or as Mr. Chief Justice Warren aptly put it: "[our duty] is to see that the waters of justice are not polluted."

Although it hurts me deeply, I am forced to the conclusion that the prosecution in this trial had something other than attaining justice foremost in its mind. In deciding this motion I have taken into consideration the prosecution's conduct throughout the entire trial. The fact that incidents of misconduct formed a pattern throughout the course of the trial leads me to the belief that this case was not prosecuted in good faith or in the spirit of justice. The waters of justice have been polluted, and dismissal, I believe, is the appropriate cure for the pollution in this case.

## 340 "the United States flag sewn to the seat of his trousers" (1974)

During the Vietnam War turmoil, counterculture adherents adopted a style of dress and nongrooming to emphasize the schism between themselves and the "establishment." Young people cast off the clothing style of their elders and sent the barbering profession into a depression. Dress and grooming codes sprang up in the nation's public schools as school officials attempted to combat the signs of cultural insurrection. One case, not countercultural in motivation, was heard in 1969, when the Supreme Court overturned the suspension of Mary Beth Tinker for wearing a black armband to school in protest over American involvement in Vietnam. The court held the wearing of the armband was "symbolic speech" so close to "pure speech" that, under the First Amendment, school officials could not restrain it. Numerous other regulations involving hair codes were upheld throughout the country, but the Supreme Court declined to examine them.

Nevertheless, the claim persisted that personal styles in dress and grooming were part of an individual's expression of political and social values and entitled to constitutional protection. In 1974, one year after American combat troops left Vietnam and four years after the commission of the crime, the Supreme Court heard Goguen's case. The court's reliance on the vagueness and overbreadth doctrines overshadowed the central issues. With this decision, the prosecutions of protesters practically came to an end.

☆ 340 *Smith v. Goguen*

415 U.S. 566 (1974).

MR. JUSTICE POWELL. . . .

I

The slender record in this case reveals little more than that Goguen wore a small cloth version of the United States flag sewn to the seat of his trousers. The flag was approximately four by six inches and was displayed at the left rear of Goguen's blue jeans.

On January 30, 1970, two police officers in Leominster, Massachusetts, saw Goguen bedecked in that fashion. The first officer encountered Goguen standing and talking with a group of persons on a public street. The group apparently was not engaged in any demonstration or other protest associated with Goguen's apparel. No disruption of traffic or breach of the peace occurred. When this officer approached Goguen to question him about the flag, the other persons present laughed. Some time later, the second officer observed Goguen in the same attire walking in the downtown business district of Leominster.

The following day the first officer swore out a complaint against Goguen under the contempt provision of the Massachusetts flag-misuse statute. The relevant part of the statute then read:

> Whoever publicly mutilates, tramples upon, defaces or treats contemptuously the flag of the United States . . . , whether such flag is public or private property . . . , shall be punished by a fine of not less than ten nor more than one hundred dollars or by imprisonment for not more than one year, or both. . . .

Despite the first six words of the statute, Goguen was not charged with any act of physical desecration. As permitted by the disjunctive structure of the portion of the statute dealing with desecration and contempt, the officer charged specifically and only that Goguen "did publicly treat contemptuously the flag of the United States. . . ." [Goguen was convicted and sentenced to six months' imprisonment.]

*            *            *

. . . Where a statute's literal scope, unaided by a narrowing state court interpretation, is capable of reaching expression sheltered by the First Amendment, the doctrine demands a greater degree of specificity than in other contexts. The statutory language at issue here, "publicly . . . treats contemptuously the flag of the United States . . . ," has such scope (verbal flag contempt), and at the relevant time was without the benefit of judicial clarification.

Flag contempt statutes have been characterized as void for lack of notice on the theory that "[w]hat is contemptuous to one man may be a work of art to another." Goguen's behavior can hardly be described as art. Immaturity or "silly conduct" probably comes closer to the mark. But we see the force of the District Court's observation that the flag has become "an object of youth fashion and high camp. . . ." As both courts below noted, casual treatment of the flag in many contexts has become a widespread contemporary phenomenon. Flag wearing in a day of relaxed clothing styles may be simply for adornment or a ploy to attract attention. It and many other current, careless uses of the flag nevertheless consti-

tute unceremonial treatment that many people may view as contemptuous. Yet in a time of widely varying attitudes and tastes for displaying something as ubiquitous as the United States flag or representations of it, it could hardly be the purpose of the Massachusetts Legislature to make criminal every informal use of the flag. The statutory language under which Goguen was charged, however, fails to draw reasonably clear lines between the kinds of nonceremonial treatment that are criminal and those that are not. Due process requires that all "be informed as to what the State commands or forbids," and that "men of common intelligence" not be forced to guess at the meaning of the criminal law. Given today's tendencies to treat the flag unceremoniously, those notice standards are not satisfied here.

*            *            *

MR. JUSTICE WHITE, concurring in the judgment.

*            *            *

It is self-evident that there is a whole range of conduct that anyone with at least a semblance of common sense would know is contemptuous conduct and that would be covered by the statute if directed at the flag. In these instances, there would be ample notice to the actor and no room for undue discretion by enforcement officers. There may be a variety of other conduct that might or might not be claimed contemptuous by the State, but unpredictability in those situations does not change the certainty in others.

I am also confident that the statute was not vague with respect to the conduct for which Goguen was arrested and convicted. It should not be beyond the reasonable comprehension of anyone who would conform his conduct to the law to realize that sewing a flag on the seat of his pants is contemptuous of the flag.

*            *            *

[Justice White concurred in the judgment of reversal on the grounds that convicting Goguen for treating the flag "contemptuously" was to punish him for communicating an idea, a direct violation of the First Amendment.]

## 341 "the difference between a criminal act and a revolutionary act is shown by what the money is used for" (1974)

On January 23, 1973, Secretary of State Henry Kissinger and North Vietnam's Le Duc Tho signed an agreement after lengthy negotiations in Paris to bring "peace with honor" to Indochina. On January 28, 1973, a cease fire went into effect; on March 29,

1973, the last American combat forces left South Vietnam. On October 10, 1973, Vice-President Spiro T. Agnew, accused of having accepted bribes while serving as governor of Maryland and as vice-president, resigned his office. In March 1974 a federal grand jury handed down indictments on counts of perjury, conspiracy, and obstruction of justice against seven Watergate defendants, including presidential aides H. R. Haldeman and John D. Ehrlichman and Attorney General John N. Mitchell. On August 9, 1974, Richard M. Nixon became the first United States president to resign his office. Gerald R. Ford, vice-president since December 6, 1973, succeeded him.

Despite these events, which absorbed the political energy of the nation, revolutionary turmoil did not end. On February 4, 1974, members of the Symbionese Liberation Army kidnapped Patricia Hearst, the nineteen-year-old granddaughter of William Randolph Hearst and daughter of *San Francisco Examiner* publisher Randolph Hearst, from her apartment in Berkeley, California. The SLA demanded $230 million in food to be distributed to the poor as ransom. After Patty Hearst adopted the name of Tania, ostensibly joined the ranks of the SLA, and appeared in a photograph of a bank holdup as one of the robbers, the federal authorities issued a warrant for her arrest. Ultimately captured, she was convicted on March 20, 1976.

Hearst was sentenced to seven years in prison. On February 1, 1979, President Jimmy Carter commuted her sentence to the time already served (22 months). Two months later, she married her former bodyguard. The SLA membership never exceeded ten, two of whom had been arrested for murder before the Hearst kidnapping. The organization effectively was extinguished when six members were killed in a gunfight with Los Angeles police on May 17, 1974.

## ☆ 341 Communiqués from the Symbionese Liberation Army

Reprinted in Les Payne, Tim Findley, and Carolyn Craven, *The Life and Death of the SLA* (New York: Ballantine Books, 1976), 332-44, 346-54.

## ☆ 341a The Goals of the Symbionese Liberation Army

1. To unite all oppressed people into a fighting force and to destroy the system of the capitalist state and all its value systems. To create in its place a system and sovereign nations that are in the total interest of its races and people, based on the true affirmation of life, love, trust, honesty, freedom and equality that is truly for all.

2. To assure the rights of all people to self-determination and the right to build their own nation and government, with representatives that have shown through their actions to be in the interest of their people. To give the right to all people to select and elect their own representatives and governments by direct vote.

3. To build a people's federated council, who will be a male and female of each people's country or sovereign nation of the Symbionese Federation of Nations, who shall be the representatives of their nations, in the forming of trade pacts and unified defense against any external enemy that may attack any of the free nations of the federation and to form other aids to each other's needs.

4. To aid and defend the cultural rights of the sovereign nations of the Symbionese Federation, and to aid each nation in the building of educational and other institutions to meet and serve this need for its people.

5. To place the control of all the institutions and industries of each nation into the hands of its people. To aid sovereign nations of the federation to build nations where work contributes concretely to the full interests and needs of its workers and the communal interest of its communities and its people and the mutual interest of all within the federation of nations.

6. To aid and defend the rights of all oppressed people to build nations which do not institute oppression and exploitation, but rather does institute the environment of freedom and defends that freedom on all levels and for all of the people, and by any means necessary.

7. To give back to all of the people their human and constitutional rights, liberty, equality, and justice and the right to bear arms in the defense of these rights.

8. To create a system where our aged are cared for with respect, love, and kindness and aided and encouraged to become assets in their own ways to their nations and to their communal community. That the life that moves around them is not a frightening and murderous one and where life is not fear, but rather one of love and feeling and unity.

9. To create a system and laws that will neither force people into nor force them to stay into personal relationships that they do not wish to stay in, and to destroy all chains instituted by legal and social laws of the capitalist state which acts as a reinforcing system to maintain this form of imprisonment.

10. To create institutions that will aid, reinforce and educate the growth of our comrade women and aid them in making a new true and better role to live in life and in the defining of themselves as a new and free people.

11. To create new forms of life and relationships that bring true meanings of love to people's relationships, and to form communes on the community

level and bring the children of the community into being the responsibility of the community, to place our children in the union of real comradeship and in the care and loving interest of the revolutionary community.

12. To destroy the prison system, which the capitalist state has used to imprison the oppressed and exploited, and thereby destroy the love, unity, and hopes of millions of lives and families. And to create in its place a system of comradeship and that of group unity and education on a communal and revolutionary level within the community, to bring home our daughters and sons, and sisters and brothers, fathers and mothers, and welcome them home with love and a new revolutionary comradeship of unity.

13. To take control of all state land and that of the capitalist class and to give back the land to the people. To form laws and codes that safeguard that no person can own the land, or sell the land, but rather the nation's people own the land and use it for their needs and interest to live. No one can own the air, the sky, the water, the trees, the birds, the sun, for all of this world belongs to the people of this earth.

14. To take control of all buildings and apartment buildings of the capitalist class and fascist government and then to totally destroy the rent system of exploitation.

15. To build a federation of nations, who shall formulate programs and unions of actions and interests that will destroy the capitalist value system and its other anti-human institutions who will be able to do this by meeting all the basic needs of all the people and their nations. For they will be able to do this because each nation will have its full control of all of its industries and institutions and does not run them for profit, but in the interest of all the people of its nation.

☆ 341b Communiqué 3

February 4, 1974
SUBJECT: Prisoners of War
TARGET: Patricia Hearst, daughter of Randolph Hearst, corporate enemy of the people
WARRANT ORDER: Arrest and protective custody: and if resistance, execution

Warrant Issued By: The Court of the People. On the aforestated date, combat elements of the United Federated Forces of the Symbionese Liberation Army armed with cyanide loaded weapons served an arrest warrant on Patricia Campbell Hearst.

It is the order of this court that the subject be arrested by combat units and removed to a protective area of safety and only upon completion of this condition to notify Unit #4 to give communications of the action. It is the directive of this court that during this action ONLY, no civilian elements be harmed if

possible, and that warning shot be given. However, if any citizens attempt to aid the authorities or interfere with the implementation of this order they shall be executed immediately.

This court hereby notifies the public and directs all combat units in the future to kill any civilian who attempts to witness or interfere with any operation conducted by the people's forces against the fascist state.

Should any attempt be made by authorities to rescue the prisoner or to arrest or harm any SLA elements, the prisoner is to be executed.

The prisoner is to be maintained in adequate physical and mental condition, and unharmed as long as these conditions are adhered to. Protective custody shall be composed of combat and medical units, to safeguard both the prisoner and her health.

All communications from this court MUST be published in full, in all newspapers, and all other forms of the media. Failure to do so will endanger the safety of the prisoner.

Further communication will follow.

SLA

DEATH TO THE FASCIST INSECT THAT PREYS UPON THE LIFE OF THE PEOPLE

☆ 341c Communiqué 4

A. We have heard that Mr. Hearst wants to save his daughter, we want to save all the children and people. In an effort to answer some of the basic needs of the people, we are asking for a symbolic gesture of good faith from this representative of the corporate state. Each person with one of the following cards is to be given $70.00 worth of meats, vegetables, and dairy products: all people with welfare cards, social security pension cards, disabled veteran cards, medical cards, parole or probation papers, and jail or bail release slips. So that all those with such cards have time and will not be forced to stand waiting in long lines, the time for distribution of this food must extend over a four-week period, beginning February 19th, on each Tuesday, Thursday, and Saturday for four successive weeks, each person with one of the listed cards can go to publicized stores and pick up their food.

*          *          *

SLA

☆ 341d Communiqué 5

[PATRICIA HEARST]

Dad, Mom, I'm making a tape to let you know that I'm still okay and to explain a few things, I hope.

*          *          *

But the SLA is really mad about certain attempts to make the feeding of food be the receiving of goods that were gotten by extortion.

They don't want people to be harassed by police or by anybody else, and I hope you can do something about that and if you can't, well, I mean they'll do something about it.

So . . . you shouldn't worry about that too much.

Also, I would like to emphasize that I am alive and that I am well and that in spite of what certain tape experts seem to think, I mean I'm fine.

It's really depressing to hear people talk about me like I'm dead. I can't explain what that's like. What it does also is that it . . . it begins to convince other people that maybe I'm dead.

If everybody is convinced that I am dead, well then it gives the FBI an excuse to come in here and try to pull me out. I'm sure that Mr. Bates understands that the FBI has to come in and get me out by force, that they won't have time to decide who not to kill. They'll just have to kill everyone.

I don't particularly want to die that way.

I hope you will realize that everything is okay and that they just have to back off for a while. There'll be plenty of time for investigating later.

I am basically an example and symbolic warning not only to you but to everyone that there are people who are not going to accept your support of other governments. . . .

It's also to show what can be done. When it's necessary the people can be fed. And to show that it's too bad it has to happen this way to make people see that there are people who need food.

Now maybe something can be done about that so that things like this won't have to happen again.

Also . . . the SLA is very annoyed about attempts by the press and by authorities to turn this into a racial issue. It's not. This is a political issue and this is a political action that they've taken.

Anyone who really reads the stated objectives of the SLA can see very clearly that this is not a racial thing. I hope there won't be any more confusion about that.

\*     \*     \*

I am being held as a prisoner of war and not as anything else and I'm being treated in accordance with international codes of war. And so you shouldn't listen or believe what anybody else says about the way I'm being treated. This is the way I'm being treated. I'm not left alone and I'm not just shoved off. I mean I'm fine.

I am not being starved and I'm not being beaten or tortured. Really.

☆ 341e Communiqué of April 18, 1974

Greetings to the people, this is Tania. On April 15 my comrades and I expropriated $10,660.02 from the Sunset branch of Hibernia Bank. Casualties could have been avoided had the persons involved kept out of the way and cooperated with the people's forces until after our departure.

\*     \*     \*

Our action of April 15 forced the corporate state to help finance the revolution. In the case of expropriation, the difference between a criminal act and a revolutionary act is shown by what the money is used for.

As for the money involved in my parents' bad faith gesture to aid the people, these funds are being used to aid the people, and to insure the survival of the people's forces in their struggle with and for the people.

\*     \*     \*

Consciousness is terrifying to the ruling class and they will do anything to discredit people who have realized that the only alternative to freedom is death and that the only way we can free ourselves of this fascist dictatorship is by fighting, not with words but with guns.

\*     \*     \*

To those people who still believe that I am brainwashed or dead, I see no reason to further defend my position. I am a soldier in the people's army. *Patria o muerte; venceremos.*

## 342 "national commitment to justice and mercy" (1974, 1977)

During the Vietnam War, thousands of young American men fled to Canada and elsewhere to avoid the Military Selective Service Act. Many others, already in uniform, deserted from the army. Motivated by the personal desire to avoid fighting in a distant and unpopular war and by religious beliefs, moral repulsion, and political opposition to America's involvement in the Southeast Asian conflict, these protestors became the largest class of political offenders since the Civil War period.

A month after taking office on September 9, 1974, President Gerald Ford announced that he had unconditionally pardoned Richard Nixon for all crimes against the United States which Nixon "ha[d] committed or may have committed" while serving as president. On September 16, 1974, President Ford, by contrast, offered a conditional amnesty to Vietnam War deserters and draft evaders on a case-by-case basis. President Jimmy Carter extended an unconditional pardon to all draft evaders, but not to deserters, on January 21, 1977, the day following his inauguration.

☆ 342 Presidential Clemency Programs for Vietnam Draft Evaders and Military Deserters

☆ 342a A Presidential Proclamation, No. 4313

39 Fed. Reg. 33293, as amended by Proc. No. 4345, 40 Fed. Reg. 8931, 10433 (Sept. 16, 1974).

PROC. NO. 4313. PROGRAM FOR RETURN OF
VIETNAM ERA DRAFT EVADERS AND MILITARY
DESERTERS

\*       \*       \*

The United States withdrew the last of its forces from the Republic of Vietnam on March 28, 1973.

In the period of its involvement in armed hostilities in Southeast Asia, the United States suffered great losses. Millions served their country, thousands died in combat, thousands more were wounded, others are still listed as missing in action.

Over a year after the last American combatant had left Vietnam, the status of thousands of our countrymen—convicted, charged, investigated or still sought . . . remains unresolved.

In furtherance of our national commitment to justice and mercy these young Americans should have the chance to contribute a share to the rebuilding of peace among ourselves and with all nations. They should be allowed the opportunity to earn return to their country, their communities, and their families, upon their agreement to a period of alternate service in the national interest, together with an acknowledgment of their allegiance to the country and its Constitution.

Desertion in time of war is a major, serious offense; failure to respond to the country's call for duty is also a serious offense. Reconciliation among our people does not require that these acts be condoned. Yet, reconciliation calls for an act of mercy to find the Nation's wounds and to heal the scars of divisiveness.

NOW, THEREFORE, I, Gerald R. Ford, President of the United States, pursuant to my powers under Article II, Sections 1, 2 and 3 of the Constitution, do hereby proclaim a program to commence immediately to afford reconciliation to Vietnam era draft evaders and military deserters upon the following terms and conditions:

1. *Draft Evaders* — An individual . . . will be relieved of prosecution and punishment for such offense [under the Selective Service law] if he:

    (i) presents himself to a United States Attorney before March 31, 1975,

    (ii) executes an agreement acknowledging his allegiance to the United States and pledging to fulfill a period of alternate service under the auspices of the Director of Selective Service, and

    (iii) satisfactorily completes such service.

The alternate service shall promote the national health, safety, or interest. No draft evader will be given the privilege of completing a period of alternate service by service in the Armed Forces.

\*       \*       \*

The period of service shall be twenty-four months, which may be reduced by the Attorney General because of mitigating circumstances.

2. *Military Deserters* — A member of the armed forces who has been administratively classified as a deserter . . . will be relieved of prosecution and punishment . . . if before March 31, 1975 he takes an oath of allegiance to the United States and executes an agreement with the Secretary of the Military Department from which he absented himself or for members of the Coast Guard, with the Secretary of Transportation, pledging to fulfill a period of alternate service under the auspices of the Director of Selective Service. The alternate service shall promote the national health, safety, or interest.

The period of service shall be twenty-four months, which may be reduced. . . .

\*       \*       \*

Each member of the armed forces who elects to seek relief through this program will receive an undesirable discharge. Thereafter, upon satisfactory completion of a period of alternate service prescribed by the Military Department or Department of Transportation, such individual will be entitled to receive, in lieu of his undesirable discharge, a clemency discharge in recognition of his fulfillment of the requirements of the program. Such clemency discharge shall not bestow entitlement to benefits administered by the Veterans Administration.

\*       \*       \*

3. *Presidential Clemency Board* — By Executive Order I have this date established a Presidential Clemency Board which will review the records of individuals within the following categories: (i) those who have been convicted of draft evasion offenses as described above, (ii) those who have received a punitive or undesirable discharge from service in the armed forces . . . or are serving sentences of confinement for such violations [of the UCMJ]. Where appropriate, the Board may recommend that clemency be conditioned upon completion of a period of alternate service. However, if any clemency discharge is recommended, such discharge shall not bestow entitlement to benefits administered by the Veterans Administration.

\*       \*       \*

IN WITNESS WHEREOF, I have hereunto set my hand this sixteenth day of September in the year of our Lord nineteen hundred seventy-four, and of the Independence of the United States of America the one hundred and ninety-ninth.

GERALD R. FORD

☆ 342b  A Presidential Proclamation, No. 4483

42 Fed. Reg. 4391 (Jan. 21, 1977).

PARDON FOR VIOLATIONS OF ACT, AUGUST 4, 1964
TO MARCH 28, 1973

Acting pursuant to the grant of authority in Article II, Section 2, of the Constitution of the United

States, I, Jimmy Carter, President of the United States, do hereby grant a full, complete and unconditional pardon to: (1) all persons who may have committed any offense between August 4, 1964 and March 28, 1973 in violation of the Military Selective Service Act or any rule or regulation promulgated thereunder; and (2) all persons heretofore convicted, irrespective of the date of conviction, of any offense committed between August 4, 1964 and March 28, 1973 in violation of the Military Selective Service Act, or any rule or regulation promulgated thereunder, restoring to them full political, civil and other rights.

This pardon does not apply to the following who are specifically excluded therefrom:

(1) All persons convicted of or who may have committed any offense in violation of the Military Selective Service Act, or any rule or regulation promulgated thereunder, involving force or violence; and

(2) All persons convicted of or who may have committed any offense in violation of the Military Selective Service Act, or any rule or regulation promulgated thereunder, in connection with duties or responsibilities arising out of employment as agents, officers or employees of the Military Selective Service system.

IN WITNESS WHEREOF, I have hereunto set my hand this 21st day of January, in the year of our Lord nineteen hundred and seventy-seven, and of the Independence of the United States of America the two hundred and first.

JIMMY CARTER

## 343 "to forge reconciliation" (1975)

One unique aspect of the American government's response to political dissidents and offenders throughout the nation's history has been the government's willingness to offer such opponents an opportunity to regain the full benefits of citizenship as soon as the flames of conflict subsided. The report of the Presidential Clemency Board appointed by President Ford discussed the issues of clemency and amnesty in American history.

### ☆343 Executive Clemency in American History

The Presidential Clemency Board's Report to the President (Washington, D.C.: U.S. Government Printing Office, 1975), 175–81.

*        *        *

Lessons can be learned from studying past clemency actions, but a note of caution is in order. Each postwar clemency has been a unique response fashioned to the circumstances of its historical period. The war

resisters of the Vietnam era are not in the same category as Southerners who were defeated on the battlefield or Jehovah's Witnesses who failed to serve during World War II. The adoption of a Lincoln program or a Truman program to resolve a present-day problem would have been no more appropriate than fashioning a program with total disregard for these precedents. President Ford's clemency program is not unmindful of programs initiated by his predecessors, yet it is distinctly tailored to the Vietnam era.

Much of the interest and concern over executive clemency stems from a fear that leniency toward draft and AWOL offenders might undermine America's future ability to mobilize and maintain a strong military force. The moral dilemma surrounding personal participation in war will always be with us, but it seems unlikely that the prospect of a clemency program modeled after President Ford's would lead anyone to evade the draft or desert the military during a future war whose military and political context will inevitably be very different from that of the Vietnam era. No one can identify any great harm ever suffered by the military as a result of past acts of executive clemency. However, the negative consequences of a universal and unconditional amnesty remain unknown inasmuch as no President has ever proclaimed a truly universal and unconditional amnesty. Australia had such an amnesty after ending its involvement in the Vietnam War, but its long-term impact is still unknown.

War and conscription have caused dissension among Americans throughout our history. From our earliest days as a nation, Presidents have acted strongly to protect national interests through military action. But they also have exercised their clemency powers to forge reconciliation by offering political outcasts and offenders an opportunity to regain the full benefits of citizenship.

President Washington acted decisively to put down the Whiskey Rebellion. Urged on by Hamilton and others, he was determined to establish the power and authority of the newly constituted Federal government. Many poverty-stricken farmers in Western Pennsylvania refused to pay a new Federal tax imposed on whiskey, rebelling when 75 of them received summonses to appear in Federal court. Several hundred rioters burned a Revenue Inspector's home. With the courts unable to enforce the laws, and with the insurrectionists ignoring a Presidential proclamation demanding adherence to the laws, Washington called on the military to quash the rebellion. The troops faced no armed opposition, and very few insurrectionists were taken into custody. Washington subsequently pardoned all offenders except two leaders who were under indictment for treason. These two were later pardoned by him after they had been convicted.

The Civil War clemency actions of Presidents

Lincoln and Johnson arose in response to a new situation in American history—the first use of significant numbers of conscripts by the U.S. Army. Draft evasion and desertion were commonplace throughout the war. The exodus to Canada by draft-liable men grew to such proportions that the borders had to be closed to them. About 88,000 deserted from the Union Army in 1864 alone. Lincoln frequently intervened to commute death sentences for desertion, partly because of his inclination for mercy, but also to further his military and political aims. Amnesty for Union deserters was predicated on their rejoining their regiments and thus being available to fight the rebels. Lincoln's early amnesty offers to supporters of the Confederacy were surely intended to undermine Jefferson Davis' army and suppress the rebellion.

Johnson's post-war clemency actions were designed to dispense the grace and favor of the government to secessionist followers, but Confederate leaders were not treated lightly. Johnson's actions were highly political. In addition to his struggle against impeachment, he continually wrestled with Congress over his program of Reconstruction. Congress unsuccessfully attempted to deprive President Johnson of his power to proclaim a general amnesty, apparently desiring to reserve such powers for itself. Nevertheless, the President issued four amnesty proclamations for former rebels before the close of his administration. President Johnson's last two proclamations were very generous, offering clemency even for the offense of treason. Civil War clemency was gradually extended to more and more individuals, but it was not until 1898 that the political disability imposed by the Fourteenth Amendment was removed for all surviving Confederates.

President Truman took great pride in his military service, and he had little sympathy for those who refused to wear the uniform. His high regard for servicemen was demonstrated by his Christmas 1945 pardon of several thousand ex-convicts who served in the military during World War II. Truman's Amnesty Board was restricted to reviewing approximately 15,000 Selective Service violations. Only three prisoners secured release from confinement as a result of Amnesty Board recommendations. The other 1,520 receiving Presidential pardons had already completed their prison sentences. During the 1952 Christmas season, Truman restored citizenship rights to approximately 9,000 peacetime deserters, but no pardon, remission, or mitigation of sentence was involved. At the sametime, Truman restored civil rights for Korean War veterans who had received civil court convictions prior to their service in the Korean War.

\*       \*       \*

President Ford's program was more universal than either Johnson's or Truman's in that it did not specifically exclude major categories of offenders. However, it did not affect as many people as Johnson's program. The 113,300 eligible persons and 21,729 applicants to President Ford's program made it the second largest in American history.

\*       \*       \*

Unlike Washington and Lincoln, President Ford did not attach any condition restraining clemency recipients' future conduct. Instead, he attached a condition of alternative service as a means of demonstrating one's commitment to national service. Like Washington and Lincoln, he required some clemency recipients to sign an oath reaffirming their allegiance. Unlike Lincoln, he did not require AWOL soldiers to return to military duty.

\*       \*       \*

An analysis of the history of executive clemency shows that different wars have produced different post-war grants of clemency. To a large extent, the Presidential policies have reflected the need for national reconciliation during the post-war periods. When there was little such need, there was little or no clemency offered. When the need was considerable—such as when Lincoln was making plans to reunite the sections during the late stages of the Civil War—the grants of executive clemency were considerable. We expect that President Ford's clemency program will be viewed in much the same manner as the Civil War programs have been.

We believe that this clemency program compares favorably with other Presidents' clemency actions, when consideration is given to the nature of benefits offered, the conditions attached, the number of individuals benefited, and the speed with which the program followed the war. If each factor is taken separately, President Ford's program does not break precedent in any fundamental way. Washington's pardon after the Whiskey Rebellion was a speedier action, but it affected only a very small number of people. Lincoln's Civil War amnesties for deserters were more clement, but he set more stringent conditions. Johnson's amnesties for Southern Secessionists benefited more individuals, but 30 years passed before all had their full rights restored. The Truman amnesty of draft evaders imposed no conditions, but it denied clemency to ninety percent of its cases.

President Ford established only two new precedents: the condition of alternative service and the issuance of a neutral Clemency Discharge. Had he announced a universal and unconditional amnesty, his program would have been much more of a break from precedent. While historians might still have viewed it as a tailored response to a unique war, its impact upon a future generation of draftees and combat troops would have been much harder to predict. These were risks well worth avoiding.

## 344 "this entire Nation has long recognized the outstanding virtues of courage, patriotism, and selfless devotion to duty" (1975)

A year after the pardon of Richard M. Nixon and the conditional clemency for the Vietnam draft evaders and deserters, Congress, by joint resolution, retroactively restored to Robert E. Lee full United States citizenship. A final settling of political accounts of the Civil War was still deemed necessary more than a century after General Lee's surrender to General Ulysses S. Grant at the Appomattox Court House in Virginia on April 9, 1865.

☆ 344 To Restore Posthumously Full Rights of Citizenship to General R. E. Lee

89 Stat. 380 (1975).

Whereas this entire Nation has long recognized the outstanding virtues of courage, patriotism, and selfless devotion to duty of General R. E. Lee, and has recognized the contribution of General Lee in healing the wounds of the War Between the States, and

Whereas, in order to further the goal of reunion of this country, General Lee, on June 13, 1865, applied to the President for amnesty and pardon and restoration of his rights as a citizen, and

Whereas this request was favorably endorsed by General Ulysses S. Grant on June 16, 1865, and

Whereas, General Lee's full citizenship was not restored to him subsequent to his request of June 13, 1865, for the reason that no accompanying oath of allegiance was submitted, and

Whereas, on October 12, 1870, General Lee died, still denied the right to hold any office and other rights of citizenship, and

Whereas a recent discovery has revealed that General Lee did in fact on October 2, 1865, swear allegiance to the Constitution of the United States and to the Union, and

Whereas it appears that General Lee thus fulfilled all of the legal as well as moral requirements incumbent upon him for restoration of his citizenship: Now, therefore, be it

*Resolved by the Senate and House of Representatives of the United States of America in Congress assembled,* That, in accordance with section 3 of amendment 14 of the United States Constitution, the legal disabilities placed upon General Lee as a result of his service as General of the Army of Northern Virginia are removed, and that General R. E. Lee is posthumously restored to the full rights of citizenship, effective June 13, 1865.

*Approved, August 5, 1975.*

## 345 "be harmonious while struggling" (1976)

As the age of protest was subsiding, many of the activists of the previous decade sought out alternative missions and lifestyles. One of the Chicago Seven defendants and a founder of the Yippie movement, Jerry Rubin departed from radicalism. His actions typified the changes that occurred in the leadership ranks of many of the dissenter and protester organizations—whether white or black, male or female. Jerry Rubin's autobiography, published in 1976 when he was thirty-seven years old, recorded his transformation from radical leader to investment counselor.

☆ 345 Uniting the Personal and the Political

Jerry Rubin, *Growing Up at Thirty-seven* (New York: E. Evans, 1976), 197-207.

During the past few years there has been a widespread feeling of powerlessness in our country, and people have put aside collective solutions in favor of individual pursuits. I have experienced the general consciousness changes within myself. Today I am more apathetic, cynical, and individualistic than I was a decade ago; nevertheless, I am still optimistic, idealistic, and believe in collective action.

Friends ask me, "Isn't your inward growth trip an escape from social reality?" Yes, it's a far cry from leading a march on the Pentagon to sitting cross-legged, counting my breaths. But there is no contradiction.

                    *        *        *

In the sixties I stressed one part of my being—the traditionally "masculine" part—the achieving "doer"—while underemphasizing the other part—the "feminine," accepting "be-er." My vision of the model human being was a totally committed person fighting against oppression, willing to sacrifice his life and freedom for the people.

In the consciousness movement of the seventies I have a new vision: a loving person, without expectations, who lives in his senses and in the moment.

These two ideals are not contradictory, although they represent different poles of my psyche. The political vision implies struggle; the psychic vision, harmony. In a synthesis I can create harmony through struggle, and be harmonious while struggling.

                    *        *        *

America is experiencing a spiritual rebirth as people discover that a materialistic existence, an ego-dominated life, is unsatisfying. We are looking for meaning in our life, pleasure in our bodies, and honest communication rather than image, money, or power. This decline in chasing after symbols and objects is eroding the morale of capitalism.

*     *     *

The know-yourself movement can be a self-indulgent, escapist, individualistic alternative to collective activity. The individual, at odds with nature and society, tries to become one with himself as a final salvation. But I don't believe anyone can attain self-perfection in a vacuum. I am no higher than the society around me. I have a responsibility to oppressed people as well as to myself.

*     *     *

The New Consciousness movement has the potential to unite spirituality and politics. There are many spiritually minded people who dismiss the physical world as illusion, just as there are many political people who deny the spiritual. More and more people today, however, are interested both in spiritual evolution *and* positive social change.

Using a spiritual approach in political ways may change people in ways we never before imagined. The future belongs to the people who have the largest view of the potential of human beings, not to those with the narrowest. A revolutionary must have the most positive view of human nature. Out of that view he acts, creates, and influences behavior.

*     *     *

I have a positive vision that America will peacefully elect a politically humanistic government. The media, the electrical hot-spring of the nation, creates awareness revolutions every second. The institutions of democracy — voting, free discussion of issues, media reporting — work for the people. America moves to the left. The fall of the empire is matched by a spiritual rebirth. The spirit of freedom when loose in the land cannot be contained.

*     *     *

In the 1960's we postponed all questions on personal growth until the revolution. But revolution is only as high as the people that make it. I had expected the revolution apocalyptically, but have since discovered that revolution is an evolutionary process. I am also a process. My personal growth and your personal growth match the growth of mass consciousness. People out of touch with bodies and souls cannot make positive change. Political activism without self-awareness perpetuates cycles of anger, competition, ego battles.

### CHAPTER 11

# Contemporary Political Conflicts and Domestic Security

———

## 1948-1985

The documents in this chapter seek mainly to inventory the laws and methods the government currently has at its disposal in combating political crime. Most of these approaches have been encountered earlier: governmental secrecy laws, resort to emergency measures, the requirement of loyalty oaths, and surveillance of suspect persons and groups. It is revealing to see these historical measures in their modern context. Since some existing measures are of earlier origin, the chronological march of this volume is broken in order that the reader have before him or her a wide range of relevant and interrelated materials and issues.

Control of information is the central focus of this chapter. On the one hand there are the old Espionage Act provisions, which penalize the dissemination of material classified by the government as sensitive to national security, as well as passport controls designed not only to keep foreign subversives out of this country but also to prevent travel abroad by suspect United States citizens. On the other hand, the major tool of the executive branch in the campaign against political crime seems to be surreptitious surveillance, electronic and otherwise, of suspect individuals and organizations, with as little adherence to the traditional standards of the Fourth Amendment requirements, such as probable cause, as possible. In this regard the executive branch's assertion of inherent extraconstitutional power to protect national security, as well as the congressional delegation of emergency powers to the president, are presented for their potential impact upon the courts, which are continually faced with challenges to these exercises of governmental authority.

Many of the materials in this chapter address the ultimate question regarding governmental response to political crime: is the particular threat posed to national security by this form of criminality sufficient to warrant and justify resort to extraconstitutional standards and powers? The historical survey previously undertaken discloses that in the war against political crime the American government has made special use of measures not available in its campaign against crime generally. These have included immigration measures, resort to loyalty oaths, preventive detention, and the imposition of martial law. The question that still remains unanswered is which, if any, extraordinary powers and standards of law can be justified as part of the government's arsenal for combating political crime. Many of the materials in this chapter relate to this question. The reader, therefore, is invited to examine all the materials, paying particular attention to the dual concern for control of dangerous political crime and the prevention of abuse of constitutional rights.

Finally, although the end of the United States' involvement in the Vietnam War and the easing of racial tensions following the new federal civil rights laws and measures has lowered the fervor of the American body politic in recent years, many causes and activists remain for whom political criminality continues as a major technique for attaining desired goals. We have included some materials on these movements both for the purpose of historical comparison and for the identification of potential sources of future political criminality.

---

## 346 "Whoever, for the purpose of obtaining information" (1948)

In 1948, Congress undertook a major revision and codification of the criminal law of the United States. The more than two-hundred-page enactment included a modified version of the Espionage Act of 1917. Congress had not repealed the provisions of that act after the conclusion of World War I, and the act remained in force throughout the twenty-five peacetime years prior to World War II, as well as through World War II.

## ☆346 The Espionage Law

62 Stat. 736–38 (1948). (Current version at 18 U.S.C. §§ 792–97.)

CHAPTER 37.—ESPIONAGE AND CENSORSHIP

\*  \*  \*

§ 791. Scope of chapter. This chapter shall apply within the admiralty and maritime jurisdiction of the United States and on the high seas, as well as within the United States [repealed 1961].

§ *792. Harboring or concealing persons.* Whoever harbors or conceals any person who he knows, or has reasonable grounds to believe or suspect, has committed, or is about to commit, an offense under sections 793 or 794 of this title, shall be fined not more than $10,000 or imprisoned not more than ten years, or both.

§ *793. Gathering, transmitting or losing defense information.* Whoever, for the purpose of obtaining information respecting the national defense with intent or reason to believe that the information is to be used to the injury of the United States, or to the advantage of any foreign nation, goes upon, enters, flies over, or otherwise obtains information concerning any vessel, aircraft, work of defense, navy yard, naval station, submarine base, fueling station, fort, battery, torpedo station, dockyard, canal, railroad, arsenal, camp, factory, mine, telegraph, telephone, wireless, or signal station, building, office, or other place connected with the national defense, owned or constructed, or in progress of construction by the United States or under the control of the United States, or of any of its officers, departments or agencies, or within the exclusive jurisdiction of the United States, or any place in which any vessel, aircraft, arms, munitions, or other materials or instruments for use in time of war are being made, prepared, repaired, or stored, under any contract or agreement with the United States, or any department or agency thereof, or with any person on behalf of the United States, or otherwise on behalf of the United States, or any other prohibited place so designated by the President by proclamation in time of war or in case of national emergency in which anything for the use of the Army or Navy is being prepared or constructed or stored, information as to which the President has determined would be prejudicial to the national defense; or

Whoever, for the purpose aforesaid, and with like intent or reason to believe, copies, takes, makes, or obtains, or attempts, to copy, take, make, or obtain, any sketch, photograph, photographic negative, blueprint, plan, map, model, instrument, appliance, document, writing, or note of anything connected with the national defense; or

Whoever, for the purpose aforesaid, receives or obtains or agrees or attempts to receive or obtain from any person, or from any source whatever, any document, writing, code book, signal book, sketch, photograph, photographic negative, blueprint, plan, map, model, instrument, appliance, or note, of anything connected with the national defense, knowing or having reason to believe, at the time he receives or obtains, or agrees or attempts to receive or obtain it, that it has been or will be obtained, taken, made or disposed of by any person contrary to the provisions of this chapter; or

Whoever, lawfully or unlawfully having possession of, access to, control over, or being intrusted with any document, writing, code book, signal book, sketch, photograph, photographic negative, blueprint, plan, map, model, instrument, appliance, or note relating to the national defense, willfully communicates or transmits or attempts to communicate or transmit the same to any person not entitled to receive it, or willfully retains the same and fails to deliver it on demand to the officer or employee of the United States entitled to receive it; or

Whoever, being intrusted with or having lawful possession or control of any document, writing, code book, signal book, sketch, photograph, photographic negative, blueprint, plan, map, model, note, or information, relating to the national defense, through gross negligence permits the same to be removed from its proper place of custody or delivered to anyone in violation of his trust, or to be lost, stolen, abstracted, or destroyed—

Shall be fined not more than $10,000 or imprisoned not more than ten years, or both.

§ *794. Gathering or delivering defense information to aid foreign government.* (a) Whoever, with intent or reason to believe that it is to be used to the injury of the United States or to the advantage of a foreign nation, communicates, delivers, or transmits, or attempts to communicate, deliver, or transmit, to any foreign government, or to any faction or party or military or naval force within a foreign country, whether recognized or unrecognized by the United States, or to any representative, officer, agent, employee, subject, or citizen thereof, either directly or indirectly, any document, writing, code book, signal book, sketch, photograph, photographic negative, blueprint, plan, map, model, note, instrument, appliance, or information relating to the national defense, shall be imprisoned not more than twenty years.

(b) Whoever violates subsection (a) in time of war shall be punished by death or by imprisonment for not more than thirty years.

(c) Whoever, in time of war, with intent that the same shall be communicated to the enemy, collects, records, publishes, or communicates, or attempts to elicit any information with respect to the movement, numbers, description, condition, or disposition of any of the armed forces, ships, aircraft, or war materials of the United States, or with respect to the plans or conduct, or supposed plans or conduct of any naval or military operations, or with respect to any works or measures undertaken for or connected with, or intended for the fortification or defense of any place, or any other information relating to the public defense, which might be useful to the enemy, shall be punished by death or by imprisonment for not more than thirty years.

(d) If two or more persons conspire to violate this section, and one or more of such persons do any act to effect the object of the conspiracy, each of the parties to such conspiracy shall be subject to the punishment provided for the offense which is the object of such conspiracy.

§ 795. *Photographing and sketching defense installations.* (a) Whenever, in the interests of national defense, the President defines certain vital military and naval installations or equipment as requiring protection against the general dissemination of information relative thereto, it shall be unlawful to make any photograph, sketch, picture, drawing, map, or graphical representation of such vital military and naval installations or equipment without first obtaining permission of the commanding officer of the military or naval post, camp, or station, or naval vessels, military and naval aircraft, and any separate military or naval command concerned, or higher authority, and promptly submitting the product obtained to such commanding officer or higher authority for censorship or such other action as he may deem necessary.

(b) Whoever violates this section shall be fined not more than $1,000 or imprisoned not more than one year, or both.

§ 796. *Use of aircraft for photographing defense installations.* Whoever uses or permits the use of an aircraft or any contrivance used, or designed for navigation or flight in the air, for the purpose of making a photograph, sketch, picture, drawing, map, or graphical representation of vital military or naval installations or equipment, in violation of section 795 of this title, shall be fined not more than $1,000 or imprisoned not more than one year, or both.

§ 797. *Publication and sale of photographs of defense installations.* On and after thirty days from the date upon which the President defines any vital military or naval installation or equipment as being within the category contemplated under section 795 of this title, whoever reproduces, publishes, sells, or gives away any photograph, sketch, picture, drawing, map, or graphical representation of the vital military or naval installations or equipment so defined, without first obtaining permission of the commanding officer of the military or naval post, camp, or station concerned, or higher authority, unless such photograph, sketch, picture, drawing, map, or graphical representation has clearly indicated thereon that it has been censored by the proper military or naval authority, shall be fined not more than $1,000 or imprisoned not more than one year, or both.

# 347 "we will meet the dangers that confront us" (1950)

The Korean conflict was not officially denominated a war but rather was defined as a United Nations police action. The United States, nevertheless, became a major contributor of troops and material. Regardless of formal definitions, the Korean action was a major event in the larger cold war between East and West. To prepare the citizenry for wartime measures, President Truman issued this proclamation of a state of emergency in 1950.

The proclamation supplied arguable authority for the executive to exercise powers and undertake measures that would be inappropriate in times of peace. President Truman partly relied on this declared national emergency as authority for seizing the steel mills and keeping them running in the face of a steelworkers' strike. In *Youngstown Sheet and Tube v. Sawyer*, 343 U.S. 479 (1952), the Supreme Court held this exercise of power to be unconstitutional in the absence of congressional authorization or a direct military threat. This emergency, like others, has never been terminated, and it provided the foundation for the Vietnam-era prosecution for the destruction of war premises (a campus ROTC building) during times of national emergency. *United States v. Achtenberg*, 459 F.2d 91 (8th Cir. 1973).

## ☆347 President Truman's Declaration of a National Emergency

Proc. No. 2914, 15 Fed. Reg. 9029 (1950).

WHEREAS recent events in Korea and elsewhere constitute a grave threat to the peace of the world and imperil the efforts of this country and those of the United Nations to prevent aggression and armed conflict; and

WHEREAS world conquest by communist imperialism is the goal of the forces of aggression that have been loosed upon the world; and

WHEREAS, if the goal of communist imperialism were to be achieved, the people of this country would no longer enjoy the full and rich life they have with God's help built for themselves and their children; they would no longer enjoy the blessings of the freedom of worshipping as they severally choose, the freedom of reading and listening to what they choose, the right of free speech including the right to criticize their Government, the right to choose those who conduct their Government, the right to engage freely in collective bargaining, the right to engage freely in their own business enterprises, and the many other freedoms and rights which are a part of our way of life; and

WHEREAS the increasing menace of the forces of communist aggression requires that the national defense of the United States be strengthened as speedily as possible:

NOW, THEREFORE, I, HARRY S. TRUMAN, President of the United States of America, do proclaim the existence of a national emergency, which requires that the military, naval, air, and civilian defenses of this country be strengthened as speedily as possible to the end that we may be able to repel any and all threats against our national security and to fulfill our responsibilities in the efforts being made through the United Nations and otherwise to bring about lasting peace.

I summon all citizens to make a united effort for the security and well-being of our beloved country and to place its needs foremost in thought and action that the full moral and material strength of the Nation may be readied for the dangers which threaten us.

I summon our farmers, our workers in industry, and our businessmen to make a mighty production effort to meet the defense requirements of the Nation and to this end to eliminate all waste and inefficiency and to subordinate all lesser interests to the common good.

I summon every person and every community to make, with a spirit of neighborliness, whatever sacrifices are necessary for the welfare of the Nation.

I summon all State and local leaders and officials to cooperate fully with the military and civilian defense agencies of the United States in the national defense program.

I summon all citizens to be loyal to the principles upon which our Nation is founded, to keep faith with our friends and allies, and to be firm in our devotion to the peaceful purposes for which the United Nations was founded.

I am confident that we will meet the dangers that confront us with courage and determination, strong in the faith that we can thereby "secure the Blessings of Liberty to ourselves and our Posterity."

HARRY S. TRUMAN

## 348 "Whoever knowingly and willfully communicates . . . to an unauthorized person" (1951)

Enacted in 1951 during the Korean hostilities, the following statute sought to protect against the dissemination of cryptographic information which was not covered clearly under the provisions of the revised Espionage Act. It prohibited any knowing and willful transmission of information concerning codes, ciphers, or cryptographic systems to the detriment of United States interests. The protected cryptographic information could be either American or foreign. This law once more granted wide discre-

tion to the executive by vesting in any United States government agency the power to designate as "classified" any information for which the agency sought limited or restricted circulation.

## ☆348 Disclosure of Classified Information

65 Stat. 719 (1951). (Current version at 18 U.S.C. § 798.)

§ 798. . . . (a) Whoever knowingly and willfully communicates, furnishes, transmits, or otherwise makes available to an unauthorized person, or publishes or uses in any manner prejudicial to the safety or interest of the United States or for the benefit of any foreign government to the detriment of the United States any classified information —

(1) concerning the nature, preparation, or use of any code, cipher, or cryptographic system of the United States or any foreign government; or

(2) concerning the design, construction, use, maintenance, or repair of any device, apparatus, or appliance used or prepared or planned for use by the United States or any foreign government for cryptographic or communication intelligence purposes; or

(3) concerning the communication intelligence activities of the United States or any foreign government; or

(4) obtained by the process of communication intelligence from the communications of any foreign government, knowing the same to have been obtained by such processes —

Shall be fined not more than $10,000 or imprisoned not more than ten years, or both.

(b) As used in subsection (a) of this section —

The term "classified information" means information which, at the time of a violation of this section, is, for reasons of national security, specifically designated by a United States Government Agency for limited or restricted dissemination or distribution;

The terms "code," "cipher," and "cryptographic system" include in their meanings, in addition to their usual meanings, any method of secret writing and any mechanical or electrical device or method used for the purpose of disguising or concealing the contents, significance, or meanings of communications;

The term "foreign government" includes in its meaning any person or persons acting or purporting to act for or on behalf of any faction, party, department, agency, bureau, or military force of or within a foreign country, or for or on behalf of any government or any person or persons purporting to act as a government within a foreign country, whether or not such government is recognized by the United States;

The term "communication intelligence" means all

procedures and methods used in the interception of communications and the obtaining of information from such communications by other than the intended recipients;

The term "unauthorized person" means any person who, or agency which, is not authorized to receive information of the categories set forth in subsection (a) of this section, by the President, or by the head of a department or agency of the United States Government which is expressly designated by the President to engage in communication intelligence activities for the United States.

(c) Nothing in this section shall prohibit the furnishing, upon lawful demand, of information to any regularly constituted committee of the Senate or House of Representatives of the United States of America, or joint committee thereof.

## 349 "until six months after the termination of the national emergency" (1953)

Certain provisions of the recodified Espionage Acts were applicable only when the United States was at war. But since war had not been declared during the Korean conflict, the acts' provisions that prohibited the destruction or defective production of war material and punished the communication of information to the enemy by death were not in force. In 1953 Congress enacted the following legislation to activate these provisions for the duration of the national emergency declared by President Truman in 1950. Since the emergency is yet to be terminated, these special wartime prohibitions continue in force. Note that this enactment incorrectly referred to Executive Order Number 2912 instead of 2914—the 1950 proclamation of the national emergency. In addition, since in 1951 Congress had enacted another identically numbered provision (18 U.S.C. § 798, dealing with cryptographic equipment), there are today two sections 798 in effect. Finally, the provisions of this enactment were probably affected or nullified by the National Emergencies Act, Pub. L. 94-412, 90 Stat. 1255 (1976) (50 U.S.C. § 1601), which purportedly terminated all "existing" national emergencies.

☆ 349 Temporary Extension of Section 798

67 Stat. 133 (1953).

*Be it enacted by the Senate and House of Representatives of the United States of America in Congress assembled,*

\* \* \*

SEC. 4. Title 18, United States Code, is hereby amended by inserting in chapter 37 thereof immedi-

ately after section 797 a new section, to be designated as section 798, as follows:

"§ *798. Temporary extension of section 794.* The provisions of section 794 of this title [punishing certain communications with foreign governments with death] in addition to coming into full force and effect in time of war shall remain in full force and effect until six months after the termination of the national emergency proclaimed by the President on December 16, 1950 (Proc. 2912 [*sic*] . . .) or such earlier date as may be prescribed by concurrent resolution of the Congress, and acts which would give rise to legal consequences and penalties under section 794 when performed during a state of war shall give rise to the same legal consequences and penalties when they are performed during the period above provided for."

## 350 "Whoever . . . willfully uses any part of the army" (1956)

The 1956 United States recodification of the laws governing the armed forces salvaged this restriction on the use of the military as a *posse comitatus* (the practice of having a county's entire population above the age of fifteen summoned by the sheriff to aid in law enforcement). During the Reconstruction era the Democrats objected to the use of federal military forces by the national government to prop up weak Republican regimes in the South. Hence they prevented passage of the annual appropriation to pay the troops. Eventually, Congress in 1878 passed this prohibition as a rider to the army appropriations measure, in order to prevent state governments from unauthorized resort to federal troops to maintain civil order. The prohibition must be viewed in light of the constitutional and legislative requirements for federal military intervention promulgated under Article IV, Section 4 of the Constitution, in which the federal government guaranteed to every state a "republican form of government" and undertook to protect each against "invasion" and "domestic violence." The sweeping terms of the act have been limited by Pub.L. 97-86, 95 Stat. 1115 (1981), 10 U.S.C. §§ 371 et seq.

☆ 350 Posse Comitatus Act

70A Stat. 626 (1956). (Current version at 18 U.S.C. 1385.)

SEC. 18. (a) Title 18, United States Code, is amended by inserting the following new section after section 1384:

"§ *1385. Use of Army and Air Force as posse comitatus.* Whoever, except in cases and under circumstances expressly authorized by the Constitution or Act of Congress, willfully uses any part of the Army or the Air Force as a posse comitatus or otherwise to execute the laws shall be fined not more than $10,000 or imprisoned not more than two years, or both. This section does not apply in Alaska."

\*       \*       \*

## 351 "extensive wiretapping carried on without legal sanctions" (1968)

In 1967, after decades of constitutional debate, the United States Supreme Court decided that the Fourth Amendment applied not only to traditional search and seizure but also to police interceptions of wire and electronic communications. Previously, police could carry out wire and electronic surveillance of suspected individuals (including political dissidents), and their targets lacked meaningful recourse. In *Katz v. United States*, 389 U.S. 347 (1967), the court held any electronic surveillance that violated a person's reasonable expectation of privacy to be unlawful, without prior judicial approval under the probable cause standards.

In 1968, crime was an important presidential campaign issue. The same year, Congress passed the Omnibus Crime Control and Safe Streets Act. Title III provided statutory guidelines that permitted the interception of communications by federal, state, and local law enforcement authorities subject to a prior court order. The act prohibited private wiretapping. The new and complicated scheme limited the nonpolitical crimes (generally "racketeering," white collar crimes, and narcotics offenses) for which courts could authorize electronic surveillance. But the act also included the classic "political" crimes, such as espionage, sabotage, and treason. The Omnibus Act's ambiguity with respect to federal eavesdropping for national security (reflected in § 2511(3)'s reference to the president's constitutional powers) soon gave rise to uncertainties regarding the role of judicial approval in such instances. The Executive's power in this regard was elaborated in the Foreign Intelligence Surveillance Act of 1978, 92 Stat. 1783, which repealed § 2511(3).

☆ 351 Authorization for Interception of Wire or Oral Communications

82 Stat. 211 (1968). (Current version at 18 U.S.C. 2510 et seq.)

### TITLE III—WIRETAPPING AND ELECTRONIC SURVEILLANCE

#### *Findings*

SEC. 801. On the basis of its own investigations and of published studies, the Congress makes the following findings:

(a) Wire communications are normally conducted through the use of facilities which form part of an interstate network. The same facilities are used for interstate and intrastate communications. There has been extensive wiretapping carried on without legal sanctions, and without the consent of any of the parties to the conversation. Electronic, mechanical, and other intercepting devices are being used to overhear oral conversations made in private, without the consent of any of the parties to such communications. The contents of these communications and evidence derived therefrom are being used by public and private parties as evidence in court and administrative proceedings. . . .

(b) In order to protect effectively the privacy of wire and oral communications, to protect the integrity of court and administrative proceedings, and to prevent the obstruction of interstate commerce, it is necessary for Congress to define on a uniform basis the circumstances and conditions under which the interception of wire and oral communications may be authorized, to prohibit any unauthorized interception of such communications, and the use of the contents thereof in evidence in courts and administrative proceedings.

(c) Organized criminals make extensive use of wire and oral communications in their criminal activities. The interception of such communications to obtain evidence of the commission of crimes or to prevent their commission is an indispensable aid to law enforcement and the administration of justice.

(d) To safeguard the privacy of innocent persons, the interception of wire or oral communications where none of the parties to the communication has consented to the interception should be allowed only when authorized by a court of competent jurisdiction and should remain under the control and supervision of the authorizing court. Interception of wire and oral communications should further be limited to certain major types of offenses and specific categories of crime with assurances that the interception is justified and that the information obtained thereby will not be misused.

Sec. 802, . . . [T]itle 18, United States Code, is amended by adding:

\*       \*       \*

"*§ 2511. Interception and disclosure of wire or oral communications prohibited.*

\*       \*       \*

"(3) Nothing contained in this chapter . . . shall limit the constitutional power of the President to take such measures as he deems necessary to protect the Nation against actual or potential attack or other hostile acts of a foreign power, to obtain foreign intelligence information deemed essential to the security of the United States, or to protect national security information against foreign intelligence activities. Nor shall anything contained in this chapter be deemed to limit the constitutional power of the President to take such measures as he deems necessary to protect the United States against the overthrow of the Government by force or other unlawful means, or against any other clear and present danger to the structure or existence of the Government. The contents of any wire or oral communication intercepted by authority of the President in the exercise of the foregoing powers may be received in evidence in any trial hearing, or other proceedings only where such interception was reasonable, and shall not be otherwise used or disclosed except as is necessary to implement that power.

\*         \*         \*

"§ 2516. *Authorization for interception of wire or oral communications.* (1) The Attorney General, or any Assistant Attorney General specially designated by the Attorney General, may authorize an application to a Federal judge of competent jurisdiction for an order authorizing or approving the interception of wire or oral communications by the Federal Bureau of Investigation, or a Federal agency having responsibility for the investigation of the offense as to which the application is made, when such interception may provide or has provided evidence of—

"(a) any offense punishable by death or by imprisonment for more than one year under sections 2274 through 2277 of title 42 of the United States Code (relating to the enforcement of the Atomic Energy Act of 1954), or under the following chapters of this title: chapter 37 (relating to espionage), chapter 105 (relating to sabotage), chapter 115 (relating to treason), or chapter 102 (relating to riots); . . .

\*         \*         \*

"(c) any offense which is punishable under the following sections of this title: section 201 (bribery of public officials and witnesses), section 224 (bribery in sporting contests), section 1084 (transmission of wagering information), section 1503 (influencing or injuring an officer, juror, or witness generally), section 1510 (obstruction of criminal investigations), section 1751 (Presidential assassinations, kidnapping, and assault), section 1951 (interference with commerce by threats or violence), section 1952 (interstate and foreign travel or transportation in aid of racketeering enterprises), section 1954 (offer, acceptance, or solicitation to influence operations of employee benefit plan), section 659 (theft from interstate shipment), section 664 (embezzlement from pension and welfare funds), or sections 2314 and 2315 (interstate transportation of stolen property);

"(d) any offense involving counterfeiting punishable under section 471, 472, or 473 of this title;

"(e) any offense involving bankruptcy fraud or the manufacture, importation, receiving, concealment, buying, selling, or otherwise dealing in narcotic drugs, marihuana, or other dangerous drugs, punishable under any law of the United States;

"(f) any offense including extortionate credit transactions under sections 892, 893, or 894 of this title; or

"(g) any conspiracy to commit any of the foregoing offenses."

\*         \*         \*

## 352 "domestic security surveillance involves different considerations from the surveillance of 'ordinary crime'" (1972)

The United States government charged three individuals with conspiracy to destroy government property and charged one with the dynamite bombing of a CIA office. The government conceded it had obtained information about this group through electronic surveillance without prior judicial approval. The defendants moved to have the government disclose the electronic surveillance information in order to suppress all government evidence obtained from the unauthorized bugging.

Relying on language in the Omnibus Crime Control and Safe Streets Act, the government stated that the executive had extraordinary powers to act without prior judicial approval in national security cases. The Supreme Court, rendering its decision three days after the arrest of the Watergate burglars, balanced the constitutional power of the president to "protect our Government against those who would subvert to overthrow it by unlawful means" against the "cherished privacy of law abiding citizens." The court rejected the contention that the executive was vested with broad national security powers and ruled that surveillance of a domestic group, having no association with a foreign power, was not a situation that might invoke a national security exception from the warrant requirement. In holding that Fourth Amendment privacy protections could not be guarded properly if the president had the sole power to authorize domestic surveillance, the court, nevertheless, left open the question of whether under the president's powers over foreign affairs he could authorize warrantless searches of persons having a "significant connection with a foreign power, its agents, or agencies."

☆ 352 *United States v. United States District Court*

407 U.S. 297 (1972).

MR. JUSTICE POWELL delivered the opinion of the Court.

\*          \*          \*

... [T]he Attorney General approved the wiretaps "to gather intelligence information deemed necessary to protect the nation from attempts of domestic organizations to attack and subvert the existing structure of the Government."

... [T]he Government asserted that the surveillance was lawful, though conducted without prior judicial approval, as a reasonable exercise of the President's power (exercised through the Attorney General) to protect the national security.

\*          \*          \*

### I

Title III of the Omnibus Crime Control and Safe Streets Act ... authorizes the use of electronic surveillance for classes of crimes carefully specified in 18 U.S.C. § 2516. Such surveillance is subject to prior court order....

\*          \*          \*

Together with the elaborate surveillance requirements in Title III, there is the following proviso, 18 U.S.C. § 2511 (3): ... *Nor shall anything contained in this chapter be deemed to limit the constitutional power of the President to take such measures as he deems necessary to protect the United States against the overthrow of the Government by force or other unlawful means, or against any other clear and present danger to the structure or existence of the Government....*

\*          \*          \*

We think the language of § 2511 (3), as well as the legislative history of the statute, refutes this interpretation. The relevant language is that "nothing contained in this chapter ... shall limit the constitutional power of the President to take such measures as he deems necessary to protect ..." against the dangers specified. At most, this is an implicit recognition that the President does have certain powers in the specified areas.... But so far as the use of the President's electronic surveillance power is concerned, the language is essentially neutral.

Section 2511 (3) certainly confers no power, as the language is wholly inappropriate for such a purpose. It merely provides that the Act shall not be interpreted to limit or disturb such power as the President may have under the Constitution. In short, Congress simply left presidential powers where it found them....

\*          \*          \*

... [V]iewing § 2511 (3) as a congressional disclaimer and expression of neutrality, we hold that the statute is not the measure of the executive authority asserted in this case. Rather, we must look to the constitutional powers of the President.

### II

... [T]he instant case requires no judgment on the scope of the President's surveillance power with respect to the activities of foreign powers, within or without this country. The Attorney General's affidavit in this case states that the surveillances were "deemed necessary to protect the nation from attempts of *domestic organizations* to attack and subvert the existing structure of Government" (emphasis supplied). There is no evidence of any involvement, directly or indirectly, of a foreign power.

Our present inquiry, though important, is therefore a narrow one....

We begin the inquiry by noting that the President of the United States has the fundamental duty, under Art. II, § 1, of the Constitution, to "preserve, protect and defend the Constitution of the United States." Implicit in that duty is the power to protect our Government against those who would subvert or overthrow it by unlawful means. In the discharge of this duty, the President—through the Attorney General—may find it necessary to employ electronic surveillance to obtain intelligence information on the plans of those who plot unlawful acts against the Government. The use of such surveillance in internal security cases has been sanctioned more or less continuously by various Presidents and Attorneys General since July 1946....

\*          \*          \*

... [U]nless Government safeguards its own capacity to function and to preserve the security of its people, society itself could become so disordered that all rights and liberties would be endangered....

But a recognition of these elementary truths does not make the employment by Government of electronic surveillance a welcome development—even when employed with restraint and under judicial supervision. There is, understandably, a deep-seated uneasiness and apprehension that this capability will be used to intrude upon cherished privacy of law-abiding citizens. We look to the Bill of Rights to safeguard this privacy. Though physical entry of the home is the chief evil against which the wording of the Fourth Amendment is directed, its broader spirit now shields private speech from unreasonable surveillance....

\*          \*          \*

### III

As the Fourth Amendment is not absolute in its terms, our task is to examine and balance the basic values at stake in this case: the duty of Government to protect the domestic security, and the potential danger posed by unreasonable surveillance to individual privacy and free expression. If the legitimate need of Government to safeguard domestic security requires the use of electronic surveillance, the question is whether the needs of citizens for privacy and free expression may not be better protected by requiring a warrant before such surveillance is undertaken. We must also ask whether a warrant requirement would unduly frustrate the efforts of Government to protect itself from acts of subversion and overthrow directed against it.

\*     \*     \*

... Fourth Amendment freedoms cannot properly be guaranteed if domestic security surveillances may be conducted solely within the discretion of the Executive Branch. The Fourth Amendment does not contemplate the executive officers of Government as neutral and disinterested magistrates. Their duty and responsibility are to enforce the laws, to investigate, and to prosecute. ... But those charged with this investigative and prosecutorial duty should not be the sole judges of when to utilize constitutionally sensitive means in pursuing their tasks. The historical judgment, which the Fourth Amendment accepts, is that unreviewed executive discretion may yield too readily to pressures to obtain incriminating evidence and overlook potential invasions of privacy and protected speech.

\*     \*     \*

... We recognize, as we have before, the constitutional basis of the President's domestic security role, but we think it must be exercised in a manner compatible with the Fourth Amendment. In this case we hold that this requires an appropriate prior warrant procedure.

We cannot accept the Government's argument that internal security matters are too subtle and complex for judicial evaluation. Courts regularly deal with the most difficult issues of our society. There is no reason to believe that federal judges will be insensitive to or uncomprehending of the issues involved in domestic security cases. Certainly courts can recognize that domestic security surveillance involves different considerations from the surveillance of "ordinary crime." If the threat is too subtle or complex for our senior law enforcement officers to convey its significance to a court, one may question whether there is probable cause for surveillance.

\*     \*     \*

... We do hold, however, that prior judicial approval is required for the type of domestic security surveillance involved in this case and that such approval may be made in accordance with such reasonable standards as the Congress may prescribe.

## V

As the surveillance of Plamondon's conversations was unlawful, because conducted without prior judicial approval, the courts below correctly held that *Alderman v. United States* is controlling and that it requires disclosure to the accused of his own impermissibly intercepted conversations. As stated in *Alderman*, "[T]he trial court can and should, where appropriate, place a defendant and his counsel under enforceable orders against unwarranted disclosure of the materials which they may be entitled to inspect."

The judgment of the Court of Appeals is hereby *Affirmed.*

## 353 " 'I do solemnly swear ... that I will uphold and defend the Constitution' " (1972)

Since our earliest history, the nation's courts have upheld the government's right to insist not only on a citizen's loyal and lawful conduct but also on an oath of loyalty to the Constitution, to be administered to public officials and employees. In 1972, the Supreme Court of the United States once more approved such a requirement. This case involved a Commonwealth of Massachusetts loyalty oath imposed on a person hired as a research sociologist by Boston State Hospital.

☆ 353 *Cole v. Richardson*

405 U.S. 676 (1972).

Mr. Chief Justice BURGER delivered the opinion of the Court.

In this appeal we review the decision of the three-judge District Court holding a Massachusetts loyalty oath unconstitutional.

... The oath is as follows:

> I do solemnly swear (or affirm) that I will uphold and defend the Constitution of the United States of America and the Constitution of the Commonwealth of Massachusetts and that I will oppose the overthrow of the government of the United States of America or of this Commonwealth by force, violence or by any illegal or unconstitutional method.

\*     \*     \*

A three-judge District Court held the oath statute unconstitutional and enjoined the appellants from applying the statute to prohibit Mrs. Richardson from working for Boston State Hospital. The District Court found ... that the "oppose the overthrow" clause was "fatally vague and unspecific," and therefore a violation of First Amendment rights. The court granted the requested injunction but denied the claim for damages.

\*     \*     \*

A review of the oath cases in this Court will put the instant oath into context. We have made clear that neither federal nor state government may condition employment on taking oaths that impinge on rights guaranteed by the First and Fourteenth Amendments respectively, as for example those relating to political beliefs. Nor may employment be conditioned on an oath that one has not engaged, or will not engage, in protected speech activities such as the following: criticizing institutions of government; discussing political doctrine that approves the overthrow of certain forms of government; and supporting candidates for political office. Employment may not be conditioned on an oath denying past, or abjuring future, associational activities within constitutional protection; such protected activities include membership in organizations having illegal purposes unless one knows of the purpose and shares a specific intent to promote the illegal purpose. . . . And, finally, an oath may not be so vague that " 'men of common intelligence must necessarily guess at its meaning and differ as to its application, [because such an oath] violates the first essential of due process of law.' " Concern for vagueness in the oath cases has been especially great because uncertainty as to an oath's meaning may deter individuals from engaging in constitutionally protected activity conceivably within the scope of the oath.

\*     \*     \*

The purpose of the oath is clear on its face. We cannot presume that the Massachusetts Legislature intended by its use of such general terms as "uphold," "defend," and "oppose" to impose obligations of specific, positive action on oath takers. Any such construction would raise serious questions whether the oath was so vague as to amount to a denial of due process.

\*     \*     \*

Since there is no constitutionally protected right to overthrow a government by force, violence, or illegal or unconstitutional means, no constitutional right is infringed by an oath to abide by the constitutional system in the future. . . .

Mr. Justice DOUGLAS, dissenting.

\*     \*     \*

I conclude that whether the First Amendment is read restrictively or literally as Jefferson would have read it, the oath which the District Court struck down is plainly unconstitutional. I would affirm its judgment.

Mr. Justice MARSHALL, with whom Mr. Justice BRENNAN joins, dissenting.

\*     \*     \*

When faced with an "imminent clear and present danger," governments may be able to compel citizens to do things that would ordinarily be beyond their authority to mandate. But, such emergency governmental power is a far cry from compelling every state employee in advance of any such danger to promise in any and all circumstances to conform speech and conduct to opposing an "overthrow" of the government. The Constitution severely circumscribes the power of government to force its citizens to perform symbolic gestures of loyalty. . . .

\*     \*     \*

Before concluding, I add one additional word about loyalty oaths in general. . . . Loyalty oaths do not have a very pleasant history in this country. Whereas they may be developed initially as a means of fostering power and confidence in government, there is a danger that they will swell "into an instrument of thought control and a means of enforcing complete political conformity." Asper, *The Long and Unhappy History of Loyalty Testing in Maryland.* Within the limits of the Constitution it is, of course, for the legislators to weigh the utility of the oaths and their potential dangers and to strike a balance. But, as a people, we should always keep in mind the words of Mr. Justice Black, concurring in *Speiser v. Randall.*

> Loyalty oaths, as well as other contemporary "security measures," tend to stifle all forms of unorthodox or unpopular thinking or expression — the kind of thought and expression which has played such a vital and beneficial role in the history of this Nation. The result is a stultifying conformity which in the end may well turn out to be more destructive to our free society than foreign agents could ever hope to be. . . . I am certain that loyalty to the United States can never be secured by the endless proliferation of "loyalty" oaths; loyalty must arise spontaneously from the hearts of people who love their country and respect their government.

Accordingly, I would affirm the decision of the District Court.

## 354 "military intrusion into civilian affairs" (1972)

Press disclosures of the army intelligence branch's interest in and surveillance of the activities of Vietnam War protesters and draft resisters led to an attempt to obtain judicial condemnation of these practices. In the opinion by Chief Justice Burger, the court refused to consider whether such activities were lawful, concluding that no injury to the interests of the plaintiffs had resulted from the army's surveillance program. Justice Douglas, nevertheless, termed the army's activities "a cancer on the body politic."

☆ 354 *Laird v. Tatum*

408 U.S. 1 (1972).

MR. CHIEF JUSTICE BURGER delivered the opinion of the Court.

Respondents brought this class action in the District Court seeking declaratory and injunctive relief on their claim that their rights were being invaded by the Department of the Army's alleged "surveillance of lawful and peaceful civilian political activity." The petitioners in response described the activity as "gathering by lawful means ... [and] maintaining and using in their intelligence activities ... information relating to potential or actual civil disturbances [or] street demonstrations." ...

\*      \*      \*

I

There is in the record a considerable amount of background information regarding the activities of which respondents complained.... A brief review of that information is helpful to an understanding of the issues.

The President is authorized by 10 U.S.C. § 331 to make use of the armed forces to quell insurrection and other domestic violence if and when the conditions described in that section obtain within one of the States. Pursuant to those provisions, President Johnson ordered federal troops to assist local authorities at the time of the civil disorders in Detroit, Michigan, in the summer of 1967 and during the disturbances that followed the assassination of Dr. Martin Luther King. Prior to the Detroit disorders, the Army had a general contingency plan for providing such assistance to local authorities, but the 1967 experience led Army authorities to believe that more attention should be given to such preparatory planning. The data-gathering system here involved is said to have been established in connection with the development of more detailed and specific contingency planning designed to permit the Army, when called upon to assist local authorities, to be able to respond effectively with a minimum of force. As the Court of Appeals observed,

> In performing this type function the Army is essentially a police force or the back-up of a local police force. To quell disturbances or to prevent further disturbances the Army needs the same tools and, most importantly, the same information to which local police forces have access. Since the Army is sent into territory almost invariably unfamiliar to most soldiers and their commanders, their need for information is likely to be greater than that of the hometown policeman.
>
>  No logical argument can be made for compelling the military to use *blind* force. When force is employed it should be intelligently directed, and

this depends upon having reliable information—in time. As Chief Justice John Marshall said of Washington, "A general must be governed by his intelligence and must regulate his measures by his information. It is his duty to obtain correct information...." So we take it as undeniable that the military, i.e., the Army, need a certain amount of information in order to perform their constitutional and statutory missions.

The system put into operation as a result of the Army's 1967 experience consisted essentially of the collection of information about public activities that were thought to have at least some potential for civil disorder, the reporting of that information to Army Intelligence headquarters at Fort Holabird, Maryland, the dissemination of these reports from headquarters to major Army posts around the country, and the storage of the reported information in a computer data bank located at Fort Holabird. The information itself was collected by a variety of means, but it is significant that the principal sources of information were the news media and publications in general circulation. Some of the information came from Army Intelligence agents who attended meetings that were open to the public and who wrote field reports describing the meetings, giving such data as the name of the sponsoring organization, the identity of speakers, the approximate number of persons in attendance, and an indication of whether any disorder occurred. And still other information was provided to the Army by civilian law enforcement agencies.

\*      \*      \*

By early 1970 Congress became concerned with the scope of the Army's domestic surveillance system; hearings on the matter were held before the Subcommittee on Constitutional Rights of the Senate Committee on the Judiciary. Meanwhile, the Army, in the course of a review of the system, ordered a significant reduction in its scope. For example, information referred to in the complaint as the "blacklist" and the records in the computer data bank at Fort Holabird were found unnecessary and were destroyed, along with other related records. One copy of all the material relevant to the instant suit was retained, however, because of the pendency of this litigation. The review leading to the destruction of these records was said at the time the District Court ruled on petitioners' motion to dismiss to be a "continuing" one and the Army's policies at that time were represented as follows in a letter from the Under Secretary of the Army to Senator Sam J. Ervin, Chairman of the Senate Subcommittee on Constitutional Rights:

> [R]eports concerning civil disturbances will be limited to matters of immediate concern to the Army—that is, reports concerning outbreaks of

violence or incidents with a high potential for violence beyond the capability of state and local police and the National Guard to control. These reports will be collected by liaison with other Government agencies and reported by teletype to the Intelligence Command. They will not be placed in a computer.... These reports are destroyed 60 days after publication or 60 days after the end of the disturbance. This limited reporting system will ensure that the Army is prepared to respond to whatever directions the President may issue in civil disturbance situations and without "watching" the lawful activities of civilians.

In briefs for petitioners filed with this Court, the Solicitor General has called our attention to certain directives issued by the Army and the Department of Defense subsequent to the District Court's dismissal of the action; these directives indicate that the Army's review of the needs of its domestic intelligence activities has indeed been a continuing one and that those activities have since been significantly reduced.

## II

... It was the view of the District Court that respondents failed to allege any action on the part of the Army that was unlawful.... The respondents' ... claim, simply stated, is that they disagree with the judgments made by the Executive Branch with respect to the type and amount of information the Army needs and that the very existence of the Army's data-gathering system produces a constitutionally impermissible chilling effect upon the exercise of their First Amendment rights. That alleged "chilling" effect may perhaps be seen as arising from respondents' very perception of the system as inappropriate to the Army's role under our form of government, or as arising from respondents' belief that it is inherently dangerous for the military to be concerned with activities in the civilian sector, or as arising from respondents' less generalized yet speculative apprehensiveness that the Army may at some future date misuse the information in some way that would cause direct harm to respondents. Allegations of a subjective "chill" are not an adequate substitute for a claim of specific present objective harm or a threat of specific future harm; "the federal courts established pursuant to Article III of the Constitution do not render advisory opinions."

Stripped to its essentials, what respondents appear to be seeking is a broad-scale investigation, conducted by themselves as private parties armed with the subpoena power of a federal district court and the power of cross-examination, to probe into the Army's intelligence-gathering activities, with the district court determining at the conclusion of that investigation the extent to which those activities

may or may not be appropriate to the Army's mission. The following excerpt from the opinion of the Court of Appeals suggests the broad sweep implicit in its holding:

> Apparently in the judgment of the civilian head of the Army not everything being done in the operation of this intelligence system was necessary to the performance of the military mission. *If the Secretary of the Army can formulate and implement such judgment based on facts within his Departmental knowledge, the United States District Court can hear evidence, ascertain the facts, and decide what, if any, further restrictions on the complained-of activities are called for* to confine the military to their legitimate sphere of activity and to protect [respondents'] allegedly infringed constitutional rights. (Emphasis added)

Carried to its logical end, this approach would have the federal courts as virtually continuing monitors of the wisdom and soundness of Executive action; such a role is appropriate for the Congress acting through its committees and the "power of the purse"; it is not the role of the judiciary, absent actual present or immediately threatened injury resulting from unlawful governmental action.

We, of course, intimate no view with respect to the propriety or desirability, from a policy standpoint, of the challenged activities of the Department of the Army; our conclusion is a narrow one, namely, that on this record the respondents have not presented a case for resolution by the courts.

The concerns of the Executive and Legislative Branches in response to disclosure of the Army surveillance activities—and indeed the claims alleged in the complaint—reflect a traditional and strong resistance of Americans to any military intrusion into civilian affairs. That tradition has deep roots in our history and found early expression, for example, in the Third Amendment's explicit prohibition against quartering soldiers in private homes without consent and in the constitutional provisions for civilian control of the military. Those prohibitions are not directly presented by this case, but their philosophical underpinnings explain our traditional insistence on limitations on military operations in peacetime. Indeed, when presented with claims of judicially cognizable injury resulting from military intrusion into the civilian sector, federal courts are fully empowered to consider claims of those asserting such injury; there is nothing in our Nation's history or in this Court's decided cases, including our holding today, that can properly be seen as giving any indication that actual or threatened injury by reason of unlawful activities of the military would go unnoticed or unremedied.

*Reversed.*

MR. JUSTICE DOUGLAS, with whom MR. JUSTICE MARSHALL concurs, dissenting.

## I

If Congress had passed a law authorizing the armed services to establish surveillance over the civilian population, a most serious constitutional problem would be presented. There is, however, no law authorizing surveillance over civilians, which in this case the Pentagon concededly had undertaken. The question is whether such authority may be implied. One can search the Constitution in vain for any such authority.

\* \* \*

[T]he Armed Services—as distinguished from the "militia"—are not regulatory agencies or bureaus that may be created as Congress desires and granted such powers as seem necessary and proper. The authority to provide rules "governing" the Armed Services means the grant of authority to the Armed Services to govern themselves, not the authority to govern civilians. Even when "martial law" is declared, as it often has been, its appropriateness is subject to judicial review.

Our tradition reflects a desire for civilian supremacy and subordination of military power. The tradition goes back to the Declaration of Independence, in which it was recited that the King "has affected to render the Military independent of and superior to the Civil power." Thus, we have the "militia" restricted to domestic use, the restriction of appropriations to the "armies" to two years, Art. I, § 8, and the grant of command over the armies and the militia when called into actual service of the United States to the President, our chief civilian officer. . . .

\* \* \*

The action in turning the "armies" loose on surveillance of civilians was a gross repudiation of our traditions. The military, though important to us, is subservient and restricted purely to military missions. . . .

The act of turning the military loose on civilians even if sanctioned by an Act of Congress, which it has not been, would raise serious and profound constitutional questions. Standing as it does only on brute power and Pentagon policy, it must be repudiated as a usurpation dangerous to the civil liberties on which free men are dependent. For, as Senator Sam Ervin has said, "[T]his claim of an inherent executive branch power of investigation and surveillance on the basis of people's beliefs and attitudes may be more of a threat to our internal security than any enemies beyond our borders."

## II

The claim that respondents have no standing to challenge the Army's surveillance of them and the other members of the class they seek to represent is too transparent for serious argument. The surveillance of the Army over the civilian sector—a part of society hitherto immune from its control—is a serious charge. It is alleged that the Army maintains files on the membership, ideology, programs, and practices of virtually every activist political group in the country, including groups such as the Southern Christian Leadership Conference, Clergy and Laymen United Against the War in Vietnam, the American Civil Liberties Union, Women's Strike for Peace, and the National Association for the Advancement of Colored People. The Army uses undercover agents to infiltrate these civilian groups and to reach into confidential files of students and other groups. The Army moves as a secret group among civilian audiences, using cameras and electronic ears for surveillance. The data it collects are distributed to civilian officials in state, federal, and local governments and to each military intelligence unit and troop command under the Army's jurisdiction (both here and abroad); and these data are stored in one or more data banks.

Those are the allegations; and the charge is that the purpose and effect of the system of surveillance is to harass and intimidate the respondents and to deter them from exercising their rights of political expression, protest, and dissent "by invading their privacy, damaging their reputations, adversely affecting their employment and their opportunities for employment, and in other ways." Their fear is that "permanent reports of their activities will be maintained in the Army's data bank, and their 'profiles' will appear in the so-called 'Blacklist' and that all of this information will be released to numerous federal and state agencies upon request."

Judge Wilkey, speaking for the Court of Appeals, properly inferred that this Army surveillance "exercises a *present inhibiting effect* on their full expression and utilization of their First Amendment rights." . . .

\* \* \*

The present controversy is not a remote, imaginary conflict. Respondents were targets of the Army's surveillance. First, the surveillance was not casual but massive and comprehensive. Second, the intelligence reports were regularly and widely circulated and were exchanged with reports of the FBI, state and municipal police departments, and the CIA. Third, the Army's surveillance was not collecting material in public records but staking out teams of agents, infiltrating undercover agents, creating command posts inside meetings, posing as press photographers and newsmen, posing as TV newsmen, posing as students, and shadowing public figures.

Finally, we know from the hearings conducted by Senator Ervin that the Army has misused or abused its reporting functions. Thus, Senator Ervin concluded that reports of the Army have been "taken from the Intelligence Command's highly inaccurate civil disturbance teletype and filed in Army dossiers on persons who have held, or were being considered for, security clearances, thus contaminating what are supposed to be investigative reports with unverified gossip and rumor. This practice directly jeopardized the employment and employment opportunities of persons seeking sensitive positions with the federal government or defense industry."

Surveillance of civilians is none of the Army's constitutional business and Congress has not undertaken to entrust it with any such function. The fact that since this litigation started the Army's surveillance may have been cut back is not an end of the matter. Whether there has been an actual cutback or whether the announcements are merely a ruse can be determined only after a hearing in the District Court. We are advised by an *amicus curiae* brief filed by a group of former Army Intelligence Agents that Army surveillance of civilians is rooted in secret programs of long standing:

> Army intelligence has been maintaining an unauthorized watch over civilian political activity for nearly 30 years. Nor is this the first time that Army intelligence has, without notice to its civilian superiors, overstepped its mission. From 1917 to 1924, the Corps of Intelligence Police maintained a massive surveillance of civilian political activity which involved the use of hundreds of civilian informants, the infiltration of civilian organizations and the seizure of dissenters and unionists, sometimes without charges. That activity was opposed—then as now—by civilian officials on those occasions when they found out about it, but it continued unabated until post-war disarmament and economies finally eliminated the bureaucracy that conducted it.

This case involves a cancer in our body politic. It is a measure of the disease which afflicts us. Army surveillance, like Army regimentation, is at war with the principles of the First Amendment. Those who already walk submissively will say there is no cause for alarm. But submissiveness is not our heritage. The First Amendment was designed to allow rebellion to remain as our heritage. The Constitution was designed to keep government off the backs of people. The Bill of Rights was added to keep the precincts of belief and expression, of the press, of political and social activities free from surveillance. The Bill of Rights was designed to keep agents of government and official eavesdroppers away from assemblies of people. The aim was to allow men to be free and independent and to assert their rights against government. There can be no influence more paralyzing of that objective than Army surveillance. When an intelligence officer looks over every nonconformist's shoulder in the library, or walks invisibly by his side in a picket line, or infiltrates his club, the American once extolled as the voice of liberty heard around the world no longer is cast in the image which Jefferson and Madison designed, but more in the Russian image.

## 355 "whenever . . . American citizens wish to meet and talk with an alien" (1972)

The authority of the government to prevent a self-confessed "revolutionary Marxist" journalist and editor from entering the United States for a six-day speaking tour, which included participation in a conference at Stanford University, was upheld in 1972. The claim that the refusal to allow an alien scholar entry into the country violated the First Amendment rights of American academics and students was considered "too much" by the court. The dissenting justices, emphasizing that Dr. Mandel's trip involved nothing but a series of scholarly conferences and lectures, characterized the exclusion as "governmental over-reacting."

☆ 355 *Kleindienst v. Mandel*

408 U.S. 753 (1972).

MR. JUSTICE BLACKMUN delivered the opinion of the Court.

The appellees have framed the issue here as follows:

> Does appellants' action in refusing to allow an alien scholar to enter the country to attend academic meetings violate the First Amendment rights of American scholars and students who had invited him?

Expressed in statutory terms, the question is whether [sections of] the Immigration and Nationality Act of 1952, providing that certain aliens "shall be ineligible to receive visas and shall be excluded from admission into the United States" unless the Attorney General, in his discretion, upon recommendation by the Secretary of State or a consular officer, waives inadmissibility and approves temporary admission, are unconstitutional as applied here in that they deprive American citizens of freedom of speech guaranteed by the First Amendment.

The challenged provisions of the statute are:

> Section 212(a). Except as otherwise provided in this Act, the following classes of aliens shall be

ineligible to receive visas and shall be excluded from admission into the United States:

\*          \*          \*

(28) Aliens who are, or at any time have been, members of any of the following classes:

\*          \*          \*

(D) Aliens not within any of the other provisions of this paragraph who advocate the economic, international, and governmental doctrines of world communism or the establishment in the United States of a totalitarian dictatorship. . . .

\*          \*          \*

(G) Aliens who write or publish . . . (v) the economic, international, and governmental doctrines of world communism or the establishment in the United States of a totalitarian dictatorship; . . . (d)

\*          \*          \*

(3) Except as provided in this subsection, an alien (A) who is applying for a nonimmigrant visa and is known or believed by the consular officer to be ineligible for such visa under one or more of the paragraphs enumerated in subsection (a) . . . may, after approval by the Attorney General of a recommendation by the Secretary of State or by the consular officer that the alien be admitted temporarily despite his inadmissibility, be granted such a visa and may be admitted into the United States temporarily as a nonimmigrant in the discretion of the Attorney General. . . .

## I

Ernest E. Mandel resides in Brussels, Belgium, and is a Belgian citizen. He is a professional journalist and is editor-in-chief of the Belgian Left Socialist weekly *La Gauche.* He is author of a two-volume work entitled *Marxist Economic Theory* published in 1969. He asserted in his visa applications that he is not a member of the Communist Party. He has described himself, however, as "a revolutionary Marxist." He does not dispute that he advocates the economic, governmental, and international doctrines of world communism.

Mandel was admitted to the United States temporarily in 1962 and again in 1968. On the first visit he came as a working journalist. On the second he accepted invitations to speak at a number of universities and colleges. On each occasion, although apparently he was not then aware of it, his admission followed a finding of ineligibility under § 212(a)(28), and the Attorney General's exercise of discretion to admit him temporarily, on recommendation of the Secretary of State, as § 212(d)(3)(A) permits.

On September 8, 1969, Mandel applied to the American Consul in Brussels for a nonimmigrant visa to enter the United States in October for a six-day period, during which he would participate in a conference on Technology and the Third World at Stanford University. He had been invited to Stanford by the Graduate Student Association there. The invitation stated that John Kenneth Galbraith would present the keynote address and that Mandel would be expected to participate in an ensuing panel discussion and to give a major address the following day. . . .

On October 23 the Consul at Brussels informed Mandel orally that his application of September 8 had been refused. This was confirmed in writing on October 30. The Consul's letter advised him of the finding of inadmissibility under § 212(a)(28) in 1962, the waivers in that year and in 1968, and the current denial of a waiver. . . . The Department of State, by a letter dated November 6 from its Bureau of Security and Consular Affairs to Mandel's New York attorney, asserted that the earlier waivers had been granted on condition that Mandel conform to his itinerary and limit his activities to the stated purposes of his trip, but that on his 1968 visit he had engaged in activities beyond the stated purposes. For this reason, it was said, a waiver "was not sought in connection with his September visa application." . . .

\*          \*          \*

Plaintiff-appellees claim that the statutes are unconstitutional on their face and as applied in that they deprive the American plaintiffs of their First and Fifth Amendment rights. Specifically, these plaintiffs claim that the statutes prevent them from hearing and meeting with Mandel in person for discussions, in contravention of the First Amendment; that § 212(a)(28) denies them equal protection by permitting entry of "rightists" but not "leftists" and that the same section deprives them of procedural due process; that § 212(d)(3)(A) is an unconstitutional delegation of congressional power to the Attorney General because of its broad terms, lack of standards, and lack of prescribed procedures. . . .

\*          \*          \*

## III

It is clear that Mandel personally, as an unadmitted and nonresident alien, had no constitutional right of entry to this country as a nonimmigrant or otherwise.

\*          \*          \*

The case, therefore, comes down to the narrow issue whether the First Amendment confers upon the appellee professors, because they wish to hear, speak, and debate with Mandel in person, the ability to determine that Mandel should be permitted to enter the country or, in other words, to compel the Attorney General to allow Mandel's admission.

\*          \*          \*

IV

\*       \*       \*

The Government . . . argues that exclusion of Mandel involves no restriction on First Amendment rights at all since what is restricted is "only action — the action of the alien in coming into this country." . . .

The Government also suggests that the First Amendment is inapplicable because appellees have free access to Mandel's ideas through his books and speeches, and because "technological developments," such as tapes or telephone hook-ups, readily supplant his physical presence. . . .

V

\*       \*       \*

Appellees' First Amendment argument would prove too much. In almost every instance of an alien excludable under § 212(a)(28), there are probably those who would wish to meet and speak to him. The ideas of most such aliens might not be so influential as those of Mandel, nor his American audience so numerous, nor the planned discussion forums so impressive. But the First Amendment does not protect only the articulate, the well known, and the popular. Were we to endorse the proposition that governmental power to withhold a waiver must yield whenever a bona fide claim is made that American citizens wish to meet and talk with an alien excludable under § 212(a)(28), one of two unsatisfactory results would necessarily ensue. Either every claim would prevail, in which case the plenary discretionary authority Congress granted the Executive becomes a nullity, or courts in each case would be required to weigh the strength of the audience's interest against that of the Government in refusing a waiver to the particular alien applicant, according to some as yet undetermined standard. . . .

\*       \*       \*

. . . In the case of an alien excludable under § 212(a)(28), Congress has delegated conditional exercise of this power to the Executive. We hold that when the Executive exercises this power negatively on the basis of a facially legitimate and bona fide reason, the courts will neither look behind the exercise of that discretion, nor test it by balancing its justification against the First Amendment interests of those who seek personal communication with the applicant. What First Amendment or other grounds may be available for attacking exercise of discretion for which no justification whatsoever is advanced is a question we neither address nor decide in this case.

*Reversed.*

MR. JUSTICE DOUGLAS, dissenting.

\*       \*       \*

Can the Attorney General under the broad discretion entrusted in him decide

that one who maintains that the earth is round can be excluded?

that no one who believes in the Darwinian theory shall be admitted?

that those who promote a Rule of Law to settle international differences rather than a Rule of Force may be barred?

that a genetic biologist who lectures on the way to create life by one sex alone is beyond the pale?

that an exponent of plate tectonics can be barred?

that one should be excluded who taught that Jesus when he arose from the Sepulcher, went east (not up) and became a teacher at Hemis Monastery in the Himalayas?

I put the issue that bluntly because national security is not involved. Nor is the infiltration of saboteurs. The Attorney General stands astride our international terminals that bring people here to bar those whose ideas are not acceptable to him. Even assuming, *arguendo*, that those on the outside seeking admission have no standing to complain, those who hope to benefit from the traveler's lectures do.

\*       \*       \*

As a matter of statutory construction, I conclude that Congress never undertook to entrust the Attorney General with the discretion to pick and choose among the ideological offerings which alien lecturers tender from our platforms, allowing those palatable to him and disallowing others. . . .

\*       \*       \*

MR. JUSTICE MARSHALL, with whom MR. JUSTICE BRENNAN joins, dissenting.

\*       \*       \*

Dr. Mandel has written about his exclusion, concluding that "[i]t demonstrates a lack of confidence" on the part of our Government "in the capacity of its supporters to combat Marxism on the battleground of ideas." He observes that he "would not be carrying any high explosives, if I had come, but only, as I did before, my revolutionary views which are well known to the public." And he wryly notes that "[i]n the nineteenth century the British ruling class, which was sure of itself, permitted Karl Marx to live as an exile in England for almost forty years."

It is undisputed that Dr. Mandel's brief trip would involve nothing but a series of scholarly conferences and lectures. . . . Nothing is served — least of all our standing in the international community — by Mandel's exclusion. In blocking his admission, the Government has departed from the basic traditions of our country, its fearless acceptance of free discussion. By now deferring to the Executive, this Court departs from its own best role as the guardian of individual liberty in the face of governmental overreaching. . . .

## 356 "states of national emergency" (1973)

The Special Senate Committee on the Termination of the National Emergency published its report in November 1973, some ten months after the agreement concluding the Vietnam War. The report focused on the emergency power statutes that delegated to the president extraordinary authority in times of national emergency. After surveying the exercise of emergency powers by various presidents, the committee summarized the existing status of the emergency power statutes and offered suggestions on how Congress and the executive could produce more effective and better coordinated procedures for the exercise of executive power in future times of war or national emergency.

The committee contrasted the increased presidential use of emergency power since Theodore Roosevelt propounded his "stewardship theory" of presidential power with the reluctance of such presidents as Taft and Wilson to exercise any power not delegated explicitly to them. The committee also reviewed Franklin D. Roosevelt's first use of emergency powers to deal with a nonmilitary emergency—the Depression. Many of the New Deal emergency measures were similar to the measures previously used only during times of war.

Recent history reflected a change in the meaning of "emergency" and an increase in presidential declarations of emergency to justify greater executive discretion. In 1973, when the Special Senate Committee published this report, four declared states of national emergency were in effect, and 470 emergency power statutes were on the books. Many of these, passed hurriedly during times of crisis, provided no congressional oversight or automatic termination.

Senator Frank Church, a member of the committee, recognized that under these powers one man in the White House, in a "plethora of particular ways," can "control the lives of all Americans . . . whenever he decides to do so without reference to Congress." Although calling for preservation of the means for a presidential exercise of emergency power when necessary, the committee recommended that Congress formally end the state of emergency then in effect. In 1976 Congress passed the National Emergencies Act, Pub. L. 94-412, 90 Stat. 1255, in an effort to better define the executive's emergency power.

☆ 356 Emergency Power Statutes: Provisions of Federal Law Now in Effect Delegating to the Executive Department Executive Extraordinary Authority in Time of National Emergency (1973)

S. Rep. No. 549, 93d Cong., 1st Sess. (1973).

### A. A BRIEF HISTORICAL SKETCH OF THE ORIGINS OF EMERGENCY POWERS NOW IN FORCE

A majority of the people of the United States have lived all of their lives under emergency rule. For 40 years, freedoms and governmental procedures guaranteed by the Constitution have, in varying degrees, been abridged by laws brought into force by states of national emergency. The problem of how a constitutional democracy reacts to great crises, however, far antedates the Great Depression. As a philosophical issue, its origins reach back to the Greek city-states and the Roman Republic. And, in the United States, actions taken by the Government in times of great crises have—from, at least, the Civil War—in important ways shaped the present phenomenon of a permanent state of national emergency.

American political theory of emergency government was derived and enlarged from John Locke, the English political-philosopher whose thought influenced the authors of the Constitution. Locke argued that the threat of national crisis—unforeseen, sudden, and potentially catastrophic—required the creation of broad executive emergency powers to be exercised by the Chief Executive in situations where the legislative authority had not provided a means or procedure of remedy. Referring to emergency power in the 14th chapter of his *Second Treatise on Civil Government* as "prerogative," Locke suggested that it:

> . . . should be left to the discretion of him that has the executive power . . . since in some governments the lawmaking power is not always in being and is usually too numerous, and so too slow for the dispatch requisite to executions, and because, also it is impossible to foresee and so by laws to provide for all accidents and necessities that may concern the public, or make such laws as will do no harm, if they are executed with an inflexible rigour on all occasions and upon all persons that may come in their way, therefore there is a latitude left to the executive power to do many things of choice which the laws do not prescribe.

To what extent the Founding Fathers adhered to this view of the executive role in emergencies is a much disputed issue. Whatever their conceptions of this role, its development in practice has been based largely on the manner in which individual President's have viewed their office and its functions. . . .

\*     \*     \*

Lincoln had drawn most heavily upon his power as Commander-in-Chief; Wilson exercised emergency power on the basis of old statutes and sweeping new legislation—thus drawing on congressional delegation as a source of authority. The most significant Wilsonian innovations were economic, including a wide array of defense and war agencies, modeled to some extent upon British wartime precedents....

Following the Allied victory, Wilson relinquished his wartime authority and asked Congress to repeal the emergency statutes, enacted to fight more effectively the war. Only a food-control measure and the 1917 Trading With the Enemy Act were retained. This procedure of terminating emergency powers when the particular emergency itself has, in fact, ended has not been consistently followed by his successors.

The next major development in the use of executive emergency powers came under Franklin D. Roosevelt. The Great Depression had already overtaken the country by the time of Roosevelt's inauguration and confronted him with a totally different crisis. This emergency, unlike those of the past, presented a nonmilitary threat. The Roosevelt administration, however, conceived the economic crisis to be a calamity equally as great as a war and employed the metaphor of war to emphasize the depression's severity. In his inaugural address, Roosevelt said: "I shall ask the Congress for the one remaining instrument to meet the crisis—broad executive power to wage a war against the emergency, as great as the power that would be given me if we were in fact invaded by a foreign foe."

\*                    \*                    \*

In his first important official act, Roosevelt proclaimed a National Bank Holiday on the basis of the 1917 Trading With the Enemy Act—itself a wartime delegation of power....

The Trading With the Enemy Act had, however, been specifically designed by its originators to meet only *wartime* exigencies. By employing it to meet the demands of the depression, Roosevelt greatly extended the concept of "emergencies" to which expansion of executive power might be applied. And in so doing, he established a pattern that was followed frequently: In time of crisis the President should utilize any statutory authority readily at hand, regardless of its original purposes, with the firm expectation of *ex post facto* congressional concurrence.

Beginning with F.D.R., then, extensive use of delegated powers exercised under an aura of crisis has become a dominant aspect of the presidency. Concomitant with this development has been a demeaning of the significance of "emergency." It became a term used to evoke public and congressional approbation, often bearing little actual relation to events....

Roosevelt and his successor, Harry S. Truman, invoked formal states of emergency to justify extensive delegations of authority during actual times of war. The Korean war, however, by the fact of its never having been officially declared a "war" as such by Congress, further diluted the concept of what constituted circumstances sufficiently critical to warrant the delegation of extraordinary authority to the President.

At the end of the Korean war, moreover, the official state of emergency was not terminated. It is not yet terminated. This may be primarily attributed to the continuance of the Cold War atmosphere which, until recent years, made the imminent threat of hostilities an accepted fact of everyday life, with "emergency" the normal state of affairs....

Besides the 1933 and Korean war emergencies, two other states of declared national emergency remain in existence. On March 23, 1970, confronted by a strike of Postal Service employees, President Nixon declared a national emergency. The following year, on August 15, 1971, Nixon proclaimed another emergency, under which he imposed stringent import controls in order to meet an international monetary crisis. Because of its general language, however, that proclamation could serve as sufficient authority to use a substantial proportion of all the emergency statutes now on the books.

Over the course of at least the last 40 years, then, Presidents have had available an enormous—seemingly expanding and never-ending—range of emergency powers. Indeed, at their fullest extent and during the height of a crisis, these "prerogative" powers appear to be virtually unlimited, confirming Locke's perceptions....

\*                    \*                    \*

The 2,000-year-old problem of how a legislative body in a democratic republic may extend extraordinary powers for use by the executive during times of great crisis and dire emergency—but do so in ways assuring both that such necessary powers will be terminated immediately when the emergency has ended and that normal processes will be resumed—has not yet been resolved in this country. Too few are aware of the existence of emergency powers and their extent, and the problem has never been squarely faced.

B. SUMMARY VIEWS OF THE PRESENT STATUS OF
EMERGENCY POWERS STATUTES

A review of the laws passed since the first state of national emergency was declared in 1933 reveals a consistent pattern of lawmaking. It is a pattern showing that the Congress, through its own actions, transferred awesome magnitudes of power to the executive ostensibly to meet the problems of governing effectively in times of great crisis. Since 1933, Congress has passed or recodified over 470 significant statutes delegating to the President powers that had been the prerogative and responsibility of the Congress since the beginning of the Republic. No charge can be sustained that the Executive branch has usurped powers belonging to the Legislative branch; on the contrary, the transfer of power has been in accord with due process of normal legislative procedures.

*          *          *

Most of the statutes pertaining to emergency powers were passed in times of extreme crisis. Bills drafted in the Executive branch were sent to Congress by the President and, in the case of the most significant laws that are on the books, were approved with only the most perfunctory committee review and virtually no consideration of their effect on civil liberties or the delicate structure of the U.S. Government of divided powers. For example, the economic measures that were passed in 1933 pursuant to the proclamation of March 5, 1933, by President Roosevelt, asserting that a state of national emergency now existed, were enacted in the most turbulent circumstances. There was a total of only 8 hours of debate in both houses. There were no committee reports; indeed, only one copy of the bill was available on the floor.

This pattern of hasty and inadequate consideration was repeated during World War II when another group of laws with vitally significant and far reaching implications was passed. It was repeated during the Korean war and, again, in most recent memory, during the debate on the Tonkin Gulf Resolution passed on August 6, 1964.

*          *          *

The repeal of almost all of the Emergency Detention Act of 1950 was a constructive and necessary step, but the following provision remains:

18 U.S.C. 1383. Restrictions in military areas and zones.
Whoever, contrary to the restrictions applicable thereto, enters, remains in, leaves, or commits any act in any military area or military zone prescribed under the authority of an Executive order of the President, by the Secretary of the Army, or by any military commander designated by the Secretary of the Army, shall, if it appears that he knew or should have known of the existence and extent of the restrictions or order and that his act was in violation thereof, be fined not more than $5,000 or imprisoned not more than one year, or both.

18 U.S.C. 1383 does not appear on its face to be an emergency power. It was used as the basis for internment of Japanese-Americans in World War II. Although it seems to be cast as a permanent power, the legislative history of the section shows that the statute was intended as a World War II emergency

power only, and was not to apply in "normal" peacetime circumstances. Two years ago, the Emergency Detention Act was repealed, yet 18 U.S.C. 1383 has almost the same effect.

Another pertinent question among many, that the Special Committee's work has revealed, concerns the statutory authority for domestic surveillance by the FBI. According to some experts, the authority for domestic surveillance appears to be based upon an Executive Order issued by President Roosevelt during an emergency period. If it is correct that no firm statutory authority exists, then it is reasonable to suggest that the appropriate committees enact proper statutory authority for the FBI with adequate provision for oversight by Congress.

What these examples suggest and what the magnitude of emergency powers affirm is that most of these laws do not provide for congressional oversight or termination. . . .

*          *          *

In the view of the Special Committee, an emergency does not now exist. Congress, therefore, should act in the near future to terminate officially the states of national emergency now in effect.

At the same time, the Special Committee is of the view that it is essential to provide the means for the Executive to act effectively in an emergency. It is reasonable to have a body of laws in readiness to delegate to the President extraordinary powers to use in times of real national emergency. The portion of the concurring opinion given by Justice Jackson in the *Youngstown Steel* case with regard to emergency powers provides sound and pertinent guidelines for the maintenance of such a body of emergency laws kept in readiness to be used in times of extreme crisis. Justice Jackson, supporting the majority opinion that the "President's power must stem either from an act of Congress or from the Constitution itself" wrote:

The appeal, however, that we declare the existence of inherent powers *ex necessitate* to meet an emergency asks us to do what many think would be wise, although it is something the forefathers omitted. They knew what emergencies were, knew the pressures they engender for authoritative action, knew, too, how they afford a ready pretext for usurpation. We may also suspect that they suspected that emergency powers would tend to kindle emergencies. Aside from suspension of the privilege of the writ of habeas corpus in time of rebellion or invasion, when the public safety may require it, they made no express provision for exercise of extraordinary authority because of a crisis. I do not think we rightfully may so amend their work, and, if we could, I am not convinced it would be wise to do so, although many modern nations have forthrightly recognized that war and economic crises may upset the normal balance between liberty and authority. Their experience with emergency powers may not be irrelevant to the argument here that we should say that the Executive, of his own volition, can invest himself with undefined emergency powers.

Germany, after the First World War, framed the Weimar Constitution, designed to secure her liberties in the Western tradition. However, the President of the Republic, without concurrence of the Reichstag, was empowered temporarily to suspend any or all individual rights if public safety and order were seriously disturbed or endangered. This proved a temptation to every government, whatever its shade of opinion, and in 13 years suspension of rights was invoked on more than 250 occasions. Finally, Hitler persuaded President Von Hindenburg to suspend all such rights, and they were never restored.

The French Republic provided for a very different kind of emergency government known as the "state of siege." It differed from the German emergency dictatorship particularly in that emergency powers could not be assumed at will by the Executive but could only be granted as a parliamentary measure. And it did not, as in Germany, result in a suspension or abrogation of law but was a legal institution governed by special legal rules and terminable by parliamentary authority.

Great Britain also has fought both World Wars under a sort of temporary dictatorship created by legislation. As Parliament is not bound by written constitutional limitations, it established a crisis government simply by delegation to its Ministers of a larger measure than usual of its own unlimited power, which is exercised under its supervision by Ministers whom it may dismiss. This has been called the "high-water mark in the voluntary surrender of liberty," but, as Churchill put it, "Parliament stands custodian of these surrendered liberties, and its most sacred duty will be to restore them in their fullness when victory has crowned our exertions and our perseverance." Thus, parliamentary controls made emergency powers compatible with freedom.

This contemporary foreign experience may be inconclusive as to the wisdom of lodging emergency powers somewhere in a modern government. But it suggests that emergency powers are consistent with free government only when their control is lodged elsewhere than in the Executive who exercises them. That is the safeguard that would be nullified by our adoption of the "inherent powers" formula. Nothing in my experience convinces me that such risks are warranted by any real necessity, although such powers would, of course, be an executive convenience.

In the practical working of our Government we already have evolved a technique within the framework of the Constitution by which normal executive powers may be considerably expanded to meet an emergency. Congress may and has granted extraordinary authorities which lie dormant in normal times but may be called into play by the Executive in war or upon proclamation of a national emergency. . . .

In view of the ease, expedition and safety with which Congress can grant and has granted large emergency powers, certainly ample to embrace this crisis, I am quite unimpressed with the argument that we should affirm possession of them without statute. Such power either has no beginning or it has no end. If it exists, it need submit to no legal restraint. I am not alarmed that it would plunge us straightway into dictatorship, but it is at least a step in that wrong direction.

\*            \*            \*

With these guidelines and against the background of experience of the last 40 years, the task that remains for the Special Committee is to determine — in close cooperation with all the Standing Committees of the Senate and all Departments, Commissions, and Agencies of the Executive branch — which of the laws now in force might be of use in a future emergency. Most important, a legislative formula needs to be devised which will provide a regular and consistent procedure by which any emergency provisions are called into force. It will also be necessary to establish a means by which Congress can exercise effective oversight over such actions as are taken pursuant to a state of national emergency as well as providing a regular and consistent procedure for the termination of such grants of authority.

## 357 "to gather political information" (1975)

At two o'clock in the morning, June 17, 1972, after discovery by a security guard, officers of the District of Columbia police arrested five men inside the Democratic Party National Headquarters in the Washington, D.C., Watergate apartment and office complex. On June 18, 1972, former attorney general John Mitchell, in his capacity as President Nixon's campaign manager, denied the men were "operating either on our behalf or with our consent." Five of the seven defendants in the case of *United States v. Barker* first pleaded guilty to seven charges arising out of the break-in. They subsequently filed motions to withdraw those pleas on the grounds that they had sincerely believed the break-ins to be part of a national security mission, and therefore had mistakenly pleaded guilty in order to protect the interests of national intelligence. Six months after the resignation of President Nixon, the Court of Appeals for the District of Columbia, sitting *en banc*, upheld trial judge John Sirica's denial of these motions. The majority and dissenting opinions reflect different attitudes toward the morality of these "foot soldiers."

☆ 357  *United States v. Barker*

514 F.2d 208 (D.C. Cir. 1975), *cert. denied*, 421 U.S. 1013 (1975).

J. SKELLY WRIGHT, Circuit Judge:

Appellants challenge denial by the District Court of their motions to withdraw guilty pleas to seven counts of an indictment arising out of the now-famous "Watergate Break-in." . . .

### I. THE PROCEEDINGS

Appellants were the foot soldiers of the Watergate Break-in. They came to the affair from the anti-Castro movement, centered in Miami's Cuban-American community, and from a long history of service in the Central Intelligence Agency (CIA) and, apparently, in other official or quasi-official agencies specializing in "clandestine" operations. In the early morning hours of June 17, 1972, District of Columbia police found them inside the headquarters of the Democratic Party's National Committee (DNC) in the Watergate office complex. They had entered surreptitiously, picking the locks; they wore rubber surgical gloves to obscure fingerprints; they had been rifling through the DNC's documents and papers and carried with them devices and tools for electronic "bugging" and "wiretapping."

Arrested with them was James McCord, a former CIA agent who was then employed as a security officer by the Committee for Re-Election of the President [Richard M. Nixon] (CRP); the next few days brought the arrest of their immediate supervisors in the bizarre enterprise: E. Howard Hunt, a former CIA agent who was then, or had recently been, employed as a "consultant" to the White House, with an office in that building; and G. Gordon Liddy, a former White House employee who was then employed as General Counsel to the Finance Committee for the Re-Election of the President (FCRP).

The purpose of the operation was to gather political information damaging to the Democratic Party and, by consequence, useful to the President's re-election effort. . . .

*       *       *

Appellants claim they pleaded guilty, suppressing their "defenses," because they honestly, though mistakenly, believed that "national security" considerations required their silence. In testing the adequacy of this explanation, we must look to the circumstances of the case.

These guilty pleas were not ill-considered or offered in haste. In its opening statement the prosecution had outlined an overwhelming case against appellants. The pleas were accepted only after an extraordinarily elaborate procedure, stretching over four days, conducted largely *in camera*, and involving two competent and loyal attorneys. . . .

*       *       *

. . . If appellants had alleged and could demonstrate that some Government official had deceived them about their "patriotic duty" to remain silent, withdrawal of their pleas might be proper. But appellants claim only that various "circumstances"—chiefly Hunt's guilty plea—gave them the *subjective impression* that someone or some agency in the Government wished them to plead guilty. There is not even a direct claim that Hunt told them as much; even if he had, the "Government" cannot be held responsible for actions taken, or rumors spread, by appellants' co-defendants. . . .

*       *       *

In sum, appellants had every chance to discover that their alleged subjective fears and beliefs were unfounded. Yet they insisted on remaining ignorant of their true situation and on "playing games" with the court. We can perceive no reasonable excuse for this course of action.

Thus we find that appellants' guilty pleas were voluntary and knowing; that on allocution appellants deliberately and repeatedly deceived the court; that withdrawal of the pleas eight months after they were entered would prejudice the Government; that appellants' supposed national security reasons for their guilty pleas were based on entirely subjective beliefs, supported only by their allegations; and that these beliefs, if indeed held, were patently unreasonable. . . . [W]e need not decide whether their new-found defenses have legal merit.

*       *       *

MACKINNON, Circuit Judge (dissenting):

*       *       *

While the average citizen may not have chosen to follow appellants' course of action in this situation, to my mind it was not unreasonable for persons with appellants' background and training to believe that they were involved in a national security affair and that it was their duty to go to prison to avoid disclosure of what they knew concerning it. Their actions in court were consistent with and can be explained by this belief. They acted to withdraw their guilty pleas only after sufficient evidence had been produced to conclusively demonstrate to them that their belief had been erroneous. . . . I conclude that this is a proper case for the court to permit withdrawal of a guilty plea when a legally valid defense is asserted.

*       *       *

Both the majority and the prosecutor recognize that these offenses are essentially political. While "custom and practice" is no defense, the political-criminal nature of the charges and the apparent prevalence of such intelligence activity should be parameters in the equation by which the criminal intent of the appellants is judged. What the majority does here, in effect, by failing to recognize the validity of their asserted defenses, is to hold these appellants criminally responsible for not specifically inquiring whether Hunt had obtained the written authorization required. . . . Hunt's representation reasonably conveyed the impression that the Watergate operation was duly authorized and approved. Greater reliance is not required to support a claim of mistake of fact or to come within the recognized exception to mistake of law.

*          *          *

WILKEY, Circuit Judge (dissenting):

*          *          *

. . . Long experience with the CIA, and in secret missions directed against the Castro regime, had taught the appellants the importance of complete reliance on, and obedience to, their supervisor. They were accustomed to operate on a "need-to-know" basis. It did not occur to them to second-guess Hunt's decisions, let alone question his authority.

*          *          *

More important, however, in the circumstances of this case, is the fact that *the appellants' dissemblance with Judge Sirica was completely in keeping with their perceived duty to keep secret the national security aspects of the Watergate operation.* Their purpose was not malicious; they could gain no tactical advantage by it. . . .

Undeniably, this evasive action by the appellants is important, but not, as the majority contends, because it shows bad faith in their dealings with the court. Rather, it provides persuasive evidence of their good faith belief that national security considerations necessitated their silence. . . .

*          *          *

. . . They knew they had a good defense. Their lawyer, Rothblatt, believed so strongly that a defense based on a lack of criminal intent would succeed that he refused to plead them guilty. Yet Hunt had told them they had no defense. In their minds, the signal was clear: the government wanted the national security aspects of the operation, and the activities of the top-secret intelligence agency of which Hunt was an official, kept under wraps. If their leader was prepared to go to jail to protect that information, certainly they were loyal and dedicated enough to follow his lead.

*          *          *

. . . Not only did the government's apparent desire deprive them of their only valid defense, but Hunt had made clear that a guilty plea was man-

dated under the circumstances. The appellants obviously did not want to go to prison, but they felt they had no choice. Theirs was the paradigm of an involuntary plea. . . . The appellants did not make a reasoned decision based on the chances of success at trial of their "national security" defense. They simple accepted that a guilty plea was required of them because the assertion of that defense was incompatible with the necessity for silence. It was not until eight months later, when the actual genesis of the Watergate operation had been revealed in full, that the appellants could make a reasoned decision. . . .

*          *          *

Thus, I conclude that the appellants have presented a valid defense to the charges against them. . . . I would direct the District Court to grant the motion and proceed with trial on the merits.

# 358 "a continuing study of dissident activity" (1975)

On December 22, 1974, the *New York Times* claimed the Central Intelligence Agency (CIA) had violated its legislative charter in conducting a "massive illegal domestic intelligence operation during the Nixon Administration against anti-war movement and other dissident groups in the United States." William Colby, director of the CIA, publicly confirmed the allegations the following month. Subsequent public outcry and the threat of broad congressional inquiries into CIA abuses led President Gerald Ford to create the Commission on CIA Activities in January 1975.

The commission's task was to assess CIA domestic operations in light of the existing statutory authority, to determine the adequacy of the existing safeguards against abuse, and to offer recommendations to the president and the director of the CIA. Headed by Vice-President Nelson Rockefeller, the presidential commission included former secretary of commerce John Connally, former secretary of the treasury C. Douglas Dillon, former solicitor general and Harvard Law School dean Erwin Griswold, AFL-CIO secretary-treasurer Lane Kirkland, former chairman of the Joint Chiefs of Staff Lyman Lemnitzer, former governor of California Ronald Reagan, and former University of Virginia president Edgar Shannon.

After an extensive investigation into CIA mail interception, infiltration of dissident groups, illegal surveillance, and White House involvement in CIA activities, the commission issued its report.

☆ 358 CIA Surveillance of Domestic Dissidents

*Report to the President by the Commission on CIA Activities within the United States* (Washington, D.C.: U.S. Government Printing Office, 1975), 9-42.

SUMMARY OF FINDINGS, CONCLUSIONS, AND
RECOMMENDATIONS

\*     \*     \*

THE CIA'S ROLE AND AUTHORITY

*Findings*

The Central Intelligence Agency was established by the National Security Act of 1947 as the nation's first comprehensive peacetime foreign intelligence service. The objective was to provide the President with coordinated intelligence, which the country lacked prior to the attack on Pearl Harbor.

\*     \*     \*

At the same time, Congress sought to assure the American public that it was not establishing a secret police which would threaten the civil liberties of Americans. It specifically forbade the CIA from exercising "police, subpoena, or law-enforcement powers or internal security functions." The CIA was not to replace the Federal Bureau of Investigation in conducting domestic activities to investigate crime or internal subversion.

\*     \*     \*

The precise scope of many of these statutory and Constitutional provisions is not easily stated. The National Security Act in particular was drafted in broad terms in order to provide flexibility for the CIA to adapt to changing intelligence needs. Such critical phrases as "internal security functions" are left undefined. The meaning of the Director's responsibility to protect intelligence sources and methods from unauthorized disclosure has also been a subject of uncertainty.

The word "foreign" appears nowhere in the statutory grant of authority, though it has always been understood that the CIA's mission is limited to matters related to foreign intelligence. This apparent statutory ambiguity, although not posing problems in practice, has troubled members of the public who read the statute without having the benefit of the legislative history and the instructions to the CIA from the National Security Council.

\*     \*     \*

Ambiguities have been partially responsible for some, though not all, of the Agency's deviations within the United States from its assigned mission. In some cases, reasonable persons will differ as to the lawfulness of the activity; in others, the absence of clear guidelines as to its authority deprived the Agency of a means of resisting pressures to engage in activities which now appear to us improper.

Greater public awareness of the limits of the CIA's domestic authority would do much to reassure the American people.

The requisite clarification can best be accomplished (*a*) through a specific amendment clarifying the National Security Act provision which delineates the permissible scope of CIA activities, as set forth in Recommendation 1, and (*b*) through issuance of an Executive Order further limiting domestic activities of the CIA, as set forth in Recommendation 2.

*Recommendation (1).* Section 403 of the National Security Act of 1947 should be amended in the form set forth in Appendix VI to this Report. These amendments, in summary, would:

    a. Make explicit that the CIA's activities must be related to *foreign* intelligence.

    b. Clarify the responsibility of the CIA to protect intelligence sources and methods from unauthorized disclosure. (The Agency would be responsible for protecting against unauthorized disclosures within the CIA, and it would be responsible for providing guidance and technical assistance to other agency and department heads in protecting against unauthorized disclosures within their own agencies and departments.)

    c. Confirm publicly the CIA's existing authority to collect foreign intelligence from willing sources within the United States, and, except as specified by the President in a published Executive Order, prohibit the CIA from collection efforts within the United States directed at securing foreign intelligence from unknowing American citizens.

*Recommendation (2).* The President should by Executive Order prohibit the CIA from the collection of information about the domestic activities of United States citizens (whether by overt or covert means), the evaluation, correlation, and dissemination of analyses or reports about such activities, and the storage of such information, with exceptions for the following categories of persons or activities:

    a. Persons presently or formerly affiliated, or being considered for affiliation, with the CIA, directly or indirectly, or others who require clearance by the CIA to receive classified information;

    b. Persons or activities that pose a clear threat to CIA facilities or personnel, provided that proper coordination with the FBI is accomplished;

    c. Persons suspected of espionage or other illegal activities relating to foreign intelligence, provided that proper coordination with the FBI is accomplished.

\*     \*     \*

SIGNIFICANT AREAS OF INVESTIGATION

*Introduction*

Domestic activities of the CIA raising substantial questions of compliance with the law have been closely examined by the Commission to determine the context in which they were performed, the pressures of the times, the relationship of the activity to the Agency's foreign intelligence assignment and to other CIA activities, the procedures used to authorize and conduct the activity, and the extent and effect of the activity.

\*        \*        \*

### 1. The CIA's Mail Intercepts: Findings

At the time the CIA came into being, one of the highest national intelligence priorities was to gain an understanding of the Soviet Union and its worldwide activities affecting our national security.

In this context, the CIA began in 1952 a program of surveying mail between the United States and the Soviet Union as it passed through a New York postal facility. In 1953 it began opening some of this mail. The program was expanded over the following two decades and ultimately involved the opening of many letters and the analysis of envelopes, or "covers," of a great many more letters.

\*        \*        \*

In the last year before the termination of this program, out of 4,350,000 items of mail sent to and from the Soviet Union, the New York intercept examined the outside of 2,300,000 of these items, photographed 33,000 envelopes, and opened 8,700.

The mail intercept was terminated in 1973 when the Chief Postal Inspector refused to allow its continuation without an up-to-date high-level approval.

The CIA also ran much smaller mail intercepts for brief periods in San Francisco between 1969 and 1971 and in the territory of Hawaii during 1954 and 1955. For a short period in 1957, mail in transit between foreign countries was intercepted in New Orleans.

### Conclusions

While in operation, the CIA's domestic mail opening programs were unlawful. United States statutes specifically forbid opening the mail.

The mail openings also raise Constitutional questions under the Fourth Amendment guarantees against unreasonable search, and the scope of the New York project poses possible difficulties with the First Amendment rights of speech and press.

Mail cover operations (examining and copying of envelopes only) are legal when carried out in compliance with postal regulations on a limited and selective basis involving matters of national security. The New York mail intercept did not meet these criteria.

\*        \*        \*

*Recommendation (13).* a. The President should instruct the Director of Central Intelligence that the CIA is not to engage again in domestic *mail openings* except with express statutory authority in time of war. (See also Recommendation 23.)

\*        \*        \*

### 3. Special Operations Group— "Operation CHAOS": Findings

The late 1960's and early 1970's were marked by widespread violence and civil disorders. . . .

Responding to Presidential requests made in the face of growing domestic disorder, the Director of Central Intelligence in August 1967 established a Special Operations Group within the CIA to collect, coordinate, evaluate and report on the extent of foreign influence on domestic dissidence.

The Group's activities, which later came to be known as Operation CHAOS, led the CIA to collect information on dissident Americans from CIA field stations overseas and from the FBI.

Although the stated purpose of the Operation was to determine whether there were any foreign contacts with American dissident groups, it resulted in the accumulation of considerable material on domestic dissidents and their activities.

During six years, the Operation compiled some 13,000 different files, including files on 7,200 American citizens. The documents in these files and related materials included the names of more than 300,000 persons and organizations, which were entered into a computerized index.

\*        \*        \*

Commencing in late 1969, Operation CHAOS used a number of agents to collect intelligence abroad on any foreign connections with American dissident groups. In order to have sufficient "cover" for these agents, the Operation recruited persons from domestic dissident groups or recruited others and instructed them to associate with such groups in this country.

Most of the Operation's recruits were not directed to collect information domestically on American dissidents. On a number of occasions, however, such information was reported by the recruits while they were developing dissident credentials in the United States, and the information was retained in the files of the Operation. On three occasions, an agent of the Operation was specifically directed to collect domestic intelligence.

No evidence was found that any Operation CHAOS agent used or was directed by the Agency to use electronic surveillance, wiretaps or break-ins in the United States against any dissident individual or group.

Activity of the Operation decreased substantially by mid-1972. The Operation was formally terminated in March 1974.

### Conclusions

Some domestic activities of Operation CHAOS unlawfully exceeded the CIA's statutory authority, even though the declared mission of gathering intelligence abroad as to foreign influence on domestic dissident activities was proper.

Most significantly, the Operation became a repository for large quantities of information on the domestic activities of American citizens. . . .

. . . [T]he accumulation of domestic data in the Operation exceeded what was reasonably required to make such an assessment and was thus improper.

The use of agents of the Operation on three occasions to gather information within the United States on strictly domestic matters was beyond the CIA's authority. . . .

\*     \*     \*

*Recommendation (15).* a. Presidents should refrain from directing the CIA to perform what are essentially internal security tasks.

b. The CIA should resist any efforts, whatever their origin, to involve it again in such improper activities.

c. The Agency should guard against allowing any component (like the Special Operations Group) to become so self-contained and isolated from top leadership that regular supervision and review are lost.

\*     \*     \*

### 4. Protection of the Agency against Threats of Violence—Office of Security: Findings

The CIA was not immune from the threats of violence and disruption during the period of domestic unrest between 1967 and 1972. . . .

The Office [of Security], from 1967 to 1970, had its field officers collect information from published materials, law enforcement authorities, other agencies and college officials before recruiters were sent to some campuses. Monitoring and communications support was provided to recruiters when trouble was expected.

The Office was also responsible, with the approval of the Director of Central Intelligence, for a program from February 1967 to December 1968, which at first monitored, but later infiltrated, dissident organizations in the Washington, D.C., area to determine if the groups planned any activities against CIA or other government installations.

\*     \*     \*

In December, 1967, the Office began a continuing study of dissident activity in the United States, using information from published and other voluntary knowledgeable sources. The Office produced weekly Situation Information Reports analyzing dissident activities and providing calendars of future events. Calendars were given to the Secret Service, but the CIA made no other disseminations outside the Agency. About 500 to 800 files were maintained on dissenting organizations and individuals. Thousands

of names in the files were indexed. Report publication was ended in late 1972, and the entire project was ended in 1973.

### Conclusions

The program under which the Office of Security rendered assistance to Agency recruiters on college campuses was justified as an exercise of the Agency's responsibility to protect its own personnel and operations. Such support activities were not undertaken for the purpose of protecting the facilities or operations of other governmental agencies, or to maintain public order or enforce laws.

The Agency should not infiltrate a dissident group for security purposes unless there is a clear danger to Agency installations, operations or personnel, and investigative coverage of the threat by the FBI and local law enforcement authorities is inadequate. The Agency's infiltration of dissident groups in the Washington area went far beyond steps necessary to protect the Agency's own facilities, personnel and operations, and therefore exceeded the CIA's statutory authority.

In addition, the Agency undertook to protect other government departments and agencies—a police function prohibited to it by statute.

\*     \*     \*

The Agency's actions in contributing funds, photographing people, activities and cars, and following people home were unreasonable under the circumstances and therefore exceeded the CIA's authority.

\*     \*     \*

*Recommendation (16).* The CIA should not infiltrate dissident groups or other organizations of Americans in the absence of a written determination by the Director of Central Intelligence that such action is necessary to meet a clear danger to Agency facilities, operations, or personnel and that adequate coverage by law enforcement agencies is unavailable.

*Recommendation (17).* All files on individuals accumulated by the Office of Security in the program relating to dissidents should be identified, and, except where necessary for a legitimate foreign intelligence activity, be destroyed at the conclusion of the current congressional investigations, or as soon thereafter as permitted by law.

\*     \*     \*

### Investigative Techniques: Findings

\*     \*     \*

Some investigations involved physical surveillance of the individuals concerned, possibly in conjunction with other methods of investigation. The last instance of physical surveillance by the Agency within the United States occurred in 1973.

The investigation disclosed the domestic use of 32 wiretaps, the last in 1965; 32 instances of bugging, the last in 1968; and 12 break-ins, the last in 1971. None of these activities was conducted under a judicial warrant, and only one with the written approval of the Attorney General.

Information from the income tax records of 16 persons was obtained from the Internal Revenue Service by the CIA in order to help determine whether the taxpayer was a security risk with possible connections to foreign groups. The CIA did not employ the existing statutory and regulatory procedures for obtaining such records from the IRS.

In 91 instances, mail covers (the photographing of the front and back of an envelope) were employed, and in 12 instances letters were intercepted and opened.

The state of the CIA records on these activities is such that it is often difficult to determine why the investigation occurred in the first place, who authorized the special coverage, and what the results were. Although there was testimony that these activities were frequently known to the Director of Central Intelligence and sometimes to the Attorney General, the files often are insufficient to confirm such information.

*Recommendation (23).* In the United States and its possessions, the CIA should not intercept wire or oral communications or otherwise engage in activities that would require a warrant if conducted by a law enforcement agency. Responsibility for such activities belongs with the FBI.

\*        \*        \*

*6. Involvement of the CIA in Improper Activities for the White House: Findings*

During 1971, at the request of various members of the White House staff, the CIA provided alias documents and disguise material, a tape recorder, camera, film and film processing to E. Howard Hunt. It also prepared a psychological profile of Dr. Daniel Ellsberg.

\*        \*        \*

Some members of the CIA's medical staff who participated in the preparation of the Ellsberg profile knew that one of its purposes was to support a public attack on Ellsberg. Except for this fact, the investigation has disclosed no evidence that the CIA knew or had reason to know that the assistance it gave would be used for improper purposes.

\*        \*        \*

*Conclusions*

Providing the assistance requested by the White House, including the alias and disguise materials, the camera and the psychological profile on Ellsberg, was not related to the performance by the

Agency of its authorized intelligence functions and was therefore improper.

\*        \*        \*

Finally, the Commission concludes that the requests for assistance by the White House reflect a pattern for actual and attempted misuse of the CIA by the Nixon administration.

\*        \*        \*

# 359  "[to] protect intelligence sources, methods, and analytical procedures" (1978)

The CIA was not the only intelligence agency whose covert activities and broad, unreviewable grants of authority gave rise to public concern. President Jimmy Carter promulgated Executive Order Number 12036 in response to the growing sentiment that the CIA, FBI, DIA (Defense Intelligence Agency), NSA (National Security Agency), and other supersecret government enterprises required clearly defined spheres of operation as well as procedural guidelines.

The executive order followed many of the Ford-appointed Commission on CIA Activity's recommendations. The order prohibited the CIA from engaging in electronic surveillance in the United States. The CIA was to conduct no intelligence activities against a United States person without a warrant, if those activities, when undertaken for law enforcement purposes, would require a warrant. One exception to the warrant requirement was the situation in which the president or the attorney general had determined probable cause existed to believe a United States citizen was a foreign agent. The order allowed mail interception and infiltration of domestic dissident groups in very limited circumstances. Nevertheless, in keeping with the continuing desire to facilitate flexibility, many unexplained or vaguely defined terms (i.e., "special activities") continued to appear throughout the order.

☆ 359  The United States' Foreign Intelligence Activities

President Jimmy Carter's Exec. Order No. 12036, 43 Fed. Reg. 3674 (Jan. 24, 1978).

SECTION 1

DIRECTION, DUTIES AND RESPONSIBILITIES WITH RESPECT TO THE NATIONAL INTELLIGENCE EFFORT

*1-1. National Security Council*

1-101. *Purpose.* The National Security Council (NSC) was established by the National Security Act of 1947 to advise the President with respect to the integration of domestic, foreign, and military policies relating to the national security. The NSC shall act as the highest Executive Branch entity that provides review of, guidance for, and direction to the conduct of all national foreign intelligence and counterintelligence activities.

\* \* \*

### 1-2. NSC Policy Review Committee

1-201. *Membership.* The NSC Policy Review Committee (PRC), when carrying out responsibilities assigned in this Order, shall be chaired by the Director of Central Intelligence and composed of the Vice President, the Secretary of State, the Secretary of the Treasury, the Secretary of Defense, the Assistant to the President for National Security Affairs, and the Chairman of the Joint Chiefs of Staff, or their designees, and other senior officials, as appropriate.

\* \* \*

### 1-3. NSC Special Coordination Committee

1-301. *Membership.* The NSC Special Coordination Committee (SCC) is chaired by the Assistant to the President for National Security Affairs and its membership includes the statutory members of the NSC and other senior officials, as appropriate.

1-302. *Special Activities.* The SCC shall consider and submit to the President a policy recommendation, including all dissents, on each special activity. When meeting for this purpose, the members of the SCC shall include the Secretary of State, the Secretary of Defense, the Attorney General, the Director of the Office of Management and Budget, the Assistant to the President for National Security Affairs, the Chairman of the Joint Chiefs of Staff, and the Director of Central Intelligence.

\* \* \*

1-604. *Protection of Sources, Methods and Procedures.* The Director of Central Intelligence shall ensure that programs are developed which protect intelligence sources, methods and analytical procedures, provided that this responsibility shall be limited within the United States to:

(a) Using a lawful means to protect against disclosure by present or former employees of the CIA or the Office of the Director of Central Intelligence, or by persons or organizations presently or formerly under contract with such entities.

\* \* \*

### SECTION 2

RESTRICTIONS ON INTELLIGENCE ACTIVITIES

### 2-1. Adherence to Law

2-101. *Purpose.* Information about the capabilities, intentions and activities of foreign powers, organizations, or persons and their agents is essential to informed decision-making in the areas of national defense and foreign relations. The measures employed to acquire such information should be responsive to legitimate governmental needs and must be conducted in a manner that preserves and respects established concepts of privacy and civil liberties.

2-102. *Principles of Interpretation.* Sections 2-201 through 2-309 set forth limitations which, in addition to other applicable laws, are intended to achieve the proper balance between protection of individual rights and acquisition of essential information. Those sections do not authorize any activity not authorized by sections 1-101 through 1-1503 and do not provide any exemption from any other law.

### 2-2. Restrictions on Certain Collection Techniques

2-201. *General Provisions.*

(a) The activities described in Sections 2-202 through 2-208 shall be undertaken only as permitted by this Order and by procedures established by the head of the agency concerned and approved by the Attorney General. Those procedures shall protect constitutional rights and privacy, ensure that information is gathered by the least intrusive means possible, and limit use of such information to lawful governmental purposes.

(b) Activities described in sections 2-202 through 2-205 for which a warrant would be required if undertaken for law enforcement rather than intelligence purposes shall not be undertaken against a United States person without a judicial warrant, unless the President has authorized the type of activity involved and the Attorney General has both approved the particular activity and determined that there is probable cause to believe that the United States person is an agent of a foreign power.

2-202. *Electronic Surveillance.* The CIA may not engage in any electronic surveillance within the United States. No agency within the Intelligence Community shall engage in any electronic surveillance directed against a United States person abroad or designed to intercept a communication sent from, or intended for receipt within, the United States except as permitted by the procedures established pursuant to section 2-201....

2-203. *Television Cameras and Other Monitoring.* No agency within the Intelligence Community shall use any electronic or mechanical device surreptitiously and continuously to monitor any person within the United States, or any United States person abroad, except as permitted by the procedures established pursuant to Section 2-201.

2-204. *Physical Searches.* No agency within the Intelligence Community except the FBI may conduct any unconsented physical searches within the United States. All such searches conducted by the FBI, as well as all such searches conducted by any agency within the Intelligence Community outside the United States and directed against United States persons, shall be undertaken only as permitted by procedures established pursuant to Section 2-201.

2-205. *Mail Surveillance.* No agency within the Intelligence Community shall open mail or examine envelopes in United States postal channels, except in accordance with applicable statutes and regulations. No agency within the Intelligence Community shall open mail of a United States person abroad except as permitted by procedures established pursuant to Section 2-201.

2-206. *Physical Surveillance.* The FBI may conduct physical surveillance directed against United States persons or others only in the course of a lawful investigation. Other agencies within the Intelligence Community may not undertake any physical surveillance directed against a United States person unless:

(a) The surveillance is conducted outside the United States and the person being surveilled is reasonably believed to be acting on behalf of a foreign power, engaging in international terrorist activities, or engaging in narcotics production or trafficking;

(b) The surveillance is conducted solely for the purpose of identifying a person who is in contact with someone who is the subject of a foreign intelligence or counterintelligence; or

(c) That person is being surveilled for the purpose of protecting foreign intelligence and counterintelligence sources and methods from unauthorized disclosure or is the subject of a lawful counterintelligence, personnel, physical or communications security investigation.

\*     \*     \*

2-207. *Undisclosed Participation in Domestic Organizations.* No employees may join, or otherwise participate in, any organization within the United States on behalf of any agency within the Intelligence Community without disclosing their intelligence affiliation to appropriate officials of the organization, except as permitted by procedures established pursuant to Section 2-201. Such procedures shall provide for disclosure of such affiliation in all cases unless the agency head or a designee approved by the Attorney General finds that non-disclosure is essential to achieving lawful purposes, and that finding is subject to review by the Attorney General. Those procedures shall further limit undisclosed participation to cases where:

(a) The participation is undertaken on behalf of the FBI in the course of a lawful investigation;

(b) The organization concerned is composed primarily of individuals who are not United States persons and is reasonably believed to be acting on behalf of a foreign power; or

(c) The participation is strictly limited in its nature, scope and duration to that necessary for other lawful purposes relating to foreign intelligence and is a type of participation approved by the Attorney General and set forth in a public document. No such participation may be undertaken for the purpose of influencing the activity of the organization or its members.

2-208. *Collection of Nonpublicly Available Information.* No agency within the Intelligence Community may collect, disseminate or store information concerning the activities of United States persons that is not available publicly, unless it does so with their consent or as permitted by procedures established pursuant to Section 2-201. . . .

\*     \*     \*

*2-3. Additional Restrictions and Limitations*

2-301. *Tax Information.* No agency within the Intelligence Community shall examine tax returns or tax information except as permitted by applicable law.

\*     \*     \*

2-305. *Prohibition on Assassination.* No person employed by or acting on behalf of the United States Government shall engage in, or conspire to engage in, assassination.

2-306. *Restrictions on Special Activities.* No component of the United States Government except an agency within the Intelligence Community may conduct any special activity. No such agency except the CIA (or the military services in wartime) may conduct any special activity unless the President determines, with the SCC's advice, that another agency is more likely to achieve a particular objective.

\*     \*     \*

## SECTION 3

OVERSIGHT OF INTELLIGENCE ORGANIZATIONS

*3-1. Intelligence Oversight Board*

3-101. *Membership.* The President's Intelligence Oversight Board (IOB) shall function within the White House. The IOB shall have three members who shall be appointed by the President and who shall be from outside the government and be qualified on the basis of ability, knowledge, diversity of background and experience. No member shall have any personal interest in any contractual relationship with any agency within the Intelligence Community. One member shall be designated by the President as chairman.

\*     \*     \*

*4-2. Definitions*

For the purposes of this Order, the following terms shall have these meanings:

4-201. *Communications security* means protective measures taken to deny unauthorized persons information derived from telecommunications of the United States Government related to national security and to ensure the authenticity of such telecommunications.

4-202. *Counterintelligence* means information gathered and activities conducted to protect against espionage and other clandestine intelligence activities, sabotage, international terrorist activities or assassinations conducted for or on behalf of foreign powers, organizations or persons, but not including personnel, physical, document, or communications security programs.

4-203. *Electronic Surveillance* means acquisition of a nonpublic communication by electronic means without the consent of a person who is a party to an electronic communication or, in the case of a nonelectronic communication, without the consent of a person who is visibly present at the place of communication, but not including the use of radio direction finding equipment solely to determine the location of a transmitter.

4-204. *Employee* means a person employed by, assigned to, or acting for an agency within the Intelligence Community.

4-205. *Foreign Intelligence* means information relating to the capabilities, intentions and activities of foreign powers, organizations or persons, but not including counterintelligence except for information on international terrorist activities.

4-206. *Intelligence* means foreign intelligence and counterintelligence.

4-207. *Intelligence Community* and *agency or agencies within the Intelligence Community* refer to the following organizations:

(a) The Central Intelligence Agency (CIA);

(b) The National Security Agency (NSA);

(c) The Defense Intelligence Agency;

(d) The Offices within the Department of Defense for the collection of specialized national foreign intelligence through reconnaissance programs;

(e) The Bureau of Intelligence and Research of the Department of State;

(f) The intelligence elements of the military services, the Federal Bureau of Investigation (FBI), the Department of the Treasury, the Department of Energy, and the Drug Enforcement Administration (DEA); and

(g) The staff elements of the Office of the Director of Central Intelligence.

4-208. *Intelligence product* means the estimates, memoranda and other reports produced from the analysis of available information.

4-209. *International terrorist activities* means any activity or activities which:

(a) involves killing, causing serious bodily harm, kidnapping, or violent destruction of property, or an attempt or credible threat to commit such acts; and

(b) appears intended to endanger a protectee of the Secret Service or the Department of State or to further political, social or economic goals by intimidating or coercing a civilian population or any segment thereof, influencing the policy of a government or international organization by intimidation or coercion, or obtaining widespread publicity for a group or its cause; and

(c) transcends national boundaries in terms of the means by which it is accomplished, the civilian population, government, or international organization it appears intended to coerce or intimidate, or the locale in which its perpetrators operate or seek asylum.

\*   \*   \*

4-212. *Special activities* means activities conducted abroad in support of national foreign policy objectives which are designed to further official United States programs and policies abroad and which are planned and executed so that the role of the United States Government is not apparent or acknowledged publicly, and functions in support of such activities, but not including diplomatic activity or the collection and production of intelligence or related support functions.

\*   \*   \*

## 360 "Notwithstanding any other law" (1978)

With the revelations concerning Vietnam and the Watergate break-in, Americans became aware of the extent of the government's surveillance of both individual citizens and their associations. The climate of surprise and shock led to attempts to curb the potential for abuses by imposing upon security agencies the "probable cause" and warrant requirements of the Constitution. Yet citizens recognized the need for the country to gather information regarding the activities of foreign powers and their agents while preventing the previous excesses.

The Foreign Intelligence Surveillance Act of 1978 authorized the government to conduct electronic surveillance without a court order if the president, through the attorney general, certified in writing that such surveillance was directly solely at communications between foreign powers or from premises under the exclusive control of a foreign power. In addition, there could exist no substantial likelihood that such surveillance would expose communications by United States citizens or permanent resident aliens. When these requirements could not be met, the act still permitted the issuance of electronic surveillance orders by a specially designated court of federal judges, appointed by the chief justice of the United States (Section 103).

In addition to the peacetime standards, the act also contained special wartime provisions regarding electronic surveillance.

## ☆ 360 Foreign Intelligence Surveillance Act

92 Stat. 1783 (1978). (Current version at 50 U.S.C. § 101 et seq.)

§ 101. Definitions

As used in this chapter:

(a) "Foreign power" means—

(1) a foreign government or any component thereof, whether or not recognized by the United States;

     *       *       *

(4) a group engaged in international terrorism or activities in preparation therefor;

     *       *       *

(c) "International terrorism" means activities that—

(1) involve violent acts or acts dangerous to human life that are a violation of the criminal laws of the United States or of any State, or that would be a criminal violation if committed within the jurisdiction of the United States or any State;

(2) appear to be intended—

(A) to intimidate or coerce a civilian population;

(B) to influence the policy of a government by intimidation or coercion; or

(C) to affect the conduct of a government by assassination or kidnapping; and

(3) occur totally outside the United States, or transcend national boundaries in terms of the means by which they are accomplished, the persons they appear intended to coerce or intimidate, or the locale in which their perpetrators operate or seek asylum.

     *       *       *

(e) "Foreign intelligence information" means—

(1) information that relates to, and if concerning a United States person is necessary to, the ability of the United States to protect against—

(A) actual or potential attack or other grave hostile acts of a foreign power or an agent of a foreign power;

(B) sabotage or international terrorism by a foreign power or an agent of a foreign power; or

(C) clandestine intelligence activities by an intelligence service or network of a foreign power or by an agent of a foreign power; or

(2) information with respect to a foreign power or foreign territory that relates to, and if

concerning a United States person is necessary to—

(A) the national defense or the security of the United States; or

(B) the conduct of the foreign affairs of the United States.

     *       *       *

(h) "Minimization procedures," with respect to electronic surveillance, means—

(1) specific procedures, which shall be adopted by the Attorney General, that are reasonably designed in light of the purpose and technique of the particular surveillance, to minimize the acquisition and retention, and prohibit the dissemination of nonpublicly available information concerning unconsenting United States persons consistent with the need of the United States to obtain, produce, and disseminate foreign intelligence information;

     *       *       *

(i) "United States person" means a citizen of the United States, an alien lawfully admitted for permanent residence. . . .

     *       *       *

§ 102. Electronic surveillance authorization without court order; certification by Attorney General; reports to congressional committees; transmittal under seal; duties and compensation of communication common carrier; applications; jurisdiction of court

(a)(1) Notwithstanding any other law, the President, through the Attorney General, may authorize electronic surveillance without a court order under this chapter to acquire foreign intelligence information for periods of up to one year if the Attorney General certifies in writing under oath that—

(A) the electronic surveillance is solely directed at—

(i) the acquisition of the contents of communications transmitted by means of communications used exclusively between or among foreign powers as defined in section 101(a)(1), (2), or (3) of this title; or

(ii) the acquisition of technical intelligence, other than the spoken communications of individuals, from property or premises under the open and exclusive control of a foreign power, as defined in section 101(a)(1), (2), or (3) of this title;

(B) there is no substantial likelihood that the surveillance will acquire the contents of any communication to which a United States person is a party; and

(C) the proposed minimization procedures with respect to such surveillance meet the definition of minimization procedures under section 101(h) of this title. . . .

(2) An electronic surveillance authorized by this subsection may be conducted only in accordance with the Attorney General's certification and the minimization procedures adopted by him. . . .

*　　　*　　　*

(b) Applications for a court order under this chapter are authorized if the President has, by written authorization, empowered the Attorney General to approve applications to the court having jurisdiction under section 103 of this title, and a judge to whom an application is made may, notwithstanding any other law, grant an order, in conformity with section 105 of this title, approving electronic surveillance of a foreign power or an agent of a foreign power for the purpose of obtaining foreign intelligence information, except that the court shall not have jurisdiction to grant any order approving electronic surveillance directed solely as described in paragraph (1)(A) of subsection (a) of this section unless such surveillance may involve the acquisition of communications of any United States person.

*　　　*　　　*

§ 104. Applications for court orders — Submission by Federal officer; approval of Attorney General; contents

(a) Each application for an order approving electronic surveillance under this chapter shall be made by a Federal officer in writing upon oath or affirmation to a judge having jurisdiction under section 103 of this title. Each application shall require the approval of the Attorney General based upon his finding that it satisfies the criteria and requirements of such application as set forth in this chapter. It shall include —

(1) the identity of the Federal officer making the application;

(2) the authority conferred on the Attorney General by the President of the United States and the approval of the Attorney General to make the application;

(3) the identity, if known, or a description of the target of the electronic surveillance;

(4) a statement of the facts and circumstances relied upon by the applicant to justify his belief that —

(A) the target of the electronic surveillance is a foreign power or an agent of a foreign power; and

(B) each of the facilities or places at which the electronic surveillance is directed is being used, or is about to be used, by a foreign power or an agent of a foreign power;

(5) a statement of the proposed minimization procedures;

(6) a detailed description of the nature of the information sought and the type of communica-

tions or activities to be subjected to the surveillance;

(7) a certification or certifications by the Assistant to the President for National Security Affairs or an executive branch official or officials designated by the President from among those executive officers employed in the area of national security or defense and appointed by the President with the advice and consent of the Senate —

(A) that the certifying official deems the information sought to be foreign intelligence information;

(B) that the purpose of the surveillance is to obtain foreign intelligence information;

(C) that such information cannot reasonably be obtained by normal investigative techniques;

(D) that designates the type of foreign intelligence information being sought according to the categories described in section 101(e) of this title; and

(E) including a statement of the basis for the certification that —

(i) the information sought is the type of foreign intelligence information designated; and

(ii) such information cannot reasonably be obtained by normal investigative techniques;

(8) a statement of the means by which the surveillance will be effected and a statement whether physical entry is required to effect the surveillance;

(9) a statement of the facts concerning all previous applications that have been made to any judge under this chapter involving any of the persons, facilities, or places specified in the application, and the action taken on each previous application;

(10) a statement of the period of time for which the electronic surveillance is required to be maintained, and if the nature of the intelligence gathering is such that the approval of the use of electronic surveillance under this chapter should not automatically terminate when the described type of information has first been obtained, a description of facts supporting the belief that additional information of the same type will be obtained thereafter; and

(11) whenever more than one electronic, mechanical or other surveillance device is to be used with respect to a particular proposed electronic surveillance, the coverage of the devices involved and what minimization procedures apply to information acquired by each device.

*　　　*　　　*

§ 105.  Issuance of order — Necessary findings

(a)  Upon an application made pursuant to section 104, the judge shall enter an ex parte order as requested or as modified approving the electronic surveillance if he finds that—

(1)  the President has authorized the Attorney General to approve applications for electronic surveillance for foreign intelligence information;

(2)  the application has been made by a Federal officer and approved by the Attorney General;

(3)  on the basis of the facts submitted by the applicant there is probable cause to believe that—

(A)  the target of the electronic surveillance is a foreign power or an agent of a foreign power: *Provided,* That no United States person may be considered a foreign power or an agent of a foreign power solely upon the basis of activities protected by the first amendment to the Constitution of the United States; and

(B)  each of the facilities or places at which the electronic surveillance is directed is being used, or is about to be used, by a foreign power or an agent of a foreign power;

(4)  the proposed minimization procedures meet the definition of minimization procedures under section 101(h) of this title. . . .

*             *             *

*Emergency Orders*

(e)  Notwithstanding any other provision of this chapter, when the Attorney General reasonably determines that—

(1)  an emergency situation exists with respect to the employment of electronic surveillance to obtain foreign intelligence information before an order authorizing such surveillance can with due diligence be obtained; and

(2)  the factual basis for issuance of an order under this chapter to approve such surveillance exists;

he may authorize the emergency employment of electronic surveillance if a judge having jurisdiction under section 103 of this title is informed by the Attorney General or his designee at the time of such authorization that the decision has been made to employ emergency electronic surveillance and if an application in accordance with this chapter is made to that judge as soon as practicable, but not more than twenty-four hours after the Attorney General authorizes such surveillance. If the Attorney General authorizes such emergency employment of electronic surveillance, he shall require that the minimization procedures required by this chapter for the issuance of a judicial order be followed. In the ab-

sence of a judicial order approving such electronic surveillance, the surveillance shall terminate when the information sought is obtained, when the application for the order is denied, or after the expiration of twenty-four hours from the time of authorization by the Attorney General, whichever is earliest. In the event that such application for approval is denied, or in any other case where the electronic surveillance is terminated and no order is issued approving the surveillance, no information obtained or evidence derived from such surveillance shall be received in evidence or otherwise disclosed in any trial, hearing, or other proceeding in or before any court, grand jury, department, office, agency, regulatory body, legislative committee, or other authority of the United States, a State, or political subdivision thereof, and no information concerning any United States person acquired from such surveillance shall subsequently be used or disclosed in any other manner by Federal officers or employees without the consent of such person, except with the approval of the Attorney General if the information indicates a threat of death or serious bodily harm to any person. . . .

*             *             *

§ 106.  Use of information — Compliance with minimization procedures; privileged communications; lawful purposes

*             *             *

*Notification of Emergency Employment of Electronic Surveillance; Contents; Postponement, Suspension or Elimination*

(j)  If an emergency employment of electronic surveillance is authorized under section 105(e) of this title and a subsequent order approving the surveillance is not obtained, the judge shall cause to be served on any United States person named in the application and on such other United States persons subject to electronic surveillance as the judge may determine in his discretion it is in the interest of justice to serve, notice of—

(1)  the fact of the application;

(2)  the period of the surveillance; and

(3)  the fact that during the period information was or was not obtained.

On an ex parte showing of good cause to the judge the serving of the notice required by this subsection may be postponed or suspended for a period not to exceed ninety days. Thereafter, on a further ex parte showing of good cause, the court shall forego ordering the serving of the notice required under this subsection.

*             *             *

§ 111.  Authorization during time of war

Notwithstanding any other law, the President, through the Attorney General, may authorize electronic surveillance without a court order under this chapter to acquire foreign intelligence information for a period not to exceed fifteen calendar days following a declaration of war by the Congress.

# 361 " 'different rules of constitutional law' " (1978)

The Church of Scientology had been the subject of extensive investigation by the United States government. Basing their action on the Tariff Act of 1930, which prohibited the importation of materials advocating treason, insurrection, or forcible resistance to the law, customs officers briefly seized and searched some documents shipped to the church from abroad. The Church of Scientology argued the statute was unconstitutional because its language was vague and unduly broad, and because it permitted a prior restraint on speech. Upholding this warrantless border search of documents, the court construed the statute narrowly to avoid the First Amendment problem, then rested its decision on the theory that the broad congressional power to regulate imports exempted such searches from traditional Fourth Amendment protections.

☆ 361 *Church of Scientology of California v. Simon*

460 F. Supp. 56 (C.D. Ca. 1978).

WILLIAM P. GRAY, District Judge.

\*　　\*　　\*

... Four cartons of papers and documents were shipped from England, via international air cargo, to Church of Scientology employees in Los Angeles County. On July 3, 1976, the Customs Inspector on duty at Los Angeles International Airport opened the cartons, briefly scanned the documents, expressed uncertainty regarding the importability of the materials, and detained the cartons for further review of their contents.

Subsequently, special customs agents more carefully reviewed the documents and, on July 7, 1976, the District Director of Customs concluded that the contents were importable. On that same day, the Church of Scientology filed suit for damages and injunctive relief. On July 13, 1976, the cartons of documents were released to the plaintiffs.

A temporary restraining order issued in this case enjoined the Customs Service from copying or disseminating copies of any of the documents contained in the cartons. The Customs Service was permitted, however, to disclose the materials to the United States Attorney, who could make one copy of documents he found appropriate for criminal evidentiary

purposes or for defense of any damage claims that the plaintiffs might assert.

\*　　\*　　\*

The plaintiffs insist that the statute is unconstitutionally overbroad, for it prohibits the importation of written materials that discuss violence as an abstract doctrine, as well as "action now" materials. It is obvious that the statute does not incorporate specifically the restrictions set forth in *Brandenberg v. Ohio*, which held that a state cannot proscribe advocacy of the use of force ". . . except where such advocacy is directed to inciting or producing imminent lawless action and is likely to incite or produce such action." Nonetheless, we read such standards into [the statute] in order to uphold its constitutionality. . . .

\*　　\*　　\*

We also reject the plaintiffs' argument that the statute permits an unconstitutional prior restraint of speech through the detention of imported materials. . . . Under the Customs Service's broad powers to restrict imports and conduct a search of materials entering the country from abroad, this temporary delay and retention of documents do not constitute a constitutional deprivation.

Finally, the plaintiffs' argument that the statute is void for vagueness must also fail. This contention relates to the scope of discretion afforded the Secretary of the Treasury to admit books of recognized literary or scientific merit. The question of an improper exercise of this discretionary power is not presented by the facts of this case, and so we need not resolve it within this decision. Thus, we hold that the statute is constitutional as applied to advocacy issues, just as it previously has been held constitutional as applied to obscenity issues.

We also hold that the search pursuant to the statute was conducted in a constitutionally valid manner. The plaintiffs argue unsuccessfully that warrantless reading of materials entering the United States from abroad is suspect. We disagree with their contentions that a warrant was needed for the original inspection and that a warrant was required once the documents were deemed importable. . . .

It is indisputable that the instant case involves a border search. The Customs Service has the statutory authority to examine materials coming into the United States, and the Supreme Court has enunciated clearly the position that the government possesses an inherent right to protect itself by stopping and examining persons and property entering the country from abroad.

In addition, the Constitution has given Congress broad, comprehensive powers to regulate commerce with foreign nations, and under this power "[i]mport restrictions and searches of persons or packages at the national borders" are justified by different "considerations and different rules of constitutional law from domestic regulations."

Under its general powers in setting import restrictions, Congress may promulgate regulations regarding the importability of obscene material and material advocating the overthrow of the government. To enforce these regulations, the Customs Service has the right to search luggage and persons at our national borders. This search necessarily involves the examination or review of the materials in question, for the customs officers must scan or peruse and perhaps even read the materials to determine whether or not they are importable.

\*          \*          \*

The instant case withstands analysis under the Ninth Circuit's "real suspicion" test. The initial search, simply as a border search, was reasonable. It appears that the customs officer developed a "real suspicion" as to the importability of the contents of the cartons as a result of this initial search. We conclude that the customs officer's real suspicion concerning the importability of the documents fulfilled the additional cause requirement, and provided the basis for the more intrusive search that subsequently took place. Thus, the actions of the customs officers were proper and the effectuation of the border search was valid.

\*          \*          \*

The plaintiffs have neither argued nor presented any credible evidence in this case that the original inspection of the documents was conducted in bad faith or that the initial . . . search was used as a guise for obtaining incriminating evidence for use against the Church of Scientology in other proceedings. Accordingly, we must conclude that the initial search was conducted in good faith and a proper inspection occurred.

\*          \*          \*

## 362 "the right to exercise exclusive jurisdiction within [the] Indian territory" (1979)

In 1946, recognizing that past policies had not been completely fair, Congress established the Indian Claims Commission to hear and determine claims by Native American individuals and tribes over the wrongful dispossession of their lands by the United States. Congress did not empower the commission to return lands wrongfully taken, but only to compensate the Native Americans with money damages for the value of the land at the time of the wrongful taking. The commission, in addition, had jurisdiction only over lands alleged to have been taken by the United States. Except for some small reservations east of the Mississippi, most of the Native Americans who remained there after the Removal of the 1830s and 1840s were under the authority, control, and trust of the states rather than the federal government.

Native American communities continued to press claims against the unlawful taking of lands by state rather than federal action. The Indian Nonintercourse Act of 1790 invalidated any sale of Indian lands to individuals or to any state unless done pursuant to "a public treaty . . . under the authority of the United States."

Despite this prohibition, in 1796 the Penobscot Nation transferred two hundred thousand acres of land to Massachusetts (the predecessor state to Maine). In return it received one hundred fifty yards of cloth for blankets, four hundred pounds of shot, one hundred pounds of powder, one hundred bushels of corn, thirteen bushels of salt, thirty-six hats, a barrel of rum, and an annual stipend of trade goods. Subsequent sales ensued, until by 1833 the three hundred remaining Penobscots were confined to one island and one town. Similarly prohibited sales were made by the Passamaquoddy Tribe beginning in 1794.

Disputes over the ownership of these lands erupted in the 1960s and gave rise to a sit-in by the Passamaquoddies in 1964. In *Joint Tribal Council of Passamaquoddy Tribe v. Morton*, 528 F.2d 270 (1st Cir. 1975), the court ordered the United States, as trustee for the Native Americans, to sue the state of Maine to enforce the claims of the Passamaquoddies. Two weeks later a similar suit commenced on behalf of the Penobscots. A cloud thus was thrown over the title to over twelve million acres of land held and occupied by 350,000 whites. Relations between the whites and the Native Americans became highly strained. The fear of the economic and political chaos that would ensue if the Native Americans were successful in their claims resulted in a land and monetary settlement between the state of Maine and the Native Americans, which Congress ratified in 1980.

Two of the Native American tribes who survived in the East thus received not only compensation, but also, like their Native American brethren in the West, now were recognized to be semi-independent political entities within the state. Some one hundred fifty years earlier, in 1829, President Jackson, in defending Georgia's sentiments against the presence of the Cherokee Nation within its boundaries, asked rhetorically: "Would the people of Maine permit the Penobscot tribe to elect an independent government within their State?" Maine's answer did not come forth until 1979.

# ☆362 Maine Indian Claims Settlement Act

Me. Rev. Stat. Ann. tit. 3a §§ 6201-10 (1979).

## § 6201. SHORT TITLE

This Act shall be known and may be cited as "AN ACT to Implement the Maine Indian Claims Settlement."

## § 6202. LEGISLATIVE FINDINGS AND DECLARATION OF POLICY

The Legislature finds and declares the following.

The Passamaquoddy Tribe, the Penobscot Nation and the Houlton Band of Maliseet Indians are asserting claims for possession of large areas of land in the State and for damages alleging that the lands in question originally were transferred in violation of the Indian Trade and Intercourse Act of 1790, 1 Stat. 137, or subsequent reenactments or versions thereof.

Substantial economic and social hardship could be created for large numbers of landowners, citizens and communities in the State, and therefore to the State as a whole, if these claims are not resolved promptly.

The claims also have produced disagreement between the Indian claimants and the State over the extent of the state's jurisdiction in the claimed areas. This disagreement has resulted in litigation and, if the claims are not resolved, further litigation on jurisdictional issues would be likely.

The Indian claimants and the State, acting through the Attorney General, have reached certain agreements which represent a good faith effort on the part of all parties to achieve a fair and just resolution of those claims which, in the absence of agreement, would be pursued through the courts for many years to the ultimate detriment of the State and all its citizens, including the Indians.

The foregoing agreement between the Indian claimants and the State also represents a good faith effort by the Indian claimants and the State to achieve a just and fair resolution of their disagreement over jurisdiction on the present Passamaquoddy and Penobscot Indian reservations and in the claimed areas. To that end, the Passamaquoddy Tribe and the Penobscot Nation have agreed to adopt the laws of the State as their own to the extent provided in this Act. The Houlton Band of the Maliseet Indians and its lands will be wholly subject to the laws of the State.

It is the purpose of this Act to implement in part the foregoing agreement.

\*      \*      \*

## § 6204. LAWS OF THE STATE TO APPLY TO INDIAN LANDS

Except as otherwise provided in this Act, all Indians, Indian nations, and tribes and bands of Indians in the State and any lands or other natural resources owned by them, held in trust for them by the United States or by any other person or entity shall be subject to the laws of the State and to the civil and criminal jurisdiction of the courts of the State to the same extent as any any other person or lands or other natural resources therein.

## § 6205. INDIAN TERRITORY

\*      \*      \*

*3. Takings under the laws of the State*

A. Prior to any taking of land for public uses within either the Passamaquoddy Indian Reservation or the Penobscot Indian Reservation, the public entity proposing the taking, or, in the event of a taking proposed by a public utility, the Public Utilities Commission, shall be required to find that there is no reasonably feasible alternative to the proposed taking. In making this finding, the public entity or the Public Utilities Commission shall compare the cost, technical feasibility, and environmental and social impact of the available alternatives, if any, with the cost, technical feasibility and environmental and social impact of the proposed taking. Prior to making this finding, the public entity or Public Utilities Commission, after notice to the affected tribe or nation, shall conduct a public hearing in the manner provided by the Maine Administrative Procedure Act, on the affected Indian reservation. The finding of the public entity or Public Utilities Commission may be appealed to the Maine Superior Court.

In the event of a taking of land for public uses within the Passamaquoddy Indian Reservation or the Penobscot Indian Reservation, the public entity or public utility making the taking shall, at the election of the affected tribe or nation, and with respect to individually allotted lands, at the election of the affected allottee or allottees, acquire by purchase or otherwise for the respective tribe, nation, allottee or allottees a parcel or parcels of land equal in value to that taken; contiguous to the affected Indian reservation; and as nearly adjacent to the parcel taken as practicable. The land so acquired shall, upon written certification to the Secretary of State by the public entity or public utility acquiring such land describing the location and boundaries thereof, be included within the Indian Reservation of the affected tribe or nation without further approval of the State. For purposes of this section, land along and adjacent to the Penobscot River shall be deemed to be contiguous to the Penobscot Indian Reservation. The acquisition of land for the Passamaquoddy Tribe or the Penobscot Nation or any allottee under this subsection shall be full compensation for any such taking. If the affected tribe, nation, allottee or allottees elect not to have a substitute parcel acquired in accordance with this subsection, the moneys received for such taking shall be reinvested. . . .

\*           \*           \*

### § 6206. POWERS AND DUTIES OF THE INDIAN TRIBES WITHIN THEIR RESPECTIVE INDIAN TERRITORIES

*1. General powers.* Except as otherwise provided in this Act, the Passamaquoddy Tribe and the Penobscot Nation, within their respective Indian territories, shall have, exercise and enjoy all the rights, privileges, powers and immunities, including, but without limitation, the power to enact ordinances and collect taxes, and shall be subject to all the duties, obligations, liabilities and limitations of a municipality of and subject to the laws of the State, provided, however, that internal tribal matters, including membership in the respective tribe or nation, the right to reside within the respective Indian territories, tribal organization, tribal government, tribal elections and the use or disposition of settlement fund income shall not be subject to regulation by the State. The Passamaquoddy Tribe and the Penobscot Nation shall designate such officers and officials as are necessary to implement and administer those laws of the State applicable to the respective Indian territories and the residents thereof. Any resident of the Passamaquoddy Indian territory or the Penobscot Indian territory who is not a member of the respective tribe or nation nonetheless shall be equally entitled to receive any municipal or governmental services provided by the respective tribe or nation or by the State, except those services which are provided exclusively to members of the respective tribe or nation pursuant to state or federal law, and shall be entitled to vote in national, state and county elections in the same manner as any tribal member residing within Indian territory.

\*           \*           \*

*3. Ordinances.* The Passamaquoddy Tribe and the Penobscot Nation each shall have the right to exercise exclusive jurisdiction within its respective Indian territory over violations by members of either tribe or nation of tribal ordinances adopted pursuant to this section or section 6207 [regulations of fish and game]. The decision to exercise or terminate the jurisdiction authorized by this section shall be made by each tribal governing body. Should either tribe or nation choose not to exercise, or to terminate its exercise of, jurisdiction as authorized by this section or section 6207, the State shall have exclusive jurisdiction over violations of tribal ordinances by members of either tribe or nation within the Indian territory of that tribe or nation. The State shall have exclusive jurisdiction over violations of tribal ordinances by persons not members of either tribe or nation.

\*           \*           \*

### § 6209. JURISDICTION OVER CRIMINAL OFFENSES, JUVENILE CRIMES, CIVIL DISPUTES AND DOMESTIC RELATIONS

*1. Exclusive jurisdiction in tribes over certain matters.* Except as provided in subsections 3 and 4, the Passamaquoddy Tribe and the Penobscot Nation shall have the right to exercise exclusive jurisdiction separate and distinct from the State over:

A. Criminal offenses against a person or property for which the maximum potential term of imprisonment does not exceed 6 months and the maximum potential fine does not exceed $500 and which are committed on the Indian reservation of the respective tribe or nation by a member of either tribe or nation against another member of either tribe or nation or against the property of another member of either tribe or nation;

B. Juvenile crimes against a person or property involving conduct which, if committed by an adult, would fall, under paragraph A, within the exclusive jurisdiction of the Passamaquoddy Tribe or the Penobscot Nation, and juvenile crimes as defined in Title 15, section 3103, subsection 1, paragraphs B to D [possession of marijuana, alcoholic beverage regulation] committed by a juvenile member of either tribe or nation on the Indian reservation of the respective tribe or nation;

C. Civil actions between members of either tribe or nation arising on the Indian reservation of the respective tribe or nation and which are cognizable as small claims under the laws of the State and civil actions against a member of either tribe or nation under Title 22, section 2383 [civil violation for possession of marijuana] involving conduct on the Indian reservation of the respective tribe or nation by a member of either tribe or nation;

D. Indian child custody proceedings to the extent authorized by applicable federal law; and

E. Other domestic relations matters including marriage, divorce and support between members of either tribe or nation both of whom reside on the Indian reservation of the respective tribe or nation.

The decision to exercise or terminate the exercise of the jurisdiction authorized by this subsection shall be made by the tribal governing body. Should either tribe or nation choose not to exercise, or choose to terminate its exercise of, jurisdiction over the criminal, juvenile, civil and domestic matters described in this subsection, the State shall have exclusive jurisdiction over those matters. Except as provided in paragraphs A and B, all laws of the State relating to criminal offenses and juvenile crimes shall apply within the Passamaquoddy and Penobscot Indian reservations and the State shall have exclusive jurisdiction over those offenses and crimes.

2. *Definitions of crimes; tribal procedures.* In exercising its exclusive jurisdiction . . . , the respective tribe or nation shall be deemed to be enforcing tribal law, provided, however, the definitions of the criminal offenses and the juvenile crimes, and the punishments applicable thereto, over which the respective tribe or nation has exclusive jurisdiction under this section, shall be governed by the laws of the State. The procedures for the establishment and operation of tribal forums created to effectuate the purpose of this section shall be governed by any and all federal statutes. . . .

\* \* \*

4. *Double jeopardy, collateral estoppel.* A prosecution for a criminal offense or juvenile crime over which the Passamaquoddy Tribe or the Penobscot Nation has exclusive jurisdiction under this section shall not bar a prosecution for a criminal offense or juvenile crime, arising out of the same conduct, over which the State has exclusive jurisdiction. A prosecution for a criminal offense or juvenile crime over which the State has exclusive jurisdiction shall not bar a prosecution for a criminal offense or juvenile crime, arising out of the same conduct, over which either tribe or nation has exclusive jurisdiction under this section. The determination of an issue of fact in a criminal or juvenile proceeding conducted in a tribal forum shall not constitute collateral estoppel in a crime or juvenile proceeding conducted in a state court. The determination of an issue of fact in a criminal or juvenile proceeding conducted in a state court shall not constitute collateral estoppel in a criminal or juvenile proceeding conducted in a tribal forum.

5. *Future Indian communities.* Any 25 or more adult members of either the Passamaquoddy Tribe or the Penobscot Nation residing within their respective Indian territory and in reasonable proximity to each other may petition the commission for designation as an "extended reservation." If the commission determines, after investigation, that the petitioning tribal members constitute an "extended reservation," the commission shall establish the boundaries of this "extended reservation" and shall recommend to the Legislature that, subject to the approval of the governing body of the tribe or nation involved, it amend this Act to extend the jurisdiction of the respective tribe or nation to the "extended reservation." The boundaries of any "extended reservation" shall not exceed those reason-

ably necessary to encompass the petitioning tribal members.

§ 6210. LAW ENFORCEMENT ON INDIAN RESERVATIONS AND WITHIN INDIAN TERRITORY

1. *Exclusive authority of tribal law enforcement officers.* Law enforcement officers appointed by the Passamaquoddy Tribe and the Penobscot Nation shall have exclusive authority to enforce, within their respective Indian territories, ordinances adopted under section 6206 and section 6207, subsection 1 and to enforce, on their respective Indian reservations, the criminal, juvenile, civil and domestic relations laws over which the Passamaquoddy Tribe or the Penobscot Nation have jurisdiction under section 6209, subsection 1.

2. *Joint authority of tribal and state law enforcement officers.* Law enforcement officers appointed by the Passamaquoddy Tribe or the Penobscot Nation shall have the authority within their respective Indian territories and state and county law enforcement officers shall have the authority within both Indian territories to enforce rules or regulations adopted by the commission under section 6207, subsection 3 and to enforce all laws of the State other than those over which the respective tribe or nation has exclusive jurisdiction under section 6209, subsection 1.

3. *Agreements for cooperation and mutual aid.* Nothing herein shall prevent the Passamaquoddy Tribe or the Penobscot Nation and any state, county or local law enforcement agency from entering into agreements for cooperation and mutual aid.

4. *Powers and training requirements.* Law enforcement officers appointed by the Passamaquoddy Tribe and the Penobscot Nation shall possess the same powers and shall be subject to the same duties, limitations and training requirements as municipal police officers under the laws of the State.

\* \* \*

# 363 "citizens . . . in open defiance" (1979)

Objections to oppressive or unfair tax systems have provided the impetus for many protest movements and insurrections in American history. Virtually everyone seeks to minimize his or her tax. Some seek shelter under exemptions granted for charitable or religious institutions. Others base their refusal to pay taxes or report income on political and constitutional grounds.

In the 1970s a small but vocal tax resistance movement began. The economic hardships of the late 1970s and early 1980s, especially in the farm belt, gave rise to such organizations as the

"Farmers' Liberation Army," the "National Freedom Movement," and the "Posse Comitatus." Some
of these organizations were committed to militant
means. In 1979, Gordon Wendall Kohl, a member of
the Posse Comitatus, had been convicted for refusing to pay federal income tax. On February 13, 1983,
two federal marshals were killed and three police officers wounded in North Dakota while attempting to
serve warrants for probation violations against him.

In *United States v. Edelson*, the court considered
a citizen's argument that his failure to disclose various items of information required by his tax return
was due to a "good motive." Making reference to
earlier decisions, which held that protest against the
war in Vietnam did not excuse filing false tax returns, the court concluded that the defendant's motives were immaterial.

☆ 363  *United States v. Edelson*

604 F.2d 232 (3d Cir. 1979).

PER CURIAM.

In recent years an increasing, if still small, number of our citizens have placed themselves in open
defiance of the Internal Revenue Code, justifying
their positions on the basis of a variety of legal theories that have, for the most part, been rejected by
the courts. The present appeal may be fairly classified as such a case and, just as our sister courts of
appeals that have considered similar arguments
have done, we reject appellant's position.

Joseph Edelson was convicted by a jury on three
counts of willful failure to file tax returns in violation
of 26 U.S.C. § 7203. On this appeal Edelson urges
that his signed income tax forms—containing only
identifying data, with the balance of the requested
information answered with bald assertions of Fifth
Amendment privilege—constitute legitimate tax returns. Edelson inserted only his name, address, occupation, and social security number on the forms.
He also provided a figure for his total income com-
puted on the basis of his interpretation of "constitutional dollars"—by which he meant those dollars
backed by silver. All other requested information
was refused, with assertions of a Fifth Amendment
privilege. Inasmuch as he filed such documents, he
argues, he may not be convicted of willful failure to
file income tax returns.

Further, even if such a use of the Fifth Amendment privilege is found to be invalid, Edelson insists
that he was entitled to have the question of his subjective "good faith" exercise of the privilege put to
the jury. Edelson claims that a good faith finding in
this respect would provide a legal justfication for his
act, and that the trial judge's charge was inadequate
in this regard.

We will affirm the judgment of the district court.

First, it is now well established that tax forms
that do not contain financial information upon which
a taxpayer's tax liability can be determined do not
constitute returns within the meaning of the Internal Revenue Code.

Second, contrary to Edelson's apparent belief,
there is no Fifth Amendment privilege negating
one's duty to file a tax return. A tax form requires
disclosure of routine information necessary for the
computation of tax liability and does not ordinarily
compel testimony about facts that might lead to a
criminal prosecution. Federal income tax information is sought in a non-accusatorial setting and is not,
as a general matter, extracted from a "highly selective group inherently suspect of criminal activities." ...

*              *              *

We find no justification for Edelson's blanket invocation of the Fifth Amendment privilege. One
who uses the Fifth Amendment to protect his refusal to provide the disclosures required in a tax return should confine that use to specific objections to
particular questions on the return for which a valid
claim of privilege exists. He may not use the Fifth
Amendment extravagantly to draw a "conjurer's
circle" around the obligation to file a return. ...

Edelson also challenges the jury instructions on
the question of his "good faith" reliance on his Fifth
Amendment rights. Even if he is adjudged to have
gone beyond any legitimate assertion of the constitutional privilege, he argues, he may not be convicted of willful failure to file tax returns inasmuch
as he sincerely believed that his actions were consistent with the law. In fact, the trial judge appears to
have put this question to the jury with considerable
precision:

*              *              *

If you find the defendant believed in good faith
that he was acting within the law, that the defendant's conduct was not marked by careless disregard as to whether he had the right to so act, you
must find the defendant not guilty for lack of
willfulness.

We can find no error in this charge. ... Insofar as
the defendant may be said to rely on a "good motive" defense,[2] the district court's instruction is in
accord with this Court's opinion in *United States v.
Malinowski* (1973).[3] As for his "good faith" argument, the trial court correctly reasoned that if
Edelson truly believed he was under no legal obligation to provide the Internal Revenue Service with
anything more than the returns he filed, he could not
be guilty of *willful* failure to file—that is, he could
not have intentionally violated a known legal duty.
As we read the instruction, this was the precise
question that was put to the jury, and it was resolved against the defendant.

Accordingly, the judgment of the district court will be affirmed.

---

2. ...

Defendant's motives in failing to file are immaterial so long as the government proves beyond a reasonable doubt that defendant was required to file a return; that he knew this obligation; and that he willfully or purposely failed to file such return. Thus defendant's arguments of good motive, i.e. protest against taxation or government use of paper money not backed by silver, or good faith but mistaken belief in the law of Fifth Amendment are material and relevant only to the statutory element of "willfulness," the specific intent which the government must establish.

3. In *Malinowski*, defendant was a college professor who had provided false information on his tax return because his taxes were used, in part, to fund the war in Vietnam, which he opposed. Malinowski reasoned that his good faith exercise of what he considered to be a First Amendment right of symbolic protest immunized him for prosecution because of his good purpose. Nonetheless, the trial court's refusal to give such a "good purpose" instruction was affirmed by this Court.

# 364 Proletarian Revolution Requires the Armed Seizure of Power (1980)

The Revolutionary Communist Party (RCP), formed in 1975, is wholly separate from the Communist Party of the United States of America. The RCP wrote its constitution and program after a split in its ranks, which focused on whether the People's Republic of China continued to maintain its socialist system after the death of Mao Tse-tung. The RCP contended that the existing Chinese government was reverting to capitalism. The RCP advocates the armed overthrow of the government and the establishment of communism in the United States. Despite all the anti-Communist government action of the 1950s, and its deep, lingering effects on many people, the ideology of overthrowing the government of the United States still has its supporters.

## ☆ 364 Constitution of the Revolutionary Communist Party of the United States

New Programme and New Constitution of the Revolutionary Communist Party, USA—Drafts for Discussion 1980 (Chicago: RCP Publications, 1980).

### GENERAL LINE OF THE REVOLUTIONARY COMMUNIST PARTY, USA

The Revolutionary Communist Party of the USA is the political party of the working class in the United States, the vanguard of the proletariat in this country, and a part of the communist movement interna-

tionally, just as the working class in the U.S. is one part of the revolutionary movement of the international proletariat.

The Revolutionary Communist Party, USA takes Marxism-Leninism, Mao Tsetung Thought as the theoretical basis guiding its thinking.

The basic programme of the Revolutionary Communist Party, USA is the complete overthrow of the bourgeoisie, the establishment of the all-around dictatorship of the proletariat in place of the dictatorship of the bourgeoisie and the triumph of socialism over capitalism in all spheres of society as the necessary transition to the ultimate aim of the Party: the realization of communism with the abolition of all class distinctions. ...

\*          \*          \*

In the United States today, rivaled as a bastion of reaction and enemy of the international proletariat only by the equally imperialist Soviet Union, the first great step of the proletarian revolution—the seizure of power by armed force—is not only a historic task that demands to be accomplished. It is also an urgent necessity, not only for the working class and the great majority of people in the U.S. itself but for the international proletariat and people of the world. It will constitute a tremendous blow against the imperialist system and reaction everywhere and will mark a tremendous leap toward the liberation of the proletariat and oppressed peoples throughout the world—toward the emancipation of mankind itself from the fetters of capitalism and every form and manifestation of class division in society.

To carry out this first, great step the Revolutionary Communist Party, USA, as the vanguard of the proletariat in the United States, must systematically and unceasingly take up the preparation of its own ranks as well as the masses for the eventual development of a revolutionary situation and then resolutely and uncompromisingly lead them in seizing the opportunity to win state power through the armed overthrow of the capitalist state in the U.S. when the conditions do ripen. Create public opinion, seize power—raise the consciousness of the masses and, when through the development of the objective situation and the work of the Party they become convinced of the necessity and possibility of proletarian revolution, organize and lead them in the armed onslaught against the military forces and political institutions of capitalism—this is the basic method through which the preparation for revolution and then the revolutionary overthrow of U.S. imperialism will be realized. It is the central task of the Revolutionary Communist Party, USA.

\*          \*          \*

As for the question of war, the only war the class-conscious proletariat in the U.S. wants to fight, the war for which the working class and masses in this country are being prepared through the work of the Revolutionary Communist Party, USA, is a revolutionary civil war to defeat and overthrow the bourgeoisie and the capitalist state and replace bourgeois dictatorship with the dictatorship of the proletariat. On a world scale, the proletariat supports the revolutionary struggles, including armed struggle as the highest form, of the workers and the oppressed peoples and nations against imperialism and reaction; it opposes the wars of plunder of the imperialists and reactionaries and actively seeks their defeat at the hands of the people. The Revolutionary Communist Party, USA will work tirelessly to educate the proletariat and masses in this country to the truth that they have no country to defend, that in a world war with the Soviet Union, while the proletariat has no interests in the victory of either imperialists, it can only welcome the defeats suffered by its own imperialist bourgeoisie — and more, that the proletariat must utilize such defeats and the weakening of the ruling class to prepare for and finally carry out its overthrow when the possibility ripens. Only this is consistent with proletarian internationalism, with the revolutionary interests of the working class and with its struggle to break free of and ultimately bury the capitalist system and all of its evils, including the monstrosity of war.

*        *        *

MEMBERSHIP

*Article 1*

Any worker or any other person involved in the revolutionary struggle who accepts the Constitution of the Party, is committed to working actively in a Party organization, to carrying out the Party's decisions and to observing Party discipline and paying Party membership dues, may become a member of the Revolutionary Communist Party, USA.

*        *        *

*Article 3*

Members of the Revolutionary Communist Party, USA must:

1. Keep constantly in mind, base themselves wholeheartedly on and dedicate their whole lives to the proletarian revolution and the historic mission of the international proletariat: the achievement of communism throughout the world;

2. Conscientiously study Marxism-Leninism, Mao Tsetung Thought, thoroughly criticize and struggle against revisionism and all forms of opportunism and fight to grasp, defend, apply and develop the correct line in opposition to the incorrect line;

3. Actively distribute the Party's press — its newspaper and other publications — as its main weapon among the masses, vigorously expose the capitalist system and the bourgeoisie, support the

outbreaks of protest and struggle of the masses, and arouse the masses to revolution;

4. Systematically apply the mass line in all their work;

5. Firmly uphold the revolutionary unity of the working class and proletarian internationalism and combat all forms of chauvinism and racism, while also struggling against nationalism and other forms of bourgeois ideology, within the Party as well as among the masses;

6. Be bold in making criticism and self-criticism;

7. Resolutely uphold the Party's discipline and take initiative in carrying out its line and policies;

8. Uphold proletarian morality.

## 365 "the barbed-wire enclosure" (1980)

On July 31, 1980, Congress created a Commission on Wartime Relocation and Internment of Civilians to study the facts surrounding the treatment of Japanese Americans during World War II. Spark Matsunaga, a decorated World War II Japanese American war veteran, was elected to the House of Representatives from Hawaii in 1962 and won a Senate seat in 1976. His testimony before the Senate Governmental Affairs Committee supported the creation of the commission. Hiroko Kamikawa Omata, born in Fresno, California, in 1920, poignantly recounted her camp experience before the committee. Jerry J. Enomoto, past president of the national Japanese American Citizens League (JACL), also testified about life in the initial assembly centers and in the more permanent relocation centers.

The JACL previously had been instrumental in persuading President Gerald Ford to rescind Executive Order 9066, President Roosevelt's document providing legal authority for the Japanese evacuation. Since the executive order was a wartime measure, it should have expired at the war's end, yet it continued in existence. On April 19, 1976, exactly thirty-four years after the order's issuance, Ford signed a proclamation rescinding it, stating, "We now know what we should have known then. Not only was the evacuation wrong, but Japanese Americans were and are loyal Americans."

☆ 365 Testimony regarding the Commission on Wartime Relocation and Internment of Civilians Act

Hearing before the Sen. Comm. on Governmental Affairs on S.1647, 96th Cong., 2d Sess. (Mar. 18, 1980).

☆ 365a Statement by Senator Spark Matsunaga

*        *        *

Some two months after the attack on Pearl Harbor, in February 1942, President Franklin D. Roosevelt issued Executive Order 9066. The Executive Order gave to the Secretary of War the authority to designate "military areas" and to exclude "any or all" persons from such areas. Penalties for the violation of such military restrictions were subsequently established by Congress in Public Law 77-503, enacted in March of that year.

Also in March, the Military Commander of the Western District (General John L. DeWitt) issued four public proclamations as follows:

> *Proclamation No. 1* divided the States of Washington, Oregon, California and Arizona into two military areas and established "restricted zones" in those States.
> *Proclamation No. 2* established four additional military areas in the States of Idaho, Montana, Nevada and Utah.
> *Proclamation No. 3* instituted a curfew in military area number one for all enemy aliens and "persons of Japanese ancestry," and placed restrictions on their travel within the military area even during non-curfew hours.
> *Proclamation No. 4* forbade all aliens of Japanese ancestry and all American-born citizens of Japanese ancestry to leave military district number one.

The first "Civilian Exclusion Order" was issued by General DeWitt on March 24, 1942 and marked the beginning of the evacuation of 120,000 Japanese Americans and their parents from the West Coast.

It is significant to note that the Military Commander of the then Territory of Hawaii, which had actually suffered an enemy attack, did not feel that it was necessary to evacuate all individuals of Japanese ancestry from Hawaii—although it is true that a number of leaders in the Japanese American community in Hawaii were sent to detention camps on the mainland.

Moreover, no Military Commander felt that it was necessary to evacuate from any area of the country all Americans of German or Italian ancestry, although the United States was also at war with Germany and Italy.

FBI Director J. Edgar Hoover, who could hardly be accused of being soft on suspected seditionists, opposed the evacuation of Japanese Americans from the West Coast, pointing out that the FBI and other law enforcement agencies were capable of apprehending any suspected saboteurs or enemy agents. Indeed, martial law was never declared in any of these western States and the federal courts and civilian law enforcement agencies continued to function normally.

\*          \*          \*

No branch of the federal government has ever undertaken a comprehensive examination of the actions taken under Executive Order 9066....

\*          \*          \*

[M]any unanswered questions remain about the detention of Japanese Americans during World War II, and there remains an "unfinished" chapter in our national history. In recent years, the issue of how to write "The End" to this sad and unsavory episode has been widely discussed in the Japanese American Community. From time to time, reports that the Japanese Americans might be preparing to request monetary reparations have been floated in the national press....

... Whether or not redress is provided, the study undertaken by the Commission will be valuable in and of itself, not only for Japanese Americans but for all Americans. Passage of S. 1647 will be just one more piece of evidence that ours is a Nation great enough to recognize and rectify its past mistakes.

Thank you very much.

☆ 365b Statement by Hiroko Kamikawa Omata

\*          \*          \*

... Both my father and mother were ... aliens not by choice but by the denial of the United States Government to allow them citizenship.

I was born in Fresno, California on July 11, 1920, which makes me a citizen of the United States.... When many restrictions were imposed on our lives because of our ancestry, I questioned the validity of being a citizen of the United States. My family and I committed no crime nor did we commit any treasonable acts. I withdrew from college.... [M]y mother, younger brother and I started to weed out the articles that were being confiscated by the United States Government. We broke all of the Japanese records, burned the Japanese books, smashed the cameras and any other item that was on the wanted list of the government. There was panic and fear. All kinds of rumors were spreading fast and with fury. We had to get rid of our car and see to it that our furniture and personal belongings were stored in a safe place.

With very short notice we were ordered to enter the Fresno Assembly Center (better known as the Fresno Race Tracks). We were never given an opportunity to have a hearing or to question the legality of the mass evacuation. We were told to take only one suit case for each person entering the center. Thus, we went like meek sheep obediently thinking that our government knew the best.

Life was primitive in the Assembly Center. For instance, the latrine was a community toilet....

My mother, father, brother and I shared one room—there were no partitions, just four army cots with mattresses filled with straw.... The food was fattening because the emphasis was on carbohydrates. Dust particles were ever present in our lives.

After six months we were herded into a train. Coaches were for the majority and the pullman cars were for the sick, the aged and the little infants. The train was guarded by M.P.'s with their guns ready to shoot anyone who tried to escape. Our destination was Jerome Relocation Center, Jerome, Arkansas. I was the last person to board the train and officially leave the State of California. The trip was long, tiring and also humiliating since we could not take care of ourselves in the way of personal hygiene. There was a small sink to wash and clean ourselves but it was inadequate for a trip that took more than four days.

Upon arriving in Jerome, we all lined up to go to the toilet since we all had diarrhea. The toilet facilities had not been completed and there was general misery. The barracks and roads were still being constructed and mud impeded our trips to the community toilet, which was a separate building from our living quarters.

Each family received a room furnished with a coal stove and the number of cots required to meet the needs of the family. That was all—no chairs, no tables, or other ordinary essentials to make life livable.

I made the best of the situation. A friend worked in the carpenter shop so he brought me some lumber. I made a small room for myself by putting up a partition. I learned to become a good carpenter. I graduated to the point where I made a chair and a bookcase. Life became a little bit more pleasant when my brother painted murals on the walls of our room.

I stayed in Jerome Relocation Center for five months and left to work at the War Relocation Authority in Washington, D.C. The thrill of leaving the barbed-wire enclosure and the gun-toting sentries was the most exhilarating experience in my life. I shall never forget the feeling of walking around free on the streets of Washington, D.C.

In the meantime, my father and mother continued to stay in the camp. My two brothers joined the army: one went to the Pacific with the Military Intelligence Service and the other went to Europe with the famed 442nd Infantry Division. In 1945, after three years of incarceration, my parents moved to Seabrook, New Jersey where they started life anew. In the early 1950's, my parents became citizens of the United States since a new law had been passed permitting them to become citizens. . . .

From 1946 to 1948, I went to Japan with the Department of the Army and found out to my great disappointment that the Japanese people considered me a foreigner. I realized then that I was truly an American, in spite of the treatment I had received by the United States Government. It fortified my belief that the United States Government had to make a formal statement, admitting its error in incarcerating its citizens and aliens.

. . . [T]here will always be a shadow over the history pages of the United States . . . unless immediate steps are taken to remedy this great injustice. I will be 60 years old in July but I hope to continue my night classes at the University of Maryland. . . . [Someday] I hope to get a B.S. degree in Business Administration. In the meantime, I shall continue to challenge the United States Government regarding the unconstitutionality of my wartime incarceration. In order for me to leave my children and their children an enduring legacy and a great faith in this country, I must appeal to you to pass Senator Inouye's bill.

\*          \*          \*

☆365c  Statement by Jerry J. Enomoto for the Japanese American Citizens League

### LIFE IN THE CAMPS

Faced with the evacuation orders, Japanese Americans had to leave their homes with only a few days' notice and could take only what they could carry with them. Property had to be hurriedly sold, abandoned, given away, left in insecure or unpredictable trusts. Crops were left unharvested. Many lost titles to homes, businesses and farmlands because taxes and mortgage payments became impossible to pay. Bank accounts had already been frozen or confiscated as "enemy assets," and there was little source of income within the camps.

\*          \*          \*

The camp life of the evacuees can be divided into two distinct periods. The first period began in March 1942 and ended later that year. It involved residence in 15 temporary detention camps scattered throughout Arizona, California, Oregon and Washington. They were mostly county fairgrounds, race tracks and livestock exhibition halls hastily converted into detention camps with barbed wire fences, searchlights and guard towers. Each camp held about 5,000 detainees, except for the Santa Anita Race Track near Los Angeles, California which held over 18,000 and Mayer, Arizona which held only 247. Living quarters for many consisted of horse stalls, some with manure still inside.

Quarters . . . were generally a bare room comprising a "family apartment," provided only with cots, blankets and mattresses (often straw-filled sacks). The apartment's only fixture was a hanging light bulb. Each family unit was separated from the adjoining one by a thin dividing partition which, "for ventilation purposes," only went part way up.

Evacuees ate communally, showered communally, defeated communally. . . . [N]o partitions had been built between toilets. . . . Protests from Caucasian church groups led, in time, to the building of partial dividing walls, but doors were never installed. . . .

In interior California camps, the hot summer sun beating down on paper-thin roofs turned living quarters into sizzling ovens, sometimes causing floors to melt.

Despite concerned efforts of humanitarian groups, the Public Health Service could not be moved to condemn the stables as unfit for human habitation though the stench became oppressive in the summer heat, especially in stables which had been merely scraped out and no floors put in. At the largest of the assembly centers, the Santa Anita Race Track, then housing over 18,000 evacuees, hospital records show that 75 percent of the illnesses came from the horse stalls.

\*     \*     \*

[Meanwhile] work crews under the supervision of Army engineers were toiling at a feverish pace to meet the near-impossible governmental deadline on relocation camps in the far interior. While most of these sprawling encampments were located on hot desert acres or on drought-parched flatlands, two of the relocation projects (Rohwer and Jerome) were taking shape on swampland areas in distant Arkansas. This marked the second period of camp life—"The Relocation Centers."

Again, with scant regard for the elderly in fragile health, rough-hewn wooden barracks—the flimsy "theater-of-operations" and meant for temporary housing of robust fighting men—had been speedily hammered together, providing only the minimum protection from the elements. Though lined on the inside with plaster board and almost totally wrapped with an overlay of black tarpaper, they afforded far from adequate protection against the icy wintry blast that swept through the warped floor boards in such northerly centers of relocation as Heart Mountain (Wyoming), Minadoka (Idaho), Topaz (Utah) and Tule Lake (California), where the mercury dipped on occasion to a numbing minus 30 degrees in the winter.

A degree of uniformity existed in the physical makeup of all centers. A bare room measuring 20 feet by 24 feet was again referred to as a "family apartment"; each accommodated a family of five to eight members; barrack end-rooms measuring 16 feet by 20 feet were set aside for smaller families. A barrack was made up of four to six such family units. Twelve to fourteen barracks, in turn, comprised a community grouping referred to as a "block." Each block housed 250-300 residents and had its own mess hall, laundry room, latrines and recreation hall.

. . . These destitute living conditions—the poor construction, the crowded and demeaning facilities—were referred to by Chief Judge William Denman of the Ninth Circuit Court of Appeals, in an opinion of August 26, 1949, in which he noted that in no federal penitentiary were conditions so poor.

\*     \*     \*

Overwhelming despair caused some detainees to commit suicide. Many more died prematurely due to inadequate medical facilities and the harsh environment.

All incoming and outgoing communications were censored, including personal letters and newspapers. All internal communications were strictly controlled by the camp administration. The Japanese language was banned at public meetings, and the Buddhist and Shinto religions were suppressed.

The detainees tried to make the dreary camps halfway tolerable by foraging scrap materials to make furniture and room partitions. They used indigenous plants to make gardens and surplus materials or adobe to build schools and recreation facilities. Detainees also operated their own camp farms, and many camps became self-sufficient in food.

Milton S. Eisenhower, associate director of the Office of War Information, in a letter dated April 22, 1943, to the President said: "My friends in the War Relocation Authority, like Secretary Ickes, are deeply distressed over the effects of the entire evacuation and the relocation program upon the Japanese-Americans, particularly upon the young citizen group. Persons in this group find themselves living in an atmosphere for which their public school and democratic teachings have not prepared them. It is hard for them to escape a conviction that their plight is due more to racial discrimination, economic motivations and wartime prejudices than to any real necessity from the military point of view for evacuation from the West Coast."

\*     \*     \*

## 366 "no governmental interest is more compelling than the security of the Nation" (1981)

Philip Agee, a CIA agent for eleven years, had been involved extensively in intelligence-gathering activities. After leaving the CIA, Agee traveled to many countries campaigning against the agency and attempting to expose its covert activities. In the process he allegedly revealed information in violation of his contract with the CIA not to make public statements about agency matters without agency approval. In 1979, Secretary of State Edmund Muskie revoked Agee's passport.

Agee claimed that the revocation of his passport was unconstitutional because it limited his freedom to travel, his exercise of free speech, and his right to criticize the government. Agee also said that his right to procedural due process was violated because the passport was revoked without a hearing. The court rejected all of Agee's arguments. Affirming the constitutionality of Muskie's actions, Justice Burger, writing for the majority, stated the former CIA agent was a threat to national security. Citing previous opinions, the court noted: "[W]hile the Constitution protects against invasions of individual rights, it is not a suicide pact."

## ☆ 366  *Haig v. Agee*

453 U.S. 280 (1981).

CHIEF JUSTICE BURGER delivered the opinion of the Court.

The question presented is whether the President, acting through the Secretary of State, has authority to revoke a passport on the ground that the holder's activities in foreign countries are causing or are likely to cause serious damage to the national security or foreign policy of the United States.

\*       \*       \*

The history of passport controls since the earliest days of the Republic shows congressional recognition of Executive authority to withhold passports on the basis of substantial reasons of national security and foreign policy....

\*       \*       \*

... Indeed, by an unbroken line of Executive Orders, regulations, instructions to consular officials, and notices to passport holders, the President and the Department of State left no doubt that likelihood of damage to national security or foreign policy of the United States was the single most important criterion in passport decisions.

\*       \*       \*

Agee argues that the only way the Executive can establish implicit congressional approval is by proof of longstanding and consistent *enforcement* of the claimed power: that is, by showing that many passports were revoked on national security and foreign policy grounds. For this proposition, he relies on *Kent* [*v. Dulles*].

\*       \*       \*

The history is clear that there have been few situations involving substantial likelihood of serious damage to the national security or foreign policy of the United States as a result of a passport holder's activities abroad, and that in the cases which have arisen, the Secretary has consistently exercised his power to withhold passports....

The Secretary has construed and applied his regulations consistently, and it would be anomalous to fault the Government because there were so few oc-

casions to exercise the announced policy and practice. Although a pattern of actual enforcement is one indicator of Executive policy, it suffices that the Executive has "openly asserted" the power at issue.

\*       \*       \*

Agee also contends that the statements of Executive policy are entitled to diminished weight because many of them concern the powers of the Executive in wartime. However, the statute provides no support for this argument. History eloquently attests that grave problems of national security and foreign policy are by no means limited to times of formally declared war.

\*       \*       \*

Agee also attacks the Secretary's action on three constitutional grounds: first, that the revocation of his passport impermissibly burdens his freedom to travel; second, that the action was intended to penalize his exercise of free speech and deter his criticism of government policies and practices; and third, that failure to accord him a prerevocation hearing violated his Fifth Amendment right to procedural due process.

In light of the express language of the passport regulations, which permits their application only in cases involving likelihood of "serious damage" to national security or foreign policy, these claims are without merit.

Revocation of a passport undeniably curtails travel, but the freedom to travel abroad with a "letter of introduction" in the form of a passport issued by the sovereign is subordinate to national security and foreign policy considerations; as such, it is subject to reasonable governmental regulation. The Court has made it plain that the *freedom* to travel outside the United States must be distinguished from the *right* to travel within the United States....

\*       \*       \*

It is "obvious and unarguable" that no governmental interest is more compelling than the security of the Nation. Protection of the foreign policy of the United States is a governmental interest of great importance, since foreign policy and national security considerations cannot neatly be compartmentalized.

\*       \*       \*

Not only has Agee jeopardized the security of the United States, but he has endangered the interests of countries other than the United States—thereby creating serious problems for American foreign relations and foreign policy. Restricting Agee's foreign travel, although perhaps not certain to prevent all of Agee's harmful activities, is the only avenue open to the Government to limit these activities.

Assuming *arguendo* that First Amendment protections reach beyond our national boundaries,

Agee's First Amendment claim has no foundation. The revocation of Agee's passport rests in part on the content of his speech: specifically, his repeated disclosures of intelligence operations and names of intelligence personnel. Long ago, however, this Court recognized that "[n]o one would question but that a government might prevent actual obstruction to its recruiting service or the publication of the sailing dates of transports or the number and location of troops." Agee's disclosures, among other things, have the declared purpose of obstructing intelligence operations and the recruiting of intelligence personnel. They are clearly not protected by the Constitution. The mere fact that Agee is also engaged in criticism of the Government does not render his conduct beyond the reach of the law.

To the extent the revocation of his passport operates to inhibit Agee, "it is an inhibition of *action*," rather than of speech (emphasis supplied). Agee is as free to criticize the United States Government as he was when he held a passport — always subject, of course, to express limits on certain rights by virtue of his contract with the Government.

On this record, the Government is not required to hold a prerevocation hearing. In *Cole v. Young* we held that federal employees who hold "sensitive" positions "where they could bring about any discernible effects on the Nation's security" may be suspended without a presuspension hearing. For the same reasons, when there is a substantial likelihood of "serious damage" to national security or foreign policy as a result of a passport holder's activities in foreign countries, the Government may take action to ensure that the holder may not exploit the sponsorship of his travels by the United States. "[W]hile the Constitution protects against invasions of individual rights, it is not a suicide pact." The Constitution's due process guarantees call for no more than what has been accorded here: a statement of reasons and an opportunity for a prompt postrevocation hearing.

We reverse the judgment of the Court of Appeals and remand for further proceedings consistent with this opinion.

*Reversed and remanded.*

JUSTICE BRENNAN, with whom JUSTICE MARSHALL joins, dissenting.

\*　　　\*　　　\*

I suspect that this case is a prime example of the adage that "bad facts make bad law." Philip Agee is hardly a model representative of our Nation. And the Executive Branch has attempted to use one of the only means at its disposal, revocation of a passport, to stop respondent's damaging statements. But just as the Constitution protects both popular and unpopular speech, it likewise protects both popular and unpopular travelers. And it is important to remember that this decision applies not only to Philip Agee, whose activities could be perceived as harming the national security, but also to other citizens who may merely disagree with Government foreign policy and express their views.

The Constitution allocates the lawmaking function to Congress, and I fear that today's decision has handed over too much of that function to the Executive. In permitting the Secretary to stop this unpopular traveler and critic of the CIA, the Court professes to rely on, but in fact departs from, the two precedents in the passport regulation area, *Zemel* and *Kent*. Of course it is always easier to fit oneself within the safe haven of *stare decisis* than boldly to overrule precedents of several decades' standing. Because I find myself unable to reconcile those cases with the decision in this case, however, and because I disagree with the Court's *sub silentio* overruling of those cases, I dissent.

# 367 "resistance against a plan to force nuclear power upon the American people" (1981)

During the summer of 1981, residents of San Luis Obispo and the Abalone Alliance of California appealed for nationwide support to block the opening of the Diablo Canyon nuclear power plant. These residents were concerned with the plant's safety, since it was located near an earthquake fault; its potentially adverse effects on water quality and conservation; and its cost and efficiency.

The Abalone Alliance sponsored protests and occupations, similar to those undertaken by the civil rights and anti-Vietnam War movements, of the plant site in 1977 and 1978. In 1981 it called for a third blockade. The alliance required all participants to take part in nonviolence training and to be willing to risk arrest.

## ☆ 367 San Luis Obispo Calls for Diablo Blockade

*Radioactive Times*, July 1981, 1-4.

Residents in the San Luis Obispo area and members of the statewide Abalone Alliance are calling on all opponents of nuclear power to join in a nonviolent blockade/encampment of the plant. A nationwide appeal for support has been issued in an attempt to prevent Diablo Canyon from ever operating.

Public hearings before the Nuclear Regulatory Commission (NRC) ended early this summer after more than ten years of legal intervention by citizens' groups. Now the NRC is poised to grant PG&E [Pacific Gas & Electric] a license to begin operating the Diablo Canyon nuclear plant located 12 miles from San Luis Obispo.

*          *          *

In March 1979, the licensing of Diablo seemed imminent despite widespread public opposition. The Abalone Alliance began planning another land and sea blockade to prevent the plant from operating. In April of 1979, the accident at Three Mile Island nuclear plant spurred public opposition and brought over 30,000 people to rallies in San Francisco and Los Angeles. On June 30, over 40,000 people came to a rally in San Luis Obispo to oppose the licensing of Diablo.

*          *          *

Recent actions by the Reagan administration and the NRC have made clear their intention to escalate the development of nuclear power. Antinuclear activists realize that the face-off in San Luis Obispo will represent more than just an effort to stop one particular nuclear plant. The blockade/encampment will be an act of resistance against a plan to force nuclear power upon the American people.

The growth of a grassroots anti-nuclear movement around the world shows that if Californians and people from across the nation join together, we can stop Diablo Canyon. More importantly, we can bring ourselves closer to a safer energy policy based on a popular voice in our energy decisions.

There is a groundswell taking place in California. This groundswell is a rapidly growing grassroots movement to prevent the licensing of the Diablo Canyon nuclear plant. Years of education, legal intervention in the regulatory process, rallies and legal actions, and nonviolent civil disobedience have sown roots of opposition to Diablo Canyon that run firm and deep.

*          *          *

When the NRC gives PG&E the go-ahead to start the plant, the Abalone Alliance, a statewide anti-nuclear network, will begin a blockade/encampment to try and prevent the plant from becoming radioactive.

All participants in the blockade must be willing to risk arrest and will have participated in Abalone Alliance "nonviolence training" sessions. People participating in the blockade/encampment, as well as individuals doing support work, will form affinity groups when they receive nonviolence preparation. For information on nonviolence preparation contact your local group.

*          *          *

... [A]s soon as PG&E attempts to load the fuel to begin "low power" testing, the Abalone Alliance will respond by initiating the blockade/encampment at the gates and on the plant site.

The Alliance has developed an "alert system" to notify affinity groups in California and nationwide exactly when the blockade must begin. People from San Luis Obispo and neighboring counties will start the action and be joined as quickly as possible by all other affinity groups.

Upon arrival in San Luis Obispo, affinity groups will be directed to briefing and camping areas. They will then proceed to "check in" areas before joining the action. Blockade/encampment participants will then enter the site through numerous land routes as well as by sea.

Some participants will aim to block the three main access roads to the plant, and others will proceed through the back country to get as close to the plant as possible.

## 368 Radicalizing Public Opinion (1981)

The Abalone Alliance compiled a sixty-page guidebook to help train participants in the organized and effective breach of the law for political purposes in preparation for the 1981 blockade of the Diablo Canyon nuclear power plant. Beginning with a history of twentieth-century nonviolent direct action in the United States and abroad, the booklet supplied forecasts of future activities and advice on methods of coping with opposition, arrest, legal process, and living in jail. Effective resort to nonviolent resistance by the antinuclear movement has resulted in the temporary occupation by protesters of nuclear power plants throughout the world and has occasionally contributed to their permanent closure.

☆ 368 Dynamics of Non-violence

Abalone Alliance, *Diablo Canyon/Encampment Handbook* (Santa Cruz, Calif: Northern California Preparers' Collective, 1980), 6–9.

HISTORY OF NON-VIOLENT MASS ACTION

*          *          *

Labor movements in this country and around the world have used non-violent action with striking effectiveness. The Industrial Workers of the World (Wobblies) in the pre-World War I period held a number of general strikes in the Northwest which radically changed the power and consciousness of labor and organized free speech confrontations in Spokane, San Diego and Fresno, among other places.

In 1937, the Flint, Michigan employees of General Motors invented the sit-down strike. After other tactics in their struggle for union recognition had failed, they voted to occupy the factories and to live inside until their demand was met. During the sit-down, all strikers met together daily to plan and organize the tasks that had to be done. The sit-downs spread rapidly to other GM plants; with the help of much outside support, the sit-down strikers achieved their goal.

The Australian dockworkers, after they had stated their opposition to uranium mining, refused to load uranium into ships bound for other countries.

\*     \*     \*

In the current anti-nuclear and environmental struggles, non-violent direct action has been a major element of campaigns waged by citizen resistance. Fisherfolk of the Japanese port of Sasebo, worried about dangers to their health and livelihood, blockaded a leaking nuclear-powered ship with their fishing boats to prevent it from docking in port. The ship was turned away and eventually forced into premature decommissioning.

In Markolsheim, France, people were angered by plans for the construction of a lead factory. From September to November 1974 they took over the site—building a friendship house, digging wells, and bringing farm animals until February 1975, when the French government was forced to withdraw the plant's permit.

\*     \*     \*

In May of 1980 several thousand Germans occupied the construction site of a waste storage facility near Gorleben. An antinuclear village on the model of Whyl was built and dubbed "The Free Republic of Wendland."

The community was brought to an end after a month when 10,000 police cleared out the 2000 Wendlanders and razed the village to the ground. The struggle against Gorleben continues.

Since the mid-seventies, tens of thousands have participated in non-violent mass actions directed against U.S. nuclear power and weapons plants including Diablo Canyon, Seabrook, Trojan, Rocky Flats, Comanche Peak and the Pentagon. These actions have proven to be effective and instrumental in raising consciousness, delaying construction or implementation of policy, as well as empowering their participants to join other social change movements.

\*     \*     \*

### DYNAMICS OF NON-VIOLENCE

When we in the anti-nuclear movement commit ourselves to non-violent campaigns, we set in motion a twofold dynamic. First, we begin to change ourselves; as we confront corporate lies, hold non-violence preparations, form new affinity groups, we gain confidence in working together. This happens both naturally and consciously, as we learn that the means by which we come together and act determine and affect our ends. The second dynamic is our effect on those outside our community, not only our governmental and corporate opponents, but the large number of uncommitted people whose support is necessary for important social change.

The antinuke movement reflects this dynamic. Its commitment to feminist process, small autonomous groups, and to strong, well-organized actions that help people brave arrest, has done more than empower its members. It asserts to neutral people that we are dedicated, that we're not going to give up or go away. We alienate some by acting, just as we perhaps exclude some who don't "believe" in consensus process—but we gain the attention and respect of many more who otherwise remain untouched by thoughts of the nuclear menace.

Potentially, everyone can act to stop nukes, because ordinary people have power. In 1977, 47 people committed civil disobedience at Diablo; the next year, ten times that many risked arrest. By acting we gain momentum—and this momentum creates grave problems for the authorities. As we gain and keep people through good process and commitment, we enlarge our choices of non-violent strategies—and limit the authorities' choices in the process.

The ideal dynamic is that of ordinary people gaining power and control over the things that matter in our lives. The means we employ—consensus decision-making, skill sharing, small groups, mutual respect and support—mirror these ends. . . . When we act violently, most of us are in unfamiliar terrain which is very familiar to police trained to respond to the cues of violence. But when we refuse to give those cues, we put the police in unfamiliar territory. Their power resides in the threat of arrest or the fear of force; and, in the power to disperse us once again and turn a collective into isolated individuals. When we stand our ground, when we show determination rather than fear of arrest or violence, we deprive them of their usual responses, and draw them into a field of conflict with rules of our choosing: non-violent rules. Violence is a relationship—when we act differently, when we combine non-violence with determination, when we treat them as potential allies or intimates, we confuse them and open them to change.

### RESPONSES TO VIOLENCE

Non-violence is not a guarantee that the authorities won't use violence. The civil rights movement in the U.S., the struggle against the British in India, and the women's suffrage struggles in the U.S. and England clearly show this.

If they do respond with violence, how does one remain non-violent in the face of riot(ing) police? The first thing is maintaining human contact with the potential assailant—whether it's a policeman, a policewoman, a counter-demonstrator, or an angry participant from "our" side. Body language is very important: keeping your hands open and at your sides, maintaining an attentive but non-aggressive stance, making predictable movements, and especially making eye contact with your opponent.

\*          \*          \*

It is crucial that affinity groups discuss, and role play, responses to potentially violent situations. For instance, an a.g. can physically surround someone being assaulted, while continuing to talk, distract, or calm the attacker. Active non-violent responses such as this are, after all, the same idea as the entire blockade, which is intervening against the corporate violence of nuclear power. This firm, collective and yet non-violent response to violence isn't restricted to one blockade, just as people's empowerment isn't restricted to one issue....

\*          \*          \*

We can show the police (among others) another model of human nature, people who are acting for nature and themselves, and this process encourages our opponents' doubts about the rightness of their actions. We can also bring about mutual respect....

In a non-violent action, then, we bring many pressures to bear on our opponent—as well as maintain more collective control over our own responses to their threats.

An integral part of this is establishing the right "feeling" during an action. Many people comment on the extraordinary tone of non-violent actions. It comes from the fact that the participants are *centered and clear* about what they are doing; about what they risk and what they can gain.

\*          \*          \*

THE POLICE AND THE NATIONAL GUARD

The police and National Guard we will face during the blockade of Diablo are as much human beings as we are, and, as humans, are susceptible to the effects of non-violence, rational communication, and love. If we approach them as foes, the interaction will take on the characteristics of a self-fulfilling prophecy, and become a hostile and possibly violent confrontation.

By dealing with the police in a positive way, we don't guarantee that they won't be brutal and obedient. But we challenge that brutality and obedience and made deviations from it possible. At the heart of all effective social change movements is the ability to affect (either to paralyze or win over) part of the repressive establishment. Only when there is large scale dissatisfaction among the forces of order does major social change become possible.

Ambivalence, even resistance, is more common among police and soldiers than most people know....

\*          \*          \*

Police from Santa Barbara, Ventura, and the Central Coast area will be at the action. National Guard units and police may come from anywhere in California. As of this writing there is no statewide collec-

tive working on outreach to these people, although there has been a great deal of communication between police in San Luis Obispo and the Abalone Alliance. It is important that this communication continue and increase; if you want to help, contact the Diablo Project Office.

## 369 "Shut Down Selective Service" (1982)

Responding to Soviet aggression in Afghanistan and to the Soviet-backed Polish government's repression of the Solidarity union, President Jimmy Carter issued an executive order in 1980 requiring young men once again to register for possible conscription into the military. With the election of Ronald Reagan as president in November of that year executive policies stiffened regarding the foreign relations and military postures of the United States.

Many in the nation objected to the military build-up and saw the new Selective Service registration requirement as a prelude to a new peacetime conscription. At the end of 1982 some five hundred thousand youths eligible for registration reportedly failed to carry out this imposed duty. The following handbill reflects the new opposition to Selective Service, reminiscent of the Vietnam era.

☆ 369  Affirm Life—Resist War

☆ 369a  A Call to Resistance at Selective Service

Resistance Campaign, Washington, D.C., October 18, 1982.

Two years ago compulsory draft registration was re-established. Since that time a strong draft resistance movement has developed. In spite of this, the government is now threatening a return of the full draft. In the past two years, in addition to registration, the SSS has reactivated draft boards, recently completed new classification and mobilization regulations and is now developing plans to deliver inductees into the armed forces. Three major draft bills are now in Congress, poised to be passed in the heat of an "international crisis" situation. In the meantime, the worsening economic situation has provided adequate numbers of soldiers for the armed forces by forcing unemployed youth into enlisting. This system of "economic conscription" particularly falls upon Black, Latino and low income youths—the same communities whose youth were placed in combat and died in disproportionate numbers during the war in Vietnam.

During this two-year period, since the reinstitution of draft registration, U.S. government policy has been moving toward war in other ways.... The U.S. has drastically increased its support of repressive dictatorships throughout the world. And, finally, the current administration has embarked on a reckless drive to achieve nuclear superiority at any cost. This same administration has repeatedly turned away from opportunities for serious disarmament initiatives.

People in the U.S., Europe and across the world have become increasingly appalled at this drive toward war. Recently, a vocal majority of people have begun to oppose the Reagan administration's foreign and military policies. However, the Reagan administration continues undaunted. The techniques used to protest, thus far, have seemed to be ineffective in changing the direction of Reagan's military policies. Those of us organizing this action believe we can no longer only *call* on the government to change its policies. Instead, we will *actively resist* the preparation for war in all its manifestations. Of these manifestations, the Selective Service System is essential in providing the unlimited numbers of troops needed to fight a prolonged intervention. The resistance movement has challenged the effectiveness of the draft registration program. At the SSS headquarters on October 18, we will take this challenge one step further by shutting down the draft registration program at its source.

To us resistance means to take control of our lives. We declare our refusal to cooperate with the preparations for war. Instead, we commit ourselves to working here at home to build a society truly based on peace and social justice. In this action we support all forms of resistance to militarism including non-registration, induction refusal, war tax resistance, counter-recruitment, and resistance of G.I.'s within the Armed Forces. Institutional violence and oppression are not confined to the armed forces. Violence pervades our society in many ways but is further reinforced and perpetuated by the military establishment. Therefore, we also support resistance to racist, sexist and anti-Lesbian and Gay violence as adamantly as we support resistance to militarism.

The trials of nonregistrants continue and the United States moves closer to war. We must take the initiative in our response.

*Join us at Selective Service on October 18.*

\* \* \*

Shut Down Selective Service October 16-18, 1982

\* \* \*

The trials of nonregistrants have recently begun. The first draft resisters are already going to prison. At the same time the Reagan Administration threatens military intervention in the Third World and has launched on a new escalation of the nuclear arms race. In this action we stand with all war resisters in their refusal to cooperate with the draft and preparations for war.

Join us on October 16-18 for a weekend of Draft Resistance events followed by a Nonviolent Civil Disobedience Action\* and Legal Picket Monday morning at Selective Service System Headquarters.

\* \* \*

Endorsers: All African Peoples Revolutionary Party; Boston Mobilization for Survival; D.C. Resistance Coalition; Hampshire Anti-Draft Coalition; Libertarian Student Network; Mass Open Resistance; Mothers and Others against the Draft; National Mobilization for Survival; National Resistance Committee; Potomac Alliance; Progressive Campus Network; Students against Militarism; Syracuse Peace Council; Upstate Resistance; War Resisters League; Washington Peace Center.

---

\*All participants must be trained in nonviolence and be part of an affinity group.

---

☆ 369b Draft Protest Results in Sixty Arrests Here

*Washington Post*, October 19, 1982, B1-2.

Washington police yesterday arrested 60 of nearly 200 antidraft demonstrators who, swaying to song and the sound of folk guitars, sought unsuccessfully to shut down the Selective Service System headquarters in Georgetown.

The protesters, ranging in age from teenagers to senior citizens, came mostly from cities throughout the Northeast....

\* \* \*

Authorities said no one was injured in the more than two-hour face-off between the protesters, representing a variety of antidraft groups organized under an umbrella group called the October 18 Resistance Campaign, and about 150 Washington and Federal Protective Service police. Some demonstrators who refused to walk to police vans were carried away on stretchers and across police night sticks.

Police set up a 50-foot-long barricade at the foot of the hill where the demonstrators, carrying signs that said "Resist Slavery, Resist the Draft" and "No Draft, No War," gathered after an early-morning march from Washington Square downtown. Starting at about 8:30, groups of the protesters attempted to cross the barricade and enter the Selective Service headquarters, where employees were arriving for work.

As the demonstrators crossed the line, they were arrested. With each arrest, cheers and rounds of applause rose from their colleagues, most dressed in jeans, sweaters and sneakers. Police estimated the crowd as about 180, while organizers said about 300 persons participated.

Inside the four-story brick building at 1023 31st St. NW, said Selective Service spokesman Joan Lamb, it was business as usual.

"We don't find any massive dissent out there [in the country] on this issue," said Selective Service director Thomas Turnage, describing antidraft protesters as an "infinitesimally small, hard core of people out there trying to make an issue out of this."

Grace Hedemann, a spokesman for the demonstration's organizers, said the day's event had been a success. "We brought the issue to the forefront," she said. "We raised the issue not only for the 13 men [who have been indicted or convicted] but for the 600,000 who have resisted."

The administration has estimated that 500,000 eligible young men have failed to register for the draft.

Outside, as the demonstration continued, someone would occasionally burn a draft registration card. The protest songs and chants provided a constant refrain, for some heightening the sense of nostalgia.

Jim Bristol of Camden, N.J., watched and remembered. A former Lutheran minister, Bristol said he refused to complete his draft registration forms 42 years ago. For that, he spent 18 months in prison and developed an affinity with the subsequent generation of young men who also refused.

"I'm glad there are more people who are opposing the draft," said Bristol, 70. "It's good to see that some are so deeply opposed that they are willing to put their bodies where their words are."

*          *          *

"I don't see this as an unpatriotic act," said Stephen Zunes, of the Mount Pleasant section of Northwest Washington. "I love my country," said the 25-year-old student.

# 370 " 'there's a victory whenever you follow your conscience' " (1982)

Enten Eller, a twenty-year-old physics major at Bridgewater College in Virginia, became the first youth to be convicted for failure to register under the newly instituted draft registration program. Prior to his trial Eller told reporters that registering would "be against God's will for my life." A member of the Church of the Brethren, a denomination historically committed to nonviolent and pacifist beliefs and action, Eller was the son of a World War II conscientious objector. Explaining his conduct to the press, the draft resister insisted his decision did not arise from any political conviction or activism. "My personal beliefs led me to this position on religious grounds only," he emphasized.

In imposing sentence the court took special no-

tice of the offender's background and motives. Both the original probation sentence and the subsequent community service sentence reflected the dilemmas of the sentencing judge. After finding Eller guilty and sentencing him to probation, in the first instance, the judge concluded: "There are many people in this room who think your action heroic—that you are a hero. I'm not passing on that one way or the other. But the defense that you raised or didn't raise here has made you an honorable person in the eyes of this court." Upon Eller's failure to comply with the probation order, which required registration, the judge once more overruled the urging of the prosecutor that severe penalties were required in order to give effect to the government's registration policy, and failed to impose imprisonment upon the youth he considered "honorable."

## ☆ 370 The Sentencing of Draft Registration Resister Enten Eller

### ☆ 370a Virginia College Senior Placed on Probation in Draft Case

*Washington Post*, August 18, 1982, A1.

Enten Eller, the clean-cut college senior who claimed God's will left him no choice, today became the first American in the 1980s convicted of failing to register for the military draft.

He was immediately sentenced to three years' probation by U.S. District Court Judge James C. Turk, who ordered the polite 20-year-old, as a condition of his sentence, to comply with the draft registration law within 90 days, or face imprisonment and a fine.

Eller said later he would continue to refuse to register.

"God has led me to this position. I need to be here," Eller told Turk during the 3½-hour, nonjury trial here in which he forbade his attorneys to defend him.

*          *          *

Eller, who had faced up to five years' imprisonment and a $10,000 fine, was sentenced by Turk today as a youth offender, meaning his sentence could be vacated if he should decide to comply with its terms.

During the trial, Assistant U.S. Attorney E. Montgomery Tucker contended that the case was not about religious or moral views or whether there should be a draft, but about Eller's "knowing, persistent, willful and continuing refusal to do an act in accordance with a law of this country."

Under questioning, Eller conceded he had written voluntarily to Selective Service officials and later to U.S. prosecutors here acknowledging that he had not registered.

"Why can't he sign [the registration form] and say it's not in any way a sign of his approval?" Turk inquired at one point of Rev. Vernard Eller, the youth's father, who is a religion professor and ordained minister in the Church of the Brethren in Le Verne, Calif.

"I've told him that. You try to tell him that," responded the father, who said he had been a conscientious objector during World War II but only after first taking the draft registration step.

Enten Eller testified he had been moved not to comply in part by what he saw as "the inequity" of receiving automatic conscientious objector status as a member of the Church of the Brethren, one of several historic pacifist denominations in the United States.

*        *        *

Two local lawyers, Arthur Strickland and Jonathan Rogers, assisted Eller in the case, but told Turk they had been frustrated by Eller's decision not to mount a legal defense. Both attorneys said they believe the draft registration statute is unconstitutional.

## ☆370b Draft Registration Resister Given Alternative Service

*Washington Post*, December 9, 1982, C1.

Enten Eller, a pacifist who said God directed him not to sign a draft registration card, was ordered today to perform two years of alternative service as punishment for his refusal to register for the standby military draft.

U.S. District Judge James C. Turk denied a request by federal prosecutors that Eller, the first registration resister convicted after the standby draft was implemented by President Carter in 1980, receive a two-year prison term.

The decision marked the latest development in a Reagan administration campaign to encourage registration among about 675,000 young men it says have failed to comply with Selective Service laws. The American Civil Liberties Union and other groups have attacked the standby draft as both illegal and unnecessary.

Turk, who clearly had little desire to imprison Eller, told reporters after today's 12-minute hearing that he found the polite, 21-year-old Bridgewater College senior "an especially unique individual. . . . He's in a funny position. He can't register for the draft. He can't bring himself to do it."

Eller told the judge as much today, apologizing for his failure to comply with the terms of an earlier sentence that directed he register. "I'm sorry I did not comply with the conditions of probation . . . but I felt I had no other choice," Eller said softly. "I hope we can work it out in a way that's acceptable not only to the government and myself but to your conscience."

The maximum penalty for failure to register is five years in prison and a $10,000 fine. Under provisions of the Youth Corrections Act, the law that Turk invoked in initially sentencing Eller last August, he could have received up to six years' incarceration.

Eller, a member of the pacifist Church of the Brethren and an honors student at the church-affiliated college near Harrisonburg, Va., has said God directed him not to sign up for the draft, a belief Turk said he found sincere.

Outside the federal courthouse here, a smiling Eller said he had been prepared to go to prison. "I had to be," he said. Asked if the judge's decision was a victory against the government, Eller replied: "I wouldn't put it in terms of a victory. If you want to put it in those terms, there's a victory whenever you follow your conscience."

Turk, who called Eller's actions "a substantial violation" of probation conditions imposed after his Aug. 17 conviction, said the young man's alternative service will be performed without pay at a Veterans Administration hospital in the Roanoke area or a similar facility.

Eller will be allowed first to complete college, the judge said. He is expected to graduate in May.

Turk had placed Eller on three years' probation, on condition he register for the draft within 90 days. Eller said after his one-day August trial he had no intention of complying with the order and he was true to his word.

*        *        *

The sole witness in today's hearing was Eller's probation officer, Jimmy Lee, who said Eller had complied with every condition of his probation, including performing community service in Harrisonburg, except to sign the draft card.

## 371 "the 'political demonstrators' and the 'opportunists' " (1982)

Political dissent, disobedience, unrest, and violence continued to manifest themselves in many arenas of American life as the nation entered the third century of its independence. Some of the conflicts were relatively new: the disagreements over the status of Puerto Rico and the controversy over America's use of nuclear power. Many of the conflicts continued in old arenas: military service, the status of labor, and the resurgent Ku Klux Klan.

At the end of 1982 the nation's capital witnessed demonstrations by and counterdemonstrations against the Klan. The reported events once more illustrated the long-existing difficulties in distinguishing between the "genuine" (the ideologically or con-scientiously motivated) political offender and the "opportunist" (the pseudo-political offender), who was using the cloak of political turmoil for selfish criminal pursuits. Writing about the latter, the late Stephen Schafer, a noted criminologist, warned: "Not all who commit crimes with the apparent mo-tive of promoting triumph of an altruistic-communal cause are genuine convictional criminals.... Many simply use the convictional ideal as an excuse for their own criminal act. Moved by love or hate, penchant for adventure, psychological deviation, justification of avoiding constructive work, or hope for gain, the pseudoconvictional offenders may join forces with the true convictional criminal.... Their targets ... [are] an individualistic goal through crime, not the service of an ideal" (Stephen Schafer, *The Political Criminal* [New York: Free Press, 1974], 154-55).

## ☆ 371  Just Hell-bent on Crime

### ☆ 371a  Klan Foes Rampage, Loot, Battle Police

*Washington Post*, November 28, 1982, A1.

Hundreds of protesters, angered when denied a con-frontation with a Ku Klux Klan group after it aban-doned a planned march yesterday, turned their rage on the city—hurling rocks and bottles at police, blocking downtown traffic and smashing store win-dows in an intense hit-and-run rampage that lasted two hours.

At least 12 officers were injured, as well as an un-determined number of the estimated 5,500 anti-Klan protesters, as police on horseback and scooters re-peatedly charged the demonstrators in an attempt to scatter them.... Police said 38 persons were arrested.

Protesters overturned an unmarked Capitol Po-lice car near Lafayette Square and smashed win-dows of several others. Shouting groups of youths smashed store windows on Vermont Avenue, 14th Street and H Street downtown, stealing cameras and bicycles from two stores.

Huge plate-glass windows at Sholl's New Cafete-ria at Vermont Avenue and K Street NW were bro-ken as startled diners fled for safety. Across the street, youths smashed several windows of the Mad-ison National Bank until police rushed up and dis-persed them.

            *            *            *

The day started peacefully with thousands of as-sorted anti-Klan protesters gathering along Penn-sylvania and Constitution avenues where members of the Alabama-based Knights of the Ku Klux Klan planned to march from the Capitol to Lafayette Square.

Other groups in counter-protests against the Klan assembled at the Ellipse, McPherson Square and the Lincoln Memorial.

Shortly after 11 a.m., about 30 to 35 Klansmen gathered in Senate Park, a broad grassy area at Constitution and Delaware avenues NW, just north of the Capitol. The park was fenced off and anti-Klan protesters were kept at a distance.

Some of the Klansmen carried their white robes in paper bags but none donned the uniforms. Three members of a Klan "security patrol," wearing black uniforms that included black helmets with shaded visors, stood protectively around the main Klan group.

Tom Robb of Arkansas, a Klan chaplain carrying a Bible, told reporters his group was protesting a bill in Congress that would grant amnesty to millions of illegal aliens who arrived here before 1977 but put controls on future immigration.

He said they also were protesting the fact that Klan Grand Wizard Don Black could not attend the rally here because of the conditions of Black's appeal bond that prevented him from leaving Louisiana. Black was convicted in 1981 of violating the federal Neutrality Act by attempting to overthrow the prime minister of the Caribbean nation of Dominica.

"The Lord will re-establish the foundation of this nation upon ... white Christianity and western civi-lization," Robb said, when reporters asked what the general goal of the organization was.

After the discussion with reporters, Robb and the other Klan members disappeared into an under-ground restroom. From there, they went to a load-ing tunnel and boarded a bus that whisked them to Lafayette Square about a mile away.

But a lone undetected Klansman made a symbolic march from Seventh Street and Constitution Ave-nue to 15th Street and Pennsylvania Avenue NW without incident, according to D.C. police.

Meanwhile, the mood was peaceful among an es-timated 5,000 anti-Klan protesters who had begun gathering as early as dawn along Constitution and Pennsylvania avenues near the Capitol.

Demonstration leaders, speaking from a large platform at the reflecting pool, denounced the Klan, the Reagan administration and capitalism with slo-gans like, "One, Two, Three, Four, Time to Finish the Civil War; Five, Six, Seven, Eight, Forward to the Workers' State."

When the demonstrators first learned that the Klan would not march past them, they began cheer-ing, "We stopped the Klan, we stopped the Klan," and poured onto Constitution Avenue as police lifted barricades and departed.

Some protesters led by far left Progressive La-bor Party organizers and the Labor/Black Mobiliza-tion to Stop the Klan, had said they wanted to have a direct confrontation with the Klan march. Now their opportunity had been taken away by the police.

Protesters began streaming northwest along Pennsylvania Avenue, many with revolutionary banners billowing in the crisp midday air. They hoped to get to Lafayette Square before the Klan rally there was completed. But police whisked the Klansmen out of the square minutes before the protesters arrived.

*　　　*　　　*

A vanguard of banner-carrying protesters, both black and white, pushed through a thin police line at 15th and H Streets and began running toward the square a block west.

A platoon of U.S. Park Police officers mounted on horses suddenly appeared and began forcing the crowd back down H Street. Rocks and bottles began to fly from the crowd, several of them hitting the officers and horses. Moments later, when the crowd failed to disperse, police threw the first tear gas of the day.

For the next two hours, police chased hit-and-run groups of protesters as they dashed through downtown streets, hurling rocks and debris at officers, blocking traffic and periodically smashing store windows.

*　　　*　　　*

During many of the fiercest exchanges between police and clusters of protesters, hundreds demonstrated peacefully in McPherson Square, ignoring the violence a block away.

☆ 371b Crowd Turns Confrontational

*Washington Post*, November 28, 1982, A1.

By the time the first canister of tear gas exploded, the Ku Klux Klan was on its way out of town.

But anti-Klan demonstrators quickly found a new target, their protest transformed into a spontaneous outburst against police that spread into sporadic looting.

For hours the rhetoric had been building as some 500 demonstrators, including hundreds of Palestinian sympathizers, marched from the Ellipse to McPherson Square and an additional 5,000 anti-Klan protesters ralled near the Capitol.

"You don't know who the Klan is. It may be your landlord. It may be the merchant you buy your food from. It may be your insurance man," Ethel Mathews of the Georgia Welfare Rights Organization warned the crowd at McPherson Square. "We are here to say . . . that we are not afraid."

Other speakers decried federal budget cutbacks, unemployment and U.S. support for Israel and South Africa.

By the time the two groups of protesters converged near Lafayette Square, the atmosphere was ripe for confrontation. It came suddenly, as the two crowds tried to push toward the park where they believed the Klan was congregated.

Officers hustled the Klansmen away, then, with helmets and nightsticks at the ready, formed a solid phalanx in front of the park, turning back a large group.

It was never clear what sparked the first blow—police said the crowd began throwing rocks when they were turned away; some protesters ran through the crowd shouting that police were beating people, though it could not be determined what incident they were referring to.

But one thing was certain: the crowd's mood changed. The chant of "Reagan and the Klan work hand in hand" quickly changed to "[t]he police and the Klan work hand in hand." Bricks, stones from the street and bottles flew in one direction; tear gas came back.

While many white police officers were pelted with rocks, black policemen bore the brunt of the crowd's anger. "You're just doing whitey's job. You ain't s——," called one black woman, her eyes watering from tear gas, to a black park policeman on horseback.

For many, the clash appeared to represent genuine frustration over the presence in Washington of a potent symbol of racism and hatred. "If people just let them walk through they might think people are afraid of them, but people aren't afraid of them anymore," said Louis Wilson of Wheaton, Md., who had brought his 4-year-old daughter to the rally.

*　　　*　　　*

Some of the demonstrators belong[ed] to groups that have a history of deliberately seeking physical confrontations with the Klan and Nazi groups. The Progressive Labor Party, for example, has repeatedly attacked Klan rallies in other cities in recent years and has vowed publicly to assault Klan and Nazi members.

Others in the crowds yesterday seemed to see the day's events as simply a cover for individual violence and crime. It became an opportunity for some youths to operate anonymously, occasionally bolting from the crowd to break into bicycle and camera shops, then disappearing back into the throng.

Individuals would from time to time move up behind a crowd of protesters, throwing rocks over their heads toward the police or toward windows of businesses and then flee, laughing as if it were a game, when the police came after them.

Police Chief Maurice Turner estimated that half of the 38 arrested yesterday had previous criminal records.

*　　　*　　　*

Before the violence broke out, some of the rally's organizers criticized Turner's public call for people to stay away from yesterday's demonstrations, and complained about the way the events were being handled. "They [the police] are out protecting the Klan, but no one is talking about safeguarding us," complained Sahu Barron, a national coordinator of the All People's Congress.

*   *   *

☆ 371c  Police Stunned by Crowd Violence in Reaction to Secret Busing of Klan

*Washington Post*, November 29, 1982, A1.

Top D.C. police officials said yesterday that they were stunned when their secret decision to keep apart a Ku Klux Klan group and militant anti-Klan demonstrators backfired Saturday and the demonstrators turned on police in a violent rampage through much of downtown.

"We knew there was a possibility they might get angry [at being duped]," said Police Chief Maurice T. Turner, "but we did not think it would turn violent."

"We just assumed that if we avoided a confrontation between the Klan and the demonstrators, we would avoid violence," said police spokesman Lt. Hiram Brewton, "but we were wrong."

Still, Turner and Assistant Chief Marty Tapscott said in separate interviews yesterday, they are satisfied they did the right thing when they bused Klan marchers to Lafayette Square through back streets rather than allow them to march down Pennsylvania Avenue, where thousands of angry protesters were waiting.

*   *   *

Police said yesterday that it was too soon to estimate the price tag of the disturbance, either in police and cleanup costs, or in damage to merchants. The scene of the violence was largely deserted yesterday, with a few businessmen sweeping broken glass and preparing to open again.

Meanwhile yesterday, Del. Walter E. Fauntroy (D-D.C.) called for a "coalition of conscience" among blacks and whites to "overcome the propaganda advantages" scored by both the Klan and anti-Klan protesters in Saturday's violence.

"The overtly racist Klan got what they wanted—widespread publicity across the nation," Fauntroy said, "and white radical organizers" [of the anti-Klan action] "got what they wanted, too—pictures of black youths looting and throwing bricks ... showing America that blacks are oppressed brick throwers."

He said "Trotskyist radicals" had gone through black neighborhoods in Washington with a sound truck, "inviting young black youths to go downtown and attack the Klan."

Fauntroy urged nonviolent means of improving conditions for blacks and other poor people, including support of the Congressional Black Caucus' economic recovery legislative package on Capitol Hill.

Turner acknowledged the violence Saturday was beyond anything police expected but said, "The situation would have been much worse if we had allowed the [Klan] march down Pennsylvania Avenue."

*   *   *

For ... two hours, skirmishing ebbed and flowed in the streets, with protesters screaming obscenities and hurling bottles, bricks and stick-mounted revolutionary banners at police. Police flailed at protesters with their nightsticks, striking many across their backs and heads.

Still other participants, mostly local young "opportunists" who had joined the fray with "criminal intent," as Turner put it, began smashing windows and looting stores. The looting, more widespread than originally reported, included stores where cameras, bicycles, clothing and jewelry were snatched.

Turner said he attempted to withdraw his officers from the streets several times but had to redeploy them to stem the looting and also to rescue isolated officers menaced by crowds.

He said the crowds consisted of two elements: the "political demonstrators" and the "opportunists," with the "opportunists" accounting for most of the arrests during the day.

"They were just hell-bent on crime," Turner said.

As for the political demonstrators, said police spokesman Brewton, "We give them permits [to march or rally] if it is not obvious they are planning violence, regardless of their politics." That is required under the U.S. Constitution, he said.

## 372  " 'They have chosen to be lawbreakers' " (1983)

That any opposition to the mandates of government, whether for political or for religious, economic, social, or racial motives, may result in criminal prosecution and punishment is demonstrated by the recent conflict between the state of Nebraska and a group of fundamentalist Christian ministers. Proclaiming adherence to higher religious imperatives, the ministers and their parishioners, who were operating "Christian schools," refused to comply with state licensing and certification requirements. After festering over a period of seven years, the legal dispute erupted in 1983. For disobeying court orders, these religiously-motivated political offenders were sentenced to jail.

☆ 372  State-Church Showdown

☆ 372a  Jailings in Nebraska

*Washington Post*, December 3, 1983, A3.

The jailing of seven parents of students at a tiny Nebraska fundamentalist Christian school that refuses to submit to state accreditation has brought a long-simmering church-state dispute to a boil.

More than 150 fundamentalist ministers from around the country converged on Louisville, Neb., this week to operate the embattled school in the basement of the Faith Baptist Church while the church pastor remains in hiding from civil authorities.

"This is a clear-cut issue of religious freedom," said Dr. H. Edward Rowe, a minister from Wheaton, Ill., who helped organize the protest. "The school is a part of the church ministry, and the state has no right to regulate it in any way. You simply have to take a stand somewhere."

The seven parents, all fathers, were jailed last week after they refused to answer any questions at a contempt-of-court hearing in Cass County Court.

Arrest warrants also have been issued against their wives, one other parent and the Rev. Everett Sileven, the church pastor, but county attorney Ray Moravec said they had gone into hiding.

"They have been forced to live out of suitcases, to run like a pack of hunted animals," said Rowe. He added that the school, which usually has 28 students in kindergarten through 12th grade, has been operating this week with just four.

The legal dispute is 7 years old. In 1981, the U.S. Supreme Court refused to hear an appeal of a Nebraska Supreme Court ruling that the state was within its rights to require that all private schools, including ones based on religion, meet basic requirements as to length of day, teacher certification and instructional materials.

Laws governing religious schools vary widely from state to state. Nebraska is one of 13 states that require teachers in such schools to be state-certified, according to a 1981 U.S. Department of Education survey.

The governance issue is still being tested in lawsuits, generally brought by fundamentalist Christian schools, in a number of states.

The schools have found no support from the Roman Catholic Church, which operates the nation's largest network of religious schools. "Heavens no, we have no problem with state certification," said Richard Duffy of the U.S. Catholic Conference.

*     *     *

But among the Christian fundamentalists, church-state separation has become a rallying cry. Last year, when Sileven was jailed on contempt charges for four months and his church was padlocked briefly in order to close the school, the Rev. Jerry Falwell, head of the Moral Majority, led a large protest rally in the small community 25 miles south of Omaha.

Rowe said that this year the ministers are putting the word out once again through their network of Christian radio and television programs. "In 1982, we generated 250,000 calls to the White House," he claimed, adding that now they are calling Nebraska state officials.

State officials are taking a dim view of the protest, especially Hugh Harlan, the official responsible for certifying private schools. . . .

"We have this infestation of fundamentalists, and they're being very immature," he said.

Harlan added that the idea of arresting parents was obviously unpleasant, but noted: "They have chosen to be lawbreakers. That's what it amounts to. They have put themselves out as martyrs for some kind of religious cause. So what do you do? You put them in jail."

Moravec, the Cass County attorney, said the seven jailed parents will appear in court again Tuesday and be asked to defend themselves against charges that they violated a court injunction against operation of the nonaccredited school.

Meantime, Rowe said the protest would continue indefinitely. It has the support of the Association of Christian Schools International, a California-based group that represents about 2,000 schools.

"It is absolutely outrageous that a parent in Nebraska who is sending his child to a school that is academically superior to a public school can be arrested for doing it," said Dr. Paul Kienel, executive director of the association.

He said that students at the Christian schools do better on standardized tests than public school students and that the accreditation standards of his association were adequate to insure quality instruction.

☆ 372b  Fight to Keep Open Church School

*Washington Times*, December 5, 1983, A3.

An Idaho congressman has promised to help nearly 200 fundamentalist-Christian ministers in their fight to keep open a tiny church school here.

"The spirit of the Lord is burning brightly and rather loudly in eastern Nebraska," Rep. George Hansen, R-Idaho, told the ministers and their followers Saturday at the Faith Baptist Church in this town south of Omaha. "And I say, 'Onward Christian Soldiers.' "

That statement and others by Rep. Hansen were interrupted by cheers and cries of "Amen, brother!"

The 30-student Faith Christian School, which is operated by the fundamentalist Faith Baptist Church, was ordered closed late last month by a county judge. The judge took the action after the school refused to hire teachers accredited by the state of Nebraska, claiming such teachers would not put sufficient emphasis on God's role in education.

*           *           *

Rep. Hansen, a Mormon, said he is a champion of "all facets of the religious community in their effort to stop government interference with religious freedom."

"The people of this country aren't going to tolerate an encroachment on those freedoms," he said. "I can't believe that, in America's heartland, seven parents have been arrested and a school has been closed because religious people want to teach their children about God."

*           *           *

"The issue is not accreditation," said Rev. Pierre Bynum, pastor of the New Covenant Church in Waldorf, Md. "The issue as we see it is interference by a state with a person's right to worship and to give his child a total religious education."

## 373  " 'God is great. God is good.' " (1984)

On June 25, 1962, the Supreme Court of the United States held, in *Engel v. Vitale*, 370 U.S. 421 (1962), that organized prayers in public schools violated the First Amendment prohibition against "establishment of religion." Despite this ruling by the country's highest judicial tribunal, prayers have continued in many schoolrooms. A recent North Carolina school survey found regular prayer recitation and Bible readings in 39 of the state's 100 counties. Notwithstanding the questioned legality of these various school prayer practices, no prosecutions have been reported, and the United States Congress has been unable to reach a consensus on a constitutional amendment that would permit some forms of organized worship in public schools.

☆ 373  Prayer in Many Schoolrooms Continues Despite '62 Ruling

*New York Times*, March 11, 1984, A1.

The 31 children in Alvenia P. Hunter's second-grade class at the Pratt Elementary School in Birmingham, Ala., began the school day Thursday as they do every day, by bowing their heads for prayer.

In unison, they recited: "O, help me please each day to find new ways of just being kind. At home, at work, at school and play, please help me now and every day. Amen."

Mrs. Hunter's class is one of many across the nation where, despite the Supreme Court's prohibition of organized prayer in the schools more than 20 years ago, students continue to recite prayers, sing hymns or read the Bible aloud.

Many more students observe a period of silence

in which they can pray if they want, a practice the Supreme Court has neither upheld nor rejected.

There is no organized worship in most of the country's public schools. In the main, educators have accepted the Supreme Court's doctrine that prayer prescribed by government or led by a teacher, a government employee, violates the First Amendment sanction against "establishment of religion."

### NO CONSENSUS IN SENATE

While some Americans, particularly fundamentalist Protestants, have sought ways around the Court's ruling, many in the Protestant, Roman Catholic and Jewish clergy have endorsed the doctrine as essential to religious freedom.

*           *           *

A spot check of schools in communities from coast to coast last week revealed practices ranging from that in Iowa, where few schools had organized prayers even before the Supreme Court outlawed them in 1962, a practice that continues, to that in North Carolina, where a survey found regular prayer recitation and Bible readings in 39 of the state's 100 counties.

Mrs. Hunter, who has been a teacher for 18 years, said she had never heard an objection to her classroom prayer from a parent or a principal. "I believe in doing things right," she said. "I have been given the strength to come here and the ability to teach. This way I am thanking my God for enabling me to come here to work."

*           *           *

### SILENT PERIODS IN DISPUTE

Jean Lancaster, who teaches the second grade at Fulwiler Elementary School in Greenville, Miss., also chooses to lead her pupils in prayer. Every day before lunch, they bow heads and recite: "God is great. God is good. Let us thank him for our food. Amen."

"If I forget to lead it, they remind me," Mrs. Lancaster said. She also said no one had ever objected to her prayer.

Much more common than organized worship in the schools are periods of silence set aside to allow children time to pray or meditate.

Nearly half the states, including New York and Connecticut, have laws that require or permit periods of silent prayer or meditation in the school day. The Federal courts have struck down such statutes as an unconstitutional subterfuge for mandating prayer in some states, including New Jersey, and have upheld them in others, where the courts said there was a difference between periods of silence and organized prayer. ... [In *Wallace v. Jaffree*, — U.S. —, 105 S. Ct. 2479 (1985), the Supreme

Court held an Alabama Statute authorizing a period of silence for "meditation or voluntary prayer" was an unconstitutional advancement of religion.]

\* \* \*

### STUDENTS' VIEWS DIFFER

Students also have varied views about silent periods. Jody Kunkel, a ninth grader at Hillcrest Junior High School in Trumbull, Conn., said: "You just stand there. There's a little fooling around, but they're basically quiet."

Isabel Copa, a Roman Catholic eighth-grader at the Pompano Beach Middle School in Florida, said that even a period of silence would be "unfair to some students who don't believe in God."

"I go to church school and we pray over there," she said. "I have friends that are all different kinds of religions. If they want to pray, they can do it at home or at church."

\* \* \*

When objections to audible prayers have been raised, the recitations have often been stopped, either by the school authorities or by the courts.

At the Joseph A. Craig Elementary School in a poor section of New Orleans a recording of Kate Smith singing the Lord's Prayer was played over the intercom every morning until someone complained last year, and the school stopped playing the record. Some of the parents and teachers think that was a serious mistake.

\* \* \*

### SOME ARE OSTRACIZED

In some places, parents who complained about prayers in the schools have been ostracized, or worse.

Three years ago, two mothers sued to stop organized prayers in the schools in Little Axe, Okla., a rural community southeast of Oklahoma City. One of the women, JoAnn Bell, a member of the Church of the Nazarene, argued that other people should not tell her children how to pray. She said last week that after she won her suit in Federal court, she was beaten by a school teacher and her home was set afire, so she moved.

\* \* \*

In Illinois, organized prayer is strictly prohibited in the schools, and some parents find that inconsistent.

"Schools," said the Rev. Leroy L. Yates, pastor of Westlawn Gospel Chapel in Chicago, "have exposure to just about any other kind of subject matter, such as marijuana, dope traffic, explicit sexual information. Why not spiritual values?" Mr. Yates's six children have all gone to the Chicago public schools.

\* \* \*

## 374 To Provide Redress for Victims (1984)

In the late 1960s and early 1970s, a vast number of United States citizens engaged in mass protest activities in an effort to arouse public awareness and produce governmental change regarding the pressing issues of the time. The protest against United States involvement in the Vietnam War and the call for full civil rights for blacks were among the activities targeted by federal law enforcement officials for disruption and possible elimination. In its now infamous COINTELPRO operation, the FBI devised a plan to disrupt systematically the protest efforts and goals. The FBI undertook the plan in conjunction with the District of Columbia Metropolitan Police Department (MPD). Under the guise of preventing national and civil disorder, these agencies employed various tactics, including printing and distributing leaflets and false press releases, sabotaging plans for peaceful demonstrations, and harassing politically active individuals.

In 1976, seven political activists from the Washington, D.C., area filed suit in federal court claiming the COINTELPRO operation violated their First Amendment rights to free speech, assembly, and association. The plaintiffs sued several FBI agents, members of the MPD, and the District of Columbia government for monetary damages resulting from the conspiracy to impede their protest efforts. The plaintiffs based their claim on 42 U.S.C. § 1985(3), which prohibits any conspiracy to deprive any person or class of persons from "the equal protection of the laws, or of equal privileges and immunities under the laws." Section 1985(3) also authorizes injured parties to recover monetary damages from each co-conspirator.

The trial court imposed fines on most defendants as compensatory damages. Some defendants also were assessed punitive damages. These fines totaled $711,937.50. On appeal, the United States Court of Appeals for the District of Columbia Circuit agreed that § 1985(3) does apply when racial bias is involved. The court found it unnecessary to determine whether conspiracies against purely political activities would fall within the protection of this law, since the activities contained in this case involved a "commingling of racial and political motives." The court upheld most of the monetary damages, thus paving the way for injured citizens to curb the activities of overzealous law enforcement officials. This unique decision reaffirmed the rights of individuals to engage in peaceful political protest free of governmental interference, at least where issues of racial justice are involved.

☆374 *Hobson v. Wilson*

737 F.2d 1 (D.C. Cir. 1984).

[EDWARDS, Circuit Judge]

\* \* \*

### THE FACTS

According to plaintiffs, the FBI defendants conspired with each other, with other FBI agents and with the District defendants to impede plaintiffs' efforts to associate with others for the purpose of publicly expressing opposition to the Vietnam War, national and local Government race relations policies, and other Government actions. Many of the defendants' activities from which plaintiffs alleged they were injured were related to COINTELPRO, an FBI program begun in 1967 and discontinued in the early 1970s. COINTELPRO had two components; one was COINTELPRO-New Left, which, as implemented, was a "vaguely defined and haphazard" operation targeting people who opposed American involvement in the Vietnam War and other related policies of the national Government; the second was COINTELPRO-Black Nationalist, which, as implemented, was directed at people seeking improvement of civil rights for Black people. The goal and strategy of these secret programs are not in doubt: a memorandum prepared and circulated by one of the FBI defendants described the COINTELPRO-New Left program as follows:

> The purpose of this program is to expose, disrupt and otherwise neutralize the activities of this group and persons connected with it. It is hoped that with this new program their violent and illegal activities may be reduced if not curtailed.

The lack of any FBI definition of "New Left" apparently resulted in the targeting of almost every anti-war group, including those involved in legitimate, non-violent activities.

The purpose of COINTELPRO-Black Nationalist basically was the same as the New Left program. An airtel dated August 25, 1967 set forth the goals as follows:

> The purpose of this new counterintelligence endeavor is to expose, disrupt, misdirect, discredit, or otherwise neutralize the activities of black nationalist, hate-type organizations and groupings, their leadership, spokesmen, membership, and supporters, and to counter their propensity for violence and civil disorder.

\* \* \*

### THE CAUSES OF ACTION

At trial, plaintiffs asserted that they were victims of three conspiracies to violate their civil rights, all actionable under 42 U.S.C. § 1985(3). They alleged that each of these conspiracies violated their First Amendment rights to assemble for peaceable political protest, to associate with others to engage in political expression, and to speak on public issues free of unreasonable Government interference. The jury returned verdicts in favor of most plaintiffs on all three conspiracy claims. One civil conspiracy, the jury found, included the five FBI defendants; a second involved certain MPD defendants and the District of Columbia; a third implicated both FBI and District defendants.

\* \* \*

### LIABILITY UNDER SECTION 1985(3)

As a threshold matter, all defendants challenge the applicability of section 1985(3) to this case, although on separate grounds. The D.C. defendants argue that the section does not apply to employees of the District of Columbia or to the municipality. The FBI defendants contend that the class-based animus necessary to a section 1985(3) action was not established. Finally, FBI defendant Jones argues that the section does not apply to federal officials or to acts occurring within the District of Columbia.

#### A. The Statutory Scheme

We begin by considering the language of, and case law relevant to, section 1985(3). The provision reads,

> If two or more persons in any State or Territory conspire or go in disguise on the highway or on the premises of another, for the purpose of depriving, either directly or indirectly, any person or class of persons of the equal protection of the laws, or of equal privileges and immunities under the laws ... [and] in any case of conspiracy set forth in this section, if one or more persons engaged therein do, or cause to be done, any act in furtherance of the object of such conspiracy, whereby another is injured in his person or property, or deprived of having and exercising any right or privilege of a citizen of the United States, the party so injured or deprived may have an action for the recovery of damages occasioned by such injury or deprivation, against any one or more of the conspirators.

\* \* \*

It is by now well-established that the provision encompasses private conspiracies, and not just actions taken under color of state law. It is equally clear that the provision does not apply to *all* conspiratorial tortious interferences with the rights of others, but only to those motivated by some class-based, invidiously discriminatory animus. Thus, the Supreme Court has added a requirement of class-based animus to the list of elements set out above.

\* \* \*

### B. Applicability of Section 1985(3) to the District of Columbia and Its Employees

The District of Columbia argues that section 1985(3) does not apply to the District of Columbia or its employees. For this proposition it offers no analytical support, but rather rests on a passing and conclusory remark in an opinion from this Circuit to the effect that section 1985 "has never been applicable to District employees." We disagree. Nothing in the statute or in Supreme Court opinions supports the view put forth by defendants. For the following reasons, we hold that the District and its employees may be sued for damages under section 1985(3).

\*       \*       \*

### C. Applicability of Section 1985(3) to Federal Officers

We turn next to consider defendant Jones' contention that section 1985(3) does not contemplate actions against federal officers. The apparent source of this argument is an antiquated decision of the Second Circuit, whose holding has repeatedly been read out of context by District Courts, and has now effectively been overruled by the Supreme Court. Accordingly, we reject Mr. Jones' argument and hold that section 1985(3) encompasses actions against federal officers, subject, of course, to considerations of qualified immunity.

\*       \*       \*

### D. Class-based Discriminatory Animus

\*       \*       \*

Given the facts of this case, it is unnecessary to decide whether purely political or other activity without any racial overtones falls within section 1985(3). The FBI conspiracy allegedly targeted plaintiffs in significant part because of their involvement in and support of civil rights. *At a minimum*, section 1985(3) reaches conspiracies motivated by animus against Blacks and those who support them.

\*       \*       \*

It is equally clear that the FBI defendants' conspiracy was directed against plaintiffs because of their participation in these very activities. Considerable testimony described efforts by the FBI to drive a wedge into this alliance between civil rights groups and peace groups.

The FBI's COINTELPRO program sought not only to "neutralize" and "disrupt" Black groups and antiwar groups separately, but also to exploit any dissension between them in an effort to deter formation of an alliance....

\*       \*       \*

We believe the foregoing amply discloses that the FBI actions were sufficiently related to matters of race to place the FBI conspiracy solidly within even the narrowest reading of section 1985(3). Section 1985(3) was "intended, perhaps more than anything else, to provide redress for victims of conspiracies impelled by a commingling of racial and political motives." We would be hard pressed to imagine a case with evidence stronger than we find here of precisely such commingled motives. Accordingly, we reject the FBI defendants' contention that plaintiffs' evidence on this element of their claim did not support the verdict.

\*       \*       \*

## 375  " 'intent to do something wrong clearly is not there' " (1984-1985)

The civil disobedience theories and tactics that were perfected in America during the campus unrest, the civil rights protests, and the anti-Vietnam war campaigns of the 1960s and early 1970s did not long remain in disuse. By the beginning of the 1980s new causes, domestic and international, were once more bringing forth American protesters to engage in what for a time had appeared as discarded practices. The new generation of protesters included not only some of the sons and daughters of movement leaders of the previous decades but also much older and more seasoned activists—including high elected local, state, and federal officials. More seasoned also was the response of the public authorities, who sought to avoid "show trials" that would further embarrass the South African government and would most likely result in acquittal verdicts by District of Columbia juries.

### ☆375  Americans Protesting South Africa's Apartheid

### ☆375a  Charges against Eleven Arrested in Embassy Sit-in Dropped

*Washington Post*, December 1, 1984, B1.

As two more congressmen and another labor leader joined a growing arrest list at the South African embassy, U.S. Attorney Joseph E. diGenova—saying the cases lacked "prosecutive merit"—dismissed charges yesterday against 11 persons arrested previously at the embassy during demonstrations to protest South Africa's apartheid policy of racial segregation.

Five cases of unlawful entry were dropped, diGenova said, because of "evidentiary problems," a reference to the embassy's decision not to press charges for sit-ins that have occurred at the Massachusetts Avenue complex. Lesser charges of congregating within 500 feet of a foreign embassy were dismissed against six others during the day after federal prosecutors determined, in a case-by-case review, that they were not worthy of prosecution.

* * *

Though diGenova would not elaborate beyond his brief statement dismissing the unlawful entry charges, sources close to the U.S. attorney's office cited several factors behind the dismissals — and speculated that charges against more defendants, including those arrested in the future, eventually will be dropped also.

There was a feeling among the prosecutors, these sources said, that the embassy charges would only result in "show trials" that would focus attention on the apartheid policies of the South African government but gain little in terms of law enforcement, even in the unlikely event that the District's predominantly black juries returned guilty verdicts.

Given an existing backlog of serious drug and other major crime cases, the Justice Department is not anxious to "clog" the courtroom with defendants arrested in a symbolic, nonviolent protest against racial oppression.

* * *

One prosecutor further described the cases as dealing with "borderline criminal activity," where "criminal intent to break the law is clear, but the intent to do something wrong clearly is not there."

This prosecutor warned, however, that the Justice Department would take a very different view with demonstrators who are violent or with those who are arrested a second time.

Two of the demonstrators arrested earlier, Rep. John Conyers Jr. (D-Mich.) and William Simons, president of the Washington Teachers Union, were charged under D.C. municipal regulations with entering a police area, which puts their cases in the hands of the D.C. corporation counsel's office.

* * *

But with D.C. Mayor Marion Barry's public endorsement of the antiapartheid campaign — he was at the protest site Thursday to offer praise and to discuss the possibility of his own arrest — there is something different about this demonstration.

"We're trying to walk a thin line and still be law enforcement officials," said one police official privately. "You can understand what's going on here. Here's the mayor standing up saying he may get arrested. He's the chief law enforcement official in the District. You can figure it out."

* * *

"Last night was my first time in jail," Yolanda King, the slain civil rights leader's 29-year-old daughter told reporters yesterday, after spending a night in jail. She said the experience heightened her respect for her father's sacrifices.

## ☆ 375b First Senator Held in Embassy Protest

*New York Times*, January 15, 1985, A13.

This was the 55th day of demonstrations against South Africa's racial policies in front of its embassy on Massachusetts Avenue in Washington's northwest sector. Once again, there were arrests.

At 4:30 P.M., Senator Lowell P. Weicker Jr., Republican of Connecticut, took his place with five other demonstrators, marched to the door of the embassy and was turned away. He then linked arms with the others and began singing the old civil rights hymn "We Shall Overcome."

The police immediately moved in, put the six protesters under arrest for demonstrating within 500 feet of an embassy and loosely cuffed their hands behind them with plastic bands. A police wagon hauled the group off to jail.

"Silence has been an ally of apartheid and this is what this demonstration is all about," Mr. Weicker said at a brief news conference shortly before he became the 190th person to be taken into custody in front of the embassy. He was the first United States Senator to be arrested in the demonstrations.

The Senator was released at 6:30 P.M. after being held for two hours. He is to appear in District of Columbia Superior Court Wednesday.

### ARRESTS BECOME ROUTINE

Arrests of demonstrators have become routine, even stylized, at the embassy over the past two months, and the handcuffing, carting off and subsequent release without trial of a prominent person like the Senator no longer draws much attention.

Still, the organizers of the demonstrations, which have spread to 14 other cities and have resulted in 459 other arrests, insist that the protests are having an effect. They say they intend to continue them indefinitely, and plan to step up other efforts to force South Africa to change its racial policies.

"We've got people signed up to demonstrate at least through February," said Randall Robinson, the head of the protest movement and director of TransAfrica, a Washington group that lobbies for African causes. Mr. Robinson said the protesters also intended to work on Capitol Hill for legislation to cut United States trade and other ties with South Africa.

* * *

For all the difficulty in judging the impact of the demonstrations, they have proved a rallying point for the activist, liberal community in this country, especially its black members.

* * *

The list of the arrested protesters contains the names of dozens of black leaders, labor leaders, community activists and legislators, many of them veterans of the earlier struggle for human rights for blacks in this country. The way the embassy demonstrations are being carried out is also a throwback to the heyday of the civil rights movement in the South, in which a favorite tactic was for groups of demonstrators to be arrested day after day.

There is one significant difference between past and present protests, however. Many of the demonstrations in the South turned violent. But there has been no violence in front of the South African Embassy.

\*       \*       \*

## 376 No Choice But to Trespass (1984)

Despite the persisting unwillingness of American courts to consider the "good faith" or "good motive" defenses of those charged with political offenses, occasional legal breakthroughs have taken place. During the university protests, and particularly the anti-Vietnam war demonstrations of the 1960s and 1970s, efforts to introduce political motive as a defense were met with judicial opposition. The courts usually held that proof of intent to break the law sufficed, and therefore evidence of the offender's underlying subjective motive for the unlawful action was not relevant. Permitting motive as a defense, it was feared, might tend to encourage widespread lawlessness for allegedly "good" causes.

The criminal law, nonetheless, has long recognized the principle of necessity as a factor to be weighed either in determining guilt or in mitigating an offender's culpability and sentence. With the return in the 1980s to a more tranquil era, a Vermont jury and court were willing to uphold the necessity defense in the case of protesters against United States policy in Central America.

### ☆376 Protesters' Unusual Defense Ends in Victory

*New York Times*, December 4, 1984, A28.

A jury's verdict acquitting 26 political protesters of trespassing charges has become a source of controversy here.

Originally, there were only trespassing charges against demonstrators in a sit-in last March at the office of United States Senator Robert T. Stafford to dramatize their opposition to United States policy in Central America. But the protesters' defense made the case unusual.

They adopted what is known in law as the necessity defense, saying, in effect, that they had no choice but to trespass.

After an emotional five-day trial that included debates on the First Amendment and international law, the jurors agreed.

The verdict was met with delight by some of those who support the defendants' views.

Ramsey Clark, the former Attorney General, who appeared as a defense witness at the trial, said the verdict was "good for Vermont." He said he hoped "it will be good for all of us."

But the verdict produced consternation among others. Some suggested that it would produce a wave of civil disobedience directed against abortion clinics or other facilities.

Kevin Bradley, the Crittenden County State's Attorney, who prosecuted the case, said the verdict was "certainly not a good situation."

The protesters' case began eight months ago when about 50 people assembled at Senator Stafford's office in Winooski. They were told they could remain there for the weekend, but that Senator Stafford would not meet with them.

When Monday dawned, they were still there. By day's end, 44 had been arrested. Some refused to give their real names and were not charged. A few were tried separately. The remaining 26 were tried as a group.

District Court Judge Frank Mahady ruled that their situation met the four requirements for the necessity defense:

> An emergency that is not the defendant's fault.
> A compelling reason for the defendant to believe he or someone else would be harmed if action isn't taken.
> No way to avoid harm without the act.
> The harm resulting from the crime is not greater than the harm the defendant is trying to prevent.

Both sides in the case agreed the judge also helped the defendants when he told the jury that in order to win a guilty verdict, the prosecution would have to prove that the protesters did not really believe the sit-in was necessary.

The necessity defense is far from common. In fact, defense lawyers could find only two instances in Vermont when it was successful, one a year ago and the second a century ago.

A woman arrested for drunken driving convinced a court in 1983 that she had to get to a hospital for treatment after her husband assaulted her. In the earlier case, a sailor who tied his boat to someone else's dock during a storm on Lake Champlain was found not to have trespassed.

Prosecutors said last week that they would not appeal the jury's verdict, but the case is far from dead.

\*       \*       \*

And protesters and their lawyers said they had received written and telephone requests from people interested in using the necessity defense. "I tell them that the most important thing is sincerity," said Jeanne Keller of Burlington, a protester. "I tell them that civil disobedience is not to be taken lightly."

# 377 Religious Fervor and Political Naïveté (1984-1985)

In a period of less than three years, from May of 1982 to January of 1985, over twenty-eight attacks of arson, bombing, and other violence were reported against abortion clinics in Florida, Virginia, Maryland, Delaware, Washington, Texas, Georgia, and California.

Early in 1985, Matt Goldsby and James Thomas Simmons, both twenty-one, confessed to the 1984 Christmas Day bombing of three Pensacola, Florida, clinics where abortions were performed. They described the bombings as "a gift to Jesus for his birthday." In an earlier public opinion poll conducted by WEAR-TV, the local ABC affiliate in Pensacola, viewers were asked, "Would your religious beliefs, under certain circumstances, lead you to violate civil law?" Fifty-eight percent of the 1,009 viewers who responded answered yes, and forty-two percent said no.

Speaking to reporters, Matt Goldsby cited the polls as evidence of public support. "Both of us are just your average young kids raised in the church," he said, describing himself and Simmons. "We have a deep respect for God and the true moral ways. We're very patriotic and, you know, we just love to hunt and fish. If we can stop this killing [of babies], whether we stopped it for a period of time or if we could stop it altogether, it would totally thrill the both of us."

The documents that follow detail the motives of various other activists and reflect the diversity of national opinion on the abortion clinic bombings.

## ☆377 God v. Caesar: The Issue of Abortion

### ☆377a Antiabortionists Share Religious Fervor, Political Naïveté

*Washington Post*, January 6, 1985, A1.

Curtis Beseda, a regular on the picket line at the Feminist Women's Health Center in Everett, Wash., decided to firebomb the clinic after watching woman after woman ignore his pleas not to have an abortion. He said he bombed the facility because he believes abortion is "the greater of two evils."

Don Benny Anderson had not been active in the antiabortion movement before setting out on a four-month campaign of violence, on orders, he said, from God and the Archangel Michael. With the aid of two young followers, Anderson formed the Army of God and set fire to two abortion clinics in Florida, bombed one in Fairfax County and kidnaped the operator of an Illinois abortion clinic.

Joseph Grace, described by a psychiatrist as a "religious political fanatic" in search of a cause, set fire to a Norfolk abortion clinic and was arrested after he fell asleep in his van a block away, his shoes still soaked with kerosene. Grace called himself a member of the Army of God, but he later admitted he knew of the group only through news reports.

Since 1982 there have been 30 bombings or fires set at abortion clinics and "pro-choice" offices across the country, including 24 last year, and the pace is intensifying. Three clinics were bombed in Pensacola, Fla., on Christmas, and a clinic in Southeast Washington was struck on New Year's Day, bringing to 17 the number of attacks on abortion-related centers since June. The Washington bombing has not been solved.

Abortion clinics have also been the target of an escalating number of acts of vandalism, death threats to employees, telephone bomb threats and other forms of harassment.

"Pro-choice" leaders maintain that at least some of the violent attacks are connected.

But federal law enforcement officials, who have made arrests in 12 of the 30 attacks, said a nationwide investigation has failed to uncover evidence that the incidents are coordinated or the work of an organized group. There is no indication that any of the seven men and two women charged or convicted in the attacks knew others who participated in attacks in other cities.

Interviews with friends, lawyers and prosecutors of the accused, and with some of the defendants themselves, suggest the attackers share many characteristics. They emerge as blue-collar, lower-to-middle-class persons who have no history of violent acts. They appear to be deeply religious and politically unsophisticated.

Motivated by antiabortion fervor and convinced they are acting "for the glory of God," as Beseda told federal investigators, they have become frustrated by the failure of the mainstream movement to stop abortions, and they are willing to risk long prison terms to achieve more immediate results.

"People get aroused when there's injustice in the land," Anderson, the Army of God leader, said last week in a telephone interview from federal prison in Oxford, Wis., where he is serving a 42-year sentence.

*          *          *

Despite 12 years of unrelenting efforts — including picketing, protest marches and lobbying for a constitutional amendment to ban abortion—and the election in 1980 of a president committed to its cause, the antiabortion movement has been unable to undo the Supreme Court's 1973 decision legalizing the controversial procedure.

\*   \*   \*

Those who attack clinics "are not wild, crazed terrorists," said Joseph M. Scheidler, executive director of the Chicago-based Pro-Life Action League. "These are people who want to put 'abortuaries' out of business ... who have decided human lives are more valuable than real estate."

\*   \*   \*

☆ 377b  Abortion Clinic Bombings

Patrick Buchanan, *Washington Times*, January 4, 1985, C1.

\*   \*   \*

Emotionally and symbolically satisfying as these blasts may be to some, it is not the buildings that are killing the children. It is the butchers who operate them. The buildings could as well be used for local health centers as for neighborhood killing houses. Also, the bombings have temporarily enabled the principal victimizers in American society—*doctors* making a hundred grand a year tearing apart and disposing of the remains of unborn children—to posture as *victims* for an indulgent press.

As Thomas Jefferson reminded us, there is a people's right to rebel, when a social or political evil becomes intolerable. But that right carries a corresponding responsibility to state one's cause, to accept the consequences. The old terrorist from Ossawatomie, the abolitionist John Brown, did not seek to evade responsibility for his raid on the federal arsenal at Harper's Ferry.

If the anti-abortion bombers believe that what they are doing is moral and necessary, why are they not standing outside the clinics when the police arrive?

But one can no more condemn the destruction of these buildings without discussing what goes on inside them than Abraham Lincoln could condemn the burning of an auction house without mentioning that, weekly, inside such structures, men, women, and children were bought and sold like so many horses and cattle.

In 20 years, a role reversal has taken place. The "coalition of conscience" that lauded the moral sensibilities of students who "sat-in" at lunch counters to protest segregation now denounce as "harassment" and "interference with constitutional rights" Right-to-Lifers who invade abortion clinics to persuade expectant mothers not to do away with their unborn children.

The old civil rights crowd is now talking property rights, while the old traditionalists are now defending the primacy of human rights.

The "pro-choice" movement wants the clinic bombings labeled terrorism; it wants the FBI to take over investigative duties from the federal Bureau of Alcohol, Tobacco and Firearms.

Perhaps it *is* terrorism to use violence to intimidate. But which is the greater terror: the destruction of two dozen buildings without loss of life in 1984, or the destruction of 1.5 million human beings because they were inconvenient to the mothers who carried them[?]

Excuse me, but an abortion is not a non-violent death. According to an anesthesiologist at Northwestern, Dr. Vincent Collins, a saline abortion causes an unborn child to "feel the same agony as an adult who has suffered burns to 80 to 90 percent of his body." Napalm is a tough way to go—especially if you're only six months old.

Men are never so eloquent, Malcolm Muggeridge reminds us, as when they are deploring the crimes of a previous generation; nor so purblind as when viewing their own.

\*   \*   \*

Something is terribly amiss when we can be so caught up in remorse over crimes committed in East[ern] Europe four decades ago while overlooking the holocaust going on within our own land, with 4,000 children being done to death every single day. The sickness is not only at the extremity of society—where the bomber resides—it is closer, much closer, to the head and heart.

☆ 377c  Pro-Life Terrorism Subverts Own Goal

Tom Diaz, *Washington Times*, January 22, 1985, A3.

Some, perhaps many, of the thousands who march down Pennsylvania Avenue in today's March for Life will have mixed emotions about the abortion clinic bombers.

But there should be no mixed emotions about such terrorists.

They deserve the unalloyed contempt and undiluted condemnation of anyone who cares about or presumes to speak for innocent life. Like all terrorists, they are fanatics who have arrogated to themselves the right to take another's life, convinced that they are doing God's will.

\*   \*   \*

The moral slope of condoning such acts is every bit as slippery as that which condones abortion itself. For it qualifies some human life as "expendable" in pursuit of a greater good.

Right-to-life advocates correctly understand the imperatives of logic that follow from the premise that an unborn child's life may be taken for the convenience of the parent. We have already seen that the next step is the elimination of children born with inconvenient "deficiencies." And old people have been told to get out of the way for our convenience.

The right to life becomes, in short, a matter of degree, a commodity held long by those with power, and short by those without. Abortion, infanticide, euthanasia.

So, too, will the bomber's blood lust grow.

When the "mere" destruction of property will not work, then will follow intentional murder, perhaps at first restricted to clinic staff.

But next will come the horrid rationale adopted by terrorists throughout the world: that lives must be taken to dramatize the problem, to cow the opposition, or—in this case—to make a visit to an abortion clinic so frightening that no one will dare go. To make an omelette, first break an egg.

In condemning the cowardly acts of terrorism worked by these midnight bombers, I am not unaware of the "Auschwitz problem."

*        *        *

It is becoming increasingly proper to ask those of us who abhor this slaughter, "Would you have turned your eyes from Auschwitz, or Dachau? What would you have done? Isn't there a point at which a higher moral law does indeed rise above the state's mere law?"

This is perhaps the most profound moral question of our time. But those who conclude that they must take direct action in defense of innocent life are mistaken when they threaten innocent life in the course of that action.

# 378  " 'the United States Government has been breaking the law' " (1985)

The 1980s were initially envisioned as a decade in which a nation tired of the turmoil of the 1960s and 1970s was to insist on political tranquillity and calm stock-taking. But the decade gave rise, instead, to its own vibrant causes and extralegal movements. Some of these causes, such as the quest for racial justice and the opposition to abortions, were primarily domestic. Others reflected America's increasing response to the world community and its problems, including South Africa's apartheid and Central America's political oppressions.

The sanctuary movement for Central America refugees brought together representatives of diverse American churches in the pursuit of proclaimed humanitarian goals. Once more, as previously during the anti-Vietnam war protests, religious motives and legal arguments were marshaled in opposition to the stance of the United States government.

☆ 378  Political Refugees or Economic Migrants?

☆ 378a  Activists Vow to Continue

*New York Times*, January 16, 1985, A1.

Despite the indictment of some of their leaders, church groups here and elsewhere said today that they would continue to give sanctuary to Central Americans they consider to be political refugees.

Supporters of the sanctuary movement, reacting to the indictment of 16 people on charges of conspiring to smuggle illegal aliens into the United States, declared they would put the Government "on trial" for its policies in Central America and in dealing with refugees.

In addition to the 16 indictments, returned by a Federal grand jury in Phoenix last week and announced Monday in Washington, more than 60 other people, mostly Salvadorans and Guatemalans who entered the United States with the sanctuary movement's help, were arrested over the weekend.

The nationwide crackdown sharply steps up the conflict between liberal church groups and the Federal Government, which says the aliens are fleeing poverty, not persecution, and do not qualify for political asylum.

Sanctuary activists argue that the United States has a moral responsibility to admit and care for refugees from Central America because American policies in that region contribute to the strife that forces them to flee their homes.

As many as 200 individual churches around the country are believed to support the movement, which has openly defied the Federal authorities. The Rev. John M. Fife of the Tucson Southside United Presbyterian Church, a central figure in the movement who is one of those indicted, vowed to continue assisting Central Americans who seek shelter in this country.

"Whenever the church has been persecuted throughout history," he said in an interview today, "it has strengthened the church, not weakened it. It is clear that our work will change, but we will continue to provide sanctuary to Central Americans who are fleeing political persecution."

*        *        *

A New York group called the Center for Constitutional Law, formed to assist antiwar protesters in the 1960's, said it was preparing a lawsuit seeking to enjoin the Government from further arrests of sanctuary activists on the legal theory that they are acting under constitutional guarantees of religious freedom.

The group said the suit would also maintain that it is the United States Government that is acting in violation of domestic and international law governing asylum for refugees.

*        *        *

☆ 378b  Not Guilty to Smuggling Aliens

*New York Times*, January 24, 1985, A10.

While nine leaders of the American sanctuary movement pleaded not guilty in Federal District Court here today to charges of illegally smuggling Central Americans into this country, about 100 refugees they helped bring in gathered in a synagogue to condemn United States policy in that part of the world.

The Central Americans, mostly from El Salvador and Guatemala, sat in a roped-off section of the Temple Emanu-El, one of 14 houses of worship here that are part of the sanctuary movement. They listened over headphones to a Spanish translation of a keynote address at a two-day symposium, delivered by the Rev. William Sloane Coffin of Riverside Church in New York City, one of about 200 churches nationally that are part of the movement.

"The real issue is human rights," Mr. Coffin said. "We must continue the sanctuary movement in its present form until Congress makes it no longer necessary to do so."

In the Federal court downtown, meanwhile, the nine leaders of the movement were released on their own recognizance after entering their not guilty pleas to 71 counts of conspiracy to smuggle and harbor illegal aliens. The nine included the Rev. John M. Fife, who publicly announced that his Tucson Southside Presbyterian Church was giving sanctuary to Central Americans he and others were helping bring into the country.

In Phoenix, four other members of sanctuary movement were arraigned on similar charges. They were also released after pleading not guilty.

Mr. Fife said after his court appearance, "It's our contention that the United States Government has been breaking the law."

The smuggling and hiding of Central Americans began secretly here in 1981, but has continued as a matter of open policy at Mr. Fife's church since March 1982.

Other churches have joined the movement, making no secret that they help transport, feed and provide shelter to people who say they are fleeing political oppression, torture and death in Central America.

The great majority of the Central American aliens who have entered this country since 1980 and then applied for political asylum have been denied it and deported.

The Government maintains that very few are actually fleeing political persecution, but rather severe economic hardship, which is not a legal reason for granting asylum.

Although more than 60 Central American aliens were arrested and named as unindicted co-conspirators in a Government crackdown on the sanctuary movement 10 days ago, the Federal authorities have not yet raided a church to arrest undocumented aliens. There is no statutory prohibition against doing so.

\* \* \*

Meanwhile, the trial of another sanctuary movement worker, Jack Elder, indicted last March on a charge of transporting three Salvadorans illegally inside this country, began today in Federal court in Corpus Christi.

Judge Hayden Head Jr. had earlier denied motions to dismiss the case on grounds that Mr. Elder acted out of religious conviction. . . .

\* \* \*

Mr. Elder's lawyer said today that he would use as a defense the sanctuary movement's contention that the Central Americans they assist actually should be admitted under the terms of the Refugee Act of 1980, and that it is the Government that is violating the law by failing to admit them.

## 379  The Unconstitutional Enforcement of Draft Registration (1985)

David Alan Wayte, one of the many hundreds of thousands of resisters of the new Selective Service registration requirements, was indicted on July 22, 1982, for failure to register. He had previously written two letters to President Reagan expressing his opposition to the law and his intention not to register. The United States District Court for the Southern District of California dismissed his indictment on the grounds that the government's policy of prosecuting only those who publicly opposed draft registration penalized the exercise of First Amendment rights by vocal draft resisters and was not permissible prosecutorial discretion. The case reached the Supreme Court.

☆379  *Wayte v. United States*

470 U.S. 598, 105 S. Ct. 1524 (1985).

Justice POWELL delivered the opinion of the Court.

The question presented is whether a passive enforcement policy under which the Government prosecutes only those who report themselves as having violated the law, or who are reported by others, violates the First and Fifth Amendments.

On July 2, 1980 . . . the President issued [a] Presidential Proclamation direct[ing] male citizens and certain male residents born during 1960 to register with the Selective Service System during the week of July 21, 1980. Petitioner fell within that class but did not register. Instead, he wrote several letters to Government officials, including the President, stating that he had not registered and did not intend to do so.

Petitioner's letters were added to a Selective Service file of young men who advised that they had failed to register or who were reported by others as having failed to register.... Selective Service adopted a policy of passive enforcement under which it would investigate and prosecute only the cases of nonregistration contained in this file. In furtherance of this policy, Selective Service sent a letter on June 17, 1981 to each reported violator who had not registered and for whom it had an address. The letter explained the duty to register ... and warned that a violation could result in criminal prosecution and specified penalties. Petitioner received a copy of this letter but did not respond.

On July 20, 1981, Selective Service transmitted to the Department of Justice, for investigation and potential prosecution, the names of petitioner and 133 other young men identified under its passive enforcement system.... [T]he Department of Justice referred the [petitioner's and other names] ... to the United States Attorney....

Pursuant to Department of Justice policy, those referred were not immediately prosecuted. Instead, the appropriate United States Attorney was required to notify identified nonregistrants by registered mail that, unless they registered within a specified time, prosecution would be considered. In addition, an FBI agent was usually sent to interview the nonregistrant before prosecution was instituted. This effort to persuade nonregistrants to change their minds became known as the "beg" policy.... Pursuant to the "beg" policy, the United States Attorney for the Central District of California sent petitioner a letter on October 15, 1981 urging him to register or face possible prosecution. Again petitioner failed to respond.

\*        \*        \*

... On June 28, 1982, FBI agents interviewed petitioner and he continued to refuse to register. Accordingly, on July 22, 1982, an indictment was returned against him for knowingly and willfully failing to register with the Selective Service....

\*        \*        \*

On November 15, 1982, the District Court dismissed the indictment....

\*        \*        \*

In our criminal justice system, the Government retains "broad discretion" as to whom to prosecute. "[S]o long as the prosecutor has probable cause to believe that the accused committed an offense defined by statute, the decision whether or not to prosecute, and what charge to file or bring before a grand jury, generally rests entirely in his discretion." This broad discretion rests largely on the rec-

ognition that the decision to prosecute is particularly ill-suited to judicial review. Such factors as the strength of the case, the prosecution's general deterrence value, the Government's enforcement priorities, and the case's relationship to the Government's overall enforcement plan are not readily susceptible to the kind of analysis the courts are competent to undertake....

[A]lthough prosecutorial discretion is broad, it is not " 'unfettered.' Selectivity in the enforcement of criminal laws is ... subject to constitutional constraints." In particular, the decision to prosecute may not be " 'deliberately based upon an unjustifiable standard such as race, religion, or other arbitrary classification,' " including the exercise of protected statutory and constitutional rights.

It is appropriate to judge selective prosecution claims according to ordinary equal protection standards. Under our prior cases, these standards require petitioner to show both that the passive enforcement system had a discriminatory effect and that it was motivated by a discriminatory purpose. All petitioner has shown here is that those eventually prosecuted, along with many not prosecuted, reported themselves as having violated the law. He has not shown that the enforcement policy selected nonregistrants for prosecution on the basis of their speech. Indeed, he could not have done so.... The Government did not prosecute those who reported themselves but later registered. Nor did it prosecute those who protested registration but did not report themselves or were not reported by others. In fact, the Government did not even investigate those who wrote letters to Selective Service criticizing registration unless their letters stated affirmatively that they had refused to comply with the law. The Government, on the other hand, did prosecute people who reported themselves or were reported by others but who did not publicly protest. These facts demonstrate that the Government treated all reported nonregistrants similarly. It did not subject vocal nonregistrants to any special burden. Indeed, those prosecuted in effect selected themselves for prosecution by refusing to register after being reported and warned by the Government.

Even if the passive policy had a discriminatory effect, petitioner has not shown that the Government intended such a result. The evidence he presented demonstrated only that the Government was aware that the passive enforcement policy would result in prosecution of vocal objectors and that they would probably make selective prosecution claims. As we have noted, however, " '[d]iscriminatory purpose' ... implies more than ... intent as awareness of consequences. It implies that the decisionmaker ... selected or reaffirmed a particular course of action at least in part 'because of,' not merely 'in spite of,' its adverse effects upon an identifiable group." In the present case, petitioner has not shown that the Government prosecuted him *because of* his protest activities. Absent such a showing, his claim of selective prosecution fails.

Petitioner also challenges the passive enforcement policy directly on First Amendment grounds. In particular, he claims that "[e]ven though the [Government's passive] enforcement policy did not overtly punish protected speech as such, it inevitably created a content-based regulatory system with a concomitantly disparate, content-based impact on nonregistrants." This Court has held that when, as here, " 'speech' and 'nonspeech' elements are combined in the same course of conduct, a sufficiently important governmental interest in regulating the nonspeech element can justify incidental limitations on First Amendment freedoms." Government regulation is justified

> if it is within the constitutional power of the Government; if it furthers an important or substantial governmental interest; if the governmental interest is unrelated to the suppression of free expression; and if the incidental restriction on alleged First Amendment freedoms is no greater than is essential to the furtherance of that interest.

In the present case, neither the first nor third condition is disputed.

There can be no doubt that the passive enforcement policy meets the second condition. Few interests can be more compelling than a nation's need to ensure its own security. It is well to remember that freedom as we know it has been suppressed in many countries. Unless a society has the capability and will to defend itself from the aggressions of others, constitutional protections of any sort have little meaning. Recognizing this fact, the Framers listed "provid[ing] for the common defence" as a motivating purpose for the Constitution and granted Congress the power to "provide for the common Defence and general Welfare of the United States." This Court, moreover, has long held that the power "to raise and support armies ... is broad and sweeping," and that the "power ... to classify and conscript manpower for military service is 'beyond question.' " With these principles in mind, the three reasons the Government offers in defense of this particular enforcement policy are sufficiently compelling to satisfy the second requirement—as to either those who reported themselves or those who were reported by others.

First, by relying on reports of nonregistration,

the Government was able to identify and prosecute violators without further delay. ... The passive enforcement program thus promoted prosecutorial efficiency. Second, the letters written to Selective Service provided strong, perhaps conclusive evidence of the nonregistrant's intent not to comply—one of the elements of the offense. Third, prosecuting visible nonregistrants was thought to be an effective way to promote general deterrence, especially since failing to proceed against publicly known offenders would encourage others to violate the law.

The passive enforcement policy also meets the final requirement of the test, for it placed no more limitation on speech than was necessary to ensure registration for the national defense. Passive enforcement not only did not subject "vocal" nonregistrants to any special burden, but also was intended to be only an interim enforcement system. Although Selective Service was engaged in developing an active enforcement program when it investigated petitioner, ... [p]assive enforcement was the only effective interim solution available to carry out the Government's compelling interest.

We think it important to note as a final matter how far the implications of petitioner's First Amendment argument would extend. Strictly speaking, his argument does not concern passive enforcement but self-reporting. The concerns he identifies would apply to all nonregistrants who report themselves even if the Selective Service engaged only in active enforcement. For example, a nonregistrant who wrote a letter informing Selective Service of his failure to register could, when prosecuted under an active system, claim that the Selective Service was prosecuting him only because of his "protest." Just as in this case, he could have some justification for believing that his letter had focused inquiry upon him. Prosecution in either context would equally "burden" his exercise of First Amendment rights. Under the petitioner's view, then, the Government could not constitutionally prosecute a self-reporter—even in an active enforcement system—unless perhaps it could prove that it would have prosecuted him without his letter. On principle, such a view would allow any criminal to obtain immunity from prosecution simply by reporting himself and claiming that he did so in order to "protest" the law. The First Amendment confers no such immunity from prosecution.

We conclude that the Government's passive enforcement system together with its "beg" policy violated neither the First nor Fifth Amendments. ...

*It is so ordered.*

### CHAPTER 12

# International Terrorism and Human Rights

---

## 1961-1985

The final chapter focuses on the growing interaction between domestic and international manifestations of political criminality, including so-called terrorism. The chapter surveys the recent developments in the American law of political criminality flowing from the international obligations and interests of the United States. In its international relations the United States has long adhered to the liberal notion of political offenders and has included the political offense exception in its extradition treaties with foreign nations. The interplay of this exception with the evolving international and domestic law punishing aircraft hijackings and assaults on foreign government officials and nationals reflects the changing international views toward political criminality. The liberal, mid-nineteenth-century world attitude is being replaced by twentieth-century impatience and condemnation, particularly with regard to violent and indiscriminate political crime.

Although political crime and terrorism by the government and its officials generally have not been covered in this collection, the volume concludes with attention to some of the connections between governmental terror and political crime. The domestic law of the United States, as previously noted, has always refused to recognize the category of political offenders. Nonetheless, both our extradition treaties and our immigration laws have manifested special concern for political refugees, although this concern often depends upon our relations with the refugee's government. Those seeking refuge from totalitarian foreign regimes have never been granted a right to refuge and asylum in this country, as is the case in many Latin American nations, but a privilege of asylum has frequently been recognized. Accordingly, a *de facto* law of political asylum and of legal obligations toward political refugees from oppressive foreign countries is gaining recognition in the United States.

For another perspective on political crime, the chapter includes materials on the development of a body of internationally declared human rights to which the United States has committed itself. To the extent that these international obligations may provide a basis for domestically enforceable rights, the right of any sovereign to define basic political and civil rights as offensive to the political order, and therefore political crime, would cease. Nevertheless, those new connections between international human rights, the political offender exception to extradition, and the ongoing antiterrorist initiatives remain unexplored in existing literature.

A related but different and innovative area of terrorism, the governmentally directed type, is included in this chapter. Finally, because of the American background of ambivalence and ambiguity regarding political criminality, the reader throughout the chapter should remain alert to the interactions between the executive, legislative, and judicial branches of the government in all areas that touch on the definition of political offenses, the combating of political crime, and the treatment of political offenders.

---

## 380 "aircraft piracy" (1961)

In 1950, a United States district court refused to exercise jurisdiction over an American citizen who committed an assault aboard an aircraft of United States registration because the attack took place above the high seas. *United States v. Cordova*, 89 F. Supp. 298 (E.D.N.Y. 1950). Congressional response produced legislation designed to extend United States jurisdiction to crimes on board aircraft owned partly or wholly by American interests if the offenses were committed on the high seas. 18 U.S.C. § 7(5).

In the aftermath of several hijackings of United States aircraft to Cuba, Congress next amended the Federal Aviation Act in 1961 to create the new crime of "air piracy." Because air piracy was recognized as a universal threat, the new law encompassed offenses ranging from murder to interference with the flight crew and extended United States jurisdiction to acts committed by foreign nationals against foreign nationals aboard aircraft of foreign registry flying over foreign states.

☆ 380  Amendments to the Federal Aviation Act

75 Stat. 466 (1961). (Amended current version at 49 U.S.C. 1472.)

AN ACT

To amend the Federal Aviation Act of 1958 to provide for the application of Federal criminal law to certain events occurring on board aircraft in air commerce.

*Be it enacted by the Senate and House of Representatives of the United States of America in Congress assembled,* That section 902 of the Federal Aviation Act of 1958 (49 U.S.C. 1472) is amended by adding at the end thereof the following new subsections:

### *"Aircraft Piracy*

"(i)(1)  Whoever commits or attempts to commit aircraft piracy, as herein defined, shall be punished—

"(A) by death if the verdict of the jury shall so recommend, or, in the case of a plea of guilty, or a plea of not guilty where the defendant has waived a trial by jury, if the court in its discretion shall so order; or

"(B) by imprisonment for not less than twenty years, if the death penalty is not imposed.

"(2) As used in this subsection, the term 'aircraft piracy' means any seizure or exercise of control, by force or violence or threat of force or violence and with wrongful intent, of an aircraft in flight in air commerce.

### *"Interference with Flight Crew Members or Flight Attendants*

"(j)  Whoever, while aboard an aircraft in flight in air commerce, assaults, intimidates, or threatens any flight crew member or flight attendant (including any steward or stewardess) of such aircraft, so as to interfere with the performance by such member or attendant of his duties or lessen the ability of such member or attendant to perform his duties, shall be fined not more than $10,000 or imprisoned not more than twenty years, or both. Whoever in the commission of any such act uses a deadly or dangerous weapon shall be imprisoned for any term of years or for life.

*          *          *

### *"Carrying Weapons Aboard Aircraft*

"(l)  Except for law enforcement officers of any municipal or State government, or the Federal Government, who are authorized or required to carry arms, and except for such other persons as may be so authorized under regulations issued by the Administrator, whoever, while aboard an aircraft being operated by an air carrier in air trans-portation, has on or about his person a concealed deadly or dangerous weapon, or whoever attempts to board such an aircraft while having on or about his person a concealed deadly or dangerous weapon, shall be fined not more than $1,000 or imprisoned not more than one year, or both.

### *"False Information*

"(m)(1)  Whoever imparts or conveys or causes to be imparted or conveyed false information, knowing the information to be false, concerning an attempt or alleged attempt being made or to be made, to do any act which would be a crime prohibited by subsection (i), (j), (k), or (l) of this section, shall be fined not more than $1,000 or imprisoned not more than one year, or both.

"(2) Whoever willfully and maliciously, or with reckless disregard for the safety of human life, imparts or conveys or causes to be imparted or conveyed false information, knowing the information to be false, concerning an attempt or alleged attempt being made or to be made, to do any act which would be a crime prohibited by subsection (i), (j), (k), or (l) of this section, shall be fined not more than $5,000 or imprisoned not more than five years, or both."

*          *          *

## 381  Acts Which Jeopardize the Safety of Aircraft or Persons (1963)

The increasing frequency of aircraft hijackings involving complex international relationships soon required more than domestic legislation. The first international agreement that attempted to control the widespread problem of aircraft hijacking was the Convention on Offenses and Certain Other Acts Committed on Board Aircraft (Tokyo, September 14, 1963). This convention pursued three major objectives: it established continuing jurisdiction over crimes committed aboard an aircraft, regardless of the aircraft's physical location, by the state of registration (Art. 3); it authorized the aircraft commander to employ reasonable measures to restrain an individual who committed or was about to commit a crime on board (Art. 6); and it set forth the duties and responsibilities of the participating states (Arts. 12 & 13). Nevertheless, Article 2 excepts political offenses from the reach of the convention.

The United States Senate and President Richard Nixon ratified this convention in 1969.

☆ 381  Convention on Offenses and Certain Other Acts Committed on Board Aircraft (Tokyo)

20 U.S.T. 2941, T.I.A.S. No. 6768 (1963).

THE STATES PARTIES TO THIS CONVENTION HAVE AGREED AS FOLLOWS:

CHAPTER I—SCOPE OF THE CONVENTION

### Article 1

1. This Convention shall apply in respect of:

(a) offences against penal law:

(b) acts which, whether or not they are offences, may or do jeopardize the safety of the aircraft or of persons or property therein or which jeopardize good order and discipline on board.

2. Except as provided in Chapter III, this Convention shall apply in respect of offences committed or acts done by a person on board any aircraft registered in a Contracting State, while that aircraft is in flight or on the surface of the high seas or of any other area outside the territory of any State.

3. For the purposes of this Convention, an aircraft is considered to be in flight from the moment when power is applied for the purpose of take-off until the moment when the landing run ends.

4. This Convention shall not apply to aircraft used in military, customs or police services.

### Article 2

Without prejudice to the provisions of Article 4 and except when the safety of the aircraft or of persons or property on board so requires, no provision of this Convention shall be interpreted as authorizing or requiring any action in respect of offences against penal laws of a political nature or those based on racial or religious discrimination.

CHAPTER II—JURISDICTION

### Article 3

1. The State of registration of the aircraft is competent to exercise jurisdiction over offences and acts committed on board.

2. Each Contracting State shall take such measures as may be necessary to establish its jurisdiction as the State of registration over offences committed on board aircraft registered in such State.

3. This Convention does not exclude any criminal jurisdiction exercised in accordance with national law.

### Article 4

A Contracting State which is not the State of registration may not interfere with an aircraft in flight in order to exercise its criminal jurisdiction over an offence committed on board except in the following cases:

(a) the offence has effect on the territory of such State;

(b) the offence has been committed by or against a national or permanent resident of such State;

(c) the offence is against the security of such State;

(d) the offence consists of a breach of any rules or regulations relating to the flight or manoeuvre of aircraft in force in such State....

\*     \*     \*

CHAPTER III—POWERS OF THE AIRCRAFT COMMANDER

### Article 5

\*     \*     \*

2. Notwithstanding the provisions of Article 1, paragraph 3, an aircraft shall, for the purposes of this Chapter, be considered to be in flight at any time from the moment when all its external doors are closed following embarkation until the moment when any such door is opened for disembarkation. In the case of a forced landing, the provisions of this Chapter shall continue to apply with respect to offences and acts committed on board until competent authorities of a State take over the responsibility for the aircraft and for the persons and property on board.

### Article 6

1. The aircraft commander may, when he has reasonable grounds to believe that a person has committed, or is about to commit, on board the aircraft, an offence or act contemplated in Article 1, paragraph 1, impose upon such person reasonable measures including restraint which are necessary:

(a) to protect the safety of the aircraft or of persons or property therein; or

(b) to maintain good order and discipline on board; or

(c) to enable him to deliver such person to competent authorities or to disembark him in accordance with the provisions of this Chapter.

2. The aircraft commander may require or authorize the assistance of other crew members and may request or authorize, but not require, the assistance of passengers to restrain any person whom he is entitled to restrain. Any crew member or passenger may also take reasonable preventive measures without such authorization when he has reasonable grounds to believe that such action is immediately necessary to protect

the safety of the aircraft, or of persons or property therein.

### Article 8

1. The aircraft commander may, in so far as it is necessary for the purpose of subparagraph (a) or (b) or paragraph 1 of Article 6, disembark in the territory of any State in which the aircraft lands any person who he has reasonable grounds to believe has committed, or is about to commit, on board the aircraft an act contemplated in Article 1, paragraph 1(b).

2. The aircraft commander shall report to the authorities of the State in which he disembarks any person pursuant to this Article, the fact of, and the reasons for, such disembarkation.

### Article 9

1. The aircraft commander may deliver to the competent authorities of any Contracting State in the territory of which the aircraft lands any person who he has reasonable grounds to believe has committed on board the aircraft an act which, in his opinion, is a serious offence according to the penal law of the State of registration of the aircraft.

2. The aircraft commander shall as soon as practicable and if possible before landing in the territory of a Contracting State with a person on board whom the aircraft commander intends to deliver in accordance with the preceding paragraph, notify the authorities of such State of his intention to deliver such person and the reasons therefor.

3. The aircraft commander shall furnish the authorities to whom any suspected offender is delivered in accordance with the provisions of this Article with evidence and information which, under the law of the State of registration of the aircraft, are lawfully in his possession.

### Article 10

For actions taken in accordance with this Convention, neither the aircraft commander, any other member of the crew, any passenger, the owner or operator of the aircraft, nor the person on whose behalf the flight was performed shall be held responsible in any proceeding on account of the treatment undergone by the person against whom the actions were taken.

CHAPTER IV—UNLAWFUL SEIZURE OF AIRCRAFT

### Article 11

1. When a person on board has unlawfully committed by force or threat thereof an act of interference, seizure or other wrongful exercise of control of an aircraft in flight or when such an act is about to be committed, Contracting States shall take all appropriate measures to restore control of the aircraft to its lawful commander or to preserve his control of the aircraft.

2. In the cases contemplated in the preceding paragraph, the Contracting State in which the aircraft lands shall permit its passengers and crew to continue their journey as soon as practicable, and shall return the aircraft and its cargo to the other persons lawfully entitled to possession.

CHAPTER V—POWERS AND DUTIES OF STATES

### Article 12

Any Contracting State shall allow the commander of an aircraft registered in another Contracting State to disembark any person pursuant to Article 8, paragraph 1.

### Article 13

1. Any Contracting State shall take delivery of any person whom the aircraft commander delivers pursuant to Article 9, paragraph 1.

2. Upon being satisfied that the circumstances so warrant, any Contracting State shall take custody or other measures to ensure the presence of any person suspected of an act contemplated in Article 11, paragraph 1 and of any person of whom it has taken delivery. The custody and other measures shall be provided in the law of the State but may only be continued for such time as is reasonably necessary to enable any criminal or extradition proceedings to be instituted.

3. Any person in custody pursuant to the previous paragraph shall be assisted in communication immediately with the nearest appropriate representative of the State of which he is a national.

4. Any Contracting State, to which a person is delivered pursuant to Article 9, paragraph 1, or in whose territory an aircraft lands following the commission of an act contemplated in Article 11, paragraph 1, shall immediately make a preliminary enquiry into the facts.

5. When a State, pursuant to this Article, has taken a person into custody, it shall immediately notify the State of registration of the aircraft and the State of nationality of the detained person and, if it considers it advisable, any other interested State of the fact that such person is in custody and of the circumstances which warrant his detention. The State which makes the preliminary enquiry contemplated in paragraph 4 of this Article shall promptly report its findings to the said States and shall indicate whether it intends to exercise jurisdiction.

\*     \*     \*

CHAPTER VI—OTHER PROVISIONS

*Article 16*

1. Offenses committed on aircraft registered in a Contracting State shall be treated, for the purpose of extradition, as if they had been committed not only in the place in which they have occurred but also in the territory of the State of registration of the aircraft.

2. Without prejudice to the provisions of the preceding paragraph, nothing in this Convention shall be deemed to create an obligation to grant extradition.

\*     \*     \*

# 382 "fear of being persecuted" (1968)

At the close of World War II, the restrictions of the United States' immigration quota system limited the country's ability to respond to the pressing needs of displaced persons and refugees in Europe. Congress therefore relaxed the quotas in the Displaced Persons Act of 1948. In 1950, Congress expanded the act for the benefit of the victims of Nazi and Communist state terror and oppression "on account of race, religion, or political opinion."

Together with this broadening of the immigration policy, new developments, both in domestic and in international law, set out to safeguard those refugees for whom no known sanctuary existed. As part of the Internal Security Act of 1950, Congress limited the discretion of the attorney general regarding deportable aliens by providing that: "No alien shall be deported to any country in which the Attorney General shall find that such alien would be subjected to physical persecution." In 1965, the provision limiting deportation was expanded further and in 1968, the United States acceded to the United Nations Convention and Protocol Relating to the Status of Refugees. It was not until 1974, however, that Congress amended the immigration and naturalization regulations to incorporate convention standards into law. In 1980 Congress once again provided measures against the deportation of aliens if the attorney general determined the deportable alien's life or freedom would be threatened. The conference committee also directed the attorney general to develop comprehensive regulations for the granting of political asylum.

☆ 382 United Nations Convention relating to the Status of Refugees

19 U.S.T. 6226, T.I.A.S. No. 6577 (1967).

\*     \*     \*

CHAPTER I: GENERAL PROVISIONS

ARTICLE 1

*Definition of the Term "Refugee"*

A. For the purposes of the present Convention, the term "refugee" shall apply to any person who:

(1) Has been considered a refugee under the Arrangements of 12 May 1926 and 30 June 1928 or under the Conventions of 28 October 1933 and 10 February 1938, the Protocol of 14 September 1939 or the Constitution of the International Refugee Organization;

Decisions of non-eligibility taken by the International Refugee Organization during the period of its activities shall not prevent the status of refugee being accorded to persons who fulfil the conditions of paragraph 2 of this section;

(2) [O]wing to well-founded fear of being persecuted for reasons of race, religion, nationality, membership of a particular social group or political opinion, is outside the country of his nationality and is unable or, owing to such fear, is unwilling to avail himself of the protection of that country; or who, not having a nationality and being outside the country of his former habitual residence as a result of such events, is unable or, owing to such fear, is unwilling to return to it.

\*     \*     \*

ARTICLE 31

*Refugees Unlawfully in the Country of Refuge*

1. The Contracting States shall not impose penalties, on account of their illegal entry or presence, on refugees who, coming directly from a territory where their life or freedom was threatened in the sense of article 1, enter or are present in their territory without authorization, provided they present themselves without delay to the authorities and show good cause for their illegal entry or presence.

2. The Contracting States shall not apply to the movements of such refugees restrictions other than those which are necessary and such restrictions shall only be applied until their status in the country is regularized or they obtain admission into another country. The Contracting States shall allow such refugees a reasonable period and all the necessary facilities to obtain admission into another country.

## ARTICLE 32

### *Expulsion*

1. The Contracting States shall not expel a refugee lawfully in their territory save on grounds of national security or public order.

2. The expulsion of such a refugee shall be only in pursuance of a decision reached in accordance with due process of law. Except where compelling reasons of national security otherwise require, the refugee shall be allowed to submit evidence to clear himself, and to appeal to and be represented for the purpose before competent authority or a person or persons specially designated by the competent authority.

3. The Contracting States shall allow such a refugee a reasonable period within which to seek legal admission into another country. The Contracting States reserve the right to apply during that period such internal measures as they may deem necessary.

## ARTICLE 33

### *Prohibition of Expulsion or Return ("Refoulement")*

1. No Contracting State shall expel or return ("refouler") a refugee in any manner whatsoever to the frontiers of territories where his life or freedom would be threatened on account of his race, religion, nationality, membership of a particular social group or political opinion.

2. The benefit of the present provision may not, however, be claimed by a refugee whom there are reasonable grounds for regarding as a danger to the security of the country in which he is, or who, having been convicted by a final judgment of a particularly serious crime, constitutes a danger to the community of that country.

*     *     *

# 383 Acts Which "undermine the confidence of the peoples of the world in the safety of civil aviation" (1970)

The 1963 Tokyo Convention failed to address several important issues regarding international hijacking. Tokyo's Article 1 referred to "offenses against penal law" and "acts which . . . jeopardize the safety of the aircraft or persons or property therein," without attempting to specify these offenses. Article 1 also limited the convention by making its applicability dependent upon the aircraft being in flight or on the surface of the high seas or outside the territory of any state. Article 16, furthermore, imposed no obligation on the participating states to extradite violators found within their territory.

The convention on the Suppression of Unlawful Seizure of Aircraft (Hijacking), The Hague, December 16, 1970, attempted to overcome some of the limitations of the Tokyo Convention. Article 1 of the Hague Convention established for the first time a definition of hijacking as the unlawful seizure of control of an aircraft in flight. Article 3 expanded the Tokyo convention definition of "in flight" to reach tarmac (airport runway) hijackings. Article 7 obligated participating states either to extradite an alleged hijacker to a state of competent jurisdiction to stand trial, or, if the requested state refused extradition (e.g., by invoking the political offense exception), to submit the alleged offender to prosecution by a competent domestic jurisdiction. The Hague Convention's emphasis on prosecution was evident in Article 8, which stated that if no extradition treaty was in force to facilitate prosecution, the convention itself could be used in lieu of such treaty. This expansion of the enforcement jurisdiction over accused hijackers was a significant step toward more effective control of air piracy. The United States Senate and President Nixon ratified this convention in 1971.

## ☆ 383 Convention on the Suppression of Unlawful Seizure of Aircraft (Hijacking) (The Hague)

22 U.S.T. 1643, T.I.A.S. No. 7192 (1970).

### PREAMBLE

THE STATES PARTIES TO THIS CONVENTION

CONSIDERING that unlawful acts of seizure or exercise of control of aircraft in flight jeopardize the safety of persons and property, seriously affect the operation of air services, and undermine the confidence of the peoples of the world in the safety of civil aviation;

CONSIDERING that the occurrence of such acts is a matter of grave concern;

CONSIDERING that, for the purpose of deterring such acts, there is an urgent need to provide appropriate measures for punishment of offenders;

HAVE AGREED AS FOLLOWS:

### *Article 1*

Any person who on board an aircraft in flight:

(a) unlawfully, by force or threat thereof, or by any other form of intimidation, seizes, or exercises control of, that aircraft, or attempts to perform any such act, or

(b) is an accomplice of a person who performs or attempts to perform any such act commits an offence (hereinafter referred to as "the offence").

### Article 2

Each Contracting State undertakes to make the offence punishable by severe penalties.

### Article 3

1. For the purposes of this Convention, an aircraft is considered to be in flight at any time from the moment when all its external doors are closed following embarkation. In the case of a forced landing, the flight shall be deemed to continue until the competent authorities take over the responsibility for the aircraft and for persons and property on board.

2. This Convention shall not apply to aircraft used in military, customs or police services.

\*          \*          \*

### Article 6

1. Upon being satisfied that the circumstances so warrant, any Contracting State in the territory of which the offender or the alleged offender is present, shall take him into custody or take other measures to ensure his presence. The custody and other measures shall be as provided in the law of that State but may only be continued for such time as is necessary to enable any criminal or extradition proceedings to be instituted.

2. Such State shall immediately make a preliminary enquiry into the facts.

3. Any person in custody pursuant to Paragraph 1 of this Article shall be assisted in communicating immediately with the nearest appropriate representative of the State of which he is a national.

\*          \*          \*

### Article 7

The Contracting State in the territory of which the alleged offender is found shall, if it does not extradite him, be obliged, without exception whatsoever and whether or not the offence was committed in its territory, to submit the case to its competent authorities for the purpose of prosecution. Those authorities shall take their decision in the same manner as in the case of any ordinary offence of a serious nature under the law of that State.

### Article 8

1. The offence shall be deemed to be included as an extraditable offence in any extradition treaty existing between Contracting States. Contracting States undertake to include the offence as an extraditable offence in every extradition treaty to be concluded between them.

2. If a Contracting State which makes extra-dition conditional on the existence of a treaty receives a request for extradition from another Contracting State with which it has no extradition treaty, it may at its option consider this Convention as the legal basis for extradition in respect of the offence. Extradition shall be subject to the other conditions provided by the law of the requested State.

3. Contracting States which do not make extradition conditional on the existence of a treaty shall recognize the offence as an extraditable offence between themselves subject to the conditions provided by the law of the requested State.

4. The offence shall be treated, for the purpose of extradition between Contracting States, as if it had been committed not only in the place in which it occurred but also in the territories of the States [having] jurisdiction [over the offense].

\*          \*          \*

### Article 10

1. Contracting States shall afford one another the greatest measure of assistance in connection with criminal proceedings brought in respect of the offence and other acts mentioned in Article 4. The law of the State requested shall apply in all cases.

2. The provisions of paragraph 1 of this Article shall not affect obligations under any other treaty, bilateral or multilateral, which governs or will govern, in whole or in part, mutual assistance in criminal matters.

\*          \*          \*

## 384 "for the purpose of deterring such acts" (1971)

Major problems continued to prevent the effective suppression and punishment of international hijacking. Under the Hague Convention, alleged offenders were to be extradited or submitted for prosecution, but no prosecution necessarily ensued. Article 2 of the Hague Convention specified that countries were to impose severe penalties on the hijacker but did not include a minimum punishment or punishment guidelines, thus permitting great discrepancies from country to country. The political offense exception remained a bar to extradition (and possible prosecution) of alleged offenders. The convention also failed to address other topics of aircraft safety, including preventive measures to help eliminate the threat of aircraft takeover and the sabotage of aircraft prior to flight. By failing to impose sanctions against countries harboring hijackers or condoning the outlawed acts, both the Tokyo and Hague conventions inadequately dealt with perhaps the most important requisite for the control of hijacking: effective international cooperation.

The third and most recent international agreement regarding hijacking, the Convention on the Suppression of Unlawful Acts Against the Safety of Civil Aviation (Sabotage) (Montreal, September 23, 1971), expanded the applicability of international regulations to the destruction of aircraft and to interference with flight operations whether the aircraft was actually in flight at the time. Article 10 encouraged participating states to establish measures for preventing the occurrence of offenses. Articles 11 and 12, calling for international assistance in bringing offenders to trial, evidenced the need for international cooperation in deterring such crimes.

Several shortcomings, nevertheless, remained in the international program for the control of aircraft hijacking. The Montreal Convention established no minimum schedule of penalties for convicted offenders. Although it acknowledged the need for preventive security measures, the convention enumerated no guidelines or minimum requirements. Furthermore, it failed to impose specific sanctions on those who condoned hijacking or harbored and refused to extradite or prosecute alleged offenders.

The United States Senate and President Richard Nixon ratified this convention in 1972.

## ☆ 384 Convention on the Suppression of Unlawful Acts against the Safety of Civil Aviation (Sabotage) (Montreal)

24 U.S.T. 568, T.I.A.S. No. 7570 (1971).

THE STATES PARTIES TO THIS CONVENTION

CONSIDERING that unlawful acts against the safety of civil aviation jeopardize the safety of persons and property, seriously affect the operation of air services, and undermine the confidence of the peoples of the world in the safety of civil aviation;

CONSIDERING that the occurrence of such acts is a matter of grave concern;

CONSIDERING that, for the purpose of deterring such acts, there is an urgent need to provide appropriate measures for punishment of offenders;

HAVE AGREED AS FOLLOWS:

### Article 1

1. Any person commits an offence if he unlawfully and intentionally:

(a) performs an act of violence against a person on board an aircraft in flight if that act is likely to endanger the safety of that aircraft; or

(b) destroys an aircraft in service or causes damage to such an aircraft which renders it incapable of flight or which is likely to endanger its safety in flight; or

(c) places or causes to be placed on an aircraft in service, by any means whatsoever, a device or substance which is likely to destroy that aircraft, or to cause damage to it which renders it incapable of flight, or to cause damage to it which is likely to endanger its safety in flight; or

(d) destroys or damages air navigation facilities or interferes with their operation, if any such act is likely to endanger the safety of aircraft in flight; or

(e) communicates information which he knows to be false, thereby endangering the safety of an aircraft in flight.

2. Any person also commits an offence if he:

(a) attempts to commit any of the offences mentioned in paragraph 1 of this Article; or

(b) is an accomplice of a person who commits or attempts to commit any such offence.

\*　　\*　　\*

### Article 11

1. Contracting States shall afford one another the greatest measure of assistance in connection with criminal proceedings brought in respect of the offences. The law of the State requested shall apply in all cases.

2. The provisions of paragraph 1 of this Article shall not affect obligations under any other treaty, bilateral or multilateral, which governs or will govern, in whole or in part, mutual assistance in criminal matters.

### Article 12

Any Contracting State having reason to believe that one of the offences mentioned in Article 1 will be committed shall, in accordance with its national law, furnish any relevant information in its possession to those States which it believes would be the States [having jurisdiction over the offense].

\*　　\*　　\*

## 385 "acts of terrorism" (1971)

Hijacking has been one of the many offenses encompassed within the broad and often loosely-used term *terrorism*. Although frequently undefined (as in the Antihijacking Act of 1974), the term is used widely by governments, the media, and individuals to describe acts of violence intended to bring about a desired political result. The United States State Department has defined terrorism as: "The threat or use of violence for political purposes by individuals or groups, whether acting for or in opposition to established governmental authority, when such actions are intended to shock or intimidate a target group wider than the immediate victims." The State Department has described international terrorism further as:

Terrorism conducted with the support of a foreign government or organization and/or directed against foreign nationals, institutions, or governments. Terrorism has involved groups seeking to overthrow specific regimes (for example, Yugoslavia and El Salvador), to rectify national or group grievances (for example, the Palestinians), or to undermine international order as an end in itself (for example, the Japanese Red Army).

Other differing definitions of international terrorism may be found in the Foreign Intelligence Surveillance Act of 1978 and in Executive Order 12036 relating to foreign intelligence operations.

Heads of state, foreign officials, and diplomats, as well as property belonging to foreign governments and their agencies, have been favorite targets of international terrorist attacks. From 1968 to 1971, approximately 72 percent of all international terrorist attacks against the United States were directed against diplomatic, government, or military officials or property. These events triggered international activity aimed at protecting these individuals.

In 1971, the Organization of American States drafted the Convention to Prevent and Punish the Acts of Terrorism Taking the Form of Crimes Against Persons and Related Extortion That Are of International Significance (Washington, D.C., February 2, 1971). The convention emphasized international cooperation in controlling terrorist attacks on "those persons to whom the state has the duty according to international law to give special protection" (Art. 1). Although the convention condemned "acts of terrorism" generally, it actually did not define terrorism. Article 1 enumerated specific "terrorist acts," including kidnapping, murder, and other assaults, as well as extortion. Article 2 specified that offenses enumerated in the convention "shall be considered common crimes of international significance regardless of motive." Therefore, an individual who committed a crime specified in the convention, whether or not politically motivated, would not be exempted from either extradition or prosecution (Art. 5).

The United States Senate and President Gerald Ford ratified the OAS Convention on October 20, 1976.

## ☆385 Convention to Prevent and Punish the Acts of Terrorism Taking the Form of Crimes against Persons and Related Extortion That Are of International Significance (Washington, D.C.)

27 U.S.T. 3949, T.I.A.S. No. 8413 (1971).

WHEREAS:

The defense of freedom and justice and respect for the fundamental rights of the individual that are recognized by the American Declaration of the Rights and Duties of Man and the Universal Declaration of Human Rights are primary duties of states;

The General Assembly of the Organization, in Resolution 4, of June 30, 1970, strongly condemned acts of terrorism, especially the kidnapping of persons and extortion in connection with that crime, which it declared to be serious common crimes;

Criminal acts against persons entitled to special protection under international law are occurring frequently, and those acts are of international significance because of the consequences that may flow from them for relations among states;

It is advisable to adopt general standards that will progressively develop international law as regards cooperation in the prevention and punishment of such acts; and

In the application of those standards the institution of asylum should be maintained and, likewise the principle of nonintervention should not be impaired,

THE MEMBER STATES OF THE ORGANIZATION OF AMERICAN STATES HAVE AGREED UPON THE FOLLOWING ARTICLES:

### Article 1

The contracting states undertake to cooperate among themselves by taking all the measures that they may consider effective, under their own laws, and especially those established in this convention, to prevent and punish acts of terrorism, especially kidnapping, murder, and other assaults against the life or physical integrity of those persons to whom the state has the duty according to international law to give special protection, as well as extortion in connection with those crimes.

### Article 2

For the purposes of this convention, kidnapping, murder, and other assaults against the life or personal integrity of those persons to whom the state has the duty to give special protection according to international law, as well as extortion in connection with those crimes, shall be considered common crimes of international significance, regardless of motive.

### Article 3

Persons who have been charged or convicted for any of the crimes referred to in Article 2 of this convention shall be subject to extradition under the provisions of the extradition treaties in force between the parties or, in the case of states that do not make extradition dependent on the existence of a treaty, in accordance with their own laws.

In any case, it is the exclusive responsibility of the state under whose jurisdiction or protection such persons are located to determine the nature of the acts and decide whether the standards of this convention are applicable.

### Article 4

Any person deprived of his freedom through the application of this convention shall enjoy the legal guarantees of due process.

\*　　　\*　　　\*

### Article 6

None of the provisions of this convention shall be interpreted so as to impair the right of asylum.

\*　　　\*　　　\*

## 386 Interference with the Conduct of Foreign Affairs (1972)

Between January and October of 1971, some seventy-nine incidents were reported world-wide involving attacks on foreign diplomats and personnel. The murder of eleven Israeli athletes at the Munich Olympic Games in 1972 further prompted congressional concern. Analogous to the situation in 1963 with respect to presidential assassins, the federal authorities had no clear-cut power to proceed against those accused of attacking foreign officials in this country. This act grants such jurisdiction in cases of murder, manslaughter, conspiracy to murder, kidnapping, assault, destruction of property, intimidation, and harassment, including picketing with such intent.

☆ 386　An Act for the Protection of Foreign Officials and Official Guests of the United States

86 Stat. 1070 (1972).

#### AN ACT

To amend title 18, United States Code, to provide for expanded protection of foreign officials, and for other purposes.

*Be it enacted by the Senate and House of Representatives of the United States of America in Congress assembled,* That this Act may be cited as the "Act for the Protection of Foreign Officials and Official Guests of the United States."

#### *Statement of Findings and Declaration of Policy*

SEC. 2. The Congress recognizes that from the beginning of our history as a nation, the police power to investigate, prosecute, and punish common crimes such as murder, kidnaping, and assault has resided in the several States, and that such power should remain with the States.

The Congress finds, however, that harassment, intimidation, obstruction, coercion, and acts of violence committed against foreign officials or their family members in the United States or against official guests of the United States adversely affect the foreign relations of the United States.

Accordingly, this legislation is intended to afford the United States jurisdiction concurrent with that of the several States to proceed against those who by such acts interfere with its conduct of foreign affairs.

#### TITLE I—MURDER OR MANSLAUGHTER OF FOREIGN OFFICIALS AND OFFICIAL GUESTS

SEC. 101. Chapter 51 of title 18, United States Code, is amended by adding at the end thereof the following new sections:

"§ *1116. Murder or manslaughter of foreign officials or official guests*

"(a) Whoever kills a foreign official or official guest shall be punished as provided under sections 1111 and 1112 of this title, except that any such person who is found guilty of murder in the first degree shall be sentenced to imprisonment for life.

"(b) For the purpose of this section 'foreign official' means—

"(1) a Chief of State or the political equivalent, President, Vice President, Prime Minister, Ambassador, Foreign Minister, or other officer of cabinet rank or above of a foreign government or the chief executive officer of an international organization, or any person who has previously served in such capacity, and any member of his family, while in the United States; and

"(2) any person of a foreign nationality who is duly notified to the United States as an officer or employee of a foreign government or international organization, and who is in the United States on official business, and any member of his family whose presence in the United States is in connection with the presence of such officer or employee."

\*　　　\*　　　\*

#### TITLE III—PROTECTION OF FOREIGN OFFICIALS AND OFFICIAL GUESTS

SEC. 301. Section 112 of title 18, United States Code, is amended to read as follows:

"§ *112. Protection of foreign officials and official guests*

\*　　　\*　　　\*

"(c) Whoever within the United States but outside the District of Columbia and within one hundred feet of any building or premises belonging to or used or occupied by a foreign government or by a foreign official for diplomatic or consular purposes, or as a mission to an international organization, or as a residence of a foreign official, or belonging to or used or occupied by an international organization for official business or residential purposes, publicly—

"(1) parades, pickets, displays any flag, banner, sign, placard, or device, or utters any word, phrase, sound, or noise, for the purpose of intimidating, coercing, threatening, or harassing any foreign official or obstructing him in the performance of his duties, or

"(2) congregates with two or more other persons with the intent to perform any of the aforesaid acts or to violate subsection (a) or (b) of this section,

shall be fined not more than $500, or imprisoned not more than six months, or both.

*      *      *

"(e) Nothing contained in this section shall be construed or applied so as to abridge the exercise of rights guaranteed under the First Amendment to the Constitution of the United States."

# 387 "crimes against diplomatic agents" (1973)

Although the 1971 Organization of American States Convention for the Protection of Diplomats was open to ratification by states outside the region, the international community saw the need for a more comprehensive international program. In 1973 the United Nations General Assembly adopted the proposed Convention on the Prevention of Crimes Against Internationally Protected Persons, Including Diplomatic Agents. Although the United States signed the convention on December 28, 1973, the Senate did not advise ratification until October 8, 1976. President Jimmy Carter ratified this agreement on March 8, 1977.

## ☆387 Convention on the Prevention and Punishment of Crimes against Internationally Protected Persons, Including Diplomatic Agents

28 U.S.T. 1975, T.I.A.S. 8532 (1973).

THE STATES PARTIES TO THIS CONVENTION,

HAVING IN MIND the purposes and principles of the Charter of the United Nations concerning the maintenance of international peace and the promotion of friendly relations and co-operation among States,

CONSIDERING that crimes against diplomatic agents and other internationally protected persons jeopardizing the safety of these persons create a serious threat to the maintenance of normal international relations which are necessary for co-operation among States,

BELIEVING that the commission of such crimes is a matter of grave concern to the international community,

CONVINCED that there is an urgent need to adopt appropriate and effective measures for the prevention and punishment of such crimes,

HAVE AGREED AS FOLLOWS:

### Article 1

For the purposes of this Convention:

1. "internationally protected person" means:

(a) a Head of State, including any member of a collegial body performing the functions of a Head of State under the constitution of the State concerned, a Head of Government or a Minister for Foreign Affairs, whenever any such person is in a foreign State, as well as members of his family who accompany him;

(b) any representative or official of a State or any official or other agent of an international organization of an intergovernmental character who, at the time when and in the place where a crime against him, his official premises, his private accommodation or his means of transport is committed, is entitled pursuant to international law to special protection from any attack on his person, freedom or dignity, as well as members of his family forming part of his household;

2. "alleged offender" means a person as to whom there is sufficient evidence to determine *prima facie* that he has committed or participated in one or more of the crimes set forth in article 2.

### Article 2

1. The intentional commission of:

(a) a murder, kidnapping or other attack upon the person or liberty of an internationally protected person;

(b) a violent attack upon the official premises, the private accommodation or the means of transport of an internationally protected person likely to endanger his person or liberty;

(c) a threat to commit any such attack;

(d) an attempt to commit any such attack; and

(e) an act constituting participation as an accomplice in any such attack shall be made by each State Party a crime under its internal law.

2. Each State Party shall make these crimes punishable by appropriate penalties which take into account their grave nature.

3. Paragraphs 1 and 2 of this article in no way derogate from the obligations of States Parties under international law to take all appropriate measures to prevent other attacks on the person, freedom or dignity of an internationally protected person.

\*        \*        \*

### Article 4

States Parties shall co-operate in the prevention of the crimes set forth in article 2, particularly by:

(a) taking all practicable measures to prevent preparations in their respective territories for the commission of those crimes within or outside their territories;

(b) exchanging information and co-ordinating the taking of administrative and other measures as appropriate to prevent the commission of those crimes.

\*        \*        \*

### Article 6

1. Upon being satisfied that the circumstances so warrant, the State Party in whose territory the alleged offender is present shall take the appropriate measures under its internal law so as to ensure his presence for the purpose of prosecution or extradition. Such measures shall be notified without delay directly or through the Secretary-General of the United Nations to:

(a) the State where the crime was committed;

(b) the State or States of which the alleged offender is a national or, if he is a stateless person, in whose territory he permanently resides;

(c) the State or States of which the internationally protected person concerned is a national or on whose behalf he was exercising his functions;

(d) all other States concerned; and

(e) the international organization of which the internationally protected person concerned is an official or an agent.

2. Any person regarding whom the measures referred to in paragraph 1 of this article are being taken shall be entitled:

(a) to communicate without delay with the nearest appropriate representative of the State of which he is a national or which is otherwise entitled to protect his rights or, if he is a stateless person, which he requests and which is willing to protect his rights; and

(b) to be visited by a representative of that State.

### Article 7

The State Party in whose territory the alleged offender is present shall, if it does not extradite him, submit, without exception whatsoever and without undue delay, the case to its competent authorities for the purpose of prosecution, through proceedings in accordance with the laws of that State.

\*        \*        \*

## 388 Sanctuaries for Terrorists Quarantined (1974)

After the ratification of the Tokyo, Hague, and Montreal conventions, United States domestic law had to be altered to conform with these international agreements. The Antihijacking Act of 1974 established United States jurisdiction over offenses committed under these conventions, thus enabling federal authorities to prosecute alleged offenders. In addition, the act attempted to deal with problems resulting from the political crime exception contained in all three international conventions. The act further authorized the president to impose sanctions against air carriers and the commerce of any foreign country that condoned hijacking or refused to comply with The Hague Convention.

Title II of the act provided for the development of detailed security measures at airports, the training of airport security personnel, and research (including behavioral research) into the phenomenon of air piracy. It empowered the secretary of transportation to limit or revoke permissions of foreign carriers if they failed to comply with minimum security standards. The 1974 act further supplemented the international conventions by prescribing criminal procedures and penalties, ranging from twenty years' imprisonment to death, for those charged with air piracy.

### ☆388 Antihijacking Act of 1974

88 Stat. 409 (1974).

#### AN ACT

To amend the Federal Aviation Act of 1958 to implement the Convention for the Suppression of Unlawful Seizure of Aircraft; to provide a more effective program to prevent aircraft piracy; and for other purposes.

*Be it enacted by the Senate and House of Representatives of the United States of America in Congress assembled,*

\*      \*      \*

SEC. 103. (a) [T]he definition of the term "aircraft piracy" is amended by striking out "threat of force or violence and" and inserting in lieu thereof "threat of force or violence, or by any other form of intimidation, and."

(b) [The Federal Aviation Act of 1958] is further amended ... by inserting ... the following new subsection:

### "Aircraft Piracy outside Special Aircraft Jurisdiction of the United States

"(n)(1) Whoever aboard an aircraft in flight outside the special aircraft jurisdiction of the United States commits 'an offense,' as defined in the Convention for the Suppression of Unlawful Seizure of Aircraft, and is afterward found in the United States shall be punished—

"(A) by imprisonment for not less than 20 years; or

"(B) if the death of another person results from the commission or attempted commission of the offense, by death or by imprisonment for life.

\*      \*      \*

SEC. 106 [49 U.S.C. §§ 1501-1503] is amended by adding ...:

### "SUSPENSION OF AIR SERVICES

"SEC. 1114. (a) Whenever the President determines that a foreign nation is acting in a manner inconsistent with the Convention for the Suppression of Unlawful Seizure of Aircraft, or if he determines that a foreign nation permits the use of territory under its jurisdiction as a base of operations or training or as a sanctuary for, or in any way arms, aids, or abets, any terrorist organization which knowingly uses the illegal seizure of aircraft or the threat thereof as an instrument of policy, he may, without notice or hearing and for as long as he determines necessary to assure the security of aircraft against unlawful seizure, suspend (1) the right of any air carrier or foreign air carrier to engage in foreign air transportation, and the right of any person to operate aircraft in foreign air commerce, to and from that foreign nation, and (2) the right of any foreign air carrier to engage in foreign air transportation, and the right of any foreign person to operate aircraft in foreign air commerce, between the United States and any foreign nation which maintains air service between itself and that foreign nation. . . .

\*      \*      \*

### "SECURITY STANDARDS IN FOREIGN AIR TRANSPORTATION

"SEC. 1115. . . .

"(b) In any case where the Secretary of Transportation, after consultation with the competent aeronautical authorities of a foreign nation, ... finds that such nation does not effectively maintain and administer security measures relating to transportation of persons or property or mail in foreign air transportation that are equal to or above the minimum standards which are established pursuant to the Convention on International Civil Aviation, he shall notify that nation of such finding and the steps considered necessary to bring the security measures of that nation to standards at least equal to the minimum standards of such convention. In the event of failure of that nation to take such steps, the Secretary of Transportation, with the approval of the Secretary of State, may withhold, revoke, or impose conditions on the operating authority of the airline or airlines of that nation."

SEC. 202. . . . [T]he Federal Aviation Act of 1958 ... is amended by adding ...:

\*      \*      \*

### "SCREENING OF PASSENGERS
#### "Procedures and Facilities

"SEC. 315. (a) The Administrator shall prescribe or continue in effect reasonable regulations requiring that all passengers and all property intended to be carried in the aircraft cabin in air transportation or intrastate air transportation be screened by weapon detecting procedures or facilities employed or operated by employees or agents of the air carrier, intrastate air carrier, or foreign air carrier prior to boarding the aircraft for such transportation. . . .

\*      \*      \*

### "AIR TRANSPORTATION SECURITY
#### "Rules and Regulations

"SEC. 316. (a)(1) The Administrator of the Federal Aviation Administration shall prescribe such reasonable rules and regulations requiring such practices, methods, and procedures, or governing the design, materials, and construction of aircraft, as he may deem necessary to protect persons and property aboard aircraft operating in air transportation or intrastate air transportation against acts of criminal violence and aircraft piracy.

"(2) In prescribing and amending rules and regulations under paragraph (1) of this subsection, the Administrator shall—

\*      \*      \*

"(B) consider whether any proposed rule or regulation is consistent with protection of passengers in air transportation or intrastate air transportation against acts of criminal violence and aircraft piracy and the public interest in the promotion of air transportation and intrastate air transportation;

"(C) to the maximum extent practicable, require uniform procedures for the inspection, detention, and search of persons and property in air transportation and intrastate air transportation to assure their safety and to assure that they will receive courteous and efficient treatment, by air carriers, their agents and employees, and by Federal, State, and local law enforcement personnel engaged in carrying out any air transportation security program established under this section. . . .

\*     \*     \*

*"Personnel*

"(b) Regulations prescribed under subsection (a) of this section shall require operators of airports regularly serving air carriers certificated by the Civil Aeronautics Board to establish air transportation security programs providing a law enforcement presence and capability at such airports adequate to insure the safety of persons traveling in air transportation or intrastate air transportation from acts of criminal violence and aircraft piracy. Such regulations shall authorize such airport operators to utilize the services of qualified State, local, and private law enforcement personnel whose services are made available by their employers. . . .

\*     \*     \*

*"Training*

"(c) The Administrator may provide training for personnel employed by him to carry out any air transportation security program established under this section and for other personnel, including State, local, and private law enforcement personnel, whose services may be utilized in carrying out any such air transportation security program. The Administrator shall prescribe uniform standards with respect to training provided personnel whose services are utilized to enforce any such air transportation security program, including State, local, and private law enforcement personnel, and uniform standards with respect to minimum qualifications for personnel eligible to receive such training.

*"Research and Development; Confidential Information*

"(d)(1) The Administrator shall conduct such research (including behavioral research) and de-

velopment as he may deem appropriate to develop, modify, test, and evaluate systems, procedures, facilities, and devices to protect persons and property aboard aircraft in air transportation or intrastate air transportation against acts of criminal violence and aircraft piracy."

\*     \*     \*

SEC. 203. [T]he Federal Aviation Act of 1958 is amended to read as follows:

*"Carrying Weapons or Explosives Aboard Aircraft*

"(l)(1) Whoever, while aboard, or while attempting to board, any aircraft in, or intended for operation in, air transportation or intrastate air transportation, has on or about his person or his property a concealed deadly or dangerous weapon, which is, or would be, accessible to such person in flight, or any person who has on or about his person, or who has placed, attempted to place, or attempted to have placed aboard such aircraft any bomb, or similar explosive or incendiary device, shall be fined not more than $1,000 or imprisoned not more than one year, or both.

"(2) Whoever willfully and without regard for the safety of human life, or with reckless disregard for the safety of human life, shall commit an act prohibited by paragraph (1) of this subsection, shall be fined not more than $5,000 or imprisoned not more than five years, or both."

\*     \*     \*

SEC. 204. [T]he Federal Aviation Act of 1958, relating to authority to refuse transportation, is amended to read as follows:

"AUTHORITY TO REFUSE TRANSPORTATION

"SEC. 1111. (a) The Administrator shall, by regulation, require any air carrier, intrastate air carrier, or foreign air carrier to refuse to transport—

"(1) any person who does not consent to a search of his person, as prescribed in section 315(a) of this Act, to determine whether he is unlawfully carrying a dangerous weapon, explosive, or other destructive substance, or

"(2) any property of any person who does not consent to a search or inspection of such property to determine whether it unlawfully contains a dangerous weapon, explosive, or other destructive substance.

Subject to reasonable rules and regulations prescribed by the Administrator, any such carrier may also refuse transportation of a passenger or property when, in the opinion of the carrier, such transportation would or might be inimical to safety of flight.

"(b) Any agreement for the carriage of persons or property in air transportation or intrastate air transportation by an air carrier, intrastate air carrier, or foreign air carrier for compensation or hire shall be deemed to include an agreement that such carriage shall be refused when consent to search such persons or inspect such property for the purposes enumerated in subsection (a) of this section is not given."

\* \* \*

# 389 "Respect for Human Rights and Fundamental Freedoms" (1975)

The international community's particular concern for political offenders was first manifested in the extradition treaties of the mid-nineteenth century, which exempted this class of offenders from extradition to countries seeking their return. The 1843 Convention for the Surrender of Criminals between the United States and France gave escaping political offenders protection against return and trial for political offenses committed at home. The international sympathy toward the political offender — who often is charged merely with the violation of laws denying him or her basic political, social, or economic justice — emerged in a dramatically different manner after World War II. The various United Nations and regional declarations and conventions on human rights sought to protect citizens against domestic prosecution as political offenders by guaranteeing a wide panorama of internationally recognized human rights.

Recent years have witnessed two distinct types of developments relating to political offenders and offenses. With regard to violent political offenses (particularly those affecting international aviation and diplomatic agents), international treaties that designate these offenses as international crimes requiring punishment by all nations have narrowed the exemption from extradition. Conversely, the lesser political offenses (consisting mostly of nonviolent protest or assertion of rights) have received international protection under a growing number of internationally proclaimed charters of human rights. The Helsinki Accord of 1975, to which both the United States and the Soviet Union are parties, gives such informal recognition to specified rights of citizens in their respective countries.

☆ 389  Helsinki Accord

Final Act of the Conference on Security and Cooperating (Helsinki, August 1, 1975)

Reprinted in 73 Dept. State Bull. 323 (1975).

\* \* \*

## VI. NON-INTERVENTION IN INTERNAL AFFAIRS

The participating States will refrain from any intervention, direct or indirect, individual or collective, in the internal or external affairs falling within the domestic jurisdiction of another participating State, regardless of their mutual relations.

\* \* \*

Accordingly, they will, inter alia, refrain from direct or indirect assistance to terrorist activities, or to subversive or other activities directed towards the violent overthrow of the regime of another participating State.

## VII. RESPECT FOR HUMAN RIGHTS AND FUNDAMENTAL FREEDOMS, INCLUDING THE FREEDOM OF THOUGHT, CONSCIENCE, RELIGION OR BELIEF

The participating States will respect human rights and fundamental freedoms, including the freedom of thought, conscience, religion or belief, for all without distinction as to race, sex, language or religion.

They will promote and encourage the effective exercise of civil, political, economic, social, cultural and other rights and freedoms all of which derive from the inherent dignity of the human person and are essential for his free and full development.

Within this framework the participating States will recognize and respect the freedom of the individual to profess and practise, alone or in community with others, religion or belief acting in accordance with the dictates of his own conscience.

The participating States on whose territory national minorities exist will respect the right of persons belonging to such minorities to equality before the law, will afford them the full opportunity for the actual enjoyment of human rights and fundamental freedoms and will, in this manner, protect their legitimate interests in this sphere.

\* \* \*

## VIII. EQUAL RIGHTS AND SELF-DETERMINATION OF PEOPLES

The participating States will respect the equal rights of peoples and their right to self-determination, acting at all times in conformity with the purposes and principles of the Charter of the United Nations and with the relevant norms of international law, including those relating to territorial integrity of States.

By virtue of the principle of equal rights and self-determination of peoples, all peoples always have the right, in full freedom, to determine, when and as they wish, their internal and external political status, without external interference, and to pursue as they wish their political, economic, social and cultural development.

# 390 "Internationally Protected Persons" (1976)

Congress passed the Act for the Prevention and Punishment of Crimes against Internationally Protected Persons to implement the Organization of American States convention and the corresponding United Nations convention, which prohibited crimes against internationally protected persons.

The 1976 act granted the United States extraterritorial jurisdiction, permitting it to prosecute an offender found within United States borders for offenses committed overseas, in compliance with Article 7 of the United Nations Convention on Crimes against Internationally Protected Persons. The act authorized the attorney general to request assistance from federal, state, or local agencies in investigating and prosecuting violations of the act. Another significant feature of the 1976 act was the prohibition of demonstrations by two or more individuals within one hundred feet of business or residential property owned by foreign governments or officials, if the demonstrators' intention was to harass, intimidate, or coerce.

In addition to murder and assault, the 1976 act extended jurisdiction to kidnapping; threats of killing, assault, or kidnapping; and extortion based upon such threats.

## ☆ 390 An Act for the Prevention and Punishment of Crimes against Internationally Protected Persons

90 Stat. 1997 (1976).

*Be it enacted by the Senate and House of Representatives of the United States of America in Congress assembled*, That this Act may be cited as the "Act for the Prevention and Punishment of Crimes against Internationally Protected Persons."

SEC. 2. Section 1116 of title 18, United States Code, is amended to read as follows:

"§ *1116. Murder or manslaughter of foreign officials, official guests, or internationally protected persons*

"(a) Whoever kills or attempts to kill a foreign official, official guest, or internationally protected person shall be punished as provided under sections 1111, 1112, and 1113 of this title, except that any such person who is found guilty of murder in the first degree shall be sentenced to imprisonment for life, and any such person who is found guilty of attempted murder shall be imprisoned for not more than twenty years.

"(b) For the purposes of this section:

\*       \*       \*

"(4) 'Internationally protected person' means—

"(A) a Chief of State or the political equivalent, head of government, or Foreign Minister whenever such person is in a country other than his own and any member of his family accompanying him; or

"(B) any other representative, officer, employee, or agent of the United States Government, a foreign government, or international organization who at the time and place concerned is entitled pursuant to international law to special protection against attack upon his person, freedom, or dignity, and any member of his family then forming part of his household.

\*       \*       \*

"(c) If the victim of an offense under subsection (a) is an internationally protected person, the United States may exercise jurisdiction over the offense if the alleged offender is present within the United States, irrespective of the place where the offense was committed or the nationality of the victim or the alleged offender. As used in this subsection, the United States includes all areas under the jurisdiction of the United States. . . .

"(d) In the course of enforcement of this section and any other sections prohibiting a conspiracy or attempt to violate this section, the Attorney General may request assistance from any Federal, State, or local agency, including the Army, Navy, and Air Force, any statute, rule, or regulation to the contrary notwithstanding."

\*       \*       \*

SEC. 5. Section 112 of title 18, United States Code, is amended to read as follows:

"§ *112. Protection of foreign officials, official guests, and internationally protected persons*

"(a) Whoever assaults, strikes, wounds, imprisons, or offers violence to a foreign official, official guest, or internationally protected person or makes any other violent attack upon the person or liberty of such person, or, if likely to endanger his person or liberty, makes a violent attack upon his official premises, private accommodation, or means of transport or attempts to commit any of the foregoing shall be fined not more than $5,000 or imprisoned not more than three years, or both. Whoever in the commission of any such act uses a deadly or dangerous weapon shall be fined not more than $10,000 or imprisoned not more than ten years, or both.

"(b) Whoever willfully—

"(1) intimidates, coerces, threatens, or harasses a foreign official or an official guest or obstructs a foreign official in the performance of his duties;

"(2) attempts to intimidate, coerce, threaten, or harass a foreign official or an official guest or obstruct a foreign official in the performance of his duties; or

"(3) within the United States but outside the District of Columbia and within one hundred feet of any building or premises in whole or in part owned, used, or occupied for official business or for diplomatic, consular, or residential purposes by—

"(A) a foreign government, including such use as a mission to an international organization;

"(B) an international organization;

"(C) a foreign official; or

"(D) an official guest;

congregates with two or more other persons with intent to violate any other provision of this section;

shall be fined not more than $500 or imprisoned not more than six months, or both.

\* \* \*

"(d) Nothing contained in this section shall be construed or applied so as to abridge the exercise of rights guaranteed under the First Amendment to the Constitution of the United States.

"(e) If the victim of an offense under subsection (a) is an internationally protected person, the United States may exercise jurisdiction over the offense if the alleged offender is present within the United States, irrespective of the place where the offense was committed or the nationality of the victim or the alleged offender. As used in this subsection, the United States includes all areas under the jurisdiction of the United States. . . .

"(f) In the course of enforcement of subsection (a) and any other sections prohibiting a conspiracy or attempt to violate subsection (a), the Attorney General may request assistance from any Federal, State, or local agency, including the Army, Navy, and Air Force, any statute, rule, or regulation to the contrary, notwithstanding."

\* \* \*

SEC. 7. Section 970 of title 18, United States Code, is amended:

\* \* \*

(b) by inserting a new subsection "(b)" as follows:

"(b) Whoever, willfully with intent to intimidate, coerce, threaten, or harass—

"(1) forcibly thrusts any part of himself or any object within or upon that portion of any building or premises located within the United States, which portion is used or occupied for official business or for diplomatic, consular, or residential purposes by—

"(A) a foreign government, including such use as a mission to an international organization;

"(B) an international organization;

"(C) a foreign official; or

"(D) an official guest; or

"(2) refuses to depart from such portion of such building or premises after a request—

"(A) by an employee of a foreign government or of an international organization, if such employee is authorized to make such request by the senior official of the unit of such government or organization which occupies such portion of such building or premises;

"(B) by a foreign official or any member of the foreign official's staff who is authorized by the foreign official to make such request; . . .

"(C) by an official guest or any member of the official guest's staff who is authorized by the official guest to make such request; or

"(D) by any person present having law enforcement powers;

shall be fined not more than $500 or imprisoned not more than six months, or both."

\* \* \*

SEC. 10. Nothing contained in this Act shall be construed to indicate an intent on the part of Congress to occupy the field in which its provisions operate to the exclusion of the laws of any State, Commonwealth, territory, possession, or the District of Columbia, on the same subject matter, nor to relieve any person of any obligation imposed by any law of any State, Commonwealth, territory, possession, or the District of Columbia, including the obligation of all persons having official law enforcement powers to take appropriate action, such as effecting arrests, for Federal as well as non-Federal violations.

\* \* \*

*Approved, October 8, 1976.*

## 391 Prohibition of Assistance (1976-1977)

The United States concern over the spread of international terrorism resulted in the ratification of international agreements against air piracy and for the protection of diplomatic personnel, as well as in the implementation of domestic legislation designed to accomplish these goals. But these efforts alone could not end this global problem. Attempting to induce other nations to develop hard-line antiterrorism stands, the United States passed the International Security Assistance and Arms Export Control Act of 1976 and the Foreign Assistance Appropriations Act of 1977, bringing its economic power to bear upon any country that condoned international terrorism or harbored terrorists. It is noteworthy that these terms remained undefined in the 1976 and 1977 legislation.

## ☆391 Amendments to the Foreign Assistance and Foreign Military Sales Act

### ☆391a Amendment of 1976—International Security Assistance and Arms Export Control Act

90 Stat. 729 (1976).

*Be it enacted by the Senate and House of Representatives of the United States of America in Congress assembled*, That this Act may be cited as the "International Security Assistance and Arms Export Control Act of 1976."

\* \* \*

PROHIBITION OF ASSISTANCE TO COUNTRIES GRANTING SANCTUARY TO INTERNATIONAL TERRORISTS

SEC. 303. Chapter 1 of part III of the Foreign Assistance Act of 1961 is amended by adding at the end thereof the following new section:

"SEC. 620A. PROHIBITION AGAINST FURNISHING ASSISTANCE TO COUNTRIES WHICH GRANT SANCTUARY TO INTERNATIONAL TERRORISTS.—(a) Except where the President finds national security to require otherwise, the President shall terminate all assistance under this Act to any government which aids or abets, by granting sanctuary from prosecution to, any individual or group which has committed an act of international terrorism and the President may not thereafter furnish assistance to such government until the end of the one year period beginning on the date of such termination, except that if during its period of ineligibility for assistance under this section such government aids or abets, by granting sanctuary from prosecution to, any other individual or group which has committed an act of international terrorism, such government's period of ineligibility shall be extended for an additional year for each such individual or group.

"(b) If the President finds that national security justifies a continuation of assistance to any government described in subsection (a), he shall report such finding to the Speaker of the House of Representatives and the Committee on Foreign Relations of the Senate."

\* \* \*

*Approved, June 30, 1976.*

### ☆391b Amendment of 1977—Foreign Assistance Appropriations Act

91 Stat. 1230 (1977).

*Be it enacted by the Senate and House of Representatives of the United States of America in Congress assembled*, That the following sums are appropriated, out of any money in the Treasury not otherwise appropriated, for Foreign Assistance and related programs for the fiscal year ending September 30, 1978, and for other purposes, namely:

TITLE I—FOREIGN ASSISTANCE ACT ACTIVITIES

\* \* \*

SEC. 509. None of the funds appropriated or otherwise made available by this Act to the Export-Import Bank and funds appropriated by this Act for direct foreign assistance may be obligated for any government which aids or abets, by granting sanctuary from prosecution to, any individual or group which has committed an act of international terrorism, unless the President of the United States finds that the national security requires otherwise.

\* \* \*

*Approved, October 31, 1977.*

## 392 "In no case shall capital punishment be inflicted for political offenses" (1977)

On June 1, 1977, the United States signed the American Convention on Human Rights (The Pact of San Jose, Costa Rica), but because the Senate has yet to ratify this document the pact has no domestic authority. The convention (in Art. 4, Sec. 4) grants special recognition to political offenses and requires differential sanctions for those committing them. Thus, if this convention were to be ratified, international treaty obligations would require that domestic American law grant a special status to political offenders.

### ☆392 Organization of American States Convention on Human Rights

Pact of San Jose, Costa Rica, 95th Cong., 2d Sess. Ex. C.D.E.F., 44-62, Feb. 27, 1978.

PREAMBLE

The American states signatory to the present Convention,

REAFFIRMING their intention to consolidate in this hemisphere, within the framework of democratic institutions, a system of personal liberty and social justice based on respect for the essential rights of man;

RECOGNIZING that the essential rights of man are not derived from one's being a national of a certain state, but are based upon attributes of the human personality, and that they therefore justify international protection in the form of a convention reinforcing or complementing the protection provided by the domestic law of the American states;

CONSIDERING that these principles have been set forth in the Charter of the Organization of American States, in the American Declaration of the Rights and Duties of Man, and in the Universal Declaration of Human Rights, and that they have been reaffirmed and refined in other international instruments, worldwide as well as regional in scope;

REITERATING that, in accordance with the Universal Declaration of Human Rights, the ideal of free men enjoying freedom from fear and want can be achieved only if conditions are created whereby everyone may enjoy his economic, social, and cultural rights, as well as his civil and political rights; and

CONSIDERING that the Third Special Inter-American Conference (Buenos Aires, 1967) approved the incorporation into the Charter of the Organization itself of broader standards with respect to economic, social, and educational rights and resolved that an inter-American convention on human rights should determine the structure, competence, and procedure of the organs responsible for these matters,

Have agreed upon the following:

PART I—STATE OBLIGATIONS AND RIGHTS
PROTECTED

\*     \*     \*

*Chapter II— Civil and Political Rights*

\*     \*     \*

*Article 4. Right to Life*

1. Every person has the right to have his life respected. This right shall be protected by law and, in general, from the moment of conception. No one shall be arbitrarily deprived of his life.

2. In countries that have not abolished the death penalty, it may be imposed only for the most serious crimes and pursuant to a final judgment rendered by a competent court and in accordance with a law establishing such punishment, enacted prior to the commission of the crime. The application of such punishment shall not be extended to crimes to which it does not presently apply.

3. The death penalty shall not be reestablished in states that have abolished it.

4. In no case shall capital punishment be inflicted for political offenses or related common crimes.

5. Capital punishment shall not be imposed upon persons who, at the time the crime was committed, were under 18 years of age or over 70 years of age; nor shall it be applied to pregnant women.

6. Every person condemned to death shall have the right to apply for amnesty, pardon, or commutation of sentence, which may be granted in all cases. Capital punishment shall not be imposed while such a petition is pending decision by the competent authority.

\*     \*     \*

## 393 International Terrorism, 1968-1978 (1979)

Although the introduction of security measures and the increase in international cooperation have greatly reduced the incidence of aircraft hijackings, other forms of terrorism have not declined. The Central Intelligence Agency prepared a research document that supplies a graphic portrayal of the various types of terrorism conducted in the period between 1968 and 1978. Note 1 to figure 1 alludes to the problems involved in defining terrorism.

☆ 393 A Research Paper: *International Terrorism in 1978*

National Foreign Assessment Center, RP 79-10149, CIA, Washington, D.C., March 1979.

(see pp. 662-63.)

## 394 " 'assisted the enemy in persecuting civil[ians]' " (1981)

Fyodor Fedorenko, a native of the Ukraine, served during World War II as an armed guard at the Nazi concentration camp in Treblinka, Poland. In 1949 he applied for admission to the United States as a displaced person, concealing his wartime activities.

Fedorenko established residence in Connecticut and "for three decades led an uneventful and law-abiding life as a factory worker." In 1970 he became an American citizen. Seven years later the government filed a petition to revoke Fedorenko's citizenship on the grounds that he had falsified his visa and naturalization application. Whether Fedorenko's wartime conduct was politically motivated never became an issue. The United States Supreme Court approved the denaturalization by holding that whether his guard service was or was not compulsory, Fedorenko was not eligible for an immigration visa under the Displaced Persons Act, and that his subsequent procurement of citizenship was illegal. On December 21, 1984, Fedorenko was deported to the Soviet Union.

(*Document 394 on p. 664*).

## ☆ 393 A Research Paper: *International Terrorism in 1978*

National Foreign Assessment Center, RP 79-10149, CIA, Washington, D.C., March 1979.

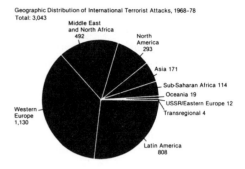

Geographic Distribution of International Terrorist Attacks, 1968-78
Total: 3,043

Middle East and North Africa 492

North America 293

Asia 171

Sub-Saharan Africa 114

Oceania 19

USSR/Eastern Europe 12

Transregional 4

Western Europe 1,130

Latin America 808

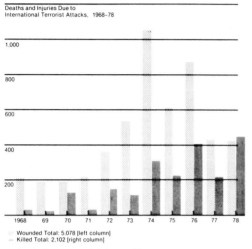

Deaths and Injuries Due to International Terrorist Attacks, 1968-78

1,000

800

600

400

200

1968  69  70  71  72  73  74  75  76  77  78

Wounded Total: 5,078 [left column]
Killed Total: 2,102 [right column]

Casualty figures are particularly susceptible to fluctuations due to inclusion of especially bloody incidents, e.g., exclusion of the 1978 explosion at a Beirut building housing Palestinian guerrilla organizations, which some reports credited to rival terrorists, would subtract 150 deaths from that year's total. Inclusion of the mass suicide/murder by the Peoples' Temple members in Guyana in November 1978 would add more than 900 deaths.

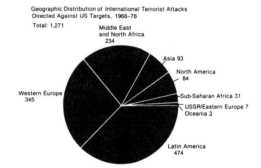

Geographic Distribution of International Terrorist Attacks Directed Against US Targets, 1968-78
Total: 1,271

Middle East and North Africa 234

Asia 93

North America 84

Sub-Saharan Africa 31

USSR/Eastern Europe 7

Oceania 3

Western Europe 345

Latin America 474

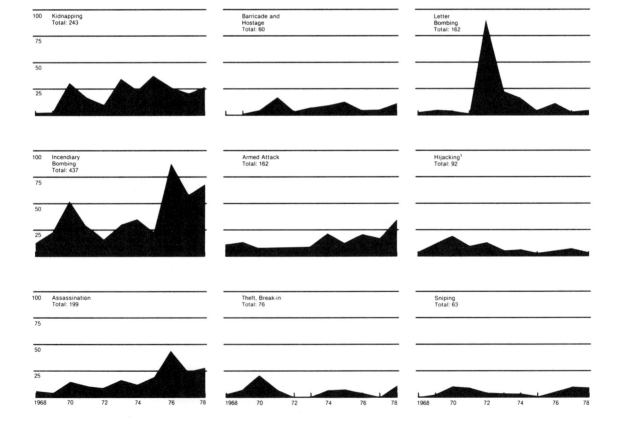

Kidnapping
Total: 243

Barricade and Hostage
Total: 60

Letter Bombing
Total: 162

Incendiary Bombing
Total: 437

Armed Attack
Total: 162

Hijacking[1]
Total: 92

Assassination
Total: 199

Theft, Break-in
Total: 76

Sniping
Total: 63

International Terrorist Attacks on US Citizens or Property 1968-78, by Category of Target

| Target | 1968 | 1969 | 1970 | 1971 | 1972 | 1973 | 1974 | 1975 | 1976 | 1977 | 1978 | Total* |
|---|---|---|---|---|---|---|---|---|---|---|---|---|
| US diplomatic officials or property | 12 | 17 | 52 | 51 | 22 | 19 | 12 | 12 | 12 | 21 | 22 | 252 (19.8) |
| US military officials or property | 4 | 2 | 38 | 36 | 11 | 12 | 12 | 9 | 33 | 40 | 30 | 197 (15.5) |
| Other US Government officials or property | 26 | 32 | 57 | 21 | 20 | 10 | 16 | 14 | 2 | 7 | 2 | 207 (16.3) |
| US business facilities or executives | 6 | 35 | 24 | 40 | 44 | 51 | 86 | 42 | 52 | 33 | 47 | 460 (36.2) |
| US private citizens | 3 | 7 | 17 | 5 | 12 | 10 | 13 | 27 | 26 | 13 | 21 | 154 (12.2) |
| Total | 51 | 93 | 188 | 153 | 109 | 102 | 139 | 104 | 125 | 84 | 122 | 1,270 |

*Figures in parentheses are percentages of the total accounted for by each category of target.

Geographic Distribution of International Terrorist Incidents, 1968-78, by Category of Attack

| | North America | Latin America | Western Europe | USSR/ Eastern Europe | Sub-Saharan Africa | Middle East/ North Africa | Asia | Oceania | Trans-regional | Total |
|---|---|---|---|---|---|---|---|---|---|---|
| Kidnaping | 2 | 133 | 23 | 0 | 39 | 33 | 11 | 2 | 0 | 243 |
| Barricade-hostage | 6 | 11 | 23 | 0 | 2 | 15 | 3 | 0 | 0 | 60 |
| Letter bombing | 14 | 9 | 78 | 0 | 14 | 6 | 37 | 0 | 4 | 162 |
| Incendiary bombing | 29 | 69 | 249 | 2 | 4 | 52 | 28 | 4 | 0 | 437 |
| Explosive bombing | 198 | 388 | 575 | 7 | 10 | 237 | 46 | 12 | 0 | 1,437 |
| Armed attack | 2 | 33 | 34 | 1 | 21 | 58 | 13 | 0 | 0 | 162 |
| Hijacking[1] | 5 | 22 | 19 | 0 | 7 | 24 | 15 | 0 | 0 | 92 |
| Assassination | 15 | 56 | 69 | 0 | 15 | 31 | 12 | 1 | 0 | 199 |
| Theft, break-in | 3 | 44 | 13 | 0 | 0 | 14 | 2 | 0 | 0 | 76 |
| Sniping | 11 | 28 | 8 | 1 | 1 | 11 | 3 | 0 | 0 | 63 |
| Other actions[2] | 8 | 15 | 39 | 1 | 1 | 11 | 1 | 0 | 0 | 76 |
| Total | 293 | 808 | 1,130 | 12 | 114 | 492 | 171 | 19 | 4 | 3,043 |

[1]Includes hijackings by means of air, sea, or land transport, but excludes numerous nonterrorist hijackings.
[2]Includes occupation of facilities without hostage seizure, shootouts with police, and sabotage.

Geographic Distribution of International Terrorist Attacks on US Citizens or Property, 1968-78, by Category of Attack

| | North America | Latin America | Western Europe | USSR/ Eastern Europe | Sub-Saharan Africa | Middle East/ North Africa | Asia | Oceania | Total |
|---|---|---|---|---|---|---|---|---|---|
| Kidnaping | 0 | 58 | 1 | 0 | 14 | 19 | 3 | 0 | 95 |
| Barricade-hostage | 3 | 2 | 1 | 0 | 0 | 6 | 1 | 0 | 13 |
| Letter bombing | 3 | 2 | 1 | 0 | 2 | 0 | 4 | 0 | 12 |
| Incendiary bombing | 6 | 60 | 130 | 1 | 3 | 41 | 21 | 4 | 266 |
| Explosive bombing | 65 | 257 | 174 | 0 | 4 | 116 | 36 | 3 | 655 |
| Armed attack | 0 | 17 | 12 | 0 | 3 | 14 | 8 | 0 | 54 |
| Hijacking[1] | 5 | 5 | 11 | 0 | 0 | 3 | 10 | 0 | 34 |
| Assassination | 2 | 23 | 5 | 0 | 5 | 14 | 5 | 0 | 54 |
| Theft, break-in | 0 | 28 | 5 | 0 | 0 | 7 | 0 | 0 | 41 |
| Sniping | 0 | 15 | 3 | 1 | 0 | 6 | 3 | 0 | 28 |
| Other actions[2] | 0 | 7 | 2 | 1 | 0 | 8 | 1 | 0 | 19 |
| Total | 84 | 474 | 245 | 3 | 31 | 234 | 93 | 7 | 1,271 |

[1]Includes hijackings by means of air or land transport, but excludes numerous nonterrorist hijackings many of which involved US aircraft.
[2]Includes occupation of facilities without hostage seizure, shootouts with police, and sabotage.

☆394 *Fedorenko v. United States*

449 U.S. 490 (1981).

JUSTICE MARSHALL delivered the opinion of the Court.

Section 340(a) of the Immigration and Nationality Act of 1952 requires revocation of United States citizenship that was "illegally procured or . . . procured by concealment of a material fact or by willful misrepresentation." The Government brought this denaturalization action, alleging that petitioner procured his citizenship illegally or by willfully misrepresenting a material fact. The District Court entered judgment for petitioner, but the Court of Appeals reversed and ordered entry of a judgment of denaturalization. We granted certiorari to resolve two questions: whether petitioner's failure to disclose, in his application for a visa to come to this country, that he had served during the Second World War as an armed guard at the Nazi concentration camp at Treblinka, Poland, rendered his citizenship revocable as "illegally procured" or procured by willful misrepresentation of a material fact, and if so, whether the District Court nonetheless possessed equitable discretion to refrain from entering judgment in favor of the Government under these circumstances.

I

A. Petitioner was born in the Ukraine in 1907. He was drafted into the Russian army in June 1941, but was captured by the Germans shortly thereafter. After being held in a series of prisoner-of-war camps, petitioner was selected to go to the German camp at Travnicki in Poland, where he received training as a concentration camp guard. In September 1942, he was assigned to the Nazi concentration camp at Treblinka in Poland, where he was issued a uniform and rifle and where he served as a guard during 1942 and 1943. The infamous Treblinka concentration camp was described by the District Court as a "human abattoir" at which several hundred thousand Jewish civilians were murdered. After an armed uprising by the inmates at Treblinka led to the closure of the camp in August 1943, petitioner was transferred to a German labor camp at Danzig and then to the German prisoner-of-war camp at Poelitz, where he continued to serve as an armed guard. Petitioner was eventually transferred to Hamburg where he served as a warehouse guard. Shortly before the British forces entered that city in 1945, petitioner discarded his uniform and was able to pass as a civilian. For the next four years, he worked in Germany as a laborer.

B. In 1948, Congress enacted the Displaced Persons Act (DPA or Act) to enable European refugees driven from their homelands by the war to emigrate to the United States without regard to traditional immigration quotas. The Act's definition of "displaced persons" [3] eligible for immigration to this country specifically excluded individuals who had "assisted the enemy in persecuting civil[ians]" or had "voluntarily assisted the enemy forces . . . in their operations. . . ." [4] Section 10 of the DPA placed the burden of proving eligibility under the Act on the person seeking admission and provided that "[a]ny person who shall willfully make a misrepresentation for the purpose of gaining admission into the United States as an eligible displaced person shall thereafter not be admissible into the United States." The Act established an elaborate system for determining eligibility for displaced person status. Each applicant was first interviewed by representatives of the International Refugee Organization of the United Nations (IRO) who ascertained that the person was a refugee or displaced person. The applicant was then interviewed by an official of the Displaced Persons Commission, who made a preliminary determination about his eligibility under the DPA. The final decision was made by one of several State Department vice consuls, who were specially trained for the task and sent to Europe to administer the Act. Thereafter, the application was reviewed by officials of the Immigration and Naturalization Service (INS) to make sure that the applicant was admissible into the United States under the standard immigration laws.

In October 1949, petitioner applied for admission to the United States as a displaced person. Petitioner falsified his visa application by lying about his wartime activities. He told the investigators from the Displaced Persons Commission that he had been a farmer in Sarny, Poland, from 1937 until March 1942, and that he had then been deported to Germany and forced to work in a factory in Poelitz until the end of the war, when he fled to Hamburg. Petitioner told the same story to the vice consul who reviewed his case and he signed a sworn statement containing these false representations as part of his application for a DPA visa. Petitioner's false statements were not discovered at the time and he was issued a DPA visa, and sailed to the United States where he was admitted for permanent residence. He took up residence in Connecticut and for three decades led an uneventful and law-abiding life as a factory worker.

In 1969, petitioner applied for naturalization at the INS office in Hartford, Conn. Petitioner did not disclose his wartime service as a concentration camp armed guard in his application, and he did not mention it in his sworn testimony to INS naturalization examiners. The INS examiners took petitioner's visa papers at face value and recommended that his citizenship application be granted. On this recommendation, the Superior Court of New Haven

County granted his petition for naturalization and he became an American citizen on April 23, 1970.

C. Seven years later, after petitioner had moved to Miami Beach and became a resident of Florida, the Government filed this action in the United States District Court for the Southern District of Florida to revoke petitioner's citizenship....

\* \* \*

Petitioner took the stand in his own behalf. He admitted his service as an armed guard at Treblinka and that he had known that thousands of Jewish inmates were being murdered there. Petitioner claimed that he was forced to serve as a guard and denied any personal involvement in the atrocities committed at the camp; he insisted that he had merely been a perimeter guard. Petitioner admitted, however, that he had followed orders and shot in the general direction of escaping inmates during the August 1943 uprising that led to closure of the camp. Petitioner maintained that he was a prisoner of war at Treblinka, although he admitted that the Russian armed guards significantly outnumbered the German soldiers at the camp, that he was paid a stipend and received a good service stripe from the Germans, and that he was allowed to leave the camp regularly but never tried to escape. Finally, petitioner conceded that he deliberately gave false statements about his wartime activities to the investigators from the Displaced Persons Commission and to the vice consul who reviewed his visa application.

The District Court entered judgment in favor of petitioner. The court found that petitioner had served as an armed guard at Treblinka and that he lied about his wartime activities when he applied for a DPA visa in 1949. The court found, however, that petitioner was forced to serve as a guard....

\* \* \*

## II

Our examination of the questions presented by this case must proceed within the framework established by two lines of prior decisions of this Court that may, at first blush, appear to point in different directions.

On the one hand, our decisions have recognized that the right to acquire American citizenship is a precious one, and that once citizenship has been acquired, its loss can have severe and unsettling consequences....

At the same time, our cases have also recognized that there must be strict compliance with all the congressionally imposed prerequisites to the acquisition of citizenship. Failure to comply with any of these conditions renders the certificate of citizenship "illegally procured," and naturalization that is unlawfully procured can be set aside....

\* \* \*

## III

\* \* \*

... Because we are unable to find any basis for an "involuntary assistance" exception in the language of § 2(a), we conclude that the District Court's construction of the Act was incorrect. The plain language of the Act mandates precisely the literal interpretation that the District Court rejected: an individual's service as a concentration camp armed guard—whether voluntary or involuntary—made him ineligible for a visa. That Congress was perfectly capable of adopting a "voluntariness" limitation where it felt that one was necessary is plain from comparing § 2(a) with § 2(b) which excludes only those individuals who "*voluntarily* assisted the enemy forces ... in their operations...." Under traditional principles of statutory construction, the deliberate omission of the word "voluntary" from § 2(a) compels the conclusion that the statute made all those who assisted in the persecution of civilians ineligible for visas....

\* \* \*

In sum, we hold that petitioner's citizenship must be revoked because it was illegally procured. Accordingly, the judgment of the Court of Appeals is affirmed.

*So ordered.*

---

3. The DPA incorporated the definition of "refugees or displaced persons" contained in Annex I to the Constitution of the International Refugee Organization of the United Nations (IRO). The IRO Constitution, 62 Stat. 3037-3055, was ratified by the United States on December 16, 1946 and became effective on August 20, 1948.

4. The IRO Constitution provided that the following persons would not be eligibile for refugee or displaced person status:

"1. War criminals, quislings and traitors.

"2. Any other persons who can be shown:

"(a) to have assisted the enemy in persecuting civil populations of countries, Members of the United Nations; or

"(b) to have voluntarily assisted the enemy forces since the outbreak of the second world war in their operations against the United Nations."

## 395 Random and Indiscriminate Violence (1981)

A major bar to effective sanctions against terrorism has been the inability of countries to prosecute escaped offenders, because host countries refuse to extradite on the grounds that the alleged crime constituted a political offense and therefore was nonextraditable. By a recent United States court decision, a Palestinian charged with planting a bomb that killed two boys and wounded thirty-six others at a bus stop in Tiberias, Israel, was returned to Israel to stand trial despite his attempts to invoke the political offense exception. The magistrate who presided at the extradition hearing developed a three-step standard for determining the political offense claim: (1) the offender's past participation and involvement with a political movement and his personal beliefs as tied to a political motive, (2) existence of a connection or link between the crime and political objectives, and (3) the relation or proportion between the crime and its method of commission and the political objective.

The magistrate concluded that although Eain was a member of a Palestine Liberation Organization faction with expressed political motives, the

> random and indiscriminate placing of an explosive near a bus stop on a public street in any trash bin ... was an isolated act of violence. The commission of these alleged offenses is so remote from the political objective that it could not reasonably have been believed by the offender to have a direct political effect on the government of Israel; nor was it directed at the government of Israel.

The Seventh Circuit Court of Appeals used a different analysis but upheld the magistrate's decision. The court also analyzed the relationship between the judicial and executive branches in considering claims of political offenses. Eain was returned to Israel to stand trial and subsequently was convicted of the offenses charged.

☆ 395 *Eain v. Wilkes*

641 F.2d 504 (7th Cir. 1981).

HARLINGTON WOOD, JR., Circuit Judge.

\*     \*     \*

[P]etitioner argues that ... the crimes of which he is accused do not fall within the terms of the treaty providing for extradition. Petitioner claims that it is apparent that the bombing was politically motivated and that political offenses of that kind are excepted from the extradition treaty....

\*     \*     \*

... [P]aragraph 4 of the Treaty [of Extradition] states that extradition shall not be granted "[w]hen the offense is regarded by the requested Party [the United States] as one of a political character or if the person sought proves that the request for his extradition has, in fact, been made with a view to trying or punishing him for an offense of a political character."

\*     \*     \*

... [S]hould the magistrate either determine that the offense charged is not within a treaty's terms or find an absence of probable cause, the magistrate cannot certify the matter to the Secretary of State for extradition. If the case *is* certified to the Secretary for completion of the extradition process it is in the Secretary's sole discretion to determine whether or not extradition should proceed further with the issuance of a warrant of surrender.

\*     \*     \*

Because petitioner's remaining arguments implicate political concerns, it is essential that we explore the significance to extradition of crimes arising in a political context. Most treaties list categories of crimes or specific offenses for which extradition may be requested. There usually are, however, exceptions to the crimes contained in the list. Many treaties include "political crimes" among those exceptions. The traditional extradition treaty language that deals with the political context of crimes excepts from the treaty crimes that are "of a political character." The Treaty involved in this case uses the traditional language, and like most other similar treaties does not further define its terms.

Petitioner notes that courts around the world have recognized analytically separate kinds of political offenses, termed "pure" and "relative." A "pure" political offense is an "act that is directed against the state but which contains none of the elements of ordinary crime," such as sedition, treason and espionage. A "relative" political offense is one "in which a common crime is so connected with a political act that the entire offense is regarded as political." Petitioner argues that he should not be extradited because the crime with which he is charged constitutes a relative political offense, and that the political overtones of the act outweigh the elements of common crime. The government, in addition to disputing petitioner's argument, urges this court to hold that the determination of the political nature of the crime is itself a political question which should be the sole responsibility of the "political branches" (i.e., Congress and the Executive) to decide, not the Judicial branch. The government also contends that the Treaty itself places sole authority to make the determination of a "political offense" in the hands of the Executive. It therefore becomes necessary to interpret the meaning of the "political offense" exception.

\*     \*     \*

The government's argument that the Political Branches should decide the question of whether the crime charged is a "political offense" under the Treaty has no basis in United States case precedent. The government's contention, however, points up an apparent anomaly in the American law of extradition. It is the settled rule that it is within the Secretary of State's sole discretion to determine whether or not a country's requisition for extradition is made with a view to try to punish the fugitive for a political crime, i.e., whether the request is a subterfuge. ... We have not found any case where an American court declined to consider the applicability of the political offense exception when it was squarely presented. If anything, one of the major criticisms leveled at American extradition law is that federal courts have tended to invoke the political acts exception in situations of common crimes mixed with political overtones upon a showing of "any connection, however feeble" to an uprising or rebellion or condition of domestic violence.

Congress originally made the determination that it is for the courts to decide how to apply the exception by making it a Judicial determination in the first instance as to whether or not the country requesting extradition had charged an individual with a crime "under the provisions of" a treaty. The Executive branch has, over the years, implicitly endorsed this approach. The present system of American extradition perhaps may have evolved as a way of providing the Executive some flexibility in decision-making by allowing it to defer to the Judiciary's decision, for example, to refuse extradition of an individual who the Secretary of State is reluctant to extradite anyway. This "permits the Executive Branch to remove itself from political and economic sanctions which might result if other nations believe the United States lax in the enforcement of its treaty obligations." With this background in mind, we consider whether the issues involved in applying the political offense exception are such that only the Executive should make the determination.

\*　　　\*　　　\*

The government stresses that courts have refused to look at the requesting country's motives to determine if extradition for a common crime is sought merely as a subterfuge for trying an individual for political crimes, even in the presence of an express provision of the treaty, such as the one in the Treaty before us. This raises the logical question of why the Executive's authority is "virtually untrammelled" in that area, but is subject to an initial decision by the Judiciary on the applicability of the political offense exception.

The different approaches taken on political offense and "subterfuge" issues are not so anomalous as the government suggests. In considering the presence of a political offense, the court determines whether the crime charged stemmed from political violence. To make that determination, the magistrate need look only to the facts supporting the extradition request for evidence as to whether or not violent political activity was unfolding at the time to which the facts relate, and of the individual's recognizable connection to that violence. Compared to that, evaluations of the motivation behind a request for extradition so clearly implicate the conduct of this country's foreign relations as to be a matter better left to the Executive's discretion. The Executive's evaluation would look at the actual operation of a government with which this country has ongoing, formal relations evidenced by the extradition treaty and imply that the government may be disingenuous. This obviously would be an embarrassing conflict over assumptions essential to our foreign relations about the integrity of governments with which the United States deals. A judicial decision, however, that establishes an American position on the honesty and integrity of a requesting foreign government is distinguishable from a judicial determination that certain events occurred and that specific acts of an individual were or were not connected to those events. The latter type of decision simply categorizes the facts involved in a given case and then construes the treaty to determine whether or not the facts fall within its ambit. Thus, the Judiciary's deference to the Executive on the "subterfuge" question is appropriate since political questions would permeate any judgment on the motivation of a foreign government.

It should be emphasized, however, that the government's argument on this point is not without some merit. If our long established extradition process is thought to need some overhauling, it is for the Congress to consider, not the courts.

### C. Extradition Request as a Subterfuge

Petitioner claims that Israel seeks his extradition on charges of common crimes in order to try him for his political beliefs. Thus, he says, he should not be extradited, even though all proceedings in Israel concerning this case have been conducted in civil, not military, court.

The determination in this case whether or not the request for extradition on common crimes amounts to a subterfuge by Israel to punish petitioner for a political offense is, as we have clearly noted, a decision within the sole province of the Secretary of State. As should be clear from our earlier discussion, petitioner's claim is without merit, since this court has no jurisdiction to determine the requesting country's motives under this Treaty.

### IV. POLITICAL OFFENSE EXCEPTION

The operative definition of "political offenses" under extradition treaties as construed by the United States limits such offenses to acts committed in the course of and incidental to a violent political disturbance such as a war, revolution or rebellion. Petitioner argues that it is apparent that the crime with which he is charged is a political offense because there was and is a conflict in Israel that involves violence, and the PLO, to which petitioner allegedly belongs, is a party to that violence.

Petitioner notes that generally the motivation of the individual in committing the alleged crime is not an issue in the extradition proceeding.... Thus, petitioner asserts that he cannot be extradited because Israel's allegation of his membership in the PLO is enough to bring his alleged role in the bombing within the scope of the political offense exception. Petitioner's characterization of the American law of extradition is facially plausible. But, like most generalizations about complex legal areas, there is much detail that petitioner's position fails to take into account.

*        *        *

... Petitioner consistently has tried to establish that there exists in Israel a state of conflict in the nature of a war, revolution or rebellion. This, he contends, establishes the propriety of using the political offense exception in this case. The magistrate refused to take judicial notice of the existence of a state of political and military conflict between Israel, its neighboring states and national liberation movements in the Middle East. The magistrate did, however, receive evidence on "the nature of the conflict in the Middle East before, during and after the 1948 proclamation of a State of Israel ... as well as the 1967 occupation by Israel of the West Bank of the country of Jordan...." It appears that the magistrate may have assumed that a conflict existed at the time of petitioner's alleged acts since her subsequent discussion on the applicability of the political offense exception went mainly to issues that usually are considered only after a determination of a violent political disturbance has been made.

There remains, however, some question as to whether that finding of a "conflict" is sufficient to establish that there exists in Israel "a violent political disturbance, such as a war, revolution or rebellion." The nature of that conflict is somewhat different than disturbances that have been considered in other cases where resistance to extradition on grounds of a political offense exception has been sustained. Those cases involved on-going, organized battles between contending armies, a situation which, given the dispersed nature of the PLO, may be distinguished. Terrorist activity seeks to promote social chaos. Modern international terrorism is a phenomenon apart from the world's experience with more conventional expressions by individuals or groups of their dissatisfaction with world order. Such terrorism does not conveniently fit the categories of conflict with which the courts and the international community have dealt in the past. An ongoing, defined clash of military forces may be significant

because that is one backdrop which may bring into sharp relief an individual act of violence. Once the circumstances move away from the context, the judiciary's task of determining what degree or type of violent disturbance permits a successful invocation of the political offense exception becomes more difficult. It also poses a different question of proof than otherwise may be involved.

For example, the evidence in this case reveals that the PLO seeks the destruction of the Israeli political structure as an incident of the expulsion of a certain population from the country, and thus directs its destructive efforts at a defined civilian populace. That, it could be argued, may be sufficient to be considered a violent political disturbance. If, however, considering the nature of the crime charged, that were all that was necessary in order to prevent extradition under the political offense exception nothing would prevent an influx of terrorists seeking a safe haven in America. Those terrorists who flee to this country would avoid having to answer to anyone anywhere for their crimes. The law is not so utterly absurd. Terrorists who have committed barbarous acts elsewhere would be able to flee to the United States and live in our neighborhoods and walk our streets forever free from any accountability for their acts. We do not need them in our society. We have enough of our own domestic criminal violence with which to contend without importing and harboring with open arms the worst that other countries have to export. We recognize the validity and usefulness of the political offense exception, but it should be applied with great care lest our country become a social jungle and an encouragement to terrorists everywhere.

The magistrate, however, understood that the finding of violent upheaval at the time an allegedly political crime occurred was not the end of the analysis under the political offense exception. She went further and found that petitioner had failed to establish that the bombing was incidental to the PLO's objectives. The magistrate held that simply noting membership in the PLO, but not tying the membership to the specific act alleged was insufficient to satisfy the burden petitioner must shoulder in order to invoke the political offense exception. Absent a direct tie between the PLO and the specific violence alleged, the act involved here, without more, was not the sort which may be reasonably "incidental to" a political disturbance. Because the bombing was not shown to be incidental to the conflict in Israel, the magistrate held that it was therefore not an act covered within the political offense exception. We agree with her conclusion.

The reason that the bombing was not "incidental to" the conflict does not lie in the motivation for the act, since, for purposes of extradition, motivation is not itself determinative of the political character of any given act. The definition of "political disturbance," with its focus on organized forms of aggression such as war, rebellion and revolution, is aimed at acts that disrupt the political structure of a State, and not the social structure that established the government. The exception does not make a random bombing intended to result in the cold-blooded murder of civilians incidental to a purpose of toppling a government, absent a direct link between the perpetrator, a political organization's political goals, and the specific act. Rather, the indiscriminate bombing of a civilian populace is not recognized as a protected political act even when the larger "political" objective of the person who sets off the bomb may be to eliminate the civilian population of a country. Otherwise, isolated acts of social violence undertaken for personal reasons would be protected simply because they occurred during a time of political upheaval, a result we think the political offense exception was not meant to produce.

\* \* \*

Anarchy presents the extreme situation of violent political activity directed at civilians and serves to highlight the considerations appropriate for this country's judiciary in construing the requirements of our extradition laws and treaties. But we emphasize that in this case, even assuming some measure of PLO involvement, we are presented with a situation that solely implicates anarchist-like activity, i.e., the destruction of a political system by undermining the social foundation of the government. The record in this case does not indicate that petitioner's alleged acts were anarchist-inspired. Yet the bombing, standing detached as it is from any substantial tie to political activity (and even if tied, as petitioner insists, to certain aspects of the PLO's strategy to achieve its goals), is so closely analogous to anarchist doctrine . . . as to be almost indistinguishable.

\* \* \*

We note that even in the nineteenth century the United States Supreme Court indicated that the civilian status of victims is of significance when courts consider the political offense exception. In *Ornelas v. Ruiz* (1896), the Court upheld a magistrate's determination that a raid on a Mexican village and its military garrison by more than a hundred men was not incidental to violent political disturbances that were occurring in Mexico at the time, as the raiders had claimed. The Court felt that the magistrate was justified in refusing to apply the political offense exception, "in view of the character of the foray, the mode of attack, the persons killed or captured, and the kind of property taken or destroyed." The applicability of *Ruiz* to the present case is even more compelling when one notes that the raiders were later tried in Mexico for their participation in the revolution

they claimed the raid had furthered. It is apparent that the Supreme Court viewed the raid as the sort of political activity that is not encompassed within the political offense exception, especially when the tie to a larger political cause was ambiguous in that specific instance.

We likewise conclude that the magistrate in this case was correct in holding that the alleged bombing directed at a civilian population was not incidental to political upheaval, however characterized, which was occurring at the time in Israel. Petitioner may not claim the benefit of the political offense exception clause contained in Article VI of the United States extradition Treaty with Israel.

\* \* \*

## 396 Seeking Political Asylum (1982)

By the summer of 1978, the numbers of "boat people" fleeing from the economic chaos and state terrorism inflicted by the Haitian regime inflated the population of southern Florida by several thousands. Faced with threatened deportations, these illegal aliens sought relief under the American immigration laws, which provide against the deportation of aliens who will be subject to political prosecution in their native countries upon their return. An evaluation of United States policy toward the Haitian refugees caused a backlog in the deportation cases against these illegal entrants. When the State Department finally concluded that the cause of the Haitian exodus was at root economic and not political, it inaugurated an accelerated deportation program for the Haitians.

Seeking to block deportations to Haiti, the refugees continued to urge that the Haitian government persecuted them for political reasons. Complicating the question of these refugees' motivation and status was the finding by the district court that very often the Tonton Macoutes, the private security force of President Duvalier, considered the act of asking for asylum in the United States an offense against the government worthy of economic reprisal, imprisonment, torture, and even death. Thus the very act of fleeing, for whatever reason, might make the refugees subject to political persecution.

☆ 396 *Haitian Refugee Center v. Smith*

676 F.2d 1023 (11th Cir. 1982).

JAMES C. HILL, Circuit Judge:

On May 9, 1979, eight black Haitian nationals and the Haitian Refugee Center (HRC), an unincorporated association seeking to assist Haitians in this country, filed a class action in federal district court on behalf of over 4,000 Haitians in the south Florida area who had sought political asylum in the United States. . . .

\*           \*           \*

. . . Briefly, the plaintiffs attacked actions taken by immigration judges in the context of deportation hearings, the manner in which asylum interviews were scheduled and conducted, and the manner in which decisions on the asylum claims were made and rendered. The plaintiffs also alleged that, through all of the enumerated practices, the defendants engaged in unlawful discrimination on the basis of national origin and denied the due process rights of the class members.

\*           \*           \*

The program of accelerated processing to which the plaintiff class was subjected by the INS — what the district court termed the "Haitian Program" — embodied the government's response to a tremendous backlog of Haitian deportation cases that had accumulated in the INS Miami district office by the summer of 1978. . . .

. . . [T]he district court found, by June of 1978 it was the perception of the INS "that the asylum process as it had been administered up to that point was the cause [of the administrative delay and consequent backlog]. In attempting to work out from under the backlog, the treatment of Haitian asylum claims would have to change."

Change it did. In July and August of 1978 a program of accelerated processing of Haitian cases was designed at the national level of the INS to resolve the "Haitian problem" in the Miami office.

Many officials provided input in the planning process. Assigned by Mario Noto, Deputy Commissioner of the INS, with the task of assessing the Haitian situation in Miami, INS Regional Commissioner Armand J. Salturelli submitted the recommendation, among others, that processing could be expedited by ceasing the practice of suspending deportation hearings upon the making of an asylum claim. Salturelli acknowledged that this would contravene Operations Instruction 108.1(f), but suggested that this provision should be cancelled or "at least be *suspended insofar as Haitians are concerned.*" One July 1978 report from the Intelligence Division of INS to the Associate Director of Enforcement advised in absolute terms that the Haitians were "economic" and not political refugees and, in belated recognition of the obvious, warned the Enforcement Division that favorable treatment of these Haitians would encourage further immigration. Associate Director of Enforcement, Charles Sava, later visited Miami to find space for holding an increased number of deportation hearings and to discuss with Miami personnel the processing of Haitians. Out of those discussions arose recommended deterrence measures, which Sava outlined in a letter to Deputy Commissioner

Noto. These included detention of arriving Haitians likely to abscond, blanket denials of work permits for Haitians, swift expulsion of Haitians from the United States, and enforcement actions against smugglers.

Planning of the Haitian program culminated in a memorandum sent on August 20, 1978 by Deputy Commissioner Noto to INS Commissioner Leonel J. Castillo. The memo explained the basic mechanics of the accelerated processing already being implemented in the Miami district office. Among the specifics set forth were the assignment of additional immigration judges to Miami, the instructions to immigration judges to effect a three-fold increase in productivity, and orders for the blanket issuance of show cause orders in all pending Haitian deportation cases.

What occurred at the district level once the policy of the Haitian program was in place was aptly described by Acting District Director Gullage. Under immense pressure from the Central Office of INS to achieve rigid numerical goals, Gullage testified: "[T]he fact was that [the Deputy Commissioner] dumped, he put the responsibility for the program on the district and he said, move it." That exhortation was reinforced personally by Deputy Commissioner Noto, who visited the Miami office in mid August 1978. He advised INS trial attorneys to cooperate with the U.S. Attorney's office in enforcement actions against smugglers, encouraging attorneys to point out "THE DIMENSIONS OF THE HAITIAN THREAT" and the fact that "these are unusual cases dealing with individuals that are threatening the community's well-being — socially & economically." Noto emphasized the importance of speed in processing Haitian cases. Responding to an inquiry on treatment of an alien's claim of the right to remain silent in deportation hearings, he commented, "When mute, go with punches and give the most publicity to it to discourage [them]," and later "When aliens refused to speak, why can't you deny [the] pol[itical] asylum request?"

In accordance with the goal of high productivity demanded of the Miami office, Gullage issued a memorandum to all personnel in the office, stating "processing of these cases cannot be delayed in any manner or in any way. All supervisory personnel are hereby ordered to take whatever action they deem necessary to keep these cases moving through the system." The Haitian cases were processed at an unprecedented rate. Prior to the Haitian program only between one and ten deportation hearings were conducted each day. During the program immigration judges held fifty-five hearings per day, or approximately eighteen per judge; at the program's peak the schedule of deportation hearings increased to as many as eighty per day.

At the show cause or deportation hearing, the immigration judges refused to suspend the hearing when an asylum claim was advanced, requiring the Haitians instead to respond to the pleadings in the show cause order and proceeding to a finding of deportability. The order entered by the judge allowed the Haitians ten days for filing an asylum claim with the district director, then ten days to request withholding of deportation from the immigration judge if the asylum deadline was not met. Failure to seek withholding in a timely manner effected automatic entry of a deportation order.

Deportation hearings were not the only matter handled during the Haitian program. Asylum interviews also were scheduled at the rate of forty per day. Immigration officers who formerly had worked at the airport were enlisted as hearing officers for these interviews. Prior to the program such interviews had lasted an hour and a half; during the program the officer devoted approximately one-half hour to each Haitian. In light of the time-consuming process of communication through interpreters, the district court concluded that only fifteen minutes of substantive dialogue took place. Consistent with the result-oriented program designed to achieve numerical goals in processing, the Travel Control section in the Miami office recorded the daily totals of asylum applications processed. The tally sheet contained space only for the total number of denials; there was no column for recording grants of asylum.

Hearings on requests for withholding deportation also were being conducted simultaneously with asylum and deportation hearings, at several different locations. It was not unusual for an attorney representing Haitians to have three hearings at the same hour in different buildings; this kind of scheduling conflict was a daily occurrence for attorneys throughout the Haitian program. The INS was fully aware that only approximately twelve attorneys were available to represent the thousands of Haitians being processed, and that scheduling made it impossible for counsel to attend the hearings. It anticipated the scheduling conflicts which in fact occurred. Nevertheless the INS decided that resolving the conflicts was "too cumbersome for us to handle" and adopted the attitude that everything would simply work out.

Under the circumstances described, we conclude that INS had knowingly made it impossible for Haitians and their attorneys to prepare and file asylum applications in a timely manner....

The results of the accelerated program adopted by INS are revealing. None of the over 4,000 Haitians processed during this program were granted asylum.

*　　　*　　　*

### III

Stating that the processing of an alien's asylum application must conform to the standards of due process, the district court held that the plaintiffs had proven a "wide variety of defects in the processing of Haitian asylum claims" which resulted in a denial of procedural due process. The government challenges that conclusion.

*　　　*　　　*

Besides protected interests, which originate in the Constitution itself, the Supreme Court has also recognized that constitutionally protected liberty or property interests may have their source in positive rules of law, enacted by the state or federal government and creating a substantive entitlement to a particular governmental benefit. In this case we conclude that Congress and the executive have created, at a minimum, a constitutionally protected right to petition our government for political asylum. Specifically, we find in the federal regulations establishing an asylum procedure—regulations duly promulgated pursuant to congressional delegation of authority to the Attorney General and having the force and effect of law—when read in conjunction with the United States' commitment to resolution of the refugee problem as expressed in the United Nations Protocol Relating to the Status of Refugees and in 8 U.S.C. § 1253(h), a clear intent to grant aliens the right to submit and the opportunity to substantiate their claim for asylum.

... [T]he United States became a party to the United Nations Protocol Relating to the Status of Refugees, which incorporates the 1951 United Nations Convention Relating to the Status of Refugees, in 1968. By accession to the Protocol the United States agreed, as stated in Article 33 of the Convention, not to deport a refugee "to frontiers or territories where his life or freedom would be threatened on account of his race, religion, nationality, membership of a particular social group or political opinion." If this commitment by the United States is to have substance at all, it must mean at least that the alien is to be allowed the opportunity to seek political asylum, even if the grant of that benefit is discretionary. Recognizing this, in 1974 the INS published the provisions found in Part 108 of Title 8 of the Code of Federal Regulations to establish the machinery by which the alien is permitted to petition for political asylum in the United States. In other words, Congress, through a designated agency, chose to implement the policy expressed in the Protocol by creating in the alien the right to submit and substantiate a claim of risk of persecution should he be deported to his country.

We concede that the right we find is but a fragile one. There is no constitutionally protected right to political asylum itself. Although fragile, the right to petition is nevertheless a valuable one to its possessor. By it he may at least send his message and be assured of the ear of the recipient. Whether this minimal entitlement be called a liberty or property interest, we think it is sufficient to invoke the guarantee of due process.

*     *     *

In determining what process is due, the Supreme Court has repeatedly emphasized that "the Due Process Clause grants the aggrieved party the opportunity to present his case and have its merits fairly judged. Thus it has become a truism that '*some* form of hearing' is required before the [individual] is finally deprived of a protected ... interest." ...

We think it strains credulity to assert that these plaintiffs were given a hearing on their asylum claims at a meaningful time and in a meaningful manner. We recognize that the constitutional adequacy of the exact timing and nature of the required hearing must be judged by balancing the competing private and governmental interests at stake. It is in light of these interests and the nature of the procedures used to process the Haitians' asylum claims that we conclude that the plaintiffs constitutionally are due more process than they received.

*     *     *

In sum, via the Haitian program, the government created conditions which negated the possibility that a Haitian's asylum hearing would be meaningful in either its timing or nature. Under such circumstances, the right to petition for political asylum was effectively denied.

We therefore find sufficient legal warrant under the Fifth Amendment for that part of the district judge's order requiring the government to submit a procedurally fair plan for the orderly reprocessing of the plaintiffs' asylum applications.

*     *     *

# 397 "warrantless electronic surveillance by the National Security Agency" (1982)

Increasingly, the United States government has added new electronic technologies to its arsenal in the campaign against political crime and criminals. Especially with regard to communications leaving or entering the country, extensive surveillance has been conducted without resort to the warrant safeguards contained in the Constitution, on the general premise that governmental authority is broader and less restricted in instances of international borders and in cases of national security.

Since the Vietnam War, antiwar activists and other dissenters have suspected their overseas communications have been intercepted indiscriminately by the country's foreign intelligence agencies and have later been reported to domestic law enforcement officers. A 1978 effort to test the constitutionality of this practice failed. The United States Court of Appeals for the District of Columbia Circuit ruled the state secrets privilege foreclosed the court from obtaining government information on whether communications had in fact been intercepted. *Halkin v. Helms*, 598 F.2d 1 (D.C. Cir. 1978).

The 1982 case of Abdeen M. Jabara, a Detroit lawyer of Arab extraction active in Arab causes, failed to resolve the question of whether the interception of international communications is exempt from the warrant requirement of the Fourth Amendment. The National Security Agency admittedly secured Jabara's international telegraphic communications without a warrant. Jabara chose not to challenge NSA's acquisition of these communications, but he objected to the agency's transfer of the data to the FBI without the issuance of a warrant. The federal court of appeals rejected Jabara's complaint on the grounds that if the NSA acquisition of the communication was lawful, the sharing of the data with the FBI, a domestic law enforcement agency, was not objectionable.

☆ 397 *Jabara v. Webster*

691 F.2d 272 (6th Cir. 1982).

BAILEY BROWN, Senior Circuit Judge.

Appellee, Abdeen M. Jabara (Jabara), a Detroit lawyer of Arab extraction, has over the years been interested and active in Arab causes. The Federal Bureau of Investigation (FBI), as a result of his activities, began an investigation of him in 1967. This investigation was not continuous and varied from time to time as to intensity and as to the technique used. The technique used by the FBI included physical surveillance by agents and informants, including his speech-making activities, inspection of Jabara's bank records, warrantless electronic surveillance by the National Security Agency (NSA), and interviews of third parties regarding Jabara. This information was maintained and disseminated by the FBI.

Jabara filed an action in district court in Detroit in October, 1972, alleging several causes of action. The defendants include the Attorney General, the Directors of the FBI and NSA in their official capacities and certain known and unknown officers and employees of the FBI and the NSA. One cause of action alleged was that Jabara's Fourth Amendment rights were violated as a result of NSA's interception of his "communications by means of warrantless electronic surveillance and/or disclosed summaries of these interceptions to the Federal Bureau of Investigation." ...

* * *

To understand the Fourth Amendment issue raised by the NSA's interception of Jabara's communications and supplying these to the FBI, all without a warrant, it is necessary briefly to describe the factual background to this claim and then to outline the contentions of the parties.

The NSA intelligence gathering operation [may be] described sufficiently for present purposes as follows:

A brief description of NSA and its functions is appropriate. NSA itself has no need for intelligence information; rather, it is a service organization which produces intelligence in response to the requirements of the Director of Central Intelligence. The mission of the NSA is to obtain intelligence from foreign electrical communications. Signals are acquired by many techniques. The process sweeps up enormous numbers of communications, not all of which can be reviewed by intelligence analysts. Using "watch-lists"—lists of words and phrases designed to identify communications of intelligence interest—NSA computers scan the mass of acquired communications to select those which may be of specific foreign intelligence interest. Only those likely to be of interest are printed out for further analysis, the remainder being discarded without reading or review. Intelligence analysts review each of the communications selected. The foreign intelligence derived from these signals is reported to the various agencies that have requested it. Only foreign communications are acquired, that is, communications having at least one foreign terminal.

On November 1, 1971, the FBI, without a warrant, requested the NSA to supply it with the contents of Jabara's telegraphic communications sent overseas, and the NSA complied by furnishing the FBI with summaries of six of such communications.

* * *

Jabara ... does not ... contend on this appeal that the interception by the NSA violated his Fourth Amendment rights; we may therefore take as a given that the information was legally in the hands of the NSA. What Jabara does contend, and the district court agreed, is that his rights were violated when the NSA turned over the information, without a warrant, to the FBI. Defendants, on the other hand, contend that, since the NSA had lawfully intercepted and had made a record of the content of Jabara's communications, the Fourth Amendment was not implicated when the FBI requested and obtained the summaries from the NSA. This is so, defendants contend, because there simply was no "search" or "seizure" when this information was turned over to another agency of the government.

Defendants still further contend that, even if there was a "search" or "seizure" when the FBI obtained the summaries from the NSA, a warrant was not required because there is a "foreign agent" exception to the warrant requirement and the foreign agent exception was applicable here since, at the time the FBI made the request for the summaries, it had reasonable cause to believe that Jabara was in fact a foreign agent. Jabara, on the other hand, contends that there is no foreign agent exception to the warrant requirement and that, in any event, at the time the FBI made the request, it had no reasonable cause to believe that he was a foreign agent.

* * *

... Since, however, we determine herein that Jabara's Fourth Amendment rights were not violated when the summaries of his overseas telegraphic messages were furnished to the FBI irrespective of whether there was reasonable cause to believe that he was a foreign agent and whether there is a foreign agent exception to the warrant requirement, we need not [reach the latter two questions.]

The district court, in determining that Jabara's Fourth Amendment rights were violated when the FBI, without a warrant, obtained the summaries of his overseas telegraphic communications, distinguished the holding of the District of Columbia Circuit in *Halkin v. Helms*. There the court held that application of the state secret privilege required dismissal of plaintiffs' claims based on alleged interception by the NSA of their overseas communications because the fact of interception need not be and was not divulged. Here, on the other hand, defendants had divulged the interception and later transmittal to the FBI. Thus, the district court reasoned, the state secret privilege was no impediment to the adjudication of Jabara's Fourth Amendment claim. . . .

As heretofore stated, Jabara does not contend on appeal that the NSA's interception of his foreign telegraphic communications violated his Fourth Amendment rights, and therefore we may take as a given the proposition that the NSA lawfully received and was in possession of the communications. From this proposition defendants argue, we think correctly, that Jabara's Fourth Amendment rights were not violated when the summaries were turned over to the FBI because this was not a "search" or "seizure" within the meaning of the amendment. . . . [In 1973 this court said]:

Evidence legally obtained by one police agency may be made available to other such agencies without a warrant, even for a use different from that for which it was originally taken.

* * *

In the instant case, Jabara's very words, summaries of which were supplied to the FBI, had been lawfully intercepted by and were in the records of the NSA. NSA therefore already had in its records, after it intercepted, all that it supplied to the FBI.

Jabara appears to argue, however, that the fact that the NSA acquired, stored and retrieved a large amount of information using sophisticated, high-technology methods and equipment should lead to the conclusion that the NSA's acquisition of Jabara's telegraphic messages was not a search and that the only search occurred when, at the request of the FBI, the NSA retrieved Jabara's messages and delivered summaries to the FBI. There are two difficulties with this argument. First, the simple fact remains that the NSA lawfully acquired Jabara's messages, and these are all that it delivered to the FBI. Second, to the extent that Jabara relies on alleged facts surrounding the methods and technology of acquisition, storage and retrieval of information, such are, as was held by the district court, subject to the state secret privilege. It was recognition of the effect of the privilege that caused the district court to limit its consideration to the question whether the targeting of Jabara's communications by the FBI, in obtaining the summaries from the NSA, was a Fourth Amendment violation irrespective of the facts surrounding the acquisition, storage and retrieval of the information by the NSA.

Jabara, however, would have us apply still another analysis in support of his contention that his Fourth Amendment rights were violated when the FBI, without a warrant, requested and received summaries of his overseas messages.... [: that of] Justice Harlan's concurring opinion in *Katz* [*v. United States* (1967)] ... that ... a reasonable expectation of privacy is the test, that the person asserting the claim must have exhibited an actual (subjective) expectation of privacy and that the expectation must be one that society is prepared to accept as reasonable.

Applying this analysis, ... we agree that Jabara exhibited an actual (subjective) expectation of privacy when he sent the telegraphic messages overseas. But the question here is whether he had an expectation of privacy that society is prepared to recognize as reasonable *after the messages had lawfully come into the possession of the NSA.* For it was *after* the messages were intercepted and within the possession of the NSA and only when they were delivered to the FBI that Jabara contends that his Fourth Amendment rights were violated. We do not believe that an expectation that information lawfully in the possession of a government agency will not be disseminated, without a warrant, to another government agency is an expectation that society is prepared to recognize as reasonable. In this connection, we believe that it is irrelevant that Jabara did not know that the NSA had intercepted his messages. To hold otherwise would in many instances require, for Fourth Amendment purposes, a succession of warrants as information, lawfully acquired, is passed from one agency to another.

We conclude, therefore, that Jabara's Fourth Amendment rights were not violated when the FBI obtained summaries of his overseas telegraphic communications from NSA and that the district court erred in granting summary judgment to Jabara and that, on the contrary, it should have granted summary judgment to defendants as to this claim.

## 398 "neither claimed nor shown to have any mercenary motive" (1983)

Political struggle and internecine vengeance often are not confined to the object territories. In 1976, Orlando Letelier, ambassador to the United States under the overthrown Allende government in Chile, and Ronnie Moffitt, his American assistant, died when a remote control bomb exploded their automobile. The investigation soon centered on a group of anti-Castro Cubans with connections to the successor Chilean regime's intelligence agency. Seven Cubans and three Chilean government officials were indicted. Chile refused to extradite the three on the grounds of insufficient evidence, but the Cubans stood trial and were found guilty. Their convictions were overturned, however, because the government obtained its evidence in part through unconstitutional activity. Upon retrial without the tainted evidence, the Cubans were acquitted of murder.

Motive in the Letelier case, political or mercenary, played little if any role in the law's response to the crime or the defendants. In *United States v. Ivic*, however, the court of appeals reversed the convictions of the Croatian terrorist defendants on one of the counts because their motive was political and not venal. The court sustained convictions on other counts but left open the question of whether the statute involved could be used where the motive of the crime was to secure money for the pursuit of political objectives.

☆ 398 *United States v. Ivic*

700 F.2d 51 (2d Cir. 1983).

FRIENDLY, Circuit Judge:

These appeals from judgments of conviction in the District Court for the Southern District of New York, after a trial before Judge Pollack and a jury, concern the terrorist activities of four Croatian nationalists from mid-November to mid-December, 1980. During this one-month period, a Joint Terrorism Task Force, made up of Special Agents of the Federal Bureau of Investigation (FBI), detectives of the New York City Police Department Arson and Explosives Section, as well as other FBI personnel, including a number of agents and translators able to understand Serbo-Croatian, conducted a large scale investigation, including the operation of four interception devices, the execution of eight search warrants, and around-the-clock physical surveillance of the four appellants and their coconspirators. This investigation culminated in the apprehension of these four appellants without the loss of life or limb or the destruction of property which the evidence demonstrated they intended. After thorough consideration of appellants' many contentions, we affirm all the convictions except those on Count One under the Racketeer Influenced and Corrupt Organizations Act ("RICO"). As to these we hold that appellants' acts and plans, however misguided, are not within RICO.

### THE FACTS

The evidence at trial showed the following: Defendants, Cale, Ivic, Sovulj, and Ivkosic were active partisans of Croatian independence, committed to the separation of Croatia from Yugoslavia.[2] ...

In the early morning hours of November 18, 1980, surveillance agents of the FBI observed Ivkosic drop off his white van at Ivic's residence [in Dobbs Ferry]. Ivic then drove the van to Astoria, in the borough of Queens, where he picked up defendant Sovulj. Together Ivic and Sovulj drove to the intersection of 43rd St. and Broadway in the same borough, arriving there at 8:20 A.M. They parked on 43rd St., just north of Broadway, and replaced the left rear glass window of the van with a cardboard screen, leaving a two-inch opening at the top. Except for a five-minute interval during which the van circled the block, Ivic and Sovulj remained inside the parked but idling van until 8:54 A.M., peering through the aperture southwards down 43rd Street. The significance of the location was that one Joseph Badurina lived with his wife and children at 32-18 43rd St., just south of Broadway. Badurina was a prominent Croatian journalist and politician, the Secretary General of the Croatian National Congress, an umbrella organization for various Croatian groups, and editor of the Congress' publication, *The Messenger*. Badurina was a strong advocate of Croatian independence but a steadfast and vocal opponent of violence. He had previously published in *The Messenger* an open letter to the Croatian community from then U.S. Attorney Robert Fiske, Jr., along with an editorial endorsing it. These views had not endeared him to those in the Croatian independence movement who favored less gentle methods: Indeed, on at least one occasion his life had been threatened in a leaflet distributed by a member of OTPOR, a Croatian separatist organization of which defendants were members.

Badurina routinely walked his young daughter to school in the morning along 43rd Street, directly passing the spot where Ivic and Sovulj sat in the idling van on the morning of November 18. His regular practice was to leave his home between 8:25 and 8:30 A.M., drop off his daughter, and return alone by 9:15 A.M. Alerted by the FBI, Badurina took a different route on November 18 and thereafter did not venture outside his home for the next four weeks.

On the mornings of November 24 and 25 and December 10, Ivic and Sovulj or, on the latter date, Ivic alone, repeated essentially the same maneuver. After the November 24 visit FBI agents followed Ivic back to Dobbs Ferry. When he exited the van, he was seen carrying a slender object, two and one half to three feet long, wrapped in some sort of white covering. Ivic cradled the object in his arm as one would a rifle.

A subsequent search of Ivkosic's van, pursuant to warrant, yielded the cardboard screen cut to fit the rear view window. The cardboard box from which the screen had been cut was found in Cale's basement, as was a loaded Dutch 30.06 semi-automatic rifle mounted with a high-powered Mayflower scope. The rifle was inside a camouflage bag, which was in turn secreted beneath white painter's dropcloths.

This and other evidence of a conspiracy to kill or otherwise injure Badurina, including statements by Sovulj to FBI agents denying ever being with Ivic in a white van anywhere in Queens, furnished the basis for Count 7 of the indictment, charging a conspiracy to violate Badurina's civil rights and also furnished a possible predicate act for the RICO count.

On November 28, 1980, Ivic and Cale talked about possible bombings. After discussing bomb construction techniques and the availability of dynamite, they identified prospective bombsites, describing one as "at the end of this avenue" and another as a "studio." ... Ivic [was observed inspecting] the premises at 19 Union Square West where the George Tomov Yugoslav Folk Dance Ensemble maintained a studio. Tomov had rented the studio for that evening to groups giving a party to celebrate Yugoslavia's Independence Day. The party had been widely advertised in the Yugoslav community and was expected to draw prominent Yugoslav officials, including the Yugoslav Ambassador to the UN and members of the Yugoslav Consulate. A search of Ivic's residence on December 12, 1980, pursuant to warrant, turned up ... assorted bomb paraphernalia and a lady's purse containing a fully operational time-bomb, consisting of 3 cartridges of 80% gelatin dynamite connected to an electric blasting cap and a clock. The time-bomb was set to explode five hours after circuitry contact was made. Thus, had the bomb been placed at the dance studio during the afternoon of November 29, it would have exploded in the middle of that evening's Independence Day festivities. Ivic did not in fact place the bomb because, as he explained later to Cale, "There was no place to park. And at the last moment you have to put that thing together, you understand?" A search of the Caron residence on Colony Street in Bridgeport on December 18, 1980, again pursuant to warrant, yielded eleven cartridges of 80% gelatin dynamite and electric blasting caps identical to the three cartridges and blasting cap in the time-bomb found . . . in Ivic's apartment. This and other evidence furnished the basis for Count 2, charging a conspiracy to transport and utilize explosives, for Count 3, a substantive count for unlawful interstate transportation and receipt of explosives, for Counts 4 and 5, charging attempts by means of explosives to damage and destroy, respectively, the vicinity of Washington Square Park and a building on Union Square West, as well as providing two possible predicates for the RICO conspiracy count.

The next bombing site selected was the Rudenjak Overseas Travel Service, a travel agency which specialized in booking trips to Yugoslavia. On the morning of December 4, Ivic surveilled the agency's office, located at 550 East 187th St. in the Bronx. Next afternoon he reported to Cale that the only effective way to destroy the agency was to leave the bomb in a garbage can outside the front display window. Cale concurred and authorized the operation, telling Ivic "I would do it. . . . There is no risk here." However, a few hours later that same day, Cale, Ivic, and Ivkosic discovered loose wires in Cale's basement. Fearing that they had been subject to electronic surveillance, they abandoned the plan. This and other evidence furnished the basis for Count 6, charging an attempt to damage and destroy, by means of explosives, a travel agency located in the Bronx, in violation of 18 U.S.C. §§ 844(i) and 2, and also provided another possible predicate for the RICO conspiracy count.

We need only add that the searches on December 12, 1980, of Cale's residence, Ivkosic's van, and Ivic's apartment yielded, in addition to the loaded Dutch 30.06 military rifle, the cardboard box and screen cut therefrom, . . . a supply of 30.06 and .38 calibre ammunition, a loaded revolver, and two copies of a pamphlet entitled "Headquarters of the Croatian Revolutionary Forces." The search of the Caron residence in Bridgeport on December 18, 1980, produced a haul which the Government characterizes as "an arsenal of weapons and ammunition" — including, in addition to the previously mentioned dynamite and blasting caps, a second Dutch military rifle virtually identical to that found in Cale's basement, a silencer, and several hundred rounds of ammunition. Also found were a copy of the same "Headquarters of the Croatian Revolutionary Forces" pamphlet and a manual detailing procedures for constructing terrorist weapons, including time-bombs.

\*     \*     \*

## THE RICO COUNT

Count 1 of the indictment entitled "Racketeering Enterprise" contains five paragraphs. The first alleged that appellants, three other individuals, and others unknown to the grand jury constituted an "enterprise" as defined by 18 U.S.C. § 1961(4). Although the statute defines this simply as including "any individual, partnership, corporation, association, or other legal entity, and any union or group of individuals associated in fact although not a legal entity," the indictment went on to say "to wit, a group of individuals associated in fact which conspired to engage in various criminal activities including acts and threats involving murder and arson as chargeable under the laws of the State of New York." The second paragraph charged that "[i]t was the primary object of this criminal enterprise" that the defendants "would and did use terror, assassination, bombings, and violence in order to foster and promote their beliefs and in order to eradicate and injure persons whom they perceived as in opposition to their beliefs." The third paragraph charged that it was "the primary means of this criminal enterprise" that defendants and their associates "would and did receive, transport, possess, conceal, stockpile, construct, and utilize explosives, blasting caps, bombs, rifles, handguns, silencers, and ammunition." The fourth paragraph charged that the defendants, "being associated with the criminal enterprise described in Paragraphs One through Three, which enterprise was engaged in and the activities of which affected interstate and foreign commerce, did unlawfully, wilfully and knowingly conspire and agree to conduct and participate, directly and indirectly, in the affairs of that enterprise through a pattern of racketeering activity: that is, through two or more acts and threats of murder and arson in violation of" certain laws of the State of New York. The fifth paragraph alleged that "[i]n conducting the affairs of their criminal enterprise through this pattern of racketeering activity, the defendants and others with whom they were associated performed the following acts and actions among others." There followed a list of 27 acts reading like the listing of overt acts usual in a garden-variety conspiracy indictment but unnecessary in a RICO conspiracy indictment.

\*     \*     \*

We find . . . the conduct charged in the indictment and proved at trial did not constitute an offense because, as the Government conceded at argument, it was neither claimed nor shown to have any mercenary motive.

\*     \*     \*

The Government's argument is simplicity itself. [Title 18 U.S.C.] section 1962(c) makes it unlawful "for any person employed by or associated with any enterprise engaged in, or the activities of which affect, interstate or foreign commerce, to conduct or participate, directly or indirectly, in the conduct of such enterprise's affairs through a pattern of racketeering activity or collection of unlawful debt," and § 1962(d) makes it unlawful for any person to conspire to violate subsections (a), (b), or (c) of § 1962. The group of Croatian nationalists to which defendants belonged fit the definition of "enterprise" inasmuch as they comprised a "group of individuals associated in fact although not a legal entity." A conspiracy to participate in the conduct of this enterprise's affairs through a "pattern of racketeering activity" would be established by showing, as to each defendant, that he agreed to further the enterprise by committing two of the State law crimes listed, in this case, murder and arson. That is all.

The Court has generally declined to adopt so simplistic an approach. . . .

\*　　　\*　　　\*

When the same word is used in the same section of an act more than once, and the meaning is clear in one place, it will be assumed to have the same meaning in other places. As it appears in subsections (a) and (b), the term "enterprise" quite clearly refers to the sort of entity in which funds can be invested and a property interest of some sort acquired, and hence the sort of entity which one joins to make money. Although perhaps somewhat wider in its reach than "business," an "enterprise," as used in these subsections, is evidently an organized profit-seeking venture. There was no charge or proof of that in this case. Defendants joined together not to make money but, as the indictment itself stated, to advance the goal of Croatian independence. They undertook to murder Badurina and to bomb the dance studio and the travel agency not to obtain money, but rather to eliminate political opponents, win publicity, or otherwise further their chosen cause. If "enterprise" in subsection (c) is given the same meaning which that term clearly has in subsections (a) and (b), then the group to which the indictment charged and the proof showed that defendants belonged is outside its scope.

Regard must be paid also to the title of the statute, "Racketeer Influenced and Corrupt Organizations." . . . In the ordinary use of language no one would choose "corrupt" as an appropriate adjective to describe members of an organization striving for the independence of their native land even by the most abhorrent means but without any desire for personal gain. Dangerous, vicious, misguided, blinded with anger, even savage and crazed, yes, but corrupt, no. . . . The words used by Congress have a familiar connotation to ordinary people as describing money-making activities about which they read in the newspaper every day. It would be stretching such words beyond permissible bounds to apply them to the terrorist ac-

tivities of misguided patriots which, although likewise subject to condemnation, are worlds removed from that of such venal organizations as gambling, narcotics, or prostitution rings. . . .

. . . No one reading these words at the time of enactment would have thought them intended to apply to Croatian terrorists seeking to murder a leader of a rival faction or to scatter death, injury and destruction through a party celebrating Yugoslav Independence Day and a travel agency booking trips to Yugoslavia. Such activity, however horrible, does not "annually drain billions of dollars from America's economy by unlawful conduct and the illegal use of force, fraud and corruption." It has nothing to do with "syndicated gambling, loan sharking, the theft and fencing of property, the importation and distribution of narcotics and other dangerous drugs, and other forms of social exploitation." . . .

\*　　　\*　　　\*

2. Croatian nationalism has roots deep in the nineteenth century, when Croatia was part of the Hapsburg Empire. The formation in 1918 of the Kingdom of Serbs, Croats, and Slovenes, renamed the Kingdom of Yugoslavia in 1929, did not fully satisfy Croatian nationalist aspirations. A nominally independent state from 1941 to 1945, Croatia has been since 1945 one of the six constituent republics of the Federal People's Republic of Yugoslavia. Separatist agitation has persisted in the post-World War II period, despite the decentralizing policies followed by the Belgrade Government. The Croats are the second largest national group in Yugoslavia, after the Serbs. Their differences with the latter are ethnic, religious (they are Roman Catholics and the Serbs Orthodox), and linguistic (though their spoken language is the same, their alphabets are different).

## 399 "causing evacuation of a building" (1978-1983)

The increase in acts of terrorism in the United States has caused many state legislatures to pass some form of antiterrorism legislation. State antiterrorism statutes can be divided into two distinct categories. First, many states have enacted statutes making terrorism a specific crime ("terrorist-specific" legislation). Terrorist-specific legislation has criminalized any terrorist threat made by a person with the purpose of causing the evacuation of a building or a place of assembly, or of disrupting public transportation in reckless disregard for the lives of other individuals. Most terrorist-specific legislation is patterned after the American Law Institute's Model Penal Code and classifies a terrorist threat as a felony. Some states have enacted legislation under the broad heading "terrorizing" and have made such criminal violations misdemeanors.

Because terrorist-specific legislation focuses on the conduct of the accused, the crime is complete when a threat is communicated to another in order to terrorize that person. Generally, courts have inferred the intent to terrorize from the circumstances surrounding the act. The following statutes of Georgia and Louisiana provide examples of terrorist-specific legislation of both the terrorist threat/felony and terrorizing/misdemeanor variety.

Second, several states have incorporated antiterrorism language into their existing criminal laws and have, thereby, criminalized terrorist activity. Generally, these states have made reference to acts of terrorism under areas of the criminal law where the likelihood of terrorist activity is greatest. For example, states have adopted the categories of terrorist activity established in the American Law Institute's Model Penal Code and have made it a crime to threaten to bomb or destroy a building by incorporating such language under their arson statutes. Other states have included, in the crime of kidnapping, the confinement of another for the purpose of terrorizing that individual. An example of a typical state statute which has incorporated the reference to terrorism is provided in the following example from New Hampshire, which prohibits criminal threatening. This statute includes the crime of terrorizing another as a criminal threat.

## ☆ 399 Domestic Antiterrorist Legislation

### ☆ 399a Terrorist-specific Legislation

La. Rev. Stat. Ann. § 14:40.1 (West 1978).

#### TERRORIZING

Terrorizing is the intentional communication of information, known by the offender to be false, that the commission of a crime of violence is imminent or in progress or that a circumstance dangerous to human life exists or is about to exist; and thereby causing any person to be in sustained fear for his or another person's safety; causing evacuation of a building, a public structure, or a facility of transportation; or causing other serious disruption to the public.

Whoever commits the offense of terrorizing shall be fined not more than five hundred dollars or imprisoned not more than six months, or both.

Ga. Code § 16-11-37 (1983).

#### TERRORISTIC THREATS AND ACTS

(a) A person commits the offense of a terroristic threat when he threatens to commit any crime of violence or to turn or damage property with the purpose of terrorizing another or of causing the evacuation of a building, place of assembly, or facility of public transportation or otherwise causing serious public inconvenience, or in reckless disregard of the risk of causing such terror or inconvenience. No person shall be convicted under this subsection on the uncorroborated testimony of the party to whom the threat is communicated.

(b) A person commits the offense of a terroristic act when:

(1) He uses a burning or flaming cross or other burning or flaming symbol or flambeau with the intent to terrorize another or another's household; or

(2) While not in the commission of a lawful act, he shoots at or throws an object at a conveyance which is being operated or which is occupied by passengers.

(c) A person convicted of the offense of a terroristic threat or act shall be punished by a fine of not more than $1,000.00 or by imprisonment for not less than one nor more than five years, or both.

### ☆ 399b Terrorism-incorporated Legislation

N.H. Rev. Stat. Ann. § 631:4 (1983).

#### CRIMINAL THREATENING

I. A person is guilty of an offense when:

(a) By physical conduct, he purposely places or attempts to place another in fear of imminent bodily injury or physical contact; or

(b) He threatens to commit any crime against the person of another with a purpose to terrorize any person; or

(c) He threatens to commit any crime of violence with a purpose to cause evacuation of a building, place of assembly, facility of public transportation or otherwise to cause serious public inconvenience, or in reckless disregard of causing such fear, terror or inconvenience; or

(d) He threatens to commit any crime against the property of another with a purpose to coerce or terrorize any person.

II. The offense is a misdemeanor, except a violation of subparagraph I(c), which is a class B felony.

\*  \*  \*

# 400 "if patriotic sacrifices [make] a terrorist, 'then I'm the greatest terrorist in the world'" (1984)

The political struggle between the United States government and Castro's Cuban regime did not come to a conclusion with the failed Bay of Pigs invasion in 1962. In United Nations forums, and in various foreign arenas (including Grenada and Nicaragua), American and Cuban interests and even personnel were engulfed in continual conflict. Manifestations of this international contest were evident also in the mainland United States, where militant anti-Communist Cuban refugees (of a total of more than six hundred thousand Cubans who arrived since Castro's accession to power) set out to combat the representatives of their native country's Marxist regime. For acts of violence and terrorism conducted within the American shores, these anti-Communist activists were convicted and harshly sanctioned. Yet this treatment was disparate from that accorded by the American government to anti-Castro volunteers who acted outside United States boundaries. Anti-Castroites who either partook in the Cuban invasion or participated in clandestine and warlike exploits against the Cuban regime and its Central American allies were frequently supported, financially as well as materially, by United States authorities.

## ☆ 400 Judge Sentences Omega 7 Leader to Life in Prison

"Anti-Castro Chief Guilty . . ."—*New York Times*, November 10, 1984, 28.

A life sentence and an additional 35 years in prison were imposed yesterday on Eduardo Arocena, a Cuban exile convicted of murder and terrorist bombings as the head of an anti-Castro group called Omega 7.

Judge Robert J. Ward, who imposed the sentence in Federal District Court in Manhattan, said the Government had presented proof that Mr. Arocena was the group's "founder, leader and chief bomb maker."

Under Federal law, the 41-year-old defendant could be eligible for parole after serving 10 years of his sentence, but authorities said he would probably be kept in prison much longer, perhaps for life.

Mr. Arocena made an impassioned speech at his sentencing, saying that if patriotic sacrifices and democratic beliefs made him a terrorist, "then I'm the greatest terrorist in the world."

"I'm an anti-Communist to the death," he exclaimed, standing in the small, crowded courtroom, with an interpreter translating his words from Spanish into English.

\*　　　\*　　　\*

The chief prosecutor, Michael L. Tabak, told Judge Ward that the Government regarded Mr. Arocena's case as "extremely important."

"He is a man who should not be on the streets as long as he is capable of making a bomb or pulling a trigger," Mr. Tabak said.

On Sept. 22, after a six-week trial, Mr. Arocena was found guilty of all the charges against him, except one bombing charge.

He was convicted of ordering the 1980 murder of an attaché at Cuba's Mission to the United Nations, Felix Garcia Rodriguez, who was shot to death in Queens. The charges against him also included trying to kill Dr. Raul Roa Kouri, Cuba's delegate to the United Nations, and bombing foreign consulates and other targets.

He was also accused of ordering the 1979 murder of a Cuban exile in New Jersey, Eulalio Jose Negrin, but that was not a Federal crime because the victim was not a foreign official.

\*　　　\*　　　\*

Mr. Tabak said in the trial that Omega 7 had committed no terrorist acts since Mr. Arocena's arrest more than a year ago.

According to the prosecutors, Mr. Tabak and Bruce A. Green, the defendant was "Omar," the Omega 7 leader who operated for years in New York, New Jersey and Florida.

"Arocena organized Omega 7 on Sept. 11, 1974, for the purpose of carrying out terrorist murders and bombings exclusively within the United States," the prosecutors said in a sentencing memorandum.

## 401 State Terrorism Accounts for Murders and Assassinations (1984-1985)

By the mid-1980s, the term *terrorism* was becoming a catchall for virtually every act of violence against United States officials, personnel, and property. Citing the growing incidence of terrorism in this country and abroad, and noting that of the nearly sixty-five hundred acts of international terrorism in the past decade approximately 40 percent had been directed against Americans, President Reagan, on March 6, 1984, sent to Congress four separate bills addressing the dangers of terrorism. These dangers, he pointed out, have increased in recent years through the emergence of state-directed or -supported terrorism. "This state terrorism," he noted, "starkly manifested in the recent spectacles of violence in Beirut, Rangoon, and Kuwait, accounts for the great majority of terrorist murders and assassinations." State-provided training, financing, and logistic support of terrorists and terrorist groups posed a severe challenge to the conduct of American foreign policy, and appropriate legislation was required to combat this evil.

Testifying before the Committee on Foreign Affairs of the United States House of Representatives, Secretary of State George P. Shultz stated on June 13, 1984:

No longer the random acts of isolated groups of local fanatics, terrorism is now a method of warfare, no less because it is undeclared and even (though not always) denied. . . .

The legislation before you represents modest but necessary steps. They are essential steps because the problem will not go away: this is certainly not the last you will hear about the problem of terrorism.

In addition to these recent enactments, other bills have been introduced into Congress. The Anti-Terrorism Act of 198-, S. 275 (1985), would make terrorism per se a federal capital offense. The Anti-Nuclear Terrorism Act of 198-, S. 274 (1985), would require all persons having access to a nuclear power station to submit to fingerprinting. And the Prohibition against Training or Support of Terrorist Organizations Act of 1984, H. R. 5613 (1984), would make it a federal offense for a United States citizen, a corporation, or a resident alien to assist or solicit assistance for any international terrorist group.

## ☆ 401 Recent United States Legislation to Combat International Terrorism

### ☆ 401a S. J. Res. 336

98 Stat. 1664.

A TIME OF REMEMBRANCE—PROCLAMATION

*Joint Resolution to Proclaim October 23, 1984, as "A Time of Remembrance" for All Victims of Terrorism Throughout the World*

Whereas the problem of terrorism has become an international concern that knows no boundaries — religious, racial, political, or national;

Whereas thousands of men, women, and children have died at the hands of terrorists in nations around the world, and today terrorism continues to claim the lives of many peace-loving individuals;

Whereas October 23, 1983, is the date on which the largest number of Americans were killed in a single act of terrorism — the bombing of the United States compound in Beirut, Lebanon, in which two hundred and forty-one United States servicemen lost their lives;

Whereas many of these victims died defending ideals of peace and freedom; and

Whereas it is appropriate to honor all victims of terrorism, and in America to console the families of victims, and to cherish the freedom that their sacrifices make possible for all Americans: Now, therefore, be it

*Resolved by the Senate and House of Representatives of the United States of America in Congress assembled.* That October 23, 1984, be proclaimed as "A Time of Remembrance," to urge all Americans to take time to reflect on the sacrifices that have been made in the pursuit of peace and freedom, and to promote active participation by the American people through the wearing of a purple ribbon, a symbol of patriotism, dignity, loyalty, and martyrdom. The President is authorized and requested to issue a proclamation calling upon the departments and agencies of the United States and interested organizations, groups, and individuals to fly United States flags at half staff throughout the world in the hope that the desire for peace and freedom take firm root in every person and every nation.

*Approved, September 28, 1984.*

### ☆ 401b 1984 Act to Combat International Terrorism

98 Stat. 2706.

*       *       *

SEC. 101. (a) Title 18 of the United States Code is amended by adding . . . :

*       *       *

"§ *3071. Information for which rewards authorized*

"With respect to acts of terrorism primarily within the territorial jurisdiction of the United States, the Attorney General may reward any individual [except government employees in performance of their official duties] who furnishes information—

"(1) leading to the arrest or conviction, in any country, of any individual or individuals for the commission of an act of terrorism against a United States person or United States property; or

"(2) leading to the arrest or conviction, in any country, of any individual or individuals for conspiring or attempting to commit an act of terrorism against a United States person or property; or

"(3) leading to the prevention, frustration, or favorable resolution of an act of terrorism against a United States person or property.

"§ *3072. Determination of entitlement; maximum amount; Presidential approval; conclusiveness*

"The Attorney General shall determine whether an individual furnishing information described in section 3071 is entitled to a reward and the amount to be paid. A reward under this section may be in an amount not to exceed $500,000. A reward of $100,000 or more may not be made without the approval of the President or the Attorney General personally. A determination made by the Attorney General or the President under this chapter shall be final and conclusive, and no court shall have power or jurisdiction to review it.

"§ *3073. Protection of identity*

"Any reward granted under this chapter shall be certified for payment by the Attorney General. If it is determined that the identity of the recipient of a reward or of the members of the recipient's immediate family must be protected, the Attorney General may take such measures in connection with the payment of the reward as deemed necessary to effect such protection.

\*        \*        \*

"§ *3076. Eligibility for witness security program*

"Any individual (and the immediate family of such individual) who furnishes information which would justify a reward by the Attorney General under this chapter or by the Secretary of State under section [102] may, in the discretion of the Attorney General, participate in the Attorney General's witness security program. . . .

"§ *3077. Definitions*

"As used in this chapter, the term—

"(1) 'act of terrorism' means an activity that—

"(A) involves a violent act or an act dangerous to human life that is a violation of the criminal laws of the United States or of any State, or that would be a criminal violation if committed within the jurisdiction of the United States or of any State; and

"(B) appears to be intended—

"(i) to intimidate or coerce a civilian population;

"(ii) to influence the policy of a government by intimidation or coercion; or

"(iii) to affect the conduct of a government by assassination or kidnaping.

"(2) 'United States person' means—

"(A) a national of the United States . . . ;

"(B) an alien lawfully admitted for permanent residence in the United States . . . ;

"(C) any person within the United States;

"(D) any employee or contractor of the United States Government, regardless of nationality, who is the victim or intended victim of an act of terrorism by virtue of that employment;

"(E) a sole proprietorship, partnership, company, or association composed principally of nationals or permanent resident aliens of the United States; and

"(F) a corporation organized under the laws of the United States, any State, the District of Columbia, or any territory or possession of the United States, and a foreign subsidiary of such corporation.

"(3) 'United States property' means any real or personal property which is within the United States or, if outside the United States, the actual or beneficial ownership of which rests in a United States person or any Federal or State governmental entity of the United States."

\*        \*        \*

AUTHORITY OF THE SECRETARY OF STATE

SEC. 102. The State Department Basic Authorities Act of 1956 is amended by redesignating existing section 36 as section 37 and by inserting the following new section 36 after section 35:

"SEC. 36. (a) The Secretary of State may pay a reward to any individual who furnishes information—

"(1) leading to the arrest or conviction, in any country, of any individual for the commission of an act of international terrorism, or

"(2) leading to the arrest or conviction, in any country, of any individual for conspiring or attempting to commit an act of international terrorism, or

"(3) leading to the prevention, frustration, or favorable resolution of an act of international terrorism,

if the act of international terrorism is against a United States person or United States property and is primarily outside the territorial jurisdiction of the United States.

"(b) A reward under this section may not exceed $500,000. A reward of $100,000 or more may not be made without the approval of the President or the Secretary of State personally.

"(c) Before making a reward under this section in a matter over which there is Federal criminal jurisdiction, the Secretary of State shall advise and consult with the Attorney General."

\*        \*        \*

INCREASING INTERNATIONAL COOPERATION TO COMBAT TERRORISM

SEC. 201. (a) The President is urged to seek more effective international cooperation in combatting international terrorism, including—

(1) severe punishment for acts of terrorism which endanger the lives of diplomatic staff, military personnel, other government personnel, or private citizens; and

(2) extradition of all terrorists and their accomplices to the country where the terrorist incident occurred or whose citizens were victims of the incident.

(b) High priority should also be given to negotiations leading to the establishment of a permanent international working group which would combat international terrorism by—

(1) promoting international cooperation among countries;

(2) developing new methods, procedures, and standards to combat international terrorism;

(3) negotiating agreements for exchanges of information and intelligence and for technical assistance; and

(4) examining the use of diplomatic immunity

and diplomatic facilities to further international terrorism.

This working group should have subgroups on appropriate matters, including law enforcement and crisis management.

SEC. 301. In light of continued terrorist incidents and given the ever increasing threat of international terrorism directed at United States missions and diplomatic personnel abroad, the Congress believes that it is imperative that the Department of State review its approach to providing security against international terrorism. Not later than February 1, 1985, the Secretary of State shall report to the Committee on Foreign Relations of the Senate and the Committee on Foreign Affairs of the House of Representatives on the findings and recommendations of the Advisory Panel on Security of United States Missions Abroad.

\*     \*     \*

### DANGER PAY

SEC. 304. In recognition of the current epidemic of worldwide terrorist activity and the courage and sacrifice of employees of United States agencies overseas, civilian as well as military, it is the sense of Congress that the provisions of section 5928 of title 5, United States Code, relating to the payment of danger pay allowance, should be more extensively utilized at United States missions abroad.

*Approved, October 19, 1984.*

⸎401c International Terrorism and Foreign Airport Security (1985)

99 Stat. 219.

PART A—INTERNATIONAL TERRORISM
GENERALLY

\*     \*     \*

### SEC. 503. PROHIBITION ON ASSISTANCE TO COUNTRIES SUPPORTING INTERNATIONAL TERRORISM

*(a) Prohibition.* — Section 620A of the Foreign Assistance Act of 1961 is amended to read as follows:

*"Sec. 620A. Prohibition on Assistance to Countries Supporting International Terrorism.* — (a) The United States shall not provide any assistance under this Act, the Agricultural Trade Development and Assistance Act of 1954, the Peace Corps Act, or the Arms Export Control Act, to any country which the President determines —

"(1) grants sanctuary from prosecution to any individual or group which has committed an act of international terrorism, or

"(2) otherwise supports international terrorism.

"(b) The President may waive the application of subsection (a) to a country if the President determines that national security or humanitarian reasons justify such waiver. . . ."

\*     \*     \*

### SEC. 504. PROHIBITION ON IMPORTS FROM AND EXPORTS TO LIBYA

*(a) Prohibition on Imports.* — Notwithstanding any other provision of law, the President may prohibit any article grown, produced, extracted, or manufactured in Libya from being imported into the United States.

*(b) Prohibition on Exports.* — Notwithstanding any other provision of law, the President may prohibit any goods or technology, including technical data or other information, subject to the jurisdiction of the United States or exported by any person subject to the jurisdiction of the United States, from being exported to Libya.

\*     \*     \*

### SEC. 505. BAN ON IMPORTING GOODS AND SERVICES FROM COUNTRIES SUPPORTING TERRORISM

*(a) Authority.* — The President may ban the importation into the United States of any good or service from any country which supports terrorism or terrorist organizations or harbors terrorists or terrorist organizations.

*(b) Consultation.* — The President, in every possible instance, shall consult with the Congress before exercising the authority granted by this section and shall consult regularly with the Congress so long as that authority is being exercised.

*(c) Reports.* — Whenever the President exercises the authority granted by this section, he shall immediately transmit to the Congress a report. . . .

### SEC. 506. INTERNATIONAL ANTI-TERRORISM COMMITTEE

The Congress calls upon the President to seek the establishment of an international committee, to be known as the International Anti-Terrorism Committee, consisting of representatives of the member countries of the North Atlantic Treaty Organization, Japan, and such other countries as may be invited and may choose to participate. The purpose of the Committee should be to focus the attention and secure the cooperation of the governments and the public of the participating countries and of other countries on the problems and responses to international terrorism, by serving as a forum at both the political and law enforcement levels.

## SEC. 507. INTERNATIONAL TERRORISM CONTROL TREATY

It is the sense of the Congress that the President should establish a process by which democratic and open societies of the world, which are those most plagued by terrorism, negotiate a viable treaty to effectively prevent and respond to terrorist attacks. Such a treaty should incorporate an operative definition of terrorism, and should establish effective close intelligence-sharing, joint counterterrorist training, and uniform laws on asylum, extradition, and swift punishment for perpetrators of terrorism. Parties to such a treaty should include, but not be limited to, those democratic nations who are most victimized by terrorism.

## SEC. 508. STATE TERRORISM

It is the sense of the Congress that all civilized nations should firmly condemn the increasing use of terrorism by certain states as an official instrument for promoting their policy goals, as evidenced by such examples as the brutal assassination of Major Arthur D. Nicholson, Junior, by a member of the Soviet armed forces.

## PART B—FOREIGN AIRPORT SECURITY

### SEC. 551. SECURITY STANDARDS FOR FOREIGN AIR TRANSPORTATION

*(a) Security at Foreign Airports.*—Section 1115 of the Federal Aviation Act of 1958 (49 U.S.C. App. 1515) is amended to read as follows:

### "SECURITY STANDARDS IN FOREIGN AIR TRANSPORTATION

#### *"Assessment of Security Measures*

"SEC. 1115. (a)(1) The Secretary of Transportation shall conduct at such intervals as the Secretary shall deem necessary an assessment of the effectiveness of the security measures maintained at those foreign airports being served by air carriers, those foreign airports from which foreign air carriers serve the United States, those foreign airports which pose a high risk of introducing danger to international air travel, and at such other foreign airports as the Secretary may deem appropriate.

\*      \*      \*

"(3) The assessment shall determine the extent to which an airport effectively maintains and administers security measures...

#### *"Consultation with the Secretary of State*

"(b) In carrying out subsection (a), the Secretary of Transportation shall consult the Secretary of State with respect to the terrorist threat which exists in each country. The Secretary of Transportation shall also consult with the Secretary of State in

order to determine which foreign airports are not under the de facto control of the government of the country in which they are located and pose a high risk of introducing danger to international air travel.

\*      \*      \*

(e)

\*      \*      \*

"(2) Subject to paragraph (1), if the Secretary of Transportation determines pursuant to this section that an airport does not maintain and administer effective security measures—

"(A) the Secretary of Transportation—

"(i) shall publish the identity of such airport in the Federal Register,

"(ii) shall cause the identity of such airport to be posted and prominently displayed at all United States airports regularly being served by scheduled air carrier operations, and

"(iii) shall notify the news media of the identity of such airport;

"(B) each air carrier and foreign air carrier providing service between the United States and such airport shall provide notice of such determination by the Secretary to any passenger purchasing a ticket for transportation between the United States and such airport, with such notice to be made by written material included on or with such ticket;

"(C) the Secretary of Transportation, after consultation with the appropriate aeronautical authorities of the foreign government concerned and each air carrier serving such airport, may,... with the approval of the Secretary of State, withhold, revoke, or impose conditions on the operating authority of any air carrier or foreign air carrier to engage in foreign air transportation utilizing such airport; and

"(D) the President may prohibit air carriers and foreign air carriers from providing service between the United States and any other foreign airport which is directly or indirectly served by aircraft flying to or from the airport with respect to which the determination is made under this section.

\*      \*      \*

*(c) Closing of Beirut International Airport.*—It is the sense of the Congress that the President is urged and encouraged to take all appropriate steps to carry forward his announced policy of seeking the effective closing of the international airport in Beirut, Lebanon, at least until such time as the Government of Lebanon has instituted measures and procedures designed to prevent the use of that airport by aircraft hijackers and other terrorists in attacking civilian airlines or their passengers, hi-

jacking their aircraft, or taking or holding their passengers hostage.

*    *    *

### SEC. 555. INTERNATIONAL CIVIL AVIATION BOYCOTT OF COUNTRIES SUPPORTING INTERNATIONAL TERRORISM

It is the sense of the Congress that the President—

(1) should call for an international civil aviation boycott with respect to those countries which the President determines—

(A) grant sanctuary from prosecution to any individual or group which has committed an act of international terrorism, or

(B) otherwise support international terrorism; and

(2) should take steps, both bilateral and multilateral, to achieve a total international civil aviation boycott with respect to those countries.

### SEC. 556. MULTILATERAL AND BILATERAL AGREEMENTS WITH RESPECT TO AIRCRAFT SABOTAGE, AIRCRAFT HIJACKING, AND AIRPORT SECURITY

The Secretary of State shall seek multilateral and bilateral agreement on strengthening enforcement measures and standards for compliance with respect to aircraft sabotage, aircraft hijacking, and airport security.

### SEC. 557. RESEARCH ON AIRPORT SECURITY TECHNIQUES FOR DETECTING EXPLOSIVES

In order to improve security at international airports, there are authorized to be appropriated to the Secretary of Transportation from the Airport and Airway Trust Fund (in addition to amounts otherwise available for such purpose) $5,000,000, without fiscal year limitation, to be used for research on and the development of airport security devices or techniques for detecting explosives.

### SEC. 558. HIJACKING OF TWA FLIGHT 847 AND OTHER ACTS OF TERRORISM

The Congress joins with all Americans in celebrating the release of the hostages taken from Trans World Airlines flight 847. It is the sense of the Congress that—

(1) purser Uli Derickson, pilot John Testrake, co-pilot Philip Maresca, flight engineer Benjamin Zimmermann, and the rest of the crew of Trans World Airlines flight 847 displayed extraordinary valor and heroism during the hostages' ordeal and therefore should be commended;

(2) the hijackers who murdered United States Navy Petty Officer Stethem should be immediately brought to justice;

(3) all diplomatic means should continue to be employed to obtain the release of the 7 United States citizens previously kidnapped and still held in Lebanon;

(4) acts of international terrorism should be universally condemned; and

(5) the Secretary of State should be supported in his efforts to gain international cooperation to prevent future acts of terrorism.

*    *    *

*Approved, August 8, 1985.*

### CHAPTER 13

# Toward the Third Millennium

1979–1997

This chapter continues to chronicle political dissidence and militance in America during the final decade and a half of the twentieth century. The reader will find that in this era some of the domestic protests documented in Chapter 11 and the international violence reviewed in Chapter 12 have escalated into open warfare, as is the natural evolution of political dissent and resistance when those in power, here or abroad, are unwilling or unable to adequately redress, in a timely manner, the underlying causes of discontent.

The reader should note also that, although a growing portion of the contemporary political strife surfacing in the United States has its roots in foreign political causes and conflicts that have been transplanted into our midst, the majority of militant incidents in the last decades represent the sprouting of either revived or new domestic anxieties, grievances, and hostilities. As one of this volume's editors noted in a different context:

> Most pundits of [today's] increasingly precarious worldwide balance between order and chaos seem to be on the wrong trail. While sundry scholars and [governmental] agencies ... keep speculating about where the next decade's or era's international arenas of conflict are likely to be, it is highly probable that the greatest contemporary and forthcoming world crises will be domestic. The escalating global disorder seems to derive from internal, rather than international, confrontations. (Nicholas N. Kittrie, *The War against Authority* [Baltimore: Johns Hopkins University Press, 1995], 1)

As we initially noted in the Introduction to this volume's revised edition, the end of the cold war and the disappearance of the Soviet Union as an external enemy (a development perceived by some as "the end of history") has allowed political dissatisfaction and paranoia to turn inward.

It is evident to the editors of this volume that a great portion of the domestic dissent, violence, and terror indeed reflects a growing American disillusionment with, or even outright hostility towards, "large," "centralized," "bureaucratic," "alien," and "international" agencies of government. At times the very legitimacy of the country's prevailing political, economic, social, cultural, and even religious order is challenged. Attacks on federal facilities

and officers, the emergence of popular antigovernmental militias, and the cropping up of new secessionist efforts, both on a statewide scale (such as in Hawaii) and in smaller "fundamentalist" or religious communities are symptoms of this growing hostility toward established authority. The conflicts of old were often driven by the desires of diverse groups to secure new rights through governmental intervention (i.e., expanding the rights of labor, safeguarding the survival of Native Americans, emancipating black Americans, granting the franchise to women, and enlarging the First Amendment). But those struggles have been eclipsed by more recent conflicts whose driving force is a desire to scale back the role and size of government. One senses a new desire to recover "natural" and "old" rights, allegedly misappropriated by government, instead of forging and securing new ones.

For all of the emerging antigovernment and antiauthority trends, the government seems to be developing a new maturity in its responses to political dissent and activism. The change has been manifested in the admission that some past sanctions against selected groups and peoples were excessive, and that remedies to help compensate or rehabilitate the victims of unnecessary or unjust political persecutions are necessary. The granting of greater autonomy to Native Americans, the institution of affirmative action for African Americans and others, the introduction of long-overdue reparations programs, and the use of civil suits and monetary damages against perpetrators of hate crimes all testify to this new trend. (These actions, when undertaken by the government, are often perceived as "special treatment" by those left out, magnifying their grievances and fueling their perceptions of abandonment.)

The country's new sensitivity is reflected also in the emerging restraint shown by governmental law enforcement agencies towards political millenialists and religious fringe communities. Compare the drawn-out sieges of Waco and Justus Township with the probable fate of a similarly placed and barricaded group of common criminals, such as bank robbers. While the outcomes of the incidents at Waco and Ruby Ridge nevertheless remain tragic in retrospect, one can only imagine the greater carnage if the authorities had moved in with lesser sensitivity. By and large, through much of this country's history, collectives of political militants have been treated deferentially (as was demonstrated in America's Civil War practice of according Southern rebels a prisoner-of-war status rather than punishing them as traitors and criminals).

Much harsher treatment has been reserved, however, for those viewed as "foreign" provocateurs, anarchists, Communists, and terrorists. The current chapter notes the new and threatening growth of imported international violence into America. The bombing of Pan Am Flight 103 over Lockerbie, Scotland, and the attack on the World Trade Center in New York City are two notable examples of the global reach of political criminality. But these international exporters of terrorism do not benefit from any public or private sympathy, however just their initial causes might have been. They are readily branded as international outlaws and terrorists, and the full force of American legal and military might is brought against them. The expanding demands for due process and the inclinations toward leniency evidenced at home are swiftly forgotten when dealing with foreign militants espousing distant grievances who seek satisfaction through violent acts on American soil or at the cost of American lives. It is because of this disparity in attitudes that advocates of America's political and civil rights remain fearful of most proposals that seek to dilute the country's traditional constitutional safeguards under the banner of the war against "international terrorism."

In the face of the current and potential growth of imported political criminality, the reader should note the increasing readiness of America's law enforcement agencies to intensify, both unilaterally and cooperatively, their war against foreign bases of political criminality. This is represented both by the expansion overseas of the jurisdiction of America's police and military agencies and by the growing collaboration between the United States and friendly foreign governments in the exchange of information, the securing of evidence, and the extradition of terrorist suspects. The "long arm" of America's law has reached out to capture foreign terrorists charged with the hijacking of a Jordanian aircraft in the Mediterranean and the endangering of an American passenger, while the United States military went into Panama to capture General Noriega, that nation's

army chief of staff and a major conspirator in the importation of drugs into the United States. In addition, the United States courts have exercised their civil jurisdiction over the alleged perpetrators of atrocities in far-off lands.

These newly emerging developments portend the increasing exposure of America's law enforcement agencies, courts, and mass media to the unique questions raised by the political offender. Not only government officials and media representatives but also the public at large increasingly face the intricate and often intriguing issues raised by this unique class of offenders, who practice an unusual admixture of politics, criminality, and warfare. As the communications and travel revolutions promise to increasingly make any local eruption of political dissent, resistance, and criminality more than one country's problem, growing national attention and deference to prevailing international norms in this arena is perhaps inevitable. Individual governments will seek, as they always have, to contain contagion by expanding available means of surveillance, monitoring mail, patrolling the borders, capturing fleeing political offenders, and censoring the Internet. As more countries are drawn into the domestic political struggles of distant nations, new transnational norms of cooperation in response to rebellion, political criminality, and terrorism, and those who support these practices (whether ideologically or materially), must be created and honored.

Simplified access to newly emerging communication techniques and global information streams might seem at first to give political dissidents greater capability to widely disperse their "subversive" ideas and attract supporters. Yet governmental monitoring of the new technologies and the emergence of more sophisticated electronic surveillance tools are likely to produce an advantage for those in power. As this edition goes to print, an emerging struggle for control over the Internet is under way. The government desires to protect the public from obscenity and other hazardous information, yet the users may have distinct wishes for their electronic realm. It must not be viewed as mere coincidence that this second edition of *The Tree of Liberty*, which opens with King Edward's attempt in 1351 to define treasonous speech, concludes with the words and deeds of a secessionist movement born on the Internet. New World Order or not, "the end of history" or not, it appears that modernity and its emerging instrumentalities pose new promises as well as threats for the future growth of the tree of liberty.

---

## 402 The County Supremacy Movement (1979-1996)

From time to time, rebellion and political conflict do not pitch an individual or a community against the government but represent instead a struggle between different layers of authority: federal, state, and local. This struggle for supremacy has been a central theme in the modern development of American federalism and has been revisited in the issue of control of federal lands in the West.

The United States government is a major landholder, especially in the Western states. The Constitution's Property and Supremacy Clauses (U.S. Const., Art. VI) have been held to vest absolute power in the federal government over all activities on and off federal lands which affect anything on them. In the early days of westward expansion, this federal ownership of and power over public lands created few problems. The public lands were open wilderness, left unregulated and up for sale.

That began to change in the 1960s. The interest in wilderness recreation, growing environmental consciousness, and shrinking privately held timber resources caused friction between the various users of public lands. Congress withdrew more land from commercial exploitation and enacted environmental legislation that restricted the use of the remainder. More than ever, control of public lands became politicized.

In 1979, during the Carter administration, forces that favored environmentalism gained power in Washington. In the West, the "Sagebrush Rebellion" ignited in response. Arizona, Colorado, Hawaii, Idaho, Nevada, New Mexico, Utah, Washington, and Wyoming enacted legislation asserting control over much of the United States public lands within their boundaries. Although these claims were never pressed, the urge for tighter federal regulation of public lands subsided. The subsequent Reagan and Bush administrations had a more lenient approach toward the traditional beneficiaries of public lands, and the "rebellion" died down.

A renewed ascendancy of environmental concerns under the Clinton administration, however, again threatened to crimp the availability of public lands for private exploitation. Old-growth timber was preserved and desert lands were removed from use to protect the spotted owl, kangaroo rat, and "pestiferous" coyote. The reintroduction of the grey wolf near federal lands leased for grazing ignited ranchers' and herders' tempers. Furthermore, the rising federal deficit caused a reassessment of the low federal charges for mining, timber, and grazing rights. Miners, loggers, and ranchers, long used to nearly free and unregulated enjoyment of public lands for private benefit, were facing restrictions on access and use, along with higher costs.

The attitudes that led to the Sagebrush Rebellion resurfaced, this time more ambitiously and militantly under the banner of the "County Supremacy Movement," or simply the "Counties Movement." Western counties began passing ordinances asserting jurisdiction over federal lands. Moreover, unlike the Sagebrush Rebellion, the ordinances were followed by direct enforcement actions by county authorities.

☆402 *United States v. Nye County, Nevada*

920 F. Supp. 1108 (D. Nev. 1996).

GEORGE, Chief Judge.

. . . In its complaint, the United States alleges that it owns and has authority to manage certain public lands within Nye County. By statute, Defendant State of Nevada claimed ownership of this public land in 1979. In late 1993, Defendant Nye County passed Resolution 93-48, declaring that Nevada owns the disputed public lands in Nye County and that only the state and the county have authority to manage the land. At the same time, Nye County passed Resolution 93-49 asserting that, with limited exceptions, Nye County owns the rights-of-way for all roads and corridors crossing the public lands. Importantly, Nye County acted upon its denial that the United States owns and has authority to manage the public lands. On July 4, 1994, Nye County reopened the Jefferson Canyon Road, . . . ignoring an order of a forest service agent to stop. Following this action, a Nye County Commissioner filed an affidavit against the federal officer, stating that the officer lacked any jurisdiction.

\*          \*          \*

Presently, the United States asserts ownership of nearly 87% of the lands in Nevada. In Nye County, the United States' assertion of ownership increases to nearly 93% of the lands. These federal lands include portions of the Humboldt and Toiyabe National Forests (administered by the Forest Service, Department of Agriculture), a portion of the Death Valley National Monument, a large part of the Nellis Air Force Range (Department of Defense), most of the Nevada Test Site (Department of Energy), and the Ash Meadows National Wildlife Refuge. The remaining federal lands are public lands administered by the Bureau of Land Management, Department of the Interior, pursuant to the Federal Land Policy and Management Act of 1976 (FLPMA). . . .

In 1979, and in response to enactment of the FLPMA, Nevada enacted a series of statutes declaring ownership of and control and jurisdiction over all "public lands" within Nevada. . . .

Nye County is a political subdivision of the State of Nevada, administered by an elected Board of Commissioners. Nye County has claimed that the United States does not own and that it lacks authority to manage public lands within its exterior boundary. In claiming that the public lands belong to Nevada, however, Nye County asserts that Nevada owns more land than Nevada itself has claimed by statute. For example, while Nevada does not claim ownership of the national forests, Nye County has asserted that Nevada owns the lands managed by the Department of Agriculture, which manages the national forests. Rather, Nye County excludes, from the public lands, only the land ceded by Nevada to the federal government for post offices and federal buildings, and the land within the Nevada Test Site. [It was not clear to the court whether Nye County ordinance also claimed the Nellis Air Force Range.]

In addition to passing Resolution 93-48 declaring that Nevada owns all public lands, Nye County passed Resolution 93-49. This resolution declared that "all ways, pathways, trails, roads, country highways, and similar travel corridors across public lands in Nye County, Nevada, whether established and maintained by usage or mechanical means, whether passable by foot, beast of burden, carts or wagons, or motorized vehicles of each and every sort, whether currently passable or impassable, that was [sic] established in the past, present, or may be established in the future, on public lands in Nye County, are hereby declared Nye County Public Roads." The resolution further declared that "All rights of way . . . across public lands that are declared Nye County Public Roads are the property of Nye County as trustee for public users thereof."

In June 1994, Nye County, through Commissioner Richard Carver, the Vice-Chairman of the Nye County Board of Commissioners who acted with authority for and on behalf of Nye County, declared that the Jefferson Canyon Road in the Toiyabe National Forest was a Nye County Public Road. As the Jefferson Canyon road had been washed out in 1983, this letter further notified the district ranger that Nye County Board of Commissioners intended to reopen and maintain the road. On July 4, 1994, Com-

missioner Carver accomplished the intent of the Board by using a county-owned bulldozer to reopen the Jefferson Canyon Road. . . . Forest Service Special Agent Dave Young stood directly in the path of the bulldozer and displayed a sign ordering the Commissioner to stop. Although Young continued to display the sign while the bulldozer was on national forest land, Commissioner Carver did not stop his activities. On July 6, 1994, Commissioner Carver filed an affidavit with the County Sheriff requesting criminal charges be brought against Young and another Forest Service employee. The Commissioner asserted that the Forest Service employees lacked any jurisdiction in Jefferson Canyon, which is clearly within the bounds of the Toiyabe National Forest. The County Sheriff forwarded the affidavit to the Nye County District Attorney, who has not yet acted upon the request for criminal prosecution.

In August 1994, Nye County informed the Bureau of Land Management by letter that the BLM could not enforce its Final Multiple Use Decisions for the Razorback and Montezuma Grazing Allotments because the BLM has not provided proof of ownership of the public lands or proof of constitutional jurisdiction.

In August 1994, Nye County, again acting through Commissioner Carver, informed the Forest Service that the San Juan and Cottonwood Canyon Roads, which were previously closed by the Forest Service and which are located in the Toiyabe National Forest, were Nye County Public Roads. In October 1994, the Nye County Board of Commissioners voted to reopen the San Juan and Cottonwood Canyon Roads. On October 15, Commissioner Carver again used a county-owned equipment to reopen San Juan Road.

The United States brought this suit against Nye County.

*          *          *

Prior to this suit, Nye County denied that the United States had any authority to manage the public lands within its boundaries. All parties, including Nye County, now agree with the Supreme Court that

> [a]bsent consent or cession a State undoubtedly retains jurisdiction over federal lands within its territory, but Congress equally surely retains the power to enact legislation respecting those lands pursuant to the Property Clause. And when Congress so acts, the federal legislation necessarily overrides conflicting state laws under the Supremacy Clause. *Kleppe v. New Mexico*, 426 U.S. 529, 543 (1976).

Nye County argues, however, that [a declaration from this court] merely recognizing that the local and federal governments have concurrent jurisdiction of public lands is virtually meaningless [and therefore the suit should be dismissed]. The court would tend to agree but for Nye County's actions establishing that, prior to this suit, Nye County refused to acknowledge the holding of *Kleppe*. Those actions indicate that, as to Nye County, a declaration is required to establish that the federal government has jurisdiction over the public lands.... Accordingly, a declaration that the federal government has power to manage and regulate the public lands within Nye County, just as it has power to regulate the public lands within New Mexico, will not be meaningless. Rather, it will resolve a dispute initiated by Nye County despite clear law to the contrary.

The court tends to agree with Nye County and Nevada that the present suit is not the appropriate vehicle to define the broad boundaries between local and federal jurisdiction over the public land in Nye County.... This limitation, however, does not preclude this court from deciding the question raised by Nye County's actions. This suit did not arise over a dispute as to the relative line between federal and local jurisdiction, but arose because Nye County disputed the existence of any federal jurisdiction. Accordingly, this court's only determination is that absent consent or cession Nevada undoubtedly retains jurisdiction over federal lands within Nye County, but Congress equally surely retains the power to enact legislation respecting those lands pursuant to the Property Clause. And when Congress so acts, the federal legislation necessarily overrides conflicting state laws under the Supremacy Clause.

[T]he United States seeks a declaration that Nye County Resolution 93-49 is unconstitutional and preempted to the extent it applies to roads and other corridors for which no valid right-of-way exists under federal law. Nye County opposes the claim, asserting that Resolution 93-49 is nothing more than a statement of opinion by the Board of Commissioners of Nye County, creating neither legal rights, duties, nor obligations. As nothing more than a statement of opinion, the County asserts the resolution is protected speech under the First Amendment.

*          *          *

Although Nye County now asserts that Resolution 93-49 created neither legal rights, duties nor obligations, Nye County plainly intended that the resolution would have the effect of law. As an attempt to formally express the opinion or will of the Board of Commissioners, the resolution offers only an example of poor writing. Other than its title, the resolution does not use any language suggesting it is an opinion, view, idea, or belief, but employs language attempting to create a legal right of Nye County in public roads.

*          *          *

In addition, Nye County has relied upon Resolution 93-49 in its chosen field of battle: the reopening

of roads.... [T]he County's ... action[s] in reopening the road[s] show that [Nye] County intended Resolution 93-49 to establish legal rights ... rather than simply state Nye County's opinion. Viewed as to the totality of circumstances, the court finds that Nye County did not pass Resolution 93-49 as a mere statement of opinion, but enacted the resolution as a law creating legal rights, obligations and duties.

*          *          *

In short, Resolution 93-49 does violate the Supremacy Clause to the extent that it applies to roads and other corridors for which no valid right-of-way exists under federal law. Therefore, for good cause shown,

*          *          *

IT IS DECLARED that, as set forth in this Court's decision, the United States owns and has the power and authority to manage and administer the [federal] public lands and National Forest System lands within Nye County, Nevada.

IT IS FURTHER DECLARED that Nye County Resolution 93-49 is invalid and unenforceable to the extent ... it applies to ways, pathways, trails, roads, county highways, and similar public travel corridors across public lands in Nye County, Nevada, for which no valid right-of-way exists or is recognized under federal law.

## 403 "Nowhere ... was I ever described as a 'traitor'" (1985)

In 1985, United States naval intelligence analyst Jonathan Pollard was arrested for passing classified satellite reconnaissance information about Iraq and Libya to Israel. Pollard, of Jewish parentage, reportedly was disturbed over the limitations placed on American intelligence-sharing with Israel after the latter destroyed the Iraqi nuclear reactor at Osirak. Pollard pled guilty to conspiracy to commit espionage, was sentenced to life in prison, and was committed to twenty-three-hours-a-day lockdown in the maximum security prison in Marion, Illinois.

The sentence did not sit well with American supporters of Israel, who continue to point out that Pollard only aided a staunch ally of the United States in a hostile region of great importance to American security interests. They also argue that life sentences should be reserved for the likes of Aldrich Ames, the CIA mole who, for mere greed, compromised United States intelligence networks in the Soviet bloc. At most, they reason, Pollard should be treated like Abdel Kader Helmy, who received a forty-six-month sentence for giving American missile and rocket secrets to Egypt in 1989. It is further believed that Pollard was betrayed by the government, which promised a milder sentence in exchange for his plea.

The courts have rejected these claims, and the United States defense intelligence establishment has stoutly maintained that Pollard's activities seriously compromised intelligence gathering capability, transferred secrets to the KGB, and cost billions of dollars by rendering useless painstakingly constructed secret databases. Pollard has been characterized as remorseless, as still possessing information that could damage United States interests, and as having tried to supply classified information to Israel from prison. Although the charge was legally insupportable, because of Israel's status as an ally, Pollard was denounced as a traitor by former secretary of defense Caspar Weinberger.

Although he has been denied clemency by the president and parole by the Bureau of Prisons, Pollard was transferred to the minimum security facility at Butner, North Carolina, after prominent world leaders intervened on his behalf and 1.5 million signatures were collected on a petition for his release in 1993.

Despite claims from Pollard that he was acting out of concern for Israeli's survival, and not for mercenary reasons, the Israeli government initially distanced itself from Pollard, claiming that the $50,000 received by him (and $300,000 deposited into a Swiss bank account) for the secrets were supplied by a "rogue operation." Later, however, the Israeli government took a more charitable stance toward Pollard. He was granted Israeli citizenship *in absentia*, and his case became a routine item on the foreign relations agenda between Israel and the United States.

## ☆403  The Case of Jonathan Pollard

### ☆403a  Appeasement of Iraq Made Me a Spy

Document at http://shamash.nysernet.org/lists/jpollard/t103.html.

*          *          *

My name is Jonathan Pollard and I am currently serving a life sentence due to my activities on behalf of Israel.

Lest you labor under a false impression . . . I want to state quite categorically that I do not consider myself to be above the law. I fully appreciate the fact that I must be punished for my activities, however justified I may have felt them to be. That being said, I do not believe that the draconian sentence meted out to me was in any way commensurate with the crime committed. Nowhere in my indictment . . . was I ever described as a "traitor," which is hardly a surprise given the fact that the operation with which I was associated actually served to strengthen America's long-term security interests in the Middle-East.

[A]ny objective examination of the record will show that no American agent, facility or program

was compromised as a result of my actions—not one. But this salient fact was conveniently overlooked by Mr. Weinberger, who felt that I deserved the death penalty for having had the audacity to make Israel "too strong."

In retrospect, perhaps one of the most [sic] things the Reagan administration did to Israel during the course of our trial was that it purposely distorted the nature of my activities in such a way so as to leave the impression that Israel had somehow become a threat to the national security of this country. So by intent the subsequent sentence I received was an arrow aimed directly at the heart of the U.S.-Israel "special relationship."

*          *          *

The problem . . . lay in the fact that many of the photos I turned over to the Israelis were of a number of Iraqi chemical weapons manufacturing plants which the Reagan administration did not want to admit existed. Why? Well, if no one knew about these facilities then the State and Defense Departments would have been spared the embarrassing task of confronting Iraq over its violation of the Geneva Protocol of 1925, which banned the use of chemical weapons in war. You have to remember . . . that at the time of my sentencing the massacre of Kurdish civilians in Halabja had not yet occurred, and what little public concern was being voiced over Iraq's apparent use of poison gas was largely ignored by the administration, which did not want to anger the Arab world by criticizing the employment of such barbaric weapons against Iran. The photos I gave Israel, though, if "compromised," would have jeopardized the administration's policy of callous indifference towards this issue, in that they constituted hard, irrefutable proof that Iraq was indeed engaged in the production and widescale use of chemical weapons manufacturing capability.

After a few days of "soul searching," the State Department finally admitted that the U.S. had intercepted some Iraqi military communications which indicated that lethal gas had, in fact, been employed against unarmed Kurdish civilians. The Iranians had astutely out maneuvered them, though, and the issue had to be "contained" before it caused a rift in U.S.-Arab relations.

*          *          *

In essence, then, what I did by passing satellite photos of the Iraqi poison gas plants to Israel was endanger the Reagan administration . . . political agenda, not the intelligence community's "sources and methods."

According to the prosecution, there were two reasons why the government refused to tell Israel about Iraq's poison gas plants:

1) fear of compromising the KH-11 [intelligence satellite] system

2) concern over the Israelis' probable reaction once they recognized the threat these facilities posed to their survival.

What the Israelis would actually have considered was a preventive attack on the Iraqi chemical-arms factories before they had become fully operational [as they had done to the nuclear reactor at Osirak].

*         *         *

So what was I supposed to do? Let Israel fend for herself? If you think that is what I should have done then how can we condemn all those . . . who during the Second World War consciously participated in the abandonment of European Jewry? Seriously . . . what would be the difference between what they did and a decision on my part to have kept silent about the Iraqi poison gas threat to Israel? I'd rather be rotting in prison than sitting shiva [prayer for the dead] for the hundreds of thousands of Israelis who could have died because of my cowardice.

JONATHAN POLLARD.

☆403b Supplemental Report on Convicted Prisoner Jonathan Pollard

Letter provided to Nicholas N. Kittrie by Dr. Morris Pollard.

Regional Commissioner
Eastern Regional Office
United States Parole Commission
April 3, 1995

Re: Supplemental Report on Convicted Prisoner Jonathan Pollard by United States Attorney

DEAR [REGIONAL COMMISSIONER]:

I write to supplement this Office's submission in the captioned matter dated April 7, 1987, a copy of which is attached hereto. I wish to . . . register this Office's strong opposition to Mr. Pollard's parole at this time. In our view, there are a number of aggravating circumstances which argue against parole in this case.

### DAMAGE TO THE NATIONAL SECURITY OF THE UNITED STATES

As a preliminary matter, I urge the members of the Parole Commission to read the unclassified supplemental affidavit, submitted by Secretary of Defense Casper [sic] Weinberger which summarizes the damage to the national security of the United States caused by Pollard in these words: "It is difficult for me, even in the so-called 'year of the spy,' to conceive of a greater harm to national security than that caused by the defendant in view of the breadth, the critical importance to the U.S., and the high sensitivity of the information he sold to Israel." In fact, some of the Sensitive Compartmented Information (SCI) that Pollard sold to the Israelis was so sensitive that the relevant intelligence agencies would not

consent to its release, even if it meant that Pollard could not be charged with conveying it to a foreign government. As a result, the indictment against Pollard was tailored to limit public disclosure of the type of information that was involved. This, in turn, has allowed Pollard since his sentencing to maintain, falsely, that the information he sold to Israel was limited to matters that directly affected the security of Israel and that its release to Israel did not harm the United States. At the time of sentencing, Chief Judge Robinson specifically referred to the damage to national security caused by Pollard which was described in the classified Weinberger Affidavit as a basis for the life sentence which the Court imposed.

### POLLARD'S CONDUCT SINCE HIS SENTENCING DEMONSTRATES THAT HE REMAINS A THREAT TO THE SECURITY OF THE UNITED STATES

Pollard has periodically claimed to recognize that his criminal acts against his country cannot be justified by his paramount loyalty to Israel. This recognition is both tardy and suspect. Pollard expressed no remorse during the post-plea debriefings conducted by United States investigators. In fact, in an early debriefing session with two members of the Federal Bureau of Investigation, Pollard stated that, given the chance, he would do it all again. . . .

Pollard's lack of true remorse is also evident from correspondence sent to a supporter while in prison. In a letter to Dr. Julian Ungar-Sargon, dated March 17, 1987, and later published in the Jerusalem Post, Pollard referred to his sentencing this way:

> . . . Although I would have preferred to have gone down flying my "true colors," the attorney stressed the fact that I had to show remorse if Anne were to stand any chance at all of receiving probation.
>
> Accordingly, I agreed to say things which burned my soul with shame, hoping that by such contrived regret the court's apparent need for a moral victory over my convictions would be satisfied.
>
> *         *         *
>
> If it's true that I have indeed enhanced Israel's military capabilities to the point where it bothers Secretary Weinberger's Saudi paymasters, then I'm quite satisfied what I did was right . . . .

*         *         *

[Pollard] will undoubtedly make the same arguments [to the Parole Commission] that he has made since his sentencing, that he did not intend to harm the United States, but only to aid Israel and that the information he sold to Israel did not in fact harm the United States. In an effort to refute these assertions, the United States would be faced with the same dilemma that it faced when drafting the original indictment: refutation of the claim that the released information was not harmful to the United States would require the release of information that the relevant intelligence agencies are still unwilling to release because of national security concerns. . . . Pollard's conduct in the past has demonstrated that he is well aware of the limitations such considerations place on the government's ability to refute his false claims and has no hesitation to exploit them to his advantage. It is likely, therefore, that Pollard will again engage in this type of cynical manipulation of the system in an effort to gain his release.

*        *        *

### THE PRECEDENT THAT PAROLE AT THIS TIME WOULD ESTABLISH IN ESPIONAGE CASES

Granting parole to Jonathan Pollard at this time would create an unfortunate and unwarranted precedent for the United States in other national security cases. . . . Despite his protestations to the contrary, it is clear that the money and gifts provided by the Israelis were significant, if not the primary factors motivating his conduct. If not for the intervention of FBI and Naval Intelligence Service agents, Pollard's espionage activities would have continued indefinitely.

*        *        *

## 404  "It's going to look good for the Klan" (1987-1995)

Civil lawsuits for money damages against hatemongers and promoters of race crimes may sometimes be more effective than criminal prosecutions in stopping such conduct. Plaintiffs in civil cases benefit from less stringent standards of evidence and proof than exist in criminal trials. Civil plaintiffs, unlike criminal prosecutors, do not need to prove their allegations beyond a reasonable doubt, civil defendants are more likely to be burdened by having to meet their own legal expenses, and, finally, civil judgments may also provide a basis for punitive sanctions.

In a civil wrongful death action, an all-white jury ordered Alabama's United Klans of America (UKA) and six of its officers to pay $7 million in damages to the mother of Michael Donald, a young black man who had been murdered by Klan members. In partial settlement of the judgment, the Klan agreed to turn over the title to its headquarters building and the surrounding six acres of land to Beulah Mae Donald.

In another civil case, a Portland, Oregon, jury awarded $12.5 million to be paid by the White Aryan Resistance (WAR) and its leaders Thomas and John Metzger, of Fallbrook, California, for the beating death of an Ethiopian native, Mulugeta Seraw. The jury found that the Metzgers had caused Seraw's

death by supplying Portland "skinheads" with an expert to teach the perpetrators beating techniques to use in attacks against blacks and Jews. Thomas Metzger, a television repairman by trade, had supported WAR by soliciting mail contributions during his appearances on radio and television talk-shows, including a syndicated cable-television show he hosted. After his judgment was affirmed on appeal, Metzger's home, vehicles, repair tools, and other possessions were auctioned off, and his mail was put under court supervision. Three-quarters of the contributions to WAR, which have fallen from $100,000 annually to $25,000, go to Seraw's son and father in Ethiopia.

The Southern Poverty Law Center, which won both judgments, concludes that civil lawsuits and the Metzger verdict, in particular, have drastically curtailed Klan and related neo-Nazi recruitment efforts and fractured the previously growing alliance between various hate groups. Although Robert Shelton, the last-known Imperial Wizard of the Alabama Klan, has declared that "The Klan is gone," one is advised to recall that the Klan has been declared dead twice before (after it was outlawed in 1871 and during the Great Depression).

## ☆404  Fighting Bigotry through Civil Damages

### ☆404a  Seeking Justice for Her Lynched Son, an Alabama Mother Ruins the Klan That Killed Him

*People*, June 8, 1987, 55.

Beulah Mae Donald's youngest son, Michael, told her he'd be back by 12:00 when he went over to his sister Betty's house, two blocks away, on that night in Alabama six years ago. "Michael had some teenage boys over there he'd play basketball with, listen to music with," Mrs. Donald recalls. "But this particular night, he didn't come home."

Mrs. Donald woke up at 2:00 a.m. and checked Michael's room. He wasn't there. She called Betty's. "They said, 'He left, Mom. We thought he was home.'" Mrs. Donald sat up the rest of the night, drinking coffee, waiting. At 6 a.m. her phone rang. An anonymous caller said that a young man's body was hanging in a tree in downtown Mobile.

Michael Donald, 19, who was working part-time in the Mobile Register mail room and studying masonry at technical college and dating two or three girls and thinking about joining the army, had been abducted at random by members of the Ku Klux Klan. He had been walking from his sister's to the corner gas station to buy a pack of cigarettes when James "Tiger" Knowles, 17, and Henry Hays, 26, forced him into their car at gunpoint. They drove him to a remote area across Mobile Bay, where they beat him with boards, ran him in circles with a rope around his neck, stomped him as he pleaded for his life. Then one stood on his face and pulled the rope tight; the other cut his throat.

Klavern 900, the Mobile unit of the United Klans of America, had decided to kill a black, any black, in retaliation for a predominantly black jury's failure to convict a black man charged with killing a white Birmingham police officer. Angered by the verdict, some Klansmen burned a cross in front of the Mobile County courthouse while Hays and Knowles set out on their murderous quest.

According to witnesses, Henry Hays's father, Bennie Jack Hays, 64, a Titan, or leader, of the UKA in southern Alabama, looked at the body strung up in a tree across the street from Henry's house and said, "That's a pretty picture. It's going to look nice on the news. It's going to look good for the Klan."

Bennie Hays didn't suspect that the grisly scene of which he spoke with such apparent satisfaction would lead, six years later, to the destruction of the UKA. He hadn't counted on the courage and tenacity of one Beulah Mae Donald.

Last month, in satisfaction of a federal court judgment for punitive damages against the UKA, Mrs. Donald, 67, took possession of the deed and keys to the racist organization's only asset, its national headquarters, a two-story office building on six acres near Tuscaloosa that may be worth $225,000. Civil rights lawyer Morris Dees calls Mrs. Donald's suit "the most significant case I've ever handled in the area of racial violence." It effectively puts the UKA—whose 2,500 members made it one of the largest of the nation's several Ku Klux Klan groups—out of business. And it sets a critical legal precedent: For the first time, a jury has held an entire Klan group liable for the acts of its members.

For Mrs. Donald, the judgment marks the end of a long, determined battle to establish the true circumstances of her son's death. From the beginning she had assured her six surviving children, "The truth will come out. We ain't gonna let it rest."

Her determination was not widely shared. On the very day that Michael's body was discovered, the Mobile County district attorney announced that the killing did not appear to have been racially motivated. Some local white politicians saw fit to denounce Mrs. Donald's attorney, state senator Michael Figures, and the head of the Mobile NAACP, Dr. Robert Gilliard, for "fanning the flames of racism" by insisting that white extremists had probably been involved. The Mobile police department launched an intensive investigation—of Michael Donald, on the theory that he must have been selling drugs or must have been involved in a love triangle.

Mrs. Donald herself did not immediately suspect the Klan. "I knew it existed, because I read about it in the newspapers," she says. "But I didn't think they were right around here."

For more than two years the killers walked the streets of Mobile undetected. But Assistant U.S. Attorney Thomas Figures, Michael Figures' brother, kept the FBI on the case. Finally, an informer supplied information on the meeting at which a lynching had been discussed. Then, in June 1983, Tiger Knowles broke down and confessed, implicating Henry Hays. Knowles is now serving life in prison for violating Donald's civil rights. Hays, convicted of murder, faces execution.

But the role of the Klan in the killing was barely touched upon in the criminal proceedings. So Dees, director of the Southern Poverty Law Center in Montgomery, suggested a civil suit for damages. Mrs. Donald readily agreed.

The suit, filed in 1984 against the United Klans of America and six present or former members of the Mobile Klavern, came to trial last February. Dees argued that the corporate Klan was liable for the acts of its members in pursuit of the organization's goal—in the words of the UKA constitution, "maintain[ing] the God-given supremacy of the White race."

The testimony of three former Klansmen linked the UKA to specific acts of violence, including the brutal beating of Freedom Riders in Birmingham in 1961, the bombing of Birmingham's 16th Street Baptist Church in 1963, which killed four Sunday-school children, and the murder of civil rights worker Viola Liuzzo near Selma in 1965.

The trial ended dramatically when defendant Tiger Knowles implored the jury to return a verdict against him and the entire Klan. "I was acting as a Klansman when I did this," he said, breaking into tears.

The Klan's attorney argued that those involved in the killing "should never be permitted to walk on the streets," but "in this country, we don't punish the organization, we punish the individuals." The all-white jury disagreed, assessing $7 million in punitive damages against the UKA as well as the six individual defendants. Mrs. Donald's lawyers say she will take one-quarter of any wages the six men earn for life, as well as Bennie Hays' house and farm. As a result of evidence developed at the civil trial, the Mobile district attorney is also expected to seek murder indictments against Klansmen Frank Cox and Bennie Hays.

Asked what Michael would say about the judgment, Mrs. Donald smiles, thinking about her baby boy. "He'd say, 'Look, Mama, we're rich!'"

She never cared about the money, and has no plans for it now, except to get herself somewhere to live, after 27 years in the stifling housing projects of northern Mobile. She never sought revenge. "Revenge is God's," she says. What she wanted was the truth. "People were telling me, 'There ain't no such thing as the Klan, Michael must have been doing something wrong,'" she says. "I'm glad it's all come to light."

☆404b  Metzger Bankroll on Way to Africa in Racial Slaying

*San Diego Union-Tribune,* January 20, 1995, A-1.

By an ironic twist of fate and law, nearly the entire bankroll of infamous white supremacist Tom Metzger is now on its way to Africa.

Soon the money that Metzger raised for his white-power crusade will go, instead, toward a black boy's future.

San Diego attorney James McElroy headed to Ethiopia this week to arrange the transfer.

It is one of the many ironies that Metzger's empire fell because of a man he never met, an African immigrant slain 1,000 miles from Metzger's Fallbrook home. A court found the former Ku Klux Klan leader responsible for that death, with a $12.5 million jury award. This trip represents the last steps toward paying the victim's family that debt, although they will receive only about 1 percent of the sum.

"This is going to be one of the greatest adventures I've ever had," McElroy said.

The fortyish civil attorney was sitting in his downtown high-rise office recently before leaving for Ethiopia's rugged highlands where, apparently, the only transportation is by donkey.

It was easy enough to get inoculations to protect him against yellow fever, typhoid and major diseases prevalent there, but he may have to deal with armed rebel factions outside the capital and land mines on the roads.

"Roughing it is not a problem," said McElroy, whose idea of vacation is a marathon bicycle-and-camping trip. "I have a problem with being shot at."

His solo voyage to Ethiopia marks one of the closing chapters in an international drama now in its seventh year.

It started in the late 1980s as racial violence and hate crimes escalated across the United States. McElroy joined the legal team that shattered Metzger's growing empire of skinheads—disaffected youths who adopted shaved heads, German-made boots, racist propaganda and violent ways.

The team used law books instead of weapons, just like the bookkeepers who brought down gangster Al Capone. Led by civil rights lawyer Morris Dees of the Southern Poverty Law Center, they sued Metzger and his son John Metzger of Fallbrook for inciting skinheads in 1988 in Oregon to beat a black man to death.

Three men pleaded guilty to charges of killing Mulugeta Seraw, a 27-year-old student from Ethiopia who left for America before his son was born in the hope of earning enough money to support his family.

The men picked their victim at random and beat him so hard with a baseball bat that they literally tore his head apart.

In a civil trial, a Portland jury found that as leaders of the White Ayran Resistance (WAR), the Metzgers were responsible for the criminal behavior of their followers. The jurors awarded $12.5 million to the dead man's family.

The victim's 13-year-old son, Henok, is poised to start collecting some of that award.

For his part, Metzger said he doesn't care if all his money goes to Africans. "I'm not against African people," Metzger maintains. "I hope he (Henok) is an African racist and builds an African separatist state."

High on Metzger's hate list are Dees and the Southern Poverty Law Center, a non-profit civil liberties organization in Alabama. Dees became famous by using the same strategy he applied to Metzger—holding leaders accountable for their followers—to the Ku Klux Klan, the Republican National Committee (for the Watergate break-in) and now Operation Rescue and other militant anti-abortion groups.

"It was a railroad job," Metzger said of his legal defeat, which he appealed to the U.S. Supreme Court. The appeal was dismissed last May.

Metzger once was considered America's most dangerous neo-Nazi, with his own skinhead version of the Hitler youth, but his financial empire apparently is nowhere near the million-dollar mark.

So far about $100,000—less than 1 percent of the jury award—has been collected from Metzger's assets, according to McElroy. But in a poor country like Ethiopia, that $100,000 will be a fortune, he said.

Meanwhile, Dees and McElroy contend the Metzgers have tumbled from the top of the white supremacist movement because of the Portland case. "I think we've done a fairly effective job of crippling the movement," said McElroy.

They calculate the Metzgers used to collect more than $100,000 a year for WAR, most of it in cash. Now their take is about a quarter of that, and most of it goes toward the judgment.

McElroy won the legal authority to collect most of the donations that come into Metzger's post office box. The Metzgers are legally barred from switching boxes.

"Metzger has been totally discredited," McElroy said. "His followers saw he was in it for the money. It came out in the trial that he used their money on himself. He paid his credit card bills with it, he bought himself a toupee."

To collect the judgment, the attorneys foreclosed on Metzger's five-bedroom house in Fallbrook, and took his television repair tools and his trailer, which he had used for recruiting. For a time, the former Grand Dragon of the Klan went on welfare and says he would do so again.

"I'll do anything to survive," he said.

Dees arranged for McElroy's fact-finding trip in Ethiopia, which he said is being paid for by private donors.

"We can never give Henok back his father, but we can do everything in our power to give him a chance in life," Dees said in a phone interview.

Once in Africa, McElroy plans to arrange for private school for Henok, possibly at the Seventh-day Adventist academy that the boy's uncle and father attended. It is a boarding school that is a five-hour walk from their village.

McElroy is taking gifts to the family, and a Walkman with tapes for the boy, including a copy of Paul Simon's "Graceland," because it mixes African music with American beats.

"I don't want to send $100,000 to some bank in Addis Ababa, or invest it somewhere until the boy turns 18," he said. "Without education, he'll just be a peasant with $200,000."

Even after the paperwork is complete and the money reaches the Seraw family, this drama will not be over for years.

McElroy won the right to continue collecting from the Metzgers' proceeds, despite being fought every step of the way. He foreclosed on the family's five-bedroom Fallbrook house, but Metzger had filed for protection under the Homestead Act and the court permitted him to keep $45,000 of the sale proceeds.

Even then, McElroy said, he was forced to spend some of the Seraw trust-fund money to make the place habitable. "The house was in shambles," he said.

Neighbors pitched in to help fix up the former Metzger home, he said, and it was sold to a woman of Mexican heritage who lives there with her children.

"I find that poetic justice," said McElroy.

## 405 "giv[ing] Indians an economic footing" (1987-1995)

The Mashantucket, or Western Pequots, were the descendants of the large and fierce Pequot Nation whose power was broken by the Mystic River Massacre of 1637 (see Doc. 16). The survivors were forced into exile among neighboring Narragansett and Mohegan tribes and, two generations later, the remnants were granted two reservations in eastern Connecticut: 280 acres for the Pawcatuck or Eastern Pequots and 2,000 acres for the Mashantucket. These reservations were placed under the control of Connecticut's colonial, and later state, "overseers."

Three hundred years after its establishment, the Mashantucket reservation had been reduced to 178 acres, inhabited by one elderly woman. The tribe had no federal recognition, and the state was considering turning the remaining part of the Pequot land into a park. But in 1975, encouraged by the successes of other eastern Native Americans in securing long-lost tribal recognition and regaining a measure of

control over their affairs (see Doc. 362), members began a movement for the resurrection of the tribe. Generating interest and attention through a lawsuit, the Mashantucket Pequots were able to find approximately two hundred people who could trace their ancestry back to a tribal roll kept by the overseers in the early twentieth century. In 1983, they gained tribal recognition through an act of Congress, which also appropriated $900,000 with which to purchase land to increase the reservation tenfold.

With their pride and land partially restored, the Mashantucket Pequots nevertheless remained impoverished as various economic enterprises undertaken by them failed. But, following President Reagan's executive order to encourage self-sufficiency for Native Americans, the Mashantucket Pequots began running a high-stakes bingo parlor. When the state of Connecticut threatened to enforce its gambling laws within the reservation, the Pequots secured a federal injunction based on the theory of tribal sovereignty that the Supreme Court adopted a year later. After more legal battles, the Mashantucket Pequots in 1992 opened Foxwoods, a hugely successful casino hotel and entertainment complex, one of the largest in the Western Hemisphere.

At the height of their power in colonial times, the Pequots are reputed to have cornered the supply of the whelk- and quahog-shell bead currency used in Indian commerce. The current-day Mashantucket Pequots are seemingly again at the economic center of the area they once dominated. That the Pequots' new ascension is propelled by the vice of gambling would have seemed more than ironic to Major John Mason, a Puritan who led the murderous seventeenth-century attack against their ancestors at Pequot Hill.

The second document deals with the issue of state control over Indian gambling activities in the Far West.

## ☆405 Reparations for Native Americans

### ☆405a The Gamble That Paid Off

Dick Dahl, *ABA Journal*, May 1995, 86.

The busloads of people who work the slot machines and roulette tables at the massive Foxwoods casino in southern Connecticut probably would never guess that they are there only because lawyers beat the odds.

The casino—by some accounts the largest in the Western hemisphere—is owned by the Mashantucket Pequot Indians, who, in less than 10 years, have gone from living hand-to-mouth to owning a nearly $800-million business.

In 1986, tribe members opened a high-stakes bingo hall that gave them a foothold in the gaming industry that has become an economic engine for many previously impoverished American Indians. After a five-year fight with the state of Connecticut, the Pequots won the right to open a casino with slot machines, which by themselves bring in $500 million annually.

This massive infusion of cash from gambling not only has boosted tribal economies across the United States, it also has changed the character of the tribal courts that traditionally have adjudicated Indian affairs. Along the way, it also has reoriented the practice of "Indian law" from poverty law to business law.

The proliferation of gambling establishments, says Kevin Gover, a lawyer in Albuquerque, N.M., and a member of the Pawnee tribe, means that "for the first time, [American Indians are] inviting large numbers of non-Indians on to their land." When that happens, of course, disputes occur—whether it is a slip-and-fall or a contractor trying to collect money.

While only 90 of the nation's 557 tribes are involved in gaming, according to the National Indian Gaming Association, their operations account for about 200 gaming sites in 19 states. Total Indian gaming revenue in 1993 was about $2.6 billion, according to Gaming and Wagering Business magazine.

In March the Coeur d'Alene tribe of Idaho announced plans to extend that reach into all 36 states that allow lotteries and the District of Columbia. The plan: a National Indian Lottery operating via toll-free telephone lines, taking payments by credit card and paying jackpots to average more than $50 million.

Those entrepreneurial ventures would have been impossible without a series of federal decisions in the 1980s, which culminated in passage of legislation in 1988. The Indian Gaming Regulatory Act defines state and Indian responsibilities by dividing gaming activity into three categories, and by establishing the National Indian Gaming Commission for oversight.

American Indians have exclusive jurisdiction over traditional Indian tribal games. They have limited jurisdiction over games such as bingo and card games, excluding blackjack. To move up to casino gambling, they must negotiate a "compact" with the state that specifies jurisdiction, sets remedies in the event of breach of contract and creates regulatory guidelines. Disputes over legality or execution of compacts are heard in federal court.

But jurisdiction over other disputes is sometimes less certain, because it is still unclear to what extent tribal courts have regulatory authority over non-Indians and their property. Likewise, lawyers representing tribes say that much of their time is taken up deciding the extent to which states can regulate tribal business affairs.

To even speak of tribal courts in a general sense may be inaccurate because each tribe is a sovereign nation with its own constitution, legal code, and tribunals (or, in some cases, none at all). Similarly, a tribe's executive power may rest with an elected tribal council or with a group of elders.

*          *          *

While tribes are sovereign nations, they are of a distinct type, says Gover. "We're not like Mexico; we're under the protection of the U.S. government. The question is: How far does the sovereignty go?"

Indian reservations were created, for the most part, as a result of treaties with the federal government. Reservation land is held in trust by the federal government, which is the trustee. As beneficiaries, Indians have many rights of ownership over the land, including the right to tax it, but any decisions to sell or encumber it need approval by the Bureau of Indian Affairs.

Land owned by Indians on the reservation is governed by federal and tribal law, but state law never applies to Indian people or their land on the reservation. Exceptions are those reservations covered by Public Law 280, which was passed in 1953, and which grants state and local governments a certain degree of criminal jurisdiction.

Tribal courts can only hear criminal matters when they involve Indians, but they are not restricted to tribal members. Criminal jurisdiction over Indians is shared by federal and tribal courts. Non-Indians, such as casino players, can be arrested by tribal police and jailed until they are turned over to state or federal authorities.

*          *          *

"Prior to the advent of gaming, I don't think any downtown firm had an Indian-law practice," says Joshua J. Kanassatega, a member of the Mille Lacs band of Chippewa and an associate in the 120-lawyer Minneapolis firm of Leonard, Street and Deinard.

Kanassatega's tribe now operates two casinos. He remembers that before they were built, and before he became a lawyer, the tribe's fortunes—and lawyers' responses to them—were a different matter. He remembers seeking out legal help for the Mille Lacs and having doors shut in his face.

*          *          *

Some American Indian lawyers, like Kanassatega, say that tribes could be doing more to exercise their sovereign power and keep their money within the tribes.

"OK, so we build roads and schools and buildings. Wonderful," Kanassatega says. "But what have we done to build an economy on those reservations? Indians could create a federal bank. They've got the power; they're sovereign nations. They can petition for a state or federal charter for a bank.

"The idea [with gaming] was to give Indians an economic footing. A foundation. You've got to create an economy. You've got to make a dollar. And the more times you get the dollar to turn around, the stronger the economy gets."

*       *       *

☆405b  *California v. Cabazon Band of Mission Indians*

480 U.S. 204 (1987).

JUSTICE WHITE delivered the opinion of the Court.

The Cabazon and Morongo Bands of Mission Indians, federally recognized Indian Tribes, occupy reservations in Riverside County, California. Each Band, pursuant to [a tribal] ordinance approved by the Secretary of the Interior, conducts bingo games on its reservation. The Cabazon Band has also opened a card club at which draw poker and other card games are played. The games are open to the public and are played predominantly by non-Indians coming onto the reservations. The games are a major source of employment for tribal members, and the profits are the Tribes' sole source of income. The State of California seeks to apply to the two [its laws which do] not entirely prohibit the playing of bingo but permits it when the games are operated and staffed by members of designated charitable organizations who may not be paid for their services. Profits must be kept in special accounts and used only for charitable purposes; prizes may not exceed $250 per game. Asserting that the bingo games on the two reservations violated . . . these restrictions, California insisted that the Tribes comply with state law. Riverside County also sought to apply its local Ordinance . . . regulating bingo, as well as its Ordinance No. 331, prohibiting the playing of draw poker and the other card games.

The Tribes sued the county in Federal District Court seeking a declaratory judgment that the [state and] county had no authority to apply [these laws] inside the reservations and an injunction against their enforcement. . . .

I

The Court has consistently recognized that Indian tribes retain "attributes of sovereignty over both their members and their territory," and that "tribal sovereignty is dependent on, and subordinate to, only the Federal Government, not the States." It is clear, however, that state laws may be applied to tribal Indians on their reservations if Congress has expressly so provided. Here, the State insists that Congress has . . . given its express consent . . . in Pub. L. 280. . . . We disagree. . . .

In Pub. L. 280, Congress expressly granted six States, including California, jurisdiction over specified areas of Indian country within the States and provided for the assumption of jurisdiction by other States. In § 2, California was granted broad criminal jurisdiction over offenses committed by or against Indians within all Indian country within the State. Section 4's grant of civil jurisdiction was more limited. In *Bryan v. Itasca County,* we interpreted § 4 to grant States jurisdiction over private civil litigation involving reservation Indians in state court, but not to grant general civil regulatory authority. We held, therefore, that Minnesota could not apply its personal property tax within the reservation. Congress' primary concern in enacting Pub. L. 280 was combating lawlessness on reservations. The Act plainly was not intended to effect total assimilation of Indian tribes into mainstream American society. We recognized that a grant to States of general civil regulatory power over Indian reservations would result in the destruction of tribal institutions and values. Accordingly, when a State seeks to enforce a law within an Indian reservation under the authority of Pub. L. 280, it must be determined whether the law is criminal in nature, and thus fully applicable to the reservation under § 2, or civil in nature, and applicable only as it may be relevant to private civil litigation in state court.

The Minnesota personal property tax at issue in *Bryan* was unquestionably civil in nature. The California bingo statute is not so easily categorized. California law permits bingo games to be conducted only by charitable and other specified organizations, and then only by their members who may not receive any wage or profit for doing so; prizes are limited and receipts are to be segregated and used only for charitable purposes. Violation of any of these provisions is a misdemeanor. California insists that these are criminal laws which Pub. L. 280 permits it to enforce on the reservations.

[I]n *Barona Group of Capitan Grande Band of Mission Indians* . . . applying what it thought to be the civil/criminal dichotomy drawn in *Bryan v. Itasca County,* the Court of Appeals drew a distinction between state "criminal/prohibitory" laws and state "civil/regulatory" laws: if the intent of a state law is generally to prohibit certain conduct, it falls within Pub. L. 280's grant of criminal jurisdiction, but if the state law generally permits the conduct at issue, subject to regulation, it must be classified as civil/regulatory and Pub. L. 280 does not authorize its enforcement on an Indian reservation. The shorthand test is whether the conduct at issue violates the State's public policy. Inquiring into the nature of [the same laws at issue here], the Court of Appeals held that it was regulatory rather than prohibitory. . . .

We are persuaded that the prohibitory/regulatory distinction is consistent with *Bryan's* construction of Pub. L. 280. It is not a bright-line rule, however; and as the Ninth Circuit itself observed, an argument of some weight may be made that the bingo statute is prohibitory rather than regulatory. But in the present case, the court reexamined the state law and reaffirmed its holding in *Barona,* and we are reluctant to disagree with that court's view of the nature and intent of the state law at issue here.

There is surely a fair basis for its conclusion.... In light of the fact that California permits a substantial amount of gambling activity, including bingo, and actually promotes gambling through its state lottery, we must conclude that California regulates rather than prohibits gambling in general and bingo in particular.

*             *             *

Accordingly, we conclude that Pub. L. 280 does not authorize California to enforce [these laws] within the Cabazon and Morongo Reservations.

*             *             *

II

Because the state and county laws at issue here are imposed directly on the Tribes that operate the games, and are not expressly permitted by Congress, the Tribes argue that the judgment below should be affirmed without more.... Our cases, however, have not established an inflexible *per se* rule precluding state jurisdiction over tribes and tribal members in the absence of express congressional consent. "[Under] certain circumstances a State may validly assert authority over the activities of non-members on a reservation, and . . . in exceptional circumstances a State may assert jurisdiction over the on-reservation activities of tribal members."

*             *             *

This case also involves a state burden on tribal Indians in the context of their dealings with non-Indians since the question is whether the State may prevent the Tribes from making available high stakes bingo games to non-Indians coming from outside the reservations. Decision in this case turns on whether state authority is pre-empted by the operation of federal law; and "[state] jurisdiction is preempted . . . if it interferes or is incompatible with federal and tribal interests reflected in federal law, unless the state interests at stake are sufficient to justify the assertion of state authority." The inquiry is to proceed in light of traditional notions of Indian sovereignty and the congressional goal of Indian self-government, including its "overriding goal" of encouraging tribal self-sufficiency and economic development.

These are important federal interests. They were reaffirmed by the President's 1983 Statement on Indian Policy. More specifically, the Department of the Interior, which has the primary responsibility for carrying out the Federal Government's trust obligations to Indian tribes, has sought to implement these policies by promoting tribal bingo enterprises.

*             *             *

These policies and actions, which demonstrate the Government's approval and active promotion of tribal bingo enterprises, are of particular relevance in this case. The Cabazon and Morongo Reservations contain no natural resources which can be exploited. The tribal games at present provide the sole source of revenues for the operation of the tribal governments and the provision of tribal services. They are also the major sources of employment on the reservations. Self-determination and economic development are not within reach if the Tribes cannot raise revenues and provide employment for their members. The Tribes' interests obviously parallel the federal interests.

California seeks to diminish the weight of these seemingly important tribal interests by asserting that the Tribes are merely marketing an exemption from state gambling laws. In *Washington v. Confederated Tribes of Colville Indian Reservation*, we held that the State could tax cigarettes sold by tribal smokeshops to non-Indians, even though it would eliminate their competitive advantage and substantially reduce revenues used to provide tribal services, because the Tribes had no right "to market an exemption from state taxation to persons who would normally do their business elsewhere." We stated that "[it] is painfully apparent that the value marketed by the smokeshops to persons coming from outside is not generated on the reservations by activities in which the Tribes have a significant interest." Here, however, the Tribes are not merely importing a product onto the reservations for immediate resale to non-Indians. They have built modern facilities which provide recreational opportunities and ancillary services to their patrons, who do not simply drive onto the reservations, make purchases and depart, but spend extended periods of time there enjoying the services the Tribes provide. The Tribes have a strong incentive to provide comfortable, clean, and attractive facilities and well-run games in order to increase attendance at the games. The tribal bingo enterprises are similar to the resort complex, featuring hunting and fishing, that the Mescalero Apache Tribe operates on its reservation through the "concerted and sustained" management of reservation land and wildlife resources. The Mescalero project generates funds for essential tribal services and provides employment for tribal members. We there rejected the notion that the Tribe is merely marketing an exemption from state hunting and fishing regulations and concluded that New Mexico could not regulate on-reservation fishing and hunting by non-Indians. Similarly, the Cabazon and Morongo Bands are generating value on the reservations through activities in which they have a substantial interest.

*             *             *

The sole interest asserted by the State to justify the imposition of its bingo laws on the Tribes is in preventing the infiltration of the tribal games by organized crime. To the extent that the State seeks to prevent any and all bingo games from being played on tribal lands while permitting regulated, off-reservation games, this asserted interest is irrelevant and the state and county laws are pre-empted. Even to the extent that the State and county seek to regulate short of prohibition, the laws are pre-empted. The State insists that the high stakes offered at tribal games are attractive to organized crime, whereas the controlled games authorized under California law are not. This is surely a legitimate concern, but we are unconvinced that it is sufficient to escape the pre-emptive force of federal and tribal interests apparent in this case. California does not allege any present criminal involvement in the Cabazon and Morongo enterprises, and the Ninth Circuit discerned none. An official of the Department of Justice has expressed some concern about tribal bingo operations, but far from any action being taken evidencing this concern—and surely the Federal Government has the authority to forbid Indian gambling enterprises—the prevailing federal policy continues to support these tribal enterprises, including those of the Tribes involved in this case.

We conclude that the State's interest in preventing the infiltration of the tribal bingo enterprises by organized crime does not justify state regulation of the tribal bingo enterprises in light of the compelling federal and tribal interests supporting them. State regulation would impermissibly infringe on tribal government, and this conclusion applies equally to the county's attempted regulation of the Cabazon card club. We therefore affirm the judgment of the Court of Appeals and remand the case for further proceedings consistent with this opinion.

*It is so ordered.*

## 406 "I think we all had to weigh in the balance the difference between lives and lies" (1987–1988)

Political criminality, as is frequently pointed out throughout this volume, is often the product of a conflict of allegiances or loyalties. Sometimes that conflict is between one's loyalty to the state and conflicting ethnic, racial, or religious commitments. The Oliver North documents portray one man's perceived loyalty to his "superiors," the executive branch, and the compelling needs of the "national interest" clashing with the United States' constitutional system of legislative and judicial checks and balances.

When it was revealed that the proceeds from secret and probably illegal arms sales to then-embargoed Iran were being funneled covertly to support the military operations of the Nicaraguan Contra-

doras against the disfavored leftist Sandinista regime in that country, investigations traced the Iran-Contra transactions to the National Security Council (NSC), a White House agency directly advising the president on foreign security matters. The activities of Marine Lt. Col. Oliver L. "Ollie" North, who was "on loan" to the agency and appeared to be at the center of the operations, were scrutinized for violations of the Boland Amendment, which made it illegal to fund the Contras. Targeted by an independent counsel conducting a criminal investigation, North was also called to testify before a joint investigation by the House and Senate. North initially invoked his Fifth Amendment right against self-incrimination, but when Congress granted him immunity from the use of his testimony in any criminal trial, North took the stand. Some of the five days of testimony is contained in Document 406a, below, in which North defends his actions in misleading Congress with respect to aiding the Contras.

North was ultimately indicted, and in preliminary motions to dismiss the indictments against him he challenged the charges on various grounds, including the assertion that he was under no obligation to tell the truth to Congress and was indeed privileged to mislead Congress and even lie to it. Documents 406b and 406c are the district court's response to that argument. North was tried and convicted for aiding and abetting the obstruction of congressional investigations and shredding NSC documents relevant to the inquiry. These convictions were reversed on appeal in 1990 because some prosecution evidence was found to have been tainted by North's immunized testimony before Congress.

Despite his involvement in the Iran-Contra scandal, North entered politics and secured the 1994 Virginia Republican Party nomination for the United States Senate, but narrowly lost in the general election. He went on to host a popular nationally syndicated radio talk-show.

## ☆406 The Iran-Contra Affair

### ☆406a Testimony of Lt. Col. Oliver North

*Joint Hearings before the Senate Select Committee on Secret Military Assistance to Iran and the Nicaraguan Opposition and the House Select Committee to Investigate Covert Arms Transactions with Iran, 100th Cong., 1st Sess. (1987), pt. 1, 165–67, 178–81, 183, 275–76, 317–18; pt. 2, 88.*

WEDNESDAY, JULY 8: AFTERNOON SESSION—2:00 PM

MR. [John] NIELDS [Counsel for the House Committee]. You're aware that there was a law of Congress passed by Congress, a statute of the United States, in effect at that time, which prohibited the use of funds available to any agency involved in intelligence activities to support, militarily or paramilitarily, the Contras?

MR. NORTH. I am not sure that I understood the way the Boland Amendment or Boland proscriptions of October 1984 read exactly the way you just said, but what I am certain is that we—[former CIA] Director [William] Casey, other lawyers—looked at that and said that the NSC staff was not proscribed doing those activities.

MR. NIELDS. In fact, you had an opinion drafted by a lawyer for—within Congress in your files saying exactly the opposite, didn't you?

MR. NORTH. I may have. I had a lot of files.

MR. NIELDS. Turn to Exhibit 106. . . . [T]he coversheet is from Vince to Ollie[.]

MR. NORTH. Yes.

MR. NIELDS. And it says, "On the chance Steve didn't give you a copy, attached is for your use."

And the attached is a memorandum dated August 8, 1985, on House of Representatives stationery from a lawyer employed by the House of Representatives, and two-thirds of the way down the page it says, "NSC is clearly a U.S. entity involved in intelligence activities, subject to the Section 8066(a) prohibition."

8066(a) is the Boland amendment, which prohibits—and it is quoted right above—funds available to the CIA, the Department of Defense, or any other agency or entity of the United States involved in intelligence activities to be obligated or expended to provide military support for the Contras.

I take it this document was in your files as of on or about August 8, 1985?

[Witness confers with his attorney.]

MR. NORTH. Well, I will believe that you found—if you tell me this was found in my files, I believe you.

I don't recall the document. I am not saying I didn't receive it. I don't know when I received it. And I will tell you that I had other people who suggested—in fact, it was suggested regularly in our media that anything like this was contrary to law.

But I will also tell you we also had opinions that said that we were fully legitimate. We had one of those from the Intelligence Oversight Board. I had the—Director Casey and I who started talking about this in 1983 and then carried it on until I left the NSC, reminded me frequently that he was a lawyer and others would remind me that he was a good one, and that it was clearly my understanding that what I was doing was legal.

MR. NIELDS. The opinion that you made reference to, the one from the Intelligence Oversight Board, had the top cut off of it in your files so that you couldn't tell who wrote it.

Can you explain why that occurred?

MR. NORTH. No.

MR. NIELDS. I take it you were aware, however, that in the summer of 1985, there were a number of press reports that raised questions about whether you were engaged in activities which violated this law, the Boland Amendment?

MR. NORTH. Yes, and I think what it focused on is that somewhere along the line there was someone who made the assumption that we in the NSC were spending part of the NSC budget to support the Nicaraguan Resistance. And we didn't.

And my understanding—and I have not read Boland, the Boland Amendments in some time, but my understanding then was that what we could not do is take and expend funds which had been made available to the CIA and the DOD [Department of Defense], etcetera, for the purpose of providing direct or indirect support for military and paramilitary operations in Nicaragua.

Now that is a memory that is over 7 months old, but I think that was what the intent was.

Certainly the way we pursued it and we made every effort not to expend U.S. Government funds to support the Nicaraguan Resistance, and thus when Director Casey suggested setting up outside entities and he gave me the name of [Major] General [Richard] Secord [USAF, ret.] as a person who could help do it, we did it as an effort to comply with the Boland prescriptions.

MR. NIELDS. And following these newspaper articles, there were various inquiries by committees of Congress?

MR. NORTH. That is correct.

MR. NIELDS. And one of them was by the House Committee on Intelligence? . . . And, indeed, you were consulted about drafting an answer to it?

\*          \*          \*

MR. NIELDS. Going to go back again now to the summer of 1986. Exhibit 122 is a resolution of inquiry. It relates to you and it seeks information about funding concerning the Contras, military advice, and asked specific questions about Robert Owen, [Major] General [John] Singlaub [USA, ret.] and a man named John Hull.

MR. NORTH. Right.

MR. NIELDS. And there came a time, did there not, when you had an interview with members of the House Intelligence Committee?

MR. NORTH. I did.

MR. NIELDS. And staff?

MR. NORTH. I don't remember if there was any staff there or not. I defer to Chairman [Lee] Hamilton [(D-Ind.)]. He convened his group in the White House Situation Room and I met with him there.

MR. NIELDS. There is a memorandum which was done by staff which is Exhibit 126.

Do you have that in front of you?

MR. NORTH. I do.

\*          \*          \*

MR. NIELDS. Then this was you personally talking to them?

MR. NORTH. It was on instructions of the National Security Advisor. I was instructed to meet with Chairman Hamilton and I believe many of the members of the Committee.

MR. NIELDS. And they were interested in finding out the answers to the questions raised by the resolution of inquiry.

MR. NORTH. Exactly.

MR. NIELDS. Your fund-raising activities?

MR. NORTH. Precisely.

MR. NIELDS. Military support for the Contras?

MR. NORTH. That's right.

MR. NIELDS. Questions about Mr. Owen, General Singlaub, and John Hull?

[Witness confers with his attorney.]

MR. NORTH. Yes.

MR. NIELDS. The beginning of this memorandum that appears to be a description of what you said during that meeting. It says from Boland Amendment on, North explained strictures to Contras.

Is that true, did you explain the strictures to the Contras?

MR. NORTH. I explained to them that there was no U.S. Government money until more was appropriated, yes.

MR. NIELDS. And it says never violated stricture, gave advice on human rights civic action program.

MR. NORTH. I did do that.

MR. NIELDS. But I take it you did considerably more, which you did not tell the committee about?

MR. NORTH. I have admitted that here before you today, knowing full well what I told the committee then. I think—and I think we can abbreviate this in hopes we can move on so that I can finish this week. I will tell you right now, counsel, and all the members here gathered that I misled the Congress. I misled—

MR. NIELDS. At that meeting?

MR. NORTH. At that meeting.

MR. NIELDS. Face to face?

MR. NORTH. Face to face.

MR. NIELDS. You made false statements to them about your activities in support of the Contras?

MR. NORTH. I did.

Furthermore, I did so with a purpose and I did so with the purpose of hopefully avoiding the very kind of thing that we have before us now, and avoiding a shut-off of help to the Nicaraguan Resistance and avoiding an elimination of the Resistance facilities in three Central American countries wherein we had promised those heads of state on my specific orders, on specific orders to me—I had gone down there and assured them of our absolute and total discretion.

MR. NIELDS. We do—

MR. NORTH. And I am admitting to you that I participated in preparation of documents for Congress that were erroneous, misleading, evasive, and wrong, and I did it again here when I appeared before that committee convened in the White House Situation Room, and I make no excuses for what I did.

I will tell you now that I am under oath and I was not then.

MR. NIELDS. We do live in a democracy, don't we?

MR. NORTH. We do, sir, thank God.

MR. NIELDS. In which it is the people, not one Marine lieutenant colonel, that get to decide the important policy decisions for the nation.

[Witness confers with his attorney.]

MR. NORTH. Yes.

MR. NIELDS. And part of the democratic process—

MR. NORTH. And I would point out that part of that answer is that this Marine lieutenant colonel was not making all of those decisions on his own. As I indicated yesterday in my testimony, Mr. Nields, I sought approval for everything that I did.

MR. NIELDS. But you denied Congress the facts.

MR. NORTH. I did.

MR. NIELDS. You denied the elected representatives of our people the facts upon which they needed to make a very important decision for this nation?

MR. NORTH. I did because of what I have just described to you as our concerns. And I did it because we have had incredible leaks from discussions with closed committees of the Congress. I was a part of, as people now know, the coordination for the mining of the harbors in Nicaragua. When that one leaked, there were American lives at stake and it leaked from a member of one of the committees, who eventually admitted it.

When there was a leak on the sensitive intelligence methods that we used to help capture the Achille Lauro terrorists, it almost wiped out that whole channel of communications.

Those kinds of things are devastating. They are devastating to the national security of the United States, and I desperately hope that one of the things that can derive from all of this ordeal is that we can find a better way by which we can communicate those things properly with the Congress.

I am not admitting that what happened in this is proper. I'm not admitting—or claiming, rather—that what I did and my role in it in communicating was proper.

MR. NIELDS. Were you instructed to do it?

MR. NORTH. I was not specifically instructed, no.

MR. NIELDS. Were you generally instructed?

MR. NORTH. Yes.

MR. NIELDS. By whom?

MR. NORTH. My superiors. I prepared—

MR. NIELDS. Who?

MR. NORTH. I prepared draft answers that they signed and sent. I would also point out—

MR. NIELDS. What superior?

MR. NORTH. Well, look who signed—I didn't sign those letters to the—to this body.

MR. NIELDS. I am talking about the last—I'm talking about the oral meeting in August of 1986.

MR. NORTH. I went down to that oral meeting

with the same kind of understanding that I prepared those memos in 1985 and other communications.

MR. NIELDS. Well you had a different boss [Vice-Admiral John Poindexter had replaced Robert McFarlane as national security adviser] and, in fairness, you ought to tell us whether he instructed you to do it, understood you to do it, knew about it afterwards, or none of those.

MR. NORTH. He did not specifically go down and say, "Ollie, lie to the committee." I told him what I had said afterwards, and he sent me a note saying, "well done." Now I would also like to point out one other thing. I deeply believe that the President of the United States is also an elected official of this land, and by the Constitution, as I understand it, he is the person charged with making and carrying out the foreign policy of this country. I believed from the moment I was engaged in this activity in 1984 that this was in furtherance of the foreign policy established by the President. I still believe that.

MR. NIELDS. Even—

MR. NORTH. I am not saying that what I did here was right. And I have just placed myself, as you know, counsel, in great jeopardy.

MR. NIELDS. Even the President—

[Witness confers with his attorney.]

MR. NIELDS. Even the President is elected by the people.

MR. NORTH. I just said that.

MR. NIELDS. And the people have the right to vote him out of office if they don't like his policies.

MR. NORTH. That is true.

MR. NIELDS. And they can't exercise that function, if the policies of the President are hidden from them?

MR. NORTH. Wait a second.... The fact is that this country does need to be able to conduct those kinds of activities, and the President ought not to be in a position, in my humble opinion, of having to go out and explain to the American people on a biweekly basis or any other kind that I, the President, am carrying out the following secret operations. It just can't be done. No nation in the world will ever help us again, and we desperately need that kind of help if we are to survive given our adversaries.

And what I am saying to you, Mr. Nields, is the American people, I think, trust that the President will indeed be conducting these kinds of activities. They trust that he will do so with a good purpose and good intent....

\*          \*          \*

MR. NORTH. Please. It was not right. It does not leave me with a good taste in my mouth. I want you to know lying does not come easy to me. I want you to know that it doesn't come easy to anybody, but I think we all had to weigh in the balance the difference between lives and lies. I had to do that on a number of occasions in both these operations, and it is not an easy thing to do.

\*          \*          \*

THURSDAY, JULY 9: AFTERNOON SESSION—2:00 PM

\*          \*          \*

MR. [Arthur] LIMAN [Counsel for the Senate Committee]. [S]ometimes you, as a military officer, are going to disagree with what the President or the Congress decide as a matter of policy, correct?

MR. NORTH. Certainly.

MR. LIMAN. And you believe very firmly in civilian control?

MR. NORTH. Absolutely.

MR. LIMAN. And you do not share the view that was expressed and retracted by your secretary that sometimes you must rise above the written law?

MR. NORTH. I do not believe in rising above the law at all, and I do not believe that I have ever stated that.

MR. LIMAN. And you haven't.

MR. NORTH. I have not.

MR. LIMAN. And when you, Colonel North, had to, in order to protect this operation and your superiors, engage in deception of Congress and deception of other members of the Executive Branch, it was particularly painful for you, in view of the Honor Code that you subscribed to at Annapolis; isn't that so?

MR. NORTH. That is correct.

\*          \*          \*

FRIDAY, JULY 10: MORNING SESSION—9:00 AM

\*          \*          \*

MR. LIMAN. Now you testified that one reason that Mr. Casey was excited about the plan for use of the residuals [from the arms sales to Iran] was that he wanted to have a funded organization that he could pull off the shelf to do other operations. Is that what in essence his view was?

\*          \*          \*

MR. NORTH. That is correct.

MR. LIMAN. Well why don't you give us a description of what he said, or as you understood it, what he meant about pulling something off the shelf?

MR. NORTH. Director Casey had in mind, as I understood it, an overseas entity that was capable of conducting operations or activities of assistance to U.S. foreign policy goals, that was a stand alone—it was—

MR. LIMAN. Self-financed?

MR. NORTH. —self-financing, independent of appropriated moneys and capable of conducting activities similar to the ones that we had conducted here. There were other countries that were suggested that might be the beneficiaries of that kind of support, other activities, to include counterterrorism.

\*          \*          \*

MR. LIMAN. Now, Director Casey was in charge of the CIA and had at his disposal an Operations Directorate, correct?

MR. NORTH. Certainly.

MR. LIMAN. And, as I understand your testimony, Director Casey was proposing to you that a CIA outside of the CIA be created. Fair?

MR. NORTH. No.

MR. LIMAN. Well, wasn't this an organization that would be able to do covert policy to advance U.S. foreign policy interests?

MR. NORTH. Well, not necessarily all covert. The Director was interested in the ability to get an existing, as he put it, off-the-shelf, self-sustaining, stand-alone entity that could perform certain activities on behalf of the United States. And as I tried to describe to the committee last night in the executive session, several of those activities were discussed with both Director Casey and with Admiral Poindexter.

Some of those were to be conducted jointly by other friendly intelligence services, but they needed money.

MR. LIMAN. Colonel—

MR. NORTH. Yes, counsel?

MR. LIMAN. You understood that the CIA is funded by the U.S. Government, correct?

MR. NORTH. That is correct.

MR. LIMAN. You understood that the U.S. Government put certain limitations on what the CIA could do, correct?

MR. NORTH. That is correct.

MR. LIMAN. And I ask you today, after all you have gone through, are you not shocked that the Director of Central Intelligence is proposing to you the creation of an organization to do these kinds of things outside of his own organization?

MR. NORTH. Counsel, I can tell you that I am not shocked. I don't see that it was necessarily inconsistent with the laws, regulations, statutes and all that obtain. I don't see that it would necessarily be unconstitutional. I don't see that it would necessarily be in any way a violation of anything that I know of. And if indeed we—the Director had chosen to use one of these entities out there to support an operation in the Middle East or South America or Africa, and an appropriate Finding were done and the appropriate activities were authorized by the Commander in Chief, or the head of state in his capacity to do so, maybe I'm overly naive, but I don't see what would be wrong with that.

MR. LIMAN. Maybe you are.

*           *           *

MONDAY, JULY 13: AFTERNOON SESSION—2:00 PM

*           *           *

MR. [Tom] FOLEY [D-Wash.]. Mr. Chairman, I'll conclude my time here. Because of the counsel's advice to his client—discourages his giving us advice,

we are left with a decision to make, and the American people are left with the decision to make, as to whether or not critical decisions of national security policy of this country, involving far-reaching impacts on our foreign policy and defense policy, can be properly undertaken in the National Security Council by a lieutenant colonel acting in response to the orders of or the acquiescence of Mr. McFarlane or Vice Admiral Poindexter, and in the absence of Presidential authority.

In a few days, Vice Admiral Poindexter will be sitting in that seat and we'll have to ask that question to him, but I think we are left with a disturbing problem that while every single matter of advice is being given by this officer on foreign policy, on national security policy, on his reactions to legal matters, what he knows most about, the internal activities of the National Security Council and his role with respect to his superiors, he will not, on the advice of counsel, give us his evaluation of whether there is not a deep defect and flaw in that policy apparatus if, in fact, the President did not know, and these policies were carried on by his subordinates without his authority.

MR. NORTH. Mr. Chairman, may I respond?

CHAIRMAN [Daniel] INOUYE [D-Haw.]. Please do.

MR. NORTH. Mr. Foley, what I deeply believe is that it is up to the Executive, and in this case, the President of the United States himself, to make whatever changes he deems appropriate in the functioning of his staff.

I do not believe then—I did not believe then and I do not believe now that it is within the purview of the legislative branch of our government to mandate those kinds of changes, that if the President sees fit to make changes in the order of his staff, the structure of his staff, the activities of his staff, that it is within his purview to do so.

REP. FOLEY. I would remind you, Colonel, that the National Security Council itself and the staff that served it was created by law, by statute, not just by the President, but by the Congress.

Thank you. Mr. Chairman.

☆406b *United States v. Oliver L. North*

708 F. Supp. 375 (D.D.C. 1988).

GESELL, United States District Judge.

*           *           *

North contends . . . that even if he was engaged in conduct that was inconsistent with the intent of the Boland Amendments, as the indictment recites, he still has not interfered with or obstructed a "lawful governmental function" by his effort to misrepresent what he was doing. The Boland Amendments are unconstitutional, he contends, because they attempt to regulate how the President should conduct foreign policy and, in any event, they were never meant to apply to the National Security Council. Thus according to North's view, his misrepresentations and evasions did not interfere with a lawful governmental function.

The difficulty with this argument is that the President and the White House staff, whatever their doubts as to the constitutional propriety of some aspects of the Boland Amendments as they applied to the NSC, were functioning in respect to pertinent aspects of this case as if they were in compliance with Boland. While any White House uncertainty may bear on North's intent under certain counts, his understanding as to the constitutionality of Boland in no way affords an excuse for his alleged misconduct or entitled him to obstruct the way the government was, in fact, functioning. The President signed the laws containing the Boland Amendments and he apparently decided to comply with relevant aspects of the Boland Amendments, and was willing to respond to Congressional committee inquiries relating to compliance with the Boland Amendments. As discussed in the Court's memorandum filed November 29, 1988, North did not refuse to answer Congressional inquiries on the grounds that Congress had no constitutional right to query National Security Council officials with respect to covert acts being conducted through employees of the NSC. In fact, he is alleged to have asserted his, and the NSC's full compliance with the Boland Amendment.

The President was free within the prerogatives of his office to comply with the prohibitions of the Boland Amendments or to resist them in whole or in part if compliance would have unduly infringed on his responsibilities in the realm of foreign relations and national security. The language of the Boland Amendments is not precise in some pertinent respects and it has many aspects, but these ambiguities are of no consequence where the Executive and the Legislative branches act in harmony. If, as Independent Counsel contends he is prepared to prove, the President, both previous and subsequent to the enactment of Boland, chose to limit the activities of the National Security Council by directives and Executive Orders that were consistent with the Boland Amendments, North's alleged unauthorized deviation from such limitations must be viewed as contrary to lawful government functions.

\*       \*       \*

☆406c  *United States v. Oliver L. North*

708 F. Supp. 380 (D.D.C. 1988).

GESELL, United States District Judge

\*       \*       \*

### B. CONSTITUTIONAL ARGUMENT.

North urges that the criminal statutes proscribing false statements within the jurisdiction of any department or agency cannot be applied to communications between an employee of the Executive Branch and Congress. North proceeds to fashion a constitutional argument, contending that the asserted primacy of the White House in foreign affairs precludes officials working for the Executive from being prosecuted for false statements made to Congress regarding foreign affairs. This argument lacks substance and it misses the point it attempts to make.

... Executive officials have a statutory obligation to provide intelligence information to this Committee on request. More generally, congressional committees act well within their authority when they seek explanation from Executive Branch officials regarding matters that may affect substantive legislative decisions. It is essential that Congress legislate based on fact, not falsifications, in the realm of foreign affairs as well as in domestic legislation.

If Congress is increasing its power in a manner that infringes upon the President's prerogatives, the President may assert executive privilege or direct a person in North's position not to answer. Deliberate falsifications are another matter, and North did not himself have executive privilege. Indeed, the inquiries were directed to McFarlane as the President's National Security Advisor regarding North's personal conduct. North did not simply refuse to answer; he affirmatively deceived Congress, and there is not the slightest suggestion in North's papers that the President instructed North to give false information. He cannot claim any sort of privilege for this. The thought that any one of the hundreds or thousands of persons working for the President can affirmatively and intentionally mislead Congress when it seeks information to perform one of its assigned functions for any reason—including self-interest or the belief that the President would approve—is unacceptable on its face. Such a disdainful view of our democratic form of government has no constitutional substance. Where, as here, power is shared among the branches, willful and deliberate deceit such as North allegedly espouses cannot be excused on constitutional grounds.

### C. POLICY ARGUMENTS.

[North] argues that requiring Executive officials to tell the truth would have a "chilling effect" that "would disrupt the orderly functioning of government." Yet the effects of not enforcing the law in these circumstances are surely worse than the consequences of enforcing it, and North's assertion ignores the requirement of criminal intent, that the false statements be made "knowingly and willfully." North seems to state that Executive Branch officials and their staffs habitually and properly lie to Congress. He thus again devalues the democratic premise that sound legislation depends on a free-flowing, accurate stream of information to Congress, from government officials who must execute the laws as enacted. Most officials no doubt find that responding truthfully to congressional inquiries is not only in keeping with our structure of shared powers, but that it is also useful to their agencies to build a trusting relationship with Congress. Whatever the practice, Congress has not accepted North's policy contentions, and Congress has set the standard.

\*       \*       \*

## 407 "bring to justice the perpetrators of terrorist attacks against Pan Am Flight 103" (1988)

Terrorist acts on international flights, an increasing problem during the 1980s and 1990s, have resulted in numerous international actions and national lawsuits. The repercussions of a bomb on a civilian flight are felt around the world. No one is safe from a terrorist's explosion because there is no way of knowing where he or she will strike next.

On December 21, 1988, Pan Am Flight 103 exploded over the village of Lockerbie in southern Scotland. After two years of investigations, the United States and the United Kingdom began to make random accusations against states, organizations, and individuals. Nearly three years later, they charged that two Libyan nationals were the culprits. Abdel Basset Ali Mohmed Al Megrahi and Al Amin Khalifa Fhima were both officers of the Libyan Intelligence Services holding positions with Libyan Arab Airlines. The two men allegedly placed a suitcase of explosives aboard the aircraft, destroying it and killing 259 passengers and crew and 11 Lockerbie residents.

After the United States and the United Kingdom proclaimed that the perpetrators were Libyan, they asked the Libyan government to deport them to either the United States or the United Kingdom to stand trial. The Libyan government refused, stating that the Libyan judicial system was an appropriate forum in which to try the alleged bombers. This refusal led to the passage of UN Security Council Resolution 883, which placed various economic and political sanctions on Libya. The Lockerbie bombing also resulted in the filing, by survivors of those killed in the bombing, of a civil suit against the Libyan government, the airline, and the terrorists in their individual capacity. The litigation is not completed as of this writing.

## ☆407 Criminal, Economic, and Civil Sanctions

### ☆407a Tightening Economic Sanctions against Libya

Statement Released by the White House, Office of the Press Secretary, December 3, 1993.

The White House, today, announced new measures to tighten economic sanctions against Libya. These measures are pursuant to the imposition by the world community of new sanctions against Libya under UN Security Council Resolution 883 and are designed to bring to justice the perpetrators of terrorist attacks against Pan Am Flight 103. . . . The actions signal that Libya cannot continue to defy justice and flout the will of the international community with impunity.

UN Security Council Resolution 883 freezes assets owned or controlled by the Government of Libya on a worldwide basis and bans provision of equipment for refining and transporting oil. It tightens the international air embargo and other measures imposed in 1992 under UN Security Council Resolution 748. It is the result of close cooperation between the United States, France, and the United Kingdom, whose citizens were the principal victims of Libyan-sponsored terrorist attacks against Pan Am Flight 103 . . . , and consultations with Russia and other friends and allies.

The President has instructed the Secretary of Commerce to reinforce our current trade embargo against Libya by prohibiting the sale from foreign countries to Libya of U.S.-origin products, including equipment for refining and transporting oil.

The President also is renewing for another year the national emergency with respect to Libya pursuant to the International Emergency Economic Powers Act. This renewal extends the current comprehensive financial and trade embargo against Libya in effect since 1986. Under these sanctions, all trade with Libya is controlled by the Department of the Treasury, and all assets owned or controlled by the Libyan Government in the United States or in possession of U.S. persons are frozen.

The United States continues to believe that still stronger measures, including a worldwide oil embargo, should be enacted if Libya continues to defy the international community. We remain determined to ensure that perpetrators of these acts of terrorism are brought to justice. The families of the victims in the murderous Lockerbie bombing and others acts of Libyan terrorism deserve nothing less.

### ☆407b Rein v. Libya

Civil Action No. 96-2077, U.S. D. Ct. E.D.N.Y. (1996).

\*       \*       \*

COMPLAINT

*Jury Trial Demanded to Extent Permitted by Law*

Plaintiffs, by their attorneys . . . as and for their Complainant, hereby allege:

1. Plaintiffs are Survivors as well as Executors, Administrators or Personal Representatives of the Estates of persons who were killed while passengers

on Pan American World Airways Flight 103 on December 21, 1988 (hereinafter "Flight 103").

2. Defendant The Socialist People's Libyan Arab Jamahiriya (hereinafter "Libya") is a foreign state and government with jurisdiction over lands located on the Mediterranean coast of North Africa.

3. The Libyan External Security Organization, a/k/a Jamahiriya Security Organization (hereinafter "JSO") is an intelligence and operational entity which operates separately from, but is an agency, instrumentality and/or organ of the Libyan government.

4. Defendant Libyan Arab Airlines (hereinafter "LAA") is an air carrier which is a separate corporate entity that operates as an agency, instrumentality and/or organ of the Libyan government, and which is majority-owned by the Libyan government.

5. Defendants Lamen Khalifa Fhima *[sic]* . . . (hereafter referred to as "Fhima"), and Abdel Basset Ali Al-Megrahi . . . (hereinafter referred to as "Megrahi"), are natural persons, subjects and citizens of the defendant Libya and agents and employees of the defendants Libya and JSO who, while acting in the scope of their agencies and employments, took conscious and affirmative steps to and did in fact place an explosive device on Flight 103.

### Jurisdiction and Venue

6. Subject matter jurisdiction exists under 28 U.S.C. Section 1330 and 28 U.S.C. Section 1331 in that plaintiffs' claims are brought pursuant to the Foreign Sovereign Immunities Act, 28 U.S.C. Section 1062 et seq., and pursuant to the Alien Tort Act, 28 U.S.C. Section 1350.

7. Venue in this action properly lies in this District Court pursuant to 28 U.S.C. Section 1391 (f) and pursuant to order of the Judicial Panel on Multidistrict Litigation dated April 4, 1989, Docket No. MDL 799, captioned In re Air Disaster at Lockerbie, Scotland on December 21, 1988.

### As and for a First Cause of Action for Wrongful Death

8. On December 21, 1988, decedents were passengers on board Flight 103, which departed from Heathrow Airport, London, England and was scheduled to arrive at John F. Kennedy International Airport in New York, New York.

9. At or about 1903 hours Greenwich Mean Time, an explosion occurred in the forward baggage compartment of Flight 103, causing the aircraft to disintegrate in mid-air and crash to the ground in and around Lockerbie, Scotland.

10. All two hundred forty-three passengers and sixteen crew members, including among them the decedents of all plaintiffs herein, perished as a result of the explosion and consequent crash.

11. The destruction of Flight 103 and deaths of plaintiffs' decedents were caused by a wilful and de-liberate act of extrajudicial killing and aircraft sabotage, in that the explosion on the aircraft was caused by the detonation of a bomb that was deliberately placed upon the aircraft by the defendants and others acting at their behest (hereafter referred to as "terrorists").

12. Defendants Fhima and Megrahi were among the group of terrorists personally responsible for the destruction of Flight 103 and the deaths of its passengers and crew.

13. Defendant Libya provided material support and resources to the terrorists, in that Libyan government agents and officials, acting in the scope of their offices, provided the terrorists with money, labor, intelligence information, equipment, and supplies, including electronic timing devices, electronic blasting caps and detonators, and explosives.

14. In addition, defendant Libya is vicariously responsible for any liability of co-defendants because defendant Libya controlled and acted in concert with the co-defendants in accomplishing the destruction of Flight 103.

15. Defendant JSO and its agents and employees were among the terrorists directly responsible for the bombing of Flight 103, and JSO cooperated with and assisted the terrorists, and/or provided material support and resources to them, in that it provided them with money, labor, intelligence information, equipment and supplies.

16. Libya's national and state-owned airline, defendant LAA, also provided material support and resources to the terrorists responsible for the bombing of Flight 103, in that its agents and officials, acting in the scope of their offices and agency, furnished the terrorists with transportation of their persons and of materials, and furnished storage facilities, baggage documents, access to airport facilities including baggage handling systems, and other assistance, with the knowledge that such would materially assist them in carrying out the Flight 103 bombing.

17. Defendants' conduct constituted a common law assault and battery under governing law, and defendants would be liable for the injuries suffered by each of the decedents, had decedents not died.

18. Defendants are liable to the decedents' estates and survivors for compensatory and punitive damages.

19. The Foreign Sovereign Immunities Act, at 28 U.S.C. Section 1605(a)(7), creates or provides for a cause of action in favor of all of the plaintiffs in this action who are United States nationals, against the defendants for their acts of torture, extrajudicial killing, aircraft sabotage and provision of material support and resources therefor.

20. Defendants' conduct also constitutes a violation of international law.

21. The Alien Tort Act, 28 U.S.C. Section 1350, creates a cause of action in favor of plaintiffs in this

action who are not nationals of the United States, and against the defendants for their violation of international law in torturing and killing the passengers and crew of Flight 103.

22. The Torture Victim Protection Act, 28 U.S.C. Section 1350, creates a cause of action for all plaintiffs in this action against the defendants, for the torture and extrajudicial killing of the decedents.

23. The plaintiffs and the estates of each decedent are entitled to recover wrongful death damages, including pecuniary losses, and damages for loss of support, consortium, society, companionship, prospective inheritance, care, love, guidance, training, education, and services, and damages for grief and mental anguish, moral damages, burial expenses and other damages.

24. By reason of the foregoing, defendants are liable to each plaintiff and each decedent's estate in the sum of TWENTY MILLION ($20,000,000) DOLLARS.

### As and for a Second Cause of Action for Survival Damages

25. Plaintiffs repeat the allegations of paragraphs 1-22 as if fully set forth at length.

26. Before their deaths, decedents suffered conscious pain and suffering and fear of their impending deaths, entitling them to compensatory damages under governing law.

27. By reason of the foregoing, defendants are liable to each of the decedent's estates in the sum of ONE MILLION ($1,000,000) DOLLARS.

### As and for a Third Cause of Action for Punitive Damages

28. Plaintiffs repeat the allegations of paragraphs 1-22 as if fully set forth at length.

29. For the reasons stated above, and pursuant to 28 U.S.C. Section 1606, defendants JSO, LAA, Fhima and Megrahi each are liable to the plaintiffs for punitive damages in the amount of TWO BILLION ($2,000,000,000) DOLLARS.

WHEREFORE, each plaintiff and estate demands judgment on the First Cause of Action against defendants in the sum of TWENTY MILLION ($20,000,000) DOLLARS, and each estate demands judgment on the Second Cause of Action against defendants in the sum of ONE MILLION ($1,000,000) DOLLARS, and all plaintiffs demand judgment on the Third Cause of Action in the total sum of TWO BILLION ($2,000,000,000) DOLLARS against each defendant, plus interest, costs, and any further relief that this Court may find just and proper.

☆407c  Who Really Blew Up Flight 103?

Document at http://hydraulix.bangor.ac.uk/nus/islam/pages/reports/flt103.html. Abridged extract from Fan Yew Teng, *The Continuing Terrorism against Libya* (Kuala Lumpur, Malaysia: Egret Publications).

On 21 December 1988, a jumbo jet, Pan Am Flight 103, blew up in the sky over Lockerbie in Scotland, killing all 259 people aboard and 11 persons on the ground. Colonel Muammer Gaddafi was held responsible. His revolution in Libya [and the exploitation of the country's oil resources have] brought high standards of living for his people and his regime maintains a strong anti-imperialist stance. However, most Muslims find his blend of Marxist-Islamic thought repulsive and his crackdown on the Islamic Movement has been bloody and brutal.

According to Jeff Jones, writing in the Summer 1990 issue of *Covert Action*, "By most accounts, investigators believe the crash was caused by a sophisticated bomb—with a time-delay barometric fuse—placed on the plane by Ahmad Jibril's Popular Front for the Liberation of Palestine-General Command (PFLP-GC), a Syrian-backed group that rejects PLO efforts to negotiate with Israel."

Jones adds, "Jibril has denied responsibility for the attack. But investigators believe that the PFLP-GC received a large payment from Iran—ABC News has reported $10 million—to carry out the attack to avenge the US downing of an Iranian airbus in which nearly 300 died on July 3, 1988."

Jones adds: "But there are many other questions percolating just beneath the surface of the investigation." Some of the questions are:

—There were, it is now known, at least four, and according to one unsubstantiated report, as many as eight, CIA and other US intelligence operatives returning from Beirut, Lebanon, aboard the plane. The Lockerbie bomb crippled US intelligence efforts in the Middle East. Were the intelligence operatives on 103 the bomb's target?

—. . . according to syndicated columnist Jack Anderson, President George Bush and British Prime Minister Margaret Thatcher held a transatlantic phone conversation some time in 1989, in which they agreed that the investigation into the crash should be "limited" in order to avoid harming the two nations' intelligence communities. Thatcher has acknowledged that the conversation took place, but denied she and Bush sought to interfere with the investigation.

In April 1990 a letter to George Bush and Margaret Thatcher, co-signed by Paul Hudson and Jim Swire, co-chairs of "U.K. Families-Flight 103," spoke of the "entirely believable published accounts (that) . . . both of you have decided to deliberately downplay the evidence and string out the investigation until the case can be dismissed as ancient history."

In Washington the President's Commission on Airline Security and Terrorism issued its report on May 15, 1990, leaving many questions about the bombing of Pan Am 103 unanswered. But it did recommend that the US should be more willing to attack suspected terrorists and the states that harbour or support them.

But as Jeff Jones comments, "Threatening military action may be a cynical means for dealing with the anger of relatives of the victims. In April 1989, during a meeting with representatives of the relatives, Bush reportedly offered the unsolicited statement that if 'the fingers (of guilt) point to state terrorism,' there would be a retaliatory strike like the one the Reagan administration launched against Libya."

\*         \*         \*

Then, suddenly in the last week of June 1991, two and a half years after the incident, *The Washington Post* carried some allegations that Libya could have been involved in the bombing of Pan Am 103.

On 1st July 1991 *The Australian* carried a report from London by James Dalrymple of *The Sunday Times* stating that there was now "proof" that Libya was behind the Lockerbie bombing. "Lord Fraser of Carmyllie, the Scottish Lord Advocate in charge of the Lockerbie inquiry, is expected to accuse Libya of involvement later this year."

\*         \*         \*

Since the tragedy in December 1988, a number of parties, as pointed out earlier, have been identified as the perpetrators. In fact, within weeks of the bombing, *The Independent* newspaper of London ran a story linking it to Mossad, the Israeli intelligence agency. Then many observers believed that it had all the markings of an Israeli terrorist operation that was to be blamed on the Palestinians or a radical Arab state in an attempt to turn world opinion against the Palestinian struggle.

However, it was not long before the "Israeli connection" quickly vanished from the headlines and the official version was that the bombing was carried out by a Palestinian organisation commissioned by Iran. Later Syria was added to the equation.

\*         \*         \*

On 14 November 1991 the United States and British governments indicted two Libyan nationals on murder charges arising from the bombing of Pan Am 103. They demanded that Libya hand over the two men—Abdel Baset Ali Mohmed al-Megrahi and Al Amin Khalifa Fhima.

The next day Libya formally denied involvement in the bombing. The Libyan Foreign Ministry in a statement "categorically denies any Libyan involvement in the mentioned incident or any knowledge by the Libyan authorities of it."

\*         \*         \*

On 22 January 1992, the United Nations Security Council passed Resolution 731 urging Libya to cooperate with international probes into the bombings of the Pan Am 103 and a French UTA jet that killed 170 people over Niger in 1989.

Out of the blue, the case of the UTA jet bombing was injected into the dispute. By "international probes," it was meant that Libya must hand over her citizens for trial in the United States, Britain and France. . . .

The United States, Britain and France, which sponsored Resolution 731 warned that if Libya refused to "co-operate," they reserved the right to ask the Security Council to impose an air and oil embargo on Libya.

\*         \*         \*

When the United States and Britain demanded that Libya should hand over the two nationals accused of being involved in the Pan Am jet bombing, Libya . . . refused to do so. Libya has no extradition treaties with these two countries.

Although Libya refused to hand over the suspects, it had agreed to co-operate in all other respects, from the very start of the controversy in mid-November 1991. It suggested that the matter should go to international arbitration. The United States and Britain refused to co-operate.

After this, all the same, Libya appointed two magistrates to look into the case. The two magistrates had asked American, British and French investigators to provide them the evidence. Again, this request was turned down.

Libya also suggested that lawyers and journalists could attend the hearings in Libya. There seemed to be no takers. Why?

\*         \*         \*

On 31 March, 1992, [the American, British and French governments] got the Security Council to vote for Resolution 748 to impose trade sanctions, flight sanctions and an arms embargo on Libya for failing to surrender six suspects in the bombings of Pan Am 103 and a French UTA jetliner.

The vote of the 15-member Council was 10 in favour, none opposed, and five abstentions: China, Cape Verde, India, Morocco and Zimbabwe. The countries that abstained argued that sanctions should be a last resort, that diplomacy should be given more time, and that action should await a ruling by the World Court.

According to an AP report, the sanctions carried the threat of the use of force. The sanctions are legally binding and can be enforced by military action because the resolution invokes Chapter 7 of the UN Charter which authorises the use of force.

Libyan Ambassador Ali Elhouderi argued before the vote that sanctions would pave the way for another air strike on Libya.

On April 5, the US government advised Americans in Libya to leave immediately. An estimated 500 to 1,000 Americans were believed to be working in Libya, mainly in the oil industry.

\*         \*         \*

[On 14 April 1992,] Malta agreed to accept the two Libyans accused of bombing Pan Am 103. This was announced by Esmat Abdel Maguid, the Secretary General of the Arab League. Earlier offers by Libya to send the two persons to a third country had been rejected by the United States and Britain.

Malta's decision was in response to a Libyan offer sent to the UN by the Arab League. The immediate response of the United States and Britain was that they did not believe the offer would be enough to avert the imposition of sanctions on Libya. In other words, they had rejected it.

\*       \*       \*

*TIME* magazine carried a special cover story on the Lockerbie affair on April 27, 1992. Titled "The Untold Story of Pan Am 103," the story was written by Roy Rowan, who had been a writer, foreign correspondent and editor for 44 years.

\*       \*       \*

In his 9-page report, Rowan concludes that provocative evidence suggests that a Syrian drug dealer may have helped to plant the bomb—and that the real targets were intelligence agents working for the CIA.

\*       \*       \*

[I]n an interview conducted by an Italian cable television network for Channel Two in New York, the Editor of *TIME* magazine confirmed the authenticity of the information and evidence which his magazine obtained and published. He said: "We are sure of the authenticity of the report published by our magazine relating to the implication of other parties in this incident." He said that the evidence furnished by the American administration accusing Libya was unconvincing and consisted merely of a small fragment of a timing device and another small piece of fabric which was said to be from the same suitcase which contained the bomb.

\*       \*       \*

# 408 "no better way to counter a flag burner's message than by saluting the flag that burns" (1989)

National flags are considered unique symbols that can evoke popular passions, move armies to valor, reduce patriots to tears, and arouse other deep responses. The willful desecration of a nation's flag is generally seen as the utmost expression of contempt for a country and its policies, and the "Stars and Stripes" has more than a few times been televised aflame in demonstrations abroad. But within the United States that scene is rare. Virtually all the states have laws that require "Old Glory" to be treated with reverence and dignity and penalize disrespectful handling of the flag.

As part of a demonstration against President Ronald Reagan during the 1984 Republican National Convention in Dallas, Texas, Gregory Lee Johnson unfurled a flag another demonstrator had taken from a flagpole outside a building, doused it with kerosene, and set it ablaze. At his trial for the crime of flag desecration, he gave his reasons: "The American flag was burned as Ronald Reagan was being renominated as President. And a more powerful statement of symbolic speech, whether you agree with it or not, couldn't have been made at that time. It's quite a juxtaposition. We had new patriotism and no patriotism." Johnson was convicted and his case reached the Supreme Court.

Noting that Johnson had not engaged in any breach of the peace (although many spectators were offended by the act, no violent retaliation was threatened), and that in this case (unlike the case excerpted in Doc. 340) the constitutionality of the flag desecration law was not under review, the Court decided that the First Amendment protected Johnson's politically motivated action from punishment.

Following the decision, bills were introduced in Congress to reverse the decision by means of a constitutional amendment. Initially, the movement gained limited support. But in 1995, the House of Representatives voted overwhelmingly for the amendment, and the Senate came just three votes shy (63–36), of the two-thirds vote necessary to send the proposal to the states for near-certain ratification, since forty-nine of the states had already petitioned Congress for the measure.

☆408  *Texas v. Johnson*

491 U.S. 397 (1989).

JUSTICE BRENNAN delivered the opinion of the Court.

\*       \*       \*

IV

It remains to consider whether the State's interest in preserving the flag as a symbol of nationhood and national unity justifies Johnson's conviction.

As in *Spence* [*v. Washington*, 418 U.S. 405 (1974)], "[w]e are confronted with a case of prosecution for the expression of an idea through activity," and "[a]ccordingly, we must examine with particular care the interests advanced by [Texas] to support its prosecution." Johnson was not, we add, prosecuted for the expression of just any idea; he was prosecuted for his expression of dissatisfaction with the policies of this country, expression situated at the core of our First Amendment values.

Moreover, Johnson was prosecuted because he knew that his politically charged expression would cause "serious offense." If he had burned the flag as a means of disposing of it because it was dirty or torn, he would not have been convicted of flag desecration under this Texas law. . . . The Texas law is thus not aimed at protecting the physical integrity of the flag in all circumstances, but is designed instead to protect it only against impairments that would cause serious offense to others. Texas concedes as much: "[The statute] reaches only those severe acts of physical abuse of the flag carried out in a way likely to be offensive. The statute mandates intentional or knowing abuse, that is, the kind of mistreatment that is not innocent, but rather is intentionally designed to seriously offend other individuals."

Whether Johnson's treatment of the flag violated Texas law thus depended on the likely communicative impact of his expressive conduct.

*      *      *

. . . Quoting extensively from the writings of this Court chronicling the flag's historic and symbolic role in our society, the State emphasizes the " 'special place' " reserved for the flag in our Nation. The State's argument is not that it has an interest simply in maintaining the flag as a symbol of *something*, no matter what it symbolizes; indeed, if that were the State's position, it would be difficult to see how that interest is endangered by highly symbolic conduct such as Johnson's. Rather, the State's claim is that it has an interest in preserving the flag as a symbol of *nationhood* and *national unity*, a symbol with a determinate range of meanings. According to Texas, if one physically treats the flag in a way that would tend to cast doubt on either the idea that nationhood and national unity are the flag's referents or that national unity actually exists, the message conveyed thereby is a harmful one and therefore may be prohibited.

If there is a bedrock principle underlying the First Amendment, it is that the government may not prohibit the expression of an idea simply because society finds the idea itself offensive or disagreeable.

We have not recognized an exception to this principle even where our flag has been involved. [We have] held that a State may not criminally punish a person for uttering words critical of the flag. . . . Nor may the government, we have held, compel conduct that would evince respect for the flag. "To sustain the compulsory flag salute we are required to say that a Bill of Rights which guards the individual's right to speak his own mind, left it open to public authorities to compel him to utter what is not in his mind."

In holding in *Barnette* [Doc. 235] that the Constitution did not leave this course open to the government, Justice Jackson described one of our society's defining principles in words deserving of their frequent repetition: "If there is any fixed star in our constitutional constellation, it is that no official, high or petty, can prescribe what shall be orthodox in politics, nationalism, religion, or other matters of

opinion or force citizens to confess by word or act their faith therein."

*      *      *

In short, nothing in our precedents suggests that a State may foster its own view of the flag by prohibiting expressive conduct relating to it. To bring its argument outside our precedents, Texas attempts to convince us that even if its interest in preserving the flag's symbolic role does not allow it to prohibit words or some expressive conduct critical of the flag, it does permit it to forbid the outright destruction of the flag. The State's argument cannot depend here on the distinction between written or spoken words and nonverbal conduct. That distinction, we have shown, is of no moment where the nonverbal conduct is expressive, as it is here, and where the regulation of that conduct is related to expression, as it is here. In addition, both *Barnette* and *Spence* involved expressive conduct, not only verbal communication, and both found that conduct protected.

Texas' focus on the precise nature of Johnson's expression, moreover, misses the point of our prior decisions: their enduring lesson, that the government may not prohibit expression simply because it disagrees with its message, is not dependent on the particular mode in which one chooses to express an idea. If we were to hold that a State may forbid flag burning wherever it is likely to endanger the flag's symbolic role, but allow it wherever burning a flag promotes that role—as where, for example, a person ceremoniously burns a dirty flag—we would be saying that when it comes to impairing the flag's physical integrity, the flag itself may be used as a symbol—as a substitute for the written or spoken word or a "short cut from mind to mind"—only in one direction. We would be permitting a State to "prescribe what shall be orthodox" by saying that one may burn the flag to convey one's attitude toward it and its referents only if one does not endanger the flag's representation of nationhood and national unity.

We never before have held that the Government may ensure that a symbol be used to express only one view of that symbol or its referents. . . . To conclude that the government may permit designated symbols to be used to communicate only a limited set of messages would be to enter territory having no discernible or defensible boundaries. . . .

There is, moreover, no indication—either in the text of the Constitution or in our cases interpreting it—that a separate juridical category exists for the American flag alone. Indeed, we would not be surprised to learn that the persons who framed our Constitution and wrote the Amendment that we now construe were not known for their reverence for the Union Jack. The First Amendment does not guarantee that other concepts virtually sacred to our Nation as a whole—such as the principle that discrimination on the basis of race is odious and destructive—will go unquestioned in the market-place of ideas. We decline, therefore, to create for the flag an exception to the joust of principles protected by the First Amendment.

It is not the State's ends, but its means, to which we object. It cannot be gainsaid that there is a special place reserved for the flag in this Nation, and thus we do not doubt that the government has a legitimate interest in making efforts to "preserv[e] the national flag as an unalloyed symbol of our country...." To say that the government has an interest in encouraging proper treatment of the flag, however, is not to say that it may criminally punish a person for burning a flag as a means of political protest. "National unity as an end which officials may foster by persuasion and example is not in question. The problem is whether under our Constitution compulsion as here employed is a permissible means for its achievement."

We are fortified in today's conclusion by our conviction that forbidding criminal punishment for conduct such as Johnson's will not endanger the special role played by our flag or the feelings it inspires....

We are tempted to say, in fact, that the flag's deservedly cherished place in our community will be strengthened, not weakened, by our holding today. Our decision is a reaffirmation of the principles of freedom and inclusiveness that the flag best reflects, and of the conviction that our toleration of criticism such as Johnson's is a sign and source of our strength. Indeed, one of the proudest images of our flag, the one immortalized in our own national anthem, is of the bombardment it survived at Fort McHenry. It is the Nation's resilience, not its rigidity, that Texas sees reflected in the flag—and it is that resilience that we reassert today.

The way to preserve the flag's special role is not to punish those who feel differently about these matters. It is to persuade them that they are wrong. "To courageous, self-reliant men, with confidence in the power of free and fearless reasoning applied through the processes of popular government, no danger flowing from speech can be deemed clear and present, unless the incidence of the evil apprehended is so imminent that it may befall before there is opportunity for full discussion. If there be time to expose through discussion the falsehood and fallacies, to avert the evil by the processes of education, the remedy to be applied is more speech, not enforced silence." And, precisely because it is our flag that is involved, one's response to the flag burner may exploit the uniquely persuasive power of the flag itself. We can imagine no more appropriate response to burning a flag than waving one's own, no better way to counter a flag burner's message than by saluting the flag that burns, no surer means of preserving the dignity even of the flag that burned than by—as one witness here did—according its remains a respectful burial. We do not consecrate the flag by punishing its desecration, for in doing so we dilute the freedom that this cherished emblem represents.

## V

Johnson was convicted for engaging in expressive conduct. The State's interest in preventing breaches of the peace does not support his conviction because Johnson's conduct did not threaten to disturb the peace. Nor does the State's interest in preserving the flag as a symbol of nationhood and national unity justify his criminal conviction for engaging in political expression. The judgment of the Texas Court of Criminal Appeals is therefore

*Affirmed.*

JUSTICE KENNEDY, concurring.

I write not to qualify the words JUSTICE BRENNAN chooses so well, for he says with power all that is necessary to explain our ruling. I join his opinion without reservation, but with a keen sense that this case, like others before us from time to time, exacts its personal toll. This prompts me to add to our pages these few remarks.

   \*   \*   \*

Our colleagues in dissent advance powerful arguments why respondent may be convicted for his expression, reminding us that among those who will be dismayed by our holding will be some who have had the singular honor of carrying the flag in battle. And I agree that the flag holds a lonely place of honor in an age when absolutes are distrusted and simple truths are burdened by unneeded apologetics.

With all respect to those views, I do not believe the Constitution gives us the right to rule as the dissenting Members of the Court urge, however painful this judgment is to announce. Though symbols often are what we ourselves make of them, the flag is constant in expressing beliefs Americans share, beliefs in law and peace and that freedom which sustains the human spirit. The case here today forces recognition of the costs to which those beliefs commit us. It is poignant but fundamental that the flag protects those who hold it in contempt.

For all the record shows, this respondent was not a philosopher and perhaps did not even possess the ability to comprehend how repellent his statements must be to the Republic itself. But whether or not he could appreciate the enormity of the offense he gave, the fact remains that his acts were speech, in both the technical and the fundamental meaning of the Constitution. So I agree with the Court that he must go free.

   \*   \*   \*

[The dissenting opinion of CHIEF JUSTICE REHNQUIST is omitted]

JUSTICE STEVENS, dissenting.

As the Court analyzes this case, it presents the

question whether the State of Texas, or indeed the Federal Government, has the power to prohibit the public desecration of the American flag. The question is unique. In my judgment rules that apply to a host of other symbols, such as state flags, armbands, or various privately promoted emblems of political or commercial identity, are not necessarily controlling. Even if flag burning could be considered just another species of symbolic speech under the logical application of the rules that the Court has developed in its interpretation of the First Amendment in other contexts, this case has an intangible dimension that makes those rules inapplicable.

A country's flag is a symbol of more than "nationhood and national unity." It also signifies the ideas that characterize the society that has chosen that emblem as well as the special history that has animated the growth and power of those ideas. . . .

So it is with the American flag. It is more than a proud symbol of the courage, the determination, and the gifts of nature that transformed 13 fledgling Colonies into a world power. It is a symbol of freedom, of equal opportunity, of religious tolerance, and of good will for other peoples who share our aspirations. The symbol carries its message to dissidents both at home and abroad who may have no interest at all in our national unity or survival.

The value of the flag as a symbol cannot be measured. Even so, I have no doubt that the interest in preserving that value for the future is both significant and legitimate. Conceivably that value will be enhanced by the Court's conclusion that our national commitment to free expression is so strong that even the United States as ultimate guarantor of that freedom is without power to prohibit the desecration of its unique symbol. But I am unpersuaded. . . . [I]n my considered judgment, sanctioning the public desecration of the flag will tarnish its value—both for those who cherish the ideas for which it waves and for those who desire to don the robes of martyrdom by burning it. . . .

It is appropriate to emphasize certain propositions that are not implicated by this case. The statutory prohibition of flag desecration does not "prescribe what shall be orthodox in politics, nationalism, religion, or other matters of opinion or force citizens to confess by word or act their faith therein." The statute does not compel any conduct or any profession of respect for any idea or any symbol.

\*          \*          \*

The Court is therefore quite wrong in blandly asserting that respondent "was prosecuted for his expression of dissatisfaction with the policies of this country, expression situated at the core of our First Amendment values." Respondent was prosecuted because of the method he chose to express his dissatisfaction with those policies. Had he chosen to spray-

paint—or perhaps convey with a motion picture projector—his message of dissatisfaction on the facade of the Lincoln Memorial, there would be no question about the power of the Government to prohibit his means of expression. The prohibition would be supported by the legitimate interest in preserving the quality of an important national asset. Though the asset at stake in this case is intangible, given its unique value, the same interest supports a prohibition on the desecration of the American flag.

## 409 "The Defendant Noriega is plainly a prisoner of war" (1990)

Those reaching the shores of the United States are frequently accompanied by an unsavory record in their former homelands. While some arrivals might be political offenders who formerly fought oppressive regimes and seek political shelter and asylum in America, others might indeed be deposed tyrants, Nazi concentration camp operators, or organized crime leaders. The Noriega document illustrates the difficulties in sorting out the status of those voluntarily entering, or forcefully brought, into the United States.

Since its 1843 extradition treaty with France (Doc. 102), the United States has adhered to the principle that as a "host" nation, it could properly refuse to extradite to a demanding country any person wanted for trial for a political offense. Nations, however, can often disagree as to the political nature of an offense or offender.

On Valentine's Day, 1988, a United States federal grand jury indicted General Manuel Antonio Noriega, commander of the Panamanian Defense Forces and de facto head of the Panamanian government, for his participation in an international drug conspiracy affecting the United States. After Panama refused to extradite General Noriega, United States troops invaded Panama on December 20, 1988, and after extensive military operations managed to capture Noriega and spirit him to the United States to face trial on the charges in a Florida federal court.

Under principles of international and United States law, Noriega raised questions about the jurisdiction of the United States court to try him. He first claimed that as the de facto head of the government of Panama, he was immune from prosecution. Second, he argued that since he was a prisoner of war, the Third Geneva Convention of 1949 prevented the court from hearing his case. Third, he urged that the court find that his kidnapping by armed forces was unlawful, which would require the court to order him repatriated.

The first argument was rejected in Document 409a, when the court decided that, even assuming that the Third Geneva Convention applied, it did not divest the court of jurisdiction to try Noriega on an extraditable offense. After his conviction, however, the court did conclude in Document 409b that he was indeed a prisoner of war and entitled to certain rights under the Third Geneva Convention of 1949. The court's rejection of Noriega's third claim foreshadowed the subsequent decision of the Supreme Court (in *United States v. Alvarez-Machain*, 112 S.Ct. 2188 (1992)), that the existence of an extradition treaty did not prevent officers of the United States from forcibly kidnapping a wanted person from foreign soil to face charges.

## ☆409  The Noriega Case

☆409a  *United States v. Noriega*

746 F. Supp. 1506 (S.D. Fla. 1990).

HOEVELER, J.

*          *          *

### II. SOVEREIGN IMMUNITY

The Court next turns to Noriega's assertion that he is immune from prosecution based on head of state immunity, the act of state doctrine, and diplomatic immunity.

#### A. Head of State Immunity

Grounded in customary international law, the doctrine of head of state immunity provides that a head of state is not subject to the jurisdiction of foreign courts, at least as to official acts taken during the ruler's term of office. The rationale behind the doctrine is to promote international comity and respect among sovereign nations by ensuring that leaders are free to perform their governmental duties without being subject to detention, arrest, or embarrassment in a foreign country's legal system.

In order to assert head of state immunity, a government official must be recognized as a head of state. Noriega has never been recognized as Panama's Head of State either under the Panamanian Constitution or by the United States. . . . [T]he Panamanian Constitution provides for an executive branch composed of the President and Ministers of State, neither of which applies to Noriega. Officially, Noriega is the *Commandante* of the Panamanian Defense Forces, but he was never elected to head Panama's government and in fact abrogated the Panamanian presidential elections of May 7, 1989. More importantly, the United States government has never accorded Noriega head of state status, but rather continued to recognize President Eric Arturo Delvalle as the legitimate leader of Panama while Noriega was in power. As this Court held in a previous case involving the Republic of Panama, the Executive's decision to recognize President Delvalle

and not the Defendant as Panama's head of state is binding on the Court. . . .

Aside from the fact that neither Panama nor the United States recognizes Noriega as a head of state. . . . [h]e nonetheless argues that he is entitled to head of state immunity as the *de facto* ruler of Panama, "regardless of the source of his power or the nature of his rule." The defendant cites numerous newspaper reports and excerpts of congressional testimony to the effect that Noriega effectively controlled Panama. In fact, this Court has previously acknowledged that, despite the official recognition of Delvalle, Noriega was the *de facto* head of Panama's government. But simply because Noriega may have in fact run the country of Panama does not mean he is entitled to head of state immunity. . . .

[T]o hold that immunity from prosecution must be granted "regardless of his source of power or nature of rule" would allow illegitimate dictators the benefit of their unscrupulous and possibly brutal seizures of power. No authority exists for such a novel extension of head of state immunity, and the Court declines to create one here. Since the United States has never recognized General Noriega as Panama's head of state, he has no claim to head of state immunity.

#### B. The Act of State Doctrine

Noriega next argues that the act of state doctrine prohibits the Court from adjudicating the legality of his official actions in Panama.

*          *          *

Although stated in terms of acts of the "State" or "sovereign," the doctrine also extends to governmental acts of State officials vested with sovereign authority.

*          *          *

In order for the act of state doctrine to apply, the defendant must establish that his activities are "acts of state," i.e., that they were taken on behalf of the state and not, as private acts, on behalf of the actor himself.

*          *          *

The Court fails to see how Noriega's alleged drug trafficking and protection of money launderers could conceivably constitute public action taken on behalf of the Panamanian state. . . . The indictment in this case charges a series of private acts committed by the defendant for his own personal financial enrichment. It does not allege, and cannot reasonably be construed to charge, that Noriega participated in a racketeering enterprise and conspired to import cocaine into the United States in furtherance of Panama's state policy or to serve some overriding national interest. The fact that Noriega is alleged to have utilized his official position to engage in criminal activity does not, as Defendant suggests, cast his actions in a public light; as we well know, government officials are as capable of exploiting their positions of power for private, selfish ends as they are for public purpose. The inquiry is not whether Noriega used his official position to engage in the challenged acts, but whether those acts were taken on behalf of Noriega instead of Panama.

Defendant does little more than state that, as the de facto ruler of Panama, his actions constitute acts of state. This sweeping position completely ignores the public/private distinction and suggests that government leaders are, as such, incapable of engaging in private, unofficial conduct.

\*      \*      \*

Yet another consideration counsels against application of the act of state doctrine to this case. Although originally couched in terms of sovereign immunity, the doctrine as presently developed does not rest on principles of international law or respect for sovereign independence. More recent interpretations of the doctrine instead emphasize the separation of powers rationale—more specifically, the need to preclude judicial encroachment in the field of [U.S.] foreign policy and international diplomacy. In questioning the validity of acts of foreign states, the judiciary may well hinder the Executive's conduct of foreign affairs and the need to speak with one voice on the world stage. No such danger is present here and in fact the opposite is true since the Executive's position is amply demonstrated by its decision to indict and prosecute the defendant.

\*      \*      \*

### C. Diplomatic Immunity

\*      \*      \*

In light of his failure to satisfy the conventional requirements for diplomatic status, Noriega relies principally on the fact that he traveled on a Panamanian diplomatic passport and was on three occasions granted an "A-2" visa by the United States. In the first place, issuance of the Panamanian diplomatic passport is a matter solely of Panamanian law and has no effect on its holder's status in another state. Though diplomatic passports issued by Panama to reflect the esteem which that nation assigned to Defendant may have obtained Noriega certain courtesies in international travel, they are without significance in international law and United States law and do not, by themselves, entitle Noriega to any internationally or domestically protected status.

Nor does the "A-2" visa establish anything of significance in the way of diplomatic immunity. The issuance of United States visas is an administrative action in connection with United States immigration law and is quite independent of the process of diplomatic accreditation. . . .

In other words, mere possession of an "A-2" visa

does not confer diplomatic immunity; other criteria, none of which are satisfied here, must be met.

\*      \*      \*

### ☆409b  *United States v. Noriega*

808 F. Supp. 791 (S.D. Fla. 1992).

HOEVELER, J.

\*      \*      \*

Before the Court are several questions, but the ultimate one appears to be whether or not the Geneva Convention prohibits incarceration in a federal penitentiary for a prisoner of war convicted of common crimes against the United States.

\*      \*      \*

### II. APPLICABILITY OF GENEVA III

Geneva III [Geneva Convention Relative to the Treatment of Prisoners of War, August 12, 1949, 6 U.S.T.S. No. 3364, 75 U.N.T.S. 135] is an international treaty designed to protect prisoners of war from inhumane treatment at the hands of their captors. Regardless of whether it is legally enforceable under the present circumstances, the treaty is undoubtedly a valid international agreement and "the law of the land" in the United States. As such, Geneva III applies to any POW captured and detained by the United States, and the U.S. government has—at minimum—an international obligation to uphold the treaty. In addition, this Court believes Geneva III is self-executing and provides General Noriega with a right of action in a U.S. court for violation of its provisions.

#### A. NORIEGA'S PRISONER OF WAR STATUS

The government has thus far obviated the need for a formal determination of General Noriega's status. . . [But a]t no time was it agreed that he was, in fact, a prisoner of war. . . .

#### Article 2

[T]he present Convention shall apply to all cases of declared war or of *any other armed conflict which may arise between two or more of the High Contracting Parties, even if the state of war is not recognized by one of them.*

The Convention shall also apply to all cases of partial or total occupation of the territory of a High Contracting Party . . . . (emphasis added [in original])

The government has characterized the deployment of U.S. Armed Forces to Panama on December 20, 1989 as the "hostilities" in Panama. However the government wishes to label it, what occurred in late 1989-early 1990 was clearly an "armed conflict" within the meaning of Article 2. Armed troops intervened in a conflict between two parties to the treaty.

\*      \*      \*

## Article 4

A. Prisoners of war, in the sense of the present Convention, are persons belonging to one of the following categories, who have fallen into the power of the enemy:

(1) Members of the armed forces of a Party to the conflict . . . .

Geneva III's definition of a POW is easily broad enough to encompass General Noriega. It is not disputed that he was the head of the PDF, and that he has "fallen into the power of the enemy." Subsection 3 of Article 4 states that captured military personnel are POWs even if they "profess allegiance to a government or an authority not recognized by the Detaining Power."

## Article 5

The present Convention shall apply to the persons referred to in Article 4 from the time they fall into the power of the enemy and until their final release and repatriation.

Should any doubt arise as to whether persons, having committed a belligerent act and having fallen into the hands of the enemy, belong to any of the categories enumerated in Article 4, such persons shall enjoy the protection of the present Convention until such time as their status has been determined by a competent tribunal.

An important issue raised by the last two words of Article 5 is, of course, what *is* a "competent tribunal"?

\*          \*          \*

[T]he Court feels and so determines it has the authority to decide the status issue presented. This is not to say that the Executive branch cannot determine this issue under other circumstances. The Court does suggest that where the Court is properly presented with the problem it is, under the law, a "competent tribunal" which can decide the issue. With that in mind, the Court finds that General Noriega is in fact a prisoner of war as defined by Geneva III, and as such must be afforded the protections established by the treaty, regardless of the type of facility in which the Bureau of Prisons chooses to incarcerate him.

### B. "LAW OF THE LAND"

The Geneva Convention applies to this case because it has been incorporated into the domestic law of the United States. A treaty becomes the "supreme law of the land" upon ratification by the United States Senate. Geneva III was ratified by a unanimous Senate vote on July 6, 1955. Thus, Geneva III is a properly ratified treaty which the United States must uphold. The government acknowledges that Geneva III is "the law of the land," but questions whether that law is binding and enforceable in U.S. courts.

### C. ENFORCEMENT

If the BOP [United States Bureau of Prisons] fails to treat Noriega according to the standard established for prisoners of war in Geneva III, what can he do to force the government to comply with the mandates of the treaty?

#### 1. Article 78 Right of Protest

There are potentially two enforcement avenues available to a POW who feels his rights under the Geneva Convention have been violated. The first is the right to complain about the conditions of confinement to the military authorities of the Detaining Power or to representatives of the Protecting Power [a neutral state monitoring treaty compliance] or humanitarian organizations. This right is established in Article 78 of Geneva III, and cannot be renounced by the POW or revoked or unnecessarily limited by the Detaining Power.

\*          \*          \*

In theory, by calling attention to violations of the Convention the prisoner of war will embarrass the government into rectifying any unacceptable conditions to which he is being subjected. However, the obvious weakness of this complaint procedure is that it has no real teeth. Incentive for the government to comply with the treaty stems from its eagerness to be looked upon favorably by others, and, it is hoped, from its desire simply to do what is proper under the circumstances. However, if we truly believe in the goals of the Convention, a more substantial and dependable method must also be available, if necessary, to protect the POW's rights. Recourse to the courts of the Detaining Power seems an appropriate measure, where available.

#### 2. Legal Action . . . in U.S. Court

A second method of enforcing the Convention would be a legal action in federal court. . . . However, the government also argues that Geneva III is not self-executing, and thus does not provide an individual the right to bring an action in a U.S. court.

\*          \*          \*

Essentially, a self-executing treaty is one that becomes domestic law of the signatory nation without implementing legislation, and provides a private right of action to individuals alleging a breach of its provisions. . . . [T]he courts have generally presumed treaties to be non-self-executing in the absence of express language to the contrary. . . .

\*          \*          \*

In the case of Geneva III, however, it is inconsistent with both the language and spirit of the treaty . . . to find that the rights established therein cannot be enforced by the individual POW in a court of law. After all, the ultimate goal of Geneva III is to ensure humane treatment of POWs—not to create some amorphous, unenforceable code of honor among the signatory nations. "It must not be forgotten that the Conventions have been drawn up first and foremost to protect individuals, and not to serve State interests."

\*      \*      \*

### III. CONTROLLING PROVISIONS OF GENEVA III

The Court's final task is to determine which provisions of Geneva III are relevant to an individual who is both a prisoner of war and a convicted felon. While these characteristics are not mutually exclusive, the combination of the two in one person creates a novel and somewhat complicated situation with respect to the application of Geneva III.

\*      \*      \*

### B. ARTICLE 108

The government has argued that the Geneva Convention "explicitly and unambiguously" authorizes the BOP to incarcerate Noriega in a penitentiary, so long as he is not treated more harshly than would be a member of the U.S. armed forces convicted of a similar offense.

\*      \*      \*

Paragraph one of Article 108 reads:

Sentences announced on prisoners of war after a conviction has become duly enforceable, shall be served in the same establishments and under the same conditions as in the case of members of the armed forces of the Detaining Power. These conditions shall in all cases conform to the requirements of health and humanity.

Pursuant, then, to paragraph one it appears that General Noriega could technically be incarcerated in a federal penitentiary without violating the Geneva Convention. However, this should not be the end of the inquiry. The real issue is whether federal penitentiaries in general or any particular federal penitentiary can afford a prisoner of war the various protections due him under the Geneva Convention.

Article 108 requires that the conditions in any facility in which a POW serves his sentence "shall in all cases conform to the requirements of health and humanity...."

In addition, Article 108 dictates that the POW must be allowed to "receive and despatch [British spelling] correspondence, to receive at least one relief parcel monthly, to take regular exercise in the open air, to have the medical care required by [his] state of health, and the spiritual assistance [he] may desire." Many of these terms are vague. For exam-

ple, what is "regular" exercise? Reasonable people may differ on what these provisions require. However, given the United States' asserted commitment to protecting POWs and promoting respect for the laws of armed conflict through liberal interpretation of the Geneva Conventions, vague or ambiguous terms should always be construed in the light most favorable to the prisoner of war.

### C. OTHER APPLICABLE ARTICLES

\*      \*      \*

The government concedes that the three Articles cited within the text of Article 108—78 *[supra]*, 87, and 126—also apply to General Noriega.

Paragraph three of Article 87 prohibits collective punishment for individual acts, corporal punishment, imprisonment in premises without daylight and, in general, any form of torture or cruelty. Again, some of these terms are vague, but because of the U.S. commitment to construing the Geneva Conventions liberally, and because it is imperative that the United States set a good example in its treatment of POWs, ambiguous terms must be construed in the light most favorable to the POW.

Article 126 creates an almost unrestricted grant of authority for representatives of the Protecting Power and international humanitarian organizations to supervise the treatment of POWs wherever and in whatever type of facility they may be held.

The government argues that Article 108's reference to Articles 78, 87, and 126 is an express limitation on Noriega's rights—that these are the *only* Articles that apply to POWs incarcerated for common crimes. Defendant counters that 108 is just a floor, so while POWs may not be treated worse than U.S. soldiers convicted of similar crimes, frequently they must be treated better. Noriega asserts that Article 108 must be read in conjunction with Article 85 which states that "prisoners of war prosecuted under the laws of the Detaining Power for acts committed prior to capture shall retain, *even if convicted,* the benefits of the present Convention" (emphasis added) [in original].

The [International Committee of the Red Cross] Commentary [on the Geneva Conventions] supports Noriega's position that he continues to be entitled to the Convention's general protections:

[T]he Convention affords important safeguards to prisoners of war confined following a judicial sentence. Some of these safeguards result from general provisions applicable to all the conditions relating to internment, such as Article 13 (humane treatment), Article 14 (respect for the person of prisoners . . .), Article 16 (equality of treatment). Other provisions refer expressly to the execution of penalties and specifically prohibit cruelty, any attack on a prisoner's honour (Article

87), and discriminatory treatment (Article 88). . . . Confinement does not involve any suppression of the principal safeguards afforded to prisoners of war by the present Convention, and the number of provisions rendered inapplicable by the fact of . . . confinement is therefore small. . . . In fact, these articles [78, 87, 126] are *among the provisions* which are not rendered inapplicable by confinement. *Because of their greater importance, however, . . . special reference was made to them.* (emphasis added) [in original]

It thus appears that a convicted POW is entitled to the basic protections of Geneva III for as long as he remains in the custody of the Detaining Power. Throughout the Commentary to Article 108, reference is made to Articles other than the three specifically named in the text. The logical conclusion is that judicial confinement serves to abrogate only those protections fundamentally inconsistent with incarceration.

*      *      *

In addition, the Court would once again note that the stated U.S. policy is to err to the benefit of the POW. In order to set the proper example and avoid diminishing the trust and respect of other nations, the U.S. government must honor its policy by placing General Noriega in a facility that can provide the full panoply of protections to which he is entitled under the Convention.

## IV. Conclusion

Considerable space has been taken to set forth conclusions which could have been stated in one or two pages. That is because of the potential importance of the question to so many and the precedentially uncharted course it spawned. The Defendant Noriega is plainly a prisoner of war under the Geneva Convention III. He is, and will be, entitled to the full range of rights under the treaty, which has been incorporated into U.S. law. Nonetheless, he can serve his sentence in a civilian prison to be designated by the Attorney General or the Bureau of Prisons . . . so long as he is afforded the full benefits of the Convention.

Whether or not those rights can be fully provided in a maximum security penitentiary setting is open to serious question. For the time being, however, that question must be answered by those who will determine Defendant's place and type of confinement. In this determination, those charged with that responsibility must keep in mind the importance to our own troops of faithful and, indeed, liberal adherence to the mandates of Geneva III. Regardless of how the government views the Defendant as a person, the implications of a failure to adhere to the Convention are too great to justify departures.

In the turbulent course of international events—the violence, deceit, and tragedies which capture the news, the relatively obscure issues in this case may seem unimportant. They are not. The implications of a less-than-strict adherence to Geneva III are serious and must temper any consideration of the questions presented.

*Done and Ordered*

## 410 "keep the flags flying" (1990-1996)

The flag folded by the main army of the Confederate States of America at Appomattox Courthouse (the site of the surrender of the Army of Northern Virginia), popularly called the "Stars and Bars," symbolizes the rebellious cause of the Confederate states and is revered by many because of its historical connections. Nevertheless, in modern times this flag has become a symbol of racial bigotry owing to its association with the Ku Klux Klan, the skinheads, and the American Nazi Party.

The state of Alabama raised the Confederate flag over its capitol in 1961, in honor of the hundredth anniversary of the Civil War. The Stars and Bars flew again in 1963, to show Governor George Wallace's determination to face down Attorney General Robert Kennedy over the issue of school desegregation. The Confederate flag still flies over Montgomery, despite the legal efforts of groups who want the symbol furled forever.

Meanwhile, a similar message was sent, in the spring of 1962, pursuant to a resolution of the all-white South Carolina General Assembly, when the Confederate flag was raised over the State House in Columbia, South Carolina, in commemoration of the Civil War Centennial. This addition to the flagpole, under the United States and the South Carolina flags, served as a powerful reminder to those still fighting against segregation and racism.

Black legislators and others offended by this symbol have challenged its continued flying with the flags of the state and federal governments over the State House dome. Others stoutly defend it as a fitting memorial to the courage of Confederate soldiers, which the South Carolina legislature recently affirmed. On May 29, 1996, two days before Memorial Day (a holiday honoring Union Civil War dead, which until recently was not officially observed in South Carolina), a white worker from out of state took matters into his own hands. While on a break from the reconstruction project on the State House, he tore and burned part of the objectionable symbol.

## ☆410  The Stars and Bars Forever?

☆410a  *National Association for the Advancement of Colored People v. Hunt*

891 F.2d 1555 (11th Cir. 1990).

JOHNSON, Circuit Judge

\*                    \*                    \*

### I. STATEMENT OF THE CASE

For some twenty years the confederate flag has flown atop the capitol dome in Montgomery, Alabama. At present, there are three flags flying on a single pole above the dome: the United States flag on top, the Alabama state flag second, and the confederate flag at the bottom.

There is no state statute authorizing or mandating the flying of the confederate flag. Alabama raised the flag on two occasions. The flag was raised in 1961 during the administration of Governor John Patterson for the purpose of commemorating the 100th anniversary of the Civil War. The flag was raised again on the morning of April 25, 1963, the day that United States Attorney General Robert F. Kennedy travelled to Montgomery to discuss with then-Governor George Wallace the governor's announced intention to block the admission of the first black students to the University of Alabama. Regardless of the reason, it is undisputed that the flying of the flag atop the capitol dome has caused much controversy.

\*                    \*                    \*

On May 20, 1988, the NAACP filed suit in the Middle District of Alabama against Governor Guy Hunt, Chief of Capitol Services Cecil Humphrey, and Director of Finance Robin Swift ("the state") seeking a declaratory judgment that the flying of the flag atop the Alabama capitol dome violates [federal law] and the First, Thirteenth, and Fourteenth Amendments to the Constitution. The NAACP sought injunctive relief requiring the state to remove the flag from the capitol and prohibiting the state from displaying the flag on capitol grounds.

\*                    \*                    \*

### II. ANALYSIS

\*                    \*                    \*

#### B. STATUTORY AND CONSTITUTIONAL CLAIMS

##### 1. Civil Rights Violations

a. Claims Raised in District Court

In order to state a cause of action . . . the NAACP must prove: (1) that the confederate flag is flown by individuals acting under the cloak of state authority and (2) that the flying of the flag deprives them of some right, privilege, or immunity secured by the Constitution or by law.

There is no dispute regarding the "under color of state law" requirement. It seems clear that a flag flown on the state capitol dome is flown under state authority. The parties dispute, however, the question of whether the NAACP has been deprived of any rights. . . . The NAACP apparently argued that the flying of the flag was "tantamount to holding public property for racially discriminatory purposes" and that it denied its members their rights to equal education, equal economic opportunity, and equal protection. Presumably the NAACP makes these claims under the Fourteenth Amendment.

Certainly the NAACP has a right to equal protection of the laws, in education and otherwise. The Fourteenth Amendment prohibits states from denying to anyone the equal protection of the laws. As the Supreme Court has stated, however, the Amendment requires equal laws, not equal results. It is true, as the NAACP points out, that a racially motivated statute may be unconstitutional even if it is facially neutral. Because there are two accounts of why Alabama flies the flag, however, it is not certain that the flag was hoisted for racially discriminatory reasons. Moreover, there is no unequal application of the state policy; all citizens are exposed to the flag. Citizens of all races are offended by its position.

Further, the NAACP has advanced many discrimination suits in federal and state courts over the 25 years since the flag was raised. Yet it has never requested that the flag be brought down as part of the equitable relief requested in any of those cases. In *Smith v. St. Tammany Parish School Bd.*, the Fifth Circuit upheld an order banning "symbols or indicia expressing the school board's or its employee's desire to maintain segregated schools. . . ." The *Smith* decision, however, was based upon the broad discretion vested in the district courts to achieve the constitutional end of desegregation. There is no legal basis for prohibiting the flying of a confederate flag on government grounds outside the realm of desegregation effort. The NAACP did not ask that the flag be removed in conjunction with desegregation attempts or other civil rights actions.

These are the only arguments advanced by the NAACP in support of their claim that the flag infringes on a protected right in violation of [the law]. When a non-movant produces no specific factual proof in support of an essential element of its case, summary judgment is appropriate.

\*                    \*                    \*

##### 2. Thirteenth Amendment Violations

The Thirteenth Amendment forbids slavery or involuntary servitude. The amendment also gives Congress the authority to enforce the prohibition by appropriate legislation. Part of this authority is the authority to legislate to eradicate badges and incidents of slavery. The NAACP's sole argument in support of its claim that the state has violated the Thirteenth Amendment is that the confederate flag, because of its inspirational power in the confederate army during the Civil War and its adoption by the Ku Klux Klan, is a "badge and vestige of slavery." Standing alone, the Thirteenth Amendment does not forbid the badges and incidents of slavery. Congress has not utilized its Thirteenth Amendment enforcement authority to pass legislation forbidding the flying of the confederate flag as a badge or incident of slavery. Because the flying of the confederate flag is not forbidden by federal statute, summary judgment was properly granted.

### 3. First Amendment Violations

\*             \*             \*

b. Free Speech

The First Amendment prohibits governments from abridging free speech. The NAACP argues that the flying of the flag violates the Free Speech Clause in two ways. First it argues that the presence of the flag chills free speech, as evidenced by appellant Reed's testimony that he has difficulty saluting the American flag atop the capitol while the confederate flag flies. The flag may indeed cause such discomfort, but there is no statute or ordinance, federal or state, absolutely prohibiting Reed or the other NAACP members from saluting the American flag. There is no threat of persecution or prosecution if they salute the American flag. Only Reed's own emotions make his speech difficult. Even the NAACP admits that "the question of whether feelings are hurt or whether speech has been chilled by government action is a question not of law, but of social sensitivity." The federal judiciary is not empowered to make decisions based on social sensitivity. Because the NAACP has advanced no proof that the flag prohibits its members from speaking or punishes them for speaking, the district court properly granted summary judgment.

Second, the NAACP argues that the flag is government speech which improperly communicates a limited set of messages. As one commentator has noted, "free speech theory has focused on the government as censor; it has had little to say about the process by which the government adds its voice to the market place." Indeed, the First Amendment protects citizens' speech only from government regulation; government speech itself is not protected by the First Amendment.

Restrictions on government speech seem to spring from one ideal: "If there is any fixed star in our constitutional constellation, it is that no official, high or petty, can prescribe what shall be orthodox in politics, nationalism, religion, or other matters of opinion or force citizens to confess by word or act

their faith therein." There are three ways in which the government's attempts to prescribe orthodoxy have been restricted. First, the government may not abridge "equality of status in the field of ideas" by granting the use of public forums to those whose views it finds acceptable while denying their use to those with controversial views. This concern is especially important when the government's dedication of a forum suppresses controversial or political speech. Second, the government may not monopolize the "marketplace of ideas," thus drowning out private sources of speech. For example, the government may not confer radio frequency monopolies on broadcasters it prefers. Finally, the government may not "compel persons to support candidates, parties, ideologies or causes that they are against." For instance, state citizens may not be compelled to use car license plates carrying messages with which they disagree.

None of these restrictions, however, is directly applicable to the present situation. The capitol dome is not public property which "by tradition or designation [is] a forum for public communication." Thus, the state may reserve the dome for its own communicative purposes as long as that reservation is reasonable and is not an effort to suppress expression because the public officials oppose the speaker's view. There is no evidence that the dome is reserved to the state in order to suppress controversial speech. Neither does the flag represent government monopolization of the marketplace of ideas.

Government communication is legitimate as long as the government does not abridge an individual's "First Amendment right to avoid becoming the courier for such message." The government of Alabama does not compel its citizens to carry or post the flag themselves, or to support whatever cause it may represent. It might appear problematic at first glance that the state is using the NAACP's tax dollars to raise and maintain the flag, and thus is forcing them to contribute to a cause repugnant to them. The Supreme Court has held [in *Abood v. Detroit Board of Education*] that union members cannot be compelled to pay dues which support causes disagreeable to them. *Abood* has never been applied to the government, however; if it were, taxation would become impossible. Neither does the state force citizens to salute the confederate flag. There is no statute, ordinance, or policy requiring citizens to salute any of the flags atop the capitol. A person may choose to salute the American flag, but such a choice does not force the individual to salute the confederate flag; the salutes are separate and distinct.

It is unfortunate that the State of Alabama chooses to utilize its property in a manner that offends a large proportion of its population, but that is a political matter which is not within our province to decide. The remedy for such a grievance lies within the democratic processes of the State of Alabama and the voting rights of all its citizens, "the restraints on which the people must often rely solely, in all representative governments."

*            *            *

☆410b  Worker Fired for Burning Flag

Lee Bandy, *The State* (Columbia, S.C.), May 31, 1996, B1.

A State House construction worker has been fired for climbing the scaffold-shrouded dome, ripping off a corner of the Confederate battle flag, carrying it to the ground and burning it.

His name was not released.

"He was an employee from the labor pool and not a permanent employee," said Louise Majors, spokeswoman for the state Budget and Control Board, which is overseeing the renovation of the State House.

She said the torn flag was immediately replaced with a new banner.

Caddell Construction Co., based in Montgomery, Ala., is obligated under its contract with the state to keep the flags flying while it restores the century-old State House, inside and outside.

Jimmy Lewis, project manager, said the fired worker violated several regulations during the Wednesday incident. He was in an area he wasn't supposed to be in, he destroyed property, and he burned material on site.

"It wouldn't have mattered to us if he had burned a 2-by-4, he would have been fired," Lewis said.

State Sen. Darrell Jackson, D-Richland, who has advocated bringing the flag down under a compromise arrangement, said he did not support what the worker did. "It might have hurt our efforts to resolve this matter peacefully," he said.

The flag-burning, Jackson noted, took place the same day the Senate voted 46-0 to authorize an African-American heritage memorial on the State House grounds and establish a [Civil War] museum.

"We showed that working together, we can achieve some things," he said.

*            *            *

# 411  "resisting those 'alien forces from Houston, Tokyo, Washington, D.C., and the Pentagon'" (1991)

In 1975, Edward Abbey, the award-winning author of *Desert Solitaire*, published *The Monkey Wrench Gang*, a romanticized novel of the exploits of four "eco-saboteurs," or "ecoteurs," who set out to defend the environment from corporate and government despoliation through their own campaign of vandalism and destruction. The book mirrored the activi-

ties of such real life environmental militants as "the Fox" of Chicago, the "Billboard Bandits" of Michigan, and the "Eco-Commandoes" in Florida.

Frustrated by the ineffectiveness of the mainstream environmental protection movement and dissatisfied by the environmental policies espoused by the Reagan administration, Dave Foreman, a former lobbyist for the Wilderness Society, helped co-found "Earth First!" in 1981. This new movement proclaimed its attitude with the slogan "No compromise in defense of Mother Earth." Although the movement (which has no "members") represents itself as being law-abiding, it encourages and inspires others to engage in "monkeywrenching." The philosophy advanced by Earth First! is that "what an individual does autonomously is his or her own business," but Foreman offered detailed instructions on how to commit ecotage in his publication *Ecodefense: A Field Guide to Monkeywrenching*.

Even though they claim not to endorse actions that are likely to be injurious to human life and security, Foreman and Earth First! have naturally been condemned as "ecoterrorists" by those threatened by their sabotage campaigns. One practice that has been particularly condemned is tree-spiking, which can result in grave physical injury to loggers and millworkers. Foreman articulates the rationale for monkeywrenching in general, and tree-spiking in particular, in his 1991 book *Confessions of an Ecowarrior*.

☆411  Monkeywrenching

Dave Foreman, *Confessions of an Ecowarrior* (New York: Harmony Books, 1991), 111-60.

THE PRINCIPLES OF MONKEYWRENCHING

*            *            *

*Monkeywrenching is individual.* Monkeywrenching is done by individuals or very small groups of people who have known each other for years. Trust and a good working relationship are essential in such groups. The more people involved, the greater the dangers of infiltration or a loose mouth. Monkeywrenchers avoid working with people they haven't known for a long time, those who can't keep their mouths closed, and those with grandiose or violent ideas (they may be police agents or dangerous crackpots).

*Monkeywrenching is targeted.* Ecodefenders pick their targets. Mindless, erratic vandalism is counterproductive as well as unethical. Monkeywrenchers know that they do not stop a specific logging sale by destroying any piece of logging equipment they come across. They make sure it belongs to the proper culprit. They ask themselves what is the most vulnerable point of a wilderness destroying project, and strike there. Senseless vandalism leads to loss of popular sympathy. . . . The Earth warrior always asks, Will monkeywrenching help or hinder the protection of this place?

*Monkeywrenching is dispersed.* Monkeywrenching is a widespread movement across the United States. Government agencies and wilderness despoilers from Maine to Hawaii know that their destruction of natural diversity may meet resistance. Nationwide monkeywrenching will hasten overall industrial retreat from wild areas.

\*            \*            \*

*Monkeywrenching is fun.* Although it is serious and potentially dangerous activity, monkeywrenching is also fun. There is a rush of excitement, a sense of accomplishment, and unparalleled camaraderie from creeping about in the night resisting those "alien forces from Houston, Tokyo, Washington, D.C., and the Pentagon." As Ed Abbey said, "Enjoy, shipmates, enjoy."

*Monkeywrenching is not revolutionary.* It does not aim to overthrow any social, political, or economic system. It is merely nonviolent self-defense of the wild. It is aimed at keeping industrial "civilization" out of natural areas and causing its retreat from areas that should be wild. It is not major industrial sabotage. Explosives, firearms, and other dangerous tools are usually avoided; they invite greater scrutiny from law enforcement agencies, repression, and loss of public support.

\*            \*            \*

*Monkeywrenching is deliberate and ethical.* Monkeywrenchers are very conscious of the gravity of what they do. They are deliberate about taking such a serious step. They are thoughtful, not cavalier. Monkeywrenchers—although nonviolent—are warriors. They are exposing themselves to possible arrest or injury. It is not a casual or flippant affair. They keep a pure heart and mind about it. They remember that they are engaged in the most moral of all actions: protecting life, defending Earth.

\*            \*            \*

IN DEFENSE OF MONKEYWRENCHING

\*            \*            \*

The arguments against monkeywrenching, and my responses, include the following:

\*            \*            \*

*Breaking the law is wrong.* There is not much room for negotiation between those who object, in principle, to breaking the laws of the state and those who believe that when higher values conflict with the laws of a political entity, one should break the laws. However, ecoteurs should carefully listen to this objection and not dismiss it out of hand. The law should *not* be broken for light or transient reasons.

If those who object to breaking the law under all circumstances were consistent, they would condemn the farmers of Lexington and Concord in 1775, as well as the demonstrators in Tiananmen Square in Beijing (which Henry Kissinger did, good ol' apologist for the supremacy of the state that he is), the Solidarity movement in Poland, Andrei Sakharov in the Soviet Union, the people of Romania who overthrew Ceausescu, and Nelson Mandela of South Africa.

Let us also remember that all of the resistance movements operating against the Nazis in Europe during World War II were acting illegally. Conversely, the Nazi atrocities were so completely legal that the allies had to write new laws hastily after World War II in order to prosecute Nazi war criminals at Nuremberg. There is obviously a difference between morality and the statutes of a government in power.

*Monkeywrenching is undemocratic, and imposes extremist beliefs on others.* An example of this argument would be, "The continued logging of ancient forests has been decided democratically through our political process. Once such a decision has been made, no one has the right to continue to oppose it, especially from outside of the law." This ignores evidence that our system is far from democratic—owing to the excessive power wielded by wealthy corporations to influence politicians through campaign donations and outright bribes, and through their advertising dollars in the media. It also ignores the fact that conservation groups, using the constitutional political process, have at times successfully halted timber sales by lawsuits in federal courts, only to have a few congressmen push legislation through Congress—without public hearings, committee hearings, or extensive debate—that prohibits citizens from challenging logging sales in the courts. Bureaucracies like the United States Forest Service are inherently undemocratic in promoting their own interests and their independence from public control.

\*            \*            \*

*Monkeywrenching threatens human beings with injury or death; it is "eco-terrorism."* Demagogues, whether editorial writers, politicians, or industry spokespersons, have found that this hysterical claim gets the most attention. This argument is directed most often against tree spiking, although it is also used against other forms of ecotage. The monkeywrencher must very carefully weigh the possibility of harm to a person from any ecotage, and must act to insure that no humans are hurt. *Ecodefense* constantly underscores this point and offers many safety suggestions—including the need for clear, direct warnings about spiked trees, [those into which] . . . large nails that can damage saws [are hammered] into trees slated to be logged. Contrary to the demagogues' claims, no one has been injured in any Monkeywrenching operation carried out by preservationists.

The true ecoterrorists are the planet-despoilers....

\*       \*       \*

*If you monkeywrench, you should take credit for your actions and accept punishment as one does for any act of civil disobedience.* Overlooked here are the fundamental differences between civil disobedience and monkeywrenching. The goal of civil disobedience in most cases is to reform society or some aspect thereof by conscientiously and nonviolently violating the law (as in a blockade), thereby appealing to the public and reasonably fair authorities with the rightness of one's cause and personal integrity. In other cases, it is to witness against evil being done, to refuse [to accept] projects destructive to nature. [Monkeywrenching thwarts destruction.] By carefully targeting logging equipment used against natural forests, ecodefenders drive up the cost of insurance for such operations. Some contractors nowadays refuse to bid on Forest Service road projects or timber sales in roadless areas because of the likelihood of damaged equipment and resulting cost overruns. Companies bidding on road construction for the Mount Graham Astronomical Observatory complex in Arizona doubled their bids because of fears of monkeywrenching and the need for round-the-clock security on site.

*Monkeywrenching gives the entire environmental movement a bad name and causes an antienvironmental backlash.* This may be the most complicated argument against monkeywrenching, and one of the most important to understand. In the larger picture, the backlash argument essentially says, "If your tactics or demands can be characterized as 'extremist,' you will besmirch those whose tactics or demands are more moderate, and you will cause a backlash that will overturn previous advances for your cause."

Dr. Martin Luther King, Jr., heard such warnings in 1955 when he began to organize civil-disobedience protests against discrimination and segregation in the South. Leaders of moderate civil-rights groups asked him not to rock the boat with excessive demands and confrontational tactics. They told him that although conditions were far from perfect, they were improved; if he asked for too much, or angered white racists, the modest gains since World War II would be rolled back. The threat of a backlash was also made by both the segregationist Southern establishment and racist poor white groups such as the Ku Klux Klan, and some carried out such threats against civil-rights workers with police brutality, murder, and assault. Fortunately, King and his compatriots had both a dream and the courage to pursue it. Had they listened to the nervous Nellies of the

moderate groups and to white racists, measures like the 1964 Civil Rights Act and the 1965 Voting Rights Act might never have been achieved.

\*       \*       \*

Let's move from defense to offense here, and consider some arguments *for* monkey wrenching. There are a number of basic arguments for ecological sabotage, several of which have solid precedents in American history and the ideas of Western civilization. You never know when you'll be called on to state your case.

\*       \*       \*

*To obtain protection denied us by a government that ignores the will of the people.* Public-opinion polls consistently demonstrate that the people want stronger protection of the environment—including clean air and water, control of toxics, protection of wilderness, forests, and wildlife—than the government will undertake. The reason for this is that our governments—local, state, and federal, including both elected officials and bureaucrats—are more influenced by corporations and a wealthy elite than by the people.

Furthermore, corporate America owns the electronic and print media, and thereby controls the presentation of the news. The advertising dollar makes some subjects taboo for news coverage and prevents presentation of effective critiques of corporate control....

Similarly, federal agencies such as the Forest Service and the Army Corps of Engineers twist environmental-reform legislation like the National Environmental Policy Act (NEPA) to their own ends. After twenty years of dealing with these agencies on projects that require formal public input and the preparation of an environmental impact statement before a decision is supposedly reached, I have seen an unbreakable pattern emerge: *Instead of using the planning process or the environmental-impact study as a tool of analysis to guide the agency to a management decision, it is used as a paper trail to justify a previously made in-house decision; instead of seeing public involvement as a means to gain outside expertise, it is seen as something to be manipulated so that it appears to support the agency decision* [emphasis in the original].

\*       \*       \*

*A political tactic.* Monkeywrenching can also be seen as a sophisticated political tactic that dramatizes ecological issues and places them before the public when they otherwise would be ignored in the media, applies pressure to resource-extraction corporations and government agencies that otherwise are able to resist "legitimate" pressure from law-abiding conservation organizations, and broadens the spectrum of environmental activism so that lobbying by mainstream groups is not considered "extremist."

Unlike the other defenses of monkeywrenching, this is not a basic defense, except in a Machiavellian sense, but is a means-to-an-end defense that complements the other defenses.

\*      \*      \*

*As a means of thwarting an unresponsive government.* Monkeywrenching is more than a collection of tools and techniques to damage machines and inhibit development. It can also be used to thwart the government and the industries that control it. America's founding fathers were believers in John Locke's characterization of government as an arrangement voluntarily entered into by free individuals in a state of nature for the common good. Modern historical and archaeological analysis presents a far different view of the emergence of the state and the nature of government from that articulated by Jefferson and Madison. These studies lead one to what I call the "Iron Law of Government": *The state, and all of its constituent elements, exists primarily to defend, with the use of lethal force if necessary, the power and status of the economic and philosophical establishment* [emphasis in the original]. This is not a statement of "ought"; it is simply one of "is."

Thus we are left with the strategy of monkeywrenching: Don't reform. Thwart. In addition to illegal ecotage, monkeywrenching can be thought of as a strategy that includes entirely legal techniques and that operates within the system, too—it is known as "paper monkeywrenching" in such cases.

\*      \*      \*

[RESPONSIBLE TREESPIKING]

The Compensation Board of British Columbia reports that in the period 1971-80 there were 175 fatalities, an average of seventeen per year, from field logging. Mill accidents also killed many people. In the state of Washington during 1988 there were twenty-eight fatalities in logging accidents. Statistics indicate that one logger in six will have his career ended by a fatal or crippling injury. Logging accidents are currently increasing in number because big timber companies busted unions in the 1980s, thereby removing or weakening union oversight of worker safety; more large timber companies are utilizing generally nonunion logging contractors who do not place a priority on safety; and companies borrow money at high interest to buy logging equipment, then maximize production for a quick return to pay back the loan, thereby causing rushed, corner-cutting working conditions.

These figures compare with one injury sustained by tree spiking—and that from an irresponsible, atypical operation. The danger to woods and mill workers comes not from tree spikers trying to defend old growth, but from large companies who rush poorly protected workers in the interest of profit for their stockholders.

Responsible tree spiking always involves warning potential logging contractors and the managing agency that a sale has been spiked. This can be done through a communique or phone call, by spray painting a large *S* or similar warning on spiked trees or on the edge of the sale area, by flagging a spike high in a tree to warn of high, unflagged spikes in other trees in the stand, or through other unmistakable means.

If such a warning is not heeded by the Forest Service or a mill operator, it becomes a matter of debate as to who is responsible if a saw encounters a spike. . . .

There is a thoroughly safe solution to the problem of spiked trees: Do not cut them down. For timber operators to be able to make that decision, though, they must be given a timely and insistent warning that the trees in a particular sale have been spiked. . . .

Is tree spiking ethical?

This is a question open to great dispute. Those who believe in the sanctity of private property, who believe that laws must never be broken, or who believe that forests are merely resources to be used by people will always argue that tree spiking is immoral.

I maintain that tree spiking can be ethical, for several reasons.

Forests are not simply collections of trees. All natural forest eco-systems (including seral forests, born in natural wildfire, and recovering second-growth forests in the East) are integrated, complex systems. Old-growth forests, the most developed and complex forest ecosystems, cannot be re-created or regrown within human time frames. Many species depend on natural forest ecosystems. These species and the community they form have value in and of themselves, not merely for the benefit of human beings. They are products of the same process of evolution that produced us, and have intrinsic value.

Current logging of old growth on Forest Service, BLM [Bureau of Land Management], and private lands represents the final mopping-up in a two-century-long campaign of genocide against the ancient forests that blanketed much of the United States.

\*      \*      \*

But is tree spiking effective? Does it work? Can it save trees?

Here we step out of our canoe onto trembling ground. Two arguments against the effectiveness of tree spiking deserve careful, even agonized, scrutiny.

The first is that tree spiking gives the anti-wilderness voices ammunition to turn the media and the public against conservationists and protection of our forests.

Despite the logical explanation of the facts of the Cloverdale incident and why tree spiking is necessary, pandering politicians will continue to use the issue of spiking to whip up sentiment against "environmeddlers," timber companies will continue to use it to elicit public sympathy, and the media will continue to misrepresent it for better copy. No matter how careful or how responsible Earth defenders are in tree spiking and in publicly defending the practice, tree spiking will be held up as proof that monkeywrenchers are more interested in trees than in workers' lives, that ecoteurs are "ecoterrorists."

*          *          *

The second argument is that tree spiking simply has not worked. . . .

There are two counterarguments to this assertion. One is that, in fact, tree spiking has stopped several timber sales in the states of Washington, Oregon, Virginia, Colorado, New Mexico, and Montana. On British Columbia's Meares Island, a massive and carefully organized spiking campaign played a role in stopping the clearcutting of the giant cedars there. . . . The other counterargument is that the timber industry, politicians, and log-town editorialists would not be weeping and wailing about tree spiking if it were not indeed effective at stopping logging.

But is tree spiking really effective? Is it of significant value in stopping the logging of our forests? Probably. In some cases. But . . . I dunno. It's like a tough piece of jerky being chewed around the campfire. You chew and you chew and you chew and nothing much happens. You work up a lot of spit, but you still have a big glob in your mouth.

I dunno.

If we accept for the sake of argument, however, that tree spiking can be effective in halting logging, that it is a tool that needs to be retained in the monkeywrencher's kit, we should take steps to defuse the political tension surrounding it.

*          *          *

# 412 "death by using dirty needles versus drug addiction by using clean needles" (1991–1993)

The United States Centers for Disease Control estimate that one-third of human immunodeficiency virus (HIV) infections occur because uninfected intravenous drug users share contaminated needles with infected users. Public health officials have concluded that making clean needles available to drug users will reduce the rate of HIV transmission, and some cities hard-hit by AIDS have instituted needle exchange programs as a public health measure. Some of the programs also make safe-sex and addiction counseling accessible for at-risk populations.

Several states and localities, however, are opposed to needle exchanges on the grounds that they promote illegal drug use. Nine states have laws that categorize hypodermic syringes as drug paraphernalia and criminalize possession and distribution except by those with documented medical needs or licenses. Although a National Research Council study found that needle swaps do not lead to a rise in intravenous drug use, existing laws prevent public health officials from instituting and maintaining needle exchange programs. In California, New York, and Massachusetts, private activist groups, such as AIDS Brigade and ACT UP, stepped into this perceived breach to offer clean needle swaps.

Police and prosecutors have frequently taken a dim view of this activity, and volunteers have been charged under the drug paraphernalia laws. Some activists have advanced the "defense of necessity," which permits a jury to find that the breach of law was justified by the public interest in avoiding a greater evil. The reactions of the two courts detailed in the documents below demonstrate the difference between a flexible response and a categorical response to political criminality.

☆412  AIDS and Necessity

☆412a  *People v. Bondowitz*

155 Misc. 2d 129, 588 N.Y.S. 2d 507 (1991).

LAURA E. DRAGER, Judge:

Defendants were each charged with one count of criminally possessing a hypodermic instrument. After a nonjury trial, this court reserved decision on its verdict.

At trial, the People presented evidence (by stipulation) that on March 6, 1990 at approximately 12:10 P.M. each defendant knowingly possessed hypodermic instruments and that no defendant had a prescription or any personal medical reason for possession of the needles.

It was further stipulated that Captain Frey of the Midtown South Task Force and several dozen officers were at Essex and Delancey Streets at that time in anticipation of the defendants' arrival to distribute hypodermic needles to other people. The police learned of the defendants' plan from a Newsday article dated March 2, 1990. The defendants were arrested on March 6th as they set up a table and removed hypodermic needles from a box. The arrests occurred within one minute of the instruments being observed in public. Captain Frey never observed anyone receive a hypodermic needle from the defendants, nor exchange a used one for a new needle.

*          *          *

The defendants admit to their knowing possession of hypodermic needles on March 6th but claim their possession of the needles was justified and, therefore, not unlawful. The defendants rely on the "necessity" provision of the justification statute.

\*　　　\*　　　\*

Application of the necessity defense to preserve the physical well-being of an individual or group of individuals is well recognized. This is true even under the strict New York statute. The drafters of that provision gave as an acceptable example of the use of the defense as "forcibly confining a person ill with a highly contagious disease for the purpose of preventing him from going to a city and possibly starting an epidemic." Historically, the defense was found at common law applicable in a number of circumstances involving the physical well-being of those concerned. From these roots there has evolved in recent cases what has come to be known as the medical necessity defense.

\*　　　\*　　　\*

[T]his court finds that under New York law a medical necessity defense requires the following: (1) the defendant acted under a reasonable belief, supported by medical evidence, that his or her action was necessary as an emergency measure to avert an imminent public or private injury; (2) the defendant's actions did not create the crisis; (3) it is clearly more desirable to avoid the public or private injury than the injury caused by violating the statute; (4) there are no available options; and (5) prior legislative action does not preclude the defense and defendant's actions are not based only upon considerations of the morality and advisability of the statute violated.

Turning to the facts in this case, this court finds it was reasonable for the defendants to believe their action necessary as an emergency measure to avert an imminent public injury. Without doubt, AIDS has created an imminent crisis in New York City. There is no dispute that use of clean needles by addicts prevents the spread of HIV infection. The defendants presented significant expert medical and public health witnesses who testified that needle exchange programs have proven successful as a means of providing addicts with clean needles which addicts will use.

\*　　　\*　　　\*

Others may not agree with this approach. The People's witness suggests that not enough is known about the long-term effects of a needle exchange program on the community and that, in any event, such a program is merely a band-aid solution. Without fundamental societal changes such as providing increased job opportunities and better education, AIDS will remain just one of a myriad of problems facing the poorer communities of this City.

. . . [T]he issue before this court is not to choose between the different policy options offered by the witnesses, nor is it necessary for defendants' efforts to be proven successful. Rather, the court must find whether it was reasonable for the defendants, relying on competent medical evidence, to engage in the conduct at issue. While defendants' actions alone would not end the epidemic, it is reasonable to believe their actions served to avert further risks of infection for some individuals. This court is satisfied that the nature of the crisis facing this City, coupled with the medical evidence offered, warranted defendants' action.

Obviously, the defendants themselves did not create the crisis. Although some might argue that addicts have brought this scourge upon themselves, that would not preclude the defendants from trying to help the addicts or to help prevent the spread of the disease by the addicts to unsuspecting sex partners or unborn children.

This court is also satisfied that the harm the defendants sought to avoid was greater than the harm in violating the statute. Hundreds of thousands of lives are at stake in the AIDS epidemic. The crime of possessing a hypodermic needle was enacted as a weapon in the war on drugs. Although law enforcement officials believe the statute essential in this fight, available evidence suggests it has had limited success. As the testimony revealed, only 11 states have statutes similar to New York's law. Despite these statutes, these states—and New York in particular—have among the highest rates of addiction and there are still plenty of dirty needles available. The defendants did not violate the drug possession laws. Rather, they violated a law that has been of limited, if any, success in preventing illegal drug use.

The distinction, in broadest terms, during this age of the AIDS crisis is death by using dirty needles versus drug addiction by using clean needles. The defendants' actions sought to avoid the greater harm.

It is equally apparent that there were no meaningful available options. As the evidence revealed, insufficient drug programs exist for the number of addicts in New York and there is no reason to believe more treatment slots will come into existence in the near future. Moreover, many addicts are not willing or able to face the need for full scale treatment and withdrawal from drugs. Providing counseling or bleach kits only would not be as direct or successful an approach. Defendants' action was not hastily considered and occurred only after the City shut its own needle exchange program.

No legislative or executive action precludes the necessity defense in this case. The hypodermic possession statute and the related public health law provision were enacted [in 1905 and 1909] to fight drug usage well before the onset of the AIDS crisis. The State Legislature has yet to consider whether to revise the hypodermic possession statute in the wake of the epidemic. Although efforts to repeal or amend the law have not been successful, without a specific vote based on consideration of the AIDS epidemic, this court cannot find legislative action to have precluded the defense in this case.

\*　　　\*　　　\*

In sum, defendants' conduct falls within the standards of the medical necessity defense. However, this court feels compelled to instill a cautionary note. A criminal case is premised on particular facts occurring on a past date. It is not the function of this court to set policy.

\*　　　\*　　　\*

That having been said, for the reasons set forth in this decision, with respect to the one count of criminally possessing a hypodermic needle, this court finds each of the defendants not guilty.

☆ 412b  *Commonwealth v. Leno*

415 Mass. 835, 616 N.E.2d 453 (1993).

ABRAMS, Justice.

Massachusetts is one of ten States that prohibit distribution of hypodermic needles without a prescription. In the face of those statutes the defendants operated a needle exchange program in an effort to combat the spread of acquired immunodeficiency syndrome (AIDS). As a result, the defendants were charged with and convicted of (1) unauthorized possession of instruments to administer controlled substances, and (2) unlawful distribution of an instrument to administer controlled substances. . . . On appeal, the defendants challenge the judge's refusal to instruct the jury on the defense of necessity. We allowed the defendants' application for direct appellate review. We affirm.

\*　　　\*　　　\*

Defendant Leno . . . started a needle exchange program in Lynn in September, 1990, after realizing that "in my own back yard . . . people were dying of AIDS . . . and this particular service was not offered to them." Leno testified that he believed that by providing clean needles to addicts he was helping to stem the spread of AIDS, he was helping addicts, especially the homeless, to reach recovery, and that he was not helping addicts continue their habit.

Defendant Robert Ingalls . . . joined Leno in operating a needle exchange program in Lynn as a matter of conscience: "I would have had a hard time with my conscience if I didn't do it without good reason. I [knew] people were dying of AIDS . . . and when [Leno] told me what he was doing, I thought well, maybe, you could save a few lives. . . . It's sort of an irresistible opportunity for me, if you can save a life."

The two defendants legally purchased new sterile needles over-the-counter in Vermont. The defendants were at a specific location on Union Street in Lynn from 5 P.M. to 7 P.M. every Wednesday evening in 1991 until they were arrested June 19. They accepted dirty needles in exchange for clean needles;

they exchanged between 150 and 200 needles each night, for fifty to sixty people. The defendants did not charge for the service or for the materials.

\*　　　\*　　　\*

The defendants do not deny that they violated the provisions of the statutes restricting the possession and distribution of hypodermic needles; rather, they contend that the judge's refusal to instruct the jury on the defense of necessity was error. We disagree.

The application of the defense [of necessity] is limited to the following circumstances: (1) the defendant is faced with a clear and imminent danger, not one which is debatable or speculative; (2) the defendant can reasonably expect that his [or her] action will be effective as the direct cause of abating the danger; (3) there is [no] legal alternative which will be effective in abating the danger; and (4) the Legislature has not acted to preclude the defense by a clear and deliberate choice regarding the values at issue. [citations omitted] . . .

We have emphasized that a person asserting the necessity defense must demonstrate that the danger motivating his or her unlawful conduct is imminent, and that he or she acted out of necessity at all times that he or she engaged in the unlawful conduct.

\*　　　\*　　　\*

The prevention of possible future harm does not excuse a current systematic violation of the law in anticipation of the eventual over-all benefit to the public. The defendants did not show that the danger they sought to avoid was clear and imminent, rather than debatable or speculative. . . . That some States prohibit the distribution of hypodermic needles without a prescription, and others do not merely indicates that the best course to take to address the long-term hazard of the spread of AIDS remains a matter of debate.

The defendants' argument is that, in their view, the prescription requirement for possession and distribution of hypodermic needles and syringes is both ineffective and dangerous. The Legislature, however, has determined that it wants to control the distribution of drug-related paraphernalia and their use in the consumption of illicit drugs. That public policy is entitled to deference by courts. Whether a statute is wise or effective is not within the province of courts. . . .

The defendants argue that the increasing number of AIDS cases constitutes a societal problem of great proportions, and that their actions were an effective means of reducing the magnitude of that problem; they assert that their possession, transportation and distribution of hypodermic needles eventually will produce an over-all reduction in the spread of HIV and in the future incidence of AIDS. The defendants' argument raises the issue of jury nullification, not the defense of necessity. We decline to require an instruction on jury nullification. "We recognize that jurors may return verdicts which do not comport with the judge's instructions. We do not accept the premise that jurors have a right to nullify the law on which they are instructed by the judge, or that the judge must inform them of their power."

*Judgments affirmed.*

[Concurrence by LIACOS, Chief Justice, omitted]

## 413 "if you see 'em, shoot 'em" (1992)

Randall Weaver, a former Green Beret and a Vietnam veteran, lived with his wife, Vicki, his four children, and his friend Kevin Harris "off the [electric and communications] grid" at Ruby Ridge in Northern Idaho. He held social and political views associated with the Christian Identity movement, and had been influenced by a Bureau of Alcohol, Tobacco, and Firearms undercover agent into selling two sawed-off shotguns. Charged with a federal weapons violation, he did not appear for trial. An arrest warrant was issued on February 20, 1991.

Weaver managed to elude the authorities until August 21, 1992, when six United States marshals trudged around Weaver's property trying to catch him. The marshals encountered Harris with Weaver's thirteen-year-old son Sammy. Accounts differ on what happened next, but Marshal William Degan was shot dead, as were Sammy and his dog. Since a federal agent had been killed, the FBI was called in, and snipers took up positions around the Weaver cabin. On August 22, as helicopters circled, an FBI sniper shot Randy Weaver as he and his sixteen-year-old daughter tried to go from the cabin to the shed where his son's body lay. As they tried to retreat, the sniper shot into the cabin, killing Vicki Weaver and injuring Harris. Harris, Weaver, and Weaver's three surviving children were finally talked out of the cabin by James "Bo" Gritz, a retired Green Beret lieutenant colonel and the founder of "Almost Heaven," a survivalist "constitutional covenant community" in central Idaho.

Weaver and Harris were tried for the death of Marshal Degan. They were acquitted of all charges except for Weaver's failure to appear for trial on the weapons trial. The jury apparently believed that the tactics of the federal agents were unreasonable and that the actions of the defendants were in large measure self-defensive. Weaver and his children sued the United States for $10 million for the wrongful death of his wife. Without admitting wrongdoing, the Justice Department settled for $3.1 million.

## ☆413 Two Versions of Ruby Ridge

### ☆413a Ruby Ridge: The Justice Report

James Bovard, *Wall Street Journal*, June 30, 1995, A14.

The 1992 confrontation between federal agents and the Randy Weaver family in Ruby Ridge, Idaho, has become one of the most controversial and widely discussed examples of the abuse of federal power. The Justice Department completed a 542-page investigation on the case last year but has not yet made the report public. However, the report was acquired by Legal Times newspaper, which this week placed the text on the Internet. The report reveals that federal officials may have acted worse than even some of their harshest critics imagined.

This case began after Randy Weaver was entrapped, as an Idaho jury concluded, by an undercover Bureau of Alcohol Tobacco and Firearms agent to sell him sawed-off shotguns.

While federal officials have claimed that the violent confrontation between the Weavers and the government began when the Weavers ambushed federal marshals, the report tells a very different story. A team of six U.S. marshals, split into two groups, trespassed onto Mr. Weaver's land on Aug. 21, 1992. One of the marshals threw rocks at the Weaver's cabin to see how much noise was required to agitate the Weavers' dogs. A few minutes later, Randy Weaver, Kevin Harris, and 13-year-old Sammy Weaver came out of the cabin and began following their dogs. Three U.S. marshals were soon tearing through the woods.

At one point, U.S. Marshal Larry Cooper "told the others that it was ['expletive deleted'] for them to continue running and that he did not want to 'run down the trail and get shot in the back.' He urged them to take up defensive positions. The others agreed. . . . William Degan . . . took a position behind a stump. . . ."

As Sammy Weaver and Kevin Harris came upon the marshals, gunfire erupted. Sammy was shot in the back and killed while running away from the scene (probably by Marshal Cooper, according to the report), and Marshal Degan was killed by Mr. Harris. The jury concluded that Mr. Harris's action was legitimate self-defense; the Justice report concluded it was impossible to know who shot first.

Several places in the report deal with the possibility of a government coverup. After the firefight between the marshals and the Weavers and Mr. Harris, the surviving marshals were taken away to rest and recuperate. The report observed, "We question the wisdom of keeping the marshals together at the condominium for several hours, while awaiting interviews with the FBI. Isolating them in that manner created the appearance and generated allegations that they were fabricating stories and colluding to cover up the true circumstances of the shootings."

After the death of the U.S. marshal, the FBI was called in. A source of continuing fierce debate across America is: Did the FBI set out to apprehend and arrest Randy Weaver and Kevin Harris—or simply to kill them? Unfortunately, the evidence from the Justice Department report is damning in the extreme on this count.

The report noted, "We have been told by observers on the scene that law enforcement personnel made statements that the matter would be handled quickly and that the situation would be 'taken down hard and fast.'" The FBI issued Rules of Engagement that declared that its snipers "can and should" use deadly force against armed males outside the cabin.

The report noted that a member of an FBI SWAT team from Denver "remembered the Rules of Engagement as 'if you see 'em, shoot 'em.'" The task force report noted, "since those Rules which contained 'should' remained in force at the crisis scene for days after the August 22 shooting, it is inconceivable to us that FBI Headquarters remained ignorant of the exact wording of the Rules of Engagement during that entire period."

The report concluded that the FBI Rules of Engagement at Ruby Ridge flagrantly violated the U.S. Constitution: "The Constitution allows no person to become 'fair game' for deadly force without law enforcement evaluating the threat that person poses, even when, as occurred here, the evaluation must be made in a split second." The report portrays the rules of engagement as practically a license to kill: "The Constitution places the decision on whether to use deadly force on the individual agent; the Rules attempted to usurp this responsibility."

FBI headquarters rejected an initial operation plan because there was no provision to even attempt to negotiate the surrender of the suspects. The plan was revised to include a negotiation provision—but subsequent FBI action made that provision a nullity. FBI snipers took their positions around the Weaver cabin a few minutes after 5 p.m. on Aug. 22. Within an hour, every adult in the cabin was either dead or severely wounded—even though they had not fired a shot at any FBI agent.

Randy Weaver, Mr. Harris, and 16-year-old Sara Weaver stepped out of the cabin a few minutes before 6 p.m. to go to the shed where Sammy's body lay. FBI sniper Lon Horiuchi shot Randy Weaver in the back. As Randy Weaver, Mr. Harris, and Sara Weaver struggled to get back into the cabin, Vicki Weaver stood in the cabin doorway holding a baby. Agent Horiuchi fired again; his bullet passed through a window in the door, hit Vicki Weaver in the head, killing her instantly, and then hit Mr. Harris in the chest. At the subsequent trial, the government claimed

that Messrs. Weaver and Harris were shot because they had threatened to shoot at a helicopter containing FBI officials. Because of insufficient evidence, the federal judge threw out the charge that Messrs. Weaver and Harris threatened the helicopter. The Justice report noted, "The SIOC [Strategic Information and Operations Center at FBI headquarters] Log indicates that shots were fired during the events of August 22. . . . We have found no evidence during this inquiry that shots were fired at any helicopter during the Ruby Ridge crisis. The erroneous entry was never corrected." (The Idaho jury found Messrs. Weaver and Harris innocent on almost all charges.)

The Justice Department task force expressed grave doubts about the wisdom of the FBI strategy: "From information received at the Marshals Service, FBI management had reason to believe that the Weaver/Harris group would respond to a helicopter in the vicinity of the cabin by coming outside with firearms. Notwithstanding this knowledge, they placed sniper/observers on the adjacent mountainside with instructions that they could and should shoot armed members of the group, if they came out of the cabin. Their use of the helicopter near the cabin invited an accusation that the helicopter was intentionally used to draw the Weaver group out of the cabin."

The task force was extremely critical of Agent Horiuchi's second shot: "Since the exchange of gunfire [the previous day], no one at the cabin had fired a shot. Indeed, they had not even returned fire in response to Horiuchi's first shot. Furthermore, at the time of the second shot, Harris and others outside the cabin were retreating, not attacking. They were not retreating to an area where they would present a danger to the public at large. . . ."

Regarding Agent Horiuchi's killing of Vicki Weaver, the task force concluded, "[B]y fixing his cross hairs on the door when he believed someone was behind it, he placed the children and Vicki Weaver at risk, in violation of even the special Rules of Engagement. . . . In our opinion he needlessly and unjustifiably endangered the persons whom he thought might be behind the door."

The Justice Department task force was especially appalled that the adults were gunned down before receiving any warning or demand to surrender: "While the operational plan included a provision for a surrender demand, that demand was not made until after the shootings. . . . The lack of a planned 'call out' as the sniper/observers deployed is significant because the Weavers were known to leave the cabin armed when vehicles or airplanes approached. The absence of such a plan subjected the Government to charges that it was setting Weaver up for attack."

☆413b The Federal Raid on Ruby Ridge, ID

*The Federal Raid on Ruby Ridge, ID: Hearings before the Subcommittee on Terrorism, Technology, and Government Information, Committee on the Judiciary,* 104th Cong. (1995), 1087 (statement of Louis J. Freeh, Director, Federal Bureau of Investigation).

\*　　　\*　　　\*

Ruby Ridge has become synonymous with tragedy, given the deaths there of a decorated Deputy United States Marshal, a young boy, and the boy's mother. It has also become synonymous with the exaggerated application of federal law enforcement. Both conclusions seem justified.

At Ruby Ridge, the FBI did not perform at the level which the American people expect or deserve from the FBI. Indeed, for the FBI, Ruby Ridge was a series of terribly flawed law enforcement operations with tragic consequences.

We know today that law enforcement overreacted at Ruby Ridge. FBI officials promulgated rules of engagement that were reasonably subject to interpretation that would permit a violation of FBI policy and the Constitution—rules that could have caused even worse consequences than actually occurred. Rules of engagement that I will never allow the FBI to use again.

\*　　　\*　　　\*

It is important to understand, however, that, in August, 1992, the FBI acted upon information that had been provided by other law enforcement agencies. Based upon that information, the FBI believed that it was facing a very grave threat in Idaho—a threat that required a prompt response. Now, with all of the benefits of hindsight, the FBI's response clearly was an overreaction. In future situations, I will make a more independent assessment of such threats before the FBI acts.

\*　　　\*　　　\*

At Ruby Ridge, the Hostage Rescue Team ("HRT") was operating in accordance with rules of engagement that were reasonably subject to interpretation that would permit a violation of FBI policy and the Constitution. Those rules said that, under certain circumstances, certain persons "can and should" be the subject of deadly force. Those rules of engagement were contrary to law and FBI policy. Moreover, some FBI SWAT personnel on-scene interpreted the rules as a "shoot-on-sight" policy—which they knew was inconsistent with the FBI's deadly force policy. Such confusion is entirely unacceptable.

According to Special Agent Lon Horiuchi, the HRT sniper who accidentally shot Mrs. Weaver, he fired two shots on August 22, 1992, both pursuant to the FBI's deadly force policy. He has testified that he did not shoot pursuant to the rules of engagement that I just mentioned.

The shot that killed Mrs. Weaver was the second that Special Agent Horiuchi fired. He testified that it was not intended for Mrs. Weaver and was not fired at her.

\*　　　\*　　　\*

Indeed, the constitutionality of Special Agent Horiuchi's second shot is a very close and very difficult question. It is not a matter that can be addressed in "black and white" terms. It cannot be answered categorically or with a high degree of certainty.

\*　　　\*　　　\*

Special Agent Horiuchi said he took the first shot only when he observed Randy Weaver raise his rifle in the direction of the helicopter. Although FBI Agents in sniper positions had observed three armed people run from the cabin and head toward the rock outcroppings, they did not shoot as those three persons moved from the cabin—because their actions were not judged to pose a threat to the safety of the agents on the scene.

The bullet that struck Mrs. Weaver was fired seconds after the first shot. It was intended for a man who Special Agent Horiuchi mistakenly believed was [Randy Weaver, whom he] had just shot. . . . Special Agent Horiuchi fired at his intended target while he was running toward the cabin and before he reached the cabin door.

Tragically, Mrs. Weaver was struck by that shot while she stood behind the open front door of the cabin.

Special Agent Horiuchi said he could not see Mrs. Weaver when he took the second shot and that he had no reason to believe that she was standing there. The shot that killed Mrs. Weaver was not even fired at or into the cabin; it travelled on a path parallel to the cabin.

\*　　　\*　　　\*

It is important to remember that two different components of the Department of Justice have reviewed the circumstances leading to Vicki Weaver's unfortunate death. Both of those components—the Office of Professional Responsibility and the Civil Rights Division—independently determined that there was no basis upon which to conclude that she had been shot intentionally or unlawfully. Both determined by their analysis that the second shot was not unconstitutional.

Special Agent Horiuchi's second shot was not criminal. Nor do I believe that a court—applying qualified immunity principles—would find any civil liability. Further, based on all of the evidence, I do not believe it was unconstitutional.

In January of this year, I disciplined or proposed discipline for twelve FBI employees for their conduct related to the incident at Ruby Ridge and the subsequent prosecution of Randy Weaver and Kevin Harris. . . . [I] relied upon a Task Force investigation that was directly supervised by the Department of Justice and a report that was written by Department of Justice attorneys—not FBI Special Agents.

I . . . determined that the twelve FBI employees did not commit any crimes or intentional misconduct. Nevertheless, I concluded that those employees had demonstrated inadequate performance, improper judgment, neglect of duty, and failure to exert proper managerial oversight. Accordingly, I imposed or proposed discipline ranging from an oral reprimand or written censure to written censure with suspension from duty. At that time, I believed the discipline imposed or proposed was commensurate with the factual basis for the imposition of that discipline.

*             *             *

With the arsenals at the disposal of criminals in our Nation today, everyone must understand that law enforcement officers have a very dangerous job to do. . . .

We take our responsibility seriously when we ask the men and women of law enforcement to put themselves in harm's way—people like Deputy United States Marshal Bill Degan. As law enforcement leaders and managers, we owe them our complete support and must strive to give them the best guidance possible.

We rely upon the men and women of law enforcement to do their best job under very difficult circumstances. In return for protecting us, we vest them with a measure of discretion and ask them to use their best judgment. Sometimes, as human nature tells us, that judgment may be imperfect and mistakes will happen.

As long as we ask them to be in the arena, to be ready in the middle of the night to take cover behind a tree or a mailbox, to put their lives and the well-being of their families in the line of fire, we must show some empathy and compassion for their human fallibility. This is particularly true as we judge with the calm, well-lighted knowledge of hindsight, far from what the Supreme Court calls "split-second judgments—in circumstances that are tense, uncertain and rapidly evolving."

☆413c  Federal Law Enforcement Reform after Waco, Ruby Ridge

Laura Murphy, document at http://www.aclu.org/news/n1024951.html.

The American Civil Liberties Union has long been concerned about improper and unlawful practices by law enforcement agencies—whether it is the FBI spying on and harassing civil rights, peace and anti-dictatorship activists, the DEA's misuse of informants and no-knock raids on the wrong families, or physical abuse by police like that captured in the Rodney King videotape.

We are, therefore, delighted to be joined today by so many other organizations—all of who have often reflected quite different perspectives. We are all united by our support for a common set of necessary reforms in federal law enforcement, regardless of which particular agency is involved or which particular political or ethnic group is under attack.

For the ACLU, the lessons of the congressional hearings on the tragedies of Waco and Ruby Ridge are not in "who shot whom" but in the recognition that there are very serious problems in federal law enforcement—problems that must be met with comprehensive solutions.

*             *             *

The 14 organizations who have signed this letter all agree that Congress must do more than merely hold hearings on Waco and Ruby Ridge. Our letter notes that, ironically, while some members of Congress were expressing deep concern about alleged civil liberties abuses at Waco, Congress was moving to enact measures to expand the unchecked powers of federal law enforcement officers.

The ACLU, the NRA, the National Black Police Association, the Gun Owners of America, the Citizens Committee for the Right to Keep and Bear Arms, the Second Amendment Foundation, the Criminal Justice Policy Foundation and the other organizations all insist that the Congress reject the so-called "counter-terrorism" bills because they will encourage additional violations of individual rights and, in addition, that the House and Senate reject any effort, including that found in the so-called crime bills, to do away with or weaken the "exclusionary rule" preventing the police from using illegally obtained evidence. From the NRA and the Citizens Committee to the ACLU, the International Association for Civilian Oversight of Law Enforcement and the National Black Police Association—we all oppose any weakening of the exclusionary rule because doing so would remove the only effective deterrence against police misconduct.

*             *             *

All of the organizations signing this letter also agree on the need for "a uniform means of permanent, independent oversight of federal law enforcement policies and practices with full redress for allegations of abuse." We further urge that Congress ensure adequate penalties for those federal law enforcement agents who engage in misconduct.

*             *             *

The fabric of a society is best bound together by a mutual sense of justice and fairness. . . . Nothing can so swiftly divide a society like the resentment and hostility that are the inevitable fruits of injustice.

# 414 "If . . . that is not terrorism, then what is?" (1992-1996)

In 1981, Alex Pacheo brought the plight of the "Silver Spring monkeys" to public attention. Pacheo had posed as a volunteer researcher and used his position to give late-night access to veterinarians in order to document the realities of the laboratory animals' lives. A national furor erupted, launching the People for the Ethical Treatment of Animals (PETA), which reached a 1996 membership of a half-million people. PETA engages in publicity stunts, such as the anti-fur "Naked" campaign featuring ads of prominent activists posing nude. It eschews violence and vandalism, but it does act as the public relations outlet for the London-based Animal Liberation Front (ALF), which has claimed credit for vandalizing laboratories, releasing animals, destroying research data, and threatening researchers. A congressional report listed 313 criminal acts attributed to animal rights activists between 1977 and mid 1993.

While organized promotion of animal welfare has been around since the Anti-Vivisectionist League was founded in Victorian England, the newcomers to the movement often part company with their philosophical predecessors. While the older organizations strive to guarantee humane treatment for animals, the animal rights activists demand that all animals be freed of any exploitation by humans. Thus farms, slaughterhouses, furriers, commercial laboratories, and zoos, as well as medical research laboratories, are among their targets. Their demand for the end of "speciesism" has often put them at odds with others, such as breeders, who are interested in the protection of biodiversity and the environment through the manipulation and support of endangered wildlife, as well as those, such as AIDS and cancer sufferers, who see in animal research a hope for relief.

The selected documents reflect political criminality and activism as being often directed not against government, but against perceived private or collective "evildoers" who might be viewed as governmentally sponsored or tolerated. The means employed by the animal rights advocates also reflect great diversity, ranging from the criminal destruction of private property to effective public opinion campaigns. The militancy of the animal rights movements finally resulted in federal intervention. Concerned over the continued vandalism and other criminal attacks against animal-handling facilities, Congress finally added the protection of the federal government to the protections extended by the thirty-two states that have enacted similar laws.

## ☆414 Animal Rights Activism

### ☆414a A Member of the Animal Liberation Front Tells Why She Broke the Law for Animals

Document at http://envirolink.org/ALF/orgs/why.html.

Karen, 38, a health care worker in a large eastern city, is one of the members of the Animal Liberation Front who broke into the Head Injury Clinical Research Center at the University of Pennsylvania in May 1984. In the most widely-publicized break-in of its kind, the A.L.F. stole more than 60 hours of videotapes of experiments and initiated an exhaustive campaign that led ultimately to the Center's closing.

For over 13 years, the Center had used hundreds of unanesthetized baboons to study the effects of head injuries. In the studies, which cost taxpayers nearly $1 million a year, baboons had their heads plastered to a machine which delivered blows as great as 1,000 times the force of gravity. Then, on Memorial Day, 1984, the A.L.F. team entered the laboratory and took the tapes, which had been made by the experimenters themselves as a part of their record-keeping routine.

The A.L.F. members left the tapes on the doorsteps of People for the Ethical Treatment of Animals' headquarters in the Maryland suburbs of Washington, D.C. PETA hastily edited them down to a 30-minute documentary, entitled "Unnecessary Fuss," which documented violations of the Animal Welfare Act, animal abuse and researchers' callous attitudes toward the baboons. Embarrassed University of Pennsylvania officials pulled political strings and Philadelphia District Attorney Edward Rendell launched an investigation to identify the A.L.F. members involved in the break-in; several PETA members were summoned to testify before a grand jury. Undaunted, PETA aggressively distributed copies of the documentary to other animal rights groups, to members of Congress and to the media.

Publicity about the baboon bashing at the University brought forth protest after protest, culminating with a four-day sit-in at offices of the National Institutes of Health in July 1985. On the fourth day of the sit-in, Health and Human Services Secretary Margaret M. Heckler ordered NIH to suspend its $1 million-a-year grant to the head injury lab.

Then, late in September after months of investigations and official reports, the University of Pennsylvania announced that "experiments in the lab have been suspended indefinitely." Within weeks, Secretary Heckler announced that funding to the lab would remain under suspension because the researchers had "failed materially to comply with the conditions of their grant with respect to the care use of non-human primates." In a separate action, NIH Director, Dr. James Wyngaarden, spelled out a list of major actions to be taken by the university before he would "consider any request for resumption of funding" for head injury studies involving non-human primates.

In this exclusive interview, Karen (last name withheld) was asked about her background and the reasons for her involvement with the Animal Liberation Front. Our interviewer deliberately took a "devil's advocate" approach in order to discuss the most frequently encountered questions about the A.L.F.

*          *          *

—*Did rescuing stray animals lead you to the A.L.F.?*

No. That was something different. For many years I was a waitress, a file clerk and so on, but I was going to school at night for a science degree. In the course of doing research in the library for a couple of papers, I read about things that were being done to animals in laboratories. I was really shocked. I had no idea whatsoever that these atrocities were going on. I could not believe it. Animals are used in the most cruel and horrible ways, and it's not as if it's being kept secret. It's right there in any medical library.

—*Could you [be] more specific as to what you learned that particularly disturbed you?*

I learned about the experiments on "learned helplessness," for example, which have been going on since the 1950's. They would give electric shocks to dogs, and they would naturally try to jump out of the box, but the escape route would be blocked. Eventually the dogs would go crazy. They would throw themselves against the wall and wind up cowering on the floor, accepting the shock and urinating on themselves. The conclusion of the researchers is that if the animal cannot escape, s/he learns to accept the shock. This has been done over and over again—at the University of Pennsylvania, among other places.

—*Would you accept the notion that some of the animal research may be valid?*

For example, the people at the UPenn head injury lab claim their research will benefit children who have suffered traumatic head injuries and brain damage. I certainly can sympathize with the parents of such children, but that still does not make this research valid. The researchers would like you to believe that if enough animals are killed, little Johnny's head will be repaired. But this is ludicrous. Considering the hundreds of millions of animals killed in research labs, we should all have eternal life by now. Very, very little has been gained from this killing that is of benefit to humans. In fact we might be farther in treating head injury victims if no animal research had been done. We've been deprived by the fact that more has not been done with human clinical studies, human autopsy studies, epidemiological studies, solid tissue cultures, computers, positive emissions tomography, and so on. Dr. Gennarelli, who was in charge of UPenn's head injury lab, even admitted that these things are not being used enough because the money is being drained off by animal research. In fact, nuclear magnetic resonance is a way to study human brain damage without using animals, but it's very expensive and the money is tied up in animal projects.

—*Are you saying that human head injury victims have not benefited at all from the kind of research that was done at UPenn?*

Absolutely. I have read every single head injury study that has been done, and not one has discussed how the human victims or the animal victims were treated after the research. The human victims and their families have been exploited and given false hope. They have been used as a shield to keep the cruelty and the money coming.

*          *          *

—*Did you know in advance about the videotapes, which were the key in shutting down the lab?*

Yes. Gennarelli mentioned the tapes in his published studies. We were very happy when we found them, but they were far worse than we had expected. The callousness and brutality were absolutely unbelievable. The researchers made fun of the animals while they were dying, and they'd beat up one animal in front of another.

You could clearly hear them say that one baboon was "off anesthesia" right before they started bashing in his/her head. You could see the animal trying to crawl off the table. One researcher said, "It looks like this one has a dislocated shoulder," and then he deliberately picked up the baboon by the arm, causing the animal excruciating pain, laughing all the while he was doing it. They were like Nazis. They didn't even do a proper neurological exam, and they left the animals unattended and tied to the operating table after the injuries.

—*How would you respond to those who say your efforts are merely condemning more animals to death since the research you disrupt is likely to be done all over again?*

We are abolitionists, and if we are successful in closing down a lab, as we did at UPenn, then obviously no more animals are going to be killed there. We also had the funding cut off from the City of Hope in Los Angeles after our break-in. They were doing cancer research, but the conditions in the animal lab were horrible. Dogs were dying unattended, and one suffocated in his own fecal matter.

—*Don't you worry about being caught and going to jail?*

I do not live in fear. I have been in on three break-ins, so I could go to jail and I'm prepared to deal with it if it happens. We are not martyrs, though, and we'd much rather stay out here, where we can do more for the animals. [Karen has no children and no husband, although she does have a boyfriend who is "supportive" of her A.L.F. activities. —Eds.[ of original document]]

*—In many of your raids, you have liberated research animals. What has happened to those animals?*

We make sure they are well cared for. We feel that by liberating animals, you are also liberating people. We are on this earth to protect animals, not to exploit them. We do not have the right to use them as if they are inanimate objects. They have a right to their own lives, which should not include slavery and torture.

*—Don't you feel you have committed an immoral act when you have destroyed property that belonged to others?*

Not when that property was used to inflict pain, suffering and death on living creatures. We have been referred to by certain critics as terrorists, but the real terrorists are those who put animals in boiling water and bash in the brains of fully conscious creatures and harm human beings by misdirecting research. If all of that is not terrorism, then what is?

☆414b People for the Ethical Treatment of Animals— Research, Investigations and Rescue

Document at http://envirolink.org/arrs/peta/95review/rir. htm.

Research, Investigations and Rescue (RIR) undercover workers found their way into laboratories, fur ranches, feedlots, animal auctions, slaughterhouses, factory farms and exotic animal shows and came out with videotape and photographs to document the abuses of animal industries. It was back-breaking, filthy and often frightening work, but the evidence gathered has saved millions of animals from abuse and agonizing death and resulted in criminal charges and convictions.

Caseworkers in the RIR office were on call 24 hours a day. Our attorneys' and caseworkers' extensive research and perseverance brought dozens of victories—everything from stopping cruel experiments on gophers to ending pigeon poisonings to persuading a Crown Books store not to put an elephant on display and preventing a golf course management board from slaughtering Canada geese.

—STOPPED! More than one million cows and bison imported from Mexico each year will be spared branding with a searing-hot iron on the tender skin of their faces. Countless others will no longer be spayed without anesthesia. PETA attorney Lucy Kaplan researched complicated laws and filed very meticulous comments with the U.S. government, proving our case against these barbarous acts.

—SAVED! Corporate giants Mobil, Texaco, Pennzoil, Phillips Petroleum, Shell and other oil companies agreed to cover their exhaust stacks after RIR showed how millions of birds and bats became trapped in the shafts and were burned alive.

\*　　　\*　　　\*

—STOPPED! Using RIR's photos of animals dying from untreated, oozing skin conditions and beating, the U.S. Department of Agriculture brought charges against Ohio's Wright State University, which paid $20,000 in fines. Some experiments were ended forever.

\*　　　\*　　　\*

—STOPPED! A Maryland fur farmer had injected minks in the chest with weedkiller for 50 years until the district attorney saw our investigators' videotape of the excruciatingly painful deaths.

—EXPOSED! Investigators revealed how, at a Florida exotic animal "training" school, big cats were beaten and starved to make them perform. The case is pending.

\*　　　\*　　　\*

—When a truck on its way to a poultry slaughterhouse overturned on a busy Virginia highway, RIR's rescue team worked through the night to help more than 3,000 injured chickens.

—CONVICTED! The U.S. government filed 41 charges of Animal Welfare Act violations against Hazleton Research Products, a Michigan company that breeds animals for pharmaceutical laboratories, after RIR investigators revealed that employees beat animals, sometimes to death. RIR's evidence also resulted in the criminal cruelty conviction of one Hazleton worker who punched rabbits with his fists and broke their hind legs.

☆414c The Animal Enterprise Protection Act of 1992

106 Stat. 928, P.L. 102-346, Aug. 26, 1992.

*Be it enacted by the Senate and House of Representatives of the United States of America in Congress assembled,*

\*　　　\*　　　\*

SEC. 2. ANIMAL ENTERPRISE TERRORISM.

(a) IN GENERAL—Title 18, United States Code, is amended by inserting after section 42 the following:

"§ 43. *Animal enterprise terrorism*

"(a) OFFENSE. Whoever—

"(1) travels in interstate or foreign commerce, or uses or causes to be used the mail or any facility in interstate or foreign commerce, for the purpose of causing physical disruption to the functioning of an animal enterprise; and

"(2) intentionally causes physical disruption to the functioning of an animal enterprise by intentionally stealing, damaging, or causing the loss of, any property (including animals or records) used by the animal enterprise, and thereby causes economic damage exceeding $10,000 to that enterprise, or conspires to do so;

shall be fined under this title or imprisoned not more than one year, or both.

"(b) Aggravated Offense.—

"(1) Serious Bodily Injury.—Whoever in the course of a violation of subsection (a) causes serious bodily injury to another individual shall be fined under this title or imprisoned not more than 10 years, or both.

"(2) Death.—Whoever in the course of a violation of subsection (a) causes the death of an individual shall be fined under this title and imprisoned for life or for any term of years.

"(c) Restitution.—An order of restitution under section 3663 of this title with respect to a violation of this section may also include restitution—

"(1) for the reasonable cost of repeating any experimentation that was interrupted or invalidated as a result of the offense; and

"(2) the loss of food production or farm income reasonably attributable to the offense.

"(d) Definitions.—As used in this section—

"(1) the term 'animal enterprise' means—

"(A) a commercial or academic enterprise that uses animals for food or fiber production, agriculture, research, or testing;

"(B) a zoo, aquarium, circus, rodeo, or lawful competitive animal event; or

"(C) any fair or similar event intended to advance agricultural arts and sciences;

"(2) the term 'physical disruption' does not include any lawful disruption that results from lawful public, governmental, or animal enterprise employee reaction to the disclosure of information about an animal enterprise;

"(3) the term 'economic damage' means the replacement costs of lost or damaged property or records, the costs of repeating an interrupted or invalidated experiment, or the loss of profits; . . . .

"(e) Non-Preemption.—Nothing in this section preempts any State law.".

*          *          *

SEC. 3. STUDY OF EFFECT OF TERRORISM ON CERTAIN ANIMAL ENTERPRISES.

(a) Study.—The Attorney General and the Secretary of Agriculture shall jointly conduct a study on the extent and effects of domestic and international terrorism on enterprises using animals for food or fiber production, agriculture, research, or testing.

*          *          *

*Approved August 26, 1992.*

## 415 "'Although the human crisis is compelling, there is no solution to be found in a judicial remedy'" (1993)

In the early 1990s, political and economic conditions in Haiti and Cuba had provoked boatloads of people to take to the seas in search of refuge in the United States. The United States' attitude to the two nationalities, however, was vastly different. Concluding that the Haitians were only fleeing economic, not political, conditions, the United States attempted to accelerate their deportation, curtailing the proceedings for ascertaining eligibility for political asylum (See Doc. 396). Cubans, however, who safely made it to Florida were accorded special treatment.

To embarrass Fidel Castro's Cuban regime by encouraging "defections from Communism," Congress had previously passed the Cuban Refugee Adjustment Act of 1966. Under this law, Cuban arrivals were made eligible for permanent residence in the United States after a one-year stay, unless otherwise excludable because of serious criminal records or other specified reasons. Cubans, unlike Haitians, were thus presumptively treated as political refugees and were accorded benefits exceeding what the standards of political asylum would require.

Despite these generous benefits, defectors and refugees from Cuba remained numerically few until the "Freedom Flotilla," or Mariel Boatlift, occurred in 1980, when Castro "opened the door" to those who wanted to leave Cuba. During the boatlift, 125,000 people, many of them hardened criminals, drug addicts, or mentally impaired persons, crossed the Florida Straits. In response, the United States became more reticent about the free entry of émigrés from Cuba, but many Cubans continued to cross over to the United States, where they continued to be favorably treated as political refugees under the 1966 act.

Haitians, however, when intercepted by the Coast Guard, were directly repatriated under a 1981 agreement between the United States and Haiti, unless their asylum claims survived a screening on board Coast Guard ships. That process changed for several months when the numbers of Haitian "boat people" mushroomed after widespread violence resulting from Haiti's 1991 military coup. Temporary facilities for processing Haitian asylum seekers were established at the United States naval facilities at Guantanamo Bay, Cuba. When these facilities were filled beyond capacity, the United States announced that it would again directly repatriate all Haitians intercepted at sea.

Even after the decline in Haitian emigration following that country's return to democracy through a United States-led intervention, the end of the Cuban refugee flow was not in sight. In the summer of 1994, when Cuba ceased interdicting small boats attempting to leave the country, the numbers of Cubans streaming to the United States began to grow dramatically. Seeking to avoid another exodus like the Mariel Boatlift, the Clinton administration announced in August that henceforth, Cubans picked up at sea would be detained at Guantanamo Bay as the Haitians had been before them. The Cuban detainees were finally allowed into the United States as part of an agreement with Cuba, similar to the one with Haiti, which the Supreme Court had previously upheld against a challenge that it violated the United Nations Convention relating to the Status of Refugees (Doc. 382).

## ☆415 *Sale v. Haitian Centers Council, Inc.*

113 S.Ct. 2549 (1993).

Justice STEVENS delivered the opinion of the Court.

The President has directed the Coast Guard to intercept vessels illegally transporting passengers from Haiti to the United States and to return those passengers to Haiti without first determining whether they may qualify as refugees. The question presented in this case is whether such forced repatriation, "authorized to be undertaken only beyond the territorial sea of the United States," violates § 243(h)(1) of the Immigration and Nationality Act of 1952 (INA or Act). We hold that neither § 243(h) nor Article 33 of the United Nations Protocol Relating to the Status of Refugees applies to action taken by the Coast Guard on the high seas.

### I

Aliens residing illegally in the United States are subject to deportation after a formal hearing. Aliens arriving at the border, or those who are temporarily paroled into the country, are subject to an exclusion hearing, the less formal process by which they, too, may eventually be removed from the United States. In either a deportation or exclusion proceeding the alien may seek asylum as a political refugee for whom removal to a particular country may threaten his life or freedom. . . . If the proof shows that it is more likely than not that the alien's life or freedom would be threatened in a particular country because of his political or religious beliefs, under § 243(h) the Attorney General must not send him to that country. The INA offers these statutory protections only to aliens who reside in or have arrived at the border of the United States. For 12 years, in one form or another, the interdiction program challenged here has prevented Haitians such as respondents from reaching our shores and invoking those protections.

On September 23, 1981, the United States and the Republic of Haiti entered into an agreement authorizing the United States Coast Guard to intercept vessels engaged in the illegal transportation of undocumented aliens to our shores. While the parties agreed to prosecute "illegal traffickers," the Haitian Government also guaranteed that its repatriated citizens would not be punished for their illegal departure. . . . On September 29, 1981, President Reagan issued a proclamation in which he characterized "the continuing illegal migration by sea of large numbers of undocumented aliens into the southeastern United States" as "a serious national problem detrimental to the interests of the United States." He therefore suspended the entry of undocumented aliens from the high seas and ordered the Coast Guard to intercept vessels carrying such aliens and to return them to their point of origin. . . .

\* \* \*

On September 30, 1991, a group of military leaders displaced the government of Jean Bertrand Aristide, the first democratically elected president in Haitian history. As the District Court stated in an uncontested finding of fact, since the military coup "hundreds of Haitians have been killed, tortured, detained without a warrant, or subjected to violence and the destruction of their property because of their political beliefs. Thousands have been forced into hiding." Following the coup the Coast Guard suspended repatriations for a period of several weeks, and the United States imposed economic sanctions on Haiti.

On November 18, 1991, the Coast Guard announced that it would resume the program of interdiction and forced repatriation.

\* \* \*

In the meantime the Haitian exodus expanded dramatically. . . .

With both the facilities at Guantanamo and available Coast Guard cutters saturated, and with the number of Haitian emigrants in unseaworthy craft increasing (many had drowned as they attempted the trip to Florida), the Government could no longer both protect our borders *and* offer the Haitians even a modified screening process. It had to choose between allowing Haitians into the United States for the screening process or repatriating them without giving them any opportunity to establish their qualifications as refugees. . . .

On May 23, 1992, President Bush adopted the second choice. After assuming office, President Clinton decided not to modify that order; it remains in effect today.

### III

Both parties argue that the plain language of § 243(h)(1) is dispositive. It reads as follows:

The Attorney General shall not deport or return any alien . . . to a country if the Attorney General determines that such alien's life or freedom would be threatened in such country on account of race, religion, nationality, membership in a particular social group, or political opinion.

Respondents emphasize the words "any alien" and "return"; neither term is limited to aliens within the United States. Respondents also contend that the 1980 amendment deleting the words "within the United States" from the prior text of § 243(h), obviously gave the statute an extraterritorial effect. This change, they further argue, was required in order to conform the statute to the text of Article 33.1 of the [United Nations] Convention [Relating to the Status of Refugees], which they find as unambiguous as the present statutory text.

Petitioners' response is that a fair reading of the INA as a whole demonstrates that sec. 243(h) does not apply to actions taken by the President or Coast Guard outside the United States; that the legislative history of the 1980 amendment supports their reading; and that both the text and the negotiating history of Article 33 of the Convention indicate that it was not intended to have any extraterritorial effect.

We shall first review the text and structure of the statute and its 1980 amendment, and then consider the text and negotiating history of the Convention.

### A. The Text and Structure of the INA

Although § 243(h)(1) refers only to the Attorney General, the Court of Appeals found it "difficult to believe that the proscription of § 243(h)(1)—returning an alien to his persecutors—was forbidden if done by the attorney general but permitted if done by some other arm of the executive branch." . . . That section, however, conveys to us a different message. It provides, in part:

> The Attorney General shall be charged with the administration and enforcement of this chapter and all other laws relating to the immigration and naturalization of aliens, *except insofar as this chapter or such laws relate to the powers, functions, and duties conferred upon the President, the Secretary of State, the officers of the Department of State, or diplomatic or consular officers.* . . . (Emphasis added [by the Court].)

> *          *          *

The reference to the Attorney General in the statutory text is significant not only because that term cannot reasonably be construed to describe either the President or the Coast Guard, but also because it suggests that it applies only to the Attorney General's normal responsibilities under the INA. . . . [W]e cannot reasonably construe § 243(h) to limit the Attorney General's [extraterritorial] actions. . . . Part V of the INA contains no reference to a possible extraterritorial application.

> *          *          *

Respondents' expansive interpretation of the word "return" raises another problem: it would make the word "deport" redundant. . . . By using both words, the statute implies an exclusively territorial application, in the context of both [deportation and exclusion] proceedings. The use of both words reflects the traditional division between the two kinds of aliens and the two kinds of hearings. We can reasonably conclude that Congress used the two words "deport or return" only to make § 243(h)'s protection available in both deportation and exclusion proceedings. Indeed, the history of the 1980 amendment confirms that conclusion.

### B. The History of the Refugee Act of 1980

. . . We [previously] explained the important distinction between "deportation" or "expulsion," on the one hand, and "exclusion," on the other:

> It is important to note at the outset that our immigration laws have long made a distinction between those aliens who have come to our shores seeking admission, such as petitioner, and those who are within the United States after an entry, irrespective of its legality. In the latter instance the Court has recognized additional rights and privileges not extended to those in the former category who are merely 'on the threshold of initial entry. . . .'

> *          *          *

The 1980 amendment erased the long-maintained distinction between deportable and excludable aliens for purposes of § 243(h). By adding the word "return" and removing the words "within the United States" from § 243(h), Congress extended the statute's protection to both types of aliens, but it did nothing to change the presumption that both types of aliens [enjoy the protection of § 243(h) only if found] within United States territory. . . .

. . . There is no change in the 1980 amendment, however, that could only be explained by an assumption that Congress also intended to provide for the statute's extraterritorial application. It would have been extraordinary for Congress to make such an important change in the law without any mention of that possible effect. Not a scintilla of evidence of such an intent can be found in the legislative history.

In sum, all available evidence about the meaning of § 243(h) . . . leads unerringly to the conclusion that it applies in only one context: the domestic procedures by which the Attorney General determines whether deportable and excludable aliens may remain in the United States.

### IV

Although the protection afforded by § 243(h) did not apply in exclusion proceedings before 1980, other provisions of the Act did authorize relief for aliens at the border seeking protection as refugees in the United States. When the United States acceded to the Protocol in 1968, therefore, the INA already offered some protection to both classes of refugees. It offered no such protection to any alien who was beyond the territorial waters of the United States, though, and we would not expect the Government to assume a burden as to those aliens without some acknowledgment of its dramatically broadened scope.... Nevertheless, because the history of the 1980 Act does disclose a general intent to conform our law to Article 33 of the Convention, it might be argued that the extraterritorial obligations imposed by Article 33 were so clear that Congress, in acceding to the Protocol, and then in amending the statute to harmonize the two, meant to give the latter a correspondingly extraterritorial effect. Or, just as the statute might have imposed an extraterritorial obligation that the Convention does not (the argument we have just rejected), the Convention might have established an extraterritorial obligation which the statute does not; under the Supremacy Clause, that broader treaty obligation might then provide the controlling rule of law. With those possibilities in mind we shall consider both the text and negotiating history of the Convention itself.

Like the text and the history of § 243(h), the text and negotiating history of Article 33 of the United Nations Convention are both completely silent with respect to the Article's possible application to actions taken by a country outside its own borders. Respondents argue that the Protocol's broad remedial goals require that a nation be prevented from repatriating refugees to their potential oppressors whether or not the refugees are within that nation's borders. In spite of the moral weight of that argument, both the text and negotiating history of Article 33 affirmatively indicate that it was not intended to have extraterritorial effect.

### A. The Text of the Convention

\*     \*     \*

The full text of Article 33 reads as follows:

### Article 33.—Prohibition of expulsion or return ('refoulement')

1. No Contracting State shall expel or return ('refouler') a refugee in any manner whatsoever to the frontiers of territories where his life or freedom would be threatened on account of his race, religion, nationality, membership of a particular social group or political opinion.

\*     \*     \*

Article 33.1 uses the words "expel or return ('refouler')" as an obvious parallel to the words "deport or return" in § 243(h)(1). There is no dispute that "expel" has the same meaning as "deport"; ... the term "return ('refouler')" refers to the exclusion of aliens who are merely "'on the threshold of initial entry.'"

This suggestion—that "return" has a legal meaning narrower than its common meaning—is reinforced by the parenthetical reference to "refouler," a French word that is not an exact synonym for the English word "return." ... [T]wo respected English-French Dictionaries ... include [in their translations of refouler] words like "repulse," "repel," "drive back," and even "expel." To the extent that they are relevant, these translations imply that "return" means a defensive act of resistance or exclusion at a border rather than an act of transporting someone to a particular destination. In the context of the Convention, to "return" means to "repulse" rather than to "reinstate."

\*     \*     \*

The drafters of the Convention and the parties to the Protocol—like the drafters of § 243(h)—may not have contemplated that any nation would gather fleeing refugees and return them to the one country they had desperately sought to escape; such actions may even violate the spirit of Article 33; but a treaty cannot impose uncontemplated extraterritorial obligations on those who ratify it through no more than its general humanitarian intent. Because the text of Article 33 cannot reasonably be read to say anything at all about a nation's actions toward aliens outside its own territory, it does not prohibit such actions.

\*     \*     \*

### V

Respondents contend that the dangers faced by Haitians who are unwillingly repatriated demonstrate that the judgment of the Court of Appeals fulfilled the central purpose of the Convention and the Refugee Act of 1980. While we must, of course, be guided by the high purpose of both the treaty and the statute, we are not persuaded that either one places any limit on the President's authority to repatriate aliens interdicted beyond the territorial seas of the United States.

It is perfectly clear that ... the President [has] ample power to establish a naval blockade that would simply deny illegal Haitian migrants the ability to disembark on our shores. Whether the President's chosen method of preventing the "attempted mass migration" of thousands of Haitians ... poses a greater risk of harm to Haitians who might otherwise face a long and dangerous return voyage, is irrelevant to the scope of his authority to take action that neither the Convention nor the statute clearly prohibits. As we have already noted, Acts of Congress normally do not have extraterritorial application unless such an intent is clearly manifested. That presumption has special force when we are construing treaty and statutory provisions that may involve foreign and military affairs for which the President has unique responsibility. We therefore find ourselves in agreement with the conclusion [that]

> This case presents a painfully common situation in which desperate people, convinced that they can no longer remain in their homeland, take desperate measures to escape. Although the human crisis is compelling, there is no solution to be found in a judicial remedy.

The judgment of the Court of Appeals is reversed.

*It is so ordered.*

Justice BLACKMUN, dissenting.

When, in 1968, the United States acceded to the United Nations Protocol Relating to the Status of Refugees, it pledged not to "return *('refouler')* a refugee in any manner whatsoever" to a place where he would face political persecution. In 1980, Congress amended our immigration law to reflect the Protocol's directives. . . .

I believe that the duty of nonreturn expressed in both the Protocol and the statute is clear. The majority finds it "extraordinary," that Congress would have intended the ban on returning "any alien" to apply to aliens at sea. That Congress would have meant what it said is not remarkable. What is extraordinary in this case is that the Executive, in disregard of the law, would take to the seas to intercept fleeing refugees and force them back to their persecutors—and that the Court would strain to sanction that conduct.

### I

I begin with the Convention, for it is undisputed that the Refugee Act of 1980 was passed to conform our law to Article 33, and that "the nondiscretionary duty imposed by sec. 243(h) parallels the United States' mandatory *non-refoulement* obligations under Article 33.1. . . ." The Convention thus constitutes the backdrop against which the statute must be understood.

### A

Article 33.1 of the Convention states categorically and without geographical limitation:

> No Contracting State shall expel or return *('refouler')* a refugee in any manner whatsoever to the frontiers of territories where his life or freedom would be threatened on account of his race, religion, nationality, membership of a particular social group or political opinion.

The terms are unambiguous. Vulnerable refugees shall not be returned. The language is clear, and the command is straightforward; that should be the end of the inquiry. . . .

\*          \*          \*

The straightforward interpretation of the duty of nonreturn is strongly reinforced by the Convention's use of the French term *"refouler."* The ordinary meaning of *"refouler,"* as the majority concedes, is "to repulse, . . . ; to drive back, to repel." Thus construed, Article 33.1 of the Convention reads: "No contracting state shall expel or [repulse, drive back, or repel] a refugee in any manner whatsoever to the frontiers of territories where his life or freedom would be threatened. . . ." That, of course, is exactly what the Government is doing. It thus is no surprise that when the French press has described the very policy challenged here, the term it has used is *"refouler."* ("Les Etats-Unis ont décidé de *refouler* directement les réfugiés recueillis par la garde cotiére." (The United States has decided [de refouler] directly the refugees picked up by the Coast Guard)).

\*          \*          \*

Article 33.1 is clear not only in what it says, but also in what it does not say: it does not include any geographical limitation. It limits only where a refugee may be sent "to," not where he may be sent from. This is not surprising, given that the aim of the provision is to protect refugees against persecution.

\*          \*          \*

### III

The Convention that the Refugee Act embodies was enacted largely in response to the experience of Jewish refugees in Europe during the period of World War II. The tragic consequences of the world's indifference at that time are well known. The resulting ban on *refoulement*, as broad as the humanitarian purpose that inspired it, is easily applicable here, the Court's protestations of impotence and regret notwithstanding.

The refugees attempting to escape from Haiti do not claim a right of admission to this country. They do not even argue that the Government has no right to intercept their boats. They demand only that the United States, land of refugees and guardian of freedom, cease forcibly driving them back to detention, abuse, and death. That is a modest plea, vindicated by the Treaty and the statute. We should not close our ears to it.

I dissent.

## 416 "We hereby reestablish our Independent and Sovereign Nation of Hawai'i" (1993)

In 1778, when the British explorer James Cook happened upon a group of Pacific islands, each inhabited by an indigenous self-governing people—the Kanaka Maoli (the real people)—he did not hesitate to rename them the Sandwich Islands. By 1810, the islands' populations were united by the conquests of Kamehameha I into the Kingdom of Hawai'i, and despite various overtures by colonial powers, the new nation won international recognition and entered into treaties with other nations, including Great Britain, France, and the United States.

In 1887, American expansionists and sugar companies, with the aid of the United States minister to Hawai'i, John L. Stevens, presented King Kalakaua the "Bayonet Constitution" to sign on pain of assassination. The document disenfranchised the local population, gave full powers to a cabinet consisting of one British and four American members, and reduced the monarch to a ceremonial figure.

In 1892, two-thirds of the natives petitioned Queen Liliuokalani for a new constitution restoring their rights. Minister Stevens retaliated by recognizing a "Provisional Government of the Kingdom of Hawai'i," led by the American businessman Sanford P. Dole, which was dominated by sugar-wealthy Americans and supported by 162 United States marines. Queen Liliuokalani refused to abdicate and issued a statement of protest (incorporated in Doc. 416a).

Although the provisional government sought annexation to the United States, it was thwarted politically. Since it failed to muster the two-thirds congressional majority needed to annex a territory, Hawai'i was acquired instead by a joint resolution that passed the Senate on July 6, 1898, after an amendment to require a vote of approval by the Kanaka Maoli was defeated. President McKinley remarked: "Annexation is not a change. It is a consummation."

Native Hawaiians have fared no better than other indigenous peoples in the United States. But they have retained no degree of authority over their communal affairs. Unlike Native Americans, Native Hawaiians have neither semiautonomy nor communally held land. (Although Congress set aside land for distribution in 1926, it was never properly allocated, and its administration was turned over to the State of Hawaii upon statehood.) Lacking the advantages provided by the mainland system of reservations, Hawai'i's natives remain less protected against the political whims of the state's nonnative majority. (Compare Docs. 362; 405.)

On the hundredth anniversary of the American takeover, Congress issued an empty acknowledgment of a wrongdoing. Equally symbolic was the gesture of the islands' Native Hawaiian governor, who refused to fly the American flag on the State House. But the lack of more concrete measures of relief has animated an increasingly militant sovereignty movement among the modern Kanaka Maoli.

## ☆416 The Fall and Rise of Hawai'i

### ☆416a Joint Resolution of Congress

P.L. 103-150, 107 Stat. 1510 (1993).

Joint Resolution [t]o acknowledge the 100th anniversary of the January 17, 1893 overthrow of the Kingdom of Hawaii, and to offer an apology to Native Hawaiians on behalf of the United States for the overthrow of the Kingdom of Hawaii.

Whereas, prior to the arrival of the first Europeans in 1778, the Native Hawaiian people lived in a highly organized, self-sufficient, subsistent social system based on communal land tenure with a sophisticated language, culture, and religion;

Whereas, a unified monarchical government of the Hawaiian Islands was established in 1810 under Kamehameha I, the first King of Hawaii;

Whereas, from 1826 until 1893, the United States recognized the independence of the Kingdom of Hawaii, extended full and complete diplomatic recognition to the Hawaiian Government, and entered into treaties and conventions with the Hawaiian monarchs to govern commerce and navigation in 1826, 1842, 1849, 1875, and 1887;

> *          *          *

Whereas, on January 14, 1893, John L. Stevens (hereafter referred to in this Resolution as the "United States Minister"), the United States Minister assigned to the sovereign and independent Kingdom of Hawaii conspired with a small group of non-Hawaiian residents of the Kingdom of Hawaii, including citizens of the United States, to overthrow the indigenous and lawful Government of Hawaii;

Whereas, in pursuance of the conspiracy to overthrow the Government of Hawaii, the United States Minister and the naval representatives of the United States caused armed naval forces of the United States to invade the sovereign Hawaiian nation on January 16, 1893, and to position themselves near the Hawaiian Government buildings and the Iolani Palace to intimidate Queen Liliuokalani and her Government;

Whereas, on the afternoon of January 17, 1893, a Committee of Safety that represented the American and European sugar planters, descendants of missionaries, and financiers deposed the Hawaiian monarchy and proclaimed the establishment of a Provisional Government;

Whereas, the United States Minister thereupon extended diplomatic recognition to the Provisional Government that was formed by the conspirators without the consent of the Native Hawaiian people or the lawful Government of Hawaii and in violation of treaties between the two nations and of international law;

Whereas, soon thereafter, when informed of the risk of bloodshed with resistance, Queen Liliuokalani issued the following statement yielding her authority to the United States Government rather than to the Provisional Government:

> I Liliuokalani, by the Grace of God and under the Constitution of the Hawaiian Kingdom, Queen, do hereby solemnly protest against any and all acts done against myself and the Constitutional Government of the Hawaiian Kingdom by certain persons claiming to have established a Provisional Government of and for this Kingdom.
>
> That I yield to the superior force of the United States of America whose Minister Plenipotentiary, His Excellency John L. Stevens, has caused United States troops to be landed at Honolulu and declared that he would support the Provisional Government.
>
> Now to avoid any collision of armed forces, and perhaps the loss of life, I do this under protest and impelled by said force yield my authority until such time as the Government of the United States shall, upon facts being presented to it, undo the action of its representatives and reinstate me in the authority which I claim as the Constitutional Sovereign of the Hawaiian Islands.
>
> Done at Honolulu this 17th day of January, A.D. 1893.;

Whereas, without the active support and intervention by the United States diplomatic and military representatives, the insurrection against the Government of Queen Liliuokalani would have failed for lack of popular support and insufficient arms;

Whereas, on February 1, 1893, the United States Minister raised the American flag and proclaimed Hawaii to be a protectorate of the United States;

\*         \*         \*

Whereas, in a message to Congress on December 18, 1893, President Grover Cleveland reported fully and accurately on the illegal acts of the conspirators, described such acts as an "act of war, committed with the participation of a diplomatic representative of the United States and without authority of Congress," and acknowledged that by such acts the government of a peaceful and friendly people was overthrown;

Whereas, President Cleveland further concluded that a "substantial wrong has thus been done which a due regard for our national character as well as the rights of the injured people requires we should endeavor to repair" and called for the restoration of the Hawaiian monarchy;

Whereas, the Provisional Government protested President Cleveland's call for the restoration of the monarchy and continued to hold state power and pursue annexation to the United States;

Whereas, the Provisional Government successfully lobbied the Committee on Foreign Relations of the Senate ( . . . the "Committee") to conduct a new

investigation into the events surrounding the overthrow of the monarchy;

Whereas, the Committee and its chairman, Senator John Morgan, conducted hearings . . . in which members of the Provisional Government justified and condoned the actions of the United States Minister and recommended annexation of Hawaii;

\*         \*         \*

Whereas, on July 4, 1894, the Provisional Government declared itself to be the Republic of Hawaii;

Whereas, on January 24, 1895, while imprisoned in Iolani Palace, Queen Liliuokalani was forced by representatives of the Republic of Hawaii to officially abdicate her throne;

Whereas, in the 1896 United States Presidential election, William McKinley replaced Grover Cleveland;

Whereas, on July 7, 1898, as a consequence of the Spanish-American War, President McKinley signed the Newlands Joint Resolution that provided for the annexation of Hawaii;

Whereas, through the Newlands Resolution, the self-declared Republic of Hawaii ceded sovereignty over the Hawaiian Islands to the United States;

Whereas, the Republic of Hawaii also ceded 1,800,000 acres of crown, government and public lands of the Kingdom of Hawaii, without the consent of or compensation to the Native Hawaiian people of Hawaii or their sovereign government;

Whereas, the Congress, through the Newlands Resolution, ratified the cession, annexed Hawaii as part of the United States, and vested title to the lands in Hawaii in the United States;

\*         \*         \*

Whereas, the indigenous Hawaiian people never directly relinquished their claims to their inherent sovereignty as a people or over their national lands to the United States, either through their monarchy or through a plebiscite or referendum;

\*         \*         \*

Whereas, the health and well-being of the Native Hawaiian people is intrinsically tied to their deep feelings and attachment to the land;

Whereas, the long-range economic and social changes in Hawaii over the nineteenth and early twentieth centuries have been devastating to the population and to the health and well-being of the Hawaiian people;

Whereas, the Native Hawaiian people are determined to preserve, develop and transmit to future generations their ancestral territory, and their cultural identity in accordance with their own spiritual and traditional beliefs, customs, practices, language, and social institutions;

\*         \*         \*

Whereas, it is proper and timely for the Congress on the occasion of the impending one hundredth anniversary of the event, to acknowledge the historic significance of the illegal overthrow of the Kingdom of Hawaii, to express its deep regret to the Native Hawaiian people, and to support the reconciliation efforts of the State of Hawaii and the United Church of Christ with Native Hawaiians; Now, therefore, be it

*Resolved by the Senate and House of Representatives of the United States of America in Congress assembled,*

SECTION 1. ACKNOWLEDGMENT AND APOLOGY.

The Congress—

(1) on the occasion of the 100th anniversary of the illegal overthrow of the Kingdom of Hawaii on January 17, 1893, acknowledges the historical significance of this event which resulted in the suppression of the inherent sovereignty of the Native Hawaiian people; . . .

(3) apologizes to Native Hawaiians on behalf of the people of the United States for the overthrow of the Kingdom of Hawaii on January 17, 1893 with the participation of agents and citizens of the United States, and the deprivation of the rights of Native Hawaiians to self-determination;

(4) expresses its commitment to acknowledge the ramifications of the overthrow of the Kingdom of Hawaii, in order to provide a proper foundation for reconciliation between the United States and the Native Hawaiian people. . . .

*SEC. 2. DEFINITIONS.*

As used in this Joint Resolution, the term "Native Hawaiians" means any individual who is a descendent of the aboriginal people who, prior to 1778, occupied and exercised sovereignty in the area that now constitutes the State of Hawaii.

*SEC. 3. DISCLAIMER.*

Nothing in this Joint Resolution is intended to serve as a settlement of any claims against the United States.

*Approved November 23, 1993*

☆416b Proclamation of Restoration of the Independence of the Sovereign Nation State of Hawai'i

Document at http://hawaii-nation.org/nation/proclamall. html.

Today, We, the Kanaka Maoli, proclaim our Right of self-determination as a People in accordance with Article 1 (2) of the United Nations Charter, and join the World Community of States as an Independent and Sovereign Nation. We hereby reestablish our Independent and Sovereign Nation of Hawai'i that was illegally taken from the Kanaka Maoli on January 17, 1893.

By virtue of our Right to self-determination, the Kanaka Maoli claim this Right to freely determine our political status and freely pursue our economic, social and cultural development in accordance with common Article 1 of the International Covenant on Civil, and Political Rights and the International Covenant on Economic, Social and Cultural Rights.

We, the Kanaka Maoli, claim our Right for our own ends, to freely control and dispose of our natural wealth and resources, including our lands and our waters, without prejudice to any obligations arising out of international economic cooperation, based upon the principle of mutual benefit and international law.

We, the Kanaka Maoli, claim all our Land, Natural Wealth, Resources, Minerals, and Waters, which have always resided and will always reside within the hands of the Kanaka Maoli, to be ours forever, originally under communal land tenure.

\*　　　\*　　　\*

In the Independent and Sovereign Nation of Hawai'i lives the Kanaka Maoli. We have resided here forever, from time immemorial. We have displaced no other people. We, the Kanaka Maoli, are the original inhabitants and occupants of these Islands. We have always been in possession of our Land and are entitled to re-establish our Independent and Sovereign Nation.

The current citizens of the Independent and Sovereign Nation of Hawai'i consist of all those who are descendants of the Kanaka Maoli prior to the arrival of the first westerners in 1778, and those persons, and their descendants who have lived in Hawai'i prior to the illegal overthrow, invasion and occupation of January 17, 1893, in the area which now constitutes the Archipelago of the Independent and Sovereign Nation of Hawai'i.

\*　　　\*　　　\*

Despite the historical injustices and abuse that have documented a dark chapter in the lives of the Kanaka Maoli, so unimaginable to the conscience of humanity and to all human life as a whole, we have come to realize that in the course of these modern times, we could never depart or separate our undying love, our connection, or our sacred ties from the Spirit of this Land, Aloha 'Aina, which is the heart and life of all living things, as taught and handed down from the ancient wise ones (Kupuna). We must protect our sacred 'Aina from such invasion and exploitation, to liberate it from alien destructive forces, and preserve and protect our Cultural Heritage for future generations, from the devastation of extinction.

We, the Kanaka Maoli, have continued to exercise, practice and occupy our lands, despite the continued subjection, domination and exploitation by the forces of the occupying foreign powers, denying us our inalienable rights to self-determination, Independence and Sovereignty. Thus have well recognized principles of International Law been violated. Thus were our national identity, land, resources, Right to Sovereignty over our Territory violated, and a peaceful people overthrown by the invasion of foreign powers, who continue to occupy, exploit and destroy our way of life.

We, the Kanaka Maoli, have united at this very historic and symbolic place, the 'Iolani Palace, wherein we remember the last days and tragic moments in our history, that have affected the safety and well-being of our people, to which our beloved Kupuna and Queen Liliuokalani and her commitment to restore the rights of our people, have been stolen. Her dedicated endurance against foreign powers who committed such acts of aggression and force, threats of fear and imprisonment, knowingly in violation of numerous treaties, agreements and principles of international customs and law, has never faltered, for the Love of her people, and those who stood on truth and justice, and shall prevail here, now and forever.

We, the Kanaka Maoli, here today in flesh and in Spirit, share that same commitment. It is the duty and obligation of every Kanaka Maoli, young and old, to stand ready to restore and defend our national rights, territorial integrity and independence, without prejudice, and reject and resist unlawful acts, injustice and complicity, violence and terrorism, against our political independence, and do summarily reject such use of violence and force against the territorial integrity of other peaceful states.

*       *       *

We call upon our Kanaka Maoli people, and upon all Nations of the World, to unite and act this day, to declare and proclaim our Inalienable Sovereignty of the Nation State of Hawai'i fully restored and functional, and to arise in the uniting of freedom and dignity in our homeland, which is the homeland of the Kanaka Maoli, now and forever.

Therefore, the Kupuna, in General Council Assembled, by the Authority recognized and vested in the Aha Kuka O Ka Ohana, in the name of the Kanaka Maoli people, to preserve and to forevermore cultivate the Heritage and Culture of the Kanaka Maoli, do solemnly publish, declare and proclaim that the Independent and Sovereign Nation of Hawai'i is free and absolved from any other political connection with any other Nation State. Those who disregard the Principles and Rule of the Law of Nations, Justice, Integrity, Morality of Character, and Humanity, by force and acts of aggression, now illegally occupy our Territory.

# 417 "tyranny under the rule of the U.S. Congress" (1993)

In 1787, the drafters of the United States Constitution reached a compromise regarding the site of the capital city of the republic. Rather than give any one state claim to being the home of the national government, the Constitution provided that a district, to be under the exclusive legislative control of Congress, be acquired from the states. Maryland and Virginia ceded portions of their territory on opposite banks of the Potomac River to create a square District of Columbia, geographically and politically poised more or less between the great divisions of the country. At the time, the District was sparsely populated. The portion of the District given by Virginia was retroceded in 1846 after a referendum by the people of what is now Arlington County, Virginia.

For most of its history, the District resembled a sleepy southern city with a small native population that swelled to accommodate the influx of politicians, lobbyists, and hangers-on when Congress was in session. Today, however, especially after the growth in government during and following the New Deal, the District has become a major metropolitan area. Like other southern cities, it enforced racial segregation until the Supreme Court acted to declare such laws unconstitutional. Meanwhile, the permanent population became first predominantly and then overwhelmingly African American. Although at the beginning the permanent residents of the District of Columbia governed themselves, Congress abolished self-rule in 1878 after financial scandals in the 1870s. Between 1878 and 1967, the District of Columbia was governed by commissioners appointed by the president. Indeed, it was not until 1961 that the ratification of the Twenty-first Amendment allowed the resident citizens of the District of Columbia to vote for the president of the United States. Following that change came nonvoting representation in Congress and, finally, legislation providing for a locally elected mayor and city council.

Nevertheless, Congress retained the constitutional authority to oversee the District through legislation. As the drug and crime problems facing any urban area, the scandals in city government, and finally financial crises became the subjects of daily headlines in the local newspapers, Congress began to flex its muscle. In response, the District's residents' abiding, but largely ignored, desire for full citizenship and statehood gained new momentum. The participation by the mayor and the District's representative to Congress in acts of civil disobedience demonstrated clearly their frustration with the orthodox methods of political change.

# ☆417  Free D.C.!

## ☆417a  Statehood Protest Results in 32 Arrests; Demonstrators Block Streets near Capitol

Kent Jenkins Jr. and Morenike Efuntade, *Washington Post*, July 2, 1993, C1.

Senior District officials, adopting a new approach in their uphill fight for D.C. statehood, embraced the nonviolent protest tactics of the civil rights movement yesterday with a demonstration that led to 32 arrests.

Jesse L. Jackson, a District lobbyist for statehood in the Senate, was among those arrested for blocking a major intersection near the Capitol yesterday morning. Chanting "Free D.C." as they were taken into custody by U.S. Capitol Police officers, the protesters promised to repeat their action once a week until the District becomes a state.

Statehood supporters had spent the last two years waging a campaign of quiet persuasion on Capitol Hill, promoting their cause through one-on-one meetings with lawmakers. That effort managed to revive the issue from legislative obscurity, but it appeared to win few converts.

Jackson, a longtime master at mustering what he has referred to as "street heat," said that a more confrontational approach would help build the political momentum needed to push statehood through the House and Senate.

Inside the Capitol, however, lawmakers predicted that the protests would have little effect....

\*          \*          \*

But Jackson said the protests were necessary to dramatize the inequity of the District's current political situation. The District's delegate to the House of Representatives does not have a full vote on the floor and the city has no representation in the Senate.

"We will fill up these jail cells for righteousness' sake," Jackson told a cheering crowd of about 100. America "cannot in good conscience fight for new states in Bosnia and not fight for statehood in Washington, D.C."

Other top D.C. officials had nothing but praise for the protest yesterday.

"You are talking to a member of the sit-in generation," said Del. Eleanor Holmes Norton (D-D.C.). "Civil disobedience is very appropriate in this case. It's a little late, frankly. We need to get people's attention."

Neither Norton nor [former] Mayor Sharon Pratt Kelly (D) was arrested yesterday, by design. Norton, who participated in part of the protest, said "my role is not to miss a vote on the House floor."

And Vada Manager, a spokesman for Kelly, said that going to jail "shouldn't be a litmus test for supporting statehood." Manager said Kelly, who spoke

yesterday at a statehood rally, had not ruled out being arrested later.

Some statehood supporters previously have hesitated to use civil disobedience to promote the issue, questioning whether it would win lawmakers' sympathy or alienate them. Plans to put the issue before the full House last year collapsed when head counts found that statehood would have lost badly.

African Americans "have never won anything in America with power lunches and negotiation," said Mark Thompson, an organizer of the event, who was arrested. "We've always had to use direct action, and we will continue with a sustained direct action movement for decolonization."

Others arrested included Florence Pendleton, another statehood lobbyist; Charles J. Moreland, the D.C. lobbyist for statehood in the House; Bishop George Augustus Stallings; and labor leader Ron Richardson. Those arrested were charged with unlawful assembly and released after paying a $50 fine.

The protest, organized by Citizens for New Columbia and the Statehood Winning Action Team (SWAT), began at 11 a.m. when protesters marched from Judiciary Square to the Longworth House Office Building to hear speeches by Kelly and others.

\*          \*          \*

Then, to the cheers of the crowd, Jackson sat down in the middle of the street. Others joined him, linking arms and creating a traffic jam.

"This is an act of conscience, an act of resistance. We must put our bodies on the line," he said.

\*          \*          \*

## ☆417b  Mayor, 37 Others Arrested after Statehood Protest

Kent Jenkins Jr., *Washington Post*, August 27, 1993, D1.

Comparing Congress to the British Crown and invoking the legacy of Martin Luther King Jr., D.C. Mayor Sharon Pratt Kelly was arrested yesterday as part of a nonviolent protest in favor of D.C. statehood.

Kelly and 37 others briefly blockaded an intersection near the Capitol at lunchtime yesterday, practicing civil disobedience to dramatize what Kelly termed Congress's "oppression" of the District.

After the mayor and a group of about 200 statehood supporters marched up Capitol Hill, Kelly and those who wanted to be arrested occupied the intersection of Independence and New Jersey avenues.

Harking back to the Boston Tea Party and the cry of "No taxation without representation," Kelly poured a large container of iced tea into the street. She and other protesters then sat down on the pavement and ignored several police warnings to leave. Police officers arrested all 38, without incident.

"Today we draw the line," Kelly said shortly before she was led away in plastic handcuffs. "We will engage in civil protest if we think the laws that govern us are unfair and un-American.... We are experiencing tyranny under the rule of the U.S. Congress."

Thus, she became the first District mayor arrested for the statehood cause.

Virtually no members of Congress witnessed the gesture. Congress is on its August recess, and the House office buildings near the protest site were almost deserted.

The carefully choreographed 90-minute demonstration, part of a once-a-week series that began two months ago, prompted unusually tight security that appeared to be aimed more at keeping Kelly safe than taking her into custody.

*       *       *

While most were hauled away in a police bus, Kelly was taken to Capitol Police headquarters alone in a squad car. She was charged with unlawful assembly, a misdemeanor, and released after posting a $50 bond. Kelly spokesman Vada Manager said she will not contest the charge.

*       *       *

... Kelly made her feelings clear in an "open letter" she issued on the subject of statehood, which portrayed the District as being occupied by a colonial power.

Under the District's local government charter, Congress has the power to overrule any law the city passes and or to change anything in the city's budget to which it objects.

"As the daughter of a judge and the mayor of the nation's capital, the last thing I ever thought I would do is be arrested," wrote Kelly, who will be up for reelection next year. "Well, for me, it looks like my day of reckoning has come. . . . As a result, I feel happier and closer to being free already."

*       *       *

But one statehood opponent who saw yesterday's event was unimpressed.

"It's ironic to have the mayor blocking her own streets," said Richard T. Dykema, the top aide to Rep. Dana Rohrabacher (R-Calif.), who serves on the House D.C. Committee. "I don't think you could find one person whose mind has been changed" because of the protests.

☆417c  Courting D.C. Statehood; Arrested Protesters Seeking Trials as Forum

Paul Duggan and James Ragland, *Washington Post*, September 2, 1993, A1.

Dozens of District statehood activists arrested in demonstrations this summer have chosen not to pay $50 fines, opting instead for a series of group "political" trials in D.C. Superior Court, where they intend to use the witness stand as a podium to advance their cause.

Eight group trials involving about 65 protesters

already have been scheduled from mid-October to mid-December, including a November trial at which 28 activists will fight misdemeanor charges of unlawful assembly. And the number of such time-consuming trials promises to grow as statehood demonstrators continue their weekly blockade of an intersection near the Capitol, where nearly 130 arrests have been made since July 1.

Exercising the right to a trial is a new tactic for statehood advocates in their evolving strategy to embarrass the federal government and put pressure on Congress by using the tools of the civil rights movement, including protest marches and acts of civil disobedience.

*       *       *

"Courtrooms have always been used as a forum for political debate," said lawyer Jordan B. Yeager, a leader of the demonstrators' legal defense team. He said the many defendants—including D.C. Council member Kevin Chavous (D-Ward 7) and Jesse L. Jackson, the District's elected statehood lobbyist in the Senate—hope to focus public attention on the statehood issue by standing trial and testifying about their cause.

*       *       *

By choosing not to pay $50 fines, the demonstrators face nonjury trials. If convicted, they could be fined $250 or jailed for 90 days.

*       *       *

☆417d  D.C. Shuns Case of Statehood Demonstrators; Move to Dismiss Charges Hailed by Supporters of the Movement

Cindy Loose, *Washington Post*, October 20, 1993, D1.

Statehood advocates celebrated what they termed a major victory and symbolic milestone yesterday after the D.C. corporation counsel moved to dismiss charges against statehood demonstrators.

"It shows the D.C. government is standing up and will no longer do the dirty work of the colonial authority," said Jordan Yeager, an attorney for 200 statehood defendants arrested during several protests over the summer that blocked a street in front of a congressional office building.

"It was historic in that the D.C. government refused to be the federal government's instrument in oppressing citizens who want to be free," said Charles J. Moreland, who was elected to lobby for statehood in the House.

*       *       *

Officials in the corporation counsel's office played down the significance of the decision not to prosecute, saying it was not political, but rather a routine attempt to avoid duplicating efforts. The U.S. attorney's office has separate but related charges pending against about 20 of the 200 demonstrators.

*      *      *

The city's decision caught the U.S. attorney's office by surprise and threw the political hot potato into its court. The office has jurisdiction over all criminal matters in the District, but cedes authority for prosecuting many misdemeanors to the city.

# 418 "We are now in the Fifth Seal" (1993)

A group of Branch Davidians, an offshoot of the Seventh Day Adventists, was led by David Koresh (né Vernon Howell), who had captivated his flock with virtuoso Bible interpretations and forecasts. One of these prophesied a final confrontation with the forces of evil, after which those chosen by God would emerge to eternal glory, purified by a wall of flames. Meanwhile, like many leaders, Koresh reveled in adulation, subordination, and sexual license within the Davidian compound at Mt. Carmel, outside Waco, Texas. He was also believed by the Bureau of Alcohol, Tobacco, and Firearms (BATF) to be stockpiling weapons and ammunition inside the compound and transforming legal semiautomatic assault rifles into illegal automatic ones.

With helicopters from the Texas National Guard, eighty-five militarily trained BATF agents went to the Davidian compound to serve arrest and search warrants. Having been tipped off, Koresh shut the door in the face of the agent serving the warrant. A firefight ensued, killing four BATF agents and five Davidians. More than twenty people on both sides were wounded.

Because federal agents had been killed, the FBI took over the operation. To effect surrender, the FBI alternately negotiated with and harassed the inhabitants of the compound. Despite signs that Koresh would eventually surrender, the FBI began a dawn assault on Koresh's "Rancho Apocalypse" on April 19, 1993, using four Bradley Fighting Vehicles and two M-60 tanks modified to inject tear gas into the compound.

Shortly after noon, fires, apparently set by the Davidians, were seen in the compound. Spreading rapidly, the fire consumed the compound in less than an hour. Koresh and seventy-three others, including twenty-one children, perished in flames as he had prophesied. Some, however, including Koresh, were found to have been killed by gunshot wounds inflicted by themselves or other sect members.

Surviving Branch Davidians from Mt. Carmel were tried for the murder of the four dead BATF agents, but they were only convicted of manslaughter by a jury that must have been troubled, as is the following analysis, by the nature of law enforcement's approach to the Davidians in the compound.

## ☆418 David Koresh and the FBI's Religious Intolerance

James D. Tabor, document at http://www.neo.com/ucalpress/whywaco/religious.html.

The FBI operation at the Branch Davidian compound outside Waco, Texas, turned out to be one of the most massive and tragic in the history of United States law enforcement. On April 19, 1993, a final assault on the Mount Carmel center by the FBI led to a fire that killed seventy-four Branch Davidians, including twenty-one children. Despite subsequent claims by the government that the outcome was unavoidable, the entire matter could have been handled differently and resolved peacefully. The FBI chose to ignore David Koresh's pronouncements about the religious significance of the events in Waco, statements that contained the only feasible solution to the crisis. The agents called to Mount Carmel could hardly have been expected to pack their Bibles, but in retrospect it would not have been such a bad idea.

*      *      *

Listening carefully to Koresh's first interviews, someone familiar with biblical texts would have perceived the situation in wholly different terms than the government[, which classified it as a "Hostage/Barricade rescue"]. To the Branch Davidians, the only "rescue" they needed was from the government itself. In their view, the federal agents represented the evil power, referred to in the book of Revelation as "Babylon." The idea of "surrendering to proper authority," as the government demanded throughout the next seven weeks, was absolutely out of the question for these believers unless they were convinced that it was what God willed.

The FBI's unwillingness to engage in a discussion of the Scriptures crippled its negotiations with Koresh. Transcripts of these conversations show that much of the time the FBI either talked down to him or failed to grasp his message. The FBI report notes that his delivery of "religious rhetoric was so strong that [the negotiators] could hardly interrupt him to discuss possible surrender." The report constantly laments that Koresh "refused to discuss any matters of substance" and merely insisted on "preaching" to negotiators. What the authorities apparently never recognized is that Koresh's preaching was to him and his followers the only matter of substance, and that a "surrender" could be worked out only through dialogue within the biblical framework in which the Branch Davidians lived. In the middle of March, Jeff Jamar, the FBI agent in charge, told the negotiators not to allow any more "Bible babble" from Koresh. This order deprived Koresh of the only means of communication he valued, effectively dooming the negotiations.

Throughout the fifty-one days, Koresh talked almost incessantly about the Seven Seals of the book of Revelation, starting on the day of the BATF raid, when he announced during a radio interview that "We are now in the Fifth Seal." (One of the FBI negotiators admitted that some of them initially thought that the Seven Seals to which Koresh referred were animals.)

The Fifth Seal in the book of Revelation takes place shortly before the cosmic judgment of God; it is the last major event leading to the end of human history. The text speaks of some of the faithful being slain, followed by a waiting period before the rest are killed. Based on the Branch Davidian interpretation of events, the killing had begun with the BATF assault on February 28. In keeping with the text, the group believed that it was supposed to wait for a "little season" until those remaining inside Mount Carmel were slain as well. Their martyrdom would lead to the Sixth Seal, which would bring about the judgment of God on the world.

It was obvious, though, that Koresh was confused by the events that had transpired. His prophetic scenario did require fulfillment of this Fifth Seal, but Koresh had taught for years that it would happen in Jerusalem, not in Waco. Furthermore, from their calculations of the "end time," the group was expecting the final confrontation to come in 1995, not in 1993. Koresh was convinced that the attack on February 28 was somehow related to the apocalypse, but he did not know precisely how, and thus he was unclear as to what he was to do. He announced that he would wait for a "word from God," which would clarify the ambiguities and uncertainties inherent in the situation outside the compound.

. . . By controlling the situation outside the compound, the government largely controlled the context and therefore unknowingly possessed the ability to influence Koresh in his interpretations, and thus in his actions. Unfortunately, by using the tactical maneuvers associated with complex Hostage/Rescue barricade situations—cutting off the compound's electricity, blaring loud music at all hours, shining searchlights in the buildings' windows, destroying Davidian vehicles—the FBI unwittingly played the perfect part of Babylon throughout the siege, validating in detail Koresh's interpretations of Scripture.

\*          \*          \*

And then, on April 14, following the Davidians' eight-day Passover celebration, and just four days before the FBI gas attack and resulting fire, Koresh received his long-awaited "word from God." He released a letter addressed to Dick DeGuerin, his lawyer, that would be his final communication to the outside world. In it he joyfully announced that the group would come out as soon as he finished writing his message on the Seven Seals. . . . In part the letter reads:

I am presently being permitted to document, in structured form, the decoded messages of the Seven Seals. Upon completion of this task, I will be free of my "waiting period." I hope to finish this as soon as possible and to stand before man to answer any and all questions regarding my actions. . . .

For seven weeks Koresh had said, consistently and incessantly, that he would not come out until he received his word from God. Then he wrote that he had received that word and that he was coming out. The FBI immediately responded to this breakthrough with ridicule. They joked about Koresh, the high school dropout, writing a book, and labeled Koresh's "word from God" nothing more than another "delay tactic." . . . The daily log in the Department of Justice report does not even mention Koresh's April 14 letter; it merely notes that "David had established a new precondition for his coming out." From the Justice report, it appears that nothing was working, that all negotiations had failed, and that the government had only one alternative—the tear-gas attack.

We now know that Koresh was indeed working on the manuscript, which he considered his divinely sanctioned task and opportunity. He worked on it as late as Sunday evening, the night before the April 19 assault, concluding his exposition of the First Seal. Those in Mount Carmel were excited and pleased by his progress, fully convinced that they would soon be able to come out peacefully. Of course, no one can ever know if Koresh would have honored his pledge to come out once the manuscript was completed. Had he been allowed to finish, though, the outcome could not have been more terrible than what actually came to pass.

## 419 "an entire town was destroyed and its residents killed or fled, never to return" (1994)

In the second half of the twentieth century, violence, riots, and looting in the nation's black ghettoes were sometimes associated with the civil rights movement, but in the first half of the century, racial mob violence was perpetrated by white mobs rampaging through African American business and residential communities. This violence often erupted following unfounded rumors of racially tainted social transgressions and offenses. Following the Wilmington, N.C., riot of 1898 (Doc. 172), many similar episodes of antiblack violence were recorded until the middle of World War II. One of these race riots, however, obliterated an entire town.

On January 1, 1923, a white woman reported being raped by a man from Rosewood, Florida, a small African American community on the Florida Gulf Coast. Frustrated at being unable to find the accused, a local white mob, drawing reinforcements from as far away as Georgia, drove the sheriff out of the county and ran amok for eight days. Rosewood, except for the white-owned general store, was overrun and set afire. Six blacks and two whites died. One victim was forced to dig his own grave; another was hanged because he could not lead the mob to the alleged assailant. A pregnant woman was shot as she crawled under her house to hide.

Rosewood's remaining inhabitants fled. When Polly Carter returned two years later to reclaim her property, she was met with a shotgun and the announcement that she possessed no property in Rosewood. She was told never to return. Rosewood, Florida, was erased from the map and mention, but not from memory.

In 1982, the *St. Petersburg Times* published an article about the mob violence in Rosewood. Survivors and relatives began speaking out, national attention was drawn to the episode, and the Florida legislature set out to investigate. On May 4, 1994, the governor of Florida signed a document appropriating $2 million to compensate the survivors of the raid and the descendants of property owners for their losses. Nine survivors, mere children in 1923, received $150,000 each, and many others shared in the reparations for losses. Rosewood stands out, however, as one example of reparations for black victims of white mob violence.

## ☆419 An Act Relating to Rosewood, Florida

1994 Fla. Laws. Ch. 359.

WHEREAS, during the month of January 1923, the African-American community of Rosewood, Florida, was destroyed, and

WHEREAS, the African-American residents of Rosewood, Florida, sustained personal and property damages, and

WHEREAS, The Rosewood Massacre was a unique tragedy in Florida's history in that the State and local government officials were on notice of the serious racial conflict in Rosewood during the entire week of January 1, 1923, and had sufficient time and opportunity to act to prevent the tragedy, and nonetheless failed to act to prevent the tragedy, an entire town was destroyed and its residents killed or fled, never to return; and the State and local government officials thereafter failed to reasonably investigate the matter, failed to bring the perpetrators to justice and failed to secure the area for the safe return of the displaced residents; and

WHEREAS, a hearing was held by the Special Master of the House of Representatives, and Arnett T. Goins, Minnie Lee Langley, Willie Evans, and Wilson Hall have shown by a preponderance of the evidence that they were present and directly affected by the violence that took place at Rosewood in January, 1923, and that they each suffered compensable damages of at least $150,000.

WHEREAS, the State of Florida recognizes an equitable obligation to redress the injuries sustained as a result of the destruction of Rosewood, Florida, NOW, THEREFORE,

Be It Enacted by the Legislature of the State of Florida:

Section 1. The facts stated in the preamble of this act are found and declared to be true.

Section 2. The Florida Department of Law Enforcement is hereby directed to investigate the crimes committed in and around Rosewood, Florida, in 1923, to determine if any criminal prosecutions may be pursued, and to report its findings to the Legislature.

Section 3. The amount of $500,000 is appropriated from the General Revenue Fund to the Office of the Attorney General for the purpose of compensating the African-American families of Rosewood, Florida, who demonstrate real property and personal property damages sustained as a result of the destruction of Rosewood, Florida, in 1923. The Attorney General in authorized to compensate each eligible family in the amount of $20,000, and, upon a finding by the Attorney General that the present-day value of real and personal property loss exceeds $20,000, the Attorney General may settle such property claims up to the amount of $100,000.

Section 4. Any African-American resident from Rosewood, Florida, living upon the effective date of this act, who was present and affected by the violence that took place at Rosewood in January, 1923, and was evacuated the week of January 1, 1923, shall be eligible for a payment of compensation from the State of Florida of up to $150,000. The Attorney General shall identify and locate eligible individuals by using records already in possession of the State of Florida and by giving notice in the newspaper. . . . The individual seeking compensation must provide the Attorney General with reasonable proof of eligibility and the extent of their damages. . . . There is hereby appropriated $1.5 million from the General Revenue Fund to implement this section. If funds are insufficient to provide maximum compensation to each eligible individual the Comptroller may prorate available funds and make a partial award to each eligible individual.

Section 5. (1) There is created a Rosewood Family Scholarship Fund for minority persons with preference given to the direct descendants of the Rosewood families, not to exceed 25 scholarships per year.

\*          \*          \*

Section 6. The state university system shall continue the research of the Rosewood incident and the history of race relations in Florida and develop materials for the educational instruction of these events.

*       *       *

*Approved by the Governor May 4, 1994*

## 420 "being necessary to the security of a free state" (1986-1996)

The Constitution of the United States provides that "[a] well-regulated militia, being necessary to the security of a free State, the right of the people to keep and bear arms shall not be infringed." These words were drafted in the midst of a revolutionary war, fought mostly by citizen soldiers. The war was followed by the hazardous westward expansion, during which a gun was a vital defense against Native Americans and predatory settlers. These images, the brave soldiers of Bunker Hill and the gunfighting of Jesse James, are ingrained in the American consciousness and have left a love of guns in many souls.

Today, some people assume that the private ownership of firearms is a leftover from this country's dangerous early years. But many still feel a need to remain armed to defend their race, religion, and personal freedoms. Antigovernment groups have armed themselves to resist perceived oppression and have formed what they term "unorganized" or "citizen militias." As of 1996, such militias had been identified in forty states and had a conservatively estimated hard-core membership of ten thousand. Although most states have laws that prohibit the formation of such private military organizations, the patriot militias argue that such laws are unconstitutional.

In addition to practicing combat techniques that were often learned through training in the armed services, these groups also proselytize in small meetings around the country, seeking to recruit members from among those disaffected with modern society, such as fundamentalist Christians; those beset by new economic anxieties, such as those whose livelihoods are threatened by environmental regulations; or those who hold similar antigovernment perspectives, such as tax protesters, National Rifle Association activists, and others on the traditional extreme political right. The issue of control over firearms and their owners, over private militias and private armies, fuels the fears of both the governments and the militia members.

☆420  Do Americans Support the Right to Take Up Arms against the Government?

☆420a  The Rise of the Militias

Daniel Junas, document at http://www.worldmedia.com/CAQ/MILITIA.HTM. Originally published in *Covert Action Quarterly*, spring 1995, 20.

Winter is harsh in western Montana. Short days, bitter cold and heavy snows enforce the isolation of the small towns and lonely ranches scattered among the broad river valleys and high peaks of the Northern Rockies. But in February 1994—the dead of winter—a wave of fear and paranoia strong enough to persuade Montanans to brave the elements swept through the region. Hundreds of people poured into meetings in small towns to hear tales of mysterious black helicopters sighted throughout the United States and foreign military equipment moving via rail and flatbed truck across the country, in preparation for an invasion by a hostile federal government aided by U.N. troops seeking to impose a New World Order.

In Hamilton (pop. 1,700), at the base of the Bitterroot Mountains dividing Idaho and Montana, 250 people showed up; 200 more gathered in Eureka (pop. 1,000), ten miles from the Canadian border. And 800 people met in Kalispell, at the foot of Glacier National Park. Meeting organizers encouraged their audiences to form citizens' militias to protect themselves from the impending military threat.

Most often, John Trochmann, a wiry, white-haired man in his fifties, led the meetings. Trochmann lives near the Idaho border in Noxon (pop. 270), a town well-suited for strategic defense. A one-lane bridge over the Clark Fork River is the only means of access, and a wall of mountains behind the town makes it a natural fortress against invasion. From this bastion, Trochmann, his brother David, and his nephew Randy run the Militia of Montana (MOM), a publicity-seeking outfit that has organized "militia support groups" and pumped out an array of written and taped tales of a sinister global conspiracy controlling the U.S. government. MOM also provides "how to" materials for organizing citizens' militias to meet this dark threat.

It is difficult to judge from attendance at public meetings how many militias and militia members there might be in Montana, or if, as is widely rumored, they are conducting military training and exercises. The same applies across the country; there is little hard information on how many are involved or what they are actually doing.

But the Trochmanns are clearly not alone in raising fears about the federal government nor in sounding the call to arms. By January, movement watchers had identified militia activity in at least 40 states, with a conservatively estimated hard-core membership of at least 10,000—and growing.

The appearance of armed militias raises the level of tension in a region already at war over environmental and land use issues.

A threat explicitly tied to militias occurred in November 1994, at a public hearing in Everett, Washington. Two men approached Ellen Gray, an Audubon Society activist. According to Gray, one of them, later identified as Darryl Lord, placed a hangman's noose on a nearby chair, saying, "This is a message for you." He also distributed cards with a picture of a hangman's noose that said, "Treason = Death" on one side, and "Eco-fascists go home" on the other. The other man told Gray, "If we can't get you at the ballot box, we'll get you with a bullet. We have a militia of 10,000." In a written statement, Lord later denied making the threat, although he admitted bringing the hangman's noose to the meeting.

As important as environmental issues are in the West, they are only part of what is driving the militia movement. The militias have close ties to the older and more broadly based "Patriot" movement, from which they emerged, and which supplies their worldview. According to Chip Berlet, an analyst at Political Research Associates in Cambridge, Massachusetts, who has been tracking the far right for over two decades, this movement consists of loosely linked organizations and individuals who perceive a global conspiracy in which key political and economic events are manipulated by a small group of elite insiders.

On the far right flank of the Patriot movement are white supremacists and anti-Semites, who believe that the world is controlled by a cabal of Jewish bankers. This position is represented by, among others, the Liberty Lobby and its weekly newspaper, the Spotlight. At the other end of this relatively narrow spectrum is the John Birch Society, which has repeatedly repudiated anti-Semitism, but hews to its own paranoid vision. For the Birchers, it is not the Rothschilds but such institutions as the Council on Foreign Relations, the Trilateral Commission, and the U.N. which secretly call the shots.

This far-right milieu is home to a variety of movements, including Identity Christians, Constitutionalists, tax protesters, and remnants of the semi-secret Posse Comitatus. Members of the Christian right who subscribe to the conspiratorial world view presented in Pat Robertson's 1991 book, The New World Order, also fall within the movement's parameters. Berlet estimates that as many as five million Americans consider themselves Patriots.

While the Patriot movement has long existed on the margins of U.S. society, it has grown markedly in recent years. Three factors have sparked that growth.

One is the end of the Cold War. For over 40 years,

the "international communist conspiracy" held plot-minded Americans in thrall. But with the collapse of the Soviet empire, their search for enemies turned toward the federal government, long an object of simmering resentment.

The other factors are economic and social. While the Patriot movement provides a pool of potential recruits for the militias, it in turn draws its members from a large and growing number of U.S. citizens disaffected from and alienated by a government that seems indifferent, if not hostile, to their interests. This predominantly white, male, and middle- and working-class sector has been buffeted by global economic restructuring, with its attendant job losses, declining real wages and social dislocations. While under economic stress, this sector has also seen its traditional privileges and status challenged by 1960s-style social movements, such as feminism, minority rights, and environmentalism.

Someone must be to blame. But in the current political context, serious progressive analysis is virtually invisible, while the Patriot movement provides plenty of answers. Unfortunately, they are dangerously wrong-headed ones.

*　　　*　　　*

## ☆420b  USA under Foreign Occupation

James Heartfield, *Living Marxism*, at http://www.junius. co.uk/LM/LM80/LM80_Oklahoma.html.

The bomb blast at the government buildings in Oklahoma that killed 164 people invited an immediate and forthright response from the president: 'Make no mistake, this was an attack on the United States, our way of life, everything we believe in.' Bill Clinton warned that 'nobody can hide any place in the world from the terrible consequences'. The FBI immediately launched an investigation into links between Oklahoma and the Muslims accused of bombing the World Trade Center in February 1993.

Within days, however, the picture had changed dramatically. All the suspects arrested were not foreign agents, but patriotic, white Americans. As attention shifted from Islamic militants to home-grown far-right groups, like the Michigan Militia, supported by prime suspect Timothy McVeigh, the president's attitude towards the bombing changed.

*　　　*　　　*

Behind the president's reaction to the bombing is an understanding that there is little agreement about what America stands for these days, and that large parts of American society are beyond the reach of the policy-making elite. Concentrating on the children killed in the bomb blast is an attempt to find something that everyone can agree on. For, while few people would support the bombing, many Americans now share the hostility to big government that seems to have been behind it. The truth is that it is easier to win a consensus behind the idea that it is bad to kill children than that it is bad to bomb government buildings.

The main suspects in the bombing are supporters of America's far-right militia movement. These people support the right to bear arms in 'well-organised militias' enshrined in the Second Amendment to the American constitution. Militia literature is fervently anti-government, some even describing Washington as the 'Zionist Occupation Government.' Less openly anti-Semitic tracts, like Pat Robertson's book *New World Order*, warn that the federal government has been taken over by the United Nations, in a conspiracy against Americans. On the ground, the militias are preparing for an invasion force made up of Los Angeles gangs like the mythical 'Crips' and 'Bloods', as well as Chinese and Russian troops that will join them in occupying America.

The militias are in reality a minority of sad and lonely misfits who play war games in the forests. But unfortunately for the US administration, the hostility to government that they embody stretches far wider. Americans do not have to share the crazy conspiracy theories of the militias to share their hatred of federal government. Throughout the country more and more people are willing to believe that, even if the administration is not literally an occupation force, it behaves like a foreign power. As the police rounded up suspects post-Oklahoma, they were amazed to find the militiamen's neighbours more interested in criticising their 'heavy-handed' arrest tactics than condemning the bombing. In every US election the candidate that makes the most aggressive attack on government is the most likely victor.

Supporters of the militias point out that their right to bear arms is enshrined in the US constitution, and protest that the president's recent restrictions on firearms are an attack on their ancient liberties. It is true that America's constitution enshrines the right of the citizen to take up arms against oppressive government. However, the current anti-government mood is of a more recent origin.

All of the revolutionary rhetoric of the far-right militias has an eerily familiar ring. Policies that today mark out the far-right militias as beyond the pale were only a few years ago part of the American mainstream. The opinions that seem outlandish today were core beliefs of the Cold War politics which, for half a century, the American authorities used against 'Soviet-inspired' subversion abroad and un-American activities at home.

\*     \*     \*

Today, however, all of the policies that used to indicate patriotism and loyalty are seen as dangerous and extreme. The thing that has changed is not the policies themselves, so much as the context in which they are put forward. The old Republican programme no longer fits the times. The Republican majority was organised around the clear project of the Cold War: free market at home and militarism abroad. Loyalty to the state was consolidated through hostility to foreigners and to supposedly foreign elements at home, like communists and America's blacks.

Five years after the collapse of the Soviet Union, American patriotism no longer has a clear focus. For Timothy McVeigh the Gulf War was nothing to be proud of. Instead of pressing on towards Baghdad, the US had stopped short, under pressure, it seemed to McVeigh, from the United Nations. Americans were willing to support the government when it meant America walking tall in the world. But increasingly it is government itself that looks like the enemy. And despite electing politicians who promise to cut taxes, taxes just keep on rising.

\*     \*     \*

☆ 420c  Leaderless Resistance

Tom Burghardt, document at http://paul.spu.edu/~sinnfein/beam.html.

The political context for the bombing of the Oklahoma City federal building can be deciphered through a careful reading of key Christian Patriot texts. The bombing is almost a textbook case of what Aryan Nations / KKK leader Louis Beam has termed "leaderless resistance." While we are appalled and horrified by the terrifying loss of life, it was only a matter of WHEN, not IF, the violent fascist underground would resort to car or truck bomb tactics. To a lesser degree and on a smaller scale, factions within the direct action anti-abortion movement have systematically applied Louis Beam's "leaderless resistance" or "phantom cell" doctrine for a number of years.

\*     \*     \*

Louis Beam's "leaderless resistance" or "phantom cell" tactic is but one of a constellation of methodologies used by fascism to achieve political goals. While we can say that the majority of adherents of Christian Patriot groups would oppose the Oklahoma City bombing, the net effect of terror sharpen[s] the social/political contradictions within capitalist society and strengthen[s] the call for authoritarian, State solutions (i.e., political repression) on all fronts. As a political methodology, a fascist "strategy of tension" relies on the psychological effects of terror to magnify the localized effects of severe loss of life so that, like a stone hurled into a pool of water, shock-waves ripple from the epicenter of the attack to the furthest reaches of the State. While Christian Patriots and other far-right forces in the U.S. are a minute proportion of the population, the ideological underpinnings of Patriot ideology [have] struck a receptive cord among millions of Americans.

The ideological fervor of thousands of "state citizens" and "freemen," and their willingness to resort to violence to achieve their political goals, spring from the same sources as the white supremacist and neo-Nazi movements throughout North America: race hatred, anti-Semitism, violent xenophobia, and their desire to create a (white) fundamentalist "Christian Republic" in the United States.

The same can be said of the demonizing rhetoric freely disseminated by "mainstream" politicos in both capitalist parties. This does not mean that the Republican Party's "Contract With America," is a "fascist" document. It does mean, however, that the draconian solutions it proposes in terms of the role of the State and civil society, call for rapid privatization in all social spheres save one—the State's immense repressive police and military apparatus.

Left and Progressive researchers have pointed to the severe danger posed by the convergence of anti-abortion extremists, armed racists, queer-bashers, anti-Semites, advocates of "state citizenship," "Wise Use" movement attacks on environmental activists and the demonizing rhetoric of the far-right's paranoid conspiracism. Though these so-called "fringe elements" have been identified as potential, and actual, sources for terrorist violence, these warnings have largely gone unheeded, even within Socialist and leftist circles.

As long as the victims themselves were "marginal" in the eyes of "mainstream media" and terrorist industry "experts," domestic right-wing terror could easily be consigned to the back pages; a quick plunge down Orwell's memory hole would do the rest.

Apparently now, the self-fulfilling prophecies of the Christian Patriots and their phantom war against the capitalist "New World Order" have come to pass, with terrifying and tragic results. What will follow, is anyone's guess.

☆ 420d  Is the Citizen Militia Lawful?

Norman Olsen, document at http://mmc.cns.net/text/lawfulmilitia.txt.

Is the citizen militia legitimate and lawful? Our Governor, the Lawmakers, and others say no. You've heard their lies. Now here are the facts:

The Second Amendment to the U.S. Constitution recognizes the inherent right of states to form militia units. That amendment reads: "A well-regulated militia, being necessary to the security of a free State, the right of the people to keep and bear arms shall not be infringed."

Not only does the Constitution allow the formation of a Federal Army, it specifically recognizes state militias, and confirms that the citizen and his personal armaments are the foundation of the citizen militia. The arming of the militia is not left to the state but to the citizen. Should the state choose to arm its citizen militia, it is free to do so under the United States Constitution (bearing in mind that the Constitution is not a document limiting the citizen, but rather one that establishes and limits the power of government). Should the state fail to arm its citizen militia, the right of the people to keep and bear arms becomes the source of the guarantee that the state will not be found defenseless in the presence of a threat to its security. It makes no sense whatsoever to look to the Constitution of the United States or that of any state for permission to form a citizen militia.

Logic demands that the power to grant permission is also the power to deny permission. Brought to its logical conclusion in this case, a state may deny the citizen the right to form a militia. If this were to happen, the state would assert itself as the principle [sic] of the contract making the people the agents. Liberty then would be dependent on the state's grant of liberty. Such a concept is foreign to American thought. While the Second Amendment to the U.S. Constitution acknowledges the existence of state militias and recognizes their necessity for the security of a free state and while it also recognizes that the right of the people to keep and bear arms shall not be infringed, the Second Amendment is not the source of the right to form a militia nor to keep and bear arms. Those rights existed in the states prior to the formation of the federal union. In fact, the right to form militias and to keep and bear arms existed from antiquity. The enumeration of those rights in the Constitution only underscores their natural occurrence and importance. The Tenth Amendment to the U.S. Constitution reads: "The Powers not delegated to the United States by the Constitution, nor prohibited by it to the States, are reserved to the States respectively, or to the people."

Ultimate power over the militia is not delegated to the United States by the Constitution nor to the states, but resides with the people. Consequently, the power of the militia remains in the hands of the people. Again, the fundamental function of the militia in society remains with the people. Therefore, the Second Amendment recognizes that the militia's existence and the security of the state rests ultimately in the people who volunteer their persons to constitute the militia and their arms to supply its firepower. The primary defense of the state rests with the citizen militia bearing its own arms. Fundamentally, it is not the state that defends the people, but the people who defend the state. . . . The militia consisting of people owning and bearing personal weapons is the very authority out of which the United States Constitution grew. This point must be emphasized. Neither the citizen's militia nor the citizen's private arsenal can be an appropriate subject for federal legislation or regulation. It was the armed militia of the American colonies whose own efforts ultimately led to the establishment of the United States of America! While some say that the right to keep and bear arms is granted to Americans by the Constitution, just the opposite is true. The federal government itself is the child of the armed citizen. We the people are the parent of the child we call government. The increasing amount of federal encroachment into the territory of the Second Amendment in particular and the Bill of Rights in general indicates the need for parental corrective action. In short, the federal government needs a good spanking to make it behave.

One other important point needs to be made. Since the Constitution is the limiting document upon the government, the government cannot become greater than the granting power, that is the servant cannot become greater than his master. Therefore, should the Chief Executive or other branch of government, or all branches together act to suspend the Constitution under a rule of martial law, all power granted to government would be canceled and defer back to the granting power, the people. Martial law shall not be possible in this country as long as the people recognize the Bill of Rights as inalienable. The present actions of this country's government have been to convince Americans that the Bill of Rights controls the people. The Bill of Rights has nothing to do with control of the people, nor control of the government established by the people. The Bill of Rights stands as immutable and unaffected by any change determined upon the Constitution by government.

In Michigan, the militia is the subject of Article III, Sec. 4. [and I presume, the constitutions of other states will echo this] "The militia shall be organized, equipped and disciplined as provided by law." The law alluded to speaks of militias of the state, to be equipped, supported and controlled by the Governor. A thoughtful consideration of this arrangement leads immediately to the question of "Who really governs the militia?" Article I, Sec. 1 of Michigan's Constitution says, (And it may be presumed that other state constitutions also say,) "All political power is inherent in the people. Government is instituted for their equal benefit, security and protection." Once again we see the inherent right of citizen militias vested in the people. The organizing and support of a state sponsored militia of the state is a power granted to the Governor. This fact is further supported by Art. I, Sec. 7, "The military shall in all cases and at all times be in strict subordination to the civil power." But which military? It cannot be the citizen militia since the agent of a contract can hold, but cannot control the principle [sic]. Therefore, the military spoken of is the military force permitted to

be formed by the state, which is the National Guard. Neither can it be the citizen militia because, like the Federal Constitution, the Constitution of Michigan is the child of vested power reserved to the people forever. There is no possible way that the Governor of this State or the Chief Executive of the United States, or any legislative body can "outlaw" the citizen's militia for to do so would rob inherent power from the people and thereby transform the limited Constitutional Republic to a government controlled state. If that were to happen, our entire form of government would cease. How then can the citizen militia be controlled? In simplest terms, it cannot be. It is the natural occurrence of the people who gather to defend against a perceived threat. Historically, citizen militias emerge when a clear and present danger exists, threatening the well-being of the people. It would stand to reason that power granted to the Governor to form a militia for the security of the people is intended to reduce the need for the citizen militia. Simply, if the National Guard did its job in securing the state, the citizen militia would not emerge. That it has emerged so dramatically seems to indicate that the people do not feel secure. Nor can the people be given promises of security. Well-being is not measured by promise, but by experience. Surely our experience has been that security is lacking, hence the emergence of the citizen militia. When safety and security are reestablished in Michigan, the citizen militia will return to its natural place, resident within the body of the people, only to emerge again when security is threatened. Security is the common desire of all mankind. We can no more control the militia than we can change the nature of men. For their safety and security, people everywhere will form militia if and when necessary.

By now it should be clear that the militia predates state and federal constitutions. Its right to exist among the citizenry cannot be subjected to legal challenge. The only effective challenge to citizen militias would be political engineering. One may envision an effort to amend both the state and federal constitution specifically abolishing the right for citizens to form militia units. Should such a venture be dared, the natural need of the citizens militia would increase, actually drawing more free people to it. By now also, one should draw the conclusion that the militia is inherent to all social, interactive people concerned about the well-being of fellow citizens. This conclusion is that which is so clearly stated in the Bill of Rights. No man-made law can abolish the citizen militia since such a law would be in fact an unlawful act designed to dissolve power vested in the people. Such an effort would reveal an intent of any tyrant to transform limited government created by the people into a government limiting the people. Most tyrants know that such a move must be well timed. It is no wonder then, that power-hungry central govern-

ment and groomed courts view the Second Amendment as applying only to organized militias, i.e. armies of the individual states, that is, the National
Guard.

To summarize: Citizen militias in Michigan are
historic lawful entities predating all federal and state
constitutions. Such militias are "grandfathered" into
the very system of government they created as
clearly revealed in both the Constitution of the
United States and that of Michigan. These constitutions grant no right to form militias, but merely
recognize the existing natural right of all people to
defend and protect themselves. The governments
created out of well armed and free people are to be
constantly obedient to the people. Any attempt to
take the means of freedom from the people is an act
of rebellion against the people. Currently in Michigan, the citizen militia is subject only to the historic
role of American militias as defined in Black's Law
Dictionary: Militia: The body of citizens in a state,
enrolled for discipline as a military force, but not
engaged in actual service except in emergencies, as
distinguished from regular troops or a standing
army. In order to conform to this definition, and to
remain able to oppose a rebellious and disobedient
government, the citizen militia must not be connected in any way with that government lest the
body politic lose its fearful countenance as the only
sure threat to a government bent on converting free
people into slaves.

*          *          *

☆420e  *Person v. Miller*

854 F.2d 656 (4th Cir. 1988).

JAMES DICKSON PHILLIPS, Circuit Judge:
   Glen Miller challenges a judgment finding him in
contempt of a court order prohibiting him from operating a paramilitary organization . . . prohibited by
North Carolina law. . . .

I

   In June 1984, Bobby Person, a black citizen of the
United States and the State of North Carolina, filed a
class action against the Carolina Knights of the Ku
Klux Klan (CKKKK), its leader, Glen Miller, and
other named and unnamed individuals associated
with the CKKKK. The suit alleged that the defendants had engaged in a series of violent and intimidating acts throughout North Carolina with the purpose of preventing black citizens and others acting in
concert with them from freely exercising their rights
under state and federal law. The district court ultimately certified a class consisting of "all black
citizens in the State of North Carolina who seek to
exercise their state and federal rights free from interference by the defendants."
   In January 1985, the parties entered into a con-

sent decree which prohibited Miller and the CKKKK
from, among other things, "operat[ing] a paramilitary organization and do[ing] other acts prohibited
by North Carolina. . . ." In September 1985 . . . the
court made the decree final as to Miller, the CKKKK,
and its successor organization, the White Patriot
Party (WPP). Miller had changed the name of the
organization after the entry of the court's order in
January 1985.
   In April 1986, Person's counsel, [the Southern
Poverty Law Center's] Morris Dees, moved, on a
supporting complaint, to cite Miller and the WPP for
criminal contempt of court. The [amended] complaint alleged that Miller and the WPP had violated
the court's order by operating a paramilitary organization and engaging in conduct violative of [N.C.
Gen. Stat. sec. 14-228.20(b)(2), which makes it a felony to assemble "with one or more persons for the
purpose of training with, practicing with, or being instructed in the use of any firearm, explosive or incendiary device, or technique capable of causing injury
or death to persons, intending to employ unlawfully
the training, practicing, instruction, or technique for
use in, or in furtherance of, a civil disorder"; and N.C.
Gen. Stat. sec. 14-10, which makes it unlawful to
"band together and assemble to muster, drill or practice any military evolutions except by virtue of the
authority of an officer recognized by law, or of an
instructor in institutions or schools in which such
evolutions form a part of the course of instructions"].
The district court ordered Miller and the WPP to
show cause why they should not be found in contempt and set a hearing for July 1986.
   Dees was initially authorized by the court to prosecute the contempt action. From the time that the
original complaint was filed until June 1986, Dees was
actively engaged in preparing the case. He filed several amendments to the original complaint, moved
the court to add various parties as defendants, one of
which was Stephen Miller, and conducted discovery.
In June 1986, counsel for Miller moved to have Dees
disqualified on the grounds that Dees would be a material witness at trial and that Dees' appointment as
prosecutor violated the North Carolina Rules of Professional Conduct and Miller's right to be prosecuted
by an impartial prosecutor as guaranteed by the Due
Process Clause.
   Noting a conflict in recent circuit court decisions
on whether counsel for an interested party could
prosecute a related criminal contempt action, the
court ordered that the prosecution would be under
the "direct supervision and control" of the United
States Attorney's Office for the Eastern District of
North Carolina. The court further ordered that Dees
could "assist the United States Attorney prior to and
during the course of the trial." Shortly after the entry of the court's order, the prosecution filed a composite complaint against Glen Miller and the WPP

which was signed by the United States Attorney for the Eastern District of North Carolina. . . .

*          *          *

[Miller] contends that the prosecution failed to show that he engaged in or ordered any acts threatening the requisite "immediate danger."

Miller's interpretation, however, would force us to rewrite § 14-288.20(b)(1) to read "immediate civil disorder." As written, the prosecution need only prove that the prohibited activities were engaged in with the intent of furthering a civil disorder at some point in time. We think that the prosecution produced ample evidence from which the jury could conclude that Miller intended that the prohibited activities were in furtherance of a plan to cause a civil disorder in the future.

Miller also argues that the prosecution did not prove that he violated § 14-10 because it did not show that the CKKKK was not authorized to conduct military evolutions or that it did not qualify for the school exemption from the prohibition on such conduct. Again, we think there was ample evidence from which the jury could find that Miller violated § 14-10.

The chief military officer of the State of North Carolina, General Charles Scott of the North Carolina National Guard, listed those organizations authorized to conduct military evolutions and the list did not include the CKKKK. He explicitly stated that neither Glen Miller, Stephen Miller, nor the WPP were to his knowledge authorized by law to conduct military operations in North Carolina. General Scott also testified that in addition to high school and college ROTC programs, the State has only one accredited military academy. Moreover, it is beyond peradventure that the school exemption to § 14-10's prohibition on engaging in military evolutions does not apply to a group like the CKKKK that is engaged in practicing guerilla warfare aimed at subverting the government.

*          *          *

*Affirmed.*

# 421 "Mr. Clinton . . . better have a bodyguard" (1994)

Presidents of the United States are often the targets not only of assassins' bullets and threats of violence but also of political invective. The first two categories are penalized by the federal criminal law—the third is protected by the First Amendment. Just where along this spectrum the sharp break in legal treatment of similar activity occurs is sometimes hard to discern.

President Clinton has, by all accounts, been the target of both physical assault and the harshest political criticism in the twentieth century. From September 1994 to May 1995 the White House was the subject of four armed attacks: a man deliberately crashing, "kamikaze" style, a light plane onto the South Lawn; a man spraying the presidential residence with twenty-nine shots from an automatic weapon; a drive-by shooting from the Ellipse; and a man with an unloaded revolver scaling the ten-foot fence and assaulting a security guard.

These events understandably have made the Secret Service jittery. Together with the April 19, 1995, bombing of the federal building in Oklahoma City, these events led the authorities to close the two-block stretch of Pennsylvania Avenue by the front door of the White House and generally step up security measures against more dangerous attacks. Should they also be increasing their scrutiny of political statements that castigate the President with colorful yet violent metaphors? How should they deal with the phenomenon of poisonous political talk-radio shows? Were the public response and the reactions of the president's protectors to the inflammatory comments of Sen. Jesse Helms (R-N.C.) appropriate? Would the United States Secret Service or other law enforcement agencies have reacted more forcibly if the same utterances were made, in private or in a public meeting, by a common citizen?

Should any attention be paid to the fact that the honorable senator was elected and is held in considerable esteem in his home state, North Carolina? Should greater senatorial sensitivity and discretion been expected in light of the fact that Sgt. William J. Kreutzer, who killed an officer and wounded eighteen soldiers in a sniper attack on October 27, 1995, and Pvt. James Burmeister, who tried to become a racist "skinhead" by randomly killing a black couple on December 6, 1995, were both stationed at Ft. Bragg, North Carolina?

## ☆421 Helms Slap "Unwise"; Senator Says "Bodyguard" Remark Was Not Meant Literally

Paul Bedard and J. Jennings Moss, *Washington Times*, November 23, 1994, A3.

President Clinton yesterday sternly rebuked Sen. Jesse Helms, the North Carolina Republican slated to head the Senate Foreign Relations Committee, for suggesting he is so unpopular with the military that he should take a bodyguard with him to North Carolina military bases.

*          *          *

In an interview published yesterday in the News and Observer in Raleigh, N.C., Mr. Helms said: "Mr. Clinton better watch out if he comes down here. He'd better have a bodyguard."

This followed an earlier Helms comment that Mr.

Clinton is "not up to" being the commander in chief of the U.S. armed forces, that men and women in the ranks do not like him, and that the peace negotiations between Israel and Syria are a fraud.

In a statement yesterday, Mr. Helms said the bodyguard remark was not meant to be taken literally.

"I made a mistake last evening which I shall not repeat," Mr. Helms said in a statement released yesterday. He made the comment in an "informal telephone interview" with a Raleigh reporter.

"I made an offhand remark in an attempt to emphasize how strongly the American people feel about the nation's declining defense capability and other issues in which the president has been involved and for which he is responsible.

"Of course, I did not expect to be taken literally."

Mr. Helms repeated his opinion that the president is an unpopular commander in chief because of his "record of draft avoidance," his efforts to open the military to homosexuals, and policies that have hurt U.S. defense capabilities.

Mr. Helms did not dispute the accuracy of the account of his remarks. . . .

Before Mr. Helms released his statement, several senators criticized his remarks about Mr. Clinton.

"I am sorry to see so much comment about the president and personal comments about the president early on [in the Republicans' control of Congress]," said Sen. Arlen Specter, Pennsylvania Republican and a likely 1996 presidential candidate. "He is the commander in chief for the next two years. . . . We owe respect to the office and the position."

Sen. Christopher J. Dodd of Connecticut, who is seeking to be the next Senate Democratic leader, said he was "deeply disturbed and appalled" by Mr. Helms' comments.

Senate GOP leader Bob Dole shook his head when asked if there was pressure to choose someone else as Foreign Relations Committee chairman. "I didn't see the entire statement," he said. "My view is that the President of the United States is welcome to come to any state."

"I think pretty much that Jesse must have said most of this probably in jest."

# 422 "'He worked very hard to be a good soldier'" (1994)

On September 15, 1994, United States Army intelligence captain Lawrence Rockwood and his unit, the Tenth Mountain Division, were ordered by President Clinton into Haiti to "restore democracy" and end local human rights abuses by Gen. Raoul Cedras's military rule. Two weeks later, disturbed by

his superiors' indifference to his reports of atrocities committed by Cedras supporters at the infamous National Penitentiary in Port-au-Prince, Captain Rockwood, in full battle gear, slipped away from his compound and traveled to the prison, where he demanded a list of still-detained prisoners from the Haitian guards still in charge. Rockwood's superior officer and other United States military personnel were summoned and took Captain Rockwood into custody.

An adherent of Tibetan Buddhism who had been deeply moved by a childhood tour of the Dachau concentration camp with his father, who had been among the Americans at the liberation of the Nazi death camp, Rockwood rejected an offer of administrative punishment for leaving his post in his attempt at an unauthorized inspection of the Haitian prison, electing instead to be court-martialed for dereliction of duty and for disobedience. He raised as his defenses the commander-in-chief's orders to stop brutality and his duty under international law to stop human rights abuses. He was acquitted of dereliction of duty but was convicted of disobedience.

In another incident, in 1993, United States Army medic Michael New was deployed to Macedonia as part of a United Nations force intended to prevent the Balkan hostilities from spreading into that region of the former Yugoslavia. Placed under the command of a Finnish general, New's unit was issued blue berets and armbands to identify them as U.N. peacekeeping forces. Specialist New refused to don the newly issued insignia, claiming that ordering him to do so was unconstitutional and illegal under United States law. Like Rockwood, he was court-martialed and given a bad conduct discharge. Both cases have sparked robust political and legal debate about the role and command of United States military forces abroad in the post-cold war era.

## ☆422 The Disobedience of Capt. Lawrence Rockwood and Spc. Michael New

### ☆422a Statement of Lawrence P. Rockwood

*Human Rights Violations in the Port-au-Prince Penitentiary: Hearing before the Subcommittee on the Western Hemisphere of the Committee on International Relations,* 104th Cong. (1995), 6 (Statement of Cpt. Lawrence Rockwood, U.S. Army).

\*          \*          \*

Last September 15, the President announced that the primary objective of the operation Uphold Democracy was "to prevent the brutal atrocities against Haitians" and, bearing in mind my military oath to the Constitution and the Commander-in-Chief I took his words at face value.

As I assumed my duties in Haiti on September 23 I was informed that 'force protection' was to be the

focus of our efforts. In spite of this, it became immediately apparent to me that the main content of the
reports that reached me centered on human rights
violations against Haitian slum residents rather than
any threats directed against our forces. This discrepancy was what triggered my week long odyssey
through all possible instances to awake interest
of the commanders and staff of the Multinational
Forces in human rights violations.

On the morning of September 25 I met with the
command's Chaplain to discuss reports on deteri-
orating human rights situation in Port-au-Prince
slums, but the chaplain did not want to get involved
in a "political" problem.

\*          \*          \*

After finding out that no inspection or regular
monitoring of prisoners being held by the Haitian
military had taken place since the arrival of U.S.
forces over two weeks ago I tried unsuccessfully to
get the Civil Military Operations Center interested
in surveying the penitentiaries.

[Lt. Rockwood recites other attempts to interest his superiors in allegations of human rights
violations.]

At this point I thought that I had exhausted all
means at my disposal to alert all sections of the Joint
Task Force [JTF] to human rights abuses in Haitian
penitentiaries. I therefore turned to the Inspector
General and deposited my complaint, which alleged
that the command had subverted [the] President's
primary mission intent concerning human rights.
The IG suggested that it be anonymous but there
was no point because by then everyone knew about
my concern for human rights. I also believed that
what I was doing was legally and morally correct,
and had no reason to hide my position as an officer
unless of course my command was prepared to act
improperly in response.

The Inspector General informed me that I have
done everything a staff officer could have possibly
done and it was not my job to pursue this further by
addressing it to the command's Chief of Staff. I was
also told that my complaint would not be brought to
the attention of General [George C.] Meade for at
least a week.

At this point I informed my immediate superior
that I feared the command could be found criminally
negligent under international law and in dereliction
of duties in carrying out the President's intent. I
reached the conclusion that the US would bear responsibility because the human rights violations
would be committed with the knowledge of the command, in the direct proximity of its forces, and by
Haitian forces with whom the US had a signed
agreement of cooperation.

I based my concern over the command's possible
criminal negligence on the historical principles rec-

ognized in the Charter of the Nuremburg Tribunal
which held commanders to be liable for failing to take
action to "prevent" war crimes. More particularly,
I was aware of the case of the United States Vs
Yamashita. General Tomoyuki Yamashita, former
commander of Japanese Forces in the Philippines
was sentenced to death in 1945 by an international
war crimes tribunal for his failure to protect American prisoners, even though he neither ordered nor
knew of their execution by his soldiers. The sentence
was upheld by the US Supreme Court. He was executed for his indifferent (although completely passive) response to human rights violations against
persons protected under customary and/or conventional international law, violations of which he had no
direct knowledge (unlike the present case where
general Meade and his staff including myself had direct and specific knowledge of human rights abuses
in the Haitian penitentiaries).

I also believed that the military Oath of Office not
only allowed me but compelled me to place loyalty to
the Constitution and the President of the United
States before obedience to my immediate superiors
who, I suspected, were indifferent to violations of the
human rights of Haitian prisoners. . . .

I was aware that the action I contemplated would
be considered directly challenging to my superiors'
conduct of the operation, but I could find no other
way to prevent ongoing human rights abuses. As a
student of military history I had in the back of my
head a precedent that guided me in this decision, a
precedent that goes back to the blackest episode of
the Vietnam war and of US army history: the My Lai
massacre. A helicopter pilot, Chief Warrant Officer
Hugh C. Thompson, who saw the massacre, ordered
his gunner to fire on US forces who were slaughtering unarmed civilians. While he acted clearly outside
the range of what is usually associated with "good
order and discipline," the Army judiciously gave him
an award rather than placing him before a court
martial. . . .

Like Thompson I had before me the theoretical
choice to do nothing or to take unconventional action
knowing that I was risking disciplinary measures.
But in practice I had no choice. I felt I had to act
because lack of such action would have meant an acquiescence on my part to the imminent and ongoing
human rights violations, and hypocrisy in the face of
duty.

\*          \*          \*

. . . In the three months between the arrival of
JTF and that date there were several sporadic visits
of persons more or less associated with the JTF: Col.
Michael Sullivan, from the 16th Military Police Brigade who in a memorandum to the Commander of
JTF-190 General Meade [wrote,] "The appalling conditions render this facility [the National Penitenti-

ary] unsuitable for human habitation, and this must be a priority in our efforts to assist Haiti in its return to democracy." Paul Browne the deputy head of the International Police Monitors (IPM) went there on October 14 and some inmates he found were in such a horrendous condition that he thought that they were in the last stage of AIDS. The Danish monitors from IPM also visited this facilities and considered it "the worst" of all confinement centers in Haiti.

The charges I am facing appear petty next to life-threatening human rights violations that continued in the Port-au-Prince National Penitentiary for 2 & ½ months after my attempted intervention.

*       *       *

☆ 422b New's Father: Pride, No Regrets; Place in History Is "a Privilege"

*Washington Times*, April 19, 1996, A6.

The father of Army Spc. Michael New came to Washington yesterday with a simple message: There's no need to feel sorry for the 22-year-old medic just because a military jury handed him a bad-conduct discharge for refusing to wear United Nations insignia.

"He's been given the opportunity to stand up with these giants of American history, and we consider that such a valuable thing, such a privilege, that we don't want your sympathy," Daniel New told a group of conservatives opposed to U.N. policies. "What we want you to do, instead, we want you to teach your children, your nephews and nieces. Your grandkids."

Spc. New is doing desk work in Germany, awaiting his division commander's review of the Jan. 24 conviction for refusing a direct order to don U.N. garb and join a peacekeeping contingent in Macedonia.

His stance has become a cause celebre within the conservative movement and brought his father the roles of newsmaker and politician. Mr. New has appeared on numerous radio talk shows and last month made an unsuccessful bid in the Texas Republican primary for a seat in Congress.

"Did I influence him? Yes," Mr. New said. "But he's his own man. He stands on his own legs. And I have to admit I've never been more inspired by perhaps any person in American history than my own son."

Mr. New told a conference sponsored by the American Sovereignty Action Project he was cool toward his son's decision to join the Army three years ago.

"We prayed every single day he would be a bright light in a dark place," said Mr. New, a missionary who, with his wife, home-schooled Michael. "And God has honored that prayer because he grew spiritually. He kept himself pure. He kept himself in the Lord. . . . He worked very hard to be a good soldier."

Spc. New contends wearing the U.N. badge and serving under a foreign commander would violate his oath of allegiance to the Constitution. His attorneys also claim the Macedonia mission is illegal because President Clinton did not get congressional approval. . . .

"The order given Michael New to deploy to Macedonia under foreign command was simply unlawful," said Lee Casey, a lawyer and former Justice Department official.

Mr. Casey said Mr. Clinton's constitutional role of commander in chief does not give him sole power to deploy forces.

Mr. Casey said it is his view that soldiers cannot be placed under the command of officers who have not been nominated by the president and confirmed by the Senate.

*       *       *

"The president should have no authority to commit troops short of a critical national survival issue," Mr. Bartlett said. "I don't know any American who wants their son or daughter fighting and dying as a U.N. soldier."

Retired Marine Corps Col. Ron Ray, Spc. New's chief defense counsel, said he plans to meet May 1 with the soldier's commanding officer in an attempt to have the sentence changed to an honorable discharge.

Conference host Cliff Kincaid circulated a Spc. New defense fund brochure that includes an Army field manual directive on "moral courage."

It states, "Stand up for your beliefs and what you know is right. Do not compromise your professional ethic or your individual values and moral principles. If you believe you are right after sober and considered judgment, hold your position."

## 423 "bringing overseas conflicts to American shores" (1994-1996)

With the bombing of the World Trade Center in February 1993, terrorism was practiced in the United States on a massive scale for the first time, according to Henry DePippo, who was responsible for the investigation and successful prosecution of those accused of the bombing. The four defendants in that case were prosecuted for violating federal statutes that prohibited bombing a motor vehicle used in interstate transportation, and for setting off a destructive device in a building used in interstate commerce. There was no federal terrorism or antiterrorism criminal statute for acts that were perpetrated here in the United States. The World Trade Center bombers were never prosecuted for "terrorism," but rather were prosecuted under other statutes that could be applied to the crime.

The bomb at the World Trade Center was a roughly 1,500- to 2,000-pound, fertilizer-based, improvised explosive. The bomb was contained within a rented van that was parked in the parking garage directly against the base of one of the Twin Towers. The hole—or the crater, as it was referred to—was roughly five stories tall and could comfortably hold two two-story homes (including land).

The bombing occurred at lunchtime on a Friday afternoon. During that day, and in fact on any given day, there are roughly one hundred thousand people in the World Trade Center complex. The bombing itself claimed the lives of six people, including a woman who was seven months pregnant. There were roughly one thousand people injured. It was the largest such single incident in United States history apart from certain battles of the Civil War. In terms of monetary damages, it cost in excess of half a billion dollars to restore the World Trade Center.

The trial of those accused of the World Trade Center bombing brought to the surface a possible worldwide network of anti-American terrorists under the leadership of Ramzi Yousef. They were brought to the United States by law enforcement agencies to be charged and convicted for crimes committed overseas, including an explosion aboard a Philippine airplane.

## ☆423  The World Trade Center Bombing and Ramzi Yousef

### ☆423a  Four for Four

John Dickerson, *Time*, March 14, 1994, 33.

To each of the 38 charges, the forewoman of the jury gave the same answer. On conspiracy to bomb buildings: "Guilty." On explosive destruction of property: "Guilty." On assault on a federal officer: "Guilty." Again and again and again: "Guilty." But when that calm recitation ended, a different kind of oratory erupted. "Injustice! We are the victims!" shouted Mohammad Salameh, one of the four men on trial, pointing at the jury and pounding his fist on the table. "Allah-Akbar (God is great)!" shouted the other defendants. "Al-Nasr lil-Islam (Victory to Islam)!" And from the gallery came a retort New Yorkers in the court could understand. Cried the brother of defendant Nidal Ayyad: "You are all f—ing liars! My brother is innocent."

It was one year and six days after the explosion that killed six people, injured more than a thousand and tore a five-story hole in the World Trade Center. After a five-month trial, a jury of eight women and four men had convicted each of the four defendants on all charges in connection with the bombing. The prosecution called the bombing the greatest terrorist attack ever to take place on American soil. The case, however, did not achieve the pyrotechnics of the crime. For five months, the jury members twisted in their leather swivel chairs while the gov-

ernment paraded 207 witnesses and more than 1,000 exhibits before them. Only once or twice did proceedings break the staid atmosphere, most notably when a prosecution witness, asked to identify two suspects, pointed to members of the jury.

Only at the end did it all come together. In a masterly six-hour summation, U.S. Attorney Henry DePippo crafted a cohesive argument out of the morass of evidence. Tracing the conspiracy back to April 1992, DePippo wove together phone calls, fingerprints, chemical analysis, chunks of metal and parking stubs into a narrative that led to the on-ramp of the B-2 parking level of the World Trade Center. Throughout the tale, he clearly delineated the roles of Mohammad Salameh, Nidal Ayyad, Mahmud Abouhalima and Ahmad Ajaj in the criminal partnership.

By the time of DePippo's summation, the four defense teams had broken ranks. During their cross-examinations of government witnesses, defense attorneys cooperated in raising doubts about each part of the prosecution's reconstruction in hopes of raising reasonable doubt about the overall story.

By the end, however, each defense lawyer was offering a distinct case for his client's acquittal. The government had built a case on "lies and deception," boomed Abouhalima's attorney in a closing argument that sounded more like a sermon. Ayyad's lawyer was less passionate, plodding through a four-hour summation that had the jurors nodding with fatigue. On one occasion, the judge fell into a deep sleep and had to be nudged awake by a court clerk.

Salameh's lawyer Robert Precht launched into a final argument that surprised his fellow attorneys. He argued that there had indeed been a plot but that his client had merely been the unwitting dupe of Ramzi Yousef, a fugitive who the government alleges was the mastermind of the conspiracy. Three days later, Salameh sent a letter to the judge saying, "I object to this summation, which I would never have agreed to had it been told me." Ajaj's lawyer immediately filed a mistrial motion claiming Precht "did more damage to Mr. Ajaj in the first six minutes of his summation than Mr. DePippo did in . . . six hours." Ajaj was in jail during the bombing and had been for six months before it happened. A defense admission of Yousef's involvement, however, fed into the prosecution's contention that Ajaj had helped Yousef get into the country to further his plot.

"The message of this verdict is twofold," said William Gavin, deputy assistant director of the FBI. "That terrorism has invaded the shores of the United States of America, and that you will be caught, prosecuted and may go to jail." The government hopes this shutout victory is a hint of what is to come. In the fall it faces what promises to be an even longer prosecution in the conspiracy case against Sheik Omar Abdel Rahman and 14 of his followers charged with plotting to blow up the U.N. and other targets in New York City. The bombing of the World Trade Center's Twin Towers is an element of that larger case, and the government also hopes to answer questions that were not found in the verdict last week: Was a larger organization behind this attack? Who ordered it? What was the motive?

But memories of the bombing have left a lingering wariness, especially against the backdrop of the trial and the massacre in Hebron. Early last week, after a van of Hasidic students in New York City was allegedly shot up by a Lebanese cabdriver, speculation spread that the deed had been part of an organized terrorist attack. At one point, the alleged gunman and two suspected accomplices were reported to be part of a terrorist ring under surveillance by both the FBI and Mossad, Israel's intelligence agency. That information proved to be false, but the fear of terrorism is now a real part of the American imagination.

☆ 423b  Federal Prosecutor Concludes in Trade Center Bombing Case

Robert Jackson, *Los Angeles Times*, February 5, 1994, A23.

In closing arguments in the World Trade Center bombing case, a federal prosecutor told jurors yesterday that the conspiracy to bomb the twin towers began five months before the blast, when one of four defendants arrived in the United States carrying bomb-making manuals and anti-American and anti-Jewish literature.

Concluding the government's 18-week case, prosecutor Henry DePippo asked the jury to convict all the foreign-born defendants for what he called "the worst terrorist act" in the nation's history. The explosion killed six persons, injured more than 1,000 others and disabled for a month one of the world's best-known landmarks.

Defense attorneys were scheduled to make their presentations Tuesday in the courtroom of U.S. District Judge Kevin T. Duffy. The jury is expected to begin its deliberations later this week.

DePippo told jurors that the government's presentation had been a lengthy one involving so many witnesses—more than 200—"because no one witness could tell the whole story."

The government has attempted to convince the jury that the plot began when Ahmad Ajaj arrived at New York's John F. Kennedy Airport in September 1992, describing himself as "a Palestinian protester" and seeking political asylum.

Immigration authorities found he had used an altered Swedish passport and employed a string of false identities. In addition, the prosecutor said, authorities discovered among his possessions bombing manuals, videos and handwritten notes indicating that he had had weapons and explosives training.

While Ajaj was jailed for immigration violations,

DePippo said, an associate, Ramzi Ahmed Yousef, entered the country on the same flight and met days later in New Jersey with two other defendants, Mohammed A. Salameh and Mahmud Abouhalima.

Yousef, who has been declared a fugitive, left the country only hours after the bombing—before authorities had linked him to the act.

DePippo said the government's evidence showed that Salameh, with whom Yousef shared an apartment, opened a joint bank account with the fourth defendant, Nidal Ayyad, a chemical engineer.

"Salameh and Ayyad opened an account with $8,500 before withdrawing most of it in cash," he said. "They then began making a slew of phone calls to chemical companies in order to buy chemicals."

In one instance, DePippo said, the men used 36 $100 bills to purchase ingredients for a 1,200-pound bomb—the one Salameh and Abouhalima drove into the trade center's underground garage in a rented van.

Abouhalima, whom federal investigators labeled the "field general" of the plot, was linked to the conspiracy through dozens of telephone calls among the defendants, the prosecutor said.

However, federal authorities never were able to trace the source of the funds deposited by Salameh and Ayyad in a Jersey City bank.

Computer disks found in Ayyad's office identified him as the author of a letter sent to New York newspapers claiming that unless the United States stopped supporting Israel more terrorist bombings would occur.

If convicted of conspiracy in the bombing, the defendants could be sentenced to life imprisonment.

☆ 423c  Was the Terrorist Who Blew Up the World Trade Centre Saddam's Man? Mask That Hides "Master Bomber"

Ian Katz and Nick Cohen, *The Observer*, September 1, 1996, 17.

The young man who rose to his feet in a Manhattan courtroom last week to sum up the defence case at the end of a three-month terror trial appeared poised and confident. Lean and darkly handsome, he wore a tan summer suit and natty tie.

Ramzi Ahmed Yousef spoke for three hours from handwritten notes. His English was faintly accented and his language a little less than lawyerly, but a casual visitor to Judge Kevin Duffy's courtroom might reasonably have concluded that he was a professional advocate rather than a criminal the Americans allege is one of the most ingenious and ambitious terrorists of modern times.

Yousef's tactic of defending himself is entirely in character. Even when FBI agents and Pakistani police officers whisked the alleged master bomb-maker from room 16 of the Su-Casa guest house in Islamabad in February 1995, his self-assurance was not disturbed. He faces life imprisonment in an American jail but the overwhelming courtroom impression is one of cockiness.

His intelligence is plain, yet the case against him implies stunning carelessness.

In the coming year, Yousef will stand trial for the central role prosecutors say he performed in planning and executing the 1993 World Trade Centre bombing that killed six people, injured more than 1,000 and shattered American complacency about terrorism.

For the past three months a Manhattan jury has been listening to evidence of an even more audacious plot to blow up, in a single period of 48 hours, 12 American airliners travelling from Asia to the United States. The plan, codenamed Project Bojinga, was foiled before it could be executed, but prosecutors say Yousef carried out a dry-run attack on a Philippines Airline jet in December 1994, in which a Japanese passenger was killed.

Yousef, 28, with two alleged accomplices, Wali Khan Amin Shah and Abdul Hakim Murad, has denied any involvement in the plot. But the jury, which will begin its deliberations this week, heard an apparently damning catalogue of evidence against the three. Filipino police officers testified how they were called to a Manila apartment in January 1995 after receiving reports of smoke, and found bomb-making ingredients and manuals.

The most compelling evidence came from a Toshiba laptop computer discovered in the apartment. With the help of experts from Microsoft, agents were able to recover files containing details of the Bojinga plan including chemical formulas, flight schedules, detonation times and fake identity documents for the three men. Investigators even claimed to have found a draft letter taking responsibility for the airline bombings. An amorous conversation recorded as a sound file on the computer's hard disk appeared to tie the computer to Yousef.

It sounds a strong case. But investigators do not know what led a man who does not appear to be a religious fundamentalist to pick targets as diverse as the World Trade Centre, Pakistani Prime Minister Benazir Bhutto and the Pope. Who bankrolled his deadly exploits? Indeed, they cannot be certain who he is.

Although Yousef is being prosecuted under the name he used when he entered the United States in September 1992, no one imagines that it is his real one. He had three passports when he was arrested in Islamabad, and Pakistani authorities say he used a host of aliases. US authorities believe his real name is Abdul Basit Karim. Critically, his fingerprints were found to match those in the Kuwaiti Interior Ministry file of a Pakistani national of that name who lived in Kuwait before the Gulf War.

Abdul Basit is believed to have been born in Kuwait. He travelled to Britain in 1986 to study A-levels at the Oxford College of Further Education. Later he studied computer-aided electronic engineering at the Swansea Institute, then known as the West Glamorgan Institute of Higher Education, graduating in 1989. During this period he travelled between Kuwait and Britain at least five times but did nothing to arouse the suspicions of British authorities.

After graduating he returned to Kuwait to work in the emirate's Planning Ministry. But in August 1990 Saddam Hussein's troops invaded and the family disappeared.

The next sighting of Abdul Basit—or Ramzi Yousef—did not come until early 1991 when he allegedly showed up in the Philippines seeking to co-operate in terrorist attacks with the local Islamic guerrilla group, Abu Sayyaf.

In September the following year, after spending time in Peshawar in Pakistan, and possibly Iraq, he arrived at New York's JFK airport travelling under an Iraqi passport in the name of Ramzi Yousef. He told immigration authorities he was a dissident and was granted temporary asylum.

US authorities say he then moved into an apartment in New Jersey with an Iraqi, Musab Yasin. Over the next six months he allegedly co-ordinated the World Trade Centre bombing, acquiring chemicals and building and planting the bomb with the help of local Muslim fundamentalists. Hours after the blast, he is believed to have slipped out of New York on a flight to Pakistan. Within weeks of the World Trade Centre attack, four of his alleged accomplices had been captured and Yousef was one of the most wanted men in the world. Yet the urbane bombmaker did not go to ground. Within months of arriving back in Pakistan he was seriously injured when a bomb allegedly designed to kill Benazir Bhutto exploded prematurely in a Karachi hotel room.

He then allegedly hatched even more ambitious plans. During 1994 he is believed to have travelled to the Philippines to hone his plot to blow up a dozen US airliners. He and his accomplices were claimed also to be planning to assassinate the Pope during his visit to Manila in January 1995.

Both plots were only foiled when reports of smoke drew police to an apartment where the men were manufacturing explosives.

But there are a number of problems with this sketchy biography, not least that Abdul Basit's height on his 1988 passport was listed as 5ft. 8in. whereas Yousef in 1992 was reckoned to be 6ft. tall. Is it possible that Abdul Basit grew four inches between the ages of 20 and 24?

The British authorities were asked for help by the FBI. CID officers from South Wales have investigated and simply do not know what to make of the case.

They and the Americans do not doubt that an Abdul Basit studied electronic engineering at the Swansea institute in the late 1980s. And photocopies of a Swansea institute library chemistry textbook were found in the Manila apartment. But the institute could not say whether the Basit in Swansea had transformed into a terrorist. In the 1980s the institute's register kept no photographic records of students. "We could not identify him," said Thomas Cadwalladr, the institute's spokesman. "There were a lot of Middle Eastern students here in the 1980s and they stuck together." One lecturer does remember Basit, but all he can say is that he seemed like a normal student. Handwriting samples and photographs of the man on trial in New York produced no positive identification.

The CID officers left three possibilities open: the 1980s Swansea Basit was the 1990s terrorist; Basit and the man using his name were both at Swansea at the same time; or Yousef stole Basit's identity with the help of the Iraqis.

The Washington-based Iraq expert Laurie Mylroie has energetically championed the last option. If true, then the World Trade Centre bombing may have been part of a clandestine bid for revenge by Saddam.

There is certainly a smattering of circumstantial evidence pointing to an Iraqi involvement in the bombing. For one thing, Yousef is understood to have been in Baghdad shortly before flying to New York in September 1992. Among New York fundamentalists he was known as "Rashid the Iraqi."

But investigators have dismissed the claim. If Yousef was an Iraqi agent, they ask, why do his fingerprints match those of Abdul Basit and what became of the real Abdul Basit? Mylroie suggests he was killed with his family during the Iraqi occupation of Kuwait and that Iraqi intelligence placed Yousef's fingerprints in his Interior Ministry file so their man would be able to adopt the Pakistani's identity at will. It is no more far-fetched than a plot to blow up 12 airliners in two days.

*     *     *

☆423d  3 Convicted of Plotting to Bomb U.S. Jets; Trial Opened Window on High-Tech Terror

Dale Russakoff, *Washington Post*, September 6, 1996, A1.

Ramzi Ahmed Yousef, the alleged terrorist mastermind accused of scripting the World Trade Center bombing, and two co-defendants were convicted here today of a high-tech conspiracy to bomb 12 U.S. jumbo jets and 4,000 passengers out of the sky over the Pacific Ocean—a plot the government described as "one of the most hideous crimes anyone ever conceived."

After a three-month trial that opened a window onto the modern age of international terrorism, a federal jury in Manhattan convicted Yousef, Abdul Hakim Murad and Wali Khan Amin Shah on all seven counts related to the foiled bombing plot, which was to unfold over a two-day period in January 1995.

Yousef, 28, also was convicted of bombing a Philippine Airlines jet in 1994, killing one passenger, as a dress rehearsal for the larger conspiracy, and Shah was convicted of attempting to escape from prison here.

All three defendants stared ahead, showing no emotion, as the jury foreman reported the verdicts and as a court clerk reread them, intoning "guilty," again and again. The jury of five women and seven men, kept anonymous for security reasons, was escorted home by court personnel and did not comment. Lawyers for all three defendants said they would appeal the verdicts.

Yousef's convictions carry three mandatory life sentences plus up to 100 years in prison and $2.25 million in fines. He is to stand trial next year on charges of orchestrating and helping to carry out the 1993 World Trade Center bombing, the event that transformed international terrorism from a distant horror to a threat facing Americans in their own communities.

The threat became even more real at mid-trial when Trans World Airlines Flight 800 exploded and crashed into the Atlantic Ocean barely 50 miles away from the courthouse here, with eerie parallels to Yousef's plot to explode planes over the Pacific.

Prosecutors and defense attorneys feared that the July 17 crash, in which all 230 people on board perished, would prejudice the jury, which was not sequestered. Criminal investigators have speculated that a miniature, time-triggered bomb similar to those devised by Yousef might have destroyed Flight 800, but so far they have uncovered no conclusive evidence to support that theory.

*     *     *

Yousef boasted to a U.S. Secret Service agent that he would have bombed a dozen planes within weeks had he not been discovered. Investigators found detailed plans of the plot in a laptop computer recovered from Yousef's Manila apartment. Five bombers were to fly on 12 U.S. jumbo jetliners in the Far East, slip bombs made using Casio digital watches under their seats, and disembark, with the bombs timed to explode when the planes were high over the Pacific en route to the West Coast.

*     *     *

The trial unfolded as a primer on the techniques of modern terrorism and of a man believed by prosecutors to be one of its most skilled practitioners. He is a multilingual professional who reportedly studied electronic engineering in Wales and was trained in explosives by the Afghan resistance movement.

*     *     *

Yousef acted as his own lawyer throughout his trial here, speaking clear, accented English, seemingly comfortable with U.S. legal jargon. He wore conservative business suits and patterned ties—although today he wore slacks and a dress shirt open at the neck—and had the confidence and carriage of an international businessman and the apparent detachment of a seasoned lawyer.

He argued to the jury that the entire case was fabricated by Philippine and Pakistani authorities to curry favor with the United States, which at that time was hunting Yousef in the World Trade Center case and considered him the world's most wanted terrorist.

Born in Pakistan, Yousef is said to have grown up in Kuwait with a Pakistani father and Palestinian mother in a neighborhood heavily populated by Palestinian exiles.

He told an Arabic language newspaper that he is Pakistani by birth, Palestinian by choice. Investigators found in his computer a manifesto pledging terror to punish Americans for their government's support of Israel.

He has traveled the globe, allegedly orchestrating plots from Manhattan to Manila—each time with different accomplices recruited from local Muslim fundamentalist networks, as well as from his circle of childhood friends.

In addition to the plots for which he has been charged, authorities have said he schemed to kill Pope John Paul II and Pakistani Prime Minister Benazir Bhutto and to fly a suicide bomber into CIA headquarters in Langley, Va.

Government officials have said they know little about who sponsored Yousef or his worldwide travels, and they are hopeful that he, Murad and Shah will now cooperate with U.S. investigators. Although Yousef appeared from the evidence in this case to be a globe-trotting, lone wolf, terrorism experts said he may in fact be a subcontractor for a foreign government, and that there are other agents like him as yet unknown to U.S. authorities.

\*       \*       \*

☆ 423e  Verdicts in Terror Trial

Christopher Wren, *New York Times*, September 6, 1996, A1.

Ramzi Ahmed Yousef, the man accused of leading terrorist cells that plotted attacks on American targets at home and abroad, was convicted with two other defendants yesterday of trying to blow up American commercial airliners in East Asia early last year.

Mr. Yousef, a 28-year-old electronics engineer, is awaiting trial on separate charges that he was the mastermind of the 1993 bombing of the World Trade Center in lower Manhattan. Whatever the outcome

of that trial, yesterday's conviction means that he and his co-defendants almost certainly will spend the rest of their lives in prison, as some of the charges carry mandatory life sentences.

Mr. Yousef's conviction was important to the Government, which views him as representing a new breed of terrorist, one intent on bringing overseas conflicts to American shores. Mr. Yousef, who said he had been born in Pakistan and raised in Kuwait, and had received explosives training in Afghanistan, brought his rage over American support of Israel to the United States, investigators said. Until his arrest in Pakistan in 1995, the United States considered him the most wanted fugitive alive, with a $2 million reward for his capture.

The jury that found him guilty yesterday in Federal District Court in Manhattan also convicted his two co-defendants, Abdul Hakim Murad and Wali Khan Amin Shah, on charges that they conspired to blow up American commercial jetliners and tried to kill Americans traveling outside the United States. Mr. Yousef was convicted separately of planting a test bomb on a Philippine Airlines jetliner bound for Tokyo that killed a Japanese passenger in late 1994.

\*       \*       \*

In the courtroom, as one guilty verdict after another was read out, the defendants sat in silence, showing no emotion. Mr. Yousef, who wore an open-necked shirt and slacks instead of his customary suit, glanced at the jury foreman and then straight ahead.

\*       \*       \*

Mr. Yousef insisted on defending himself throughout the trial, relegating Mr. Kulcsar, his court-appointed lawyer, to the role of legal adviser. His decision allowed Mr. Yousef to address the jurors without being cross-examined by Government prosecutors, but it failed to win the jury's sympathy.

\*       \*       \*

The convictions conclude a case that has dragged on for 14 weeks, weathering the backlash of the explosion of the T.W.A. flight [800] on July 17. Judge Duffy pressed ahead with the trial after determining that the jurors were not affected by unproved speculation that Mr. Yousef or his supporters might have had some hand in the crash, whose cause has not been determined.

But Mr. Murad's lawyer, Clover M. Barrett, observed that the T.W.A. crash "is not a small thing, and I think it had an impact on the jury."

\*       \*       \*

The trial was unusual for a Federal court because the crimes of which the defendants were convicted took place halfway around the world, primarily in the Philippines. But Judge Duffy accepted the Government's contention that a nexus existed to the United States because the defendants were accused of planning to attack American jetliners and kill Americans overseas.

The charges were originally part of a broader indictment that also accuses Mr. Yousef and two other men, Eyad Ismoil and Abdul Rahman Yasin, of helping to bomb the World Trade Center. Four other Muslim men have already been sentenced to life in prison for their roles in the bombing, which killed six people and injured hundreds more.

To simplify the 20-count indictment, Judge Duffy created the current trial for the 9 counts relating to the airline bombing conspiracy, and deferred the other 11 counts concerning the World Trade Center bombing for the subsequent trial.

Mr. Yousef's plan to single out American airliners called for five terrorists each to smuggle bombs aboard a succession of United States commercial airliners departing from cities around East Asia. The conspirators would get off at the first stop, leaving bombs timed to explode in midair as the airliners flew on to other Asian cities or back to the United States. Some terrorists would follow up by planting more bombs on later flights. Then, all five men would make their way separately back to Pakistan.

*        *        *

To rehearse the operation, a practice bomb was detonated in the Greenbelt Theater in Manila on the night of Dec. 1, 1994, the authorities said. Another bomb was concealed aboard Philippine Airlines Flight 434 from Manila to Tokyo 10 days later. Mr. Yousef, who was identified by a flight attendant who testified at the trial, boarded Flight 434 in Manila but got off at the southern Philippine city of Cebu. The bomb, hidden under Seat 26K, exploded on the way to Tokyo, killing the Japanese passenger, Haruki Ikegami. The pilot managed to land the damaged Boeing 747 safely in Okinawa.

According to investigators, Mr. Yousef's specialty was making bombs from innocuous-looking articles that could be smuggled through airport security—a digital wristwatch modified to serve as a timer, or a plastic contact-lens solution bottle filled with liquid components for nitroglycerine.

When Mr. Yousef was arrested on Feb. 7, 1995, in the Pakistani capital of Islamabad, law enforcement agents said they found more bomb-making ingredients in his hotel room. He was extradited the next day to the United States.

A motive was offered in a draft letter found in the computer. It threatened attacks against American targets "in response to the financial, political and military assistance given to the Jewish State in the occupied land of Palestine by the American Government."

But Judge Duffy instructed the jurors to "please remember that political beliefs are not on trial here" and "neither are religious beliefs."

## 424 " 'There are manifold restraints to which every person is necessarily subject for the common good' " (1995)

When the Supreme Court affirmed in 1992 a woman's right to seek medical assistance in obtaining an early abortion (*Planned Parenthood of Southeastern Pennsylvania v. Casey*, 505 U.S. 833 (1992)), the frequency and severity of violence against abortion clinics and their staffs increased. In March 1993 Michael Griffin shot and killed Dr. David Gunn outside a Pensacola, Florida, abortion clinic. On August 19 of that year, an Oregon abortion protester, Rochelle Shannon, traveled to Wichita, Kansas, and shot an abortion provider, Dr. George Tiller, three times at close range.

Criminal attacks upon clinics had heretofore seemingly been timed to avoid serious threat to life or limb. The shootings were a serious escalation of the violence. But the reactions of many antiabortion spokespeople remained ambivalent, as they had been to the earlier disruptions at and vandalism against the clinics.

In March 1994 Congress passed the Freedom of Access to Clinic Entrances (FACE) Act to prohibit, and impose federal penalties for, the disruptive tactics used by antiabortion "sidewalk counselors" outside the clinics. FACE was immediately challenged by abortion opponents as violating their constitutional rights of free speech and free exercise of religion. The Fourth Circuit Court of Appeals addressed the constitutional challenges to FACE. The Supreme Court declined to review the appellate outcome.

### ☆424 *American Life League, Inc. v. Reno*

47 F.3d 642 (4th Cir.), *cert. denied*, 116 S.Ct. 55 (1995).

Michael, Circuit Judge:

Plaintiffs, the American Life League, Inc. and five individuals, all actively opposed to abortion, appeal from a judgment upholding the validity of the Freedom of Access to Clinic Entrances Act of 1994 (the Access Act or Act). We affirm.

*        *        *

II.

Congress passed the Access Act in response to protracted and nationwide violence and access obstruction at facilities providing abortions. Between 1977 and early 1993, more than 1,000 acts of violence against abortion providers and more than 6,000 clinic blockades were reported in the United States. "These acts included at least 36 bombings, 81 arsons, 131 death threats, 84 assaults, two kidnappings, 327 clinic invasions, and one [now five] murder[s]." Congress concluded that state and local law

enforcement agencies were often unable and sometimes unwilling to protect the patients and staffs of
these clinics from violence and severe disruption.

The Access Act aims to protect and promote public safety and health "by establishing Federal criminal penalties and civil remedies for certain violent,
threatening, obstructive and destructive conduct
that is intended to injure, intimidate or interfere
with persons seeking to obtain or provide reproductive health services." To that end the Act provides
criminal and civil penalties against anyone who:

> (1) by force or threat of force or by physical
> obstruction, intentionally injures, intimidates or
> interferes with or attempts to injure, intimidate
> or interfere with any person because that person
> is or has been, or in order to intimidate such per-
> son or any other person or any class of persons
> from, obtaining or providing reproductive health
> services; . . . or
>
> (3) intentionally damages or destroys the
> property of a facility, or attempts to do so, be-
> cause such facility provides reproductive health
> services. . . .

*       *       *

We turn now to plaintiffs' several challenges to
the Act.

*       *       *

## IV.

### A.

The Constitution ordains that "Congress shall
make no law . . . abridging the freedom of speech."
Plaintiffs claim that the Access Act abridges this
freedom.

We begin our consideration of plaintiffs' freedom
of speech claims by repeating the elements of a basic
offense under the Act. A violator must (1) "by force
or threat of force or by physical obstruction," (2) "intentionally injure[ ], intimidate[ ], or interfere[ ] . . .
with any person," (3) "because that person [the vic-
tim] is . . . obtaining or providing reproductive health
services."

The government's first defense is that the Act
does not implicate the First Amendment at all;
rather, it regulates conduct that is outside the First
Amendment. According to the government, the Act
leaves plaintiffs free to engage in any form of protected speech they choose.

In many respects the government is correct. The
Access Act does not prohibit protestors from praying, chanting, counseling, carrying signs, distributing handbills or otherwise expressing opposition to
abortion, so long as these activities are carried out in
a non-violent, non-obstructive manner. What the Act
does prohibit is force, the threat of force and physi-

cal obstruction intended to deprive someone of the
lawful right to use or provide reproductive health
services.

The use of force or violence is outside the scope of
First Amendment protection. True threats of force
also lie outside the First Amendment. Finally, certain physical obstructions, such as a blockade of
pedestrian traffic, are not protected by the First
Amendment.

Thus, the Act does target unprotected activities.
But the Act cannot escape First Amendment scrutiny entirely. The Act might incidentally affect some
conduct with protected expressive elements, such as
peaceful but obstructive picketing. The right to
peaceful protest lies near the heart of the freedom of
speech. Accordingly, we examine the Act under the
First Amendment.

### B.

The first step in our First Amendment inquiry
is to determine whether the Act is content and
viewpoint neutral. Plaintiffs argue that the Act is a
content- or viewpoint-based restriction because it
outlaws conduct for its anti-abortion message. If
plaintiffs are correct, then we subject the Act to
strict scrutiny. To pass this test a law must be necessary to serve compelling governmental interests by
the least restrictive means available. If plaintiffs are
incorrect, if the Act is content and viewpoint neutral,
then we subject it to intermediate scrutiny. To pass
this test a law must be narrowly tailored to serve
substantial governmental interests.

The neutrality inquiry does not focus on the motive of the violator. Rather, a statute regulating
expressive conduct is neutral if it is justified without reference to the content of the violator's message
or point of view. Congress's purpose is the main
consideration.

*       *       *

[T]he Act was not passed to outlaw conduct because it expresses an idea. Instead, Congress passed
the Act to promote public safety and health. . . .

Plaintiffs insist that these lofty statements of
purpose and construction are subterfuge. They say
Congress really intended to "suppress only the anti-
abortion side of a fierce national debate." This argument ignores the Act's substantive provisions. These
unambiguous provisions do not target any message
based on content or viewpoint.

The Act protects reproductive health services
and those who use and provide them. Reproductive
health services embrace "medical, surgical, counseling, or referral services relating to the human reproductive system." The Act thus protects access to
all reproductive health services, including both abortion and services connected with carrying a fetus to
term. It applies, for example, to facilities opposing

abortion and to facilities offering pregnant women counseling about alternatives to abortion. For example, AAA Women for Choice, Inc., a facility run by plaintiff Patricia Lohman, would be protected. AAA Women for Choice offers "counsel, comfort and alternatives other than abortion to pregnant women."

Moreover, the Act punishes anyone who engages in the prohibited conduct. For example, anyone who, with the requisite intent, blocks a person from entering a facility to obtain or provide reproductive health services violates the Act. The viewpoint of the obstructer is irrelevant. The Act forbids the obstructive conduct not because of the content of any message that conduct might convey, but because of its harmful effects.

Plaintiffs press on and say that the Act's apparent neutrality is not enough. They charge that the inclusion of protection for anti-abortion services is a ruse to make the Act look neutral. In reality, they argue, the Act aims to suppress the anti-abortion movement. . . .

This lack-of-neutrality argument overlooks the distinction between what the Act does and does not regulate. Again, the Act does not prohibit peaceful protestors from praying, chanting, counseling, carrying signs, distributing handbills, or otherwise expressing their opposition to abortion. What the Act does prohibit is force, the threat of force, and physical obstruction, when carried out because a person is using or providing reproductive health services. The "because" or motive element does not render the Act content or viewpoint based. As we explain below, the Act's motive requirement simply narrows its reach, and this narrowing is within congressional prerogative.

In *Wisconsin v. Mitchell*, the Supreme Court upheld a Wisconsin law that enhanced the sentence for the crime of aggravated battery when the defendant intentionally selected his victim *because* of the victim's race. Just like plaintiffs here, the defendant argued that he was being punished for his motive for acting. The unanimous Supreme Court rejected that argument, saying "[m]otive plays the same role under the Wisconsin statute as it does under the federal and state anti-discrimination laws, which we have previously upheld against constitutional challenge." The Court reasoned that "the penalty-enhancement statute [was] aimed at conduct unprotected by the First Amendment." Thus, Wisconsin's statute did not target conduct on the basis of its expressive elements. *Mitchell*'s conclusion was consistent with the Supreme Court's prior recognition that "where government does not target conduct on the basis of its expressive content, acts are not shielded from regulation merely because they express a discriminatory idea or philosophy."

*       *       *

### C.

Intermediate scrutiny is required when a statute potentially regulates conduct that has protected expressive elements. The intermediate scrutiny test was first enunciated by the Supreme Court in [*United States v. O'Brien*, Doc. 309].

O'Brien was convicted under a federal statute which made it a crime to destroy a draft card knowingly. In the Supreme Court O'Brien argued that his "act of burning his [draft card] was protected 'symbolic speech' within the First Amendment." The Supreme Court upheld the conviction, noting that Congress could regulate conduct that has an expressive element, given sufficient justification. . . . The Court then laid down a test for reviewing a statute, such as the Access Act, that may incidentally affect speech as it regulates conduct. Under *O'Brien*'s test such a statute passes constitutional muster "if it [1] furthers an important or substantial governmental interest; if [2] the governmental interest is unrelated to the suppression of free expression; and if [3] the incidental restriction on alleged First Amendment freedoms is no greater than is essential to the furtherance of that interest."

### 1.

*O'Brien*'s first prong asks whether the Act furthers important or substantial government interests. For easier discussion we group the several interests suggested by the government.

One group relates to protecting public health, safety and commerce. This interest includes protecting patients and staff from violence and harm and protecting reproductive health facilities from physical destruction or damage. It also includes protecting interstate patient traffic and the interstate market for the services of doctors, nurses, counselors, and other staff.

A second group of interests relates to protecting women and men from violence and threats in the exercise of their rights. The Supreme Court has recognized that government "has a strong interest in protecting a woman's freedom to seek lawful medical or counseling services in connection with her pregnancy." This freedom includes the constitutional right to terminate a pregnancy. . . . They should be able to use reproductive health facilities to exercise this right.

Together, or separately, these interests are significant. The government has a substantial interest in acting to protect them, as Congress did by passing the Access Act.

### 2.

*O'Brien* next asks whether the government's interests relate to suppressing free expression. This analysis is essentially the same as the content- and viewpoint-neutrality test we applied earlier. . . . We believe this analysis is sufficient for the Act to pass the second prong of the *O'Brien* test.

### 3.

Under *O'Brien*'s third prong we consider whether the incidental restriction on alleged First Amendment freedoms is no greater than required to meet the government's interests. . . . The statute must not "burden substantially more speech than is necessary to further the government's legitimate interests."

The Act meets this standard. Much of the conduct (force and violence) outlawed under the Act lacks any protected expressive element at all. Of course, peaceful but obstructive protesting, which plaintiffs argue has expressive elements, could run afoul of the Act. For example, protesters blocking a clinic door as they pray might violate the Act's prohibition on physical obstruction. However, such a violation would be simply a consequence of the government's lawful aim to protect access to reproductive health services. And the Act proscribes no more expressive conduct than necessary to protect safe and reliable access to reproductive health services. After all, the Act leaves open ample alternative means for communication. In a non-violent, nonobstructive manner, protestors may still stand outside reproductive health facilities and express their anti-abortion message. They may still proclaim their views and make their pleas by voice, signs, handbills, symbolic gestures and other expressive means.

### 4.

In sum, the Access Act serves substantial government interests such as preventing violence, preserving public access to reproductive health services, and protecting citizens in their exercise of constitutional rights. It is not aimed at expression, and it is narrowly tailored. It passes *O'Brien*'s test.

### D.

Plaintiffs next assert that the Act is unconstitutionally overbroad and vague. They claim that "thousands of persons who daily engage in peaceful activities around abortion clinics now risk arrest [and] prosecution" for exercising their First Amendment rights. They specifically point to "sign-carrying . . . and rosary-carrying processions outside clinics." Plaintiffs' argument is this: the Act's alleged overbreadth and vagueness will have a "chilling effect" on such activities.

\*          \*          \*

Even though the Act might be applied to some protected expression, such as peaceful picketing, that picketing would be prohibited only in the most narrow and justifiable circumstances. Under the Act, "physical obstruction" involves intentionally "rendering impassable ingress or egress from a facility . . . or rendering passage to or from such a facility . . . unreasonably difficult or hazardous." Thus, it is difficult to see how the Act is substantially overbroad in relation to its legitimate scope of outlawing violence and barriers to access.

The vagueness doctrine is concerned with clarity. A statute is unconstitutionally vague if it does not give a "person of ordinary intelligence a reasonable opportunity to know what is prohibited. . . ." The vagueness doctrine protects both free speech and due process values.

The Access Act's anti-obstruction provisions closely resemble a statute the Supreme Court upheld against a vagueness challenge in *Cameron v. Johnson*. In *Cameron* arrested civil rights protestors challenged Mississippi's Anti-Picketing Law, which provided:

> 1. It shall be unlawful for any person, singly or in concert with others, to engage in picketing or mass demonstrations in such a manner as to obstruct or unreasonably interfere with free ingress or egress to and from any public premises. . . .

The Supreme Court rejected the vagueness challenge on the grounds that the terms "obstruct," "unreasonably" and "interfere with" were perfectly clear, widely used, and well understood. According to the Court, the statute "precisely delineates its reach in words of common understanding."

\*          \*          \*

We conclude that the Access Act is neither overbroad nor vague.

\*          \*          \*

### V.

Plaintiffs' last claims concern protections afforded religion. Specifically, they argue that the Access Act offends the First Amendment's Free Exercise Clause. . . .

### A.

The Free Exercise Clause provides that "Congress shall make no law . . . prohibiting the free exercise" of religion. The clause forbids government from adopting laws designed to suppress religious belief or practice. However, a neutral, generally applicable law does not offend the Free Exercise Clause, even if the law has an incidental effect on religious practice.

Relying on *Church of Lukumi Babalu Aye*, plaintiffs claim that the Access Act violates the Free Exercise Clause. They say it aims to restrict nonviolent protest because of the protestors' religious motivation. In *Church of Lukumi Babalu Aye* the Supreme Court examined city ordinances aimed at suppressing the Santeria religion. The ordinances prohibited ritual animal slaughter, a Santeria religious practice. The ordinances carefully outlawed *only* animal sacrifice and the possession of animals for sacrificial purposes. They did not outlaw hunting, fishing, or the killing of animals for food. In short, the ordinances accomplished a religious gerrymander. They singled out religious practices for discriminatory treatment. The Supreme Court subjected the ordinances to the same level of exacting (strict) scrutiny it applies to content-based restrictions on speech. The ordinances were held unconstitutional.

By contrast, the Access Act punishes conduct for the harm it causes, not because the conduct is religiously motivated. By necessity, then, the Act does not punish religious belief. It proscribes violent, forceful or threatening conduct without regard to expressive content or viewpoint. Under the Act it makes no difference whether a violator acts on the basis of religious conviction or temporal views. The same conduct is outlawed for all. Therefore, the Act is a generally applicable law, neutral toward religion. It does not offend the First Amendment's Free Exercise Clause.

*      *      *

VI.

"There are manifold restraints to which every person is necessarily subject for the common good. On any other basis organized society could not exist with safety to its members." In passing the Access Act, Congress acted to ensure that violence and aggressive obstruction are not used as means of settling what has become a loud and vexing public dispute.

The Access Act strikes a balance among competing rights holders. It protects those who seek or provide reproductive health services without suppressing robust debate about abortion. Those opposed to abortion or to any other reproductive health service retain the freedom to express their deeply-held moral or religious views in a peaceful, nonobstructive way.

The district court's order dismissing the complaint is affirmed.

*Affirmed*

## 425 "the alleged atrocities are actionable" (1995)

The 1989 breach of the Berlin Wall signaled the collapse of the Soviet bloc. Distinct national and ethnic groups within the former Communist satellites began to assert themselves. In 1991, Yugoslavia, the most pluralistic and independent member of the Communist nations of Europe, came apart, as four of its six constituent republics—Slovenia, Macedonia, Bosnia-Hercegovina, and Croatia—declared their independence from the Serb-dominated central government.

Left alone, Serbia and Montenegro reconstituted themselves as the Federal Republic of Yugoslavia. Slovenia established itself relatively peacefully, but civil war broke out in Bosnia and Croatia, as each of their composite communities (the Eastern Rite Serbians, the Roman Catholic Croatians, and the largely Muslim Bosnians) embarked on programs of "ethnic cleansing." The objective of these pogroms was to "purify" the ethnic composition of claimed territory by razing villages, usurping tenements, forcing migrations, and imprisoning, raping, and killing ethnically distinct inhabitants. The process was decried by all nations and likened to the genocide of the Holocaust.

In 1996, a war crimes tribunal, patterned after the Nuremberg tribunal in post-World War II Germany, opened at the Hague to try international human rights violators from the former Yugoslavia. Not satisfied with the slow perambulations of international law, victims of ethnic cleansing meanwhile invoked the United States' obscure Alien Tort Act of 1789 to assert the jurisdiction of the federal courts to try civilly in the United States some foreign offenders for the personal injuries and atrocities inflicted by them in the distant Balkans.

### ☆425 *Kadic v. Karadzic*

70 F.3d 232 (2d Cir. 1995), *cert. denied* 116 S.Ct. 2524 (1996).

JON O. NEWMAN, Chief Judge:

Most Americans would probably be surprised to learn that victims of atrocities committed in Bosnia are suing the leader of the insurgent Bosnian-Serb forces in a United States District Court in Manhattan. Their claims seek to build upon the foundation of this Court's [1980] decision in *Filartiga v. Pena-Irala*, which recognized the important principle that the venerable Alien Tort Act, enacted in 1789 but rarely invoked since then, validly creates federal court jurisdiction for suits alleging torts committed anywhere in the world against aliens in violation of the law of nations. The pending appeals pose additional significant issues as to the scope of the Alien Tort Act....

*      *      *

For the reasons set forth below, we hold that ... [defendant] Karadzic may be found liable for genocide, war crimes, and crimes against humanity in his private capacity and for other violations in his capacity as a state actor, and that he is not immune from service of process. We therefore reverse and remand.

## BACKGROUND

The plaintiffs-appellants are Croat and Muslim citizens of the internationally recognized nation of Bosnia-Herzegovina, formerly a republic of Yugoslavia. Their complaints, which we accept as true for purposes of this appeal, allege that they are victims, and representatives of victims, of various atrocities, including brutal acts of rape, forced prostitution, forced impregnation, torture, and summary execution, carried out by Bosnian-Serb military forces as part of a genocidal campaign conducted in the course of the Bosnian civil war. Karadzic, formerly a citizen of Yugoslavia and now a citizen of Bosnia-Herzegovina, is the President of a three-man presidency of the self-proclaimed Bosnian-Serb republic within Bosnia-Herzegovina, sometimes referred to as "Srpska," which claims to exercise lawful authority, and does in fact exercise actual control, over large parts of the territory of Bosnia-Herzegovina. In his capacity as President, Karadzic possesses ultimate command authority over the Bosnian-Serb military forces, and the injuries perpetrated upon plaintiffs were committed as part of a pattern of systematic human rights violations that was directed by Karadzic and carried out by the military forces under his command. The complaints allege that Karadzic acted in an official capacity either as the titular head of Srpska or in collaboration with the government of the recognized nation of the former Yugoslavia and its dominant constituent republic, Serbia.

The two groups of plaintiffs ... sought compensatory and punitive damages....

\*          \*          \*

Without notice or a hearing, the District Court ... dismissed both actions for lack of subject-matter jurisdiction.... [T]he Court concluded that "acts committed by non-state actors do not violate the law of nations." Finding that "the current Bosnian-Serb warring military faction does not constitute a recognized state," and that "the members of Karadzic's faction do not act under the color of any recognized state law," the Court concluded that "the acts alleged in the instant actions, while grossly repugnant, cannot be remedied through [the Alien Tort Act]." The Court did not consider the plaintiffs' alternative claim that Karadzic acted under color of law by acting in concert with the Serbian Republic of the former Yugoslavia, a recognized nation.

\*          \*          \*

## DISCUSSION

Though the District Court dismissed for lack of subject-matter jurisdiction, the parties have briefed not only that issue but also the threshold issues of personal jurisdiction and justiciability under the political question doctrine. Karadzic urges us to affirm on any one of these three grounds. We consider each in turn.

### I. SUBJECT-MATTER JURISDICTION

Appellants allege three statutory bases for the subject-matter jurisdiction of the District Court—the Alien Tort Act, the Torture Victim Act, and the general federal-question jurisdictional statute.

### A. The Alien Tort Act

1. General Application to Appellants' Claims
The Alien Tort Act provides:

> The district courts shall have original jurisdiction of any civil action by an alien for a tort only, committed in violation of the law of nations or a treaty of the United States.

Our decision in *Filartiga* established that this statute confers federal subject-matter jurisdiction when the following three conditions are satisfied: (1) an alien sues (2) for a tort (3) committed in violation of the law of nations (i.e., international law). The first two requirements are plainly satisfied here, and the only disputed issue is whether plaintiffs have pleaded violations of international law.

\*          \*          \*

*Filartiga* established that courts ascertaining the content of the law of nations "must interpret international law not as it was in 1789, but as it has evolved and exists among the nations of the world today." We find the norms of contemporary international law by "'consulting the works of jurists, writing professedly on public law; or by the general usage and practice of nations; or by judicial decisions recognizing and enforcing that law.'" If this inquiry discloses that the defendant's alleged conduct violates "well-established, universally recognized norms of international law," as opposed to "idiosyncratic legal rules," then federal jurisdiction exists under the Alien Tort Act.

Karadzic contends that appellants have not alleged violations of the norms of international law because such norms bind only states and persons acting under color of a state's law, not private individuals. In making this contention, Karadzic advances the contradictory positions that he is not a state actor, even as he asserts that he is the President of the self-proclaimed Republic of Srpska. For their part, the Kadic appellants also take somewhat inconsistent positions in pleading defendant's role as President of Srpska, and also contending that "Karadzic is not an official of any government."

[District Court] Judge Leisure accepted Karadzic's contention that "acts committed by non-state actors do not violate the law of nations," and considered him to be a non-state actor. The Judge appears to have deemed state action required primarily on the basis of cases determining the need for state action as to claims of official torture, without consideration of the substantial body of law, discussed below, that renders private individuals liable for some international law violations.

We do not agree that the law of nations, as understood in the modern era, confines its reach to state action. Instead, we hold that certain forms of conduct violate the law of nations whether undertaken by those acting under the auspices of a state or only as private individuals. An early example of the application of the law of nations to the acts of private individuals is the prohibition against piracy. In [1844], the Supreme Court observed that pirates were *"hostis humani generis"* (an enemy of all mankind) in part because they acted "without. . . any pretense of public authority." Later examples are prohibitions against the slave trade and certain war crimes.

The liability of private persons for certain violations of customary international law and the availability of the Alien Tort Act to remedy such violations was early recognized by the Executive Branch in an opinion of Attorney General Bradford in reference to acts of American citizens aiding the French fleet to plunder British property off the coast of Sierra Leone in 1795. The Executive Branch has emphatically restated in this litigation its position that private persons may be found liable under the Alien Tort Act for acts of genocide, war crimes, and other violations of international humanitarian law.

The Restatement (Third) of the Foreign Relations Law of the United States (1986) proclaims: "Individuals may be held liable for offenses against international law, such as piracy, war crimes, and genocide." The Restatement is careful to identify those violations that are actionable when committed by a state, and a more limited category of violations of "universal concern. . . ." [T]he inclusion of piracy and slave trade from an earlier era and aircraft hijacking from the modern era demonstrates that the offenses of "universal concern" include those capable of being committed by non-state actors. . . .

Karadzic disputes the application of the law of nations to any violations committed by private individuals. . . . *Filartiga* involved an allegation of torture committed by a state official. . . . We had no occasion to consider whether international law violations other than torture are actionable against private individuals, and nothing in Filartiga purports to preclude such a result.

*     *     *

### 2. Specific Application of Alien Tort Act to Appellants' Claims

In order to determine whether the offenses alleged by the appellants in this litigation are violations of the law of nations that may be the subject of Alien Tort Act claims against a private individual, we must make a particularized examination of these offenses, mindful of the important precept that "evolving standards of international law govern who is within the [Alien Tort Act's] jurisdictional grant." In making that inquiry, it will be helpful to group the appellants' claims into three categories: (a) genocide, (b) war crimes, and (c) other instances of inflicting death, torture, and degrading treatment.

(a) *Genocide.* In the aftermath of the atrocities committed during the Second World War, the condemnation of genocide as contrary to international law quickly achieved broad acceptance by the community of nations. In 1946, the General Assembly of the United Nations declared that genocide is a crime under international law that is condemned by the civilized world, whether the perpetrators are "private individuals, public officials or statesmen." The General Assembly also affirmed the principles of Article 6 of the Agreement and Charter Establishing the Nuremberg War Crimes Tribunal for punishing "'persecutions on political, racial, or religious grounds,'" regardless of whether the offenders acted "'as individuals or as members of organizations.'"

The Convention on the Prevention and Punishment of the Crime of Genocide . . . defines "genocide" to mean any of the following acts committed with intent to destroy, in whole or in part, a national, ethnical, racial or religious group, as such:

(a) Killing members of the group;
(b) Causing serious bodily or mental harm to members of the group;
(c) Deliberately inflicting on the group conditions of life calculated to bring about its physical destruction in whole or in part;
(d) Imposing measures intended to prevent births with the group;
(e) Forcibly transferring children of the group to another group.

Convention on Genocide art. II. Especially pertinent to the pending appeal, the Convention makes clear that "persons committing genocide . . . shall be punished, *whether they are constitutionally responsible rulers, public officials or private individuals.*" (emphasis added). These authorities unambiguously reflect that, from its incorporation into international law, the proscription of genocide has applied equally to state and non-state actors.

*     *     *

Appellants' allegations that Karadzic personally planned and ordered a campaign of murder, rape, forced impregnation, and other forms of torture designed to destroy the religious and ethnic groups of Bosnian Muslims and Bosnian Croats clearly state a violation of the international law norm proscribing genocide, regardless of whether Karadzic acted under color of law or as a private individual. The

District Court has subject-matter jurisdiction over these claims pursuant to the Alien Tort Act.

(b) *War crimes.* Plaintiffs also contend that the acts of murder, rape, torture, and arbitrary detention of civilians, committed in the course of hostilities, violate the law of war. Atrocities of the types alleged here have long been recognized in international law as violations of the law of war. Moreover, international law imposes an affirmative duty on military commanders to take appropriate measures within their power to control troops under their command for the prevention of such atrocities.

After the Second World War, the law of war was codified in the four Geneva Conventions. . . . Common article 3, which is substantially identical in each of the four Conventions, applies to "armed conflicts not of an international character" and binds "each Party to the conflict . . . to apply, as a minimum, the following provisions":

> Persons taking no active part in the hostilities . . . shall in all circumstances be treated humanely, without any adverse distinction founded on race, colour, religion or faith, sex, birth or wealth, or any other similar criteria.
>
> To this end, the following acts are and shall remain prohibited at any time and in any place whatsoever with respect to the above-mentioned persons:
>
> (a) violence to life and person, in particular murder of all kinds, mutilation, cruel treatment and torture;
>
> (b) taking of hostages;
>
> (c) outrages upon personal dignity, in particular humiliating and degrading treatment;
>
> (d) the passing of sentences and carrying out of executions without previous judgment pronounced by a regularly constituted court. . . .

Geneva Convention I art. 3(1). Thus, under the law of war as codified in the Geneva Conventions, all "parties" to a conflict—which includes insurgent military groups—are obliged to adhere to these most fundamental requirements of the law of war.

The offenses alleged by the appellants, if proved, would violate the most fundamental norms of the law of war embodied in common article 3, which binds parties to internal conflicts regardless of whether they are recognized nations or roving hordes of insurgents. The liability of private individuals for committing war crimes has been recognized since World War I and was confirmed at Nuremberg after World War II. . . . The District Court has jurisdiction pursuant to the Alien Tort Act over appellants' claims of war crimes and other violations of international humanitarian law.

(c) *Torture and summary execution.* In *Filartiga*, we held that official torture is prohibited by universally accepted norms of international law. . . . However, torture and summary execution—when not perpetrated in the course of genocide or war crimes—are proscribed by international law only when committed by state officials or under color of law.

. . . It suffices to hold at this stage that the alleged atrocities are actionable under the Alien Tort Act, without regard to state action, to the extent that they were committed in pursuit of genocide or war crimes, and otherwise may be pursued against Karadzic to the extent that he is shown to be a state actor. Since the meaning of the state action requirement for purposes of international law violations will likely arise on remand and has already been considered by the District Court, we turn next to that requirement.

3. The State Action Requirement for International Law Violations

In dismissing plaintiffs' complaints for lack of subject-matter jurisdiction, the District Court concluded that the alleged violations required state action and that the "Bosnian-Serb entity" headed by Karadzic does not meet the definition of a state. . . .

*        *        *

The customary international law of human rights, such as the proscription of official torture, applies to states without distinction between recognized and unrecognized states. It would be anomalous indeed if non-recognition by the United States, which typically reflects disfavor with a foreign regime—sometimes due to human rights abuses—had the perverse effect of shielding officials of the unrecognized regime from liability for those violations of international law norms that apply only to state actors.

Appellants' allegations entitle them to prove that Karadzic's regime satisfies the criteria for a state, for purposes of those international law violations requiring state action. Srpska is alleged to control defined territory, control populations within its power, and to have entered into agreements with other governments. It has a president, a legislature, and its own currency. These circumstances readily appear to satisfy the criteria for a state in all aspects of international law. . . .

(b) *Acting in concert with a foreign state.* Appellants also sufficiently alleged that Karadzic acted under color of law insofar as they claimed that he acted in concert with the former Yugoslavia, the statehood of which is not disputed. The "color of law" jurisprudence of [United States law, see Doc. 146b] is a relevant guide to whether a defendant has engaged in official action for purposes of jurisdiction under the Alien Tort Act. A private individual acts under color of law within the meaning of [United States law] when he acts together with state officials or with significant state aid. The appellants are entitled to prove their allegations that Karadzic acted under color of law of Yugoslavia by acting in concert with Yugoslav officials or with significant Yugoslavian aid.

\*     \*     \*

### III. JUSTICIABILITY

We recognize that cases of this nature might pose special questions concerning the judiciary's proper role when adjudication might have implications in the conduct of this nation's foreign relations. We do not read *Filartiga* to mean that the federal judiciary must always act in ways that risk significant interference with United States foreign relations. To the contrary, we recognize that suits of this nature can present difficulties that implicate sensitive matters of diplomacy historically reserved to the jurisdiction of the political branches.

\*     \*     \*

In the pending appeal, we need have no concern that interference with important governmental interests warrants rejection of appellants' claims. . . . [The United States Department of State has indicated in a letter] that Karadzic was not immune from suit as an invitee of the United Nations. . . . In a "Statement of Interest," signed by the Solicitor General [of the United States] and the State Department's Legal Adviser, the United States has expressly disclaimed any concern that the political question doctrine should be invoked to prevent the litigation of these lawsuits: "Although there might be instances in which federal courts are asked to issue rulings under the Alien Tort Statute . . . that might raise a political question, this is not one of them." Though even an assertion of the political question doctrine by the Executive Branch, entitled to respectful consideration, would not necessarily preclude adjudication, the Government's reply to our inquiry reinforces our view that adjudication may properly proceed.

\*     \*     \*

Finally, we note that at this stage of the litigation no party has identified a more suitable forum, and we are aware of none. Though the Statement of the United States suggests the general importance of considering the doctrine of *forum non conveniens*, it seems evident that the courts of the former Yugoslavia, either in Serbia or war-torn Bosnia, are not now available to entertain plaintiffs' claims, even if circumstances concerning the location of witnesses and documents were presented that were sufficient to overcome the plaintiffs' preference for a United States forum.

### CONCLUSION

The judgment of the District Court dismissing appellants' complaints for lack of subject-matter jurisdiction is reversed, and the cases are remanded for further proceedings in accordance with this opinion.

## 426  "The fight will go on" (1995-1996)

After the horrors of the Holocaust were revealed during the liberation of Europe and the Nuremberg trials, those who succeeded the Nazi regime vowed that such atrocities would never be perpetrated in Germany again. To that end, in their Basic Law, the German people placed limitations upon political freedoms. These restrictions have been used to outlaw a neo-Nazi party in the early 1950s and a Communist party in 1956. These provisions, and their corresponding penal statutes, were little used until a rash of violence against foreigners erupted in the economic hard times following the reunification of East and West Germany.

These crackdowns on burgeoning neo-Nazi sentiments, however, brought little relief from the flood of Nazi paraphernalia and propaganda coming from the United States. But in 1995, Danish authorities arrested Gary Rex Lauck, the "Farm Belt Fuehrer," who had operated a mail-order export business out of Lincoln, Nebraska. After being extradited to Germany, he was convicted of inciting racial hatred and disseminating material forbidden under German laws passed to effect German constitutional limitations on political expression. He was sentenced to four years in jail, but his lawyers vowed an appeal, claiming that Germany cannot punish him for activities in the United States which are protected by the First Amendment to the Constitution.

## ☆426  United States Exports Neo-Naziism

### ☆426a  Basic Law for the Federal Republic of Germany

Donald Kommers, *The Constitutional Jurisprudence of the Federal Republic of Germany* (Durham, N.C.: Duke University Press, 1989), 505.

#### PREAMBLE

Conscious of their responsibility before God and men,

Animated by the resolve to serve world peace as an equal partner in a united Europe, the German people have adopted, by virtue of their constituent power, this Basic Law.

\*     \*     \*

#### I. BASIC RIGHTS

*Article 1 (Protection of Human Dignity)*

(1) Human dignity is inviolable. To respect and protect it is the duty of all state authority.

(2) The German people therefore acknowledge inviolable and inalienable human rights as the basis of every community, of peace and of justice in the world.

\*     \*     \*

*Article 5 (Freedom of Expression)*

(1) Everyone has the right freely to express and disseminate his opinion in speech, writing, and pictures and freely to inform himself from generally accessible sources. Freedom of the press and freedom of reporting by means of broadcasts and films are guaranteed. There shall be no censorship.

\* \* \*

*Article 8 (Freedom of Assembly)*

(1) All Germans have the right to assemble peaceably and unarmed without prior notification or permission.

\* \* \*

*Article 9 (Freedom of Association)*

(1) All Germans shall have the right to form associations and corporations.

\* \* \*

*Article 18 (Forfeiture of Basic Rights)*

Whoever abuses freedom of expression of opinion, in particular freedom of the press (paragraph (1) of Article 5), freedom of teaching (paragraph (3) of Article 5), freedom of assembly (Article 8), freedom of association (Article 9) . . . in order to combat the free democratic basic order shall forfeit these basic rights. Such forfeiture and the extent thereof shall be determined by the Federal Constitutional Court.

\* \* \*

*Article 21 (Political Parties)*

(1) The political parties shall participate in the formation of the political will of the people. They may be freely established. Their internal organization shall conform to democratic principles. . . .

(2) Parties that, by reason of their aims or the behavior of their adherents seek to impair or abolish the free democratic basic order or to endanger the existence of the Federal Republic of Germany are unconstitutional. The Federal Constitutional Court shall decide on the question of unconstitutionality.

\* \* \*

☆426b  Nebraska's Nazi

Document at http://net.unl.edu/~swi/pers/nazi.html.

Gary Lauck is in prison in Germany. In March, 1995, police in Europe arrested Lauck and extradited him to Germany. On August 22, 1996, he was convicted of inciting racial hatred and disseminating illegal propaganda. Lauck was sentenced to four years in jail. After the sentence was imposed, Lauck spoke to the media for the first time, shouting, "Neither the Communists nor the Nazis would ever have dared kidnap an American citizen. The fight will go on." Lauck maintained that he was prosecuted for acts that are protected by the U.S. Constitution's free speech protections.

\* \* \*

Gary Lauck was born in Milwaukee. When he was 11, his family moved to Lincoln where his father taught engineering at the University of Nebraska. When he became politically active, Gary changed his name to Gerhard. And at the age of 19, he established the NSDAP/AO [Nationalsozialistische Deutsche Arbeiterpartei Auslands- und Aufbauorganisation] named after Hitler's Nazi party.

\* \* \*

According to corporate records on file with the Nebraska Secretary of State's office, in 1974 Lauck created the non-profit Socialist Workers Party using his German language name. The articles of incorporation state the group promotes the study of Germany by means of cooperation with other political organizations not created for propaganda purposes. State records on file reveal Lauck also controls a for-profit corporation, R.J.G. Engineering. Lauck is listed as a consultant. Both the non-profit Nazi party and the engineering firm share much in common. Both have Lauck, his mother, and a woman in Indiana listed as officers. Both list this home in south central Lincoln as their official business address.

\* \* \*

In the four years since the Berlin Wall fell and Germany reunited, the neo-Nazi movement has become increasingly vocal. Germany, fearful of its recent history of fascism, bans the symbols of its Nazi past—Swastikas and hate literature. Those who market such paraphernalia are not welcome . . . so Gary Lauck [was] banned from entering Germany even while his own newspapers brag of his secret visits.

\* \* \*

Lauck lives undisturbed and almost unnoticed with his wife in Syracuse, [Nebraska,] a town that perhaps coincidentally boasts of its annual Octoberfest. He likes to be able to keep a low profile here so he does little to build a higher profile Nazi party in his home state.

[Lauck explains that] "Nebraska is not a good agitation potential for two reasons. One is it's economically prosperous. I know that might sound almost callous but it is, compared to most parts of the country. Second it's too white. The people in Nebraska, they turn on TV and they see TV presenting black people as being just like you and me, but they happen to have dark skin. And the ones you meet in Nebraska, outside of maybe Omaha or parts of Omaha, are basically decent middle-class people so they believe it. But that's the exception to the rule. You cannot agitate on these issues when people don't have anything going on. Basically you're not going to support a revolutionary struggle unless the situation is really bad, and it's just not bad here."

*          *          *

[Before his German conviction] Lauck pledge[d] to continue to run his Nazi propaganda machine from his hometown. His Nebraska neighbors and the first amendment of the constitution allow[ed] him to publish his hate literature within the law and without hassle.

## ☆426c  Lauck Gets Prison Term in Germany: Neo-Nazi's Publishing Continues in Lincoln

Toni Heinzl, *Omaha World-Herald*, August 23, 1996, 1.

The arrest and prosecution of Gary Lauck, Nebraska's most notorious neo-Nazi, has hurt but not stopped his Lincoln publishing business, German authorities said.

Lauck has shipped his hate publications, T-shirts and buttons to Germany and around the world for two decades.

Lauck, a self-proclaimed Adolf Hitler admirer, was sentenced to four years in jail Thursday on conviction of inciting racial hatred and disseminating illegal propaganda in Germany.

*          *          *

His lawyer, Hans-Otto Sieg, immediately said he will appeal the sentence on grounds that the so-called Farm Belt Fuehrer's Nebraska-based mail order exports are legal in the United States despite Germany's laws punishing neo-Nazi propaganda and paraphernalia.

He argued that Germany has no right to tell an American citizen what to do in the United States. Lauck, who prefers to be addressed as Gerhard, sports a Hitler-like toothbrush mustache and speaks English with a German accent but is a resident of Nebraska.

*          *          *

German officials . . . were pleased by the verdict, capping two decades of efforts to interrupt Lauck's thriving exports of neo-Nazi propaganda literature, cassettes, arm bands, records, swastikas and other symbols in 10 European languages to more than 30 countries.

In contravention of German laws, Lauck's materials slander Jews and other "non-Aryans," praise Hitler, advocate restoration of his Third Reich and deny the Holocaust.

*          *          *

. . . Lincoln Mayor Mike Johanns also won't shed a tear about Lauck's conviction. He said Lauck kept such a low profile in the city that he seemed virtually nonexistent in public life, yet he gave the city and the state a ton of bad publicity. . . . "He brought us a zillion dollars worth of bad publicity. It's been a source of frustration for many years." The Nebraska Legislature and the Lincoln City Council passed resolutions distancing themselves from Lauck and the hateful ideas for which he stands, Johanns said.

## ☆426d  Defiant U.S. Neo-Nazi Jailed by German Court

Andrew Gray, Reuters North American Wire, August 22, 1996.

A Hamburg court sentenced U.S. neo-Nazi leader Gary Lauck on Thursday to four years in prison for pumping banned extremist propaganda into Germany from his base in the United States.

Lauck, from Lincoln, Nebraska, yelled a tirade of abuse at the court after his conviction for inciting racial hatred.

"The struggle will go on," the 43-year-old shouted in German before being escorted out by security guards.

Lauck's lawyer vowed he would appeal against the court's decision, arguing that his client should have been set free because he had not committed any offence under German law.

The German government hailed the conviction as a major victory in the fight against neo-Nazism. Lauck's worldwide network has been the main source of anti-Semitic propaganda material flowing into Germany since the 1970s.

"Lauck possessed a well-oiled propaganda machine, honed during more than 20 years," presiding judge Guenter Bertram told the court.

"He set up a propaganda cannon and fired it at Germany," said Bertram, who also read out extracts from Lauck's material praising Hitler as "the greatest of all leaders" and describing the Nazi slaughter of millions of Jews as a myth.

Eager to put Lauck behind bars quickly and avoid a long and complex trial, prosecutor Bernd Mauruschat limited his charges to offences since 1994. He had demanded a five-year jail term but said he was satisfied with the court's sentence.

Publishing and distributing neo-Nazi material is illegal in Germany but Lauck's defence team had argued that U.S. freedom of speech laws meant he was free to produce his swastika-covered books, magazines, videos and flags in his homeland.

Interior Minister Manfred Kanther said in a statement he "welcomed the prosecution and conviction of one of the ringleaders of international neo-Nazism and biggest distributers of vicious racist publications."

"It is high time he was behind bars," the opposition Social Democrats said in a statement.

Lauck, dressed in a sober blue suit and sporting his trademark Hitleresque black moustache, showed no sign of emotion as Bertram spent more than an hour reading out the verdict and explaining the court's decision.

But as Lauck was about to be led away, he turned to reporters and blurted out a virtually incomprehensible quick-fire diatribe against the court.

"Neither the National Socialists (Nazis) nor the

communists dared to kidnap an American citizen," he shouted, in an oblique reference to his extradition to Germany from Denmark. "That's the truth."

His attorney, Hans-Otto Sieg, told reporters outside the courtroom that the judges had not explained how a German court could judge someone for actions carried out in the United States.

Bertram said Lauck was obsessed by Nazism and devoted his life to leading his National Socialist German Workers' Party Foreign Organisation (NSDAP-AO), which derives its name from the full German title of Hitler's Nazi party.

During the three-month trial, the court dealt mainly with issues of the NSDAP-AO's "NS Kampfruf" ("National Socialist Battle Cry") magazine, filled with references to Aryan supremacy and defamatory statements about Jews.

The court rejected Sieg's argument that Lauck's extradition from Denmark, where he was arrested in March last year at the request of German authorities, was illegal.

Lauck was also convicted of disseminating the symbols of anti-constitutional organisations.

He will probably be free in around two and a half years. The court ruled that the 15 months he has spent in custody since his arrest should be subtracted from his prison term.

## 427 "McVeigh came to symbolize our nation's worst fears" (1995–1997)

At 9:01 A.M. on April 19, 1995, a rental truck packed with fertilizer mixed with diesel fuel exploded outside the Alfred P. Murrah Federal Building in Oklahoma City, Oklahoma. The bomb killed 168 people, including nineteen children in a day-care center that caught the brunt of the explosion. The building was heavily damaged and had to be razed after all hope of rescuing survivors was given up. The blast was the deadliest terrorist attack in United States history. Initial speculation, recalling the 1993 New York World Trade Center bombing by Muslim fundamentalists, focused on foreign terrorist groups, but the arrest of Timothy McVeigh and Terry Nichols shortly after the explosion raised the possibility that responsibility lay somewhere within the domestic phenomena of the patriot militias and other antigovernment associations. The intuitive connection was strengthened with the realization that the bombing occurred on the second anniversary of the FBI's assault on the compound of the Branch Davidian sect in Waco, Texas (see Doc. 418), and by the T-shirt McVeigh was wearing at the time of his arrest. The front of the shirt portrayed Abraham Lincoln accompanied by the words of his assassin, John Wilkes Booth: "Sic Semper Tyrannis." The rear

quoted Thomas Jefferson's famous words "The tree of liberty must be refreshed from time to time with blood of patriots and tyrants."

The Waco disaster and the Ruby Ridge incident (see Doc. 413) had given credibility among antigovernment groups to the view that the perfidious and hostile United States government, prophesied in the 1979 apocalyptic novel *The Turner Diaries*, by William Pierce (writing under the pseudonym Andrew Macdonald), had begun to wage war against its own people. Timothy McVeigh was reported to have been an especial fan of the book and is alleged in the criminal complaint against him to have been "so agitated by the deaths of the Branch Davidians . . . that he personally visited the site [and] . . . expressed extreme anger at the federal government." McVeigh and Nichols had some association with the Michigan Militia, one of the many organized militias around the country (see Doc. 420). Terry Nichols has shown his belief in the dictates of the Freeman Movement (see Doc. 429), as shown by his declaration reproduced below (Doc. 427c).

The role of the media in the Oklahoma City bombing, and in political criminality generally, cannot be underestimated. Often, media coverage is a major objective of the offender. Moreover, the media's power to "demonize" or rally support for alleged offenders is well recognized. In the case of McVeigh and Nichols, the media coverage that saturated the Oklahoma City area forced the trial to move to Denver. McVeigh was sentenced to death in June 1997. As this book goes to press, Nichols is being tried.

☆427 Documents regarding the Oklahoma City Bombing

☆427a *United States v. McVeigh*

Criminal Complaint No. M-95-98-H, U.S. D. Ct., W.D. Okla. (1995).

### AFFIDAVIT

I, HENRY C. GIBBONS, being duly sworn, do hereby state that I am an agent with the Federal Bureau of Investigation, having been so employed for 26 years and as such am vested with the authority to investigate violations of federal laws, including Title 18, United States Code, Section 844 (f). Further, the Affiant states as follows:

1. The following information has been received by the Federal Bureau of Investigation over the period from April 19 through April 21, 1995;

2. On April 19, 1995, a massive explosion detonated outside the Alfred P. Murrah building in Oklahoma City, Oklahoma, at approximately 9:00 a.m.

                    *         *         *

6. On April 20, 1995, the FBI interviewed three witnesses who were near the scene of the explosion

at Alfred P. Murrah Federal Building prior to the determination of the explosives. The three witnesses were shown a copy of the composite drawing of Unsub [Unidentified Subject] #1 and identified him as closely resembling a person the witnesses had seen in front of the Alfred P. Murrah Building where the explosion occurred on April 19, 1995. The witnesses advised the FBI that they observed a person identified as Unsub #1 at approximately 8:40 a.m. on April 19, 1995, when they entered the building. They again observed Unsub #1 at approximately 8:55 a.m., still in front of the 5th Road entrance of the building when they departed just minutes before the explosion.

7. The Alfred P. Murrah building is used by various agencies of the United States. . . .

8. The composite drawings were shown to employees at various motels and commercial establishments in the Junction City, Kansas, vicinity. Employees of the Dreamland Motel in Junction City, Kansas, advised FBI agents that an individual resembling Unsub #1 depicted in the composite drawings had been a guest at the Motel from April 14 through April 18, 1995. This individual had registered at the Motel under the name of Tim McVeigh, listed his automobile as bearing an Oklahoma license plate with an illegible plate number, and provided a Michigan address, on North Van Dyke Road in Decker, Michigan. The individual was seen driving a car described as a Mercury from the 1970's.

*       *       *

11. A relative of James Nichols reports to the FBI that Tim McVeigh is a friend and associate of James Nichols, who has worked and resided at the farm on North Van Dyke Road in Decker. . . . This relative further reports that she had heard that James Nichols had been involved in constructing bombs in approximately November 1994, and that he possessed large quantities of fuel oil and fertilizer.

12. On April 21, 1995, a former co-worker of Tim McVeigh's reported to the FBI that he had seen the composite drawing of Unsub #1 on the television and recognized the drawing to be a former co-worker, Tim McVeigh. He further advised that McVeigh was known to hold extreme rightwing views, was a military veteran, and was particularly agitated about the conduct of the federal government in Waco, Texas, in 1993. In fact, the co-worker further reports that McVeigh had been so agitated about the deaths of the Branch Davidians in Waco, Texas, on April 19, 1993, that he personally visited the site. After visiting the site, McVeigh expressed extreme anger at the federal government and advised that the Government should never had done what it did. He further advised that the last known address he had for McVeigh is 1711 Stockton Hill Road, #206, Kingman, Arizona.

13. On April 21, 1994, investigators learned that a Timothy McVeigh was arrested at 10:30 a.m. on April 19, 1995, in Perry, Oklahoma, for not having a license tag and for possession of a weapon approximately 1½ hours after the detonation of the explosive device at the Alfred P. Murrah Federal Building in Oklahoma City, Oklahoma. Perry, Oklahoma, is approximately a 1½ hour drive from Oklahoma City, Oklahoma. McVeigh, who has been held in custody since his arrest on April 19, 1995, listed his home address as 3616 North Van Dyke Road, Decker, Michigan. He listed James Nichols of Decker, Michigan, as a reference. McVeigh was stopped driving a yellow 1977 Mercury Marquis.

14. The detonation of the explosive in front of the Alfred P. Murrah Federal Building constitutes a violation of 18 U.S.C. Section 844(f), which makes it a crime to maliciously damage or destroy by means of an explosive any building or real property, in whole or in part owned, possessed or used by the United States, or any Department, or agency thereof.

*       *       *

☆427b  Defendant Timothy McVeigh's Motion for Media Access

Criminal Action No. 96-CR-68-M, U.S. D. Ct., D. Col. (1996).

### I. INTRODUCTION

Defendant Timothy James McVeigh, by counsel, respectfully requests the Court to authorize and permit Mr. McVeigh, a pre-trial detainee, to have reasonable access to members of the local, Oklahoma, national, and European media as specified herein, including the opportunity to participate in one videotaped interview with either Barbara Walters, Diane Sawyer, Tom Brokaw, Dan Rather, Susan Candiotti or Jack Bowen, and a videotaped interview with the BBC-TV (Documentary Division) "BBC."

### II. DISCUSSION

A. Factual Background: Virtually every aspect of the April 19, 1995, Oklahoma City bombing has generated unprecedented public interest worldwide and a corresponding surfeit of international media attention. As this Court's Memorandum Opinion and Order on Motion for Change of Venue held, a fair and impartial trial in Oklahoma was impossible. . . . Evidence produced at the venue hearing demonstrated that an overwhelming percentage of Americans believe Mr. McVeigh to be guilty of the Oklahoma City bombing. Indeed, this Court found that the publicity concerning Mr. McVeigh (and Mr. Nichols) had "demonized" the Defendant. Lengthy articles appearing in the New York Times, The Washington Post and the Dallas Morning News have presented false, misleading, or half truths concerning the Defendant's background. A purported biography by Brandon

Stickney will be released in September by a well known publishing house, and the demonization continues. The description of the book, as published in Publisher's Weekly indicates that it will be harsh in its treatment of Mr. McVeigh and clearly one-sided, and present an unfair representation of his youth and early years. The television Channel A & E produced, filmed and showed an hour long biography of Mr. McVeigh, and that video biography is now available in book stores across the United States in video cassettes. Both CNN and ABC News likewise did lengthy video biographies or purported biographies of Mr. McVeigh. Morris Dees has authored a book, Gathering Storm, which contains an entire chapter arguing Mr. McVeigh's guilt and outlining how his lawyer can save his life if he will only follow Morris Dees' crusade against the author of The Turner Diaries, William Pierce. Dees, a lawyer, promoted his book actively in Denver. All of these films, books and television presentations, have received widespread publicity. Many of them have relied upon interviews with individuals who would not recognize Mr. McVeigh if he walked in the room today, but for the publicity surrounding this case. These interviews, which have been published, have had the effect of "chilling" family, former employers, and former colleagues in the military from a willingness to testify or to assist the Defendant until recently when after repeated efforts by defense investigators, some, but not all, family members, former employers, and military colleagues are now willing to give a more balanced picture of Mr. McVeigh. The juggernaut of guilt, supported in part, by the media has made the work of the Defendant much greater. . . .

From the beginning of counsel's appointment, radio and television stations and newspapers from Brazil, Israel, Hong Kong, Great Britain, the United States, France, Germany, and worldwide services such as the Associated Press and Reuters have requested interviews with Mr. McVeigh. Mr. McVeigh has granted only four (4) interviews to print media. These interviews were submitted for approval to the Bureau of Prisons before the interview and in each case approval was granted during various periods of time when different judges had control of the case. A Newsweek interview was granted in the late Spring of 1995, a Time Magazine interview on the first anniversary of the bombing, and approximately two weeks later an interview with the Times of London (Sunday edition). . . .

In an attempt to set the balance true and dispel the demonization effects, counsel for Mr. McVeigh, has in addition permitted various members of the media to talk to Mr. McVeigh, off-the-record, at the El Reno Federal Correctional Institution. These individuals who have talked with Mr. McVeigh agreed that the conversations were off-the-record, not for publication, not for attribution, that Mr. McVeigh

could not discuss the facts of the case or his strategy, and that Mr. McVeigh would neither be tape recorded nor filmed, and no reference could even be made publicly to the fact that the reporter had met with Mr. McVeigh. Reporters and/or media which were granted this limited opportunity to talk to Mr. McVeigh, without exception, honored the written requirements. . . .

\*            \*            \*

This defense effort has sought to humanize Mr. McVeigh and stop the rush to judgment of guilt by undermining the inaccurate impression of Mr. McVeigh conveyed throughout the world. . . .

We live in a time in which we as a nation are peculiarly vulnerable to anger and hatred, a time in which we have a marked tendency to identify certain people as enemies, then seek to eliminate them.

The government took advantage of this attitude from the day the Murrah Building was bombed: Most people felt anger, bewilderment, and fear over what happened in Oklahoma City. Tim McVeigh was then accused as the person primarily responsible. He was portrayed—falsely—as a person who refused to answer the questions of law enforcement officers and who asserted he was a prisoner of war—a person who hated the government for its actions at Waco and Ruby Ridge, whose hatred grew to encompass anyone associated with the government, and who was willing to and did kill many people as reprisal for what he perceived as the government's misdeeds. Mr. McVeigh was then marginalized. He was characterized as an aberration, "All American Monster" as the title of a recent biography suggests, as a person who lived alone and embittered on the fringes of society, not bound by relationships to other human beings, seething in misplaced and deluded anger at the federal government, as a "loser" whose own inadequacies produced the tragedy.

Through this process, Tim McVeigh came to symbolize our nation's worst fears, our own worst enemy. Who he was portrayed to be readily confirmed the accusations of guilt. Very quickly, Mr. McVeigh was tried, convicted (before the first piece of evidence was admitted at trial) and condemned in the minds of many, and he became "the most hated man in America." If there was ever an accused tried and convicted in the media, it was Tim McVeigh.

This is the process of demonization about which we have complained from the time we became Mr. McVeigh's counsel. The Court recognized it as a reason for changing venue from the Western District of Oklahoma to the District of Colorado. It is insidious and can never be fully overcome. In the few cautious attempts counsel for Mr. McVeigh have made to allow the national media access to Mr. McVeigh, counsel have been accused of "dressing him up"—trying to portray him, falsely, as a likeable, fully human young man, rather than allowing him to be seen as the demon that he really is.

If Mr. McVeigh is to receive a fair trial, one of the things that must be done is to present information that will begin to counter the false view that he is a demon. Allowing limited access to him for interview on a respected, nationally televised program will contribute to such a process. It can be accomplished without transgressing in any way the Court's guidelines for media contact. Moreover, it can serve the same goal—assuring a fair trial—that the Court sought to serve in its media contact Order.

Shortly after counsel was appointed, and he became aware of the worldwide interest in Mr. McVeigh, counsel was approached by Mr. Neil Grant of the BBC Television, Documentary Division, and ask[ed] whether counsel would permit the BBC-TV to film an interview with Mr. McVeigh, with counsel, and some footage of counsel at work as a part of an overall one or two hour documentary on this case.

\* \* \*

3. The BBC-TV advised counsel that it was filming for history, not for news and that sensationalism and conflict, were being avoided, and that the BBC-TV wished that 25 or 50 years from now its documentary would survive as a balanced, proportioned, and accurate account of what the BBC-TV described as an "unprecedented" criminal trial in the United States.

4. Meetings with the BBC's personnel convinced counsel of their resourcefulness, professionalism and integrity and on that basis, counsel recommended to Mr. McVeigh that he cooperate with the understanding that (1) Judge Matsch's guidelines must be followed, (2) the program would not be released to an American broadcasting unit in advance of the trial, and (3) that it would not be shown in the United Kingdom before the commencement of the trial.

\* \* \*

Aside from the proposed BBC-TV program, which is a documentary, counsel was also besieged with requests for media interviews with Mr. McVeigh which would be shown in this country. Counsel met with all those who requested such interviews including Diane Sawyer, Dan Rather, Peter Jennings, Tom Brokaw and Barbara Walters. Each of their representatives met with Mr. McVeigh, as indicated above, and in addition, Harry Smith, Tom Brokaw, Barbara Walters and Diane Sawyer met personally with Mr. McVeigh.

Mr. McVeigh, on his own election, has decided that he would choose one from among the following individuals, subject to Court authorization, to conduct one (1) national television interview: Barbara Walters of ABC, Diane Sawyer of ABC, Susan Candiotti of CNN, Dan Rather of CBS, Tom Brokaw of NBC, and Jack Bowen of Fox Television. Counsel has concurred.

\* \* \*

Warden Perrill has indicated, informally, no objection whatsoever to the interview[s].

We believe that the public interest is served by such interviews. . . . The possibility for exploitation, politically, or in a more dangerous and adventuresome ways, by those who believe that Mr. McVeigh is a "political prisoner" and that the federal government is "evil" simply cannot be discounted. Public safety is not an unimportant consideration and access to Mr. McVeigh by television is an important contribution to the confidence of the public and to circumstances in which Mr. McVeigh is being held.

\* \* \*

B. Legal Standards: As a pre-trial detainee, Mr. McVeigh retains at least those constitutional rights that are enjoyed by convicted prisoners. Thus, Mr. McVeigh has "a First Amendment right to be free from governmental interference with [his] contacts with the press if that interference is based on the content of the speech or proposed speech." Nonetheless, Mr. McVeigh recognizes that the First Amendment is not violated by denying a prisoner permission to conduct a face-to-face interview with a television news program if doing so would disrupt the orderly operation of the prison.

Mr. McVeigh need not rely upon the Constitution, however, because federal regulations and United States Department of Justice policies both recognize and regulate inmates' rights to contact with news media, including interviews which are videotaped for subsequent broadcasts.

☆427c Affidavit of Terry Nichols

Document at http://www.courttv.com/casefiles/oklahoma/documents/nicholstax.html.

AFFIDAVIT

I, Terry L. Nichols do Lawfully Affirm as follows this date:

1. I am a NATURAL-BORN, FREE adult Citizen of the State of Michigan by birth, thus of America, and an inhabitant of the State of Kansas, thankfully endowed by our Creator God with Unalienable Rights enumerated in America's founding organic documents, which I have never with knowingly intelligent acts waived. . . . The foregoing, including my STATUS and Unalienable Rights, are not negotiable. My Status, in accord, is stated for all in 1:2:3, 2:1:5, 3:2:1 and 4:2:1 of the U.S. Constitution.

2. Recent diligent studies have convinced me . . . that a shrewd and criminal Constructive Fraud has been perpetrated upon America by government under counterfeit "color of law. . . ."

4. Due to such shrewd entrapments, over the years I have unwittingly signed many of the related documents or contracts, some even under the "per-

jury" jurat as was supposedly required. With American Law on this Citizen's side, I hereby REVOKE all such signatures and render them null and void. . . .

5. With this accurate knowledge, I Lawfully "squarely challenge" the fraudulent usurping octopus of JURISDICTION/AUTHORITY which does not apply to me. . . . It is therefore now mandatory for any personnel of Article 1:8:17-18's so-called "IRS," for example, to first prove its "jurisdiction" if any over me before any further procedures can take place in my regard; or else its personnel and accomplices willfully violating this can and shall be personally charged as citizens under Title 18 U.S. Criminal Codes 241, 242, 1001 and/or otherwise. In fairness it can be added that "IRS" agents have no written, Lawful "Delegation of Authority" to my knowledge and that their so-called "Form 1040" appears to be a bootleg document, lacking both a required OMB number and an expiration date.

6. With all of the above in mind, it appears that this private Citizen is by Law as "Foreign" and "Non-Resident Alien" to the Article 1:8: 17-18's Washington, D.C., as to another country and thus shall feel free to use its forms when and as useful (e.g. W-8 "Certificate of FOREIGN STATUS," 1040 NR for "U.S. Non-Resident Alien Income Tax Return" Refunds, and IRS Code Section 402(n) to cancel "Withholding").

FURTHER THE AFFIANT SAITH NOT on this Date of 16 March 1994

TERRY L. NICHOLS
*Rt. 3 Box 83*
*Marion, Kansas*

☆427d  The Oklahoma City Bombing Trial
Transcripts: Friday, June 13, 1997 Sentencing
Verdict

Document at http://www.cnn.com/US/9703/okc.trial/transcripts/june/061397.pm.html.

IN THE UNITED STATES DISTRICT COURT FOR THE
DISTRICT OF COLORADO, CRIMINAL ACTION NO.
96-CR-68, UNITED STATES OF AMERICA, PLAINTIFF,
VS. TIMOTHY JAMES MCVEIGH, DEFENDANT.

Proceedings before the HONORABLE RICHARD P. MATSCH, Judge, United States District Court for the District of Colorado, commencing at 3:20 p.m., on the 13th day of June, 1997, in Chambers C-234, United States Courthouse, Denver, Colorado.

*          *          *

(In open court at 3:20 p.m.)

THE COURT: Please be seated.

The jury has informed that they have arrived at their findings and recommendation. I caution all present to avoid any reaction to these findings and the recommendation, either audibly or visibly. And if anyone violates that, we'll have to remove them.

*          *          *

THE COURT: Members of the jury, have you arrived at your special findings and recommendation?

JURORS: Yes.

THE COURT: If the foreman will please hand that to Mr. Manspeaker, who will hand it to me.

Members of the jury, you will please listen to the reading of your Special Findings Form A. These findings apply to all 11 counts.

Under Section I, Intent to Cause Death:

Question (1) The defendant intentionally killed the victims. Answer: Yes.

(2) The defendant intentionally inflicted serious body injury that resulted in the death of the victims. Answer: Yes.

*          *          *

Section II, Statutory Aggravating Factors:

(1) The deaths or injuries resulting in death occurred during the commission of an offense under 18 United States Code Section 844(d), transportation of explosives in interstate commerce for certain purposes. Answer: Yes.

(2) The defendant, in the commission of the offenses, knowingly created a grave risk of death to one or more persons in addition to the victims of the offense. Answer: Yes.

(3) The defendant committed the offenses after substantial planning and premeditation to cause the death of one or more persons and to commit an act of terrorism. Answer: Yes.

*          *          *

Third section, Non-statutory Aggravating Factors:

(1) The offenses committed by the defendant resulted in the deaths of 168 persons. Answer: Yes.

(2) In committing the offenses, the defendant caused serious physical and emotional injury, including maiming, disfigurement, and permanent disability to numerous individuals. Answer: Yes.

(3) That by committing the offenses, the defendant caused severe injuries and losses suffered by the victims' families. Answer: Yes.

Mitigating factors in Section IV:

(1) Timothy McVeigh believed deeply in the ideals upon which the United States was founded. Number of jurors who so find: Zero.

(2) Timothy McVeigh believed that the ATF and FBI were responsible for the deaths of everyone who lost their lives at Mt. Carmel, near Waco, Texas, between February 28 and April 19, 1993. Number of jurors who so find: 12.

*          *          *

(3) Timothy McVeigh believed that federal law enforcement agents murdered Sammy Weaver and Vicki Weaver near Ruby Ridge, Idaho, in August, 1992. Number of jurors who so find: 12.

(4) Timothy McVeigh believed that the increasing use of military-style force and tactics by federal law enforcement agencies against American citizens threatened an approaching police state. Number of jurors who so find: 12.

(5) Timothy McVeigh's belief that federal law enforcement agencies failed to take responsibilities for their actions at Ruby Ridge and Waco and failed to punish those persons responsible added to his growing concerns regarding the existence of a police state and a loss of constitutional liberties. Number of jurors who so find: 12.

(6) Timothy McVeigh served honorably and with great distinction in the United States Army from May, 1988, until December, 1991. Number of jurors who so find: 10.

*       *       *

(10) Timothy McVeigh is a patient and effective teacher when he is working in a supervisory role. Number of jurors who so find: 12.

(11) Timothy McVeigh is a good and loyal friend. Number of jurors who so find. Zero.

(12) Over the course of his life, Timothy McVeigh has done good deeds for and helped others, including a number of strangers who needed assistance. Number of jurors who so find: 4.

(13) Timothy McVeigh has no prior criminal record. Number of jurors who so find: 12.

*       *       *

Recommendation, V:

The jury has considered whether the aggravating factors found to exist sufficiently outweigh any mitigating factor or factors found to exist, or in the absence of any mitigating factors, whether the aggravating factors are themselves sufficient to justify a sentence of death. Based upon this consideration, the jury recommends by unanimous vote that the following sentence be imposed:

The defendant, Timothy James McVeigh, shall be sentenced to death.

*       *       *

THE COURT: Members of the jury, the Court will, as I instructed you in the instructions, sentence in accordance with your recommendation, sentencing the defendant to death. The sentence will be imposed at a hearing at a later time.

*       *       *

THE COURT: Members of the jury, you have now discharged your duty in this case, having rendered first of all your verdict with respect to the charges and then, of course, these findings and recommendation with respect to the sentence. Before excusing you from the courtroom, however, there are some things that I want to say to you and do wish to say them publicly.

First of all, I want to thank you on behalf of all of the people of the United States. You have served your country and you have served the system, as we've so often referred to it; but the system is really the democratic system that is our form of government, wherein people are brought together from all walks of life and background and given the responsibility for making the decision. And you have done that.

Now, it may be a matter for you now or at some later time to wonder: Did we do the right thing?

The answer to that question is yes, you did the right thing, not because I believe it one way or the other but because you did it. And that is what we rely upon, 12 people coming together, hearing the evidence, following the law, and reaching the decision.

So therefore, it is done. And you, as the jurors, are the final authority. You are not answerable to anyone for your verdict and your sentencing decision. No one of you can change it or undermine it or impeach it by anything that you may say or do after this. The decision is final.

Now, obviously, this decision will be commented upon, both your verdict and your recommendation. And that, as you well know, is a part of living in a free society.

## 428 "a haunting image with horrific . . . implications" (1995-1996)

In the 1960s, during the height of the Civil Rights movement in the South, a common counterattack resorted to by white supremacists was to set fire to black churches, which traditionally served as a source of spiritual strength and as the centers for the organization of black communities. One firebombing resulted in the deaths of four young girls at the Sixteenth Street Baptist Church in Birmingham, Alabama, in 1963. With the legal dismantling of official segregation, marked by the passage of the Civil Rights Act of 1964, and the widespread public discrediting of racism, relative peace returned to those places of worship.

As political winds have recently shifted away from support for such civil rights measures as "affirmative action" in higher education and employment, and the forces of economic, social, and political discontent have been in ascendance, the burning of southern black churches has risen dramatically, totaling twenty-four in June 1996. Authorities have not been able to uncover any network of racially motivated arsonists, and they believe the incidents to be isolated. The suspicion remains, nonetheless, that virulent racism may be fueling these conflagrations. Responding to the rash of fires, Congress unanimously passed the Church Arson Prevention Act of 1996, P.L. 104-155 (H.R. 3525), on July 3, 1996.

## ☆428  Church Burnings

### ☆428a  Bureau of Alcohol, Tobacco, and Firearms Fact Sheet

BUREAU OF ALCOHOL, TOBACCO AND FIREARMS, ARSON AND EXPLOSIVES DIVISION, ARSON ENFORCEMENT BRANCH, DATE: JUNE 11, 1996

#### *Church Fire Fact Sheet*

Number of active church fire investigations at predominantly African American churches in the southeast United States, since January 1995: . . . . . . . . . *24*

In 1995 . . . . . . . . . . . . . . . . . . . . . . . . . *5*

In 1996 . . . . . . . . . . . . . . . . . . . . . . . . *19*

*Fires by State* (Including Those Solved by Arrest)

| Tennessee | 6 | South Carolina | 6 |
| Louisiana | 5 | Alabama | 5 |
| Mississippi | 3 | North Carolina | 3 |
| Georgia | 1 | Virginia | 1 |

Number of predominantly African American church fire investigations in the southeast United States, since January 1995, that have been solved by arrest: *6*

Number of persons arrested: . . . . . . . . . . . . . . . . . . . *8*

\*          \*          \*

Number of open ATF church fire investigations nationwide since January 1995 (all churches): . . . . . . *49*

In 1995 . . . . . . . . . . . . . . . . . . . . . . . . . *12*

In 1996 . . . . . . . . . . . . . . . . . . . . . . . . *37*

Number of ATF church fire investigations nationwide since October 1991 (all churches): . . . . . . . . *145*

\*          \*          \*

### ☆428b  Statements on Introduced Bills and Joint Resolutions

104th Cong., 2d Sess., 142 *Cong. Rec.* S6146, June 12, 1996.

THE CHURCH ARSON PREVENTION ACT OF 1996

Mr. HOLLINGS. Mr. President, I rise today to introduce a bill aimed at providing a mechanism for Federal law enforcement to combat the most recent scourge to sweep across the Southeast. I am talking about the burnings of black churches that have been making such dramatic headlines lately. The burning of houses of worship have been taking place for the past 5 or 6 years, but this particular outbreak of fires has all the characteristics of an epidemic. Not since the sixties have I been witness to such blatant intolerance and hatred, such utterly despicable acts of American citizens against their fellow Americans as . . . I have seen over these past few weeks. I turn on the news and see a burning church, a haunting image with horrific symbolic and practical implications, and I say this must stop. Not just this specific rash of crime, but the whole trend toward violence and intolerance in our society. We as Americans have fought too hard to let racial or religious intolerance once again pollute our democracy.

This morning I accompanied President Clinton as he traveled to South Carolina. I welcome his strong presence in the midst of this unsettling trend, and moreover I welcome the message he brought to my home State. This country is stronger than the forces of hatred that would divide us. We will rebuild, and we will punish those responsible for these episodes of destruction.

To fight against the forces of divisiveness, we must pull together as a community. In the South, that means rebuilding, it means congregations of churches all over America picking a Sunday and dedicating their collections to rebuild these burned churches. Here in the Government, it means using every means within our power to make sure that this never happens again.

As of this moment, we don't have legislation that adequately addresses this brand of criminal behavior. The investigations by Federal authorities, and their ability to prosecute these cases have been limited by the current law. The bill I propose will remove the impediments to bringing Federal cases, and give the Attorney General an effective, and necessary weapon with which to combat these crimes. Section 247 of Title 18, United States Code, makes it a crime to damage religious property or to obstruct persons in the free exercise of religious beliefs. I propose to amend this by requiring only that the offense is in or affects interstate or foreign commerce. Congress will be effectively granting jurisdiction over all conduct which may be reached under the interstate commerce clause of the constitution.

Additionally, the bill eliminates the $10,000 threshold for fire damages to grant Federal jurisdiction in cases where there is only minimal damage. This way, desecration or defacement of houses of worship can be prosecuted. . . .

I urge the Senate to act quickly and adopt this provision. As I understand a similar measure is making its way through the House, the Senate should also act in an expeditious manner to ensure the Federal Government has the necessary authority to combat this tragic epidemic.

More importantly, this country must come together, leave racial intolerance behind, and insure that we end this type of bigotry.

\*          \*          \*

## 429  My Free Man Status (1996)

The economic crises of the mid and late eighties saw many farm families displaced when their homes and properties were foreclosed due to mortgage defaults or they were forced by tax liens to sell long-held family homesteads. Snarled in inescapable legal and financial complexities, people were primed to reject the legal and banking structures as corrupt and un-American. They were ripe for seduction by the promise that the "Our One Supreme Court, Common Law Venue" movement offered an easy way out of their troubles.

Adherents of the "Our One Supreme Court" movement weave a pseudo-legal theory that "proves" that the United States government has no jurisdiction outside of the District of Columbia and that the Federal Reserve Bank is unconstitutional. State law is also tainted by having been usurped by the "bogus" United States through submission to congressional authority and laws.

As a result, obedience to federal and state law is optional for those who reclaim their "Sovereign Free Man Character," or status, in a proceeding before any of the several self-created "common law courts." For contrary to the implications of its name, "Our One Supreme Court" exists any time twelve or more Freemen declare it to be in session. After Free Man Status is obtained and advertised, Freemen often discard any evidence of prior compliance with law—car registrations, drivers' and marriage licenses (the marriage remains valid, only its licensure is disavowed), and local permits. They also refuse to pay taxes, except with specie that they issue as "sovereigns" in their own right (see Doc. 427c).

Moreover, Our One Supreme Court claims the power to intervene in regular judicial proceedings and to issue money judgments against government officials who "oppress" the people. Once these judgment liens are filed, they can create financial havoc for the hapless official until they are removed. In 1996, the Freemen of the self-proclaimed "Justus Township," near Jordan, Montana, were indicted for bank fraud relating to passing bad checks under the guise of Our One Supreme Court judgment liens. One justice of the Ohio Supreme Court has termed these tactics "paper terrorism."

Sharing similar beliefs and adherents with the Patriot Militia and Christian Identity movements, the Freemen have usually sought relief through bizarre and unfathomable legal documents and maneuvers, as demonstrated in the case below. Yet the Freemen's association with more militant activists has made them subject to particular law enforcement sensitivity. Fearing another debacle like those at Ruby Ridge and Waco, the FBI treated the presumably armed Montana Freemen of Justus Township with uncharacteristic caution in 1996, permitting negotiations through a leader of the "Montana Militia" and bringing about a surrender only after a standoff lasting more than eighty days.

## ☆429  Our One Supreme Court, Common Law Venue

### ☆429a  Free Man Declaration

Various newspapers.

I, [name of person], do hereby announce publicly my Free Man Status [Character]. Failure of any private party to make proof of why I should not have my Free Man Status [Character], within seventy-two hours of this notice, shall be forever barred from making any claim(s) to the contrary as presented in this Common Law venue quiet title cause of action, original exclusive. [Name and address of person].

### ☆429b  *United States v. Greenstreet*

912 F. Supp. 224 (N.D. Tex. 1996).

Mary Lou Robinson, District Judge

*          *          *

#### I. BACKGROUND

This case stems from the filing of five UCC-1 financing statements against three U.S. Department of Agriculture employees named as "debtors." The financing statements were filed in Dallam and Randall counties by Defendant Greenstreet and Lawrence Wayne Garth, deceased. None of the federal employees named in the statements were, or ever had been, indebted to either Greenstreet or Garth.

It appears that as a form of retribution, retaliation, or harassment, Defendant Greenstreet and Mr. Garth caused financing statements to be filed against specific Farmers Home Administration (FmHA) employees. Both Greenstreet and Garth had financed property through the FmHA in the past. Greenstreet defaulted on a promissory note; therefore, his land was foreclosed upon and subsequently sold. Garth was convicted of conversion of property pledged to the FmHA. He was sentenced by this Court in 1985 to serve two years in a federal correctional institution.

Defendant Greenstreet has filed several documents with the Court since this matter was initiated against him. The filings have routinely been voluminous and difficult to comprehend. Apparently, Mr. Greenstreet is of the opinion that "Our One Supreme Court, Republic of Texas, in and for Dallam County" maintains exclusive jurisdiction over the case. He has challenged the Court's jurisdiction and venue, and moved the Court to dismiss the case against him. Mr. Greenstreet's requests were denied.

On October 31, 1995, the United States of America moved that this Court grant it summary judgment. Defendant Greenstreet responded by filing a document entitled "Notice of No Venue to This Statutory, Admiralty Court." Parsing the Response's imprecise, vague, argumentative, conclusory, and sometimes unintelligible prose, this Court gleans that Mr. Greenstreet objects to the Government's position on the following grounds. First, Greenstreet reasserts that this Court lacks jurisdiction over his case and that venue is improper. Further, he maintains that since no one filed a claim of any right, title, or interest in the property he formerly owned in accordance with an Order from "Our One Supreme Court" for the Republic of Texas, he should thus prevail by default. Additionally, Greenstreet argues that since all relevant issues have already been adjudicated by a court of "superior and competent jurisdiction" (common law court for the Republic of Texas), any action now brought by the Plaintiff should be barred by the doctrine of *res judicata*. Finally, Greenstreet contends that Plaintiff's motion should be dismissed as contemptuous, as it is in violation of prior court orders issued by Our One Supreme Court for the Republic of Texas. To support his position, Defendant Greenstreet filed findings of fact signed by 12 "jurors" which resulted from his action to quiet title before a court of common law venue.

*      *      *

### III. DISCUSSION

Because the purported financing statements fail to comply with the requisites of law, they are void and of no legal consequence. As a preliminary matter, the federal employees burdened by the financing statements at issue do not fall within Texas' . . . definition of a "debtor." There is no evidence before the Court that the federal employees, burdened by the fraudulently filed UCC-1 statements, owed payment or other performance to Defendant Greenstreet or Mr. Garth for any obligation secured.

Furthermore, the federal employees named in the financing statements never signed the documents filed against them. Generally, a debtor's signature is necessary for a financing statement to be valid. . . . The presence of a debtor's signature provides an indispensable concession to authenticity and a deterrent to inaccurate or malicious filings. As a result, the financing statements at issue are without legal effect and should be removed from the county clerks' records.

Apparently, in an attempt to circumvent the signature requirement, Defendant Greenstreet and Mr. Garth attached to the UCC-1 statements the signature page of letters or other documents previously signed by the alleged debtors. The UCC-1 financing statements in this case do not even purport to contain the signatures of the alleged debtors. . . . The addition of documents evincing the signature of the alleged debtors amounts to a crude compliance attempt at best and a forgery at worst.

Basically, there is absolutely no evidence to support the belief that a security agreement exists between the federal employees named in the financing statements and either Mr. Garth or Mr. Greenstreet.

Messrs. Greenstreet and Garth's conduct illustrates a disregard for the legal system and should be considered reprehensible. They abused the system by filing fraudulent documents. Mr. Greenstreet compounded the abuse by subsequently flooding the Court with frivolous pleadings. Their actions were costly and inconvenient to many. Although there is little federal case law precisely addressing the specific conduct Greenstreet engaged in before this Court, his tactics are unfortunately not uncommon. As a consequence, more attention to Greenstreet's activity is warranted.

Greenstreet argues that he is of "Freeman Character" and "of the white Preamble Citizenship and not one of the 14th Amendment legislated enfranchised De Facto colored races." He further claims that he is a "white Preamble natural sovereign Common Law De Jure Citizen of the Republic/State of Texas." As a result, he concludes that he is a sovereign, not subject to the jurisdiction of this Court. Greenstreet's argument is entirely frivolous. Except for documents allegedly issued from the common law court Greenstreet claims is superior to this Court, no support for his position exists. Greenstreet provides no acceptable authority or cogent analysis to support his contention that this Court lacks personal jurisdiction over him. Accordingly, this Court finds Greenstreet's argument lacking in justification.

Likewise, Greenstreet failed to support his position that this Court lacks subject matter jurisdiction. . . . Mr. Greenstreet's contentions to the contrary are simply misstatements of the law. Greenstreet "removed" this case to Our One Supreme Court for the Republic of Texas. Thus, he argues, this Court lacks concurrent subject matter jurisdiction in "Common Law Venue." His position is without merit. . . . [T]his Court holds that the mythical judiciary described as Our One Supreme Court for the Republic of Texas does not exist. As a result, this Court rejects Defendant Greenstreet's subject matter jurisdictional arguments.

Accordingly, this Court also rejects Greenstreet's attempt to defeat the Plaintiff's motion for summary judgment based on rulings or orders from the mythical common law court he feels is superior to this Court. Thus, Greenstreet is not entitled to a default judgment because of Plaintiff's non-compliance with orders from a fictitious court. Similarly, Greenstreet will not benefit from a *res judicata* defense or from his attempt to prove that the Plaintiff's motion is contemptuous. On balance, the authority Greenstreet relies upon has absolutely no legal value.

Perhaps the most bizarre basis for Greenstreet's position rests on the theory that the American system of currency is illegal and unconstitutional. Liberally construing the language of his pleadings before the Court, Greenstreet apparently believes that he has never been provided with funding (i.e. "lawful money") from the FmHA, under their contract, because it failed to give him money in silver or gold. . . . Greenstreet contends that federal reserve notes are not legal tender, because they violate Article 1, Section 10, of the United States Constitution. Defendant Greenstreet's argument centers around his view that "the Congress of the United States of America declared a partial NATIONAL BANKRUPTCY on June 5, 1933, under H.J.R. 192 which abrogated the gold clause and deprived the American Citizens of their Constitutional Article 1, Section 10, lawful money" and that the "COINAGE ACT OF 1965 deprived the American Citizens of their required and mandated . . . silver coinage." Thus, Greenstreet extrapolates, until he is given funds in silver or gold, he will not consider any past payment to have been acceptable or satisfactory. Attacking the legitimacy of federal reserve notes is not a novel argument. Others have asserted such claims; however, they have been summarily rejected. This Court will also reject Mr. Greenstreet's coinage arguments. The Court believes that Defendant's position is simply irrational.

Finally, Defendant Greenstreet's response to Plaintiff's motion for summary judgment identifies this Court as an "Admiralty Court" without further discussing his allegation. If his reference is to be construed as a jurisdictional challenge, his motion is denied. Others have attempted to persuade the judiciary that fringe on an American flag denotes a court of admiralty. In light of the fact that this Court has such a flag in its courtroom, the issue is addressed. The concept behind the theory the proponent asserts is that if a courtroom is adorned with a flag which happens to be fringed around the edges, such decor indicates that the court is one of admiralty jurisdiction exclusively. To think that a fringed flag adorning the courtroom somehow limits this Court's jurisdiction is frivolous. Unfortunately for Defendant Greenstreet, decor is not a determinant for jurisdiction.

\* \* \*

The evidence before the Court clearly demonstrates that the financing statements filed by Defendant Greenstreet and Mr. Garth are fraudulent. The UCC-1 Statements at issue are deficient technically and substantively. Mr. Greenstreet came forward with no understandable evidence to defeat Plaintiff's properly supported motion for summary judgment. Accordingly, Plaintiff is entitled to relief in this matter.

\* \* \*

#### IV. CONCLUSION

Litigants such as Mr. Greenstreet should not be underestimated. They are often motivated and know how to work the system. Unfortunately, the honest taxpayer is victimized as a result. Tactics such as declaring oneself a sovereign, turning to common law courts, challenging the jurisdiction of state and federal trial courts, and contending that federal reserve notes are not legal tender are favorites among these litigants. Such arguments, however, are time consuming for courts to process and routinely futile.

\* \* \*

Mr. Greenstreet's improper tactics failed to overcome Plaintiff's properly supported motion for summary judgment. As a result, judgment is appropriately entered against the defendants. . . . Mr. Greenstreet is hereby cautioned that if he continues to take legal positions which are not supported by existing law, severe monetary sanctions may result, his *pro se* status notwithstanding. Hopefully, litigants like Mr. Greenstreet will be unwilling to pay to harass the government in the future.

*It is so ordered.*

## 430 "a serious and deadly problem" (1996)

The Antiterrorism and Effective Death Penalty Act was introduced by Senator Robert Dole (R.-Kans.) and signed into law by President Clinton on April 24, 1996. Following the explosion of Pan Am Flight 103 at Lockerbie, Scotland, the World Trade Center bombing in New York City, and, finally, the bombing of the federal building in Oklahoma City, the new law was seeking to remedy the "irreparable harm" caused "to the psyche of all Americans" by these disasters. Public opinion polls demonstrated a considerable increase of the fear of future terroristic activity, whether undertaken from abroad or originated by domestic malcontents.

Responding to the growing sophistication of the infrastructure and technical skills of the terrorist underground, and aware that some sympathizers as well as nations were providing terrorist organizations with both material support and safe havens, the new act sought to fortify the antiterrorism force. The act articulated the finding of Congress that "international terrorism is a serious and deadly problem which threatens the vital interests of the United States" and furthermore that it "is among the most serious transnational threats faced by the United States and its allies, far eclipsing the dangers posed by population growth and pollution."

The Antiterrorism Act set out, therefore, among other measures, to increase international cooperation in curbing fundraising by those affiliated with terrorism, to enhance the security measures employed by the aviation industry worldwide, to improve methods for detecting plastic explosives, in-

creasingly used for sabotaging aircraft and other facilities, and to expand the reach of the United States
by increasing its law enforcement jurisdiction over
selected crimes committed abroad. Particularly significant is Section 221 of the new act, which offers
American victims of specified terrorism activities
(including torture, aircraft sabotage, and hostage
taking) access to United States courts in their quest
for money damages against foreign countries
deemed as "state sponsors of terrorism" found responsible for such acts committed overseas. This exception to the traditional international law principle
of "foreign sovereign immunity" once more demonstrates the growing United States resort to civil
penalties in the struggle against foreign as well as
domestic terrorism, violence, and bigotry.

## ☆430  Combating International and Domestic Terrorism

### ☆430a  Antiterrorism and Effective Death Penalty Act of 1996

P.L. 104-132, 110 Stat. 1214 (1996).

An Act to deter terrorism, provide justice for victims, provide for an effective death penalty, and for
other purposes.

*Be it enacted by the Senate and House of Repre-
sentatives of the United States of America in Congress assembled,*

#### Section 1. Short Title.

This Act may be cited as the "Antiterrorism and
Effective Death Penalty Act of 1996."

*          *          *

#### Sec. 221. Jurisdiction for Lawsuits against Terrorist States.

(a) Exception to Foreign Sovereign Immunity for
Certain Cases.—Section 1605 of title 28, United
States Code, is amended—

    (1) in subsection (a)—

*          *          *

    (C) by adding at the end the following new
paragraph:

      "(7) [A foreign state shall not be immune from
the jurisdiction of courts of the United States in
any case] in which money damages are sought
against a foreign state for personal injury or
death that was caused by an act of torture, extrajudicial killing, aircraft sabotage, hostage taking,
or the provision of material support or resources
(as defined in section 2339A of title 18) for such an
act if such act or provision of material support is
engaged in by an official, employee, or agent of
such foreign state while acting within the scope of
his or her office, employment, or agency, except

that the court shall decline to hear a claim under
this paragraph—

    "(A) if the foreign state was not desig-
nated as a state sponsor of terrorism under
section 6(j) of the Export Administration
Act . . . at the time the act occurred, unless
later so designated as a result of such act; and

    "(B) even if the foreign state is or was so
designated, if—

      "(i) the act occurred in the foreign
state against which the claim has been
brought and the claimant has not afforded
the foreign state a reasonable opportunity to arbitrate the claim in accordance with accepted international rules of
arbitration; or

      "(ii) the claimant or victim was not a
national of the United States (as that
term is defined in section 101 (a) (22) of
the Immigration and Nationality Act)
when the act upon which the claim is
based occurred."; and

(2) by adding at the end [of 28 U.S.C. § 1605]
the following:

"(e) For purposes of paragraph (7) of subsection
(a)—

    "(1) the terms 'torture' and 'extrajudicial kill-
ing' have the meaning given those terms in section
3 of the Torture Victim Protection Act of 1991;

    "(2) the term 'hostage taking' has the meaning
given that term in Article 1 of the International
Convention Against the Taking of Hostages; and

    "(3) the term 'aircraft sabotage' has the mean-
ing given that term in Article 1 of the Convention
for the Suppression of Unlawful Acts Against the
Safety of Civil Aviation.

*          *          *

#### TITLE III—INTERNATIONAL TERRORISM PROHIBITIONS

##### SUBTITLE A—PROHIBITION ON INTERNATIONAL TERRORIST FUNDRAISING

#### Sec. 301. Findings and Purpose.

(a) Findings.—The Congress finds that—

    (1) international terrorism is a serious and
deadly problem that threatens the vital interests
of the United States;

    (2) the Constitution confers upon Congress
the power to punish crimes against the law of nations and to carry out the treaty obligations of the
United States, and therefore Congress may by
law impose penalties relating to the provision of
material support to foreign organizations engaged in terrorist activity;

    (3) the power of the United States over immi-
gration and naturalization permits the exclusion

from the United States of persons belonging to international terrorist organizations;

(4) international terrorism affects the interstate and foreign commerce of the United States by harming international trade and market stability, and limiting international travel by United States citizens as well as foreign visitors to the United States;

(5) international cooperation is required for an effective response to terrorism, as demonstrated by the numerous multilateral conventions in force providing universal prosecutive jurisdiction over persons involved in a variety of terrorist acts, including hostage taking, murder of an internationally protected person, and aircraft piracy and sabotage;

(6) some foreign terrorist organizations, acting through affiliated groups or individuals, raise significant funds within the United States, or use the United States as a conduit for the receipt of funds raised in other nations; and

(7) foreign organizations that engage in terrorist activity are so tainted by their criminal conduct that any contribution to such an organization facilitates that conduct.

(b) Purpose.—The purpose of this subtitle is to provide the Federal Government the fullest possible basis, consistent with the Constitution, to prevent persons within the United States, or subject to the jurisdiction of the United States, from providing material support or resources to foreign organizations that engage in terrorist activities.

\* \* \*

*Sec. 303. Prohibition on Terrorist Fundraising.*

(a) In General.—Chapter 113B of title 18, United States Code, is amended by adding at the end the following new section:

"Sec. 2339B. Providing material support or resources to designated foreign terrorist organizations

"(a) Prohibited Activities.—

"(1) Unlawful conduct.—Whoever, within the United States or subject to the jurisdiction of the United States, knowingly provides material support or resources to a foreign terrorist organization, or attempts or conspires to do so, shall be fined under this title or imprisoned not more than 10 years, or both.

\* \* \*

*Sec. 322. Foreign Air Travel Safety.*

Section 44906 of title 49, United States Code, is amended to read as follows:

"Sec. 44906. Foreign air carrier security programs

"The Administrator of the Federal Aviation Administration shall continue in effect the requirement . . . that a foreign air carrier must adopt and use a security program approved by the Administrator. The Administrator shall not approve a security program of a foreign air carrier under . . . any . . . regulation, unless the security program requires the foreign air carrier in its operations to and from airports in the United States to adhere to the identical security measures that the Administrator requires air carriers serving the same airports to adhere to. The foregoing requirement shall not be interpreted to limit the ability of the Administrator to impose additional security measures on a foreign air carrier or an air carrier when the Administrator determines that a specific threat warrants such additional measures. The Administrator shall prescribe regulations to carry out this section.".

\* \* \*

*Sec. 324. Findings.*

The Congress finds that—

(1) international terrorism is among the most serious transnational threats faced by the United States and its allies, far eclipsing the dangers posed by population growth or pollution;

(2) the President should continue to make efforts to counter international terrorism a national security priority;

(3) because the United Nations has been an inadequate forum for the discussion of cooperative, multilateral responses to the threat of international terrorism, the President should undertake immediate efforts to develop effective multilateral responses to international terrorism as a complement to national counter terrorist efforts;

(4) the President should use all necessary means, including covert action and military force, to disrupt, dismantle, and destroy international infrastructure used by international terrorists, including overseas terrorist training facilities and safe havens;

(5) the Congress deplores decisions to ease, evade, or end international sanctions on state sponsors of terrorism, including the recent decision by the United Nations Sanctions Committee to allow airline flights to and from Libya despite Libya's noncompliance with United Nations resolutions; and

(6) the President should continue to undertake efforts to increase the international isolation of state sponsors of international terrorism, including efforts to strengthen international sanctions, and should oppose any future initiatives to ease sanctions on Libya or other state sponsors of terrorism.

*Sec. 325. Prohibition on Assistance to Countries
That Aid Terrorist States.*

The Foreign Assistance Act of 1961 (22 U.S.C. 151 et seq.) is amended by adding immediately after section 620F the following new section:

*"Sec. 620G. Prohibition on assistance to countries
that aid terrorist states.*

"(a) Withholding of Assistance.—The President shall withhold assistance under this Act to the government of any country that provides assistance to the government of any other country for which the Secretary of State has made a determination under section 620A.

"(b) Waiver.—Assistance prohibited by this section may be furnished to a foreign government described in subsection (a) if the President determines that furnishing such assistance is important to the national interests of the United States and, not later than 15 days before obligating such assistance, furnishes a report to the appropriate committees of Congress including—

"(1) a statement of the determination;

"(2) a detailed explanation of the assistance to be provided;

"(3) the estimated dollar amount of the assistance; and

"(4) an explanation of how the assistance furthers United States national interests.".

\*        \*        \*

TITLE VI—IMPLEMENTATION OF PLASTIC EXPLOSIVES CONVENTION

*Sec. 601. Findings and Purposes.*

(a) Findings.—The Congress finds that—

(1) plastic explosives were used by terrorists in the bombings of Pan American Airlines flight number 103 in December 1988 and UTA flight number 722 in September 1989;

(2) plastic explosives can be used with little likelihood of detection for acts of unlawful interference with civil aviation, maritime navigation, and other modes of transportation;

(3) the criminal use of plastic explosives places innocent lives in jeopardy, endangers national security, affects domestic tranquility, and gravely affects interstate and foreign commerce;

(4) the marking of plastic explosives for the purpose of detection would contribute significantly to the prevention and punishment of such unlawful acts; and

(5) for the purpose of deterring and detecting such unlawful acts, the Convention on the Marking of Plastic Explosives for the Purpose of Detection, Done at Montreal on 1 March 1991, requires each contracting State to adopt appropri-

ate measures to ensure that plastic explosives are duly marked and controlled.

(b) Purpose.—The purpose of this title is to fully implement the Convention on the Marking of Plastic Explosives for the Purpose of Detection, Done at Montreal on 1 March 1991.

*Sec. 602. Definitions.*

\*        \*        \*

"(q) 'Plastic explosive' means an explosive material in flexible or elastic sheet form formulated with one or more high explosives which in their pure form has a vapor pressure less than $10^{-4}$ Pa at a temperature of 25 degrees C., is formulated with a binder material, and is as a mixture malleable or flexible at normal room temperature."

\*        \*        \*

TITLE VII—CRIMINAL LAW MODIFICATIONS TO COUNTER TERRORISM

SUBTITLE A—CRIMES AND PENALTIES

*Sec. 701. Increased Penalty for Conspiracies
Involving Explosives.*

Section 844 of title 18, United States Code, is amended by adding at the end the following new subsection:

"(n) Except as otherwise provided in this section, a person who conspires to commit any offense defined in this chapter shall be subject to the same penalties (other than the penalty of death) as the penalties prescribed for the offense the commission of which was the object of the conspiracy.".

*Sec. 702. Acts of Terrorism Transcending National
Boundaries.*

(a) Offense.—Chapter 113B of title 18, United States Code, relating to terrorism, is amended by inserting after section 2332a the following new section:

"SEC. 2332b. Acts of terrorism transcending
national boundaries

"(a) Prohibited Acts.—

"(1) Offenses.—Whoever, involving conduct transcending national boundaries and in a circumstance described in subsection (b)—

"(A) kills, kidnaps, maims, commits an assault resulting in serious bodily injury, or assaults with a dangerous weapon any person within the United States; or

"(B) creates a substantial risk of serious bodily injury to any other person by destroying or damaging any structure, conveyance, or other real or personal property within the United States or by attempting or conspiring to destroy or damage any structure, conveyance, or other real or personal property within the United States [shall be punished with imprisonment for 10 years to life or with death (depending on the harm done) consecutive to any other penalty and without the option of parole];

*       *       *

### Sec. 709. Determination of Constitutionality of Restricting the Dissemination of Bomb-Making Instructional Materials.

(a) Study.—The Attorney General, in consultation with such other officials and individuals as the Attorney General considers appropriate, shall conduct a study concerning—

(1) the extent to which there is available to the public material in any medium (including print, electronic, or film) that provides instruction on how to make bombs, destructive devices, or weapons of mass destruction;

(2) the extent to which information gained from such material has been used in incidents of domestic or international terrorism;

(3) the likelihood that such information may be used in future incidents of terrorism;

(4) the application of Federal laws in effect on the date of enactment of this Act to such material;

(5) the need and utility, if any, for additional laws relating to such material; and

(6) an assessment of the extent to which the first amendment protects such material and its private and commercial distribution.

(b) Report.—

(1) Requirement.—Not later than 180 days after the date of enactment of this Act, the Attorney General shall submit to the Congress a report that constrains the results of the study required by this section.

(2) Availability.—The Attorney General shall make the report submitted under this subsection available to the public.

SUBTITLE B—CRIMINAL PROCEDURES

### Sec. 721. Clarification and Extension of Criminal Jurisdiction over Certain Terrorism Offenses Overseas.

(a) Aircraft Piracy.—Section 46502(b) of title 49, United States Code, is amended—

(1) in paragraph (1), by striking "[the requirement that the defendant be] later found in the United States"; [and]

(2) so that paragraph (2) reads as follows:

"(2) There is jurisdiction over the offense in paragraph (1) if—

"(A) a national of the United States was aboard the aircraft;

"(B) an offender is a national of the United States; or

"(C) an offender is afterwards found in the United States. . . ."

*       *       *

☆430b  Statement on Signing the Antiterrorism and Effective Death Penalty Act

32 *Weekly Comp. Pres. Doc.* 719 (April 26, 1996).

*       *       *

I first transmitted antiterrorism legislation to the Congress in February 1995. Most of the proposals in that legislation, the "Omnibus Counter Terrorism Act of 1995," were aimed at fighting international terrorism. After the tragedy in Oklahoma City, I asked Federal law enforcement agencies to reassess their needs and determine which tools would help them meet the new challenge of domestic terrorism. They produced, and I transmitted to the Congress, the "Antiterrorism Amendments Act of 1995" in May 1995.

Together, these two proposals took a comprehensive approach to fighting terrorism both at home and abroad. I am pleased that the Congress included most of the provisions of these proposals in this legislation. As a result, our law enforcement officials will have tough new tools to stop terrorists before they strike and to bring them to justice if they do. . . .

*       *       *

By enacting this legislation, the United States remains in the forefront of the international effort to fight terrorism through tougher laws and resolute enforcement. Nevertheless, as strong as this bill is, it should have been stronger. For example, I asked the Congress to give U.S. law enforcement increased wiretap authority in terrorism cases, including the power to seek multi-point wiretaps, enabling police to follow a suspected terrorist from phone to phone, and authority for the kind of emergency wiretaps available in organized crime cases. But the Congress refused. After I proposed that the Secretary of the Treasury consider the inclusion of taggants in explosive materials, so that bombs can be traced more easily to the bomb makers, the Congress exempted black and smokeless powder—two of the most commonly used substances in improvised explosive devices.

I asked that law enforcement be given increased access to hotel, phone and other records in terrorism cases. I asked for a mandatory penalty for those who knowingly transfer a firearm for use in a violent felony. I asked for a longer statute of limitations to allow law enforcement more time to prosecute terrorists who use weapons such as machine guns, sawed-off shotguns, and explosive devices. But the Congress stripped each of these provisions out of the bill. And when I asked for a ban on cop-killer bullets, the Congress delivered only a study, which will delay real action to protect our Nation's police officers.

I intend to keep urging the Congress to give our law enforcement officials all the tools they need and deserve to carry on the fight against international and domestic terrorism. This is no time to give the criminals a break.

*        *        *

WILLIAM J. CLINTON
*The White House*
*April 26, 1996*

## 431 "In order to get our message before the public ... we've had to kill people" (1978–1996)

On May 26, 1978, a package exploded in the hands of a Northwestern University police officer. Nearly a year later, a bomb disguised as a cigar box injured a graduate student at Northwestern's Technological Institute. Six months after that, a bomb in the cargo hold of an American Airlines flight exploded, and the FBI formed the UNABOM (*UN*iversity/*A*irline *BOM*ber) task force.

Four more bombs were mailed between 1980 and 1982, injuring an airline executive and two university employees. The "Unabomber" then took a three-year hiatus to perfect his bomb-building. Between 1985 and 1987, he struck five more times, causing a fatality for the first time. After the World Trade Center explosion in February 1993, he dispatched four bombs, injuring two and killing two, the last explosion occurring just five days after the Oklahoma City bombing. The Unabomber's focus had also widened over the years. In addition to universities and airlines, his targets included computer stores, an advertising executive, and a timber industry lobbyist.

In addition to a bomb mailed on April 24, 1995, the Unabomber also sent out four unarmed letters, two of which appear below. These communications were unusual, since only one letter had been previously received from the Unabomber. After the April 1995 flurry, the number of Unabomber writings increased, including a meticulously hand-edited "manifesto" of thirty-five thousand words in 232 numbered paragraphs (excerpts of which appear in Doc. 431d below). The manifesto displayed a Luddite philosophy and reflected analytical and critical training and familiarity with sociological literature and jargon.

The manifesto was to be the Unabomber's undoing. Theodore Kaczynski, a reclusive mathematician, was arrested by the FBI on explosives charges at his backwoods cabin outside of Lincoln, Montana. His brother had recognized his writing style and alerted the authorities.

### ☆431  The Unabomber

### ☆431a  Text of Letter Purportedly Sent Dec. 11, 1985

*San Francisco Examiner*, July 2, 1995.

The bomb that crippled the right arm of a graduate student in electrical engineering and damaged a computer lab of U. of Cal. Berkeley last May was planted by a terrorist group called the Freedom Club.

We are also responsible for some earlier bombing attempts; among others, the bomb that injured a professor in the computer science building at U. of Cal., the mail bomb that injured the secretary of computer expert Patrick Fischer at Vanderbilt University 3 1/2 years ago, and the fire bomb planted in the Business School at U. of Utah, which never went off....

We have waited until now to announce ourselves because our earlier bombs were embarrassingly ineffectual. The injuries they inflicted were relatively minor. In order to influence people, a terrorist group must show a certain amount of success.

When we finally realized that the amount of smokeless powder needed to blow up anyone or anything was too large to be practical, we decided to take a couple of years off to learn something about explosives and develop an effective bomb.

### ☆431b  Letter to the *New York Times*, Received April 24, 1995

*Portland Oregonian*, April 27, 1995.

This is a message from the terrorist group FC.

We blew up Thomas Mosser last December because he was a Burston-Marsteller executive. Among other misdeeds, Burston-Marsteller helped Exxon clean up its public image after the Exxon Valdez incident. But we attacked Burston-Marsteller less for its specific misdeeds than on general principles. Burston-Marsteller is about the biggest organization in the public relations field. This means that its business is the development of techniques for manipulating people's attitudes. It was for this more than for its actions in specific cases that we sent a bomb to an executive of this company.

Some news reports have made the misleading statement that we have been attacking universities or scholars. We have nothing against universities or scholars as such. All the university people whom we have attacked have been specialists in technical fields. (We consider certain areas of applied psychology, such as behavior modification, to be technical fields.) We would not want anyone to think that we have any desire to hurt professors who study archaeology, history, literature or harmless stuff like that. The people we are out to get are the scientists and engineers, especially in critical fields like computers and genetics.

Why do we announce our goals only now, through we made our first bomb some seventeen years ago? Our early bombs were too ineffectual to attract much public attention or give encouragement to those who hate the system. We found by experience that gunpowder bombs, if small enough to be carried inconspicuously, were too feeble to do much damage, so we took a couple of years off to do some experimenting. We learned how to make pipe bombs that were powerful enough, and we used these in a couple of successful bombings as well as in some unsuccessful ones.

*        *        *

Clearly we are in a position to do a great deal of damage. And it doesn't appear that the FBI is going to catch us any time soon. The FBI is a joke.

The people who are pushing all this growth and progress garbage deserve to be severely punished. But our goal is less to punish them than to propagate ideas. Anyhow we are getting tired of making bombs. It's no fun having to spend all your evenings and weekends preparing dangerous mixtures, filing trigger mechanisms out of scraps of metal or searching the sierras for a place isolated enough to test a bomb. So we offer a bargain.

We have a long article, between 29,000 and 37,000 words, that we want to have published. If you can get it published according to our requirements we will permanently desist from terrorist activities. It must be published in the New York Times, Time or Newsweek, or in some other widely read, nationally distributed periodical. Because of its length we suppose it will have to be serialized. Alternatively, it can be published as a small book, but the book must be well publicized and made available at a moderate price in bookstores nationwide and in at least some places abroad. Whoever agrees to publish the material will have exclusive rights to reproduce it for a period of six months and will be welcome to any profits they may make from it. After six months from the first appearance of the article or book it must become public property, so that anyone can reproduce or publish it. (If material is serialized, first instalment becomes public property six months after appearance of first instalment, second instalment, etc.) We must have the right to publish in the New York Times, Time or Newsweek, each year for three years after the appearance of our article or book, three thousand words expanding or clarifying our material or rebutting criticisms of it.

How do you know that we will keep our promise to desist from terrorism if our conditions are met? It will be to our advantage to keep our promise. We want to win acceptance for certain ideas. If we break our promise people will lose respect for us and so will be less likely to accept the ideas.

Our offer to desist from terrorism is subject to three qualifications. First: Our promise to desist will not take effect until all parts of our article or book have appeared in print. Second: If the authorities should succeed in tracking us down and an attempt is made to arrest any of us, or even to question us in connection with the bombings, we reserve the right to use violence. Third: We distinguish between ter-

rorism and sabotage. By terrorism we mean actions motivated by a desire to influence the development of a society and intended to cause injury or death to human beings. By sabotage we mean similarly motivated actions intended to destroy property without injuring human beings. The promise we offer is to desist from terrorism. We reserve the right to engage in sabotage.—FC

☆431c  Letter to Dr. David Gelernter, Received April 24, 1995

*Fresno Bee*, April 27, 1995.

Dr. Gelernter:

People with advanced degrees aren't as smart as they think they are. If you'd had any brains you would have realized that there are a lot of people out there who resent bitterly the way techno-nerds like you are changing the world and you wouldn't have been dumb enough to open an unexpected package from an unknown source.

In the epilog of your book, "Mirror Worlds," you tried to justify your research by claiming that the developments you describe are inevitable, and that any college person can learn enough about computers to compete in a computer-dominated world. Apparently, people without a college degree don't count. In any case, being informed about computers won't enable anyone to prevent invasion of privacy (through computers), genetic engineering (to which computers make an important contribution), environmental degradation through excessive economic growth (computers make an important contribution to economic growth) and so forth.

As for the inevitability argument, if the developments you describe are inevitable, they are not inevitable in the way that old age and bad weather are inevitable. They are inevitable only because techno-nerds like you make them inevitable. If there were no computer scientists there would be no progress in computer science. If you claim you are justified in pursuing your research because the developments involved are inevitable, then you may as well say that theft is inevitable, therefore we shouldn't blame thieves.

But we do not believe that progress and growth are inevitable. We'll have more to say about that later. FC

P.S. Warren Hoge of the New York Times can confirm that this letter does come from FC.

☆431d  The Unabomber's Manifesto: *Industrial Society and Its Future*

*Washington Post*, August 2, 1995, A16.

INTRODUCTION

1. The industrial revolution and its consequences have been a disaster for the human race. They

have . . . destabilized society, have made life unfulfill-
ing, have subjected human beings to indignities,
have led to widespread psychological suffering . . .
and have inflicted severe damage on the natural
world. . . .

2. The industrial-technological system may survive . . . only at the cost of permanently reducing
human beings and many other living organisms to
engineered products and mere cogs in the social machine. . . . [I]f it is to break down it had best break
down sooner rather than later.

*         *         *

4. We therefore advocate a revolution against the
industrial system. . . . This is not to be a POLITICAL
revolution. Its object will be to overthrow not governments but the economic and technological basis of
the present society. . . .

### THE PSYCHOLOGY OF MODERN LEFTISM

*         *         *

9. [T]wo psychological tendencies that underlie
modern leftism we call feelings of inferiority and
oversocialization. . . . By "feelings of inferiority" we
mean . . . low self-esteem, feelings of powerlessness,
depressive tendencies, defeatism, guilt, self-hatred,
etc. . . .

### THE FEELINGS OF INFERIORITY

*         *         *

16. Words like "self-confidence," "self-reliance,"
"initiative," "enterprise," "optimism," etc., play little
role in the liberal and leftist vocabulary. The leftist is
anti-individualistic, pro-collectivist. He wants society to solve everyone's problems for them. . . . The
leftist is antagonistic to the concept of competition
because, deep inside, he feels like a loser. . . .

*         *         *

19. His feelings of inferiority are so ingrained that
he cannot conceive of himself as individually strong
and valuable. Hence the collectivism of the leftist.
He can feel strong only as a member of a large organization or a mass movement with which he identifies himself.

*         *         *

### OVERSOCIALIZATION

*         *         *

26. Oversocialization can lead to low self-esteem,
a sense of powerlessness, defeatism, guilt, etc. One of
the most important means by which our society so-
cializes children is by making them feel ashamed of
behavior or speech that is contrary to society's expectations. If this is overdone, or if a particular child
is especially susceptible to such feelings, he ends by
feeling ashamed of HIMSELF. . . . The majority of
people engage in a significant amount of naughty behavior. They lie, they commit petty thefts, they

break traffic laws, they goof off at work, they hate
someone, they say spiteful things or they use some
underhanded trick to get ahead of the other guy. The
oversocialized person cannot do these things, or if
he does do them he generates in himself a sense of
shame and self-hatred. The oversocialized person
cannot even experience, without guilt, thoughts or
feelings that are contrary to the accepted morality;
he cannot think "unclean" thoughts. . . .

*         *         *

### THE POWER PROCESS

*         *         *

33. Human beings have a need (probably based in
biology) for something that we will call the "power
process." This is closely related to the need for power
(which is widely recognized) but is not quite the same
thing. The power process has four elements. The
three most clear-cut of these we call goal, effort and
attainment of goal. (Everyone needs to have goals
whose attainment requires effort, and needs to succeed in attaining at least some of his goals). The
fourth element is more difficult to define and may not
be necessary for everyone. We call it autonomy. . . .

*         *         *

### SURROGATE ACTIVITIES

*         *         *

39. We use the term "surrogate activity" to designate an activity that is directed toward an artificial
goal that people set up for themselves merely in
order to have some goal to work toward, or let us say,
merely for the sake of the "fulfilment" that they get
from pursuing the goal. . . .

40. In modern industrial society only minimal effort is necessary to satisfy one's physical needs. It is
enough to go through a training program to acquire
some petty technical skill, then come to work on time
and exert the very modest effort needed to hold a job.
The only requirements are a moderate amount of intelligence and, most of all, simple OBEDIENCE. . . .
[M]odern society is full of surrogate activities. These
include scientific work, athletic achievement, humanitarian work, artistic and literary creation, climbing
the corporate ladder, acquisition of money and material goods far beyond the point at which they cease
to give any additional physical satisfaction, and social activism when it addresses issues that are not
important for the activist personally, as in the case of
white activists who work for the rights of nonwhite
minorities. . . .

*         *         *

### SOURCES OF SOCIAL PROBLEMS

*         *         *

46. We attribute the social and psychological
problems of modern society to the fact that society

requires people to live under conditions radically different from those under which the human race evolved and to behave in ways that conflict with the patterns of behavior that the human race developed while living under the earlier conditions. It is clear from what we have already written that we consider lack of opportunity to properly experience the power process as the most important of the abnormal conditions to which modern society subjects people. . . .

\*                  \*                  \*

49. For primitive societies the natural world (which usually changes only slowly) provided a stable framework and therefore a sense of security. In the modern world it is human society that dominates nature rather than the other way around, and modern society changes very rapidly owing to technological change. Thus there is no stable framework. . . .

DISRUPTION OF THE POWER PROCESS IN MODERN
SOCIETY

59. We divide human drives into three groups: (1) those drives that can be satisfied with minimal effort; (2) those that can be satisfied but only at the cost of serious effort; (3) those that cannot be adequately satisfied no matter how much effort one makes. The power process is the process of satisfying the drives of the second group. The more drives there are in the third group, the more there is frustration, anger, eventually defeatism, depression, etc.

60. In primitive societies, physical necessities generally fall into group 2: They can be obtained, but only at the cost of serious effort. But modern society tends to guaranty the physical necessities to everyone in exchange for only minimal effort, hence physical needs are pushed into group 1. . . .

\*                  \*                  \*

62. Social needs, such as sex, love and status, often remain in group 2 in modern society, depending on the situation of the individual. But, except for people who have a particularly strong drive for status, the effort required to fulfill the social drives [is] insufficient to satisfy adequately the need for the power process.

63. So certain artificial needs have been created that fall into group 2, hence serve the need for the power process. Advertising and marketing techniques have been developed that make many people feel they need things that their grandparents never desired or even dreamed of. It requires serious effort to earn enough money to satisfy these artificial needs, hence they fall into group 2. Modern man must satisfy his need for the power process largely through pursuit of the artificial needs created by the advertising and marketing industry. . . .

\*                  \*                  \*

69. It is true that primitive man is powerless against some of the things that threaten him; disease

for example. But he can accept the risk of disease stoically. It is part of the nature of things, it is no one's fault, unless it is the fault of some imaginary, impersonal demon. But threats to the modern individual tend to be MAN-MADE. They are not the result of chance but are IMPOSED on him by other persons whose decisions he, as an individual, is unable to influence. Consequently he feels frustrated, humiliated and angry.

70. Thus primitive man for the most part has his security in his own hands (either as an individual or as a member of a SMALL group) whereas the security of modern man is in the hands of persons or organizations that are too remote or too large for him to be able personally to influence them. So modern man's drive for security tends to fall into groups 1 and 3; in some areas (food, shelter etc.) his security is assured at the cost of only trivial effort, whereas in other areas he CANNOT attain security. . . .

\*                  \*                  \*

76. In response to the arguments of this section someone will say, "Society must find a way to give people the opportunity to go through the power process." For such people the value of the opportunity is destroyed by the very fact that society gives it to them. What they need is to find or make their own opportunities. As long as the system GIVES them their opportunities it still has them on a leash. To attain autonomy they must get off that leash.

HOW SOME PEOPLE ADJUST

\*                  \*                  \*

86. But even if most people in industrial-technological society were well satisfied, we (FC) would still be opposed to that form of society, because (among other reasons) we consider it demeaning to fulfill one's need for the power process through surrogate activities or through identification with an organization, rather than through pursuit of real goals.

\*                  \*                  \*

THE NATURE OF FREEDOM

93. We are going to argue that industrial-technological society cannot be reformed in such a way as to prevent it from progressively narrowing the sphere of human freedom. But, because "freedom" is a word that can be interpreted in many ways, we must first make clear what kind of freedom we are concerned with.

94. By "freedom" we mean the opportunity to go through the power process, with real goals not the artificial goals of surrogate activities, and without interference, manipulation or supervision from anyone, especially from any large organization. Freedom means being in control (either as an individual or as a member of a SMALL group) of the life-and-death issues of one's existence; food, clothing, shelter

and defense against whatever threats there may be in one's environment. Freedom means having power; not the power to control other people but the power to control the circumstances of one's own life. . . .

95. It is said that we live in a free society because we have a certain number of constitutionally guaranteed rights. But these are not as important as they seem. The degree of personal freedom that exists in a society is determined more by the economic and technological structure of the society than by its laws or its forms of government.

96. [C]onsider for example . . . freedom of the press. . . . The mass media are mostly under the control of large organizations that are integrated into the system. Anyone who has a little money can have something printed, or can distribute it on the Internet or in some such way, but what he has to say will be swamped by the vast volume of material put out by the media. . . . Take us (FC) for example. If we had never done anything violent and had submitted the present writings to a publisher, they probably would not have been accepted. If they had been accepted and published, they probably would not have attracted many readers, because it's more fun to watch the entertainment put out by the media than to read a sober essay. Even if these writings had had many readers, most of those readers would soon have forgotten what they had read as their minds were flooded by the mass of material to which the media expose them. In order to get our message before the public with some chance of making a lasting impression, we've had to kill people.

97. Constitutional rights are useful up to a point, but they do not serve to guarantee much more than what might be called the bourgeois conception of freedom. According to the bourgeois conception, a "free" man is essentially an element of a social machine and has only a certain set of prescribed and delimited freedoms; freedoms that are designed to serve the needs of the social machine more than those of the individual.

\*            \*            \*

TECHNOLOGY IS MORE POWERFUL SOCIAL FORCE
THAN THE ASPIRATION FOR FREEDOM

\*            \*            \*

125. It is not possible to make a LASTING compromise between technology and freedom, because technology is by far the more powerful social force and continually encroaches on freedom through RE-PEATED compromise.

\*            \*            \*

STRATEGY

180. The technophiles are taking all of us on an utterly reckless ride into the unknown. Many people understand something of what technological prog-

ress is doing to us yet take a passive attitude toward it because they think it is inevitable. But we (FC) don't think it is inevitable. We think it can be stopped. . . .

181. [T]he two main tasks for the present are to promote social stress and instability in industrial society and to develop and propagate an ideology that opposes technology and the industrial system. When the system becomes sufficiently stressed and unstable, a revolution against technology may be possible. . . .

182. [W]e have no illusions about the feasibility of creating a new, ideal form of society. Our goal is only to destroy the existing form of society. . . .

183. But an ideology, in order to gain enthusiastic support, must have a positive ideal as well as a negative one; it must be FOR something as well as AGAINST something. The positive ideal that we propose is Nature. That is, WILD nature: those aspects of the functioning of the earth and its living things that are independent of human management and free of human interference and control. And with wild nature we include human nature, by which we mean those aspects of the functioning of the human individual that are not subject to regulation by organized society but are products of chance, or free will, or God (depending on your religious or philosophical opinions). . . .

\*            \*            \*

193. The kind of revolution we have in mind will not necessarily involve an armed uprising AGAINST any government. It may or may not involve physical violence, but it will not be a POLITICAL revolution. Its focus will be on technology and economics, not politics.

\*            \*            \*

195. The revolution must be international and worldwide. It cannot be carried out on a nation-by-nation basis. . . .

\*            \*            \*

206. With regard to revolutionary strategy, the only point on which we absolutely insist are that the single overriding goal must be the elimination of modern technology, and that no other goal can be allowed to compete with this one. For the rest, revolutionaries should take an empirical approach. If experience indicates that some of the recommendations made in the foregoing paragraphs are not going to give good results, then those recommendations should be discarded.

\*            \*            \*

THE DANGER OF LEFTISM

\*            \*            \*

214. To avoid this, a movement that exalts nature and opposes technology must take a resolutely anti-leftist stance and must avoid all collaboration with leftists. Leftism is in the long run inconsistent with

the wild nature, with human freedom and with the elimination of modern technology. Leftism is collectivist; it seems to bind together the entire world (both nature and the human race) into a unified whole. But this implies management of nature and of human life by organized society, and it requires advanced technology.... Above all, leftism is driven by the need for power, and the leftist seeks power on a collective basis, through identification, with a mass movement or an organization. Leftism is unlikely ever to give up technology, because technology is too valuable a source of collective power.

215. The anarchist too seeks power, but he seeks it on an individual or small-group basis; he wants individuals and small groups to be able to control the circumstances of their own lives. He opposes technology because it makes small groups dependent on large organizations.

*     *     *

217. In earlier revolutions, leftists of the most power-hungry type, repeatedly, have first cooperated with non-leftist revolutionaries, as well as with leftists of a more libertarian inclination, and later have double-crossed them to seize power for themselves. Robespierre did this in the French Revolution, the Bolsheviks did it in the Russian Revolution, the communists did it in Spain in 1938 and Castro and his followers did it in Cuba. Given the past history of leftism, it would be utterly foolish for non-leftists revolutionaries today to collaborate with leftists.

*     *     *

230. The more dangerous leftists, that is, those who are most power-hungry, are often characterized by arrogance or by a dogmatic approach to ideology. However, the most dangerous leftists of all may be certain oversocialized types who avoid irritating displays of aggressiveness and refrain from advertising their leftism, but work quietly and unobtrusively to promote collectivist values, "enlightened" psychological techniques for socializing children, dependence of the individual on the system, and so forth. These crypto-leftists (as we may call them) approximate certain bourgeois types as far as practical action is concerned, but differ from them in psychology, ideology and motivation. The ordinary bourgeois tries to bring people under control of the system in order to protect his way of life, or he does so simply because his attitudes are conventional. The crypto-leftist tries to bring people under control of the system because he is a True Believer in a collectivistic ideology. The crypto-leftist is differentiated from the average leftist of the oversocialized type by the fact that his rebellious impulse is weaker and he is more securely socialized. He is differentiated from the ordinary well-socialized bourgeois by the fact that there is some deep lack within him that makes it necessary for him to devote himself to a cause and

immerse himself in a collectivity. And maybe his (well-sublimated) drive for power is stronger than that of the average bourgeois.

FINAL NOTE

231. Throughout this article we've made imprecise statements and statements that ought to have had all sorts of qualifications and reservations attached to them; and some of our statements may be flatly false. Lack of sufficient information and the need for brevity made it impossible for us to formulate our assertions more precisely or add all the necessary qualifications. And of course in a discussion of this kind one must rely heavily on intuitive judgment, and that can sometimes be wrong. So we don't claim that this article expresses more than a crude approximation to the truth.

*     *     *

## 432 "We cannot separate the air that chokes from the air upon which wings beat" (1996)

Governments have long attempted to combat the spread of unorthodox ideas that challenge their authority. By prohibiting associations of dissenters and curbing the promulgation and dissemination of their words, government officials have sought to suppress the propagation of criticism and revolutionary thought as manifestations of sedition.

The dissidents' greatest challenge, in turn, has been to expand their ranks through meetings, speeches, and publications large and small. The instruments and institutions of public communications—the church, the labor hall, the political rally, the poster, the press, and other mass media (whether legitimate or underground)—have served as the constant battlefields between those in power and those striving for empowerment.

As the twentieth century draws to a close, a new medium—cyberspace, or the Internet—has blossomed as a free, popular, and anarchic means of accessing the hearts and minds of people all over the globe. No longer can authoritarian regimes control the information flow to their peoples. Now the people from the far-flung corners of the world can share sentiments, strategies, and support for political change.

Governments have recently begun to try and assert themselves. A popular Internet service suspended operations to Germany after officials complained of the distribution to Germans of information that was illegal under German law.

In 1996, old wire-fraud laws are being pressed into service against unauthorized hackers, and the Congress passed a massive telecommunications reform act placing restrictions on the content of information in cyberspace. While these governmental controls were being challenged in court, a new cyberspace "declaration of independence" flashed around the world.

## ☆432 Declaration of Independence from Cyberspace

Document at http://www.eff.org/barlow.

Yesterday, that great invertebrate in the White House signed into the law the Telecom "Reform" Act of 1996, while Tipper Gore took digital photographs of the proceedings to be included in a book called "24 Hours in Cyberspace."

I had also been asked to participate in the creation of this book by writing something appropriate to the moment. Given the atrocity that this legislation would seek to inflict on the Net, I decided it was as good a time as any to dump some tea in the virtual harbor.

After all, the Telecom "Reform" Act, passed in the Senate with only 5 dissenting votes, makes it unlawful, and punishable by a $250,000 [fine] to say "shit" online. Or, for that matter, to say any of the other 7 dirty words prohibited in broadcast media. Or to discuss abortion openly. Or to talk about any bodily function in any but the most clinical terms.

It attempts to place more restrictive constraints on the conversation in Cyberspace than presently exist in the Senate cafeteria, where I have dined and heard colorful indecencies spoken by United States senators on every occasion I did.

This bill was enacted upon us by people who haven't the slightest idea who we are or where our conversation is being conducted. It is, as my good friend and Wired Editor Louis Rossetto put it, as though "the illiterate could tell you what to read."

Well, fuck them.

Or, more to the point, let us now take our leave of them. They have declared war on Cyberspace. Let us show them how cunning, baffling, and powerful we can be in our own defense.

\* \* \*

I do hope this cry will echo across Cyberspace, changing and growing and self-replicating, until it becomes a great shout equal to the idiocy they have just inflicted upon us.

I give you . . .

### A DECLARATION OF THE INDEPENDENCE OF CYBERSPACE

Governments of the Industrial World, you weary giants of flesh and steel, I come from Cyberspace, the new home of Mind. On behalf of the future, I ask you of the past to leave us alone. You are not welcome among us. You have no sovereignty where we gather.

We have no elected government, nor are we likely to have one, so I address you with no greater authority than that with which liberty itself always speaks. I declare the global social space we are building to be naturally independent of the tyrannies you seek to impose on us. You have no moral right to rule us nor do you possess any methods of enforcement we have true reason to fear.

Governments derive their just powers from the consent of the governed. You have neither solicited nor received ours. We did not invite you. You do not know us, nor do you know our world. Cyberspace does not lie within your borders. Do not think that you can build it, as though it were a public construction project. You cannot. It is an act of nature and it grows itself through our collective actions.

You have not engaged in our great and gathering conversation, nor did you create the wealth of our marketplaces. You do not know our culture, our ethics, or the unwritten codes that already provide our society more order than could be obtained by any of your impositions.

\* \* \*

Our identities have no bodies, so, unlike you, we cannot obtain order by physical coercion. We believe that from ethics, enlightened self-interest, and the commonweal, our governance will emerge. Our identities may be distributed across many of your jurisdictions. The only law that all our constituent cultures would generally recognize is the Golden Rule. We hope we will be able to build our particular solutions on that basis. . . .

In the United States, you have today created a law, the Telecommunications Reform Act, which repudiates your own Constitution and insults the dreams of Jefferson, Washington, Mill, Madison, de Tocqueville, and Brandeis. These dreams must now be born anew in us.

You are terrified of your own children, since they are natives in a world where you will always be immigrants. Because you fear them, you entrust your bureaucracies with the parental responsibilities you are too cowardly to confront yourselves. In our world, all the sentiments and expressions of humanity, from the debasing to the angelic, are parts of a seamless whole, the global conversation of bits. We cannot separate the air that chokes from the air upon which wings beat.

In China, Germany, France, Russia, Singapore, Italy and the United States, you are trying to ward off the virus of liberty by erecting guard posts at the frontiers of Cyberspace. These may keep out the contagion for a small time, but they will not work in a world that will soon be blanketed in bit-bearing media.

\* \* \*

These increasingly hostile and colonial measures place us in the same position as those previous lovers of freedom and self-determination who had to reject the authorities of distant, uninformed powers. We must declare our virtual selves immune to your sovereignty, even as we continue to consent to your rule over our bodies. We will spread ourselves across the Planet so that no one can arrest our thoughts.

We will create a civilization of the Mind in Cyberspace. May it be more humane and fair than the world your governments have made before.

*Davos, Switzerland*
*February 8, 1996*

*********************************

JOHN PERRY BARLOW, Cognitive Dissident
Co-Founder, Electronic Frontier Foundation

## 433 A Leader in the Quest for Civil Rights and Justice (1996–1997)

Only a few of those leading or taking part in America's rebellions, protests, and civil disobedience have had their names recorded by history. Many more have been mere anonymous soldiers in the country's perpetual struggle between established authority and the quest for greater liberty and autonomy. Many of those struggling for change have been young, poor, and uneducated. Some have seen their goals attained, others have not. Many had to pay dearly for their daring; many had been socially ostracized for their quests. Only few have been eventually vindicated. The story of Ola Mae Quarterman-Clemons is a small tribute to the thousands of others who have struggled for justice yet whose names remain totally unknown.

### ☆433 Ola Mae Quarterman-Clemons's Protest

### ☆433a H.R. 1195, Georgia House of Representatives

Document at http://www.State.Ga.US/legis/1995_96/leg/fulltext/hr1195.htm.

A RESOLUTION

Recognizing and commending Ola Mae Quarterman-Clemons; and for other purposes.

WHEREAS, Ola Mae Quarterman-Clemons was born in Worth County, attended public schools in Dougherty County, graduated from Monroe High School in Albany, and attended Albany State College; and

WHEREAS, she was a devoted wife and is the mother of Galvester Clemons; and

WHEREAS, she is a Christian woman and a believer who was baptized into the Antioch Missionary Baptist Church family; and

WHEREAS, on January 12, 1962, Ola Mae Quarterman-Clemons, a student at Albany State College, re-fused the request of an Albany bus driver that she move from her seat to the back of the bus; and

WHEREAS, she was convicted of disorderly conduct and sentenced to 30 days in jail for exercising her rights as a citizen; and

WHEREAS, upon her release from jail, she was expelled from Albany State College, where she was a freshman; and

WHEREAS, her actions, her courage, and her insistence in exercising her rights as a citizen have led to the enjoyment of the rights of citizenship by countless others and made her a leader in the quest for civil rights and justice.

NOW, THEREFORE, BE IT RESOLVED BY THE HOUSE OF REPRESENTATIVES that the members of this body recognize and commend Ola Mae Quarterman-Clemons for her bravery, for her leadership, and for the important role which she has played in the history of the civil rights movement in Albany and the State of Georgia.

BE IT FURTHER RESOLVED that the Clerk of the House of Representatives is authorized and directed to transmit an appropriate copy of this resolution to Ola Mae Quarterman-Clemons.

### ☆433b Still a Freedom Movement Casualty after 32 Years

Rick Bragg, *New York Times*, July 31, 1997, A14.

A hero of the freedom movement marches still, but only across clean, quiet grounds, through hallways of vacant stares and dreamy, narcotic smiles.

In what history refers to as the Albany Movement, an 18-year-old college freshman named Ola Mae Quarterman defied the racism that gripped southern Georgia in 1962. When a driver ordered her to the back of a bus, she told him, "I'll sit where I want." A judge gave her 30 days.

Heroes are made this way. The legend of Rosa Parks, a living legend of the civil rights movement after the 1955 Montgomery bus boycott, was born in such a way.

*     *     *

Ms. Quarterman, like many others who took such risks, has paid a price for her moment in history. She was ostracized, she said, not only by an angry white community but also by some in the black establishment who opposed the civil rights movement. She was expelled from a black college, Albany State. Later, when she needed work, no one would hire her.

Bitter disappointment, aggravated by a difficult childbirth that left her weak and ill, was finally too much for her. Her mind drowned in its own sadness.

"I had a nervous breakdown in 1965," she said recently, walking in hot summer sunlight at Central State Hospital, the state's psychiatric hospital. "I've been here ever since."

*     *     *

While there is no scientific link between the events of 1962 and her condition, which has been diagnosed as chronic paranoid schizophrenia, she wonders what her future would have been if her so-fleeting glory had not been snuffed out so soon, so completely.

\*          \*          \*

"What America has done with the civil rights movement is to pick who they want to represent what happened," said Jane Austin-Taylor, who owns the Austin-Taylor Mortuary in Albany. "Those were the people on stage. They weren't the ones bearing the brunt" of retaliation inside the community.

\*          \*          \*

While Ms. Quarterman's name has been lost in the civil rights struggle as a whole, it does appear briefly in some chapters about Albany. In a chapter from his book "Bearing the Cross" (Random House, 1987), David J. Garrow wrote:

"On Friday, Jan. 12, an 18-year-old black student, Ola Mae Quarterman, was arrested for refusing to move to the back of an Albany city bus and for allegedly saying 'damn.'"

She knew what she was risking that day.

She had picked what seemed like a million miles of cotton to make enough money to go to college in Albany. She desperately wanted to break free of the cycle of stoop labor so many others traveled, season after season.

"I just wanted to better myself," she said.

She wanted to major in sociology and counsel people with troubles. She wanted to dress nice and have fellowship at the Baptist church on Sundays—and sometimes on Wednesdays.

\*          \*          \*

Ms. Quarterman ignored the dangers. She traveled around the southern part of the state, registering people to vote. She was captivated by Dr. King's speeches and the words of other less famous men and women who spoke from pulpits and picket lines about a world on the brink of momentous change.

"She was always outspoken, what we used to call a fighter," said Arthur Searles Sr., the retired editor and publisher of The Albany Southwest Georgian and a leader of that movement. . . .

Her moment in history happened, oddly enough, almost by accident. The Albany Movement had not even planned a boycott or sit-in on city buses on Jan. 12.

It was not even so much that she wanted to sit in the front of the bus, or that she disliked the back.

"I just wanted to see the scenery," Ms. Quarterman said, and the only window seat, on that day she stepped on board from East Society Street, was in the front. She took it.

Some drivers did not mind, but this one did. He ordered her to the back.

"I said, 'I paid my damn 10 cents and I'll sit where I want,'" she said. "Then he stuck his finger in my face. I don't like nobody to stick their finger in my face. I said, 'Get your damn finger out of my face.' Just like that."

The driver, apparently, had never been talked to that way by a black person.

"He said I cussed him out," she said. "But I didn't."

The driver stopped the bus and found a police officer.

"The policeman said, 'Come on, Ola Mae,' and locked me up," she said.

She was charged with disorderly conduct but was also chastised for being disrespectful to the driver and for cursing. She refused to pay a $102 fine and served her 30 days in a jail.

Her arrest moved the leaders of the movement to boycott the city's bus lines, which largely served black people. Bus service came almost to a halt as Ms. Quarterman became the boycott's figurehead.

"That was the beginning of it," said Mr. Searles, who handled public relations for the movement.

But it was also, in many ways, the end of everything.

Instead of being embraced, even exalted, the young Ms. Quarterman's fame was brief and brittle.

The college president expelled Ms. Quarterman because she had disobeyed him. Four other students who were ousted for the same reason got scholarships to other colleges, in part because of that involvement. But Ms. Quarterman was somehow passed over, although her grades were excellent.

\*          \*          \*

As the civil rights movement waned in Albany, Ms. Quarterman found that she was unwelcome, and not only in white circles.

\*          \*          \*

Looking for something to belong to, she married and had a baby, a healthy boy. But complications with the birth left her bedridden. It was, she said, the last bit of pain she could absorb.

\*          \*          \*

She can leave here if she wants, and she talks about going back to Albany someday. But she is comfortable in her routine here. She works. She prays. She plays hooky from work some days, a friend said, tattling on her, to get her hair done.

She needs to look good. After so long, she is getting attention.

Two years ago, Ms. Austin-Taylor, trying to set right what she saw as a great wrong, held the reception for Ms. Quarterman. A limousine picked her up at Milledgeville and drove her to Albany. People there shook her hand and gave her plaques and roses. She loved the attention.

Last year, the Georgia Legislature honored Ms. Quarterman with Resolution No. 1195, which declared her "a leader in the quest for civil rights and justice." It is official now.

## 434 "They have lived their lives and gotten away with it" (1997)

On September 15, 1963, a bomb exploded in the Sixteenth Street Baptist Church in Birmingham, Alabama, killing four young African American girls. The Federal Bureau of Investigation was brought in to solve the case. After netting only one suspect, and amid suspicions that J. Edgar Hoover's FBI was deliberately hampering its own case, the investigation was quietly suspended. However, on July 10, 1997, Attorney General Janet Reno announced the Department of Justice's intent to reopen the long-suspended investigation.

With the passage of time and the accompanying changes in public opinion and public policy, historical acts of rebellion, dissent, and political criminality (by citizens as well as through governmental abuse of power) frequently assume new perspectives. John Brown's antislavery revolt in Harpers Ferry, for which he was sentenced to death and executed, became a rallying point during the Civil War and is still viewed as an act of heroism today. The Federal confinement of Japanese Americans during World War II was followed less than fifty years later by a congressional apology as well as a reparation program for those abused by the unnecessary United States military and political zeal (see Doc. 365).

The case of the Birmingham bombing illustrates a change in the United States national perspective and attitude toward those who resorted to indiscriminate violence against others who merely sought to pursue the civil and human rights they considered themselves entitled to under the United States Constitution. Thirty-three years after the bombing, the attitudes in Birmingham and Washington have undergone a sea-change, and what was once viewed as a local tragedy to be hushed up has now become a national crime to be vigorously and publicly revisited.

### ☆434 Bomb Probe Stirs Memories in Birmingham; Reno Vows Thoroughness in Reopening 1963 Case

Donald P. Baker, *Washington Post*, July 11, 1997, A3.

The physical damage caused by a bomb that ripped into the Sixteenth Street Baptist Church in 1963 and killed four young black girls here has long been repaired.

And the city torn asunder during the civil rights era of the 1960s—and called "the most thoroughly segregated city in America" by the Rev. Martin Luther King Jr.—is now a different place.

But the Justice Department's announcement that it will reopen the investigation of the church bombing, an act that became a symbol of white separatist hatred, has drawn a lot of interest and some skepticism here. Ku Klux Klan member Robert Edward Chambliss was the only person tried for the attack. He was convicted in 1977 and died 12 years ago in prison at age 81. But many people here have long believed that others were involved, sometimes even naming names.

Although Justice Department officials refused today to reveal what new information they have received that is leading them to reopen the case, Attorney General Janet Reno said, "We are pursuing it in every way possible. When something that horrible occurs, I just want to make sure we do everything humanly possible, and do it the right way, so that the people who do that sort of thing are held accountable."

Denise McNair, 11, Cynthia Wesley, 14, Carole Robertson, 14, and Addie Mae Collins, 14, were killed on Sept. 15, 1963, when 19 sticks of dynamite were detonated outside the restroom where the girls were changing clothes for a special program at the church.

How the federal government's renewed interest in the church attack is carried out will determine the effect the new investigation has on the community, said the Rev. Christopher M. Hamlin, who has been pastor of the church for seven years. He said he has heard stories of how the FBI botched—some say on purpose—the original investigation.

"I hope it's done expeditiously," Hamlin said of the government's reopening of the case. "If so, people will feel good. But if it is dragged out, it could make things worse. There is still a lot of suspicion of the FBI here."

Hamlin said that today, "Birmingham is a wonderful place to live."

With a population of 265,000, two-thirds of whom are black, the city has had a black mayor for 17 years. Chris McNair, the father of the youngest victim of the bombing, is one of two blacks on the five-member board of commissioners for Jefferson County, which includes Birmingham, has a population of 660,000 and is two-thirds white. The 500-member Sixteenth Street Baptist Church, meanwhile, has become a popular tourist attraction to people of all colors—as is a city-owned civil rights museum across the street.

\*　　　\*　　　\*

The bombing, which occurred about two weeks after the 1963 civil rights March on Washington, prompted introspection and action by whites and blacks in Birmingham.

One group that arose from the debris was Operation New Birmingham, whose community-affairs committee still meets regularly—sometimes at the church—to discuss racial problems in the city.

Sheldon Schaffer, an economist who is a co-chair of the panel, said today that "a bunch of good things have happened" over the years in what boosters now call "The Magic City." Schaffer cited increased opportunities for employment for blacks, in an economy where unemployment is 3.3 percent.

*   *   *

Ahmed Obgfemi, a transplanted New Yorker who directs the Malcolm X Center for Self-Determination here, is among those skeptical of the new probe.

"The FBI has new information? Who are you kidding?" he said, referring to a 1980 news report that then-FBI Director J. Edgar Hoover allegedly barred the prosecution of five members of the Ku Klux Klan as accomplices in the case, despite assurances by the FBI office here that it had strong evidence against them.

Any accomplices he had, Obgfemi said, "are probably 85 or 90 years old by now. They have lived their lives and gotten away with it."

*   *   *

None of the families of the girls killed in the bombing commented today. A plaque in the church, bearing the smiling faces of the four, says: "May men learn to replace bitterness and violence with love and understanding."

## 435 "These men are at war" (1997)

In July 1997, three Idaho men were convicted on federal charges stemming from bombings and bank robberies described by the prosecutors as "domestic terrorism." After a four-week trial and eight hours of jury deliberations, the three men, Verne Jay Merrell, fifty-one years old, Charles Barbee, forty-five, and Robert S. Berry, forty-three, were convicted and faced life in prison without parole.

The federal prosecutors charged that the defendants were the masked men in military-style camouflage who had detonated a pipe bomb outside the *Spokesman-Review* newspaper office moments before a local bank was robbed and bombed on April 1, 1996. The three men were also charged with the bombing of a Planned Parenthood office on July 12, 1997, shortly before the same bank was robbed again. Although no one was injured in either blast, about $108 was taken in the two robberies.

The defendants, who denied their guilt, claimed that they were being singled out for prosecution because of their political views and activism. They admitted to being members of an antigovernment, secessionist, and religious paramilitary group whose members believed, among other things, that the charging of interest on loans is evil and punishable by death. The closing arguments to the jury by Asso-

ciate United States Attorney Joe Harrington sought to address the defendants' claims of political discrimination as well as their assertions of justification.

## ☆435  Warriors of Yahweh

### ☆435a  Instructions Given to the Jury by Chief United States District Judge Wm. Fremming Nielsen, 21st day of July, 1997

*United States v. Merrell,* Docket No. CR 96-0257-WFN (E.D. Wash. 1997).

UNITED STATES OF AMERICA, Plaintiff, -vs- VERNE JAY MERRELL, aka Jay Merrell, aka Thomas C. James, aka Carl Avery Martell CHARLES HARRISON BARBEE, and ROBERT SHERMAN BERRY, aka Jim Preston, aka Scott Westmann, aka Bryron Vurmullien, Defendants.

*   *   *

INSTRUCTION NO. 4.

. . . Remember that the defendants are on trial only for the crimes charged, not for their beliefs and not for anything else. You should consider evidence about the acts, statements, and intentions of others, or evidence about other acts of the Defendants, only as they relate to the charges against these Defendants. In [other] words, you must give separate and individual consideration to each charge against each Defendant.

INSTRUCTION NO. 5.

The law presumes a defendant to be innocent of a crime. This is not an idle presumption. It is a true presumption of innocence. Thus, a defendant, although accused, begins the trial with a clean slate—with no evidence against him or her. The law permits nothing but legal evidence presented before the jury to be considered in support of a charge against a defendant.

The burden is always upon the Government to prove guilt by proof beyond a reasonable doubt. This burden never shifts to a defendant. The law never imposes upon a defendant the burden or duty of calling any witnesses or producing any evidence.

A reasonable doubt is a doubt based upon reason and common sense, and may arise from a careful and impartial consideration of the evidence, or from lack of evidence. It is not required, however, that the Government prove guilt beyond all possible doubt. Proof beyond a reasonable doubt is proof that leaves you firmly convinced that a defendant is guilty.

If after a careful and impartial consideration of all the evidence you are not convinced beyond a reasonable doubt that the Defendant is guilty, it is your duty to find the Defendant not guilty. On the other hand, if after a careful and impartial consideration of all the evidence you are convinced beyond a reasonable doubt that the Defendant is guilty, it is your duty to find the Defendant guilty.

\*     \*     \*

### INSTRUCTION NO. 21.

There are two kinds of evidence: direct and circumstantial. Direct evidence is direct proof of a fact, such as testimony of an eyewitness. Circumstantial evidence is indirect evidence, that is, proof of a chain of facts from which you could find that another fact exists, even though it has not been proven directly. You are entitled to consider both kinds of evidence and the law permits you to give equal weight to both. It is for you to decide whether a fact has been proven by circumstantial evidence and how much weight to give to any evidence. You are permitted to conclude from the facts which you find have been proven, such reasonable inferences as seem justified by reason and common sense.

\*     \*     \*

### INSTRUCTION NO. 25.

You have heard evidence that a Defendant has previously been convicted of a felony. You may consider that evidence only as it may affect the Defendant's believability as a witness. You may not consider a prior conviction as evidence of guilt of the crime for which the Defendant is now on trial.

\*     \*     \*

### INSTRUCTION NO. 28.

You have heard testimony that Christopher Davidson, a witness, has received benefits, reward and immunity from the Government in connection with this case. You should examine Christopher Davidson's testimony with greater caution than that of an ordinary witness. In evaluating that testimony, you should consider the extent to which it may have been influenced by the receipt of these benefits from the Government.

\*     \*     \*

### INSTRUCTION NO. 30.

The punishment provided by law for the offenses charged in the Indictment is a matter exclusively within the province of the Court, and should never be considered by the jury in any way in arriving at an impartial verdict as to whether any Defendant is guilty or not guilty.

\*     \*     \*

[Topper S. Baker, Official Court Reporter]

☆435b  Closing Argument of Joseph Harrington, Assistant US Attorney, Spokane, Washington

United States v. Merrell, Docket No. CR 96-0257-WFN (E.D. Wash. 1997).

{Monday, July 21, 1997}

THE COURT: \* \* \* \* \* On behalf of the Government, Mr. Harrington.

MR. HARRINGTON: May it please the Court and counsel. . . .

\*     \*     \*

As . . . [you were] told . . . during opening statements, this case is about violent armed men who terrorized the Spokane Valley in the spring and summer of 1996.

This is my opportunity to talk to you about the evidence, about the law, and how the evidence applies to the law as Judge Nielsen has just instructed you.

I want to talk to you a bit about the evidence. I am not going to talk about all of the evidence, because I am operating off of some of my notes, but you as a collective body of twelve have a much better recollection of the testimony, the witnesses' testimony and the physical items of evidence that were admitted during the trial.

\*     \*     \*

The bottom line is, you are a twelve-member jury . . . on a fact-finding mission. That is really what your duty is here. When you go back to deliberate, you are going to be on a fact-finding mission to determine what the truth of this case really is.

In connection with that mission that you are on, the Court has given you some instructions and those are legal tools. Those legal tools are going to avail you of an opportunity to analyze the facts and apply the law.

\*     \*     \*

What I would like to do now is just sort of tell you where I am going.

\*     \*     \*

First, I want to talk about things that are undisputed in the case. Something we can look at—that you can look at and make a determination that really there is no contest and there is really not a requirement to spend a lot of time deliberating because the facts are just undisputed. Given facts.

Second thing I want to talk about is the MO. You know, MO is short for the Latin word modus operandi. It means the method of operation, a criminal's standard operating procedure.

I want to talk about the MO that links the crimes that occurred on April 1st, 1996 and the crimes that occurred on July 12th, 1996.

And then I am going to talk—I want to talk to you about how the MO that links the crime is also the MO that links these three defendants to those crimes.

\*     \*     \*

First, undisputed facts.

\*     \*     \*

The U.S. Bank—a bomb was exploded at the U.S. Bank and there was also a bomb that exploded at the

Planned Parenthood. All of those things, those are evidences that you heard during the course of the case and there is really no dispute.

There was no dispute that the property at the Spokesman Review and the Planned Parenthood, that building is used in interstate commerce. No dispute.

*         *         *

No question that a crime of violence occurred. No question that firearms and pipe bombs were carried and those firearms and pipe bombs were carried in connection with a crime of violence.

*         *         *

The only issue that has been [disputed] is who done it, and that, I would suggest, is going to be the main thrust of your jury deliberations. Who [has] done it is really the essence of your fact-finding mission.

Who done it? First thing we want to do is look at the MO that connected the crimes, that links the crimes together.

*         *         *

Let's talk the MO. First, there is stolen vans. The vans are stolen outside of the target city. April 1st, the van is stolen from Barrell Bender out in Ellensburg, a white Chevy conversion van, 1992.

That van is a little unusual, because it is not a brand new van, it is an older used van with license plates. No need to steal any license plates on that van, but a conversion van nonetheless.

A van is used on July 12th, a white conversion van, stolen this time away from the target city, this time near the SeaTac Airport.

*         *         *

The vans are ultimately recovered. Both have, on April 1st and July 12th, have the back seat removed allowing for easier access in and out.

*         *         *

There is more MO. There is a bombing prior to the bank robberies on April 1st and July 12th. The bombings occurred at sensitive locations and were used as either a diversion or a way to send a message.

The Spokesman Review bomb on April 1st could have been a vendetta for [previously published] articles, or it could have been a way to send a message.

When you get back in the jury deliberation room, look at the letter that was left there and [its] first words are, "Publish and conceal not," and who better to publish this Biblical rhetoric than the Spokesman Review, the local newspaper.

The Planned Parenthood, a sensitive location, consistent with people who have beliefs about the wrongness of abortion, and you know how these three defendants believe about abortion.

*         *         *

They didn't leave fingerprints, but what they did is they left their MO, their standard criminal operat-

ing procedure at these crimes. Their MO links the crimes committed on April 1st with the crimes that were committed on July 12th, and it links—those crimes are linked to the ambassadors of Yahweh.

By the way, I want to mention this in passing. You know, Yahweh is really a sacred, venerated Biblical term. It is something that is a holy and sacred name that is used in the Bible and somehow there has been an implication that that name carries with it some bad connotations and I don't want you to believe that, it is not the name itself, it is the way the name is used.

Here there is ambassadors of Yahweh and it appears that this ambassadorship, this reference to Yahweh has somehow been twisted. The use of the Biblical references . . . has been twisted and used to justify violent criminal acts and those violent criminal acts are connected because they are the same MO and those MO's link the crimes of April 1st and July 12th.

*         *         *

Charles Harrison Barbee is no altar boy, no matter how you spell alter.

Robert Sherman Berry is anything but a hardworking mechanic, and Vernon Jay Merrell is certainly not holier than thou.

These men are at war. They are at war with today's purported Babylonic society. They are waging a war against society and they believe if their war breaks the United States' law, they will justify their actions based on their Biblical interpretations.

They are intolerant to abortion clinics. They don't believe in usury. They believe any charging of interest is an act punishable by death.

They don't believe in corporations, insurance companies, and even the court systems. They are false idols, according to these defendants, and they also believe that stealing from corporations and insurance companies is justified by their Biblical views, but most importantly, they believe that violent acts against this Babylonic society is justified by their Biblical views.

*         *         *

[Topper S. Baker, Official Court Reporter]

## 436 "I've Reduced the Guilt Somewhat" (1997)

Most rebels and political protestors engage in the pursuit of a single and short-term cause. Few become career political offenders, dedicating a major segment of their life to a broad and continuous struggle for political, social, or economic reform. In jail at age seventy-three, Philip Berrigan, a former Catholic priest, has become a symbol for persistent resistance to what he considers the main American evil: militarism. Going back to his 1967 dumping of bottles of blood over drawers of Selective Service files in the Baltimore Customs House, Berrigan has spent nearly half of his life battling the nation's military establishment. "I'm a recidivist," he says.

## ☆436 Swords to Plowshares

### ☆436a Prince of Peace Plowshares: The Saga (Philip Berrigan)

Electronic mail provided by Elizabeth MacAllister (Jonah House, Baltimore, Md.) to Dr. Nicholas Kittrie

        *        *        *

It doesn't get any easier—my fifth Plowshares, and it doesn't get easier. The last days before D-Day are the worst—one is on a form of countdown—resisting the passage of time, numbering the days and hours. Fear dogs one, always a companion; always lending its peculiar misery. Fear of leaving Elizabeth, our family and community, fear of the war-makers, and the security given weapons over people; fear of the numbing travel (650 miles plus); fear of injury or worse; fear of kangaroo courts and jails. Fear of the unknown.

        *        *        *

Why? Why risk liberty, limb, or life to act this way? Both sincere people and dilettantes will ask the question. They know, as we know, that the Navy will mop up our blood, repair its hell-ship and, eventually, put it on imperial patrol. They know, as we know, that the empire hasn't blinked over more than fifty Plowshares, and that it is a more efficient killer now than when the first Plowshares happened in 1980.

So why do what we did? Even sympathizers will tell us that Plowshares looks ridiculous now, a sermon to the converted, ignored by government and media, the public no longer listening. Most Americans would agree that Plowshares is a Theatre of the Absurd.

So why? Our answers come from both faith and sanity. Because God forbid us (persons and governments) to kill. Because God commands us to love our enemies, even protect them when others threaten. Because the God of the Bible is an unarmed, nonviolent God, who enjoins us to be perfect, and therefore, disarmed. Because Christ Our Lord went to his death rather than pick up the sword.

As for sanity—nuclear weapons have made war obsolete, for those interested in sane conduct—we disarm or we are socially helpless. Nuclear weapons and the empire's wars are killing us and humankind—killing us spiritually, ecologically, socially. They are indeed, the taproot of violence. Nuclear weapons and war dominate foreign and domestic policy. Our government is helpless to disarm. Therefore, the people must.

The federal government has now indicted us.

Warrants for our arrest have been issued—federal marshals hunt us. We will return to the Bath Iron Works once, twice, and then, the marshals will take us and remand us to jail. Later, in all likelihood, we will face a gag rule in court, and have all reference to God or the empire's warmaking or divine and international law suppressed.

No matter. We gamble on reconciliation, knowing that only the weaponless can greet a sister or brother. And believing (knowing) that reconciliation will happen in God's time—that we will become what we are, children of God, sisters and brothers of one another. So Isaiah is not blowing smoke in the second chapter of his prophecy. The Messiah has come; God has instructed us in her ways so that we may walk in her paths, and the nations have begun disarmament.

"One nation shall not raise the sword against another, nor shall they train for war again."
(Is. 2:4)

### ☆436b One Man's War

Paula Span, *Washington Post*, July 28, 1997, C01

Understand that Philip Berrigan does not enjoy being in jail. Not even in this small county jail—cleaner and quieter than most—where he and four compatriots await sentencing for damaging a Navy destroyer in a peace protest last winter.

He manages. A former Josephite priest, he wears a wooden crucifix hung around his neck with green dental floss, other sorts of cords being forbidden to inmates. He reads the Bible for "spiritual nourishment," Noam Chomsky to help hone his arguments against militarism, paperback mysteries to help settle him into sleep at night. He writes to his children, saying how proud he is of them and how sorry he was to miss his daughter Frida's and son Jerry's college graduation ceremonies this spring.

As he waits, he sometimes hears from old friends, veterans like himself of the Catholic peace movement that flowered in the '60s. He should stop courting prison sentences with acts of civil disobedience, they tell him. He and his brother Daniel, the Jesuit poet and onetime fugitive, can be advisers and elders now, and leave the front lines to the younger activists they helped inspire. Philip, after all, is nearing 74.

A futile argument. "You can't very well take it easy and give up and go back to normalcy," he says. "There's no reason to say, 'Look, I've done my bit.' You've never done your bit." Which is why he and a cadre of fellow activists from the Plowshares movement—a reference to what the Old Testament says swords should be beaten into—cut through a shipyard gate in nearby Bath last Ash Wednesday and strode aboard the USS Sullivans, an Aegis-class guided-missile destroyer.

A former athlete and an Army veteran, Berrigan

is barrel-chested in his orange prison jumpsuit. His voice remains hearty; so does his laugh. To speak with him in the jail's cinder block interview room feels like visiting your feisty, silver-haired grandfather behind bars.

"I'm as strong as a horse," he announces, almost bragging. In his cell, "I work out every day. I do push-ups and sit-ups and stretches of all kinds. Put the old carcass through some paces."

This by way of explaining that he can handle a hefty federal prison sentence. Fifteen years is the maximum for conspiracy and destruction of government property, the charges on which he was convicted, but Berrigan figures five years is more likely. Some of the others will get lighter sentences, but "I'm a recidivist," Berrigan says. True enough: He estimates that he's spent more than seven years behind bars for various crimes committed in the name of peace, starting with the destruction of draft records in 1967.

*          *          *

At 4:30 on a bleak, snowy February morning, six people in parkas and boots snipped through a lock with bolt-cutters and entered the Bath Iron Works, a 40-minute drive north of Portland. One of the country's oldest and busiest shipyards, its huge cranes tower over the small New England town on the banks of the Kennebec River. The U.S. Navy is its only customer.

The protesters carried plastic baby bottles filled with their own blood, collected by a helpful medical professional, and ordinary household hammers. Almost ordinary: Susan Crane, 53 and a former California high school teacher, had wood-burned "Love Your Enemies" into two of the handles.

The destroyer they boarded, named for five Iowa brothers who died when their ship was torpedoed in World War II, was merely the one closest to the gate. But the Sullivans, unknown to the protesters, had been officially turned over to the Navy as it neared completion. That meant that damaging it, even "symbolically," constituted destruction of government property, a federal crime. It also meant that instead of being nearly deserted, as the group expected, the ship was occupied by more than 300 sailors.

*          *          *

Berrigan never got past the gangplank. Neither did 35-year-old Mark Colville, a member of a Catholic Worker community that ministers to the poor in New Haven, Conn., or activist Thomas Lewis-Borbely, 56, of Worcester, Mass. The statement they attempted to read was torn from their hands; their hammers and bottles were tossed overboard. "The sailors were running around with shotguns and handguns," Berrigan remembers. "They were frantic." They had no ammunition, it was later revealed, but the protesters didn't know that.

The other three had darted off in different directions. Steven Baggarly, at 31 the youngest of the group and a member of a Catholic Worker community in Norfolk, sprinted up a ladder to the ship's launching-system deck along with Crane. As they hammered at the missile hatches—to symbolize the turning of weapons to peaceful uses—"the sound rang out through the snow," Crane recalls. "Every cell of my body was happy." They were soon grabbed and wrestled onto the icy deck.

[T]he Rev. Stephen Kelly, the sixth member of the group, managed to slip into the starboard entry and was hurrying through the dark ship, encountering locked doors and dead ends. "It was like going through a maze," says Kelly, 48, a Jesuit priest who had already done time, along with Crane, for damaging a Trident missile at a California defense plant. Finding the door to the bridge open, he threw blood on the navigational charts and equipment, hammered at instruments (but avoided breaking glass as "excessive"), left a dent on a table top. Two sailors with guns arrived and ordered him down onto the deck. "I think what I'll do is kneel and pray for you," Kelly said. It was all over within half an hour.

If the action had a ritualized quality, with the protesters reciting the Lord's Prayer as they waited to be arrested, so did the trial in May. Outside the stone courthouse in downtown Portland, scores of supporters drummed, chanted and sang. One scrambled up a pillar to unfurl a banner and had to be removed by a firetruck's cherry picker. More than a dozen were arrested.

But inside, the defendants were stymied. Assistant U.S. Attorney Helene Kazanjian prevented them from introducing a "necessity defense"—a claim that their action was necessary to prevent greater harm—or invoking the principles of international law. At one point, when the judge ruled that they could not call an expert on that subject as a witness, the defendants turned their backs and began to recite Bible verses; they were herded from the courtroom, shouting "Thou shalt not kill," to watch the trial's conclusion on closed-circuit TV.

The Plowshares people, acting as their own attorneys, acknowledged committing the acts they were accused of. But they wanted to explain their motivation: the brutality of "hellships," as they call destroyers; the social costs of U.S. arms policies; the moral imperative to resist. Kazanjian, on the other hand, saw simple vandalism. The Navy initially estimated the damage, including a biohazard cleanup of spilled blood, at $80,000—a paltry sum for an $853 million ship, but more than enough to qualify as a felony. "If we ask juries to isolate people out—'We acquit you because we like your religious or political beliefs'—that's very dangerous," Kazanjian says.

It took the jury just two hours to convict all six defendants. Four were offered release on personal recognizance (Crane and Kelly, who hadn't complied with their release conditions after the Trident episode, were ineligible), but only one defendant accepted. Berrigan, Colville and Baggarly refused. They would not promise to avoid lawbreaking or to stay away from the Bath Iron Works and so, since February, they have been inmates here. Nor will they accept probation when they are sentenced this month or next.

"What we did was right," Colville says. "We're not going to pretend that it wasn't."

*     *     *

On a sunny noon, as workers finishing the first shift come streaming out of the yard's main gate carrying their lunch boxes—"Through These Gates Pass the Best Shipbuilders in the World," a sign proclaims—it's hard to find one sympathetic to the Plowshares ethos. The trespassers broke the law, the workers say. They don't approve.

Fred Cooper, pipe fitter: "If they don't like the way things are, they should go to the ballot box."

Ron Hiscock, welder: "Our best defense is a strong offense, and making it into plowshares isn't necessarily the best solution."

Dave Hall, electrician: "It was perceived as an act of aggression and destruction."

Did the protest change anyone's mind about building weapons? "Maybe somewhere," Hall says. "But not in this town."

Phil Berrigan, who is committed but not delusional, knows that his actions no longer carry the jolt they did decades back, when he and his brother made the cover of Time. He doesn't claim that the world has become more peaceful (nuclear weapons treaties, he says, are "mostly window dressing"). He thinks the "war machine" might be even more powerful if he and his confreres hadn't acted, but how can one know for sure?

It comes down to doing what they think Christians are commanded to do, the Plowshares people say, whether their efforts produce measurable results or not. In the '70s, early theorists of the women's movement declared that the personal is political; in the Plowshares movement, the political is also personal.

"It's taken me out of the complicity loop," Berrigan says of his long history of crime and punishment. Otherwise, "I'd be contributing to the madness. I'd be silent in the face of this doomsday enterprise." With his hammers and blood and his small group of colleagues—there may be 100 or so men and women around the country committed to this style of civil disobedience—"I've reduced the guilt somewhat."

*     *     *

# 437 "I pray reinforcements arrive . . ." (1997)

A small group of disgruntled and ideologically motivated residents of remote west Texas came to national attention at the end of 1995 by proclaiming not their intent to secede from the United States, but their legally articulated assertion that, initially, the state of Texas was unlawfully incorporated into the American union.

Seeking originally to pursue their claim through court actions and negotiations with the president and other federal authorities, the representatives of the new "Republic of Texas" eventually allegedly resorted to kidnapping and other criminal activities.

What is unique to the Texas story is that dissidents represented themselves not as the presenters of individual grievances but as collective, international claimants representing one sovereign (albeit occupied) country against another. The group also represented itself as a military force, seeking for itself the standing usually accorded to lawful belligerents in the international law of war. The stance of the leaders of the Texas Republic supplies a real and current case study illustrating the analytical approach seen in the Introduction to this volume, which portrayed political criminality as a composite of unorthodox crime, unorthodox politics, and unorthodox warfare.

☆437 The Standoff at Fort Davis

☆437a Plans and Powers of the Provisional Government of the Republic of Texas, December 13, 1995

Document at http://208.129.178.21/provgov.htm.

### PREAMBLE

We the People of the Republic of Texas by the grace and beneficence of God do ordain and reestablish its lawful position among the sovereign nations of the earth in accordance with Common Law under the laws of nations, and by these acts, reestablish the Government of the Republic of Texas by this its provisional mode. This act formally dissolves the military rule which has existed over its soil since 1861.

### PRAYER

It is with solemn resolve and respect that the People of the Republic of Texas will vow in their commitment towards their American kindred relations and to all the people of the various states within the Union of the united States of America. To act with whatever aid is possible in salvaging their lands and sovereignty. With all prayer, the People of the Republic of Texas shall, where possible, help in fostering world peace and friendship and respect to all cultures and religions as private and sacred to all human beings. It is to that end that we and our posterity are now committed.

### ARTICLE 1. THE LAWS OF NATIONS

In accordance with the laws of nations and by the acts now perfected by the Political Subdivision of the Republic of Texas known as The Davis Mountains Land Commission, by and through the acts of the citizens, have now brought about the re-constitution of the lawful de jure Government of Texas. It is to that perfection that this provisional government is now hereby instituted to serve until, in accordance with the Original Petition of the People of the land territory of the Davis Mountains and Big Bend, a proper Constitutional Convention is convened and a fully operational Government is in place in accordance with the June 9, 1995, Petition.

### ARTICLE 2. CONSTITUTIONAL BASIS

The Provisional Government of the Republic of Texas and its agents and agencies hereby adopt and incorporate as a basis of its constitutional foundation the plans and powers of the Provisional Government of Texas of November 13, 1835; the Declaration of Independence of March 2, 1836; the Constitution of the Republic of Texas dated March 17, 1836; the Constitution of the Republic of Texas dated December 29, 1845, as amended January 16, 1850, as amended August 29, 1994, January 27, 1995, and June 9, 1995; and finally, anything in these plans and powers consistent with the Common Law.

### ARTICLE 3. BOUNDARIES OF THE NATION

That by the institution of this Provisional Government, the previous acts of the Republic of Texas in Commonwealth holding known as the 1850 Compromise are hereby affirmed. The Republic of Texas shall not extend any boundaries past those which are the present-day Texas boundaries and by this act dissolves any boundary claims or attachments claimed in the name of the state of Texas by the united States of America in the Gulf of Mexico or along its border with the Republic of Mexico.

### ARTICLE 4. CREATION OF GOVERNMENT

There is hereby created a Provisional Transitional Government of Texas whose Executive branch shall consist of a President and Vice-President, and of a General Council which will act in the place of Congress. All members shall be elected from the Transitional Government Convention so called. Thereafter any vacancies will be filled by the elected body of the Council.

\*          \*          \*

### ARTICLE 6. POWERS OF THE GENERAL COUNCIL

The duties of the General Council shall be to devise ways and means to assist the President in the discharge of his functions; to help develop and implement a plan for the transition of existing de facto Government operating on the soil of Texas into one uniform body, the Republic of Texas; to provide for this plan to encompass privatization, decentralization, deregulation, and the elimination of all excess waste; and in the final steps to in-place a limited Government, in order to move to the highest point possible in self government. The Council shall pass no law except in their opinion in case of emergency; they shall pursue the most energetic measures possible in accomplishing all goals. Two-thirds of the members of the General Council shall form a quorum to do business.

The General Council shall have the power to levy taxes on all franchised corporate, foreign de facto governments operating upon the soil of Texas for the benefit of commerce.

The President and the General Council shall have the power to hear and judge all cases usual in high Courts of Admiralty, agreeable to the law of nations with respect to political questions at law.

The President and the General Council shall have the right to make treaties and to authorize its Ambassadors, Foreign Ministers, or Consul Generals to effect whatever steps they may deem necessary to establish diplomatic relations under the laws of nations.

There shall be elected the following positions to the General Council from the floor of the Convention:

President
Vice-President
Secretary of the Council
Treasurer
Auditor
Secretary of Defense
Chief Ambassador and Consul General
Counsel General
Secretary of Judicial Affairs
Secretary of Commerce and Trade
Secretary of Agriculture, Environment, and Community Survivability
Secretary of Science and Technologies
Secretary of Plans, Powers, Constitution, and Convention

### ARTICLE 7. DUTIES AND RESPONSIBILITIES OF OFFICERS

The duties and responsibilities of Officers shall be consistent with this Section and with the Common Law; the Articles of Section One and Two shall be the fundamental control.

#### DUTIES AND POWERS OF POSITIONS OF THE GENERAL COUNCIL

##### *President*

The President shall serve in the position of Chief Executive for the Republic of Texas and shall be the

Chief Spokesman for the Republic. He shall be governed by this document and subsequent attachments and in accordance with the Common Law.

\*         \*         \*

☆437b  Diplomatic Notice of Perfection of International Relations between the United States of America and the "Republic of Texas," April 21, 1996

Document at http://208.129.178.21/dnpir.htm.

Pursuant to Treaty dated April 25, 1838, declared in force on October 13, 1838

To: The President and Congress of the UNITED STATES of AMERICA
William Jefferson Clinton, President
Albert Gore, Vice President
Robert Dole, for the Senate
Newt Gingrich, for the House

GREETINGS:

\*         \*         \*

The executive and legislative branches of the government of the UNITED STATES OF AMERICA are hereby placed upon lawful notice in accordance with the law of nations to the following; and in pursuance of this notice, lawful demand is hereby made and this notice posted and filed with various nations of the world, demanding that the UNITED STATES OF AMERICA comply with the law of nations and its own requisite treaties of operations and foreign relations law in respect to the reestablished nation of Texas and the rights of its Citizens and People upon the foundations of its creation as a nation on November 13, 1835, as amended March 2, 1836, and March 17, 1836, and in conjunction with a now recertified treaty between the united States of America and the Republic of Texas dated April 25, 1838, as perfected on October 13, 1838.

POLITICAL AND JUDICIAL NOTICE OF DOCUMENTS AND EXHIBITS OF RECORD UNDER THE LAW OF NATIONS

By this diplomatic notice under the law of nations, you are to take political and judicial notice of the below referenced and incorporated documents of record in the reclamation of the independence of the nation of Texas, known as the Republic of Texas, as of November 13, 1835. . . .

\*         \*         \*

1. That no clause of perpetuity or the right of annexation of a foreign nation ever existed in the Constitution of the united States of America or within the Constitution of the Republic of Texas in 1845 to perfect a permanent union in accord with the law of nations either then or now in effect in accordance with the Foreign Relations Law of the United States with respect to a Joint Resolution dated March 1, 1845.

\*         \*         \*

4. That the Republic of Texas after the Civil War became a captured nation of war under reconstruction and war powers, and thus remained until by acts of the Sovereign aggregate body of Citizens as described in the preamble to the Texas Constitution of December 29, 1845, in a political subdivision so declared and operational, by acts in convention under the law of nations, the People and Citizens of the Republic of Texas did lawfully dissolve the war powers acts, and did so by reconstituting the common law for remedy under a provisional government and developing a foundational court system and full national character of government for the nation of Texas;

\*         \*         \*

Mr. President and Congress, . . . [w]e have come peacefully and have highest respect for all concerned, but if you fail to regard this as a valid notice in perfecting international relations and continue to plunder the lives and property of our Citizens and People on the Soil of Texas, and refuse to make proper arrangements for vacating the Soil of Texas and relinquishing your operations to the existing coalition government by and through the existing STATE OF TEXAS de facto government, we will regard your continued presence as acts of war involving war crimes against our Citizens and People, and will move in international means of remedy against your government on the Soil of Texas.

Executed this the twenty-first day of April, 1996, the one hundred and sixtieth anniversary of the Battle of San Jacinto.

[Signed]
RICHARD LANCE MCLAREN
Chief Ambassador and Consul General
Republic of Texas

☆437c  Declaration and Proclamation of the Independence and Reclamation of the Republic of Texas, a Sovereign Nation State Body Politic, to All Nations of the World, June 13, 1996

Document at http://208.129.178.21/doi0613.htm.

\*         \*         \*

EXPLICIT NOTICE

International notice is hereby given that the nation of Texas, its People and its government, known as the Republic of Texas, will not be responsible for the generated and illusory debt created by the United States or its entity State of Texas by and through the acts of March 9, 1933, as amended; and in accordance with its previous acts in color of March 1, 1845, the United States did not accept the debts of the Republic of Texas.

3. All companies or corporations, whether domes-

tic or non-domestic, doing business on the soil of Texas, are now deemed to be unincorporated and will be governed by the rules of common law, just equity in parity, and private accountability, thus extinguishing the previous doctrine of limited liability.

4. All banks operating on the soil of Texas shall be given the right to convert to a lawful bank of specie operation and/or of the nature of commodity or barter.

5. The assets and natural resources of the Republic of Texas may be monetized for value and treasury notes may be issued for a medium of exchange.

6. All United States federal agents and employees who are displaced due to the acts of independence of the nation of Texas shall be given fair and equal opportunities at all transitional positions in the Republic of Texas.

7. All existing military armaments, equipment, and facilities on, over, or under the soil and waters of Texas are hereby deemed the property of the People of the Republic of Texas, and an immediate notification is to be served on all base commanders, advising that these properties will be absorbed into the Texas defense system, and that all excess military hardware not conducive to the status of Texas as a neutral and non-aggressive nation, including any nuclear weapons, will be immediately eliminated or destroyed.

8. The Texas State Bar Association is hereby dissolved, and shall have no charter or incorporation or any legal tie to courts of the Republic of Texas or to any operation in transition for the extradition of cases from the absorbed former Texas state courts. This does not limit the right of the former attorneys' association to reorganize and operate as a common law guild for purposes of legal education and setting standards for their private membership.

9. The absorbed Texas state legislature shall be given the right to quorum, and from their standing membership, except those members who are ineligible for reelection, will elect and fill positions currently vacant on the General Council of the Provisional Government, to serve until the conclusion of the constitutional convention and the election of a new governmental body.

10. In order to warrant a peaceful and orderly transition and to bring immediate relief to the over-burdened Citizens and businesses of Texas that are in economic slavery, the following are proper:

A. All U.S. federal taxes of any kind are hereby abolished on the soil of Texas.

B. All property and ad valorem taxes of any kind are hereby eliminated.

C. All use and excise taxes imposed to fund agencies of the absorbed State of Texas shall be continued in full force and effect for 120 days while the determination of the status of each

agency is made, pursuant to the Transitional Plan of January 7, 1996.

D. The sales tax of the absorbed State of Texas shall be extended for a period of 120 days until the implementation of import and export taxes and tariffs and the establishment of Texas as a free trade zone for its People.

\*　　　\*　　　\*

[Signed]
Archie Huel Lowe
President
Republic of Texas

*Attest*

[Signed]
Richard Lance McLaren
Chief Ambassador and Consul General
Republic of Texas

☆437d  Cyber-Savvy "Texians" Are Papered into a Corner of the Southwest

Sue Anne Pressley, *Washington Post*, March 12, 1997, A3.

Deep within this mountain forest of juniper and pine, Richard McLaren is hiding away in his crowded, computer-lit cabin. He is, he says, the ambassador-at-large for the Republic of Texas—and he and his band of "paper warriors" will not be ignored.

McLaren, 43, is involved in one of the more curious standoffs in recent Texas history. On one side is the self-proclaimed Republic of Texas, not just a separatist group with paramilitary connections, but, as he sees it, a boldly reclaimed country that must be recognized. On the other side are state and federal authorities, who are waiting patiently to arrest him. McLaren has said he will defend his "embassy" against foreign invaders, and neither side seems eager for a confrontation.

"The news media keeps asking, 'Oh, are you going to shoot a federal marshal, blah blah blah?' " he said. "Well, let me ask you, if a foreign country was on your soil, what would the Marine guard do? You tell me.

"They have no course against us but by violent force, and if they do that, they'll have the rest of the world on them. Because we have spent an extensive amount of time developing foreign relations, doing the main key things we have to do to make the Republic of Texas a reality."

The setting for this strange controversy is one of the most isolated spots in the country, a starkly beautiful land of tourists, ranchers and recluses in far southwest Texas. A four-hour drive from the nearest airport, surrounded by the 7,000-foot peaks of the Davis Mountains, it has the look of a western storybook.

Here, McLaren lives in a crude metal-sided cabin, surrounded by perhaps a dozen supporters, although he claims to have at least 10,000 sympathizers, mainly through the Internet. And, while reporters are almost always welcome, McLaren's armed bodyguards and his threats of violence have kept law enforcement officials at a careful distance.

McLaren and his group have managed to make their presence felt throughout Texas, however. In Austin, they have laid claim through warrants to the pink-stoned state capital, served Gov. George W. Bush (R) with papers demanding he vacate his office immediately, and filed a lien on all the state's assets.

In January, Bush grew irritated at the mess their "bogus" liens, which can make it difficult to sell property, began to create. He declared a state of emergency, enabling state lawmakers to bypass normal procedures and quickly pass a law making the filing of unofficial court judgments and liens a criminal act. Bush acted at the request of Texas Attorney General Dan Morales, who has been a special target of the group [see Doc. 429].

*          *          *

McLaren's claim for the Republic of Texas is based on a complex and confusing melange of historic documents and international law. But it boils down to the belief that Texas was illegally annexed by Congress in 1845, and nothing short of a vote by its citizens—in an area that includes parts of Kansas, Wyoming, Colorado, Oklahoma and New Mexico—can ever restore it to the Union. Until then, he and his supporters have concocted what seems like an elaborate game of Play Country, with a provisional government, a passport office and a court that continues to condemn state and local officials.

Taking a dim view of this premise, Ron Dusek, Morales's spokesman, scoffed that the Republic of Texas is "simply a social group that has no more authority than the Moose Lodge. They are a novelty."

*          *          *

Nor does the local sheriff seem perturbed about McLaren's activities: "He's just a nut with the press and a fax machine," said Steve Bailey, sheriff of Jeff Davis County. "Both keep him fed. If the press would go away, he'd come down out of the mountains and go to the store and buy some groceries."

All this trouble stems from someone who is not even a native Texan. McLaren, a tall, lanky man who wears tweed jackets with his blue jeans and calls to mind an obsessed philosophy teacher, smarts at this particular point. But, he reasons that "if freedom runs in your blood, you're a Texian," as he refers to the republic's citizens.

While he was growing up in Missouri, his revolutionary spirit surfaced quite early. "I've never been nonviolent," he said. "In elementary school, I used to get beat up—I stood up for the underdog. That was kind of hard for me, I was small. Finally, after the third time of getting beat up, I told the guy who was

doing it, 'Let me tell you, boy, you're going to go to sleep one night and they're going to have to come pick up the pieces.' And after that, they let me alone, they knew I was serious."

A high school graduate who is "self-educated," McLaren said he has worked "in agriculture most of my life, and done a number of things. I was in the car business for a while. I sold insurance. I wrote automobile manuals." His immersion in litigation began in 1985 when he discovered that, because of a dispute with the developer, there was no clear title to his land or to that belonging to other residents of the sprawling development where he lives, the Davis Mountain Resorts.

*          *          *

Several months ago, Dusek said, state officials became more concerned about the group when it began to attract the attention of militias throughout the state. While McLaren claims no arsenal, he speaks enthusiastically of the "defense force system" he is organizing to defend his reclaimed country. A shooting incident around Thanksgiving alarmed neighbors—McLaren said his security chief, Chris Leonard, was simply taking target practice—and mail service was briefly disrupted in the development because it seemed too dangerous for the postal carrier to venture into the mountains.

But Dusek and other officials say they are mindful of the lessons of Waco, and that no one wants to repeat that tragic 1993 standoff involving David Koresh and the Branch Davidians.

"Waco has a great influence on how we are handling this. . . . We're not going to go risking people's lives over this particular silly notion," Dusek said.

*          *          *

☆437e  Republic of Texas Press Release, May 1, 1997

Document at http://208.129.178.21/pr0501.htm.

The situation near Fort Davis appears to be intensifying. Information from eyewitnesses is beginning to show discrepancies in what is being reported publicly and what is actually taking place.

Law enforcement presence is intensifying, with over 200 officers on or near the scene at this time.

There is also a buildup of United States federal law enforcement personnel in the area. The official position is that federal personnel are there as observers only, but their increasing numbers make this seem unlikely. Law enforcement stated early in the week that they had cut off telephone communications, and they are now stating that they have shut off electricity.

Despite efforts by the Republic of Texas Provisional Government to convince both sides of this standoff that this be resolved peacefully, concerns are mounting that law enforcement may be staging a massive armed confrontation.

The Republic of Texas does not condone criminal activity, whether that criminal activity be done by a Citizen or by the Government. We therefore offer the following points for consideration:

\*       \*       \*

—Agents of the FBI, ATF, and other federal agencies known to be in the area are agents of the corporate United States. Law enforcement has made statements to Citizens that the FBI is "in charge." If this is true, the United States is not acting as an observer as has been reported, but as an active participant. There have been no crimes charged under United States law, and the United States has no jurisdiction for participating in this action. Their actions are in violation of the boundary treaty of 1838 between the Republic of Texas and the United States.

—While we cannot and do not support the actions of Mr. McLaren and his followers on April 27, we also cannot and will not tolerate a massive military-style assault against any Citizen of the Republic of Texas. We are aware of the type of force that can be brought to bear by agents of the corporate government, and of their disregard for basic human rights.

\*       \*       \*

We continue to implore both Mr. McLaren and the local Sheriff to work quickly to resolve this issue peacefully, before this situation can escalate. Tremendous attention is focused on Texas, and all of us want this situation resolved peacefully in a proper court of law.

For further details, visit the Republic of Texas web site on the Internet at "www.republic-of-texas.com" or "Texas.by.net"....

☆437f  Separatists End Texas Standoff as 5 Surrender

Sam Howe Verhovek, *New York Times*, May 4, 1997, 1.

The seven-day standoff between Texas authorities and an armed separatist group ended this afternoon when the group's leader, who had vowed to wage an Alamo-style fight to the death, walked out of his trailer with three other members and surrendered here in the high desert of West Texas.

The leader, Richard L. McLaren, dressed in boots, jeans, a tweed coat and a cowboy hat, gave himself up after a "military style ceremony," at which he and his followers laid down their arms, said Mike Cox, a spokesman for the state Department of Public Safety.

\*       \*       \*

The surrender under a brilliant sun came a few hours after Evelyn McLaren walked out of the trailer and gave herself up to the authorities. She married Mr. McLaren last December in a ceremony sanctioned only by the laws of the secessionist group, known as the Republic of Texas, which holds that Texas was illegally annexed by the United States in 1845 and thus remains an independent nation. Ms. McLaren, . . . a former postal worker from Fort Worth, Tex., surrendered after an emotional appeal here from two of her daughters.

"Please, please, don't make us bring your two-and-a-half-year-old grandson to your funeral," said one daughter, Julie Hopkins, 29, of Fort Worth.

Mr. McLaren's lawyer, Terence O'Rourke, said tonight that the state authorities and his client had negotiated a signed agreement calling for a "Texas-wide cease-fire" in the war that Mr. McLaren declared last Sunday. He said that Mr. McLaren would be given an opportunity to state his case, including his contention that he should be given diplomatic immunity, before a Federal judge.

But, said Mr. Cox: "There is no agreement other than they agreed to come out peacefully and they agreed to cease fire. There were no promises on the part of the Department of Public Safety."

\*       \*       \*

More than a few neighbors expressed disappointment that Mr. McLaren, who has long been widely detested here for his legal confrontations with town residents, was not killed during the siege.

Without question, the bizarre standoff here had many elements of farce, or perhaps those of a bad B-movie. At the same time, though, it was handled by the state as a deadly serious affair, in which it had said it was determined to serve criminal warrants on at least five of the six people inside the trailer with minimal violence or risk to its officers.

The Republic of Texas members "must be held accountable for breaking the law," Texas Gov. George W. Bush said Friday. "They're kidnapping people in the state of Texas with guns."

It was clear that the state authorities were immensely pleased that the standoff appeared to be coming to a peaceful end. . . .

Around the country, law-enforcement authorities have been haunted by the legacy of the botched and deadly Federal assaults on a white separatist in Ruby Ridge, Idaho, in 1992, whose unarmed wife was killed by a Federal sniper, and on the Branch Davidians near Waco in 1993, more than 80 of whom perished in a fire after Federal Bureau of Investigation tanks punched open their compound and inserted tear gas.

Like last year's 81-day standoff with the Freemen of Montana, which ended with a surrender and without a single shot fired, the operation by Texas authorities may well be cited as a model for dealing with armed antigovernment belligerents. At the same time, though, some critics suggested this week that the hands-off treatment might encourage other groups and that the state should have acted more quickly and forcefully to root out the rebels.

As the week wore on, Mr. McLaren's rhetoric had grown increasingly belligerent.

*     *     *

On the evening of Friday, May 2, he sent out a letter that bore overtones of a plea sent out by Col. William Barrett Travis, the commander of the Texans at the Alamo, who all died in 1838 after a 13-day seige by Mexican forces in San Antonio.

"Everyone has chosen to stay and hold the sovereign soil of the Republic and its foreign missions," wrote Mr. McLaren. "I pray reinforcements arrive before they overrun the embassy."

*     *     *

The five group members who surrendered were placed in the Presidio County jail in Marfa, 21 miles southwest of Fort Davis tonight awaiting a bail hearing. Mr. McLaren is likely to be charged with conspiracy to commit kidnapping and assault and a variety of other crimes. If convicted, he could spend the rest of his life in prison.

# Bibliography

Abalone Alliance. *Diablo Canyon/Encampment Handbook.* Santa Cruz, Calif.: Northern California Preparers' Collective, 1980.

Abbey, Edward. *The Monkey Wrench Gang.* Philadelphia: Lippincott, 1975.

Abels, Jules. *Man on Fire: John Brown and the Cause of Liberty.* New York: Macmillan, 1971.

Abernathy, Thomas P. *The Burr Conspiracy.* New York: Oxford University Press, 1954.

*The Acts of Assembly Now in Force in the Colony of Virginia, 1661-1769.* Williamsburg: Rind, Purdie, and Dixon, 1769.

Adams, C. F., ed. *The Works of John Adams.* Vols. 3, 7-10, *Official Letters, Messages and Public Papers, Correspondence.* 1851, 1854 eds. Reprint. New York: AMS Press, 1971.

Adams, James Truslow. *The Epic of America.* Garden City, N.Y.: Blue Ribbon Books, 1941.

Agee, Philip, and Wolf, Louis, eds. *Dirty Work: The CIA in Western Europe.* Secaucus, N.J.: Stuart, 1978.

Albright, Joseph. *What Makes Spiro Run: The Life and Times of Spiro T. Agnew.* New York: Dodd, Mead, 1972.

Alexander, James. *A Brief Narrative of the Case and Trial of John Peter Zenger.* Cambridge, Mass.: Harvard University Press, Belknap Press, 1963.

Alexander, Yonah; Browne, Marjorie A.; and Nanes, Allan S., eds. *Control of Terrorism: International Documents.* New York: Crane, Russak, 1979.

Ali, Tariq, ed. *The New Revolutionaries: A Handbook of the International Radical Left.* New York: Morrow, 1969.

Alinsky, Saul D. *Reveille for Radicals.* Chicago: University of Chicago Press, 1946.

Allen, Francis A. *The Crimes of Politics: Political Dimensions of Criminal Justice.* Cambridge, Mass.: Harvard University Press, 1974.

Allen, W. *Governor Chamberlain's Administration in South Carolina.* New York: Negro Universities Press, 1969.

Anderson, Eric. *Race and Politics in North Carolina, 1872-1901.* Baton Rouge: Louisiana State University Press, 1981.

Andrews, Charles McLean, ed. *Narratives of the Insurrections, 1675-1690.* New York: Scribner, 1915.

Anthony, Earl. *Picking Up the Gun: A Report on the Black Panthers.* New York: Dial Press, 1970.

Aptheker, Herbert. *American Negro Slave Revolts.* New York: International Publishers, 1978.

Arber, E. *Travels and Works of Captain John Smith.* New York: Burt Franklin, 1910.

Archer, Jules. *Treason in America: Disloyalty versus Dissent.* New York: Hawthorn Books, 1971.

Arendt, Hannah. *On Revolution.* New York: Viking Press, 1970.

Arens, Richard, and Lasswell, Harold D. *In Defense of Public Order: The Emerging Field of Sanction Law.* New York: Columbia University Press, 1961.

Avrich, Paul. *The Haymarket Tragedy.* Princeton: Princeton University Press, 1984.

Babcox, Deborah; Babcox, Peter; and Abel, Bob, eds. *The Conspiracy.* New York: Dell, 1969.

Bailyn, Bernard. *The Ideological Origins of the American Revolution.* Cambridge, Mass.: Harvard University Press, 1967.

Bakeless, John. *Turncoats, Traitors, and Heroes.* New York: Lippincott, 1959.

Baldwin, Leland Dewitt. *Whiskey Rebels: The Story of a Frontier Uprising.* Pittsburgh: University of Pittsburgh Press, 1939.

Banner, James M. *To the Hartford Convention: The Federalists and the Origins of Party Politics in Massachusetts, 1789-1815.* New York: Knopf, 1970.

Barnes, Gilbert Hobbs. *The Antislavery Impulse, 1830-1844.* New York: Harcourt Brace & World, 1964.

Barsh, Russel Lawrence, and Henderson, James Youngblood. *The Road.* Berkeley and Los Angeles: University of California Press, 1980.

Barton, William E. *The Life of Abraham Lincoln.* Indianapolis: Bobbs-Merrill, 1925.

Baskir, Laurence M., and Strauss, William A. *Chance and Circumstance: The Draft, the War, and the Vietnam Generation.* New York: Knopf, 1978.

Basler, R. P., ed. *The Collected Works of Abraham Lincoln.* Vols. 4-8. New Brunswick, N.J.: Rutgers University Press, 1959.

Bassiouni, M. Cheriff, ed. *International Terrorism and Political Crimes.* Springfield, Ill.: Charles C Thomas, 1975.

Beck, Carl. *Contempt of Congress: A Study of the Prosecutions Initiated by the Committee on Un-American Activities, 1945-1957.* New Orleans: Hauser Press, 1959.

Becker, Carl Lotus. *The Eve of the Revolution: A Chronicle of the Breach with England.* New Haven: Yale University Press, 1918.

———. *The Declaration of Independence: A Study in the History of Political Ideas.* 3d ed. Reprint. New York: Vintage Books, 1958.

Becker, Theodore L., ed. *Political Trials.* Indianapolis: Bobbs-Merrill, 1971.

Bedau, Hugo Adam, ed. *Civil Disobedience: Theory and Practice.* New York: Pegasus, 1969.

Belfrage, Cedric. *The American Inquisition, 1945-1960.* Indianapolis: Bobbs-Merrill, 1973.

Belknap, Michal R. *Cold War Political Justice: The Smith Act, the Communist Party and American Civil Liberties.* Westport, Conn.: Greenwood Press, 1977.

Bell, Derrick, ed. *Shades of Brown: New Perspectives on School Desegregation.* New York: Teachers College Press, Columbia University, 1980.

Bell, Jason S. "Violation of International Law and Doomed United States Policy: An Analysis of the Cuban Democracy Act." 25 *U. Miami Inter-Am. L. Rev.* 77 (1993).

Bemis, Samuel Flagg. *The Diplomacy of the American Revolution.* Bloomington: Indiana University Press, 1957.

Ben-Dak, Joseph D., ed. *The Future of Collective Violence: Societal and International Perspectives.* Lund: Student Litteratur, 1974.

Bennett, Lerone. *Before the Mayflower: A History of the Negro in America, 1619-1966.* 3d ed. Chicago: Johnson, 1966.

Bentley, Eric, ed. *Thirty Years of Treason: Excerpts from Hearings before the House Committee on Un-American Activities, 1938-1968.* New York: Viking Press, 1971.

Berrigan, Daniel. *The Trial of the Catonsville Nine.* Boston: Beacon Press, 1970.

———. *The Dark Night of Resistance.* Garden City, N.Y.: Doubleday, 1971.

Berrigan, Daniel, and Coles, Robert. *The Geography of Faith.* New York: Bantam Books, 1972.

Berrigan, Philip. *Prison Journals of a Priest Revolutionary.* New York: Holt, Rinehart and Winston, 1969.

Blanchard, Dallas A., and Prewitt, Terry J. *Religious Violence and Abortion: The Gideon Project.* Gainesville: University Press of Florida, 1993.

Blaustein, Albert P. *Desegregation and the Law: The Meaning and Effect of the School Desegregation Cases.* New Brunswick, N.J.: Rutgers University Press, 1957.

Blaustein, Albert P., and Zangrando, Robert, eds. *Civil Rights and the American Negro: A Documentary History.* New York: Trident Press, 1968.

Blumenthal, Monica D.; Kahn, Robert L.; Andrews, Frank M.; and Head, Kendra B. *Justifying Violence: Attitudes of American Men.* Ann Arbor: Institute for Social Research, University of Michigan, 1975.

Blumenthal, Walter Hart. *American Indians Dispossessed.* 1955 ed. Reprint. New York: Arno Press, 1975.

Boesel, David, and Rossi, Peter H. *Cities under Siege: An Anatomy of the Ghetto Riots, 1964-1968.* New York: Basic Books, 1971.

*The Book of the General Laws of the Inhabitants of the Jurisdiction of New Plymouth.* Boston: Samuel Green, 1685.

Boorstin, Daniel J. *The Americans: The Colonial Experience.* New York: Random House, 1958.

Bowers, Claude G. *Jefferson and Hamilton: The Struggle for Democracy in America.* Boston: Houghton Mifflin, 1926.

Boyd, J., ed. *The Papers of Thomas Jefferson.* Princeton: Princeton University Press, 1950.

Brackenridge, Henry M. *History of the Western Insurrection in Western Pennsylvania, Commonly Called the Whiskey Insurrection, 1794.* Pittsburgh: W. S. Haven, 1859.

Bradford, William. *Of Plymouth Plantation, 1620-1647.* 1898 ed. Reprint. New York: Knopf, 1953.

Breen, T. H. *Puritans and Adventurers: Change and Persistence in Early America.* New York: Oxford University Press, 1980.

Breitman, G., ed. *Malcolm X Speaks.* New York: Grove Press, 1965.

Bremer, Arthur. *An Assassin's Diary.* New York: Harper's Magazine Press, 1972.

Brinton, Crane. *The Anatomy of Revolution.* New York: Random House, 1952.

———. *A Decade of Revolution, 1789-1799.* New York: Harper & Row, 1963.

Brissenden, Paul F. *The I.W.W.: A Study of American Syndicalism.* 2d ed. New York: Columbia University, 1920.

Brock, William R. *An American Crisis: Congress and Reconstruction, 1865-1867.* New York: St. Martin's Press, 1963.

Brodie, Fawn M. *Thomas Jefferson: An Intimate History.* New York: Bantam Books, 1974.

Brogan, D. W. *The American Character*. New York: Random House, 1956.

Brooks, Thomas R. *Toil and Trouble: A History of American Labor*. New York: Dell, 1964.

Brower, Brock. *Other Loyalties*. New York: Atheneum, 1968.

Brown, Ralph S. *Loyalty and Security: Employment Tests in the United States*. New Haven: Yale University Press, 1958.

Brown, Richard M. *Strain of Violence*. New York: Oxford University Press, 1975.

Brown, W., ed. *Proceedings and Acts of the General Assembly of Maryland, January 1637-1658*. Baltimore: Press of Isaac Friedenwald, 1883.

Brownlie, Ian. *The Law Relating to Public Order*. London: Butterworth, 1968.

Bryan, George S. *The Spy in America*. Philadelphia: Lippincott, 1943.

Buckley, William F. *The Committee and Its Critics: A Calm Review of the House Committee on Un-American Activities*. New York: Putnam, 1962.

Buckman, Peter. *The Limits of Protest*. Indianapolis: Bobbs-Merrill, 1970.

Buncher, Judith F., ed. *The CIA and the Security Debate, 1975-1976*. New York: Facts on File, 1977.

Bunzel, John H. *Anti-Politics in America*. New York: Vintage Books, 1970.

Burke, Edmund. *Reflections on the Revolution in France*. Baltimore: Penguin Books, 1969.

Burton, Anthony. *Revolutionary Violence*. New York: Crane, Russak, 1978.


Calhoon, Robert McCluer. *The Loyalists in Revolutionary America, 1760-1781*. New York: Harcourt Brace Jovanovich, 1973.

Califano, Joseph A., Jr. *The Student Revolution: A Global Confrontation*. New York: Norton, 1970.

Cameron, Jenks. *The Development of Governmental Forest Control in the United States*. 1928; reprint, New York: DaCapo Press, 1972.

Campbell, James S.; Sahid, Joseph R.; and Stang, David P. *Law and Order Reconsidered*. Washington, D.C.: U.S. Government Printing Office, 1969.

Campbell, Stanley W. *The Slave Catchers: Enforcement of the Fugitive Slave Law, 1850-1860*. Chapel Hill: University of North Carolina Press, 1970.

Camus, Albert. *Resistance, Rebellion, and Death*. New York: Random House, 1960.

Canby, Courtland. *Lincoln and the Civil War: A Profile and a History*. New York: Braziller, 1960.

Candler, A., ed. *The Confederate Records of the State of Georgia*. Atlanta: C. P. Byrd, 1909.

Carlson, Peter. *Roughneck: The Life and Times of Big Bill Haywood*. New York: Norton, 1983.

Carmichael, Stokely. *Stokely Speaks: Black Power Back to Pan-Africanism*. New York: Random House, 1971.

Carter, H.; Stone, W.; and Gould, M., eds. *Reports of the Proceedings and Debates of the Convention of 1821*. New York: Da Capo Press, 1970.

Catton, William B. *Two Roads to Sumter*. New York: McGraw-Hill, 1963.

Caute, David. *The Great Fear: The Anti-Communist Purge under Truman and Eisenhower*. New York: Simon & Schuster, 1978.

Chafee, Zechariah. *How Human Rights Got into the Constitution*. Boston: Boston University Press, 1952.

Chalmers, David M. *Hooded Americanism: The First Century of the Ku Klux Klan, 1865-1965*. Garden City, N.Y.: Doubleday, 1965.

*The Chicago Martyrs: The Famous Speeches of Eight Anarchists in Judge Gary's Court*. San Francisco: Free Society, 1899.

Chomsky, Noam, et al. *Trials of the Resistance*. New York: Vintage Books, 1970.

Clavir, Judy, and Spitzer, John, eds. *The Conspiracy Trial*. Indianapolis: Bobbs-Merrill, 1970.

Cleaver, Eldridge. *Soul on Ice*. New York: Dell, 1972.

Clinard, Marshall B., and Quinney, Richard. *Criminal Behavior Systems: A Typology*. New York: Holt, Rinehart and Winston, 1967.

Cohen, Nathan, ed. *The Los Angeles Riots: A Psychological Study*. New York: Praeger, 1970.

Commager, H. S., ed. *Documents of American History*. New York: Meredith Corp., 1973.

Commins, S., ed. *Basic Writings of George Washington*. New York: Random House, 1948.

Commission on CIA Activities within the United States. *Report to the President by the Commission on CIA Activities within the United States*. Washington, D.C.: U.S. Government Printing Office, 1975.

Commons, J. R., and Gillmore, E., eds. *A Documentary History of American Industrial Society*. Vol. 4. New York: Russell & Russell, 1958.

Connery, Robert H., ed. *Urban Riots: Violence and Social Change*. New York: Vintage Books, 1969.

Cook, Adrian. *The Armies of the Streets: The New York City Draft Riots of 1863*. Lexington: University Press of Kentucky, 1974.

Cooper, T., ed. *Statutes of South Carolina, 1682-1716.* Vol. 2. Columbia, S.C.: A. S. Johnston, 1837.

Cooper, William J. *The Conservative Regime: South Carolina, 1877-1890.* Baltimore: Johns Hopkins Press, 1968.

Cornell, J. *The Trial of Ezra Pound: A Documented Account of the Treason Case by the Defendant's Lawyer.* New York: John Day, 1966.

Cover, Robert. *Justice Accused: Antislavery and the Judicial Process.* New Haven: Yale University Press, 1975.

Crelinsten, Ronald D.; Laberge-Altmejd, Danielle; and Szabo, Denis. *Terrorism and Criminal Justice.* Lexington, Mass.: Heath, 1978.

Crook, Wilfred H. "The Revolutionary Logic of the General Strike." *American Political Science Review* 28 (1934): 655-63.

Currie, David P. *The Constitution of the Federal Republic of Germany.* Chicago: University of Chicago Press, 1994.

Cushing, J. D., ed. *The Earliest Laws of the New Haven and Connecticut Colonies, 1639-1673.* Wilmington, Del.: Michael Glazier, 1977.

——. *Laws of the Province of Maryland (1718).* Wilmington, Del.: Michael Glazier, 1977.

——. *Rhode Island Colony Laws, 1647-1719.* Wilmington, Del.: Michael Glazier, 1977.


Daniels, Roger. *The Bonus March: An Episode of the Great Depression.* Westport, Conn.: Greenwood Press, 1971.

Darvall, Frank O. *Popular Disturbances and Public Order in Regency England.* London: Oxford University Press, 1934.

David, H. *The History of the Haymarket Affair.* New York: Farrar & Rinehart, 1936.

Davis, Allen F., and Woodman, Harold D., eds. *Conflict and Consensus in Modern American History.* Lexington, Mass.: Heath, 1980.

Davis, Angela Y. *If They Come in the Morning.* New York: Joseph Okpaku, 1971.

Davis, David B. *The Fear of Conspiracy: Images of Un-American Subversion from the Revolution to the Present.* Ithaca: Cornell University Press, 1971.

Davis, D. *The Billy Mitchell Affair.* New York: Random House, 1967.

Davis, William W. H. *The Fries Rebellion, 1798-1799: An Armed Resistance to the House Tax Law, Passed by Congress, July 9, 1798, in Bucks and Northampton Counties, Pennsylvania.* Doylestown, Pa.: Doylestown, 1899.

Dawson, Frank Griffith, and Head, Ivan L. *International Law, National Tribunals, and the Rights of Aliens.* New York: Procedural Aspects of International Law Institute, 1971.

Debo, Angie. *The Road to Disappearance.* Norman: University of Oklahoma Press, 1941.

——. *A History of the Indians of the United States.* Norman: University of Oklahoma Press, 1971.

Debray, Regis. *Revolution in the Revolution: Armed Struggle and Political Struggle in Latin America.* New York: Grove Press, 1967.

Dell, Christopher. *Lincoln and the War Democrats: The Grand Erosion of Conservative Tradition.* Rutherford, N.J.: Fairleigh Dickinson University Press, 1975.

Dellinger, Dave. *Revolutionary Nonviolence.* New York: Doubleday, 1971.

Deloria, Vine. *A Brief History of the Federal Responsibility to the American Indians.* Washington, D.C.: U.S. Government Printing Office, 1979.

Deloria, Vine, and Lytle, Clifford M. *American Indians, American Justice.* Austin: University of Texas Press, 1983.

De Silva, Peer. *Sub Rosa: The CIA and the Uses of Intelligence.* New York: Times Books, 1978.

Dillon, Martin, and Lehane, Denis. *Political Murder in Northern Ireland.* Middlesex: Penguin Books, 1973.

Dobrouir, William A. *Justice in Time of Crisis.* Washington, D.C.: U.S. Government Printing Office, 1969.

Donner, Frank J. *The Age of Surveillance.* New York: Knopf, 1980.

Dowell, Eldridge F. *A History of Criminal Syndicalism Legislation in the United States.* New York: Da Capo Press, 1969.

Dubofsky, Melvyn. *We Shall Be All: A History of the Industrial Workers of the World.* Chicago: Quadrangle Books, 1969.

Dubois, W. E. B. *John Brown.* New York: International Publishers, 1962.

Duff, John B., and Mitchell, Peter M., eds. *The Nat Turner Rebellion: The Historical Event and the Modern Controversy.* New York: Harper & Row, 1971.

Dwight, T. *History of the Hartford Convention.* 1833 ed. Reprint. New York: Da Capo Press, 1970.

Eddowes, Michael. *The Oswald File*. New York: C. N. Potter, 1977.

Edelman, Murray. *The Symbolic Uses of Politics*. Urbana: University of Illinois Press, 1970.

Edwards, Samuel. *Rebel! A Biography of Tom Paine*. New York: Praeger, 1974.

Ehrlich, Walter. *They Have No Rights: Dred Scott's Struggle for Freedom*. Westport, Conn.: Greenwood Press, 1979.

Ehrmann, Herbert. *The Case That Will Not Die: Commonwealth vs. Sacco and Vanzetti*. Boston: Little, Brown, 1969.

Elliot, J., ed. *Debates in the Several State Conventions on the Adoption of the Federal Constitution*. 5 vols. Philadelphia: Lippincott, 1907.

Elliot, John D., and Gibson, Leslie K., eds. *Contemporary Terrorism: Selected Readings*. Gaithersburg, Md.: International Association of Chiefs of Police, 1978.

Ellis, George William, and Morris, John E. *King Philip's War*. New York: Grafton Press, 1906.

Emerson, Thomas I. *The System of Freedom of Expression*. New York: Random House, 1970.

Emerson, Thomas I.; Haber, David; and Dorsen, Norman, eds. *Political and Civil Rights in the United States*. Boston: Little, Brown, 1967.

Endleman, Shalom, ed. *Violence in the Streets*. Chicago: Quadrangle Books, 1968.

Erm, Rene, II. "The 'Wise Use' Movement: The Constitutionality of Local Action on Federal Lands under the Preemption Doctrine." 30 *Idaho L. Rev.* 631 (1993-94).

Ernst, Morris L. *The First Freedom*. New York: Macmillan, 1946.


Fall, Bernard B., ed. *Ho Chi Minh on Revolution*. New York: Praeger, 1968.

Fanon, Frantz. *The Wretched of the Earth*. New York: Grove Press, 1968.

Farrell, William R. *The U.S. Government Response to Terrorism*. Boulder, Colo.: Westview Press, 1982.

Fehrenbacker, Don E. *The Dred Scott Case: Its Significance in American Law and Politics*. New York: Oxford University Press, 1978.

——. *Slavery, Law, and Politics: The Dred Scott Case in Historical Perspective*. New York: Oxford University Press, 1981.

Ferber, Michael. *The Resistance*. Boston: Beacon Press, 1971.

Feuerlicht, Roberta S. *Justice Crucified: The Story of Sacco and Vanzetti*. New York: McGraw-Hill, 1977.

*Fifty Mutinies, Rebellions, and Revolutions*. London: Odhams Press, n.d.

Filler, Louis. *The Crusade against Slavery, 1830-1860*. New York: Harper & Row, 1960.

Filler, Louis, and Guttmann, Allen, eds. *The Removal of the Cherokee Nation: Manifest Destiny or National Dishonor?* Problems in American Civilization, vol. 48. Boston: Heath, 1962.

Fink, Leon. *Workingmen's Democracy: The Knights of Labor and American Politics*. Urbana: University of Illinois Press, 1983.

Finn, James, ed. *A Conflict of Loyalties*. New York: Western Publishing, 1968.

Fleming, W. L., ed. *The Ku Klux Klan: Its Origin, Growth, and Disbandment*. New York: Neale, 1905.

Fleming, W. L., ed. *Documents Relating to Reconstruction*. Morgantown: University of West Virginia, 1904.

Flynn, Elizabeth Gurley. *The Rebel Girl: An Autobiography, My First Life (1906-1926)*. New York: International Publishers, 1979.

Foner, Eric. *Nothing but Freedom: Emancipation and Its Legacy*. Baton Rouge: Louisiana State University Press, 1983.

Foner, Philip S. *History of the Labor Movement in the United States*. New York: International Publishers, 1947.

——. *The Case of Joe Hill*. New York: International Publishers, 1975.

——, ed. *The Black Panthers Speak*. Philadelphia: Lippincott, 1970.

Foreman, Dave. *Confessions of an Ecowarrior*. New York: Harmony Books, 1991.

Foreman, Dave, and Haywood, Bill, eds. *Ecodefense: A Field Guide to Monkeywrenching*. 3d ed. Chico, Calif.: Abbzug Press, 1993.

Force, P., ed. *American Archives: 4th series*. Vol. 3. Washington, D.C.: M. St. Clair Clarke & P. Force, 1853.

Force, W. C., ed. *Writings of George Washington*. New York: Putnam, 1889.

Ford, Gerald R., and Stiles, John R. *Portrait of the Assassin*. New York: Ballantine Books, 1966.

Ford, W. C., ed. *Journals of the Continental Congress*. 34 vols. Washington, D.C.: U.S. Government Printing Office, 1906.

Ford, W. J. *Resistance Movements and International Law*. Geneva: 1967, 1968.

Foreman, Grant. *Indian Removal: The Emigration of the Five Civilized Tribes of Indians*. Norman: University of Oklahoma Press, 1966.

Fortas, Abe. *Concerning Dissent and Civil Disobedience*. New York: New American Library, 1968.

Fraenkel, O. K. *The Sacco-Vanzetti Case*. New York: Knopf, 1931.

Frankfurter, M. D., and Jackson, G., eds. *The Letters of Sacco and Vanzetti*. New York: Viking Press, 1928.

Fritz, Henry E. *The Movement for Indian Assimilation, 1860-1890*. Philadelphia: University of Pennsylvania Press, 1963.

Fromm, Erich. *Escape from Freedom*. 1941 ed. Reprint. New York: Avon Books, 1969.

Frost, R. *The Mooney Case*. Stanford: Stanford University Press, 1968.

Furniss, Norman F. *The Mormon Conflict, 1850-1859*. New Haven: Yale University Press, 1966.


Gage, Thomas. *The Correspondence of General Thomas Gage*. Edited by Clarence Edwin Carter. 2 vols. New Haven: Yale University Press, 1931-33.

Gambill, Edward L. *Conservative Ordeal: Northern Democrats and Reconstruction, 1865-1868*. Ames: Iowa State University Press, 1981.

Gambs, John S. *The Decline of the I. W. W.* New York: Columbia University Press, 1932.

Garrison, W., and Garrison, F. *William Lloyd Garrison, 1805-1879: The Story of His Life Told by His Children*. 4 vols. 1884-89 ed. Reprint. New York: Arno Press, 1969.

Gates, Paul W. *History of Public Land Law Development*. North Stratford, N.H.: Ayer Publishers, 1972.

Gaylin, Willard. *In the Service of Their Country: War Resisters in Prison*. New York: Grosset & Dunlap, 1970.

Gellhorn, Walter. *Security, Loyalty, and Science*. Ithaca: Cornell University Press, 1950.

Gentry, Curt. *Frame-Up: The Incredible Case of Tom Mooney and Warren Billings*. New York: Norton, 1967.

Gerhardt, James M. *The Draft and Public Policy: Issues in Military Manpower Procurement, 1945-1970*. Columbus: Ohio State University Press, 1971.

Geschwender, James A. *The Black Revolt*. Englewood Cliffs, N.J.: Prentice-Hall, 1971.

Gillette, William. *Retreat from Reconstruction, 1869-1879*. Baton Rouge: Louisiana State University Press, 1982.

Goldman, E. *Anarchism and Other Essays*. Port Washington, N.Y.: Kennikat Press, 1969.

Goldstein, Alvin H. *The Unquiet Death of Julius and Ethel Rosenberg*. New York: Lawrence Hill, 1975.

Goldstein, Robert J. *Political Repression in Modern America*. Cambridge, Mass.: Schenkman, 1977.

Goodell, Charles E. *Political Prisoners in America*. New York: Random House, 1973.

Goodman, Walter. *The Committee: The Extraordinary Career of the House Committee on Un-American Activities*. New York: Farrar, Straus & Giroux, 1968.

Goodspeed, D. J. *The Conspirators: A Study of the Coup d'Etat*. New York: Viking Press, 1962.

Graglia, Lino A. *Disaster by Decree: The Supreme Court Decisions on Race and the Schools*. Ithaca: Cornell University Press, 1976.

Graham, Hugh Davis, and Gurr, Ted Robert. *Violence in America: Historical and Comparative Perspectives*. Washington, D.C.: U.S. Government Printing Office, 1969.

Grathwohl, Larry, as told to Frank Reagan. *Bringing down America: An FBI Informer with the Weathermen*. New Rochelle, N.Y.: Arlington House, 1976.

Greenberg, Douglas. *Crime and Law Enforcement in the Colony of New York, 1691-1761*. Ithaca: Cornell University Press, 1976.

Greene, Jack P., ed. *Colonies to Nation, 1763-1789: A Documentary History of the American Revolution*. New York: Norton, 1975.

Grey, Zane. *To the Last Man*. New York: Harper & Bros., 1921.

*Guerrilla War in the U.S.A. Scanlan's Monthly*, January 1971.

Gurr, Ted Robert. *Why Men Rebel*. Princeton: Princeton University Press, 1971.

———. *Rogues, Rebels, and Reformers: A Political History of Urban Crime and Conflict*. Beverly Hills, Calif.: Sage, 1976.

Gusfield, Joseph R. *Protest, Reform, and Revolt*. New York: Wiley, 1970.

Guttmann, Allen, ed. *Communism, the Courts, and the Constitution*. Boston: Heath, 1964.


Halperin, Morton H. *The Lawless State: The Crimes of the U.S. Intelligence Agencies*. New York: Penguin Books, 1976.

Hansen, Klaus J. *Quest for Empire: The Political Kingdom of God and the Council of Fifty in Mormon History*. East Lansing: Michigan State University Press, 1967.

Hanser, Richard. *A Noble Treason*. New York: Putnam, 1979.

Hardt, Scott W. "Federal Land Management in the Twenty-first Century: From Wise Use to Wise Stewardship." 18 *Harv. Env. L. Rev.* 345 (1994).

Hartogs, Dr. Renatus, and Artzt, Eric. *Violence: Causes and Solutions*. New York: Dell, 1970.

Haskins, George Lee. *Law and Authority in Early Massachusetts: A Study in Tradition and Design.* New York: Macmillan, 1960.

Havens, Murray Clark; Leiden, Carl; and Schmitt, Karl M. *The Politics of Assassination.* Englewood Cliffs, N.J.: Prentice-Hall, 1970.

Hayden, Tom. *Trial.* New York: Holt, Rinehart and Winston, 1970.

Haywood, William D. *The Autobiography of Big Bill Haywood.* New York: International Publishers, 1974.

Heffner, R., ed. *A Documentary History of the United States.* New York: Mentor, 1952.

Hendel, Samuel, ed. *The Politics of Confrontation.* New York: Meredith Corp., 1971.

Hendrick, Burton J. *Statesmen of the Lost Cause: Jefferson Davis and His Cabinet.* Boston: Little, Brown, 1939.

——. *Lincoln's War Cabinet.* Garden City, N.Y.: Doubleday, 1961.

Hening, W., ed. *Virginia Statutes at Large.* Vol. 1, *Virginia Statutes at Large, 1619-1660.* Vol. 2, *Virginia Statutes at Large, 1660-1682.* Vol. 3, *Virginia Statutes at Large, 1682-1710.* 1823 ed. Reprint. Charlottesville: University Press of Virginia, 1969.

Hennacy, A., ed. *Two Agitators: Peter Maurin—Ammon Hennacy.* New York: Catholic Worker, 1959.

Henty, G. A. *Through the Fray: A Tale of the Luddite Riots.* New York: Hurst, c. 1890.

Higham, John. *Strangers in the Land: Patterns of American Nativism, 1860-1925.* New York: Atheneum, 1965.

Hofstadter, Richard, and Wallace, Michael, eds. *American Violence: A Documentary History.* New York: Knopf, 1970.

Holden, Matthew, Jr. *The Politics of the Black "Nation."* New York: Chandler, 1973.

Holt, Thomas. *Black over White: Negro Political Leadership in South Carolina during Reconstruction.* Urbana: University of Illinois Press, 1977.

Honderich, Ted. *Three Essays on Political Violence.* Oxford: Basil Blackwell, 1976.

Hoopes, Townsend. *The Limits of Intervention.* New York: McKay, 1970.

Horn, Stanley F. *Invisible Empire: The Story of the Ku Klux Klan, 1866-1871.* Montclair, N.J.: Patterson Smith, 1969.

Horowitz, Irving Louis, ed. *The Anarchists.* New York: Dell, 1970.

Hubbard, David G. *The Skyjacker.* New York: Macmillan, 1971.

Huffman, James L., "The Inevitability of Private Rights in Public Lands." 65 *U. Colo. L. Rev.* 241 (1994).

Hughes, Rupert. *George Washington: The Rebel and the Patriot, 1762-1777.* New York: Morrow, 1927.

Humphrey, Hubert H., ed. *School Desegregation: Documents and Commentaries.* New York: Crowell, 1962.

Hurd, Rollin C. *A Treatise on the Right of Personal Liberty and on the Writ of Habeas Corpus.* 2d ed., rev., with notes by Frank H. Hurd. New York: Da Capo Press, 1972.

Hurst, Charles G. *Passport to Freedom: Education, Humanism, and Malcolm X.* Hamden, Conn.: Linnet Books, 1972.

Hurwood, Bernhardt J. *Society and the Assassin: A Background Book on Political Murder.* New York: Parents Magazine Press, 1970.

Hyams, Edward. *Terrorists and Terrorism.* New York: St. Martin's Press, 1975.

Hyman, Harold M. *Era of the Oath: Northern Loyalty Tests during the Civil War and Reconstruction.* Philadelphia: University of Pennsylvania Press, 1954.

——. *To Try Men's Souls: Loyalty Tests in American History.* Berkeley and Los Angeles: University of California Press, 1959.

Hyneman, Charles S., and Lutz, Donald S., eds. *American Political Writings during the Founding Era.* Indianapolis: Liberty Press, 1983.


Inglis, Brian. *Roger Casement.* London: Hodder Paperbacks, 1974.

Irons, Peter H. *Justice at War.* New York: Oxford University Press, 1983.


Jackson, Curtis, and Galli, Marcia J. *A History of the Bureau of Indian Affairs and Its Activities among Indians.* San Francisco: R & E Research Associates, 1977.

Jackson, George. *Soledad Brother: The Prison Letters of George Jackson.* New York: Bantam Books, 1970.

Jackson, Kenneth T. *The Ku Klux Klan in the City, 1915-1930.* New York: Oxford University Press, 1977.

Jacobs, Harold, ed. *Weatherman.* Berkeley: Ramparts Press, 1971.

Jacobs, Wilbur R. *Dispossessing the American Indian: Indians and Whites on the Colonial Frontier.* New York: Scribner, 1972.

James, Edward T., ed. *The American Plutarch: Eighteen Lives Selected from the Dictionary of American Biography.* New York: Scribner, 1964.

Jameson, John Franklin, ed. *Essays in the Constitutional History of the United States in the Formative Period, 1775-1789, by Graduates and Former Members of The Johns Hopkins University*. Boston: Houghton Mifflin, 1889.

Johnson, F. Roy, *The Nat Turner Slave Insurrection*. Murfreesboro, N.C.: Johnson Publishing Co., 1966.

Josephy, Alvin M., Jr. *Red Power*. New York: McGraw-Hill, 1971.

———. *The Patriot Chiefs*. New York: Penguin Books, 1978.

Joughin, Louis, and Morgan, E. M. *The Legacy of Sacco and Vanzetti*. New York: Harcourt, Brace, 1948.

Joyner, Nancy D. *Aerial Hijacking as an International Crime*. Dobbs Ferry, N.Y.: Oceana Publications, 1974.


Kaiser, R. B. *RFK Must Die*. New York: Dutton, 1970.

Karalekas, Anne. *History of the Central Intelligence Agency*. Laguna Hills, Calif.: Aegean Park Press, 1977.

Kariel, Henry S. *The Decline of American Pluralism*. Stanford: Stanford University Press, 1967.

Katkov, George. *The Trial of Bukharin*. London: B. T. Batsford, 1969.

Keller, Allan. *Thunder at Harper's Ferry*. Englewood Cliffs, N.J.: Prentice-Hall, 1958.

Kennedy, Robert F. *The Enemy Within*. New York: Popular Library, 1960.

Kimmel, Stanley. *The Mad Booths of Maryland*. 2d ed., rev. and enl. New York: Dover, 1969.

King, Dan. *The Life and Times of Thomas Wilson Dorr, with Outlines of the Political History of Rhode Island*. Freeport, N.Y.: Books for Libraries Press, 1969.

King, Duane H., ed. *The Cherokee Indian Nation: A Troubled History*. Knoxville: University of Tennessee Press, 1979.

King, Martin Luther, Jr. *Why We Can't Wait*. New York: Harper & Row, 1963.

Kirchheimer, Otto. *Political Justice*. Princeton: Princeton University Press, 1961.

Kirkham, James; Levy, Sheldon G.; and Crotty, William J. *Assassination and Political Violence*. Vol. 8 of *The National Commission on the Causes and Prevention of Violence Staff Study Series*. Washington, D.C.: U.S. Government Printing Office, 1969.

Kittrie, Nicholas N. "Reconciling the Irreconcilable: The Quest for Internationl Agreement over Political Crime and Terrorism." In *The Year Book of World Affairs, 1978*. London: Stevens & Sons, 1978.

Kommers, Donald P. *The Constitutional Jurisprudence of the Federal Republic of Germany*. Durham, N.C.: Duke University Press, 1989.

Konitz, Milton R. *A Century of Civil Rights*. New York: Columbia University Press, 1961.

Kornbluh, Joyce L., ed. *Rebel Voices: An I. W. W. Anthology*. Ann Arbor: University of Michigan Press, 1964.

Kraditor, Aileen S. *The Ideas of the Woman Suffrage Movement, 1890-1920*. New York: Columbia University Press, 1965.

———. *Means and Ends in American Abolitionism: Garrison and His Critics on Strategy and Tactics, 1834—1850*. New York: Pantheon Books, 1969.

Kutler, Stanley I. *The American Inquisition: Justice and Injustice in the Cold War*. New York: Hill & Wang, 1982.


Labaree, Benjamin W. *The Boston Tea Party*. New York: Oxford University Press, 1964.

Lane, Mark. *Rush to Judgment: A Critique of the Warren Commission's Inquiry into the Murders of President John F. Kennedy, Officer J. D. Tippit, and Lee Harvey Oswald*. New York: Holt, Rinehart and Winston, 1966.

Larsen, Otto N., ed. *Violence and the Mass Media*. New York: Harper & Row, 1968.

Lattimore, Owen. *Ordeal by Slander*. Boston: Little, Brown, 1950.

Lauber, Almon Wheeler. *Indian Slavery in Colonial Times within the Present Limits of the United States*. New York: Columbia University, 1913.

*Laws of the Colonial and State Governments, Relating to Indians and Indian Affairs, 1633-1831, Inclusive: With an Appendix Containing the Proceedings of the Congress of the Confederation and the Laws of Congress from 1800 to 1830 on the same subject*. 1932 ed. Reprint. Standfordville, N.Y.: E. M. Coleman, 1979.

*Laws of the State of New York*. Vol. 1, *1777-1784*. Albany: Weed, Parsons, 1886.

Lawson, J. D., ed. *American State Trials*. Vol. 15. St. Louis: Thomas Lawbook Co., 1856.

Leach, Douglas Edward. *Flintlock and Tomahawk: New England in King Philip's War*. New York: Macmillan, 1958.

Leary, Timothy. *Flashbacks: An Autobiography*. Boston: Houghton Mifflin, 1983.

Leary, William L., ed. *The Central Intelligence Agency: History and Documents*. University, Ala.: University of Alabama Press, 1984.

Lee, R. Alton. *Truman and Taft-Hartley: A Question of Mandate*. Lexington: University of Kentucky Press, 1966.

Leech, Margaret. *In The Days of McKinley*. New York: Harper & Bros., 1959.

Lehey, John D. "Unraveling the Sagebrush Rebellion: Law, Politics, and Federal Lands." 14 *U. Cal. Dav. L. Rev.* 317 (1980).

Levy, Leonard W. *The Law of the Commonwealth of Chief Justice Shaw.* New York: Harper & Row, 1957.

——. *Legacy of Suppression: Freedom of Speech in Early American History.* Cambridge, Mass.: Harvard University Press, Belknap Press, 1960.

Lewis, Anthony. *Gideon's Trumpet.* New York: Vintage Books, 1964.

Lewy, Guenter. *The Federal Loyalty Security Program: The Need for Reform.* Washington, D.C.: American Enterprise Institute for Public Policy Research, 1983.

Lieberman, Jethro K. *How the Government Breaks the Law.* New York: Stein & Day, 1972.

Lindner, Robert. *Must You Conform?* New York: Holt, Rinehart and Winston, 1956.

Linton, Calvin D., ed. *The Bicentennial Almanac.* New York: Thomas Nelson, 1975.

Lipset, Seymour M. *Political Man: The Social Bases of Politics.* Garden City, N.Y.: Doubleday, 1963.

Lisio, Donald J. *The President and Protest: Hoover, Conspiracy, and the Bonus Riot.* Columbia: University of Missouri Press, 1974.

Liston, Robert A. *Dissent in America.* New York: McGraw-Hill, 1971.

Littlefield, Daniel F. *Africans and Creeks: From the Colonial Period to the Civil War.* Westport, Conn.: Greenwood Press, 1979.

Lockridge, Kenneth A. *Settlement and Unsettlement in Early America: The Crisis of Political Legitimacy before the Revolution.* New York: Cambridge University Press, 1981.

Lockwood, Lee. *Conversation with Eldridge Cleaver.* New York: Dell, 1970.

Lowi, Theodore, ed. *The Politics of Disorder.* New York: Norton, 1974.

——, ed. *The End of Liberalism: The Second Republic of the United States.* New York: Norton, 1979.

Lucas, Jim. *Agnew: Profile in Conflict.* New York: Universal Publishing, 1970.

Lumpkin, Wilson. *The Removal of the Cherokee Indians from Georgia.* New York: Dodd, Mead, 1907.

Lundberg, Ferdinand. *Cracks in the Constitution.* Secaucus, N.J.: Stuart, 1980.

Lutz, Alma. *Susan B. Anthony: Rebel, Crusader, Humanitarian.* Boston: Beacon Press, 1959.

Lynd, S., ed. *Nonviolence in America: A Documentary History.* New York: Bobbs-Merrill, 1966.


Mabee, Carleton. *Black Freedom.* London: Macmillan, 1970.

McCague, James. *The Second Rebellion: The Story of the New York City Draft Riots of 1863.* New York: Dial Press, 1968.

McCaleb, Walter F. *The Aaron Burr Conspiracy; and, A New Light on Aaron Burr.* 2 vols in 1. 1903 ed., enl. New York: Argosy-Antiquarian, 1966.

McDonald, Forrest. *Alexander Hamilton: A Biography.* New York: Norton, 1982.

McHenry, Robert, ed. *Liberty's Women.* Springfield, Mass.: Merriam, 1980.

Mackenzie, Compton. *Certain Aspects of Moral Courage.* Garden City, N.Y.: Doubleday, 1962.

Macknight, Gerald. *The Terrorist Mind.* Indianapolis: Bobbs-Merrill, 1974.

McDougall, Mary Lynn, ed. *The Working Class in Modern Europe.* Lexington, Mass.: Heath, 1975.

McLellan, Vin, and Avery, Paul. *The Voices of Guns: The Definitive and Dramatic Story of the Twenty-Two-Month Career of the Symbionese Liberation Army, One of the Most Bizarre Chapters in the History of the American Left.* New York: Putnam, 1977.

McPherson, E., ed. *The Political History of the United States during the Great Rebellion.* Washington, D.C.: Philip and Solomons, 1865.

McPherson, James M. *Ordeal by Fire: The Civil War and Reconstruction.* New York: Knopf, 1981.

Madison, James, and Jefferson, Thomas. *Resolutions of Virginia and Kentucky.* Richmond, Va.: Shepherd, 1835.

Major, John. *The New Deal.* London: Longmans, Green, 1968.

Major, Reginald. *Justice in the Round: The Trial of Angela Davis.* New York: Third Press, 1973.

Malcolm X, and Haley, Alex. *The Autobiography of Malcolm X.* New York: Grove Press, 1969.

Malone, Dumas. *Jefferson the Virginian.* Boston: Little, Brown, 1948.

Marchetti, Victor, and Marks, John D. *The CIA and the Cult of Intelligence.* New York: Dell, 1974.

Marine, Gene. *The Black Panthers.* New York: New American Library, 1969.

Mark, Irving. *Agrarian Conflicts in Colonial New York, 1711-1775.* 2d ed. Port Washington, N.Y.: I. J. Friedman, 1965.

Martin, James Kirby. *Men in Rebellion.* New York: Macmillan, 1973.

Marx, Karl. *The Civil War in France.* Peking: Foreign Languages Press, 1966.

Mason, Alpheus T. *The States Rights Debate: Antifederalism and the Constitution.* 2d ed. New York: Oxford University Press, 1972.

Masotti, Louis H., and Bowen, Don R., eds. *Riots and Rebellion: Civil Violence in the Urban Community.* Beverly Hills, Calif.: Sage, 1968.

Mayo, Bernard, ed. *Jefferson Himself: The Personal Narrative of a Many-Sided American.* Charlottesville: University Press of Virginia, 1976.

Mazlish, Bruce; Kaledin, Arthur D.; and Ralston, David B., eds. *Revolution: A Reader.* New York: Macmillan, 1971.

Meltzer, Milton. *Hunted Like a Wolf: The Story of the Seminole War.* New York: Farrar, Straus & Giroux, 1972.

Merrill, W. M., ed. *The Letters of William Lloyd Garrison.* 6 vols. Cambridge, Mass.: Harvard University Press, Belknap Press, 1971-1981.

Methuin, Eugene H. *The Riot Makers.* New Rochelle, N.Y.: Arlington House, 1970.

Middlekauff, Robert, ed. *Bacon's Rebellion.* Chicago: Rand McNally, 1964.

Miller, Helen Hill. *The Case for Liberty.* Chapel Hill: University of North Carolina Press, 1965.

Miller, John C. *Crisis in Freedom: The Alien and Sedition Acts.* Boston: Little, Brown, 1951.

Miller, Michael V., and Gilmore, Susan, eds. *Revolution at Berkeley.* New York: Dell, 1965.

Miller, Sally M. *Victor Berger and the Promise of Constructive Socialism, 1910-1920.* Westport, Conn.: Greenwood Press, 1973.

Miner, Craig H., and Unrau, William E. *The End of Indian Kansas: A Study of Cultural Revolution, 1854-1871.* Lawrence: Regents Press of Kansas, 1978.

Minor, Clarence E. *The Ratification of the Federal Constitution by the State of New York.* New York: Columbia University Press, 1921.

Minot, G. R. *History of the Insurrection in Massachusetts.* Boston: James W. Burditt, 1810.

*Mississippi Violence vs. Human Rights.* Atlanta: Committee for the Distribution of the Mississippi Story, 1963.

Mitchell, Broadus. *The Price of Independence: A Realistic View of the American Revolution.* New York: Oxford University Press, 1974.

Mitford, Jessica. *The Trial of Dr. Spock.* New York: Random House, 1970.

Mode, P., ed. *Source Book and Bibliographical Guide for American Church History.* Menasha, Wis.: George Banta, 1921.

Montgomery, Robert H. *Sacco-Vanzetti: The Murder and the Myth.* New York: Devin-Adair, 1960.

Montross, Lynn. *The Reluctant Rebels: The Story of the Continental Congress, 1774-1789.* New York: Harper, 1950.

Moore, Barrington, Jr. *Social Origins of Dictatorship and Democracy.* Boston: Beacon Press, 1969.

Moore, F., ed. *The Rebellion Record.* 12 vols. New York: Putnam, 1861-63.

Morgan, David. *Suffragists and Democrats: The Politics of Woman Suffrage in America.* East Lansing: Michigan State University Press, 1972.

Morgan, Edmund Sears, ed. *Prologue to Revolution: Sources and Documents on the Stamp Act Crisis, 1764-1766.* Chapel Hill: University of North Carolina Press, 1959.

Morison, Samuel Eliot; Merk, Frederick; and Freidel, Frank. *Dissent in Three American Wars.* Cambridge, Mass.: Harvard University Press, 1970.

Morris, Richard B. *Seven Who Shaped Our Destiny: The Founding Fathers as Revolutionaries.* New York: Harper & Row, 1973.

Motley, James B. *U.S. Strategy to Counter Domestic Political Terrorism.* Washington, D.C.: National Defense University Press, 1983.

Mowry, George E. *The Era of Theodore Roosevelt and the Birth of Modern America, 1900-1912.* New York: Harper & Row, 1962.

Muller, Charles G. *The Proudest Day: Macdonough on Lake Champlain.* New York: John Day, 1960.

Mullin, Gerald W. *Flight and Rebellion: Slave Resistance in Eighteenth-Century Virginia.* New York: Oxford University Press, 1975.

Muse, Benjamin. *Ten Years of Prelude: The Story of Integration since the Supreme Court's 1954 Decision.* New York: Viking Press, 1964.

Myles, W., ed. *The State Papers and Other Public Writings of Herbert Hoover.* Garden City, N.Y.: Doubleday, Doran, 1934.


Nammack, Georgiana. *Fraud, Politics, and the Dispossession of the Indians: The Iroquois Frontier in the Colonial Period.* Norman: University of Oklahoma Press, 1969.

Nash, Howard P. *Andrew Johnson: Congress and Reconstruction.* Rutherford, N.J.: Fairleigh Dickinson University Press, 1972.

National Advisory Commission on Civil Disorders. *Report of the National Advisory Commission on Civil Disorders.* New York: Bantam Books, 1968.

National Advisory Commission on Civil Disorders. *Supplemental Studies for the National Advisory Commission on Civil Disorders.* Washington, D.C.: U.S. Government Printing Office, 1968.

National Commission on the Causes and Prevention of Violence Task Force on Law and Law Enforcement. *Rights in Concord.* Washington, D.C.: U.S. Government Printing Office, 1969.

National Commission on the Causes and Prevention of Violence. *To Establish Justice, to Insure Domestic Tranquillity.* Washington, D.C.: U.S. Government Printing Office, 1969.

Nelson, Jack, and Ostrow, Ronald J. *The FBI and the Berrigans: The Making of a Conspiracy.* New York: Coward, McCann & Geoghegan, 1972.

Nelson, Truman J. *Documents of Upheaval: Selections from William Lloyd Garrison's "The Liberator," 1831-1865.* New York: Hill & Wang, 1966.

Newman, Graeme. *Understanding Violence.* New York: Harper & Row, 1979.

Nichols, David A. *Lincoln and the Indians: Civil War Policy and Politics.* Columbia: University of Missouri Press, 1978.

Nicolay, J., and Hay, J., eds. *Complete Works of Lincoln.* 12 vols. New York: F. D. Tandy, 1905.

Niles, Hezekiah. *Chronicles of the American Revolution.* Edited by Alden T. Vaughn. (Reprint of Niles, *Principles and Acts of the Revolution in America,* 1822.) Grosset & Dunlap, 1965.

Nizer, Louis. *The Implosion Conspiracy.* Garden City, N.Y.: Doubleday, 1973.

North, Oliver L., et al. *Taking the Stand.* Edited by Daniel Schorr. New York: Pocket Books, 1987.

Nozick, Robert. *Anarchy, State, and Utopia.* New York: Basic Books, 1974.


Oates, Stephen B. *To Purge This Land with Blood: A Biography of John Brown.* New York: Harper & Row, 1970.

———. *The Fires of Jubilee: Nat Turner's Fierce Rebellion.* New York: Harper & Row, 1975.

O'Gorman, Ned, ed. *Prophetic Voices.* New York: Random House, 1969.

Overstreet, Harry, and Overstreet, Bonaro. *The Strange Tactics of Extremism.* New York: Norton, 1964.


Palmer, Stuart. *The Violent Society.* New Haven, Conn.: College and University Press Services, 1972.

Parker, J. A. *Angela Davis.* New Rochelle, N.Y.: Arlington House, 1973.

Parker, W., ed. *Letters and Addresses of Thomas Jefferson.* New York: United Book Publishing Co., 1905.

Parry, Albert. *Terrorism from Robespierre to Arafat.* New York: Vanguard Press, 1976.

Payne, Les, and Findley, Tim. *The Life and Death of the SLA.* New York: Ballantine Books, 1976.

Peare, Catherine Owens. *William Penn: A Biography.* Ann Arbor: University of Michigan Press, 1956.

———. *The Woodrow Wilson Story: An Idealist in Politics.* New York: Crowell, 1963.

Pekelis, Alexander H. *Law and Social Action.* Ithaca: Cornell University Press, 1950.

Perkus, Cathy, ed. *Cointelpro: The FBI's Secret War on Political Freedom.* New York: Monad Press, 1975.

Philbrick, Herbert A. *I Led Three Lives.* Washington, D.C.: Capitol Hill Press, 1972.

Phillips, Donald E. *Student Protest, 1960-1969: An Analysis of the Issues and Speeches.* Washington, D.C.: University Press of America, 1980.

Pierce, William L. [Andrew Macdonald]. *The Turner Diaries.* Hillsboro, W. Va.: National Vanguard, 1979.

Pinkney, Alphonso. *The American Way of Violence.* New York: Random House, 1972.

Pitman, B., ed. *The Assassination of President Lincoln and the Trial of the Conspirators.* Cincinnati: Moore, Wilstach & Baldwin, 1865.

Plechanoff, George. *Anarchism and Socialism.* Translated by Eleanor Marx Aveling. London: Twentieth Century Press, 1906.

Poore, B. P., ed. *The Federal and State Constitutions, Colonial Charters, and Other Organic Laws of the United States.* Washington, D.C.: U.S. Government Printing Office, 1877.

Powderly, T. V. *Thirty Years of Labor.* Columbus, Ohio: Excelsior, 1980.

Powers, E. *Crime and Punishment in Early Massachusetts, 1620-1692.* Boston: Beacon Press, 1966.

Powers, Thomas. *Diana: The Making of a Terrorist.* Boston: Houghton Mifflin, 1971.

*The Presidential Clemency Board's Report to the President.* Washington, D.C.: U.S. Government Printing Office, 1975.

President's Commission on Campus Unrest. *The Report of the President's Commission on Campus Unrest.* New York: Avon Books, 1971.

Preston, William, Jr. *Aliens and Dissenters.* New York: Harper & Row, 1966.

Price, Glenn W. *Origins of the War with Mexico: The Polk-Stockton Intrigue.* Austin: University of Texas Press, 1970.

Priest, Loring B. *Uncle Sam's Stepchildren: The Reformation of United States Indian Policy, 1865-1887.* New Brunswick, N.J.: Rutgers University Press, 1942.

Prucha, Francis Paul, ed. *Documents of United States Indian Policy*. Lincoln: University of Nebraska Press, 1975.

Rable, George C. *But There Was No Peace: The Role of Violence in the Politics of Reconstruction*. Athens: University of Georgia Press, 1984.

Radosh, Ronald, and Milton, Joyce. *The Rosenberg File: A Search for the Truth*. New York: Holt, Rinehart and Winston, 1983.

Randall, James G. *Constitutional Problems under Lincoln*. Urbana: University of Illinois Press, 1951.

Rapoport, David C. *Assassination and Terrorism*. Toronto: T. H. Best, 1971.

Raschhofer, Hermann. *Political Assassination*. Tübingen: Fritz Schlichtenmayer, 1964.

Reed, Scott W. "The County Supremacy Movement: Mendacious Myth Marketing." 30 *Idaho L. Rev.* 525 (1993-94).

Reich, Charles A. *The Greening of America*. New York: Random House, 1970.

Reid, John P. *In a Defiant Stance*. University Park: Pennsylvania State University Press, 1977.

Renshaw, Patrick. *The Wobblies: The Story of Syndicalism in the United States*. Garden City, N.Y.: Anchor Books, 1968.

*Report of the President's Commission on the Assassination of President John F. Kennedy*. Washington, D.C.: U.S. Government Printing Office, 1964.

*Report to the President by the Commission on CIA Activities within the United States*. Washington, D.C.: U.S. Government Printing Office, 1975.

Revolutionary Communist Party, USA. *Revolution and Counter-Revolution*. Chicago: RCP Publications, 1978.

——. *News Programme and New Constitution of the Revolutionary Communist Party, USA*. Chicago: RCP Publications, 1980.

Richardson, J., ed. *A Compilation of Messages and Papers of the Confederacy*. 2 vols. Nashville: United States Publishing Co., 1905.

Richardson, J., ed. *A Compilation of the Messages and Papers of the Presidents*. 20 vols. New York: Bureau of National Literature, 1897-1917.

Rivera, Mario A. *Decision and Structure: United States Refugee Policy in the Mariel Crisis*. Lanham, Md.: University Press of Maryland, 1991.

Robertson, A. H., ed. *Human Rights in National and International Law*. Manchester: Manchester University Press, 1968.

Roebuck, Julian, and Weeber, Stanley C. *Political Crime in the United States*. New York: Praeger, 1978.

Rojo, Ricardo. *My Friend Che*. New York: Grove Press, 1968.

Rosenberg, Charles E. *The Trial of the Assassin Guiteau: Psychiatry and Law in the Gilded Age*. Chicago: University of Chicago Press, 1968.

Rostow, Eugene V., ed. *Is Law Dead?* New York: Simon & Schuster, 1971.

Roszak, Theodore. *The Cult of Information: A Neo-Luddite Treatise on Higher Technology, Artificial Intelligence, and the True Art of Thinking*. 2d ed. Berkeley: University of California Press, 1994.

Rozwenc, Edwin C., ed. *The Causes of the American Civil War*. Boston: Heath, 1965.

Rubenstein, Richard E. *Rebels in Eden: Mass Political Violence in the United States*. Boston: Little, Brown, 1970.

Rubin, Jerry. *Growing Up at Thirty-seven*. New York: M. Evans, 1976.

Ruchames, L. *John Brown: The Making of a Revolutionary*. New York: Grosset & Dunlap, 1969.

Rushton, Reginald M. *The Rushton Report: Right-Wing Extremism in the Federal Republic of Germany, 1973-1995*. Diss., Department of German Studies, University of Birmingham, U.K., June 1995. Available at http://www.almanac.bc.ca/web/people/z/zundel-ernst/rushton-report.html.

Ruthland, Robert A. *The Ordeal of the Constitution: The Antifederalists and the Ratification Struggle of 1787-1788*. Norman: University of Oklahoma Press, 1966.

Said, Abdul A., and Collier, Daniel M. *Revolutionism*. Boston: Allyn & Bacon, 1971.

St. George, M., and Dennis, L. *A Trial on Trial: The Great Sedition Trial of 1944*. National Civil Rights Committee, 1946.

Sale, Kirkpatrick. *Rebels against the Future: The Luddites and Their War on the Industrial Revolution*. Reading, Mass.: Addison-Wesley, 1995.

Salisbury, H., ed. *The Eloquence of Protest: Voices of the 70's*. Boston: Houghton Mifflin, 1972.

Sandburg, Carl. *Abraham Lincoln: The War Years*. New York: Harcourt, Brace, 1939.

Sanders, Ronald. *Lost Tribes and Promised Lands*. Boston: Little, Brown, 1978.

Sargent, W. *The Loyalist Poetry of the Revolution*. Boston: Milford House, 1972.

Saunders, W., ed. *The Colonial Records of North Carolina*. 10 vols. Raleigh: Josephus Daniel, 1890.

Schafer, Stephen. *The Political Criminal*. New York: Free Press, 1974.

Scheer, Robert, ed. *Eldridge Cleaver*. New York: Random House, 1969.

Schiff, Zeev, and Rothstein, Raphael. *Fedayeen*. New York: McKay, 1972.

Schindler, D., and Toman, J., eds. *The Laws of Armed Conflicts*. Alphen aan den Rijn, The Netherlands: Sijthoff & Noordhoff, 1981.

Schlissel, Lillian, ed. *Conscience in America: A Documentary History of Conscientious Objection in America, 1757-1967*. New York: Dutton, 1968.

Schneebeck, Richard. "State Participation in Federal Policy for the Yellowstone Ecosystem: A Meaningful Solution or Business as Usual." 21 *Land & Water L. Rev.* 397 (1986).

Schwartz, David C. *Political Alienation and Political Behavior*. Chicago: Aldine, 1973.

Seidman, Joel. *Sit Down*. New York: League for Industrial Democracy, 1937.

*1777-80 Maryland Laws*. Annapolis: Frederick Green, 1777.

Shaw, Peter. *The Character of John Adams*. New York: Norton, 1976.

Shearer, I. A. *Extradition in International Law*. Manchester: Manchester University Press, 1971.

Sheehan, Bernard W. *Seeds of Extinction: Jeffersonian Philanthropy and the American Indian*. New York: Norton, 1974.

Shoham, Shlomo. *Crime and Social Deviation*. Chicago: Henry Regnery, 1966.

Short, James F., Jr., and Wolfgang, Marvin E., eds. *Collective Violence*. Chicago: Aldine-Atherton, 1972.

Shuman, Samuel I., ed. *Law and Disorder: The Legitimation of Direct Action as an Instrument of Social Policy*. Detroit: Wayne State University Press, 1971.

Silver, David M. *Lincoln's Supreme Court*. Urbana: University of Illinois Press, 1956.

Simkins, Francis B., and Woody, Robert H. *South Carolina during Reconstruction*. Chapel Hill: University of North Carolina Press, 1932.

Sims, Patsy. *The Klan*. New York: Stein & Day, 1978.

Sink, John M. *Political Criminal Trials: How to Defend Them*. New York: Clark Boardman, 1974.

Sirica, John J. *To Set the Record Straight: The Break-in, The Tapes, The Conspirators, The Pardon*. New York: Norton, 1979.

Skolnick, Jerome H. *The Politics of Protest*. New York: Ballantine Books, 1970.

Smith, Colin. *Carlos: Portrait of a Terrorist*. London: André Deutsch, 1976.

Smith, Gibbs M. *Joe Hill*. Salt Lake City: University of Utah Press, 1969.

Snow, Peter, and Phillips, David. *The Arab Hijack War*. New York: Ballantine Books, 1971.

Sonn, Richard D. *Anarchism*. New York: Twayne, 1992.

Sowell, Thomas. *Civil Rights: Rhetoric or Reality?* New York: Morrow, 1984.

Stanton, E.; Anthony, S.; and Gage, M., eds. *History of Woman Suffrage*. 6 vols. New York: Fowler & Wells, 1881.

Stein, Leon. *The Pullman Strike*. New York: Arno Press, 1969.

Steinberg, Peter L. *The Great "Red Menace": United States Prosecution of American Communists, 1949-1952*. Westport, Conn.: Greenwood Press, 1984.

Stephenson, C., and Marcham, F., eds. *Sources of English Constitutional History*. New York: Harper & Bros., 1937.

Stevens, D. *Jailed for Freedom*. New York: Boni and Liveright, 1920.

Stewart, James Brewer. *Holy Warriors: The Abolitionists and American Slavery*. New York: Hill & Wang, 1976.

Stone, Irving. *Clarence Darrow for the Defense*. Garden City, N.Y.: Garden City Publishing Co., 1943.

Stormer, John A. *None Dare Call It Treason*. Florissant, Mo.: Liberty Bell Press, 1964.

Styron, William. *The Confessions of Nat Turner*. New York: Random House, 1967.

Summers, Marvin, ed. *Free Speech and Political Protest*. Boston: Heath, 1967.

Szatmary, David P. *Shays's Rebellion: The Making of an Agrarian Insurrection*. Amherst: University of Massachusetts Press, 1980.

Tannenbaum, Frank. *Darker Phases of the South*. New York: Putnam, 1924.

Tatum, Laurie. *Our Red Brothers and the Peace Policy of President Ulysses S. Grant*. Philadelphia: J. C. Winston, 1899.

Taylor, Telford. *Grand Inquest*. New York: Ballantine Books, 1961.

Theoharis, Athan G., ed. *Beyond the Hiss Case: The FBI, Congress, and the Cold War*. Philadelphia: Temple University Press, 1982.

Thomas, Donald, ed. *Treason and Libel*. Vol. 1 of *State Trials*. Boston: Routledge & Kegan Paul, 1972.

Thomas, Gordon, and Witts, Max Morgan. *The Voyage of the Damned*. New York: Stein & Day, 1974.

Thomas, N. *The Conscientious Objector in America*. New York: B. W. Heubsch, 1923.

Thomis, Malcolm I., ed. *Luddism in Nottinghamshire*. London: Phillimore, 1972.

Thompson, E. P. *The Making of the English Working Class*. New York: Pantheon Books, 1963.

Thompson, Francis H. *The Frustration of Politics: Truman, Congress, and the Loyalty Issue, 1945-1953*. Rutherford, N.J.: Fairleigh Dickinson University Press, 1979.

Thompson, Henry T. *Ousting the Carpetbagger from South Carolina*. Columbia, S.C.: Press of the R. J. Bryan Co., 1926.

Thoreau, Henry David. *"Walden" and the "Essay on Civil Disobedience."* New York: Lancer Books, 1968.

Thornton, J. W., ed. *The Pulpit of the American Revolution: Or the Political Sermons of the Period of 1776*. Boston: Gould & Lincoln, 1860.

Thorpe, F., ed. *Federal and State Constitutions*. 7 vols. 59th Cong., 2d sess., 1906. H. Doc. 357. Washington, D.C.: U.S. Government Printing Office, 1909.

Toch, Hans. *Violent Men*. Chicago: Aldine, 1969.

Toplin, Robert Brent. *Unchallenged Violence*. Westport, Conn.: Williamhouse-Regency, 1975.

Trager, James, ed. *The People's Chronology: A Year-by-Year Record of Human Events from Prehistory to the Present*. New York: Holt, Rinehart and Winston, 1979.

Tragle, Henry I. *The Southampton Slave Revolt of 1831: A Compilation of Source Material*. Amherst: University of Massachusetts Press, 1971.

Turk, Austin T. *Political Criminality*. Beverly Hills, Calif.: Sage, 1982.

Turner, Nat. *The Confession, Trial, and Execution of Nat Turner, The Negro Insurrectionist*. 1881 ed. Reprint. New York: AMS Press, 1975.

Turner, William W., and Christian, John G. *The Assassination of Robert F. Kennedy: The Conspiracy and the Cover-Up, 1968-1978*. New York: Random House, 1978.

Tyler, Alice Felt. *Freedom's Ferment*. New York: Harper & Row, 1961.

Tyler, Lyman S. *Indian Affairs: A Study of the Changes in Policy of the United States toward Indians*. Provo, Utah: Institute of American Studies, Brigham Young University, 1964.

——. *A History of Indian Policy*. Washington, D.C.: Bureau of Indian Affairs, 1973.

Tyler, Lyon Gardiner, ed. *Narratives of Early Virginia, 1606-1625*. New York: Barnes & Noble, 1952.


Ulam, Adam B. *The Unfinished Revolution*. New York: Random House, 1964.

U.S. Commission on Wartime Relocation and Internment of Civilians. *Personal Justice Denied: Report of the Commission on Wartime Relocation and Internment of Civilians*. Washington, D.C.: U.S. Government Printing Office, 1983.

U.S. Congress. House. Committee on Internal Security. *Terrorism*, pts. 1 & 2. 93d Cong., 2d sess. Washington, D.C.: U.S. Government Printing Office, 1974.

U.S. Congress. Senate. Subcommittee to Investigate the Administration of the Internal Security Act and Other Internal Security Laws of the Committee on the Judiciary. *Communist Global Subversion and American Security*. 92d Cong., 2d sess. Committee Print. Washington, D.C.: U.S. Government Printing Office, 1972.

U.S. Library of Congress. Legislative Reference Service. *Internal Security and Subversion: Principal State Laws and Cases*. Washington, D.C.: U.S. Government Printing Office, 1965.

Upton, L. F. S., ed. *Revolutionary versus Loyalist: The First American Civil War, 1774-1784*. Waltham, Mass.: Blaisdell, 1968.

Useem, Michael. *Conscription, Protest, and Social Conflict: The Life and Death of a Draft Resistance Movement*. New York: Wiley, 1973.

Utley, Robert M., and Washburn, Wilcomb E. *The American Heritage History of the Indian Wars*. New York: American Heritage, 1977.


Van Doren, Carl C. *Secret History of the American Revolution: An Account of the Conspiracies of Benedict Arnold and Numerous Others, Drawn from the Secret Service Papers of the British Headquarters in North America, Now for the First Time Examined and Made Public*. New York: Viking Press, 1941.

Viorst, Milton. *Fire in the Streets: America in the 1960s*. New York: Simon & Schuster, 1979.


Walker, Daniel. *Rights in Conflict*. New York: New American Library, 1968.

The Walker Report to the National Commission on The Causes and Prevention of Violence. *Rights in Conflict*. New York: Bantam Books, 1968.

Ward, Barbara. *Faith and Freedom*. Garden City, N.Y.: Doubleday, 1958.

Ware, Norman J. *The Labor Movement in the United States, 1860-1895: A Study in Democracy*. New York: Appleton, 1929.

Warfield, Ethelbert D. *The Kentucky Resolutions of 1798: An Historical Study*. New York: Putnam, 1894.

Warne, Colston E. *The Pullman Boycott of 1894*. Boston: Heath, 1955.

Wasby, Stephen L.; D'Amato, Anthony A.; and Metrailer, Rosemary. *Desegregation from Brown to Alexander: An Exploration of Supreme Court Strategies*. Carbondale: Southern Illinois University Press, 1977.

Washburn, Wilcomb E. *The Governor and the Rebel: A History of Bacon's Rebellion in Virginia*. Chapel Hill: University of North Carolina Press, 1957.

——. *The American Indian and The United States: A Documentary History*. New York: Random House, 1973.

Webb, Stephen Saunders. *1676, the End of American Independence*. New York: Knopf, 1984.

Weber, David R., ed. *Civil Disobedience in America*. Ithaca: Cornell University Press, 1978.

Weglyn, Michi. *Years of Infamy: The Untold Story of America's Concentration Camps*. New York: Morrow, 1976.

Weichmann, L. A. *A True History of the Assassination of Abraham Lincoln and of the Conspiracy of 1865*. New York: Knopf, 1975.

Weinberg, A., ed. *Attorney for the Damned*. New York: Simon & Schuster, 1957.

Weyl, Nathaniel. *Treason*. Washington, D.C.: Public Affairs Press, 1950.

Whittaker, Charles E., and Griffin, William Sloane, Jr. *Law and Order and Civil Disobedience*. Washington, D.C.: American Enterprise Institute for Public Policy Research, 1967.

Whitten, Woodrow C. *Criminal Syndicalism and the Law in California, 1919-1927*. Philadelphia: American Philosophical Society, 1969.

Wilbur, William H. *The Making of George Washington*. Deland, Fla.: Patriotic Education, 1973.

Williams, Roger Neville. *The New Exiles: American War Resisters in Canada*. New York: Liveright, 1971.

Wills, Garry. *The Second Civil War: Arming for Armageddon*. New American Library, 1968.

Wolfenstein, Victor E. *The Victims of Democracy: Malcolm X and the Black Revolution*. Berkeley and Los Angeles: University of California Press, 1981.

Wright, Esmond. *Fabric of Freedom, 1763-1800*. New York: Hill & Wang, 1964.


Yarmolinsky, Adam; Liebman, Lance; and Schelling, Corinne S., eds. *Race and Schooling in the City*. Cambridge, Mass.: Harvard University Press, 1981.

Young, Alfred F., ed. *Dissent: Explorations in the History of American Radicalism*. De Kalb: Northern Illinois University Press, 1968.


Zimmerman, Bill. *Airlift to Wounded Knee*. Chicago: Swallow Press, 1976.

Zinn, Howard. *Disobedience and Democracy*. New York: Random House, 1968.

Zobel, Hiller B. *The Boston Massacre*. New York: Norton, 1970.

# Concordance and User's Guide

All numbers refer to documents.

Abortion  377, 424

Advocacy of Unlawful Acts or Disobedience to Law  36, 96, 99, 105, 108, 111, 133, 174, 175, 186, 194, 195, 197, 204, 207, 211, 213, 220, 223, 227, 228, 229, 234, 246, 247, 250, 251, 255, 256, 257, 258, 259, 261, 262, 271, 272, 275, 276, 277, 279, 280, 282, 283, 286, 287, 291, 294, 296, 304, 311, 319, 320, 337, 361, 372, 373, 375, 376, 377, 378, 400, 406, 411, 412, 422, 429, 432

Air Piracy. *See* Piracy.

Aliens  67, 70, 76, 82, 97, 146, 164, 175, 176, 186, 199, 200, 202, 204, 206, 212, 226, 227, 229, 232, 240, 245, 249, 251, 252, 254, 291, 355, 376, 378, 382, 394, 396, 397, 398, 401, 407, 409, 415, 423, 425, 430

Allegiance. *See* Citizenship and Allegiance

Americanism. *See* Citizenship and Allegiance

Amnesty, Pardon, and Mercy  18, 63, 64, 65, 69, 72, 74, 75, 76, 83, 114, 127, 140, 142, 143, 144, 154, 177, 187, 205, 242, 253, 257, 284, 307, 321, 324, 325, 328, 341, 342, 343, 344, 375, 396, 403

Anarchy  63, 103, 163, 164, 174, 175, 176, 178, 179, 187, 191, 196, 199, 204, 207, 212, 254, 316

Anti-Communism. *See* Communism and Socialism

Antitrust Laws. *See* Labor

Antiwar  47, 48, 82, 121, 130, 133, 178, 186, 190, 191, 192, 193, 194, 197, 198, 199, 200, 203, 228, 234, 240, 242, 300, 301, 303, 304, 307, 309, 310, 312, 315, 316, 319, 321, 322, 323, 325, 326, 332, 337, 338, 341, 342, 343, 376, 422, 436

Assassination  16, 99, 136, 159, 174, 175, 177, 178, 186, 253, 264, 298, 299, 300, 302, 314, 317, 323, 336, 386, 387, 390, 400, 421

Assembly  20, 60, 67, 87, 105, 138, 155, 163, 174, 184, 201, 223, 300, 306, 307, 308, 320, 324, 371, 375, 389, 424

Association  16, 87, 96, 97, 99, 100, 105, 138, 146, 158, 166, 174, 175, 180, 184, 195, 211, 214, 227, 229, 230, 245, 250, 251, 252, 256, 258, 259, 261, 262, 265, 266, 272, 274, 277, 279, 283, 284, 285, 287, 291, 292, 293, 319, 324, 328, 354, 355, 367, 376, 424, 429

Bar, Admission to. *See* Restraints on Officeholding and Profession of Law

Bible. *See* Religion

Bills of Attainder, Outlawry, and Registration  17, 18, 140, 176, 210, 220, 227, 241, 250, 251, 252, 256, 262, 283, 290, 292, 393, 399, 401, 429

Blacks, Slavery, and Civil Rights  14, 16, 21, 23, 28, 56, 61, 85, 87, 90, 93, 94, 96, 99, 100, 103, 104, 105, 108, 109, 110, 111, 113, 115, 116, 117, 118, 119, 126, 127, 129, 136, 138, 141, 145, 146, 150, 152, 155, 156, 172, 186, 210, 221, 276, 285, 295, 296, 297, 298, 299, 300, 301, 304, 305, 306, 307, 308, 313, 317, 318, 320, 322, 323, 324, 325, 333, 338, 371, 374, 375, 377, 398, 417, 419, 428, 433, 434

Bombing. *See* Terrorism

Boycott. *See* Extralegal Coercion of Others

Bureaucracy Protests. *See* Tax and Bureaucracy Protests

Capitalism. *See* Labor

Censorship. *See* Free Speech and Press

Citizenship and Allegiance  3, 4, 9, 20, 27, 32, 37, 38, 43, 44, 46, 48, 53, 108, 109, 113, 128, 133, 136, 140, 145, 146, 150, 151, 153, 154, 155, 162, 165, 166, 188, 194, 200, 204, 206, 218, 227, 232, 235, 236, 238, 239, 240, 245, 246, 250, 251, 262, 272, 283, 286, 299, 303, 304, 318, 321, 325, 340, 344, 347, 352, 357, 364, 365, 369, 372, 377, 394, 400, 402, 403, 406, 416, 417, 418, 420

Civil Disobedience  109, 151, 152, 167, 168, 169, 186, 188, 189, 190, 191, 193, 226, 237, 269, 300, 304, 306, 309, 310, 312, 315, 316, 319, 321, 327, 329, 332, 338, 367, 369, 370, 375, 376, 378, 379, 410, 412, 414, 417, 424

Civil Rights. *See* Blacks, Slavery, and Civil Rights

Classified Information. *See* National (State) and Internal Security

Clemency. *See* Amnesty, Pardon, and Mercy

Communism and Socialism  179, 186, 191, 193, 194, 195, 196, 198, 199, 200, 202, 204, 207, 211, 212, 213, 223, 227, 228, 234, 241, 246, 247, 248, 250, 251, 252, 254, 255, 256, 257, 259, 261, 262, 265, 266, 269, 271, 272, 273, 274, 277, 278, 279, 280, 281, 283, 284, 285, 286, 287, 288, 289, 290, 291, 292, 293, 294, 299, 313, 318, 333, 347, 355, 364, 400, 420, 431

Compulsory Registration. *See* Bills of Attainder, Outlawry, and Registration

Confiscation. *See* Forfeiture and Confiscation

Conscientious Objection. *See* Antiwar

Conscription  29, 53, 82, 121, 130, 140, 178, 188, 190, 191, 192, 193, 194, 197, 200, 303, 305, 309, 310, 312, 319, 326, 332, 342, 343, 369, 370, 379

Consent of the Governed  4, 31, 32, 33, 39, 45, 73, 76, 106, 148, 165, 204, 218, 223, 255, 300, 305, 325, 333, 341, 345, 362, 375, 402, 417, 420, 429, 432

Conspiracy  30, 40, 48, 67, 77, 78, 97, 99, 125, 139, 146, 155, 163, 167, 168, 169, 171, 175, 179, 184, 187, 192, 197, 199, 209, 211, 229, 234, 241, 251, 255, 257, 262, 271, 284, 299, 319, 328, 351, 352, 400, 423

Courts. *See* Judicial Authority and the Powers of the Judiciary

Criminal Anarchy. *See* Anarchy

Curfew  16, 236

Cyberspace, 432, 437

Demonstrations. *See* Strikes and Direct Action

Denaturalization. *See* Exile, Exclusion, and Emigration

Denunciation  11, 38, 40, 47, 48, 59, 105, 111, 192, 401

Deportation. *See* Exile, Exclusion, and Emigration

Domestic Security. *See* National (State) and Internal Security

Draft Resistance. *See* Conscription

Due Process of Law. *See* Procedural Rights

Eavesdropping. *See* Extraordinary Surveillance

Economic Pains and Penalties  3, 20, 35, 39, 132, 134, 143,

# Table of Cases

All numbers refer to documents.

# Proper Name Index

All numbers refer to documents.

*Permissions for documents.*

Documents 130b, 135, 159, 161, 225: Copyright © 1970 by Alfred A. Knopf, Inc. Reprinted by permission of the publisher.

Document 136b: Copyright © 1975 by Floyd E. Risvold. Reprinted by permission of Alfred A. Knopf, Inc.

Document 208: Copyright © by Burke Davis. Reprinted by permission of Random House, Inc.

Documents 171, 177, 210: © 1957 renewed © 1985 by Arthur Weinberg. Reprinted by permission of Simon & Schuster.

Document 298: Copyright © 1965. Reprinted by permission of Grove Press, Inc.

Documents 300 a, b: Reprinted by permission of the Sterling Lord Agency, Inc. Copyright © 1965 by Michael V. Miller and Susan Gilmore.

Document 307c: Copyright © 1971 by the *New York Times*. Reprinted by permission.

Document 313: Copyright © 1971 by Macmillan Publishing Co. Reprinted by permission of Macmillan Publishing Co.

Document 316: Copyright © 1967, 1968, 1970 by Philip Berrigan. Reprinted by permission of Henry Holt & Co.

Document 318: Reprinted with permission from *Weatherman*, Ramparts Press, Palo Alto, Calif. 94303. Copyright © 1970 by Ramparts Press.

Document 321: Reprinted with permission from the *New York Review of Books*. Copyright © 1969 by Francine Gray.

Document 324: Copyright © 1970 by the *New York Times*. Reprinted by permission.

Documents 314a-e: Copyright © 1976 by Les Payne, Tim Findley, and Carolyn Craven. Reprinted by permission of Ballantine Books, a division of Random House, Inc.

Document 345: Copyright © 1978 by Jerry Rubin. Reprinted by permission of the publisher, M. Evans & Co., Inc., New York, N.Y.

Documents 369b, 370a, b, 371a-c, 372a, 375a, 377a: Copyright © the *Washington Post*.

Documents 373, 376, 400: Copyright © 1984 by the *New York Times*. Reprinted by permission.

Documents 375b, 378a, b: Copyright © 1985 by the *New York Times*. Reprinted by permission.

Document 404a. Reprinted from the June 8, 1987 issue of *People* Weekly Magazine by special permission; © 1987, Time Inc.

Document 404b. Reprinted by permission of the *San Diego Union-Tribune*.

Document 405a. "The Gamble That Paid Off," by Dick Dahl, *ABA Journal*, May 1995. Reprinted by permission of the *ABA Journal*.

Document 410b. Reprinted by permission of *The State* (Columbia, S.C.)

Document 411. From *Confessions of an Eco-Warrior*, by David Foreman. Copyright © 1991 by David Foreman. Reprinted by permission of Crown Publishers, Inc.

Document 413a. Reprinted by permission of the *Wall Street Journal*.

Document 413c. Reprinted by permission of the American Civil Liberties Union.

Document 417a. © 1993 *The Washington Post*. Reprinted with permission.

Document 417b. © 1993 *The Washington Post*. Reprinted with permission.

Document 417c. © 1993 *The Washington Post*. Reprinted with permission.

Document 417d. © 1993 *The Washington Post*. Reprinted with permission.

Document 418. Adapted from James D. Tabor and Eugene V. Gallagher, *Why Waco? Cults and the Battle for Religious Freedom in America* (Berkeley: University of California Press, 1995). Copyright © 1995 The Regents of the University of California. Reprinted by permission of the University of California Press and James Tabor.

Document 420a. This article was adapted from *CovertAction Quarterly* (issue no. 52, spring 1995), 1500 Massachusetts Avenue #732, Washington, DC 20005, phone: (202) 331-9763. Annual subscriptions in the U.S. are $22; Canada $27; Europe $33. The issue of *Covert Action*, containing the full text of the article with footnotes, is available from *CAQ* for $8 in the U.S. and $12.00 other.

Document 420c. Reprinted by permission of Tom Burghardt.

Document 421. Reprinted from the *Washington Times*.

Document 422b. Reprinted from the *Washington Times*.

Document 423a. ©1994 Time Inc. Reprinted by permission.

Document 423b. Copyright, 1994, *Los Angeles Times*. Reprinted by permission.

Document 423c. © 1996 *The Observer.*

Document 423d. © 1996 *The Washington Post*. Reprinted with permission.

Document 423e. Copyright © 1996 by The New York Times Co. Reprinted by permission.

Document 426c. Reprinted by permission of *Omaha World-Herald*.

Document 426d. Reprinted by permission of Reuters.

Document 427c. Reprinted by permission of the Courtroom Television Network.
Document 433b. Copyright © 1997 by The New York Times Co. Reprinted by permission.
Document 434. © 1997 *The Washington Post.* Reprinted with permission.
Document 436a. Reprinted by permission of Philip Berrigan.
Document 436b. © 1997 *The Washington Post.* Reprinted with permission.
Document 437d. © 1997 *The Washington Post.* Reprinted with permission.
Document 437f. Copyright © 1997 by The New York Times Co. Reprinted by permission.

*Photographic credits.*

Documents 4, 5, 17, 19, 35, 45, 52, 61, 88, 95 (of Chief Osceola), 98 (from the Broadside Collection), 114, 116, 124, 130, 131, 134, 136, 145, 151, 158, 159, 163, 177, 188, 194, 212, 215, 231, 244, 305, 339: Prints and Photographs, Library of Congress.
Documents 178, 251, 297: Still Photos, National Archives.
Document 95 (of the Trail of Tears): Woolaroc Museum, Bartlesville, Oklahoma.
Document 185: Archives of Labor and Urban Affairs, Wayne State University.
Document 333: Washington, D.C. Public Library.
Document 371: Gamma Liaison Agency, New York City.

Library of Congress Cataloging-in-Publication Data

The tree of liberty : a documentary history of rebellion and political crime
    in America / edited by Nicholas N. Kittrie and Eldon D. Wedlock, Jr. —
    Rev. ed.
        p.    cm.
    "A legal, historical, social, and psychological inquiry into rebellions
    and political crimes, their causes, suppression, and punishment in the
    United States."
    Includes bibliographical references (p.    ) and index.
    ISBN 0-8018-5812-7 (alk. paper)
    (ISBN 0-8018-5643-4, pbk. vol. 1; ISBN 0-8018-5811-9, pbk. vol. 2)
    1. Political crimes and offenses—United States—History—Sources.
2. Criminal law—United States—History—Sources.    I. Kittrie,
Nicholas N., 1928-    .  II. Wedlock, Eldon D.
    KF9390.A7T74    1998
    345.73'0231—dc21                                                    97-31380
                                                                          CIP